AF412698

The
Selected Works
of
Thoreau

The
Selected Works
of
Thoreau

Cambridge Edition

Revised and with a New Introduction
by Walter Harding

Houghton Mifflin Company Boston

Library of Congress Cataloging in Publication Data

Thoreau, Henry David, 1817–1862.
    The selected works of Thoreau.

    Texts from Thoreau in the present edition are those
originally published in 1937 in Works, selected and
edited by H. S. Canby.
    Includes bibliographical references and index.
    I. Harding, Walter R., ed.   II. Title.
PS3042.H3 1975   818'.3'09   74-30151
ISBN 0-395-20430-5

Printed in the United States of America

v   10   9   8   7   6   5   4   3

EDITOR'S NOTE

The original Cambridge Edition of the Works of Thoreau was edited by Henry Seidel Canby in 1937. So felicitous was his choice of selections from Thoreau's writings that there has been no need to modify them and they have been left just as they were. His texts were based on the twenty-volume edition of *The Writings of Thoreau*, which were edited by Francis H. Allen and Bradford Torrey and published by Houghton Mifflin in 1906 as the Manuscript or Walden Edition, and which have long been accepted by Thoreau scholars as the standard edition.

The type of the 1937 edition has been renewed, darkened and enlarged. A new biographical and critical introduction replaces Canby's as do introductory notes to each of the selections. The bibliographical note has been brought up to date and an index of titles has been added.

W. H.

CONTENTS

INTRODUCTION

HENRY THOREAU was born in Concord, Massachusetts, some eighteen miles northwest of Boston, on July 12, 1817, the only one of the so-called "Concord school of writers" who was a native of that town. His paternal grandfather had come to America from the English Channel isle of Jersey shortly before the Revolution and established himself as a moderately prosperous businessman first in Boston and then in Concord. The earlier Thoreaus were French protestants who fled their country after the revocation of the Edict of Nantes in 1685. Thoreau's maternal grandmother, Mary Jones, came from a wealthy and prominent Tory family and as a young lady in the American Revolution once aided two of her Loyalist brothers to escape from Concord jail to safety in Canada. Her husband, the Reverend Asa Dunbar, was a Harvard graduate, a clergyman in Salem, Massachusetts, and later a lawyer in Keene, New Hampshire. His sudden death at forty-one left his family in poverty. Thoreau's father, in the early years of his marriage, was a merchant who tottered continually on the verge of bankruptcy because he was too easygoing and kindhearted to force his customers to pay their bills. Thoreau's mother was a regal, cultured woman, dominant in the home, always engaged in good causes, and anxious to raise her family to the social status and prestige of her ancestors. For a long time she conducted a boarding house to bolster the family income. Her love of nature and her intellectual interests undoubtedly were formative influences on her children. Independence, initiative, and individualism were traits common to many of Thoreau's ancestors and these characteristics coalesced in Henry.

Henry was the third of four children. Helen, the eldest, was an incipient bluestocking who encouraged her brother's intellectual interests and taught school to help put him through college. Like her mother, she was active in the Abolitionist movement. She and Henry had much in common, but she contracted the scourge of their time, tuberculosis, faded into invalidism, and died in 1849. John, the second child, was the gregarious and outgoing member of the family. He was a born raconteur and a leader in any social gathering from childhood on. Most of Concord quite naturally thought him by far the more promising of the two Thoreau boys, but in actuality his intellectuality was fairly superficial and he lacked the high seriousness of his younger brother. Henry, however, worshipped him, and when John died tragically of lockjaw in 1842, it was a traumatic experience for Henry. He could never thereafter mention John's name without tears coming to his eyes. Sophia, the youngest of the family, taught school briefly, dabbled in painting and music, and under Henry's influence developed an interest in botany, collecting a large herbarium of Concord's wildflowers. After Henry's death she very capably managed the family business and considered herself the nurturer and protector of Henry's posthumous reputation.

In Thoreau's childhood Concord was a quiet farming town of two thousand marked by neither outstanding wealth nor outrageous poverty. (The Thoreaus, or at least Mrs. Thoreau, may have thought of themselves at times as poverty stricken, but it was at most a genteel poverty.) Henry himself was a shy, quiet, conscientious lad who was so solemn his schoolmates called him "Judge." Even at this early age he could show his independence by refusing, on invitation, to play with the children of the most elite family in town because "I did not want to." His preference was to wander alone along the banks of the rivers or pick huckleberries in the fields. Concord public schools were probably as good if not better than most schools of the time, but Mrs. Thoreau, anxious to see that her children got the best, enrolled them all in the private Concord Academy, at considerable family financial strain, and there Henry received a solid training in the classics.

In 1823 Thoreau's father embarked upon the manufacturing of pencils. Although only moderately successful at first, it did eventually put the family on a firmer financial foundation so that when Henry was sixteen, the family felt able to enroll him at Harvard College. His college years were for the most part quiet, he spending most of his spare time absorbing the contents of the college library on his own. Although he did not participate in a massive student rebellion of his freshman year, he spoke out sturdily to the faculty in defense of those who did. Much has been made of the fact that he wore a green coat when the college rules required black, but a more likely explanation than rebelliousness is that he simply could not afford a new coat. In his junior year he taught school for a few months in Canton, Massachusetts, to recoup his dwindling finances. Later he was forced to drop out for a time because of ill health, probably the first attack of tuberculosis that was to plague his life. But despite these two extended absences, he maintained a better-than-average standing and at his graduation in 1837 was asked to deliver one of the honors papers, wherein he advocated:

> The order of things should be somewhat reversed; the seventh should be man's day of toil, wherein to earn his living by the sweat of his brow; and the other six his Sabbath of the affections and the soul, — in which to range this widespread garden, and drink in the soft influences and sublime revelations of nature.

This was a philosophy that was undoubtedly dismissed as impractical and even heretical by most of his audience, but which accurately foreshadowed his own plan of life in later years.

Henry was prone to belittle the value of his education at Harvard. When Ralph Waldo Emerson once remarked to him that Harvard taught all the branches of learning, he quickly replied, "Yes, but none of the roots." It is true that the curriculum in those days was dull and unimaginative and the teaching chiefly by rote, yet Harvard's faculty, student body, and library opened his intellectual horizons as they hardly could have been in Concord alone and prepared him for the ferment of Transcendentalism that soon attracted him.

Ralph Waldo Emerson had moved to Concord while Thoreau was away at college, but they quickly became acquainted upon his return and developed a deep and rewarding friendship. Emerson was fourteen years Thoreau's elder and already well established as an intellectual leader of his time. He found in Thoreau the potential of the young "American Scholar" he called for and a sturdy down-to-earthness that he himself never achieved. Thoreau, on his part, found in Emerson a mentor, one who preached the idealism that Henry was devoting himself to living and who urged and encouraged him to embark on a literary career.

Emerson quickly introduced his young friend into the circle of the Transcendentalists — Bronson Alcott, Margaret Fuller, George Ripley, Theodore Parker, Ellery Channing, and the others. Thoreau found their acceptance of an anti-Lockean idealism, their rejection of materialism, their fostering of creative individualism, and their concern for the moral problems of their day akin to his own innermost feelings. He felt at home with many of them as he had with few others. While others gradually drifted away, he remained true to the Transcendentalist principles throughout his life, not because he consciously adapted himself to their beliefs, but because their beliefs and his own innately coincided. It would not be unfair to say that of all the Transcendentalists he was the most thoroughly transcendental at heart and in practice.

Thoreau was offered a teaching position in the public schools when he returned from Harvard, but he resigned in less than two weeks after a member of the school board insisted that he practice corporal punishment. Since the country was in the midst of a harsh depression, Thoreau was unsuccessful in finding another job and finally in the early summer of 1838 opened a private school in the family's home where he could teach in a manner to please himself and promptly introduced many of the methods we now term "progressive education." The school was a quick success and he shortly asked his brother John to join him in the teaching. They never lacked for pupils and the school was given up in 1841 only because John's health precluded his teaching further and Henry, anxious to turn to new fields, was unwilling to carry on alone.

When Emerson found Thoreau at loose ends, he invited him to join his household, suggesting that if he would take care of the handiwork such as snow-shoveling, lawn-mowing, and furniture repair at which Emerson was notoriously inept and Thoreau adept, he could have free board and room and — most important — time to devote to writing. Thoreau quickly accepted and as a result of Emerson's largesse began turning out articles and poems for the Transcendentalist *Dial* and other magazines. In 1843 Emerson arranged for Henry to tutor his brother William Emerson's sons on Staten Island, hoping thus to make him acquainted with the lions of the literary world — the editors and publishers and critics of New York City. Thoreau did win the lifelong friendship and encouragement of Horace Greeley, editor of the nation's most prestigious newspaper, the *Tribune*, who acted thereafter as his chief literary agent. But he was lonesome and homesick on Staten Island and after seven months returned to Concord, there to settle down, except for occasional brief excursions, for the rest of his life.

Although Thoreau was later to become noted for his caustic comments on marriage as an institution and women in general (Kicking a skunk cabbage one day, he said, "There's what I think of marriage."), he did participate briefly if rather abortively in a romance in 1840 with Ellen Sewall, the daughter of a Unitarian minister in Scituate, Massachusetts. Henry took her on walks and boat rides, wrote her several sentimental love poems and eventually proposed marriage. She apparently would have been happy to accept but was forbidden by her father who would have none of an associate of the "radical" Ralph Waldo Emerson as a son-in-law. Ellen a few years later married a man closer to her father's taste but retained her friendship with Henry to the end.

In the late summer of 1839 Henry and his brother had taken a short vacation jaunt by rowboat on the Concord and Merrimack Rivers. With John's death Henry determined to write up that excursion as a memorial to his brother, but somehow he never seemed to find the time to do it. When Emerson purchased some acreage on the shores of Walden Pond, a mile and a half south of Concord village, Thoreau seized the opportunity and with Emerson's permission in the spring of 1845 built himself a sturdy little ten-by-fifteen-foot cabin where he could live the simple life and devote himself to writing his book. Since his wants were simple and his necessities few, he was able to support himself with only six weeks of labor a year. The remainder of his time he could devote himself to writing and to what was becoming more and more of an obsession with him — the observation of nature and the recording of its phenomena. Rarely a day went by that he did not spend as much as five hours walking through the fields and woods of Concord or boating, swimming, or skating on its ponds and rivers. In his two years, two months, and two days at Walden Pond Thoreau wrote not only his memorial volume, *A Week on the Concord and Merrimack Rivers,* but also the first draft of his account of his life at the pond, *Walden.* The former, after numerous vicissitudes was published in 1849; the latter, not until 1854.

Concord was a focal point of antislavery activity in the 1840's and all of Henry's family were involved in it. Their home was often used as a station on the underground railroad smuggling escaped slaves to freedom in Canada. Nearly every New England antislavery leader dined at one time or another at the Thoreau family table. Thoreau himself was often a "conductor" on the underground railroad. But that was not solving the problem. He should work at eliminating slavery itself. In 1843, as an act of open protest, he began refusing to pay his poll tax. For some unknown reason, it was late in July of 1846, while Thoreau was at Walden Pond, before Samuel Staples, the local constable, arrested him and put him in jail, first, as a friend, even offering to pay the taxes for him. When the next morning Staples came down to the jail to release him because during the night someone —

probably Thoreau's Aunt Maria — had paid the taxes, Thoreau at first refused to leave, arguing that he himself had not paid the taxes and still wanted to protest slavery. Only when Staples threatened to eject him bodily did Henry leave. So many were the questions of his townsmen at his "strange behavior," that Thoreau finally delivered a lecture at the Concord Lyceum explaining his position. In 1849 Elizabeth Peabody published the lecture in her short-lived periodical *Aesthetic Papers*, and thus the essay that was later to be titled "Civil Disobedience" got into print.

In the late summer of 1847 Emerson decided to go abroad on a lecture tour and, hesitating to leave his wife and three small children home alone for an extended period of time, persuaded Thoreau to leave the Walden cabin and return to the Emerson household to live in his absence. Although Thoreau thus gave up Walden Pond, he did not abandon the pattern of simple living he had adopted there. For the remainder of his life he continued to devote his mornings to writing, his afternoons to observing nature, and his evenings to reading and conversation. Approximately six weeks of each year he spent in earning a living — surveying, pencil-making, or doing odd jobs. He was never so proud as to think manual labor beneath him.

Although the manuscript of *A Week* circulated widely among publishers, no one was interested in publishing it except at the author's expense. Finally in 1849 he persuaded James Munroe & Co. of Boston to bring it out in an edition of one thousand copies, he guaranteeing them against financial loss. The book failed and not only did Thoreau have to reimburse Munroe, but neither Munroe nor any other publisher would then consider publishing *Walden*. Failing to be discouraged, Thoreau sat down and re-wrote *Walden*, not just once, but seven separate times, adding, subtracting, rewording and polishing it until it became the masterpiece we now know. Finally the new Boston firm of Ticknor & Fields had the foresight to publish it in the summer of 1854. Although it was by no means a best-seller, it was generally well reviewed, sold off the first printing of two thousand copies in a little under five years, and established the foundation for Thoreau's later fame.

Shortly after his return to Concord from college Thoreau began lecturing once or twice a season before the Concord Lyceum. His early lectures, such as "Sir Walter Raleigh," were written specifically for the Lyceum. Later he began using it as a testing place for essays he intended to publish elsewhere. Gradually it became the laboratory out of which grew his books. Large portions of *A Week* and *Walden* were tried out first on the lecture platform. By the late 1840's he began to receive invitations to lecture in other Massachusetts towns and in the 1850's his circuit extended pretty widely throughout New England and even into New Jersey and Pennsylvania. Although he sometimes fulminated at his audiences' imperceptiveness, he could, at times at least, arouse them to tears or laughter.

In a search for good topics for his lectures, he began taking trips to points such as the dunes of Cape Cod, the woods of northern Maine, and the cities of Quebec, sometimes alone, sometimes with a companion such as the poet Ellery Channing, who had over the years become his closest friend. Each of these "excursions," as he liked to call them, he wrote up in light-hearted detail and they quickly became the most popular of his lectures. Later they formed the bases for his posthumous books *The Maine Woods, Cape Cod,* and the briefer and less successful *Yankee in Canada.*

In the late 1840's an opportunity to collect specimens for Louis Agassiz's zoological studies at Harvard developed Thoreau's interest in a scientific study of the flora and fauna of his native Concord. He began to gather what few natural history handbooks were then available, to acquire a telescope, to start his own herbarium, and to accumulate data on the arrival and nesting of birds, the budding of flowers, and the leafing of trees. At times the data he gathered tended to overwhelm him and he lamented that he was becoming bogged down in detail, that his interest in nature was becoming more scientific at the expense of the aesthetic and emotional. Fortunately however he never lost his joy in nature and his sense of wonder. He retained his youthful enthusiasm to the very end and that enthusiasm shines through the pages of his journal, giving us some of his greatest writing.

From childhood Thoreau had been fascinated by the American Indians. He gathered their artifacts from the fields of Concord and learned to detect where their village sites had been. On his trips to Maine he made a point of hiring Indian guides so that he could get to know them personally. He read every book on the Indian he could lay hands on and took eleven large volumes of notes on them. It was his intent to write a book about them, but unfortunately he never got around to it. The furthest he got was to draw up a table of contents. His final illness cut his work short. But also as he grew better acquainted with the Indian, he became disillusioned. He had idealized him as a "noble savage" who lived in perfect communion with Nature.

In real life the Indian proved to have no cultural nor aesthetic interests. He was interested only in where his next day's food was coming from. Thoreau was deeply disappointed and disillusioned.

In 1857 and again early in 1859 Thoreau met John Brown who visited Concord in his efforts to raise funds for his antislavery activities. Thoreau was much impressed by his intensity and his sincerity. When in October of 1859 word was received of Brown's attack on Harpers Ferry, most abolitionists feared Brown had gone too far and would create a backlash against their activities. Thoreau, however, who had had no advance knowledge of Brown's plans, was the first to come to Brown's defense. He called a meeting in Concord town hall and delivered an impassioned "Plea for Captain John Brown" that won many of his audience to Brown's cause. It is important to note however that Thoreau was not so much endorsing Brown's violence as praising his courage in giving his life for his principles.

In the late 1850's Thoreau through surveying woodlots developed a particular interest in the study of tree growth. He worked out a theory to explain the apparently spontaneous alternation of deciduous and evergreen trees in the woods and he discovered the significance of tree-growth patterns both in studying the climate of an area and in identifying the source of a piece of lumber. He started work on a book tentatively titled "Notes on Fruits and Seeds." One cold, snowy day in early December of 1860, spent charting tree ring patterns in a newly lumbered woodlot on Fair Haven Hill, he caught a cold that soon worsened into bronchitis and in turn opened the tubercular lesions in his lungs that had plagued his life. Doctors told him his only hope was to move to a different climate. In May of 1861, accompanied by young Horace Mann, Jr., the son of the famous educator, he traveled out to Minnesota, hoping to find surcease, but it was soon obvious that he would not recover. He returned to Concord in two months and, accepting his fate, set to work to put as many of his unpublished manuscripts in final form as he could. His last months were marked by cheerfulness and peace. Sam Staples, the jailer, said he "never saw a man dying with so much pleasure and peace." When his orthodox Aunt Louisa Dunbar asked if Thoreau had made his peace with God, he replied, "I did not know we had ever quarrelled." He died on the morning of May 6, 1862; his last words — "moose" and "Indian" — showing his concern for the *Maine Woods* manuscripts he had been working on to the very end. Emerson, preaching the funeral sermon three days later, said, "His soul was made for the noblest society; he had in a short life exhausted the capabilities of this world; wherever there is knowledge, wherever there is beauty, he will find a home." He now rests in Sleepy Hollow Cemetery in Concord only a few steps from the graves of his friends, Emerson, Hawthorne, Bronson Alcott, and Ellery Channing.

In his own day, when he was noticed at all, Thoreau was usually dismissed as a second-rate imitator of his friend, neighbor, and mentor Ralph Waldo Emerson. Few of his contemporaries imagined he would ever be remembered beyond his lifetime. Of the two books he had published in his lifetime, as we have seen, *A Week* had been a complete failure and *Walden* had seemingly created little more than a passing flurry. At his death in 1862 both were out of print. Yet, ironically, within a few weeks of his death, both were back in print, and within four years five posthumous volumes — *Excursions, The Maine Woods, Cape Cod, Letters to Various Persons,* and *A Yankee in Canada, with Anti-Slavery and Reform Papers* had all been published. Their sale over the years was steady, but not spectacular.

Just as interest in Thoreau seemed to be building he had the misfortune of receiving what we would now call bad publicity. In 1865 James Russell Lowell published a lengthy essay-review in the influential *North American Review* of Thoreau's posthumously published works. The two men had known each other but had clashed when Lowell arbitrarily censored one of Thoreau's *Maine Woods* essays for its appearance in the *Atlantic Monthly* in 1858 and Thoreau denounced his actions in no uncertain terms. Lowell used his essay-review as a means of retaliation. He dismissed Thoreau as a poor imitator of Emerson, charged that he was not an observer by nature, "had not a healthy mind," and "had no humor." As preposterous as these charges seem now, Lowell's prestige in his day was such that his pronouncements were accepted as gospel. Then in 1880 Robert Louis Stevenson in a widely read article in the *Cornhill Magazine* denounced Thoreau as "a skulker." Although a few years later Stevenson issued a recantation stating that he had based his charge on misinformation, the damage had already been done. But ironically it was Thoreau's closest friend, Ralph Waldo Emerson, who unwittingly did the greatest damage. Looking upon Thoreau primarily as a Stoic he greatly overemphasized Thoreau's negative characteristics both in the funeral sermon he preached in 1862, which reached wide circulation in the *Atlantic Monthly* and in Emerson's collected works, and in his editing of Thoreau's letters in 1865. (Thoreau's sister Sophia protested she did not even recognize her brother in the latter volume.) And so the utterly false legend grew that Thoreau was a cold, inhuman misanthrope and few bothered to read his works for themselves to see if the charges were true.

However, from 1881 to 1892, his friend H. G. O. Blake published the four volumes of extracts from his Journals, *Early Spring in Massachusetts, Summer, Winter,* and *Autumn,* emphasizing his comments on natural history and a renewed interest in Thoreau as a nature writer was aroused. His publishers were encouraged in 1894 to bring out an eleven-volume collected edition of his works and in 1906 an expanded twenty-volume edition including a transcript of virtually the entire journal. Thoreau was beginning to attract a small but ardently devoted coterie of followers.

In England just before the turn of the century Henry Salt and some of the early British Labour Party leaders became interested in Thoreau, not as a nature writer, but as an economist, a philosopher of the simple life. But it was not until the great depression of the 1930's that this facet of Thoreau attracted any considerable interest in his own country. Then, when people were suddenly forced by economic circumstance to get down to the essentials, Thoreau the simplifier became fashionable. But the interest in Thoreau did not fade away with the end of the depression. By the 1940's his name had become standard on every list of great American authors, and with the surge of internationalism after World War II, *Walden* was translated into every major foreign language. By the turbulent years of the 1960's "Civil Disobedience" had become an international handbook of revolution. His name had become a household word.

What is the basis of Thoreau's fame today? It is impossible to isolate one single cause. His appeal is multifaceted. When one finds him quoted approvingly by people as diverse as Mahatma Gandhi, Loren Eiseley, Emma Goldman, Sinclair Lewis, Robert Lowell, Ernest Hemingway, John F. Kennedy, Edwin Way Teale, Lord Tweedsmuir, Gene Tunney, Martin Luther King, Malcolm X, George Bernard Shaw, Robert Frost, and Franklin Delano Roosevelt, one realizes just how broad his appeal is.

Thoreau has always had an appeal as a nature writer. Although he did make some distinctive scientific contributions such as in his theory of the succession of forest trees and in his collecting of natural history data in his journals, it is as a student of man's relation to nature that he makes his greatest contribution. His vignettes of the wild life of the

New England landscape are beautifully and lovingly drawn with none of the sentimentality that so often mars nature writing. More important is his understanding of the essentiality of nature to man. In a day when most men looked upon nature as something to destroy and defeat, Thoreau realized that man, Antaeus-like, was absolutely dependent upon nature not only for his material goods, but even more for his spiritual resources. His was one of the earliest voices to speak out for the conservation of natural resources and for the establishment of local, state, and national parks and to contend that man separated from nature, as in our cities, becomes debased, maladjusted, and ill. We all need regular contact with nature, he maintains. One word of caution, however, must be observed. Thoreau is not a Rousseauean primitivist. He does not ask for a return to the life of the savage, but rather to the simple life. He was fully aware and appreciative of the accomplishments of civilization and ready to take advantage of them. It was typical of him that when he decided to become a surveyor, he bought the best instruments available and read every book on surveying that he could lay hands on. What did disturb him was that altogether too often we permit ourselves to become the tools of our machines rather than their masters. We forget that machines are means to ends and not ends in themselves. Just because a telephone has been invented does not mean that we must subject ourselves to its every command nor tie ourselves down to the range of its ring. A telephone properly put to use can extend endlessly our means of communication. But we do not have to become slaves to it.

What disturbed Thoreau even more were the misuses to which we put the tools of our civilization. We put a cable across the Atlantic but instead of using it to bring our greatest thinkers closer together, we devoted it to such trivia as the fact that "Princess Adelaide has the whooping cough." We develop railroads, or jets, in order to get to the cities an hour sooner, and then proceed to waste the hour when we get there. Thoreau did not want to abandon the advantages of civilization; he simply wanted them put to better use. One should remember that Thoreau himself did not flee from civilization. His cabin at Walden Pond was only a mile and a half from home and less than twenty miles from the metropolitan center of Boston. There was rarely a day when he was at Walden when either he did not walk into the village to visit his friends and family or that he in turn was not visited by them. On one occasion when in the wilds of northern Maine he came upon a professional hermit, a man who had truly withdrawn from civilization,

Thoreau confessed that such a life was not for him. He needed society as much as nature. What he was trying to achieve was an appropriate and workable balance between the two.

Thoreau was a century ahead of his time in realizing the problems that the growing complexity of our civilization would and did produce. "Simplify, simplify, simplify" may not have seemed a vital message in the mid-nineteenth century, but it has become essential today if we are to survive. We can no longer embrace the universe, as Walt Whitman would say. Unless we become selective in our interests, our actions, our endorsements, we are likely to drown in trivia or become schizophrenic. Thoreau points out the only viable solution — to decide individually what it is we really want in life and then have the courage to say "No" to all else. Thoreau wanted to become a writer, so he stripped his life to the essentials at Walden Pond and thus was able to follow his career. It is important to realize that he does not advocate everyone's going to a Walden Pond. "I would not have anyone adopt *my* mode of living on any account," he says in *Walden*. He would not have us imitate *his* choice, but rather make our own. It is not necessary to go to Concord or even to the woods to find our personal Walden. Thoreau did not leave his native area to find his. Walden is a state of mind far more than it is a geographical location. Thoreau dwelt on the shores of Walden Pond for only two years; when he returned to the village in 1847, he brought his Walden with him. Our Waldens are where we can find personal fulfillment as Thoreau found his.

Thoreau's philosophy is the epitome of individualism. We cannot become Thoreauvians by imitating Thoreau but by becoming ourselves. Society today is essentially conformist. It would mold all men in one pattern. But Thoreau says we cannot become men unless we break out of the pattern and become ourselves. We cannot lead our neighbor's lives nor can our parents lead ours. We have only one life to live and that must be our own. Like Thoreau, when we come to die, we want to know that we have lived. A few weeks before he died Thoreau wrote that he regretted nothing about his life. He asks, will we be able to say the same?

On the surface Thoreau's life pattern may seem blatantly egotistic and self-centered. There is no question but that he had a great deal of self-confidence. Any creative artist has to in order to maintain the drive to create. But we must remember that Thoreau was a Transcendentalist among Transcendentalists. And fundamental to the Transcendental way of life is a belief in the spirit of God within each man. They believed they were not self-reliant, but god-reliant. They believed that only by following the voice within could they achieve success — not materialistic success, but the far greater success of a fulfilled life:

> If one listens to the faintest but constant suggestions of his genius, which are certainly true, he sees not to what extremes, or even insanity, it may lead him; and yet that way, as he grows more resolute and faithful, his road lies . . . If the day and night are such that you greet them with joy, and life emits a fragrance like flowers and sweet-scented herbs, is more elastic, more starry, more immortal — that is your success . . .

Or again:

> I learned this, at least, by my experiment; that if one advances confidently in the direction of his dreams, and endeavors to live the life which he has imagined, he will meet with a success unexpected in common hours. He will put some things behind, will pass an invisible boundary; new, universal, and more liberal laws will begin to establish themselves around and within him; or the old laws be expanded, and interpreted in his favor in a more liberal sense, and he will live with the license of a higher order of beings.

He asks us to have the courage of our convictions and predicts our success if we have that courage. He urges us that if we have built our castles in the air, that we should now build our foundations under them.

Thoreau was a radical in the sense that he liked to get down to the root of things. Gifted with an independent mind, he had faith in the value of questioning all things. And once he started questioning, he often found himself coming to conclusions quite different from those generally accepted. As a true Transcendentalist, he does not try to impose his conclusions on others. He is neither doctrinaire nor dogmatic. What he does do however is attempt to get his fellow man to think and to question. As he states in his epigraph to *Walden*, he brags "as lustily as chanticleer in the morning, standing on his roost, if only to wake [his] neighbors up." Hyperbole is one of his major tools, for by overstating his case he hopes to stir his somnolent reader into thought. At the beginning of "Civil Disobedience," for example, he shouts at us that "that government is best which governs not at all," but once he has stirred us up with that statement, he modifies his position to the more modest proposal, "I ask for, not at once no government, but *at once* a better government." Unquestionably some readers are turned off by his technique, but for the majority it does serve Thoreau's purpose of getting them to think and to question what they had thought unquestionable.

At first glance some of Thoreau's proposals seem topsy-turvy. When he tells us that the Bible had things backward, that we should work one day a week and rest six instead of the reverse, our first reaction is to snort, "Preposterous." But when we see how he worked out that formula in his own life, we realize it is not so nonsensical after all. It is a pattern that we all could well adopt. Of course those who do not think Thoreau's proposition through may immediately jump to the conclusion that it is a lazy man's proposal, ignoring the fact that Thoreau did not waste the six days of each week but rather devoted them to that which he could do best — writing. And out of that came three million words of some of the best prose in our language. Such productivity is not that of the lazy.

Because Thoreau is so often critical of society and of his fellow man, one might easily get the impression that he was a misanthrope. Indeed there were those who were certain that he was. As a matter of fact, while he was often disappointed in mankind, he was at heart an almost incurable optimist, convinced that man could create a heaven here on earth if only he would devote himself wholeheartedly to the effort. He was not only convinced that man *could*, but also that eventually man *would*. Note that every single one of his major works — *Walden*, *A Week*, "Civil Disobedience," and "Life Without Principle," for example — ends on an exceedingly optimistic note: "The sun is but a morning star."

A word should be said about the relationship of Thoreau and his neighbor, friend, and mentor, Ralph Waldo Emerson. It was Emerson, already a nationally famous author when the two became acquainted in 1837, who so perceptively recognized Thoreau's potential abilities, encouraged him to embark upon a literary career, and then exerted every effort to help him along the way. There is little doubt but that Thoreau would not have devoted himself to the pen had it not been for Emerson. During their lifetimes, their contemporaries made much of the fact and, perhaps blinded by the almost overwhelming brilliance of Emerson's personality, regularly dismissed Thoreau as nothing more than a pale imitator of his mentor. Although Emerson realized the frequent similarity of their ideas and acknowledged it in the privacy of his unpublished journal, he also recognized Thoreau's originality and publicly came to the defense of Thoreau's reputation on many an occasion. He was one of the first to recognize the sturdiness of Thoreau's style and said, "In reading him, I find the same thought, the same spirit that is in me, but he takes a step beyond, and illustrates by excellent images that which I should have conveyed in a sleepy generality. 'Tis as if I went into a gymnasium, and saw youths leap, climb, and swing with a force unapproachable, — though their feats are only continuations of my initial grapplings and jumps." Now in the twentieth century Thoreau seems to have superseded Emerson in popularity because those "excellent images" of his style speak more to our generation than the "sleepy generalities" of Emerson. Compare the concreteness of *Walden* to the abstractness of "Self-Reliance," and one readily sees the difference.

Another major difference between the two is in the use of form. As Thomas Carlyle once commented on Emerson's essays, they are a collection of duck shot in a canvas bag. Emerson accumulates ideas rather than develops them. His essays can be started anywhere and even read backward as well as forward. Early critics, knowing of the kinship of the two men, assumed the same to be true of Thoreau. It is only in comparatively recent years that critics have become aware of the fact that Thoreau's techniques were very different. His ideas are carefully developed rather than accumulated. Each chapter, each paragraph, and even each sentence is in its precise place for a carefully calculated reason and cannot be moved without damage to the structure as a whole. He knit his books together very consciously, using a cycle of the seasons in *Walden* and the structure of the calendar in *A Week*, for example, as unifying devices. In *Cape Cod* he melded three different journeys into one. In smaller units he used geography, chronology, contrast, and connectives to tie his works together. Few if any of these devices can be found in Emerson.

There is a feeling today that Thoreau put into practice what Emerson only preached. Emerson was a great sayer, but Thoreau was both a sayer and a doer. We must not belittle Emerson, however, for his contribution and his influence were great. Undoubtedly for some future generation whose stylistic tastes have changed from our own he will speak strongly again.

For our day, though, Thoreau is the stylist *par excellence*. He was the first in the nineteenth century to speak the diction and the vocabulary of the twentieth. One need only read any of his contemporaries to see the difference. There is rarely a sentence of his that does not have the feel of our day. He avoided the archaisms of both his day and ours. He caught the rhythm of the modern sentence. Even when expressing abstract ideas he couched them in the concrete language we today prefer.

Thoreau's is a remarkable vocabulary — remarkable in both its size and its precision. Reading him is a vocabulary-stretching experience. The joy of it is that his word usage is utilitarian rather than ostentatious. Each word is chosen with precision and on those occasions when we think he has misfired, we discover upon checking the dictionary that he has gone back to a root meaning of the word that we were not even aware of — for example, his use of "with-drawing room" in *Walden*.

Thoreau is an inverterate punster, as true word-lovers always are. It would be difficult to find a page of his without a pun — or two, or three, or four, or five. Occasionally they are there for the pure fun of it, as when in *Walden* he speaks of the unlucky fishermen as Coenobites ("See, no bites"), but more typically his puns are used either to emphasize his meanings or to give a humorous edge to his criticism. ("It [articles for popular magazines] must be submitted to the D.D.'s. I would it were the chickadee-dees.") Humor pervades Thoreau and one can be sure that if he does not see it, he is missing or misinterpreting what Thoreau is saying. The humor is by no means limited to puns but ranges from hyperbole to slapstick. It can be both sardonic and merry. Often it is topsy-turvy. But, as with the puns, it is usually there for a purpose. Like Mark Twain and Bernard Shaw, Thoreau realized that criticism dipped in humor was often more effective.

In recent years the symbol hunters have had a field day with Thoreau. There is no question but that he offers them fair hunting ground. As a literary artist he made conscious and effective use of the symbol and the metaphor. F. O. Matthiessen, in his masterly *American Renaissance*, has demonstrated how effectively, for example, Thoreau makes use of the symbolism of re-birth in *Walden*. But nonetheless a word of caution is necessary, for there are those who would find symbols everywhere whether they are there or not. Thus more than one fanciful critic has found all sorts of esoteric Zen symbolism in Thoreau, overlooking the fact that none of the literature of Zen was available in English until after Thoreau's death. (This is not to say that there are not interesting parallels between Thoreau and Zen, but of influence there is none.)

While it is interesting to analyze Thoreau's artistry, for he was a true architect of prose, we must not forget that artistry was for him a means, not an end. Art for art's sake would have been meaningless to him. He wrote primarily to convey a message. Henry Thoreau is the voice of conscience for our day, for his day, for all days. He asks not to listen to him, but to the voice within ourselves. That is why he seems such a prickly, erinaceous porcupine to many, for one's conscience is not always easy to live with, particularly if one begins to pay attention to it. But that is also why he speaks so strongly to our day, for now more than ever before we need to heed the voice of conscience.

WALTER HARDING

The
Selected Works
of
Thoreau

1 . SELECTIONS FROM THE JOURNAL

"What are you doing now?" he asked. "Do you keep a journal?" So I
make my first entry to-day.

THUS on October 22, 1837, two months after he graduated from Harvard and
returned to Concord, Thoreau, at the instigation of his new friend and neighbor
Ralph Waldo Emerson, began the journal that was to continue with almost
daily entries for more than twenty-four years, filling nearly forty large manuscript volumes with more than two million words, one of the most thorough
and complete life-records of a man's thought and growth in our history.

At Emerson's suggestion he began the journal primarily as a conscious step
toward a writing career. It was to be used as a source book for his to-be-written
publishable works and, somewhat incidentally, a commonplace book (that is,
a sort of anthology of favorite quotations from his reading — quotations that
might prove useful to insert into his lectures and essays). As he once noted:

> From all points of the compass, from the earth beneath and the heavens
> above, have come these inspirations and been entered duly in the order of
> their arrival in the journal. Thereafter, when the time arrived, they were
> winnowed into lectures, and again, in due time, from lectures into essays.

Because he followed that plan, a great part of Thoreau's early journals through
the 1840's are lost to us. He literally tore them apart to create his early essays
and his first two books, *A Week* and *Walden*.[1] When the journals literally fell
to pieces because of his mutilations, he then went through and copied what he
liked of the remnants, labeling them "Gleanings or what time has not reaped
of my journal." Thus we cannot consider what is left of the early journals to
be any more than fragments. The early journal is dull and aphoristic to any
but the most enthusiastic Thoreauvian. Scholars read it to understand the

---

[1] Through some very ingenious detective work, by studying inks, and papers,
and matching torn sheets in the working papers for his books and essays, some of
our young scholars, led primarily by Thomas Blanding, are just now finding that
they are able to recreate whole sections of these destroyed journals.

development of Thoreau's intellect; for that it is invaluable. There is little aesthetic pleasure in reading it.

But in late 1850 Thoreau began to find a new purpose for his journal. It was no longer to be primarily a source book for his other writings (although he still continued to use it occasionally for that purpose). He began to see it as a work of art in itself. It became no longer a means, but an end. On those more and more rare occasions when he did use it for a source book, he copied out those sections he wished to use rather than clipping them out. Thus the journal from that point on has its own integrity. And gradually it developed new characteristics. The entries became much longer. They became much less abstract. Commonplace book quotations disappeared almost completely. The entries began to develop a continuity. Thoreau himself became the central character, though in an artistic rather than an egotistic sense. It contains some of his very best writing and sustains that high level over long periods. It is a master work, but an extremely long one. Because of that tremendous length, the number of people who will read it in its entirety is inevitably limited in these days of rush and hurly-burly. But the true Thoreau connoisseur will not be deflected. I know of one couple who have read the entire journal aloud to each other and I envy them that experience. I know of a surprisingly large number of others (and I include myself among that group) who have read it through not only once, but two, three, four, or five times, and have found each reading more worthwhile than the one before — one of the true tests of a masterpiece.

In a volume of this sort, however, it is of course impossible to include even an extended section from the journal. What has been done here is to excerpt a series of selections, trying to give at least the flavor of the journal as a whole, hoping that it will whet the reader's appetite and tempt him to start on the full journal someday. The journal was first published in a fourteen-volume edition edited in 1906 by Bradford Torrey and Francis H. Allen as part of the twenty-volume Walden Edition of Thoreau's writings.

I. MYSELF

Oct. 22, 1837. 'What are you doing now?' he asked. 'Do you keep a journal?' So I make my first entry today.

June 4, 1839. I sit here this fourth of June, looking out on men and nature from this that I call my perspective window, through which all things are seen in their true relations. This is my upper empire, bounded by four walls, viz., three of boards yellow-washed, facing the north, west, and south, respectively, and the fourth of plaster, likewise yellow-washed, fronting the sunrise — to say nothing of the purlieus and outlying provinces, unexplored as yet but by rats.

June 22, 1839. I have within the last few days come into contact with a pure, uncompromising spirit, that is somewhere wandering in the atmosphere, but settles not positively anywhere. Some persons carry about them the air and conviction of virtue, though they themselves are unconscious of it, and are even backward to appreciate it in others. Such it is impossible not to love; still is their loveliness, as it were, independent of them, so that you seem not to lose it when they are absent, for when they are near it is like an invisible presence which attends you.

That virtue we appreciate is as much ours as another's. We see so much only as we possess.

March 21, 1840. The world is a fit theatre today in which any part may be acted. There is this moment proposed to me every kind of life that men lead anywhere, or that imagination can paint. By another spring I may be a mail-carrier in Peru, or a South African planter, or a Siberian exile, or a Greenland whaler, or a settler on the Columbia River, or a Canton merchant, or a soldier in Florida, or a mackerel-fisher off Cape Sable, or a Robinson Crusoe in the Pacific, or a silent navigator of any sea. So wide is the choice of parts, what a pity if the part of Hamlet be left out!

I am freer than any planet; no complaint reaches round the world. I can move away from public opinion, from government, from religion, from education, from society. Shall I be reckoned a ratable poll in the county of Middlesex, or be rated at one spear under the palm trees of Guinea? Shall I raise corn and potatoes in Massachusetts, or figs and olives in Asia Minor? sit out the day in my office in State Street, or ride it out on the steppes of Tartary? For my Brobdingnag I may sail to Patagonia; for my Lilliput, to Lapland. In Arabia and Persia, my day's adventures may surpass the Arabian Nights' Entertainments. I may be a logger on the head waters of the Penobscot, to be recorded in fable hereafter as an amphibious river-god, by as sounding a name as Triton or Proteus; carry furs from Nootka to China, and so be more renowned than Jason and his golden fleece; or go on a South Sea exploring expedition, to be hereafter recounted along with the periplus of Hanno. I may repeat the adventures of Marco Polo or Mandeville.

These are but few of my chances, and how many more things may I do with which there are none to be compared!

April 22, 1840. I cannot turn on my heel in a carpeted room. What a gap in the morning is a breakfast! A supper supersedes the sunset. . . .

Will not one thick garment suffice for three thin ones? Then I shall be less compound, and can lay my hand on myself in the dark.

June 21, 1840. I never feel that I am inspired unless my body is also. It too spurns a tame and commonplace life. They are fatally mistaken who think, while they strive with their minds, that they may suffer their bodies to stagnate in luxury or sloth. The body is the first proselyte the Soul makes. Our life is but the Soul made known by its fruits, the body. The whole duty of man may be expressed in one line — Make to yourself a perfect body.

June 25, 1840. Let me see no other conflict but with prosperity. If my path run on before me level and smooth, it is all a mirage; in reality it is steep and arduous as a chamois pass. I will not let the years roll over me like a Juggernaut car.

Jan. 23, 1841. The gods delight in stillness; they say, 'St — 'st. My truest, serenest moments are too still for emotion; they have woollen feet. In all our lives we live under the hill, and if we are not gone we live there still.

Jan. 25, 1841. We should strengthen, and beautify, and industriously mould our bodies to be fit companions of the soul — assist them to grow up like trees, and be agreeable and wholesome objects in nature. I think if I had had the disposal of this soul of man, I should have bestowed it sooner on some antelope of the plains than upon this sickly and sluggish body.

Feb. 3, 1841. We are constantly invited to be what we are; as to something worthy and noble. I never waited but for myself to come round; none ever detained me, but I lagged or tagged after myself.

March 3, 1841. As for these communities, I think I had rather keep bachelor's hall in hell than go to board in heaven. Do you think your virtue will be boarded with you? It will never live on the interest of your money, depend upon it. The boarder has no home. In heaven I hope to bake my own bread and clean my own linen. The tomb is the only boarding-house in which a hundred are served at once. In the catacomb we may dwell together and prop one another without loss.

March 27, 1841. I must not lose any of my freedom by being a farmer and landholder. Most who enter on·any profession are doomed men. The world might as well sing a dirge over them forthwith. The farmer's muscles are rigid. He can do one thing long, not many well. His pace seems determined henceforth; he never quickens it. A very rigid Nemesis is his fate. When the right wind blows or a star calls, I can leave this arable and grass ground, without making a will or settling my estate. I would buy a farm as freely as a silken streamer. Let me not think my front windows must face east henceforth because a particular hill slopes that way. My life must undulate still. I will not feel that my wings are clipped when once I have settled on ground which the law calls my own, but find new pinions grown to the old, and talaria to my feet beside.

[Dec.] 13, 1841. We constantly anticipate repose. Yet it surely can only be the repose that is in entire and healthy activity. It must be a

repose without rust. What is leisure but opportunity for more complete and entire action? Our energies pine for exercise. That time we spend in our duties is so much leisure, so that there is no man but has sufficient of it.

I make my own time, I make my own terms. I cannot see how God or Nature can ever get the start of me.

March 28, 1842. How often must one feel, as he looks back on his past life, that he has gained a talent but lost a character! My life has got down into my fingers. My inspiration at length is only so much breath as I can breathe.

April 30, 1851. Does not the history of chivalry and knight-errantry suggest or point to another relation to woman than leads to marriage, yet an elevating and all-absorbing one, perchance transcending marriage? As yet men know not one another, nor does man know woman.

I am sure that the design of my maker when he has brought me nearest to woman was not the propagation, but rather the maturation, of the species. Man is capable of a love of woman quite transcending marriage.

June 11, 1851. Ah, that life that I have known! How hard it is to remember what is most memorable! We remember how we itched, not how our hearts beat. I can sometimes recall to mind the quality, the immortality, of my youthful life, but in memory is the only relation to it.

July 6, 1851. There is some advantage in being the humblest, cheapest, least dignified man in the village, so that the very stable boys shall damn you. Methinks I enjoy that advantage to an unusual extent. There is many a coarsely.well-meaning fellow, who knows only the skin of me, who addresses me familiarly by my Christian name. I get the whole good of him and lose nothing myself. There is 'Sam,' the jailer — whom I never call Sam, however — who exclaimed last evening: 'Thoreau, are you going up the street pretty soon? Well, just take a couple of these handbills along and drop one in at Hoar's piazza and one at Holbrook's, and I'll do as much for you another time.' I am not above being used, aye abused, sometimes.

July 16, 1851. Methinks my present experience is nothing; my past experience is all in all. I think that no experience which I have today comes up to, or is comparable with, the experiences of my boyhood. And not only this is true, but as far back as I can remember I have unconsciously referred to the experiences of a previous state of existence, 'For life is a forgetting,' etc. Formerly, methought, nature developed as I developed, and grew up with me. My life was ecstasy. In youth, before I lost any of my senses, I can remember that I was all alive, and inhabited my body with inexpressible satisfaction; both its weariness and its refreshment were sweet to me. This earth was the most glorious musical instrument, and I was audience to its strains. To have such sweet impressions made on us, such ecstasies begotten of the breezes! I can remember how I was astonished. I said to myself — I said to others — 'There comes into my mind such an indescribable, infinite, all-absorbing, divine, heavenly pleasure, a sense of elevation and expansion, and [I] have had nought to do with it. I perceive that I am dealt with by superior powers. This is a pleasure, a joy, an existence which I have not procured myself. I speak as a witness on the stand, and tell what I have perceived.' The morning and the evening were sweet to me, and I led a life aloof from society of men. I wondered if a mortal had ever known what I knew. I looked in books for some recognition of a kindred experience, but, strange to say, I found none. Indeed, I was slow to discover that other men had had this experience, for it had been possible to read books and to associate with men on other grounds. The maker of me was improving me. When I detected this interference I was profoundly moved. For years I marched as to a music in comparison with which the military music of the streets is noise and discord. I was daily intoxicated, and yet no man could call me intemperate. With all your science can you tell how it is, and whence it is, that light comes into the soul?

Jan. 22, 1852. When a man asks me a question, I look him in the face. If I do not see any inquiry there, I cannot answer it. A man asked me about the coldness of this winter compared with others last night. I looked at him. His face expressed no more curiosity or relationship to me than a custard pudding. I made him a random answer. I put him off till he was in earnest. He wanted to make conversation.

Jan. 26, 1852. Obey the spur of the moment. These accumulated it is that make the impulse and the impetus of the life of genius. These are the spongioles or rootlets by which its trunk is fed. If you neglect the moments, if you cut off your fibrous roots, what but a languishing life is to be expected? Let the spurs of countless moments goad us incessantly into life. I feel the spur of the moment thrust deep into my side. The present is an inexorable rider. . . .

The truest account of heaven is the fairest, and I will accept none which disappoints expectation. It is more glorious to expect a better, than to enjoy a worse.

My life as essentially belongs to the present as that of a willow tree in the spring. Now, now, its catkins expand, its yellow bark shines, its sap flows; now or never must you make whistles of it. Get the day to back you; let it back you and the night.

April 11, 1852. (I hear the sound of the piano below as I write this, and feel as if the winter in me were at length beginning to thaw, for my spring has been even more backward than nature's. For a month past life has been a thing incredible to me. None but the kind gods can make me sane. If only they will let their south winds blow on me! I ask to be melted. You can only ask of the metals that they be tender to the fire that *melts* them. To naught else can they be tender.)

Aug. 24, 1852. Like cuttlefish we conceal ourselves, we darken the atmosphere in which we move; we are not transparent. I pine for one to whom I can speak my *first thoughts;* thoughts which represent me truly, which are no better and no worse than I; thoughts which have the bloom on them, which alone can be sacred and divine. Our sin and shame prevent our expressing even the innocent thoughts we have. I know of no one to whom I can be transparent instinctively. I live the life of the cuttlefish; another appears, and the element in which I move is tinged and I am concealed. My first thoughts are azure; there is a bloom and a dew on them; they are papillaceous feelers which I put out, tender, innocent. Only to a friend can I expose them. To all parties, though they be youth and maiden, if they are transparent to each other, and their thoughts can be expressed, there can be no further nakedness. I cannot be surprised by an intimacy which reveals the outside, when it has shown me the inside. The result of a full communication of our thoughts would be the immediate neglect of those coverings which a false modesty wears.

Jan. 3, 1853. I have a room all to myself; it is nature. It is a place beyond the jurisdiction of human governments. Pile up your books, the records of sadness, your saws and your laws. Nature is glad outside, and her merry worms within will ere long topple them down. There is a prairie beyond your laws. Nature is a prairie for outlaws. There are two worlds, the post-office and nature. I know them both. I continually forget mankind and their institutions, as I do a bank.

March 21, 1853. It is a genial and reassuring day; the mere warmth of the west wind amounts almost to balminess. The softness of the air mollifies our own dry and congealed substance. I sit down by a wall to see if I can muse again. We become, as it were, pliant and ductile again to strange but memorable influences; we are led a little way by our genius. We are affected like the earth, and yield to the elemental tenderness; winter breaks up within us; the frost is coming out of me, and I am heaved like the road; accumulated masses of ice and snow dissolve, and thoughts like a freshet pour down unwonted channels.

June 22, 1853. I long for wildness, a nature which I cannot put my foot through, woods where the wood thrush forever sings, where the hours are early morning ones, and there is dew on the grass, and the day is forever unproved, where I might have a fertile unknown for a soil about me. I would go after the cows, I would watch the flocks of Admetus there forever, only for my board and clothes. A New Hampshire everlasting and unfallen.

Sept. 12, 1853. It occurred to me when I awoke this morning, feeling regret for intemperance of the day before in eating fruit, which had dulled my sensibilities, that man was to be treated as a musical instrument, and if any viol was to be made of sound timber and kept well tuned always, it was he, so that when the bow of events is drawn across him he may vibrate and resound in perfect harmony. A sensitive soul will be continually trying its strings to see if they are in tune. A man's body must be rasped down exactly to a shaving. It is of far more importance than the wood of a Cremona violin.

Nov. 12, 1853. I cannot but regard it as a kindness in those who have the steering of me that, by the want of pecuniary wealth, I have been nailed down to this my native region so long and steadily, and made to study and love this spot of earth more and more. What would signify in comparison a thin and diffused love and knowledge of the whole earth instead, got by wandering? The traveller's is but a barren and comfortless condition. Wealth will not buy a man a home in nature — house nor farm there. The man of business does not by his business earn a residence in nature, but is denaturalized rather. What is a farm, house and land, office or shop, but a settlement in nature under the most favorable conditions? It is insignificant, and a merely negative good fortune, to be provided with thick garments against cold and wet, an unprofitable, weak, and defensive condition, compared with being able to extract some exhilaration, some warmth even, out of cold and wet themselves, and to clothe them with our sympathy. The rich man buys woollens and furs, and sits naked and shivering still in spirit, besieged by cold and wet. But the poor Lord of Creation, cold and wet he makes to warm him, and be his garments.

Dec. 22, 1853. Surveying the last three days. They have not yielded much that I am aware of. All I find is old boundmarks, and the slowness and dullness of farmers reconfirmed. They even complain that I walk too fast for them. Their legs have become stiff from toil. This coarse and hurried outdoor work compels me to live grossly or be inattentive to my diet; that is the worst of it. Like work, like diet; that, I find, is the rule. Left to my chosen pursuits, I should never drink tea nor coffee, nor eat meat. The diet of any class or generation is the natural result of its employment and locality. It is remarkable how unprofitable it is for the most part to talk with farmers. They commonly stand on their good behavior and attempt to moralize or philosophize in a serious conversation. Sportsmen and loafers are better company. For society a man must not be too *good* or well-disposed, to spoil his natural disposition. The bad are frequently good enough to let you see how bad they are, but the good as frequently endeavor [to] get between you and themselves.

I have dined out five times and tea'd once within a week. Four times there was tea on the dinner-table, always meat, but once baked beans, always pie, but no puddings. I suspect tea has taken the place of cider with farmers. I am reminded of Haydon the painter's experience when he went about painting the nobility. I go about to the houses of the farmers and squires in like manner. This is my portrait-painting — when I would fain be employed on higher subjects. I have offered myself much more earnestly as a lecturer than a surveyor. Yet I do not get any employment as a lecturer; was not invited to lecture once last winter, and only once (without pay) this winter. But I can get surveying enough, which a hundred others in this county can do as well as I, though it is not boasting much to say that a hundred others in New England cannot lecture as well as I on my themes. But they who do not make the highest demand on you shall rue it. It is because they make a low demand on themselves. All the while that they use only your humbler faculties, your higher unemployed faculties, like an invisible cimetar, are cutting them in twain. Woe be to the generation that lets any higher faculty in its midst go unemployed! That is to deny God and know him not, and he, accordingly, will know not of them.

May 10, 1854. In Boston yesterday an ornithologist said significantly, 'If you held the bird in your hand —;' but I would rather hold it in my affections.

May 23, 1854. How many springs shall I continue to see the common sucker (*Catostomus Bostoniensis*) floating dead on our river! Will not Nature select her types from a new fount? The vignette of the year.

This earth which is spread out like a map around me is but the lining of my inmost soul exposed. In me is the sucker that I see. No wholly extraneous object can compel me to recognize it. I am guilty of suckers.

Aug. 2, 1854. My attic chamber has compelled me to sit below with the family at evening for a month. I feel the necessity of deepening the stream of my life; I must cultivate privacy. It is very dissipating to be with people too much. As C. says, it takes the edge off a man's thoughts to have been much in society. I cannot spare my moonlight and my mountains for the best of man I am likely to get in exchange.

Aug. 31, 1856, P.M. There sits one by the shore who wishes to go with me, but I cannot think of it. I must be fancy-free. There is no such mote in the sky as a man who is not perfectly transparent to you — who has any opacity. I would rather attend to him earnestly for half an hour, on shore or elsewhere, and then dismiss him. He thinks I could merely take him into my boat and then not mind him. He does not realize that I should by the same act take him into my mind, where there is no room for him, and my bark would surely founder in such a voyage as I was contemplating. I know very well that I should never reach that expansion of the river I have in my mind, with him aboard with his broad terrene qualities. He would sink my bark (not to another sea) and never know it. I could better carry a heaped load of meadow mud and sit on the tholepins. There would be more room for me, and I should reach that expansion of the river nevertheless....

Some are so inconsiderate as to ask to walk or sail with me regularly every day — I have known such — and think that, because there will be six inches or a foot between our bodies, we shall not interfere! These things are settled by fate. The good ship sails — when she is ready. For freight or passage apply to —?? Ask my friend where. What is getting into a man's carriage when it is full, compared with putting your foot in his mouth and popping right into his mind without considering whether it is occupied or not? If I remember aright, it was only on condition *that you were asked*, that you were to go with a man one mile or twain. Suppose a man asks, not you to go with him, but to go with you! Often, I would rather undertake to shoulder a barrel of pork and carry it a mile than take into my company a man. It would not be so heavy a weight upon my mind. I could put it down and only feel my *back* ache for it.

Oct. 18, 1856. Men commonly exaggerate the theme. Some themes they think are significant and others insignificant. I feel that my life is very homely, my pleasures very cheap. Joy and sorrow, success and failure, grandeur and meanness, and indeed most words in the English language do not mean for me what they do for my neighbors. I see that my neighbors look with compassion on me, that they think it is a mean and unfortunate destiny which makes me to walk in these fields and woods so much and sail on this river alone. But so long as I find here the only real elysium, I cannot hesitate in my choice. My work is writing, and I do not hesitate, though I know that no subject is too trivial for me, tried by ordinary standards; for, ye fools, the theme is nothing, the life is everything. All that interests the reader is the depth and intensity of the life excited. We touch our subject but by a point which has no breadth, but the pyramid of our experience, or our interest in it, rests on us by a broader or narrower base. That is, man is all in all, Nature nothing, but as she draws him out and reflects him. Give me simple, cheap, and homely themes.

Dec. 5, 1856. My themes shall not be far-fetched. I will tell of homely every-day phenomena and adventures. Friends! Society! It seems to me that I have an abundance of it, there is so much that I rejoice and sympathize with, and men, too, that I never speak to but only know and think of. What you call bareness and poverty is to me simplicity. God could not be unkind to me if he should try. I love the winter, with its imprisonment and its cold, for it compels the prisoner to try new fields and resources. I love to have the river closed up for a season and a pause put to my boating, to be obliged to get my boat in. I shall launch it again in the spring with so much more pleasure. This is an advantage in point of abstinence and moderation compared with the seaside boating, where the boat ever lies on the shore. I love best to have each thing in its season only, and enjoy doing without it at all other times. It is the greatest of all advantages to enjoy no advantage at all. I find it invariably true, the poorer I am, the richer I am. What you consider my disadvantage, I consider my advantage. While you are pleased to get knowledge and culture in many ways, I am delighted to think that I am getting rid of them. I have never got over my surprise that I should have been born into the most estimable place in all the world, and in the very nick of time, too.

Jan. 7, 1857. There is nothing so sanative, so poetic, as a walk in the woods and fields even now, when I meet none abroad for pleasure. Nothing so inspires me and excites such serene and profitable thought. The objects are elevating. In the street and in society I am almost invariably cheap and dissipated, my life is unspeakably mean. No amount of gold or respectability would in the least redeem it — dining with the Governor or a member of Congress!! But alone in distant woods or fields, in unpretending sprout-lands or pastures tracked by rabbits, even in a bleak and, to most, cheerless day, like this, when a villager would be thinking of his inn, I come to myself, I once more feel myself grandly related, and that cold and solitude are friends of mine. I suppose that this value, in my case, is equivalent to what others get by churchgoing and prayer. I come to my solitary woodland walk as the homesick go home. I thus dispose of the superfluous and see things as they are, grand and beautiful. I have told many that I walk every day about half the daylight, but I think they do not believe it. I wish to get the Concord, the Massachusetts, the America, out of my head and be sane a part of every day. If there are missionaries for the heathen, why not send them to me? I wish to know something; I wish to be made better. I wish to forget, a considerable part of every day, all mean, narrow, trivial men (and this requires usually to forego and forget all personal relations so long), and therefore I come out to these solitudes, where the problem of existence is simplified. I get away a mile or two from the town into the stillness and solitude of nature, with rocks, trees, weeds, snow about me. I enter some glade in the woods, perchance, where a few weeds and dry leaves alone lift themselves above the surface of the snow, and it is as if I had come to an open window. I see out and around myself. Our *skylights* are thus far away from the ordinary resorts of men. I am not satisfied with ordinary windows. I must have a true *skylight*. My true skylight is on the outside of the village. I am not thus expanded, recreated, enlightened, when I meet a company of men. It chances that the sociable, the town and county, or the farmers' club does not prove a skylight to me. I do not invariably find myself translated under those circumstances. They bore me. The man I meet with is not often so instructive as the silence he breaks. This stillness, solitude, wildness of nature is a kind of thoroughwort, or boneset, to my intellect. This is what I go out to seek. It is as if I always met in those places some grand, serene, immortal, infinitely encouraging, though invisible, companion, and walked with him. There at last my nerves are steadied, my senses and my mind do their office. I am aware that most of my neighbors would think it a hardship to be compelled to linger here one hour, especially this bleak day, and yet I receive this sweet and ineffable compensation for it. It is the most agreeable thing I do. Truly, my coins are uncurrent with them. . . . But away out of the town, on Brown's scrub oak lot, which was sold the other day for six dollars an acre, I have company such as England cannot buy, nor afford.

Aug. 9, 1858. The mind tastes but few flavors in the course of a year. We are visited by but few thoughts which are worth entertaining, and we chew the cud of these unceasingly. What ruminant spirits we are! I remember well the flavor of that rusk which I bought in New York two or three months ago and ate in the cars for my supper. A fellow-passenger, too, pretended to praise it, and yet, O man of little faith! he took a regular supper at Springfield. They cannot make such in Boston. The mere fragrance, rumor, and reminiscence of life is all that we get, for the most part. If I am visited by a thought, I chew that cud each successive morning, as long as there is any flavor in it. Until my keepers shake down some fresh fodder. Our genius is like a brush which only once in many months is freshly dipped into the paint-pot. It becomes so dry that though we apply it incessantly, it fails to tinge our earth and sky. Applied to the same spot incessantly, it at length imparts no color to it.

Dec. 19, 1859. When a man is young and his constitution and body have not acquired firmness, *i.e.*, before he has arrived at middle age, he is not an assured inhabitant of the earth, and his compensation is that he is not quite earthy, there is something peculiarly tender and divine about him. His sentiments and his weakness, nay, his very sickness and the greater uncertainty of his fate, seem to ally him to a noble race of beings, to whom he in part belongs, or with whom he is in communication. The young man is a demigod; the grown man, alas! is commonly a mere mortal. He is but half here, he knows not the men of this world, the powers that be. They know him not. Prompted by the reminiscence of that other sphere from which he so lately arrived, his actions are unintelligible to his seniors. He bathes in light. He is interesting as a stranger from another sphere. He really thinks and talks about a larger sphere of existence than this world. It takes him forty years to accommodate himself to the carapax of this world. This is the age of poetry. Afterward he may be the president of a bank, and go the way of all flesh. But a man of settled views, whose thoughts are few and hardened like his bones, is truly mortal, and his only resource is to say his prayers.

II. WHAT I LIVED FOR

Dec. 26, 1841. Sin, I am sure, is not in overt acts or, indeed, in acts of any kind, but is in proportion to the time which has come behind us and displaced eternity — that degree to which our elements are mixed with the elements of the world. The whole duty of life is contained in the question how to respire and aspire both at once.

Dec. 31, 1841. There is a singular health for me in those words Labrador and East Main which no desponding creed recognizes. How much more than federal are these States! If there were no other vicissitudes but the seasons, with their attendant and consequent changes, our interest would never flag. Much more is a-doing than Congress wots of in the winter season. What journal do the persimmon and buckeye keep, or the sharp-shinned hawk? What is transpiring from summer to winter in the Carolinas, and the Great Pine Forest, and the Valley of the Mohawk? The merely political aspect of the land is never very cheering. Men are degraded when considered as the members of a political organization. As a nation the people never utter one great and healthy word. From this side all nations present only the symptoms of disease. I see but Bunker's Hill and Sing Sing, the District of Columbia and Sullivan's Island, with a few avenues connecting them. But paltry are all these beside one blast of the east or south wind which blows over them all.

[1837–47.] It has not been my design to live cheaply, but only to live as I could, not devoting much time to getting a living. I made the most of what means were already got.

[1837–47.] Almost any man knows how to earn money, but not one in a million knows how to spend it. If he had known so much as this, he would never have earned it.

Feb. 27, 1851. The lecturer is wont to describe the Nineteenth Century, the American [of] the last generation, in an off-hand and triumphant strain, wafting him to paradise, spreading his fame by steam and telegraph, recounting the number of wooden stopples he has whittled. But who does not perceive that this is not a sincere or pertinent account of any man's or nation's life? It is the hip-hip-hurrah and mutual-admiration-society style. Cars go by, and we know their substance as well as their shadow. They stop and we get into them. But those sublime thoughts passing on high do not stop, and we never get into them. Their conductor is not like one of us.

Sept. 7, 1851. The scenery, when it is truly seen, reacts on the life of the seer. How to live. How to get the most life. As if you were to teach the young hunter how to entrap his game. How to extract its honey from the flower of the world. That is my every-day business. I am as busy as a bee about it. I ramble over all fields on that errand, and am never so happy as when I feel myself heavy with honey and wax. I am like a bee searching the livelong day for the sweets of nature. Do I not impregnate and intermix the flowers, produce rare and finer varieties by transferring my eyes from one to another? I do as naturally and as joyfully, with my own humming music, seek honey all the day. ... The art of spending a day. If it is possible that we may be addressed, it behooves us to be attentive. If by watching all day and all night I may detect some trace of the Ineffable, then will it not be worth the while to watch? Watch and pray without ceasing, but not necessarily in sadness. Be of good cheer. Those Jews were too sad: to another people a still deeper revelation may suggest only joy. Don't I know what gladness is? Is it but the reflex of sadness, its back side? In the Hebrew gladness, I hear but too distinctly still the sound of sadness retreating. Give me a gladness which has never given place to sadness.

Dec. 28, 1852. It is worth the while to apply what wisdom one has to the conduct of his life, surely. I find myself oftenest wise in little things and foolish in great ones. That I may accomplish some particular petty affair well, I live my whole life coarsely. A broad margin of leisure is as beautiful in a man's life as in a book. Haste makes waste, no less in life than in housekeeping. Keep the time, observe the hours of the universe, not of the cars. What are threescore years and ten hurriedly and coarsely lived to moments of divine leisure in which your life is coincident with the life of the universe? We live too fast and coarsely, just as we eat too fast, and do not know the true savor of our food. We consult our will and understanding and the expectation of men, not our genius. I can impose upon myself tasks which will crush me for life and prevent all expansion, and this I am but too inclined to do.

March 5, 1853. The secretary of the Association for the Advancement of Science requests me, as he probably has thousands of others, by a printed circular letter from Washington the other day, to fill the blank against certain questions, among which the most important one was what branch of science I was specially interested in, using the term science in the most comprehensive sense possible. Now, though I could state to a select few that department of human inquiry which engages me, and should be rejoiced at an opportunity to do so, I felt that it would be to make myself the laughing-stock of the scientific community to describe or attempt to describe to them that branch of science which specially interests me, inasmuch as they do not believe in a science which deals with the higher law. So I was obliged to speak to their condition and describe to them that poor part of me which alone they can understand. The fact is I am a mystic, a transcendentalist, and a natural philosopher to boot. Now I think of it, I should have told them at once that I was a transcendentalist. That would have been the shortest way of telling them that they would not understand my explanations.

May 10, 1853. He is the richest who has most use for nature as raw material of tropes and symbols with which to describe his life. If these gates of golden willows affect me, they correspond to the beauty and promise of some experience on which I am entering. If I am overflowing with life, am rich in experience for which I lack expression, then nature will be my language full of poetry — all nature will *fable*, and every natural phenomenon be a myth. The man of science, who is not seeking for expression but for a fact to be expressed merely, studies nature as a dead language. I pray for such inward experience as will make nature significant.

Sept. 1, 1853. The savage lives simply through ignorance and idleness or laziness, but the philosopher lives simply through wisdom. In the case of the savage, the accompaniment of simplicity is idleness with its attendant vices, but in the case of the philosopher, it is the highest employment and development. The fact for the savage, and for the mass of mankind, is that it is better to plant, weave, and build than do nothing or worse; but the fact for the philosopher, or a nation loving wisdom, is that it is most important to cultivate the highest faculties and spend as little time as possible in planting, weaving, building, etc. It depends upon the height of your standard, and no doubt through manual labor as a police men are educated up to a certain level. The simple style is bad for the savage because he does worse than to obtain the luxuries of life; it is good for the philosopher because he does better than to work for them. The question is whether you can bear freedom. At present the vast majority of men, whether black or white, require the discipline of labor which enslaves them for their good. If the Irishman did not shovel all day, he would get drunk and quarrel. But the philosopher does not require the same discipline; if he shovelled all day, we should receive no elevating suggestions from him.

Jan. 1, 1854. The snow is the great betrayer. It not only shows the track of mice, otters, etc., etc., which else we should rarely, if ever, see, but the tree sparrows are more plainly seen against its white ground, and they in turn are attracted by the dark weeds it reveals. It also drives the crows and other birds out of the woods to the villages for food. We might expect to find in the snow the footprint of a life superior to our own, of which no zoölogy takes cognizance. Is there no trace of a nobler life than that of an otter or an escaped convict to be looked for in it? Shall we suppose that is the only life that has been abroad in the night? It is only the savage that can see the track of no higher life than an otter's. Why do the vast snow plains give us pleasure, the twilight of the bent and half-buried woods? Is not all there consonant with virtue, justice, purity, courage, magnanimity; and does not all this amount to the track of a higher life than the otter's, a life which has not gone by and left a footprint merely,[1] but is there with its beauty, its music, its perfume, its sweetness, to exhilarate and re-create us? Where there is a perfect government of the world according to the highest laws, is there no trace of intelligence there, whether in the snow, or the earth, or in ourselves? No other trail but such as a dog can scent? Is there none which an angel can detect and follow? None to guide a man on his pilgrimage, which water will not conceal? Is there no odor of sanctity to be perceived? Is its trail too old? Have mortals lost the scent? The great game for mighty hunters as soon as the first snow falls is Purity, for, earlier than any rabbit or fox, it is abroad, and its trail may be detected by curs of lowest degree. Did this great snow come to reveal the track merely of some timorous hare, or of the Great Hare, whose track no hunter has seen? Is there no trace nor suggestion of Purity to be detected? If one could detect the meaning of the snow, would he not be on the trail of some higher life that has been abroad in the night? Are there not hunters who seek for something higher than foxes, with judgment more discriminating than the senses of fox-hounds, who rally to a nobler music than that of the hunting-horn? As there is contention among the fishermen who shall be the first to reach the pond as soon as the ice will bear, in spite of the cold, as the hunters are for-

---

[1] But all that we see is the impress of its spirit.

ward to take the field as soon as the first snow has fallen, so the observer, or he who would make the most of his life for discipline, must be abroad early and late, in spite of cold and wet, in pursuit of nobler game, whose traces are then most distinct. A life [1] which, pursued, does not earth itself, does not burrow downward but upward, which takes not to the trees but to the heavens as its home, which the hunter pursues with winged thoughts and aspirations — these the dogs that tree it — rallying his pack with the bugle notes of undying faith, and returns with some worthier trophy than a fox's tail, a life which we seek, not to destroy it, but to save our own. Is the great snow of use to the hunter only, and not to the saint, or him who is earnestly building up a life? Do the Indian and hunter only need snow-shoes, while the saint sits indoors in embroidered slippers?

May 6, 1854. There is no such thing as pure *objective* observation. Your observation, to be interesting, *i.e.* to be significant, must be *subjective*. The sum of what the writer of whatever class has to report is simply some human experience, whether he be poet or philosopher or man of science. The man of most science is the man most alive, whose life is the greatest event. Senses that take cognizance of outward things merely are of no avail. It matters not where or how far you travel — the farther commonly the worse — but how much alive you are. If it is possible to conceive of an event outside to humanity, it is not of the slightest significance, though it were the explosion of a planet. Every important worker will report what life there is in him. . . . All that a man has to say or do that can possibly concern mankind, is in some shape or other to tell the story of his love — to sing, and, if he is fortunate and keeps alive, he will be forever in love. This alone is to be alive to the extremities.

Nov. 5, 1855. I hate the present modes of living and getting a living. Farming and shopkeeping and working at a trade or profession are all odious to me. I should relish getting my living in a simple, primitive fashion. The life which society proposes to me to live is so artificial and complex — bolstered up on many weak supports, and sure to topple down at last — that no man surely can ever be inspired to live it, and only 'old fogies' ever praise it. At best some think it their duty to live it. I believe in the infinite joy and satisfaction of helping myself and others to the extent of my ability. But what is the use in trying to live simply, raising what you eat, making what you wear, building what you inhabit, burning what you cut or dig, when those to whom you

---

[1] H. G. O. Blake's transcription of this passage (Concord ed., X, p. 91) adds 'which we seek not to destroy, but to make our own.'

are allied insanely want and will have a thousand other things which neither you nor they can raise and nobody else, perchance, will pay for? The fellow-man to whom you are yoked is a steer that is ever bolting right the other way.

Nov. 18, 1855. Instead of walking in the wood-market amid sharp-visaged teamsters, I float over dark reflecting waters in which I see mirrored the stumps on the bank, and am dazzled by the beauty of a summer duck. Though I should get no wood, I should get a beauty perhaps more valuable. The price of this my wood, however high, is the very thing which I delight to pay. What I obtain with the most labor — the most water-logged and heaviest wood which I fish up from the bottom and split and dry — warms the most. The greater, too, the distance from which I have conveyed it, the more I am warmed by it in my thought. All the intervening shores glow and are warmed by it as it passes, or as I repass them in my mind. And yet men will cut their wood with sorrow, and burn it with lucifer matches. This was where I drove my team afield, and, instead of the grey-fly, I heard the wood tortoises even yet rustling through the sedge to the water, or the gray squirrel coursing from maple to maple.

March 11, 1856. When it was proposed to me to go abroad, rub off some rust, and *better my condition* in a worldly sense, I fear lest my life will lose some of its homeliness. If these fields and streams and woods, the phenomena of nature here, and the simple occupations of the inhabitants should cease to interest and inspire me, no culture or wealth would atone for the loss. I fear the dissipation that travelling, going into society, even the best, the enjoyment of intellectual luxuries, imply. If Paris is much in your mind, if it is more and more to you, Concord is less and less, and yet it would be a wretched bargain to accept the proudest Paris in exchange for my native village. At best, Paris could only be a school in which to learn to live here, a stepping-stone to Concord, a school in which to fit for this university. I wish so to live ever as to derive my satisfactions and inspirations from the commonest events, every-day phenomena, so that what my senses hourly perceive, my daily walk, the conversation of my neighbors, may inspire me, and I may dream of no heaven but that which lies about me. A man may acquire a taste for wine or brandy, and so lose his love for water, but should we not pity him?

Aug. 30, 1856. Our employment generally is tinkering, mending the old worn-out teapot of society. Our stock in trade is solder. Better for me, says my genius, to go cranberrying this afternoon for the *Vaccinium*

Oxycoccus in Gowing's Swamp, to get but a pocketful and learn its peculiar flavor, aye, and the flavor of Gowing's Swamp and of *life* in New England, than to go consul to Liverpool and get I don't know how many thousand dollars for it, with no such flavor. Many of our days should be spent, not in vain expectations and lying on our oars, but in carrying out deliberately and faithfully the hundred little purposes which every man's genius must have suggested to him. Let not your life be wholly without an object, though it be only to ascertain the flavor of a cranberry, for it will not be only the quality of an insignificant berry that you will have tasted, but the flavor of your life to that extent, and it will be such a sauce as no wealth can buy.

Both a conscious and an unconscious life are good. Neither is good exclusively, for both have the same source. The wisely conscious life springs out of an unconscious suggestion. I have found my account in travelling in having prepared beforehand a list of questions which I would get answered, not trusting to my interest at the moment, and can then travel with the most profit. Indeed, it is by obeying the suggestions of a higher light within you that you escape from yourself and, in the transit, as it were see with the unworn sides of your eye, travel totally new paths. What is that pretended life that does not take up a claim, that does not occupy ground, that cannot build a causeway to its objects, that sits on a bank looking over a bog, singing its desires?

Oct. 26, 1857. These regular phenomena of the seasons get at last to be — they were *at first*, of course — simply and plainly phenomena or phases of my life. The seasons and all their changes are in me. I see not a dead eel or floating snake, or a gull, but it rounds my life and is like a line or accent in its poem. Almost I believe the Concord would not rise and overflow its banks again, were I not here. After a while I learn what my moods and seasons are. I would have nothing subtracted. I can imagine nothing added. My moods are thus periodical, not two days in my year alike. The perfect correspondence of Nature to man, so that he is at home in her! . . .

Those sparrows, too, are thoughts I have. They come and go; they flit by quickly on their migrations, uttering only a faint *chip*, I know not whither or why exactly. One will not rest upon its twig for me to scrutinize it. The whole copse will be alive with my rambling thoughts, bewildering me by their very multitude, but they will be all gone directly without leaving me a feather. My loftiest thought is somewhat like an eagle that suddenly comes into the field of view, suggesting great things and thrilling the beholder, as if it were bound hitherward with a message for me; but it comes no nearer, but circles and soars away, growing dimmer, disappointing me, till it is lost behind a cliff or a cloud.

Nov. 18, 1857. In one light, these are old and worn-out fields that I ramble over, and men have gone to law about them long before I was born, but I trust that I ramble over them in a new fashion and redeem them.

March 25, 1859. A score of my townsmen have been shooting and trapping musquash and mink of late. Some have got nothing else to do. If they should strike for higher wages now, instead of going to the clam-banks, as the Lynn shoemakers propose, they would go to shooting musquash. They are gone all day; early and late they scan the rising tide; stealthily they set their traps in remote swamps, avoiding one another. Am not I a trapper too, early and late scanning the rising flood, ranging by distant woodsides, setting my traps in solitude, and baiting them as well as I know how, that I may catch life and light, that my intellectual part may taste some venison and be invigorated, that my nakedness may be clad in some wild, furry warmth?

III. CONCORD

Jan. 21, 1838. Such is beauty ever — neither here nor there, now nor then — neither in Rome nor in Athens, but wherever there is a soul to admire. If I seek her elsewhere because I do not find her at home, my search will prove a fruitless one.

July 11, 1839. At length we leave the river and take to the road which leads to the hilltop, if by any means we may spy out what manner of earth we inhabit. East, west, north, and south, it is farm and parish, this world of ours. One may see how at convenient, eternal intervals men have settled themselves, without thought for the universe. How little matters it all they have built and delved there in the valley! It is after all but a feature in the landscape. Still the vast impulse of nature breathes over all. The eternal winds sweep across the interval *today,* bringing mist and haze to shut out their works. Still the crow caws from Nawshawtuct to Annursnack, as no feeble tradesman nor smith may do. And in all swamps the hum of mosquitoes drowns this modern hum of industry.

June 20, 1850. And then for my afternoon walks I have a garden, larger than any artificial garden that I have read of and far more attractive to me — mile after mile of embowered walks, such as no nobleman's grounds can boast, with animals running free and wild therein as from the first — varied with land and water prospect, and, above all, so retired that it is extremely rare that I meet a single wanderer in its mazes. No gardener is seen therein, no gates nor [*sic*]. You may wander away to solitary bowers and brooks and hills.

July 20, 1851. A thunder-shower in the night. Thunder near at hand, though louder, is a more trivial and earthly sound than at a distance; likened to sounds of men. The clap which waked me last night was as if some one was moving lumber in an upper apartment, some vast hollow hall, tumbling it down and dragging it over the floor; and ever and anon the lightning filled the damp air.with light, like some vast glow-worm in the fields of ether opening its wings.

The river, too, steadily yields its crop. In louring days it is remarkable how many villagers resort to it. It is of more worth than many gardens. I meet one, late in the afternoon, going to the river with his basket on his arm and his pole in hand, not ambitious to catch pickerel this time, but he thinks he may perhaps get a mess of small fish. These [*sic*] kind of values are real and important, though but little appreciated, and he is not a wise legislator who underrates them and allows the bridges to be built low so as to prevent the passage of small boats. The town is but little conscious how much interest it has in the river, and might vote it away any day thoughtlessly. There is always to be seen either some unshaven wading man, an old mower of the river meadows, familiar with water, vibrating his long pole over the lagoons of the off-shore pads, or else some solitary fisher, in a boat behind the willows, like a mote in the sunbeams reflecting the light; and who can tell how many a mess of river fish is daily cooked in the town? They are an important article of food to many a poor family.

Aug. 23, 1851. Our little river reaches are not to be forgotten. I noticed that seen northward on the Assabet from the Causeway Bridge near the second stone bridge. There was [a] man in a boat in the sun, just disappearing in the distance round a bend, lifting high his arms and dipping his paddle as if he were a vision bound to land of the blessed — far off, as in picture. When I see Concord to purpose, I see it as if it were not real but painted, and what wonder if I do not

speak to *thee?* I saw a snake by the roadside and touched him with my
foot to see if he were alive. He had a toad in his jaws, which he was
preparing to swallow with his jaws distended to three times his width,
but he relinquished his prey in haste and fled; and I thought, as the
toad jumped leisurely away with his slime-covered hind-quarters
glistening in the sun, as if I, his deliverer, wished to interrupt his meditations — without a shriek or fainting — I thought what a healthy
indifference he manifested. Is not this the broad earth still? he said.

Aug. 31, 1851. With what sober joy I stand to let the water drip from
me and feel my fresh vigor, who have been bathing in the same tub
which the muskrat uses! Such a medicated bath as only nature furnishes. A fish leaps, and the dimple he makes is observed now. How
ample and generous was nature! My inheritance is not narrow. Here
is no other this evening. Those resorts which I most love and frequent,
numerous and vast as they are, are as it were given up to me, as much
as if I were an autocrat or owner of the world, and by my edicts excluded men from my territories. Perchance there is some advantage
here not enjoyed in older countries. There are said to be two thousand
inhabitants in Concord, and yet I find such ample space and verge,
even miles of walking every day in which I do not meet nor see a human
being, and often not very recent traces of them. So much of man as
there is in your mind, there will be in your eye. Methinks that for a
great part of the time, as much as it is possible, I walk as one possessing
the advantages of human culture, fresh from society of men, but turned
loose into the woods, the only man in nature, walking and meditating to
a great extent as if man and his customs and institutions were not. The
catbird, or the jay, is sure of the whole of your ear now. Each noise
is like a stain on pure glass. The rivers now, these great blue subterranean heavens, reflecting the supernal skies and red-tinted clouds.

Aug. 31, 1851. I talked of buying Conantum once, but for want of
money we did not come to terms. But I have farmed it in my own
fashion every year since.

Nov. 7, 1851. Close by we found Long Pond, in Wayland, Framingham, and Natick, a great body of water with singularly sandy, shelving,
caving, undermined banks; and there we ate our luncheon. The mayflower leaves we saw there, and the *Viola pedata* in blossom. We went
down it a mile or two on the east side through the woods on its high
bank, and then dined, looking far down to what seemed the Boston
outlet (opposite to its natural outlet), where a solitary building stood
on the shore. It is a wild and stretching loch, where yachts might sail

— Cochituate. It was not only larger but wilder and more novel than I had expected. In some respects unlike New England. I could hardly have told in what part of the world I was, if I had been carried there blindfolded. Yet some features, at least the composition of the soil, were familiar. The glorious sandy banks far and near, caving and sliding — far sandy slopes, the forts of the land — where you see the naked flesh of New England, her garment being blown aside like that of the priests (of the Levites?) when they ascend to the altar. Seen through this November sky, these sands are dear to me, worth all the gold of California, suggesting Pactolus, while the Saxonville factory-bell sounds o'er the woods. That sound perchance it is that whets my vision. The shore suggests the seashore, and two objects at a distance near the shore look like seals on a sand-bar. Dear to me to lie in, this sand; fit to preserve the bones of a race for thousands of years to come. And this is my home, my native soil; and I am a New-Englander. Of thee, O earth, are my bone and sinew made; to thee, O sun, am I brother. . . . To this dust my body will gladly return as to its origin. Here have I my habitat. I am of thee.

Nov. 8, 1851. Ah, those sun-sparkles on Dudley Pond in this November air! what a heaven to live in! Intensely brilliant, as no artificial light I have seen, like a dance of diamonds. Coarse mazes of a diamond dance seen through the trees. All objects shine today, even the sportsmen seen at a distance, as if a cavern were unroofed, and its crystals gave entertainment to the sun. This great seesaw of brilliants, the ἀνήριθμον γέλασμα. . . . When I saw the bare sand at Cochituate I felt my relation to the soil. These are *my* sands not yet run out. Not yet will the fates turn the glass. This air have I title to taint with my decay. In this clean sand my bones will gladly lie. Like *Viola pedata*, I shall be ready to bloom again here in my Indian summer days. Here ever springing, never dying, with perennial root I stand; for the winter of the land is warm to me. While the flowers bloom again as in the spring, shall I pine? When I see her sands exposed, thrown up from beneath the surface, it touches me inwardly, it reminds me of my origin; for I am such a plant, so native to New England, methinks, as springs from the sand cast up from below.

Jan. 27, 1852. As I stand under the hill beyond J. Hosmer's and look over the plains westward toward Acton and see the farmhouses nearly half a mile apart, few and solitary, in these great fields between these stretching woods, out of the world, where the children have to go far to school; the still, stagnant, heart-eating, life-everlasting, and gone-to-seed country, so far from the post-office where the weekly paper comes, wherein the new-married wife cannot live for loneliness, and the young man has to depend upon his horse for society; see young J. Hosmer's house, whither he returns with his wife in despair after living in the city — I standing in Tarbell's road, which he alone cannot break out — the world in winter for most walkers reduced to a sled track winding far through the drifts, all springs sealed up and no digressions; where the old man thinks he may possibly afford to rust it out, not having long to live, but the young man pines to get nearer the post-office and the Lyceum, is restless and resolves to go to California, because the depot is a mile off (he hears the rattle of the cars at a distance and thinks the world is going by and leaving him); where rabbits and partridges multiply, and muskrats are more numerous than ever, and none of the farmer's sons are willing to be farmers, and the apple trees are decayed, and the cellar-holes are more numerous than the houses, and the rails are covered with lichens, and the old maids wish to sell out and move into the village, and have waited twenty years in vain for this purpose and never finished but one room in the house, never plastered nor painted, inside or out, lands which the Indian was long since dispossessed [of], and now the farms are run out, and what were forests are grain-fields, what were grain-fields, pastures; dwellings which only those Arnolds of the wilderness, those *coureurs de bois*, the baker and the butcher visit, to which at least the latter penetrates for the annual calf — and as he returns the cow lows after; — whither the villager never penetrates, but in huckleberry time, perchance, and if he does not, who does? — where some men's breaths smell of rum, having smuggled in a jugful to alleviate their misery and solitude; where the owls give a regular serenade; — I say, standing there and seeing these things, I cannot realize that this is that hopeful young America which is famous throughout the world for its activity and enterprise, and this is the most thickly settled and Yankee part of it. What must be the condition of the *old* world! The *sphagnum* must by this time have concealed it from the eye.

July 25, 1852. From Fair Haven Hill, the sun having risen, I see great wreaths of fog far northeast, revealing the course of the river, a noble sight, as it were the river elevated, or rather the ghost of the ample stream that once flowed to ocean between these now distant uplands in another geological period, filling the broad meadows — the dews saved to the earth by this great Musketaquid condenser, refrigerator. And now the rising sun makes glow with downiest white the ample wreaths, which rise higher than the highest trees. The farmers that lie slumbering on this their day of rest, how little do they know of this stupendous pageant! The bright, fresh aspect of the woods glistening with moisture when the early sun falls on them. (As I came along, the whole earth resounded with the crowing of cocks, from the eastern unto the western horizon, and as I passed a yard, I saw a white rooster on the topmost rail of a fence pouring forth his challenges for destiny to come on. This salutation was travelling round the world; some six hours since had resounded through England, France, and Spain; then the sun passed over a belt of silence where the Atlantic flows, except a clarion here and there from some cooped-up cock upon the waves, till greeted with a general all-hail along the Atlantic shore.) Looking now from the rocks, the fog is a perfect sea over the great Sudbury meadows in the southwest, commencing at the base of this Cliff and reaching to the hills south of Wayland, and further still to Framingham, through which only the tops of the higher hills are seen as islands, great bays of the sea, many miles across, where the largest fleets would find ample room and in which countless farms and farmhouses are immersed. The fog rises highest over the channel of the river and over the ponds in the woods which are thus revealed. I clearly distinguish where White Pond lies by this sign, and various other ponds, methinks, to which I have walked ten or twelve miles distant, and I distinguish the course of the Assabet far in the west and southwest beyond the woods. Every valley is densely packed with the downy vapor. What levelling on a great scale is done thus for the eye! The fog rises to the top of Round Hill in the Sudbury meadows, whose sunburnt yellow grass makes it look like a low sand-bar in the ocean, and I can judge thus pretty accurately what hills are higher than this by their elevation above the surface of the fog. Every meadow and watercourse makes an arm of this bay. The primeval banks make thus a channel which only the fogs of late summer and autumn fill. The Wayland hills make a sort of promontory or peninsula like some Nahant. As I look across thither, I think of the sea monsters that swim in that sea and of the wrecks that strew the bottom, many fathom deep, where, in an hour, when this sea dries up, farms will smile and farmhouses be revealed. A certain thrilling vastness or wasteness it now suggests. This is one of those ambrosial, white, ever-memorable fogs presaging fair weather. It produces the most picturesque and grandest effects as it rises, and travels hither and thither, enveloping and concealing trees and forests and hills. It is lifted up now into quite a little white mountain over Fair Haven Bay, and, even on its skirts, only the tops of the highest pines are seen above it, and all adown the river it has an uneven outline like a rugged mountain ridge; in one place some rainbow tints, and far, far in the south horizon, near the further verge of the sea (over Saxonville?) it is heaved up into great waves, as if there were breakers there. In the meanwhile the wood thrush and the jay and the robin sing around me here, and birds are heard singing from the midst of the fog. And in one short hour this sea will all evaporate and the sun be reflected from farm windows on its green bottom.

Jan. 7, 1855. The delicious soft, spring-suggesting air — how it fills my veins with life! Life becomes again credible to me. A certain dormant life awakes in me, and I begin to love nature again. Here is my Italy, my heaven, my New England. I understand why the Indians hereabouts placed heaven in the southwest — the soft south.

Jan. 22, 1856. I have attended the felling and, so to speak, the funeral of this old citizen of the town — I who commonly do not attend funerals — as it became me to do. I was the chief if not the only mourner there. I have taken the measure of his grandeur; have spoken a few words of eulogy at his grave, remembering the maxim *de mortuis nil nisi bonum* (in this case *magnum*). But there were only the choppers and the passers-by to hear me. Further the town was not represented; the fathers of the town, the selectmen, the clergy were not there. But I have not known a fitter occasion for a sermon of late. Travellers whose journey was for a short time delayed by its prostrate body were forced to pay it some attention and respect, but the axe-boys had climbed upon it like ants, and commenced chipping at it before it had fairly ceased groaning. There was a man already bargaining for some part. How have the mighty fallen! Its history extends back over more than half the whole history of the town. Since its kindred could not conveniently attend, I attended. Methinks its fall marks an epoch in the history of the town. It has passed away together with the clergy of the old school and the stage-coach which used to rattle beneath it. Its virtue was that it steadily grew and expanded from year to year to the very last. How much of old Concord falls with it! The town clerk will not chronicle its fall. I will, for it is of greater moment to the town than that of many a human inhabitant would be. Instead of erecting a monument to it, we take all possible pains to obliterate its stump, the only monument of a tree which is commonly allowed to stand. Another link that bound us to the past is broken. How much of old Concord was cut away with it! A few such elms would alone constitute a township. They might claim to send a representative to the General Court to look after their interests, if a fit one could be found, a native American one in a true and worthy sense, with catholic principles. Our town has lost some of its venerableness. No longer will our eyes rest on its massive gray trunk, like a vast Corinthian column by the wayside; no longer shall we walk in the shade of its lofty, spreading dome. It is as if you had laid the axe at the feet of some venerable Buckley or Ripley. You have laid the axe, you have made fast your tackle, to one of the king-posts of the town. I feel the whole building wracked by it. Is it not sacrilege to cut down the tree which has so long looked over Concord beneficently?

Nov. 1, 1858. As the afternoons grow shorter, and the early evening drives us home to complete our chores, we are reminded of the shortness of life, and become more pensive, at least in this twilight of the year. We are prompted to make haste and finish our work before the night comes. I leaned over a rail in the twilight on the Walden road, waiting for the evening mail to be distributed, when such thoughts visited me. I seemed to recognize the November evening as a familiar thing come round again, and yet I could hardly tell whether I had ever known it or only divined it. The November twilights just begun! It appeared like a part of a panorama at which I sat spectator, a part with which I was perfectly familiar just coming into view, and I foresaw how it would look and roll along, and prepared to be pleased. Just such a piece of art merely, though infinitely sweet and grand, did it appear to me, and just as little were any active duties required of me. We are independent on all that we see. The hangman whom I have *seen* cannot hang me. The earth which I have *seen* cannot bury me. Such doubleness and distance does sight prove. Only the rich and such as are troubled with ennui are implicated in the maze of phenomena. You cannot see anything until you are clear of it. The long railroad causeway through the meadows west of me, the still twilight in which hardly a cricket was heard,[1] the dark bank of clouds in the horizon long after sunset, the villagers crowding to the post-office, and the hastening home to supper by candlelight, had I not seen all this before! What new sweet was I to extract from it? Truly they mean that we shall learn our lesson well. Nature gets thumbed like an old spelling-book. The alms-house and Frederick were still as last November. I was no nearer, methinks, nor further off from my friends. Yet I sat the bench with perfect contentment, unwilling to

---

[1] Probably too cool for any these evenings; only in the afternoon.

exchange the familiar vision that was to be unrolled for any treasure or heaven that could be imagined. Sure to keep just so far apart in our orbits still, in obedience to the laws of attraction and repulsion, affording each other only steady but indispensable starlight. It was as if I was promised the greatest novelty the world has ever seen or shall see, though the utmost possible novelty would be the difference between me and myself a year ago. This alone encouraged me, and was my fuel for the approaching winter. That we may behold the panorama with this slight improvement or change, this is what we sustain life for with so much effort from year to year.

Nov. 8, 1858. I stand in Ebby Hubbard's yellow birch swamp, admiring some gnarled and shaggy picturesque old birches there, which send out large knee-like limbs near the ground, while the brook, raised by the late rain, winds fuller than usual through the rocky swamp. I thought with regret how soon these trees, like the black birches that grew on the hill near by, would be all cut off, and there would be almost nothing of the old Concord left, and we should be reduced to read old deeds in order to be reminded of such things — deeds, at least, in which some old and revered bound trees are mentioned. These will be the only proof at last that they ever existed. Pray, farmers, keep some old woods to match the old deeds. Keep them for history's sake, as specimens of what the township was. Let us not be reduced to a mere paper evidence, to deeds kept in a chest or secretary, when not so much as the bark of the paper birch will be left for evidence, about its decayed stump.

Sept. 8, 1859. The 7th, 8th, and 9th, the State muster is held here. The only observation I have to make is that [Concord] is fuller of dust and more uninhabitable than I ever knew it to be before. Not only the walls, fences, and houses are thickly covered with dust, but the fields and meadows and bushes; and the pads in the river for half a mile from the village are white with it. From a mile or two distant you see a cloud of dust over the town and extending thence to the muster-field. I went to the store the other day to buy a bolt for our front door, for, as I told the storekeeper, the Governor was coming here. 'Aye,' said he, 'and the Legislature too.' 'Then I will take two bolts,' said I. He said that there had been a steady demand for bolts and locks of late, for our protectors were coming. The surface of the roads for three to six inches in depth is a light and dry powder like ashes.

Sept. 16, 1859. Again and again I am surprised to observe what an interval there is, in what is called civilized life, between the shell and the inhabitant of the shell — what a disproportion there is between the life of man and his conveniences and luxuries. The house is neatly painted, has many apartments. You are shown into the sitting-room, where is a carpet and couch and mirror and splendidly bound Bible, daguerreotypes, ambrotypes, photographs of the whole family even, on the mantelpiece. One could live here more deliciously and improve his divine gifts better than in a cave surely. In the bright and costly saloon man will not be starving or freezing or contending with vermin surely, but he will be meditating a divine song or a heroic deed, or perfuming the atmosphere by the very breath of his natural and healthy existence. As the parlor is preferable to the cave, so will the life of its occupant be more godlike than that of the dweller in the cave. I called at such a house this afternoon, the house of one who in Europe would be called an operative. The woman was not in the third heavens, but in the third kitchen, as near the wood-shed or to outdoors and to the cave as she could instinctively get, for there she belonged — a coarse scullion or wench, not one whit superior, but in fact inferior, to the squaw in a wigwam — and the master of the house, where was he? He was drunk somewhere, on some mow or behind some stack, and I could not see him. He had been having a spree. If he had been as sober as he may be tomorrow, it would have been essentially the same; for refinement is not in him, it is only in his house — in the appliances which he did not invent. So is it in the Fifth Avenue and all over the civilized world. There is nothing but confusion in our New England life. The hogs are in the parlor. This man and his wife — and how many like them! — should have sucked their claws in some hole in a rock, or lurked like gypsies in the outbuildings of some diviner race. They've got into the wrong boxes; they rained down into these houses by mistake, as it is said to rain toads sometimes. They wear these advantages helter-skelter and without appreciating them, or to satisfy a vulgar taste, just as savages wear the dress of civilized men, just as that Indian chief walked the streets of New Orleans clad in nothing but a gaudy military coat which his Great Father had given him. Some philanthropists trust that the houses will civilize the inhabitants at last. The mass of men, just like savages, strive always after the outside, the clothes and finery of civilized life, the blue beads and tinsel and centre-tables. It is a wonder that any load ever gets moved, men are so prone to put the cart before the horse.

Oct. 15, 1859. Each town should have a park, or rather a primitive forest, of five hundred or a thousand acres, where a stick should never be cut for fuel, a common possession forever, for instruction and recreation. We hear of cow-commons and ministerial lots, but we want *men*-commons and lay lots, inalienable forever. Let us keep the New World *new*, preserve all the advantages of living in the country. There is meadow and pasture and wood-lot for the town's poor. Why not a forest and huckleberry-field for the town's rich? All Walden Wood might have been preserved for our park forever, with Walden in its midst, and the Easterbrooks Country, an unoccupied area of some four square miles, might have been our huckleberry-field. If any owners of these tracts are about to leave the world without natural heirs who need or deserve to be specially remembered, they will do wisely to abandon their possession to all, and not will them to some individual who perhaps has enough already. As some give to Harvard College or another institution, why might not another give a forest or huckleberry-field to Concord? A town is an institution which deserves to be remembered. We boast of our system of education, but why stop at schoolmasters and schoolhouses? We are all schoolmasters, and our schoolhouse is the universe. To attend chiefly to the desk or schoolhouse while we neglect the scenery in which it is placed is absurd. If we do not look out we shall find our fine schoolhouse standing in a cow-yard at last.

Oct. 17, 1859. What I put into my pocket, whether berry or apple, generally has to keep company with an arrowhead or two. I hear the latter chinking against a key as I walk. These are the perennial crop of Concord fields. If they were sure it would pay, we should see farmers raking the fields for them. . . .

Nov. 23, 1860. At first, perchance, there would be an abundant crop of rank garden weeds and grasses in the cultivated land — and rankest of all in the cellar-holes — and of pinweed, hardhack, sumach, blackberry, thimble-berry, raspberry, etc., in the fields and pastures. Elm, ash, maples, etc., would grow vigorously along old garden limits and main streets. Garden weeds and grasses would soon disappear. Huckleberry and blueberry bushes, lambkill, hazel, sweet-fern, barberry, elder, also shad-bush, choke-berry, andromeda, and thorns, etc., would rapidly prevail in the deserted pastures. At the same time the wild cherries, birch, poplar, willows, checkerberry would reëstablish themselves. Finally the pines, hemlock, spruce, larch, shrub oak, oaks, chestnut, beech, and walnuts would occupy the site of Concord once more. The apple and perhaps all exotic trees and shrubs and a great part of the indigenous ones named above would have disappeared, and the laurel and yew would to some extent be an underwood here, and perchance the red man once more thread his way through the mossy, swamp-like, primitive wood.

IV. MY FRIENDS AND NEIGHBORS

Feb. 22. [1845–1847]. Emerson does not consider things in respect to their essential utility, but an important partial and relative one, as works of art perhaps. His probes pass one side of their centre of gravity. His exaggeration is of a part, not of the whole.

[1837–47.] Not only must men talk, but for the most part must talk about talk — even about books, or dead and buried talk. Sometimes my friend expects a few periods from me. Is he exorbitant? He thinks it is my turn now. Sometimes my companion thinks he has said a good thing, but I don't see the difference. He looks just as he did before. Well, it is no loss. I suppose he has plenty more. . . .

Sometimes I have listened so attentively and with so much interest to the whole expression of a man that I did not hear one word he was saying, and saying too with the more vivacity observing my attention.

But a man may be an object of interest to me though his tongue is pulled out by the roots.

Nov. 24, 1850. I have certain friends whom I visit occasionally, but I commonly part from them early with a certain bitter-sweet sentiment. That which we love is so mixed and entangled with that we hate in one another that we are more grieved and disappointed, aye, and estranged from one another, by meeting than by absence. Some men may be my acquaintances merely, but one whom I have been accustomed to regard, to idealize, to have dreams about as a friend, and mix up intimately with myself, can never degenerate into an acquaintance. I must know him on that higher ground or not know him at all. We do not confess and explain, because we would fain be so intimately related as to understand each other without speech. Our friend must be broad. His must be an atmosphere coextensive with the universe, in which we can expand and breathe. For the most part we are smothered and stifled by one another. I go and see my friend and try his atmosphere. If our atmospheres do not mingle, if we repel each other strongly, it is of no use to stay.

July 30, 1851. Talked with Webster's nearest neighbor, Captain Hewit, whose small farm he surrounds and endeavors in vain to buy. A fair specimen of a retired Yankee sea-captain turned farmer. Proud of the quantity of carrots he had raised on a small patch. It was better husbandry than Webster's. He told a story of his buying a cargo for his owners at St. Petersburg just as peace was declared in the last war. These men are not so remarkable for anything as the quality of hardness. The very fixedness and rigidity of their jaws and necks express a sort of adamantine hardness. This is what they have learned by contact with the elements. The man who does not grow rigid with years and experience! Where is he? What avails it to grow hard merely? The harder you are, the more brittle really, like the bones of the old. How much rarer and better to grow mellow! A sort of stone fruit the man bears commonly; a bare stone it is, without any sweet and mellow pericarp around it. It is like the peach which has dried to the stone as the season advanced; it is dwindled to a dry stone with its almond. In presence of one of these hard men I think: 'How brittle! How easily you would crack! What a poor and lame conclusion!' I can think of nothing but a stone in his head. Truly genial men do not grow [hard]. It is the result of despair, this attitude of resistance. They behave like men already driven to the wall.

Sept. 4, 1851. I have no doubt but that, as is the master, such in course of time tend to become his herds and flocks as well as dogs. One man's oxen will be clever and solid, another's mischievous, another's mangy — in each case like their respective owners. No doubt man impresses his own character on the beasts which he tames and employs; they are not only humanized, but they acquire his particular human nature. How much oxen are like farmers generally, and cows like farmers' wives! and young steers and heifers like farmers' boys and girls! The farmer acts on the ox, and the ox reacts on the farmer. They do not meet half-way, it is true, but they do meet at a distance from the centre of each proportionate to each one's intellectual power. The farmer is ox-like in his thought, in his walk, in his strength, in his trustworthiness, in his taste.

Sept. 21, 1851. The retirement in which Green has lived for nearly eighty years in Carlisle is a retirement very different from and much greater than that in which the pioneer dwells at the West; for the latter dwells within sound of the surf of those billows of migration which are breaking on the shores around him, or near him, of the West, but those billows have long since swept over the spot which Green inhabits, and left him in the calm sea. There is somewhat exceedingly pathetic to think of in such a life as he must have lived — with no more to redeem it — such a life as an average Carlisle man may be supposed to live drawn out to eighty years. And he has died, perchance, and there is nothing but the mark of his cider-mill left. Here was the cider-mill, and there the orchard, and there the hog-pasture; and so men lived, and ate, and drank, and passed away — like vermin. Their long life was mere duration. As respectable is the life of the woodchucks, which perpetuate their race in the orchard still. That is the life of these *select-men* (!) spun out. They will be forgotten in a few years, even by such as themselves, like vermin. They will be known only like Kibbe, who is said to have been a large man who weighed two hundred and fifty, who had five or six heavy daughters who rode to Concord meeting-house on horseback, taking turns — they were so heavy that only one could ride at once. What, then, would redeem such a life? We only know that they ate, and drank, and built barns, and died and were buried, and still, perchance, their tombstones cumber the ground. But if I could know that there was ever entertained over their cellar-hole some divine thought, which came as a messenger of the gods, that he who resided here acted once in his life from a noble impulse, rising superior to his grovelling and penurious life, if only a single verse of poetry or of poetic prose had ever been written or spoken or conceived here beyond a doubt, I should not think it in vain that man had lived here. It would to some extent be true then that God had lived here. That all his life he lived only as a farmer — as the most valuable stock only on a farm — and in no moments as a man!

Sept. 28, 1851. What honest, homely, earth-loving, unaspiring houses they used to live in! Take that on Conantum for instance — so low you can put your hand on the eaves behind. There are few whose pride could stoop to enter such a house today. And then the broad chimney, built for comfort, not for beauty, with no coping of bricks to catch the eye, no alto or basso relievo.

Sept. 29, 1851. Found Hosmer carting out manure from under his barn to make room for the winter. He said he was tired of farming, he was too old. Quoted Webster as saying that he had never eaten the bread of idleness for a single day, and thought that Lord Brougham might have said as much with truth while he was in the opposition, but he did not know that he could say as much of himself. However, he did not wish to be idle, he merely wished to rest.

Oct. 4, 1851. Minott is, perhaps, the most poetical farmer — who most realizes to me the poetry of the farmer's life — that I know. He does nothing with haste and drudgery, but as if he loved it. He makes the most of his labor, and takes infinite satisfaction in every part of it. He is not looking forward to the sale of his crops or any pecuniary profit, but he is paid by the constant satisfaction which his labor yields him. He has not too much land to trouble him — too much work to do — no hired man nor boy — but simply to amuse himself and live. He cares not so much to raise a large crop as to do his work well. He knows every pin and nail in his barn. If another linter is to be floored, he lets no hired man rob him of that amusement, but he goes slowly to the woods and, at his leisure, selects a pitch pine tree, cuts it, and hauls it or gets it hauled to the mill; and so he knows the history of his barn floor.

Nov. 13, 1851. Just spent a couple of hours (eight to ten) with Miss Mary Emerson at Holbrook's. The wittiest and most vivacious woman that I know, certainly that woman among my acquaintance whom it is most profitable to meet, the least frivolous, who will most surely provoke to good conversation and the expression of what is in you. She is singular, among women at least, in being really and perseveringly interested to know what thinkers think. She relates herself surely to the intellectual where she goes. It is perhaps her greatest praise and peculiarity that she, more surely than any other woman, gives her companion occasion to utter his best thought. In spite of her own biases, she can entertain a large thought with hospitality, and is not prevented by any intellectuality in it, as women commonly are. In short, she is a genius, as woman seldom is, reminding you less often of her sex than any woman whom I know. In that sense she is capable of a masculine appreciation of poetry and philosophy. I never talked with any other woman who I thought accompanied me so far in describing a poetic experience.

Nov. 14, 1851. In the evening went to a party. It is a bad place to go to — thirty or forty persons, mostly young women, in a small room, warm and noisy. Was introduced to two young women. The first one was as lively and loquacious as a chickadee; had been accustomed to the society of watering-places, and therefore could get no refreshment out of such a dry fellow as I. The other was said to be pretty-looking, but I rarely look people in their faces, and, moreover, I could not hear what she said, there was such a clacking — could only see the motion of her lips when I looked that way. I could imagine better places for conversation, where there should be a certain degree of silence surrounding you, and less than forty talking at once. Why, this afternoon, even,

I did better. There was old Mr. Joseph Hosmer and I ate our luncheon of cracker and cheese together in the woods. I heard all he said, though it was not much, to be sure, and he could hear me. And then he talked out of such a glorious repose, taking a leisurely bite at the cracker and cheese between his words; and so some of him was communicated to me, and some of me to him, I trust.

These parties, I think, are a part of the machinery of modern society, that young people may be brought together to form marriage connections.

Nov. 16, 1851. It is remarkable that the highest intellectual mood which the world tolerates is the perception of the truth of the most ancient revelations, now in some respects out of date; but any direct revelation, any original thoughts, it hates like virtue. The fathers and the mothers of the town would rather hear the young man or young woman at their tables express reverence for some old statement of the truth than utter a direct revelation themselves. They don't want to have any prophets born into their families — damn them! So far as thinking is concerned, surely original thinking is the divinest thing. Rather we should reverently watch for the least motions, the least scintillations, of thought in this sluggish world, and men should run to and fro on the occasion more than at an earthquake. We check and repress the divinity that stirs within us, to fall down and worship the divinity that is dead without us. I go to see many a good man or good woman, so called, and utter freely that thought which alone it was given to me to utter; but there was a man who lived a long, long time ago, and his name was Moses, and another whose name was Christ, and if your thought does not, or does not appear to, coincide with what they said, the good man or the good woman has no ears to hear you. They think they love God! It is only his old clothes, of which they make scarecrows for the children. Where will they come nearer to God than in those very children?

Dec. 17, 1851. One of the best men I know often offends me by uttering made words — the very best words, of course, or dinner speeches, most smooth and gracious and fluent repartees, a sort of talking to Buncombe, a dash of polite conversation, a graceful bending, as if I were Master Slingsby of promising parts, from the University. O would you but be simple and downright! Would you but cease your palaver! It is the misfortune of being a gentleman and famous. The conversation of gentlemen after dinner! One of the best of men and wisest, to whom this diabolical formality will adhere. Repeating himself, shampooing himself! Passing the time of day, as if he were just introduced! No words are so tedious. Never a natural or simple word or yawn. It produces an appearance of phlegm and stupidity in me the auditor. I am suddenly the closest and most phlegmatic of mortals, and the conversation comes to naught. Such speeches as an ex-Member of Congress might make to an ex-Member of Parliament.

Dec. 31, 1851. I observed this afternoon the old Irishwoman at the shanty in the woods, sitting out on the hillside, bareheaded, in the rain and on the icy though thawing ground, knitting. She comes out, like the ground squirrel, at the least intimation of warmer weather. She will not have to go far to be buried, so close she lives to the earth, while I walk still in a greatcoat and under an umbrella. Such Irish as these are naturalizing themselves at a rapid rate, and threaten at last to displace the Yankees, as the latter have the Indians. The process of acclimation is rapid with them; they draw long breaths in the American sick-room. What must be the philosophy of life to that woman, ready to flow down the slope with the running sand! Ah, what would I not give for her point of view! She does not use any *th's* in her style. Yet I fear that even she may have learned to lie.

Dec. 31, 1851. This night I heard Mrs. S—— lecture on womanhood. The most important fact about the lecture was that a woman said it, and in that respect it was suggestive. Went to see her afterward, but the interview added nothing to the previous impression, rather subtracted. She was a woman in the too common sense after all. You had to fire small charges: I did not have a finger in once, for fear of blowing away all her works and so ending the game. You had to substitute courtesy for sense and argument. It requires nothing less than a chivalric feeling to sustain a conversation with a lady. I carried her lecture for her in my pocket wrapped in her handkerchief; my pocket exhales cologne to this moment. The championess of woman's rights still asks you to be a ladies' man. I can't fire a salute, even, for fear some of the guns may be shotted. I had to unshot all the guns in truth's battery and fire powder and wadding only. Certainly the heart is only for rare occasions; the intellect affords the most unfailing entertainment. It would only do to let her feel the wind of the ball. I fear that to the last woman's lectures will demand mainly courtesy from man.

Jan. 16, 1852. Channing has great respect for McKean, he stands on so low a level. Says he's great for conversation. He never says anything, hardly answers a question, but keeps at work; never exaggerates, nor uses an exclamation, and does as he agrees to. He appears to have got his shoulder to the wheel of the universe. But the other day he went greater lengths with me, as he and Barry were sawing down a pine, both kneeling of necessity. I said it was wet work for the knees in the snow. He observed, looking up at me, 'We pray without ceasing.'

Jan. 30, 1852. I doubt if Emerson could trundle a wheelbarrow through the streets, because it would be out of character. One needs to have a comprehensive character.

Feb. 9, 1852. Met Sudbury Haines on the river before the Cliffs, come a-fishing. Wearing an old coat, much patched, with many colors. He represents the Indian still. The very patches in his coat and his improvident life do so. I feel that he is as essential a part, nevertheless, of our community as the lawyer in the village. He tells me that he caught three pickerel here the other day that weighed seven pounds all together. It is the old story. The fisherman is a natural story-teller. No man's imagination plays more pranks than his, while he is tending his reels and trotting from one to another, or watching his cork in summer. He is ever waiting for the sky to fall. He has sent out a venture. He has a ticket in the lottery of fate, and who knows what it may draw? He ever expects to catch a bigger fish yet. He is the most patient and believing of men. Who else will stand so long in wet places? When the haymaker runs to shelter, he takes down his pole and bends his steps to the river, glad to have a leisure day. He is more like an inhabitant of nature. The weather concerns him. He is an observer of her phenomena.

Aug. 24, 1852. How happens it that I find myself making such an enormous demand on men and so constantly disappointed? Are my friends aware how disappointed I am? Is it all my fault? Have I no heart? Am I incapable of expansion and generosity? I shall accuse myself of everything else sooner. I have never met with a friend who furnished me sea-room. I have only tacked a few times and come to anchor — not sailed — made no voyage, carried no venture. Do they think me eccentric because I refuse this chicken's meat, this babe's food?

Jan. 1, 1853. After talking with Uncle Charles the other night about the worthies of this country, Webster and the rest, as usual, considering who were geniuses and who not, I showed him up to bed, and when I had got into bed myself, I heard his chamber door opened, after eleven o'clock, and he called out, in an earnest, stentorian voice, loud enough to wake the whole house, 'Henry! was John Quincy Adams a genius?' 'No, I think not,' was my reply. 'Well, I didn't think he was,' answered he.

May 24, 1853, P.M. — Talked, or tried to talk, with R. W. E. Lost my time — nay, almost my identity. He, assuming a false opposition where there was no difference of opinion, talked to the wind — told me what I knew — and I lost my time trying to imagine myself somebody else to oppose him.

June 17, 1853. Here have been three ultra-reformers, lecturers on Slavery, Temperance, the Church, etc., in and about our house and Mrs. Brooks's the last three or four days — A. D. Foss, once a Baptist minister in Hopkinton, N.H.; Loring Moody, a sort of travelling pattern-working chaplain; and H. C. Wright, who shocks all the old women with his infidel writings. Though Foss was a stranger to the others, you would have thought them old and familiar cronies. (They happened here together by accident.) They addressed each other constantly by their Christian names, and rubbed you continually with the greasy cheeks of their kindness. They would not keep their distance, but cuddle up and lie spoon-fashion with you, no matter how hot the weather nor how narrow the bed — chiefly ——.[1] I was awfully pestered with his benignity; feared I should get greased all over with it past restoration; tried to keep some starch in my clothes. He wrote a book called 'A Kiss for a Blow,' and he behaved as if there were no alternative between these, or as if I had given him a blow. I would have preferred the blow, but he was bent on giving me the kiss, when there was neither quarrel nor agreement between us. I wanted that he should straighten his back, smooth out those ogling wrinkles of benignity about his eyes, and, with a healthy reserve, pronounce something in a downright manner. It was difficult to keep clear of his slimy benignity, with which he sought to cover you before he swallowed you and took you fairly into his bowels. It would have been far worse than the fate of Jonah. I do not wish to get any nearer to a man's bowels than usual. They lick you as a cow her calf. They would fain wrap you about with their bowels. —— addressed me as 'Henry' within one minute from the time I first laid eyes on him, and when I spoke, he said with drawling, sultry sympathy, 'Henry, I know all you would say; I understand you perfectly; you need not explain anything to me'; and to another, 'I am going to dive into Henry's inmost depths.' I said, 'I trust you will not strike your head against the bottom.' He could tell in a dark room, with his eyes blinded and in perfect stillness, if there was one there whom he loved. One of the most attractive things about

---

[1] In the original journal Thoreau had crossed out the 'chiefly' and substituted 'wholly' in pencil.

the flowers is their beautiful reserve. The truly beautiful and noble puts its lover, as it were, at an infinite distance, while it attracts him more strongly than ever. I do not like the men who come so near me with their bowels. It is the most disagreeable kind of snare to be caught in. Men's bowels are far more slimy than their brains. They must be ascetics indeed who approach you by this side. What a relief to have heard the ring of one healthy reserved tone! With such a forgiving disposition, as if he were all the while forgiving you for existing. Considering our condition or *habit* of soul — maybe corpulent and asthmatic — maybe dying of atrophy, with all our bones sticking out — is it kindness to embrace a man? They lay their sweaty hand on your shoulder, or your knee, to magnetize you.

Aug. 10, 1853. Alcott spent the day with me yesterday. He spent the day before with Emerson. He observed that he had got his wine and now he had come after his venison. Such was the compliment he paid me. The question of a livelihood was troubling him. He knew of nothing which he could do for which men would pay him. He could not compete with the Irish in cradling grain. His early education had not fitted him for a clerkship. He had offered his services to the Abolition Society, to go about the country and speak for freedom as their agent, but they declined him. This is very much to their discredit; they should have been forward to secure him. Such a connection with him would confer unexpected dignity on their enterprise. But they cannot tolerate a man who stands by a head above them. They are as bad — Garrison and Phillips, etc. — as the overseers and faculty of Harvard College. They require a man who will train well *under* them. Consequently they have not in their employ any but small men — trainers.

Nov. 17, 1855. It is interesting to me to talk with Rice, he lives so thoroughly and satisfactorily to himself. He has learned that rare art of living, the very elements of which most professors do not know. His life has been not a failure but a success. Seeing me going to sharpen some plane-irons, and hearing me complain of the want of tools, he said that I ought to have a chest of tools. But I said it was not worth the while. I should not use them enough to pay for them. 'You would use them more, if you had them,' said he. 'When I came to do a piece of work I used to find commonly that I wanted a certain tool, and I made it a rule first always to make that tool. I have spent as much as $3000 thus on my tools.' Comparatively speaking, his life is a success; not such a failure as most men's. He gets more out of any enterprise than his neighbors, for he helps himself more and hires less. Whatever pleasure there is in it he enjoys. By good sense and calculation he has become rich and has invested his property well, yet practices a fair and neat economy, dwells not in untidy luxury. It costs him less to live, and he gets more out of life, than others. To get his living, or keep it, is not a hasty or disagreeable toil. He works slowly but surely, enjoying the sweet of it. He buys a piece of meadow at a profitable rate, works at it in pleasant weather, he and his son, when they are inclined, goes a-fishing or a-bee-hunting or a-rifle-shooting quite as often, and thus the meadow gets redeemed, and potatoes get planted, perchance, and he is very sure to have a good crop stored in his cellar in the fall, and some to sell. He always has the best of potatoes there. In the same spirit in which he and his son tackle up their Dobbin (he never keeps a fast horse) and go a-spearing or a-fishing through the ice, they also tackle up and go to their Sudbury farm to hoe or harvest a little, and when they return they bring home a load of stumps in their hay-rigging, which impeded their labors, but, perchance, supply them with their winter wood. All the woodchucks they shoot or trap in the bean-field are brought home also. And thus their life is a long sport and they know not what hard times are.

Dec. 1, 1856. I see the old pale-faced farmer out again on his sled now for the five-thousandth time — Cyrus Hubbard, a man of a certain New England probity and worth, immortal and natural, like a natural product, like the sweetness of a nut, like the toughness of hickory. He, too, is a redeemer for me. How superior actually to the faith he professes! He is not an office-seeker. What an institution, what a revelation is a man! We are wont foolishly to think that the creed which a man professes is more significant than the fact he is. It matters not how hard the conditions seemed, how mean the world, for a man is a prevalent force and a new law himself. He is a system whose law is to be observed. The old farmer condescends to countenance still this nature and order of things. It is a great encouragement that an honest man makes this world his abode. He rides on the sled drawn by oxen, world-wise, yet comparatively so young, as if they had seen scores of winters. The farmer spoke to me, I can swear, clean, cold, moderate as the snow. He does not melt the snow where he treads. Yet what a faint impression that encounter may make on me after all! Moderate, natural, true, as if he were made of earth, stone, wood, snow. I thus meet in this universe kindred of mine, composed of these elements. I see men like frogs; their peeping I partially understand.

Dec. 2, 1856. Saw Melvin's lank bluish-white black-spotted hound, and Melvin with his gun near, going home at eve. He follows hunting, praise be to him, as regularly in our tame fields as the farmers follow farming. Persistent Genius! How I respect him and thank him for him! [*sic*] I trust the Lord will provide us with another Melvin when he is gone. How good in him to follow his own bent, and not continue at the Sabbath-school all his days! What a wealth he thus becomes in the neighborhood! Few know how to take the census. I thank my stars for Melvin. I think of him with gratitude when I am going to sleep, grateful that he exists — that Melvin who is such a trial to his mother. Yet he is agreeable to me as a tinge of russet on the hillside. I would fain give thanks morning and evening for my blessings. Awkward, gawky, loose-hung, dragging his legs after him. He is my contemporary and neighbor. He is one tribe, I am another, and we are not at war.

Dec. 3, 1856. How I love the simple, reserved countrymen, my neighbors, who mind their own business and let me alone, who never waylaid nor shot at me, to my knowledge, when I crossed their fields, though each one has a gun in his house! For nearly twoscore years I have known, at a distance, these long-suffering men, whom I never spoke to, who never spoke to me, and now feel a certain tenderness for them, as if this long probation were but the prelude to an eternal friendship. What a long trial we have withstood, and how much more admirable we are to each other, perchance, than if we had been bedfellows! I am not only grateful because Veias, and Homer, and Christ, and Shakespeare have lived, but I am grateful for Minott, and Rice, and Melvin, and Goodwin, and Puffer even. I see Melvin all alone filling his sphere, in russet suit, which no other could fill or suggest. He takes up as much room in nature as the most famous.

Feb. 28, 1857. It is a singular infatuation that leads men to become clergymen in regular, or even irregular, standing. I pray to be introduced to new men, at whom I may stop short and taste their peculiar sweetness. But in the clergyman of the most liberal sort I see no perfectly independent human nucleus, but I seem to see some indistinct scheme hovering about, to which he has lent himself, to which he belongs. It is a very fine cobweb in the lower stratum of the air, which stronger wings do not even discover. Whatever he may say, he does not know that one day is as good as another. Whatever he may say, he does not know that a man's creed can never be written, that there are no particular expressions of belief that deserve to be prominent. He dreams of a certain sphere to be filled by him, something less in diameter than a great circle, maybe not greater than a hogshead. All the staves are got out, and his sphere is already hooped. What's the use of talking to him? When you spoke of sphere-music he thought only of a thumping on his cask. If he doesn't know something that nobody else does, that nobody told him, then he's a telltale. What great interval is there between him who is caught in Africa and made a plantation slave of in the South, and him who is caught in New England and made a Unitarian minister of? In course of time they will abolish the one form of servitude, and, not long after, the other. I do not see the necessity for a man's getting into a hogshead and so narrowing his sphere, nor for his putting his head into a halter. Here's a man who can't butter his own bread, and he has just combined with a thousand like him to make a dipped toast for all eternity!

April 16, 1857. About a month ago, at the post-office, Abel Brooks, who is pretty deaf, sidling up to me, observed in a loud voice which all could hear, 'Let me see, your society is pretty large, ain't it?' 'Oh, yes, large enough,' said I, not knowing what he meant. 'There's Stewart belongs to it, and Collier, he's one of them, and Emerson, and my boarder' (Pulsifer), 'and Channing, I believe, I think he goes there.' 'You mean the *walkers*; don't you?' 'Ye-es, I call you the Society. All go to the woods; don't you?' 'Do you miss any of your wood?' I asked. 'No, I hain't worried any yet. I believe you're a pretty clever set, as good as the average,' etc., etc.

Telling Sanborn of this, he said that, when he first came to town and boarded at Holbrook's, he asked H. how many religious societies there were in town. H. said that there were three — the Unitarian, the Orthodox, and the Walden Pond Society.

Oct. 7, 1857. I do not know how to entertain one who can't take long walks. The first thing that suggests itself is to get a horse to draw them, and that brings us at once into contact with stablers and dirty harness, and I do not get over my ride for a long time. I give up my forenoon to them and get along pretty well, the very elasticity of the air and promise of the day abetting me, but they are as heavy as dumplings by mid-afternoon. If they can't walk, why won't they take an honest nap and let me go in the afternoon? But, come two o'clock, they alarm me by an evident disposition to sit. In the midst of the most glorious Indian-summer afternoon, there they sit, breaking your chairs and wearing out the house, with their backs to the light, taking no note of the lapse of time.

Nov. 6, 1857. Minott is a very pleasing figure in nature. He improves every scenery — he and his comrades, Harry Hooper, John Wyman,

Oliver Williams, etc. If he gets into a pond-hole he disturbs it no more than a water-spirit for me.

Nov. 7, 1857. Minott adorns whatever part of nature he touches; whichever way he walks he transfigures the earth for me. If a common man speaks of Walden Pond to me, I see only a shallow, dull-colored body of water without reflections or peculiar color, but if Minott speaks of it, I see the green water and reflected hills at once, for he *has been* there. I hear the rustle of the leaves from woods which he goes through.

Aug. 6, 1858. Emerson is gone to the Adirondack country with a hunting party. Eddy says he has carried a double-barrelled gun, one side for shot, the other for ball, for Lowell killed a bear there last year. But the story on the Mill-Dam is that he has taken a gun which throws shot from one end and ball from the other!

Jan. 22, 1859. The energy and excitement of the musquash-hunter even, not despairing of life, but keeping the same rank and savage hold on it that his predecessors have for so many generations, while so many are sick and despairing, even this is inspiriting to me. Even these deeds of death are interesting as evidences of life, for life will still prevail in spite of all accidents. I have a certain faith that even musquash are immortal and not born to be killed by Melvin's double-B (?) shot. . . . The musquash-hunter (last night), with his increased supply of powder and shot and boat turned up somewhere on the bank, now that the river is rapidly rising, dreaming of his exploits today in shooting musquash, of the great pile of dead rats that will weigh down his boat before night, when he will return wet and weary and weather-beaten to his hut with an appetite for his supper and for much sluggish (punky) social inter-course with his fellows — even he, dark, dull, and battered flint as he is, is an inspired man to his extent now, perhaps the most inspired by this freshet of any, and the Musketaquid Meadows cannot spare him. There are poets of all kinds and degrees, little known to each other. The Lake School is not the only or the principal one. They love various things. Some love beauty, and some love rum. Some go to Rome, and some go a-fishing, and are sent to the house of correction once a month. They keep up their fires by means unknown to me. I know not their comings and goings. How can I tell what violets they watch for? I know them wild and ready to risk all when their muse invites. The most sluggish will be up early enough then, and face any amount of wet and cold. I meet these gods of the river and woods with sparkling faces (like Apollo's) late from the house of correction, it may be carrying whatever mystic and forbidden bottles or other vessels concealed, while the dull regular priests are steering their parish rafts in a prose mood. What care I to see galleries full of representations of heathen gods, when I can see natural living ones by an infinitely superior artist, without perspective tube? If you read the Rig Veda, oldest of books, as it were, describing a very primitive people and condition of things, you hear in their prayers of a still older, more primitive and aboriginal race in their midst and round about, warring on them and seizing their flocks and herds, infesting their pastures. Thus is it in another sense in all communities, and hence the prisons and police.

I hear these guns going today, and I must confess they are to me a springlike and exhilarating sound, like the cock-crowing, though each one may report the death of a musquash. This, methinks, or the like of this, with whatever mixture of dross, is the real morning or evening hymn that goes up from these vales today, and which the stars echo. This is the best sort of glorifying of God and enjoying him that at all prevails here today, without any clarified butter or sacred ladles.

As a mother loves to see her child imbibe nourishment and expand, so God loves to see his children thrive on the nutriment he has furnished them. In the musquash-hunters I see the Almouchicois still pushing swiftly over the dark stream in their canoes. These aboriginal men cannot be repressed, but under some guise or other they survive and reappear continually. Just as simply as the crow picks up the worms which all over the fields have been washed out by the thaw, these men pick up the musquash that have been washed out the banks. And to serve such ends men plow and sail, and powder and shot are made, and the grocer exists to retail them, though he may think himself much more the deacon of some church.

2 . A WEEK ON THE CONCORD AND MERRIMACK RIVERS

PREFATORY NOTE

IN THE LATE summer of 1839, Thoreau and his brother John took a two-week vacation from their teaching duties and embarked in their homemade rowboat on a voyage on the Concord and Merrimack Rivers, with a week's interlude for a hike through the White Mountains. Almost immediately upon their return Henry apparently decided to write a short travel essay on this excursion, but when John died suddenly and tragically of lockjaw in January of 1842, Henry recast his plans and determined to expand the essay to a book-length memorial tribute to John. Worldly duties kept him from his task for a time. But when in the fall of 1844 his friend Emerson bought a small parcel of land on the shore of Walden Pond about a mile and a half southeast of the village of Concord, Henry saw his opportunity. Gaining permission from Emerson, he built a small cabin on the land — what his friend Ellery Channing called "a wooden inkstand" — and there set about devoting himself wholeheartedly to writing. By the spring of 1847 the manuscript was sufficiently ready to circulate among the publishers. But to his dismay, not a publisher was interested unless he, Thoreau, were willing to underwrite the cost himself. Finally by the spring of 1849, by promising to reimburse them for any losses they might incur, he persuaded James Munroe & Co. of Boston to publish an edition of one thousand copies. It was an immediate failure, receiving few reviews and those few chiefly negative. He was forced to earn money elsewhere to compensate Munroe. The book had cost him $290. His total income on it was fifteen dollars. On October 27, 1853, he recorded in his journal:

> For a year or two past, my *publisher*, falsely so called, has been writing from time to time to ask what disposition should be made of the copies of "A Week on the Concord and Merrimack Rivers" still on hand, and at last suggesting that he had use for the room they occupied in his cellar. So I had them all sent to me here, and they have arrived to-day by express, filling the man's wagon, — 706 copies out of an edition of 1000 which I bought of Munroe four years ago and have been ever since paying for, and have not quite paid for yet. The wares are sent to me at last, and I

have an opportunity to examine my purchase. They are something more substantial than fame, as my back knows, which has borne them up two flights of stairs to a place similar to that to which they trace their origin. Of the remaining two hundred and ninety and odd, seventy-five were given away, the rest sold. I have now a library of nearly nine hundred volumes, over seven hundred of which I wrote myself.

Though the original journey had taken two weeks, Thoreau confines his account to the seven days spent on the rivers, thus the title "A Week." The account of the voyage itself is smooth-flowing, vivid, and highly interesting. Not particularly profound, it makes pleasant summer hammock reading, creating an idyllic picture of rural America of yesteryear, contrasting strikingly with the depressed, over-populated, and vastly polluted areas the valleys of the Concord and Merrimack have become. A number of authors of our day, among them Edwin Way Teale and Raymond Mungo, have retraced Thoreau's route and have invariably been sickened by the havoc wrought by our generation. Fortunately the ecologists are now hard at work and water lilies and fish, for many years absent from the rivers, are beginning a slow return.

A Week has its aficionados — H. M. Tomlinson, for example, once declared it the best travel book ever written — but others find it strangely unsatisfying. One of the better known Thoreau scholars has confessed he was never able to read it through. Its basic flaw is that it is two books in one — the travel narrative and an intrusive anthology of selections from Thoreau's portfolio, ranging from poems and translations from the Greek to essays on subjects as varied as Chaucer, local history, friendship, and religion, inserted into the narrative either to make it book length or to get the shorter works into print — one is never quite sure which. Either book would be satisfactory in itself, but they do not blend well together. As James Russell Lowell complained, you come upon the inserts in the narrative like snags in the current of the river. In this version of *A Week*, abridged by Henry S. Canby, then, only the travel narrative is given, and, I believe, a more readable edition results. Two samples of the selections omitted here may be found in Section Eight, below: "The Christian Fable" and "Friendship."

A Week was first published in 1849 by James Munroe & Co. of Boston. A heavily revised and corrected edition was published by Ticknor & Fields in 1868.

CONCORD RIVER

Beneath low hills, in the broad interval
Through which at will our Indian rivulet
Winds mindful still of sannup and of squaw,
Whose pipe and arrow oft the plough unburies,
Here in pine houses built of new-fallen trees,
Supplanters of the tribe, the farmer dwell.

EMERSON.

THE Musketaquid, or Grass-ground River, though probably as old as the Nile or Euphrates, did not begin to have a place in civilized history until the fame of its grassy meadows and its fish attracted settlers out of England in 1635, when it received the other but kindred name of CONCORD from the first plantation on its banks, which appears to have been commenced in a spirit of peace and harmony. It will be Grass-ground River as long as grass grows and water runs here; it will be Concord River only while men lead peaceable lives on its banks. To an extinct race it was grass-ground, where they hunted and fished; and it is still perennial grass-ground to Concord farmers, who own the Great Meadows, and get the hay from year to year. 'One branch of it,' according to the historian of Concord, for I love to quote so good authority, 'rises in the south part of Hopkinton, and another from a pond and a large cedar-swamp in Westborough,' and flowing between Hopkinton and Southborough, through Framingham, and between Sudbury and Wayland, where it is sometimes called Sudbury River, it enters Concord at the south part of the town, and after receiving the North or Assabet River, which has its source a little farther to the north and west, goes out at the northeast angle, and, flowing between Bedford and Carlisle, and through Billerica, empties into the Merrimack at Lowell. In Concord, it is in summer from four to fifteen feet deep, and from one hundred to three hundred feet wide, but in the spring freshets, when it overflows its banks, it is in some places nearly a mile wide. Between Sudbury and Wayland the meadows acquire their greatest breadth, and when covered with water, they form a handsome chain of shallow vernal lakes, resorted to by numerous gulls and ducks. Just above Sherman's Bridge, between these towns, is the largest expanse; and when the wind blows freshly in a raw March day, heaving up the surface into dark and sober billows or regular swells, skirted as it is in the distance with alder swamps and smoke-like maples, it looks like a smaller Lake Huron, and is very pleasant and exciting for a landsman to row or sail over. The farmhouses along the Sudbury shore, which rises gently to a considerable height, command fine water prospects at this season. The shore is more flat on the Wayland side, and this town is the greatest loser by the flood. Its farmers tell me that thousands of acres are flooded now, since the dams have been erected, where they remember to have seen the white honeysuckle or clover growing once, and they could go dry with shoes only in summer. Now there is nothing but blue-joint and sedge and cut-grass there, standing in water all the year round. For a long time, they made the most of the driest season to get their hay, working sometimes till nine o'clock at night, sedulously paring with their scythes in the twilight round the hummocks left by the ice; but now it is not worth the getting when they can come at it, and they look sadly round to their woodlots and upland as a last resource.

It is worth the while to make a voyage up this stream, if you go no farther than Sudbury, only to see how much country there is in the rear of us: great hills, and a hundred brooks, and farmhouses, and barns, and haystacks, you never saw before, and men everywhere; Sudbury, that is *Southborough* men, and Wayland, and Nine-Acre-Corner men, and Bound Rock, where four towns bound on a rock in the river, Lincoln, Wayland, Sudbury, Concord. Many waves are there agitated by the wind, keeping nature fresh, the spray blowing in your face, reeds and rushes waving; ducks by the hundred, all uneasy in the surf, in the raw wind, just ready to rise, and now going off with a clatter and a whistling like riggers straight for Labrador, flying against the stiff gale with reefed wings, or else circling round first, with all their paddles briskly moving, just over the surf, to reconnoitre you before they leave these parts; gulls wheeling overhead, muskrats swimming for dear life, wet and cold, with no fire to warm them by that you know of, their labored homes rising here and there like haystacks; and countless mice and moles and winged titmice along the sunny, windy shore; cran-berries tossed on the waves and heaving up on the beach, their little red skiffs beating about among the alders; — such healthy natural tumult as proves the last day is not yet at hand. And there stand all around the alders, and birches, and oaks, and maples, full of glee and sap, holding in their buds until the waters subside. You shall perhaps run aground on Cranberry Island, only some spires of last year's pipe-grass above water to show where the danger is, and get as good a freezing there as anywhere on the Northwest Coast. I never voyaged so far in all my life. You shall see men you never heard of before, whose names you don't know, going away down through the meadows with long ducking guns, with water-tight boots wading through the fowl-meadow grass, on bleak, wintry, distant shores, with guns at half-cock; and they shall see teal — blue-winged, green-winged — sheldrakes, whistlers, black ducks, ospreys, and many other wild and noble sights before night, such as they who sit in parlors never dream of. You shall see rude and sturdy, experienced and wise men, keeping their castles, or teaming up their summer's wood, or chopping alone in the woods; men fuller of talk and rare adventure in the sun and wind and rain, than a chestnut is of meat, who were out not only in '75 and 1812, but have been out every day of their lives; greater men than Homer, or Chaucer, or Shakespeare, only they never got time to say so; they never took to the way of writing. Look at their fields, and imagine what they might write, if ever they should put pen to paper. Or what have they not written on the face of the earth already, clearing, and burning, and scratching, and harrowing, and plowing, and subsoiling, in and in, and out and out, and over and over, again and again, erasing what they had already written for want of parchment.

As yesterday and the historical ages are past, as the work of today is present, so some flitting perspectives and demi-experiences of the life that is in nature are in time veritably future, or rather outside to time, perennial, young, divine, in the wind and rain which never die.

> The respectable folks —
> Where dwell they?
> They whisper in the oaks,
> And they sigh in the hay;
> Summer and winter, night and day,
> Out on the meadow, there dwell they.
> They never die,
> Nor snivel nor cry,
> Nor ask our pity
> With a wet eye.
> A sound estate they ever mend,
> To every asker readily lend;

> To the ocean wealth,
> To the meadow health,
> To Time his length,
> To the rocks strength,
> To the stars light,
> To the weary night,
> To the busy day,
> To the idle play;
> And so their good cheer never ends,
> For all are their debtors, and all their friends.

Concord River is remarkable for the gentleness of its current, which is scarcely perceptible, and some have referred to its influence the proverbial moderation of the inhabitants of Concord, as exhibited in the Revolution, and on later occasions. It has been proposed that the town should adopt for its coat of arms a field verdant, with the Concord circling nine times round. I have read that a descent of an eighth of an inch in a mile is sufficient to produce a flow. Our river has, probably, very near the smallest allowance. The story is current, at any rate, though I believe that strict history will not bear it out, that the only bridge ever carried away on the main branch, within the limits of the town, was driven up-stream by the wind. But wherever it makes a sudden bend it is shallower and swifter, and asserts its title to be called a river. Compared with the other tributaries of the Merrimack, it appears to have been properly named Musketaquid, or Meadow River, by the Indians. For the most part, it creeps through broad meadows, adorned with scattered oaks, where the cranberry is found in abundance, covering the ground like a moss-bed. A row of sunken dwarf willows borders the stream on one or both sides, while at a greater distance the meadow is skirted with maples, alders, and other fluviatile trees, overrun with the grape-vine, which bears fruit in its season, purple, red, white, and other grapes. Still farther from the stream, on the edge of the firm land, are seen the gray and white dwellings of the inhabitants. According to the valuation of 1831, there were in Concord two thousand one hundred and eleven acres, or about one seventh of the whole territory, in meadow; this standing next in the list after pasturage and unimproved lands; and, judging from the returns of previous years, the meadow is not reclaimed so fast as the woods are cleared.

Let us here read what old Johnson says of these meadows in his 'Wonder-Working Providence,' which gives the account of New England from 1628 to 1652, and see how matters looked to him. He says of the Twelfth Church of Christ gathered at Concord: 'This town is seated upon a fair fresh river, whose rivulets are filled with fresh marsh, and her streams with fish, it being a branch of that large river of Merrimack. Allwifes and shad in their season come up to this town, but salmon and dace cannot come up, by reason of the rocky falls, which causeth their meadows to lie much covered with water, the which these people, together with their neighbor town, have several times essayed to cut through but cannot, yet it may be turned another way with an hundred pound charge as it appeared.' As to their farming he says: 'Having laid out their estate upon cattle at 5 to 20 pound a cow, when they came to winter them with inland hay, and feed upon such wild fother as was never cut before, they could not hold out the winter, but, ordinarily the first or second year after their coming up to a new plantation, many of their cattle died.' And this from the same author: 'Of the Planting of the 19th Church in the Mattachusets' Government, called Sudbury:' 'This year [does he mean 1654?] the town and church of Christ at Sudbury began to have the first foundation stones laid, taking up her station in the inland country, as her elder sister Concord had formerly done, lying further up the same river, being furnished with great plenty of fresh marsh, but, it lying very low is much indamaged with land floods, Insomuch that when the summer proves wet they lose part of their hay; yet are they so sufficiently provided that they take in cattle of other towns to winter.'

The sluggish artery of the Concord meadows steals thus unobserved through the town, without a murmur or a pulse-beat, its general course from southwest to northeast, and its length about fifty miles; a huge volume of matter, ceaselessly rolling through the plains and valleys of the substantial earth with the moccasined tread of an Indian warrior, making haste from the high places of the earth to its ancient reservoir. The murmurs of many a famous river on the other side of the globe reach even to us here, as to more distant dwellers on its banks; many a poet's stream, floating the helms and shields of heroes on its bosom. The Xanthus or Scamander is not a mere dry channel and bed of a mountain torrent, but fed by the ever-flowing springs of fame:

> 'And thou Simois, that as an arrowe, clere
> Through Troy rennest, aie downward to the sea;' —

and I trust that I may be allowed to associate our muddy but much abused Concord River with the most famous in history.

> 'Sure there are poets which did never dream
> Upon Parnassus, nor did taste the stream
> Of Helicon; we therefore may suppose
> Those made not poets, but the poets those.'

The Mississippi, the Ganges, and the Nile, those journeying atoms from the Rocky Mountains, the Himmaleh, and Mountains of the Moon, have a kind of personal importance in the annals of the world. The heavens are not yet drained over their sources, but the Mountains of the Moon still send their annual tribute to the Pasha without fail, as they did to the Pharaohs, though he must collect the rest of his revenue at the point of the sword. Rivers must have been the guides which conducted the footsteps of the first travelers. They are the constant lure, when they flow by our doors, to distant enterprise and adventure; and, by a natural impulse, the dwellers on their banks will at length accompany their currents to the lowlands of the globe, or explore at their invitation the interior of continents. They are the natural highways of all nations, not only leveling the ground and removing obstacles from the path of the traveler, quenching his thirst and bearing him on their bosoms, but conducting him through the most interesting scenery, the most populous portions of the globe, and where the animal and vegetable kingdoms attain their greatest perfection.

I had often stood on the banks of the Concord, watching the lapse of the current, an emblem of all progress, following the same law with the system, with time, and all that is made; the weeds at the bottom gently bending down the stream, shaken by the watery wind, still planted where their seeds had sunk, but ere long to die and go down likewise; the shining pebbles, not yet anxious to better their condition, the chips and weeds, and occasional logs and stems of trees that floated past, fulfilling their fate, were objects of singular interest to me, and at last I resolved to launch myself on its bosom and float whither it would bear me.

SATURDAY

Come, come, my lovely fair, and let us try
Those rural delicacies.
QUARLES, *Christ's Invitation to the Soul.*

AT LENGTH, on Saturday, the last day of August, 1839, we two, brothers, and natives of Concord, weighed anchor in this river port; for Concord, too, lies under the sun, a port of entry and departure for the bodies as well as the souls of men; one shore at least exempted from all duties but such as an honest man will gladly discharge. A warm, drizzling rain had obscured the morning, and threatened to delay our voyage, but at length the leaves and grass were dried, and it came out a mild afternoon, as serene and fresh as if Nature were maturing some greater scheme of her own. After this long dripping and oozing from every pore, she began to respire again more healthily than ever. So with a vigorous shove we launched our boat from the bank, while the flags and bulrushes courtesied a God-speed, and dropped silently down the stream.

Our boat, which had cost us a week's labor in the spring, was in form like a fisherman's dory, fifteen feet long by three and a half in breadth at the widest part, painted green below, with a border of blue, with reference to the two elements in which it was to spend its existence. It had been loaded the evening before at our door, half a mile from the river, with potatoes and melons, from a patch which we had cultivated, and a few utensils; and was provided with wheels in order to be rolled around falls, as well as with two sets of oars, and several slender poles for shoving in shallow places, and also two masts, one of which served for a tent-pole at night; for a buffalo-skin was to be our bed, and a tent of cotton cloth our roof. It was strongly built, but heavy, and hardly of better model than usual. If rightly made, a boat would be a sort of amphibious animal, a creature of two elements, related by one half its structure to some swift and shapely fish, and by the other to some strong-winged and graceful bird. The fish shows where there should be the greatest breadth of beam and depth in the hold; its fins direct where to set the oars, and the tail gives some hint for the form and position of the rudder. The bird shows how to rig and trim the sails, and what form to give to the prow, that it may balance the boat and divide the air and water best. These hints we had but partially obeyed. But the eyes, though they are no sailors, will never be satisfied with any model, however fashionable, which does not answer all the requisitions of art. However, as art is all of a ship but the wood, and yet the wood alone will rudely serve the purpose of a ship, so our boat, being of wood, gladly availed itself of the old law that the heavier shall float the lighter, and though a dull water-fowl, proved a sufficient buoy for our purpose.

> 'Were it the will of Heaven, an osier bough
> Were vessel safe enough the seas to plough.'

Some village friends stood upon a promontory lower down the stream to wave us a last farewell; but we, having already performed these shore rites, with excusable reserve, as befits those who are embarked on unusual enterprises, who behold but speak not, silently glided past the firm lands of Concord, both peopled cape and lonely summer meadow, with steady sweeps. And yet we did unbend so far as to let our guns speak for us, when at length we had swept out of sight, and thus left the woods to ring again with their echoes; and it may be many russet-clad children, lurking in those broad meadows, with the bittern and the woodcock and the rail, though wholly concealed by brakes and hardhack and meadow-sweet, heard our salute that afternoon.

We were soon floating past the first regular battle-ground of the Revolution, resting on our oars between the still visible abutments of that 'North Bridge' over which in April, 1775, rolled the first faint tide of that war which ceased not till, as we read on the stone on our right, it 'gave peace to these United States.' As a Concord poet has sung:

> 'By the rude bridge that arched the flood,
>> Their flag to April's breeze unfurled,
> Here once the embattled farmers stood
>> And fired the shot heard round the world.
>
> 'The foe long since in silence slept;
>> Alike the conqueror silent sleeps;
> And Time the ruined bridge has swept
>> Down the dark stream which seaward creeps.'

Our reflections had already acquired a historical remoteness from the scenes we had left, and we ourselves essayed to sing:

> Ah, 'tis in vain the peaceful din
>> That wakes the ignoble town,
> Not thus did braver spirits win
>> A patriot's renown.
>
> There is one field beside this stream
>> Wherein no foot does fall,
> But yet it beareth in my dream
>> A richer crop than all.
>
> Let me believe a dream so dear,
>> Some heart beat high that day,
> Above the petty Province here,
>> And Britain far away;
>
> Some hero of the ancient mould,
>> Some arm of knightly worth,
> Of strength unbought, and faith unsold,
>> Honored this spot of earth;

Who sought the prize his heart described,
    And did not ask release,
Whose free-born valor was not bribed
    By prospect of a peace.

The men who stood on yonder height
    That day are long since gone;
Not the same hand directs the fight
    And monumental stone.

Ye were the Grecian cities then,
    The Romes of modern birth,
Where the New England husbandmen
    Have shown a Roman worth.

In vain I search a foreign land
    To find our Bunker Hill,
And Lexington and Concord stand
    By no Laconian rill.

With such thoughts we swept gently by this now peaceful pasture-ground, on waves of Concord, in which was long since drowned the din of war.

But since we sailed
Some things have failed,
And many a dream
Gone down the stream.

Here then an aged shepherd dwelt,
Who to his flock his substance dealt,
And ruled them with a vigorous crook,
By precept of the sacred Book;
But he the pierless bridge passed o'er,
And solitary left the shore.

Anon a youthful pastor came,
Whose crook was not unknown to fame,
His lambs he viewed with gentle glance,
Spread o'er the country's wide expanse,
And fed with 'Mosses from the Manse.'
Here was our Hawthorne in the dale,
And here the shepherd told his tale.

That slight shaft had now sunk behind the hills, and we had floated round the neighboring bend, and under the new North Bridge between Ponkawtasset and the Poplar Hill, into the Great Meadows, which,

like a broad moccasin-print, have leveled a fertile and juicy place in
nature.

> On Ponkawtasset, since we took our way
> Down this still stream to far Billericay,
> A poet wise has settled, whose fine ray
> Doth often shine on Concord's twilight day.
>
> Like those first stars, whose silver beams on high,
> Shining more brightly as the day goes by,
> Most travelers cannot at first descry,
> But eyes that wont to range the evening sky,
>
> And know celestial lights, do plainly see,
> And gladly hail them, numbering two or three;
> For lore that's deep must deeply studied be,
> As from deep wells men read star-poetry.
>
> These stars are never paled, though out of sight,
> But like the sun they shine forever bright;
> Ay, *they* are suns, though earth must in its flight
> Put out its eyes that it may see their light.
>
> Who would neglect the least celestial sound,
> Or faintest light that falls on earthly ground,
> If he could know it one day would be found
> That star in Cygnus whither we are bound,
> And pale our sun with heavenly radiance round?

Gradually the village murmur subsided, and we seemed to be embarked on the placid current of our dreams, floating from past to future
as silently as one awakes to fresh morning or evening thoughts. We
glided noiselessly down the stream, occasionally driving a pickerel or
a bream from the covert of the pads, and the smaller bittern now and
then sailed away on sluggish wings from some recess in the shore, or the
larger lifted itself out of the long grass at our approach, and carried its
precious legs away to deposit them in a place of safety. The tortoises
also rapidly dropped into the water, as our boat ruffled the surface
amid the willows, breaking the reflections of the trees. The banks had
passed the height of their beauty, and some of the brighter flowers
showed by their faded tints that the season was verging towards the
afternoon of the year; but this sombre tinge enhanced their sincerity,
and in the still unabated heats they seemed like the mossy brink of some
cool well. The narrow-leaved willow (*Salix Purshiana*) lay along the
surface of the water in masses of light green foliage, interspersed with

the large balls of the button-bush. The small rose-colored polygonum raised its head proudly above the water on either hand, and flowering at this season and in these localities, in front of dense fields of the white species which skirted the sides of the stream, its little streak of red looked very rare and precious. The pure white blossoms of the arrowhead stood in the shallower parts, and a few cardinals on the margin still proudly surveyed themselves reflected in the water, though the latter, as well as the pickerel-weed, was now nearly out of blossom. The snake-head (*Chelone glabra*) grew close to the shore, while a kind of coreopsis, turning its brazen face to the sun, full and rank, and a tall dull-red flower (*Eupatorium purpureum*, or trumpet-weed) formed the rear rank of the fluvial array. The bright-blue flowers of the soapwort gentian were sprinkled here and there in the adjacent meadows, like flowers which Proserpine had dropped, and still farther in the fields or higher on the bank were seen the purple gerardia, the Virginian rhexia, and drooping neottia or ladies'-tresses; while from the more distant waysides which we occasionally passed, and banks where the sun had lodged, was reflected still a dull-yellow beam from the ranks of tansy, now past its prime. In short, Nature seemed to have adorned herself for our departure with a profusion of fringes and curls, mingled with the bright tints of flowers, reflected in the water. But we missed the white water-lily, which is the queen of river flowers, its reign being over for this season. He makes his voyage too late, perhaps, by a true water clock who delays so long. Many of this species inhabit our Concord water. I have passed down the river before sunrise on a summer morning, between fields of lilies still shut in sleep; and when, at length, the flakes of sunlight from over the bank fell on the surface of the water, whole fields of white blossoms seemed to flash open before me, as I floated along, like the unfolding of a banner, so sensible is this flower to the influence of the sun's rays.

As we were floating through the last of these familiar meadows, we observed the large and conspicuous flowers of the hibiscus, covering the dwarf willows and mingled with the leaves of the grape, and wished that we could inform one of our friends behind of the locality of this somewhat rare and inaccessible flower before it was too late to pluck it; but we were just gliding out of sight of the village spire before it occurred to us that the farmer in the adjacent meadow would go to church on the morrow, and would carry this news for us; and so by the Monday, while we should be floating on the Merrimack, our friend would be reaching to pluck this blossom on the bank of the Concord.

After a pause at Ball's Hill, the St. Anne's of Concord voyageurs, not to say any prayer for the success of our voyage, but to gather the few berries which were still left on the hills, hanging by very slender threads, we weighed anchor again, and were soon out of sight of our native village. The land seemed to grow fairer as we withdrew from it. Far away to the southwest lay the quiet village, left alone under its elms and buttonwoods in mid-afternoon; and the hills, notwithstanding their blue, ethereal faces, seemed to cast a saddened eye on their old playfellows; but, turning short to the north, we bade adieu to their familiar outlines, and addressed ourselves to new scenes and adventures. Naught was familiar but the heavens, from under whose roof the voyageur never passes; but with their countenance, and the acquaintance we had with river and wood, we trusted to fare well under any circumstances.

From this point the river runs perfectly straight for a mile or more to Carlisle Bridge, which consists of twenty wooden piers, and when we looked back over it, its surface was reduced to a line's breadth, and appeared like a cobweb gleaming in the sun. Here and there might be seen a pole sticking up, to mark the place where some fisherman had enjoyed unusual luck, and in return had consecrated his rod to the deities who preside over these shallows. It was full twice as broad as before, deep and tranquil, with a muddy bottom, and bordered with willows, beyond which spread broad lagoons covered with pads, bulrushes, and flags.

Late in the afternoon we passed a man on the shore fishing with a long birch pole, its silvery bark left on, and a dog at his side, rowing so near as to agitate his cork with our oars, and drive away luck for a season; and when we had rowed a mile as straight as an arrow, with our faces turned towards him, and the bubbles in our wake still visible on the tranquil surface, there stood the fisher still with his dog, like statues under the other side of the heavens, the only objects to relieve the eye in the extended meadow; and there would he stand abiding his luck, till he took his way home through the fields at evening with his fish. Thus, by one bait or another, Nature allures inhabitants into all her recesses. This man was the last of our townsmen whom we saw, and we silently through him bade adieu to our friends.

The characteristics and pursuits of various ages and races of men are always existing in epitome in every neighborhood. The pleasures of my earliest youth have become the inheritance of other men. This man is still a fisher, and belongs to an era in which I myself have lived.

Perchance he is not confounded by many knowledges, and has not sought out many inventions; but how to take many fishes before the sun sets, with his slender birchen pole and flaxen line, that is invention enough for him. It is good even to be a fisherman in summer and in winter. Some men are judges, these August days, sitting on benches, even till the court rises; they sit judging there honorably, between the seasons and between meals, leading a civil, politic life, arbitrating in the case of Spaulding *versus* Cummings, it may be, from highest noon till the red vesper sinks into the west. The fisherman, meanwhile, stands in three feet of water, under the same summer's sun, arbitrating in other cases between muck-worm and shiner, amid the fragrance of water-lilies, mint, and pontederia, leading his life many rods from the dry land, within a pole's length of where the larger fishes swim. Human life is to him very much like a river,

> 'renning aie downward to the sea.'

This was his observation. His honor made a great discovery in bailments.

I can just remember an old brown-coated man who was the Walton of this stream, who had come over from Newcastle, England, with his son — the latter a stout and hearty man who had lifted an anchor in his day. A straight old man he was, who took his way in silence through the meadows, having passed the period of communication with his fellows; his old experienced coat, hanging long and straight and brown as the yellow pine bark, glittering with so much smothered sunlight, if you stood near enough, no work of art but naturalized at length. I often discovered him unexpectedly amid the pads and the gray willows when he moved, fishing in some old country method — for youth and age then went a-fishing together — full of incommunicable thoughts, perchance about his own Tyne and Northumberland. He was always to be seen in serene afternoons haunting the river, and almost rustling with the sedge; so many sunny hours in an old man's life, entrapping silly fish; almost grown to be the sun's familiar; what need had he of hat or raiment any, having served out his time, and seen through such thin disguises? I have seen how his coeval fates rewarded him with the yellow perch, and yet I thought his luck was not in proportion to his years; and I have seen when, with slow steps and weighed down with aged thoughts, he disappeared with his fish under his low-roofed house on the skirts of the village. I think nobody else saw him; nobody else remembers him now, for he soon after died, and migrated to new Tyne streams. His fishing was not a sport, nor solely a means of subsistence, but a sort of solemn sacrament and withdrawal from the world, just as the aged read their Bibles.

Whether we live by the seaside, or by the lakes and rivers, or on the prairie, it concerns us to attend to the nature of fishes, since they are not phenomena confined to certain localities only, but forms and phases of the life in nature universally dispersed. The countless shoals which annually coast the shores of Europe and America are not so interesting to the student of nature as the more fertile law itself, which deposits their spawn on the tops of mountains and on the interior plains; the fish principle in nature, from which it results that they may be found in water in so many places, in greater or less numbers. The natural historian is not a fisherman who prays for cloudy days and good luck merely; but as fishing has been styled 'a contemplative man's recreation,' introducing him profitably to woods and water, so the fruit of the naturalist's observations is not in new genera or species, but in new contemplations still, and science is only a more contemplative man's recreation. The seeds of the life of fishes are everywhere disseminated, whether the winds waft them, or the waters float them, or the deep earth holds them; wherever a pond is dug, straightway it is stocked with this vivacious race. They have a lease of nature, and it is not yet out. The Chinese are bribed to carry their ova from province to province in jars or in hollow reeds, or the water-birds to transport them to the mountain tarns and interior lakes. There are fishes wherever there is a fluid medium, and even in clouds and in melted metals we detect their semblance. Think how in winter you can sink a line down straight in a pasture through snow and through ice, and pull up a bright, slippery, dumb, subterranean silver or golden fish! It is curious, also, to reflect how they make one family, from the largest to the smallest. The least minnow that lies on the ice as bait for pickerel looks like a huge sea-fish cast up on the shore. In the waters of this town there are about a dozen distinct species, though the inexperienced would expect many more.

It enhances our sense of the grand security and serenity of nature to observe the still undisturbed economy and content of the fishes of this century, their happiness a regular fruit of the summer. The fresh-water sun-fish, bream, or ruff (*Pomotis vulgaris*), as it were without ancestry, without posterity, still represents the fresh-water sun-fish in nature. It is the most common of all, and seen on every urchin's string; a simple and inoffensive fish, whose nests are visible all along the shore, hollowed in the sand, over which it is steadily poised through the summer hours on waving fin. Sometimes there are twenty or thirty nests in the space of a few rods, two feet wide by half a foot in depth, and made with no little labor, the weeds being removed, and the sand shoved up on the sides, like a bowl. Here it may be seen early in summer assiduously brooding, and driving away minnows and larger fishes, even its own species, which would disturb its ova, pursuing them a few feet, and circling round swiftly to its nest again; the minnows, like young sharks, instantly entering the empty nests, meanwhile, and swallowing the spawn, which is attached to the weeds and to the bottom, on the sunny side. The spawn is exposed to so many dangers that a very small proportion can ever become fishes, for beside being the constant prey of birds and fishes, a great many nests are made so near the shore, in shallow water, that they are left dry in a few days, as the river goes down. These and the lamprey's are the only fishes' nests that I have observed, though the ova of some species may be seen floating on the surface. The breams are so careful of their charge that you may stand close by in the water and examine them at your leisure. I have thus stood over them half an hour at a time, and stroked them familiarly without frightening them, suffering them to nibble my fingers harmlessly, and seen them erect their dorsal fins in anger when my hand approached their ova, and have even taken them gently out of the water with my hand; though this cannot be accomplished by a sudden movement, however dexterous, for instant warning is conveyed to them through their denser element, but only by letting the fingers gradually close about them as they are poised over the palm, and with the utmost gentleness raising them slowly to the surface. Though stationary, they kept up a constant sculling or waving motion with their fins, which is exceedingly graceful, and expressive of their humble happiness; for unlike ours, the element in which they live is a stream which must be constantly resisted. From time to time they nibble the weeds at the bottom or overhanging their nests, or dart after a fly or a worm. The dorsal fin, besides answering the purpose of a keel, with the anal, serves to keep the fish upright, for in shallow water, where this is not covered, they fall on their sides. As you stand thus stooping over the bream in its nest, the edges of the dorsal and caudal fins have a singular dusty golden reflection, and its eyes, which stand out from the head, are transparent and colorless. Seen in its native element, it is a very beautiful and compact fish, perfect in all its parts, and looks like a brilliant coin fresh from the mint. It is a perfect jewel of the river, the green, red, coppery, and golden reflections of its mottled sides being the con-centration of such rays as struggle through the floating pads and flowers to the sandy bottom, and in harmony with the sunlit brown and yellow pebbles. Behind its watery shield it dwells far from many accidents inevitable to human life.

There is also another species of bream found in our river, without the red spot on the operculum, which, according to M. Agassiz, is un-described.

The common perch (*Perca flavescens*, which name describes well the gleaming, golden reflections of its scales as it is drawn out of the water, its red gills standing out in vain in the thin element) is one of the hand-somest and most regularly formed of our fishes, and at such a moment as this reminds us of the fish in the picture which wished to be restored to its native element until it had grown larger; and indeed most of this species that are caught are not half grown. In the ponds there is a light-colored and slender kind, which swim in shoals of many hundreds in the sunny water, in company with the shiner, averaging not more than six or seven inches in length, while only a few larger specimens are found in the deepest water, which prey upon their weaker brethren. I have often attracted these small perch to the shore at evening, by rippling the water with my fingers, and they may sometimes be caught while attempting to pass inside your hands. It is a tough and heedless fish, biting from impulse, without nibbling, and from impulse refraining to bite, and sculling indifferently past. It rather prefers the clear water and sandy bottoms, though here it has not much choice. It is a true fish, such as the angler loves to put into his basket or hang at the top of his willow twig, in shady afternoons along the banks of the stream. So many unquestionable fishes he counts, and so many shiners, which he counts and then throws away. Old Josselyn in his 'New England's Rarities,' published in 1672, mentions the Perch or River Partridge.

The chivin, dace, roach, cousin trout, or whatever else it is called (*Leuciscus pulchellus*), white and red, is always an unexpected prize, which, however, any angler is glad to hook for its rarity; — a name that reminds us of many an unsuccessful ramble by swift streams, when the wind rose to disappoint the fisher. It is commonly a silvery soft-scaled fish, of graceful, scholarlike, and classical look, like many a picture in an English book. It loves a swift current and a sandy bottom, and bites inadvertently, yet not without appetite for the bait. The min-nows are used as bait for pickerel in the winter. The red chivin, according to some, is still the same fish, only older, or with its tints deepened as they think by the darker water it inhabits, as the red clouds swim in the twilight atmosphere. He who has not hooked the red chivin is not yet a complete angler. Other fishes, methinks, are slightly amphibious, but this is a denizen of the water wholly. The cork goes dancing down the swift-rushing stream, amid the weeds and sands, when suddenly, by a coincidence never to be remembered, emerges this fabulous inhabitant of another element, a thing heard of but not seen, as if it were the instant creation of an eddy, a true product of the running stream. And this bright cupreous dolphin was spawned and has passed its life beneath the level of your feet in your native fields. Fishes, too, as well as birds and clouds, derive their armor from the mine. I have heard of mackerel visiting the copper banks at a particular season; this fish, perchance, has its habitat in the Coppermine River. I have caught white chivin of great size in the Aboljacknagesic, where it empties into the Penobscot, at the base of Mount Ktaadn, but no red ones there. The latter variety seems not to have been sufficiently observed.

The dace (*Leuciscus argenteus*) is a slight silvery minnow, found generally in the middle of the stream where the current is most rapid, and frequently confounded with the last named.

The shiner (*Leuciscus chrysoleucus*) is a soft-scaled and tender fish, the victim of its stronger neighbors, found in all places, deep and shallow, clear and turbid; generally the first nibbler at the bait, but, with its small mouth and nibbling propensities, not easily caught. It is a gold or silver bit that passes current in the river, its limber tail dimpling the surface in sport or flight. I have seen the fry, when frightened by something thrown into the water, leap out by dozens, together with the dace, and wreck themselves upon a floating plank. It is the little light-infant of the river, with body armor of gold or silver spangles, slipping, gliding its life through with a quirk of the tail, half in the water, half in the air, upward and ever upward with flitting fin to more crystalline tides, yet still abreast of us dwellers on the bank. It is almost dissolved by the summer heats. A slighter and lighter-colored shiner is found in one of our ponds.

The pickerel (*Esox reticulatus*), the swiftest, wariest, and most ravenous of fishes, which Josselyn calls the Fresh-Water or River Wolf, is very common in the shallow and weedy lagoons along the sides of the stream. It is a solemn, stately, ruminant fish, lurking under the shadow of a pad at noon, with still, circumspect, voracious eye, motionless as a jewel set in water, or moving slowly along to take up its position, darting from time to time at such unlucky fish or frog or insect as comes within its range, and swallowing it at a gulp. I have caught one which had swallowed a brother pickerel half as large as itself, with the tail still visible in its mouth, while the head was already digested in its stomach. Sometimes a striped snake, bound to greener meadows across the stream, ends its undulatory progress in the same receptacle. They are so greedy and impetuous that they are frequently caught by being entangled in the line the moment it is cast. Fishermen also distinguish the brook pickerel, a shorter and thicker fish than the former.

The horned pout (*Pimelodus nebulosus*), sometimes called Minister, from the peculiar squeaking noise it makes when drawn out of the water, is a dull and blundering fellow, and, like the eel, vespertinal in his habits and fond of the mud. It bites deliberately, as if about its business. They are taken at night with a mass of worms strung on a thread, which catches in their teeth, sometimes three or four, with an eel, at one pull. They are extremely tenacious of life, opening and shutting their mouths for half an hour after their heads have been cut off; a bloodthirsty and bullying race of rangers, inhabiting the fertile river bottoms, with ever a lance in rest, and ready to do battle with their nearest neighbor. I have observed them in summer, when every other one had a long and bloody scar upon his back, where the skin was gone, the mark, perhaps, of some fierce encounter. Sometimes the fry, not an inch long, are seen darkening the shore with their myriads.

The suckers (*Catostomi Bostonienses* and *tuberculati*), common and horned, perhaps on an average the largest of our fishes, may be seen in shoals of a hundred or more, stemming the current in the sun, on their mysterious migrations, and sometimes sucking in the bait which the fisherman suffers to float toward them. The former, which sometimes grow to a large size, are frequently caught by the hand in the brooks, or like the red chivin are jerked out by a hook fastened firmly to the end of a stick, and placed under their jaws. They are hardly known to the mere angler, however, not often biting at his baits, though the spearer carries home many a mess in the spring. To our village eyes, these shoals have a foreign and imposing aspect, realizing the fertility of the seas.

The common eel, too (*Muræna Bostoniensis*), the only species of eel known in the State, a slimy, squirming creature, informed of mud, still squirming in the pan, is speared and hooked up with various success. Methinks it too occurs in picture, left after the deluge, in many a meadow high and dry.

In the shallow parts of the river, where the current is rapid and the bottom pebbly, you may sometimes see the curious circular nests of the lamprey eel (*Petromyzon Americanus*), the American stone-sucker, as large as a cart-wheel, a foot or two in height, and sometimes rising half a foot above the surface of the water. They collect these stones, of the size of a hen's egg, with their mouths, as their name implies, and are said to fashion them into circles with their tails. They ascend falls by clinging to the stones, which may sometimes be raised by lifting the fish by the tail. As they are not seen on their way down the streams, it is thought by fishermen that they never return, but waste away and die, clinging to rocks and stumps of trees for an indefinite period; a tragic feature in the scenery of the river bottoms worthy to be remembered with Shakespeare's description of the sea-floor. They are rarely seen in our waters at present, on account of the dams, though they are taken in great quantities at the mouth of the river in Lowell. Their nests, which are very conspicuous, look more like art than anything in the river.

If we had leisure this afternoon, we might turn our prow up the brooks in quest of the classical trout and the minnows. Of the last alone, according to M. Agassiz, several of the species found in this town are yet undescribed. These would, perhaps, complete the list of our finny contemporaries in the Concord waters.

Salmon, shad, and alewives were formerly abundant here, and taken in weirs by the Indians, who taught this method to the whites, by whom they were used as food and as manure, until the dam and afterward the canal at Billerica, and the factories at Lowell, put an end to their migrations hitherward; though it is thought that a few more enterprising shad may still occasionally be seen in this part of the river. It is said, to account for the destruction of the fishery, that those who at that time represented the interests of the fishermen and the fishes, remembering between what dates they were accustomed to take the grown shad, stipulated that the dams should be left open for that season only, and the fry, which go down a month later, were consequently stopped and destroyed by myriads. Others say that the fish-ways were not properly constructed. Perchance, after a few thousands of years, if the fishes will be patient, and pass their summers elsewhere meanwhile, nature will have leveled the Billerica dam, and the Lowell factories, and the Grass-ground River run clear again, to be explored by new migratory shoals, even as far as the Hopkinton pond and Westborough swamp.

One would like to know more of that race, now extinct, whose seines lie rotting in the garrets of their children, who openly professed the trade of fishermen, and even fed their townsmen creditably, not skulking through the meadows to a rainy afternoon sport. Dim visions we still get of miraculous draughts of fishes, and heaps uncountable by the riverside, from the tales of our seniors sent on horseback in their childhood from the neighboring towns, perched on saddle-bags, with instructions to get the one bag filled with shad, the other with alewives. At least one memento of those days may still exist in the memory of this generation, in the familiar appellation of a celebrated train-band of this town, whose untrained ancestors stood creditably at Concord North Bridge. Their captain, a man of piscatory tastes, having duly warned his company to turn out on a certain day, they, like obedient soldiers, appeared promptly on parade at the appointed time, but, unfortunately, they went undrilled, except in the manœuvres of a soldier's wit and unlicensed jesting, that May day; for their captain, forgetting his own appointment, and warned only by the favorable aspect of the heavens, as he had often done before, went a-fishing that afternoon, and his company thenceforth was known to old and young, grave and gay, as 'The Shad,' and by the youths of this vicinity this was long regarded as the proper name of all the irregular militia in Christendom. But, alas! no record of these fishers' lives remains that we know, unless it be one brief page of hard but unquestionable history, which occurs in Day Book No. 4, of an old trader of this town, long since dead, which shows pretty plainly what constituted a fisherman's stock in trade in those days. It purports to be a Fisherman's Account Current, probably for the fishing season of the year 1805, during which months he purchased daily rum and sugar, sugar and rum, N. E. and W. I., 'one cod line,' 'one brown mug,' and 'a line for the seine;' rum and sugar, sugar and rum, 'good loaf sugar,' and 'good brown,' W. I. and N. E., in short and uniform entries to the bottom of the page, all carried out in pounds, shillings, and pence, from March 25 to June 5, and promptly settled by receiving 'cash in full' at the last date. But perhaps not so settled altogether. These were the necessaries of life in those days; with salmon, shad, and alewives, fresh and pickled, he was thereafter independent on the groceries. Rather a preponderance of the fluid elements; but such is the fisherman's nature. I can faintly remember to have seen this same fisher in my earliest youth, still as near the river as he could get, with uncertain undulatory step, after so many things had gone down-stream, swinging a scythe in the meadow, his bottle like a serpent hid in the grass; himself as yet not cut down by the Great Mower.

Surely the fates are forever kind, though Nature's laws are more immutable than any despot's, yet to man's daily life they rarely seem rigid, but permit him to relax with license in summer weather. He is not harshly reminded of the things he may not do. She is very kind and liberal to all men of vicious habits, and certainly does not deny them quarter; they do not die without priest. Still they maintain life along the way, keeping this side the Styx, still hearty, still resolute, 'never better in their lives;' and again, after a dozen years have elapsed, they start up from behind a hedge, asking for work and wages for able-bodied men. Who has not met such

> 'a beggar on the way,
> Who sturdily could gang?...
> Who cared neither for wind nor wet,
> In lands where'er he past?'

> 'That bold adopts each house he views, his own;
> Makes every purse his checquer, and, at pleasure,
> Walks forth, and taxes all the world, like Cæsar;' —

as if consistency were the secret of health, while the poor inconsistent aspirant man, seeking to live a pure life, feeding on air, divided against himself, cannot stand, but pines and dies after a life of sickness, on beds of down.

The unwise are accustomed to speak as if some were not sick; but methinks the difference between men in respect to health is not great enough to lay much stress upon. Some are reputed sick and some are not. It often happens that the sicker man is the nurse to the sounder.

Shad are still taken in the basin of Concord River, at Lowell, where they are said to be a month earlier than the Merrimack shad, on account of the warmth of the water. Still patiently, almost pathetically, with instinct not to be discouraged, not to be *reasoned* with, revisiting their old haunts, as if their stern fates would relent, and still met by the Corporation with its dam. Poor shad! where is thy redress? When Nature gave thee instinct, gave she thee the heart to bear thy fate? Still wandering the sea in thy scaly armor to inquire humbly at the mouths of rivers if man has perchance left them free for thee to enter. By countless shoals loitering uncertain meanwhile, merely stemming the tide there, in danger from sea foes in spite of thy bright armor, awaiting new instructions, until the sands, until the water itself, tell thee if it be so or not. Thus by whole migrating nations, full of instinct, which is thy faith, in this backward spring, turned adrift, and perchance knowest not where men do *not* dwell, where there are *not* factories, in these days. Armed with no sword, no electric shock, but mere shad, armed only with innocence and a just cause, with tender dumb mouth only forward, and scales easy to be detached. I for one am with thee, and who knows what may avail a crowbar against that Billerica dam? — Not despairing when whole myriads have gone to feed those sea monsters during thy suspense, but still brave, indifferent, on easy fin there, like shad reserved for higher destinies. Willing to be decimated for man's behoof after the spawning season. Away with the superficial and selfish *philanthropy* of men — who knows what admirable virtue of fishes may be below low-water-mark, bearing up against a hard destiny, not admired by that fellow-creature who alone can appreciate it! Who hears the fishes when they cry? It will not be forgotten by some memory that we were contemporaries. Thou shalt ere long have thy way up the rivers, up all the rivers of the globe, if I am not mistaken. Yea, even thy dull watery dream shall be more than realized. If it were not so, but thou wert to be overlooked at first and at last, then would not I take their heaven. Yes, I say so, who think I know better than thou canst. Keep a stiff fin, then, and stem all the tides thou mayst meet.

At length it would seem that the interests, not of the fishes only, but of the men of Wayland, of Sudbury, of Concord, demand the leveling of that dam. Innumerable acres of meadow are waiting to be made dry land, wild native grass to give place to English. The farmers stand with scythes whet, waiting the subsiding of the waters, by gravitation, by evaporation, or otherwise, but sometimes their eyes do not rest, their wheels do not roll, on the quaking meadow ground during the haying season at all. So many sources of wealth inaccessible. They rate the loss hereby incurred in the single town of Wayland alone as equal to the expense of keeping a hundred yoke of oxen the year round. One year, as I learn, not long ago, the farmers standing ready to drive their teams afield as usual, the water gave no signs of falling; without new attraction in the heavens, without freshet or visible cause, still standing stagnant at an unprecedented height. All hydrometers were at fault; some trembled for their English, even. But speedy emissaries revealed the unnatural secret, in the new float-board, wholly a foot in width, added to their already too high privileges by the dam proprietors. The hundred yoke of oxen, meanwhile, standing patient, gazing wishfully meadowward, at that inaccessible waving native grass, uncut but by the great mower Time, who cuts so broad a swath, without so much as a wisp to wind about their horns.

That was a long pull from Ball's Hill to Carlisle Bridge, sitting with our faces to the south, a slight breeze rising from the north; but nevertheless water still runs and grass grows, for now, having passed the bridge between Carlisle and Bedford, we see men haying far off in the meadow, their heads waving like the grass which they cut. In the distance the wind seemed to bend all alike. As the night stole over, such a freshness was wafted across the meadow that every blade of cut grass seemed to teem with life. Faint purple clouds began to be reflected in the water, and the cow-bells tinkled louder along the banks, while, like sly water-rats, we stole along nearer the shore, looking for a place to pitch our camp.

At length, when we had made about seven miles, as far as Billerica, we moored our boat on the west side of a little rising ground which in the spring forms an island in the river. Here we found huckleberries still hanging upon the bushes, where they seemed to have slowly ripened for our especial use. Bread and sugar, and cocoa boiled in river water, made our repast, and as we had drank in the fluvial prospect all day, so now we took a draft of the water with our evening meal to propitiate the river gods, and whet our vision for the sights it was to behold. The sun was setting on the one hand, while our eminence was contributing its shadow to the night on the other. It seemed insensibly to grow lighter as the night shut in, and a distant and solitary farmhouse was revealed, which before lurked in the shadows of the noon. There was no other house in sight, nor any cultivated field. To the right and left, as far as the horizon, were straggling pine woods with their plumes against the sky, and across the river were rugged hills, covered with shrub oaks, tangled with grape-vines and ivy, with here and there a gray rock jutting out from the maze. The sides of these cliffs, though a quarter of a mile distant, were almost heard to rustle while we looked at them, it was such a leafy wilderness; a place for fauns and satyrs, and where bats hung all day to the rocks, and at evening flitted over the water, and fireflies husbanded their light under the grass and leaves against the night. When we had pitched our tent on the hillside, a few rods from the shore, we sat looking through its triangular door in the twilight at our lonely mast on the shore just seen above the alders, and hardly yet come to a standstill from the swaying of the stream; the first encroachment of commerce on this land. There was our port, our Ostia. That straight, geometrical line against the water and the sky stood for the last refinements of civilized life, and what of sublimity there is in history was there symbolized.

For the most part, there was no recognition of human life in the night; no human breathing was heard, only the breathing of the wind. As we sat up, kept awake by the novelty of our situation, we heard at intervals foxes stepping about over the dead leaves, and brushing the dewy grass close to our tent, and once a musquash fumbling among the potatoes and melons in our boat; but when we hastened to the shore we could detect only a ripple in the water ruffling the disk of a star. At intervals we were serenaded by the song of a dreaming sparrow or the throttled cry of an owl; but after each sound which near at hand broke the stillness of the night, each crackling of the twigs, or rustling among the leaves, there was a sudden pause, and deeper and more conscious silence, as if the intruder were aware that no life was rightfully abroad at that hour. There was a fire in Lowell, as we judged, this night, and we saw the horizon blazing, and heard the distant alarm-bells, as it were a faint tinkling music borne to these woods. But the most constant and memorable sound of a summer's night, which we did not fail to hear every night afterward, though at no time so incessantly and so favorably as now, was the barking of the house-dogs, from the loudest and hoarsest bark to the faintest aerial palpitation under the eaves of heaven, from the patient but anxious mastiff to the timid and wakeful terrier, at first loud and rapid, then faint and slow, to be imitated only in a whisper; wow-wow-wow-wow — wo — wo — w — w. Even in a retired and uninhabited district like this, it was a sufficiency of sound for the ear of night, and more impressive than any music. I have heard the voice of a hound, just before daylight, while the stars were shining, from over the woods and river, far in the horizon, when it sounded as sweet and melodious as an instrument. The hounding of a dog pursuing a fox or other animal in the horizon may have first suggested the notes of the hunting-horn to alternate with and relieve the lungs of the dog. This natural bugle long resounded in the woods of the ancient world before the horn was invented. The very dogs that sullenly bay the moon from farm-yards in these nights excite more heroism in our breasts than all the civil exhortations or war sermons of the age. 'I would rather be a dog, and bay the moon,' than many a Roman that I know. The night is equally indebted to the clarion of the cock, with wakeful hope, from the very setting of the sun, prematurely ushering in the dawn. All these sounds, the crowing of cocks, the baying of dogs, and the hum of insects at noon, are the evidence of nature's health or *sound* state. Such is the never-failing beauty and accuracy of language, the most perfect art in the world; the chisel of a thousand years retouches it.

At length the antepenultimate and drowsy hours drew on, and all sounds were denied entrance to our ears.

> Who sleeps by day and walks by night,
> Will meet no spirit, but some sprite.

SUNDAY

> The river calmly flows,
> Through shining banks, through lonely glen,
> Where the owl shrieks, though ne'er the cheer of men
> Has stirred its mute repose,
> Still if you should walk there, you would go there again.
>
> CHANNING.

The Indians tell us of a beautiful river lying far to the south, which they call Merrimack. — SIEUR DE MONTS, *Relations of the Jesuits*, 1604.

IN THE morning the river and adjacent country were covered with a dense fog, through which the smoke of our fire curled up like a still subtiler mist; but before we had rowed many rods, the sun arose and the fog rapidly dispersed, leaving a slight steam only to curl along the surface of the water. It was a quiet Sunday morning, with more of the auroral rosy and white than of the yellow light in it, as if it dated from earlier than the fall of man, and still preserved a heathenish integrity:

> An early unconverted Saint,
> Free from noontide or evening taint,
> Heathen without reproach,
> That did upon the civil day encroach,
> And ever since its birth
> Had trod the outskirts of the earth.

But the impressions which the morning makes vanish with its dews, and not even the most 'persevering mortal' can preserve the memory of its freshness to midday. As we passed the various islands or what were islands in the spring, rowing with our backs down-stream, we gave names to them. The one on which we had camped we called Fox Island, and one fine densely wooded island surrounded by deep water and overrun by grape-vines, which looked like a mass of verdure and of flowers cast upon the waves, we named Grape Island. From Ball's Hill to Billerica meeting-house, the river was still twice as broad as in Concord, a deep, dark, and dead stream, flowing between gentle hills and sometimes cliffs, and well wooded all the way. It was a long woodland lake bordered with willows. For long reaches we could see neither house nor cultivated field, nor any sign of the vicinity of man. Now we coasted along some shallow shore by the edge of a dense palisade of bulrushes, which straightly bounded the water as if clipped by art, reminding us of the reed forts of the East-Indians of which we had read; and now the bank, slightly raised, was overhung with graceful grasses and various species of brake, whose downy stems stood closely grouped and naked as in a vase, while their heads spread several feet on either side. The dead limbs of the willow were rounded and adorned by the climbing mikania (*Mikania scandens*), which filled every crevice in the leafy bank, contrasting agreeably with the gray bark of its supporter and the balls of the button-bush. The water willow (*Salix Purshiana*), when it is of large size and entire, is the most graceful and ethereal of our trees. Its masses of light-green foliage, piled one upon another to the height of twenty or thirty feet, seemed to float on the surface of the water, while the slight gray stems and the shore were hardly visible between them. No tree is so wedded to the water, and harmonizes so well with still streams. It is even more graceful than the weeping willow, or any pendulous trees which dip their branches in the stream instead of being buoyed up by it. Its limbs curved outward over the surface as if attracted by it. It had not a New England but an Oriental character, reminding us of trim Persian gardens, of Haroun Alraschid, and the artificial lakes of the East.

As we thus dipped our way along between fresh masses of foliage overrun with the grape and smaller flowering vines, the surface was so calm, and both air and water so transparent, that the flight of a kingfisher or robin over the river was as distinctly seen reflected in the water below as in the air above. The birds seemed to flit through submerged groves, alighting on the yielding sprays, and their clear notes to come up from below. We were uncertain whether the water floated the land, or the land held the water in its bosom. It was such a season, in short, as that in which one of our Concord poets sailed on its stream, and sung its quiet glories.

> 'There is an inward voice, that in the stream
> Sends forth its spirit to the listening ear,
> And in a calm content it floweth on,
> Like wisdom, welcome with its own respect.
> Clear in its breast lie all these beauteous thoughts,
> It doth receive the green and graceful trees,
> And the gray rocks smile in its peaceful arms.'

And more he sung, but too serious for our page. For every oak and birch, too, growing on the hilltop, as well as for these elms and willows, we knew that there was a graceful ethereal and ideal tree making down from the roots, and sometimes Nature in high tides brings her mirror to its foot and makes it visible. The stillness was intense and almost conscious, as if it were a natural Sabbath, and we fancied that the morning was the evening of a celestial day. The air was so elastic and crystalline that it had the same effect on the landscape that a glass has on a picture, to give it an ideal remoteness and perfection. The landscape was clothed in a mild and quiet light, in which the woods and fences checkered and partitioned it with new regularity, and rough and uneven fields stretched away with lawn-like smoothness to the horizon, and the clouds, finely distinct and picturesque, seemed a fit drapery to hang over fairyland. The world seemed decked for some holiday or prouder pageantry, with silken streamers flying, and the course of our lives to wind on before us like a green lane into a country maze, at the season when fruit-trees are in blossom.

Why should not our whole life and its scenery be actually thus fair and distinct? All our lives want a suitable background. They should at least, like the life of the anchorite, be as impressive to behold as objects in the desert, a broken shaft or crumbling mound against a limitless horizon. Character always secures for itself this advantage, and is thus distinct and unrelated to near or trivial objects, whether things or persons. On this same stream a maiden once sailed in my boat, thus unattended but by invisible guardians, and as she sat in the prow there was nothing but herself between the steersman and the sky. I could then say with the poet —

> 'Sweet falls the summer air
> Over her frame who sails with me;
> Her way like that is beautifully free,
> Her nature far more rare,
> And is her constant heart of virgin purity.'

At evening, still the very stars seem but this maiden's emissaries and reporters of her progress.

> Low in the eastern sky
> Is set thy glancing eye;
> And though its gracious light
> Ne'er riseth to my sight,
> Yet every star that climbs
> Above the gnarled limbs
>   Of yonder hill,
> Conveys thy gentle will.
>
> Believe I knew thy thought,
> And that the zephyrs brought
> Thy kindest wishes through,
> As mine they bear to you,
> That some attentive cloud
> Did pause amid the crowd
>   Over my head,
> While gentle things were said.
>
> Believe the thrushes sung,
> And that the flower-bells rung,
> That herbs exhaled their scent,
> And beasts knew what was meant,
> The trees a welcome waved,
> And lakes their margins laved,
>   When thy free mind
> To my retreat did wind.
>
> It was a summer eve,
> The air did gently heave
> While yet a low-hung cloud
> Thy eastern skies did shroud;
> The lightning's silent gleam,
> Startling my drowsy dream,
>   Seemed like the flash
> Under thy dark eyelash.
>
> Still will I strive to be
> As if thou wert with me;
> Whatever path I take,
> It shall be for thy sake,
> Of gentle slope and wide,
> As thou wert by my side,
>   Without a root
> To trip thy gentle foot.

> I'll walk with gentle pace,
> And choose the smoothest place,
> And careful dip the oar,
> And shun the winding shore,
> And gently steer my boat
> Where water-lilies float,
>   And cardinal-flowers
> Stand in their sylvan bowers.

It required some rudeness to disturb with our boat the mirror-like surface of the water, in which every twig and blade of grass was so faithfully reflected; too faithfully indeed for art to imitate, for only Nature may exaggerate herself. The shallowest still water is unfathomable. Wherever the trees and skies are reflected, there is more than Atlantic depth, and no danger of fancy running aground. We notice that it required a separate intention of the eye, a more free and abstracted vision, to see the reflected trees and the sky, than to see the river bottom merely; and so are there manifold visions in the direction of every object, and even the most opaque reflect the heavens from their surface. Some men have their eyes naturally intended to the one and some to the other object.

> 'A man that looks on glass,
>   On it may stay his eye,
> Or, if he pleaseth, through it pass,
>   And the heavens espy.'

Two men in a skiff, whom we passed hereabouts, floating buoyantly amid the reflections of the trees, like a feather in mid-air, or a leaf which is wafted gently from its twig to the water without turning over, seemed still in their element, and to have very delicately availed themselves of the natural laws. Their floating there was a beautiful and successful experiment in natural philosophy, and it served to ennoble in our eyes the art of navigation; for as birds fly and fishes swim, so these men sailed. It reminded us how much fairer and nobler all the actions of man might be, and that our life in its whole economy might be as beautiful as the fairest works of art or nature.

The sun lodged on the old gray cliffs, and glanced from every pad; the bulrushes and flags seemed to rejoice in the delicious light and air; the meadows were a-drinking at their leisure; the frogs sat meditating, all Sabbath thoughts, summing up their week, with one eye out on the golden sun, and one toe upon a reed, eying the wondrous universe in which they act their part; the fishes swam more staid and soberly, as maidens go to church; shoals of golden and silver minnows rose to the surface to behold the heavens, and then sheered off into more sombre aisles; they swept by as if moved by one mind, continually gliding past each other, and yet preserving the form of their battalion unchanged, as if they were still embraced by the transparent membrane which held the spawn; a young band of brethren and sisters trying their new fins; now they wheeled, now shot ahead, and when we drove them to the shore and cut them off, they dexterously tacked and passed underneath the boat. Over the old wooden bridges no traveler crossed, and neither the river nor the fishes avoided to glide between the abutments.

Here was a village not far off behind the woods, Billerica, settled not long ago, and the children still bear the names of the first settlers in this late 'howling wilderness;' yet to all intents and purposes it is as old as Fernay or as Mantua, an old gray town where men grow old and sleep already under moss-grown monuments — outgrow their usefulness. This is ancient Billerica (Villarica?), now in its dotage, named from the English Billericay, and whose Indian name was Shawshine. I never heard that it was young. See, is not nature here gone to decay, farms all run out, meeting-house grown gray and racked with age? If you would know of its early youth, ask those old gray rocks in the pasture. It has a bell that sounds sometimes as far as Concord woods; I have heard that — ay, hear it now. No wonder that such a sound startled the dreaming Indian, and frightened his game, when the first bells were swung on trees, and sounded through the forest beyond the plantations of the white man; but today I like best the echo amid these cliffs and woods. It is no feeble imitation, but rather its original, or as if some rural Orpheus played over the strain again to show how it should sound.

> Dong, sounds the brass in the east,
> As if to a funeral feast,
> But I like that sound the best
> Out of the fluttering west.
>
> The steeple ringeth a knell,
> But the fairies' silvery bell
> Is the voice of that gentle folk,
> Or else the horizon that spoke.
>
> Its metal is not of brass,
> But air, and water, and glass,
> And under a cloud it is swung,
> And by the wind it is rung.

> When the steeple tolleth the noon,
> It soundeth not so soon,
> Yet it rings a far earlier hour,
> And the sun has not reached its tower.

On the other hand, the road runs up to Carlisle, city of the woods, which, if it is less civil, is the more natural. It does well hold the earth together. It gets laughed at because it is a small town, I know, but nevertheless it is a place where great men may be born any day, for fair winds and foul blow right on over it without distinction. It has a meeting-house and horse-sheds, a tavern and a blacksmith's shop, for centre, and a good deal of wood to cut and cord yet. And

> 'Bedford, most noble Bedford,
> I shall not thee forget.'

History has remembered thee; especially that meek and humble petition of thy old planters, like the wailing of the Lord's own people, 'To the gentlemen, the selectmen' of Concord, praying to be erected into a separate parish. We can hardly credit that so plaintive a psalm resounded but little more than a century ago along these Babylonish waters. 'In the extreme difficult seasons of heat and cold,' said they, 'we were ready to say of the Sabbath, Behold what a weariness is it.' 'Gentlemen, if our seeking to draw off proceed from any disaffection to our present Reverend Pastor, or the Christian Society with whom we have taken such sweet counsel together, and walked unto the house of God in company, then hear us not this day; but we greatly desire, if God please, to be eased of our burden on the Sabbath, the travel and fatigue thereof, that the word of God may be nigh to us, near to our houses and in our hearts, that we and our little ones may serve the Lord. We hope that God, who stirred up the spirit of Cyrus to set forward temple work, has stirred us up to ask, and will stir you up to grant, the prayer of our petition; so shall your humble petitioners ever pray, as in duty bound' — And so the temple work went forward here to a happy conclusion. Yonder in Carlisle the building of the temple was many wearisome years delayed, not that there was wanting of Shittim wood, or the gold of Ophir, but a site therefor convenient to all the worshipers; whether on 'Buttrick's Plain,' or rather on 'Poplar Hill.' It was a tedious question.

In this Billerica solid men must have lived, select from year to year; a series of town clerks, at least; and there are old records that you may search. Some spring the white man came, built him a house, and made a clearing here, letting in the sun, dried up a farm, piled up the old gray stones in fences, cut down the pines around his dwelling, planted orchard seeds brought from the old country, and persuaded the civil apple-tree to blossom next to the wild pine and the juniper, shedding its perfume in the wilderness. Their old stocks still remain. He culled the graceful elm from out the woods and from the riverside, and so refined and smoothed his village plot. He rudely bridged the stream, and drove his team afield into the river meadows, cut the wild grass, and laid bare the homes of beaver, otter, muskrat, and with the whetting of his scythe scared off the deer and bear. He set up a mill, and fields of English grain sprang in the virgin soil. And with his grain he scattered the seeds of the dandelion and the wild trefoil over the meadows, mingling his English flowers with the wild native ones. The bristling burdock, the sweet-scented catnip, and the humble yarrow planted themselves along his woodland road, they, too, seeking 'freedom to worship God' in their way. And thus he plants a town. The white man's mullein soon reigned in Indian corn-fields, and sweet-scented English grasses clothed the new soil. Where, then, could the red man set his foot? The honey-bee hummed through the Massachusetts woods, and sipped the wild-flowers round the Indian's wigwam, perchance unnoticed, when, with prophetic warning, it stung the red child's hand, forerunner of that industrious tribe that was to come and pluck the wild-flower of his race up by the root.

The white man comes, pale as the dawn, with a load of thought, with a slumbering intelligence as a fire raked up, knowing well what he knows, not guessing but calculating; strong in community, yielding obedience to authority; of experienced race; of wonderful, wonderful common sense; dull but capable, slow but persevering, severe but just, of little humor but genuine; a laboring man, despising game and sport; building a house that endures, a framed house. He buys the Indian's moccasins and baskets, then buys his hunting-grounds, and at length forgets where he is buried and plows up his bones. And here town records, old, tattered, time-worn, weather-stained chronicles, contain the Indian sachem's mark perchance, an arrow or a beaver, and the few fatal words by which he deeded his hunting-grounds away. He comes with a list of ancient Saxon, Norman, and Celtic names, and strews them up and down this river — Framingham, Sudbury, Bedford, Carlisle, Billerica, Chelmsford — and this is New Angle-land, and these are the New West Saxons, whom the red men call, not Angle-ish or English, but Yengeese, and so at last they are known for Yankees.

When we were opposite to the middle of Billerica, the fields on either hand had a soft and cultivated English aspect, the village spire being seen over the copses which skirt the river, and sometimes an orchard straggled down to the water-side, though, generally, our course this forenoon was the wildest part of our voyage. It seemed that men led a quiet and very civil life there. The inhabitants were plainly cultivators of the earth, and lived under an organized political government. The schoolhouse stood with a meek aspect, entreating a long truce to war and savage life. Every one finds by his own experience, as well as in history, that the era in which men cultivate the apple, and the amenities of the garden, is essentially different from that of the hunter and forest life, and neither can displace the other without loss. We have all had our day-dreams, as well as more prophetic nocturnal vision; but as for farming, I am convinced that my genius dates from an older era than the agricultural. I would at least strike my spade into the earth with such careless freedom but accuracy as the woodpecker his bill into a tree. There is in my nature, methinks, a singular yearning toward all wildness. I know of no redeeming qualities in myself but a sincere love for some things, and when I am reproved I fall back on to this ground. What have I to do with plows? I cut another furrow than you see. Where the off ox treads, there is it not, it is farther off; where the nigh ox walks, it will not be, it is nigher still. If corn fails, my crop fails not, and what are drought and rain to me? The rude Saxon pioneer will sometimes pine for that refinement and artificial beauty which are English, and love to hear the sound of such sweet and classical names as the Pentland and Malvern Hills, the Cliffs of Dover and the Trosachs, Richmond, Derwent, and Winandermere, which are to him now instead of the Acropolis and Parthenon, of Baiæ, and Athens, with its sea-walls, and Arcadia and Tempe.

> Greece, who am I that should remember thee,
> Thy Marathon and thy Thermopylæ?
> Is my life vulgar, my fate mean,
> Which on these golden memories can lean?

We are apt enough to be pleased with such books as Evelyn's Sylva, Actearium, and Kalendarium Hortense, but they imply a relaxed nerve in the reader. Gardening is civil and social, but it wants the vigor and freedom of the forest and the outlaw. There may be an excess of cultivation as well as of anything else, until civilization becomes pathetic. A highly cultivated man — all whose bones can be bent! whose heaven-born virtues are but good manners! The young pines springing up in the corn-fields from year to year are to me a refreshing fact. We talk of civilizing the Indian, but that is not the name for his improvement. By the wary independence and aloofness of his dim forest life he preserves his intercourse with his native gods, and is admitted from time to time to a rare and peculiar society with Nature. He has glances of starry recognition to which our saloons are strangers. The steady illumination of his genius, dim only because distant, is like the faint but satisfying light of the stars compared with the dazzling but ineffectual and short-lived blaze of candles. The Society-Islanders had their day-born gods, but they were not supposed to be 'of equal antiquity with the *atua fauau po*, or night-born gods.' It is true, there are the innocent pleasures of country life, and it is sometimes pleasant to make the earth yield her increase, and gather the fruits in their season; but the heroic spirit will not fail to dream of remoter retirements and more rugged paths. It will have its garden-plots and its *parterres* elsewhere than on the earth, and gather nuts and berries by the way for its subsistence, or orchard fruits with such heedlessness as berries. We would not always be soothing and taming nature, breaking the horse and the ox, but sometimes ride the horse wild and chase the buffalo. The Indian's intercourse with Nature is at least such as admits of the greatest independence of each. If he is somewhat of a stranger in her midst, the gardener is too much of a familiar. There is something vulgar and foul in the latter's closeness to his mistress, something noble and cleanly in the former's distance. In civilization, as in a southern latitude, man degenerates at length, and yields to the incursion of more northern tribes,

> 'Some nation yet shut in
> With hills of ice.'

There are other, savager and more primeval aspects of nature than our poets have sung. It is only white man's poetry. Homer and Ossian even can never revive in London or Boston. And yet, behold how these cities are refreshed by the mere tradition, or the imperfectly transmitted fragrance and flavor of these wild fruits. If we could listen but for an instant to the chant of the Indian muse, we should understand why he will not exchange his savageness for civilization. Nations are not whimsical. Steel and blankets are strong temptations; but the Indian does well to continue Indian.

After sitting in my chamber many days, reading the poets, I have been out early on a foggy morning and heard the cry of an owl in a neighboring wood as from a nature behind the common, unexplored by science or by literature. None of the feathered race has yet realized my youthful conceptions of the woodland depths. I had seen the red Election-birds brought from their recesses on my comrades' string, and fancied that their plumage would assume stranger and more dazzling colors, like the tints of evening, in proportion as I advanced farther into the darkness and solitude of the forest. Still less have I seen such strong and wilderness tints on any poet's string.

These modern ingenious sciences and arts do not affect me as those more venerable arts of hunting and fishing, and even of husbandry in its primitive and simple form; as ancient and honorable trades as the sun and moon and winds pursue, coeval with the faculties of man, and invented when these were invented. We do not know their John Gutenberg, or Richard Arkwright, though the poets would fain make them to have been gradually learned and taught. According to Gower,

> 'And Iadahel, as saith the boke,
>   Firste made nette, fishes toke.
> Of huntyng eke he fond the chace,
> Whiche nowe is knowe in many place;
> A tent of clothe, with corde and stake,
> He sette up first, and did it make.'

Also, Lydgate says:

> 'Jason first sayled, in story it is tolde,
> Toward Colchos, to wynne the flees of golde,
> Ceres the Goddess fond first the tilthe of londe;
>
> .   .   .   .
>
> Also, Aristeus fonde first the usage
> Of mylke, and cruddis, and of honey swote;
> Peryodes, for grete avauntage,
> From flyntes smote fuyre, daryng in the roote.'

We read that Aristeus 'obtained of Jupiter and Neptune, that the pestilential heat of the dog-days, wherein was great mortality, should be mitigated with wind.' This is one of those dateless benefits conferred on man which have no record in our vulgar day, though we still find some similitude to them in our dreams, in which we have a more liberal and juster apprehension of things, unconstrained by habit, which is then in some measure put off, and divested of memory, which we call history.

According to fable, when the island of Ægina was depopulated by sickness, at the instance of Æacus, Jupiter turned the ants into men, that is, as some think, he made men of the inhabitants who lived meanly like ants. This is perhaps the fullest history of those early days extant. . . .[1]

As we said before, the Concord is a dead stream, but its scenery is the more suggestive to the contemplative voyager, and this day its water was fuller of reflections than our pages even. Just before it reaches the falls in Billerica, it is contracted, and becomes swifter and shallower, with a yellow pebbly bottom, hardly passable for a canal-boat, leaving the broader and more stagnant portion above like a lake among the hills. All through the Concord, Bedford, and Billerica meadows we had heard no murmur from its stream, except where some tributary runnel tumbled in,

> Some tumultuous little rill,
>   Purling round its storied pebble,
> Tinkling to the selfsame tune,
> From September until June,
>   Which no drought doth e'er enfeeble.
>
> Silent flows the parent stream,
>   And if rocks do lie below,
> Smothers with her waves the din,
> As it were a youthful sin,
>   Just as still, and just as slow.

But now at length we heard this staid and primitive river rushing to her fall, like any rill. We here left its channel, just above the Billerica Falls, and entered the canal, which runs, or rather is conducted, six miles through the woods to the Merrimack, at Middlesex; and as we did not care to loiter in this part of our voyage, while one ran along the tow-path drawing the boat by a cord, the other kept it off the shore with a pole, so that we accomplished the whole distance in little more than an hour. This canal, which is the oldest in the country, and has even an antique look beside the more modern railroads, is fed by the Concord, so that we were still floating on its familiar waters. It is so much water which the river *lets* for the advantage of commerce. There appeared some want of harmony in its scenery, since it was not of equal date with the woods and meadows through which it is led, and we missed the conciliatory influence of time on land and water; but in the lapse of ages, Nature will recover and indemnify herself, and gradually plant fit shrubs and flowers along its borders. Already the kingfisher sat upon a pine over the water, and the bream and pickerel

[1] Pp. 58–61 (Walden Edition) on The Nature of Fable, omitted.

swam below. Thus all works pass directly out of the hands of the architect into the hands of Nature, to be perfected.

It was a retired and pleasant route, without houses or travelers, except some young men who were lounging upon a bridge in Chelmsford, who leaned impudently over the rails to pry into our concerns, but we caught the eye of the most forward, and looked at him till he was visibly discomfited. Not that there was any peculiar efficacy in our look, but rather a sense of shame left in him which disarmed him.

It is a very true and expressive phrase, 'He looked daggers at me,' for the first pattern and prototype of all daggers must have been a glance of the eye. First, there was the glance of Jove's eye, then his fiery bolt; then, the material gradually hardening, tridents, spears, javelins; and finally, for the convenience of private men, daggers, krisses, and so forth, were invented. It is wonderful how we get about the streets without being wounded by these delicate and glancing weapons, a man can so nimbly whip out his rapier, or without being noticed carry it unsheathed. Yet it is rare that one gets seriously looked at.

As we passed under the last bridge over the canal, just before reaching the Merrimack, the people coming out of church paused to look at us from above, and apparently, so strong is custom, indulged in some heathenish comparisons; but we were the truest observers of this sunny day. According to Hesiod,

> 'The seventh is a holy day,
> For then Latona brought forth golden-rayed Apollo,'

and by our reckoning this was the seventh day of the week, and not the first. I find among the papers of an old Justice of the Peace and Deacon of the town of Concord, this singular memorandum, which is worth preserving as a relic of an ancient custom. After reforming the spelling and grammar, it runs as follows: 'Men that traveled with teams on the Sabbath, December 18, 1803, were Jeremiah Richardson and Jonas Parker, both of Shirley. They had teams with rigging such as is used to carry barrels, and they were traveling westward. Richardson was questioned by the Hon. Ephraim Wood, Esq., and he said that Jonas Parker was his fellow-traveler, and he further said that a Mr. Longley was his employer, who promised to bear him out.' We were the men that were gliding northward, this September 1, 1839, with still team, and rigging not the most convenient to carry barrels, unquestioned by any squire or church deacon, and ready to bear ourselves out if need were. In the latter part of the seventeenth century, according to the historian of Dunstable, 'Towns were directed to erect "*a cage*" near the meeting-house, and in this all offenders against the sanctity of the Sabbath were confined.' Society has relaxed a little from its strictness, one would say, but I presume that there is not less *religion* than formerly. If the *ligature* is found to be loosened in one part, it is only drawn the tighter in another.

You can hardly convince a man of an error in a lifetime, but must content yourself with the reflection that the progress of science is slow. If he is not convinced, his grandchildren may be. The geologists tell us that it took one hundred years to prove that fossils are organic, and one hundred and fifty more to prove that they are not to be referred to the Noachian deluge. I am not sure but I should betake myself in extremities to the liberal divinities of Greece, rather than to my country's God. Jehovah, though with us he has acquired new attributes, is more absolute and unapproachable, but hardly more divine, than Jove. He is not so much of a gentleman, not so gracious and catholic, he does not exert so intimate and genial an influence on nature, as many a god of the Greeks. I should fear the infinite power and inflexible justice of the almighty mortal hardly as yet apotheosized, so wholly masculine, with no sister Juno, no Apollo, no Venus, nor Minerva, to intercede for me, θυμῷ φιλέουσά τε, κηδομένη τε. The Grecian are youthful and erring and fallen gods, with the vices of men, but in many important respects essentially of the divine race. In my Pantheon, Pan still reigns in his pristine glory, with his ruddy face, his flowing beard, and his shaggy body, his pipe and his crook, his nymph Echo, and his chosen daughter Iambe; for the great god Pan is not dead, as was rumored. No god ever dies. Perhaps of all the gods of New England and of ancient Greece, I am most constant at his shrine.

It seems to me that the god that is commonly worshiped in civilized countries is not at all divine, though he bears a divine name, but is the overwhelming authority and respectability of mankind combined. Men reverence one another, not yet God. If I thought that I could speak with discrimination and impartiality of the nations of Christendom, I should praise them, but it tasks me too much. They seem to be the most civil and humane, but I may be mistaken. Every people have gods to suit their circumstances; the Society Islanders had a god called Toahitu, 'in shape like a dog; he saved such as were in danger of falling from rocks and trees.' I think that we can do without him, as we have not much climbing to do. Among them a man could make himself a god out of a piece of wood in a few minutes, which would frighten him out of his wits.

I fancy that some indefatigable spinster of the old school, who had the supreme felicity to be born in 'days that tried men's souls,' hearing this, may say with Nestor, another of the old school, 'But you are younger than I. For time was when I conversed with greater men than you. For not at any time have I seen such men, nor shall see them, as Perithous, and Dryas, and ποιμένα λαῶν,' that is probably Washington, sole 'Shepherd of the People.' And when Apollo has now six times rolled westward, or seemed to roll, and now for the seventh time shows his face in the east, eyes wellnigh glazed, long glassed, which have fluctuated only between lamb's wool and worsted, explore ceaselessly some good sermon book. For six days shalt thou labor and do all thy knitting, but on the seventh, forsooth, thy reading. Happy we who can bask in this warm September sun, which illumines all creatures, as well when they rest as when they toil, not without a feeling of gratitude; whose life is as blameless, how blameworthy soever it may be, on the Lord's Mona-day as on his Suna-day.

There are various, nay, incredible faiths; why should we be alarmed at any of them? What man believes, God believes. Long as I have lived, and many blasphemers as I have heard and seen, I have never yet heard or witnessed any direct and conscious blasphemy or irreverence; but of indirect and habitual, enough. Where is the man who is guilty of direct and personal insolence to Him that made him? . . .[1]

By noon we were let down into the Merrimack through the locks at Middlesex, just above Pawtucket Falls, by a serene and liberal-minded man, who came quietly from his book, though his duties, we supposed, did not require him to open the locks on Sunday. With him we had a just and equal encounter of the eyes, as between two honest men.

The movements of the eyes express the perpetual and unconscious courtesy of the parties. It is said that a rogue does not look you in the face, neither does an honest man look at you as if he had his reputation to establish. I have seen some who did not know when to turn aside their eyes in meeting yours. A truly confident and magnanimous spirit is wiser than to contend for the mastery in such encounters. Serpents alone conquer by the steadiness of their gaze. My friend looks me in the face and sees me, that is all.

The best relations were at once established between us and this man, and though few words were spoken, he could not conceal a visible interest in us and our excursion. He was a lover of the higher mathe-

---

[1] Pages 67–80 (Walden edition) on The Christian Fable, omitted. See pp. 747–54 of this edition.

matics, as we found, and in the midst of some vast sunny problem, when we overtook him and whispered our conjectures. By this man we were presented with the freedom of the Merrimack. We now felt as if we were fairly launched on the ocean stream of our voyage, and were pleased to find that our boat would float on Merrimack water. We began again busily to put in practice those old arts of rowing, steering, and paddling. It seemed a strange phenomenon to us that the two rivers should mingle their waters so readily, since we had never associated them in our thoughts.

As we glided over the broad bosom of the Merrimack, between Chelmsford and Dracut, at noon, here a quarter of a mile wide, the rattling of our oars was echoed over the water to those villages, and their 'slight sounds to us. Their harbors lay as smooth and fairy-like as the Lida, or Syracuse, or Rhodes, in our imagination, while, like some strange roving craft, we flitted past what seemed the dwellings of noble home-staying men, seemingly as conspicuous as if on an eminence, or floating upon a tide which came up to those villagers' breasts. At a third of a mile over the water we heard distinctly some children repeating their catechism in a cottage near the shore, while in the broad shallows between, a herd of cows stood lashing their sides, and waging war with the flies.

Two hundred years ago, other catechizing than this was going on here; for here came the Sachem Wannalancet and his people, and sometimes Tahatawan, our Concord Sachem, who afterwards had a church at home, to catch fish at the falls; and here also came John Eliot, with the Bible and Catechism, and Baxter's 'Call to the Unconverted,' and other tracts, done into the Massachusetts tongue, and taught them Christianity meanwhile. 'This place' says Gookin, referring to Wamesit, 'being an ancient and capital seat of Indians, they came to fish; and this good man takes this opportunity to spread the net of the gospel, to fish for their souls.' 'May 5, 1674,' he continues, 'according to our usual custom, Mr. Eliot and myself took our journey to Wamesit, or Pawtuckett; and arriving there that evening, Mr. Eliot preached to as many of them as could be got together, out of Matt. xxii, 1–14, the parable of the marriage of the king's son. We met at the wigwam of one called Wannalancet, about two miles from the town, near Pawtuckett falls, and bordering upon Merrimak river. This person, Wannalancet, is the eldest son of old Pasaconaway, the chiefest sachem of Pawtuckett. He is a sober and grave person, and of years, between fifty and sixty. He hath been always loving and friendly to the English.'

As yet, however, they had not prevailed on him to embrace the Christian religion. 'But at this time,' says Gookin, 'May 6, 1674' — 'after some deliberation and serious pause, he stood up, and made a speech to this effect: "I must acknowledge I have, all my days, used to pass in an old canoe, [alluding to his frequent custom to pass in a canoe upon the river,] and now you exhort me to change and leave my old canoe, and embark in a new canoe, to which I have hitherto been unwilling; but now I yield up myself to your advice, and enter into a new canoe, and do engage to pray to God hereafter."' One 'Mr. Richard Daniel, a gentleman that lived in Billerica,' who with other 'persons of quality' was present, 'desired brother Eliot to tell the sachem from him, that it may be, while he went in his old canoe, he passed in a quiet stream; but the end thereof was death and destruction to soul and body. But now he went into a new canoe, perhaps he would meet with storms and trials, but yet he should be encouraged to persevere, for the end of his voyage would be everlasting rest.' 'Since that time, I hear this sachem doth persevere, and is a constant and diligent hearer of God's word, and sanctifieth the Sabbath, though he doth travel to Wamesit meeting every Sabbath, which is above two miles; and though sundry of his people have deserted him, since he subjected to the gospel, yet he continues and persists.'[1]

Already, as appears from the records, 'At a General Court held at Boston in New England, the 7th of the first month, 1643–44,' 'Wassamequin, Nashoonon, Kutchamaquin, Massaconomet, and Squaw Sachem, did voluntarily submit themselves' to the English; and among other things did 'promise to be willing from time to time to be instructed in the knowledge of God.' Being asked 'not to do any unnecessary work on the Sabbath day, especially within the gates of Christian towns,' they answered, 'It is easy to them; they have not much to do on any day, and they can well take their rest on that day.' 'So,' says Winthrop, in his Journal, 'we causing them to understand the articles, and all the ten commandments of God, and they freely assenting to all, they were solemnly received, and then presented the Court with twenty-six fathom more of wampom; and the Court gave each of them a coat of two yards of cloth, and their dinner; and to them and their men, every of them, a cup of sack at their departure; so they took leave and went away.'

What journeyings on foot and on horseback through the wilderness, to preach the gospel to these minks and muskrats! who first, no doubt,

[1] Gookin's *Hist. Coll. of the Indians in New England*, 1674.

listened with their red ears out of a natural hospitality and courtesy, and afterward from curiosity or even interest, till at length there 'were praying Indians,' and, as the General Court wrote to Cromwell, the 'work is brought to this perfection that some of the Indians themselves can pray and prophesy in a comfortable manner.'

It was in fact an old battle and hunting ground through which we had been floating, the ancient dwelling-place of a race of hunters and warriors. Their weirs of stone, their arrowheads and hatchets, their pestles, and the mortars in which they pounded Indian corn before the white man had tasted it, lay concealed in the mud of the river bottom. Tradition still points out the spots where they took fish in the greatest numbers, by such arts as they possessed. It is a rapid story the historian will have to put together. Miantonimo — Winthrop — Webster. Soon he comes from Montaup to Bunker Hill, from bear-skins, parched corn, bows and arrows, to tiled roofs, wheat-fields, guns and swords. Pawtucket and Wamesit, where the Indians resorted in the fishing season, are now Lowell, the city of spindles and Manchester of America, which sends its cotton cloth round the globe. Even we youthful voyagers had spent a part of our lives in the village of Chelmsford, when the present city, whose bells we heard, was its obscure north district only, and the giant weaver was not yet fairly born. So old are we; so young is it.

We were thus entering the State of New Hampshire on the bosom of the flood formed by the tribute of its innumerable valleys. The river was the only key which could unlock its maze, presenting its hills and valleys, its lakes and streams, in their natural order and position. The Merrimack, or Sturgeon River, is formed by the confluence of the Pemigewasset, which rises near the Notch of the White Mountains, and the Winnipiseogee, which drains the lake of the same name, signifying 'The Smile of the Great Spirit.' From their junction it runs south seventy-eight miles to Massachusetts, and thence east thirty-five miles to the sea. I have traced its stream from where it bubbles out of the rocks of the White Mountains above the clouds, to where it is lost amid the salt billows of the ocean on Plum Island beach. At first it comes on murmuring to itself by the base of stately and retired mountains, through moist primitive woods whose juices it receives, where the bear still drinks it, and the cabins of settlers are far between, and there are few to cross its stream; enjoying in solitude its cascades still unknown to fame; by long ranges of mountains of Sandwich and of Squam, slumbering like tumuli of Titans, with the peaks of Moose-hillock, the Haystack, and Kearsarge reflected in its waters; where the maple and the raspberry, those lovers of the hills, flourish amid temperate dews; — flowing long and full of meaning, but untranslatable as its name Pemigewasset, by many a pastured Pelion and Ossa, where unnamed muses haunt, tended by Oreads, Dryads, Naiads, and receiving the tribute of many an untasted Hippocrene. There are earth, air, fire, and water — very well, this is water and down it comes.

> Such water do the gods distill,
> And pour down every hill
>   For their New England men;
> A draught of this wild nectar bring,
> And I'll not taste the spring
>   Of Helicon again.

Falling all the way, and yet not discouraged by the lowest fall. By the law of its birth never to become stagnant, for it has come out of the clouds, and down the sides of precipices worn in the flood, through beaver-dams broke loose, not splitting but splicing and mending itself, until it found a breathing-place in this low land. There is no danger now that the sun will steal it back to heaven again before it reach the sea, for it has a warrant even to recover its own dews into its bosom again with interest at every eve.

It was already the water of Squam and Newfound Lake and Winnipiseogee, and White Mountain snow dissolved, on which we were floating, and Smith's and Baker's and Mad Rivers, and Nashua and Souhegan and Piscataquoag, and Suncook and Soucook and Contoocook, mingled in incalculable proportions, still fluid, yellowish, restless all, with an ancient, ineradicable inclination to the sea.

So it flows on down by Lowell and Haverhill, at which last place it first suffers a sea change, and a few masts betray the vicinity of the ocean. Between the towns of Amesbury and Newbury it is a broad, commercial river, from a third to half a mile in width, no longer skirted with yellow and crumbling banks, but backed by high green hills and pastures, with frequent white beaches on which the fishermen draw up their nets. I have passed down this portion of the river in a steamboat, and it was a pleasant sight to watch from its deck the fishermen dragging their seines on the distant shore, as in pictures of a foreign strand. At intervals you may meet with a schooner laden with lumber, standing up to Haverhill, or else lying at anchor or aground, waiting for wind or tide; until, at last, you glide under the famous Chain Bridge, and are landed at Newburyport. Thus she who at first was 'poore of waters, naked of renowne,' having received so many fair tributaries, as was said of the Forth,

> 'Doth grow the greater still, the further downe;
> Till that abounding both in power and fame,
> She long doth strive to give the sea her name;'

or if not her name, in this case, at least the impulse of her stream. From the steeples of Newburyport you may review this river stretching far up into the country, with many a white sail glancing over it like an inland sea, and behold, as one wrote who was born on its head-waters, 'Down out at its mouth, the dark inky main blending with the blue above. Plum Island, its sand ridges scolloping along the horizon like the sea-serpent, and the distant outline broken by many a tall ship, leaning, *still*, against the sky.'

Rising at an equal height with the Connecticut, the Merrimack reaches the sea by a course only half as long, and hence has no leisure to form broad and fertile meadows, like the former, but is hurried along rapids, and down numerous falls, without long delay. The banks are generally steep and high, with a narrow interval reaching back to the hills, which is only rarely or partially overflown at present, and is much valued by the farmers. Between Chelmsford and Concord, in New Hampshire, it varies from twenty to seventy-five rods in width. It is probably wider than it was formerly, in many places, owing to the trees having been cut down, and the consequent wasting away of its banks. The influence of the Pawtucket Dam is felt as far up as Cromwell's Falls, and many think that the banks are being abraded and the river filled up again by this cause. Like all our rivers, it is liable to freshets, and the Pemigewasset has been known to rise twenty-five feet in a few hours. It is navigable for vessels of burden about twenty miles; for canal-boats, by means of locks, as far as Concord in New Hampshire, about seventy-five miles from its mouth; and for smaller boats to Plymouth, one hundred and thirteen miles. A small steamboat once plied between Lowell and Nashua, before the railroad was built, and one now runs from Newburyport to Haverhill.

Unfitted to some extent for the purposes of commerce by the sand-bar at its mouth, see how this river was devoted from the first to the service of manufactures. Issuing from the iron region of Franconia, and flowing through still uncut forests, by inexhaustible ledges of granite, with Squam, and Winnipiseogee, and Newfound, and Massa-besic Lakes for its mill-ponds, it falls over a succession of natural dams, where it has been offering its *privileges* in vain for ages, until at last the Yankee race came to *improve* them. Standing at its mouth, look up its sparkling stream to its source — a silver cascade which falls all the way from the White Mountains to the sea — and behold a city on each successive plateau, a busy colony of human beaver around every fall. Not to mention Newburyport and Haverhill, see Lawrence, and Lowell, and Nashua, and Manchester, and Concord, gleaming one above the other. When at length it has escaped from under the last of the factories, it has a level and unmolested passage to the sea, a mere *waste water*, as it were, bearing little with it but its fame; its pleasant course revealed by the morning fog which hangs over it, and the sails of the few small vessels which transact the commerce of Haverhill and Newburyport. But its real vessels are railroad cars, and its true and main stream, flowing by an iron channel farther south, may be traced by a long line of vapor amid the hills, which no morning wind ever disperses, to where it empties into the sea at Boston. This side is the louder murmur now. Instead of the scream of a fish hawk scaring the fishes, is heard the whistle of the steam-engine, arousing a country to its progress.

This river too was at length discovered by the white man, 'trending up into the land,' he knew not how far, possibly an inlet to the South Sea. Its valley, as far as the Winnipiseogee, was first surveyed in 1652. The first settlers of Massachusetts supposed that the Connecticut, in one part of its course, ran northwest, 'so near the great lake as the Indians do pass their canoes into it over land.' From which lake and the 'hideous swamps' about it, as they supposed, came all the beaver that was traded between Virginia and Canada — and the Potomac was thought to come out of or from very near it. Afterward the Connecticut came so near the course of the Merrimack that, with a little pains, they expected to divert the current of the trade into the latter river, and its profits from their Dutch neighbors into their own pockets.

Unlike the Concord, the Merrimack is not a dead but a living stream, though it has less life within its waters and on its banks. It has a swift current, and, in this part of its course, a clayey bottom, almost no weeds, and comparatively few fishes. We looked down into its yellow water with the more curiosity, who were accustomed to the Nile-like blackness of the former river. Shad and alewives are taken here in their season, but salmon, though at one time more numerous than shad, are now more rare. Bass, also, are taken occasionally; but locks and dams have proved more or less destructive to the fisheries. The shad make their appearance early in May, at the same time with the blossoms of the pyrus, one of the most conspicuous early flowers, which is for this reason called the shad-blossom. An insect called the shad-fly also appears at the same time, covering the houses and fences. We are told that 'their greatest run is when the apple-trees are in full blossom. The old shad return in August; the young, three or four inches long, in September. These are very fond of flies.' A rather picturesque and luxurious mode of fishing was formerly practiced on the Connecticut, at Bellows Falls, where a large rock divides the stream. 'On the steep sides of the island rock,' says Belknap, 'hang several arm-chairs, fastened to ladders, and secured by a counterpoise, in which fishermen sit to catch salmon and shad with dipping nets.' The remains of Indian weirs, made of large stones, are still to be seen in the Winnipiseogee, one of the head-waters of this river.

It cannot but affect our philosophy favorably to be reminded of these shoals of migratory fishes, of salmon, shad, alewives, marsh-bankers, and others, which penetrate up the innumerable rivers of our coast in the spring, even to the interior lakes, their scales gleaming in the sun; and again, of the fry which in still greater numbers wend their way downward to the sea. 'And is it not pretty sport,' wrote Captain John Smith, who was on this coast as early as 1614, 'to pull up twopence, six-pence, and twelvepence, as fast as you can haul and veer a line?' 'And what sport doth yield a more pleasing content, and less hurt or charge, than angling with a hook, and crossing the sweet air from isle to isle, over the silent streams of a calm sea?'

On the sandy shore, opposite the Glass-house village in Chelmsford, at the Great Bend, where we landed to rest us and gather a few wild plums, we discovered the *Campanula rotundifolia*, a new flower to us, the harebell of the poets, which is common to both hemispheres, growing close to the water. Here, in the shady branches of an apple tree on the sand, we took our nooning, where there was not a zephyr to disturb the repose of this glorious Sabbath day, and we reflected serenely on the long past and successful labors of Latona.

> 'So silent is the cessile air,
> That every cry and call,
> The hills, and dales, and forest fair
> Again repeats them all.

> 'The herds beneath some leafy trees,
>   Amidst the flowers they lie,
> The stable ships upon the seas
>   Tend up their sails to dry.'

As we thus rested in the shade, or rowed leisurely along, we had recourse, from time to time, to the Gazetteer, which was our Navigator, and from its bald natural facts extracted the pleasure of poetry. Beaver River comes in a little lower down, draining the meadows of Pelham, Windham, and Londonderry. The Scotch Irish settlers of the latter town, according to this authority, were the first to introduce the potato into New England, as well as the manufacture of linen cloth.

Everything that is printed and bound in a book contains some echo at least of the best that is in literature. Indeed, the best books have a use, like sticks and stones, which is above or beside their design, not anticipated in the preface, not concluded in the appendix. Even Virgil's poetry serves a very different use to me today from what it did to his contemporaries. It has often an acquired and accidental value merely, proving that man is still man in the world. It is pleasant to meet with such still lines as,

> 'Jam laeto turgent in palmite gemmae;'
> Now the buds swell on the joyful stem.

> 'Strata jacent passim sua quaeque sub arbore poma;'
> The apples lie scattered everywhere, each under its tree.

In an ancient and dead language, any recognition of living nature attracts us. These are such sentences as were written while grass grew and water ran. It is no small recommendation when a book will stand the test of mere unobstructed sunshine and daylight.[1]

Enough has been said in these days of the charm of fluent writing. We hear it complained of some works of genius that they have fine thoughts, but are irregular and have no flow. But even the mountain peaks in the horizon are, to the eye of science, parts of one range. We should consider that the flow of thought is more like a tidal wave than a prone river, and is the result of a celestial influence, not of any declivity in its channel. The river flows because it runs down hill, and flows the faster, the faster it descends. The reader who expects to float down-stream for the whole voyage may well complain of nauseating swells and choppings of the sea when his frail shore craft gets amidst

---

[1] Pages 93–105 (Walden Edition) on Poetry, omitted.

the billows of the ocean stream, which flows as much to sun and moon as lesser streams to it. But if we would appreciate the flow that is in these books, we must expect to feel it rise from the page like an exhalation, and wash away our critical brains like burr millstones, flowing to higher levels above and behind ourselves. There is many a book which ripples on like a freshet, and flows as glibly as a mill-stream sucking under a causeway; and when their authors are in the full tide of their discourse, Pythagoras and Plato and Jamblichus halt beside them. Their long, stringy, slimy sentences are of that consistency that they naturally flow and run together. They read as if written for military men, for men of business, there is such a dispatch in them. Compared with these, the grave thinkers and philosophers seem not to have got their swaddling-clothes off; they are slower than a Roman army in its march, the rear camping tonight where the van camped last night. The wise Jamblichus eddies and gleams like a watery slough.

> 'How many thousands never heard the name
> Of Sidney, or of Spenser, or their books!
> And yet brave fellows, and presume of fame,
> And seem to bear down all the world with looks!'

The ready writer seizes the pen and shouts, 'Forward! Alamo and Fanning!' and after rolls the tide of war. The very walls and fences seem to travel. But the most rapid trot is no flow after all; and thither, reader, you and I, at least, will not follow.

A perfectly healthy sentence, it is true, is extremely rare. For the most part we miss the hue and fragrance of the thought; as if we could be satisfied with the dews of the morning or evening without their colors, or the heavens without their azure. The most attractive sentences are, perhaps, not the wisest, but the surest and roundest. They are spoken firmly and conclusively, as if the speaker had a right to know what he says, and if not wise, they have at least been well learned. Sir Walter Raleigh might well be studied, if only for the excellence of his style, for he is remarkable in the midst of so many masters. There is a natural emphasis in his style, like a man's tread, and a breathing space between the sentences, which the best of modern writing does not furnish.. His chapters are like English parks, or say rather like a Western forest, where the larger growth keeps down the underwood, and one may ride on horseback through the openings. All the distinguished writers of that period possess a greater vigor and naturalness than the more modern — for it is allowed to slander our own time — and when we read a quotation from one of them in the midst of a modern author, we seem to have come suddenly upon a greener ground, a greater depth and strength of soil. It is as if a green bough were laid across the page, and we are refreshed as by the sight of fresh grass in midwinter or early spring. You have constantly the warrant of life and experience in what you read. The little that is said is eked out by implication of the much that was done. The sentences are verdurous and blooming as evergreen and flowers, because they are rooted in fact and experience, but our false and florid sentences have only the tints of flowers without their sap or roots. All men are really most attracted by the beauty of plain speech, and they even write in a florid style in imitation of this. They prefer to be misunderstood rather than to come short of its exuberance. Hussein Effendi praised the epistolary style of Ibrahim Pasha to the French traveler Botta, because of 'the difficulty of understanding it; there was,' he said, 'but one person at Jidda who was capable of understanding and explaining the Pasha's correspondence.' A man's whole life is taxed for the least thing well done. It is its net result. Every sentence is the result of a long probation. Where shall we look for standard English but to the words of a standard man? The word which is best said came nearest to not being spoken at all, for it is cousin to a deed which the speaker could have better done. Nay, almost it must have taken the place of a deed by some urgent necessity, even by some misfortune, so that the truest writer will be some captive knight, after all. And perhaps the fates had such a design, when, having stored Raleigh so richly with the substance of life and experience, they made him a fast prisoner, and compelled him to make his words his deeds, and transfer to his expression the emphasis and sincerity of his action.

Men have a respect for scholarship and learning greatly out of proportion to the use they commonly serve. We are amused to read how Ben Jonson engaged that the dull masks with which the royal family and nobility were to be entertained should be 'grounded upon antiquity and solid learning.' Can there be any greater reproach than an idle learning? Learn to split wood, at least. The necessity of labor and conversation with many men and things to the scholar is rarely well remembered; steady labor with the hands, which engrosses the attention also, is unquestionably the best method of removing palaver and sentimentality out of one's style, both of speaking and writing. If he has worked hard from morning till night, though he may have grieved, that he could not be watching the train of his thoughts during that time, yet the few hasty lines which at evening record his day's experience will be more musical and true than his freest but idle fancy could have furnished. Surely the writer is to address a world of laborers, and such therefore must be his own discipline. He will not idly dance at his work who has wood to cut and cord before nightfall in the short days of winter; but every stroke will be husbanded, and ring soberly through the wood; and so will the strokes of that scholar's pen, which at evening record the story of the day, ring soberly, yet cheerily, on the ear of the reader, long after the echoes of his axe have died away. The scholar may be sure that he writes the tougher truth for the calluses on his palms. They give firmness to the sentence. Indeed, the mind never makes a great and successful effort, without a corresponding energy of the body. We are often struck by the force and precision of style to which hard-working men, unpracticed in writing, easily attain when required to make the effort. As if plainness and vigor and sincerity, the ornaments of style, were better learned on the farm and in the workshop than in the schools. The sentences written by such rude hands are nervous and tough, like hardened thongs, the sinews of the deer, or the roots of the pine. As for the graces of expression, a great thought is never found in a mean dress; but though it proceed from the lips of the Wolofs, the nine Muses and the three Graces will have conspired to clothe it in fit phrase. Its education has always been liberal, and its implied wit can endow a college. The world, which the Greeks called Beauty, has been made such by being gradually divested of every ornament which was not fitted to endure. The Sibyl, 'speaking with inspired mouth, smileless, inornate, and unperfumed, pierces through centuries by the power of the god.' The scholar might frequently emulate the propriety and emphasis of the farmer's call to his team, and confess that if that were written it would surpass his labored sentences. Whose are the truly *labored* sentences? From the weak and flimsy periods of the politician and literary man, we are glad to turn even to the description of work, the simple record of the month's labor in the farmer's almanac, to restore our tone and spirits. A sentence should read as if its author, had he held a plow instead of a pen, could have drawn a furrow deep and straight to the end. The scholar requires hard and serious labor to give an impetus to his thought. He will learn to grasp the pen firmly so, and wield it gracefully and effectively, as an axe or a sword. When we consider the weak and nerveless periods of some literary men, who perchance in feet and inches come up to the standard of their race, and are not deficient in girth also, we are amazed at the immense sacrifice of thews and sinews. What! these proportions, these bones — and this their work! Hands which could have felled an ox have hewed this fragile matter which would not have tasked a lady's fingers! Can this be a stalwart man's work, who has a marrow in his back and a tendon Achilles in his heel? They who set up the blocks of Stonehenge did somewhat, if they only laid out their strength for once, and stretched themselves.

Yet, after all, the truly efficient laborer will not crowd his day with work, but will saunter to his task, surrounded by a wide halo of ease and leisure, and then do but what he loves best. He is anxious only about the fruitful kernels of time. Though the hen should sit all day, she could lay only one egg, and, besides, would not have picked up materials for another. Let a man take time enough for the most trivial deed, though it be but the paring of his nails. The buds swell imperceptibly, without hurry or confusion, as if the short spring days were an eternity.

> Then spend an age in whetting thy desire,
> Thou need'st not *hasten* if thou dost *stand fast*.

Some hours seem not to be occasion for any deed, but for resolves to draw breath in. We do not directly go about the execution of the purpose that thrills us, but shut our doors behind us and ramble with prepared mind, as if the half were already done. Our resolution is taking root or hold on the earth then, as seeds first send a shoot downward which is fed by their own albumen, ere they send one upward to the light.

There is a sort of homely truth and naturalness in some books which is very rare to find, and yet looks cheap enough. There may be nothing lofty in the sentiment, or fine in the expression, but it is careless country talk. Homeliness is almost as great a merit in a book as in a house, if the reader would abide there. It is next to beauty, and a very high art. Some have this merit only. The scholar is not apt to make his most familiar experience come gracefully to the aid of his expression. Very few men can speak of Nature, for instance, with any truth. They overstep her modesty, somehow or other, and confer no favor. They do not speak a good word for her. Most cry better than they speak, and you can get more nature out of them by pinching than by addressing them. The surliness with which the woodchopper speaks of his woods, handling them as indifferently as his axe, is better than the mealy-mouthed enthusiasm of the lover of nature. Better that the primrose by the river's brim be a yellow primrose, and nothing more, than that it be something less. Aubrey relates of Thomas Fuller that his was 'a very working head, insomuch that, walking and meditating before dinner, he would eat up a penny loaf, not knowing that he did it. His natural memory was very great, to which he added the art of memory. He would repeat to you forwards and backwards all the signs from Ludgate to Charing Cross.' He says of Mr. John Hales, that 'he loved Canarie,' and was buried 'under an altar monument of black marble . . . with a too long epitaph;' of Edmund Halley, that he 'at sixteen could make a dial, and then, he said, he thought himself a brave fellow;' of William Holder, who wrote a book upon his curing one Popham who was deaf and dumb, 'he was beholding to no author; did only consult with nature.' For the most part, an author consults only with all who have written before him upon a subject, and his book is but the advice of so many. But a good book will never have been forestalled, but the topic itself will in one sense be new, and its author, by consulting with nature, will consult not only with those who have gone before, but with those who may come after. There is always room and occasion enough for a true book on any subject; as there is room for more light the brightest day, and more rays will not interfere with the first.

We thus worked our way up this river, gradually adjusting our thoughts to novelties, beholding from its placid bosom a new nature and new works of men, and, as it were with increasing confidence, finding nature still habitable, genial, and propitious to us; not following any beaten path, but the windings of the river, as ever the nearest way for us. Fortunately we had no business in this country. The Concord had rarely been a river, or *rivus*, but barely *fluvius*, or between *fluvius* and *lacus*. This Merrimack was neither *rivus* nor *fluvius* nor *lacus*, but rather *amnis* here, a gently swelling and stately rolling flood approaching the sea. We could even sympathize with its buoyant tide, going to seek its fortune in the ocean, and, anticipating the time when 'being received within the plain of its freer water,' it should 'beat the shores for banks,'

> 'campoque recepta
> Liberioris aquae, pro ripis litora pulsant.'

At length we doubled a low shrubby islet, called Rabbit Island, subjected alternately to the sun and to the waves, as desolate as if it lay some leagues within the icy sea, and found ourselves in a narrower part of the river, near the sheds and yards for picking the stone known as the Chelmsford granite, which is quarried in Westford and the neighboring towns. We passed Wicasuck Island, which contains seventy acres or more, on our right, between Chelmsford and Tyngsborough.

This was a favorite residence of the Indians. According to the History of Dunstable, 'About 1663, the eldest son of Passaconaway [Chief of the Penacooks] was thrown into jail for a debt of £45, due to John Tinker, by one of his tribe, and which he had promised verbally should be paid. To relieve him from his imprisonment, his brother Wanna-lancet and others, who owned Wicasuck Island, sold it and paid the debt.' It was, however, restored to the Indians by the General Court in 1665. After the departure of the Indians in 1683, it was granted to Jonathan Tyng in payment for his services to the colony, in maintaining a garrison at his house. Tyng's house stood not far from Wicasuck Falls. Gookin, who, in his Epistle Dedicatory to Robert Boyle, apologizes for presenting his 'matter clothed in a wilderness dress,' says that, on the breaking out of Philip's war in 1675, there were taken up by the Christian Indians and the English in Marlborough, and sent to Cambridge, seven 'Indians belonging to Narragansett, Long Island, and Pequod, who had all been at work about seven weeks with one Mr. Jonathan Tyng, of Dunstable, upon Merrimack River; and, hearing of the war, they reckoned with their master, and getting their wages, conveyed themselves away without his privity, and, being afraid, marched secretly through the woods, designing to go to their own country.' However, they were released soon after. Such were the hired men in those days. Tyng was the first permanent settler of Dunstable, which then embraced what is now Tyngsborough and many other towns. In the winter of 1675, in Philip's war, every other settler left the town, but 'he,' says the historian of Dunstable, 'fortified his house; and, although "obliged to send to Boston for his food," sat himself down in the midst of his savage enemies, alone, in the wilderness, to defend his home. Deeming his position an important one for the defense of the frontiers, in February, 1676, he petitioned the Colony for aid,' humbly showing, as his petition runs, that, as he lived 'in the uppermost house on Merrimac river, lying open to ye enemy, yet being so seated that it is, as it were, a watch-house to the neighboring towns,' he could render important service to his country if only he had some assistance, 'there being,' he said, 'never an inhabitant left in the town but myself.' Wherefore he requests that their 'Honors would be pleased to order him *three or four men* to help garrison his said house,' which they did. But methinks that such a garrison would be weakened by the addition of a man.

> 'Make bandog thy scout watch to bark at a thief,
> Make courage for life, to be capitain chief;
> Make trap-door thy bulwark, make bell to begin,
> Make gunstone and arrow show who is within.'

Thus he earned the title of first permanent settler. In 1694 a law was passed 'that every settler who deserted a town for fear of the Indians should forfeit all his rights therein.' But now, at any rate, as I have frequently observed, a man may desert the fertile frontier territories of truth and justice, which are the State's best lands, for fear of far more insignificant foes, without forfeiting any of his civil rights therein. Nay, townships are granted to deserters, and the General Court, as I am sometimes inclined to regard it, is but a deserters' camp itself.

As we rowed along near the shore of Wicasuck Island, which was then covered with wood, in order to avoid the current, two men, who looked as if they had just run out of Lowell, where they had been waylaid by the Sabbath, meaning to go to Nashua, and who now found themselves in the strange, natural, uncultivated, and unsettled part of the globe which intervenes, full of walls and barriers, a rough and uncivil place to them, seeing our boat moving so smoothly up the stream, called out from the high bank above our heads to know if we would take them as passengers, as if this were the street they had missed; that they might sit and chat and drive away the time, and so at last find themselves in Nashua. This smooth way they much preferred. But our boat was crowded with necessary furniture, and sunk low in the water, and more-over required to be worked, for even *it* did not progress against the stream without effort; so we were obliged to deny them passage. As we glided away with even sweeps, while the fates scattered oil in our course, the sun now sinking behind the alders on the distant shore, we could still see them far off over the water, running along the shore and climb-ing over the rocks and fallen trees like insects — for they did not know any better than we that they were on an island — the unsympathizing river ever flowing in an opposite direction; until, having reached the entrance of the island brook, which they had probably crossed upon the locks below, they found a more effectual barrier to their progress. They seemed to be learning much in a little time. They ran about like ants on a burning brand, and once more they tried the river here, and once more there, to see if water still indeed was not to be walked on, as if a new thought inspired them, and by some peculiar disposition of the limbs they could accomplish it. At length sober common sense seemed to have resumed its sway, and they concluded that what they had so long heard must be true, and resolved to ford the shallower stream. When nearly a mile distant we could see them stripping off their clothes and preparing for this experiment; yet it seemed likely that a new dilemma would arise, they were so thoughtlessly throwing away their clothes on the wrong side of the stream, as in the case of the country-man with his corn, his fox, and his goose, which had to be transported one at a time. Whether they got safely through, or went round by the locks, we never learned. We could not help being struck by the seeming, though innocent, indifference of Nature to these men's necessities, while elsewhere she was equally serving others. Like a true benefactress, the secret of her service is unchangeableness. Thus is the busiest merchant, though within sight of his Lowell, put to pilgrim's shifts, and soon comes to staff and scrip and scallop-shell.

We, too, who held the middle of the stream, came near experiencing a pilgrim's fate, being tempted to pursue what seemed a sturgeon or larger fish, for we remembered that this was the Sturgeon River, its dark and monstrous back alternately rising and sinking in midstream. We kept falling behind, but the fish kept his back well out, and did not dive, and seemed to prefer to swim against the stream, so, at any rate, he would not escape us by going out to sea. At length, having got as near as was convenient, and looking out not to get a blow from his tail, now the bow-gunner delivered his charge, while the stern-man held his ground. But the halibut-skinned monster, in one of these swift-gliding pregnant moments, without ever ceasing his bobbing up and down, saw fit, without a chuckle or other prelude, to proclaim himself a huge imprisoned spar, placed there as a buoy, to warn sailors of sunken rocks. So, each casting some blame upon the other, we withdrew quickly to safer waters.

The Scene-shifter saw fit here to close the drama of this day without regard to any unities which we mortals prize. Whether it might have proved tragedy, or comedy, or tragi-comedy, or pastoral, we cannot tell. This Sunday ended by the going down of the sun, leaving us still on the waves. But they who are on the water enjoy a longer and brighter twilight than they who are on the land, for here the water, as well as the atmosphere, absorbs and reflects the light, and some of the day seems to have sunk down into the waves. The light gradually forsook the deep water, as well as the deeper air, and the gloaming came to the fishes as well as to us, and more dim and gloomy to them, whose day is a perpetual twilight, though sufficiently bright for their weak and watery eyes. Vespers had already rung in many a dim and watery chapel down below, where the shadows of the weeds were extended in length over the sandy floor. The vespertinal pout had already begun to flit on leathern fin, and the finny gossips withdrew from the fluvial street to creeks and coves, and other private haunts, excepting a few of stronger fin, which anchored in the stream, stemming the tide even in their dreams. Meanwhile, like a dark evening cloud, we were wafted over the cope of their sky, deepening the shadows on their deluged fields.

Having reached a retired part of the river where it spread out to sixty rods in width, we pitched our tent on the east side, in Tyngsborough, just above some patches of the beach plum, which was now nearly ripe, where the sloping bank was a sufficient pillow, and with the bustle of sailors making the land, we transferred such stores as were required from boat to tent, and hung a lantern to the tent-pole, and so our house was ready. With a buffalo spread on the grass, and a blanket for our covering, our bed was soon made. A fire crackled merrily before the entrance, so near that we could tend it without stepping abroad, and when we had supped, we put out the blaze, and closed the door, and with the semblance of domestic comfort, sat up to read the Gazetteer, to learn our latitude and longitude, and write the journal of the voyage, or listened to the wind and the rippling of the river till sleep overtook us. There we lay under an oak on the bank of the stream, near to some farmer's cornfield, getting sleep, and forgetting where we were; a great blessing, that we are obliged to forget our enterprises every twelve hours. Minks, muskrats, meadow mice, woodchucks, squirrels, skunks, rabbits, foxes, and weasels, all inhabit near, but keep very close while you are there. The river sucking and eddying away all night down toward the marts and the seaboard, a great wash and freshet, and no small enterprise to reflect on. Instead of the Scythian vastness of the Billerica night, and its wild musical sounds, we were kept awake by the boisterous sport of some Irish laborers on the railroad, wafted to us over the water, still unwearied and unresting on this seventh day, who would not have done with whirling up and down the track with ever-increasing velocity and still reviving shouts, till late in the night.

One sailor was visited in his dreams this night by the Evil Destinies, and all those powers that are hostile to human life, which constrain and oppress the minds of men, and make their path seem difficult and narrow, and beset with dangers, so that the most innocent and worthy enterprises appear insolent and a tempting of fate, and the gods go not with us. But the other happily passed a serene and even ambrosial or immortal night, and his sleep was dreamless, or only the atmosphere of pleasant dreams remained, a happy, natural sleep until the morning; and his cheerful spirit soothed and reassured his brother, for whenever they meet, the Good Genius is sure to prevail.

MONDAY

I thynke for to touche also
The worlde whiche neweth everie daie,
So as I can, so as I maie.

GOWER.

The hye sheryfe of Notynghame,
    Hym holde in your mynde.

Robin Hood Ballads.

His shoote it was but loosely shott,
    Yet flewe not the arrowe in vaine,
For it mett one of the sheriffe's men,
    And William a Trent was slaine.

Robin Hood Ballads.

Gazed on the Heavens for what he missed on Earth.

Britannia's Pastorals.

WHEN the first light dawned on the earth, and the birds awoke, and the brave river was heard rippling confidently seaward, and the nimble early rising wind rustled the oak leaves about our tent, all men, having reinforced their bodies and their souls with sleep, and cast aside doubt and fear, were invited to unattempted adventures.

'All courageous knichtis
Agains the day dichtis
The breest-plate that bricht is,
    To feght with their foue.

The stoned steed stampis
Throw curage and crampis,
Syne on the land lampis;
    The night is neir gone.'

One of us took the boat over to the opposite shore, which was flat and accessible, a quarter of a mile distant, to empty it of water and wash out the clay, while the other kindled a fire and got breakfast ready. At an early hour we were again on our way, rowing through the fog as before, the river already awake, and a million crisped waves come forth to meet the sun when he should show himself. The countrymen, recruited by their day of rest, were already stirring, and had begun to cross the ferry on the business of the week. This ferry was as busy as a beaver dam, and all the world seemed anxious to get across the Merrimack River at this particular point, waiting to get set over — children with their two cents done up in paper, jail-birds broke loose and constable with warrant, travelers from distant lands to distant lands, men and women to whom the Merrimack River was a bar. There stands a gig in the gray morning, in the mist, the impatient traveler pacing the wet shore with whip in hand, and shouting through the fog after the regardless Charon and his retreating ark, as if he might throw that passenger overboard and return forthwith for himself; he will compensate him. He is to break his fast at some unseen place on the opposite side. It may be Ledyard or the Wandering Jew. Whence, pray, did he come out of the foggy night? and whither through the sunny day will he go? We observe only his transit; important to us, forgotten by him, transiting all day. There are two of them. Maybe they are Virgil and Dante. But when they crossed the Styx, none were seen bound up or down the stream, that I remember. It is only a *transjectus*, a transitory voyage, like life itself, none but the long-lived gods bound up or down the stream. Many of these Monday men are ministers, no doubt, reseeking their parishes with hired horses, with sermons in their valises all read and gutted, the day after never with them. They cross each other's routes all the country over like woof and warp, making a garment of loose texture; vacation now for six days. They stop to pick nuts and berries, and gather apples, by the wayside at their leisure. Good religious men, with the love of men in their hearts, and the means to pay their toll in their pockets. We got over this ferry chain without scraping, rowing athwart the tide of travel — no toll for us that day.

The fog dispersed, and we rowed leisurely along through Tyngsborough, with a clear sky and a mild atmosphere, leaving the habitations of men behind, and penetrating yet farther into the territory of ancient Dunstable. It was from Dunstable, then a frontier town, that the famous Captain Lovewell, with his company, marched in quest of the Indians on the 18th of April, 1725. He was the son of 'an ensign in the army of Oliver Cromwell, who came to this country, and settled at Dunstable, where he died at the great age of one hundred and twenty years.' In the words of the old nursery tale, sung about a hundred years ago,

> 'He and his valiant soldiers did range the woods full wide,
> And hardships they endured to quell the Indian's pride.'

In the shaggy pine forest of Pequawket they met the 'rebel Indians,' and prevailed, after a bloody fight, and a remnant returned home to enjoy the fame of their victory. A township called Lovewell's Town, but now, for some reason, or perhaps without reason, Pembroke, was granted them by the State.

> 'Of all our valiant English, there were but thirty-four,
> And of the rebel Indians, there were about four-score;
> And sixteen of our English did safely home return,
> The rest were killed and wounded, for which we all must mourn.

> 'Our worthy Capt. Lovewell among them there did die,
> They killed Lieut. Robbins, and wounded good young Frye,
> Who was our English Chaplin; he many Indians slew,
> And some of them he scalped while bullets round him flew.'

Our brave forefathers have exterminated all the Indians, and their degenerate children no longer dwell in garrisoned houses nor hear any war-whoop in their path. It would be well, perchance, if many an 'English Chaplin' in these days could exhibit as unquestionable trophies of his valor as did 'good young Frye.' We have need to be as sturdy pioneers still as Miles Standish, or Church, or Lovewell. We are to follow on another trail, it is true, but one as convenient for ambushes. What if the Indians are exterminated, are not savages as grim prowling about the clearings today?

> 'And braving many dangers and hardships in the way,
> They safe arrived at Dunstable the thirteenth (?) day of May.'

But they did not all 'safe arrive in Dunstable the thirteenth,' or the fifteenth, or the thirtieth 'day of May.' Eleazer Davis and Josiah Jones, both of Concord — for our native town had seven men in this fight — Lieutenant Farwell, of Dunstable, and Jonathan Frye, of Andover, who were all wounded, were left behind, creeping toward the settlements. 'After traveling several miles, Frye was left and lost,' though a more recent poet has assigned him company in his last hours.

> 'A man he was of comely form,
> Polished and brave, well learned and kind;
> Old Harvard's learned halls he left
> Far in the wilds a grave to find.

> 'Ah! now his blood-red arm he lifts;
>   His closing lids he tries to raise;
> And speak once more before he dies,
>   In supplication and in praise.
>
> 'He prays kind Heaven to grant success,
>   Brave Lovewell's men to guide and bless,
> And when they've shed their heart-blood true,
>   To raise them all to happiness.
>
> .   .   .   .
>
> 'Lieutenant Farwell took his hand,
>   His arm around his neck he threw,
> And said, "Brave Chaplain, I could wish
>   That Heaven had made me die for you.'

Farwell held out eleven days. 'A tradition says,' as we learn from the History of Concord, 'that arriving at a pond with Lieut. Farwell, Davis pulled off one of his moccasins, cut it in strings, on which he fastened a hook, caught some fish, fried and ate them. They refreshed him, but were injurious to Farwell, who died soon after.' Davis had a ball lodged in his body, and his right hand shot off; but on the whole, he seems to have been less damaged than his companions. He came into Berwick after being out fourteen days. Jones also had a ball lodged in his body, but he likewise got into Saco after fourteen days, though not in the best condition imaginable. 'He had subsisted,' says an old journal, 'on the spontaneous vegetables of the forest; and cranberries which he had eaten came out of wounds he had received in his body.' This was also the case with Davis. The last two reached home at length, safe if not sound, and lived many years in a crippled state to enjoy their pension.

But alas! of the crippled Indians, and their adventures in the woods,

> 'For as we are informed, so thick and fast they fell,
> Scarce twenty of their number at night did get home well,'

how many balls lodged with them, how fared their cranberries, what Berwick or Saco they got into, and finally what pension or township was granted them, there is no journal to tell.

It is stated in the History of Dunstable that just before his last march, Lovewell was warned to beware of the ambuscades of the enemy, but 'he replied, "that he did not care for them," and bending down a small elm beside which he was standing into a bow, declared "that he would treat the Indians in the same way." This elm is still standing [in Nashua], a venerable and magnificent tree.'

Meanwhile, having passed the Horseshoe Interval in Tyngsborough, where the river makes a sudden bend to the northwest — for our reflections have anticipated our progress somewhat — we were advancing farther into the country and into the day, which last proved almost as golden as the preceding, though the slight bustle and activity of the Monday seemed to penetrate even to this scenery. Now and then we had to muster all our energy to get round a point, where the river broke rippling over rocks, and the maples trailed their branches in the stream, but there was generally a backwater or eddy on the side, of which we took advantage. The river was here about forty rods wide and fifteen feet deep. Occasionally one ran along the shore, examining the country, and visiting the nearest farmhouses, while the other followed the windings of the stream alone, to meet his companion at some distant point, and hear the report of his adventures; how the farmer praised the coolness of his well, and his wife offered the stranger a draught of milk, or the children quarreled for the only transparency in the window that they might get sight of the man at the well. For though the country seemed so new, and no house was observed by us, shut in between the banks that sunny day, we did not have to travel far to find where men inhabited, like wild bees, and had sunk wells in the loose sand and loam of the Merrimack. There dwelt the subject of the Hebrew scriptures, and the Esprit des Lois, where a thin, vaporous smoke curled up through the noon. All that is told of mankind, of the inhabitants of the Upper Nile, and the Sunderbunds, and Timbuctoo, and the Orinoko, was experience here. Every race and class of men was represented. According to Belknap, the historian of New Hampshire, who wrote sixty years ago, here too, perchance, dwelt 'new lights' and free-thinking men even then. 'The people in general throughout the State,' it is written, 'are professors of the Christian religion in some form or other. There is, however, a sort of *wise men* who pretend to reject it; but they have not yet been able to substitute a better in its place.'

The other voyageur, perhaps, would in the mean while have seen a brown hawk, or a woodchuck, or a musquash creeping under the alders.

We occasionally rested in the shade of a maple or a willow, and drew forth a melon for our refreshment, while we contemplated at our leisure the lapse of the river and of human life; and as that current, with its floating twigs and leaves, so did all things pass in review before us, while far away in cities and marts on this very stream, the old routine was proceeding still. There is, indeed, a tide in the affairs of men, as the poet says, and yet as things flow they circulate, and the ebb always balances the flow. All streams are but tributary to the ocean, which itself does not stream, and the shores are unchanged, but in longer periods than man can measure. Go where we will, we discover infinite change in particulars only, not in generals. When I go into a museum and see the mummies wrapped in their linen bandages, I see that the lives of men began to need reform as long ago as when they walked the earth. I come out into the streets, and meet men who declare that the time is near at hand for the redemption of the race. But as men lived in Thebes, so do they live in Dunstable today. 'Time drinketh up the essence of every great and noble action which ought to be performed, and is delayed in the execution.' So says Veeshnoo Sarma; and we perceive that the schemers return again and again to common sense and labor. Such is the evidence of history.

> 'Yet I doubt not through the ages one increasing purpose runs,
>   And the thoughts of men are widened with the process of the Suns.'

There are secret articles in our treaties with the gods, of more importance than all the rest, which the historian can never know.

There are many skillful apprentices, but few master workmen. On every hand we observe a truly wise practice, in education, in morals, and in the arts of life, the embodied wisdom of many an ancient philosopher. Who does not see that heresies have some time prevailed, that reforms have already taken place? All this worldly wisdom might be regarded as the once unamiable heresy of some wise man. Some interests have got a footing on the earth which we have not made sufficient allowance for. Even they who first built these barns and cleared the land thus, had some valor. The abrupt epochs and chasms are smoothed down in history as the inequalities of the plain are concealed by distance. But unless we do more than simply learn the trade of our time, we are but apprentices, and not yet masters of the art of life.

Now that we are casting away these melon seeds, how can we help feeling reproach? He who eats the fruit should at least plant the seed; ay, if possible, a better seed than that whose fruit he has enjoyed. Seeds, there are seeds enough which need only be stirred in with the soil where they lie, by an inspired voice or pen, to bear fruit of a divine flavor. O thou spendthrift! Defray thy debt to the world; eat not the seed of institutions, as the luxurious do, but plant it rather, while thou devourest the pulp and tuber for thy subsistence; that so, perchance, one variety may at last be found worthy of preservation.

There are moments when all anxiety and stated toil are becalmed in the infinite leisure and repose of nature. All laborers must have their nooning, and at this season of the day, we are all, more or less, Asiatics, and give over all work and reform. While lying thus on our oars by the side of the stream, in the heat of the day, our boat held by an osier put through the staple in its prow, and slicing the melons, which are a fruit of the East, our thoughts reverted to Arabia, Persia, and Hindostan, the lands of contemplation and dwelling-places of the ruminant nations. In the experience of this noontide we could find some apology even for the instinct of the opium, betel, and tobacco chewers. Mount Sabér, according to the French traveler and naturalist Botta, is celebrated for producing the Kát-tree, of which 'the soft tops of the twigs and tender leaves are eaten,' says his reviewer, 'and produce an agreeable soothing excitement, restoring from fatigue, banishing sleep, and disposing to the enjoyment of conversation.' We thought that we might lead a dignified Oriental life along this stream as well, and the maple and alders would be our Kát-trees.

It is a great pleasure to escape sometimes from the restless class of Reformers. What if these grievances exist? So do you and I. Think you that sitting hens are troubled with ennui these long summer days, sitting on and on in the crevice of a hay-loft, without active employment? By the faint crackling in distant barns, I judge that Dame Nature is interested still to know how many eggs her hens lay. The Universal Soul, as it is called, has an interest in the stacking of hay, the foddering of cattle, and the draining of peat-meadows. Away in Scythia, away in India, it makes butter and cheese. Suppose that all farms *are* run out, and we youths must buy old land and bring it to, still everywhere the relentless opponents of reform bear a strange resemblance to ourselves; or, perchance, they are a few old maids and bachelors, who sit round the kitchen hearth and listen to the singing of the kettle. 'The oracles often give victory to our choice, and not to the order alone of the mundane periods. As, for instance, when they say that our voluntary sorrows germinate in us as the growth of the particular life we lead.' The reform which you talk about can be undertaken any morning before unbarring our doors. We need not call any convention. When two neighbors begin to eat corn bread, who before ate wheat, then the gods smile from ear to ear, for it is very pleasant to them. Why do you not try it? Don't let me hinder you.

There are theoretical reformers at all times, and all the world over, living on anticipation. Wolff, traveling in the deserts of Bokhara, says,

'Another party of derveeshes came to me and observed, "The time will come when there shall be no difference between rich and poor, between high and low, when property will be in common, even wives and children." ' But forever I ask of such, What then? The derveeshes in the deserts of Bokhara and the reformers in Marlboro' Chapel sing the same song. 'There's a good time coming, boys,' but, asked one of the audience, in good faith, 'Can you fix the date?' Said I, 'Will you help it along?'

The nonchalance and *dolce-far-niente* air of nature and society hint at infinite periods in the progress of mankind. The States have leisure to laugh from Maine to Texas at some newspaper joke, and New England shakes at the double-entendres of Australian circles, while the poor reformer cannot get a hearing.

Men do not fail commonly for want of knowledge, but for want of prudence to give wisdom the preference. What we need to know in any case is very simple. It is but too easy to establish another durable and harmonious routine. Immediately all parts of nature consent to it. Only make something to take the place of something, and men will behave as if it was the very thing they wanted. They *must* behave, at any rate, and will work up any material. There is always a present and extant life, be it better or worse, which all combine to uphold. We should be slow to mend, my friends, as slow to require mending, 'Not hurling, according to the oracle, a transcendent foot towards piety.' The language of excitement is at best picturesque merely. You must be calm before you can utter oracles. What was the excitement of the Delphic priestess compared with the calm wisdom of Socrates — or whoever it was that was wise? Enthusiasm is a supernatural serenity.

> 'Men find that action is another thing
>   Than what they in discoursing papers read;
> The world's affairs require in managing
>   More arts than those wherein you clerks proceed.'

As in geology, so in social institutions, we may discover the causes of all past change in the present invariable order of society. The greatest appreciable physical revolutions are the work of the light-footed air, the stealthy-paced water, and the subterranean fire. Aristotle said, 'As time never fails, and the universe is eternal, neither the Tanais nor the Nile can have flowed forever.' We are independent of the change we detect. The longer the lever, the less perceptible its motion. It is the slowest pulsation which is the most vital. The hero then will know how to wait, as well as to make haste. All good abides with him who waiteth *wisely*; we shall sooner overtake the dawn by remaining here than by hurrying over the hills of the west. Be assured that every man's success is in proportion to his *average* ability. The meadow flowers spring and bloom where the waters annually deposit their slime, not where they reach in some freshet only. A man is not his hope, nor his despair, nor yet his past deed. We know not yet what we have done, still less what we are doing. Wait till evening, and other parts of our day's work will shine than we had thought at noon, and we shall discover the real purport of our toil. As when the farmer has reached the end of the furrow and looks back, he can tell best where the pressed earth shines most.

To one who habitually endeavors to contemplate the true state of things, the political state can hardly be said to have any existence whatever. It is unreal, incredible, and insignificant to him, and for him to endeavor to extract the truth from such lean material is like making sugar from linen rags, when sugar-cane may be had. Generally speaking, the political news, whether domestic or foreign, might be written today for the next ten years with sufficient accuracy. Most revolutions in society have not power to interest, still less alarm us; but tell me that our rivers are drying up, or the genus pine dying out in the country, and I might attend. Most events recorded in history are more remarkable than important, like eclipses of the sun and moon, by which all are attracted, but whose effects no one takes the trouble to calculate.

But will the government never be so well administered, inquired one, that we private men shall hear nothing about it? 'The king answered: At all events, I require a prudent and able man, who is capable of managing the state affairs of my kingdom. The ex-minister said: The criterion, O Sire! of a wise and competent man is, that he will not meddle with such like matters.' Alas that the ex-minister should have been so nearly right!

In my short experience of human life, the *outward* obstacles, if there were any such, have not been living men, but the institutions of the dead. It is grateful to make one's way through this latest generation as through dewy grass. Men are as innocent as the morning to the unsuspicious.

> 'And round about good morrows fly,
> As if day taught humanity.'

Not being Reve of this Shire,

> 'The early pilgrim blythe he hailed,
> That o'er the hills did stray,
> And many an early husbandman,
> That he met on the way;'

thieves and robbers all, nevertheless. I have not so surely foreseen that any Cossack or Chippeway would come to disturb the honest and simple commonwealth, as that some monster institution would at length embrace and crush its free members in its scaly folds; for it is not to be forgotten, that while the law holds fast the thief and murderer, it lets itself go loose. When I have not paid the tax which the State demanded for that protection which I did not want, itself has robbed me; when I have asserted the liberty it presumed to declare, itself has imprisoned me. Poor creature! if it knows no better I will not blame it. If it cannot live but by these means, I can. I do not wish, it happens, to be associated with Massachusetts, either in holding slaves or in conquering Mexico. I am a little better than herself in these respects. As for Massachusetts, that huge she Briareus, Argus, and Colchian Dragon conjoined, set to watch the Heifer of the Constitution and the Golden Fleece, we would not warrant our respect for her, like some compositions, to preserve its qualities through all weathers. Thus it has happened, that not the Arch Fiend himself has been in my way, but these toils which tradition says were originally spun to obstruct him. They are cobwebs and trifling obstacles in an earnest man's path, it is true, and at length one even becomes attached to his unswept and undusted garret. I love man — kind, but I hate the institutions of the dead unkind. Men execute nothing so faithfully as the wills of the dead, to the last codicil and letter. *They* rule this world, and the living are but their executors. Such foundation too have our lectures and our sermons, commonly. They are all *Dudleian*; and piety derives its origin still from that exploit of *pius Æneas*, who bore his father, Anchises, on his shoulders from the ruins of Troy. Or, rather, like some Indian tribes, we bear about with us the mouldering relics of our ancestors on our shoulders. If, for instance, a man asserts the value of individual liberty over the merely political commonweal, his neighbor still tolerates him, that is, he who is *living near* him, sometimes even sustains him, but never the State. Its officer, as a living man, may have human virtues and a thought in his brain, but as the tool of an institution, a jailer or constable it may be, he is not a whit superior to his prison key or his staff. Herein is the tragedy: that men doing outrage to their proper natures, even those called wise and good, lend themselves to perform the office of inferior and brutal ones. Hence come war and slavery in; and what else may not come in by this opening? But certainly there are modes by which a man may put bread into his mouth which will not prejudice him as a companion and neighbor.

> 'Now turn again, turn again, said the pindér,
>> For a wrong way you have gone,
>> For you have forsaken the king's highway,
>> And made a path over the corn.'

Undoubtedly, countless reforms are called for because society is not animated, or instinct enough with life, but in the condition of some snakes which I have seen in early spring, with alternate portions of their bodies torpid and flexible, so that they could wriggle neither way. All men are partially buried in the grave of custom, and of some we see only the crown of the head above ground. Better are the physically dead, for they more lively rot. Even virtue is no longer such if it be stagnant. A man's life should be constantly as fresh as this river. It should be the same channel, but a new water every instant.

> 'Virtues as rivers pass,
> But still remains that virtuous man there was.'

Most men have no inclination, no rapids, no cascades, but marshes, and alligators, and miasma instead. We read that when, in the expedition of Alexander, Onesicritus was sent forward to meet certain of the Indian sect of Gymnosophists, and he had told them of those new philosophers of the West, Pythagoras, Socrates, and Diogenes, and their doctrines, one of them, named Dandamis, answered that 'they appeared to him to have been men of genius, but to have lived with too passive a regard for the laws.' The philosophers of the West are liable to this rebuke still. 'They say that Lieou-hia-hoei and Chao-lien did not sustain to the end their resolutions, and that they dishonored their character. Their language was in harmony with reason and justice; while their acts were in harmony with the sentiments of men.'

Chateaubriand said: 'There are two things which grow stronger in the breast of man, in proportion as he advances in years — the love of country and religion. Let them be never so much forgotten in youth, they sooner or later present themselves to us arrayed in all their charms, and excite in the recesses of our hearts an attachment justly due to their beauty.' It may be so. But even this infirmity of noble minds marks the gradual decay of youthful hope and faith. It is the allowed infidelity of age. There is a saying of the Wolofs, 'He who was born first has the greatest number of old clothes;' consequently M. Chateaubriand has more old clothes than I have. It is comparatively a faint and reflected beauty that is admired, not an essential and intrinsic one. It is because the old are weak, feel their mortality, and think that they have measured the strength of man. They will not boast; they will be frank and humble. Well, let them have the few poor comforts they can keep. Humility is still a very human virtue. They look back on life, and so see not into the future. The prospect of the young is forward and unbounded, mingling the future with the present. In the declining day the thoughts make haste to rest in darkness, and hardly look forward to the ensuing morning. The thoughts of the old prepare for night and slumber. The same hopes and prospects are not for him who stands upon the rosy mountain-tops of life, and him who expects the setting of his earthly day.

I must conclude that Conscience, if that be the name of it, was not given us for no purpose, or for a hindrance. However flattering order and expediency may look, it is but the repose of a lethargy, and we will choose rather to be awake, though it be stormy, and maintain ourselves on this earth, and in this life, as we may, without signing our death-warrant. Let us see if we cannot stay here, where He has put us, on his own conditions. Does not his law reach as far as his light? The expedients of the nations clash with one another; only the absolutely right is expedient for all. . . .[1]

While engaged in these reflections, thinking ourselves the only navigators of these waters, suddenly a canal-boat, with its sail set, glided round a point before us, like some huge river beast, and changed the scene in an instant; and then another and another glided into sight, and we found ourselves in the current of commerce once more. So we threw our rinds in the water for the fishes to nibble, and added our breath to the life of living men. Little did we think, in the distant garden in which we had planted the seed and reared this fruit, where it would be eaten. Our melons lay at home on the sandy bottom of the Merrimack, and our potatoes in the sun and water at the bottom of the boat looked like a fruit of the country. Soon, however, we were delivered from this fleet of junks, and possessed the river in solitude, once more rowing steadily upward through the noon, between the territories

---

[1] Pages 139–150 (Walden Edition) on Sophocles and on The Scriptures of Mankind, omitted.

of Nashua on the one hand and Hudson, once Nottingham, on the other. From time to time we scared up a kingfisher or a summer duck, the former flying rather by vigorous impulses than by steady and patient steering with that short rudder of his, sounding his rattle along the fluvial street.

Ere long another scow hove in sight, creeping down the river; and hailing it, we attached ourselves to its side, and floated back in company, chatting with the boatmen, and obtaining a draught of cooler water from their jug. They appeared to be green hands from far among the hills, who had taken this means to get to the seaboard, and see the world; and would possibly visit the Falkland Isles, and the China seas, before they again saw the waters of the Merrimack, or, perchance, they would not return this way forever. They had already embarked the private interests of the landsman in the larger venture of the race, and were ready to mess with mankind, reserving only the till of a chest to themselves. But they too were soon lost behind a point, and we went croaking on our way alone. What grievance has its root among the New Hampshire hills? we asked; what is wanting to human life here, that these men should make haste to the antipodes? We prayed that their bright anticipations might not be rudely disappointed.

> Though all the fates should prove unkind,
> Leave not your native land behind.
> The ship, becalmed, at length stands still;
> The steed must rest beneath the hill;
> But swiftly still our fortunes pace
> To find us out in every place.
> The vessel, though her masts be firm,
> Beneath her copper bears a worm;
> Around the cape, across the line,
> Till fields of ice her course confine;
> It matters not how smooth the breeze,
> How shallow or how deep the seas,
> Whether she bears Manilla twine,
> Or in her hold Madeira wine,
> Or China teas, or Spanish hides,
> In port or quarantine she rides;
> Far from New England's blustering shore,
> New England's worm her hulk shall bore,
> And sink her in the Indian seas,
> Twine, wine, and hides, and China teas.

We passed a small desert here on the east bank, between Tyngsborough and Hudson, which was interesting and even refreshing to our eyes in the midst of the almost universal greenness. This sand was indeed somewhat impressive and beautiful to us. A very old inhabitant, who was at work in a field on the Nashua side, told us that he remembered when corn and grain grew there, and it was a cultivated field. But at length the fishermen — for this was a fishing-place — pulled up the bushes on the shore, for greater convenience in hauling their seines, and when the bank was thus broken, the wind began to blow up the sand from the shore, until at length it had covered about fifteen acres several feet deep. We saw near the river, where the sand was blown off down to some ancient surface, the foundation of an Indian wigwam exposed, a perfect circle of burnt stones, four or five feet in diameter, mingled with fine charcoal, and the bones of small animals which had been preserved in the sand. The surrounding sand was sprinkled with other burnt stones on which their fires had been built, as well as with flakes of arrowhead stone, and we found one perfect arrowhead. In one place we noticed where an Indian had sat to manufacture arrowheads out of quartz, and the sand was sprinkled with a quart of small glass-like chips about as big as a fourpence, which he had broken off in his work. Here, then, the Indians must have fished before the whites arrived. There was another similar sandy tract about half a mile above this.

Still the noon prevailed, and we turned the prow aside to bathe, and recline ourselves under some buttonwoods, by a ledge of rocks, in a retired pasture sloping to the water's edge and skirted with pines and hazels, in the town of Hudson. . . .[1]

Suddenly a boatman's horn was heard echoing from shore to shore, to give notice of his approach to the farmer's wife with whom he was to take his dinner, though in that place only muskrats and kingfishers seemed to hear. The current of our reflections and our slumbers being thus disturbed, we weighed anchor once more.

As we proceeded on our way in the afternoon, the western bank became lower, or receded farther from the channel in some places, leaving a few trees only to fringe the water's edge; while the eastern rose abruptly here and there into wooded hills fifty or sixty feet high. The bass (*Tilia Americana*), also called the lime or linden, which was a new tree to us, overhung the water with its broad and rounded leaf, interspersed with clusters of small hard berries now nearly ripe, and

[1] Pages 153–165 (Walden Edition) on The Scriptures of Mankind and on History, omitted.

made an agreeable shade for us sailors. The inner bark of this genus is the bast, the material of the fisherman's matting, and the ropes and peasant's shoes of which the Russians make so much use, and also of nets and a coarse cloth in some places. According to poets, this was once Philyra, one of the Oceanides. The ancients are said to have used its bark for the roofs of cottages, for baskets, and for a kind of paper called Philyra. They also made bucklers of its wood, 'on account of its flexibility, lightness, and resiliency.' It was once much used for carving, and is still in demand for sounding-boards of pianofortes and panels of carriages, and for various uses for which toughness and flexibility are required. Baskets and cradles are made of the twigs. Its sap affords sugar, and the honey made from its flowers is said to be preferred to any other. Its leaves are in some countries given to cattle, a kind of chocolate has been made of its fruit, a medicine has been prepared from an infusion of its flowers, and finally, the charcoal made of its wood is greatly valued for gunpowder.

The sight of this tree reminded us that we had reached a strange land to us. As we sailed under this canopy of leaves, we saw the sky through its chinks, and, as it were, the meaning and idea of the tree stamped in a thousand hieroglyphics on the heavens. The universe is so aptly fitted to our organization that the eye wanders and reposes at the same time. On every side there is something to soothe and refresh this sense. Look up at the tree-tops, and see how finely Nature finishes off her work there. See how the pines spire without end higher and higher, and make a graceful fringe to the earth. And who shall count the finer cobwebs that soar and float away from their utmost post, and the myriad insects that dodge between them? Leaves are of more various forms than the alphabets of all languages put together; of the oaks alone there are hardly two alike, and each expresses its own character.

In all her products, Nature only develops her simplest germs. One would say that it was no great stretch of invention to create birds. The hawk which now takes his flight over the top of the wood was at first, perchance, only a leaf which fluttered in its aisles. From rustling leaves she came in the course of ages to the loftier flight and clear carol of the bird.

Salmon Brook comes in from the west under the railroad, a mile and a half below the village of Nashua. We rowed up far enough into the meadows which border it to learn its piscatorial history from a haymaker on its banks. He told us that the silver eel was formerly abundant here, and pointed to some sunken creels at its mouth. This man's memory and imagination were fertile in fishermen's tales of floating isles in bottomless ponds, and of lakes mysteriously stocked with fishes, and would have kept us till nightfall to listen, but we could not afford to loiter in this roadstead, and so stood out to our sea again. Though we never trod in those meadows, but only touched their margin with our hands, we still retain a pleasant memory of them.

Salmon Brook, whose name is said to be a translation from the Indian, was a favorite haunt of the aborigines. Here, too, the first white settlers of Nashua planted, and some dents in the earth where their houses stood and the wrecks of ancient apple trees are still visible. About one mile up this stream stood the house of old John Lovewell, who was an ensign in the army of Oliver Cromwell, and the father of 'famous Captain Lovewell.' He settled here before 1690, and died about 1754, at the age of one hundred and twenty years. He is thought to have been engaged in the famous Narragansett swamp fight, which took place in 1675, before he came here. The Indians are said to have spared him in succeeding wars on account of his kindness to them. Even in 1700 he was so old and gray-headed that his scalp was worth nothing, since the French governor offered no bounty for such. I have stood in the dent of his cellar on the bank of the brook, and talked there with one whose grandfather had — whose father might have — talked with Lovewell. Here also he had a mill in his old age, and kept a small store. He was remembered by some who were recently living, as a hale old man who drove the boys out of his orchard with his cane. Consider the triumphs of the mortal man, and what poor trophies it would have to show, to wit: He cobbled shoes without glasses at a hundred, and cut a handsome swath at a hundred and five! Lovewell's house is said to have been the first which Mrs. Dustan reached on her escape from the Indians. Here, probably, the hero of Pequawket was born and bred. Close by may be seen the cellar and the gravestone of Joseph Hassell, who, as is elsewhere recorded, with his wife Anna, and son Benjamin, and Mary Marks, 'were slain by our Indian enemies on September 2, [1691], in the evening.' As Gookin observed on a previous occasion, 'The Indian rod upon the English backs had not yet done God's errand.' Salmon Brook near its mouth is still a solitary stream, meandering through woods and meadows, while the then uninhabited mouth of the Nashua now resounds with the din of a manufacturing town.

A stream from Otternic Pond in Hudson comes in just above Salmon Brook, on the opposite side. There was a good view of Uncannunuc, the most conspicuous mountain in these parts, from the bank here, seen rising over the west end of the bridge above. We soon after passed the village of Nashua, on the river of the same name, where there is a covered bridge over the Merrimack. The Nashua, which is one of the largest tributaries, flows from Wachusett Mountain, through Lancaster, Groton, and other towns, where it has formed well-known elm-shaded meadows, but near its mouth it is obstructed by falls and factories, and did not tempt us to explore it.

Far away from here, in Lancaster, with another companion, I have crossed the broad valley of the Nashua, over which we had so long looked westward from the Concord hills without seeing it to the blue mountains in the horizon. So many streams, so many meadows and woods and quiet dwellings of men had lain concealed between us and those Delectable Mountains; — from yonder hill on the road to Tyngsborough you may get a good view of them. There where it seemed uninterrupted forest to our youthful eyes, between two neighboring pines in the horizon, lay the valley of the Nashua, and this very stream was even then winding at its bottom, and then, as now, it was here silently mingling its waters with the Merrimack. The clouds which floated over its meadows and were born there, seen far in the west, gilded by the rays of the setting sun, had adorned a thousand evening skies for us. But as it were by a turf wall this valley was concealed, and in our journey to those hills it was first gradually revealed to us. Summer and winter our eyes had rested on the dim outline of the mountains, to which distance and indistinctness lent a grandeur not their own, so that they served to interpret all the allusions of poets and travelers. Standing on the Concord Cliffs, we thus spoke our mind to them:

> With frontier strength ye stand your ground,
> With grand content ye circle round,
> Tumultuous silence for all sound,
> Ye distant nursery of rills,
> Monadnock and the Peterborough Hills;
> Firm argument that never stirs,
> Outcircling the philosophers —
> Like some vast fleet,
> Sailing through rain and sleet,
> Through winter's cold and summer's heat;
>
> Still holding on upon your high emprise,
> Until ye find a shore amid the skies;
> Not skulking close to land,
> With cargo contraband,

For they who sent a venture out by ye
Have set the Sun to see
Their honesty.
Ships of the line, each one,
Ye westward run,
Convoying clouds,
Which cluster in your shrouds,
Always before the gale,
Under a press of sail,
With weight of metal all untold —
I seem to feel ye in my firm seat here,
Immeasurable depth of hold,
And breadth of beam, and length of running gear.

Methinks ye take luxurious pleasure
In your novel Western leisure;
So cool your brows and freshly blue,
As Time had naught for ye to do;
For ye lie at your length,
An unappropriated strength,
Unhewn primeval timber,
For knees so stiff, for masts so limber;
The stock of which new earths are made,
One day to be our *Western* trade,
Fit for the stanchions of a world
Which through the seas of space is hurled.

While we enjoy a lingering ray,
Ye still o'ertop the western day,
Reposing yonder on God's croft
Like solid stacks of hay;
So bold a line as ne'er was writ
On any page by human wit;
The forest glows as if
An enemy's camp-fires shone
Along the horizon,
Or the day's funeral pyre
Were lighted there;

Edged with silver and with gold,
The clouds hang o'er in damask fold,
And with such depth of amber light
The west is dight,
Where still a few rays slant,
That even Heaven seems extravagant.
Watatic Hill
Lies on the horizon's sill

Like a child's toy left overnight,
And other duds to left and right,
On the earth's edge, mountains and trees
Stand as they were on air graven,
Or as the vessels in a haven
Await the morning breeze.
I fancy even
Through your defiles windeth the way to heaven;
And yonder still, in spite of history's page,
Linger the golden and the silver age;
Upon the laboring gale
The news of future centuries is brought,
And of new dynasties of thought,
From your remotest vale.

But special I remember thee,
Wachusett, who like me
Standest alone without society.
Thy far blue eye,
A remnant of the sky.
Seen through the clearing or the gorge,
Or from the windows of the forge,
Doth leaven all it passes by.
Nothing is true
But stands 'tween me and you,
Thou Western pioneer,
Who know'st not shame nor fear,
By venturous spirit driven
Under the eaves of heaven;
And canst expand thee there,
And breathe enough of air?
Even beyond the West
Thou migratest,
Into unclouded tracts,
Without a pilgrim's axe,
Cleaving thy road on high
With thy well-tempered brow,
And mak'st thyself a clearing in the sky.
Upholding heaven, holding down earth,
Thy pastime from thy birth;
Not steadied by the one, nor leaning on the other,
May I approve myself thy worthy brother!

At length, like Rasselas and other inhabitants of happy valleys, we had resolved to scale the blue wall which bounded the western horizon, though not without misgivings that thereafter no visible fairyland would exist for us. But it would be long to tell of our adventures, and we have no time this afternoon, transporting ourselves in imagination up this hazy Nashua valley, to go over again that pilgrimage. We have since made many similar excursions to the principal mountains of New England and New York, and even far in the wilderness, and have passed a night on the summit of many of them. And now, when we look again westward from our native hills, Wachusett and Monadnock have retreated once more among the blue and fabulous mountains in the horizon, though our eyes rest on the very rocks on both of them where we have pitched our tent for a night, and boiled our hasty-pudding amid the clouds.

As late as 1724 there was no house on the north side of the Nashua, but only scattered wigwams and grisly forests between this frontier and Canada. In September of that year, two men who were engaged in making turpentine on that side — for such were the first enterprises in the wilderness — were taken captive and carried to Canada by a party of thirty Indians. Ten of the inhabitants of Dunstable, going to look for them, found the hoops of their barrel cut, and the turpentine spread on the ground. I have been told by an inhabitant of Tyngsborough, who had the story from his ancestors, that one of these captives, when the Indians were about to upset his barrel of turpentine, seized a pine knot and, flourishing it, swore so resolutely that he would kill the first who touched it, that they refrained, and when at length he returned from Canada he found it still standing. Perhaps there was more than one barrel. However this may have been, the scouts knew by marks on the trees, made with coal mixed with grease, that the men were not killed, but taken prisoners. One of the company, named Farwell, perceiving that the turpentine had not done spreading, concluded that the Indians had been gone but a short time, and they accordingly went in instant pursuit. Contrary to the advice of Farwell, following directly on their trail up the Merrimack, they fell into an ambuscade near Thornton's Ferry, in the present town of Merrimack, and nine were killed, only one, Farwell, escaping after a vigorous pursuit. The men of Dunstable went out and picked up their bodies, and carried them all down to Dunstable and buried them. It is almost word for word as in the Robin Hood ballad:

> 'They carried these foresters into fair Nottingham,
>   As many there did know,
> They digged them graves in their churchyard,
>   And they buried them all a-row.'

Nottingham is only the other side of the river, and they were not exactly all a-row. You may read in the churchyard at Dunstable, under the

'Memento Mori,' and the name of one of them, how they 'departed this life,' and

> 'This man with seven more that lies in
> this grave was slew all in a day by
> the Indians.'

The stones of some others of the company stand around the common grave with their separate inscriptions. Eight were buried here, but nine were killed, according to the best authorities.

> 'Gentle river, gentle river,
>   Lo, thy streams are stained with gore,
> Many a brave and noble captain
>   Floats along thy willowed shore.
>
> 'All beside thy limpid waters,
>   All beside thy sands so bright,
> *Indian* Chiefs and Christian warriors
>   Joined in fierce and mortal fight.'

It is related in the History of Dunstable that on the return of Farwell the Indians were engaged by a fresh party, which they compelled to retreat, and pursued as far as the Nashua, where they fought across the stream at its mouth. After the departure of the Indians, the figure of an Indian's head was found carved by them on a large tree by the shore, which circumstance has given its name to this part of the village of Nashville — the 'Indian Head.' 'It was observed by some judicious,' says Gookin, referring to Philip's War, 'that at the beginning of the war the English soldiers made a nothing of the Indians, and many spake words to this effect, that one Englishman was sufficient to chase ten Indians; many reckoned it was no other but *Veni, vidi, vici.*' But we may conclude that the judicious would by this time have made a different observation.

Farwell appears to have been the only one who had studied his profession, and understood the business of hunting Indians. He lived to fight another day, for the next year he was Lovewell's lieutenant at Pequawket, but that time, as we have related, he left his bones in the wilderness. His name still reminds us of twilight days and forest scouts on Indian trails, with an uneasy scalp; — an indispensable hero to New England. As the more recent poet of Lovewell's fight has sung, halting a little but bravely still,

> 'Then did the crimson streams that flowed
>   Seem like the waters of the brook,
> That brightly shine, that loudly dash,
>   Far down the cliffs of Agiochook.'

These battles sound incredible to us. I think that posterity will doubt if such things ever were — if our bold ancestors who settled this land were not struggling rather with the forest shadows, and not with a copper-colored race of men. They were vapors, fever and ague of the unsettled woods. Now, only a few arrowheads are turned up by the plow. In the Pelasgic, the Etruscan, or the British story, there is nothing so shadowy and unreal.

It is a wild and antiquated looking graveyard, overgrown with bushes, on the highroad, about a quarter of a mile from and overlooking the Merrimack, with a deserted mill-stream bounding it on one side, where lie the earthly remains of the ancient inhabitants of Dunstable. We passed it three or four miles below here. You may read there the names of Lovewell, Farwell, and many others whose families were distinguished in Indian warfare. We noticed there two large masses of granite more than a foot thick and rudely squared, lying flat on the ground over the remains of the first pastor and his wife.

It is remarkable that the dead lie everywhere under stones,

'Strata jacent passim *suo* quaeque sub' *lapide* —

corpora, we might say, if the measure allowed. When the stone is a slight one, it does not oppress the spirits of the traveler to meditate by it; but these did seem a little heathenish to us; and so are all large monuments over men's bodies, from the Pyramids down. A monument should at least be 'star-y-pointing,' to indicate whither the spirit is gone, and not prostrate, like the body it has deserted. There have been some nations who could do nothing but construct tombs, and these are the only traces which they have left. They are the heathen. But why these stones, so upright and emphatic, like exclamation-points? What was there so remarkable that lived? Why should the monument be so much more enduring than the fame which it is designed to perpetuate — a stone to a bone? 'Here lies' — 'Here lies;' — why do they not sometimes write, There rises? Is it a monument to the body only that is intended? 'Having reached the term of his *natural* life;' — would it not be truer to say, Having reached the term of his *unnatural* life? The rarest quality in an epitaph is truth. If any character is given, it should be as severely true as the decision of the three judges below, and not the partial testimony of friends. Friends and contemporaries should supply only the name and date, and leave it to posterity to write the epitaph.

> Here lies an honest man,
> Rear-Admiral Van.

> Faith, then ye have
> Two in one grave,
> For in his favor,
> Here too lies the Engraver.

Fame itself is but an epitaph; as late, as false, as true. But they only are the true epitaphs which Old Mortality retouches.

A man might well pray that he may not taboo or curse any portion of nature by being buried in it. For the most part, the best man's spirit makes a fearful sprite to haunt his grave, and it is therefore much to the credit of Little John, the famous follower of Robin Hood, and reflecting favorably on his character, that his grave was 'long celebrous for the yielding of excellent whetstones.' I confess that I have but little love for such collections as they have at the Catacombs, Père la Chaise, Mount Auburn, and even this Dunstable graveyard. At any rate, nothing but great antiquity can make graveyards interesting to me. I have no friends there. It may be that I am not competent to write the poetry of the grave. The farmer who has skimmed his farm might perchance leave his body to Nature to be plowed in, and in some measure restore its fertility. We should not retard but forward her economies.

Soon the village of Nashua was out of sight, and the woods were gained again, and we rowed slowly on before sunset, looking for a solitary place in which to spend the night. A few evening clouds began to be reflected in the water, and the surface was dimpled only here and there by a muskrat crossing the stream. We camped at length near Penichook Brook, on the confines of what is now Nashville, by a deep ravine, under the skirts of a pine wood, where the dead pine leaves were our carpet, and their tawny boughs stretched overhead. But fire and smoke soon tamed the scene; the rocks consented to be our walls, and the pines our roof. A woodside was already the fittest locality for us.

The wilderness is near as well as dear to every man. Even the oldest villages are indebted to the border of wild wood which surrounds them, more than to the gardens of men. There is something indescribably inspiriting and beautiful in the aspect of the forest skirting and oc-

casionally jutting into the midst of new towns, which, like the sand-
heaps of fresh fox-burrows, have sprung up in their midst. The very
uprightness of the pines and maples asserts the ancient rectitude and
vigor of nature. Our lives need the relief of such a background, where
the pine flourishes and the jay still screams.

We had found a safe harbor for our boat, and as the sun was setting
carried up our furniture, and soon arranged our house upon the bank,
and while the kettle steamed at the tent door, we chatted of distant
friends and of the sights which we were to behold, and wondered which
way the towns lay from us. Our cocoa was soon boiled, and supper set
upon our chest, and we lengthened out this meal, like old voyageurs,
with our talk. Meanwhile we spread the map on the ground, and read
in the Gazetteer when the first settlers came here and got a township
granted. Then, when supper was done and we had written the journal
of our voyage, we wrapped our buffaloes about us and lay down with
our heads pillowed on our arms, listening awhile to the distant baying
of a dog, or the murmurs of the river, or to the wind, which had not
gone to rest:

> The western wind came lumbering in,
> Bearing a faint Pacific din,
> Our evening mail, swift at the call
> Of its Postmaster-General;
> Laden with news from Californ',
> Whate'er transpired hath since morn,
> How wags the world by brier and brake
> From hence to Athabasca Lake; —

or half awake and half asleep, dreaming of a star which glimmered
through our cotton roof. Perhaps at midnight one was awakened by
a cricket shrilly singing on his shoulder, or by a hunting spider in his
eye, and was lulled asleep again by some streamlet purling its way along
at the bottom of a wooded and rocky ravine in our neighborhood. It
was pleasant to lie with our heads so low in the grass, and hear what
a tinkling, ever-busy laboratory it was. A thousand little artisans beat
on their anvils all night long.

Far in the night, as we were falling asleep on the bank of the Merrimack, we heard some tyro beating a drum incessantly, in preparation
for a country muster, as we learned, and we thought of the line,

> 'When the drum beat at dead of night.'

We could have assured him that his beat would be answered, and the
forces be mustered. Fear not, thou drummer of the night; we too will

be there. And still he drummed on in the silence and the dark. This stray sound from a far-off sphere came to our ears from time to time, far, sweet, and significant, and we listened with such an unprejudiced sense as if for the first time we heard at all. No doubt he was an insignificant drummer enough, but his music afforded us a prime and leisure hour, and we felt that we were in season wholly. These simple sounds related us to the stars. Ay, there was a logic in them so convincing that the combined sense of mankind could never make me doubt their conclusions. I stop my habitual thinking, as if the plow had suddenly run deeper in its furrow through the crust of the world. How can I go on, who have just stepped over such a bottomless skyline in the bog of my life? Suddenly old Time winked at me — Ah, you know me, you rogue — and news had come that IT was well. That ancient universe is in such capital health, I think undoubtedly it will never die. Heal yourselves, doctors; by God I live.

> Then idle Time ran gadding by
> And left me with Eternity alone;
> I hear beyond the range of sound,
> I see beyond the verge of sight —

I see, smell, taste, hear, feel, that everlasting Something to which we are allied, at once our maker, our abode, our destiny, our very Selves; the one historic truth, the most remarkable fact which can become the distinct and uninvited subject of our thought, the actual glory of the universe; the only fact which a human being cannot avoid recognizing, or in some way forget or dispense with.

> It doth expand my privacies
> To all, and leave me single in the crowd.

I have seen how the foundations of the world are laid, and I have not the least doubt that it will stand a good while.

> Now chiefly is my natal hour,
> And only now my prime of life.
> I will not doubt the love untold,
> Which not my worth nor want hath bought,
> Which wooed me young and wooes me old,
> And to this evening hath me brought.

What are ears? what is Time? that this particular series of sounds called a strain of music, an invisible and fairy troop which never brushed the dew from any mead, can be wafted down through the centuries from Homer to me, and he have been conversant with that same aerial and mysterious charm which now so tingles my ears? What a fine communication from age to age, of the fairest and noblest thoughts, the aspirations of ancient men, even such as were never communicated by speech, is music! It is the flower of language, thought colored and curved, fluent and flexible, its crystal fountain tinged with the sun's rays, and its purling ripples reflecting the grass and the clouds. A strain of music reminds me of a passage of the Vedas, and I associate with it the idea of infinite remoteness, as well as of beauty and serenity, for to the senses that is farthest from us which addresses the greatest depth within us. It teaches us again and again to trust the remotest and finest as the divinest instinct, and makes a dream our only real experience. We feel a sad cheer when we hear it, perchance because we that hear are not one with that which is heard.

> Therefore a torrent of sadness deep
> Through the strains of thy triumph is heard to sweep.

The sadness is ours. The Indian poet Calidas says in the Sacontala: 'Perhaps the sadness of men on seeing beautiful forms and hearing sweet music arises from some faint remembrance of past joys, and the traces of connections in a former state of existence.' As polishing expresses the vein in marble, and grain in wood, so music brings out what of heroic lurks anywhere. The hero is the sole patron of music. That harmony which exists naturally between the hero's moods and the universe, the soldier would fain imitate with drum and trumpet. When we are in health, all sounds fife and drum for us; we hear the notes of music in the air, or catch its echoes dying away when we awake in the dawn. Marching is when the pulse of the hero beats in unison with the pulse of Nature, and he steps to the measure of the universe; then there is true courage and invincible strength.

Plutarch says that 'Plato thinks the gods never gave men music, the science of melody and harmony, for mere delectation or to tickle the ear; but that the discordant parts of the circulations and beauteous fabric of the soul, and that of it that roves about the body, and many times, for want of tune and air, breaks forth into many extravagances and excesses, might be sweetly recalled and artfully wound up to their former consent and agreement.'

Music is the sound of the universal laws promulgated. It is the only assured tone. There are in it such strains as far surpass any man's faith in the loftiness of his destiny. Things are to be learned which it will be worth the while to learn. Formerly I heard these

RUMORS FROM AN ÆOLIAN HARP

There is a vale which none hath seen,
Where foot of man has never been,
Such as here lives with toil and strife,
An anxious and a sinful life.

There every virtue has its birth,
Ere it descends upon the earth,
And thither every deed returns,
Which in the generous bosom burns.

There love is warm, and youth is young,
And poetry is yet unsung,
For Virtue still adventures there,
And freely breathes her native air.

And ever, if you hearken well,
You still may hear its vesper bell,
And tread of high-souled men go by,
Their thoughts conversing with the sky.

According to Jamblichus, 'Pythagoras did not procure for himself a thing of this kind through instruments or the voice, but employing a certain ineffable divinity, and which it is difficult to apprehend, he extended his ears and fixed his intellect in the sublime symphonies of the world, he alone hearing and understanding, as it appears, the universal harmony and consonance of the spheres, and the stars that are moved through them, and which produce a fuller and more intense melody than anything effected by mortal sounds.'

Traveling on foot very early one morning due east from here about twenty miles, from Caleb Harriman's tavern in Hampstead toward Haverhill, when I reached the railroad in Plaistow, I heard at some distance a faint music in the air like an Æolian harp, which I immediately suspected to proceed from the cord of the telegraph vibrating in the just awakening morning wind, and applying my ear to one of the posts I was convinced that it was so. It was the telegraph harp singing its message through the country, its message sent not by men, but by gods. Perchance, like the statue of Memnon, it resounds only in the morning, when the first rays of the sun fall on it. It was like the first lyre or shell heard on the seashore — that vibrating cord high in the air over

the shores of earth. So have all things their higher and their lower uses.
I heard a fairer news than the journals ever print. It told of things
worthy to hear, and worthy of the electric fluid to carry the news of, not
of the price of cotton and flour, but it hinted at the price of the world
itself and of things which are priceless, of absolute truth and beauty.

Still the drum rolled on, and stirred our blood to fresh extravagance
that night. The clarion sound and clang of corselet and buckler were
heard from many a hamlet of the soul, and many a knight was arming
for the fight behind the encamped stars.

> 'Before each van
> Prick forth the aery knights, and couch their spears
> Till thickest legions close; with feats of arms
> From either end of Heaven the welkin burns.'

Away! away! away! away!
　Ye have not kept your secret well,
I will abide that other day,
　Those other lands ye tell.

Has time no leisure left for these,
　The acts that ye rehearse?
Is not eternity a lease
　For better deeds than verse?

'Tis sweet to hear of heroes dead,
　To know them still alive,
But sweeter if we earn their bread,
　And in us they survive.

Our life should feed the springs of fame
　With a perennial wave,
As ocean feeds the babbling founts
　Which find in it their grave.

Ye skies, drop gently round my breast,
　And be my corselet blue,
Ye earth, receive my lance in rest,
　My faithful charger you;

Ye stars, my spear-heads in the sky,
　My arrow-tips ye are;
I see the routed foemen fly,
　My bright spears fixèd are.

> Give me an angel for a foe,
>   Fix now the place and time,
> And straight to meet him I will go
>   Above the starry chime.
>
> And with our clashing bucklers' clang
>   The heavenly spheres shall ring,
> While bright the northern lights shall hang
>   Beside our tourneying.
>
> And if she lose her champion true,
>   Tell Heaven not despair,
> For I will be her champion new,
>   Her fame I will repair.

There was a high wind this night, which we afterwards learned had been still more violent elsewhere, and had done much injury to the corn-fields far and near; but we only heard it sigh from time to time, as if it had no license to shake the foundations of our tent; the pines murmured, the water rippled, and the tent rocked a little, but we only laid our ears closer to the ground, while the blast swept on to alarm other men, and long before sunrise we were ready to pursue our voyage as usual.

TUESDAY

> On either side the river lie
> Long fields of barley and of rye,
> That clothe the wold and meet the sky;
> And through the fields the road runs by
>   To many-towered Camelot. — TENNYSON.

LONG before daylight we ranged abroad, hatchet in hand, in search of fuel, and made the yet slumbering and dreaming wood resound with our blows. Then with our fire we burned up a portion of the loitering night, while the kettle sang its homely strain to the morning star. We tramped about the shore, waked all the muskrats, and scared up the bittern and birds that were asleep upon their roots; we hauled up and upset our boat, and washed it and rinsed out the clay, talking aloud as if it were broad day, until at length, by three o'clock, we had completed our preparations and were ready to pursue our voyage as usual; so, shaking the clay from our feet, we pushed into the fog.

Though we were enveloped in mist as usual, we trusted that there was a bright day behind it.

Ply the oars! away! away!
In each dewdrop of the morning
Lies the promise of a day.

Rivers from the sunrise flow,
Springing with the dewy morn;
Voyageurs 'gainst time do row,
Idle noon nor sunset know,
Ever even with the dawn.

Belknap, the historian of this State, says that 'in the neighborhood of fresh rivers and ponds, a whitish fog in the morning lying over the water is a sure indication of fair weather for that day; and when no fog is seen, rain is expected before night.' That which seemed to us to invest the world was only a narrow and shallow wreath of vapor stretched over the channel of the Merrimack from the seaboard to the mountains. More extensive fogs, however, have their own limits. I once saw the day break from the top of Saddle-back Mountain in Massachusetts, above the clouds. As we cannot distinguish objects through this dense fog, let me tell this story more at length.

I had come over the hills on foot and alone in serene summer days, plucking the raspberries by the wayside, and occasionally buying a loaf of bread at a farmer's house, with a knapsack on my back which held a few traveler's books and a change of clothing, and a staff in my hand. I had that morning looked down from the Hoosack Mountain, where the road crosses it, on the village of North Adams in the valley three miles away under my feet, showing how uneven the earth may sometimes be, and making it seem an accident that it should ever be level and convenient for the feet of man. Putting a little rice and sugar and a tin cup into my knapsack at this village, I began in the afternoon to ascend the mountain, whose summit is three thousand six hundred feet above the level of the sea, and was seven or eight miles distant by the path. My route lay up a long and spacious valley called the Bellows, because the winds rush up or down it with violence in storms, sloping up to the very clouds between the principal range and a lower mountain. There were a few farms scattered along at different elevations, each commanding a fine prospect of the mountains to the north, and a stream ran down the middle of the valley, on which, near the head, there was a mill. It seemed a road for the pilgrim to enter upon who would climb to the gates of heaven. Now I crossed a hayfield, and now over the brook on a slight bridge, still gradually ascending all the while with a sort of awe, and filled with indefinite expectations as to what kind of inhabitants and what kind of nature I should come to at last. It now seemed some advantage that the earth was uneven, for one could not imagine a more noble position for a farmhouse than this vale afforded, farther from or nearer to its head, from a glenlike seclusion overlooking the country at a great elevation between these two mountain walls.

It reminded me of the homesteads of the Huguenots, on Staten Island, off the coast of New Jersey. The hills in the interior of this island, though comparatively low, are penetrated in various directions by similar sloping valleys on a humble scale, gradually narrowing and rising to the centre, and at the head of these the Huguenots, who were the first settlers, placed their houses quite within the land, in rural and sheltered places, in leafy recesses where the breeze played with the poplar and the gum-tree, from which, with equal security in calm and storm, they looked out through a widening vista, over miles of forest and stretching salt marsh, to the Huguenot's Tree, an old elm on the shore, at whose root they had landed, and across the spacious outer bay of New York to Sandy Hook and the Highlands of Neversink, and thence over leagues of the Atlantic, perchance to some faint vessel in the horizon, almost a day's sail on her voyage to that Europe whence they had come. When walking in the interior there, in the midst of rural scenery, where there was as little to remind me of the ocean as amid the New Hampshire hills, I have suddenly, through a gap, a cleft or 'clove road,' as the Dutch settlers called it, caught sight of a ship under full sail, over a field of corn, twenty or thirty miles at sea. The effect was similar, since I had no means of measuring distances, to seeing a painted ship passed backwards and forwards through a magic lantern.

But to return to the mountain. It seemed as if he must be the most singular and heavenly-minded man whose dwelling stood highest up the valley. The thunder had rumbled at my heels all the way, but the shower passed off in another direction, though if it had not, I half believed that I should get above it. I at length reached the last house but one, where the path to the summit diverged to the right, while the summit itself rose directly in front. But I determined to follow up the valley to its head, and then find my own route up the steep as the shorter and more adventurous way. I had thoughts of returning to this house, which was well kept and so nobly placed, the next day, and perhaps remaining a week there, if I could have entertainment. Its mistress was a frank and hospitable young woman, who stood before me in a dishabille, busily and unconcernedly combing her long black hair while she talked, giving her head the necessary toss with each sweep of the comb, with lively, sparkling eyes, and full of interest in that lower world from which I had come, talking all the while as familiarly as if she had known me for years, and reminding me of a cousin of mine. She at first had taken me for a student from Williamstown, for they went by in parties, she said, either riding or walking, almost every pleasant day, and were a pretty wild set of fellows; but they never went by the way I was going. As I passed the last house, a man called out to know what I had to sell, for, seeing my knapsack, he thought that I might be a peddler who was taking this unusual route over the ridge of the valley into South Adams. He told me that it was still four or five miles to the summit by the path which I had left, though not more than two in a straight line from where I was, but that nobody ever went this way; there was no path, and I should find it as steep as the roof of a house. But I knew that I was more used to woods and mountains than he, and went along through his cow-yard, while he, looking at the sun, shouted after me that I should not get to the top that night. I soon reached the head of the valley, but as I could not see the summit from this point, I ascended a low mountain on the opposite side, and took its bearing with my compass. I at once entered the woods, and began to climb the steep side of the mountain in a diagonal direction, taking the bearing of a tree every dozen rods. The ascent was by no means difficult or unpleasant, and occupied much less time than it would have taken to follow the path. Even country people, I have observed, magnify the difficulty of traveling in the forest, and especially among mountains. They seem to lack their usual common sense in this. I have climbed several higher mountains without guide or path, and have found, as might be expected, that it takes only more time and patience commonly than to travel the smoothest highway. It is very rare that you meet with obstacles in this world which the humblest man has not faculties to surmount. It is true we may come to a perpendicular precipice, but we need not jump off, nor run our heads against it. A man may jump down his own cellar stairs, or dash his brains out against his chimney, if he is mad. So far as my experience goes, travelers generally exaggerate the difficulties of the way. Like most evil, the difficulty is imaginary; for what's the hurry? If a person lost would conclude that after all he is not lost, he is not beside himself, but standing in his own old shoes on the very spot where he is, and that for the time being he will live there; but the places that have known him, *they* are lost — how much anxiety and danger would vanish. I am not alone if I stand by myself. Who knows where in space this globe is rolling? Yet we will not give ourselves up for lost, let it go where it will.

I made my way steadily upward in a straight line, through a dense undergrowth of mountain laurel, until the trees began to have a scraggy and infernal look, as if contending with frost goblins, and at length I reached the summit, just as the sun was setting. Several acres here had been cleared, and were covered with rocks and stumps, and there was a rude observatory in the middle which overlooked the woods. I had one fair view of the country before the sun went down, but I was too thirsty to waste any light in viewing the prospect, and set out directly to find water. First, going down a well-beaten path for half a mile through the low, scrubby wood, till I came to where the water stood in the tracks of the horses which had carried travelers up, I lay down flat, and drank these dry, one after another, a pure, cold, spring-like water, but yet I could not fill my dipper, though I contrived little siphons of grass stems, and ingenious aqueducts on a small scale; it was too slow a process. Then, remembering that I had passed a moist place near the top, on my way up, I returned to find it again, and here, with sharp stones and my hands, in the twilight, I made a well about two feet deep, which was soon filled with pure cold water, and the birds too came and drank at it. So I filled my dipper, and, making my way back to the observatory, collected some dry sticks, and made a fire on some flat stones which had been placed on the floor for that purpose, and so I soon cooked my supper of rice, having already whittled a wooden spoon to eat it with.

I sat up during the evening, reading by the light of the fire the scraps of newspapers in which some party had wrapped their luncheon — the prices current in New York and Boston, the advertisements, and the singular editorials which some had seen fit to publish, not foreseeing under what critical circumstances they would be read. I read these things at a vast advantage there, and it seemed to me that the advertisements, or what is called the business part of a paper, were greatly the best, the most useful, natural, and respectable. Almost all the opinions and sentiments expressed were so little considered, so shallow and flimsy, that I thought the very texture of the paper must be weaker in that part and tear the more easily. The advertisements and the prices current were more closely allied to nature, and were respectable in some measure as tide and meteorological tables are; but the reading-matter, which I remembered was most prized down below, unless it was some humble record of science, or an extract from some old classic, struck me as strangely whimsical, and crude, and one-idea'd, like a school-boy's theme, such as youths write and after burn. The opinions were of that kind that are doomed to wear a different aspect tomorrow, like last year's fashions; as if mankind were very green indeed, and would be ashamed of themselves in a few years, when they had outgrown this verdant period. There was, moreover, a singular disposition to wit and humor, but rarely the slightest real success; and the apparent success was a terrible satire on the attempt; the Evil Genius of man laughed the loudest at his best jokes. The advertisements, as I have said, such as were serious, and not of the modern quack kind, suggested pleasing and poetic thoughts; for commerce is really as interesting as nature. The very names of the commodities were poetic, and as suggestive as if they had been inserted in a pleasing poem — Lumber, Cotton, Sugar, Hides, Guano, Logwood. Some sober, private, and original thought would have been grateful to read there, and as much in harmony with the circumstances as if it had been written on a mountain-top; for it is of a fashion which never changes, and as respectable as hides and logwood, or any natural product. What an inestimable companion such a scrap of paper would have been, containing some fruit of a mature life! What a relic! What a recipe! It seemed a divine invention, by which not mere shining coin, but shining and current thoughts, could be brought up and left there.

As it was cold, I collected quite a pile of wood and lay down on a board against the side of the building, not having any blanket to cover me, with my head to the fire, that I might look after it, which is not the Indian rule. But as it grew colder towards midnight, I at length encased myself completely in boards, managing even to put a board on top of me, with a large stone on it, to keep it down, and so slept comfortably. I was reminded, it is true, of the Irish children, who inquired what their neighbors did who had no door to put over them in winter nights as they had; but I am convinced that there was nothing very strange in the inquiry. Those who have never tried it can have no idea how far a door, which keeps the single blanket down, may go toward making one comfortable. We are constituted a good deal like chickens, which, taken from the hen, and put in a basket of cotton in the chimney-corner, will often peep till they die, nevertheless; but if you put in a book, or anything heavy, which will press down the cotton, and feel like the hen, they go to sleep directly. My only companions were the mice, which came to pick up the crumbs that had been left in those scraps of paper; still, as everywhere, pensioners on man, and not un-wisely improving this elevated tract for their habitation. They nibbled what was for them; I nibbled what was for me. Once or twice in the night, when I looked up, I saw a white cloud drifting through the windows, and filling the whole upper story.

This observatory was a building of considerable size, erected by the students of Williamstown College, whose buildings might be seen by daylight gleaming far down in the valley. It would be no small ad-vantage if every college were thus located at the base of a mountain, as good at least as one well-endowed professorship. It were as well to be educated in the shadow of a mountain as in more classical shades. Some will remember, no doubt, not only that they went to the college, but that they went to the mountain. Every visit to its summit would, as it were, generalize the particular information gained below, and subject it to more catholic tests.

I was up early and perched upon the top of this tower to see the day-break, for some time reading the names that had been engraved there, before I could distinguish more distant objects. An 'untamable fly' buzzed at my elbow with the same nonchalance as on a molasses hogs-head at the end of Long Wharf. Even there I must attend to his stale humdrum. But now I come to the pith of this long digression. As the light increased, I discovered around me an ocean of mist, which by chance reached up exactly to the base of the tower, and shut out every vestige of the earth, while I was left floating on this fragment of the wreck of a world, on my carved plank, in cloudland; a situation which required no aid from the imagination to render it impressive. As the light in the east steadily increased, it revealed to me more clearly the new world into which I had risen in the night, the new *terra firma* per-chance of my future life. There was not a crevice left through which the trivial places we name Massachusetts or Vermont or New York could be seen, while I still inhaled the clear atmosphere of a July morning — if it were July there. All around beneath me was spread for a hundred miles on every side, as far as the eye could reach, an undulating country of clouds, answering in the varied swell of its surface to the terrestrial world it veiled. It was such a country as we might set in dreams, with all the delights of paradise. There were immense snowy pastures, apparently smooth shaven and firm, and shady vales between the vaporous mountains; and far in the horizon I could see where some luxurious misty timber jutted into the prairie, and trace the windings of a watercourse, some unimagined Amazon or Orinoko, by the misty trees on its brink. As there was wanting the symbol, so there was not the substance of impurity, no spot nor stain. It was a favor for which to be forever silent to be shown this vision. The earth beneath had become such a flitting thing of lights and shadows as the clouds had been before. It was not merely veiled to me, but it had passed away like the phantom of a shadow, σκιᾶς ὄναρ, and this new platform was gained. As I had climbed above storm and cloud, so by successive days' journeys I might reach the region of eternal day, beyond the tapering shadow of the earth; ay,

> 'Heaven itself shall slide,
> And roll away like melting stars that glide
> Along their oily threads.'

But when its own sun began to rise on this pure world, I found myself a dweller in the dazzling halls of Aurora, into which poets have had but a partial glance over the eastern hills, drifting amid the saffron-colored clouds, and playing with the rosy fingers of the Dawn, in the very path of the Sun's chariot, and sprinkled with its dewy dust, enjoying the benignant smile, and near at hand the far-darting glances of the god. The inhabitants of earth behold commonly but the dark and shadowy under side of heaven's pavement; it is only when seen at a favorable angle in the horizon, morning or evening, that some faint streaks of the rich lining of the clouds are revealed. But my muse would fail to convey an impression of the gorgeous tapestry by which I was surrounded, such as men see faintly reflected afar off in the chambers of the east. Here, as on earth, I saw the gracious god

> 'Flatter the mountain-tops with sovereign eye,
> .   .   .   .
> Gilding pale streams with heavenly alchemy.'

But never here did 'Heaven's sun' stain himself.

But, alas, owing, as I think, to some unworthiness in myself, my private sun did stain himself, and

> 'Anon permit the basest clouds to ride
> With ugly wrack on his celestial face' —

for before the god had reached the zenith the heavenly pavement rose and embraced my wavering virtue, or rather I sank down again into that 'forlorn world,' from which the celestial sun had hid his visage,

> 'How may a worm that crawls along the dust,
> Clamber the azure mountains, thrown so high,
> And fetch from thence thy fair idea just,
> That in those sunny courts doth hidden lie,
> Clothed with such light as blinds the angel's eye?
>   How may weak mortal ever hope to file
>   His unsmooth tongue, and his deprostrate style?
> Oh, raise thou from his corse thy now entombed exile!

In the preceding evening I had seen the summits of new and yet higher mountains, the Catskills, by which I might hope to climb to heaven again, and had set my compass for a fair lake in the southwest, which lay in my way, for which I now steered, descending the mountain by my own route, on the side opposite to that by which I had ascended, and soon found myself in the region of cloud and drizzling rain, and the inhabitants affirmed that it had been a cloudy and drizzling day wholly.

But now we must make haste back before the fog disperses to the blithe Merrimack water.

> Since that first 'Away! away!'
>   Many a lengthy reach we've rowed,
> Still the sparrow on the spray
> Hastes to usher in the day
>   With her simple stanza'd ode.

We passed a canal-boat before sunrise, groping its way to the seaboard, and, though we could not see it on account of the fog, the few dull, thumping, stertorous sounds which we heard impressed us with a sense of weight and irresistible motion. One little rill of commerce already awake on this distant New Hampshire river. The fog, as it required more skill in the steering, enhanced the interest of our early voyage, and made the river seem indefinitely broad. A slight mist, through which objects are faintly visible, has the effect of expanding even ordinary streams, by a singular mirage, into arms of the sea or inland lakes. In the present instance, it was even fragrant and invigorating, and we enjoyed it as a sort of earlier sunshine, or dewy and embryo light.

> Low-anchored cloud,
> Newfoundland air,
> Fountain-head and source of rivers,
> Dew-cloth, dream drapery,
> And napkin spread by fays;
> Drifting meadow of the air,
> Where bloom the daisied banks and violets,
> And in whose fenny labyrinth
> The bittern booms and heron wades;
> Spirit of lakes and seas and rivers,
> Bear only perfumes and the scent
> Of healing herbs to just men's fields!

The same pleasant and observant historian whom we quoted above says that 'In the mountainous parts of the country, the ascent of vapors, and their formation into clouds, is a curious and entertaining object. The vapors are seen rising in small columns like smoke from many chimneys. When risen to a certain height, they spread, meet, condense, and are attracted to the mountains, where they either distill in gentle dews, and replenish the springs, or descend in showers, accompanied with thunder. After short intermissions, the process is repeated many times in the course of a summer day, affording to travelers a lively illustration of that is observed in the Book of Job, "They are wet with the showers of the mountains." '

Fogs and clouds which conceal the overshadowing mountains lend the breadth of the plains to mountain vales. Even a small-featured country acquires some grandeur in stormy weather when clouds are seen drifting between the beholder and the neighboring hills. When, in traveling toward Haverhill through Hampstead in this State, on the height of land between the Merrimack and the Piscataqua or the sea, you commence the descent eastward, the view toward the coast is so distant and unexpected, though the sea is invisible, that you at first suppose the unobstructed atmosphere to be a fog in the lowlands concealing hills of corresponding elevation to that you are upon; but it is the mist of prejudice alone, which the winds will not disperse. The most stupendous scenery ceases to be sublime when it becomes distinct, or in other words limited, and the imagination is no longer encouraged to exaggerate it. The actual height and breadth of a mountain or a waterfall are always ridiculously small; they are the imagined only that content us. Nature is not made after such a fashion as we would have her. We piously exaggerate her wonders, as the scenery around our home.

Such was the heaviness of the dews along this river that we were generally obliged to leave our tent spread over the bows of the boat till the sun had dried it, to avoid mildew. We passed the mouth of Penichook Brook, a wild salmon stream, in the fog, without seeing it. At length the sun's rays struggled through the mist and showed us the pines on shore dripping with dew, and springs trickling from the moist banks,

> 'And now the taller sons, whom Titan warms,
> Of unshorn mountains blown with easy winds,
> Dandle the morning's childhood in their arms,
> And, if they chanced to slip the prouder pines,
> The under corylets did catch their shines,
> To gild their leaves.'

We rowed for some hours between glistening banks before the sun had dried the grass and leaves, or the day had established its character. Its serenity at last seemed the more profound and secure for the denseness of the morning's fog. The river became swifter, and the scenery more pleasing than before. The banks were steep 'and clayey for the most part, and trickling with water, and where a spring oozed out a few feet above the river the boatmen had cut a trough out of a slab with their axes, and placed it so as to receive the water and fill their jugs conveniently. Sometimes this purer and cooler water, bursting out from under a pine or a rock, was collected into a basin close to the edge of and level with the river, a fountain-head of the Merrimack. So near along life's stream are the fountains of innocence and youth making fertile its sandy margin; and the voyageur will do well to replenish his vessels often at these uncontaminated sources. Some youthful spring, perchance, still empties with tinkling music into the oldest river, even when it is falling into the sea, and we imagine that its music is distinguished by the river-gods from the general lapse of the stream, and falls sweeter on their ears in proportion as it is nearer to the ocean. As the evaporations of the river feed thus these unsuspected springs which filter through its banks, so, perchance, our aspirations fall back again in springs on the margin of life's stream to refresh and purify it. The yellow and tepid river may float his scow, and cheer his eye with its reflections and its ripples, but the boatman quenches his thirst at this small rill alone. It is this purer and cooler element that chiefly sustains his life. The race will long survive that is thus discreet.

Our course this morning lay between the territories of Merrimack, on the west, and Litchfield, once called Brenton's Farm, on the east, which townships were anciently the Indian Naticook. Brenton was a fur-trader among the Indians, and these lands were granted to him in 1656. The latter township contains about five hundred inhabitants, of whom, however, we saw none, and but few of their dwellings. Being on the river, whose banks are always high and generally conceal the few houses, the country appeared much more wild and primitive than to the traveler on the neighboring roads. The river is by far the most attractive highway, and those boatmen who have spent twenty or twenty-five years on it must have had a much fairer, more wild and memorable experience than the dusty and jarring one of the teamster who has driven, during the same time, on the roads which run parallel with the stream. As one ascends the Merrimack he rarely sees a village, but for the most part alternate wood and pasture lands, and sometimes a field of corn or potatoes, of rye or oats or English grass, with a few straggling apple trees, and, at still longer intervals, a farmer's house. The soil, excepting the best of the interval, is commonly as light and sandy as a patriot could desire. Sometimes this forenoon the country appeared in its primitive state, and as if the Indian still inhabited it, and, again, as if many free, new settlers occupied it, their slight fences straggling down to the water's edge; and the barking of dogs, and even the prattle of children, were heard, and smoke was seen to go up from some hearthstone, and the banks were divided into patches of pasture, mowing, tillage, and woodland. But when the river spread out broader, with an uninhabited islet, or a long, low, sandy shore which ran on single and devious, not answering to its opposite, but far off as if it were seashore or single coast, and the land no longer nursed the river in its bosom, but they conversed as equals, the rustling leaves with rippling leaves, and few fences were seen, but high oak woods on one side, and large herds of cattle, and all tracks seemed to point to one centre behind some statelier grove — we imagined that the river flowed through an extensive manor, and that the few inhabitants were retainers to a lord, and a feudal state of things prevailed.

When there was a suitable reach, we caught sight of the Goffstown mountain, the Indian Uncannunuc, rising before us on the west side. It was a calm and beautiful day, with only a slight zephyr to ripple the surface of the water, and rustle the woods on shore, and just warmth enough to prove the kindly disposition of Nature to her children. With buoyant spirits and vigorous impulses we tossed our boat rapidly along into the very middle of this forenoon. The fish hawk sailed and screamed overhead. The chipping or striped squirrel, *Sciurus striatus* (*Tamias Lysteri*, Aud.), sat upon the end of some Virginia fence or rider reaching over the stream, twirling a green nut with one paw, as in a lathe, while the other held it fast against its incisors as chisels. Like an independent russet leaf, with a will of its own, rustling whither it could; now under the fence, now over it, now peeping at the voyageurs through a crack with only its tail visible, now at its lunch deep in the toothsome kernel, and now a rod off playing at hide-and-seek, with the nut stowed away in its chaps, where were half a dozen more besides, extending its cheeks to a ludicrous breadth — as if it were devising through what safe valve of frisk or somerset to let its superfluous life escape; the stream passing harmlessly off, even while it sits, in constant electric flashes through its tail. And now with a chuckling squeak it dives into the root of a hazel, and we see no more of it. Or the larger red squirrel, or chickaree, sometimes called the Hudson Bay squirrel (*Sciurus Hudsonius*), gave warning of our approach by that peculiar alarum of his, like the winding up of some strong clock, in the top of a pine tree, and dodged behind its stem, or leaped from tree to tree with such caution and adroitness, as if much depended on the fidelity of his scout, running along the white pine boughs sometimes twenty rods by our side, with such speed, and by such unerring routes, as if it were some well-worn familiar path to him; and presently, when we have passed, he returns to his work of cutting off the pine cones, and letting them fall to the ground.

We passed Cromwell's Falls, the first we met with on this river, this forenoon, by means of locks, without using our wheels. These falls are the Nesenkeag of the Indians. Great Nesenkeag Stream comes in on the right just above, and Little Nesenkeag some distance below, both in Litchfield. We read in the Gazetteer, under the head of Merrimack, that 'the first house in this town was erected on the margin of the river [soon after 1665] for a house of traffic with the Indians. For some time one Cromwell carried on a lucrative trade with them, weighing their furs with his foot, till, enraged at his supposed or real deception, they formed the resolution to murder him. This intention being communicated to Cromwell, he buried his wealth and made his escape. Within a few hours after his flight, a party of the Penacook tribe arrived, and, not finding the object of their resentment, burnt his habitation.' Upon the top of the high bank here, close to the river, was still to be seen his cellar, now overgrown with trees. It was a convenient spot for such a traffic, at the foot of the first falls above the settlements, and commanding a pleasant view up the river, where he could see the Indians coming down with their furs. The lock-man told us that his shovel and tongs had been plowed up here, and also a stone with his name on it. But we will not vouch for the truth of this story. In the New Hampshire Historical Collections for 1815 it says, 'Some time after, pewter was found in the well, and an iron pot and trammel in the sand; the latter are preserved.' These were the traces of the white trader. On the opposite bank, where it jutted over the stream cape-wise, we picked up four arrowheads, and a small Indian tool made of stone, as soon as we had climbed it, where plainly there had once stood a wigwam of the Indians with whom Cromwell traded, and who fished and hunted here before he came.

As usual, the gossips have not been silent respecting Cromwell's buried wealth, and it is said that some years ago a farmer's plow, not far from here, slid over a flat stone which emitted a hollow sound, and, on its being raised, a small hole six inches in diameter was discovered, stoned about, from which a sum of money was taken. The lock-man told us another similar story about a farmer in a neighboring town, who had been a poor man, but who suddenly bought a good farm, and was well to do in the world, and, when he was questioned, did not give a satisfactory account of the matter; how few, alas, could! This caused his hired man to remember that one day, as they were plowing together, the plow struck something, and his employer, going back to look, con-cluded not to go round again, saying that the sky looked rather lower-ing, and so put up his team. The like urgency has caused many things to be remembered which never transpired. The truth is, there is money buried everywhere, and you have only to go to work to find it.

Not far from these falls stands an oak tree, on the interval, about a quarter of a mile from the river, on the farm of a Mr. Lund, which was pointed out to us as the spot where French, the leader of the party which went in pursuit of the Indians from Dunstable, was killed. Farwell dodged them in the thick woods near. It did not look as if men had ever had to run for their lives on this now open and peaceful interval.

Here, too, was another extensive desert by the side of the road in Litchfield, visible from the bank of the river. The sand was blown off in some places to the depth of ten or twelve feet, leaving small grotesque hillocks of that height, where there was a clump of bushes firmly rooted. Thirty or forty years ago, as we were told, it was a sheep-pasture, but the sheep, being worried by the fleas, began to paw the ground, till they broke the sod, and so the sand began to blow, till now it had extended over forty or fifty acres. This evil might easily have been remedied, at first, by spreading birches with their leaves on over the sand, and fastening them down with stakes, to break the wind. The fleas bit the sheep, and the sheep bit the ground, and the sore had spread to this extent. It is astonishing what a great sore a little scratch breedeth. Who knows but Sahara, where caravans and cities are buried, began with the bite of an African flea? This poor globe, how it must itch in many places! Will no god be kind enough to spread a salve of birches over its sores? Here, too, we noticed where the Indians had gathered a heap of stones, perhaps for their council-fire, which, by their weight having prevented the sand under them from blowing away, were left on the summit of a mound. They told us that arrowheads, and also bullets of lead and iron, had been found here. We noticed several other sandy tracts in our voyage; and the course of the Merrimack can be traced from the nearest mountain by its yellow sand-banks, though the river itself is for the most part invisible. Lawsuits, as we hear, have in some cases grown out of these causes. Railroads have been made through certain irritable districts, breaking their sod, and so have set the sand to blowing, till it has converted fertile farms into deserts, and the company has had to pay the damages.

This sand seemed to us the connecting link between land and water. It was a kind of water on which you could walk, and you could see the ripple-marks on its surface, produced by the winds, precisely like those at the bottom of a brook or lake. We had read that Mussulmans are permitted by the Koran to perform their ablutions in sand when they cannot get water, a necessary indulgence in Arabia, and we now understood the propriety of this provision.

Plum Island, at the mouth of this river, to whose formation, perhaps, these very banks have sent their contribution, is a similar desert of drifting sand, of various colors, blown into graceful curves by the wind. It is a mere sand-bar exposed, stretching nine miles parallel to the coast, and, exclusive of the marsh on the inside, rarely more than half a mile wide. There are but half a dozen houses on it, and it is almost without a tree, or a sod, or any green thing with which a countryman is familiar. The thin vegetation stands half buried in sand, as in drifting snow. The only shrub, the beach plum, which gives the island its name, grows but a few feet high; but this is so abundant that parties of a hundred at once come from the mainland and down the Merrimack in September, pitch their tents, and gather the plums, which are good to eat raw and to preserve. The graceful and delicate beach pea, too, grows abundantly amid the sand, and several strange moss-like and succulent plants. The island for its whole length is scalloped into low hills, not more than twenty feet high, by the wind, and, excepting a faint trail on the edge of the marsh, is as trackless as Sahara. There are dreary bluffs of sand and valleys plowed by the wind, where you might expect to discover the bones of a caravan. Schooners come from Boston to load with the sand for masons' uses, and in a few hours the wind obliterates all traces of their work. Yet you have only to dig a foot or two anywhere to come to fresh water; and you are surprised to learn that woodchucks abound here, and foxes are found, though you see not where they can burrow or hide themselves. I have walked down the whole length of its broad beach at low tide, at which time alone you can find a firm ground to walk on, and probably Massachusetts does not furnish a more grand and dreary walk. On the seaside there are only a distant sail and a few coots to break the grand monotony. A solitary stake stuck up, or a sharper sand-hill than usual, is remarkable as a landmark for miles; while for music you hear only the ceaseless sound of the surf, and the dreary peep of the beach-birds.

There were several canal-boats at Cromwell's Falls passing through the locks, for which we waited. In the forward part of one stood a brawny New Hampshire man, leaning on his pole, bareheaded and in shirt and trousers only, a rude Apollo of a man, coming down from 'that vast uplandish country' to the main; of nameless age, with flaxen hair and vigorous, weather-bleached countenance, in whose wrinkles the sun still lodged, as little touched by the heats and frosts and withering cares of life as a maple of the mountain; an undressed, unkempt, uncivil man, with whom we parleyed awhile, and parted not without a sincere interest in one another. His humanity was genuine and instinctive, and his rudeness only a manner. He inquired, just as we were passing out of earshot, if we had killed anything, and we shouted after him that we had shot a *buoy*, and could see him for a long while scratching his head in vain to know if he had heard aright.

There is reason in the distinction of civil and uncivil. The manners are sometimes so rough a rind that we doubt whether they cover any core or sap-wood at all. We sometimes meet uncivil men, children of Amazons, who dwell by mountain paths, and are said to be inhospitable to strangers; whose salutation is as rude as the grasp of their brawny hands, and who deal with men as unceremoniously as they are wont to deal with the elements. They need only to extend their clearings, and let in more sunlight, to seek out the southern slopes of the hills, from which they may look down on the civil plain or ocean, and temper their diet duly with the cereal fruits, consuming less wild meat and acorns, to become like the inhabitants of cities. A true politeness does not result from any hasty and artificial polishing, it is true, but grows naturally in characters of the right grain and quality, through a long fronting of men and events, and rubbing on good and bad fortune. Perhaps I can tell a tale to the purpose while the lock is filling — for our voyage this forenoon furnishes but few incidents of importance.

Early one summer morning I had left the shores of the Connecticut, and for the livelong day traveled up the bank of a river, which came in from the west; now looking down on the stream, foaming and rippling through the forest a mile off, from the hills over which the road led, and now sitting on its rocky brink and dipping my feet in its rapids, or bathing adventurously in mid-channel. The hills grew more and more frequent, and gradually swelled into mountains as I advanced, hemming in the course of the river, so that at last I could not see where it came from, and was at liberty to imagine the most wonderful meanderings and descents. At noon I slept on the grass in the shade of a maple, where the river had found a broader channel than usual, and was spread out shallow, with frequent sand-bars exposed. In the names of the towns I recognized some which I had long ago read on teamsters' wagons, that had come from far up country; quiet uplandish towns, of mountainous fame. I walked along, musing and enchanted, by rows of sugar maples, through the small and uninquisitive villages, and sometimes was pleased with the sight of a boat drawn up on a sand-bar, where there appeared no inhabitants to use it. It seemed, however, as essential to the river as a fish, and to lend a certain dignity to it. It was like the trout of mountain streams to the fishes of the sea, or like the young of the land crab born far in the interior, who have never yet heard the sound of the ocean's surf. The hills approached nearer and nearer to the stream, until at last they closed behind me, and I found myself just before nightfall in a romantic and retired valley, about half a mile in length, and barely wide enough for the stream at its bottom. I thought that there could be no finer site for a cottage among mountains. You could anywhere run across the stream on the rocks, and its constant murmuring would quiet the passions of mankind forever.

Suddenly the road, which seemed aiming for the mountain-side, turned short to the left, and another valley opened, concealing the former, and of the same character with it. It was the most remarkable and pleasing scenery I had ever seen. I found here a few mild and hospitable inhabitants, who, as the day was not quite spent, and I was anxious to improve the light, directed me four or five miles farther on my way to the dwelling of a man whose name was Rice, who occupied the last and highest of the valleys that lay in my path, and who, they said, was a rather rude and uncivil man. But 'what is a foreign country to those who have science? Who is a stranger to those who have the habit of speaking kindly?'

At length, as the sun was setting behind the mountains in a still darker and more solitary vale, I reached the dwelling of this man. Except for the narrowness of the plain, and that the stones were solid granite, it was the counterpart of that retreat to which Belphœbe bore the wounded Timias,

> 'In a pleasant glade,
> With mountains round about environed,
> And mighty woods, which did the valley shade,
> And like a stately theatre it made,
> Spreading itself into a spacious plain;
> And in the midst a little river played
> Amongst the pumy stones which seemed to plain,
> With gentle murmur, that his course they did restrain.'

I observed, as I drew near, that he was not so rude as I had anticipated, for he kept many cattle, and dogs to watch them, and I saw where he had made maple sugar on the sides of the mountains, and above all distinguished the voices of children mingling with the murmur of the torrent before the door. As I passed his stable, I met one whom I supposed to be a hired man, attending to his cattle, and I inquired if they entertained travelers at that house. 'Sometimes we do,' he answered gruffly, and immediately went to the farthest stall from me, and I perceived that it was Rice himself whom I had addressed. But pardoning this incivility to the wildness of the scenery, I bent my steps to the house. There was no sign-post before it, nor any of the usual invitations to the traveler, though I saw by the road that many went and came there, but the owner's name only was fastened to the outside; a sort of implied and sullen invitation, as I thought. I passed from room to room without meeting anyone, till I came to what seemed the guests' apartment, which was neat, and even had an air of refinement about it, and I was glad to find a map against the wall which would direct me on my journey on the morrow. At length I heard a step in a distant apartment, which was the first I had entered, and went to see if the landlord had come in; but it proved to be only a child, one of those whose voices I had heard, probably his son, and between him and me stood in the doorway a large watch-dog, which growled at me, and looked as if he would presently spring, but the boy did not speak to him; and when I asked for a glass of water, he briefly said, 'It runs in the corner.' So I took a mug from the counter and went out of doors, and searched round the corner of the house, but could find neither well nor spring, nor any water but the stream which ran all along the front. I came back, therefore, and, setting down the mug, asked the child if the stream was good to drink; whereupon he seized the mug, and, going to the corner of the room, where a cool spring which issued from the mountain behind trickled through a pipe into the apartment, filled it, and drank, and gave it to me empty again, and, calling to the dog, rushed out of doors. Ere long some of the hired men made their appearance, and drank at the spring, and lazily washed themselves and combed their hair in silence, and some sat down as if weary, and fell asleep in their seats. But all the while I saw no women, though I sometimes heard a bustle in that part of the house from which the spring came.

At length Rice himself came in, for it was now dark, with an ox-whip in his hand, breathing hard, and he too soon settled down into his seat not far from me, as if, now that his day's work was done, he had no farther to travel, but only to digest his supper at his leisure. When I asked him if he could give me a bed, he said there was one ready, in such a tone as implied that I ought to have known it, and the less said about that the better. So far so good. And yet he continued to look at me as if he would fain have me say something further like a traveler. I remarked that it was a wild and rugged country he inhabited, and worth coming many miles to see. 'Not so very rough neither,' said he, and appealed to his men to bear witness to the breadth and smoothness of his fields, which consisted in all of one small interval, and to the size of his crops; 'and if we have some hills,' added he, 'there's no better pasturage anywhere.' I then asked if this place was the one I had heard of, calling it by a name I had seen on the map, or if it was a certain other; and he answered, gruffly, that it was neither the one nor the other; that he had settled it and cultivated it, and made it what it was, and I could know nothing about it. Observing some guns and other

implements of hunting hanging on brackets around the room, and his
hounds now sleeping on the floor, I took occasion to change the discourse, and inquired if there was much game in that country, and he
answered this question more graciously, having some glimmering of
my drift; but when I inquired if there were any bears, he answered impatiently that he was no more in danger of losing his sheep than his
neighbors; he had tamed and civilized that region. After a pause,
thinking of my journey on the morrow, and the few hours of daylight in
that hollow and mountainous country, which would require me to be
on my way betimes, I remarked that the day must be shorter by an hour
there than on the neighboring plains; at which he gruffly asked what
I knew about it, and affirmed that he had as much daylight as his
neighbors; he ventured to say, the days were longer there than where
I lived, as I should find if I stayed; that in some way, I could not be
expected to understand how, the sun came over the mountains half
an hour earlier, and stayed half an hour later there than on the neighboring plains. And more of like sort he said. He was, indeed, as rude
as a fabled satyr. But I suffered him to pass for what he was — for
why should I quarrel with nature? — and was even pleased at the
discovery of such a singular natural phenomenon. I dealt with him as
if to me all manners were indifferent, and he had a sweet, wild way with
him. I would not question nature, and I would rather have him as he
was than as I would have him. For I had come up here not for sympathy, or kindness, or society, but for novelty and adventure, and to see
what nature had produced here. I therefore did not repel his rudeness,
but quite innocently welcomed it all, and knew how to appreciate it,
as if I were reading in an old drama a part well sustained. He was
indeed a coarse and sensual man, and, as I have said, uncivil, but he had
his just quarrel with nature and mankind, I have no doubt, only he
had no artificial covering to his ill-humors. He was earthy enough, but
yet there was good soil in him, and even a long-suffering Saxon probity
at bottom. If you could represent the case to him, he would not let the
race die out in him, like a red Indian.

At length I told him that he was a fortunate man, and I trusted
that he was grateful for so much light; and, rising, said I would take
a lamp, and that I would pay him then for my lodging, for I expected
to recommence my journey even as early as the sun rose in his country;
but he answered in haste, and this time civilly, that I should not fail
to find some of his household stirring, however early, for they were no
sluggards, and I could take my breakfast with them before I started, it

I chose; and as he lighted the lamp I detected a gleam of true hospitality and ancient civility, a beam of pure and even gentle humanity, from his bleared and moist eyes. It was a look more intimate with me, and more explanatory, than any words of his could have been if he had tried to his dying day. It was more significant than any Rice of those parts could even comprehend, and long anticipated this man's culture — a glance of his pure genius, which did not much enlighten him, but did impress and rule him for the moment, and faintly constrain his voice and manner. He cheerfully led the way to my apartment, stepping over the limbs of his men, who were asleep on the floor in an intervening chamber, and showed me a clean and comfortable bed. For many pleasant hours after the household was asleep I sat at the open window, for it was a sultry night, and heard the little river

> 'Amongst the pumy stones, which seemed to plain,
>   With gentle murmur, that his course they did restrain.'

But I arose as usual by starlight the next morning, before my host, or his men, or even his dogs, were awake; and, having left a ninepence on the counter, was already halfway over the mountain with the sun before they had broken their fast.

Before I had left the country of my host, while the first rays of the sun slanted over the mountains, as I stopped by the wayside to gather some raspberries, a very old man, not far from a hundred, came along with a milking-pail in his hand, and turning aside began to pluck the berries near me:

> 'His reverend locks
> In comelye curles did wave;
> And on his aged temples grew
> The blossoms of the grave.'

But when I inquired the way, he answered in a low, rough voice, without looking up or seeming to regard my presence, which I imputed to his years; and presently, muttering to himself, he proceeded to collect his cows in a neighboring pasture; and when he had again returned near to the wayside, he suddenly stopped, while his cows went on before, and, uncovering his head, prayed aloud in the cool morning air, as if he had forgotten this exercise before, for his daily bread, and also that He who letteth his rain fall on the just and on the unjust, and without whom not a sparrow falleth to the ground, would not neglect the stranger (meaning me), and with even more direct and personal applications, though mainly according to the long-established formula common to lowlanders and the inhabitants of mountains. When he had done praying, I made bold to ask him if he had any cheese in his hut which he would sell me, but he answered without looking up, and in the same low and repulsive voice as before, that they did not make any, and went to milking. It is written, 'The stranger who turneth away from a house with disappointed hopes, leaveth there his own offenses, and departeth, taking with him all the good actions of the owner.'

Being now fairly in the stream of this week's commerce, we began to meet with boats more frequently, and hailed them from time to time with the freedom of sailors. The boatmen appeared to lead an easy and contented life, and we thought that we should prefer their employment ourselves to many professions which are much more sought after. They suggested how few circumstances are necessary to the well-being and serenity of man, how indifferent all employments are, and that any may seem noble and poetic to the eyes of men, if pursued with sufficient buoyancy and freedom. With liberty and pleasant weather, the simplest occupation, any unquestioned country mode of life which detains us in the open air, is alluring. The man who picks peas steadily for a living is more than respectable, he is even envied by his shop-worn neighbors. We are as happy as the birds when our Good Genius permits us to pursue any outdoor work, without a sense of dissipation. Our penknife glitters in the sun; our voice is echoed by yonder wood; if an oar drops, we are fain to let it drop again.

The canal-boat is of very simple construction, requiring but little ship-timber, and, as we were told, costs about two hundred dollars. They are managed by two men. In ascending the stream they use poles fourteen or fifteen feet long, pointed with iron, walking about one third the length of the boat from the forward end. Going down, they commonly keep in the middle of the stream, using an oar at each end; or if the wind is favorable they raise their broad sail, and have only to steer. They commonly carry down wood or bricks — fifteen or sixteen cords of wood, and as many thousand bricks, at a time — and bring back stores for the country, consuming two or three days each way between Concord and Charlestown. They sometimes pile the wood so as to leave a shelter in one part where they may retire from the rain. One can hardly imagine a more healthful employment, or one more favorable to contemplation and the observation of nature. Unlike the mariner, they have the constantly varying panorama of the shore to relieve the monotony of their labor, and it seemed to us that as they thus glided noiselessly from town to town, with all their furniture about them, for their very homestead is a movable, they could comment on the character of the inhabitants with greater advantage and security to themselves than the traveler in a coach, who would be unable to indulge in such broadsides of wit and humor in so small a vessel for fear of the recoil. They are not subject to great exposure, like the lumberers of Maine, in any weather, but inhale the healthfulest breezes, being slightly incumbered with clothing, frequently with the head and feet bare. When we met them at noon, as they were leisurely descending the stream, their busy commerce did not look like toil, but rather like some ancient Oriental game still played on a large scale, as the game of chess, for instance, handed down to this generation. From morning till night, unless the wind is so fair that his single sail will suffice without other labor than steering, the boatman walks backwards and forwards on the side of his boat, now stooping with his shoulder to the pole, then drawing it back slowly to set it again, meanwhile moving steadily forward through an endless valley and an ever-changing scenery, now distinguishing his course for a mile or two, and now shut in by a sudden turn of the river in a small woodland lake. All the phenomena which surround him are simple and grand, and there is something impressive, even majestic, in the very motion he causes, which will naturally be communicated to his own character, and he feels the slow, irresistible movement under him with pride, as if it were his own energy.

The news spread like wildfire among us youths, when formerly, once in a year or two, one of these boats came up the Concord River, and was seen stealing mysteriously through the meadows and past the village. It came and departed as silently as a cloud, without noise or dust, and was witnessed by few. One summer day this huge traveler might be seen moored at some meadow's wharf, and another summer day it was not there. Where precisely it came from, or who these men were who knew the rocks and soundings better than we who bathed there, we could never tell. We knew some river's bay only, but they took rivers from end to end. They were a sort of fabulous rivermen to us. It was inconceivable by what sort of mediation any mere landsman could hold communication with them. Would they heave to, to gratify his wishes? No, it was favor enough to know faintly of their destination, or the time of their possible return. I have seen them in the summer, when the stream ran low, mowing the weeds in mid-channel, and with hayers' jests cutting broad swaths in three feet of water, that they might make a passage for their scow, while the grass in long windrows was carried down the stream, undried by the rarest hay weather. We admired unweariedly how their vessel would float, like a huge chip, sustaining so many casks of lime, and thousands of bricks, and such heaps of iron ore, with wheelbarrows aboard, and that, when we stepped on it, it did not yield to the pressure of our feet. It gave us confidence in the prevalence of the law of buoyancy, and we imagined to what infinite uses it might be put. The men appeared to lead a kind of life on it, and it was whispered that they slept aboard. Some affirmed that it carried sail, and that such winds blew here as filled the sails of vessels on the ocean; which again others much doubted. They had been seen to sail across our Fair Haven Bay by lucky fishers who were out, but unfortunately others were not there to see. We might then say that our river was navigable — why not? In after years I read in print, with no little satisfaction, that it was thought by some that, with a little expense in removing rocks and deepening the channel, 'there might be a profitable inland navigation.' *I* then lived somewhere to tell of.

Such is Commerce, which shakes the cocoanut and bread-fruit tree in the remotest isle, and sooner or later dawns on the duskiest and most simple-minded savage. If we may be pardoned the digression, who can help being affected at the thought of the very fine and slight, but positive relation, in which the savage inhabitants of some remote isle stand to the mysterious white mariner, the child of the sun? — as if *we* were to have dealings with an animal higher in the scale of being than ourselves. It is a barely recognized fact to the natives that he exists, and has his home far away somewhere, and is glad to buy their fresh fruits with his superfluous commodities. Under the same catholic sun glances his white ship over Pacific waves into their smooth bays, and the poor savage's paddle gleams in the air.

> Man's little acts are grand,
> Beheld from land to land,
> There as they lie in time,
> Within their native clime.
>   Ships with the noontide weigh,
>   And glide before its ray
>   To some retired bay,
>   Their haunt,
>   Whence, under tropic sun,
>   Again they run,
>   Bearing gum Senegal and Tragicant.
> For this was ocean meant,
> For this the sun was sent,
> And moon was lent,
> And winds in distant caverns pent.

Since our voyage the railroad on the bank has been extended, and there is now but little boating on the Merrimack. All kinds of produce and stores were formerly conveyed by water, but now nothing is carried up the stream, and almost wood and bricks alone are carried down, and these are also carried on the railroad. The locks are fast wearing out, and will soon be impassable, since the tolls will not pay the expense of repairing them, and so in a few years there will be an end of boating on this river. The boating at present is principally between Merrimack and Lowell, or Hooksett and Manchester. They make two or three trips in a week, according to wind and weather, from Merrimack to Lowell and back, about twenty-five miles each way. The boatman comes singing in to shore late at night, and moors his empty boat, and gets his supper and lodging in some house near at hand, and again early in the morning, by starlight perhaps, he pushes away up-stream, and, by a shout, or the fragment of a song, gives notice of his approach to the lock-man, with whom he is to take his breakfast. If he gets up to his wood-pile before noon he proceeds to load his boat, with the help of his single 'hand,' and is on his way down again before night. When he gets to Lowell he unloads his boat, and gets his receipt for his cargo, and, having heard the news at the public house at Middlesex or else-where, goes back with his empty boat and his receipt in his pocket to the owner, and to get a new load. We were frequently advertised of their approach by some faint sound behind us, and looking round saw them a mile off, creeping stealthily up the side of the stream like alliga-tors. It was pleasant to hail these sailors of the Merrimack from time to time, and learn the news which circulated with them. We imagined that the sun shining on their bare heads had stamped a liberal and public character on their most private thoughts.

The open and sunny interval still stretched away from the river some-times by two or more terraces, to the distant hill-country, and when we climbed the bank, we commonly found an irregular copse-wood skirting the river, the primitive having floated down-stream long ago to ———, the 'King's navy.' Sometimes we saw the river road a quarter or half a mile distant, and the parti-colored Concord stage, with its cloud of dust, its van of earnest traveling faces, and its rear of dusty trunks, reminding us that the country had its places of rendezvous for restless Yankee men. There dwelt along at considerable distances on this interval a quiet agricultural and pastoral people, with every house its well, as we sometimes proved, and every household, though never so still and remote it appeared in the noontide, its dinner about these times. There they lived on, those New England people, farmer lives, father and grandfather and great-grandfather, on and on without noise, keeping up tradition, and expecting, beside fair weather and abundant harvests, we did not learn what. They were contented to live, since it was so contrived for them, and where their lines had fallen.

> Our uninquiring corpses lie more low
> Than our life's curiosity doth go.

Yet these men had no need to travel to be as wise as Solomon in all his glory, so similar are the lives of men in all countries, and fraught with the same homely experiences. One half the world *knows* how the other half lives.

About noon we passed a small village in Merrimack at Thornton's Ferry, and tasted of the waters of Naticook Brook on the same side, where French and his companions, whose grave we saw in Dunstable, were ambuscaded by the Indians. The humble village of Litchfield, with its steepleless meeting-house, stood on the opposite or east bank, near where a dense grove of willows backed by maples skirted the shore. There also we noticed some shagbark trees, which, as they do not grow in Concord, were as strange a sight to us as the palm would be, whose fruit only we have seen. Our course now curved gracefully to the north, leaving a low, flat shore on the Merrimack side, which forms a sort of harbor for canal-boats. We observed some fair elms and particularly large and handsome white maples standing conspicuously on this interval; and the opposite shore, a quarter of a mile below, was covered with young elms and maples six inches high, which had probably sprung from the seeds which had been washed across.

Some carpenters were at work here mending a scow on the green and sloping bank. The strokes of their mallets echoed from shore to shore, and up and down the river, and their tools gleamed in the sun a quarter of a mile from us, and we realized that boat-building was as ancient and honorable an art as agriculture, and that there might be a naval as well as a pastoral life. The whole history of commerce was made manifest in that scow turned bottom upward on the shore. Thus did men begin to go down upon the sea in ships; *quaeque diu steterant in montibus altis, Fluctibus ignotis insultavêre carinae;* 'and keels which had long stood on high mountains careered insultingly (*insultavêre*) over unknown waves.' [1]

[1] Ovid, *Met.* I, 133.

We thought that it would be well for the traveler to build his boat on the bank of a stream, instead of finding a ferry or a bridge. In the Adventures of Henry the fur-trader, it is pleasant to read that when with his Indians he reached the shore of Ontario, they consumed two days in making two canoes of the bark of the elm tree, in which to transport themselves to Fort Niagara. It is a worthy incident in a journey, a delay as good as much rapid traveling. A good share of our interest in Xenophon's story of his retreat is in the manœuvres to get the army safely over the rivers, whether on rafts of logs or fagots, or sheepskins blown up. And where could they better afford to tarry meanwhile than on the banks of a river?

As we glided past at a distance, these outdoor workmen appeared to have added some dignity to their labor by its very publicness. It was a part of the industry of nature, like the work of hornets and mud wasps.

> The waves slowly beat,
> Just to keep the noon sweet,
> And no sound is floated o'er,
> Save the mallet on shore,
> Which echoing on high
> Seems a-calking the sky.

The haze, the sun's dust of travel, had a Lethean influence on the land and its inhabitants, and all creatures resigned themselves to float upon the inappreciable tides of nature.

> Woof of the sun, ethereal gauze,
> Woven of Nature's richest stuffs,
> Visible heat, air-water, and dry sea,
> Last conquest of the eye;
> Toil of the day displayed, sun-dust,
> Aerial surf upon the shores of earth,
> Ethereal estuary, frith of light,
> Breakers of air, billows of heat,
> Fine summer spray on inland seas;
> Bird of the sun, transparent-winged
> Owlet of noon, soft-pinioned,
> From heath or stubble rising without song,
> Establish thy serenity o'er the fields.

The routine which is in the sunshine and the finest days, as that which has conquered and prevailed, commends itself to us by its very antiquity and apparent solidity and necessity. Our weakness needs it, and our strength uses it. We cannot draw on our boots without bracing ourselves against it. If there were but one erect and solid-standing tree in the woods, all creatures would go to rub against it and make sure of their footing. During the many hours which we spend in this waking sleep, the hand stands still on the face of the clock, and we grow like corn in the night. Men are as busy as the brooks or bees, and postpone everything to their business; as carpenters discuss politics between the strokes of the hammer while they are shingling a roof. . . .[1]

During the heat of the day, we rested on a large island a mile above the mouth of this river, pastured by a herd of cattle, with steep banks and scattered elms and oaks, and a sufficient channel for canal-boats on each side. When we made a fire to boil some rice for our dinner, the flames spreading amid the dry grass, and the smoke curling silently upward and casting grotesque shadows on the ground, seemed phenomena of the noon, and we fancied that we progressed up the stream without effort, and as naturally as the wind and tide went down, not outraging the calm days by unworthy bustle or impatience. The woods on the neighboring shore were alive with pigeons, which were moving south, looking for mast, but now, like ourselves, spending their noon in the shade. We could hear the slight, wiry, winnowing sound of their wings as they changed their roosts from time to time, and their gentle and tremulous cooing. They sojourned with us during the noontide, greater travelers far than we. You may frequently discover a single pair sitting upon the lower branches of the white pine in the depths of the wood, at this hour of the day, so silent and solitary, and with such a hermitlike appearance, as if they had never strayed beyond its skirts, while the acorn which was gathered in the forests of Maine is still undigested in their crops. We obtained one of these handsome birds, which lingered too long upon its perch, and plucked and broiled it here with some other game, to be carried along for our supper; for, beside the provisions which we carried with us, we depended mainly on the river and forest for our supply. It is true, it did not seem to be putting this bird to its right use to pluck off its feathers, and extract its entrails, and broil its carcass on the coals; but we heroically persevered, nevertheless, waiting for further information. The same regard for Nature which excited our sympathy for her creatures nerved our hands to carry through what we had begun. For we would be honorable to the party we deserted; we would fulfill fate, and so at length, perhaps,

[1] Pages 230–235 (Walden Edition) on Fur-Traders and Indians, omitted.

detect the secret innocence of these incessant tragedies which Heaven
allows.

> 'Too quick resolves do resolution wrong.
> What, part so soon to be divorced so long?
> Things to be done are long to be debated;
> Heaven is not day'd, Repentance is not dated.'

We are double-edged blades, and every time we whet our virtue the
return stroke straps our vice. Where is the skillful swordsman who can
give clean wounds, and not rip up his work with the other edge?

Nature herself has not provided the most graceful end for her creatures. What becomes of all these birds that people the air and forest
for our solacement? The sparrows seem always *chipper*, never infirm.
We do not see their bodies lie about. Yet there is a tragedy at the end
of each one of their lives. They must perish miserably; not one of them
is translated. True, 'not a sparrow falleth to the ground without our
Heavenly Father's knowledge,' but they do fall, nevertheless.

The carcasses of some poor squirrels, however, the same that frisked
so merrily in the morning, which we had skinned and emboweled for
our dinner, we abandoned in disgust, with tardy humanity, as too
wretched a resource for any but starving men. It was to perpetuate
the practice of a barbarous era. If they had been larger, our crime had
been less. Their small red bodies, little bundles of red tissue, mere
gobbets of venison, would not have 'fattened fire.' With a sudden
impulse we threw them away, and washed our hands, and boiled some
rice for our dinner. 'Behold the difference between the one who eateth
flesh, and him to whom it belonged! The first hath a momentary enjoyment, whilst the latter is deprived of existence!' 'Who would commit so
great a crime against a poor animal, who is fed only by the herbs which
grow wild in the woods, and whose belly is burnt up with hunger?' We
remembered a picture of mankind in the hunter age, chasing hares
down the mountains; O me miserable! Yet sheep and oxen are but
larger squirrels, whose hides are saved and meat is salted, whose souls
perchance are not so large in proportion to their bodies.

There should always be some flowering and maturing of the fruits
of nature in the cooking process. Some simple dishes recommend themselves to our imaginations as well as palates. In parched corn, for
instance, there is a manifest sympathy between the bursting seed and
the more perfect developments of vegetable life. It is a perfect flower
with its petals, like the houstonia or anemone. On my warm hearth
these cerealian blossoms expanded; here is the bank whereon they grew.

Perhaps some such visible blessing would always attend the simple and wholesome repast. . . .[1]

Late in the afternoon, for we had lingered long on the island, we raised our sail for the first time, and for a short hour the southwest wind was our ally; but it did not please Heaven to abet us long. With one sail raised we swept slowly up the eastern side of the stream, steering clear of the rocks, while, from the top of a hill which formed the opposite bank, some lumberers were rolling down timber to be rafted down the stream. We could see their axes and levers gleaming in the sun, and the logs came down with a dust and a rumbling sound, which was reverberated through the woods beyond us on our side, like the roar of artillery. But Zephyr soon took us out of sight and hearing of his commerce. Having passed Read's Ferry, and another island called McGaw's Island, we reached some rapids called Moore's Falls, and entered on 'that section of the river, nine miles in extent, converted, by law, into the Union Canal, comprehending in that space six distinct falls; at each of which, and at several intermediate places, work has been done.' After passing Moore's Falls by means of locks, we again had recourse to our oars, and went merrily on our way, driving the small sandpiper from rock to rock before us, and sometimes rowing near enough to a cottage on the bank, though they were few and far between, to see the sunflowers, and the seed-vessels of the poppy, like small goblets filled with the water of Lethe, before the door, but without disturbing the sluggish household behind. Thus we held on, sailing or dipping our way along with the paddle up this broad river, smooth and placid, flowing over concealed rocks, where we could see the pickerel lying low in the transparent water, eager to double some distant cape, to make some great bend as in the life of man, and see what new perspective would open; looking far into a new country, broad and serene, the cottages of settlers seen afar for the first time, yet with the moss of a century on their roofs, and the third or fourth generation in their shadows. Strange was it to consider how the sun and the summer, the buds of spring and the seared leaves of autumn, were related to these cabins along the shore; how all the rays which paint the landscape radiate from them, and the flight of the crow and the gyrations of the hawk have reference to their roofs. Still the ever rich and fertile shores accompanied us, fringed with vines and alive with small birds and frisking squirrels, the edge of some farmer's field or widow's wood-lot, or wilder, perchance, where the

[1] Pages 238–244 (Walden Edition) on Anacreon, omitted.

muskrat, the little medicine of the river, drags itself along stealthily over the alder leaves and mussel shells, and man and the memory of man are banished far.

At length the unwearied, never-sinking shore, still holding on without break, with its cool copses and serene pasture-grounds, tempted us to disembark; and we adventurously landed on this remote coast, to survey it, without the knowledge of any human inhabitant probably to this day. But we still remember the gnarled and hospitable oaks which grew even there for our entertainment, and were no strangers to us, the lonely horse in his pasture, and the patient cows, whose path to the river, so judiciously chosen to overcome the difficulties of the way, we followed, and disturbed their ruminations in the shade; and, above all, the cool, free aspect of the wild apple trees, generously proffering their fruit to us, though still green and crude — the hard, round, glossy fruit, which, if not ripe, still was not poison, but New English too, brought hither, its ancestors, by ours once. These gentler trees imparted a half-civilized and twilight aspect to the otherwise barbarian land. Still farther on we scrambled up the rocky channel of a brook, which had long served nature for a sluice there, leaping like it from rock to rock, through tangled woods, at the bottom of a ravine, which grew darker and darker, and more and more hoarse the murmurs of the stream, until we reached the ruins of a mill, where now the ivy grew, and the trout glanced through the crumbling flume; and there we imagined what had been the dreams and speculations of some early settler. But the waning day compelled us to embark once more, and redeem this wasted time with long and vigorous sweeps over the rippling stream.

It was still wild and solitary, except that at intervals of a mile or two the roof of a cottage might be seen over the bank. This region, as we read, was once famous for the manufacture of straw bonnets of the Leghorn kind, of which it claims the invention in these parts; and occasionally some industrious damsel tripped down to the water's edge, to put her straw a-soak, as it appeared, and stood awhile to watch the retreating voyageurs, and catch the fragment of a boat-song which we had made, wafted over the water.

> Thus, perchance, the Indian hunter,
>   Many a lagging year agone,
> Gliding o'er thy rippling waters,
>   Lowly hummed a natural song.

> Now the sun's behind the willows,
> Now he gleams along the waves;
> Faintly o'er the wearied billows
> Come the spirits of the braves.

Just before sundown we reached some more falls in the town of Bedford, where some stone-masons were employed repairing the locks in a solitary part of the river. They were interested in our adventure, especially one young man of our own age, who inquired at first if we were bound up to ' 'Skeag;' and when he had heard our story, and examined our outfit, asked us other questions, but temperately still, and always turning to his work again, though as if it were become his duty. It was plain that he would like to go with us, and, as he looked up the river, many a distant cape and wooded shore were reflected in his eye, as well as in his thoughts. When we were ready he left his work, and helped us through the locks with a sort of quiet enthusiasm; telling us that we were at Coos Falls, and we could still distinguish the strokes of his chisel for many sweeps after we had left him.

We wished to camp this night on a large rock in the middle of the stream, just above these falls, but the want of fuel, and the difficulty of fixing our tent firmly, prevented us; so we made our bed on the mainland opposite, on the west bank, in the town of Bedford, in a retired place, as we supposed, there being no house in sight.

WEDNESDAY

Man is man's foe and destiny. — COTTON.

EARLY this morning, as we were rolling up our buffaloes and loading our boat amid the dew, while our embers were still smoking, the masons who worked at the locks, and whom we had seen crossing the river in their boat the evening before while we were examining the rock, came upon us as they were going to their work, and we found that we had pitched our tent directly in the path to their boat. This was the only time that we were observed on our camping-ground. Thus, far from the beaten highways and the dust and din of travel, we beheld the country privately, yet freely, and at our leisure. Other roads do some violence to Nature, and bring the traveler to stare at her, but the river steals into the scenery it traverses without intrusion, silently creating and adorning it, and is as free to come and go as the zephyr.

As we shoved away from this rocky coast, before sunrise, the smaller bittern, the genius of the shore, was moping along its edge, or stood probing the mud for its food, with ever an eye on us, though so demurely at work, or else he ran along over the wet stones like a wrecker in his storm-coat, looking out for wrecks of snails and cockles. Now away he goes, with a limping flight, uncertain where he will alight, until a rod of clear sand amid the alders invites his feet; and now our steady approach compels him to seek a new retreat. It is a bird of the oldest Thalesian school, and no doubt believes in the priority of water to the other elements; the relic of a twilight antediluvian age which yet inhabits these bright American rivers with us Yankees. There is something venerable in this melancholy and contemplative race of birds, which may have trodden the earth while it was yet in a slimy and imperfect state. Perchance their tracks, too, are still visible on the stones. It still lingers into our glaring summers, bravely supporting its fate without sympathy from man, as if it looked forward to some second advent of which *he* has no assurance. One wonders if, by its patient study by rocks and sandy capes, it has wrested the whole of her secret from Nature yet. What a rich experience it must have gained, standing on one leg and looking out from its dull eye so long on sunshine and rain, moon and stars! What could it tell of stagnant pools and reeds and dank night-fogs! It would be worth the while to look closely into the eye which has been open and seeing at such hours, and in such solitudes its dull, yellowish, greenish eye. Methinks my own soul must be a bright invisible green. I have seen these birds stand by the half dozen together in the shallower water along the shore, with their bills thrust into the mud at the bottom, probing for food, the whole head being concealed, while the neck and body formed an arch above the water.

Cohass Brook, the outlet of Massabesic Pond — which last is five or six miles distant, and contains fifteen hundred acres, being the largest body of fresh water in Rockingham County — comes in near here from the east. Rowing between Manchester and Bedford, we passed, at an early hour, a ferry and some falls, called Goff's Falls, the Indian Cohasset, where there is a small village, and a handsome green islet in the middle of the stream. From Bedford and Merrimack have been boated the bricks of which Lowell is made. About twenty years before, as they told us, one Moore, of Bedford, having clay on his farm, contracted to furnish eight millions of bricks to the founders of that city within two years. He fulfilled his contract in one year, and since then bricks have been the principal export from these towns. The farmers found thus a market for their wood, and when they had brought a load to the kilns, they could cart a load of bricks to the shore, and so make a profitable day's work of it. Thus all parties were benefited. It was worth the while to see the place where Lowell was 'dug out.' So, likewise, Manchester is being built of bricks made still higher up the river at Hooksett.

There might be seen here on the bank of the Merrimack, near Goff's Falls, in what is now the town of Bedford, famous 'for hops and for its fine domestic manufactures,' some graves of the aborigines. The land still bears this scar here, and time is slowly crumbling the bones of a race. Yet, without fail, every spring, since they first fished and hunted here, the brown thrasher has heralded the morning from a birch or alder spray, and the undying race of reed-birds still rustles through the withering grass. But these bones rustle not. These mouldering elements are slowly preparing for another metamorphosis, to serve new masters, and what was the Indian's will ere long be the white man's sinew.

We learned that Bedford was not so famous for hops as formerly, since the price is fluctuating, and poles are now scarce. Yet if the traveler goes back a few miles from the river, the hop kilns will still excite his curiosity.

There were few incidents in our voyage this forenoon, though the river was now more rocky and the falls more frequent than before. It was a pleasant change, after rowing incessantly for many hours, to lock ourselves through in some retired place — for commonly there was no lock-man at hand — one sitting in the boat, while the other, sometimes with no little labor and heave-yo-ing, opened and shut the gates, waiting patiently to see the locks fill. We did not once use the wheels which we had provided. Taking advantage of the eddy, we were sometimes floated up to the locks almost in the face of the falls; and, by the same cause, any floating timber was carried round in a circle and repeatedly drawn into the rapids before it finally went down the stream. These old gray structures, with their quiet arms stretched over the river in the sun, appeared like natural objects in the scenery, and the kingfisher and sandpiper alighted on them as readily as on stakes or rocks.

We rowed leisurely up the stream for several hours, until the sun had got high in the sky, our thoughts monotonously beating time to our oars. For outward variety there was only the river and the receding shores, a vista continually opening behind and closing before us, as we sat with our backs upstream; and, for inward, such thoughts as the muses grudgingly lent us. We were always passing some low, inviting shore, or some over-hanging bank, on which, however, we never landed.

> Such near aspects had we
> Of our life's scenery.

It might be seen by what tenure men held the earth. The smallest stream is *mediterranean* sea, a smaller ocean creek within the land, where men may steer by their farm bounds and cottage lights. For my own part, but for the geographers, I should hardly have known how large a portion of our globe is water, my life has chiefly passed within so deep a cove. Yet I have sometimes ventured as far as to the mouth of my Snug Harbor. From an old ruined fort on Staten Island, I have loved to watch all day some vessel whose name I had read in the morning through the telegraph glass, when she first came upon the coast, and her hull heaved up and glistened in the sun, from the moment when the pilot and most adventurous news-boats met her, past the Hook, and up the narrow channel of the wide bay, till she was boarded by the health officer, and took her station at quarantine, or held on her un-questioned course to the wharves of New York. It was interesting, too, to watch the less adventurous newsman, who made his assault as the vessel swept through the Narrows, defying plague and quarantine law, and, fastening his little cockboat to her huge side, clambered up and disappeared in the cabin. And then I could imagine what momentous news was being imparted by the captain, which no American ear had ever heard, that Asia, Africa, Europe — were all sunk; for which at length he pays the price, and is seen descending the ship's side with his bundle of newspapers, but not where he first got up, for these arrivers do not stand still to gossip; and he hastes away with steady sweeps to dis-pose of his wares to the highest bidder, and we shall ere long read some-thing startling — 'By the latest arrival,' — 'by the good ship ——.' On Sunday I beheld, from some interior hill, the long procession of vessels getting to sea, reaching from the city wharves through the Narrows, and past the Hook, quite to the ocean stream, far as the eye could reach, with stately march and silken sails, all counting on lucky voyages, but each time some of the number, no doubt, destined to go to Davy's locker, and never come on this coast again. And, again, in the evening of a pleasant day, it was my amusement to count the sails in sight. But as the setting sun continually brought more and more to light, still farther in the horizon, the last count always had the advantage, till, by the time the last rays streamed over the sea, I had doubled and trebled my first number; though I could no longer class them all under the several heads of ships, barks, brigs, schooners, and sloops, but most were faint generic *vessels* only. And then the temperate twilight, perchance, revealed the floating home of some sailor whose thoughts were already alienated from this American coast, and directed towards the Europe of our dreams. I have stood upon the same hilltop, when a thunder-shower, rolling down from the Catskills and Highlands, passed over the island, deluging the land; and, when it had suddenly left us in sunshine, have seen it overtake successively, with its huge shadow and dark, descending wall of rain, the vessels in the bay. Their bright sails were suddenly drooping and dark, like the sides of barns, and they seemed to shrink before the storm; while still far beyond them on the sea, through this dark veil, gleamed the sunny sails of those vessels which the storm had not yet reached. And at midnight, when all around and overhead was darkness, I have seen a field of trembling, silvery light far out on the sea, the reflection of the moonlight from the ocean, as if beyond the precincts of our night, where the moon traversed a cloudless heaven — and sometimes a dark speck in its midst, where some fortunate vessel was pursuing its happy voyage by night.

But to us river sailors the sun never rose out of ocean waves, but from some green coppice, and went down behind some dark mountain line. We, too, were but dwellers on the shore, like the bittern of the morning; and our pursuit, the wrecks of snails and cockles. Nevertheless, we were contented to know the better one fair particular shore.

> My life is like a stroll upon the beach,
>   As near the ocean's edge as I can go;
> My tardy steps its waves sometimes o'erreach,
>   Sometimes I stay to let them overflow.
>
> My sole employment 'tis, and scrupulous care,
>   To place my gains beyond the reach of tides,
> Each smoother pebble, and each shell more rare,
>   Which ocean kindly to my hand confides.
>
> I have but few companions on the shore,
>   They scorn the strand who sail upon the sea,
> Yet oft I think the ocean they've sailed o'er
>   Is deeper known upon the strand to me.

> The middle sea contains no crimson dulse,
>   Its deeper waves cast up no pearls to view,
>   Along the shore my hand is on its pulse,
>   And I converse with many a shipwrecked crew.

The small houses which were scattered along the river at intervals of a mile or more were commonly out of sight to us, but sometimes, when we rowed near the shore, we heard the peevish note of a hen, or some slight domestic sound, which betrayed them. The lock-men's houses were particularly well placed, retired, and high, always at falls or rapids, and commanding the pleasantest reaches of the river — for it is generally wider and more lake-like just above a fall — and there they wait for boats. These humble dwellings, homely and sincere, in which a hearth was still the essential part, were more pleasing to our eyes than palaces or castles would have been. In the noon of these days, as we have said, we occasionally climbed the banks and approached these houses, to get a glass of water and make acquaintance with their inhabitants. High in the leafy bank, surrounded commonly by a small patch of corn and beans, squashes and melons, with sometimes a graceful hopyard on one side, and some running vine over the windows, they appeared like beehives set to gather honey for a summer. I have not read of any Arcadian life which surpasses the actual luxury and serenity of these New England dwellings. For the outward gilding, at least, the age is golden enough. As you approach the sunny doorway, awakening the echoes by your steps, still no sound from these barracks of repose, and you fear that the gentlest knock may seem rude to the Oriental dreamers. The door is opened, perchance, by some Yankee-Hindoo woman, whose small-voiced but sincere hospitality, out of the bottomless depths of a quiet nature, has traveled quite round to the opposite side, and fears only to obtrude its kindness. You step over the white-scoured floor to the bright 'dresser' lightly, as if afraid to disturb the devotions of the household — for Oriental dynasties appear to have passed away since the dinner-table was last spread here — and thence to the frequented curb, where you see your long-forgotten, unshaven face at the bottom, in juxtaposition with new-made butter and the trout in the well. 'Perhaps you would like some molasses and ginger,' suggests the faint noon voice. Sometimes there sits the brother who follows the sea, their representative man; who knows only how far it is to the nearest port, no more distances, all the rest is sea and distant capes — patting the dog, or dandling the kitten in arms that were stretched by the cable and the oar, pulling against Boreas or the trade-winds. He looks up at the stranger, half pleased, half astonished, with a mariner's eye, as if he were a dolphin within cast. If men will believe it, *sua si bona norint*, there are no more quiet Tempes, nor more poetic and Arcadian lives, than may be lived in these New England dwellings. We thought that the employment of their inhabitants by day would be to tend the flowers and herds, and at night, like the shepherds of old, to cluster and give names to the stars from the river banks.

We passed a large and densely wooded island this forenoon, between Short's and Griffith's Falls, the fairest which we had met with, with a handsome grove of elms at its head. If it had been evening, we should have been glad to camp there. Not long after, one or two more were passed. The boatmen told us that the current had recently made important changes here. An island always pleases my imagination, even the smallest, as a small continent and integral portion of the globe. I have a fancy for building my hut on one. Even a bare, grassy isle, which I can see entirely over at a glance, has some undefined and mysterious charm for me. There is commonly such a one at the junction of two rivers, whose currents bring down and deposit their respective sands in the eddy at their confluence, as it were the womb of a continent. By what a delicate and far-stretched contribution every island is made! What an enterprise of Nature thus to lay the foundations of and to build up the future continent, of golden and silver sands and the ruins of forests, with ant-like industry. Pindar gives the following account of the origin of Thera, whence, in after times, Libyan Cyrene was settled by Battus. Triton, in the form of Eurypylus, presents a clod to Euphemus, one of the Argonauts, as they are about to return home.

> 'He knew of our haste,
> And immediately seizing a clod
> With his right hand, strove to give it
> As a chance stranger's gift.
> Nor did the hero disregard him, but leaping on the shore,
> Stretching hand to hand,
> Received the mystic clod.
> But I hear it sinking from the deck,
> Go with the sea brine
> At evening, accompanying the watery sea.
> Often indeed I urged the careless
> Menials to guard it, but their minds forgot.
> And now in this island the imperishable seed of spacious Libya
> Is spilled before its hour.'

It is a beautiful fable, also related by Pindar, how Helius, or the Sun, looked down into the sea one day — when perchance his rays were first reflected from some increasing, glittering sand-bar — and saw the fair and fruitful island of Rhodes

> 'springing up from the bottom,
> Capable of feeding many men, and suitable for flocks;'

and at the nod of Zeus,

> 'The island sprang from the watery
> Sea; and the genial Father of penetrating beams,
> Ruler of fire-breathing horses, has it.'

The shifting islands! who would not be willing that his house should be undermined by such a foe! The inhabitant of an island can tell what currents formed the land which he cultivates; and his earth is still being created or destroyed. There before his door, perchance, still empties the stream which brought down the material of his farm ages before, and is still bringing it down or washing it away — the graceful, gentle robber!

Not long after this we saw the Piscataquoag, or Sparkling Water, emptying in on our left, and heard the Falls of Amoskeag above. Large quantities of lumber, as we read in the Gazetteer, were still annually floated down the Piscataquoag to the Merrimack, and there are many fine mill privileges on it. Just above the mouth of this river we passed the artificial falls where the canals of the Manchester Manufacturing Company discharge themselves into the Merrimack. They are striking enough to have a name, and, with the scenery of a Bashpish, would be visited from far and near. The water falls thirty or forty feet over seven or eight steep and narrow terraces of stone, probably to break its force, and is converted into one mass of foam. This canal water did not seem to be the worse for the wear, but foamed and fumed as purely, and boomed as savagely and impressively, as a mountain torrent, and, though it came from under a factory, we saw a rainbow here. These are now the Amoskeag Falls, removed a mile down-stream. But we did not tarry to examine them minutely, making haste to get past the village here collected, and out of hearing of the hammer which was laying the foundation of another Lowell on the banks. At the time of our voyage Manchester was a village of about two thousand inhabitants, where we landed for a moment to get some cool water, and where an inhabitant told us that he was accustomed to go across the river into Goffstown for his water. But now, as I have been told, and indeed have witnessed, it contains fourteen thousand inhabitants. From a hill on the road between Goffstown and Hooksett, four miles distant, I have seen a thunder-shower pass over, and the sun break out and shine on a city there, where I had landed nine years before in the fields; and there was waving the flag of its Museum, where 'the only perfect skeleton of a Greenland or river whale in the United States' was to be seen, and I also read in its directory of a 'Manchester Athenæum and Gallery of the Fine Arts.'

According to the Gazetteer, the descent of Amoskeag Falls, which are the most considerable in the Merrimack, is fifty-four feet in half a mile. We locked ourselves through here with much ado, surmounting the successive watery steps of this river's staircase in the midst of a crowd of villagers, jumping into the canal to their amusement, to save our boat from upsetting, and consuming much river water in our service. Amoskeag, or Namaskeak, is said to mean 'great fishing-place.' It was hereabouts that the Sachem Wannalancet resided. Tradition says that his tribe, when at war with the Mohawks, concealed their provisions in the cavities of the rocks in the upper part of these falls. The Indians, who hid their provisions in these holes, and affirmed 'that God had cut them out for that purpose,' understood their origin and use better than the Royal Society, who in their Transactions, in the last century, speaking of these very holes, declare that 'they seem plainly to be artificial.' Similar 'pot-holes' may be seen at the Stone Flume on this river, on the Ottaway, at Bellows Falls on the Connecticut, and in the limestone rock at Shelburne Falls on Deerfield River in Massachusetts, and more or less generally about all falls. Perhaps the most remarkable curiosity of this kind in New England is the well-known Basin on the Pemigewasset, one of the headwaters of this river, twenty by thirty feet in extent and proportionably deep, with a smooth and rounded brim, and filled with a cold, pellucid, and greenish water. At Amoskeag the river is divided into many separate torrents and trickling rills by the rocks, and its volume is so much reduced by the drain of the canals that it does not fill its bed. There are many pot-holes here on a rocky island which the river washes over in high freshets. As at Shelburne Falls, where I first observed them, they are from one foot to four or five in diameter, and as many in depth, perfectly round and regular, with smooth and gracefully curved brims, like goblets. Their origin is apparent to the most careless observer. A stone which the current has washed down, meeting with obstacles, revolves as on a pivot where it lies, gradually sinking in the course of centuries deeper and deeper into the rock, and in new freshets receiving the aid of fresh stones, which are drawn into this trap and doomed to revolve there for an indefinite period, doing

Sisyphus-like penance for stony sins, until they either wear out or wear through the bottom of their prison, or else are released by some revolution of nature.   There lie the stones of various sizes, from a pebble to a foot or two in diameter, some of which have rested from their labor only since the spring, and some higher up which have lain still and dry for ages — we noticed some here at least sixteen feet above the present level of the water — while others are still revolving, and enjoy no respite at any season.   In one instance, at Shelburne Falls, they have worn quite through the rock, so that a portion of the river leaks through in anticipation of the fall.   Some of these pot-holes at Amoskeag, in a very hard brownstone, had an oblong, cylindrical stone of the same material loosely fitting them.   One, as much as fifteen feet deep and seven or eight in diameter, which was worn quite through to the water, had a huge rock of the same material, smooth but of irregular form, lodged in it.   Everywhere there were the rudiments or the wrecks of a dimple in the rock; the rocky shells of whirlpools.   As if by force of example and sympathy after so many lessons, the rocks, the hardest material, had been endeavoring to whirl or flow into the forms of the most fluid.   The finest workers in stone are not copper or steel tools, but the gentle touches of air and water working at their leisure with a liberal allowance of time.

Not only have some of these basins been forming for countless ages, but others exist which must have been completed in a former geological period.   In deepening the Pawtucket Canal, in 1822, the workmen came to ledges with pot-holes in them, where probably was once the bed of the river, and there are some, we are told, in the town of Canaan in this State, with the stones still in them, on the height of land between the Merrimack and Connecticut, and nearly a thousand feet ·above these rivers, proving that the mountains and the rivers have changed places.   There lie the stones which completed their revolutions perhaps before thoughts began to revolve in the brain of man.   The periods of Hindoo and Chinese history, though they reach back to the time when the race of mortals is confounded with the race of gods, are as nothing compared with the periods which these stones have inscribed. That which commenced a rock when time was young shall conclude a pebble in the unequal contest. With such expense of time and natural forces are our very paving-stones produced.   They teach us lessons, these dumb workers; verily there are 'sermons in stones, and books in the running brooks.'   In these very holes the Indians hid their provisions; but now there is no bread, but only its old neighbor stones at the bottom.

Who knows how many races they have served thus? By as simple a law, some accidental bylaw, perchance, our system itself was made ready for its inhabitants.

These, and such as these, must be our antiquities, for lack of human vestiges. The monuments of heroes and the temples of the gods which may once have stood on the banks of this river are now, at any rate, returned to dust and primitive soil. The murmur of unchronicled nations has died away along these shores, and once more Lowell and Manchester are on the trail of the Indian.

The fact that Romans once inhabited her reflects no little dignity on Nature herself; that from some particular hill the Roman once looked out on the sea. She need not be ashamed of the vestiges of her children. How gladly the antiquary informs us that their vessels penetrated into this frith, or up that river of some remote isle! Their military monuments still remain on the hills and under the sod of the valleys. The oft-repeated Roman story is written in still legible characters in every quarter of the Old World, and but today, perchance, a new coin is dug up whose inscription repeats and confirms their fame. Some 'Judæa Capta,' with a woman mourning under a palm tree, with silent argument and demonstration confirms the pages of history.

> 'Rome living was the world's sole ornament;
> And dead is now the world's sole monument.
>
> . . . .
>
> With her own weight down pressèd now she lies,
> And by her heaps her hugeness testifies.'

If one doubts whether Grecian valor and patriotism are not a fiction of the poets, he may go to Athens and see still upon the walls of the temple of Minerva the circular marks made by the shields taken from the enemy in the Persian war, which were suspended there. We have not far to seek for living and unquestionable evidence. The very dust takes shape and confirms some story which we had read. As Fuller said, commenting on the zeal of Camden, 'A broken urn is a whole evidence; or an old gate still surviving out of which the city is run out.' When Solon endeavored to prove that Salamis had formerly belonged to the Athenians, and not to the Megareans, he caused the tombs to be opened, and showed that the inhabitants of Salamis turned the faces of their dead to the same side with the Athenians, but the Megareans to the opposite side. There they were to be interrogated.

Some minds are as little logical or argumentative as nature; they can offer no reason or 'guess,' but they exhibit the solemn and in-controvertible fact. If a historical question arises, they cause the tombs to be opened. Their silent and practical logic convinces the reason and the understanding at the same time. Of such sort is always the only pertinent question and the only satisfactory reply.

Our own country furnishes antiquities as ancient and durable, and as useful, as any; rocks at least as well covered with lichens, and a soil which, if it is virgin, is but virgin mould, the very dust of nature. What if we cannot read Rome or Greece, Etruria or Carthage, or Egypt or Babylon, on these; are our cliffs bare? The lichen on the rocks is a rude and simple shield which beginning and imperfect Nature suspended there. Still hangs her wrinkled trophy. And here, too, the poet's eye may still detect the brazen nails which fastened Time's inscriptions, and if he has the gift, decipher them by this clue. The walls that fence our fields, as well as modern Rome, and not less the Parthenon itself, are all built of *ruins*. Here may be heard the din of rivers, and ancient winds which have long since lost their names sought through our woods — the first faint sounds of spring, older than the summer of Athenian glory, the titmouse lisping in the wood, the jay's scream, and bluebird's warble, and the hum of

<blockquote>'bees that fly
About the laughing blossoms of sallowy.'</blockquote>

Here is the gray dawn for antiquity, and our tomorrow's future should be at least paulo-post to theirs which we have put behind us. There are the red maple and birchen leaves, old runes which are not yet deciphered; catkins, pine cones, vines, oak leaves, and acorns; the very things themselves, and not their forms in stone — so much the more ancient and venerable. And even to the current summer there has come down tradition of a hoary-headed master of all art, who once filled every field and grove with statues and godlike architecture, of every design which Greece has lately copied; whose ruins are now mingled with the dust, and not one block remains upon another. The century sun and unwearied rain have wasted them, till not one frag-ment from that quarry now exists; and poets perchance will feign that gods sent down the material from heaven.

What though the traveler tell us of the ruins of Egypt, are we so sick or idle that we must sacrifice our America and today to some man's ill-remembered and indolent story? Carnac and Luxor are but names, or if their skeletons remain, still more desert sand and at length a wave of the Mediterranean Sea are needed to wash away the filth that

attaches to their grandeur. Carnac! Carnac! here is Carnac for me.
I behold the columns of a larger and purer temple.

> This is my Carnac, whose unmeasured dome
> Shelters the measuring art and measurer's home.
> Behold these flowers, let us be up with time,
> Not dreaming of three thousand years ago,
> Erect ourselves and let those columns lie,
> Not stoop to raise a foil against the sky.
> Where is the spirit of that time but in
> This present day, perchance the present line?
> Three thousand years ago are not agone,
> They are still lingering in this summer morn,
> And Memnon's Mother sprightly greets us now,
> Wearing her youthful radiance on her brow.
> If Carnac's columns still stand on the plain,
> To enjoy our opportunities they remain.

In these parts dwelt the famous Sachem Pasaconaway, who was seen by Gookin 'at Pawtucket, when he was about one hundred and twenty years old.' He was reputed a wise man and a powwow, and restrained his people from going to war with the English. They believed 'that he could make water burn, rocks move, and trees dance, and metamorphose himself into a flaming man; that in winter he could raise a green leaf out of the ashes of a dry one, and produce a living snake from the skin of a dead one, and many similar miracles.' In 1660, according to Gookin, at a great feast and dance, he made his farewell speech to his people, in which he said that as he was not likely to see them met together again, he would leave them this word of advice, to take heed how they quarreled with their English neighbors, for though they might do them much mischief at first, it would prove the means of their own destruction. He himself, he said, had been as much an enemy to the English at their first coming as any, and had used all his arts to destroy them, or at least to prevent their settlement, but could by no means effect it. Gookin thought that he 'possibly might have such a kind of spirit upon him as was upon Balaam, who, in Numbers xxiii. 23, said, "Surely, there is no enchantment against Jacob, neither is there any divination against Israel." ' His son Wannalancet carefully followed his advice, and when Philip's war broke out, he withdrew his followers to Penacook, now Concord in New Hampshire, from the scene of the war. On his return afterwards, he visited the minister of Chelmsford, and, as is stated in the history of that town, 'wished to know whether Chelmsford had suffered much during the war; and being informed that it had not, and that God should be thanked for it, Wannalancet replied, "Me next." '

Manchester was the residence of John Stark, a hero of two wars, and survivor of a third, and at his death the last but one of the American generals of the Revolution. He was born in the adjoining town of Londonderry, then Nutfield, in 1728. As early as 1752, he was taken prisoner by the Indians while hunting in the wilderness near Baker's River; he performed notable service as a captain of rangers in the French war; commanded a regiment of the New Hampshire militia at the battle of Bunker Hill; and fought and won the battle of Bennington in 1777. He was past service in the last war, and died here in 1822, at the age of ninety-four. His monument stands upon the second bank of the river, about a mile and a half above the falls, and commands a prospect several miles up and down the Merrimack. It suggested how much more impressive in the landscape is the tomb of a hero than the dwellings of the inglorious living. Who is most dead — a hero by whose monument you stand, or his descendants of whom you have never heard?

The graves of Pasaconaway and Wannalancet are marked by no monument on the bank of their native river.

Every town which we passed, if we may believe the Gazetteer, had been the residence of some great man. But though we knocked at many doors, and even made particular inquiries, we could not find that there were any now living. Under the head of Litchfield we read:

'The Hon. Wyseman Clagett closed his life in this town.' According to another, 'He was a classical scholar, a good lawyer, a wit, and a poet.' We saw his old gray house just below Great Nesenkeag Brook. — Under the head of Merrimack: 'Hon. Mathew Thornton, one of the signers of the Declaration of American Independence, resided many years in this town.' His house too we saw from the river. — 'Dr. Jonathan Gove, a man distinguished for his urbanity, his talents and professional skill, resided in this town [Goffstown]. He was one of the oldest practitioners of medicine in the county. He was many years an active member of the legislature.' — 'Hon. Robert Means, who died January 24, 1823, at the age of 80, was for a long period a resident in Amherst. He was a native of Ireland. In 1764 he came to this country, where, by his industry and application to business, he acquired a large property, and great respect.' — 'William Stinson [one of the first settlers of Dunbarton], born in Ireland, came to Londonderry with his father. He was much respected and was a useful man. James Rogers was from

Ireland, and father to Major Robert Rogers. He was shot in the woods, being mistaken for a bear.' — 'Rev. Matthew Clark, second minister of Londonderry, was a native of Ireland, who had in early life been an officer in the army, and distinguished himself in the defense of the city of Londonderry, when besieged by the army of King James II., A.D. 1688–89. He afterwards relinquished a military life for the clerical profession. He possessed a strong mind, marked by a considerable degree of eccentricity. He died January 25, 1735, and was borne to the grave, at his particular request, by his former companions in arms, of whom there were a considerable number among the early settlers of this town; several of them had been made free from taxes throughout the British dominions by King William, for their bravery in that memorable siege.' — Colonel George Reid and Captain David M'Clary, also citizens of Londonderry, were 'distinguished and brave' officers. — 'Major Andrew M'Clary, a native of this town [Epsom], fell at the battle of Breed's Hill.' Many of these heroes, like the illustrious Romans, were plowing when the news of the massacre at Lexington arrived, and straightway left their plows in the furrow, and repaired to the scene of action. Some miles from where we now were, there once stood a guide-post on which were the words, '3 miles to Squire MacGaw's.'

But, generally speaking, the land is now, at any rate, very barren of men, and we doubt if there are as many hundreds as we read of. It may be that we stood too near.

Uncannunuc Mountain in Goffstown was visible from Amoskeag, five or six miles westward. It is the northeasternmost in the horizon which we see from our native town, but seen from there is too ethereally blue to be the same which the like of us have ever climbed. Its name is said to mean 'The Two Breasts,' there being two eminences some distance apart. The highest, which is about fourteen hundred feet above the sea, probably affords a more extensive view of the Merrimack valley and the adjacent country than any other hill, though it is some-what obstructed by woods. Only a few short reaches of the river are visible, but you can trace its course far down-stream by the sandy tracts on its banks.

A little south of Uncannunuc, about sixty years ago, as the story goes, an old woman who went out to gather pennyroyal tripped her foot in the bail of a small brass kettle in the dead grass and bushes. Some say that flints and charcoal and some traces of a camp were also found. This kettle, holding about four quarts, is still preserved and used to dye thread in. It is supposed to have belonged to some old

French or Indian hunter, who was killed in one of his hunting or scouting excursions, and so never returned to look after his kettle.

But we were most interested to hear of the pennyroyal; it is soothing to be reminded that wild nature produced anything ready for the use of man. Men know that *something* is good. One says that it is yellow dock, another that it is bittersweet, another that it is slippery-elm bark, burdock, catnip, calamint, elecampane, thoroughwort, or pennyroyal. A man may esteem himself happy when that which is his food is also his medicine. There is no kind of herb, but somebody or other says that it is good. I am very glad to hear it. It reminds me of the first chapter of Genesis. But how should they know that it is good? That is the mystery to me. I am always agreeably disappointed; it is incredible that they should have found it out. Since all things are good, men fail at last to distinguish which is the bane and which the antidote. There are sure to be two prescriptions diametrically opposite. Stuff a cold and starve a cold are but two ways. They are the two practices, both always in full blast. Yet you must take advice of the one school as if there was no other. In respect to religion and the healing art, all nations are still in a state of barbarism. In the most civilized countries the priest is still but a Powwow, and the physician a Great Medicine. Consider the deference which is everywhere paid to a doctor's opinion. Nothing more strikingly betrays the credulity of mankind than medicine. Quackery is a thing universal, and universally successful. In this case it becomes literally true that no imposition is too great for the credulity of men. Priests and physicians should never look one another in the face. They have no common ground, nor is there any to mediate between them. When the one comes, the other goes. They could not come together without laughter, or a significant silence, for the one's profession is a satire on the other's, and either's success would be the other's failure. It is wonderful that the physician should ever die, and that the priest should ever live. Why is it that the priest is never called to consult with the physician? Is it because men believe practically that matter is independent of spirit? But what is quackery? It is commonly an attempt to cure the diseases of a man by addressing his body alone. There is need of a physician who shall minister to both soul and body at once, that is, to man. Now he falls between two stools.

After passing through the locks, we had poled ourselves through the canal here, about half a mile in length, to the boatable part of the river. Above Amoskeag the river spreads out into a lake reaching a mile or two without a bend. There were many canal-boats here bound up to

Hooksett, about eight miles, and as they were going up empty, with a fair wind, one boatman offered to take us in tow if we would wait. But when we came alongside, we found that they meant to take us on board, since otherwise we should clog their motions too much; but as our boat was too heavy to be lifted aboard, we pursued our way up the stream, as before, while the boatmen were at their dinner, and came to anchor at length under some alders on the opposite shore, where we could take our lunch. Though far on one side, every sound was wafted over to us from the opposite bank, and from the harbor of the canal, and we could see everything that passed. By and by came several canal-boats, at intervals of a quarter of a mile, standing up to Hooksett with a light breeze, and one by one disappeared round a point above. With their broad sails set, they moved slowly up the stream in the sluggish and fitful breeze, like one-winged antediluvian birds, and as if impelled by some mysterious counter-current. It was a grand motion, so slow and stately, this 'standing out,' as the phrase is, expressing the gradual and steady progress of a vessel, as if it were by mere rectitude and disposition, without shuffling. Their sails, which stood so still, were like chips cast into the current of the air, to show which way it set. At length the boat which we had spoken came along, keeping the middle of the stream, and when within speaking distance, the steersman called out ironically to say that if we could come alongside now, he would take us in tow; but not heeding his taunt, we still loitered in the shade till we had finished our lunch, and when the last boat had disappeared round the point with flapping sail, for the breeze had now sunk to a zephyr, with our own sails set, and plying our oars, we shot rapidly up the stream in pursuit, and as we glided close alongside, while they were vainly invoking Æolus to their aid, we returned their compliment by proposing, if they would throw us a rope, to 'take them in tow,' to which these Merrimack sailors had no suitable answer ready. Thus we gradually overtook and passed each boat in succession until we had the river to ourselves again. . . .[1]

Having rowed five or six miles above Amoskeag before sunset, and reached a pleasant part of the river, one of us landed to look for a farm-house, where we might replenish our stores, while the other remained cruising about the stream, and exploring the opposite shores to find a suitable harbor for the night. In the mean while the canal-boats

[1] Pages 274–307 (Walden edition) on Friendship, omitted. See pp. 754–72 of this edition.

began to come round a point in our rear, poling their way along close to the shore, the breeze having quite died away. This time there was no offer of assistance, but one of the boatmen only called out to say as the truest revenge for having been the losers in the race, that he had seen a wood duck, which we had scared up, sitting on a tall, white pine, half a mile down-stream; and he repeated the assertion several times, and seemed really chagrined at the apparent suspicion with which this information was received. But there sat the summer duck still, undisturbed by us.

By and by the other voyageur returned from his inland expedition, bringing one of the natives with him, a little flaxen-headed boy, with some tradition, or small edition, of Robinson Crusoe in his head, who had been charmed by the account of our adventures, and asked his father's leave to join us. He examined, at first from the top of the bank, our boat and furniture, with sparkling eyes, and wished himself already his own man. He was a lively and interesting boy, and we should have been glad to ship him; but Nathan was still his father's boy, and had not come to years of discretion.

We had got a loaf of home-made bread, and musk and water melons for dessert. For this farmer, a clever and well-disposed man, cultivated a large patch of melons for the Hooksett and Concord markets. He hospitably entertained us the next day, exhibiting his hop-fields and kiln and melon-patch, warning us to step over the tight rope which surrounded the latter at a foot from the ground, while he pointed to a little bower at one corner, where it connected with the lock of a gun ranging with the line, and where, as he informed us, he sometimes sat in pleasant nights to defend his premises against thieves. We stepped high over the line, and sympathized with our host's on the whole quite human, if not humane, interest in the success of his experiment. That night especially thieves were to be expected, from rumors in the atmosphere, and the priming was not wet. He was a Methodist man, who had his dwelling between the river and Uncannunuc Mountain; who there belonged, and stayed at home there, and by the encouragement of distant political organizations, and by his own tenacity, held a property in his melons, and continued to plant. We suggested melon seeds of new varieties and fruit of foreign flavor to be added to his stock. We had come away up here among the hills to learn the impartial and unbribable beneficence of Nature. Strawberries and melons grow as well in one man's garden as another's, and the sun lodges as kindly under his hillside — when we had imagined that she inclined rather to some few earnest and faithful souls whom we know.

We found a convenient harbor for our boat on the opposite or east shore, still in Hooksett, at the mouth of a small brook which emptied into the Merrimack, where it would be out of the way of any passing boat in the night — for they commonly hug the shore if bound upstream, either to avoid the current or touch the bottom with their poles — and where it would be accessible without stepping on the clayey shore. We set one of our largest melons to cool in the still water among the alders at the mouth of this creek, but when our tent was pitched and ready, and we went to get it, it had floated out into the stream, and was nowhere to be seen. So taking the boat in the twilight, we went in pursuit of this property, and at length, after long straining of the eyes, its green disk was discovered far down the river, gently floating seaward with many twigs and leaves from the mountains that evening, and so perfectly balanced that it had not keeled at all, and no water had run in at the tap which had been taken out to hasten its cooling.

As we sat on the bank eating our supper, the clear light of the western sky fell on the eastern trees, and was reflected in the water, and we enjoyed so serene an evening as left nothing to describe. For the most part we think that there are few degrees of sublimity, and that the highest is but little higher than that which we now behold; but we are always deceived. Sublimer visions appear, and the former pale and fade away. We are grateful when we are reminded by interior evidence of the permanence of universal laws; for our faith is but faintly remembered, indeed, is not a remembered assurance, but a use and enjoyment of knowledge. It is when we do not have to believe, but come into actual contact with Truth, and are related to her in the most direct and intimate way. Waves of serener life pass over us from time to time, like flakes of sunlight over the fields in cloudy weather. In some happier moment, when more sap flows in the withered stalk of our life, Syria and India stretch away from our present as they do in history. All the events which make the annals of the nations are but the shadows of our private experiences. Suddenly and silently the eras which we call history awake and glimmer in us, and *there* is room for Alexander and Hannibal to march and conquer. In short, the history which we read is only a fainter memory of events which have happened in our own experience. Tradition is a more interrupted and feebler memory.

This world is but canvas to our imaginations. I see men with infinite pains endeavoring to realize to their bodies, what I, with at least equal pains, would realize to my imagination — its capacities; for certainly there is a life of the mind above the wants of the body, and independent of it. Often the body is warmed, but the imagination is torpid; the body is fat, but the imagination is lean and shrunk. But what avails all other wealth if this is wanting? 'Imagination is the air of mind,' in which it lives and breathes. All things are as I am. Where is the House of Change? The past is only so heroic as we see it. It is the canvas on which our idea of heroism is painted, and so, in one sense, the dim prospectus of our future field. Our circumstances answer to our expectations and the demand of our natures. I have noticed that if a man thinks that he needs a thousand dollars, and cannot be convinced that he does not, he will commonly be found to have them; if he lives and thinks, a thousand dollars will be forthcoming, though it be to buy shoe-strings with. A thousand mills will be just as slow to come to one who finds it equally hard to convince himself that he needs *them*.

> Men are by birth equal in this, that given
> Themselves and their condition, they are even.

I am astonished at the singular pertinacity and endurance of our lives. The miracle is, that what is *is*, when it is so difficult, if not impossible, for anything else to be; that we walk on in our particular paths so far, before we fall on death and fate, merely because we must walk in some path; that every man can get a living, and so few can do anything more. So much only can I accomplish ere health and strength are gone, and yet this suffices. The bird now sits just out of gunshot. I am never rich in money, and I am never meanly poor. If debts are incurred, why, debts are in the course of events canceled, as it were, by the same law by which they were incurred. I heard that an engagement was entered into between a certain youth and a maiden, and then I heard that it was broken off, but I did not know the reason in either case. We are hedged about, we think, by accident and circumstance; now we creep as in a dream, and now again we run, as if there were a fate in it, and all things thwarted or assisted. I cannot change my clothes but when I do, and yet I do change them, and soil the new ones. It is wonderful that this gets done, when some admirable deeds which I could mention do not get done. Our particular lives seem of such fortune and confident strength and durability as piers of solid rock thrown forward into the tide of circumstance. When every other path would fail, with singular and unerring confidence we advance on our particular course. What risks we run! famine and fire and pestilence, and the thousand forms of a cruel fate — and yet every man lives till he — dies. How

did he manage that? Is there no immediate danger? We wonder
superfluously when we hear of a somnambulist walking a plank securely
— we have walked a plank all our lives up to this particular string-piece
where we are. My life will wait for nobody, but is being matured still
without delay, while I go about the streets, and chaffer with this man
and that to secure it a living. It is as indifferent and easy meanwhile
as a poor man's dog, and making acquaintance with its kind. It will cut
its own channel like a mountain stream, and by the longest ridge is not
kept from the sea at last. I have found all things thus far, persons and
inanimate matter, elements and seasons, strangely adapted to my
resources. No matter what imprudent haste in my career; I am permitted to be rash. Gulfs are bridged in a twinkling, as if some unseen
baggage train carried pontoons for my convenience, and while from the
heights I scan the tempting but unexplored Pacific Ocean of Futurity,
the ship is being carried over the mountains piecemeal on the backs of
mules and llamas, whose keel shall plow its waves, and bear me to the
Indies. Day would not dawn if it were not for

THE INWARD MORNING

Packed in my mind lie all the clothes
   Which outward nature wears,
And in its fashion's hourly change
   It all things else repairs.

In vain I look for change abroad,
   And can no difference find,
Till some new ray of peace uncalled
   Illumes my inmost mind.

What is it gilds the trees and clouds,
   And paints the heavens so gay,
But yonder fast-abiding light
   With its unchanging ray?

Lo, when the sun streams through the wood,
   Upon a winter's morn,
Where'er his silent beams intrude
   The murky night is gone.

How could the patient pine have known
   The morning breeze would come,
Or humble flowers anticipate
   The insect's noonday hum —

Till the new light with morning cheer
   From far streamed through the aisles,
And nimbly told the forest trees
   For many stretching miles?

I've heard within my inmost soul
   Such cheerful morning news,
In the horizon of my mind
   Have seen such orient hues,

As in the twilight of the dawn,
   When the first birds awake,
Are heard within some silent wood,
   Where they the small twigs break,

Or in the eastern skies are seen,
   Before the sun appears,
The harbingers of summer heats
   Which from afar he bears.

Whole weeks and months of my summer life slide away in thin volumes like mist and smoke, till at length, some warm morning, perchance, I see a sheet of mist blown down the brook to the swamp, and I float as high above the fields with it. I can recall to mind the stillest summer hours, in which the grasshopper sings over the mulleins, and there is a valor in that time the bare memory of which is armor that can laugh at any blow of fortune. For our lifetime the strains of a harp are heard to swell and die alternately, and death is but 'the pause when the blast is recollecting itself.'

We lay awake a long while listening to the murmurs of the brook, in the angle formed by whose bank with the river our tent was pitched, and there was a sort of man interest in its story, which ceases not in freshet or in drought the livelong summer, and the profounder lapse of the river was quite drowned by its din. But the rill, whose

   'Silver sands and pebbles sing
   Eternal ditties with the spring,'

is silenced by the first frosts of winter, while mightier streams, on whose bottom the sun never shines, clogged with sunken rocks and the ruins of forests, from whose surface comes up no murmur, are strangers to the icy fetters which bind fast a thousand contributory rills.

I dreamed this night of an event which had occurred long before.

It was a difference with a Friend, which had not ceased to give me pain, though I had no cause to blame myself. But in my dream ideal justice was at length done me for his suspicions, and I received that compensation which I had never obtained in my waking hours. I was unspeakably soothed and rejoiced, even after I awoke, because in dreams we never deceive ourselves, nor are deceived, and this seemed to have the authority of a final judgment.

We bless and curse ourselves. Some dreams are divine, as well as some waking thoughts. Donne sings of one

> 'Who dreamt devoutlier than most use to pray.'

Dreams are the touchstones of our characters. We are scarcely less afflicted when we remember some unworthiness in our conduct in a dream, than if it had been actual, and the intensity of our grief, which is our atonement, measures the degree by which this is separated from an actual unworthiness. For in dreams we but act a part which must have been learned and rehearsed in our waking hours, and no doubt could discover some waking consent thereto. If this meanness had not its foundation in us, why are we grieved at it? In dreams we see ourselves naked and acting out our real characters, even more clearly than we see others awake. But an unwavering and commanding virtue would compel even its most fantastic and faintest dreams to respect its everwakeful authority; as we are accustomed to say carelessly, we should never have *dreamed* of such a thing. Our truest life is when we are in dreams awake.

> 'And, more to lulle him in his slumber soft,
> A trickling streame from high rock tumbling downe,
> And ever-drizzling raine upon the loft,
> Mixt with a murmuring winde, much like the sowne
> Of swarming bees, did cast him in a swowne,
> No other noyse, nor people's troublous cryes,
> As still are wont t'annoy the walled towne,
> Might there be heard; but careless Quiet lyes
> Wrapt in eternall silence farre from enemyes.'

THURSDAY

He trode the unplanted forest floor, whereon
The all-seeing sun for ages hath not shone;
Where feeds the moose, and walks the surly **bear,**
And up the tall mast runs the woodpecker.
. . . .
Where darkness found him he lay glad at night;
There the red morning touched him with its light.
. . . .
Go where he will, the wise man is at home,
His hearth the earth — his hall the azure dome;
Where his clear spirit leads him, there's his **road,**
By God's own light illumined and foreshowed.

EMERSON.

WHEN we awoke this morning, we heard the faint, deliberate, and ominous sound of raindrops on our cotton roof. The rain had pattered all night, and now the whole country wept, the drops falling in the river, and on the alders, and in the pastures, and instead of any bow in the heavens, there was the trill of the hair-bird all the morning. The cheery faith of this little bird atoned for the silence of the whole woodland choir beside. When we first stepped abroad, a flock of sheep, led by their rams, came rushing down a ravine in our rear, with heedless haste and unreserved frisking, as if unobserved by man, from some higher pasture where they had spent the night, to taste the herbage by the riverside; but when their leaders caught sight of our white tent through the mist, struck with sudden astonishment, with their fore feet braced, they sustained the rushing torrent in their rear, and the whole flock stood stock-still, endeavoring to solve the mystery in their sheepish brains. At length, concluding that it boded no mischief to them, they spread themselves out quietly over the field. We learned afterward that we had pitched our tent on the very spot which a few summers before had been occupied by a party of Penobscots. We could see rising before us through the mist a dark conical eminence called Hooksett Pinnacle, a landmark to boatmen, and also Uncannunuc Mountain, broad off on the west side of the river.

This was the limit of our voyage, for a few hours more in the rain would have taken us to the last of the locks, and our boat was too heavy to be dragged around the long and numerous rapids which would occur. On foot, however, we continued up along the bank, feeling our way with a stick through the showery and foggy day, and climbing over the slippery logs in our path with as much pleasure and buoyancy as in brightest sunshine; scenting the fragrance of the pines and the wet clay under our feet, and cheered by the tones of invisible waterfalls; with visions of toadstools, and wandering frogs, and festoons of moss hanging from the spruce trees, and thrushes flitting silent under the leaves; our road still holding together through that wettest of weather, like faith, while we confidently followed its lead. We managed to keep our thoughts dry, however, and only our clothes were wet. It was altogether a cloudy and drizzling day, with occasional brightenings in the mist, when the trill of the tree sparrow seemed to be ushering in sunny hours.

'Nothing that naturally happens to man can *hurt* him, earthquakes and thunder-storms not excepted,' said a man of genius, who at this time lived a few miles farther on our road. When compelled by a shower to take shelter under a tree, we may improve that opportunity for a more minute inspection of some of Nature's works. I have stood under a tree in the woods half a day at a time, during a heavy rain in the summer, and yet employed myself happily and profitably there prying with microscopic eye into the crevices of the bark or the leaves of the fungi at my feet. 'Riches are the attendants of the miser; and the heavens rain plenteously upon the mountains.' I can fancy that it would be a luxury to stand up to one's chin in some retired swamp a whole summer day, scenting the wild honeysuckle and bilberry blows, and lulled by the minstrelsy of gnats and mosquitoes! A day passed in the society of those Greek sages, such as described in the Banquet of Xenophon, would not be comparable with the dry wit of decayed cranberry vines, and the fresh Attic salt of the moss-beds. Say twelve hours of genial and familiar converse with the leopard frog; the sun to rise behind alder and dogwood, and climb buoyantly to his meridian of two hands' breadth, and finally sink to rest behind some bold western hummock. To hear the evening chant of the mosquito from a thousand green chapels, and the bittern begin to boom from some concealed fort like a sunset gun! Surely one may as profitably be soaked in the juices of a swamp for one day as pick his way dry-shod over sand. Cold and damp — are they not as rich experience as warmth and dryness?

At present, the drops come trickling down the stubble while we lie drenched on a bed of withered wild oats, by the side of a bushy hill; and the gathering in of the clouds, with the last rush and dying breath of the wind, and then the regular dripping of twigs and leaves the country over, enhance the sense of inward comfort and sociableness. The birds draw closer and are more familiar under the thick foliage, seemingly composing new strains upon their roots against the sunshine. What were the amusements of the drawing-room and the library in comparison, if we had them here? We should still sing as of old,

> My books I'd fain cast off, I cannot read;
> 'Twixt every page my thoughts go stray at large
> Down in the meadow, where is richer feed,
> And will not mind to hit their proper targe.
>
> Plutarch was good, and so was Homer too,
> Our Shakespeare's life were rich to live again;
> What Plutarch read, that was not good nor true,
> Nor Shakespeare's books, unless his books were men.
>
> Here while I lie beneath this walnut bough,
> What care I for the Greeks or for Troy town,
> If juster battles are enacted now
> Between the ants upon this hummock's crown?
>
> Bid Homer wait till I the issue learn,
> If red or black the gods will favor most,
> Or yonder Ajax will the phalanx turn,
> Struggling to heave some rock against the host.
>
> Tell Shakespeare to attend some leisure hour,
> For now I've business with this drop of dew,
> And see you not, the clouds prepare a shower —
> I'll meet him shortly when the sky is blue.
>
> This bed of herd's-grass and wild oats was spread
> Last year with nicer skill than monarchs use,
> A clover tuft is pillow for my head,
> And violets quite overtop my shoes.
>
> And now the cordial clouds have shut all in,
> And gently swells the wind to say all's well,
> The scattered drops are falling fast and thin,
> Some in the pool, some in the flower-bell.
>
> I am well drenched upon my bed of oats;
> But see that globe come rolling down its stem;
> Now like a lonely planet there it floats,
> And now it sinks into my garment's hem.

> Drip, drip the trees for all the country round,
> And richness rare distills from every bough,
> The wind alone it is makes every sound,
> Shaking down crystals on the leaves below.
>
> For shame the sun will never show himself,
> Who could not with his beams e'er melt me so,
> My dripping locks — they would become an elf,
> Who in a beaded coat does gayly go.

The Pinnacle is a small wooded hill which rises very abruptly to the height of about two hundred feet, near the shore at Hooksett Falls. As Uncannunuc Mountain is perhaps the best point from which to view the valley of the Merrimack, so this hill affords the best view of the river itself. I have sat upon its summit, a precipitous rock only a few rods long, in fairer weather, when the sun was setting and filling the river valley with a flood of light. You can see up and down the Merrimack several miles each way. The broad and straight river, full of light and life, with its sparkling and foaming falls, the islet which divides the stream, the village of Hooksett on the shore almost directly under your feet, so near that you can converse with its inhabitants or throw a stone into its yards, the woodland lake at its western base, and the mountains in the north and northeast, make a scene of rare beauty and completeness, which the traveler should take pains to behold.

We were hospitably entertained in Concord, New Hampshire, which we persisted in calling *New* Concord, as we had been wont, to distinguish it from our native town, from which we had been told that it was named and in part originally settled. This would have been the proper place to conclude our voyage, uniting Concord with Concord by these meandering rivers, but our boat was moored some miles below its port.

The richness of the intervals at Penacook, now Concord, New Hampshire, had been observed by explorers, and, according to the historian of Haverhill, in the 'year 1726, considerable progress was made in the settlement, and a road was cut through the wilderness from Haverhill to Penacook. In the fall of 1727, the first family, that of Captain Ebenezer Eastman, moved into the place. His team was driven by Jacob Shute, who was by birth a Frenchman, and he is said to have been the first person who drove a team through the wilderness. Soon after, says tradition, one Ayer, a lad of eighteen, drove a team consisting of ten yoke of oxen to Penacook, swam the river, and ploughed a portion of the interval. He is supposed to have been the first person who ploughed land in that place. After he had completed his work, he started on his return at sunrise, drowned a yoke of oxen while recrossing the river, and arrived at Haverhill about midnight. The crank of the first saw-mill was manufactured in Haverhill, and carried to Penacook on a horse.'

But we found that the frontiers were not this way any longer. This generation has come into the world fatally late for some enterprises. Go where we will on the *surface* of things, men have been there before us. We cannot now have the pleasure of erecting the *last* house; that was long ago set up in the suburbs of Astoria City, and our boundaries have literally been run to the South Sea, according to the old patents. But the lives of men, though more extended laterally in their range, are still as shallow as ever. Undoubtedly, as a Western orator said, 'Men generally live over about the same surface; some live long and narrow, and others live broad and short;' but it is all superficial living. A worm is as good a traveler as a grasshopper or a cricket, and a much wiser settler. With all their activity these do not hop away from drought nor forward to summer. We do not avoid evil by fleeing before it, but by rising above or diving below its plane; as the worm escapes drought and frost by boring a few inches deeper. The frontiers are not east or west, north or south; but wherever a man *fronts* a fact, though that fact be his neighbor, there is an unsettled wilderness between him and Canada, between him and the setting sun, or, farther still, between him and *it*. Let him build himself a log house with the bark on where he is, *fronting* IT, and wage there an Old French war for seven or seventy years, with Indians and Rangers, or whatever else may come between him and the reality, and save his scalp if he can.

We now no longer sailed or floated on the river, but trod the unyielding land like pilgrims. Sadi tells who may travel; among others, 'A common mechanic, who can earn a subsistence by the industry of his hand, and shall not have to stake his reputation for every morsel of bread, as philosophers have said.' He may travel who can subsist on the wild fruits and game of the most cultivated country. A man may travel fast enough and earn his living on the road. I have at times been applied to, to do work when on a journey; to do tinkering and repair clocks, when I had a knapsack on my back. A man once applied to me to go into a factory, stating conditions and wages, observing that I succeeded in shutting the window of a railroad car in which we were traveling, when the other passengers had failed. 'Hast thou not heard of a Sufi, who was hammering some nails into the sole of his sandal; an officer of cavalry took him by the sleeve, saying, Come along and shoe my horse.' Farmers have asked me to assist them in haying when I was passing their fields. A man once applied to me to mend his umbrella, taking me for an umbrella-mender, because, being on a journey, I carried an umbrella in my hand while the sun shone. Another wished to buy a tin cup of me, observing that I had one strapped to my belt, and a sauce-pan on my back. The cheapest way to travel, and the way to travel the farthest in the shortest distance, is to go afoot, carrying a dipper, a spoon, and a fish line, some Indian meal, some salt, and some sugar. When you come to a brook or a pond, you can catch fish and cook them; or you can boil a hasty-pudding; or you can buy a loaf of bread at a farmer's house for fourpence, moisten it in the next brook that crosses the road, and dip it into your sugar — this alone will last you a whole day; — or, if you are accustomed to heartier living, you can buy a quart of milk for two cents, crumb your bread or cold pudding into it, and eat it with your own spoon out of your own dish. Any one of these things I mean, not all together. I have traveled thus some hundreds of miles without taking any meal in a house, sleeping on the ground when convenient, and found it cheaper, and in many respects more profitable, than staying at home. So that some have inquired why it would not be best to travel always. But I never thought of traveling simply as a means of getting a livelihood. A simple woman down in Tyngsborough, at whose house I once stopped to get a draught of water, when I said, recognizing the bucket, that I had stopped there nine years before for the same purpose, asked if I was not a traveler, supposing I had been traveling ever since, and had now come round again; that traveling was one of the professions, more or less productive, which her husband did not follow. But continued traveling is far from productive. It begins with wearing away the soles of the shoes, and making the feet sore, and ere long it will wear a man clean up, after making his heart sore into the bargain. I have observed that the after life of those who have traveled much is very pathetic. True and sincere traveling is no pastime, but it is as serious as the grave, or any part of the human journey, and it requires a long probation to be broken into it. I do not speak of those that travel sitting, the sedentary travelers whose legs hang dangling the while, mere idle symbols of the fact, any more than when we speak of sitting hens we mean those that sit standing, but I mean those to whom traveling is life for the legs, and death too, at last. The traveler must be born again on the road, and earn a passport from the elements, the principal powers that be for him.

He shall experience at last that old threat of his mother fulfilled, that he shall be skinned alive. His sores shall gradually deepen themselves that they may heal inwardly, while he gives no rest to the sole of his foot, and at night weariness must be his pillow, that so he may acquire experience against his rainy days. So was it with us.

Sometimes we lodged at an inn in the woods, where trout-fishers from distant cities had arrived before us, and where, to our astonishment, the settlers dropped in at nightfall to have a chat and hear the news, though there was but one road, and no other house was visible — as if they had come out of the earth. There we sometimes read old newspapers, who never before read new ones, and in the rustle of their leaves heard the dashing of the surf along the Atlantic shore, instead of the sough of the wind among the pines. But then walking had given us an appetite even for the least palatable and nutritious food. . . .[1]

Suns rose and set and found us still on the dank forest path which meanders up the Pemigewasset, now more like an otter's or a marten's trail, or where a beaver had dragged his trap, than where the wheels of travel raise a dust; where towns begin to serve as gores, only to hold the earth together. The wild pigeon sat secure above our heads, high on the dead limbs of naval pines, reduced to a robin's size. The very yards of our hostelries inclined upon the skirts of mountains, and, as we passed, we looked up at a steep angle at the stems of maples waving in the clouds.

Far up in the country — for we would be faithful to our experience — in Thornton, perhaps, we met a soldier lad in the woods, going to muster in full regimentals, and holding the middle of the road; deep in the forest, with shouldered musket and military step, and thoughts of war and glory all to himself. It was a sore trial to the youth, tougher than many a battle, to get by us creditably and with soldier-like bearing. Poor man! He actually shivered like a reed in his thin military pants, and by the time we had got up with him, all the sternness that becomes the soldier had forsaken his face, and he skulked past as if he were driving his father's sheep under a sword-proof helmet. It was too much for him to carry any extra armor then, who could not easily dispose of his natural arms. And for his legs, they were like heavy artillery in boggy places; better to cut the traces and forsake them. His greaves chafed and wrestled one with another for want of other foes. But he did get by and get off with all his munitions, and lived to fight another

[1] Pages 327–333 (Walden Edition), on Persius, omitted.

day; and I do not record this as casting any suspicion on his honor and real bravery in the field.

Wandering on through notches which the streams had made, by the side and over the brows of hoar hills and mountains, across the stumpy, rocky, forested, and bepastured country, we at length crossed on prostrate trees over the Amonoosuck, and breathed the free air of Unappropriated Land. Thus, in fair days as well as foul, we had traced up the river to which our native stream is a tributary, until from Merrimack it became the Pemigewasset that leaped by our side, and when we had passed its fountain-head, the Wild Amonoosuck, whose puny channel was crossed at a stride, guiding us toward its distant source among the mountains, at length, without its guidance, we were enabled to reach the summit AGIOCOCHOOK.

'Sweet day, so cool, so calm, so bright,
The bridal of the earth and sky,
The dew shall weep thy fall tonight,
For thou must die.' — HERBERT.

When we returned to Hooksett, a week afterward, the melon man, in whose corn-barn we had hung our tent and buffaloes and other things to dry, was already picking his hops, with many women and children to help him. We bought one watermelon, the largest in his patch, to carry with us for ballast. It was Nathan's, which he might sell if he wished, having been conveyed to him in the green state, and owned daily by his eyes. After due consultation with 'Father,' the bargain was concluded — we to buy it at a venture on the vine, green or ripe, our risk, and pay 'what the gentleman pleased.' It proved to be ripe; for we had had honest experience in selecting this fruit.

Finding our boat safe in its harbor, under Uncannunuc Mountain, with a fair wind and the current in our favor, we commenced our return voyage at noon, sitting at our ease and conversing, or in silence watching for the last trace of each reach in the river as a bend concealed it from our view. As the season was further advanced, the wind now blew steadily from the north, and with our sail set we could occasionally lie on our oars without loss of time. The lumbermen throwing down wood from the top of the high bank, thirty or forty feet above the water, that it might be sent downstream, paused in their work to watch our retreating sail. By this time, indeed, we were well known to the boatmen, and were hailed as the Revenue Cutter of the stream. As we sailed rapidly down the river, shut in between two mounds of earth, the sounds of this timber rolled down the bank enhanced the silence and vastness of the noon, and we fancied that only the primeval echoes were awakened. The vision of a distant scow just heaving in sight round a headland also increased by contrast the solitude.

Through the din and desultoriness of noon, even in the most Oriental city, is seen the fresh and primitive and savage nature, in which Scythians and Ethiopians and Indians dwell. What is echo, what are light and shade, day and night, ocean and stars, earthquake and eclipse, there? The works of man are everywhere swallowed up in the immensity of nature. The Ægean Sea is but Lake Huron still to the Indian. Also there is all the refinement of civilized life in the woods under a sylvan garb. The wildest scenes have an air of domesticity and homeliness even to the citizen, and when the flicker's cackle is heard in the clearing, he is reminded that civilization has wrought but little change there. Science is welcome to the deepest recesses of the forest, for there too nature obeys the same old civil laws. The little red bug on the stump of a pine — for it the wind shifts and the sun breaks through the clouds. In the wildest nature, there is not only the material of the most cultivated life, and a sort of anticipation of the last result, but a greater refinement already than is ever attained by man. There is papyrus by the riverside, and rushes for light, and the goose only flies overhead, ages before the studious are born or letters invented, and that literature which the former suggest, and even from the first have rudely served, it may be man does not yet use them to express. Nature is prepared to welcome into her scenery the finest work of human art, for she is herself an art so cunning that the artist never appears in his work.

Art is not tame, and Nature is not wild, in the ordinary sense. A perfect work of man's art would also be wild or natural in a good sense. Man tames Nature only that he may at last make her more free even than he found her, though he may never yet have succeeded.

With this propitious breeze, and the help of our oars, we soon reached the Falls of Amoskeag, and the mouth of the Piscataquoag, and recognized, as we swept rapidly by, many a fair bank and islet on which our eyes had rested in the upward passage. Our boat was like that which Chaucer describes in his Dream, in which the knight took his departure from the island,

> 'To journey for his marriage,
> And returne with such an host,
> That wedded might be least and most....

> Which barge was as a man's thought,
> After his pleasure to him brought,
> The queene herselfe accustomed aye
> In the same barge to play,
> It needeth neither mast ne rother,
> I have not heard of such another,
> No maister for the governaunce,
> Hie sayled by thought and pleasaunce,
> Without labour, east and west,
> Alle was one, calme or tempest.'

So we sailed this afternoon, thinking of the saying of Pythagoras, though we had no peculiar right to remember it, 'It is beautiful when prosperity is present with intellect, and when sailing as it were with a prosperous wind, actions are performed looking to virtue; just as a pilot looks to the motions of the stars.' All the world reposes in beauty to him who preserves equipoise in his life, and moves serenely on his path without secret violence; as he who sails down a stream, he has only to steer, keeping his bark in the middle, and carry it round the falls. The ripples curled away in our wake, like ringlets from the head of a child, while we steadily held on our course, and under the bows we watched

> 'The swaying soft,
> Made by the delicate wave parted in front,
> As through the gentle element we move
> Like shadows gliding through untroubled realms.'

The forms of beauty fall naturally around the path of him who is in the performance of his proper work; as the curled shavings drop from the plane, and borings cluster around the auger. Undulation is the gentlest and most ideal of motions, produced by one fluid falling on another. Rippling is a more graceful flight. From a hill-top you may detect in it the wings of birds endlessly repeated. The two waving lines which represent the flight of birds appear to have been copied from the ripple.

The trees made an admirable fence to the landscape, skirting the horizon on every side. The single trees and the groves left standing on the interval appeared naturally disposed, though the farmer had con-sulted only his convenience, for he too falls into the scheme of Nature. Art can never match the luxury and superfluity of Nature. In the former all is seen; it cannot afford concealed wealth, and is niggardly in comparison; but Nature, even when she is scant and thin outwardly, satisfies us still by the assurance of a certain generosity at the roots. In swamps, where there is only here and there an evergreen tree amid the quaking moss and cranberry beds, the bareness does not suggest poverty. The single spruce, which I had hardly noticed in gardens, attracts me in such places, and now first I understand why men try to make them grow about their houses. But though there may be very perfect specimens in front-yard plots, their beauty is for the most part ineffectual there, for there is no such assurance of kindred wealth beneath and around them, to make them show to advantage. As we have said, Nature is a greater and more perfect art, the art of God; though, referred to herself, she is genius; and there is a similarity between her operations and man's art even in the details and trifles. When the overhanging pine drops into the water, by the sun and water, and the wind rubbing it against the shore, its boughs are worn into fantastic shapes, and white and smooth, as if turned in a lathe. Man's art has wisely imitated those forms into which all matter is most inclined to run, as foliage and fruit. A hammock swung in a grove assumes the exact form of a canoe, broader or narrower, and higher or lower at the ends, as more or fewer persons are in it, and it rolls in the air with the motion of the body, like a canoe in the water. Our art leaves its shavings and its dust about; her art exhibits itself even in the shavings and the dust which we make. She has perfected herself by an eternity of practice. The world is well kept; no rubbish accumulates; the morning air is clear even at this day, and no dust has settled on the grass. Behold how the evening now steals over the fields, the shadows of the trees creeping farther and farther into the meadow, and ere long the stars will come to bathe in these retired waters. Her undertakings are secure and never fail. If I were awakened from a deep sleep, I should know which side of the meridian the sun might be by the aspect of nature, and by the chirp of the crickets, and yet no painter can paint this difference. The landscape contains a thousand dials which indicate the natural divisions of time, the shadows of a thousand styles point to the hour.

> 'Not only o'er the dial's face
>   This silent phantom day by day,
> With slow, unseen, unceasing pace
>   Steals moments, months, and years away;
> From hoary rock and aged tree,
>   From proud Palmyra's mouldering walls,
> From Teneriffe, towering o'er the sea,
>   From every blade of grass it falls.'

It is almost the only game which the trees play at, this tit-for-tat, now this side in the sun, now that, the drama of the day. In deep ravines under the eastern sides of cliffs, Night forwardly plants her foot even at noonday, and as Day retreats she steps into his trenches, skulking from tree to tree, from fence to fence, until at last she sits in her citadel and draws out her forces into the plain. It may be that the forenoon is brighter than the afternoon, not only because of the greater transparency of its atmosphere, but because we naturally look most into the west, as forward into the day, and so in the forenoon see the sunny side of things, but in the afternoon the shadow of every tree.

The afternoon is now far advanced, and a fresh and leisurely wind is blowing over the river, making long reaches of bright ripples. The river has done its stint, and appears not to flow, but lie at its length reflecting the light, and the haze over the woods is like the inaudible panting, or rather the gentle perspiration of resting nature, rising from a myriad of pores into the attenuated atmosphere.

On the thirty-first day of March, one hundred and forty-two years before this, probably about this time in the afternoon, there were hurriedly paddling down this part of the river, between the pine woods which then fringed these banks, two white women and a boy, who had left an island at the mouth of the Contoocook before daybreak. They were slightly clad for the season, in the English fashion, and handled their paddles unskillfully, but with nervous energy and determination, and at the bottom of their canoe lay the still bleeding scalps of ten of the aborigines. They were Hannah Dustan, and her nurse, Mary Neff, both of Haverhill, eighteen miles from the mouth of this river, and an English boy, named Samuel Lennardson, escaping from captivity among the Indians. On the 15th of March previous, Hannah Dustan had been compelled to rise from childbed, and half dressed, with one foot bare, accompanied by her nurse, commence an uncertain march, in still inclement weather, through the snow and the wilderness. She had seen her seven elder children flee with their father, but knew not of their fate. She had seen her infant's brains dashed out against an apple tree, and had left her own and her neighbors' dwellings in ashes. When she reached the wigwam of her captor, situated on an island in the Merrimack, more than twenty miles above where we now are, she had been told that she and her nurse were soon to be taken to a distant Indian settlement, and there made to run the gauntlet naked. The family of this Indian consisted of two men, three women, and seven children, besides an English boy, whom she found a prisoner among them. Having determined to attempt her escape, she instructed the boy to inquire of one of the men, how he should dispatch an enemy in the quickest manner, and take his scalp. 'Strike 'em there,' said he, placing his finger on his temple, and he also showed him how to take off the scalp. On the morning of the 31st she arose before daybreak, and awoke her nurse and the boy, and taking the Indians' tomahawks, they killed them all in their sleep, excepting one favorite boy, and one squaw who fled wounded with him to the woods. The English boy struck the Indian who had given him the information, on the temple, as he had been directed. They then collected all the provision they could find, and took their master's tomahawk and gun, and scuttling all the canoes but one, commenced their flight to Haverill, distant about sixty miles by the river. But after having proceeded a short distance, fearing that her story would not be believed if she should escape to tell it, they returned to the silent wigwam, and taking off the scalps of the dead, put them into a bag as proofs of what they had done, and then, retracing their steps to the shore in the twilight, recommenced their voyage.

Early this morning this deed was performed, and now, perchance, these tired women and this boy, their clothes stained with blood, and their minds racked with alternate resolution and fear, are making a hasty meal of parched corn and moose-meat, while their canoe glides under these pine roots whose stumps are still standing on the bank. They are thinking of the dead whom they have left behind on that solitary isle far up the stream, and of the relentless living warriors who are in pursuit. Every withered leaf which the winter has left seems to know their story, and in its rustling to repeat it and betray them. An Indian lurks behind every rock and pine, and their nerves cannot bear the tapping of a woodpecker. Or they forget their own dangers and their deeds in conjecturing the fate of their kindred, and whether, if they escape the Indians, they shall find the former still alive. They do not stop to cook their meals upon the bank, nor land, except to carry their canoe about the falls. The stolen birch forgets its master and does them good service, and the swollen current bears them swiftly along with little need of the paddle, except to steer and keep them warm by exercise. For ice is floating in the river; the spring is opening; the muskrat and the beaver are driven out of their holes by the flood; deer gaze at them from the bank; a few faint-singing forest birds, perchance, fly across the river to the northernmost shore; the fishhawk sails and screams overhead, and geese fly over with a startling clangor; but they do not observe these things, or they speedily forget them. They do not smile or chat all day. Sometimes they pass an Indian grave surrounded by its paling on the bank, or the frame of a wigwam, with a few coals left behind, or the withered stalks still rustling in the Indian's solitary corn-field on the interval. The birch stripped of its bark, or the charred stump where a tree has been burned down to be made into a canoe — these are the only traces of man, a fabulous wild man to us. On either side, the primeval forest stretches away uninterrupted to Canada, or to the 'South Sea;' to the white man a drear and howling wilderness, but to the Indian a home, adapted to his nature, and cheerful as the smile of the Great Spirit.

While we loiter here this autumn evening, looking for a spot retired enough, where we shall quietly rest tonight, they thus, in that chilly March evening, one hundred and forty-two years before us, with wind and current favoring, have already glided out of sight, not to camp, as we shall, at night, but while two sleep, one will manage the canoe, and the swift stream bear them onward to the settlements, it may be, even to old John Lovewell's house on Salmon Brook tonight.

According to the historian, they escaped as by a miracle all roving bands of Indians, and reached their homes in safety, with their trophies, for which the General Court paid them fifty pounds. The family of Hannah Dustan all assembled alive once more, except the infant whose brains were dashed out against the apple tree, and there have been many who in later time have lived to say that they have eaten of the fruit of that apple tree.

This seems a long while ago, and yet it happened since Milton wrote his Paradise Lost. But its antiquity is not the less great for that, for we do not regulate our historical time by the English standard, nor did the English by the Roman, nor the Roman by the Greek. 'We must look a long way back,' says Raleigh, 'to find the Romans giving laws to nations, and their consuls bringing kings and princes bound in chains to Rome in triumph; to see men go to Greece for wisdom, or Ophir for gold; when now nothing remains but a poor paper remembrance of their former condition.' And yet, in one sense, not so far back as to find the Penacooks and Pawtuckets using bows and arrows and hatchets of stone, on the banks of the Merrimack. From this September after-noon, and from between these now cultivated shores, those times seemed more remote than the dark ages. On beholding an old picture of Concord, as it appeared but seventy-five years ago, with a fair open prospect and a light on trees and river, as if it were broad noon, I find that I had not thought the sun shone in those days, or that men lived in broad daylight then. Still less do we imagine the sun shining on hill and valley during Philip's war, on the war-path of Church or Philip, or later of Lovewell or Paugus, with serene summer weather, but they must have lived and fought in a dim twilight or night.

The age of the world is great enough for our imaginations, even according to the Mosaic account, without borrowing any years from the geologist. From Adam and Eve at one leap sheer down to the deluge, and then through the ancient monarchies, through Babylon and Thebes, Brahma and Abraham, to Greece and the Argonauts; whence we might start again with Orpheus, and the Trojan war, the Pyramids and the Olympic games, and Homer and Athens, for our stages; and after a breathing space at the building of Rome, continue our journey down through Odin and Christ to — America. It is a wearisome while. And yet the lives of but sixty old women, such as live under the hill, say of a century each, strung together, are sufficient to reach over the whole ground. Taking hold of hands they would span the interval from Eve to my own mother. A respectable tea-party merely — whose gossip would be Universal History. The fourth old woman from myself suckled Columbus — the ninth was nurse to the Norman Conqueror — the nineteenth was the Virgin Mary — the twenty-fourth the Cu-mæan Sibyl — the thirtieth was at the Trojan war and Helen her name — the thirty-eighth was Queen Semiramis — the sixtieth was Eve, the mother of mankind. So much for the

> 'Old woman that lives under the hill,
> And if she's not gone she lives there still.'

It will not take a very great-granddaughter of hers to be in at the death of Time.

We can never safely exceed the actual facts in our narratives. Of pure invention, such as some suppose, there is no instance. To write a true work of fiction even is only to take leisure and liberty to describe some things more exactly as they are. A true account of the actual is the rarest poetry, for common sense always takes a hasty and superficial view. Though I am not much acquainted with the works of Goethe, I should say that it was one of his chief excellences as a writer, that he was satisfied with giving an exact description of things as they appeared to him, and their effect upon him. Most travelers have not self-respect enough to do this simply, and make objects and events stand around them as the centre, but still imagine more favorable positions and rela-tions than the actual ones, and so we get no valuable report from them at all. In his 'Italian Travels' Goethe jogs along at a snail's pace, but always mindful that the earth is beneath and the heavens are above him. His Italy is not merely the fatherland of lazzaroni and virtuosi, and scene of splendid ruins, but a solid turf-clad soil, daily shined on by the sun, and nightly by the moon. Even the few showers are faithfully recorded. He speaks as an unconcerned spectator, whose object is faithfully to describe what he sees, and that, for the most part, in the order in which he sees it. Even his reflections do not interfere with his descriptions. In one place he speaks of himself as giving so glowing and truthful a description of an old tower to the peasants who had gathered around him, that they who had been born and brought up in the neighborhood must needs look over their shoulders, 'that,' to use his own words, 'they might behold with their eyes, what I had praised to their ears' — 'and I had added nothing, not even the ivy which for centuries had decorated the walls.' It would thus be possible for inferior minds to produce invaluable books, if this very moderation were not the evidence of superiority; for the wise are not so much wiser than others as respecters of their own wisdom. Some, poor in spirit, record plaintively only what has happened to them; but others how they have happened to the universe, and the judgment which they have awarded to circumstances. Above all, he possessed a hearty good-will to all men, and never wrote a cross or even careless word. On one occasion the post-boy sniveling, 'Signor, perdonate, questa è la mia patria,' he confesses that 'to me poor northerner came something tear-like into the eyes.'

Goethe's whole education and life were those of the artist. He lacks the unconsciousness of the poet. In his autobiography he describes accurately the life of the author of Wilhelm Meister. For as there is in that book, mingled with a rare and serene wisdom, a certain pettiness or exaggeration of trifles, wisdom applied to produce a constrained and partial and merely well-bred man — a magnifying of the theatre till life itself is turned into a stage, for which it is our duty to study our parts well, and conduct with propriety and precision — so in the autobiography, the fault of his education is, so to speak, its merely artistic completeness. Nature is hindered, though she prevails at last in making an unusually catholic impression on the boy. It is the life of a city boy, whose toys are pictures and works of art, whose wonders are the theatre and kingly processions and crownings. As the youth studied minutely the order and the degrees in the imperial procession, and suffered none of its effect to be lost on him, so the man aimed to secure a rank in society which would satisfy his notion of fitness and respectability. He was defrauded of much which the savage boy enjoys. Indeed, he himself has occasion to say in this very autobiography, when at last he escapes into the woods without the gates: 'Thus much is certain, that only the undefinable, wide-expanding feelings of youth and of uncultivated nations are adapted to the sublime, which, whenever it may be excited in us through external objects, since it is either formless, or else moulded into forms which are incomprehensible, must surround us with a grandeur which we find above our reach.' He further says of himself: 'I had lived among painters from my childhood, and had accustomed myself to look at objects, as they did, with reference to art.' And this was his practice to the last. He was even too *well-bred* to be thoroughly bred. He says that he had had no intercourse with the lowest class of his towns-boys. The child should have the advantage of ignorance as well as of knowledge, and is fortunate if he gets his share of neglect and exposure.

'The laws of Nature break the rules of Art.'

The Man of Genius may at the same time be, indeed is commonly, an Artist, but the two are not to be confounded. The Man of Genius, referred to mankind, is an originator, an inspired or demonic man, who produces a perfect work in obedience to laws yet unexplored. The artist is he who detects and applies the law from observation of the works of Genius, whether of man or nature. The Artisan is he who merely applies the rules which others have detected. There has been no man of pure Genius, as there has been none wholly destitute of Genius.

Poetry is the mysticism of mankind.

The expressions of the poet cannot be analyzed; his sentence is one word, whose syllables are words. There are indeed no *words* quite worthy to be set to his music. But what matter if we do not hear the words always, if we hear the music?

Much verse fails of being poetry because it was not written exactly at the right crisis, though it may have been inconceivably near to it. It is only by a miracle that poetry is written at all. It is not recoverable thought, but a hue caught from a vaster receding thought.

A poem is one undivided, unimpeded expression fallen ripe into literature, and it is undividedly and unimpededly received by those for whom it was matured.

If you can speak what you will never hear, if you can write what you will never read, you have done rare things.

The work we choose should be our own
God lets alone.

The unconsciousness of man is the consciousness of God.

Deep are the foundations of sincerity. Even stone walls have their foundation below the frost.

What is produced by a free stroke charms us, like the forms of lichens and leaves. There is a certain perfection in accident which we never consciously attain. Draw a blunt quill filled with ink over a sheet of paper, and fold the paper before the ink is dry, transversely to this line, and a delicately shaded and regular figure will be produced, in some respects more pleasing than an elaborate drawing.

The talent of composition is very dangerous — the striking out the heart of life at a blow, as the Indian takes off a scalp. I feel as if my life had grown more outward when I can express it.

On his journey from Brenner to Verona, Goethe writes: 'The Tees flows now more gently, and makes in many places broad sands. On the land, near to the water, upon the hillsides, everything is so closely planted one to another, that you think they must choke one another — vineyards, maize, mulberry-trees, apples, pears, quinces, and nuts. The dwarf elder throws itself vigorously over the walls. Ivy grows with strong stems up the rocks, and spreads itself wide over them, the lizard glides through the intervals, and everything that wanders to and fro reminds one of the loveliest pictures of art. The women's tufts of hair bound up, the men's bare breasts and light jackets, the excellent oxen which they drive home from market, the little asses with their loads — everything forms a living animated Heinrich Roos. And now that it is evening, in the mild air a few clouds rest upon the mountains, in the heavens more stand still than move, and immediately after sunset the chirping of crickets begins to grow more loud; then one feels for once at home in the world, and not as concealed or in exile. I am contented as though I had been born and brought up here, and were now returning from a Greenland or whaling voyage. Even the dust of my Fatherland, which is often whirled about the wagon, and which for so long a time I had not seen, is greeted. The clock-and-bell jingling of the crickets is altogether lovely, penetrating, and agreeable. It sounds bravely when roguish boys whistle in emulation of a field of such songstresses. One fancies that they really enhance one another. Also the evening is perfectly mild as the day.

'If one who dwelt in the south, and came hither from the south, should hear of my rapture hereupon, he would deem me very childish. Alas! what I here express I have long known while I suffered under an unpropitious heaven, and now may I joyful feel this joy as an exception, which we should enjoy everforth as an eternal necessity of our nature.'

Thus we 'sayled by thought and pleasaunce,' as Chaucer says, and all things seemed with us to flow; the shore itself and the distant cliffs were dissolved by the undiluted air. The hardest material seemed to obey the same law with the most fluid, and so indeed in the long run it does. Trees were but rivers of sap and woody fibre, flowing from the atmosphere, and emptying into the earth by their trunks, as their roots flowed upward to the surface. And in the heavens there were rivers of stars, and milky ways, already beginning to gleam and ripple over our heads. There were rivers of rock on the surface of the earth, and rivers of ore in its bowels, and our thoughts flowed and circulated, and this portion of time was but the current hour. Let us wander where we will, the universe is built round about us, and we are central still. If we look into the heavens they are concave, and if we were to look into a gulf as bottomless, it would be concave also. The sky is curved downward to the earth in the horizon, because we stand on the plain. I draw down its skirts. The stars so low there seem loath to depart, but by a circuitous path to be remembering me, and returning on their steps.

We had already passed by broad daylight the scene of our encampment at Coos Falls, and at length we pitched our camp on the west bank, in the northern part of Merrimack, nearly opposite to the large island on which we had spent the noon in our way up the river.

There we went to bed that summer evening, on a sloping shelf in the bank, a couple of rods from our boat, which was drawn up on the sand, and just behind a thin fringe of oaks which bordered the river; without having disturbed any inhabitants but the spiders in the grass, which came out by the light of our lamp, and crawled over our buffaloes. When we looked out from under the tent, the trees were seen dimly through the mist, and a cool dew hung upon the grass, which seemed to rejoice in the night, and with the damp air we inhaled a solid fragrance. Having eaten our supper of hot cocoa and bread and watermelon, we soon grew weary of conversing, and writing in our journals, and putting out the lantern which hung from the tentpole, fell asleep.

Unfortunately, many things have been omitted which should have been recorded in our journal; for though we made it a rule to set down all our experiences therein, yet such a resolution is very hard to keep, for the important experience rarely allows us to remember such obligations, and so indifferent things get recorded, while that is frequently neglected. It is not easy to write in a journal what interests us at any time, because to write it is not what interests us.

Whenever we awoke in the night, still eking out our dreams with half-awakened thoughts, it was not till after an interval, when the wind breathed harder than usual, flapping the curtains of the tent, and causing its cords to vibrate, that we remembered that we lay on the bank of the Merrimack, and not in our chamber at home. With our heads so low in the grass, we heard the river whirling and sucking, and lapsing downward, kissing the shore as it went, sometimes rippling louder than usual, and again its mighty current making only a slight limpid, trickling sound, as if our water-pail had sprung a leak, and the water were flowing into the grass by our side. The wind, rustling the oaks and hazels, impressed us like a wakeful and inconsiderate person up at midnight, moving about, and putting things to rights, occasionally stirring up whole drawers full of leaves at a puff. There seemed to be a great haste and preparation throughout Nature, as for a distinguished visitor; all her aisles had to be swept in the night by a thousand hand-maidens, and a thousand pots to be boiled for the next day's feasting — such a whispering bustle, as if ten thousand fairies made their fingers fly, silently sewing at the new carpet with which the earth was to be clothed, and the new drapery which was to adorn the trees. And then the wind would lull and die away, and we like it fell asleep again.

FRIDAY

The Boteman strayt
Held on his course with stayed stedfastnesse,
Ne ever shroncke, ne ever sought to bayt
His tryed armes for toylesome wearinesse;
But with his oares did sweepe the watry wildernesse.

SPENSER.

Summer's robe grows
Dusky, and like an oft-dyed garment shows. — DONNE.

As WE lay awake long before daybreak, listening to the rippling of the river and the rustling of the leaves, in suspense whether the wind blew up or down the stream, was favorable or unfavorable to our voyage, we already suspected that there was a change in the weather, from a freshness as of autumn in these sounds. The wind in the woods sounded like an incessant waterfall dashing and roaring amid rocks, and we even felt encouraged by the unusual activity of the element. He who hears the rippling of rivers in these degenerate days will not utterly despair. That night was the turning-point in the season. We had gone to bed in summer, and we awoke in autumn; for summer passes into autumn in some unimaginable point of time, like the turning of a leaf.

We found our boat in the dawn just as we had left it, and as if waiting for us, there on the shore, in autumn, all cool and dripping with dew, and our tracks still fresh in the wet sand around it, the fairies all gone or concealed. Before five o'clock we pushed it into the fog, and, leaping in, at one shove were out of sight of the shores, and began to sweep downward with the rushing river, keeping a sharp lookout for rocks. We could see only the yellow gurgling water, and a solid bank of fog on every side, forming a small yard around us. We soon passed the mouth of the Souhegan, and the village of Merrimack, and as the mist gradually rolled away, and we were relieved from the trouble of watching for rocks, we saw by the flitting clouds, by the first russet tinge on the hills, by the rushing river, the cottages on shore, and the shore itself, so coolly fresh and shining with dew, and later in the day, by the hue

of the grape-vine, the goldfinch on the willow, the flickers flying in
flocks, and when we passed near enough to the shore, as we fancied,
by the faces of men, that the fall had commenced. The cottages looked
more snug and comfortable, and their inhabitants were seen only for
a moment, and then went quietly in and shut the door, retreating inward to the haunts of summer.

> 'And now the cold autumnal dews are seen
>   To cobweb ev'ry green;
> And by the low-shorn rowens doth appear
>   The fast-declining year.'

We heard the sigh of the first autumnal wind, and even the water
had acquired a grayer hue. The sumach, grape, and maple were
already changed, and the milkweed had turned to a deep, rich yellow.
In all woods the leaves were fast ripening for their fall; for their full
veins and lively gloss mark the ripe leaf and not the sered one of the poets;
and we knew that the maples stripped of their leaves among the earliest,
would soon stand like a wreath of smoke along the edge of the meadow.
Already the cattle were heard to low wildly in the pastures and along
the highways, restlessly running to and fro, as if in apprehension of the
withering of the grass and of the approach of winter. Our thoughts, too,
began to rustle.

As I pass along the streets of our village of Concord on the day of
our annual Cattle-Show, when it usually happens that the leaves of the
elms and buttonwoods begin first to strew the ground under the breath
of the October wind, the lively spirits in their sap seem to mount as
high as any plow-boy's let loose that day; and they lead my thoughts
away to the rustling woods, where the trees are preparing for their
winter campaign. This autumnal festival, when men are gathered in
crowds in the streets as regularly and by as natural a law as the leaves
cluster and rustle by the wayside, is naturally associated in my mind
with the fall of the year. The low of cattle in the streets sounds like
a hoarse symphony or running bass to the rustling of the leaves. The
wind goes hurrying down the country, gleaning every loose straw that
is left in the fields, while every farmer lad too appears to scud before it —
having donned his best pea-jacket and pepper-and-salt waistcoat, his
unbent trousers, outstanding rigging of duck or kerseymere or corduroy,
and his furry hat withal — to country fairs and cattle-shows, to that
Rome among the villages where the treasures of the year are gathered.
All the land over they go leaping the fences with their tough, idle palms,
which have never learned to hang by their sides, amid the low of

calves and the bleating of sheep — Amos, Abner, Elnathan, Elbridge,

'From steep pine-bearing mountains to the plain.'

I love these sons of earth, every mother's son of them, with their great hearty hearts rushing tumultuously in herds from spectacle to spectacle, as if fearful lest there should not be time between sun and sun to see them all, and the sun does not wait more than in haying time.

'Wise Nature's darlings, they live in the world
Perplexing not themselves how it is hurled.'

Running hither and thither with appetite for the coarse pastimes of the day, now with boisterous speed at the heels of the inspired negro from whose larynx the melodies of all Congo and Guinea Coast have broke loose into our streets; now to see the procession of a hundred yoke of oxen, all as august and grave as Osiris, or the droves of neat cattle and milch cows as unspotted as Isis or Io. Such as had no love for Nature

'at all,
Came lovers home from this great festival.'

They may bring their fattest cattle and richest fruits to the fair, but they are all eclipsed by the show of men. These are stirring autumn days, when men sweep by in crowds, amid the rustle of leaves like migrating finches; this is the true harvest of the year, when the air is but the breath of men, and the rustling of leaves is as the trampling of the crowd. We read nowadays of the ancient festivals, games, and processions of the Greeks and Etruscans with a little incredulity, or at least with little sympathy; but how natural and irrepressible in every people is some hearty and palpable greeting of Nature! The Corybantes, the Bacchantes, the rude primitive tragedians with their procession and goat-song, and the whole paraphernalia of the Panathenæa, which appear so antiquated and peculiar, have their parallel now. The husbandman is always a better Greek than the scholar is prepared to appreciate, and the old custom still survives, while antiquarians and scholars grow gray in commemorating it. The farmers crowd to the fair today in obedience to the same ancient law, which Solon or Lycurgus did not enact, as naturally as bees swarm and follow their queen.

It is worth the while to see the country's people, how they pour into the town, the sober farmer folk, now all agog, their very shirt and coat collars pointing forward — collars so broad as if they had put their shirts on wrong end upward, for the fashions always tend to superfluity — and with an unusual springiness in their gait, jabbering earnestly to one another. The more supple vagabond, too, is sure to appear on the least rumor of such a gathering, and the next day to disappear, and go into his hole like the seventeen-year locust, in an ever-shabby coat, though finer than the farmer's best, yet never dressed; come to see the sport, and have a hand in what is going — to know 'what's the row,' if there is any; to be where some men are drunk, some horses race, some cockerels fight; anxious to be shaking props under a table and above all to see the 'striped pig.' He especially is the creature of the occasion. He empties both his pockets and his character into the stream, and swims in such a day. He dearly loves the social slush. There is no reserve of soberness in him.

I love to see the herd of men feeding heartily on coarse and succulent pleasures, as cattle on the husks and stalks of vegetables. Though there are many crooked and crabbed specimens of humanity among them, run all to thorn and rind, and crowded out of shape by adverse circumstances, like the third chestnut in the bur, so that you wonder to see some heads wear a whole hat, yet fear not that the race will fail or waver in them; like the crabs which grow in hedges, they furnish the stocks of sweet and thrifty fruits still. Thus is nature recruited from age to age, while the fair and palatable varieties die out, and have their period. This is that mankind. How cheap must be the material of which so many men are made!

The wind blew steadily down the stream, so that we kept our sails set, and lost not a moment of the forenoon by delays, but from early morning until noon were continually dropping downward. With our hands on the steering-paddle, which was thrust deep into the river, or bending to the oar, which indeed we rarely relinquished, we felt each palpitation in the veins of our steed, and each impulse of the wings which drew us above. The current of our thoughts made as sudden bends as the river, which was continually opening new prospects to the east or south, but we are aware that rivers flow most rapidly and shallowest at these points. The steadfast shores never once turned aside for us, but still trended as they were made; why then should we always turn aside for them?

A man cannot wheedle nor overawe his Genius. It requires to be conciliated by nobler conduct than the world demands or can appreciate. These winged thoughts are like birds, and will not be handled; even hens will not let you touch them like quadrupeds. Nothing was ever so unfamiliar and startling to a man as his own thoughts.

To the rarest genius it is the most expensive to succumb and conform to the ways of the world. Genius is the worst of lumber, if the poet would float upon the breeze of popularity. The bird of paradise is obliged constantly to fly against the wind, lest its gay trappings, pressing close to its body, impede its free movements.

He is the best sailor who can steer within the fewest points of the wind, and extract a motive power out of the greatest obstacles. Most begin to veer and tack as soon as the wind changes from aft, and as within the tropics it does not blow from all points of the compass, there are some harbors which they can never reach.

The poet is no tender slip of fairy stock, who requires peculiar institutions and edicts for his defense, but the toughest son of earth and of Heaven, and by his greater strength and endurance his fainting companions will recognize the God in him. It is the worshipers of beauty, after all, who have done the real pioneer work of the world.

The poet will prevail to be popular in spite of his faults, and in spite of his beauties too. He will hit the nail on the head, and we shall not know the shape of his hammer. He makes us free of his hearth and heart, which is greater than to offer one the freedom of a city.

Great men, unknown to their generation, have their fame among the great who have preceded them, and all true wordly fame subsides from their high estimate beyond the stars.

Orpheus does not hear the strains which issue from his lyre, but only those which are breathed into it; for the original strain precedes the sound, by as much as the echo follows after. The rest is the perquisite of the rocks and trees and beasts.

When I stand in a library where is all the recorded wit of the world, but none of the recording, a mere accumulated, and not truly cumulative treasure; where immortal works stand side by side with anthologies which did not survive their month, and cobweb and mildew have already spread from these to the binding of those; and happily I am reminded of what poetry is — I perceive that Shakespeare and Milton did not foresee into what company they were to fall. Alas! that so soon the work of a true poet should be swept into such a dust-hole!

The poet will write for his peers alone. He will remember only that he saw truth and beauty from his position, and expect the time when a vision as broad shall overlook the same field as freely.

We are often prompted to speak our thoughts to our neighbors, or the single travelers whom we meet on the road, but poetry is a communication from our home and solitude addressed to all Intelligence.

It never whispers in a private ear. Knowing this we may understand those sonnets said to be addressed to particular persons, or 'To a Mistress's Eyebrow.' Let none feel flattered by them. For poetry write love, and it will be equally true.

No doubt it is an important difference between men of genius or poets, and men not of genius, that the latter are unable to grasp and confront the thought which visits them. But it is because it is too faint for expression, or even conscious impression. What merely quickens or retards the blood in their veins and fills their afternoons with pleasure, they know not whence, conveys a distinct assurance to the finer organization of the poet.

We talk of genius as if it were a mere knack, and the poet could only express what other men conceived. But in comparison with his task, the poet is the least talented of any; the writer of prose has more skill. See what talent the smith has. His material is pliant in his hands. When the poet is most inspired, is stimulated by an *aura* which never even colors the afternoons of common men, then his talent is all gone, and he is no longer a poet. The gods do not grant him any skill more than another. They never put their gifts into his hands, but they encompass and sustain him with their breath.

To say that God has given a man many and great talents frequently means that he has brought his heavens down within reach of his hands.

When the poetic frenzy seizes us, we run and scratch with our pen, intent only on worms, calling our mates around us, like the cock, and delighting in the dust we make, but do not detect where the jewel lies, which, perhaps, we have in the mean time cast to a distance, or quite covered up again.

The poet's body even is not fed like other men's, but he sometimes tastes the genuine nectar and ambrosia of the gods, and lives a divine life. By the healthful and invigorating thrills of inspiration his life is preserved to a serene old age.

Some poems are for holidays only. They are polished and sweet, but it is the sweetness of sugar, and not such as toil gives to sour bread. The breath with which the poet utters his verse must be that by which he lives.

Great prose, of equal elevation, commands our respect more than great verse, since it implies a more permanent and level height, a life more pervaded with the grandeur of the thought. The poet often only makes an irruption, like a Parthian, and is off again, shooting while he retreats; but the prose writer has conquered like a Roman, and settled colonies.

The true poem is not that which the public read. There is always a poem not printed on paper, coincident with the production of this, stereotyped in the poet's life. It is *what he has become through his work.* Not how is the idea expressed in stone, or on canvas or paper, is the question, but how far it has obtained form and expression in the life of the artist. His true work will not stand in any prince's gallery.

> My life has been the poem I would have writ,
> But I could not both live and utter it.

THE POET'S DELAY

> In vain I see the morning rise,
>   In vain observe the western blaze,
> Who idly look to other skies,
>   Expecting life by other ways.
>
> Amidst such boundless wealth without,
>   I only still am poor within,
> The birds have sung their summer out,
>   But still my spring does not begin.
>
> Shall I then wait the autumn wind,
>   Compelled to seek a milder day,
> And leave no curious nest behind,
>   No woods still echoing to my lay?...[1]

While we sailed fleetly before the wind, with the river gurgling under our stern, the thoughts of autumn coursed as steadily through our minds, and we observed less what was passing on the shore than the dateless associations and impressions which the season awakened, anticipating in some measure the progress of the year.

> I hearing get, who had but ears,
>   And sight, who had but eyes before,
> I moments live, who lived but years,
>   And truth discern, who knew but learning's lore.

Sitting with our faces now up-stream, we studied the landscape by degrees, as one unrolls a map — rock, tree, house, hill, and meadow assuming new and varying positions as wind and water shifted the scene, and there was variety enough for our entertainment in the metamorphoses of the simplest objects. Viewed from this side the scenery appeared new to us.

The most familiar sheet of water, viewed from a new hilltop, yields

---

[1] Pages 366–371 (Walden Edition), on Ossian, omitted.

a novel and unexpected pleasure. When we have traveled a few miles, we do not recognize the profiles even of the hills which overlook our native village, and perhaps no man is quite familiar with the horizon as seen from the hill nearest to his house, and can recall its outline distinctly when in the valley. We do not commonly know, beyond a short distance, which way the hills range which take in our houses and farms in their sweep. As if our birth had at first sundered things, and we had been thrust up through into nature like a wedge, and not till the wound heals and the scar disappears do we begin to discover where we are, and that nature is one and continuous everywhere. It is an important epoch when a man who has always lived on the east side of a mountain, and seen it in the west, travels round and sees it in the east. Yet the universe is a sphere whose centre is wherever there is intelligence. The sun is not so central as a man. Upon an isolated hilltop, in an open country, we seem to ourselves to be standing on the boss of an immense shield, the immediate landscape being apparently depressed below the more remote, and rising gradually to the horizon, which is the rim of the shield — villas, steeples, forests, mountains, one above another, till they are swallowed up in the heavens. The most distant mountains in the horizon appear to rise directly from the shore of that lake in the woods by which we chance to be standing, while from the mountain-top, not only this, but a thousand nearer and larger lakes are equally unobserved.

Seen through this clear atmosphere, the works of the farmer, his plowing and reaping, had a beauty to our eyes which he never saw. How fortunate were we who did not own an acre of these shores, who had not renounced our title to the whole! One who knew how to appropriate the true value of this world would be the poorest man in it. The poor rich man! all he has is what he has bought. What I see is mine. I am a large owner in the Merrimack intervals.

> Men dig and dive but cannot my wealth spend,
> Who yet no partial store appropriate,
> Who no armed ship into the Indies send,
> To rob me of my orient estate.

He is the rich man, and enjoys the fruits of riches, who summer and winter forever can find delight in his own thoughts. Buy a farm! What have I to pay for a farm which a farmer will take?

When I visit again some haunt of my youth, I am glad to find that nature wears so well. The landscape is indeed something real, and solid, and sincere, and I have not put my foot through it yet. There is a pleasant tract on the bank of the Concord, called Conantum, which I have in my mind — the old deserted farmhouse, the desolate pasture with its bleak cliff, the open wood, the river-reach, the green meadow in the midst, and the moss-grown wild-apple orchard — places where one may have many thoughts and not decide anything. It is a scene which I can not only remember, as I might a vision, but when I will can bodily revisit, and find it even so, unaccountable, yet unpretending in its pleasant dreariness. When my thoughts are sensible of change, I love to see and sit on rocks which I *have* known, and pry into their moss, and see unchangeableness so established. I not yet gray on rocks forever gray, I no longer green under the evergreens. There is something even in the lapse of time by which time recovers itself.

As we have said, it proved a cool as well as breezy day, and by the time we reached Penichook Brook we were obliged to sit muffled in our cloaks, while the wind and current carried us along. We bounded swiftly over the rippling surface, far by many cultivated lands and ends of fences which divided innumerable farms, with hardly a thought for the various lines which they separated; now by long rows of alders or groves of pines or oaks, and now by some homestead where the women and children stood outside to gaze at us, till we had swept out of their sight, and beyond the limit of their longest Saturday ramble. We glided past the mouth of the Nashua, and not long after, of Salmon Brook, without more pause than the wind.

> Salmon Brook,
> Penichook,
> Ye sweet waters of my brain,
> When shall I look,
> Or cast the hook,
> In your waves again?
>
> Silver eels,
> Wooden creels,
> These the baits that still allure,
> And dragon-fly
> That floated by,
> May they still endure?

The shadows chased one another swiftly over wood and meadow, and their alternation harmonized with our mood. We could distinguish the clouds which cast each one, though never so high in the heavens. When a shadow flits across the landscape of the soul where is the substance? Probably, if we were wise enough, we should see to what virtue we are indebted for any happier moment we enjoy. No doubt we have earned it at some time, for the gifts of Heaven are never quite gratuitous. The constant abrasion and decay of our lives makes the soil of our future growth. The wood which we now mature, when it becomes virgin mould, determines the character of our second growth, whether that be oaks or pines. Every man casts a shadow; not his body only, but his imperfectly mingled spirit. This is his grief. Let him turn which way he will, it falls opposite to the sun; short at noon, long at eve. Did you never see it? But, referred to the sun, it is widest at its base, which is no greater than his own capacity. The divine light is diffused almost entirely around us, and by means of the refraction of light, or else by a certain self-luminousness, or, as some will have it, transparency, if we preserve ourselves untarnished, we are able to enlighten our shaded side. At any rate, our darkest grief has that bronze color of the moon eclipsed. There is no ill which may not be dissipated, like the dark, if you let in a stronger light upon it. Shadows, referred to the source of light, are pyramids whose bases are never greater than those of the substances which cast them, but light is a spherical congeries of pyramids, whose very apexes are the sun itself, and hence the system shines with uninterrupted light. But if the light we use is but a paltry and narrow taper, most objects will cast a shadow wider than themselves.

The places where we had stopped or spent the night in our way up the river had already acquired a slight historical interest for us; for many upward days' voyaging were unraveled in this rapid downward passage. When one landed to stretch his limbs by walking, he soon found himself falling behind his companion, and was obliged to take advantage of the curves, and ford the brooks and ravines in haste, to recover his ground. Already the banks and the distant meadows wore a sober and deepened tinge, for the September air had shorn them of their summer's pride.

> 'And what's a life? The flourishing array
> Of the proud summer meadow, which today
> Wears her green plush, and is tomorrow hay.'

The air was really the 'fine element' which the poets describe. It had a finer and sharper grain, seen against the russet pastures and meadows, than before, as if cleansed of the summer's impurities.

Having passed the New Hampshire line and reached the Horeshoe Interval in Tyngsborough, where there is a high and regular second bank, we climbed up this in haste to get a nearer sight of the autumnal flowers, asters, goldenrod, and yarrow, and blue-curls (*Trichostema dichotomum*), humble roadside blossoms, and, lingering still, the harebell and the *Rhexia Virginica*. The last, growing in patches of lively pink flowers on the edge of the meadows, had almost too gay an appearance for the rest of the landscape, like a pink ribbon on the bonnet of a Puritan woman. Asters and goldenrods were the livery which nature wore at present. The latter alone expressed all the ripeness of the season, and shed their mellow lustre over the fields, as if the now declining summer's sun had bequeathed its hues to them. It is the floral solstice a little after mid-summer, when the particles of golden light, the sun-dust, have, as it were, fallen like seeds on the earth, and produced these blossoms. On every hillside, and in every valley, stood countless asters, coreopses, tansies, goldenrods, and the whole race of yellow flowers, like Brahminical devotees, turning steadily with their luminary from morning till night.

> 'I see the goldenrod shine bright,
>   As sun-showers at the birth of day,
> A golden plume of yellow light,
>   That robs the Day-god's splendid ray.
>
> 'The aster's violet rays divide
>   The bank with many stars for me,
> And yarrow in blanch tints is dyed,
>   As moonlight floats across the sea.
>
> 'I see the emerald woods prepare
>   To shed their vestiture once more,
> And distant elm-trees spot the air
>   With yellow pictures softly o'er.
> . . . .
> 'No more the water-lily's pride
>   In milk-white circles swims content,
> No more the blue-weed's clusters ride
>   And mock the heavens' element.
> . . . .
> 'Autumn, thy wreath and mine are blent
>   With the same colors, for to me
> A richer sky than all is lent,
>   While fades my dream-like company.
>
> 'Our skies glow purple, but the wind
>   Sobs chill through green trees and bright grass,
> Today shines fair, and lurk behind
>   The times that into winter pass.

> 'So fair we seem, so cold we are,
>   So fast we hasten to decay,
> Yet through our night glows many a star,
>   That still shall claim its sunny day.'

So sang a Concord poet once.

There is a peculiar interest belonging to the still later flowers, which abide with us the approach of winter. There is something witchlike in the appearance of the witch-hazel, which blossoms late in October and in November, with its irregular and angular spray and petals like furies' hair, or small ribbon streamers. Its blossoming, too, at this irregular period, when other shrubs have lost their leaves, as well as blossoms, looks like witches' craft. Certainly it blooms in no garden of man's. There is a whole fairy-land on the hillside where it grows.

Some have thought that the gales do not at present waft to the voyager the natural and original fragrance of the land, such as the early navigators described, and that the loss of many odoriferous native plants, sweet-scented grasses and medicinal herbs, which formerly sweetened the atmosphere, and rendered it salubrious — by the grazing of cattle and the rooting of swine — is the source of many diseases which now prevail; the earth, say they, having been long subjected to extremely artificial and luxurious modes of cultivation, to gratify the appetite, converted into a stye and hotbed, where men for profit increase the ordinary decay of nature.

According to the record of an old inhabitant of Tyngsborough, now dead, whose farm we were now gliding past, one of the greatest freshets on this river took place in October, 1785, and its height was marked by a nail driven into an apple tree behind his house. One of his descendants has shown this to me, and I judged it to be at least seventeen or eighteen feet above the level of the river at the time. According to Barber, the river rose twenty-one feet above the common high-water mark at Bradford in the year 1818. Before the Lowell and Nashua railroad was built, the engineer made inquiries of the inhabitants along the banks as to how high they had known the river to rise. When he came to this house he was conducted to the apple tree, and as the nail was not then visible, the lady of the house placed her hand on the trunk where she said that she remembered the nail to have been from her childhood. In the meanwhile the old man put his arm inside the tree, which was hollow, and felt the point of the nail sticking through, and it was exactly opposite to her hand. The spot is now plainly marked by a notch in the bark. But as no one else remembered the river to have risen so high as this, the engineer disregarded this statement, and I learn that there has since been a freshet which rose within nine inches of the rails at Biscuit Brook, and such a freshet as that of 1785 would have covered the railroad two feet deep.

The revolutions of nature tell as fine tales, and make as interesting revelations, on this river's banks, as on the Euphrates or the Nile. This apple tree, which stands within a few rods of the river, is called 'Elisha's apple tree,' from a friendly Indian who was anciently in the service of Jonathan Tyng, and, with one other man, was killed here by his own race in one of the Indian wars — the particulars of which affair were told us on the spot. He was buried close by, no one knew exactly where, but in the flood of 1785, so great a weight of water standing over the grave caused the earth to settle where it had once been disturbed, and when the flood went down, a sunken spot, exactly of the form and size of the grave, revealed its locality; but this was now lost again, and no future flood can detect it; yet, no doubt, nature will know how to point it out in due time, if it be necessary, by methods yet more searching and unexpected. Thus there is not only the crisis when the spirit ceases to inspire and expand the body, marked by a fresh mound in the churchyard, but there is also a crisis when the body ceases to take up room as such in nature, marked by a fainter depression in the earth.

We sat awhile to rest us here upon the brink of the western bank, surrounded by the glossy leaves of the red variety of the mountain laurel, just above the head of Wicasuck Island, where we could observe some scows which were loading with clay from the opposite shore, and also overlook the grounds of the farmer, of whom I have spoken, who once hospitably entertained us for a night. He had on his pleasant farm, besides an abundance of the beach plum, or *Prunus littoralis*, which grew wild, the Canada plum under cultivation, fine Porter apples, some peaches and large patches of musk and water melons, which he culti-vated for the Lowell market. Elisha's apple tree, too, bore a native fruit, which was prized by the family; he raised the blood peach, which, as he showed us with satisfaction, was more like the oak in the color of its bark and in the setting of its branches, and was less liable to break down under the weight of the fruit, or the snow, than other varieties. It was of slower growth, and its branches strong and tough. There, also, was his nursery of native apple trees, thickly set upon the bank, which cost but little care, and which he sold to the neighboring farmers when they were five or six years old. To see a single peach upon its stem makes an impression of paradisaical fertility and luxury. This reminded us even of an old Roman farm, as described by Varro: 'Cæsar Vopiscus Ædilicius, when he pleaded before the Censors, said that the grounds of Rosea were the garden (*sumen*, the tidbit) of Italy, in which a pole being left would not be visible the day after, on account of the growth of the herbage.' This soil may not have been remarkably fertile, yet at this distance we thought that this anecdote might be told of the Tyngsborough farm.

When we passed Wicasuck Island, there was a pleasure boat containing a youth and a maiden on the island brook, which we were pleased to see, since it proved that there were some hereabouts to whom our excursion would not be wholly strange. Before this, a canal-boatman, of whom we made some inquiries respecting Wicasuck Island, and who told us that it was disputed property, suspected that we had a claim upon it, and though we assured him that all this was news to us, and explained, as well as we could, why we had come to see it, he believed not a word of it, and seriously offered us one hundred dollars for our title. The only other small boats which we met with were used to pick up driftwood. Some of the poorer class along the stream collect, in this way, all the fuel which they require. While one of us landed not far from this island to forage for provisions among the farm-houses whose roofs we saw — for our supply was now exhausted — the other, sitting in the boat, which was moored to the shore, was left alone to his reflections.

If there is nothing new on the earth, still the traveler always has a resource in the skies. They are constantly turning a new page to view. The wind sets the types on this blue ground, and the inquiring may always read a new truth there. There are things there written with such fine and subtle tinctures, paler than the juice of limes, that to the diurnal eye they leave no trace, and only the chemistry of night reveals them. Every man's daylight firmament answers in his mind to the brightness of the vision in his starriest hour.

These continents and hemispheres are soon run over, but an always unexplored and infinite region makes off on every side from the mind, further than to sunset, and we can make no highway or beaten track into it, but the grass immediately springs up in the path, for we travel there chiefly with our wings.

Sometimes we see objects as through a thin haze, in their eternal relations, and they stand like Palenque and the Pyramids, and we

wonder who set them up, and for what purpose. If we see the reality in
things, of what moment is the superficial and apparent longer? What
are the earth and all its interests beside the deep surmise which pierces
and scatters them? While I sit here listening to the waves which ripple
and break on this shore, I am absolved from all obligation to the past,
and the council of nations may reconsider its votes. The grating of
a pebble annuls them. Still occasionally in my dreams I remember
that rippling water.

> Oft as I turn me on my pillow o'er
> I hear the lapse of waves upon the shore,
> Distinct as if it were at broad noonday,
> And I were drifting down from Nashua.

With a bending sail we glided rapidly by Tyngsborough and Chelmsford, each holding in one hand half of a tart country apple pie which
we had purchased to celebrate our return, and in the other a fragment
of the newspaper in which it was wrapped, devouring these with divided
relish, and learning the news which had transpired since we sailed.
The river here opened into a broad and straight reach of great length,
which we bounded merrily over before a smacking breeze, with a devil-
may-care look in our faces, and our boat a white bone in its mouth, and
a speed which greatly astonished some scow boatmen whom we met.
The wind in the horizon rolled like a flood over valley and plain, and
every tree bent to the blast, and the mountains like school-boys turned
their cheeks to it. They were great and current motions, the flowing
sail, the running stream, the waving tree, the roving wind. The north
wind stepped readily into the harness which we had provided, and
pulled us along with good will. Sometimes we sailed as gently and
steadily as the clouds overhead, watching the receding shores and the
motions of our sail; the play of its pulse so like our own lives, so thin
and yet so full of life, so noiseless when it labored hardest, so noisy and
impatient when least effective; now bending to some generous impulse
of the breeze, and then fluttering and flapping with a kind of human
suspense. It was the scale on which the varying temperature of distant
atmospheres was graduated, and it was some attraction for us that the
breeze it played with had been out of doors so long. Thus we sailed,
not being able to fly, but as next best, making a long furrow in the fields
of the Merrimack toward our home, with our wings spread, but never
lifting our heel from the watery trench; gracefully plowing homeward
with our brisk and willing team, wind and stream, pulling together,
the former yet a wild steer, yoked to his more sedate fellow. It was very

near flying, as when the duck rushes through the water with an impulse of her wings, throwing the spray about her before she can rise. How we had stuck fast if drawn up but a few feet on the shore!

When we reached the great bend just above Middlesex, where the river runs east thirty-five miles to the sea, we at length lost the aid of this propitious wind, though we contrived to make one long and judicious tack carry us nearly to the locks of the canal. We were here locked through at noon by our old friend, the lover of the higher mathematics, who seemed glad to see us safe back again through so many locks; but we did not stop to consider any of his problems, though we could cheerfully have spent a whole autumn in this way another time, and never have asked what his religion was. It is so rare to meet with a man outdoors who cherishes a worthy thought in his mind, which is independent of the labor of his hands. Behind every man's busy-ness there should be a level of undisturbed serenity and industry, as within the reef encircling a coral isle there is always an expanse of still water, where the depositions are going on which will finally raise it above the surface.

The eye which can appreciate the naked and absolute beauty of a scientific truth is far more rare than that which is attracted by a moral one. Few detect the morality in the former, or the science in the latter. Aristotle defined art to be Λόγος τοῦ ἔργου ἄνευ ὕλης, *The principle of the work without the wood;* but most men prefer to have some of the wood along with the principle; they demand that the truth be clothed in flesh and blood and the warm colors of life. They prefer the partial statement because it fits and measures them and their commodities best. But science still exists everywhere as the sealer of weights and measures at least.

We have heard much about the poetry of mathematics, but very little of it has yet been sung. The ancients had a juster notion of their poetic value than we. The most distinct and beautiful statement of any truth must take at last the mathematical form. We might so simplify the rules of moral philosophy, as well as of arithmetic, that one formula would express them both. All the moral laws are readily translated into natural philosophy, for often we have only to restore the primitive meaning of the words by which they are expressed, or to attend to their literal instead of their metaphorical sense. They are already *supernatural* philosophy. The whole body of what is now called moral or ethical truth existed in the golden age as abstract science. Or, if we prefer, we may say that the laws of Nature are the purest morality. The Tree of Knowledge is a Tree of Knowledge of good and evil. He is not a true man of science who does not bring some sympathy to his studies, and expect to learn something by behavior as well as by application. It is childish to rest in the discovery of mere coincidences, or of partial and extraneous laws. The study of geometry is a petty and idle exercise of the mind, if it is applied to no larger system than the starry one. Mathematics should be mixed not only with physics but with ethics, *that* is *mixed* mathematics. The fact which interests us most is the life of the naturalist. The purest science is still biographical. Nothing will dignify and elevate science while it is sundered so wholly from the moral life of its devotee, and he professes another religion than it teaches, and worships at a foreign shrine. Anciently the faith of a philosopher was identical with his system, or, in other words, his view of the universe.

My friends mistake when they communicate facts to me with so much pains. Their presence, even their exaggerations and loose statements, are equally good facts for me. I have no respect for facts even except when I would use them, and for the most part I am independent of those which I hear, and can afford to be inaccurate, or, in other words, to substitute more present and pressing facts in their place.

The poet uses the results of science and philosophy, and generalizes their widest deductions.

The process of discovery is very simple. An unwearied and systematic application of known laws to nature causes the unknown to reveal themselves. Almost any *mode* of observation will be successful at last, for what is most wanted is method. Only let something be determined and fixed around which observation may rally. How many new relations a foot-rule alone will reveal, and to how many things still this has not been applied! What wonderful discoveries have been and may still be made with a plumb-line, a level, a surveyor's compass, a thermometer, or a barometer! Where there is an observatory and a telescope, we expect that any eyes will see new worlds at once. I should say that the most prominent scientific men of our country, and perhaps of this age, are either serving the arts and not pure science, or are performing faithful but quite subordinate labors in particular departments. They make no steady and systematic approaches to the central fact. A discovery is made, and at once the attention of all observers is distracted to that, and it draws many analogous discoveries in its train; as if their work were not already laid out for them, but they had been lying on their oars. There is wanting constant and accurate observation with enough of theory to direct and discipline it.

But, above all, there is wanting genius. Our books of science, as they improve in accuracy, are in danger of losing the freshness and vigor and readiness to appreciate the real laws of Nature, which is a marked merit in the ofttimes false theories of the ancients. I am attracted by the slight pride and satisfaction, the emphatic and even exaggerated style, in which some of the older naturalists speak of the operations of Nature, though they are better qualified to appreciate than to discriminate the facts. Their assertions are not without value when disproved. If they are not facts, they are suggestions for nature herself to act upon. 'The Greeks,' says Gesner, 'had a common proverb (Ααγὸς καθεῦδον), a sleeping hare, for a dissembler or counterfeit; because the hare sees when she sleeps; for this is an admirable and rare work of Nature, that all the residue of her bodily parts take their rest, but the eye standeth continually sentinel.'

Observation is so wide awake, and facts are being so rapidly added to the sum of human experience, that it appears as if the theorizer would always be in arrears, and were doomed forever to arrive at imperfect conclusions; but the power to perceive a law is equally rare in all ages of the world, and depends but little on the number of facts observed. The senses of the savage will furnish him with facts enough to set him up as a philosopher. The ancients can still speak to us with authority, even on the themes of geology and chemistry, though these studies are thought to have had their birth in modern times. Much is said about the progress of science in these centuries. I should say that the useful results of science had accumulated, but that there had been no accumulation of knowledge, strictly speaking, for posterity; for knowledge is to be acquired only by a corresponding experience. How can we *know* what we are *told* merely? Each man can interpret another's experience only by his own. We read that Newton discovered the law of gravitation, but how many who have heard of his famous discovery have recognized the same truth that he did? It may be not one. The revelation which was then made to him has not been superseded by the revelation made to any successor.

We see the *planet* fall,
And that is all.

In a review of Sir James Clark Ross's 'Antarctic Voyage of Discovery,' there is a passage which shows how far a body of men are commonly impressed by an object of sublimity, and which is also a good instance of the step from the sublime to the ridiculous. After describing the discovery of the Antarctic Continent, at first seen a hundred miles distant over fields of ice — stupendous ranges of mountains from seven and eight to twelve and fourteen thousand feet high, covered with eternal snow and ice, in solitary and inaccessible grandeur, at one time the weather being beautifully clear, and the sun shining on the icy landscape; a continent whose islands only are accessible, and these exhibited 'not the smallest trace of vegetation,' only in a few places the rocks protruding through their icy covering, to convince the beholder that land formed the nucleus, and that it was not an iceberg — the practical British reviewer proceeds thus, sticking to his last: 'On the 22d of January, afternoon, the Expedition made the latitude of 74° 20', and by 7^h P.M., having ground [ground! where did they get ground?] to believe that they were then in a higher southern latitude than had been attained by that enterprising seaman, the late Captain James Weddel, and therefore higher than all their predecessors, an extra allowance of grog was issued to the crews as a reward for their perseverance.'

Let not us sailors of late centuries take upon ourselves any airs on account of our Newtons and our Cuviers; we deserve an extra allowance of grog only.

We endeavored in vain to persuade the wind to blow through the long corridor of the canal, which is here cut straight through the woods, and were obliged to resort to our old expedient of drawing by a cord. When we reached the Concord, we were forced to row once more in good earnest, with neither wind nor current in our favor, but by this time the rawness of the day had disappeared, and we experienced the warmth of a summer afternoon. This change in the weather was favorable to our contemplative mood, and disposed us to dream yet deeper at our oars, while we floated in imagination farther down the stream of time, as we had floated down the stream of the Merrimack, to poets of a milder period than had engaged us in the morning. Chelmsford and Billerica appeared like old English towns, compared with Merrimack and Nashua, and many generations of civil poets might have lived and sung here....[1]

A true poem is distinguished not so much by a felicitous expression,

[1] Pages 391–400 (Walden Edition), on Chaucer, omitted.

or any thought it suggests, as by the atmosphere which surrounds it. Most have beauty of outline merely, and are striking as the form and bearing of a stranger; but true verses come toward us indistinctly, as the very breath of all friendliness, and envelop us in their spirit and fragrance. Much of our poetry has the very best manners, but no character. It is only an unusual precision and elasticity of speech, as if its author had taken, not an intoxicating draught, but an electuary. It has the distinct outline of sculpture, and chronicles an early hour. Under the influence of passion all men speak thus distinctly, but wrath is not always divine.

There are two classes of men called poets. The one cultivates life, the other art — one seeks food for nutriment, the other for flavor; one satisfies hunger, the other gratifies the palate. There are two kinds of writing, both great and rare — one that of genius, or the inspired, the other of intellect and taste, in the intervals of inspiration. The former is above criticism, always correct, giving the law to criticism. It vibrates and pulsates with life forever. It is sacred, and to be read with reverence, as the works of nature are studied. There are few instances of a sustained style of this kind; perhaps every man has spoken words, but the speaker is then careless of the record. Such a style removes us out of personal relations with its author; we do not take his words on our lips, but his sense into our hearts. It is the stream of inspiration, which bubbles out, now here, now there, now in this man, now in that. It matters not through what ice-crystals it is seen, now a fountain, now the ocean stream running underground. It is in Shakespeare, Alpheus, in Burns, Arethuse; but ever the same. The other is self-possessed and wise. It is reverent of genius, and greedy of inspiration. It is conscious in the highest and the least degree. It consists with the most perfect command of the faculties. It dwells in a repose as of the desert, and objects are as distinct in it as oases or palms in the horizon of sand. The train of thought moves with subdued and measured step, like a caravan. But the pen is only an instrument in its hand, and not instinct with life, like a longer arm. It leaves a thin varnish or glaze over all its work. The works of Goethe furnish remarkable instances of the latter.

There is no just and serene criticism as yet. Nothing is considered simply as it lies in the lap of eternal beauty, but our thoughts, as well as our bodies, must be dressed after the latest fashions. Our taste is too delicate and particular. It says nay to the poet's work, but never yea to his hope. It invites him to adorn his deformities, and not to cast them off by expansion, as the tree its bark. We are a people who live in a bright light, in houses of pearl and porcelain, and drink only light wines, whose teeth are easily set on edge by the least natural sour. If we had been consulted, the backbone of the earth would have been made, not of granite, but of Bristol spar. A modern author would have died in infancy in a ruder age. But the poet is something more than a scald, 'a smoother and polisher of language'; he is a Cincinnatus in literature, and occupies no west end of the world. Like the sun, he will indifferently select his rhymes, and with a liberal taste weave into his verse the planet and the stubble.

In these old books the stucco has long since crumbled away, and we read what was sculptured in the granite. They are rude and massive in their proportions, rather than smooth and delicate in their finish. The workers in stone polish only their chimney ornaments, but their pyramids are roughly done. There is a soberness in a rough aspect, as of unhewn granite, which addresses a depth in us, but a polished surface hits only the ball of the eye. The true finish is the work of time, and the use to which a thing is put. The elements are still polishing the pyramids. Art may varnish and gild, but it can do no more. A work of genius is rough-hewn from the first, because it anticipates the lapse of time, and has an ingrained polish, which still appears when fragments are broken off, an essential quality of its substance. Its beauty is at the same time its strength, and it breaks with a lustre.

The great poem must have the stamp of greatness as well as its essence. The reader easily goes within the shallowest contemporary poetry, and informs it with all the life and promise of the day, as the pilgrim goes within the temple, and hears the faintest strains of the worshipers; but it will have to speak to posterity, traversing these deserts, through the ruins of its outmost walls, by the grandeur and beauty of its proportions.

But here on the stream of the Concord, where we have all the while been bodily, Nature, who is superior to all styles and ages, is now, with pensive face, composing her poem Autumn, with which no work of man will bear to be compared.

In summer we live out of doors, and have only impulses and feelings, which are all for action, and must wait commonly for the stillness and longer nights of autumn and winter before any thought will subside; we are sensible that behind the rustling leaves, and the stacks of grain, and the bare clusters of the grape, there is the field of a wholly new life, which no man has lived; that even this earth was made for more mysterious and nobler inhabitants than men and women. In the hues of October sunsets, we see the portals to other mansions than those which we occupy, not far off geographically,

> 'There is a place beyond that flaming hill,
> From whence the stars their thin appearance shed,
> A place beyond all place, where never ill,
> Nor impure thought was ever harbored.'

Sometimes a mortal feels in himself Nature — not his Father but his Mother stirs within him, and he becomes immortal with her immortality. From time to time she claims kindredship with us, and some globule from her veins steals up into our own.

> I am the autumnal sun,
> With autumn gales my race is run;
> When will the hazel put forth its flowers,
> Or the grape ripen under my bowers?
> When will the harvest or the hunter's moon
> Turn my midnight into mid-noon?
> I am all sere and yellow,
> And to my core mellow.
> The mast is dropping within my woods,
> The winter is lurking within my moods,
> And the rustling of the withered leaf
> Is the constant music of my grief.

To an unskillful rhymer the Muse thus spoke in prose:

The moon no longer reflects the day, but rises to her absolute rule, and the husbandman and hunter acknowledge her for their mistress. Asters and goldenrods reign along the way, and the life-everlasting withers not. The fields are reaped and shorn of their pride, but an inward verdure still crowns them. The thistle scatters its down on the pool, and yellow leaves clothe the vine, and naught disturbs the serious life of men. But behind the sheaves, and under the sod, there lurks a ripe fruit, which the reapers have not gathered, the true harvest of the year, which it bears forever, annually watering and maturing it, and man never severs the stalk which bears this palatable fruit.

Men nowhere, east or west, live yet a *natural* life, round which the vine clings, and which the elm willingly shadows. Man would desecrate it by his touch, and so the beauty of the world remains veiled to him. He needs not only to be spiritualized but *naturalized,* on the soil of earth. Who shall conceive what kind of roof the heavens might extend over him, what seasons minister to him, and what employment dignify his life! Only the convalescent raise the veil of nature. An immortality in his life would confer immortality on his abode. The winds should be his breath, the seasons his moods, and he should impart of his serenity to Nature herself. But such as we know him he is ephemeral like the scenery which surrounds him, and does not aspire to an enduring existence. When we come down into the distant village, visible from the mountain-top, the nobler inhabitants with whom we peopled it have departed, and left only vermin in its desolate streets. It is the imagination of poets which puts those brave speeches into the mouths of their heroes. They may feign that Cato's last words were

> 'The earth, the air and seas I know, and all
> The joys and horrors of their peace and wars;
> And now will view the Gods' state and the stars,'

but such are not the thoughts nor the destiny of common men. What is this heaven which they expect, if it is no better than they expect? Are they prepared for a better than they can now imagine? Where is the heaven of him who dies on a stage, in a theatre? Here or nowhere is our heaven.

> 'Although we see celestial bodies move
> Above the earth, the earth we till and love.'

We can conceive of nothing more fair than something which we have experienced. 'The remembrance of youth is a sigh.' We linger in man-hood to tell the dreams of our childhood, and they are half forgotten ere we have learned the language. We have need to be earth-born as well as heaven-born, γηγενεῖς, as was said of the Titans of old, or in a better sense than they. There have been heroes for whom this world seemed expressly prepared, as if creation had at last succeeded; whose daily life was the stuff of which our dreams are made, and whose presence enhanced the beauty and ampleness of Nature herself. Where they walked,

> 'Largior hic campos aether et lumine vestit
> Purpureo: Solemque suum, sua sidera norunt.'

'Here a more copious air invests the fields, and clothes with purple light; and they know their own sun and their own stars.' We love to hear some men speak, though we hear not what they say; the very air they breathe is rich and perfumed, and the sound of their voices falls on the ear like the rustling of leaves or the crackling of the fire. They stand many deep. They have the heavens for their abettors, as those who have never stood from under them, and they look at the stars with an answering ray. Their eyes are like glowworms, and their motions

graceful and flowing, as if a place were already found for them, like
rivers flowing through valleys. The distinctions of morality, of right
and wrong, sense and nonsense, are petty, and have lost their significance, beside these pure primeval natures. When I consider the clouds
stretched in stupendous masses across the sky, frowning with darkness
or glowing with downy light, or gilded with the rays of the setting sun,
like the battlements of a city in the heavens, their grandeur appears
thrown away on the meanness of my employment; the drapery is
altogether too rich for such poor acting. I am hardly worthy to be
a suburban dweller outside those walls.

> 'Unless above himself he can
> Erect himself, how poor a thing is man!'

With our music we would fain challenge transiently another and
finer sort of intercourse than our daily toil permits. The strains come
back to us amended in the echo, as when a friend reads our verse. Why
have they so painted the fruits, and freighted them with such fragrance
as to satisfy a more than animal appetite?

> 'I asked the schoolman, his advice was free,
> But scored me out too intricate a way.'

These things imply, perchance, that we live on the verge of another and
purer realm, from which these odors and sounds are wafted over to us.
The borders of our plot are set with flowers, whose seeds were blown
from more Elysian fields adjacent. They are the pot-herbs of the gods.
Some fairer fruits and sweeter fragrances wafted over to us betray
another realm's vicinity. There, too, does Echo dwell, and there is the
abutment of the rainbow's arch.

> A finer race and finer fed
> Feast and revel o'er our head,
> And we titmen are only able
> To catch the fragments from their table.
> Theirs is the fragrance of the fruits,
> While we consume the pulp and roots.
> What are the moments that we stand
> Astonished on the Olympian land!

We need pray for no higher heaven than the pure senses can furnish,
a *purely* sensuous life. Our present senses are but the rudiments of what
they are destined to become. We are comparatively deaf and dumb
and blind, and without smell or taste or feeling. Every generation
makes the discovery that its divine vigor has been dissipated, and each

sense and faculty misapplied and debauched. The ears were made, not for such trivial uses as men are wont to suppose, but to hear celestial sounds. The eyes were not made for such groveling uses as they are now put to and worn out by, but to behold beauty now invisible. May we not *see* God? Are we to be put off and amused in this life, as it were with a mere allegory? Is not Nature, rightly read, that of which she is commonly taken to be the symbol merely? When the common man looks into the sky, which he has not so much profaned, he thinks it less gross than the earth, and with reverence speaks of 'the Heavens,' but the seer will in the same sense speak of 'the Earths,' and his Father who is in them. 'Did not he that made that which is *within* make that which is *without* also?' What is it, then, to educate but to develop these divine germs called the senses? for individuals and states to deal magnanimously with the rising generation, leading it not into temptation — not teach the eye to squint, nor attune the ear to profanity. But where is the instructed teacher? Where are the *normal* schools?

A Hindoo sage said, 'As a dancer, having exhibited herself to the spectator, desists from the dance, so does Nature desist, having manifested herself to soul. Nothing, in my opinion, is more gentle than Nature; once aware of having been seen, she does not again expose herself to the gaze of soul.'

It is easier to discover another such a new world as Columbus did, than to go within one fold of this which we appear to know so well; the land is lost sight of, the compass varies, and mankind mutiny; and still history accumulates like rubbish before the portals of nature. But there is only necessary a moment's sanity and sound senses, to teach us that there is a nature behind the ordinary, in which we have only some vague preëmption right and western reserve as yet. We live on the outskirts of that region. Carved wood, and floating boughs, and sunset skies are all that we know of it. We are not to be imposed on by the longest spell of weather. Let us not, my friends, be wheedled and cheated into good behavior to earn the salt of our eternal porridge, whoever they are that attempt it. Let us wait a little, and not purchase any clearing here, trusting that richer bottoms will soon be put up. It is but thin soil where we stand; I have felt my roots in a richer ere this. I have seen a bunch of violets in a glass vase, tied loosely with a straw, which reminded me of myself.

> I am a parcel of vain strivings tied
>   By a chance bond together,

Dangling this way and that, their links
Were made so loose and wide,
            Methinks
For milder weather.

A bunch of violets without their roots,
And sorrel intermixed,
Encircled by a wisp of straw
Once coiled about their shoots,
            The law
By which I'm fixed.

A nosegay which Time clutched from out
Those fair Elysian fields,
With weeds and broken stems, in haste,
Doth make the rabble rout
            That waste
The day he yields.

And here I bloom for a short hour unseen,
Drinking my juices up,
With no root in the land
To keep my branches green,
            But stand
In a bare cup.

Some tender buds were left upon my stem
In mimicry of life,
But ah! the children will not know,
Till time has withered them,
            The woe
With which they're rife.

But now I see I was not plucked for naught,
And after in life's vase
Of glass set while I might survive,
But by a kind hand brought
            Alive
To a strange place.

That stock thus thinned will soon redeem its hours,
And by another year,
Such as God knows, with freer air,
More fruits and fairer flowers
            Will bear,
While I droop here.

This world has many rings, like Saturn, and we live now on the outmost of them all. None can say deliberately that he inhabits the same sphere, or is contemporary, with the flower which his hands have plucked, and though his feet may seem to crush it, inconceivable spaces and ages separate them, and perchance there is no danger that he will hurt it. What do the botanists know? Our lives should go between the lichen and the bark. The eye may see for the hand, but not for the mind. We are still being born, and have as yet but a dim vision of sea and land, sun, moon, and stars, and shall not see clearly till after nine days at least. That is a pathetic inquiry among travelers and geographers after the site of ancient Troy. It is not near where they think it is. When a thing is decayed and gone, how indistinct must be the place it occupied!

The anecdotes of modern astronomy affect me in the same way as do those faint revelations of the Real which are vouchsafed to men from time to time, or rather from eternity to eternity. When I remember the history of that faint light in our firmament which we call Venus, which ancient men regarded, and which most modern men still regard, as a bright spark attached to a hollow sphere revolving about our earth, but which we have discovered to be *another world,* in itself — how Copernicus, reasoning long and patiently about the matter, predicted confidently concerning it, before yet the telescope had been invented, that if ever men came to see it more clearly than they did then, they would discover that it had phases like our moon, and that within a century after his death the telescope was invented, and that prediction verified, by Galileo — I am not without hope that we may, even here and now, obtain some accurate information concerning that OTHER WORLD which the instinct of mankind has so long predicted. Indeed, all that we call science, as well as all that we call poetry, is a particle of such information, accurate as far as it goes, though it be but to the confines of the truth. If we can reason so accurately, and with such wonderful confirmation of our reasoning, respecting so-called material objects and events infinitely removed beyond the range of our natural vision, so that the mind hesitates to trust its calculations even when they are confirmed by observation, why may not our speculations penetrate as far into the immaterial starry system, of which the former is but the outward and visible type? Surely, we are provided with senses as well fitted to penetrate the spaces of the real, the substantial, the eternal, as these outward are to penetrate the material universe. Veias, Menu, Zoroaster, Socrates, Christ, Shakespeare, Swedenborg — these are some of our astronomers.

There are perturbations in our orbits produced by the influences of outlying spheres, and no astronomer has ever yet calculated the elements of that undiscovered world which produces them. I perceive in the common train of my thoughts a natural and uninterrupted sequence, each implying the next, or, if interruption occurs, it is occasioned by a new object being presented to my *senses*. But a steep, and sudden, and by these means unaccountable transition is that from a comparatively narrow and partial, what is called common-sense view of things, to an infinitely expanded and liberating one, from seeing things as men describe them, to seeing them as men cannot describe them. This implies a sense which is not common, but rare in the wisest man's experience; which is sensible or sentient of more than common.

In what inclosures does the astronomer loiter! His skies are shoal, and imagination, like a thirsty traveler, pants to be through their desert. The roving mind impatiently bursts the fetters of astronomical orbits, like cobwebs in a corner of its universe, and launches itself to where distance fails to follow, and law, such as science has discovered, grows weak and weary. The mind knows a distance and a space of which all those sums combined do not make a unit of measure — the interval between that which *appears* and that which *is*. I know that there are many stars, I know that they are far enough off, bright enough, steady enough in their orbits — but what are they all worth? They are more waste land in the West — star territory — to be made slave States, perchance, if we colonize them. I have interest but for six feet of star, and that interest is transient. Then farewell to all ye bodies, such as I have known ye.

Every man, if he is wise, will stand on such bottom as will sustain him, and if one gravitates downward more strongly than another, he will not venture on those meads where the latter walks securely, but rather leave the cranberries which grow there unraked by himself. Perchance, some spring, a higher freshet will float them within his reach, though they may be watery and frost-bitten by that time. Such shriveled berries I have seen in many a poor man's garret, ay, in many a church-bin and state-coffer, and with a little water and heat they swell again to their original size and fairness, and added sugar enough, stead mankind for sauce to this world's dish.

What is called common sense is excellent in its department, and as invaluable as the virtue of conformity in the army and navy — for there must be subordination — but uncommon sense, that sense which is common only to the wisest, is as much more excellent as it is more rare. Some aspire to excellence in the subordinate department, and may God speed them. What Fuller says of masters of colleges is universally applicable, that 'a little alloy of dullness in a master of a college makes him fitter to manage secular affairs.'

> 'He that wants faith, and apprehends a grief
> Because he wants it, hath a true belief;
> And he that grieves because his grief's so small,
> Has a true grief, and the best Faith of all.'

Or be encouraged by this other poet's strain:

> 'By them went Fido, marshal of the field:
> Weak was his mother when she gave him day;
> And he at first a sick and weakly child,
> As e'er with tears welcomed the sunny ray;
> Yet when more years afford more growth and might,
> A champion stout he was, and puissant knight,
> As ever came in field, or shone in armor bright.
>
> 'Mountains he flings in seas with mighty hand;
> Stops and turns back the sun's impetuous course;
> Nature breaks Nature's laws at his command;
> No force of Hell or Heaven withstands his force;
> Events to come yet many ages hence,
> He present makes, by wondrous prescience;
> Proving the senses blind by being blind to sense.'

'Yesterday, at dawn,' says Hafiz, 'God delivered me from all worldly affliction; and amidst the gloom of night presented me with the water of immortality.'

In the life of Sadi by Dowlat Shah occurs this sentence: 'The eagle of the immaterial soul of Shaikh Sadi shook from his plumage the dust of his body.'

Thus thoughtfully we were rowing homeward to find some autumnal work to do, and help on the revolution of the seasons. Perhaps Nature would condescend to make use of us even without our knowledge, as when we help to scatter her seeds in our walks, and carry burs and cockles on our clothes from field to field.

> All things are current found
> On earthly ground,
> Spirits and elements
> Have their descents.

> Night and day, year on year,
> High and low, far and near,
> These are our own aspects,
> These are our own regrets.
>
> Ye gods of the shore,
> Who abide evermore,
> I see your far headland,
> Stretching on either hand;
>
> I hear the sweet evening sounds
> From your undecaying grounds;
> Cheat me no more with time,
> Take me to your clime.

As it grew later in the afternoon, and we rowed leisurely up the gentle stream, shut in between fragrant and blooming banks, where we had first pitched our tent, and drew nearer to the fields where our lives had passed, we seemed to detect the hues of our native sky in the southwest horizon. The sun was just setting behind the edge of a wooded hill, so rich a sunset as would never have ended but for some reason unknown to men, and to be marked with brighter colors than ordinary in the scroll of time. Though the shadows of the hills were beginning to steal over the stream, the whole river valley undulated with mild light, purer and more memorable than the noon. For so day bids farewell even to solitary vales uninhabited by man. Two herons (*Ardea herodias*), with their long and slender limbs relieved against the sky, were seen traveling high over our heads — their lofty and silent flight, as they were wending their way at evening, surely not to alight in any marsh on the earth's surface, but, perchance, on the other side of our atmosphere, a symbol for the ages to study, whether impressed upon the sky or sculptured amid the hieroglyphics of Egypt. Bound to some northern meadow, they held on their stately, stationary flight, like the storks in the picture, and disappeared at length behind the clouds. Dense flocks of blackbirds were winging their way along the river's course, as if on a short evening pilgrimage to some shrine of theirs, or to celebrate so fair a sunset.

> 'Therefore, as doth the pilgrim, whom the night
> Hastes darkly to imprison on his way,
> Think on thy home, my soul, and think aright
> Of what's yet left thee of life's wasting day:
> Thy sun posts westward, passed is thy morn,
> And twice it is not given thee to be born.'

The sun-setting presumed all men at leisure, and in a contemplative mood; but the farmer's boy only whistled the more thoughtfully as he drove his cows home from pasture, and the teamster refrained from cracking his whip, and guided his team with a subdued voice. The last vestiges of daylight at length disappeared, and as we rowed silently along with our backs toward home through the darkness, only a few stars being visible, we had little to say, but sat absorbed in thought, or in silence listened to the monotonous sound of our oars, a sort of rudimental music, suitable for the ear of Night and the acoustics of her dimly lighted halls;

'Pulsae referunt ad sidera valles,'

and the valleys echoed the sound to the stars.

As we looked up in silence to those distant lights, we were reminded that it was a rare imagination which first taught that the stars are worlds, and had conferred a great benefit on mankind. It is recorded in the Chronicle of Bernaldez that in Columbus's first voyage the natives 'pointed towards the heavens, making signs that they believed that there was all power and holiness.' We have reason to be grateful for celestial phenomena, for they chiefly answer to the ideal in man. The stars are distant and unobtrusive, but bright and enduring as our fairest and most memorable experiences. 'Let the immortal depth of your soul lead you, but earnestly extend your eyes upwards.'

As the truest society approaches always nearer to solitude, so the most excellent speech finally falls into Silence. Silence is audible to all men, at all times, and in all places. She is when we hear inwardly, sound when we hear outwardly. Creation has not displaced her, but is her visible framework and foil. All sounds are her servants, and purveyors, proclaiming not only that their mistress is, but is a rare mistress, and earnestly to be sought after. They are so far akin to Silence that they are but bubbles on her surface, which straightway burst, an evidence of the strength and prolificness of the under-current; a faint utterance of Silence, and then only agreeable to our auditory nerves when they contrast themselves with and relieve the former. In proportion as they do this, and are heighteners and intensifiers of the Silence, they are harmony and purest melody.

Silence is the universal refuge, the sequel to all dull discourses and all foolish acts, a balm to our every chagrin, as welcome after satiety as after disappointment; that background which the painter may not daub, be he master or bungler, and which, however awkward a figure we may have made in the foreground, remains ever our inviolable asylum, where no indignity can assail, no personality disturb us.

The orator puts off his individuality, and is then most eloquent when most silent. He listens while he speaks, and is a hearer along with his audience. Who has not hearkened to her infinite din? She is Truth's speaking-trumpet, the sole oracle, the true Delphi and Dodona, which kings and courtiers would do well to consult, nor will they be balked by an ambiguous answer. For through her all revelations have been made, and just in proportion as men have consulted her oracle within, they have obtained a clear insight, and their age has been marked as an enlightened one. But as often as they have gone gadding abroad to a strange Delphi and her mad priestess, their age has been dark and leaden. Such were garrulous and noisy eras, which no longer yield any sound, but the Grecian or silent and melodious era is ever sounding and resounding in the ears of men.

A good book is the plectrum with which our else silent lyres are struck. We not unfrequently refer the interest which belongs to our own unwritten sequel to the written and comparatively lifeless body of the work. Of all books this sequel is the most indispensable part. It should be the author's aim to say once and emphatically, 'He said,' ἔφη. This is the most the bookmaker can attain to. If he make his volume a mole whereon the waves of Silence may break, it is well.

It were vain for me to endeavor to interpret the Silence. She cannot be done into English. For six thousand years men have translated her with what fidelity belonged to each, and still she is little better than a sealed book. A man may run on confidently for a time, thinking he has her under his thumb, and shall one day exhaust her, but he too must at last be silent, and men remark only how brave a beginning he made; for when he at length dives into her, so vast is the disproportion of the told to the untold that the former will seem but the bubble on the surface where he disappeared. Nevertheless, we will go on, like those Chinese cliff swallows, feathering our nests with the froth which may one day be bread of life to such as dwell by the seashore.

We had made about fifty miles this day with sail and oar, and now, far in the evening, our boat was grating against the bulrushes of its native port, and its keel recognized the Concord mud, where some semblance of its outline was still preserved in the flattened flags which had scarce yet erected themselves since our departure; and we leaped gladly on shore, drawing it up and fastening it to the wild apple tree, whose stem still bore the mark which its chain had worn in the chafing of the spring freshets.

3. WALDEN

WALDEN is Thoreau's masterpiece and by far the most popular of all his works.
It is an account of the two years, two months, and two days he spent living in a
cabin of his own construction on the shores of Walden Pond about a mile and a
half south of the village of Concord from July 4, 1845 until September 6, 1847.
Originally written, for the most part, as a series of lectures to explain to his
fellow townsmen why he, a college graduate, spent his time living in the woods
communing with Nature rather than following a regular profession, it was so
well received on the lecture platform that he worked it over, polishing and
revising it through eight separate complete drafts until after many delays
(occasioned chiefly by the failure of his first book, *A Week on the Concord and Merrimack Rivers*) he persuaded the firm of Ticknor & Fields of Boston (Houghton
Mifflin's direct ancestor) to publish it in 1854. It took five years to sell the
first edition of two thousand copies, but once it was brought back into print
a few weeks after his death in 1862, it has never since gone out of print, has
been published in nearly two hundred different editions, has probably sold
more copies than any other book-length American literary work of nonfiction,
and has been translated into virtually every major modern language.

Despite its popularity, *Walden* is a book that is very easily misread — a fact
that Thoreau himself was well aware of. It was for this reason that he prefaced
the book with an epigraph that is too often overlooked or ignored. It warns,
"I do not propose to write an ode to dejection, but to brag as lustily as chanticleer in the morning, standing on his roost, if only to wake my neighbors up."
He is deliberately trying to wake his readers up from their lives of quiet
desperation. He goads and needles to get his readers to think. Hyperbole is
one of his favorite literary devices and irony another. One must be careful
therefore about always taking him literally. He, for example, is not being
bloodthirsty — as I find an occasional student thinking — when he says, "I
could spit a Mexican with a good relish," but bitterly ironic. I do not mean
to denigrate or undercut what he is saying, for despite his use of humorous and

exaggerative devices, he is deadly serious in his purpose. One should simply keep in mind that Thoreau is an artist who often uses literary devices to get his message across.

Because Thoreau is a literary artist, it has become the fashion to do a great deal of symbol hunting in *Walden*. There is no question but that he did make use of symbols. F. O. Matthiessen, in his masterly *American Renaissance*, demonstrates conclusively how effectively Thoreau made use of such symbols of rebirth as the purification ceremonies of the Indians and the Mexicans, the mysterious apple-tree table bug, and, on a much broader scale, the coming of spring to Walden Pond to underline his major theme of the necessity for every man to undergo a spiritual rebirth. And his famous statement in "Economy" about losing a hound, a bay horse and a turtle dove, has so intrigued his readers that a whole book could be filled with the scholarship written on that one paragraph alone. But, on the other hand, one must be careful not to read in a symbolism that was not there.

One very real contribution modern scholars have made to our appreciation of the artistry of the book is their study of the construction, the architecture of *Walden*. Thoreau was very much concerned with the unity of *Walden*. He telescoped the narrative of his two years' experience into one to better unify it. He carefully alternated wit and high seriousness. He balanced chapters against each other for both subject matter and style. He interlocked each chapter, each paragraph, each sentence so skillfully that none can be moved without damage to the whole. *Walden* is not a book to condense or excerpt. It is a carefully constructed unit.

Although *Walden* can be read as a nature book, a guide to the simple life, a satirical criticism of the foibles of our civilization, or simply as a superbly artistic piece of prose, it is best read as a spiritual autobiography, a *Pilgrim's Progress* to the good life. Henry David Thoreau was constantly in search for the higher values of life. While far from orthodox, he was a deeply religious man. In his chapter on "Reading," he says, "How many a man has dated a new era in his life from the reading of a book," and *Walden* has been just such a book for many people. It can open the doors to a new life if read perceptively. Thomas Wentworth Higginson many years ago said that *Walden* was one of the few books worth reading again every year. If one really reads it once, he will find he must return to it again and again.

I DO NOT PROPOSE TO WRITE AN ODE TO DEJECTION, BUT TO BRAG AS LUSTILY AS CHANTICLEER IN THE MORNING, STANDING ON HIS ROOST, IF ONLY TO WAKE MY NEIGHBORS UP.

I. ECONOMY

WHEN I wrote the following pages, or rather the bulk of them, I lived alone, in the woods, a mile from any neighbor, in a house which I had built myself, on the shore of Walden Pond, in Concord, Massachusetts, and earned my living by the labor of my hands only. I lived there two years and two months. At present I am a sojourner in civilized life again.

I should not obtrude my affairs so much on the notice of my readers if very particular inquiries had not been made by my townsmen concerning my mode of life, which some would call impertinent, though they do not appear to me at all impertinent, but, considering the circumstances, very natural and pertinent. Some have asked what I got to eat; if I did not feel lonesome; if I was not afraid; and the like. Others have been curious to learn what portion of my income I devoted to charitable purposes; and some, who have large families, how many poor children I maintained. I will therefore ask those of my readers who feel no particular interest in me to pardon me if I undertake to answer some of these questions in this book. In most books, the *I*, or first person, is omitted; in this it will be retained; that, in respect to egotism, is the main difference. We commonly do not remember that it is, after all, always the first person that is speaking. I should not talk so much about myself if there were anybody else whom I knew as well. Unfortunately, I am confined to this theme by the narrowness of my experience. Moreover, I, on my side, require of every writer, first or last, a simple and sincere account of his own life, and not merely what he has heard of other men's lives; some such account as he would send to his kindred from a distant land; for if he has lived sincerely, it must have been in a distant land to me. Perhaps these pages are more particularly addressed to poor students. As for the rest of my readers, they will accept such portions as apply to them. I trust that none will stretch the seams in putting on the coat, for it may do good service to him whom it fits.

I would fain say something, not so much concerning the Chinese and Sandwich Islanders as you who read these pages, who are said to live in New England; something about your condition, especially your outward condition or circumstances in this world, in this town, what it is, whether it is necessary that it be as bad as it is, whether it cannot be improved as well as not. I have travelled a good deal in Concord; and everywhere, in shops, and offices, and fields, the inhabitants have appeared to me to be doing penance in a thousand remarkable ways. What I have heard of Bramins sitting exposed to four fires and looking in the face of the sun; or hanging suspended, with their heads downward, over flames; or looking at the heavens over their shoulders 'until it becomes impossible for them to resume their natural position, while from the twist of the neck nothing but liquids can pass into the stomach;' or dwelling, chained for life, at the foot of a tree; or measuring with their bodies, like caterpillars, the breadth of vast empires; or standing on one leg on the tops of pillars — even these forms of conscious penance are hardly more incredible and astonishing than the scenes which I daily witness. The twelve labors of Hercules were trifling in comparison with those which my neighbors have undertaken; for they were only twelve, and had an end; but I could never see that these men slew or captured any monster or finished any labor. They have no friend Iolaus to burn with a hot iron the root of the hydra's head, but as soon as one head is crushed, two spring up.

I see young men, my townsmen, whose misfortune it is to have inherited farms, houses, barns, cattle, and farming tools; for these are more easily acquired than got rid of. Better if they had been born in the open pasture and suckled by a wolf, that they might have seen with clearer eyes what field they were called to labor in. Who made them serfs of the soil? Why should they eat their sixty acres, when man is condemned to eat only his peck of dirt? Why should they begin digging their graves as soon as they are born? They have got to live a man's life, pushing all these things before them, and get on as well as they can. How many a poor immortal soul have I met well-nigh crushed and smothered under its load, creeping down the road of life, pushing before it a barn seventy-five feet by forty, its Augean stables never cleansed, and one hundred acres of land, tillage, mowing, pasture, and wood-lot! The portionless, who struggle with no such unnecessary inherited encumbrances, find it labor enough to subdue and cultivate a few cubic feet of flesh.

But men labor under a mistake. The better part of the man is soon plowed into the soil for compost. By a seeming fate, commonly called necessity, they are employed, as it says in an old book, laying up treasures which moth and rust will corrupt and thieves break through and steal. It is a fool's life, as they will find when they get to the end of it, if not before. It is said that Deucalion and Pyrrha created men by throwing stones over their heads behind them:

> Inde genus durum sumus, experiensque laborum,
> Et documenta damus quâ simus origine nati.

Or, as Raleigh rhymes it in his sonorous way,

> 'From thence our kind hard-hearted is, enduring pain and care,
> Approving that our bodies of a stony nature are.'

So much for a blind obedience to a blundering oracle, throwing the stones over their heads behind them, and not seeing where they fell.

Most men, even in this comparatively free country, through mere ignorance and mistake, are so occupied with the factitious cares and superfluously coarse labors of life that its finer fruits cannot be plucked by them. Their fingers, from excessive toil, are too clumsy and tremble too much for that. Actually, the laboring man has not leisure for a true integrity day by day; he cannot afford to sustain the manliest relations to men; his labor would be depreciated in the market. He has no time to be anything but a machine. How can he remember well his ignorance — which his growth requires — who has so often to use his knowledge? We should feed and clothe him gratuitously sometimes, and recruit him with our cordials, before we judge of him. The finest qualities of our nature, like the bloom on fruits, can be preserved only by the most delicate handling. Yet we do not treat ourselves nor one another thus tenderly.

Some of you, we all know, are poor, find it hard to live, are sometimes, as it were, gasping for breath. I have no doubt that some of you who read this book are unable to pay for all the dinners which you have actually eaten, or for the coats and shoes which are fast wearing or are already worn out, and have come to this page to spend borrowed or stolen time, robbing your creditors of an hour. It is very evident what mean and sneaking lives many of you live, for my sight has been whetted by experience; always on the limits, trying to get into business and trying to get out of debt, a very ancient slough, called by the Latins *aes alienum*, another's brass, for some of their coins were made of brass; still living, and dying, and buried by this other's brass; always promising to pay, promising to pay, tomorrow, and dying today, insolvent; seeking to curry favor, to get custom, by how many modes, only not state-prison offences; lying, flattering, voting, contracting yourselves into a nutshell of civility or dilating into an atmosphere of thin and vaporous generosity, that you may persuade your neighbor to let you make his shoes, or his hat, or his coat, or his carriage, or import his groceries for him; making yourselves sick, that you may lay up something against a sick day, something to be tucked away in an old chest, or in a stocking behind the plastering, or, more safely, in the brick bank; no matter where, no matter how much or how little.

I sometimes wonder that we can be so frivolous, I may almost say, as to attend to the gross but somewhat foreign form of servitude called Negro Slavery, there are so many keen and subtle masters that enslave both North and South. It is hard to have a Southern overseer; it is worse to have a Northern one; but worst of all when you are the slave-driver of yourself. Talk of a divinity in man! Look at the teamster on the highway, wending to market by day or night; does any divinity stir within him? His highest duty to fodder and water his horses! What is his destiny to him compared with the shipping interests? Does not he drive for Squire Make-a-stir? How godlike, how immortal, is he? See how he cowers and sneaks, how vaguely all the day he fears, not being immortal nor divine, but the slave and prisoner of his own opinion of himself, a fame won by his own deeds. Public opinion is a weak tyrant compared with our own private opinion. What a man thinks of himself, that it is which determines, or rather indicates, his fate. Self-emancipation even in the West Indian provinces of the fancy and imagination — what Wilberforce is there to bring that about? Think, also, of the ladies of the land weaving toilet cushions against the last day, not to betray too green an interest in their fates! As if you could kill time without injuring eternity.

The mass of men lead lives of quiet desperation. What is called resignation is confirmed desperation. From the desperate city you go into the desperate country, and have to console yourself with the bravery of minks and muskrats. A stereotyped but unconscious despair is concealed even under what are called the games and amusements of mankind. There is no play in them, for this comes after work. But it is a characteristic of wisdom not to do desperate things.

When we consider what, to use the words of the catechism, is the chief end of man, and what are the true necessaries and means of life, it appears as if men had deliberately chosen the common mode of living because they preferred it to any other. Yet they honestly think there is no choice left. But alert and healthy natures remember that the sun rose clear. It is never too late to give up our prejudices. No way of thinking or doing, however ancient, can be trusted without proof. What everybody echoes or in silence passes by as true today may turn out to be falsehood tomorrow, mere smoke of opinion, which some had trusted for a cloud that would sprinkle fertilizing rain on their fields. What old people say you cannot do, you try and find that you can. Old deeds for old people, and new deeds for new. Old people did not know enough once, perchance, to fetch fresh fuel to keep the fire a-going; new people put a little dry wood under a pot, and are whirled round the globe with the speed of birds, in a way to kill old people, as the phrase is. Age is no better, hardly so well, qualified for an instructor as youth, for it has not profited so much as it has lost. One may almost doubt if the wisest man has learned anything of absolute value by living. Practically, the old have no very important advice to give the young, their own experience has been so partial, and their lives have been such miserable failures, for private reasons, as they must believe; and it may be that they have some faith left which belies that experience, and they are only less young than they were. I have lived some thirty years on this planet, and I have yet to hear the first syllable of valuable or even earnest advice from my seniors. They have told me nothing, and probably cannot tell me anything to the purpose. Here is life, an experiment to a great extent untried by me; but it does not avail me that they have tried it. If I have any experience which I think valuable, I am sure to reflect that this my Mentors said nothing about.

One farmer says to me, 'You cannot live on vegetable food solely, for it furnishes nothing to make bones with;' and so he religiously devotes a part of his day to supplying his system with the raw material of bones; walking all the while he talks behind his oxen, which, with vegetable-made bones, jerk him and his lumbering plow along in spite of every obstacle. Some things are really necessaries of life in some circles, the most helpless and diseased, which in others are luxuries merely, and in others still are entirely unknown.

The whole ground of human life seems to some to have been gone over by their predecessors, both the heights and the valleys, and all things to have been cared for. According to Evelyn, 'the wise Solomon prescribed ordinances for the very distances of trees; and the Roman prætors have decided how often you may go into your neighbor's land to gather the acorns which fall on it without trespass, and what share belongs to that neighbor.' Hippocrates has even left directions how we should cut our nails; that is, even with the ends of the fingers, neither shorter nor longer. Undoubtedly the very tedium and ennui which presume to have exhausted the variety and the joys of life are as old as Adam. But man's capacities have never been measured; nor are we to judge of what he can do by any precedents, so little has been tried. Whatever have been thy failures hitherto, 'be not afflicted, my child, for who shall assign to thee what thou hast left undone?'

We might try our lives by a thousand simple tests; as, for instance, that the same sun which ripens my beans illumines at once a system of earths like ours. If I had remembered this it would have prevented some mistakes. This was not the light in which I hoed them. The stars are the apexes of what wonderful triangles! What distant and different beings in the various mansions of the universe are contemplating the same one at the same moment! Nature and human life are as various as our several constitutions. Who shall say what prospect life offers to another? Could a greater miracle take place than for us to look through each other's eyes for an instant? We should live in all the ages of the world in an hour; ay, in all the worlds of the ages. History, Poetry, Mythology! — I know of no reading of another's experience so startling and informing as this would be.

The greater part of what my neighbors call good I believe in my soul to be bad, and if I repent of anything, it is very likely to be my good behavior. What demon possessed me that I behaved so well? You may say the wisest thing you can, old man — you who have lived seventy years, not without honor of a kind — I hear an irresistible voice which invites me away from all that. One generation abandons the enterprises of another like stranded vessels.

I think that we may safely trust a good deal more than we do. We may waive just so much care of ourselves as we honestly bestow elsewhere. Nature is as well adapted to our weakness as to our strength. The incessant anxiety and strain of some is a well-nigh incurable form of disease. We are made to exaggerate the importance of what work we do; and yet how much is not done by us! or, what if we had been taken sick? How vigilant we are! determined not to live by faith if we can avoid it; all the day long on the alert, at night we unwillingly say our prayers and commit ourselves to uncertainties. So thoroughly and sincerely are we compelled to live, reverencing our life, and denying the possibility of change. This is the only way, we say; but there are as many ways as there can be drawn radii from one centre. All change is a miracle to contemplate; but it is a miracle which is taking place every instant. Confucius said, 'To know that we know what we know, and that we do not know what we do not know, that is true knowledge.' When one man has reduced a fact of the imagination to be a fact to his understanding, I foresee that all men will at length establish their lives on that basis.

Let us consider for a moment what most of the trouble and anxiety which I have referred to is about, and how much it is necessary that we be troubled, or at least careful. It would be some advantage to live a primitive and frontier life, though in the midst of an outward civilization, if only to learn what are the gross necessaries of life and what methods have been taken to obtain them; or even to look over the old day-books of the merchants, to see what it was that men most commonly bought at the stores, what they stored, that is, what are the grossest groceries. For the improvements of ages have had but little influence on the essential laws of man's existence: as our skeletons, probably, are not to be distinguished from those of our ancestors.

By the words, *necessary of life*, I mean whatever, of all that man obtains by his own exertions, has been from the first, or from long use has become, so important to human life that few, if any, whether from savageness, or poverty, or philosophy, ever attempt to do without it. To many creatures there is in this sense but one necessary of life, Food. To the bison of the prairie it is a few inches of palatable grass, with water to drink; unless he seeks the Shelter of the forest or the mountain's shadow. None of the brute creation requires more than Food and Shelter. The necessaries of life for man in this climate may, accurately enough, be distributed under the several heads of Food, Shelter, Clothing, and Fuel; for not till we have secured these are we prepared to entertain the true problems of life with freedom and a prospect of success. Man has invented, not only houses, but clothes and cooked food; and possibly from the accidental discovery of the warmth of fire, and the consequent use of it, at first a luxury, arose the present necessity to sit by it. We observe cats and dogs acquiring the same second nature. By proper Shelter and Clothing we legitimately retain our own internal heat; but with an excess of these, or of Fuel, that is, with an external heat greater than our own internal, may not cookery properly be said to begin? Darwin, the naturalist, says of the inhabitants of Tierra del Fuego, that while his own party, who were well clothed and sitting close to a fire, were far from too warm, these naked savages, who were farther off, were observed, to his great surprise, 'to be streaming with perspiration at undergoing such a roasting.' So, we are told, the New Hollander goes naked with impunity, while the European shivers in his clothes. Is it impossible to combine the hardiness of these savages with the intellectualness of the civilized man? According to Liebig, man's body is a stove, and food the fuel which keeps up the internal combustion in the lungs. In cold weather we eat more, in warm less. The animal heat is the result of a slow combustion, and disease and death take place when this is too rapid; or for want of fuel, or from some defect in the draught, the fire goes out. Of course the vital heat is not to be confounded with fire; but so much for analogy. It appears, therefore, from the above list, that the expression, *animal life,* is nearly synonymous with the expression, *animal heat;* for while Food may be regarded as the Fuel which keeps up the fire within us — and Fuel serves only to prepare that Food or to increase the warmth of our bodies by addition from without — Shelter and Clothing also serve only to retain the *heat* thus generated and absorbed.

The grand necessity, then, for our bodies, is to keep warm, to keep the vital heat in us. What pains we accordingly take, not only with our Food, and Clothing, and Shelter, but with our beds, which are our night-clothes, robbing the nests and breasts of birds to prepare this shelter within a shelter, as the mole has its bed of grass and leaves at the end of its burrow! The poor man is wont to complain that this is a cold world; and to cold, no less physical than social, we refer directly a great part of our ails. The summer, in some climates, makes possible to man a sort of Elysian life. Fuel, except to cook his Food, is then unnecessary; the sun is his fire, and many of the fruits are sufficiently cooked by its rays; while Food generally is more various, and more easily obtained, and Clothing and Shelter are wholly or half unnecessary. At the present day, and in this country, as I find by my own experience, a few implements, a knife, an axe, a spade, a wheelbarrow, etc., and for the studious, lamplight, stationery, and access to a few books, rank next to necessaries, and can all be obtained at a trifling cost. Yet some, not wise, go to the other side of the globe, to barbarous and unhealthy regions, and devote themselves to trade for ten or twenty years, in order that they may live — that is, keep comfortably warm — and die in New England at last. The luxuriously rich are not simply kept comfortably warm, but unnaturally hot; as I implied before, they are cooked, of course *à la mode.*

Most of the luxuries, and many of the so-called comforts of life, are not only not indispensable, but positive hindrances to the elevation of mankind. With respect to luxuries and comforts, the wisest have ever lived a more simple and meagre life than the poor. The ancient philosophers, Chinese, Hindoo, Persian, and Greek, were a class than which none has been poorer in outward riches, none so rich in inward. We know not much about them. It is remarkable that *we* know so much of them as we do. The same is true of the more modern reformers and benefactors of their race. None can be an impartial or wise observer of human life but from the vantage ground of what *we* should call voluntary poverty. Of a life of luxury the fruit is luxury, whether in agriculture, or commerce, or literature, or art. There are nowadays professors of philosophy, but not philosophers. Yet it is admirable to profess because it was once admirable to live. To be a philosopher is not merely to have subtle thoughts, nor even to found a school, but so to love wisdom as to live according to its dictates, a life of simplicity, independence, magnanimity, and trust. It is to solve some of the problems of life, not only theoretically, but practically. The success of great scholars and thinkers is commonly a courtier-like success, not kingly, not manly. They make shift to live merely by conformity, practically as their fathers did, and are in no sense the progenitors of a noble race of men. But why do men degenerate ever? What makes families run out? What is the nature of the luxury which enervates and destroys nations? Are we sure that there is none of it in our own lives? The philosopher is in advance of his age even in the outward form of his life. He is not fed, sheltered, clothed, warmed, like his contemporaries. How can a man be a philosopher and not maintain his vital heat by better methods than other men?

When a man is warmed by the several modes which I have described, what does he want next? Surely not more warmth of the same kind, as more and richer food, larger and more splendid houses, finer and more abundant clothing, more numerous, incessant, and hotter fires, and the like. When he has obtained those things which are necessary to life, there is another alternative than to obtain the superfluities; and that is, to adventure on life now, his vacation from humbler toil having commenced. The soil, it appears, is suited to the seed, for it has sent its radicle downward, and it may now send its shoot upward also with confidence. Why has man rooted himself thus firmly in the earth, but that he may rise in the same proportion into the heavens above? — for the nobler plants are valued for the fruit they bear at last in the air and light, far from the ground, and are not treated like the humbler esculents, which, though they may be biennials, are cultivated only till they have perfected their root, and often cut down at top for this purpose, so that most would not know them in their flowering season.

I do not mean to prescribe rules to strong and valiant natures, who will mind their own affairs whether in heaven or hell, and perchance build more magnificently and spend more lavishly than the richest, without ever impoverishing themselves, not knowing how they live — if, indeed, there are any such, as has been dreamed; nor to those who find their encouragement and inspiration in precisely the present condition of things, and cherish it with the fondness and enthusiasm of lovers — and, to some extent, I reckon myself in this number; I do not speak to those who are well employed, in whatever circumstances, and they know whether they are well employed or not; — but mainly to the mass of men who are discontented, and idly complaining of the hardness of their lot or of the times, when they might improve them. There are some who complain most energetically and inconsolably of any, because they are, as they say, doing their duty. I also have in my mind that seemingly wealthy, but most terribly impoverished class of all, who have accumulated dross, but know not how to use it, or get rid of it, and thus have forged their own golden or silver fetters.

If I should attempt to tell how I have desired to spend my life in years past, it would probably surprise those of my readers who are somewhat acquainted with its actual history; it would certainly astonish those who know nothing about it. I will only hint at some of the enterprises which I have cherished.

In any weather, at any hour of the day or night, I have been anxious to improve the nick of time, and notch it on my stick too; to stand on the meeting of two eternities, the past and future, which is precisely the present moment; to toe that line. You will pardon some obscurities, for there are more secrets in my trade than in most men's, and yet not voluntarily kept, but inseparable from its very nature. I would gladly tell all that I know about it, and never paint 'No Admittance' on my gate.

I long ago lost a hound, a bay horse, and a turtle-dove, and am still on their trail. Many are the travellers I have spoken concerning them, describing their tracks and what calls they answered to. I have met one or two who had heard the hound, and the tramp of the horse, and even seen the dove disappear behind a cloud, and they seemed as anxious to recover them as if they had lost them themselves.

To anticipate, not the sunrise and the dawn merely, but, if possible, Nature herself! How many mornings, summer and winter, before yet any neighbor was stirring about his business, have I been about mine! No doubt, many of my townsmen have met me returning from this enterprise, farmers starting for Boston in the twilight, or woodchoppers going to their work. It is true, I never assisted the sun materially in his rising, but, doubt not, it was of the last importance only to be present at it.

So many autumn, ay, and winter days, spent outside the town, trying to hear what was in the wind, to hear and carry it express! I well-nigh sunk all my capital in it, and lost my own breath into the bargain, running in the face of it. If it had concerned either of the political parties, depend upon it, it would have appeared in the Gazette with the earliest intelligence. At other times watching from the observatory of some cliff or tree, to telegraph any new arrival; or waiting at evening on the hill-tops for the sky to fall, that I might catch something, though I never caught much, and that, manna-wise, would dissolve again in the sun.

For a long time I was reporter to a journal, of no very wide circulation, whose editor has never yet seen fit to print the bulk of my contributions, and, as is too common with writers, I got only my labor for my pains. However, in this case my pains were their own reward.

For many years I was self-appointed inspector of snow-storms and rain-storms, and did my duty faithfully; surveyor, if not of highways, then of forest paths and all across-lot routes, keeping them open, and ravines bridged and passable at all seasons, where the public heel had testified to their utility.

I have looked after the wild stock of the town, which give a faithful herdsman a good deal of trouble by leaping fences; and I have had an eye to the unfrequented nooks and corners of the farm; though I did not always know whether Jonas or Solomon worked in a particular field today; that was none of my business. I have watered the red huckleberry, the sand cherry and the nettle-tree, the red pine and the black ash, the white grape and the yellow violet, which might have withered else in dry seasons.

In short, I went on thus for a long time (I may say it without boasting), faithfully minding my business, till it became more and more evident that my townsmen would not after all admit me into the list of town officers, nor make my place a sinecure with a moderate allowance. My accounts, which I can swear to have kept faithfully, I have, indeed, never got audited, still less accepted, still less paid and settled. However, I have not set my heart on that.

Not long since, a strolling Indian went to sell baskets at the house of a well-known lawyer in my neighborhood. 'Do you wish to buy any baskets?' he asked. 'No, we do not want any,' was the reply. 'What!' exclaimed the Indian as he went out the gate, 'do you mean to starve us?' Having seen his industrious white neighbors so well off — that the lawyer had only to weave arguments, and, by some magic, wealth and standing followed — he had said to himself: I will go into business; I will weave baskets; it is a thing which I can do. Thinking that when he had made the baskets he would have done his part, and then it would be the white man's to buy them. He had not discovered that it was necessary for him to make it worth the other's while to buy them, or at least make him think that it was so, or to make something else which it would be worth his while to buy. I too had woven a kind of basket of a delicate texture, but I had not made it worth any one's while to buy them. Yet not the less, in my case, did I think it worth my while to weave them, and instead of studying how to make it worth men's while to buy my baskets, I studied rather how to avoid the necessity of selling them. The life which men praise and regard as successful is but one kind. Why should we exaggerate any one kind at the expense of the others?

Finding that my fellow-citizens were not likely to offer me any room in the court house, or any curacy or living anywhere else, but I must shift for myself, I turned my face more exclusively than ever to the woods, where I was better known. I determined to go into business at once, and not wait to acquire the usual capital, using such slender means as I had already got. My purpose in going to Walden Pond was not to live cheaply nor to live dearly there, but to transact some private business with the fewest obstacles; to be hindered from accomplishing which for want of a little common sense, a little enterprise and business talent, appeared not so sad as foolish.

I have always endeavored to acquire strict business habits; they are indispensable to every man. If your trade is with the Celestial Empire, then some small counting house on the coast, in some Salem harbor, will be fixture enough. You will export such articles as the country affords, purely native products, much ice and pine timber and a little granite, always in native bottoms. These will be good ventures. To oversee all the details yourself in person; to be at once pilot and captain, and owner and underwriter; to buy and sell and keep the accounts; to read every letter received, and write or read every letter sent; to superintend the discharge of imports night and day; to be upon many parts of the coast almost at the same time — often the richest freight will be discharged upon a Jersey shore; — to be your own telegraph, unweariedly sweeping the horizon, speaking all passing vessels bound coastwise; to keep up a steady despatch of commodities, for the supply of such a distant and exorbitant market; to keep yourself informed of the state of the markets, prospects of war and peace everywhere, and anticipate the tendencies of trade and civilization — taking advantage of the results of all exploring expeditions, using new passages and all improvements in navigation; — charts to be studied, the position of reefs and new lights and buoys to be ascertained, and ever, and ever, the logarithmic tables to be corrected, for by the error of some calculator the vessel often splits upon a rock that should have reached a friendly pier — there is the untold fate of La Pérouse; — universal science to be kept pace with, studying the lives of all great discoverers and navigators, great adventurers and merchants, from Hanno and the Phœnicians down to our day; in fine, account of stock to be taken from time to time, to know how you stand. It is a labor to task the faculties of a man — such problems of profit and loss, of interest, of tare and tret, and gauging of all kinds in it, as demand a universal knowledge.

I have thought that Walden Pond would be a good place for business, not solely on account of the railroad and the ice trade; it offers advantages which it may not be good policy to divulge; it is a good port and a good foundation. No Neva marshes to be filled; though you must everywhere build on piles of your own driving. It is said that a flood-tide, with a westerly wind, and ice in the Neva, would sweep St. Petersburg from the face of the earth.

As this business was to be entered into without the usual capital, it may not be easy to conjecture where those means, that will still be indispensable to every such undertaking, were to be obtained. As for Clothing, to come at once to the practical part of the question, perhaps we are led oftener by the love of novelty and a regard for the opinions of men, in procuring it, than by a true utility. Let him who has work to do recollect that the object of clothing is, first, to retain the vital heat, and secondly, in this state of society, to cover nakedness, and he may judge how much of any necessary or important work may be accomplished without adding to his wardrobe. Kings and queens who wear a suit but once, though made by some tailor or dressmaker to their majesties, cannot know the comfort of wearing a suit that fits. They are no better than wooden horses to hang the clean clothes on. Every day our garments become more assimilated to ourselves, receiving the impress of the wearer's character, until we hesitate to lay them aside without such delay and medical appliances and some such solemnity even as our bodies. No man ever stood the lower in my estimation for having a patch in his clothes; yet I am sure that there is greater anxiety, commonly, to have fashionable, or at least clean and unpatched clothes, than to have a sound conscience. But even if the rent is not mended, perhaps the worst vice betrayed is improvidence. I sometimes try my acquaintances by such tests as this — Who could wear a patch, or two extra seams only, over the knee? Most behave as if they believed that their prospects for life would be ruined if they should do it. It would be easier for them to hobble to town with a broken leg than with a broken pantaloon. Often if an accident happens to a gentleman's legs, they can be mended; but if a similar accident happens to the legs of his pantaloons, there is no help for it; for he considers, not what is truly respectable, but what is respected. We know but few men, a great many coats and breeches. Dress a scarecrow in your last shift, you standing shiftless by, who would not soonest salute the scarecrow? Passing a cornfield the other day, close by a hat and coat on a stake, I recognized the owner of the farm. He was only a little more weather-beaten than when I saw him last. I have heard of a dog that barked at every stranger who approached his master's premises with clothes on, but was easily quieted by a naked thief. It is an interesting question how far men would retain their relative rank if they were divested of their clothes. Could you, in such a case, tell surely of any company of civilized men which belonged to the most respected class? When Madam Pfeiffer, in her adventurous travels round the world, from east to west, had got so near home as Asiatic Russia, she says that she felt the necessity of wearing other than a travelling dress, when she went to meet the authorities, for she 'was now in a civilized country, where . . . people are judged of by their clothes.' Even in our democratic New

England towns the accidental possession of wealth, and its manifestation in dress and equipage alone, obtain for the possessor almost universal respect. But they who yield such respect, numerous as they are, are so far heathen, and need to have a missionary sent to them. Beside, clothes introduced sewing, a kind of work which you may call endless; a woman's dress, at least, is never done.

A man who has at length found something to do will not need to get a new suit to do it in; for him the old will do, that has lain dusty in the garret for an indeterminate period. Old shoes will serve a hero longer than they have served his valet — if a hero ever has a valet — bare feet are older than shoes, and he can make them do. Only they who go to soirées and legislative halls must have new coats, coats to change as often as the man changes in them. But if my jacket and trousers, my hat and shoes, are fit to worship God in, they will do; will they not? Who ever saw his old clothes — his old coat, actually worn out, resolved into its primitive elements, so that it was not a deed of charity to bestow it on some poor boy, by him perchance to be bestowed on some poorer still, or shall we say richer, who could do with less? I say, beware of all enterprises that require new clothes, and not rather a new wearer of clothes. If there is not a new man, how can the new clothes be made to fit? If you have any enterprise before you, try it in your old clothes. All men want, not something to *do with*, but something to *do*, or rather something to *be*. Perhaps we should never procure a new suit, however ragged or dirty the old, until we have so conducted, so enterprised or sailed in some way, that we feel like new men in the old, and that to retain it would be like keeping new wine in old bottles. Our moulting season, like that of the fowls, must be a crisis in our lives. The loon retires to solitary ponds to spend it. Thus also the snake casts its slough, and the caterpillar its wormy coat, by an internal industry and expansion; for clothes are but our outmost cuticle and mortal coil. Otherwise we shall be found sailing under false colors, and be inevitably cashiered at last by our own opinion, as well as that of mankind.

We don garment after garment, as if we grew like exogenous plants by addition without. Our outside and often thin and fanciful clothes are our epidermis, or false skin, which partakes not of our life, and may be stripped off here and there without fatal injury; our thicker garments, constantly worn, are our cellular integument, or cortex; but our shirts are our liber, or true bark, which cannot be removed without girdling and so destroying the man. I believe that all races at some seasons wear something equivalent to the shirt. It is desirable that a man be clad so simply that he can lay his hands on himself in the dark, and that he live in all respects so compactly and preparedly that, if an enemy take the town, he can, like the old philosopher, walk out the gate empty-handed without anxiety. While one thick garment is, for most purposes, as good as three thin ones, and cheap clothing can be obtained at prices really to suit customers; while a thick coat can be bought for five dollars, which will last as many years, thick pantaloons for two dollars, cowhide boots for a dollar and a half a pair, a summer hat for a quarter of a dollar, and a winter cap for sixty-two and a half cents, or a better be made at home at a nominal cost, where is he so poor that, clad in such a suit, *of his own earning*, there will not be found wise men to do him reverence?

When I ask for a garment of a particular form, my tailoress tells me gravely, 'They do not make them so now,' not emphasizing the 'They' at all, as if she quoted an authority as impersonal as the Fates, and I find it difficult to get made what I want, simply because she cannot believe that I mean what I say, that I am so rash. When I hear this oracular sentence, I am for a moment absorbed in thought, emphasizing to myself each word separately that I may come at the meaning of it, that I may find out by what degree of consanguinity *They* are related to *me*, and what authority they may have in an affair which affects me so nearly; and, finally, I am inclined to answer her with equal mystery, and without any more emphasis of the 'they' — 'It is true, they did not make them so recently, but they do now.' Of what use this measuring of me if she does not measure my character, but only the breadth of my shoulders, as it were a peg to hang the coat on? We worship not the Graces, nor the Parcæ, but Fashion. She spins and weaves and cuts with full authority. The head monkey at Paris puts on a traveller's cap, and all the monkeys in America do the same. I sometimes despair of getting anything quite simple and honest done in this world by the help of men. They would have to be passed through a powerful press first, to squeeze their old notions out of them, so that they would not soon get upon their legs again; and then there would be some one in the company with a maggot in his head, hatched from an egg deposited there nobody knows when, for not even fire kills these things, and you would have lost your labor. Nevertheless, we will not forget that some Egyptian wheat was handed down to us by a mummy.

On the whole, I think that it cannot be maintained that dressing has in this or any country risen to the dignity of an art. At present men make shift to wear what they can get. Like shipwrecked sailors, they put on what they can find on the beach, and at a little distance, whether of space or time, laugh at each other's masquerade. Every generation laughs at the old fashions, but follows religiously the new. We are amused at beholding the costume of Henry VIII, or Queen Elizabeth, as much as if it was that of the King and Queen of the Cannibal Islands. All costume off a man is pitiful or grotesque. It is only the serious eye peering from and the sincere life passed within it which restrain laughter and consecrate the costume of any people. Let Harlequin be taken with a fit of the colic and his trappings will have to serve that mood too. When the soldier is hit by a cannon-ball, rags are as becoming as purple.

The childish and savage taste of men and women for new patterns keeps how many shaking and squinting through kaleidoscopes that they may discover the particular figure which this generation requires today. The manufacturers have learned that this taste is merely whimsical. Of two patterns which differ only by a few threads more or less of a particular color, the one will be sold readily, the other lie on the shelf, though it frequently happens that after the lapse of a season the latter becomes the most fashionable. Comparatively, tattooing is not the hideous custom which it is called. It is not barbarous merely because the printing is skin-deep and unalterable.

I cannot believe that our factory system is the best mode by which men may get clothing. The condition of the operatives is becoming every day more like that of the English; and it cannot be wondered at, since, as far as I have heard or observed, the principal object is, not that mankind may be well and honestly clad, but, unquestionably, that the corporations may be enriched. In the long run men hit only what they aim at. Therefore, though they should fail immediately, they had better aim at something high.

As for a Shelter, I will not deny that this is now a necessary of life, though there are instances of men having done without it for long periods in colder countries than this. Samuel Laing says that 'the Laplander in his skin dress, and in a skin bag which he puts over his head and shoulders, will sleep night after night on the snow . . . in a degree of cold which would extinguish the life of one exposed to it in any woollen clothing.' He had seen them asleep thus. Yet he adds, 'They are not hardier than other people.' But, probably, man did not live long on the earth without discovering the convenience which there is in a house, the domestic comforts, which phrase may have originally signified the satisfactions of the house more than of the family; though these must be extremely partial and occasional in those climates where the house is associated in our thoughts with winter or the rainy season chiefly, and two thirds of the year, except for a parasol, is unnecessary. In our climate, in the summer, it was formerly almost solely a covering at night. In the Indian gazettes a wigwam was the symbol of a day's march, and a row of them cut or painted on the bark of a tree signified that so many times they had camped. Man was not made so large limbed and robust but that he must seek to narrow his world, and wall in a space such as fitted him. He was at first bare and out of doors; but though this was pleasant enough in serene and warm weather, by daylight, the rainy season and the winter, to say nothing of the torrid sun, would perhaps have nipped his race in the bud if he had not made haste to clothe himself with the shelter of a house. Adam and Eve, according to the fable, wore the bower before other clothes. Man wanted a home, a place of warmth, or comfort, first of physical warmth, then the warmth of the affections.

We may imagine a time when, in the infancy of the human race, some enterprising mortal crept into a hollow in a rock for shelter. Every child begins the world again, to some extent, and loves to stay outdoors, even in wet and cold. It plays house, as well as horse, having an instinct for it. Who does not remember the interest with which, when young, he looked at shelving rocks, or any approach to a cave? It was the natural yearning of that portion of our most primitive ancestor which still survived in us. From the cave we have advanced to roofs of palm leaves, of bark and boughs, of linen woven and stretched, of grass and straw, of boards and shingles, of stones and tiles. At last, we know not what it is to live in the open air, and our lives are domestic in more senses than we think. From the hearth the field is a great distance. It would be well, perhaps, if we were to spend more of our days and nights without any obstruction between us and the celestial bodies, if the poet did not speak so much from under a roof, or the saint dwell there so long. Birds do not sing in caves, nor do doves cherish their innocence in dovecots.

However, if one designs to construct a dwelling-house, it behooves him to exercise a little Yankee shrewdness, lest after all he find himself in a workhouse, a labyrinth without a clue, a museum, an almshouse, a prison, or a splendid mausoleum instead. Consider first how slight a shelter is absolutely necessary. I have seen Penobscot Indians, in this town, living in tents of thin cotton cloth, while the snow was nearly a foot deep around them, and I thought that they would be glad to have it deeper to keep out the wind. Formerly, when how to get my living honestly, with freedom left for my proper pursuits, was a question which vexed me even more than it does now, for unfortunately I am become somewhat callous, I used to see a large box by the railroad, six feet long by three wide, in which the laborers locked up their tools at night; and it suggested to me that every man who was hard pushed might get such a one for a dollar, and, having bored a few auger holes in it, to admit the air at least, get into it when it rained and at night, and hook down the lid, and so have freedom in his love, and in his soul be free. This did not appear the worst, nor by any means a despicable alternative. You could sit up as late as you pleased, and, whenever you got up, go abroad without any landlord or house-lord dogging you for rent. Many a man is harassed to death to pay the rent of a larger and more luxurious box who would not have frozen to death in such a box as this. I am far from jesting. Economy is a subject which admits of being treated with levity, but it cannot so be disposed of. A comfortable house for a rude and hardy race, that lived mostly out of doors, was once made here almost entirely of such materials as Nature furnished ready to their hands. Gookin, who was superintendent of the Indians subject to the Massachusetts Colony, writing in 1674, says, 'The best of their houses are covered very neatly, tight and warm, with barks of trees, slipped from their bodies at those seasons when the sap is up, and made into great flakes, with pressure of weighty timber, when they are green. . . . The meaner sort are covered with mats which they make of a kind of bulrush, and are also indifferently tight and warm, but not so good as the former. . . . Some I have seen, sixty or a hundred feet long and thirty feet broad. . . . I have often lodged in their wigwams, and found them as warm as the best English houses.' He adds that they were commonly carpeted and lined within with well-wrought embroidered mats, and were furnished with various utensils. The Indians had advanced so far as to regulate the effect of the wind by a mat suspended over the hole in the roof and moved by a string. Such a lodge was in the first instance constructed in a day or two at most, and taken down and put up in a few hours; and every family owned one, or its apartment in one.

In the savage state every family owns a shelter as good as the best, and sufficient for its coarser and simpler wants; but I think that I speak within bounds when I say that, though the birds of the air have their nests, and the foxes their holes, and the savages their wigwams, in modern civilized society not more than one half the families own a shelter. In the large towns and cities, where civilization especially

prevails, the number of those who own a shelter is a very small fraction
of the whole. The rest pay an annual tax for this outside garment of
all, become indispensable summer and winter, which would buy a village
of Indian wigwams, but now helps to keep them poor as long as they
live. I do not mean to insist here on the disadvantage of hiring compared with owning, but it is evident that the savage owns his shelter
because it costs so little, while the civilized man hires his commonly
because he cannot afford to own it; nor can he, in the long run, any
better afford to hire. But, answers one, by merely paying this tax the
poor civilized man secures an abode which is a palace compared with
the savage's. An annual rent of from twenty-five to a hundred dollars
(these are the country rates) entitles him to the benefit of the improvements of centuries, spacious apartments, clean paint and paper, Rum-
ford fireplace, back plastering, Venetian blinds, copper pump, spring
lock, a commodious cellar, and many other things. But how happens
it that he who is said to enjoy these things is so commonly a *poor* civilized
man, while the savage, who has them not, is rich as a savage? If it is
asserted that civilization is a real advance in the condition of man —
and I think that it is, though only the wise improve their advantages —
it must be shown that it has produced better dwellings without making
them more costly; and the cost of a thing is the amount of what I will
call life which is required to be exchanged for it, immediately or in the
long run. An average house in this neighborhood costs perhaps eight
hundred dollars, and to lay up this sum will take from ten to fifteen
years of the laborer's life, even if he is not encumbered with a family —
estimating the pecuniary value of every man's labor at one dollar a day,
for if some receive more, others receive less; — so that he must have
spent more than half his life commonly before *his* wigwam will be
earned. If we suppose him to pay a rent instead, this is but a doubtful
choice of evils. Would the savage have been wise to exchange his wigwam for a palace on these terms?

It may be guessed that I reduce almost the whole advantage of
holding this superfluous property as a fund in store against the future,
so far as the individual is concerned, mainly to the defraying of funeral
expenses. But perhaps a man is not required to bury himself. Nevertheless this points to an important distinction between the civilized man
and the savage; and, no doubt, they have designs on us for our benefit,
in making the life of a civilized people an *institution*, in which the life
of the individual is to a great extent absorbed, in order to preserve and
perfect that of the race. But I wish to show at what a sacrifice this

advantage is at present obtained, and to suggest that we may possibly so live as to secure all the advantage without suffering any of the disadvantage. What mean ye by saying that the poor ye have always with you, or that the fathers have eaten sour grapes, and the children's teeth are set on edge?

'As I live, saith the Lord God, ye shall not have occasion any more to use this proverb in Israel.

'Behold all souls are mine; as the soul of the father, so also the soul of the son is mine: the soul that sinneth, it shall die.'

When I consider my neighbors, the farmers of Concord, who are at least as well off as the other classes, I find that for the most part they have been toiling twenty, thirty, or forty years, that they may become the real owners of their farms, which commonly they have inherited with encumbrances, or else bought with hired money — and we may regard one third of that toil as the cost of their houses — but commonly they have not paid for them yet. It is true, the encumbrances sometimes outweigh the value of the farm, so that the farm itself becomes one great encumbrance, and still a man is found to inherit it, being well acquainted with it, as he says. On applying to the assessors, I am surprised to learn that they cannot at once name a dozen in the town who own their farms free and clear. If you would know the history of these homesteads, inquire at the bank where they are mortgaged. The man who has actually paid for his farm with labor on it is so rare that every neighbor can point to him. I doubt if there are three such men in Concord. What has been said of the merchants, that a very large majority, even ninety-seven in a hundred, are sure to fail, is equally true of the farmers. With regard to the merchants, however, one of them says pertinently that a great part of their failures are not genuine pecuniary failures, but merely failures to fulfil their engagements, because it is inconvenient; that is, it is the moral character that breaks down. But this puts an infinitely worse face on the matter, and suggests, beside, that probably not even the other three succeed in saving their souls, but are perchance bankrupt in a worse sense than they who fail honestly. Bankruptcy and repudiation are the spring-boards from which much of our civilization vaults and turns its somersets, but the savage stands on the unelastic plank of famine. Yet the Middlesex Cattle Show goes off here with *éclat* annually, as if all the joints of the agricultural machine were suent.

The farmer is endeavoring to solve the problem of a livelihood by a formula more complicated than the problem itself. To get his shoestrings he speculates in herds of cattle. With consummate skill he has set his trap with a hair springe to catch comfort and independence, and then, as he turned away, got his own leg into it. This is the reason he is poor; and for a similar reason we are all poor in respect to a thousand savage comforts, though surrounded by luxuries. As Chapman sings,

'The false society of men —
—— — for earthly greatness
All heavenly comforts rarefies to air.'

And when the farmer has got his house, he may not be the richer but the poorer for it, and it be the house that has got him. As I understand it, that was a valid objection urged by Momus against the house which Minerva made, that she 'had not made it movable, by which means a bad neighborhood might be avoided;' and it may still be urged, for our houses are such unwieldy property that we are often imprisoned rather than housed in them; and the bad neighborhood to be avoided is our own scurvy selves. I know one or two families, at least, in this town, who, for nearly a generation, have been wishing to sell their houses in the outskirts and move into the village, but have not been able to accomplish it, and only death will set them free.

Granted that the *majority* are able at last either to own or hire the modern house with all its improvements. While civilization has been improving our houses, it has not equally improved the men who are to inhabit them. It has created palaces, but it was not so easy to create noblemen and kings. And *if the civilized man's pursuits are no worthier than the savage's, if he is employed the greater part of his life in obtaining gross necessaries and comforts merely, why should he have a better dwelling than the former ?*

But how do the poor *minority* fare? Perhaps it will be found that just in proportion as some have been placed in outward circumstances above the savage, others have been degraded below him. The luxury of one class is counterbalanced by the indigence of another. On the one side is the palace, on the other are the almshouse and 'silent poor.' The myriads who built the pyramids to be the tombs of the Pharaohs were fed on garlic, and it may be were not decently buried themselves. The mason who finishes the cornice of the palace returns at night perchance to a hut not so good as a wigwam. It is a mistake to suppose that, in a country where the usual evidences of civilization exist, the condition of a very large body of the inhabitants may not be as degraded as that of savages. I refer to the degraded poor, not now to the degraded rich.

To know this I should not need to look farther than to the shanties which everywhere border our railroads, that last improvement in civilization; where I see in my daily walks human beings living in sties, and all winter with an open door, for the sake of light, without any visible, often imaginable, wood-pile, and the forms of both old and young are permanently contracted by the long habit of shrinking from cold and misery, and the development of all their limbs and faculties is checked. It certainly is fair to look at that class by whose labor the works which distinguish this generation are accomplished. Such too, to a greater or less extent, is the condition of the operatives of every denomination in England, which is the great workhouse of the world. Or I could refer you to Ireland, which is marked as one of the white or enlightened spots on the map. Contrast the physical condition of the Irish with that of the North American Indian, or the South Sea Islander, or any other savage race before it was degraded by contact with the civilized man. Yet I have no doubt that that people's rulers are as wise as the average of civilized rulers. Their condition only proves what squalidness may consist with civilization. I hardly need refer now to the laborers in our Southern States who produce the staple exports of this country, and are themselves a staple production of the South. But to confine myself to those who are said to be in *moderate* circumstances.

Most men appear never to have considered what a house is, and are actually though needlessly poor all their lives because they think that they must have such a one as their neighbors have. As if one were to wear any sort of coat which the tailor might cut out for him, or, gradually leaving off palm-leaf hat or cap of woodchuck skin, complain of hard times because he could not afford to buy him a crown! It is possible to invent a house still more convenient and luxurious than we have, which yet all would admit that man could not afford to pay for. Shall we always study to obtain more of these things, and not sometimes to be content with less? Shall the respectable citizen thus gravely teach, by precept and example, the necessity of the young man's providing a certain number of superfluous glow-shoes, and umbrellas, and empty guest chambers for empty guests, before he dies? Why should not our furniture be as simple as the Arab's or the Indian's? When I think of the benefactors of the race, whom we have apotheosized as messengers from heaven, bearers of divine gifts to man, I do not see in my mind any retinue at their heels, any carload of fashionable furniture. Or what if I were to allow — would it not be a singular allowance? — that our furniture should be more complex than the Arab's, in proportion as we are morally and intellectually his superiors! At present our houses are cluttered and defiled with it, and a good housewife would sweep out the greater part into the dust hole, and not leave her morning's work undone. Morning work! By the blushes of Aurora and the music of Memnon, what should be man's *morning work* in this world? I had three pieces of limestone on my desk, but I was terrified to find that they required to be dusted daily, when the furniture of my mind was all undusted still, and I threw them out the window in disgust. How, then, could I have a furnished house? I would rather sit in the open air, for no dust gathers on the grass, unless where man has broken ground.

It is the luxurious and dissipated who set the fashions which the herd so diligently follow. The traveller who stops at the best houses, so called, soon discovers this, for the publicans presume him to be a Sardanapalus, and if he resigned himself to their tender mercies he would soon be completely emasculated. I think that in the railroad car we are inclined to spend more on luxury than on safety and convenience, and it threatens without attaining these to become no better than a modern drawing-room, with its divans, and ottomans, and sunshades, and a hundred other oriental things, which we are taking west with us, invented for the ladies of the harem and the effeminate natives of the Celestial Empire, which Jonathan should be ashamed to know the names of. I would rather sit on a pumpkin and have it all to myself than be crowded on a velvet cushion. I would rather ride on earth in an ox cart, with a free circulation, than go to heaven in the fancy car of an excursion train and breathe a *malaria* all the way.

The very simplicity and nakedness of man's life in the primitive ages imply this advantage, at least, that they left him still but a sojourner in nature. When he was refreshed with food and sleep, he contemplated his journey again. He dwelt, as it were, in a tent in this world, and was either threading the valleys, or crossing the plains, or climbing the mountain-tops. But lo! men have become the tools of their tools. The man who independently plucked the fruits when he was hungry is become a farmer; and he who stood under a tree for shelter, a housekeeper. We now no longer camp as for a night, but have settled down on earth and forgotten heaven. We have adopted Christianity merely as an improved method of *agri*-culture. We have built for this world a family mansion, and for the next a family tomb. The best works of art are the expression of man's struggle to free himself from this condition, but the effect of our art is merely to make this low state comfortable and that higher state to be forgotten. There is actually no place in this village for a work of *fine* art, if any had come down to us, to stand, for our lives, our houses and streets, furnish no proper pedestal for it. There is not a nail to hang a picture on, nor a shelf to receive the bust of a hero or a saint. When I consider how our houses are built and paid for, or not paid for, and their internal economy managed and sustained, I wonder that the floor does not give way under the visitor while he is admiring the gewgaws upon the mantelpiece, and let him through into the cellar, to some solid and honest though earthy foundation. I cannot but perceive that this so-called rich and refined life is a thing jumped at, and I do not get on in the enjoyment of the *fine* arts which adorn it, my attention being wholly occupied with the jump; for I remember that the greatest genuine leap, due to human muscles alone, on record, is that of certain wandering Arabs, who are said to have cleared twenty-five feet on level ground. Without factitious support, man is sure to come to earth again beyond that distance. The first question which I am tempted to put to the proprietor of such great impropriety is, Who bolsters you? Are you one of the ninety-seven who fail, or the three who succeed? Answer me these questions, and then perhaps I may look at your bawbles and find them ornamental. The cart before the horse is neither beautiful nor useful. Before we can adorn our houses with beautiful objects the walls must be stripped, and our lives must be stripped, and beautiful housekeeping and beautiful living be laid for a foundation: now, a taste for the beautiful is most cultivated out of doors, where there is no house and no housekeeper.

Old Johnson, in his 'Wonder-Working Providence,' speaking of the first settlers of this town, with whom he was contemporary, tells us that 'they burrow themselves in the earth for their first shelter under some hillside, and, casting the soil aloft upon timber, they make a smoky fire against the earth, at the highest side.' They did not 'provide them houses,' says he, 'till the earth, by the Lord's blessing, brought forth bread to feed them,' and the first year's crop was so light that 'they were forced to cut their bread very thin for a long season.' The secretary of the Province of New Netherland, writing in Dutch, in 1650, for the information of those who wished to take up land there, states more particularly that 'those in New Netherland, and especially in New England, who have no means to build farmhouses at first according to their wishes, dig a square pit in the ground, cellar fashion, six or seven feet deep, as long and as broad as they think proper, case the earth inside with wood all round the wall, and line the wood with the bark of trees or something else to prevent the caving in of the earth; floor this cellar with plank, and wainscot it overhead for a ceiling, raise a roof of spars clear up, and cover the spars with bark or green sods, so that they can live dry and warm in these houses with their entire families for two, three, and four years, it being understood that partitions are run through those cellars which are adapted to the size of the family. The wealthy and principal men in New England, in the beginning of the colonies, commenced their first dwelling-houses in this fashion for two reasons: firstly, in order not to waste time in building, and not to want food the next season; secondly, in order not to discourage poor laboring people whom they brought over in numbers from Fatherland. In the course of three or four years, when the country became adapted to agriculture, they built themselves handsome houses, spending on them several thousands.'

In this course which our ancestors took there was a show of prudence at least, as if their principle were to satisfy the more pressing wants first. But are the more pressing wants satisfied now? When I think of acquiring for myself one of our luxurious dwellings, I am deterred, for, so to speak, the country is not yet adapted to *human* culture, and we are still forced to cut our *spiritual* bread far thinner than our forefathers did their wheaten. Not that all architectural ornament is to be neglected even in the rudest periods; but let our houses first be lined with beauty, where they come in contact with our lives, like the tenement of the shellfish, and not overlaid with it. But, alas! I have been inside one or two of them, and know what they are lined with.

Though we are not so degenerate but that we might possibly live in a cave or a wigwam or wear skins today, it certainly is better to accept the advantages, though so dearly bought, which the invention and industry of mankind offer. In such a neighborhood as this, boards and shingles, lime and bricks, are cheaper and more easily obtained than suitable caves, or whole logs, or bark in sufficient quantities, or even well-tempered clay or flat stones. I speak understandingly on this subject, for I have made myself acquainted with it both theoretically and practically. With a little more wit we might use these materials so as to become richer than the richest now are, and make our civilization a blessing. The civilized man is a more experienced and wiser savage. But to make haste to my own experiment.

Near the end of March, 1845, I borrowed an axe and went down to the woods by Walden Pond, nearest to where I intended to build my house, and began to cut down some tall, arrowy white pines, still in their youth, for timber. It is difficult to begin without borrowing, but perhaps it is the most generous course thus to permit your fellow-men to have an interest in your enterprise. The owner of the axe, as he released his hold on it, said that it was the apple of his eye; but I returned it sharper than I received it. It was a pleasant hillside where I worked, covered with pine woods, through which I looked out on the pond, and a small open field in the woods where pines and hickories were springing up. The ice in the pond was not yct dissolved, though there were some open spaces, and it was all dark-colored and saturated with water. There were some slight flurries of snow during the days that I worked there; but for the most part when I came out on to the railroad, on my way home, its yellow sand-heap stretched away gleaming in the hazy atmosphere, and the rails shone in the spring sun, and I heard the lark and pewee and other birds already come to commence another year with us. They were pleasant spring days, in which the winter of man's discontent was thawing as well as the earth, and the life that had lain torpid began to stretch itself. One day, when my axe had come off and I had cut a green hickory for a wedge, driving it with a stone, and had placed the whole to soak in a pond-hole in order to swell the wood, I saw a striped snake run into the water, and he lay on the bottom, apparently without inconvenience, as long as I stayed there, or more than a quarter of an hour; perhaps because he had not yet fairly come out of the torpid state. It appeared to me that for a like reason men remain in their present low and primitive condition; but if they should feel the influence of the spring of springs arousing them, they would of necessity rise to a higher and more ethereal life. I had previously seen the snakes in frosty mornings in my path with portions of their bodies still numb and inflexible, waiting for the sun to thaw them. On the 1st of April it rained and melted the ice, and in the early part of the day, which was very foggy, I heard a stray goose groping about over the pond and cackling as if lost, or like the spirit of the fog.

So I went on for some days cutting and hewing timber, and also studs and rafters, all with my narrow axe, not having many communicable or scholar-like thoughts, singing to myself,

> Men say they know many things;
> But lo! they have taken wings —
> The arts and sciences,
> And a thousand appliances;
> The wind that blows
> Is all that anybody knows.

I hewed the main timbers six inches square, most of the studs on two sides only, and the rafters and floor timbers on one side, leaving the rest of the bark on, so that they were just as straight and much stronger than sawed ones. Each stick was carefully mortised or tenoned by its stump, for I had borrowed other tools by this time. My days in the woods were not very long ones; yet I usually carried my dinner of bread and butter, and read the newspaper in which it was wrapped, at noon, sitting amid the green pine boughs which I had cut off, and to my bread was imparted some of their fragrance, for my hands were covered with a thick coat of pitch. Before I had done I was more the friend than the foe of the pine tree, though I had cut down some of them, having become better acquainted with it. Sometimes a rambler in the wood was attracted by the sound of my axe, and we chatted pleasantly over the chips which I had made.

By the middle of April, for I made no haste in my work, but rather made the most of it, my house was framed and ready for the raising. I had already bought the shanty of James Collins, an Irishman who worked on the Fitchburg Railroad, for boards. James Collins' shanty was considered an uncommonly fine one. When I called to see it he was not at home. I walked about the outside, at first unobserved from within, the window was so deep and high. It was of small dimensions, with a peaked cottage roof, and not much else to be seen, the dirt being raised five feet all around as if it were a compost heap. The roof was the soundest part, though a good deal warped and made brittle by the sun. Doorsill there was none, but a perennial passage for the hens under the door-board. Mrs. C. came to the door and asked me to view it from the inside. The hens were driven in by my approach. It was dark, and had a dirt floor for the most part, dank, clammy, and aguish, only here a board and there a board which would not bear removal. She lighted a lamp to show me the inside of the roof and the walls, and also that the board floor extended under the bed, warning me not to step into the cellar, a sort of dust hole two feet deep. In her own words, they were 'good boards overhead, good boards all around, and a good window' — of two whole squares originally, only the cat had passed out that way lately. There was a stove, a bed, and a place to sit, an infant in the house where it was born, a silk parasol, gilt-framed looking-glass, and a patent new coffee-mill nailed to an oak sapling, all told. The bargain was soon concluded, for James had in the meanwhile returned. I to pay four dollars and twenty-five cents tonight, he to vacate at five tomorrow morning, selling to nobody else meanwhile:

I to take possession at six. It were well, he said, to be there early, and anticipate certain indistinct but wholly unjust claims on the score of ground rent and fuel. This he assured me was the only encumbrance. At six I passed him and his family on the road. One large bundle held their all — bed, coffee-mill, looking-glass, hens — all but the cat; she took to the woods and became a wild cat, and, as I learned afterward, trod in a trap set for woodchucks, and so became a dead cat at last.

I took down this dwelling the same morning, drawing the nails, and removed it to the pond-side by small cartloads, spreading the boards on the grass there to bleach and warp back again in the sun. One early thrush gave me a note or two as I drove along the woodland path. I was informed treacherously by a young Patrick that neighbor Seeley, an Irishman, in the intervals of the carting, transferred the still tolerable, straight, and drivable nails, staples, and spikes to his pocket, and then stood when I came back to pass the time of day, and look freshly up, unconcerned, with spring thoughts, at the devastation; there being a dearth of work, as he said. He was there to represent spectatordom, and help make this seemingly insignificant event one with the removal of the gods of Troy.

I dug my cellar in the side of a hill sloping to the south, where a woodchuck had formerly dug his burrow, down through sumach and blackberry roots, and the lowest stain of vegetation, six feet square by seven deep, to a fine sand where potatoes would not freeze in any winter. The sides were left shelving, and not stoned; but the sun having never shone on them, the sand still keeps its place. It was but two hours' work. I took particular pleasure in this breaking of ground, for in almost all latitudes men dig into the earth for an equable temperature. Under the most splendid house in the city is still to be found the cellar where they store their roots as of old, and long after the superstructure has disappeared posterity remark its dent in the earth. The house is still but a sort of porch at the entrance of a burrow.

At length, in the beginning of May, with the help of some of my acquaintances, rather to improve so good an occasion for neighborliness than from any necessity, I set up the frame of my house. No man was ever more honored in the character of his raisers than I. They are destined, I trust, to assist at the raising of loftier structures one day. I began to occupy my house on the 4th of July, as soon as it was boarded and roofed, for the boards were carefully feather-edged and lapped, so that it was perfectly impervious to rain, but before boarding I laid the foundation of a chimney at one end, bringing two cartloads of stones up

the hill from the pond in my arms. I built the chimney after my hoeing
in the fall, before a fire became necessary for warmth, doing my cooking
in the meanwhile out of doors on the ground, early in the morning:
which mode I still think is in some respects more convenient and agreeable than the usual one. When it stormed before my bread was baked,
I fixed a few boards over the fire, and sat under them to watch my
loaf, and passed some pleasant hours in that way. In those days, when
my hands were much employed, I read but little, but the least scraps of
paper which lay on the ground, my holder, or tablecloth, afforded me
as much entertainment, in fact answered the same purpose as the Iliad.

It would be worth the while to build still more deliberately than I did,
considering, for instance, what foundation a door, a window, a cellar,
a garret, have in the nature of man, and perchance never raising any
superstructure until we found a better reason for it than our temporal
necessities even. There is some of the same fitness in a man's building
his own house that there is in a bird's building its own nest. Who knows
but if men constructed their dwellings with their own hands, and provided food for themselves and families simply and honestly enough, the
poetic faculty would be universally developed, as birds universally sing
when they are so engaged? But alas! we do like cowbirds and cuckoos,
which lay their eggs in nests which other birds have built, and cheer no
traveller with their chattering and unmusical notes. Shall we forever
resign the pleasure of construction to the carpenter? What does archi
tecture amount to in the experience of the mass of men? I never in all
my walks came across a man engaged in so simple and natural an
occupation as building his house. We belong to the community. It
is not the tailor alone who is the ninth part of a man; it is as much the
preacher, and the merchant, and the farmer. Where is this division
of labor to end? and what object does it finally serve? No doubt another
may also think for me; but it is not therefore desirable that he should
do so to the exclusion of my thinking for myself.

True, there are architects so called in this country, and I have heard
of one at least possessed with the idea of making architectural ornaments
have a core of truth, a necessity, and hence a beauty, as if it were a
revelation to him. All very well perhaps from his point of view, but
only a little better than the common dilettantism. A sentimental reformer in architecture, he began at the cornice, not at the foundation.
It was only how to put a core of truth within the ornaments, that every
sugarplum, in fact, might have an almond or caraway seed in it —

though I hold that almonds are most wholesome without the sugar —
and not how the inhabitant, the indweller, might build truly within
and without, and let the ornaments take care of themselves. What
reasonable man ever supposed that ornaments were something outward
and in the skin merely — that the tortoise got his spotted shell, or the
shell-fish its mother-o'-pearl tints, by such a contract as the inhabitants
of Broadway their Trinity Church? But a man has no more to do with
the style of architecture of his house than a tortoise with that of its shell:
nor need the soldier be so idle as to try to paint the precise *color* of his
virtue on his standard. The enemy will find it out. He may turn pale
when the trial comes. This man seemed to me to lean over the cornice,
and timidly whisper his half truth to the rude occupants who really
knew it better than he. What of architectural beauty I now see, I know
has gradually grown from within outward, out of the necessities and
character of the indweller, who is the only builder — out of some unconscious truthfulness, and nobleness, without ever a thought for the
appearance and whatever additional beauty of this kind is destined
to be produced will be preceded by a like unconscious beauty of life.
The most interesting dwellings in this country, as the painter knows,
are the most unpretending, humble log huts and cottages of the poor
commonly; it is the life of the inhabitants whose shells they are, and
not any peculiarity in their surfaces merely, which makes them *picturesque;* and equally interesting will be the citizen's suburban box, when
his life shall be as simple and as agreeable to the imagination, and there
is as little straining after effect in the style of his dwelling. A great
proportion of architectural ornaments are literally hollow, and a
September gale would strip them off, like borrowed plumes, without
injury to the substantials. They can do without *architecture* who have
no olives nor wines in the cellar. What if an equal ado were made
about the ornaments of style in literature, and the architects of our
bibles spent as much time about their cornices as the architects of our
churches do? So are made the *belles-lettres* and the *beaux-arts* and their
professors. Much it concerns a man, forsooth, how a few sticks are
slanted over him or under him, and what colors are daubed upon his
box. It would signify somewhat, if, in any earnest sense, *he* slanted
them and daubed it; but the spirit having departed out of the tenant,
it is of a piece with constructing his own coffin — the architecture of
the grave — and 'carpenter' is but another name for 'coffin-maker.'
One man says, in his despair or indifference to life, take up a handful
of the earth at your feet, and paint your house that color. Is he thinking

of his last and narrow house? Toss up a copper for it as well. What an abundance of leisure he must have! Why do you take up a handful of dirt? Better paint your house your own complexion; let it turn pale or blush for you. An enterprise to improve the style of cottage architecture! When you have got my ornaments ready, I will wear them.

Before winter I built a chimney, and shingled the sides of my house, which were already impervious to rain, with imperfect and sappy shingles made of the first slice of the log, whose edges I was obliged to straighten with a plane.

I have thus a tight shingled and plastered house, ten feet wide by fifteen long, and eight-feet posts, with a garret and' a closet, a large window on each side, two trap-doors, one door at the end, and a brick fireplace opposite. The exact cost of my house, paying the usual price for such materials as I used, but not counting the work, all of which was done by myself, was as follows; and I give the details because very few are able to tell exactly what their houses cost, and fewer still, if any, the separate cost of the various materials which compose them:

Boards	. $8 03½,	mostly shanty boards.
Refuse shingles for roof and sides	. 4 00	
Laths	. 1 25	
Two second-hand windows with glass	. 2 43	
One thousand old brick	. 4 00	
Two casks of lime	. 2 40	That was high.
Hair	. 0 31	More than I needed.
Mantle-tree iron	. 0 15	
Nails	. 3 90	
Hinges and screws	. 0 14	
Latch	. 0 10	
Chalk	. 0 01	
Transportation	. 1 40	{ I carried a good part on my back.
In all	$28 12½	

These are all the materials, excepting the timber, stones, and sand, which I claimed by squatter's right. I have also a small woodshed adjoining, made chiefly of the stuff which was left after building the house.

I intend to build me a house which will surpass any on the main street in Concord in grandeur and luxury, as soon as it pleases me as much and will cost me no more than my present one.

I thus found that the student who wishes for a shelter can obtain one for a lifetime at an expense not greater than the rent which he now pays annually. If I seem to boast more than is becoming, my excuse is that I brag for humanity rather than for myself; and my shortcomings and inconsistencies do not affect the truth of my statement. Notwithstanding much cant and hypocrisy — chaff which I find it difficult to separate from my wheat, but for which I am as sorry as any man — I will breathe freely and stretch myself in this respect, it is such a relief to both the moral and physical system; and I am resolved that I will not through humility become the devil's attorney. I will endeavor to speak a good word for the truth. At Cambridge College the mere rent of a student's room, which is only a little larger than my own, is thirty dollars each year, though the corporation had the advantage of building thirty-two side by side and under one roof, and the occupant suffers the inconvenience of many and noisy neighbors, and perhaps a residence in the fourth story. I cannot but think that if we had more true wisdom in these respects, not only less education would be needed, because, forsooth, more would already have been acquired, but the pecuniary expense of getting an education would in a great measure vanish. Those conveniences which the student requires at Cambridge or elsewhere cost him or somebody else ten times as great a sacrifice of life as they would with proper management on both sides. Those things for which the most money is demanded are never the things which the student most wants. Tuition, for instance, is an important item in the term bill, while for the far more valuable education which he gets by associating with the most cultivated of his contemporaries no charge is made. The mode of founding a college is, commonly, to get up a subscription of dollars and cents, and then, following blindly the principles of a division of labor to its extreme — a principle which should never be followed but with circumspection — to call in a contractor who makes this a subject of speculation, and he employs Irishmen or other operatives actually to lay the foundations, while the students that are to be are said to be fitting themselves for it; and for these oversights successive generations have to pay. I think that it would be *better than this*, for the students, or those who desire to be benefited by it, even to lay the foundation themselves. The student who secures his coveted leisure and retirement by systematically shirking any labor necessary to man obtains but an ignoble and unprofitable leisure, defrauding himself of the experience which alone can make leisure fruitful. 'But,' says one, 'you do not mean that the students should go to work with their hands instead of their heads?' I do not mean that exactly, but I mean something which he might think a good deal like that; I mean that they should not *play* life, or *study* it merely, while the community supports them at this expensive game, but earnestly *live* it from beginning to end. How could youths better learn to live than by at once trying the experiment of living? Methinks this would exercise their minds as much as mathematics. If I wished a boy to know something about the arts and sciences, for instance, I would not pursue the common course, which is merely to send him into the neighborhood of some professor, where anything is professed and practised but the art of life; — to survey the world through a telescope or a microscope, and never with his natural eye; to study chemistry, and not learn how his bread is made, or mechanics, and not learn how it is earned; to discover new satellites to Neptune, and not detect the motes in his eyes, or to what vagabond he is a satellite himself; or to be devoured by the monsters that swarm all around him, while contemplating the monsters in a drop of vinegar. Which would have advanced the most at the end of a month — the boy who had made his own jackknife from the ore which he had dug and smelted, reading as much as would be necessary for this — or the boy who had attended the lectures on metallurgy at the Institute in the meanwhile, and had received a Rodgers penknife from his father? Which would be most likely to cut his fingers?... To my astonishment I was informed on leaving college that I had studied navigation! — why, if I had taken one turn down the harbor I should have known more about it. Even the *poor* student studies and is taught only *political* economy, while that economy of living which is synonymous with philosophy is not even sincerely professed in our colleges. The consequence is, that while he is reading Adam Smith, Ricardo, and Say, he runs his father in debt irretrievably.

As with our colleges, so with a hundred 'modern improvements;' there is an illusion about them; there is not always a positive advance. The devil goes on exacting compound interest to the last for his early share and numerous succeeding investments in them. Our inventions are wont to be pretty toys, which distract our attention from serious things. They are but improved means to an unimproved end, an end which it was already but too easy to arrive at; as railroads lead to Boston or New York. We are in great haste to construct a magnetic telegraph from Maine to Texas; but Maine and Texas, it may be, have nothing important to communicate. Either is in such a predicament as the man who was earnest to be introduced to a distinguished deaf woman, but when he was presented, and one end of her ear trumpet was put into his hand, had nothing to say. As if the main object were to talk fast and not to talk sensibly. We are eager to tunnel under the Atlantic and bring the Old World some weeks nearer to the New; but perchance the first news that will leak through into the broad, flapping American ear will be that the Princess Adelaide has the whooping cough. After all, the man whose horse trots a mile in a minute does not carry the most important messages; he is not an evangelist, nor does he come round eating locusts and wild honey. I doubt if Flying Childers ever carried a peck of corn to mill.

One says to me, 'I wonder that you do not lay up money; you love to travel; you might take the cars and go to Fitchburg today and see the country.' But I am wiser than that. I have learned that the swiftest traveller is he that goes afoot. I say to my friend, Suppose we try who will get there first. The distance is thirty miles; the fare ninety cents. That is almost a day's wages. I remember when wages were sixty cents a day for laborers on this very road. Well, I start now on foot, and get there before night; I have travelled at that rate by the week together. You will in the meanwhile have earned your fare, and arrive there some time tomorrow, or possibly this evening, if you are lucky enough to get a job in season. Instead of going to Fitchburg, you will be working here the greater part of the day. And so, if the railroad reached round the world, I think that I should keep ahead of you; and as for seeing the country and getting experience of that kind, I should have to cut your acquaintance altogether.

Such is the universal law, which no man can ever outwit, and with regard to the railroad even we may say it is as broad as it is long. To make a railroad round the world available to all mankind is equivalent to grading the whole surface of the planet. Men have an indistinct notion that if they keep up this activity of joint stocks and spades long enough all will at length ride somewhere, in next to no time, and for nothing; but though a crowd rushes to the depot, and the conductor shouts 'All aboard!' when the smoke is blown away and the vapor condensed, it will be perceived that a few are riding, but the rest are run over — and it will be called, and will be, 'A melancholy accident.' No doubt they can ride at last who shall have earned their fare, that is, if they survive so long, but they will probably have lost their elasticity and desire to travel by that time. This spending of the best part of one's life earning money in order to enjoy a questionable liberty during the least valuable part of it reminds me of the Englishman who went to India to make a fortune first, in order that he might return to England and live the life of a poet. He should have gone up garret at once.

'What!' exclaim a million Irishmen starting up from all the shanties in the land, 'is not this railroad which we have built a good thing?' Yes, I answer, *comparatively* good, that is, you might have done worse; but I wish, as you are brothers of mine, that you could have spent your time better than digging in this dirt.

Before I finished my house, wishing to earn ten or twelve dollars by some honest and agreeable method, in order to meet my unusual expenses, I planted about two acres and a half of light and sandy soil near it chiefly with beans, but also a small part with potatoes, corn, peas, and turnips. The whole lot contains eleven acres, mostly growing up to pines and hickories, and was sold the preceding season for eight dollars and eight cents an acre. One farmer said that it was 'good for nothing but to raise cheeping squirrels on.' I put no manure whatever on this land, not being the owner, but merely a squatter, and not expecting to cultivate so much again, and I did not quite hoe it all once. I got out several cords of stumps in plowing, which supplied me with fuel for a long time, and left small circles of virgin mould, easily distinguishable through the summer by the greater luxuriance of the beans there. The dead and for the most part unmerchantable wood behind my house, and the driftwood from the pond, have supplied the remainder of my fuel. I was obliged to hire a team and a man for the plowing, though I held the plow myself. My farm outgoes for the first season were, for implements, seed, work, etc., \$14.72½. The seed corn was given me. This never costs anything to speak of, unless you plant more than enough. I got twelve bushels of beans, and eighteen bushels of potatoes, beside some peas and sweet corn. The yellow corn and turnips were too late to come to anything. My whole income from the farm was

	\$23 44
Deducting the outgoes	14 72½
There are left	\$8 71½

beside produce consumed and on hand at the time this estimate was made of the value of \$4.50 — the amount on hand much more than balancing a little grass which I did not raise. All things considered, that is, considering the importance of a man's soul and of today, notwithstanding the short time occupied by my experiment, nay, partly even because of its transient character, I believe that that was doing better than any farmer in Concord did that year.

The next year I did better still, for I spaded up all the land which I required, about a third of an acre, and I learned from the experience of both years, not being in the least awed by many celebrated works on husbandry, Arthur Young among the rest, that if one would live simply and eat only the crop which he raised, and raise no more than he ate, and not exchange it for an insufficient quantity of more luxurious and expensive things, he would need to cultivate only a few rods of ground, and that it would be cheaper to spade up that than to use oxen to plow it, and to select a fresh spot from time to time than to manure the old, and he could do all his necessary farm work as it were with his left hand at odd hours in the summer; and thus he would not be tied to an ox, or horse, or cow, or pig, as at present. I desire to speak impartially on this point, and as one not interested in the success or failure of the present economical and social arrangements. I was more independent than any farmer in Concord, for I was not anchored to a house or farm, but could follow the bent of my genius, which is a very crooked one, every moment. Beside being better off than they already, if my house had been burned or my crops had failed, I should have been nearly as well off as before.

I am wont to think that men are not so much the keepers of herds as herds are the keepers of men, the former are so much the freer. Men and oxen exchange work; but if we consider necessary work only, the oxen will be seen to have greatly the advantage, their farm is so much the larger. Man does some of his part of the exchange work in his six weeks of haying, and it is no boy's play. Certainly no nation that lived simply in all respects, that is, no nation of philosophers, would commit so great a blunder as to use the labor of animals. True, there never was and is not likely soon to be a nation of philosophers, nor am I certain it is desirable that there should be. However, *I* should never have broken a horse or bull and taken him to board for any work he might do for me, for fear I should become a horseman or a herds-man merely; and if society seems to be the gainer by so doing, are we certain that what is one man's gain is not another's loss, and that the stable-boy has equal cause with his master to be satisfied? Granted that some public works would not have been constructed without this aid, and let man share the glory of such with the ox and horse; does it follow that he could not have accomplished works yet more worthy of himself in that case? When men begin to do, not merely unnecessary or artistic, but luxurious and idle work, with their assistance, it is inevitable that a few do all the exchange work with the oxen, or, in other words, become the slaves of the strongest. Man thus not only works for the animal within him, but, for a symbol of this, he works for the animal without him. Though we have many substantial houses of brick or stone, the prosperity of the farmer is still measured by the degree to which the barn overshadows the house. This town is said to have the largest houses for oxen, cows, and horses hereabouts, and it is not behindhand in its public buildings; but there are very few halls for free worship or free speech in this county. It should not be by their architecture, but why not even by their power of abstract thought, that nations should seek to commemorate themselves? How much more admirable the Bhagvat-Geeta than all the ruins of the East! Towers and temples are the luxury of princes. A simple and independent mind does not toil at the bidding of any prince. Genius is not a retainer to any emperor, nor is its material silver, or gold, or marble, except to a trifling extent. To what end, pray, is so much stone hammered? In Arcadia, when I was there, I did not see any hammering stone. Nations are possessed with an insane ambition to perpetuate the memory of themselves by the amount of hammered stone they leave. What if equal pains were taken to smooth and polish their manners? One piece of good sense would be more memorable than a monument as high as the moon. I love better to see stones in place. The grandeur of Thebes was a vulgar grandeur. More sensible is a rod of stone wall that bounds an honest man's field than a hundred-gated Thebes that has wandered farther from the true end of life. The religion and civilization which are barbaric and heathenish build splendid temples; but what you might call Christianity does not. Most of the stone a nation hammers goes toward its tomb only. It buries itself alive. As for the Pyramids, there is nothing to wonder at in them so much as the fact that so many men could be found degraded enough to spend their lives constructing a tomb for some ambitious booby, whom it would have been wiser and manlier to have drowned in the Nile, and then given his body to the dogs. I might possibly invent some excuse for them and him, but I have no time for it. As for the religion and love of art of the builders, it is much the same all the world over, whether the building be an Egyptian temple or the United States Bank. It costs more than it comes to. The mainspring is vanity, assisted by the love of garlic and bread and butter. Mr. Balcom, a promising young architect, designs it on the back of his Vitruvius, with hard pencil and ruler, and the job is let out to Dobson & Sons, stonecutters. When the thirty centuries begin to look down on it, mankind begin to look up at it. As for your high towers and monuments, there was a crazy fellow once in this town who undertook to dig through to China, and he got so far that, as he said, he heard the Chinese pots and kettles rattle; but I think that I shall not go out of my way to admire the hole which he made. Many are concerned about the monuments of the West and the East — to know who built them. For my part, I should like to know who in those days did not build them — who were above such trifling. But to proceed with my statistics.

By surveying, carpentry, and day-labor of various other kinds in the village in the meanwhile, for I have as many trades as fingers, I had earned $13.34. The expense of food for eight months, namely, from July 4th to March 1st, the time when these estimates were made, though I lived there more than two years — not counting potatoes, a little green corn, and some peas, which I had raised, nor considering the value of what was on hand at the last date — was

Rice	.$1 73½	
Molasses	. 1 73	Cheapest form of the saccharine.
Rye meal	. 1 04¾	
Indian meal	. 0 99¾	Cheaper than rye.
Pork	. 0 22	
Flour	. 0 88	{ Costs more than Indian meal, both money and trouble. }
Sugar	. 0 80	
Lard	. 0 65	
Apples	. 0 25	
Dried apple	. 0 22	
Sweet potatoes	. 0 10	
One pumpkin	. 0 6	
One watermelon	. 0 2	
Salt	. 0 3	

(right margin bracket: All experiments which failed.)

Yes, I did eat $8.74, all told; but I should not thus unblushingly publish my guilt, if I did not know that most of my readers were equally guilty with myself, and that their deeds would look no better in print. The next year I sometimes caught a mess of fish for my dinner, and once I went so far as to slaughter a woodchuck which ravaged my bean-field — effect his transmigration, as a Tartar would say — and devour him, partly for experiment's sake; but though it afforded me a momentary enjoyment, notwithstanding a musky flavor, I saw that the longest use would not make that a good practice, however it might seem to have your woodchucks ready dressed by the village butcher.

Clothing and some incidental expenses within the same dates, though little can be inferred from this item, amounted to

$$\$8\ 40¾$$

Oil and some household utensils 2 00

So that all the pecuniary outgoes, excepting for washing and mending, which for the most part were done out of the house, and their bills have not yet been received — and these are all and more than all the ways by which money necessarily goes out in this part of the world — were

House	$28 12½
Farm one year	14 72½
Food eight months	8 74
Clothing, etc., eight months	8 40¾
Oil, etc., eight months	2 00
In all	$61 99¾

I address myself now to those of my readers who have a living to get. And to meet this I have for farm produce sold

	$23 44
Earned by day-labor	13 34
In all	$36 78

which subtracted from the sum of the outgoes leaves a balance of $25.21¾ on the one side — this being very nearly the means with which I started, and the measure of expenses to be incurred — and on the other, beside the leisure and independence and health thus secured, a comfortable house for me as long as I choose to occupy it.

These statistics, however accidental and therefore uninstructive they may appear, as they have a certain completeness, have a certain value also. Nothing was given me of which I have not rendered some account. It appears from the above estimate, that my food alone cost me in money about twenty-seven cents a week. It was, for nearly two years after this, rye and Indian meal without yeast, potatoes, rice, a very little salt pork, molasses, and salt; and my drink, water. It was fit that I should live on rice, mainly, who love so well the philosophy of India. To meet the objections of some inveterate cavillers, I may as well state, that if I dined out occasionally, as I always had done, and I trust shall have opportunities to do again, it was frequently to the detriment of my domestic arrangements. But the dining out, being, as I have stated, a constant element, does not in the least affect a comparative statement like this.

I learned from my two years' experience that it would cost incredibly little trouble to obtain one's necessary food, even in this latitude; that a man may use as simple a diet as the animals, and yet retain health and strength. I have made a satisfactory dinner, satisfactory on several accounts, simply off a dish of purslane (*Portulaca oleracea*) which I gathered in my cornfield, boiled and salted. I give the Latin on account of the savoriness of the trivial name. And pray what more can a reasonable man desire, in peaceful times, in ordinary noons, than a sufficient number of ears of green sweet corn boiled, with the addition of salt? Even the little variety which I used was a yielding to the demands of appetite, and not of health. Yet men have come to such a pass that they frequently starve, not for want of necessaries, but for want of luxuries; and I know a good woman who thinks that her son lost his life because he took to drinking water only.

The reader will perceive that I am treating the subject rather from an economic than a dietetic point of view, and he will not venture to put my abstemiousness to the test unless he has a well-stocked larder.

Bread I at first made of pure Indian meal and salt, genuine hoe-cakes, which I baked before my fire out of doors on a shingle or the end of a stick of timber sawed off in building my house; but it was wont to get smoked and to have a piny flavor. I tried flour also; but have at last found a mixture of rye and Indian meal most convenient and agreeable. In cold weather it was no little amusement to bake several small loaves of this in succession, tending and turning them as carefully as an Egyptian his hatching eggs. They were a real cereal fruit which I ripened, and they had to my senses a fragrance like that of other noble fruits, which I kept in as long as possible by wrapping them in cloths. I made a study of the ancient and indispensable art of bread-making, consulting such authorities as offered, going back to the primitive days and first invention of the unleavened kind, when from the wildness of nuts and meats men first reached the mildness and refinement of this diet, and travelling gradually down in my studies through that accidental souring of the dough which, it is supposed, taught the leavening process, and through the various fermentations thereafter, till I came to 'good, sweet, wholesome bread,' the staff of life. Leaven, which some deem the soul of bread, the *spiritus* which fills its cellular tissue, which is religiously preserved like the vestal fire — some precious bottleful, I suppose, first brought over in the Mayflower, did the business for America, and its influence is still rising, swelling, spreading, in cerealian billows over the land — this seed I regularly and faithfully procured from the village, till at length one morning I forgot the rules, and scalded my yeast; by which accident I discovered that even this was not indispensable — for my discoveries were not by the synthetic but analytic process — and I have gladly omitted it since, though most housewives earnestly assured me that safe and wholesome bread without yeast might not be, and elderly people prophesied a speedy decay of the vital forces. Yet I find it not to be an essential ingredient, and after going without it for a year am still in the land of the living; and I am glad to escape the trivialness of carrying a bottleful in my pocket, which would sometimes pop and discharge its contents to my discomfiture. It is simpler and more respectable to omit it. Man is an animal who more than any other can adapt himself to all climates and circumstances. Neither did I put any sal-soda, or other acid or alkali, into my bread. It would seem that I made it according to the recipe which Marcus Porcius Cato gave about two centuries before Christ. 'Panem depsticium sic facito. Manus mortariumque bene lavato. Farinam in mortarium indito, aquae paulatim addito, subigitoque pulchre. Ubi bene subegeris, defingito, coquitoque sub testu.' Which I take to mean, 'Make kneaded bread thus. Wash your hands and trough well. Put the meal into the trough, add water gradually, and knead it thoroughly. When you have kneaded it well, mould it, and bake it under a cover,' that is, in a baking-kettle. Not a word about leaven. But I did not always use this staff of life. At one time, owing to the emptiness of my purse, I saw none of it for more than a month.

Every New Englander might easily raise all his own breadstuffs in this land of rye and Indian corn, and not depend on distant and fluctuating markets for them. Yet so far are we from simplicity and independence that, in Concord, fresh and sweet meal is rarely sold in the shops, and hominy and corn in a still coarser form are hardly used by any. For the most part the farmer gives to his cattle and hogs the grain of his own producing, and buys flour, which is at least no more wholesome, at a greater cost, at the store. I saw that I could easily raise my bushel or two of rye and Indian corn, for the former will grow on the poorest land, and the latter does not require the best, and grind them in a hand-mill, and so do without rice and pork; and if I must have some concentrated sweet, I found by experiment that I could make a very good molasses either of pumpkins or beets, and I knew that I needed only to set out a few maples to obtain it more easily still, and while these were growing I could use various substitutes beside those which I have named. 'For,' as the Forefathers sang,

> 'we can make liquor to sweeten our lips
> Of pumpkins and parsnips and walnut-tree chips.'

Finally, as for salt, that grossest of groceries, to obtain this might be a fit occasion for a visit to the seashore, or, if I did without it altogether,

I should probably drink the less water. I do not learn that the Indians ever troubled themselves to go after it.

Thus I could avoid all trade and barter, so far as my food was concerned, and having a shelter already, it would only remain to get clothing and fuel. The pantaloons which I now wear were woven in a farmer's family — thank Heaven there is so much virtue still in man; for I think the fall from the farmer to the operative as great and memorable as that from the man to the farmer; — and in a new country, fuel is an encumbrance. As for a habitat, if I were not permitted still to squat, I might purchase one acre at the same price for which the land I cultivated was sold — namely, eight dollars and eight cents. But as it was, I considered that I enhanced the value of the land by squatting on it.

There is a certain class of unbelievers who sometimes ask me such questions as, if I think that I can live on vegetable food alone; and to strike at the root of the matter at once — for the root is faith — I am accustomed to answer such, that I can live on board nails. If they cannot understand that, they cannot understand much that I have to say. For my part, I am glad to hear of experiments of this kind being tried; as that a young man tried for a fortnight to live on hard, raw corn on the ear, using his teeth for all mortar. The squirrel tribe tried the same and succeeded. The human race is interested in these experiments, though a few old women who are incapacitated for them, or who own their thirds in mills, may be alarmed.

My furniture, part of which I made myself — and the rest cost me nothing of which I have not rendered an account — consisted of a bed, a table, a desk, three chairs, a looking-glass three inches in diameter, a pair of tongs and andirons, a kettle, a skillet, and a frying-pan, a dipper, a wash-bowl, two knives and forks, three plates, one cup, one spoon, a jug for oil, a jug for molasses, and a japanned lamp. None is so poor that he need sit on a pumpkin. That is shiftlessness. There is a plenty of such chairs as I like best in the village garrets to be had for taking them away. Furniture! Thank God, I can sit and I can stand without the aid of a furniture warehouse. What man but a philosopher would not be ashamed to see his furniture packed in a cart and going up country exposed to the light of heaven and the eyes of men, a beggarly account of empty boxes? That is Spaulding's furniture. I could never tell from inspecting such a load whether it belonged to a so-called rich man or a poor one; the owner always seemed poverty-stricken. Indeed, the more you have of such things the poorer you are. Each load looks as if it contained the contents of a dozen shanties; and if one shanty is poor, this is a dozen times as poor. Pray, for what do we *move* ever but to get rid of our furniture, our *exuviæ*; at last to go from this world to another newly furnished, and leave this to be burned? It is the same as if all these traps were buckled to a man's belt, and he could not move over the rough country where our lines are cast without dragging them — dragging his trap. He was a lucky fox that left his tail in the trap. The muskrat will gnaw his third leg off to be free. No wonder man has lost his elasticity. How often he is at a dead set! 'Sir, if I may be so bold, what do you mean by a dead set?' If you are a seer, whenever you meet a man you will see all that he owns, ay, and much that he pretends to disown, behind him, even to his kitchen furniture and all the trumpery which he saves and will not burn, and he will appear to be harnessed to it and making what headway he can. I think that the man is at a dead set who has got through a knot-hole or gate-way where his sledge load of furniture cannot follow him. I cannot but feel compassion when I hear some trig, compact-looking man, seemingly free, all girded and ready, speak of his 'furniture,' as whether it is insured or not. 'But what shall I do with my furniture?' My gay butterfly is entangled in a spider's web then. Even those who seem for a long while not to have any, if you inquire more narrowly you will find have some stored in somebody's barn. I look upon England today as an old gentleman who is travelling with a great deal of baggage, trumpery which has accumulated from long housekeeping, which he has not the courage to burn; great trunk, little trunk, bandbox, and bundle. Throw away the first three at least. It would surpass the powers of a well man nowadays to take up his bed and walk, and I should certainly advise a sick one to lay down his bed and run. When I have met an immigrant tottering under a bundle which contained his all — looking like an enormous wen which had grown out of the nape of his neck — I have pitied him, not because that was his all, but because he had all *that* to carry. If I have got to drag my trap, I will take care that it be a light one and do not nip me in a vital part. But perchance it would be wisest never to put one's paw into it.

I would observe, by the way, that it costs me nothing for curtains, for I have no gazers to shut out but the sun and moon, and I am willing that they should look in. The moon will not sour milk nor taint meat of mine, nor will the sun injure my furniture or fade my carpet; and if he is sometimes too warm a friend, I find it still better economy to retreat behind some curtain which nature has provided, than to add a single item to the details of housekeeping. A lady once offered me a mat, but as I had no room to spare within the house, nor time to spare within or without to shake it, I decline it, preferring to wipe my feet on the sod before my door. It is best to avoid the beginnings of evil.

Not long since I was present at the auction of a deacon's effects, for his life had not been ineffectual:

'The evil that men do lives after them.'

As usual, a great proportion was trumpery which had begun to accumulate in his father's day. Among the rest was a dried tapeworm. And now, after lying half a century in his garret and other dust holes, these things were not burned; instead of a *bonfire*, or purifying destruction of them, there was an *auction*, or increasing of them. The neighbors eagerly collected to view them, bought them all, and carefully transported them to their garrets and dust holes, to lie there till their estates are settled, when they will start again. When a man dies he kicks the dust.

The customs of some savage nations might, perchance, be profitably imitated by us, for they at least go through the semblance of casting their slough annually; they have the idea of the thing, whether they have the reality or not. Would it not be well if we were to celebrate such a 'busk,' or 'feast of first fruits,' as Bartram describes to have been the custom of the Mucclasse Indians? 'When a town celebrates the busk,' says he, 'having previously provided themselves with new clothes, new pots, pans, and other household utensils and furniture, they collect all their worn out clothes and other despicable things, sweep and cleanse their houses, squares, and the whole town, of their filth, which with all the remaining grain and other old provisions they cast together into one common heap, and consume it with fire. After having taken medicine, and fasted for three days, all the fire in the town is extinguished. During this fast they abstain from the gratification of every appetite and passion whatever. A general amnesty is proclaimed; all malefactors may return to their town.'

'On the fourth morning, the high priest, by rubbing dry wood together, produces new fire in the public square, from whence every habitation in the town is supplied with the new and pure flame.'

They then feast on the new corn and fruits, and dance and sing for three days, 'and the four following days they receive visits and rejoice with their friends from neighboring towns who have in like manner purified and prepared themselves.'

The Mexicans also practised a similar purification at the end of every fifty-two years, in the belief that it was time for the world to come to an end.

I have scarcely heard of a truer sacrament, that is, as the dictionary defines it, 'outward and visible sign of an inward and spiritual grace,' than this, and I have no doubt that they were originally inspired directly from Heaven to do thus, though they have no Biblical record of the revelation.

For more than five years I maintained myself thus solely by the labor of my hands, and I found that, by working about six weeks in a year, I could meet all the expenses of living. The whole of my winters, as well as most of my summers, I had free and clear for study. I have thoroughly tried school-keeping, and found that my expenses were in proportion, or rather out of proportion, to my income, for I was obliged to dress and train, not to say think and believe, accordingly, and I lost my time into the bargain. As I did not teach for the good of my fellow-men, but simply for a livelihood, this was a failure. I have tried trade; but I found that it would take ten years to get under way in that, and that then I should probably be on my way to the devil. I was actually afraid that I might by that time be doing what is called a good business. When formerly I was looking about to see what I could do for a living, some sad experience in conforming to the wishes of friends being fresh in my mind to tax my ingenuity, I thought often and seriously of picking huckleberries; that surely I could do, and its small profits might suffice — for my greatest skill has been to want but little — so little capital it required, so little distraction from my wonted moods, I foolishly thought. While my acquaintances went unhesitatingly into trade or the professions, I contemplated this occupation as most like theirs; ranging the hills all summer to pick the berries which came in my way, and thereafter carelessly dispose of them; so, to keep the flocks of Admetus. I also dreamed that I might gather the wild herbs, or carry evergreens to such villagers as loved to be reminded of the woods, even to the city, by hay-cart loads. But I have since learned that trade curses everything it handles; and though you trade in messages from heaven, the whole curse of trade attaches to the business.

As I preferred some things to others, and especially valued my freedom, as I could fare hard and yet succeed well, I did not wish to spend my time in earning rich carpets or other fine furniture, or delicate cookery, or a house in the Grecian or the Gothic style just yet. If there are any to whom it is no interruption to acquire these things, and who know how to use them when acquired, I relinquish to them the pursuit. Some are 'industrious,' and appear to love labor for its own sake, or perhaps because it keeps them out of worse mischief; to such I have at present nothing to say. Those who would not know what to do with more leisure than they now enjoy, I might advise to work twice as hard as they do — work till they pay for themselves, and get their free papers. For myself I found that the occupation of a day-laborer was the most independent of any, especially as it required only thirty or forty days in a year to support one. The laborer's day ends with the going down of the sun, and he is then free to devote himself to his chosen pursuit, independent of his labor; but his employer, who speculates from month to month, has no respite from one end of the year to the other.

In short, I am convinced, both by faith and experience, that to maintain one's self on this earth is not a hardship but a pastime, if we will live simply and wisely; as the pursuits of the simpler nations are still the sports of the more artificial. It is not necessary that a man should earn his living by the sweat of his brow, unless he sweats easier than I do.

One young man of my acquaintance, who has inherited some acres, told me that he thought he should live as I did, *if he had the means.* I would not have any one adopt *my* mode of living on any account; for, beside that before he has fairly learned it I may have found out another for myself, I desire that there may be as many different persons in the world as possible; but I would have each one be very careful to find out and pursue *his own* way, and not his father's or his mother's or his neighbor's instead. The youth may build or plant or sail, only let him not be hindered from doing that which he tells me he would like to do. It is by a mathematical point only that we are wise, as the sailor or the fugitive slave keeps the polestar in his eye; but that is sufficient guidance for all our life. We may not arrive at our port within a calculable period, but we would preserve the true course.

Undoubtedly, in this case, what is true for one is truer still for a thousand, as a large house is not proportionally more expensive than a small one, since one roof may cover, one cellar underlie, and one wall separate several apartments. But for my part, I preferred the solitary dwelling. Moreover, it will commonly be cheaper to build the whole yourself than to convince another of the advantage of the common wall; and when you have done this, the common partition, to be much cheaper, must be a thin one, and that other may prove a bad neighbor, and also not keep his side in repair. The only coöperation which is commonly possible is exceedingly partial and superficial; and what little true coöperation there is, is as if it were not, being a harmony inaudible to men. If a man has faith, he will coöperate with equal faith everywhere; if he has not faith, he will continue to live like the rest of the world, whatever company he is joined to. To coöperate in the highest as well as the lowest sense, means *to get our living together*. I heard it proposed lately that two young men should travel together over the world, the one without money, earning his means as he went, before the mast and behind the plow, the other carrying a bill of exchange in his pocket. It was easy to see that they could not long be companions or coöperate, since one would not *operate* at all. They would part at the first interesting crisis in their adventures. Above all, as I have implied, the man who goes alone can start today; but he who travels with another must wait till that other is ready, and it may be a long time before they get off.

But all this is very selfish, I have heard some of my townsmen say. I confess that I have hitherto indulged very little in philanthropic enterprises. I have made some sacrifices to a sense of duty, and among others have sacrificed this pleasure also. There are those who have used all their arts to persuade me to undertake the support of some poor family in the town; and if I had nothing to do — for the devil finds employment for the idle — I might try my hand at some such pastime as that. However, when I have thought to indulge myself in this respect, and lay their Heaven under an obligation by maintaining certain poor persons in all respects as comfortably as I maintain myself, and have even ventured so far as to make them the offer, they have one and all unhesitatingly preferred to remain poor. While my townsmen and women are devoted in so many ways to the good of their fellows, I trust that one at least may be spared to other and less humane pursuits. You must have a genius for charity as well as for anything else. As for Doing-good, that is one of the professions which are full. Moreover, I have tried it fairly, and, strange as it may seem, am satisfied that it does not agree with my constitution. Probably I should not consciously and deliberately forsake my particular calling to do the good which society demands of me, to save the universe from annihilation; and I believe that a like but infinitely greater steadfastness elsewhere is all that now preserves it. But I would not stand between any man and his genius; and to him who does this work, which I decline, with his whole heart and soul and life, I would say, Persevere, even if the world call it doing evil, as it is most likely they will.

I am far from supposing that my case is a peculiar one; no doubt many of my readers would make a similar defence. At doing something — I will not engage that my neighbors shall pronounce it good — I do not hesitate to say that I should be a capital fellow to hire; but what that is, it is for my employer to find out. What *good* I do, in the common sense of that word, must be aside from my main path, and for the most part wholly unintended. Men say, practically, Begin where you are and such as you are, without aiming mainly to become of more worth, and with kindness aforethought go about doing good. If I were to preach at all in this strain, I should say rather, Set about being good. As if the sun should stop when he had kindled his fires up to the splendor of a moon or a star of the sixth magnitude, and go about like a Robin Goodfellow, peeping in at every cottage window, inspiring lunatics, and tainting meats, and making darkness visible, instead of steadily increasing his genial heat and beneficence till he is of such brightness that no mortal can look him in the face, and then, and in the meanwhile too, going about the world in his own orbit, doing it good, or rather, as a truer philosophy has discovered, the world going about him getting good. When Phaëton, wishing to prove his heavenly birth by his beneficence, had the sun's chariot but one day, and drove out of the beaten track, he burned several blocks of houses in the lower streets of heaven, and scorched the surface of the earth, and dried up every spring, and made the great desert of Sahara, till at length Jupiter hurled him headlong to the earth with a thunderbolt, and the sun, through grief at his death, did not shine for a year.

There is no odor so bad as that which arises from goodness tainted. It is human, it is divine, carrion. If I knew for a certainty that a man was coming to my house with the conscious design of doing me good, I should run for my life, as from that dry and parching wind of the African deserts called the simoom, which fills the mouth and nose and ears and eyes with dust till you are suffocated, for fear that I should get some of his good done to me — some of its virus mingled with my blood. No — in this case I would rather suffer evil the natural way. A man is not a good *man* to me because he will feed me if I should be starving, or warm me if I should be freezing, or pull me out of a ditch if I should ever fall into one. I can find you a Newfoundland dog that will do as much. Philanthropy is not love for one's fellow-man in the broadest sense. Howard was no doubt an exceedingly kind and worthy man in his way, and has his reward; but, comparatively speaking, what are a hundred Howards to *us*, if their philanthropy do not help *us* in our best estate, when we are most worthy to be helped? I never heard of a philanthropic meeting in which it was sincerely proposed to do any good to me, or the like of me.

The Jesuits were quite balked by those Indians who, being burned at the stake, suggested new modes of torture to their tormentors. Being superior to physical suffering, it sometimes chanced that they were superior to any consolation which the missionaries could offer; and the law to do as you would be done by fell with less persuasiveness on the ears of those who, for their part, did not care how they were done by, who loved their enemies after a new fashion, and came very near freely forgiving them all they did.

Be sure that you give the poor the aid they most need, though it be your example which leaves them far behind. If you give money, spend yourself with it, and do not merely abandon it to them. We make curious mistakes sometimes. Often the poor man is not so cold and hungry as he is dirty and ragged and gross. It is partly his taste, and not merely his misfortune. If you give him money, he will perhaps buy more rags with it. I was wont to pity the clumsy Irish laborers who cut ice on the pond, in such mean and ragged clothes, while I shivered in my more tidy and somewhat more fashionable garments, till, one bitter cold day, one who had slipped into the water came to my house to warm him, and I saw him strip off three pairs of pants and two pairs of stockings ere he got down to the skin, though they were dirty and ragged enough, it is true, and that he could afford to refuse the *extra* garments which I offered him, he had so many *intra* ones. This ducking was the very thing he needed. Then I began to pity myself, and I saw that it would be a greater charity to bestow on me a flannel shirt than a whole slop-shop on him. There are a thousand hacking at the branches of evil to one who is striking at the root, and it may be that he who bestows the largest amount of time and money on the needy is doing the most by his mode of life to produce that misery which he strives in vain to relieve. It is the pious slave-breeder devoting the proceeds of every tenth slave to buy a Sunday's liberty for the rest. Some show their kindness to the poor by employing them in their kitchens. Would they not be kinder if they employed themselves there? You boast of spending a tenth part of your income in charity; maybe you should spend the nine tenths so, and done with it. Society recovers only a tenth part of the property then. Is this owing to the generosity of him in whose possession it is found, or to the remissness of the officers of justice?

Philanthropy is almost the only virtue which is sufficiently appreciated by mankind. Nay, it is greatly overrated; and it is our selfishness which overrates it. A robust poor man, one sunny day here in Concord, praised a fellow-townsman to me, because, as he said, he was kind to the poor; meaning himself. The kind uncles and aunts of the race are more esteemed than its true spiritual fathers and mothers. I once heard a reverend lecturer on England, a man of learning and intelligence, after enumerating her scientific, literary, and political worthies, Shakespeare, Bacon, Cromwell, Milton, Newton, and others, speak next of her Christian heroes, whom, as if his profession required it of him, he elevated to a place far above all the rest, as the greatest of the great. They were Penn, Howard, and Mrs. Fry. Every one must feel the falsehood and cant of this. The last were not England's best men and women; only, perhaps, her best philanthropists.

I would not subtract anything from the praise that is due to philanthropy, but merely demand justice for all who by their lives and works are a blessing to mankind. I do not value chiefly a man's uprightness and benevolence, which are, as it were, his stem and leaves. Those plants of whose greenness withered we make herb tea for the sick serve but a humble use, and are most employed by quacks. I want the flower and fruit of a man; that some fragrance be wafted over from him to me, and some ripeness flavor our intercourse. His goodness must not be a partial and transitory act, but a constant superfluity, which costs him nothing and of which he is unconscious. This is a charity that hides a multitude of sins. The philanthropist too often surrounds mankind with the remembrance of his own castoff griefs as an atmosphere, and calls it sympathy. We should impart our courage, and not our despair, our health and ease, and not our disease, and take care that this does not spread by contagion. From what southern plains comes up the voice of wailing? Under what latitudes reside the heathen to whom we would send light? Who is that intemperate and brutal man whom we would redeem? If anything ail a man, so that he does not perform his functions, if he have a pain in his bowels even — for that is the seat of sympathy — he forthwith sets about reforming — the world. Being a microcosm himself, he discovers — and it is a true discovery, and he is the man to make it — that the world has been eating green apples; to his eyes, in fact, the globe itself is a great green apple, which there is danger awful to think of that the children of men will nibble before it is ripe; and straightway his drastic philanthropy seeks out the Esquimau and the Patagonian, and embraces the populous Indian and Chinese villages; and thus, by a few years of philanthropic activity, the powers in the meanwhile using him for their own ends, no doubt, he cures himself of his dyspepsia, the globe acquires a faint blush on one or both of its cheeks, as if it were beginning to be ripe, and life loses its crudity and is once more sweet and wholesome to live. I never dreamed of any enormity greater than I have committed. I never knew, and never shall know, a worse man than myself.

I believe that what so saddens the reformer is not his sympathy with his fellows in distress, but, though he be the holiest son of God, is his private ail. Let this be righted, let the spring come to him, the morning rise over his couch, and he will forsake his generous companions without apology. My excuse for not lecturing against the use of tobacco is, that I never chewed it, that is a penalty which reformed tobacco-chewers have to pay; though there are things enough I have chewed which I could lecture against. If you should ever be betrayed into any of these philanthropies, do not let your left hand know what your right hand does, for it is not worth knowing. Rescue the drowning and tie your shoestrings. Take your time, and set about some free labor.

Our manners have been corrupted by communication with the saints. Our hymn-books resound with a melodious cursing of God and enduring Him forever. One would say that even the prophets and redeemers had rather consoled the fears than confirmed the hopes of man. There is nowhere recorded a simple and irrepressible satisfaction with the gift of life, any memorable praise of God. All health and success does me good, however far off and withdrawn it may appear; all disease and failure helps to make me sad and does me evil, however much sympathy it may have with me or I with it. If, then, we would indeed restore mankind by truly Indian, botanic, magnetic, or natural means, let us first be as simple and well as Nature ourselves, dispel the clouds which hang over our own brows, and take up a little life into our pores. Do not stay to be an overseer of the poor, but endeavor to become one of the worthies of the world.

I read in the Gulistan, or Flower Garden, of Sheik Sadi of Shiraz, that 'they asked a wise man, saying: Of the many celebrated trees which the Most High God has created lofty and umbrageous, they call none azad, or free, excepting the cypress, which bears no fruit; what mystery is there in this? He replied: Each has its appropriate produce, and appointed season, during the continuance of which it is fresh and blooming, and during their absence dry and withered; to neither of which states is the cypress exposed, being always flourishing; and of this nature are the azads, or religious independents. — Fix not thy heart on that which is transitory; for the Dijlah, or Tigris, will continue to flow through Bagdad after the race of caliphs is extinct: if thy hand has plenty, be liberal as the date tree; but if it affords nothing to give away, be an azad, or free man, like the cypress.'

COMPLEMENTAL VERSES

THE PRETENSIONS OF POVERTY

Thou dost presume too much, poor needy wretch,
To claim a station in the firmament
Because thy humble cottage, or thy tub,
Nurses some lazy or pedantic virtue
In the cheap sunshine or by shady springs,
With roots and pot-herbs; where thy right hand,
Tearing those humane passions from the mind,
Upon whose stocks fair blooming virtues flourish,
Degradeth nature, and benumbeth sense,
And, Gorgon-like, turns active men to stone.
We not require the dull society
Of your necessitated temperance,
Or that unnatural stupidity
That knows nor joy nor sorrow; nor your forc'd
Falsely exalted passive fortitude
Above the active. This low abject brood,
That fix their seats in mediocrity,
Become your servile minds; but we advance
Such virtues only as admit excess,
Brave, bounteous acts, regal magnificence,
All-seeing prudence, magnanimity
That knows no bound, and that heroic virtue
For which antiquity hath left no name,

> But patterns only, such as Hercules,
> Achilles, Theseus. Back to thy loath'd cell;
> And when thou seest the new enlightened sphere,
> Study to know but what those worthies were.
>
> T. CAREW

II. WHERE I LIVED, AND WHAT I LIVED FOR

AT A certain season of our life we are accustomed to consider every spot as the possible site of a house. I have thus surveyed the country on every side within a dozen miles of where I live. In imagination I have bought all the farms in succession, for all were to be bought, and I knew their price. I walked over each farmer's premises, tasted his wild apples, discoursed on husbandry with him, took his farm at his price, at any price, mortgaging it to him in my mind; even put a higher price on it — took everything but a deed of it — took his word for his deed, for I dearly love to talk — cultivated it, and him too to some extent, I trust, and withdrew when I had enjoyed it long enough, leaving him to carry it on. This experience entitled me to be regarded as a sort of real-estate broker by my friends. Wherever I sat, there I might live, and the landscape radiated from me accordingly. What is a house but a *sedes*, a seat? — better if a country seat. I discovered many a site for a house not likely to be soon improved, which some might have thought too far from the village, but to my eyes the village was too far from it. Well, there I might live, I said; and there I did live, for an hour, a summer and a winter life; saw how I could let the years run off, buffet the winter through, and see the spring come in. The future inhabitants of this region, wherever they may place their houses, may be sure that they have been anticipated. An afternoon sufficed to lay out the land into orchard, wood-lot, and pasture, and to decide what fine oaks or pines should be left to stand before the door, and whence each blasted tree could be seen to the best advantage; and then I let it lie, fallow perchance, for a man is rich in proportion to the number of things which he can afford to let alone.

My imagination carried me so far that I even had the refusal of several farms — the refusal was all I wanted — but I never got my fingers burned by actual possession. The nearest that I came to actual possession was when I bought the Hollowell place, and had begun to sort my seeds, and collected materials with which to make a wheelbarrow to carry it on or off with; but before the owner gave me a deed of it, his wife — every man has such a wife — changed her mind and wished to keep it, and he offered me ten dollars to release him. Now, to speak the truth, I had but ten cents in the world, and it surpassed my arithmetic to tell, if I was that man who had ten cents, or who had a farm, or ten dollars, or all together. However, I let him keep the ten dollars and the farm too, for I had carried it far enough; or rather, to be generous, I sold him the farm for just what I gave for it, and, as he was not a rich man, made him a present of ten dollars, and still had my ten cents, and seeds, and materials for a wheelbarrow left. I found thus that I had been a rich man without any damage to my poverty. But I retained the landscape, and I have since annually carried off what it yielded without a wheelbarrow. With respect to landscapes,

> 'I am monarch of all I *survey*,
> My right there is none to dispute.'

I have frequently seen a poet withdraw, having enjoyed the most valuable part of a farm, while the crusty farmer supposed that he had got a few wild apples only. Why, the owner does not know it for many years when a poet has put his farm in rhyme, the most admirable kind of invisible fence, has fairly impounded it, milked it, skimmed it, and got all the cream, and left the farmer only the skimmed milk.

The real attractions of the Hollowell farm, to me, were: its complete retirement, being about two miles from the village, half a mile from the nearest neighbor, and separated from the highway by a broad field; its bounding on the river, which the owner said protected it by its fogs from frosts in the spring, though that was nothing to me; the gray color and ruinous state of the house and barn, and the dilapidated fences, which put such an interval between me and the last occupant; the hollow and lichen-covered apple trees, gnawed by rabbits, showing what kind of neighbors I should have; but above all, the recollection I had of it from my earliest voyages up the river, when the house was concealed behind a dense grove of red maples, through which I heard the house-dog bark. I was in haste to buy it, before the proprietor finished getting out some rocks, cutting down the hollow apple trees, and grubbing up some young birches which had sprung up in the pasture, or, in short, had made any more of his improvements. To enjoy these advantages I was ready to carry it on; like Atlas, to take the world on my shoulders — I never heard what compensation he received for that — and do all those things which had no other motive or excuse but that I might pay for it and be unmolested in my possession of it; for I knew all the while that it would yield the most abundant crop of the kind I wanted, if I could only afford to let it alone. But it turned out as I have said.

All that I could say, then, with respect to farming on a large scale — I have always cultivated a garden — was, that I had had my seeds ready. Many think that seeds improve with age. I have no doubt that time discriminates between the good and the bad; and when at last I shall plant, I shall be less likely to be disappointed. But I would say to my fellows, once for all, As long as possible live free and uncommitted. It makes but little difference whether you are committed to a farm or the county jail.

Old Cato, whose 'De Re Rustâ' is my 'Cultivator,' says — and the only translation I have seen makes sheer nonsense of the passage — 'When you think of getting a farm turn it thus in your mind, not to buy greedily; nor spare your pains to look at it, and do not think it enough to go round it once. The oftener you go there the more it will please you, if it is good.' I think I shall not buy greedily, but go round and round it as long as I live, and be buried in it first, that it may please me the more at last.

The present was my next experiment of this kind, which I purpose to describe more at length, for convenience putting the experience of two years into one. As I have said, I do not propose to write an ode to dejection, but to brag as lustily as chanticleer in the morning, standing on his roost, if only to wake my neighbors up.

When first I took up my abode in the woods, that is, began to spend my nights as well as days there, which, by accident, was on Independence Day, or the Fourth of July, 1845, my house was not finished for winter, but was merely a defence against the rain, without plastering or chimney, the walls being of rough, weather-stained boards, with wide chinks, which made it cool at night. The upright white hewn studs and freshly planed door and window casings gave it a clean and airy look, especially in the morning, when its timbers were saturated with dew, so that I fancied that by noon some sweet gum would exude from them. To my imagination it retained throughout the day more or less of this auroral character, reminding me of a certain house on a mountain which I had visited a year before. This was an airy and unplastered cabin, fit to entertain a travelling god, and where a goddess might trail her garments. The winds which passed over my dwelling were such as sweep over the ridges of mountains, bearing the broken strains, or celestial parts only, of terrestrial music. The morning wind forever blows, the poem of creation is uninterrupted; but few are the ears that hear it. Olympus is but the outside of the earth every-where.

The only house I had been the owner of before, if I except a boat, was a tent, which I used occasionally when making excursions in the summer, and this is still rolled up in my garret; but the boat, after passing from hand to hand, has gone down the stream of time. With this more substantial shelter about me, I had made some progress toward settling in the world. This frame, so slightly clad, was a sort of crystallization around me, and reacted on the builder. It was suggestive somewhat as a picture in outlines. I did not need to go outdoors to take the air, for the atmosphere within had lost none of its freshness. It was not so much within-doors as behind a door where I sat, even in the rainiest weather. The Harivansa says, 'An abode without birds is like a meat without seasoning.' Such was not my abode, for I found myself suddenly neighbor to the birds; not by having imprisoned one, but having caged myself near them. I was not only nearer to some of those which commonly frequent the garden and the orchard, but to those wilder and more thrilling songsters of the forest which never, or rarely, serenade a villager — the wood thrush, the veery, the scarlet tanager, the field sparrow, the whip-poor-will, and many others.

I was seated by the shore of a small pond, about a mile and a half south of the village of Concord and somewhat higher than it, in the midst of an extensive wood between that town and Lincoln, and about two miles south of that our only field known to fame, Concord Battle Ground; but I was so low in the woods that the opposite shore, half a mile off, like the rest, covered with wood, was my most distant horizon. For the first week, whenever I looked out on the pond it impressed me like a tarn high up on the side of a mountain, its bottom far above the surface of other lakes, and, as the sun arose, I saw it throwing off its nightly clothing of mist, and here and there, by degrees, its soft ripples or its smooth reflecting surface was revealed, while the mists, like ghosts, were stealthily withdrawing in every direction into the woods, as at the breaking up of some nocturnal conventicle. The very dew seemed to hang upon the trees later into the day than usual, as on the sides of mountains.

This small lake was of most value as a neighbor in the intervals of a gentle rain-storm in August, when, both air and water being perfectly still, but the sky overcast, mid-afternoon had all the serenity of evening, and the wood thrush sang around, and was heard from shore to shore. A lake like this is never smoother than at such a time; and the clear portion of the air above it being shallow and darkened by clouds, the water, full of light and reflections, becomes a lower heaven itself so much the more important. From a hill-top near by, where the wood had been recently cut off, there was a pleasing vista southward across the pond, through a wide indentation in the hills which form the shore there, where their opposite sides sloping toward each other suggested a stream flowing out in that direction through a wooded valley, but stream there was none. That way I looked between and over the near green hills to some distant and higher ones in the horizon, tinged with blue. Indeed, by standing on tiptoe I could catch a glimpse of some of the peaks of the still bluer and more distant mountain ranges in the northwest, those true-blue coins from heaven's own mint, and also of some portion of the village. But in other directions, even from this point, I could not see over or beyond the woods which surrounded me. It is well to have some water in your neighborhood, to give buoyancy to and float the earth. One value even of the smallest well is, that when you look into it you see that earth is not continent but insular. This is as important as that it keeps butter cool. When I looked across the pond from this peak toward the Sudbury meadows, which in time of flood I distinguished elevated perhaps by a mirage in their seething valley, like a coin in a basin, all the earth beyond the pond appeared like a thin crust insulated and floated even by this small sheet of intervening water, and I was reminded that this on which I dwelt was but *dry land*.

Though the view from my door was still more contracted, I did not feel crowded or confined in the least. There was pasture enough for my imagination. The low shrub oak plateau to which the opposite shore arose stretched away toward the prairies of the West and the steppes of Tartary, affording ample room for all the roving families of men. 'There are none happy in the world but beings who enjoy freely a vast horizon' — said Damodara, when his herds required new and larger pastures.

Both place and time were changed, and I dwelt nearer to those parts of the universe and to those eras in history which had most attracted me.

Where I lived was as far off as many a region viewed nightly by astronomers. We are wont to imagine rare and delectable places in some remote and more celestial corner of the system, behind the constellation of Cassiopeia's Chair, far from noise and disturbance. I discovered that my house actually had its site in such a withdrawn, but forever new and unprofaned, part of the universe. If it were worth the while to settle in those parts near to the Pleiades or the Hyades, to Aldebaran or Altair, then I was really there, or at an equal remoteness from the life which I had left behind, dwindled and twinkling with as fine a ray to my nearest neighbor, and to be seen only in moonless nights by him. Such was that part of creation where I had squatted;

> 'There was a shepherd that did live,
> And held his thoughts as high
> As were the mounts whereon his flocks
> Did hourly feed him by.'

What should we think of the shepherd's life if his flocks always wandered to higher pastures than his thoughts?

Every morning was a cheerful invitation to make my life of equal simplicity, and I may say innocence, with Nature herself. I have been as sincere a worshipper of Aurora as the Greeks. I got up early and bathed in the pond; that was a religious exercise, and one of the best things which I did. They say that characters were engraven on the bathing tub of King Tching-thang to this effect: 'Renew thyself completely each day; do it again, and again, and forever again.' I can understand that. Morning brings back the heroic ages. I was as much affected by the faint hum of a mosquito making its invisible and unimaginable tour through my apartment at earliest dawn, when I was sitting with door and windows open, as I could be by any trumpet that ever sang of fame. It was Homer's requiem; itself an Iliad and Odyssey in the air, singing its own wrath and wanderings. There was something cosmical about it; a standing advertisement, till forbidden, of the everlasting vigor and fertility of the world. The morning, which is the most memorable season of the day, is the awakening hour. Then there is least somnolence in us; and for an hour, at least, some part of us awakes which slumbers all the rest of the day and night. Little is to be expected of that day, if it can be called a day, to which we are not awakened by our Genius, but by the mechanical nudgings of some servitor, are not awakened by our own newly acquired force and aspirations from within, accompanied by the undulations of celestial music, instead of factory bells, and a fragrance filling the air — to a higher life than we fell asleep from; and thus the darkness bear its fruit, and prove itself to be good, no less than the light. That man who does not believe that each day contains an earlier, more sacred, and auroral hour than he has yet profaned, has despaired of life, and is pursuing a descending and darkening way. After a partial cessation of his sensuous life, the soul of man, or its organs rather, are reinvigorated each day, and his Genius tries again what noble life it can make. All memorable events, I should say, transpire in morning time and in a morning atmosphere. The Vedas say, 'All intelligences awake with the morning.' Poetry and art, and the fairest and most memorable of the actions of men, date from such an hour. All poets and heroes, like Memnon, are the children of Aurora, and emit their music at sunrise. To him whose elastic and vigorous thought keeps pace with the sun, the day is a perpetual morning. It matters not what the clocks say or the attitudes and labors of men. Morning is when I am awake and there is a dawn in me. Moral reform is the effort to throw off sleep. Why is it that men give so poor an account of their day if they have not been slumbering? They are not such poor calculators. If they had not been overcome with drowsiness, they would have performed something. The millions are awake enough for physical labor; but only one in a million is awake enough for effective intellectual exertion, only one in a hundred millions to a poetic or divine life. To be awake is to be alive. I have never yet met a man who was quite awake. How could I have looked him in the face?

We must learn to reawaken and keep ourselves awake, not by mechanical aids, but by an infinite expectation of the dawn, which does not forsake us in our soundest sleep. I know of no more encouraging fact than the unquestionable ability of man to elevate his life by a conscious endeavor. It is something to be able to paint a particular picture, or to carve a statue, and so to make a few objects beautiful; but it is far more glorious to carve and paint the very atmosphere and medium through which we look, which morally we can do. To affect the quality of the day, that is the highest of arts. Every man is tasked to make his life, even in its details, worthy of the contemplation of his most elevated and critical hour. If we refused, or rather used up, such paltry information as we get, the oracles would distinctly inform us how this might be done.

I went to the woods because I wished to live deliberately, to front only the essential facts of life, and see if I could not learn what it had to teach, and not, when I came to die, discover that I had not lived. I did not wish to live what was not life, living is so dear; nor did I wish to practise resignation, unless it was quite necessary. I wanted to live deep and suck out all the marrow of life, to live so sturdily and Spartan-like as to put to rout all that was not life, to cut a broad swath and shave close, to drive life into a corner, and reduce it to its lowest terms, and, if it proved to be mean, why then to get the whole and genuine meanness of it, and publish its meanness to the world; or if it were sublime, to know it by experience, and be able to give a true account of it in my next excursion. For most men, it appears to me, are in a strange uncertainty about it, whether it is of the devil or of God, and have *somewhat hastily* concluded that it is the chief end of man here to 'glorify God and enjoy him forever.'

Still we live meanly, like ants; though the fable tells us that we were long ago changed into men; like pygmies we fight with cranes; it is error upon error, and clout upon clout, and our best virtue has for its occasion a superfluous and evitable wretchedness. Our life is frittered away by detail. An honest man has hardly need to count more than his ten fingers, or in extreme cases he may add his ten toes, and lump the rest. Simplicity, simplicity, simplicity! I say, let your affairs be as two or three, and not a hundred or a thousand; instead of a million count half a dozen, and keep your accounts on your thumb-nail. In the midst of this chopping sea of civilized life, such are the clouds and storms and quicksands and thousand-and-one items to be allowed for, that a man has to live, if he would not founder and go to the bottom and not make his port at all, by dead reckoning, and he must be a great calculator indeed who succeeds. Simplify, simplify. Instead of three meals a day, if it be necessary eat but one; instead of a hundred dishes, five; and reduce other things in proportion. Our life is like a German Confederacy, made up of petty states, with its boundary forever fluctuating, so that even a German cannot tell you how it is bounded at any moment. The nation itself, with all its so-called internal improvements, which, by the way are all external and superficial, is just such an unwieldy and overgrown establishment, cluttered with furniture and tripped up by its own traps, ruined by luxury and heedless expense, by want of calculation and a worthy aim, as the million households in the land; and the only cure for it, as for them, is in a rigid economy, a stern and more than Spartan simplicity of life and elevation of purpose. It lives too fast. Men think that it is essential that the *Nation* have commerce, and export ice, and talk through a telegraph, and ride thirty miles an hour, without a doubt, whether *they* do or not; but whether we should live like baboons or like men, is a little uncertain. If we do not get out sleepers, and forge rails, and devote days and nights to the work, but go to tinkering upon our *lives* to improve *them*, who will build railroads? And if railroads are not built, how shall we get to heaven in season? But if we stay at home and mind our business, who will want railroads? We do not ride on the railroad; it rides upon us. Did you ever think what those sleepers are that underlie the railroad? Each one is a man, an Irishman, or a Yankee man. The rails are laid on them, and they are covered with sand, and the cars run smoothly over them. They are sound sleepers, I assure you. And every few years a new lot is laid down and run over; so that, if some have the pleasure of riding on a rail, others have the misfortune to be ridden upon. And when they run over a man that is walking in his sleep, a supernumerary sleeper in the wrong position, and wake him up, they suddenly stop the cars, and make a hue and cry about it, as if this were an exception. I am glad to know that it takes a gang of men for every five miles to keep the sleepers down and level in their beds as it is, for this is a sign that they may sometime get up again.

Why should we live with such hurry and waste of life? We are determined to be starved before we are hungry. Men say that a stitch in time saves nine, and so they take a thousand stitches today to save nine tomorrow. As for *work*, we haven't any of any consequence. We have the Saint Vitus' dance, and cannot possibly keep our heads still. If I should only give a few pulls at the parish bell-rope, as for a fire, that is, without setting the bell, there is hardly a man on his farm in the outskirts of Concord, notwithstanding that press of engagements which was his excuse so many times this morning, nor a boy, nor a woman, I might almost say, but would forsake all and follow that sound, not mainly to save property from the flames, but, if we will confess the truth, much more to see it burn, since burn it must, and we, be it known, did not set it on fire — or to see it put out, and have a hand in it, if that is done as handsomely; yes, even if it were the parish church itself. Hardly a man takes a half-hour's nap after dinner, but when he wakes he holds up his head and asks, 'What's the news?' as if the rest of mankind had stood his sentinels. Some give directions to be waked every half-hour, doubtless for no other purpose; and then, to pay for it, they tell what they have dreamed. After a night's sleep the news is as indispensable as the breakfast. 'Pray tell me anything new that has happened to a man anywhere on this globe' — and he reads it over his coffee and rolls, that a man has had his eyes gouged out this morning on the Wachito River; never dreaming the while that he lives in the dark unfathomed mammoth cave of this world, and has but the rudiment of an eye himself.

For my part, I could easily do without the post-office. I think that there are very few important communications made through it. To speak critically, I never received more than one or two letters in my life — I wrote this some years ago — that were worth the postage. The penny-post is, commonly, an institution through which you seriously offer a man that penny for his thoughts which is so often safely offered in jest. And I am sure that I never read any memorable news in a newspaper. If we read of one man robbed, or murdered, or killed by accident, or one house burned, or one vessel wrecked, or one steamboat blown up, or one cow run over on the Western Railroad, or one mad dog killed, or one lot of grasshoppers in the winter — we never need read of another. One is enough. If you are acquainted with the principle, what do you care for a myriad instances and applications? To a philosopher all *news*, as it is called, is gossip, and they who edit and read it are old women over their tea. Yet not a few are greedy after this gossip. There was such a rush, as I hear, the other day at one of the offices to learn the foreign news by the last arrival, that several large squares of plate glass belonging to the establishment were broken by the pressure — news which I seriously think a ready wit might write a twelvemonth, or twelve years, beforehand with sufficient accuracy. As for Spain, for instance, if you know how to throw in Don Carlos and the Infanta, and Don Pedro and Seville and Granada, from time to time in the right proportions — they may have changed the names a little since I saw the papers — and serve up a bull-fight when other entertainments fail, it will be true to the letter, and give us as good an idea of the exact state or ruin of things in Spain as the most succinct and lucid reports under this head in the newspapers: and as for England, almost the last significant scrap of news from that quarter was the revolution of 1649; and if you have learned the history of her crops for an average year, you never need attend to that thing again, unless your speculations are of a merely pecuniary character. If one may judge who rarely looks into the newspapers, nothing new does ever happen in foreign parts, a French revolution not excepted.

What news! how much more important to know what that is which was never old! 'Kieou-he-yu (great dignitary of the state of Wei) sent a man to Khoung-tseu to know his news. Khoung-tseu caused the messenger to be seated near him, and questioned him in these terms:

What is your master doing? The messenger answered with respect: My master desires to diminish the number of his faults, but he cannot come to the end of them. The messenger being gone, the philosopher remarked: What a worthy messenger! What a worthy messenger!' The preacher, instead of vexing the ears of drowsy farmers on their day of rest at the end of the week — for Sunday is the fit conclusion of an ill-spent week, and not the fresh and brave beginning of a new one — with this one other draggle-tail of a sermon, should shout with thundering voice, 'Pause! Avast! Why so seeming fast, but deadly slow?'

Shams and delusions are esteemed for soundest truths, while reality is fabulous. If men would steadily observe realities only, and not allow themselves to be deluded, life, to compare it with such things as we know, would be like a fairy tale and the Arabian Nights' Entertainments. If we respected only what is inevitable and has a right to be, music and poetry would resound along the streets. When we are unhurried and wise, we perceive that only great and worthy things have any permanent and absolute existence, that petty fears and petty pleasures are but the shadow of the reality. This is always exhilarating and sublime. By closing the eyes and slumbering, and consenting to be deceived by shows, men establish and confirm their daily life of routine and habit everywhere, which still is built on purely illusory foundations. Children, who play life, discern its true law and relations more clearly than men, who fail to live it worthily, but who think that they are wiser by experience, that is, by failure. I have read in a Hindoo book, that 'there was a king's son, who, being expelled in infancy from his native city, was brought up by a forester, and, growing up to maturity in that state, imagined himself to belong to the barbarous race with which he lived. One of his father's ministers having discovered him, revealed to him what he was, and the misconception of his character was removed, and he knew himself to be a prince. So soul,' continues the Hindoo philosopher, 'from the circumstances in which it is placed, mistakes its own character, until the truth is revealed to it by some holy teacher, and then it knows itself to be *Brahme*.' I perceive that we inhabitants of New England live this mean life that we do because our vision does not penetrate the surface of things. We think that that *is* which *appears* to be. If a man should walk through this town and see only the reality, where, think you, would the 'Mill-dam' go to? If he should give us an account of the realities he beheld there, we should not recognize the place in his description. Look at a meeting-house, or a court-house, or a jail, or a shop, or a dwelling-house, and say what that thing really is before a true gaze, and they would all go to pieces in your account of them. Men esteem truth remote, in the outskirts of the system, behind the farthest star, before Adam and after the last man. In eternity there is indeed something true and sublime. But all these times and places and occasions are now and here. God himself culminates in the present moment, and will never be more divine in the lapse of all the ages. And we are enabled to apprehend at all what is sublime and noble only by the perpetual instilling and drenching of the reality that surrounds us. The universe constantly and obediently answers to our conceptions; whether we travel fast or slow, the track is laid for us. Let us spend our lives in conceiving then. The poet or the artist never yet had so fair and noble a design but some of his posterity at least could accomplish it.

Let us spend one day as deliberately as Nature, and not be thrown off the track by every nutshell and mosquito's wing that falls on the rails. Let us rise early and fast, or break fast, gently and without perturbation; let company come and let company go, let the bells ring and the children cry — determined to make a day of it. Why should we knock under and go with the stream? Let us not be upset and over-whelmed in that terrible rapid and whirlpool called a dinner, situated in the meridian shallows. Weather this danger and you are safe, for the rest of the way is down hill. With unrelaxed nerves, with morning vigor, sail by it, looking another way, tied to the mast like Ulysses. If the engine whistles, let it whistle till it is hoarse for its pains. If the bell rings, why should we run? We will consider what kind of music they are like. Let us settle ourselves, and work and wedge our feet down-ward through the mud and slush of opinion, and prejudice, and tradi-tion, and delusion, and appearance, that alluvion which covers the globe, through Paris and London, through New York and Boston and Concord, through Church and State, through poetry and philosophy and religion, till we come to a hard bottom and rocks in place, which we can call *reality*, and say, This is, and no mistake; and then begin, having a *point d'appui*, below freshet and frost and fire, a place where you might found a wall or a state, or set a lamp-post safely, or perhaps a gauge, not a Nilometer, but a Realometer, that future ages might know how deep a freshet of shams and appearances had gathered from time to time. If you stand right fronting and face to face to a fact, you will see the sun glimmer on both its surfaces, as if it were a cimeter, and feel its sweet edge dividing you through the heart and marrow, and so you will happily conclude your mortal career. Be it life or death, we crave only reality. If we are really dying, let us hear the rattle in our throats and feel cold in the extremities; if we are alive, let us go about our business.

Time is but the stream I go a-fishing in. I drink at it; but while I drink I see the sandy bottom and detect how shallow it is. Its thin current slides away, but eternity remains. I would drink deeper; fish in the sky, whose bottom is pebbly with stars. I cannot count one. I know not the first letter of the alphabet. I have always been regretting that I was not as wise as the day I was born. The intellect is a cleaver; it discerns and rifts its way into the secret of things. I do not wish to be any more busy with my hands than is necessary. My head is hands and feet. I feel all my best faculties concentrated in it. My instinct tells me that my head is an organ for burrowing, as some creatures use their snout and fore paws, and with it I would mine and burrow my way through these hills. I think that the richest vein is somewhere hereabouts; so by the divining-rod and thin rising vapors I judge; and here I will begin to mine.

III. READING

WITH a little more deliberation in the choice of their pursuits, all men would perhaps become essentially students and observers, for certainly their nature and destiny are interesting to all alike. In accumulating property for ourselves or our posterity, in founding a family or a state, or acquiring fame even, we are mortal; but in dealing with truth we are immortal, and need fear no change nor accident. The oldest Egyptian or Hindoo philosopher raised a corner of the veil from the statue of the divinity; and still the trembling robe remains raised, and I gaze upon as fresh a glory as he did, since it was I in him that was then so bold, and it is he in me that now reviews the vision. No dust has settled on that robe; no time has elapsed since that divinity was revealed. That time which we really improve, or which is improvable, is neither past, present, nor future.

My residence was more favorable, not only to thought, but to serious reading, than a university; and though I was beyond the range of the ordinary circulating library, I had more than ever come within the influence of those books which circulate round the world, whose sentences were first written on bark, and are now merely copied from time to time on to linen paper. Says the poet Mîr Camar Uddin Mast, 'Being seated, to run through the region of the spiritual world; I have had this advantage in books. To be intoxicated by a single glass of wine; I have experienced this pleasure when I have drunk the liquor of the esoteric doctrines.' I kept Homer's Iliad on my table through the summer, though I looked at his page only now and then. Incessant labor with my hands, at first, for I had my house to finish and my beans to hoe at the same time, made more study impossible. Yet I sustained myself by the prospect of such reading in future. I read one or two shallow books of travel in the intervals of my work, till that employment made me ashamed of myself, and I asked where it was then that *I* lived.

The student may read Homer or Æschylus in the Greek without danger of dissipation or luxuriousness, for it implies that he in some measure emulate their heroes, and consecrate morning hours to their pages. The heroic books, even if printed in the character of our mother tongue, will always be in a language dead to degenerate times; and we must laboriously seek the meaning of each word and line, conjecturing a larger sense than common use permits out of what wisdom and valor and generosity we have. The modern cheap and fertile press, with all its translations, has done little to bring us nearer to the heroic writers of antiquity. They seem as solitary, and the letter in which they are printed as rare and curious, as ever. It is worth the expense of youthful days and costly hours, if you learn only some words of an ancient language, which are raised out of the trivialness of the street, to be perpetual suggestions and provocations. It is not in vain that the farmer remembers and repeats the few Latin words which he has heard. Men sometimes speak as if the study of the classics would at length make way for more modern and practical studies; but the adventurous student will always study classics, in whatever language they may be written and however ancient they may be. For what are the classics but the noblest recorded thoughts of man? They are the only oracles which are not decayed, and there are such answers to the most modern inquiry in them as Delphi and Dodona never gave. We might as well omit to study Nature because she is old. To read well, that is, to read true books in a true spirit, is a noble exercise, and one that will task the reader more than any exercise which the customs of the day esteem. It requires a training such as the athletes underwent, the steady intention almost of the whole life to this object. Books must be read as deliberately and reservedly as they were written. It is not enough even to be able to speak the language of that nation by which they are written, for there is a memorable interval between the spoken and the written language, the language heard and the language read. The one is commonly transitory, a sound, a tongue, a dialect merely, almost brutish, and we learn it unconsciously, like the brutes, of our mothers. The other is the maturity and experience of that; if that is our mother tongue, this is our father tongue, a reserved and select expression, too significant to be heard by the ear, which we must be born again in order to speak. The crowds of men who merely *spoke* the Greek and Latin tongues in the Middle Ages were not entitled by the accident of birth to *read* the works of genius written in those languages; for these were not written in that Greek or Latin which they knew, but in the select language of literature. They had not learned the nobler dialects of Greece and Rome, but the very materials on which they were written were waste paper to them, and they prized instead a cheap contemporary literature. But when the several nations of Europe had acquired distinct though rude written languages of their own, sufficient for the purposes of their rising literatures, then first learning revived, and scholars were enabled to discern from that remoteness the treasures of antiquity. What the Roman and Grecian multitude could not *hear*, after the lapse of ages a few scholars *read*, and a few scholars only are still reading it.

However much we may admire the orator's occasional bursts of eloquence, the noblest written words are commonly as far behind or above the fleeting spoken language as the firmament with its stars is behind the clouds. *There* are the stars, and they who can may read them. The astronomers forever comment on and observe them. They are not exhalations like our daily colloquies and vaporous breath. What is called eloquence in the forum is commonly found to be rhetoric in the study. The orator yields to the inspiration of a transient occasion, and speaks to the mob before him, to those who can *hear* him; but the writer, whose more equable life is his occasion, and who would be distracted by the event and the crowd which inspire the orator, speaks to the intellect and heart of mankind, to all in any age who can *understand* him.

No wonder that Alexander carried the Iliad with him on his expeditions in a precious casket. A written word is the choicest of relics. It is something at once more intimate with us and more universal than any other work of art. It is the work of art nearest to life itself. It may be translated into every language, and not only be read but actually breathed from all human lips; — not be represented on canvas or in marble only, but be carved out of the breath of life itself. The symbol of an ancient man's thought becomes a modern man's speech. Two thousand summers have imparted to the monuments of Grecian literature, as to her marbles, only a maturer golden and autumnal tint, for they have carried their own serene and celestial atmosphere into all lands to protect them against the corrosion of time. Books are the treasured wealth of the world and the fit inheritance of generations and nations. Books, the oldest and the best, stand naturally and rightfully on the shelves of every cottage. They have no cause of their own to plead, but while they enlighten and sustain the reader his common sense will not refuse them. Their authors are a natural and irresistible aristocracy in every society, and, more than kings or emperors, exert an influence on mankind. When the illiterate and perhaps scornful trader has earned by enterprise and industry his coveted leisure and independence, and is admitted to the circles of wealth and fashion, he turns inevitably at last to those still higher but yet inaccessible circles of intellect and genius, and is sensible only of the imperfection of his culture and the vanity and insufficiency of all his riches, and further proves his good sense by the pains which he takes to secure for his children that intellectual culture whose want he so keenly feels; and thus it is that he becomes the founder of a family.

Those who have not learned to read the ancient classics in the language in which they were written must have a very imperfect knowledge of the history of the human race; for it is remarkable that no transcript of them has ever been made into any modern tongue, unless our civilization itself may be regarded as such a transcript. Homer has never yet been printed in English, nor Æschylus, nor Virgil even — works as refined, as solidly done, and as beautiful almost as the morning itself; for later writers, say what we will of their genius, have rarely, if ever, equalled the elaborate beauty and finish and the lifelong and heroic literary labors of the ancients. They only talk of forgetting them who never knew them. It will be soon enough to forget them when we have the learning and the genius which will enable us to attend to and appreciate them. That age will be rich indeed when those relics which we call Classics, and the still older and more than classic but even less known Scriptures of the nations, shall have still further accumulated, when the Vaticans shall be filled with Vedas and Zendavestas and Bibles, with Homers and Dantes and Shakespeares, and all the centuries to come shall have successively deposited their trophies in the forum of the world. By such a pile we may hope to scale heaven at last.

The works of the great poets have never yet been read by mankind, for only great poets can read them. They have only been read as the multitude read the stars, at most astrologically, not astronomically. Most men have learned to read to serve a paltry convenience, as they have learned to cipher in order to keep accounts and not be cheated in trade; but of reading as a noble intellectual exercise they know little or nothing; yet this only is reading, in a high sense, not that which lulls us as a luxury and suffers the nobler faculties to sleep the while, but what we have to stand on tip-toe to read and devote our most alert and wakeful hours to.

I think that having learned our letters we should read the best that is in literature, and not be forever repeating our a-b-abs, and words of one syllable, in the fourth or fifth classes, sitting on the lowest and fore-most form all our lives. Most men are satisfied if they read or hear read, and perchance have been convicted by the wisdom of one good book, the Bible, and for the rest of their lives vegetate and dissipate their faculties in what is called easy reading. There is a work in several vol-umes in our Circulating Library entitled 'Little Reading,' which I thought referred to a town of that name which I had not been to. There are those who, like cormorants and ostriches, can digest all sorts of this, even after the fullest dinner of meats and vegetables, for they suffer nothing to be wasted. If others are the machines to provide this provender, they are the machines to read it. They read the nine thou-sandth tale about Zebulon and Sophronia, and how they loved as none had ever loved before, and neither did the course of their true love run smooth — at any rate, how it did run and stumble, and get up again and go on! how some poor unfortunate got up on to a steeple, who had better never have gone up as far as the belfry; and then, having need-lessly got him up there, the happy novelist rings the bell for all the world to come together and hear, O dear! how he did get down again! For my part, I think that they had better metamorphose all such aspiring heroes of universal noveldom into man weather-cocks, as they used to put heroes among the constellations, and let them swing round there till they are rusty, and not come down at all to bother honest men with their pranks. The next time the novelist rings the bell I will not stir though the meeting-house burn down. 'The Skip of the Tip-Toe-Hop, a Romance of the Middle Ages, by the celebrated author of "Tittle-Tol-Tan," to appear in monthly parts; a great rush; don't all come together.' All this they read with saucer eyes, and erect and primitive curiosity, and with unwearied gizzard, whose corrugations even yet need no sharpening, just as some little four-year-old bencher his two-cent gilt-covered edition of Cinderella — without any improvement, that I can see, in the pronunciation, or accent, or emphasis, or any more skill in extracting or inserting the moral. The result is dulness of sight, a stagnation of the vital circulations, and a general deliquium and sloughing off of all the intellectual faculties. This sort of gingerbread is baked daily and more sedulously than pure wheat or rye-and-Indian in almost every oven, and finds a surer market.

The best books are not read even by those who are called good readers. What does our Concord culture amount to? There is in this town, with a very few exceptions, no taste for the best or for very good books even in English literature, whose words all can read and spell. Even the college-bred and so-called liberally educated men here and elsewhere have really little or no acquaintance with the English classics; and as for the recorded wisdom of mankind, the ancient classics and Bibles, which are accessible to all who will know of them, there are the feeblest efforts anywhere made to become acquainted with them. I know a woodchopper, of middle age, who takes a French paper, not for news as he says, for he is above that, but to 'keep himself in practice,' he being a Canadian by birth; and when I ask him what he considers the best thing he can do in this world, he says, beside this, to keep up and add to his English. This is about as much as the college-bred generally do or aspire to do, and they take an English paper for the purpose. One who has just come from reading perhaps one of the best English books will find how many with whom he can converse about it? Or suppose he comes from reading a Greek or Latin classic in the original, whose praises are familiar even to the so-called illiterate; he will find nobody at all to speak to, but must keep silence about it. Indeed, there is hardly the professor in our colleges, who, if he has mastered the difficulties of the language, has proportionally mastered the difficulties of the wit and poetry of a Greek poet, and has any sympathy to impart to the alert and heroic reader; and as for the sacred Scriptures, or Bibles of mankind, who in this town can tell me even their titles? Most men do not know that any nation but the Hebrews have had a scripture. A man, any man, will go considerably out of his way to pick

up a silver dollar; but here are golden words, which the wisest men of
antiquity have uttered, and whose worth the wise of every succeeding
age have assured us of; — and yet we learn to read only as far as Easy
Reading, the primers and class-books, and when we leave school, the
'Little Reading,' and story-books, which are for boys and beginners;
and our reading, our conversation and thinking, are all on a very low
level, worthy only of pygmies and manikins.

I aspire to be acquainted with wiser men than this our Concord soil
has produced, whose names are hardly known here. Or shall I hear the
name of Plato and never read his book? As if Plato were my townsman
and I never saw him — my next neighbor and I never heard him speak
or attended to the wisdom of his words. But how actually is it? His
Dialogues, which contain what was immortal in him, lie on the next
shelf, and yet I never read them. We are underbred and low-lived and
illiterate; and in this respect I confess I do not make any very broad
distinction between the illiterateness of my townsman who cannot read
at all and the illiterateness of him who has learned to read only what
is for children and feeble intellects. We should be as good as the worthies
of antiquity, but partly by first knowing how good they were. We are
a race of tit-men, and soar but little higher in our intellectual flights
than the columns of the daily paper.

It is not all books that are as dull as their readers. There are probably
words addressed to our condition exactly, which, if we could really hear
and understand, would be more salutary than the morning or the spring
to our lives, and possibly put a new aspect on the face of things for us.
How many a man has dated a new era in his life from the reading of
a book! The book exists for us, perchance, which will explain our
miracles and reveal new ones. The at present unutterable things we
may find somewhere uttered. These same questions that disturb and
puzzle and confound us have in their turn occurred to all the wise men;
not one has been omitted; and each has answered them, according to
his ability, by his words and his life. Moreover, with wisdom we shall
learn liberality. The solitary hired man on a farm in the outskirts of
Concord, who has had his second birth and peculiar religious experience, and is driven as he believes into silent gravity and exclusiveness
by his faith, may think it is not true; but Zoroaster, thousands of years
ago, travelled the same road and had the same experience; but he,
being wise, knew it to be universal, and treated his neighbors accordingly, and is even said to have invented and established worship among
men. Let him humbly commune with Zoroaster then, and through the

liberalizing influence of all the worthies, with Jesus Christ himself, and let 'our church' go by the board.

We boast that we belong to the Nineteenth Century and are making the most rapid strides of any nation. But consider how little this village does for its own culture. I do not wish to flatter my townsmen, nor to be flattered by them, for that will not advance either of us. We need to be provoked — goaded like oxen, as we are, into a trot. We have a comparatively decent system of common schools, schools for infants only; but excepting the half-starved Lyceum in the winter, and latterly the puny beginning of a library suggested by the State, no school for ourselves. We spend more on almost any article of bodily aliment or ailment than on our mental aliment. It is time that we had uncommon schools, that we did not leave off our education when we begin to be men and women. It is time that villages were universities, and their elder inhabitants the fellows of universities, with leisure — if they are, indeed, so well off — to pursue liberal studies the rest of their lives. Shall the world be confined to one Paris or one Oxford forever? Cannot students be boarded here and get a liberal education under the skies of Concord? Can we not hire some Abélard to lecture to us? Alas! what with foddering the cattle and tending the store, we are kept from school too long, and our education is sadly neglected. In this country, the village should in some respects take the place of the nobleman of Europe. It should be the patron of the fine arts. It is rich enough. It wants only the magnanimity and refinement. It can spend money enough on such things as farmers and traders value, but it is thought Utopian to propose spending money for things which more intelligent men know to be of far more worth. This town has spent seventeen thousand dollars on a town-house, thank fortune or politics, but probably it will not spend so much on living wit, the true meat to put into that shell, in a hundred years. The one hundred and twenty-five dollars annually subscribed for a Lyceum in the winter is better spent than any other equal sum raised in the town. If we live in the Nineteenth Century, why should we not enjoy the advantages which the Nineteenth Century offers? Why should our life be in any respect provincial? If we will read newspapers, why not skip the gossip of Boston and take the best newspaper in the world at once? — not be sucking the pap of 'neutral family' papers, or browsing 'Olive-Branches' here in New England. Let the reports of all the learned societies come to us, and we will see if they know anything. Why should we leave it to Harper & Brothers and Redding & Co. to select our reading? As the nobleman of cultivated taste surrounds himself with whatever conduces to his culture — genius — learning — wit — books — paintings — statuary — music — philosophical instruments, and the like; so let the village do — not stop short at a pedagogue, a parson, a sexton, a parish library, and three selectmen, because our Pilgrim forefathers got through a cold winter once on a bleak rock with these. To act collectively is according to the spirit of our institutions; and I am confident that, as our circumstances are more flourishing, our means are greater than the nobleman's. New England can hire all the wise men in the world to come and teach her, and board them round the while, and not be provincial at all. That is the *uncommon* school we want. Instead of noblemen, let us have noble villages of men. If it is necessary, omit one bridge over the river, go round a little there, and throw one arch at least over the darker gulf of ignorance which surrounds us.

IV. SOUNDS

But while we are confined to books, though the most select and classic, and read only particular written languages, which are themselves but dialects and provincial, we are in danger of forgetting the language which all things and events speak without metaphor, which alone is copious and standard. Much is published, but little printed. The rays which stream through the shutter will be no longer remembered when the shutter is wholly removed. No method nor discipline can supersede the necessity of being forever on the alert. What is a course of history or philosophy, or poetry, no matter how well selected, or the best society, or the most admirable routine of life, compared with the discipline of looking always at what is to be seen? Will you be a reader, a student merely, or a seer? Read your fate, see what is before you, and walk on into futurity.

I did not read books the first summer; I hoed beans. Nay, I often did better than this. There were times when I could not afford to sacrifice the bloom of the present moment to any work, whether of the head or hands. I love a broad margin to my life. Sometimes, in a summer morning, having taken my accustomed bath, I sat in my sunny doorway from sunrise till noon, rapt in a revery, amidst the pines and hickories and sumachs, in undisturbed solitude and stillness, while the birds sang around or flitted noiseless through the house, until by the sun falling in at my west window, or the noise of some traveller's wagon on the distant highway, I was reminded of the lapse of time. I grew in those seasons like corn in the night, and they were far better than any work of the hands would have been. They were not time subtracted from my life, but so much over and above my usual allowance. I realized what the Orientals mean by contemplation and the forsaking of works. For the most part, I minded not how the hours went. The day advanced as if to light some work of mine; it was morning, and lo, now it is evening, and nothing memorable is accomplished. Instead of singing like the birds, I silently smiled at my incessant good fortune. As the sparrow had its trill, sitting on the hickory before my door, so had I my chuckle or suppressed warble which he might hear out of my nest. My days were not days of the week, bearing the stamp of any heathen deity, nor were they minced into hours and fretted by the ticking of a clock; for I lived like the Puri Indians, of whom it is said that 'for yesterday, today, and tomorrow they have only one word, and they express the variety of meaning by pointing backward for yesterday, forward for tomorrow, and overhead for the passing day.' This was sheer idleness to my fellow-townsmen, no doubt; but if the birds and flowers had tried me by their standard, I should not have been found wanting. A man must find his occasions in himself, it is true. The natural day is very calm, and will hardly reprove his indolence.

I had this advantage, at least, in my mode of life, over those who were obliged to look abroad for amusement, to society and the theatre, that my life itself was become my amusement and never ceased to be novel. It was a drama of many scenes and without an end. If we were always, indeed, getting our living, and regulating our lives according to the last and best mode we had learned, we should never be troubled with ennui. Follow your genius closely enough, and it will not fail to show you a fresh prospect every hour. Housework was a pleasant pastime. When my floor was dirty, I rose early, and, setting all my furniture out of doors on the grass, bed and bedstead making but one budget, dashed water on the floor, and sprinkled white sand from the pond on it, and then with a broom scrubbed it clean and white; and by the time the villagers had broken their fast the morning sun had dried my house sufficiently to allow me to move in again, and my meditations were almost uninterrupted. It was pleasant to see my whole household effects out on the grass, making a little pile like a gypsy's pack, and my three-legged table, from which I did not remove the books and pen and ink, standing amid the pines and hickories. They seemed glad to get out themselves, and as if unwilling to be brought in. I was sometimes tempted to stretch an awning over them and take my seat there. It was worth the while to see the sun shine on these things, and hear the free wind blow on them; so much more interesting most familiar objects look out of doors than in the house. A bird sits on the next bough, life-everlasting grows under the table, and blackberry vines run round its legs; pine cones, chestnut burs, and strawberry leaves are strewn about. It looked as if this was the way these forms came to be transferred to our furniture, to tables, chairs, and bedsteads — because they once stood in their midst.

My house was on the side of a hill, immediately on the edge of the larger wood, in the midst of a young forest of pitch pines and hickories, and half a dozen rods from the pond, to which a narrow footpath led down the hill. In my front yard grew the strawberry, blackberry, and life-everlasting, johnswort and goldenrod, shrub oaks and sand cherry, blueberry and groundnut. Near the end of May, the sand cherry (*Cerasus pumila*) adorned the sides of the path with its delicate flowers arranged in umbels cylindrically about its short stems, which last, in the fall, weighed down with goodsized and handsome cherries, fell over in wreaths like rays on every side. I tasted them out of compliment to Nature, though they were scarcely palatable. The sumach (*Rhus glabra*) grew luxuriantly about the house, pushing up through the embankment which I had made, and growing five or six feet the first season. Its broad pinnate tropical leaf was pleasant though strange to look on. The large buds, suddenly pushing out late in the spring from dry sticks which had seemed to be dead, developed themselves as by magic into graceful green and tender boughs, an inch in diameter; and sometimes, as I sat at my window, so heedlessly did they grow and tax their weak joints, I heard a fresh and tender bough suddenly fall like a fan to the ground, when there was not a breath of air stirring, broken off by its own weight. In August, the large masses of berries, which, when in flower, had attracted many wild bees, gradually assumed their bright velvety crimson hue, and by their weight again bent down and broke the tender limbs.

As I sit at my window this summer afternoon, hawks are circling about my clearing; the tantivy of wild pigeons, flying by twos and threes athwart my view, or perching restless on the white pine boughs behind my house, gives a voice to the air; a fish hawk dimples the glassy surface of the pond and brings up a fish; a mink steals out of the marsh before my door and seizes a frog by the shore; the sedge is bending under the weight of the reed-birds flitting hither and thither; and for the last half-hour I have heard the rattle of railroad cars, now dying away and then reviving like the beat of a partridge, conveying travellers from Boston to the country. For I did not live so out of the world as that boy who, as I hear, was put out to a farmer in the east part of the town, but ere long ran away and came home again, quite down at the heel and homesick. He had never seen such a dull and out-of-the-way place; the folks were all gone off; why, you couldn't even hear the whistle! I doubt if there is such a place in Massachusetts now:

> 'In truth, our village has become a butt
> For one of those fleet railroad shafts, and o'er
> Our peaceful plain its soothing sound is — Concord.'

The Fitchburg Railroad touches the pond about a hundred rods south of where I dwell. I usually go to the village along its causeway, and am, as it were, related to society by this link. The men on the freight trains, who go over the whole length of the road, bow to me as to an old acquaintance, they pass me so often, and apparently they take me for an employee; and so I am. I too would fain be a track-repairer somewhere in the orbit of the earth.

The whistle of the locomotive penetrates my woods summer and winter, sounding like the scream of a hawk sailing over some farmer's yard, informing me that many restless city merchants are arriving within the circle of the town, or adventurous country traders from the other side. As they come under one horizon, they shout their warning to get off the track to the other, heard sometimes through the circles of two towns. Here come your groceries, country; your rations, country-men! Nor is there any man so independent on his farm that he can say them nay. And here's your pay for them! screams the countryman's whistle; timber like long battering-rams going twenty miles an hour against the city's walls, and chairs enough to seat all the weary and heavy-laden that dwell within them. With such huge and lumbering civility the country hands a chair to the city. All the Indian huckle-berry hills are stripped, all the cranberry meadows are raked into the city. Up comes the cotton, down goes the woven cloth; up comes the silk, down goes the woollen; up come the books, but down goes the wit that writes them.

When I meet the engine with its train of cars moving off with planetary motion — or, rather, like a comet, for the beholder knows not if with that velocity and with that direction it will ever revisit this system, since its orbit does not look like a returning curve — with its steam cloud like a banner streaming behind in golden and silver wreaths, like many a downy cloud which I have seen, high in the heavens, unfolding its masses to the light — as if this travelling demigod, this cloud-compeller, would ere long take the sunset sky for the livery of his train; when I hear the iron horse make the hills echo with his snort like thunder, shaking the earth with his feet, and breathing fire and smoke from his nostrils (what kind of winged horse or fiery dragon they will put into the new Mythology I don't know), it seems as if the earth had got a race now worthy to inhabit it. If all were as it seems, and men made the elements their servants for noble ends! If the cloud that hangs over the engine were the perspiration of heroic deeds, or as beneficent as that which floats over the farmer's fields, then the elements and Nature herself would cheerfully accompany men on their errands and be their escort.

I watch the passage of the morning cars with the same feeling that I do the rising of the sun, which is hardly more regular. Their train of clouds stretching far behind and rising higher and higher, going to heaven while the cars are going to Boston, conceals the sun for a minute and casts my distant field into the shade, a celestial train beside which the petty train of cars which hugs the earth is but the barb of the spear. The stabler of the iron horse was up early this winter morning by the light of the stars amid the mountains, to fodder and harness his steed. Fire, too, was awakened thus early to put the vital heat in him and get him off. If the enterprise were as innocent as it is early! If the snow lies deep, they strap on his snowshoes, and, with the giant plow, plow a furrow from the mountains to the seaboard, in which the cars, like a following drill-barrow, sprinkle all the restless men and floating merchandise in the country for seed. All day the fire-steed flies over the country, stopping only that his master may rest, and I am awakened by his tramp and defiant snort at midnight, when in some remote glen in the woods he fronts the elements incased in ice and snow; and he will reach his stall only with the morning star, to start once more on his travels without rest or slumber. Or perchance, at evening, I hear him in his stable blowing off the superfluous energy of the day, that he may calm his nerves and cool his liver and brain for a few hours of iron slumber. If the enterprise were as heroic and commanding as it is protracted and unwearied!

Far through unfrequented woods on the confines of towns, where once only the hunter penetrated by day, in the darkest night dart these bright saloons without the knowledge of their inhabitants; this moment stopping at some brilliant station-house in town or city, where a social crowd is gathered, the next in the Dismal Swamp, scaring the owl and fox. The startings and arrivals of the cars are now the epochs in the village day. They go and come with such regularity and precision, and their whistle can be heard so far, that the farmers set their clocks by them, and thus one well-conducted institution regulates a whole country. Have not men improved somewhat in punctuality since the railroad was invented? Do they not talk and think faster in the depot than they did in the stage-office? There is something electrifying in the atmosphere of the former place. I have been astonished at the miracles it has wrought; that some of my neighbors, who, I should have prophesied, once for all, would never get to Boston by so prompt a conveyance, are on' hand when the bell rings. To do things 'railroad fashion' is now the byword; and it is worth the while to be warned so often and so sincerely by any power to get off its track. There is no stopping to read the riot act, no firing over the heads of the mob, in this case. We have constructed a fate, an *Atropos*, that never turns aside. (Let that be the name of your engine.) Men are advertised that at a certain hour and minute these bolts will be shot toward particular points of the compass; yet it interferes with no man's business, and the children go to school on the other track. We live the steadier for it. We are all educated thus to be sons of Tell. The air is full of invisible bolts. Every path but your own is the path of fate. Keep on your own track, then.

What recommends commerce to me is its enterprise and bravery. It does not clasp its hands and pray to Jupiter. I see these men every day go about their business with more or less courage and content, doing more even than they suspect, and perchance better employed than they could have consciously devised. I am less affected by their heroism who stood up for half an hour in the front line at Buena Vista, than by the steady and cheerful valor of the men who inhabit the snow-plow for their winter quarters; who have not merely the three-o'-clock-in-the-morning courage, which Bonaparte thought was the rarest, but whose courage does not go to rest so early, who go to sleep only when the storm sleeps or the sinews of their iron steed are frozen. On this morning of the Great Snow, perchance, which is still raging and chilling men's blood, I hear the muffled tone of their engine bell from out the fog bank of their chilled breath, which announces that the cars *are com-*

ing, without long delay, notwithstanding the veto of a New England northeast snow-storm, and I behold the plowmen covered with snow and rime, their heads peering above the mould-board which is turning down other than daisies and the nests of field mice, like bowlders of the Sierra Nevada, that occupy an outside place in the universe.

Commerce is unexpectedly confident and serene, alert, adventurous, and unwearied. It is very natural in its methods withal, far more so than many fantastic enterprises and sentimental experiments, and hence its singular success. I am refreshed and expanded when the freight train rattles past me, and I smell the stores which go dispensing their odors all the way from Long Wharf to Lake Champlain, reminding me of foreign parts, of coral reefs, and Indian oceans, and tropical climes, and the extent of the globe. I feel more like a citizen of the world at the sight of the palm-leaf which will cover so many flaxen New England heads the next summer, the Manilla hemp and cocoanut husks, the old junk, gunny bags, scrap iron, and rusty nails. This car-load of torn sails is more legible and interesting now than if they should be wrought into paper and printed books. Who can write so graphically the history of the storms they have weathered as these rents have done? They are proof-sheets which need no correction. Here goes lumber from the Maine woods, which did not go out to sea in the last freshet, risen four dollars on the thousand because of what did go out or was split up; pine, spruce, cedar — first, second, third, and fourth qualities, so lately all of one quality, to wave over the bear, and moose, and caribou. Next rolls Thomaston lime, a prime lot, which will get far among the hills before it gets slacked. These rags in bales, of all hues and qualities, the lowest condition to which cotton and linen descend, the final result of dress — of patterns which are now no longer cried up, unless it be in Milwaukee, as those splendid articles, English, French, or American prints, ginghams, muslins, etc., gathered from all quarters both of fashion and poverty, going to become paper of one color or a few shades only, on which, forsooth, will be written tales of real life, high and low, and founded on fact! This closed car smells of salt fish, the strong New England and commercial scent, reminding me of the Grand Banks and the fisheries. Who has not seen a salt fish, thoroughly cured for this world, so that nothing can spoil it, and putting the perseverance of the saints to the blush? with which you may sweep or pave the streets, and split your kindlings, and the teamster shelter himself and his lading against sun, wind, and rain behind it — and the trader, as a Concord trader once did, hang it up by his door for a sign when he commences business, until at last his oldest customer cannot tell surely whether it be animal, vegetable, or mineral, and yet it shall be as pure as a snowflake, and if it be put into a pot and boiled, will come out an excellent dunfish for a Saturday's dinner. Next Spanish hides, with the tails still preserving their twist and the angle of elevation they had when the oxen that wore them were careering over the pampas of the Spanish Main — a type of all obstinacy, and evincing how almost hopeless and incurable are all constitutional vices. I confess, that practically speaking, when I have learned a man's real disposition, I have no hopes of changing it for the better or worse in this state of existence. As the Orientals say, 'A cur's tail may be warmed, and pressed, and bound round with ligatures, and after a twelve years' labor bestowed upon it, still it will retain its natural form.' The only effectual cure for such inveteracies as these tails exhibit is to make glue of them, which I believe is what is usually done with them, and then they will stay put and stick. Here is a hogshead of molasses or of brandy directed to John Smith, Cuttingsville, Vermont, some trader among the Green Mountains, who imports for the farmers near his clearing, and now perchance stands over his bulkhead and thinks of the last arrivals on the coast, how they may affect the price for him, telling his customers this moment, as he has told them twenty times before this morning, that he expects some by the next train of prime quality. It is advertised in the Cuttingsville Times.

While these things go up other things come down. Warned by the whizzing sound, I look up from my book and see some tall pine, hewn on far northern hills, which has winged its way over the Green Mountains and the Connecticut, shot like an arrow through the township within ten minutes, and scarce another eye beholds it; going

> 'to be the mast
> Of some great ammiral.'

And hark! here comes the cattle-train bearing the cattle of a thousand hills, sheepcots, stables, and cow-yards in the air, drovers with their sticks, and shepherd boys in the midst of their flocks, all but the mountain pastures, whirled along like leaves blown from the mountains by the September gales. The air is filled with the bleating of calves and sheep, and the hustling of oxen, as if a pastoral valley were going by, When the old bell-wether at the head rattles his bell, the mountains do indeed skip like rams and the little hills like lambs. A carload of drovers, too, in the midst, on a level with their droves now, their vocation gone, but still clinging to their useless sticks as their badge of office. But their dogs, where are they? It is a stampede to them; they are quite thrown out; they have lost the scent. Methinks I hear them barking behind the Peterboro' Hills, or panting up the western slope of the Green Mountains. They will not be in at the death. Their vocation, too, is gone. Their fidelity and sagacity are below par now. They will slink back to their kennels in disgrace, or perchance run wild and strike a league with the wolf and the fox. So is your pastoral life whirled past and away. But the bell rings, and I must get off the track and let the cars go by;

> What's the railroad to me?
> I never go to see
> Where it ends.
>
> It fills a few hollows,
> And makes banks for the swallows,
> It sets the sand a-blowing,
> And the blackberries a-growing,

but I cross it like a cart-path in the woods. I will not have my eyes put out and my ears spoiled by its smoke and steam and hissing.

Now that the cars are gone by and all the restless world with them, and the fishes in the pond no longer feel their rumbling, I am more alone than ever. For the rest of the long afternoon, perhaps, my meditations are interrupted only by the faint rattle of a carriage or team along the distant highway.

Sometimes, on Sundays, I heard the bells, the Lincoln, Acton, Bedford, or Concord bell, when the wind was favorable, a faint, sweet, and, as it were, natural melody, worth importing into the wilderness. At a sufficient distance over the woods this sound acquires a certain vibratory hum, as if the pine needles in the horizon were the strings of a harp which it swept. All sound heard at the greatest possible distance produces one and the same effect, a vibration of the universal lyre, just as the intervening atmosphere makes a distant ridge of earth interesting to our eyes by the azure tint it imparts to it. There came to me in this case a melody which the air had strained, and which had conversed with every leaf and needle of the wood, that portion of the sound which the elements had taken up and modulated and echoed from vale to vale The echo is, to some extent, an original sound, and therein is the magic and charm of it. It is not merely a repetition of what was worth repeating in the bell, but partly the voice of the wood; the same trivial words and notes sung by a wood-nymph.

At evening, the distant lowing of some cow in the horizon beyond the woods sounded sweet and melodious, and at first I would mistake it for the voices of certain minstrels by whom I was sometimes serenaded, who might be straying over hill and dale; but soon I was not unpleasantly disappointed when it was prolonged into the cheap and natural music of the cow. I do not mean to be satirical, but to express my appreciation of those youths' singing, when I state that I perceived clearly that it was akin to the music of the cow, and they were at length one articulation of Nature.

Regularly at half-past seven, in one part of the summer, after the evening train had gone by, the whip-poor-wills chanted their vespers for half an hour, sitting on a stump by my door, or upon the ridge-pole of the house. They would begin to sing almost with as much precision as a clock, within five minutes of a particular time, referred to the setting of the sun, every evening. I had a rare opportunity to become acquainted with their habits. Sometimes I heard four or five at once in different parts of the wood, by accident one a bar behind another, and so near me that I distinguished not only the cluck after each note, but often that singular buzzing sound like a fly in a spider's web, only proportionally louder. Sometimes one would circle round and round me in the woods a few feet distant as if tethered by a string, when probably I was near its eggs. They sang at intervals throughout the night, and were again as musical as ever just before and about dawn.

When other birds are still, the screech owls take up the strain, like mourning women their ancient u-lu-lu. Their dismal scream is truly Ben Jonsonian. Wise midnight hags! It is no honest and blunt tu-whit tu-who of the poets, but, without jesting, a most solemn graveyard ditty, the mutual consolations of suicide lovers remembering the pangs and the delights of supernal love in the infernal groves. Yet I love to hear their wailing, their doleful responses, trilled along the woodside; reminding me sometimes of music and singing birds; as if it were the dark and tearful side of music, the regrets and sighs that would fain be sung. They are the spirits, the low spirits and melancholy forebodings, of fallen souls that once in human shape night-walked the earth and did the deeds of darkness, now expiating their sins with their wailing hymns or threnodies in the scenery of their transgressions. They give me a new sense of the variety and capacity of that nature which is our common dwelling. *Oh-o-o-o-o that I never had been bor-r-r-r-n!* sighs one on this side of the pond, and circles with the restlessness of despair to some new perch on the gray oaks. Then — *that I never had been bor-r-r-r-n!* echoes another on the farther side with tremulous sincerity, and — *bor-r-r-r-n!* comes faintly from far in the Lincoln woods.

I was also serenaded by a hooting owl. Near at hand you could fancy it the most melancholy sound in Nature, as if she meant by this to stereotype and make permanent in her choir the dying moans of a human being — some poor weak relic of mortality who has left hope behind, and howls like an animal, yet with human sobs, on entering the dark valley, made more awful by a certain gurgling melodiousness — I find myself beginning with the letters *gl* when I try to imitate it — expressive of a mind which has reached the gelatinous, mildewy stage in the mortification of all healthy and courageous thought. It reminded me of ghouls and idiots and insane howlings. But now one answers from far woods in a strain made really melodious by distance — *Hoo hoo hoo, hoorer hoo;* and indeed for the most part it suggested only pleasing associations, whether heard by day or night, summer or winter.

I rejoice that there are owls. Let them do the idiotic and maniacal hooting for men. It is a sound admirably suited to swamps and twilight woods which no day illustrates, suggesting a vast and undeveloped nature which men have not recognized. They represent the stark twilight and unsatisfied thoughts which all have. All day the sun has shone on the surface of some savage swamp, where the single spruce stands hung with usnea lichens, and small hawks circulate above, and the chickadee lisps amid the evergreens, and the partridge and rabbit skulk beneath; but now a more dismal and fitting day dawns, and a different race of creatures awakes to express the meaning of Nature there.

Late in the evening I heard the distant rumbling of wagons over bridges — a sound heard farther than almost any other at night — the baying of dogs, and sometimes again the lowing of some disconsolate cow in a distant barn-yard. In the meanwhile all the shore rang with the trump of bullfrogs, the sturdy spirits of ancient wine-bibbers and wassailers, still unrepentant, trying to sing a catch in their Stygian lake — if the Walden nymphs will pardon the comparison, for though there are almost no weeds, there are frogs there — who would fain keep up the hilarious rules of their old festal tables, though their voices have waxed hoarse and solemnly grave, mocking at mirth, and the wine has lost its flavor, and become only liquor to distend their paunches, and sweet intoxication never comes to drown the memory of the past, but mere saturation and waterloggedness and distention. The most aldermanic, with his chin upon a heart-leaf, which serves for a napkin to his drooling chaps, under this northern shore quaffs a deep draught of the once scorned water, and passes round the cup with the ejaculation *tr-r-r-oonk, tr-r-r-oonk, tr-r-r-oonk!* and straightway comes over the water from some distant cove the same password repeated, where the next in seniority and girth has gulped down to his mark; and when this observance has made the circuit of the shores, then ejaculates the master of ceremonies, with satisfaction, *tr-r-r-oonk!* and each in his turn repeats the same down to the least distended, leakiest, and flabbiest paunched, that there be no mistake; and then the bowl goes round again and again, until the sun disperses the morning mist, and only the patriarch is not under the pond, but vainly bellowing *troonk* from time to time, and pausing for a reply.

I am not sure that I ever heard the sound of cock-crowing from my clearing, and I thought that it might be worth the while to keep a cockerel for his music merely, as a singing bird. The note of this once wild Indian pheasant is certainly the most remarkable of any bird's, and if they could be naturalized without being domesticated, it would soon become the most famous sound in our woods, surpassing the clangor of the goose and the hooting of the owl; and then imagine the cackling of the hens to fill the pauses when their lords' clarions rested! No wonder that man added this bird to his tame stock — to say nothing of the eggs and drumsticks. To walk in a winter morning in a wood where these birds abounded, their native woods, and hear the wild cockerels crow on the trees, clear and shrill for miles over the resounding earth, drowning the feebler notes of other birds — think of it! It would put nations on the alert. Who would not be early to rise, and rise earlier and earlier every successive day of his life, till he became unspeakably healthy, wealthy, and wise? This foreign bird's note is celebrated by the poets of all countries along with the notes of their native songsters. All climates agree with brave Chanticleer. He is more indigenous even than the natives. His health is ever good, his lungs are sound, his spirits never flag. Even the sailor on the Atlantic and Pacific is awakened by his voice; but its shrill sound never roused me from my slumbers. I kept neither dog, cat, cow, pig, nor hens, so that you would have said there was a deficiency of domestic sounds; neither the churn, nor the spinning-wheel, nor even the singing of the kettle, nor the hissing of the urn, nor children crying, to comfort one. An old-fashioned man would have lost his senses or died of ennui before this. Not even rats in the wall, for they were starved out, or rather were never baited in — only squirrels on the roof and under the floor, a whip-poor-will on the ridge-pole, a blue jay screaming beneath the window, a hare or woodchuck under the house, a screech owl or a cat owl behind it, a flock of wild geese or a laughing loon on the pond, and a fox to bark in the night. Not even a lark or an oriole, those mild plantation birds, ever visited my clearing. No cockerels to crow nor hens to cackle in the yard. No yard! but unfenced nature reaching up to your very sills. A young forest growing up under your windows, and wild sumachs and blackberry vines breaking through into your cellar; sturdy pitch pines rubbing and creaking against the shingles for want of room, their roots reaching quite under the house. Instead of a scuttle or a blind blown off in the gale — a pine tree snapped off or torn up by the roots behind your house for fuel. Instead of no path to the front-yard gate in the Great Snow — no gate — no front-yard — and no path to the civilized world.

V. SOLITUDE

THIS is a delicious evening, when the whole body is one sense, and imbibes delight through every pore. I go and come with a strange liberty in Nature, a part of herself. As I walk along the stony shore of the pond in my shirt-sleeves, though it is cool as well as cloudy and windy, and I see nothing special to attract me, all the elements are unusually congenial to me. The bullfrogs trump to usher in the night, and the note of the whip-poor-will is borne on the rippling wind from over the water. Sympathy with the fluttering alder and poplar leaves almost takes away my breath; yet, like the lake, my serenity is rippled but not ruffled. These small waves raised by the evening wind are as remote from storm as the smooth reflecting surface. Though it is now dark, the wind still blows and roars in the wood, the waves still dash, and some creatures lull the rest with their notes. The repose is never complete. The wildest animals do not repose, but seek their prey now; the fox, and skunk, and rabbit, now roam the fields and woods without fear. They are Nature's watchmen — links which connect the days of animated life.

When I return to my house I find that visitors have been there and left their cards, either a bunch of flowers, or a wreath of evergreen, or a name in pencil on a yellow walnut leaf or a chip. They who come rarely to the woods take some little piece of the forest into their hands to play with by the way, which they leave, either intentionally or accidentally. One has peeled a willow wand, woven it into a ring, and dropped it on my table. I could always tell if visitors had called in my absence, either by the bended twigs or grass, or the print of their shoes, and generally of what sex or age or quality they were by some slight trace left, as a flower dropped, or a bunch of grass plucked and thrown away, even as far off as the railroad, half a mile distant, or by the lingering odor of a cigar or pipe. Nay, I was frequently notified of the passage of a traveller along the highway sixty rods off by the scent of his pipe.

There is commonly sufficient space about us. Our horizon is never quite at our elbows. The thick wood is not just at our door, nor the pond, but somewhat is always clearing, familiar and worn by us, appropriated and fenced in some way, and reclaimed from Nature. For what reason have I this vast range and circuit, some square miles of unfrequented forest, for my privacy, abandoned to me by men? My nearest neighbor is a mile distant, and no house is visible from any place but the hill-tops within half a mile of my own. I have my horizon bounded by woods all to myself; a distant view of the railroad where it touches the pond on the one hand, and of the fence which skirts the woodland road on the other. But for the most part it is as solitary where I live as on the prairies. It is as much Asia or Africa as New England. I have, as it were, my own sun and moon and stars, and a little world all to myself. At night there was never a traveller passed my house, or knocked at my door, more than if I were the first or last man; unless it were in the spring, when at long intervals some came from the village to fish for pouts — they plainly fished much more in the Walden Pond of their own natures, and baited their hooks with darkness — but they soon retreated, usually with light baskets, and left 'the world to darkness and to me,' and the black kernel of the night was never profaned by any human neighborhood. I believe that men are generally still a little afraid of the dark, though the witches are all hung, and Christianity and candles have been introduced.

Yet I experienced sometimes that the most sweet and tender, the most innocent and encouraging society may be found in any natural object, even for the poor misanthrope and most melancholy man. There can be no very black melancholy to him who lives in the midst of nature and has his senses still. There was never yet such a storm but it was Æolian music to a healthy and innocent ear. Nothing can rightly compel a simple and brave man to a vulgar sadness. While I enjoy the friendship of the seasons I trust that nothing can make life a burden to me. The gentle rain which waters my beans and keeps me in the house today is not drear and melancholy, but good for me too. Though it prevents my hoeing them, it is of far more worth than my hoeing. If it should continue so long as to cause the seeds to rot in the ground and destroy the potatoes in the low lands, it would still be good for the grass on the uplands, and, being good for the grass, it would be good for me. Sometimes, when I compare myself with other men, it seems as if I were more favored by the gods than they, beyond any deserts that I am conscious of; as if I had a warrant and surety at their hands which my fellows have not, and were especially guided and guarded. I do not flatter myself, but if it be possible they flatter me. I have never felt lonesome, or in the least oppressed by a sense of solitude, but once, and that was a few weeks after I came to the woods, when, for an hour, I doubted if the near neighborhood of man was not essential to a serene and healthy life. To be alone was something unpleasant. But I was at the same time conscious of a slight insanity in my mood, and seemed to foresee my recovery. In the midst of a gentle rain while these thoughts prevailed, I was suddenly sensible of such sweet and beneficent society in Nature, in the very pattering of the drops, and in every sound and sight around my house, an infinite and unaccountable friendliness all at once like an atmosphere sustaining me, as made the fancied advantages of human neighborhood insignificant, and I have never thought of them since. Every little pine needle expanded and swelled with sympathy and befriended me. I was so distinctly made aware of the presence of something kindred to me, even in scenes which we are accustomed to call wild and dreary, and also that the nearest of blood to me and humanest was not a person nor a villager, that I thought no place could ever be strange to me again.

> 'Mourning untimely consumes the sad;
> Few are their days in the land of the living,
> Beautiful daughter of Toscar.'

Some of my pleasantest hours were during the long rain-storms in the spring or fall, which confined me to the house for the afternoon as well as the forenoon, soothed by their ceaseless roar and pelting; when an early twilight ushered in a long evening in which many thoughts had time to take root and unfold themselves. In those driving northeast rains which tried the village houses so, when the maids stood ready with mop and pail in front entries to keep the deluge out, I sat behind my door in my little house, which was all entry, and thoroughly enjoyed its protection. In one heavy thunder-shower the lightning struck a large pitch pine across the pond, making a very conspicuous and perfectly regular spiral groove from top to bottom, an inch or more deep, and four or five inches wide, as you would groove a walking-stick. I passed it again the other day, and was struck with awe on looking up and beholding that mark, now more distinct than ever, where a terrific and resistless bolt came down out of the harmless sky eight years ago. Men frequently say to me, 'I should think you would feel lonesome down there, and want to be nearer to folks, rainy and snowy days and nights especially.' I am tempted to reply to such — This whole earth which we inhabit is but a point in space. How far apart, think you, dwell the two most distant inhabitants of yonder star, the breadth of whose disk cannot be appreciated by our instruments? Why should I feel lonely? is not our planet in the Milky Way? This which you put seems to me not to be the most important question. What sort of space is that which separates a man from his fellows and makes him solitary? I have found that no exertion of the legs can bring two minds much nearer to one another. What do we want most to dwell near to? Not to many men surely, the depot, the post-office, the bar-room, the meeting-house, the school-house, the grocery, Beacon Hill, or the Five Points, where men most congregate, but to the perennial source of our life, whence in all our experience we have found that to issue, as the willow stands near the water and sends out its roots in that direction. This will vary with different natures, but this is the place where a wise man will dig his cellar. . . . I one evening overtook one of my townsmen, who has accumulated what is called 'a handsome property' — though I never got a *fair* view of it — on the Walden road, driving a pair of cattle to market, who inquired of me how I could bring my mind to give up so many of the comforts of life. I answered that I was very sure I liked it passably well; I was not joking. And so I went home to my bed, and left him to pick his way through the darkness and the mud to Brighton — or Bright-town — which place he would reach some time in the morning.

Any prospect of awakening or coming to life to a dead man makes indifferent all times and places. The place where that may occur is always the same, and indescribably pleasant to all our senses. For the most part we allow only outlying and transient circumstances to make our occasions. They are, in fact, the cause of our distraction. Nearest to all things is that power which fashions their being. *Next* to us the grandest laws are continually being executed. *Next* to us is not the workman whom we have hired, with whom we love so well to talk, but the workman whose work we are.

'How vast and profound is the influence of the subtile powers of Heaven and of Earth!'

'We seek to perceive them, and we do not see them; we seek to hear them, and we do not hear them; identified with the substance of things, they cannot be separated from them.'

'They cause that in all the universe men purify and sanctify their hearts, and clothe themselves in their holiday garments to offer sacrifices and oblations to their ancestors. It is an ocean of subtile intelligences. They are everywhere, above us, on our left, on our right; they environ us on all sides.'

We are the subjects of an experiment which is not a little interesting to me. Can we not do without the society of our gossips a little while under these circumstances — have our own thoughts to cheer us? Confucius says truly, 'Virtue does not remain as an abandoned orphan; it must of necessity have neighbors.'

With thinking we may be beside ourselves in a sane sense. By a conscious effort of the mind we can stand aloof from actions and their consequences; and all things, good and bad, go by us like a torrent. We are not wholly involved in Nature. I may be either the driftwood in the stream, or Indra in the sky looking down on it. I *may* be affected by a theatrical exhibition; on the other hand, I *may not* be affected by an actual event which appears to concern me much more. I only know myself as a human entity; the scene, so to speak, of thoughts and affections; and am sensible of a certain doubleness by which I can stand as remote from myself as from another. However intense my experience, I am conscious of the presence and criticism of a part of me, which, as it were, is not a part of me, but spectator, sharing no experience, but taking note of it, and that is no more I than it is you. When the play, it may be the tragedy, of life is over, the spectator goes his way. It was a kind of fiction, a work of the imagination only, so far as he was concerned. This doubleness may easily make us poor neighbors and friends sometimes.

I find it wholesome to be alone the greater part of the time. To be in company, even with the best, is soon wearisome and dissipating. I love to be alone. I never found the companion that was so companionable as solitude. We are for the most part more lonely when we go abroad among men than when we stay in our chambers. A man thinking or working is always alone, let him be where he will. Solitude is not measured by the miles of space that intervene between a man and his fellows. The really diligent student in one of the crowded hives of Cambridge College is as solitary as a dervis in the desert. The farmer can work alone in the field or the woods all day, hoeing or chopping, and not feel lonesome, because he is employed; but when he comes home at night he cannot sit down in a room alone, at the mercy of his thoughts, but must be where he can 'see the folks,' and recreate, and, as he thinks, remunerate himself for his day's solitude; and hence he wonders how the student can sit alone in the house all night and most of the day without ennui and 'the blues;' but he does not realize that the student, though in the house, is still at work in *his* field, and chopping in *his* woods, as the farmer in his, and in turn seeks the same recreation and society that the latter does, though it may be a more condensed form of it.

Society is commonly too cheap. We meet at very short intervals, not having had time to acquire any new value for each other. We meet at meals three times a day, and give each other a new taste of that old musty cheese that we are. We have had to agree on a certain set of rules, called etiquette and politeness, to make this frequent meeting tolerable and that we need not come to open war. We meet at the post-office, and at the sociable, and about the fireside every night; we live thick and are in each other's way, and stumble over one another, and I think that we thus lose some respect for one another. Certainly less frequency would suffice for all important and hearty communications. Consider the girls in a factory — never alone, hardly in their dreams. It would be better if there were but one inhabitant to a square mile, as where I live. The value of a man is not in his skin, that we should touch him.

I have heard of a man lost in the woods and dying of famine and exhaustion at the foot of a tree, whose loneliness was relieved by the grotesque visions with which, owing to bodily weakness, his diseased imagination surrounded him, and which he believed to be real. So also, owing to bodily and mental health and strength, we may be continually cheered by a like but more normal and natural society, and come to know that we are never alone.

I have a great deal of company in my house; especially in the morning, when nobody calls. Let me suggest a few comparisons, that some one may convey an idea of my situation. I am no more lonely than the loon in the pond that laughs so loud, or than Walden Pond itself. What company has that lonely lake, I pray? And yet it has not the blue devils, but the blue angels in it, in the azure tint of its waters. The sun is alone, except in thick weather, when there sometimes appear to be two, but one is a mock sun. God is alone — but the devil, he is far from being alone; he sees a great deal of company; he is legion. I am no more lonely than a single mullein or dandelion in a pasture, or a bean leaf, or sorrel, or a horse-fly, or a humblebee. I am no more lonely than the Mill Brook, or a weathercock, or the north star, or the south wind, or an April shower, or a January thaw, or the first spider in a new house.

I have occasional visits in the long winter evenings, when the snow falls fast and the wind howls in the wood, from an old settler and original proprietor, who is reported to have dug Walden Pond, and stoned it, and fringed it with pine woods; who tells me stories of old time and of new eternity; and between us we manage to pass a cheerful evening with social mirth and pleasant views of things, even without apples or cider — a most wise and humorous friend, whom I love much, who keeps himself more secret than ever did Goffe or Whalley; and though he is thought to be dead, none can show where he is buried. An elderly dame, too, dwells in my neighborhood, invisible to most persons, in whose odorous herb garden I love to stroll sometimes, gathering simples and listening to her fables; for she has a genius of unequalled fertility, and her memory runs back farther than mythology, and she can tell me the original of every fable, and on what fact every one is founded, for the incidents occurred when she was young. A ruddy and lusty old dame, who delights in all weathers and seasons, and is likely to outlive all her children yet.

The indescribable innocence and beneficence of Nature — of sun and wind and rain, of summer and winter — such health, such cheer, they afford forever! and such sympathy have they ever with our race, that all Nature would be affected, and the sun's brightness fade, and the winds would sigh humanely, and the clouds rain tears, and the woods shed their leaves and put on mourning in midsummer, if any man should ever for a just cause grieve. Shall I not have intelligence with the earth? Am I not partly leaves and vegetable mould myself?

What is the pill which will keep us well, serene, contented? Not my or thy great-grandfather's, but our great-grandmother Nature's universal, vegetable, botanic medicines, by which she has kept herself young always, outlived so many old Parrs in her day, and fed her health with their decaying fatness. For my panacea, instead of one of those quack vials of a mixture dipped from Acheron and the Dead Sea, which come out of those long shallow black-schooner looking wagons which we sometimes see made to carry bottles, let me have a draught of undiluted morning air. Morning air! If men will not drink of this at the fountain-head of the day, why, then, we must even bottle up some and sell it in the shops, for the benefit of those who have lost their subscription ticket to morning time in this world. But remember, it will not keep quite till noonday even in the coolest cellar, but drive out the stopples long ere that and follow westward the steps of Aurora. I am no worshipper of Hygeia, who was the daughter of that old herb-doctor Æsculapius, and who is represented on monuments holding a serpent in one hand, and in the other a cup out of which the serpent sometimes drinks; but rather of Hebe, cup-bearer to Jupiter, who was the daughter of Juno and wild lettuce, and who had the power of restoring gods and men to the vigor of youth. She was probably the only thoroughly sound-conditioned, healthy, and robust young lady that ever walked the globe, and wherever she came it was spring.

VI. VISITORS

I THINK that I love society as much as most, and am ready enough to fasten myself like a bloodsucker for the time to any full-blooded man that comes in my way. I am naturally no hermit, but might possibly sit out the sturdiest frequenter of the bar-room, if my business called me thither.

I had three chairs in my house; one for solitude, two for friendship, three for society. When visitors came in larger and unexpected numbers there was but the third chair for them all, but they generally economized the room by standing up. It is surprising how many great men and women a small house will contain. I have had twenty-five or thirty souls, with their bodies, at once under my roof, and yet we often parted without being aware that we had come very near to one another. Many of our houses, both public and private, with their almost innumerable apartments, their huge halls and their cellars for the storage of wines and other munitions of peace, appear to be extravagantly large for their inhabitants. They are so vast and magnificent that the latter seem to be only vermin which infest them. I am surprised when the herald blows his summons before some Tremont or Astor or Middlesex House, to see come creeping out over the piazza for all inhabitants a ridiculous mouse, which soon again slinks into some hole in the pavement.

One inconvenience I sometimes experienced in so small a house, the difficulty of getting to a sufficient distance from my guest when we began to utter the big thoughts in big words. You want room for your thoughts to get into sailing trim and run a course or two before they make their port. The bullet of your thought must have overcome its lateral and ricochet motion and fallen into its last and steady course before it reaches the ear of the hearer, else it may plow out again through the side of his head. Also, our sentences wanted room to unfold and form their columns in the interval. Individuals, like nations, must have suitable broad and natural boundaries, even a considerable neutral ground, between them. I have found it a singular luxury to talk across the pond to a companion on the opposite side. In my house we were so near that we could not begin to hear — we could not speak low enough to be heard; as when you throw two stones into calm water so near that they break each other's undulations. If we are merely loquacious and loud talkers, then we can afford to stand very near together, cheek by jowl, and feel each other's breath; but if we speak reservedly and thought-fully, we want to be farther apart, that all animal heat and moisture may have a chance to evaporate. If we would enjoy the most intimate society with that in each of us which is without, or above, being spoken to, we must not only be silent, but commonly so far apart bodily that we cannot possibly hear each other's voice in any case. Referred to this standard, speech is for the convenience of those who are hard of hearing; but there are many fine things which we cannot say if we have to shout. As the conversation began to assume a loftier and grander tone, we gradually shoved our chairs farther apart till they touched the wall in opposite corners, and then commonly there was not room enough.

My 'best' room, however, my withdrawing room, always ready for company, on whose carpet the sun rarely fell, was the pine wood behind my house. Thither in summer days, when distinguished guests came,

I took them, and a priceless domestic swept the floor and dusted the furniture and kept the things in order.

If one guest came he sometimes partook of my frugal meal, and it was no interruption to conversation to be stirring a hasty-pudding, or watching the rising and maturing of a loaf of bread in the ashes, in the meanwhile. But if twenty came and sat in my house there was nothing said about dinner, though there might be bread enough for two, more than if eating were a forsaken habit; but we naturally practised abstinence; and this was never felt to be an offence against hospitality, but the most proper and considerate course. The waste and decay of physical life, which so often needs repair, seemed miraculously retarded in such a case, and the vital vigor stood its ground. I could entertain thus a thousand as well as twenty; and if any ever went away disappointed or hungry from my house when they found me at home, they may depend upon it that I sympathized with them at least. So easy is it, though many housekeepers doubt it, to establish new and better customs in the place of the old. You need not rest your reputation on the dinners you give. For my own part, I was never so effectually deterred from frequenting a man's house, by any kind of Cerberus whatever, as by the parade one made about dining me, which I took to be a very polite and roundabout hint never to trouble him so again. I think I shall never revisit those scenes. I should be proud to have for the motto of my cabin those lines of Spenser which one of my visitors inscribed on a yellow walnut leaf for a card:

> 'Arrivèd there, the little house they fill,
> Ne looke for entertainment where none was;
> Rest is their feast, and all things at their will:
> The noblest mind the best contentment has.'

When Winslow, afterward governor of the Plymouth Colony, went with a companion on a visit of ceremony to Massasoit on foot through the woods, and arrived tired and hungry at his lodge, they were well received by the king, but nothing was said about eating that day. When the night arrived, to quote their own words — 'He laid us on the bed with himself and his wife, they at the one end and we at the other, it being only planks laid a foot from the ground and a thin mat upon them. Two more of his chief men, for want of room, pressed by and upon us; so that we were worse weary of our lodging than of our journey.' At one o'clock the next day Massasoit 'brought two fishes that he had shot,' about thrice as big as a bream. 'These being boiled, there were at least forty looked for a share in them; the most eat of them. This meal only we had in two nights and a day; and had not one of us bought a partridge, we had taken our journey fasting.' Fearing that they would be light-headed for want of food and also sleep, owing to 'the savages' barbarous singing, (for they use to sing themselves asleep,)' and that they might get home while they had strength to travel, they departed. As for lodging, it is true they were but poorly entertained, though what they found an inconvenience was no doubt intended for an honor; but as far as eating was concerned, I do not see how the Indians could have done better. They had nothing to eat themselves, and they were wiser than to think that apologies could supply the place of food to their guests; so they drew their belts tighter and said nothing about it. Another time when Winslow visited them, it being a season of plenty with them, there was no deficiency in this respect.

As for men, they will hardly fail one anywhere. I had more visitors while I lived in the woods than at any other period of my life; I mean that I had some. I met several there under more favorable circumstances than I could anywhere else. But fewer came to see me on trivial business. In this respect, my company was winnowed by my mere distance from town. I had withdrawn so far within the great ocean of solitude, into which the rivers of society empty, that for the most part, so far as my needs were concerned, only the finest sediment was deposited around me. Beside, there were wafted to me evidences of unexplored and uncultivated continents on the other side.

Who should come to my lodge this morning but a true Homeric or Paphlagonian man — he had so suitable and poetic a name that I am sorry I cannot print it here — a Canadian, a woodchopper and postmaker, who can hole fifty posts in a day, who made his last supper on a woodchuck which his dog caught. He, too, has heard of Homer, and, 'if it were not for books,' would 'not know what to do rainy days,' though perhaps he has not read one wholly through for many rainy seasons. Some priest who could pronounce the Greek itself taught him to read his verse in the Testament in his native parish far away; and now I must translate to him, while he holds the book, Achilles' reproof to Patroclus for his sad countenance. — 'Why are you in tears, Patroclus, like a young girl?'

> 'Or have you alone heard some news from Phthia?
> They say that Menœtius lives yet, son of Actor,
> And Peleus lives, son of Æacus, among the Myrmidons,
> Either of whom having died, we should greatly grieve.'

He says, 'That's good.' He has a great bundle of white oak bark under his arm for a sick man, gathered this Sunday morning. 'I suppose there's no harm in going after such a thing today,' says he. To him Homer was a great writer, though what his writing was about he did not know. A more simple and natural man it would be hard to find. Vice and disease, which cast such a sombre moral hue over the world, seemed to have hardly any existence for him. He was about twenty-eight years old, and had left Canada and his father's house a dozen years before to work in the States, and earn money to buy a farm with at last, perhaps in his native country. He was cast in the coarsest mould; a stout but sluggish body, yet gracefully carried, with a thick sunburnt neck, dark bushy hair, and dull sleepy blue eyes, which were occasionally lit up with expression. He wore a flat gray cloth cap, a dingy wool-colored greatcoat, and cow-hide boots. He was a great consumer of meat, usually carrying his dinner to his work a couple of miles past my house — for he chopped all summer — in a tin pail; cold meats, often cold woodchucks, and coffee in a stone bottle which dangled by a string from his belt; and sometimes he offered me a drink. He came along early, crossing my bean-field, though without anxiety or haste to get to his work, such as Yankees exhibit. He wasn't a-going to hurt himself. He didn't care if he only earned his board. Frequently he would leave his dinner in the bushes, when his dog had caught a woodchuck by the way, and go back a mile and a half to dress it and leave it in the cellar of the house where he boarded, after deliberating first for half an hour whether he could not sink it in the pond safely till night fall — loving to dwell long upon these themes. He would say, as he went by in the morning, 'How thick the pigeons are! If working every day were not my trade, I could get all the meat I should want by hunting — pigeons, woodchucks, rabbits, partridges — by gosh! I could get all I should want for a week in one day.'

He was a skilful chopper, and indulged in some flourishes and ornaments in his art. He cut his trees level and close to the ground, that the sprouts which came up afterward might be more vigorous and a sled might slide over the stumps; and instead of leaving a whole tree to support his corded wood, he would pare it away to a slender stake or splinter which you could break off with your hand at last.

He interested me because he was so quiet and solitary and so happy withal; a well of good humor and contentment which overflowed at his eyes. His mirth was without alloy. Sometimes I saw him at his work in the woods, felling trees, and he would greet me with a laugh of inexpressible satisfaction, and a salutation in Canadian French, though he spoke English as well. When I approached him he would suspend his work, and with half-suppressed mirth lie along the trunk of a pine which he had felled, and, peeling off the inner bark, roll it up into a ball and chew it while he laughed and talked. Such an exuberance of animal spirits had he that he sometimes tumbled down and rolled on the ground with laughter at anything which made him think and tickled him. Looking round upon the trees he would exclaim — 'By George! I can enjoy myself well enough here chopping; I want no better sport.' Sometimes, when at leisure, he amused himself all day in the woods with a pocket pistol, firing salutes to himself at regular intervals as he walked. In the winter he had a fire by which at noon he warmed his coffee in a kettle; and as he sat on a log to eat his dinner the chickadees would sometimes come round and alight on his arm and peck at the potato in his fingers; and he said that he 'liked to have the little *fellers* about him.'

In him the animal man chiefly was developed. In physical endurance and contentment he was cousin to the pine and the rock. I asked him once if he was not sometimes tired at night, after working all day; and he answered, with a sincere and serious look, 'Gorrappit, I never was tired in my life.' But the intellectual and what is called spiritual man in him were slumbering as in an infant. He had been instructed only in that innocent and ineffectual way in which the Catholic priests teach the aborigines, by which the pupil is never educated to the degree of consciousness, but only to the degree of trust and reverence, and a child is not made a man, but kept a child. When Nature made him, she gave him a strong body and contentment for his portion, and propped him on every side with reverence and reliance, that he might live out his threescore years and ten a child. He was so genuine and unsophisticated that no introduction would serve to introduce him, more than if you introduced a woodchuck to your neighbor. He had got to find him out as you did. He would not play any part. Men paid him wages for work, and so helped to feed and clothe him; but he never exchanged opinions with them. He was so simply and naturally humble — if he can be called humble who never aspires — that humility was no distinct quality in him, nor could he conceive of it. Wiser men were demigods to him. If you told him that such a one was coming, he did as if he thought that anything so grand would expect nothing of himself, but take all the responsibility on itself, and let him be forgotten still. He never heard the sound of praise. He particularly reverenced the writer and the preacher. Their performances were miracles. When I told him that I wrote considerably, he thought for a long time that it was merely the handwriting which I meant, for he could write a remarkably good hand himself. I sometimes found the name of his native parish handsomely written in the snow by the highway, with the proper French accent, and knew that he had passed. I asked him if he ever wished to write his thoughts. He said that he had read and written letters for those who could not, but he never tried to write thoughts — no, he could not, he could not tell what to put first, it would kill him, and then there was spelling to be attended to at the same time!

I heard that a distinguished wise man and reformer asked him if he did not want the world to be changed; but he answered with a chuckle of surprise in his Canadian accent, not knowing that the question had ever been entertained before, 'No, I like it well enough.' It would have suggested many things to a philosopher to have dealings with him. To a stranger he appeared to know nothing of things in general; yet I sometimes saw in him a man whom I had not seen before, and I did not know whether he was as wise as Shakespeare or as simply ignorant as a child, whether to suspect him of a fine poetic consciousness or of stupidity. A townsman told me that when he met him sauntering through the village in his small close-fitting cap, and whistling to himself, he reminded him of a prince in disguise.

His only books were an almanac and an arithmetic, in which last he was considerably expert. The former was a sort of cyclopædia to him, which he supposed to contain an abstract of human knowledge, as indeed it does to a considerable extent. I loved to sound him on the various reforms of the day, and he never failed to look at them in the most simple and practical light. He had never heard of such things before. Could he do without factories? I asked. He had worn the home-made Vermont gray, he said, and that was good. Could he dispense with tea and coffee? Did this country afford any beverage beside water? He had soaked hemlock leaves in water and drank it, and thought that was better than water in warm weather. When I asked him if he could do without money, he showed the convenience of money in such a way as to suggest and coincide with the most philosophical accounts of the origin of this institution, and the very derivation of the word *pecunia*. If an ox were his property, and he wished to get needles and thread at the store, he thought it would be inconvenient and impossible soon to go on mortgaging some portion of the creature each time to that amount. He could defend many institutions better than any philosopher, because, in describing them as they concerned him, he gave the true reason for their prevalence, and speculation had not suggested to him any other. At another time, hearing Plato's definition of a man — a biped without feathers — and that one exhibited a cock plucked and called it Plato's man, he thought it an important difference that the *knees* bent the wrong way. He would sometimes exclaim, 'How I love to talk! By George, I could talk all day!' I asked him once, when I had not seen him for many months, if he had got a new idea this summer. 'Good Lord,' said he, 'a man that has to work as I do, if he does not forget the ideas he has had, he will do well. May be the man you hoe with is inclined to race; then, by gorry, your mind must be there; you think of weeds.' He would sometimes ask me first on such occasions, if I had made any improvement. One winter day I asked him if he was always satisfied with himself, wishing to suggest a substitute within him for the priest without, and some higher motive for living. 'Satisfied!' said he; 'some men are satisfied with one thing, and some with another. One man, perhaps, if he has got enough, will be satisfied to sit all day with his back to the fire and his belly to the table, by George!' Yet I never, by any manœuvring, could get him to take the spiritual view of things; the highest that he appeared to conceive of was a simple expediency, such as you might expect an animal to appreciate; and this, practically, is true of most men. If I suggested any improvement in his mode of life, he merely answered, without expressing any regret, that it was too late. Yet he thoroughly believed in honesty and the like virtues.

There was a certain positive originality, however slight, to be detected in him, and I occasionally observed that he was thinking for himself and expressing his own opinion, a phenomenon so rare that I would any day walk ten miles to observe it, and it amounted to the re-origination of many of the institutions of society. Though he hesitated, and perhaps failed to express himself distinctly, he always had a presentable thought behind. Yet his thinking was so primitive and immersed in his animal life, that, though more promising than a merely learned man's, it rarely ripened to anything which can be reported. He suggested that there might be men of genius in the lowest grades of life, however permanently humble and illiterate, who take their own view always, or do not pretend to see at all; who are as bottomless even as Walden Pond was thought to be, though they may be dark and muddy.

Many a traveller came out of his way to see me and the inside of my house, and, as an excuse for calling, asked for a glass of water. I told them that I drank at the pond, and pointed thither, offering to lend them a dipper. Far off as I lived, I was not exempted from the annual visitation which occurs, methinks, about the first of April, when everybody is on the move; and I had my share of good luck, though there were some curious specimens among my visitors. Half-witted men from the almshouse and elsewhere came to see me; but I endeavored to make them exercise all the wit they had, and make their confessions to me; in such cases making wit the theme of our conversation; and so was compensated. Indeed, I found some of them to be wiser than the so-called *overseers* of the poor and selectmen of the town, and thought it was time that the tables were turned. With respect to wit, I learned that there was not much difference between the half and the whole. One day, in particular, an inoffensive, simpleminded pauper, whom with others I had often seen used as fencing stuff, standing or sitting on a bushel in the fields to keep cattle and himself from straying, visited me, and expressed a wish to live as I did. He told me, with the utmost simplicity and truth, quite superior, or rather *inferior*, to anything that is called humility, that he was 'deficient in intellect.' These were his words. The Lord had made him so, yet he supposed the Lord cared as much for him as for another. 'I have always been so,' said he, 'from my childhood; I never had much mind; I was not like other children; I am weak in the head. It was the Lord's will, I suppose.' And there he was to prove the truth of his words. He was a metaphysical puzzle to me. I have rarely met a fellow-man on such promising ground — it was so simple and sincere and so true all that he said. And, true enough, in proportion as he appeared to humble himself was he exalted. I did not know at first but it was the result of a wise policy. It seemed that from such a basis of truth and frankness as the poor weak-headed pauper had laid, our intercourse might go forward to something better than the intercourse of sages.

I had some guests from those not reckoned commonly among the town's poor, but who should be; who are among the world's poor, at any rate; guests who appeal, not to your hospitality, but to your *hospitalality;* who earnestly wish to be helped, and preface their appeal with the information that they are resolved, for one thing, never to help themselves. I require of a visitor that he be not actually starving, though he may have the very best appetite in the world, however he got it. Objects of charity are not guests. Men who did not know when their visit had terminated, though I went about my business again, answering

them from greater and greater remoteness. Men of almost every degree
of wit called on me in the migrating season. Some who had more wits
than they knew what to do with; run-away slaves with plantation
manners, who listened from time to time, like the fox in the fable, as if
they heard the hounds a-baying on their track, and looked at me
beseechingly, as much as to say,

'O Christian, will you send me back?'

One real runaway slave, among the rest, whom I helped to forward
toward the north star. Men of one idea, like a hen with one chicken,
and that a duckling; men of a thousand ideas, and unkempt heads, like
those hens which are made to take charge of a hundred chickens, all
in pursuit of one bug, a score of them lost in every morning's dew —
and become frizzled and mangy in consequence; men of ideas instead
of legs, a sort of intellectual centipede that made you crawl all over.
One man proposed a book in which visitors should write their names,
as at the White Mountains; but, alas! I have too good a memory to
make that necessary.

I could not but notice some of the peculiarities of my visitors. Girls
and boys and young women generally seemed glad to be in the woods.
They looked in the pond and at the flowers, and improved their time.
Men of business, even farmers, thought only of solitude and employment, and of the great distance at which I dwelt from something or
other; and though they said that they loved a ramble in the woods
occasionally, it was obvious that they did not. Restless committed men,
whose time was all taken up in getting a living or keeping it; ministers
who spoke of God as if they enjoyed a monopoly of the subject, who
could not bear all kinds of opinions; doctors, lawyers, uneasy housekeepers who pried into my cupboard and bed when I was out — how
came Mrs. —— to know that my sheets were not as clean as hers? —
young men who had ceased to be young, and had concluded that it was
safest to follow the beaten track of the professions — all these generally
said that it was not possible to do so much good in my position. Ay!
there was the rub. The old and infirm and the timid, of whatever age
or sex, thought most of sickness, and sudden accident and death; to
them life seemed full of danger — what danger is there if you don't think
of any? — and they thought that a prudent man would carefully select
the safest position, where Dr. B. might be on hand at a moment's
warning. To them the village was literally a *com-munity*, a league for
mutual defence, and you would suppose that they would not go

a-huckleberrying without a medicine chest. The amount of it is, if a man is alive, there is always *danger* that he may die, though the danger must be allowed to be less in proportion as he is dead-and-alive to begin with. A man sits as many risks as he runs. Finally, there were the self-styled reformers, the greatest bores of all, who thought that I was forever singing,

> This is the house that I built;
> This is the man that lives in the house that I built;

but they did not know that the third line was,

> These are the folks that worry the man
> That lives in the house that I built.

I did not fear the hen-harriers, for I kept no chickens; but I feared the men-harriers rather.

I had more cheering visitors than the last. Children come a-berrying, railroad men taking a Sunday morning walk in clean shirts, fishermen and hunters, poets and philosophers; in short, all honest pilgrims, who came out to the woods for freedom's sake, and really left the village behind, I was ready to greet with — 'Welcome, Englishmen! welcome, Englishmen!' for I had had communication with that race.

VII. THE BEAN-FIELD

MEANWHILE my beans, the length of whose rows, added together, was seven miles already planted, were impatient to be hoed, for the earliest had grown considerably before the latest were in the ground; indeed they were not easily to be put off. What was the meaning of this so steady and self-respecting, this small Herculean labor, I knew not. I came to love my rows, my beans, though so many more than I wanted. They attached me to the earth, and so I got strength like Antæus. But why should I raise them? Only Heaven knows. This was my curious labor all summer — to make this portion of the earth's surface, which had yielded only cinquefoil, blackberries, johnswort, and the like, before, sweet wild fruits and pleasant flowers, produce instead this pulse. What shall I learn of beans or beans of me? I cherish them,

I hoe them, early and late I have an eye to them; and this is my day's work. It is a fine broad leaf to look on. My auxiliaries are the dews and rains which water this dry soil, and what fertility is in the soil itself, which for the most part is lean and effete. My enemies are worms, cool days, and most of all woodchucks. The last have nibbled for me a quarter of an acre clean. But what right had I to oust johnswort and the rest, and break up their ancient herb garden? Soon, however, the remaining beans will be too tough for them, and go forward to meet new foes.

When I was four years old, as I well remember, I was brought from Boston to this my native town, through these very woods and this field, to the pond. It is one of the oldest scenes stamped on my memory. And now tonight my flute has waked the echoes over that very water. The pines still stand here older than I; or, if some have fallen, I have cooked my supper with their stumps, and a new growth is rising all around, preparing another aspect for new infant eyes. Almost the same johnswort springs from the same perennial root in this pasture, and even I have at length helped to clothe that fabulous landscape of my infant dreams, and one of the results of my presence and influence is seen in these bean leaves, corn blades, and potato vines.

I planted about two acres and a half of upland; and as it was only about fifteen years since the land was cleared, and I myself had got out two or three cords of stumps, I did not give it any manure; but in the course of the summer it appeared by the arrowheads which I turned up in hoeing, that an extinct nation had anciently dwelt here and planted corn and beans ere white men came to clear the land, and so, to some extent, had exhausted the soil for this very crop.

Before yet any woodchuck or squirrel had run across the road, or the sun had got above the shrub oaks, while all the dew was on, though the farmers warned me against it — I would advise you to do all your work if possible while the dew is on — I began to level the ranks of haughty weeds in my bean-field and throw dust upon their heads. Early in the morning I worked barefooted, dabbling like a plastic artist in the dewy and crumbling sand, but later in the day the sun blistered my feet. There the sun lighted me to hoe beans, pacing slowly backward and forward over that yellow gravelly upland, between the long green rows, fifteen rods, the one end terminating in a shrub oak copse where I could rest in the shade, the other in a blackberry field where the green berries deepened their tints by the time I had made another bout. Removing the weeds, putting fresh soil about the bean stems, and encouraging this weed which I had sown, making the yellow soil express its summer thought in bean leaves and blossoms rather than in wormwood and piper and millet grass, making the earth say beans instead of grass — this was my daily work. As I had little aid from horses or cattle, or hired men or boys, or improved implements of husbandry, I was much slower, and became much more intimate with my beans than usual. But labor of the hands, even when pursued to the verge of drudgery, is perhaps never the worst form of idleness. It has a constant and imperishable moral, and to the scholar it yields a classic result. A very *agricola laboriosus* was I to travellers bound westward through Lincoln and Wayland to nobody knows where; they sitting at their ease in gigs, with elbows on knees, and reins loosely hanging in festoons; I the home-staying, laborious native of the soil. But soon my homestead was out of their sight and thought. It was the only open and cultivated field for a great distance on either side of the road, so they made the most of it; and sometimes the man in the field heard more of travellers' gossip and comment than was meant for his ear: 'Beans so late! peas so late!' — for I continued to plant when others had begun to hoe — the ministerial husbandman had not suspected it. 'Corn, my boy, for fodder; corn for fodder.' 'Does he *live* there?' asks the black bonnet of the gray coat; and the hard-featured farmer reins up his grateful dobbin to inquire what you are doing where he sees no manure in the furrow, and recommends a little chip dirt, or any little waste stuff, or it may be ashes or plaster. But here were two acres and a half of furrows, and only a hoe for cart and two hands to draw it — there being an aversion to other carts and horses — and chip dirt far away. Fellow-travellers as they rattled by compared it aloud with the fields which they had passed, so that I came to know how I stood in the agricultural world. This was one field not in Mr. Colman's report. And, by the way, who estimates the value of the crop which nature yields in the still wilder fields unimproved by man? The crop of *English* hay is carefully weighed, the moisture calculated, the silicates and the potash; but in all dells and pond-holes in the woods and pastures and swamps grows a rich and various crop only unreaped by man. Mine was, as it were, the connecting link between wild and cultivated fields; as some states are civilized, and others half-civilized, and others savage or barbarous, so my field was, though not in a bad sense, a half-cultivated field. They were beans cheerfully returning to their wild and primitive state that I cultivated, and my hoe played the *Ranz des Vaches* for them.

Near at hand, upon the topmost spray of a birch, sings the brown thrasher — or red mavis, as some love to call him — all the morning, glad of your society, that would find out another farmer's field if yours were not here. While you are planting the seed, he cries — 'Drop it, drop it — cover it up, cover it up — pull it up, pull it up, pull it up.' But this was not corn, and so it was safe from such enemies as he. You may wonder what his rigmarole, his amateur Paganini performances on one string or on twenty, have to do with your planting, and yet prefer it to leached ashes or plaster. It was a cheap sort of top dressing in which I had entire faith.

As I drew a still fresher soil about the rows with my hoe, I disturbed the ashes of unchronicled nations who in primeval years lived under these heavens, and their small implements of war and hunting were brought to the light of this modern day. They lay mingled with other natural stones, some of which bore the marks of having been burned by Indian fires, and some by the sun, and also bits of pottery and glass brought hither by the recent cultivators of the soil. When my hoe tinkled against the stones, that music echoed to the woods and the sky, and was an accompaniment to my labor which yielded an instant and immeasurable crop. It was no longer beans that I hoed, nor I that hoed beans; and I remembered with as much pity as pride, if I remembered at all, my acquaintances who had gone to the city to attend the oratorios. The nighthawk circled overhead in the sunny afternoons — for I sometimes made a day of it — like a mote in the eye, or in heaven's eye, falling from time to time with a swoop and a sound as if the heavens were rent, torn at last to very rags and tatters, and yet a seamless cope remained; small imps that fill the air and lay their eggs on the ground on bare sand or rocks on the tops of hills, where few have found them; graceful and slender like ripples caught up from the pond, as leaves are raised by the wind to float in the heavens; such kindredship is in nature. The hawk is aerial brother of the wave which he sails over and surveys, those his perfect air-inflated wings answering to the elemental unfledged pinions of the sea. Or sometimes I watched a pair of hen-hawks circling high in the sky, alternately soaring and descending, approaching and leaving one another, as if they were the embodiment of my own thoughts. Or I was attracted by the passage of wild pigeons from this wood to that, with a slight quivering winnowing sound and carrier haste; or from under a rotten stump my hoe turned up a sluggish portentous and outlandish spotted salamander, a trace of Egypt and the Nile, yet our contemporary. When I paused to lean on my hoe, these sounds and sights I heard and saw anywhere in the row, a part of the inexhaustible entertainment which the country offers.

On gala days the town fires its great guns, which echo like popguns to these woods, and some waifs of martial music occasionally penetrate thus far. To me, away there in my bean-field at the other end of the town, the big guns sounded as if a puffball had burst; and when there was a military turnout of which I was ignorant, I have sometimes had a vague sense all the day of some sort of itching and disease in the horizon, as if some eruption would break out there soon, either scarlatina or canker-rash, until at length some more favorable puff of wind, making haste over the fields and up the Wayland road, brought me information of the 'trainers.' It seemed by the distant hum as if somebody's bees had swarmed, and that the neighbors, according to Virgil's advice, by a faint *tintinnabulum* upon the most sonorous of their domestic utensils, were endeavoring to call them down into the hive again. And when the sound died quite away, and the hum had ceased, and the most favorable breezes told no tale, I knew that they had got the last drone of them all safely into the Middlesex hive, and that now their minds were bent on the honey with which it was smeared.

I felt proud to know that the liberties of Massachusetts and of our fatherland were in such safe keeping; and as I turned to my hoeing again I was filled with an inexpressible confidence, and pursued my labor cheerfully with a calm trust in the future.

When there were several bands of musicians, it sounded as if all the village was a vast bellows and all the buildings expanded and collapsed alternately with a din. But sometimes it was a really noble and inspiring strain that reached these woods, and the trumpet that sings of fame, and I felt as if I could spit a Mexican with a good relish — for why should we always stand for trifles? — and looked round for a woodchuck or a skunk to exercise my chivalry upon. These martial strains seemed as far away as Palestine, and reminded me of a march of crusaders in the horizon, with a slight tantivy and tremulous motion of the elm tree tops which overhang the village. This was one of the *great* days; though the sky had from my clearing only the same everlastingly great look that it wears daily, and I saw no difference in it.

It was a singular experience that long acquaintance which I cultivated with beans, what with planting, and hoeing, and harvesting, and threshing, and picking over and selling them — the last was the hardest of all — I might add eating, for I did taste. I was determined to know beans. When they were growing, I used to hoe from five o'clock in the morning till noon, and commonly spent the rest of the day about other affairs. Consider the intimate and curious acquaintance one makes with various kinds of weeds — it will bear some iteration in the account, for there was no little iteration in the labor — disturbing their delicate organizations so ruthlessly, and making such invidious distinctions with his hoe, levelling whole ranks of one species, and sedulously cultivating another. That's Roman wormwood — that's pigweed — that's sorrel — that's piper-grass — have at him, chop him up, turn his roots upward to the sun, don't let him have a fibre in the shade, if you do he'll turn himself t'other side up and be as green as a leek in two days. A long war, not with cranes, but with weeds, those Trojans who had sun and rain and dews on their side. Daily the beans saw me come to their rescue armed with a hoe, and thin the ranks of their enemies, filling up the trenches with weedy dead. Many a lusty crest-waving Hector, that towered a whole foot above his crowding comrades, fell before my weapon and rolled in the dust.

Those summer days which some of my contemporaries devoted to the fine arts in Boston or Rome, and others to contemplation in India, and others to trade in London or New York, I thus, with the other farmers of New England, devoted to husbandry. Not that I wanted beans to eat, for I am by nature a Pythagorean, so far as beans are concerned, whether they mean porridge or voting, and exchanged them for rice; but, perchance, as some must work in fields if only for the sake of tropes and expression, to serve a parable-maker one day. It was on the whole a rare amusement, which, continued too long, might have become a dissipation. Though I gave them no manure, and did not hoe them all once, I hoed them unusually well as far as I went, and was paid for it in the end, 'there being in truth,' as Evelyn says, 'no compost or lætation whatsoever comparable to this continual motion, repastination, and turning of the mould with the spade.' 'The earth,' he adds elsewhere, 'especially if fresh, has a certain magnetism in it, by which it attracts the salt, power, or virtue (call it either) which gives it life, and is the logic of all the labor and stir we keep about it, to sustain us; all dungings and other sordid temperings being but the vicars succedaneous to this improvement.' Moreover, this being one of those 'worn-out and exhausted lay fields which enjoy their sabbath,' had perchance, as Sir Kenelm Digby thinks likely, attracted 'vital spirits' from the air. I harvested twelve bushels of beans.

But to be more particular, for it is complained that Mr. Colman has reported chiefly the expensive experiments of gentlemen farmers, my outgoes were,

For a hoe	$0 54	
Plowing, harrowing, and furrowing	7 50	Too much.
Beans for seed	3 12½	
Potatoes "	1 33	
Peas "	0 40	
Turnip seed	0 06	
White line for crow fence	0 02	
Horse cultivator and boy three hours	1 00	
Horse and cart to get crop	0 75	
In all	$14 72½	

My income was (patremfamilias vendacem, non emacem esse oportet), from

Nine bushels and twelve quarts of beans sold	$16 94
Five " large potatoes	2 50
Nine " small	2 25
Grass	1 00
Stalks	0 75
In all	$23 44
Leaving a pecuniary profit, as I have elsewhere said, of	$8 71½

This is the result of my experience in raising beans: Plant the common small white bush bean about the first of June, in rows three feet by eighteen inches apart, being careful to select fresh round and unmixed seed. First look out for worms, and supply vacancies by planting anew. Then look out for woodchucks, if it is an exposed place, for they will nibble off the earliest tender leaves almost clean as they go; and again, when the young tendrils make their appearance, they have notice of it, and will shear them off with both buds and young pods, sitting erect like a squirrel. But above all harvest as early as possible, if you would escape frosts and have a fair and salable crop; you may save much loss by this means.

This further experience also I gained: I said to myself, I will not plant beans and corn with so much industry another summer, but such seeds, if the seed is not lost, as sincerity, truth, simplicity, faith, innocence, and the like, and see if they will not grow in this soil, even with less toil and manurance, and sustain me, for surely it has not been exhausted for these crops. Alas! I said this to myself; but now another summer is gone, and another, and another, and I am obliged to say to you, Reader, that the seeds which I planted, if indeed they *were* the seeds of those virtues, were wormeaten or had lost their vitality, and so did not come up. Commonly men will only be brave as their fathers were brave, or timid. This generation is very sure to plant corn and beans each new year precisely as the Indians did centuries ago and taught the first settlers to do, as if there were a fate in it. I saw an old man the other day, to my astonishment, making the holes with a hoe for the seventieth time at least, and not for himself to lie down in! But why should not the New Englander try new adventures, and not lay so much stress on his grain, his potato and grass crop, and his orchards — raise other crops than these? Why concern ourselves so much about our beans for seed, and not be concerned at all about a new generation of men? We should really be fed and cheered if when we met a man we were sure to see that some of the qualities which I have named, which we all prize more than those other productions, but which are for the most part broadcast and floating in the air, had taken root and grown in him. Here comes such a subtile and ineffable quality, for instance, as truth or justice, though the slightest amount or new variety of it, along the road. Our ambassadors should be instructed to send home such seeds as these, and Congress help to distribute them over all the land. We should never stand upon ceremony with sincerity. We should never cheat and insult and banish one another by our meanness, if there were present the kernel of worth and friendliness. We should not meet thus in haste. Most men I do not meet at all, for they seem not to have time; they are busy about their beans. We would not deal with a man thus plodding ever, leaning on a hoe or a spade as a staff between his work, not as a mushroom, but partially risen out of the earth, something more than erect, like swallows alighted and walking on the ground:

> 'And as he spake, his wings would now and then
> Spread, as he meant to fly, then close again —'

so that we should suspect that we might be conversing with an angel. Bread may not always nourish us; but it always does us good, it even takes stiffness out of our joints, and makes us supple and buoyant, when we knew not what ailed us, to recognize any generosity in man or Nature, to share any unmixed and heroic joy.

Ancient poetry and mythology suggest, at least, that husbandry was once a sacred art; but it is pursued with irreverent haste and heedlessness by us, our object being to have large farms and large crops merely. We have no festival, nor procession, nor ceremony, not excepting our cattle-shows and so-called Thanksgivings, by which the farmer expresses a sense of the sacredness of his calling, or is reminded of its sacred origin. It is the premium and the feast which tempt him. He sacrifices not to Ceres and the Terrestrial Jove, but to the infernal Plutus rather. By avarice and selfishness, and a grovelling habit, from which none of us is free, of regarding the soil as property, or the means of acquiring property chiefly, the landscape is deformed, husbandry is degraded with us, and the farmer leads the meanest of lives. He knows Nature but as a robber. Cato says that the profits of agriculture are particularly pious or just (*maximeque pius quaestus*), and according to Varro the old Romans 'called the same earth Mother and Ceres, and thought that they who cultivated it led a pious and useful life, and that they alone were left of the race of King Saturn.'

We are wont to forget that the sun looks on our cultivated fields and on the prairies and forests without distinction. They all reflect and absorb his rays alike, and the former make but a small part of the glorious picture which he beholds in his daily course. In his view the earth is all equally cultivated like a garden. Therefore we should receive the benefit of his light and heat with a corresponding trust and magnanimity. What though I value the seed of these beans, and harvest that in the fall of the year? This broad field which I have looked at so long looks not to me as the principal cultivator, but away from me to influences more genial to it, which water and make it green. These beans have results which are not harvested by me. Do they not grow for woodchucks partly? The ear of wheat (in Latin *spica*, obsoletely *speca*, from *spe*, hope) should not be the only hope of the husbandman; its kernel or grain (*granum* from *gerendo*, bearing) is not all that it bears. How, then, can our harvest fail? Shall I not rejoice also at the abundance of the weeds whose seeds are the granary of the birds? It matters little comparatively whether the fields fill the farmer's barns. The true husbandman will cease from anxiety, as the squirrels manifest no concern whether the woods will bear chestnuts this year or not, and finish his labor with every day, relinquishing all claim to the produce of his fields, and sacrificing in his mind not only his first but his last fruits also.

VIII. THE VILLAGE

AFTER hoeing, or perhaps reading and writing, in the forenoon, I usually bathed again in the pond, swimming across one of its coves for a stint, and washed the dust of labor from my person, or smoothed out the last wrinkle which study had made, and for the afternoon was absolutely free. Every day or two I strolled to the village to hear some of the gossip which is incessantly going on there, circulating either from mouth to mouth, or from newspaper to newspaper, and which, taken in homœopathic doses, was really as refreshing in its way as the rustle of leaves and the peeping of frogs. As I walked in the woods to see the birds and squirrels, so I walked in the village to see the men and boys; instead of the wind among the pines I heard the carts rattle. In one direction from my house there was a colony of muskrats in the river meadows; under the grove of elms and buttonwoods in the other horizon was a village of busy men, as curious to me as if they had been prairie-dogs, each sitting at the mouth of its burrow, or running over to a neighbor's to gossip. I went there frequently to observe their habits. The village appeared to me a great news room; and on one side, to support it, as once at Redding & Company's on State Street, they kept nuts and raisins, or salt and meal and other groceries. Some have such a vast appetite for the former commodity, that is, the news, and such sound digestive organs, that they can sit forever in public avenues without stirring, and let it simmer and whisper through them like the Etesian winds, or as if inhaling ether, it only producing numbness and insensibility to pain — otherwise it would often be painful to hear — without affecting the consciousness. I hardly ever failed, when I rambled through the village, to see a row of such worthies, either sitting on a ladder sunning themselves, with their bodies inclined forward and their eyes glancing along the line this way and that, from time to time, with a voluptuous expression, or else leaning against a barn with their hands in their pockets, like caryatides, as if to prop it up. They, being commonly out of doors, heard whatever was in the wind. These are the coarsest mills, in which all gossip is first rudely digested or cracked up before it is emptied into finer and more delicate hoppers within doors. I observed that the vitals of the village were the grocery, the bar-room, the post-office, and the bank; and, as a necessary part of the machinery, they kept a bell, a big gun, and a fire-engine, at convenient places; and the houses were so arranged as to make the most of mankind, in lanes and fronting one another, so that every traveller had to run the gauntlet, and every man, woman, and child might get a lick at him. Of course, those who were stationed nearest to the head of the line, where they could most see and be seen, and have the first blow at him, paid the highest prices for their places; and the few straggling inhabitants in the outskirts, where long gaps in the line began to occur, and the traveller could get over walls or turn aside into cow-paths, and so escape, paid a very slight ground or window tax. Signs were hung out on all sides to allure him; some to catch him by the appetite, as the tavern and victualling cellar; some by the fancy, as the dry goods store and the jeweller's; and others by the hair or the feet or the skirts, as the barber, the shoe-maker, or the tailor. Besides, there was a still more terrible standing invitation to call at every one of these houses, and company expected about these times. For the most part I escaped wonderfully from these dangers, either by proceeding at once boldly and without deliberation to the goal, as is recommended to those who run the gauntlet, or by keeping my thoughts on high things, like Orpheus, who, 'loudly singing the praises of the gods to his lyre, drowned the voices of the Sirens, and kept out of danger.' Sometimes I bolted suddenly, and nobody could tell my whereabouts, for I did not stand much about gracefulness, and never hesitated at a gap in a fence. I was even accustomed to make an irruption into some houses, where I was well entertained, and after learning the kernels and very last sieveful of news — what had subsided, the prospects of war and peace, and whether the world was likely to hold together much longer — I was let out through the rear avenues, and so escaped to the woods again.

It was very pleasant, when I stayed late in town, to launch myself into the night, especially if it was dark and tempestuous, and set sail from some bright village parlor or lecture room, with a bag of rye or Indian meal upon my shoulder, for my snug harbor in the woods, having made all tight without and withdrawn under hatches with a merry crew of thoughts, leaving only my outer man at the helm, or even tying up the helm when it was plain sailing. I had many a genial thought by the cabin fire 'as I sailed.' I was never cast away nor distressed in any weather, though I encountered some severe storms. It is darker in the woods, even in common nights, than most suppose. I frequently had to look up at the opening between the trees above the path in order to learn my route, and, where there was no cart-path, to feel with my feet the faint track which I had worn, or steer by the known relation of particular trees which I felt with my hands, passing between two pines for instance, not more than eighteen inches apart, in the midst of the woods, invariably, in the darkest night. Sometimes, after coming home thus late in a dark and muggy night, when my feet felt the path which my eyes could not see, dreaming and absent-minded all the way, until I was aroused by having to raise my hand to lift the latch, I have not been able to recall a single step of my walk, and I have thought that perhaps my body would find its way home if its master should forsake it, as the hand finds its way to the mouth without assistance. Several times, when a visitor chanced to stay into evening, and it proved a dark night, I was obliged to conduct him to the cart-path in the rear of the house, and then point out to him the direction he was to pursue, and in keeping which he was to be guided rather by his feet than his eyes. One very dark night I directed thus on their way two young men who had been fishing in the pond. They lived about a mile off through the woods, and were quite used to the route. A day or two after one of them told me that they wandered about the greater part of the night, close by their own premises, and did not get home till toward morning, by which time, as there had been several heavy showers in the meanwhile, and the leaves were very wet, they were drenched to their skins. I have heard of many going astray even in the village streets, when the darkness was so thick that you could cut it with a knife, as the saying is. Some who live in the outskirts, having come to town a-shopping in their wagons, have been obliged to put up for the night; and gentlemen and ladies making a call have gone half a mile out of their way, feeling the sidewalk only with their feet, and not knowing when they turned. It is a surprising and memorable, as well as valuable experience, to be lost in the woods any time. Often in a snow-storm, even by day, one will come out upon a well-known road and yet find it impossible to tell which way leads to the village. Though he knows that he has travelled it a thousand times, he cannot recognize a feature in it, but it is as strange to him as if it were a road in Siberia. By night, of course, the perplexity is infinitely greater In our most trivial walks, we are constantly, though unconsciously, steering like pilots by certain well-known beacons and headlands, and if we go beyond our usual course we still carry in our minds the bearing of some neighboring cape; and not till we are completely lost, or turned round — for a man needs only to be turned round once with his eyes shut in this world to be lost — do we appreciate the vastness and strangeness of nature. Every man has to learn the points of compass again as often as he awakes, whether from sleep or any abstraction. Not till we are lost, in other words not till we have lost the world, do we begin to find ourselves, and realize where we are and the infinite extent of our relations.

One afternoon, near the end of the first summer, when I went to the village to get a shoe from the cobbler's, I was seized and put into jail, because, as I have elsewhere related, I did not pay a tax to, or recognize the authority of, the State which buys and sells men, women, and children, like cattle, at the door of its senate-house. I had gone down to the woods for other purposes. But, wherever a man goes, men will pursue and paw him with their dirty institutions, and, if they can, constrain him to belong to their desperate odd-fellow society. It is true, I might have resisted forcibly with more or less effect, might have run 'amok' against society; but I preferred that society should run 'amok' against me, it being the desperate party. However, I was released the next day, obtained my mended shoe, and returned to the woods in season to get my dinner of huckleberries on Fair Haven Hill. I was never molested by any person but those who represented the State. I had no lock nor bolt but for the desk which held my papers, not even a nail to put over my latch or windows. I never fastened my door night or day, though I was to be absent several days; not even when the next fall I spent a fortnight in the woods of Maine. And yet my house was more respected than if it had been surrounded by a file of soldiers. The tired rambler could rest and warm himself by my fire, the literary amuse himself with the few books on my table, or the curious, by opening my closet door, see what was left of my dinner, and what prospect I had of a supper. Yet, though many people of every class came this way to the pond, I suffered no serious inconvenience from these sources, and I never missed anything but one small book, a volume of Homer, which perhaps was improperly gilded, and this I trust a soldier of our camp has found by this time. I am convinced, that if all men were to live as simply as I then did, thieving and robbery would be unknown. These take place only in communities where some have got more than is sufficient while others have not enough. The Pope's Homers would soon get properly distributed.

'Nec bella.fuerunt,
Faginus astabat dum scyphus ante dapes.'

'Nor wars did men molest,
When only beechen bowls were in request.'

'You who govern public affairs, what need have you to employ punishments? Love virtue, and the people will be virtuous. The virtues of a superior man are like the wind; the virtues of a common man are like the grass; the grass, when the wind passes over it, bends.'

IX. THE PONDS

Sometimes, having had a surfeit of human society and gossip, and worn out all my village friends, I rambled still farther westward than I habitually dwell, into yet more unfrequented parts of the town, 'to fresh woods and pastures new,' or, while the sun was setting, made my supper of huckleberries and blueberries on Fair Haven Hill, and laid up a store for several days. The fruits do not yield their true flavor to the purchaser of them, nor to him who raises them for the market. There is but one way to obtain it, yet few take that way. If you would know the flavor of huckleberries, ask the cow-boy or the partridge. It is a vulgar error to suppose that you have tasted huckleberries who never plucked them. A huckleberry never reaches Boston; they have not been known there since they grew on her three hills. The ambrosial and essential part of the fruit is lost with the bloom which is rubbed off in the market cart, and they become mere provender. As long as Eternal Justice reigns, not one innocent huckleberry can be transported thither from the country's hills.

Occasionally, after my hoeing was done for the day, I joined some impatient companion who had been fishing on the pond since morning, as silent and motionless as a duck or a floating leaf, and, after practising various kinds of philosophy, had concluded commonly, by the time I arrived, that he belonged to the ancient sect of Cœnobites. There was one older man, an excellent fisher and skilled in all kinds of wood-craft, who was pleased to look upon my house as a building erected for the convenience of fishermen; and I was equally pleased when he sat in my doorway to arrange his lines. Once in a while we sat together on the pond, he at one end of the boat, and I at the other; but not many words passed between us, for he had grown deaf in his later years, but he occasionally hummed a psalm, which harmonized well enough with my philosophy. Our intercourse was thus altogether one of unbroken harmony, far more pleasing to remember than if it had been carried on by speech. When, as was commonly the case, I had none to commune with, I used to raise the echoes by striking with a paddle on the side of my boat, filling the surrounding woods with circling and dilating sound, stirring them up as the keeper of a menagerie his wild beasts, until I elicited a growl from every wooded vale and hillside.

In warm evenings I frequently sat in the boat playing the flute, and saw the perch, which I seem to have charmed, hovering around me, and the moon travelling over the ribbed bottom, which was strewed with the wrecks of the forest. Formerly I had come to this pond adventurously, from time to time, in dark summer nights, with a companion, and, making a fire close to the water's edge, which we thought attracted the fishes, we caught pouts with a bunch of worms strung on a thread, and when we had done, far in the night, threw the burning brands high into the air like skyrockets, which, coming down into the pond, were quenched with a loud hissing, and we were suddenly groping in total darkness. Through this, whistling a tune, we took our way to the haunts of men again. But now I had made my home by the shore.

Sometimes, after staying in a village parlor till the family had all retired, I have returned to the woods, and, partly with a view to the next day's dinner, spent the hours of midnight fishing from a boat by moonlight, serenaded by owls and foxes, and hearing, from time to time, the creaking note of some unknown bird close at hand. These experiences were very memorable and valuable to me — anchored in forty feet of water, and twenty or thirty rods from the shore, surrounded sometimes by thousands of small perch and shiners, dimpling the surface with their tails in the moonlight, and communicating by a long flaxen line with mysterious nocturnal fishes which had their dwelling forty feet below, or sometimes dragging sixty feet of line about the pond as I drifted in the gentle night breeze, now and then feeling a slight vibration along it, indicative of some life prowling about its extremity, of dull uncertain blundering purpose there, and slow to make up its mind. At length you slowly raise, pulling hand over hand, some horned pout squeaking and squirming to the upper air. It was very queer, especially in dark nights, when your thoughts had wandered to vast and cosmogonal themes in other spheres, to feel this faint jerk, which came to interrupt your dreams and link you to Nature again. It seemed as if I might next cast my line upward into the air, as well as downward into this element, which was scarcely more dense. Thus I caught two fishes as it were with one hook.

The scenery of Walden is on a humble scale, and, though very beautiful, does not approach to grandeur, nor can it much concern one who has not long frequented it or lived by its shore; yet this pond is so remarkable for its depth and purity as to merit a particular description. It is a clear and deep green well, half a mile long and a mile and three quarters in circumference, and contains about sixty-one and a half acres; a perennial spring in the midst of pine and oak woods, without any visible inlet or outlet except by the clouds and evaporation. The surrounding hills rise abruptly from the water to the height of forty to eighty feet, though on the southeast and east they attain to about one hundred and one hundred and fifty feet respectively, within a quarter and a third of a mile. They are exclusively woodland. All our Concord waters have two colors at least; one when viewed at a distance, and another, more proper, close at hand. The first depends more on the light, and follows the sky. In clear weather, in summer, they appear blue at a little distance, especially if agitated, and at a great distance all appear alike. In stormy weather they are sometimes of a dark slate-color. The sea, however, is said to be blue one day and green another without any perceptible change in the atmosphere. I have seen our river, when, the landscape being covered with snow, both water and ice were almost as green as grass. Some consider blue 'to be the color of pure water, whether liquid or solid.' But, looking directly down into our waters from a boat, they are seen to be of very different colors. Walden is blue at one time and green at another, even from the same point of view. Lying between the earth and the heavens, it partakes of the color of both. Viewed from a hilltop it reflects the color of the sky; but near at hand it is of a yellowish tint next the shore where you can see the sand, then a light green, which gradually deepens to a uniform dark green in the body of the pond. In some lights, viewed even from a hilltop, it is of a vivid green next the shore. Some have referred this to the reflection of the verdure; but it is equally green there against the railroad sandbank, and in the spring, before the leaves are expanded, and it may be simply the result of the prevailing blue mixed with the yellow of the sand. Such is the color of its iris. This is that portion, also, where in the spring, the ice being warmed by the heat of the sun reflected from the bottom, and also transmitted through the earth, melts first and forms a narrow canal about the still frozen middle. Like the rest of our waters, when much agitated, in clear weather, so that the surface of the waves may reflect the sky at the right angle, or because there is more light mixed with it, it appears at a little distance of a darker blue than the sky itself; and at such a time, being on its surface, and looking with divided vision, so as to see the reflection, I have discerned a matchless and indescribable light blue, such as watered or changeable silks and sword blades suggest, more cerulean than the sky itself, alternating with the original dark green on the opposite sides of the waves, which last appeared but muddy in comparison. It is a vitreous greenish blue, as I remember it, like those patches of the winter sky seen through cloud vistas in the west before sundown. Yet a single glass of its water held up to the light is as colorless as an equal quantity of air. It is well known that a large plate of glass will have a green tint, owing, as the makers say, to its 'body,' but a small piece of the same will be colorless. How large a body of Walden water would be required to reflect a green tint I have never proved. The water of our river is black or a very dark brown to one looking directly down on it, and, like that of most ponds, imparts to the body of one bathing in it a yellowish tinge; but this water is of such crystalline purity that the body of the bather appears of an alabaster whiteness, still more unnatural, which, as the limbs are magnified and distorted withal, produces a monstrous effect, making fit studies for a Michael Angelo.

The water is so transparent that the bottom can easily be discerned at the depth of twenty-five or thirty feet. Paddling over it, you may see, many feet beneath the surface, the schools of perch and shiners, perhaps only an inch long, yet the former easily distinguished by their transverse bars, and you think that they must be ascetic fish that find a subsistence there. Once, in the winter, many years ago, when I had been cutting holes through the ice in order to catch pickerel, as I stepped ashore I tossed my axe back on to the ice, but, as if some evil genius had directed it, it slid four or five rods directly into one of the holes, where the water was twenty-five feet deep. Out of curiosity, I lay down on the ice and looked through the hole, until I saw the axe a little on one side, standing on its head, with its helve erect and gently swaying to and fro with the pulse of the pond; and there it might have stood erect and swaying till in the course of time the handle rotted off, if I had not disturbed it. Making another hole directly over it with an ice chisel which I had, and cutting down the longest birch which I could find in the neighborhood with my knife, I made a slip-noose, which I attached to its end, and, letting it down carefully, passed it over the knob of the handle, and drew it by a line along the birch, and so pulled the axe out again.

The shore is composed of a belt of smooth rounded white stones like paving-stones, excepting one or two short sand beaches, and is so steep that in many places a single leap will carry you into water over your head; and were it not for its remarkable transparency, that would be the last to be seen of its bottom till it rose on the opposite side. Some think it is bottomless. It is nowhere muddy, and a casual observer would say that there were no weeds at all in it; and of noticeable plants, except in the little meadows recently overflowed, which do not properly belong to it, a closer scrutiny does not detect a flag nor a bulrush, nor even a lily, yellow or white, but only a few small heart-leaves and potamogetons, and perhaps a water-target or two; all which however a bather might not perceive; and these plants are clean and bright like the element they grow in. The stones extend a rod or two into the water, and then the bottom is pure sand, except in the deepest parts, where there is usually a little sediment, probably from the decay of the leaves which have been wafted on to it so many successive falls, and a bright green weed is brought up on anchors even in midwinter.

We have one other pond just like this, White Pond, in Nine Acre Corner, about two and a half miles westerly; but, though I am acquainted with most of the ponds within a dozen miles of this centre, I do not know a third of this pure and well-like character. Successive nations perchance have drank at, admired, and fathomed it, and passed away, and still its water is green and pellucid as ever. Not an intermitting spring! Perhaps on that spring morning when Adam and Eve were driven out of Eden Walden Pond was already in existence, and even then breaking up in a gentle spring rain accompanied with mist and a southerly wind, and covered with myriads of ducks and geese, which had not heard of the fall, when still such pure lakes sufficed them. Even then it had commenced to rise and fall, and had clarified its waters and colored them of the hue they now wear, and obtained a patent of Heaven to be the only Walden Pond in the world and distiller of celestial dews. Who knows in how many unremembered nations' literatures this has been the Castalian Fountain? or what nymphs presided over it in the Golden Age? It is a gem of the first water which Concord wears in her coronet.

Yet perchance the first who came to this well have left some trace of their footsteps. I have been surprised to detect encircling the pond, even where a thick wood has just been cut down on the shore, a narrow shelf-like path in the steep hillside, alternately rising and falling, approaching and receding from the water's edge, as old probably as the race of man here, worn by the feet of aboriginal hunters, and still from time to time unwittingly trodden by the present occupants of the land. This is particularly distinct to one standing on the middle of the pond in winter, just after a light snow has fallen, appearing as a clear undulating white line, unobscured by weeds and twigs, and very obvious a quarter of a mile off in many places where in summer it is hardly distinguishable close at hand. The snow reprints it, as it were, in clear white type alto-relievo. The ornamented grounds of villas which will one day be built here may still preserve some trace of this.

The pond rises and falls, but whether regularly or not, and within what period, nobody knows, though, as usual, many pretend to know. It is commonly higher in the winter and lower in the summer, though not corresponding to the general wet and dryness. I can remember when it was a foot or two lower, and also when it was at least five feet higher, than when I lived by it. There is a narrow sand-bar running into it, with very deep water on one side, on which I helped boil a kettle of chowder, some six rods from the main shore, about the year 1824, which it has not been possible to do for twenty-five years; and, on the other hand, my friends used to listen with incredulity when I told them, that a few years later I was accustomed to fish from a boat in a secluded cove in the woods, fifteen rods from the only shore they knew, which place was long since converted into a meadow. But the pond has risen steadily for two years, and now, in the summer of '52, is just five feet higher than when I lived there, or as high as it was thirty years ago, and fishing goes on again in the meadow. This makes a difference of level, at the outside, of six or seven feet; and yet the water shed by the surrounding hills is insignificant in amount, and this overflow must be referred to causes which affect the deep springs. This same summer the pond has begun to fall again. It is remarkable that this fluctuation, whether periodical or not, appears thus to require many years for its accomplishment. I have observed one rise and a part of two falls, and I expect that a dozen or fifteen years hence the water will again be as low as I have ever known it. Flint's Pond, a mile eastward, allowing for the disturbance occasioned by its inlets and outlets, and the smaller intermediate ponds also, sympathize with Walden, and recently attained their greatest height at the same time with the latter. The same is true, as far as my observation goes, of White Pond.

This rise and fall of Walden at long intervals serves this use at least; the water standing at this great height for a year or more, though it makes it difficult to walk round it, kills the shrubs and trees which have sprung up about its edge since the last rise — pitch pines, birches, alders, aspens, and others — and, falling again, leaves an unobstructed shore; for, unlike many ponds and all waters which are subject to a daily tide, its shore is cleanest when the water is lowest. On the side of the pond next my house a row of pitch pines, fifteen feet high, has been killed and tipped over as if by a lever, and thus a stop put to their encroachments; and their size indicates how many years have elapsed since the last rise to this height. By this fluctuation the pond asserts its title to a shore, and thus the *shore* is *shorn*, and the trees cannot hold it by right of possession. These are the lips of the lake, on which no beard grows. It licks its chaps from time to time. When the water is at its height, the alders, willows, and maples send forth a mass of fibrous red roots several feet long from all sides of their stems in the water, and to the height of three or four feet from the ground, in the effort to maintain themselves; and I have known the high blueberry bushes about the shore, which commonly produce no fruit, bear an abundant crop under these circumstances.

Some have been puzzled to tell how the shore became so regularly paved. My townsmen have all heard the tradition — the oldest people tell me that they heard it in their youth — that anciently the Indians were holding a pow-wow upon a hill here, which rose as high into the heavens as the pond now sinks deep into the earth, and they used much profanity, as the story goes, though this vice is one of which the Indians were never guilty, and while they were thus engaged the hill shook and suddenly sank, and only one old squaw, named Walden, escaped, and from her the pond was named. It has been conjectured that when the hill shook these stones rolled down its side and became the present shore. It is very certain, at any rate, that once there was no pond here, and now there is one; and this Indian fable does not in any respect conflict with the account of that ancient settler whom I have mentioned, who remembers so well when he first came here with his divining-rod, saw a thin vapor rising from the sward, and the hazel pointed steadily downward, and he concluded to dig a well here. As for the stones, many still think that they are hardly to be accounted for by the action of the waves on these hills; but I observe that the surrounding hills are remarkably full of the same kind of stones, so that they have been obliged to pile them up in walls on both sides of the railroad cut nearest the pond; and, moreover, there are most stones where the shore is most abrupt; so that, unfortunately, it is no longer a mystery to me. I detect the paver. If the name was not derived from that of some English locality — Saffron Walden, for instance — one might suppose that it was called originally *Walled-in* Pond.

The pond was my well ready dug. For four months in the year its water is as cold as it is pure at all times; and I think that it is then as good as any, if not the best, in the town. In the winter, all water which is exposed to the air is colder than springs and wells which are protected from it. The temperature of the pond water which had stood in the room where I sat from five o'clock in the afternoon till noon the next day, the sixth of March, 1846, the thermometer having been up to 65° or 70° some of the time, owing partly to the sun on the roof, was 42°, or one degree colder than the water of one of the coldest wells in the village just drawn. The temperature of the Boiling Spring the same day was 45°, or the warmest of any water tried, though it is the coldest that I know of in summer, when, beside, shallow and stagnant surface water is not mingled with it. Moreover, in summer, Walden never becomes so warm as most water which is exposed to the sun, on account of its depth. In the warmest weather I usually placed a pailful in my cellar, where it became cool in the night, and remained so during the day; though I also resorted to a spring in the neighborhood. It was as good when a week old as the day it was dipped, and had no taste of the pump. Whoever camps for a week in summer by the shore of a pond, needs only bury a pail of water a few feet deep in the shade of his camp to be independent of the luxury of ice.

There have been caught in Walden pickerel, one weighing seven pounds — to say nothing of another which carried off a reel with great velocity, which the fisherman safely set down at eight pounds because he did not see him — perch and pouts, some of each weighing over two pounds, shiners, chivins or roach (*Leuciscus pulchellus*), a very few breams, and a couple of eels, one weighing four pounds — I am thus particular because the weight of a fish is commonly its only title to fame, and these are the only eels I have heard of here; — also, I have a faint recollection of a little fish some five inches long, with silvery sides and a greenish back, somewhat dace-like in its character, which I mention here chiefly to link my facts to fable. Nevertheless, this pond is not very fertile in fish. Its pickerel, though not abundant, are its chief boast. I have seen at one time lying on the ice pickerel of at least three different kinds: a long and shallow one, steel-colored, most like those caught in the river; a bright golden kind, with greenish reflections and remarkably deep, which is the most common here; and another, golden-colored, and shaped like the last, but peppered on the sides with small dark brown or black spots, intermixed with a few faint blood-red ones, very much like a trout. The specific name *reticulatus* would not apply to this; it should be *guttatus* rather. These are all very firm fish, and weigh more than their size promises. The shiners, pouts, and perch also, and indeed all the fishes which inhabit this pond, are much cleaner, handsomer, and firmer-fleshed than those in the river and most other ponds, as the water is purer, and they can easily be distinguished from them. Probably many ichthyologists would make new varieties of some of them. There are also a clean race of frogs and tortoises, and a few mussels in it; muskrats and minks leave their traces about it, and occasionally a travelling mud-turtle visits it. Sometimes, when I pushed off my boat in the morning, I disturbed a great mud-turtle which had secreted himself under the boat in the night. Ducks and geese frequent it in the spring and fall, the white-bellied swallows (*Hirundo bicolor*) skim over it, and the peetweets (*Totanus macularius*) 'teeter' along its stony shores all summer. I have sometimes disturbed a fish hawk sitting on a white pine over the water; but I doubt if it is ever profaned by the wind of a gull, like Fair Haven. At most, it tolerates one annual loon. These are all the animals of consequence which frequent it now.

You may see from a boat, in calm weather, near the sandy eastern shore, where the water is eight or ten feet deep, and also in some other parts of the pond, some circular heaps half a dozen feet in diameter by a foot in height, consisting of small stones less than a hen's egg in size, where all around is bare sand. At first you wonder if the Indians could have formed them on the ice for any purpose, and so, when the ice melted, they sank to the bottom; but they are too regular and some of them plainly too fresh for that. They are similar to those found in rivers; but as there are no suckers nor lampreys here, I know not by what fish they could be made. Perhaps they are the nests of the chivin. These lend a pleasing mystery to the bottom.

The shore is irregular enough not to be monotonous. I have in my mind's eye the western, indented with deep bays, the bolder northern, and the beautifully scalloped southern shore, where successive capes overlap each other and suggest unexplored coves between. The forest has never so good a setting, nor is so distinctly beautiful, as when seen from the middle of a small lake amid hills which rise from the water's edge; for the water in which it is reflected not only makes the best foreground in such a case, but, with its winding shore, the most natural and agreeable boundary to it. There is no rawness nor imperfection in its edge there, as where the axe has cleared a part, or a cultivated field abuts on it. The trees have ample room to expand on the water side, and each sends forth its most vigorous branch in that direction. There Nature has woven a natural selvage, and the eye rises by just gradations from the low shrubs of the shore to the highest trees. There are few traces of man's hand to be seen. The water laves the shore as it did a thousand years ago.

A lake is the landscape's most beautiful and expressive feature. It is earth's eye; looking into which the beholder measures the depth of his own nature. The fluviatile trees next the shore are the slender eyelashes which fringe it, and the wooded hills and cliffs around are its overhanging brows.

Standing on the smooth sandy beach at the east end of the pond, in a calm September afternoon, when a slight haze makes the opposite shore-line indistinct, I have seen whence came the expression, 'the glassy surface of a lake.' When you invert your head, it looks like a thread of finest gossamer stretched across the valley, and gleaming against the distant pine woods, separating one stratum of the atmosphere from another. You would think that you could walk dry under it to the opposite hills, and that the swallows which skim over might perch on it. Indeed, they sometimes dive below the line, as it were by mistake, and are undeceived. As you look over the pond westward you are obliged to employ both your hands to defend your eyes against the reflected as well as the true sun, for they are equally bright; and if, between the two, you survey its surface critically, it is literally as smooth as glass, except where the skater insects, at equal intervals scattered over its whole extent, by their motions in the sun produce the finest imaginable sparkle on it, or, perchance, a duck plumes itself, or, as I have said, a swallow skims so low as to touch it. It may be that in the distance a fish describes an arc of three or four feet in the air, and there is one bright flash where it emerges, and another where it strikes the water; sometimes the whole silvery arc is revealed; or here and there, perhaps, is a thistle-down floating on its surface, which the fishes dart at and so dimple it again. It is like molten glass cooled but not congealed, and the few motes in it are pure and beautiful like the imperfections in glass. You may often detect a yet smoother and darker water, separated from the rest as if by an invisible cobweb, boom of the water nymphs, resting on it. From a hilltop you can see a fish leap in almost any part; for not a pickerel or shiner picks an insect from this smooth surface but it manifestly disturbs the equilibrium of the whole lake. It is wonderful with what elaborateness this simple fact is advertised — this piscine murder will out — and from my distant perch I distinguish the circling undulations when they are half a dozen rods in diameter. You can even detect a water-bug (*Gyrinus*) ceaselessly progressing over the smooth surface a quarter of a mile off; for they furrow the water slightly, making a conspicuous ripple bounded by two diverging lines, but the skaters glide over it without rippling it perceptibly. When the surface is considerably agitated there are no skaters nor water-bugs on it, but apparently, in calm days, they leave their havens and adventurously glide forth from the shore by short impulses till they completely cover it. It is a soothing employment, on one of those fine days in the fall when all the warmth of the sun is fully appreciated, to sit on a stump on such a height as this, overlooking the pond, and study the dimpling circles which are incessantly inscribed on its otherwise invisible surface amid the reflected skies and trees. Over this great expanse there is no disturbance but it is thus at once gently smoothed away and assuaged, as, when a vase of water is jarred, the trembling circles seek the shore and all is smooth again. Not a fish can leap or an insect fall on the pond but it is thus reported in circling dimples, in lines of beauty, as it were the constant welling up of its fountain, the gentle pulsing of its life, the heaving of its breast. The thrills of joy and thrills of pain are undistinguishable. How peaceful the phenomena of the lake! Again the works of man shine as in the spring. Ay, every leaf and twig and stone and cobweb sparkles now at mid-afternoon as when covered with dew in a spring morning. Every motion of an oar or an insect produces a flash of light; and if an oar falls, how sweet the echo!

In such a day, in September or October, Walden is a perfect forest mirror, set round with stones as precious to my eye as if fewer or rarer. Nothing so fair, so pure, and at the same time so large, as a lake, perchance, lies on the surface of the earth. Sky water. It needs no fence. Nations come and go without defiling it. It is a mirror which no stone can crack, whose quicksilver will never wear off, whose gilding Nature continually repairs; no storms, no dust, can dim its surface ever fresh; — a mirror in which all impurity presented to it sinks, swept and dusted by the sun's hazy brush — this the light dust-cloth — which retains no breath that is breathed on it, but sends its own to float as clouds high above its surface, and be reflected in its bosom still.

A field of water betrays the spirit that is in the air. It is continually receiving new life and motion from above. It is intermediate in its nature between land and sky. On land only the grass and trees wave, but the water itself is rippled by the wind. I see where the breeze dashes across it by the streaks or flakes of light. It is remarkable that we can look down on its surface. We shall, perhaps, look down thus on the surface of air at length, and mark where a still subtler spirit sweeps over it.

The skaters and water-bugs finally disappear in the latter part of October, when the severe frosts have come; and then and in November, usually, in a calm day, there is absolutely nothing to ripple the surface. One November afternoon, in the calm at the end of a rain-storm of several days' duration, when the sky was still completely overcast and the air was full of mist, I observed that the pond was remarkably smooth, so that it was difficult to distinguish its surface; though it no longer reflected the bright tints of October, but the sombre November colors of the surrounding hills. Though I passed over it as gently as possible, the slight undulations produced by my boat extended almost as far as I could see, and gave a ribbed appearance to the reflections. But, as I was looking over the surface, I saw here and there at a distance a faint glimmer, as if some skater insects which had escaped the frosts might be collected there, or, perchance, the surface, being so smooth, betrayed where a spring welled up from the bottom. Paddling gently to one of these places, I was surprised to find myself surrounded by myriads of small perch, about five inches long, of a rich bronze color in the green water, sporting there, and constantly rising to the surface and dimpling it, sometimes leaving bubbles on it. In such transparent and seemingly bottomless water, reflecting the clouds, I seemed to be floating through the air as in a balloon, and their swimming impressed me as a kind of flight or hovering, as if they were a compact flock of birds passing just beneath my level on the right or left, their fins, like sails, set all around them. There were many such schools in the pond, apparently improving the short season before winter would draw an icy shutter over their broad skylight, sometimes giving to the surface an appearance as if a slight breeze struck it, or a few rain-drops fell there. When I approached carelessly and alarmed them, they made a sudden plash and rippling with their tails, as if one had struck the water with a brushy bough, and instantly took refuge in the depths. At length the wind rose, the mist increased, and the waves began to run, and the perch leaped much higher than before, half out of water, a hundred black points, three inches long, at once above the surface. Even as late as the fifth of December, one year, I saw some dimples on the surface, and thinking it was going to rain hard immediately, the air being full of mist, I made haste to take my place at the oars and row homeward; already the rain seemed rapidly increasing, though I felt none on my cheek, and I anticipated a thorough soaking. But suddenly the dimples ceased, for they were produced by the perch, which the noise of my oars had scared into the depths, and I saw their schools dimly disappearing; so I spent a dry afternoon after all.

An old man who used to frequent this pond nearly sixty years ago, when it was dark with surrounding forests, tells me that in those days he sometimes saw it all alive with ducks and other water-fowl, and that there were many eagles about it. He came here a-fishing, and used an old log canoe which he found on the shore. It was made of two white pine logs dug out and pinned together, and was cut off square at the ends. It was very clumsy, but lasted a great many years before it became water-logged and perhaps sank to the bottom. He did not know whose it was; it belonged to the pond. He used to make a cable for his anchor of strips of hickory bark tied together. An old man, a potter, who lived by the pond before the Revolution, told him once that there was an iron chest at the bottom, and that he had seen it. Sometimes it would come floating up to the shore; but when you went toward it, it would go back into deep water and disappear. I was pleased to hear of the old log canoe, which took the place of an Indian one of the same material but more graceful construction, which perchance had first been a tree on the bank, and then, as it were, fell into the water, to float there for a generation, the most proper vessel for the lake. I remember that when I first looked into these depths there were many large trunks to be seen indistinctly lying on the bottom, which had either been blown over formerly, or left on the ice at the last cutting, when wood was cheaper; but now they have mostly disappeared.

When I first paddled a boat on Walden, it was completely surrounded by thick and lofty pine and oak woods, and in some of its coves grapevines had run over the trees next the water and formed bowers under which a boat could pass. The hills which form its shores are so steep, and the woods on them were then so high, that, as you looked down from the west end, it had the appearance of an amphitheatre for some kind of sylvan spectacle. I have spent many an hour, when I was younger, floating over its surface as the zephyr willed, having paddled my boat to the middle, and lying on my back across the seats, in a summer forenoon, dreaming awake, until I was aroused by the boat touching the sand, and I arose to see what shore my fates had impelled me to; days when idleness was the most attractive and productive industry. Many a forenoon have I stolen away, preferring to spend thus the most valued part of the day; for I was rich, if not in money, in sunny hours and summer days, and spent them lavishly; nor do I regret that I did not waste more of them in the workshop or the teacher's desk. But since I left those shores the woodchoppers have still further laid them waste, and now for many a year there will be no more rambling through the aisles of the wood, with occasional vistas through which you see the water. My Muse may be excused if she is silent henceforth. How can you expect the birds to sing when their groves are cut down?

Now the trunks of trees on the bottom, and the old log canoe, and the dark surrounding woods, are gone, and the villagers, who scarcely know where it lies, instead of going to the pond to bathe or drink, are thinking to bring its water, which should be as sacred as the Ganges at least, to the village in a pipe, to wash their dishes with! — to earn their Walden by the turning of a cock or drawing of a plug! That devilish Iron Horse, whose ear-rending neigh is heard throughout the town, has muddied the Boiling Spring with his foot, and he it is that has browsed off all the woods on Walden shore, that Trojan horse, with a thousand men in his belly, introduced by mercenary Greeks! Where is the country's champion, the Moore of Moore Hall, to meet him at the Deep Cut and thrust an avenging lance between the ribs of the bloated pest?

Nevertheless, of all the characters I have known, perhaps Walden wears best, and best preserves its purity. Many men have been likened to it, but few deserve that honor. Though the woodchoppers have laid bare first this shore and then that, and the Irish have built their sties by it, and the railroad has infringed on its border, and the ice-men have skimmed it once, it is itself unchanged, the same water which my youthful eyes fell on; all the change is in me. It has not acquired one permanent wrinkle after all its ripples. It is perennially young, and I may stand and see a swallow dip apparently to pick an insect from its surface as of yore. It struck me again tonight, as if I had not seen it almost daily for more than twenty years — Why, here is Walden, the same woodland lake that I discovered so many years ago; where a forest

was cut down last winter another is springing up by its shore as lustily
as ever; the same thought is welling up to its surface that was then; it
is the same liquid joy and happiness to itself and its Maker, ay, and it
may be to me. It is the work of a brave man surely, in whom there was
no guile! He rounded this water with his hand, deepened and clarified
it in his thought, and in his will bequeathed it to Concord. I see by its
face that it is visited by the same reflection; and I can almost say,
Walden, is it you?

> It is no dream of mine,
> To ornament a line;
> I cannot come nearer to God and Heaven
> Than I live to Walden even.
> I am its stony shore,
> And the breeze that passes o'er;
> In the hollow of my hand
> Are its water and its sand,
> And its deepest resort
> Lies high in my thought.

The cars never pause to look at it; yet I fancy that the engineers and
firemen and brakemen, and those passengers who have a season ticket
and see it often, are better men for the sight. The engineer does not forget at night, or his nature does not, that he has beheld this vision of
serenity and purity once at least during the day. Though seen but
once, it helps to wash out State Street and the engine's soot. One proposes that it be called 'God's Drop.'

I have said that Walden has no visible inlet nor outlet, but it is on
the one hand distantly and indirectly related to Flint's Pond, which is
more elevated, by a chain of small ponds coming from that quarter,
and on the other directly and manifestly to Concord River, which is
lower, by a similar chain of ponds through which in some other geological period it may have flowed, and by a little digging, which God for-
bid, it can be made to flow thither again. If by living thus reserved and
austere, like a hermit in the woods, so long, it has acquired such wonderful purity, who would not regret that the comparatively impure waters
of Flint's Pond should be mingled with it, or itself should ever go to
waste its sweetness in the ocean wave?

Flint's, or Sandy Pond, in Lincoln, our greatest lake and inland sea,
lies about a mile east of Walden. It is much larger, being said to contain one hundred and ninety-seven acres, and is more fertile in fish;

but it is comparatively shallow, and not remarkably pure. A walk through the woods thither was often my recreation. It was worth the while, if only to feel the wind blow on your cheek freely, and see the waves run, and remember the life of mariners. I went a-chestnutting there in the fall, on windy days, when the nuts were dropping into the water and were washed to my feet; and one day, as I crept along its sedgy shore, the fresh spray blowing in my face, I came upon the mouldering wreck of a boat, the sides gone, and hardly more than the impression of its flat bottom left amid the rushes; yet its model was sharply defined, as if it were a large decayed pad, with its veins. It was as impressive a wreck as one could imagine on the seashore, and had as good a moral. It is by this time mere vegetable mould and un-distinguishable pond shore, through which rushes and flags have pushed up. I used to admire the ripple marks on the sandy bottom, at the north end of this pond, made firm and hard to the feet of the wader by the pressure of the water, and the rushes which grew in Indian file, in waving lines, corresponding to these marks, rank behind rank, as if the waves had planted them. There also I have found, in considerable quantities, curious balls, composed apparently of fine grass or roots, of pipewort perhaps, from half an inch to four inches in diameter, and perfectly spherical. These wash back and forth in shallow water on a sandy bottom, and are sometimes cast on the shore. They are either solid grass, or have a little sand in the middle. At first you would say that they were formed by the action of the waves, like a pebble; yet the smallest are made of equally coarse materials, half an inch long, and they are produced only at one season of the year. Moreover, the waves, I suspect, do not so much construct as wear down a material which has already acquired consistency. They preserve their form when dry for an indefinite period.

Flint's Pond! Such is the poverty of our nomenclature. What right had the unclean and stupid farmer, whose farm abutted on this sky water, whose shores he has ruthlessly laid bare, to give his name to it? Some skin-flint, who loved better the reflecting surface of a dollar, or a bright cent, in which he could see his own brazen face; who regarded even the wild ducks which settled in it as trespassers; his fingers grown into crooked and horny talons from the long habit of grasping harpy-like; — so it is not named for me. I go not there to see him nor to hear of him; who never *saw* it, who never bathed in it, who never loved it, who never protected it, who never spoke a good word for it, nor thanked God that He had made it. Rather let it be named from the fishes that swim in it, the wild fowl or quadrupeds which frequent it, the wild flowers which grow by its shores, or some wild man or child the thread of whose history is interwoven with its own; not from him who could show no title to it but the deed which a like-minded neighbor or legislature gave him — him who thought only of its money value; whose presence perchance cursed all the shores; who exhausted the land around it, and would fain have exhausted the waters within it; who regretted only that it was not English hay or cranberry meadow — there was nothing to redeem it, forsooth, in his eyes — and would have drained and sold it for the mud at its bottom. It did not turn his mill, and it was no *privilege* to him to behold it. I respect not his labors, his farm where everything has its price, who would carry the landscape, who would carry his God, to market, if he could get anything for him; who goes to market *for* his god as it is; on whose farm nothing grows free, whose fields bear no crops, whose meadows no flowers, whose trees no fruits, but dollars; who loves not the beauty of his fruits, whose fruits are not ripe for him till they are turned to dollars. Give me the poverty that enjoys true wealth. Farmers are respectable and interesting to me in proportion as they are poor — poor farmers. A model farm! where the house stands like a fungus in a muckheap, chambers for men, horses, oxen, and swine, cleansed and uncleansed, all contiguous to one another! Stocked with men! A great grease-spot, redolent of manures and buttermilk! Under a high state of cultivation, being manured with the hearts and brains of men! As if you were to raise your potatoes in the churchyard! Such is a model farm.

No, no; if the fairest features of the landscape are to be named after men, let them be the noblest and worthiest men alone. Let our lakes receive as true names at least as the Icarian Sea, where 'still the shore' a 'brave attempt resounds.'

Goose Pond, of small extent, is on my way to Flint's; Fair Haven, an expansion of Concord River, said to contain some seventy acres, is a mile southwest; and White Pond, of about forty acres, is a mile and a half beyond Fair Haven. This is my lake country. These, with Concord River, are my water privileges; and night and day, year in year out, they grind such grist as I carry to them.

Since the wood-cutters, and the railroad, and I myself have profaned Walden, perhaps the most attractive, if not the most beautiful, of all our lakes, the gem of the woods, is White Pond; — a poor name from its commonness, whether derived from the remarkable purity of its waters or the color of its sands. In these as in other respects, however, it is a lesser twin of Walden. They are so much alike that you would say they must be connected under ground. It has the same stony shore, and its waters are of the same hue. As at Walden, in sultry dogday weather, looking down through the woods on some of its bays which are not so deep but that the reflection from the bottom tinges them, its waters are of a misty bluish-green or glaucous color. Many years since I used to go there to collect the sand by cartloads, to make sandpaper with, and I have continued to visit it ever since. One who frequents it proposes to call it Virid Lake. Perhaps it might be called Yellow Pine Lake, from the following circumstance. About fifteen years ago you could see the top of a pitch pine, of the kind called yellow pine hereabouts, though it is not a distinct species, projecting above the surface in deep water, many rods from the shore. It was even supposed by some that the pond had sunk, and this was one of the primitive forest that formerly stood there. I find that even so long ago as 1792, in a 'Topographical Description of the Town of Concord,' by one of its citizens, in the Collections of the Massachusetts Historical Society, the author, after speaking of Walden and White Ponds, adds, 'In the middle of the latter may be seen, when the water is very low, a tree which appears as if it grew in the place where it now stands, although the roots are fifty feet below the surface of the water; the top of this tree is broken off, and at that place measures fourteen inches in diameter.' In the spring of '49 I talked with the man who lives nearest the pond in Sudbury, who told me that it was he who got out this tree ten or fifteen years before. As near as he could remember, it stood twelve or fifteen rods from the shore, where the water was thirty or forty feet deep. It was in the winter, and he had been getting out ice in the forenoon, and had resolved that in the afternoon, with the aid of his neighbors, he would take out the old yellow pine. He sawed a channel in the ice toward the shore, and hauled it over and along and out on to the ice with oxen; but, before he had gone far in his work, he was surprised to find that it was wrong end upward, with the stumps of the branches pointing down, and the small end firmly fastened in the sandy bottom. It was about a foot in diameter at the big end, and he had expected to get a good saw-log, but it was so rotten as to be fit only for fuel, if for that. He had some of it in his shed then. There were marks of an axe and of woodpeckers on the butt. He thought that it might have been a dead tree on the shore, but was finally blown over into the pond, and after the top had become water-logged, while the butt-end was still dry and light, had drifted out and sunk wrong end up. His father, eighty years old, could not remember when it was not there. Several pretty large logs may still be seen lying on the bottom, where, owing to the undulation of the surface, they look like huge water snakes in motion.

This pond has rarely been profaned by a boat, for there is little in it to tempt a fisherman. Instead of the white lily, which requires mud, or the common sweet flag, the blue flag (*Iris versicolor*) grows thinly in the pure water, rising from the stony bottom all around the shore, where it is visited by hummingbirds in June; and the color both of its bluish blades and its flowers and especially their reflections, is in singular harmony with the glaucous water.

White Pond and Walden are great crystals on the surface of the earth, Lakes of Light. If they were permanently congealed, and small enough to be clutched, they would, perchance, be carried off by slaves, like precious stones, to adorn the heads of emperors; but being liquid, and ample, and secured to us and our successors forever, we disregard them, and run after the diamond of Kohinoor. They are too pure to have a market value; they contain no muck. How much more beautiful than our lives, how much more transparent than our characters, are they! We never learned meanness of them. How much fairer than the pool before the farmer's door, in which his ducks swim! Hither the clean wild ducks come. Nature has no human inhabitant who appreciates her. The birds with their plumage and their notes are in harmony with the flowers, but what youth or maiden conspires with the wild luxuriant beauty of Nature? She flourishes most alone, far from the towns where they reside. Talk of heaven! ye disgrace earth.

X. BAKER FARM

Sometimes I rambled to pine groves, standing like temples, or like fleets at sea, full-rigged, with wavy boughs, and rippling with light, so soft and green and shady that the Druids would have forsaken their oaks to worship in them; or to the cedar wood beyond Flint's Pond, where the trees, covered with hoary blue berries, spiring higher and higher, are fit to stand before Valhalla, and the creeping juniper covers the ground with wreaths full of fruit; or to swamps where the usnea lichen hangs in festoons from the white spruce trees, and toadstools, round tables of the swamp gods, cover the ground, and more beautiful fungi adorn the stumps, like butterflies or shells, vegetable winkles; where the swamp-pink and dogwood grow, the red alder berry glows like eyes of imps, the waxwork grooves and crushes the hardest woods in its folds, and the wild holly berries make the beholder forget his home with their beauty, and he is dazzled and tempted by nameless other wild forbidden fruits, too fair for mortal taste. Instead of calling on some scholar, I paid many a visit to particular trees, of kinds which are rare in this neighborhood, standing far away in the middle of some pasture, or in the depths of a wood or swamp, or on a hilltop; such as the black birch, of which we have some handsome specimens two feet in diameter; its cousin, the yellow birch, with its loose golden vest, perfumed like the first; the beech, which has so neat a bole and beautifully lichen-painted, perfect in all its details, of which, excepting scattered specimens, I know but one small grove of sizable trees left in the township, supposed by some to have been planted by the pigeons that were once baited with beechnuts near by; it is worth the while to see the silver grain sparkle when you split this wood; the bass; the hornbeam; the *Celtis occidentalis*, or false elm, of which we have but one well-grown; some taller mast of a pine, a shingle tree, or a more perfect hemlock than usual, standing like a pagoda in the midst of the woods; and many others I could mention. These were the shrines I visited both summer and winter.

Once it chanced that I stood in the very abutment of a rainbow's arch, which filled the lower stratum of the atmosphere, tinging the grass and leaves around, and dazzling me as if I looked through colored crystal. It was a lake of rainbow light, in which, for a short while, I lived like a dolphin. If it had lasted longer it might have tinged my employments and life. As I walked on the railroad causeway, I used to wonder at the halo of light around my shadow, and would fain fancy myself one of the elect. One who visited me declared that the shadows of some Irishmen before him had no halo about them, that it was only natives that were so distinguished. Benvenuto Cellini tells us in his memoirs, that, after a certain terrible dream or vision which he had during his confinement in the castle of St. Angelo a resplendent light appeared over the shadow of his head at morning and evening, whether he was in Italy or France, and it was particularly conspicuous when the grass was moist with dew. This was probably the same phenomenon to which I have referred, which is especially observed in the morning, but also at other times, and even by moonlight. Though a constant one, it is not commonly noticed, and, in the case of an excitable imagination like Cellini's, it would be basis enough for superstition. Beside, he tells us that he showed it to very few. But are they not indeed distinguished who are conscious that they are regarded at all?

I set out one afternoon to go a-fishing to Fair Haven, through the woods, to eke out my scanty fare of vegetables. My way led through Pleasant Meadow, an adjunct of the Baker Farm, that retreat of which a poet has since sung, beginning,

> 'Thy entry is a pleasant field,
> Which some mossy fruit trees yield
> Partly to a ruddy brook,
> By gliding musquash undertook,
> And mercurial trout,
> Darting about.'

I thought of living there before I went to Walden. I 'hooked' the apples, leaped the brook, and scared the musquash and the trout. It was one of those afternoons which seem indefinitely long before one, in which many events may happen, a large portion of our natural life, though it was already half spent when I started. By the way there came up a shower, which compelled me to stand half an hour under a pine, piling boughs over my head, and wearing my handkerchief for a shed; and when at length I had made one cast over the pickerelweed, standing up to my middle in water, I found myself suddenly in the shadow of a cloud, and the thunder began to rumble with such emphasis that I could do no more than listen to it. The gods must be proud, thought I, with such forked flashes to rout a poor unarmed fisherman. So I made haste for shelter to the nearest hut, which stood half a mile from any road, but so much the nearer to the pond, and had long been un-inhabited:

> "And here a poet builded,
> In the completed years,
> For behold a trivial cabin
> That to destruction steers."

So the Muse fables. But therein, as I found, dwelt now John Field, an Irishman, and his wife, and several children, from the broad-faced boy who assisted his father at his work, and now came running by his side from the bog to escape the rain, to the wrinkled, sibyl-like, cone-headed infant that sat upon its father's knee as in the palaces of nobles, and looked out from its home in the midst of wet and hunger inquisitively upon the stranger, with the privilege of infancy, not knowing but it was the last of a noble line, and the hope and cynosure of the world, instead of John Field's poor starveling brat. There we sat together under that part of the roof which leaked the least, while it showered and thundered without. I had sat there many times of old before the ship was built that floated his family to America. An honest, hard-working, but shiftless man plainly was John Field; and his wife, she too was brave to cook so many successive dinners in the recesses of that lofty stove; with round greasy face and bare breast, still thinking to improve her condition one day; with the never absent mop in one hand, and yet no effects of it visible anywhere. The chickens, which had also taken shelter here from the rain, stalked about the room like members of the family, too humanized, methought, to roast well. They stood and looked in my eye or pecked at my shoe significantly. Meanwhile my host told me his story, how hard he worked 'bogging' for a neighboring farmer, turning up a meadow with a spade or bog hoe at the rate of ten dollars an acre and the use of the land with manure for one year, and his little broad-faced son worked cheerfully at his father's side the while, not knowing how poor a bargain the latter had made. I tried to help him with my experience, telling him that he was one of my nearest neighbors, and that I too, who came a-fishing here, and looked like a loafer, was getting my living like himself; that I lived in a tight, light, and clean house, which hardly cost more than the annual rent of such a ruin as his commonly amounts to; and how, if he chose, he might in a month or two build himself a palace of his own; that I did not use tea, nor coffee, nor butter, nor milk, nor fresh meat, and so did not have to work to get them; again, as I did not work hard, I did not have to eat hard, and it cost me but a trifle for my food; but as he began with tea, and coffee, and butter, and milk, and beef, he had to work hard to pay for them, and when he had worked hard he had to eat hard again to repair the waste of his system — and so it was as broad as it was long, indeed it was broader than it was long, for he was discontented and wasted his life into the bargain; and yet he had rated it as a gain in coming to America, that here you could get tea, and coffee, and meat every day. But the only true America is that country where you are at liberty to pursue such a mode of life as may enable you to do without these, and where the state does not endeavor to compel you to sustain the slavery and war and other superfluous expenses which directly or indirectly result from the use of such things. For I purposely talked to him as if he were a philosopher, or desired to be one. I should be glad if all the meadows on the earth were left in a wild state, if that were the consequence of men's beginning to redeem themselves. A man will not need to study history to find out what is best for his own culture. But alas! the culture of an Irishman is an enterprise to be undertaken with a sort of moral bog hoe. I told him, that as he worked so hard at bogging, he required thick boots and stout clothing, which yet were soon soiled and worn out, but I wore light shoes and thin clothing, which cost not half so much, though he might think that I was dressed like a gentleman (which, however, was not the case), and in an hour or two, without labor, but as a recreation, I could, if I wished, catch as many fish as I should want for two days, or earn enough money to support me a week. If he and his family would live simply, they might all go a-huckleberrying in the summer for their amusement. John heaved a sigh at this, and his wife stared with arms a-kimbo, and both appeared to be wondering if they had capital enough to begin such a course with, or arithmetic enough to carry it through. It was sailing by dead reckoning to them, and they saw not clearly how to make their port so; therefore I suppose they still take life bravely, after their fashion, face to face, giving it tooth and nail, not having skill to split its massive columns with any fine entering wedge, and rout it in detail; — thinking to deal with it roughly, as one should handle a thistle. But they fight at an overwhelming disadvantage — living, John Field, alas! without arithmetic, and failing so.

'Do you ever fish?' I asked. 'Oh yes, I catch a mess now and then when I am lying by; good perch I catch.' 'What's your bait?' 'I catch shiners with fishworms, and bait the perch with them.' 'You'd better go now, John,' said his wife, with glistening and hopeful face; but John demurred.

The shower was now over, and a rainbow above the eastern woods promised a fair evening; so I took my departure. When I had got without I asked for a drink, hoping to get a sight of the well bottom, to complete my survey of the premises; but there, alas! are shallows and quicksands, and rope broken withal, and bucket irrecoverable. Meanwhile the right culinary vessel was selected, water was seemingly distilled, and after consultation and long delay passed out to the thirsty one — not yet suffered to cool, not yet to settle. Such gruel sustains life here, I thought; so, shutting my eyes, and excluding the motes by a skilfully directed undercurrent, I drank to genuine hospitality the heartiest draught I could. I am not squeamish in such cases when manners are concerned.

As I was leaving the Irishman's roof after the rain, bending my steps again to the pond, my haste to catch pickerel, wading in retired meadows, in sloughs and bog-holes, in forlorn and savage places, appeared for an instant trivial to me who had been sent to school and college; but as I ran down the hill toward the reddening west, with the rainbow over my shoulder, and some faint tinkling sounds borne to my ear through the cleansed air, from I know not what quarter, my Good Genius seemed to say — Go fish and hunt far and wide day by day — farther and wider — and rest thee by many brooks and hearth-sides without misgiving. Remember thy Creator in the days of thy youth. Rise free from care before the dawn, and seek adventures. Let the noon find thee by other lakes, and the night overtake thee everywhere at home. There are no larger fields than these, no worthier games than may here be played. Grow wild according to thy nature, like these sedges and brakes, which will never become English hay. Let the thunder rumble; what if it threaten ruin to farmers' crops? that is not its errand to thee. Take shelter under the cloud, while they flee to carts and sheds. Let not to get a living be thy trade, but thy sport. Enjoy the land, but own it not. Through want of enterprise and faith men are where they are, buying and selling, and spending their lives like serfs.

O Baker Farm!

> 'Landscape where the richest element
> Is a little sunshine innocent.' . . .

> 'No one runs to revel
> On thy rail-fenced lea.' . . .

> 'Debate with no man hast thou,
>   With questions art never perplexed,
> As tame at the first sight as now,
>   In thy plain russet gabardine dressed.' . . .

> 'Come ye who love,
>   And ye who hate,
> Children of the Holy Dove,
>   And Guy Faux of the state,
> And hang conspiracies
> From the tough rafters of the trees!'

Men come tamely home at night only from the next field or street, where their household echoes haunt, and their life pines because it breathes its own breath over again; their shadows, morning and evening, reach farther than their daily steps. We should come home from far, from adventures, and perils, and discoveries every day, with new experience and character.

Before I had reached the pond some fresh impulse had brought out John Field, with altered mind, letting go 'bogging' ere this sunset. But he, poor man, disturbed only a couple of fins while I was catching a fair string, and he said it was his luck; but when we changed seats in the boat luck changed seats too. Poor John Field! — I trust he does not read this, unless he will improve by it — thinking to live by some derivative old-country mode in this primitive new country — to catch perch with shiners. It is good bait sometimes, I allow. With his horizon all his own, yet he a poor man, born to be poor, with his inherited Irish poverty or poor life, his Adam's grandmother and boggy ways, not to rise in this world, he nor his posterity, till their wading webbed bog-trotting feet get *talaria* to their heels.

XI. HIGHER LAWS

As I came home through the woods with my string of fish, trailing my pole, it being now quite dark, I caught a glimpse of a woodchuck stealing across my path, and felt a strange thrill of savage delight, and was strongly tempted to seize and devour him raw; not that I was hungry then, except for that wildness which he represented. Once or twice, however, while I lived at the pond, I found myself ranging the woods, like a half-starved hound, with a strange abandonment, seeking some kind of venison which I might devour, and no morsel could have been too savage for me. The wildest scenes had become unaccountably familiar. I found in myself, and still find, an instinct toward a higher, or, as it is named, spiritual life, as do most men, and another toward a primitive rank and savage one, and I reverence them both. I love the wild not less than the good. The wildness and adventure that are in fishing still recommended it to me. I like sometimes to take rank hold on life and spend my day more as the animals do. Perhaps I have owed to this employment and to hunting, when quite young, my closest acquaintance with Nature. They early introduce us to and detain us in scenery with which otherwise, at that age, we should have little acquaintance. Fishermen, hunters, woodchoppers, and others, spending their lives in the fields and woods, in a peculiar sense a part of Nature themselves, are often in a more favorable mood for observing her, in the intervals of their pursuits, than philosophers or poets even, who approach her with expectation. She is not afraid to exhibit herself to them. The traveller on the prairie is naturally a hunter, on the head waters of the Missouri and Columbia a trapper, and at the Falls of St. Mary a fisherman. He who is only a traveller learns things at second-hand and by the halves, and is poor authority. We are most interested when science reports what those men already know practically or instinctively, for that alone is a true *humanity*, or account of human experience.

They mistake who assert that the Yankee has few amusements, because he has not so many public holidays, and men and boys do not play so many games as they do in England, for here the more primitive but solitary amusements of hunting, fishing, and the like have not yet given place to the former. Almost every New England boy among my contemporaries shouldered a fowling-piece between the ages of ten and fourteen; and his hunting and fishing grounds were not limited, like the preserves of an English nobleman, but were more boundless even than those of a savage. No wonder, then, that he did not oftener stay to play on the common. But already a change is taking place, owing, not to an increased humanity, but to an increased scarcity of game, for perhaps the hunter is the greatest friend of the animals hunted, not excepting the Humane Society.

Moreover, when at the pond, I wished sometimes to add fish to my fare for variety. I have actually fished from the same kind of necessity that the first fishers did. Whatever humanity I might conjure up against it was all factitious, and concerned my philosophy more than my feelings. I speak of fishing only now, for I had long felt differently about fowling, and sold my gun before I went to the woods. Not that I am less humane than others, but I did not perceive that my feelings were much affected. I did not pity the fishes nor the worms. This was habit. As for fowling, during the last years that I carried a gun my excuse was that I was studying ornithology, and sought only new or rare birds. But I confess that I am now inclined to think that there is a finer way of studying ornithology than this. It requires so much closer attention to the habits of the birds, that, if for that reason only, I have been willing to omit the gun. Yet notwithstanding the objection on the score of humanity, I am compelled to doubt if equally valuable sports are ever substituted for these; and when some of my friends have asked me anxiously about their boys, whether they should let them hunt, I have answered, yes — remembering that it was one of the best parts of my education — *make* them hunters, though sportsmen only at first, if possible, mighty hunters at last, so that they shall not find game large enough for them in this or any vegetable wilderness — hunters as well as fishers of men. Thus far I am of the opinion of Chaucer's nun, who

> 'yave not of the text a pulled hen
> That saith that hunters ben not holy men.'

There is a period in the history of the individual, as of the race, when the hunters are the 'best men,' as the Algonquins called them. We cannot but pity the boy who has never fired a gun; he is no more humane, while his education has been sadly neglected. This was my answer with respect to those youths who were bent on this pursuit, trusting that they would soon outgrow it. No humane being, past the thoughtless age of boyhood, will wantonly murder any creature which holds its life by the same tenure that he does. The hare in its extremity cries like a child. I warn you, mothers, that my sympathies do not always make the usual phil*anthropic* distinctions.

Such is oftenest the young man's introduction to the forest, and the most original part of himself. He goes thither at first as a hunter and fisher, until at last, if he has the seeds of a better life in him, he distinguishes his proper objects, as a poet or naturalist it may be, and leaves the gun and fish-pole behind. The mass of men are still and always young in this respect. In some countries a hunting parson is no uncommon sight. Such a one might make a good shepherd's dog, but is far from being the Good Shepherd. I have been surprised to consider that the only obvious employment, except wood-chopping, ice-cutting, or the like business, which ever to my knowledge detained at Walden Pond for a whole half-day any of my fellow-citizens, whether fathers or children of the town, with just one exception, was fishing. Commonly they did not think that they were lucky, or well paid for their time, unless they got a long string of fish, though they had the opportunity of seeing the pond all the while. They might go there a thousand times before the sediment of fishing would sink to the bottom and leave their purpose pure; but no doubt such a clarifying process would be going on all the while. The Governor and his Council faintly remember the pond, for they went a-fishing there when they were boys; but now they are too old and dignified to go a-fishing, and so they know it no more forever. Yet even they expect to go to heaven at last. If the legislature regards it, it is chiefly to regulate the number of hooks to be used there; but they know nothing about the hook of hooks with which to angle for the pond itself, impaling the legislature for a bait. Thus, even in civilized communities, the embryo man passes through the hunter stage of development.

I have found repeatedly, of late years, that I cannot fish without falling a little in self-respect. I have tried it again and again. I have skill at it, and, like many of my fellows, a certain instinct for it, which revives from time to time, but always when I have done I feel that it would have been better if I had not fished. I think that I do not mistake. It is a faint intimation, yet so are the first streaks of morning. There is unquestionably this instinct in me which belongs to the lower orders of creation; yet with every year I am less a fisherman, though without more humanity or even wisdom; at present I am no fisherman at all. But I see that if I were to live in a wilderness I should again be tempted to become a fisher and hunter in earnest. Beside, there is something essentially unclean about this diet and all flesh, and I began to see where house-work commences, and whence the endeavor, which costs so much, to wear a tidy and respectable appearance each day, to keep the house sweet and free from all ill odors and sights. Having been my own butcher and scullion and cook, as well as the gentleman for whom the dishes were served up, I can speak from an unusually complete experience. The practical objection to animal food in my case was its uncleanness; and besides, when I had caught and cleaned and cooked and eaten my fish, they seemed not to have fed me essentially. It was insignificant and unnecessary, and cost more than it came to. A little bread or a few potatoes would have done as well, with less trouble and filth. Like many of my contemporaries, I had rarely for many years used animal food, or tea, or coffee, etc.; not so much because of any ill effects which I had traced to them, as because they were not agreeable to my imagination. The repugnance to animal food is not the effect of experience, but is an instinct. It appeared more beautiful to live low and fare hard in many respects; and though I never did so, I went far enough to please my imagination. I believe that every man who has ever been earnest to preserve his higher or poetic faculties in the best condition has been particularly inclined to abstain from animal food, and from much food of any kind. It is a significant fact, stated by entomologists — I find it in Kirby and Spence — that 'some insects in their perfect state, though furnished with organs of feeding, make no use of them;' and they lay it down as 'a general rule, that almost all insects in this state eat much less than in that of larvæ. The voracious caterpillar when transformed into a butterfly . . . and the gluttonous maggot when become a fly' content themselves with a drop or two of honey or some other sweet liquid. The abdomen under the wings of the butterfly still represents the larva. This is the tidbit which tempts his insectivorous fate. The gross feeder is a man in the larva state; and there are whole nations in that condition, nations without fancy or imagination, whose vast abdomens betray them.

It is hard to provide and cook so simple and clean a diet as will not offend the imagination; but this, I think, is to be fed when we feed the body; they should both sit down at the same table. Yet perhaps this may be done. The fruits eaten temperately need not make us ashamed of our appetites, nor interrupt the worthiest pursuits. But put an extra condiment into your dish, and it will poison you. It is not worth the while to live by rich cookery. Most men would feel shame if caught preparing with their own hands precisely such a dinner, whether of animal or vegetable food, as is every day prepared for them by others. Yet till this is otherwise we are not civilized, and, if gentlemen and ladies, are not true men and women. This certainly suggests what change is to be made. It may be vain to ask why the imagination will not be reconciled to flesh and fat. I am satisfied that it is not. Is it not a reproach that man is a carnivorous animal? True, he can and does live, in a great measure, by preying on other animals; but this is a miserable way — as any one who will go to snaring rabbits, or slaughtering lambs, may learn — and he will be regarded as a benefactor of his race who shall teach man to confine himself to a more innocent and wholesome diet. Whatever my own practice may be, I have no doubt that it is a part of the destiny of the human race, in its gradual improvement, to leave off eating animals, as surely as the savage tribes have left off eating each other when they came in contact with the more civilized.

If one listens to the faintest but constant suggestions of his genius, which are certainly true, he sees not to what extremes, or even insanity, it may lead him; and yet that way, as he grows more resolute and faithful, his road lies. The faintest assured objection which one healthy man feels will at length prevail over the arguments and customs of mankind.

No man ever followed his genius till it misled him. Though the result were bodily weakness, yet perhaps no one can say that the consequences were to be regretted, for these were a life in conformity to higher principles. If the day and the night are such that you greet them with joy, and life emits a fragrance like flowers and sweet-scented herbs, is more elastic, more starry, more immortal — that is your success. All nature is your congratulation, and you have cause momentarily to bless yourself. The greatest gains and values are farthest from being appreciated. We easily come to doubt if they exist. We soon forget them. They are the highest reality. Perhaps the facts most astounding and most real are never communicated by man to man. The true harvest of my daily life is somewhat as intangible and indescribable as the tints of morning or evening. It is a little star-dust caught, a segment of the rainbow which I have clutched.

Yet, for my part, I was never unusually squeamish; I could sometimes eat a fried rat with a good relish, if it were necessary. I am glad to have drunk water so long, for the same reason that I prefer the natural sky to an opium-eater's heaven. I would fain keep sober always; and there are infinite degrees of drunkenness. I believe that water is the only drink for a wise man; wine is not so noble a liquor; and think of dashing the hopes of a morning with a cup of warm coffee, or of an evening with a dish of tea! Ah, how low I fall when I am tempted by them! Even music may be intoxicating. Such apparently slight causes destroyed Greece and Rome, and will destroy England and America. Of all ebriosity, who does not prefer to be intoxicated by the air he breathes? I have found it to be the most serious objection to coarse labors long continued, that they compelled me to eat and drink coarsely also. But to tell the truth, I find myself at present somewhat less particular in these respects. I carry less religion to the table, ask no blessing; not because I am wiser than I was, but, I am obliged to confess, because, however much it is to be regretted, with years I have grown more coarse and indifferent. Perhaps these questions are entertained only in youth, as most believe of poetry. My practice is 'nowhere,' my opinion is here. Nevertheless I am far from regarding myself as one of those privileged ones to whom the Ved refers when it says, that 'he who has true faith in the Omnipresent Supreme Being may eat all that exists,' that is, is not bound to inquire what is his food, or who prepares it; and even in their case it is to be observed, as a Hindoo commentator has remarked, that the Vedant limits this privilege to 'the time of distress.'

Who has not sometimes derived an inexpressible satisfaction from his food in which appetite had no share? I have been thrilled to think that I owed a mental perception to the commonly gross sense of taste, that I have been inspired through the palate, that some berries which I had eaten on a hillside had fed my genius. 'The soul not being mistress of herself,' says Thseng-tseu, 'one looks, and one does not see; one listens, and one does not hear; one eats, and one does not know the savor of food.' He who distinguishes the true savor of his food can never be a glutton; he who does not cannot be otherwise. A puritan may go to his brown-bread crust with as gross an appetite as ever an alderman to his turtle. Not that food which entereth into the mouth defileth a man, but the appetite with which it is eaten. It is neither the quality nor the quantity, but the devotion to sensual savors; when that which is eaten is not a viand to sustain our animal, or inspire our spiritual life, but food for the worms that possess us. If the hunter has a taste for mud-turtles, muskrats, and other such savage tidbits, the fine lady indulges a taste for jelly made of a calf's foot, or for sardines from over the sea, and they are even. He goes to the mill-pond, she to her preserve-pot. The wonder is how they, how you and I, can live this slimy, beastly life, eating and drinking.

Our whole life is startlingly moral. There is never an instant's truce between virtue and vice. Goodness is the only investment that never fails. In the music of the harp which trembles round the world it is the insisting on this which thrills us. The harp is the travelling patterer for the Universe's Insurance Company, recommending its laws, and our little goodness is all the assessment that we pay. Though the youth at last grows indifferent, the laws of the universe are not indifferent, but are forever on the side of the most sensitive. Listen to every zephyr for some reproof, for it is surely there, and he is unfortunate who does not hear it. We cannot touch a string or move a stop but the charming moral transfixes us. Many an irksome noise, go a long way off, is heard as music, a proud, sweet satire on the meanness of our lives.

We are conscious of an animal in us, which awakens in proportion as our higher nature slumbers. It is reptile and sensual, and perhaps cannot be wholly expelled; like the worms which, even in life and health, occupy our bodies. Possibly we may withdraw from it, but never change its nature. I fear that it may enjoy a certain health of its own; that we may be well, yet not pure. The other day I picked up the lower jaw of a hog, with white and sound teeth and tusks, which suggested that there was an animal health and vigor distinct from the spiritual. This creature succeeded by other means than temperance and purity.

'That in which men differ from brute beasts,' says Mencius, 'is a thing very inconsiderable; the common herd lose it very soon; superior men preserve it carefully.' Who knows what sort of life would result if we had attained to purity? If I knew so wise a man as could teach me purity I would go to seek him forthwith. 'A command over our passions, and over the external senses of the body, and good acts, are declared by the Ved to be indispensable in the mind's approximation to God.' Yet the spirit can for the time pervade and control every member and function of the body, and transmute what in form is the grossest sensuality into purity and devotion. The generative energy, which, when we are loose, dissipates and makes us unclean, when we are continent invigorates and inspires us. Chastity is the flowering of man; and what are called Genius, Heroism, Holiness, and the like, are but various fruits which succeed it. Man flows at once to God when the channel of purity is open. By turns our purity inspires and our impurity casts us down. He is blessed who is assured that the animal is dying out in him day by day, and the divine being established. Perhaps there is none but has cause for shame on account of the inferior and brutish nature to which he is allied. I fear that we are such gods or demigods only as fauns and satyrs, the divine allied to beasts, the creatures of appetite, and that, to some extent, our very life is our disgrace.

> 'How happy's he who hath due place assigned
> To his beasts and disafforested his mind!
>
> . . . .
>
> Can use his horse, goat, wolf, and ev'ry beast,
> And is not ass himself to all the rest!
> Else man not only is the herd of swine,
> But he's those devils too which did incline
> Them to a headlong rage, and made them worse.'

All sensuality is one, though it takes many forms; all purity is one. It is the same whether a man eat, or drink, or cohabit, or sleep sensually. They are but one appetite, and we only need to see a person do any one of these things to know how great a sensualist he is. The impure can neither stand nor sit with purity. When the reptile is attacked at one mouth of his burrow, he shows himself at another. If you would be chaste, you must be temperate. What is chastity? How shall a man know if he is chaste? He shall not know it. We have heard of this virtue, but we know not what it is. We speak conformably to the rumor which we have heard. From exertion come wisdom and purity; from sloth ignorance and sensuality. In the student sensuality is a sluggish habit of mind. An unclean person is universally a slothful one, one who sits by a stove, whom the sun shines on prostrate, who reposes without being fatigued. If you would avoid uncleanness, and all the sins, work earnestly, though it be at cleaning a stable. Nature is hard to be overcome, but she must be overcome. What avails it that you are Christian, if you are not purer than the heathen, if you deny yourself no more, if you are not more religious? I know of many systems of religion esteemed heathenish whose precepts fill the reader with shame, and provoke him to new endeavors, though it be to the performance of rites merely.

I hesitate to say these things, but it is not because of the subject — I care not how obscene my *words* are — but because I cannot speak of them without betraying my impurity. We discourse freely without shame of one form of sensuality, and are silent about another. We are so degraded that we cannot speak simply of the necessary functions of human nature. In earlier ages, in some countries, every function was reverently spoken of and regulated by law. Nothing was too trivial for the Hindoo lawgiver, however offensive it may be to modern taste. He teaches how to eat, drink, cohabit, void excrement and urine, and the like, elevating what is mean, and does not falsely excuse himself by calling these things trifles.

Every man is the builder of a temple, called his body, to the god he worships, after a style purely his own, nor can he get off by hammering marble instead. We are all sculptors and painters, and our material is our own flesh and blood and bones. Any nobleness begins at once to refine a man's features, any meanness or sensuality to imbrute them.

John Farmer sat at his door one September evening, after a hard day's work, his mind still running on his labor more or less. Having bathed, he sat down to re-create his intellectual man. It was a rather cool evening, and some of his neighbors were apprehending a frost. He had not attended to the train of his thoughts long when he heard some one playing on a flute, and that sound harmonized with his mood. Still he thought of his work; but the burden of his thought was, that though this kept running in his head, and he found himself planning and contriving it against his will, yet it concerned him very little. It was no more than the scurf of his skin, which was constantly shuffled off. But the notes of the flute came home to his ears out of a different sphere from that he worked in, and suggested work for certain faculties which slumbered in him. They gently did away with the street, and the village, and the state in which he lived. A voice said to him — Why do you stay here and live this mean moiling life, when a glorious existence is possible for you? Those same stars twinkle over other fields than these. — But how to come out of this condition and actually migrate thither? All that he could think of was to practise some new austerity, to let his mind descend into his body and redeem it, and treat himself with ever increasing respect.

XII. BRUTE NEIGHBORS

Sometimes I had a companion in my fishing, who came through the village to my house from the other side of the town, and the catching of the dinner was as much a social exercise as the eating of it.

Hermit. I wonder what the world is doing now. I have not heard so much as a locust over the sweet-fern these three hours. The pigeons are all asleep upon their roosts — no flutter from them. Was that a farmer's noon horn which sounded from beyond the woods just now? The hands are coming in to boiled salt beef and cider and Indian bread. Why will men worry themselves so? He that does not eat need not work. I wonder how much they have reaped. Who would live there where a body can never think for the barking of Bose? And oh, the housekeeping! to keep bright the devil's door-knobs, and scour his tubs this bright day! Better not keep a house. Say, some hollow tree; and then for morning calls and dinner-parties! Only a woodpecker tapping. Oh, they swarm; the sun is too warm there; they are born too far into life for me. I have water from the spring, and a loaf of brown bread on the shelf. — Hark! I hear a rustling of the leaves. Is it some ill-fed village hound yielding to the instinct of the chase? or the lost pig which is said to be in these woods, whose tracks I saw after the rain? It comes on apace; my sumachs and sweetbriers tremble. — Eh, Mr. Poet, is it you? How do you like the world today?

Poet. See those clouds; how they hang! That's the greatest thing I have seen today. There's nothing like it in old paintings, nothing like it in foreign lands — unless when we were off the coast of Spain. That's a true Mediterranean sky. I thought, as I have my living to get, and have not eaten today, that I might go a-fishing. That's the true industry for poets. It is the only trade I have learned. Come, let's along.

Hermit. I cannot resist. My brown bread will soon be gone. I will go with you gladly soon, but I am just concluding a serious meditation. I think that I am near the end of it. Leave me alone, then, for a while. But that we may not be delayed, you shall be digging the bait meanwhile. Angleworms are rarely to be met with in these parts, where the soil was never fattened with manure; the race is nearly extinct. The sport of digging the bait is nearly equal to that of catching the fish, when one's appetite is not too keen; and this you may have all to yourself today. I would advise you to set in the spade down yonder among the ground-nuts, where you see the johnswort waving. I think that I may warrant you one worm to every three sods you turn up, if you look well in among the roots of the grass, as if you were weeding. Or, if you choose to go farther, it will not be unwise, for I have found the increase of fair bait to be very nearly as the squares of the distances.

Hermit alone. Let me see; where was I? Methinks I was nearly in this frame of mind; the world lay about at this angle. Shall I go to heaven or a-fishing? If I should soon bring this meditation to an end, would another so sweet occasion be likely to offer? I was as near being resolved into the essence of things as ever I was in my life. I fear my thoughts will not come back to me. If it would do any good, I would whistle for them. When they make us an offer, is it wise to say, We will think of it? My thoughts have left no track, and I cannot find the path again. What was it that I was thinking of? It was a very hazy day. I will just try these three sentences of Confut-see; they may fetch that state about again. I know not whether it was the dumps or a budding ecstasy. Mem. There never is but one opportunity of a kind.

Poet. How now, Hermit, is it too soon? I have got just thirteen whole ones, beside several which are imperfect or undersized; but they will do for the smaller fry; they do not cover up the hook so much. Those village worms are quite too large; a shiner may make a meal off one without finding the skewer.

Hermit. Well, then, let's be off. Shall we to the Concord? There's good sport there if the water be not too high.

Why do precisely these objects which we behold make a world? Why has man just these species of animals for his neighbors; as if nothing but a mouse could have filled this crevice? I suspect that Pilpay & Co. have put animals to their best use, for they are all beasts of burden, in a sense, made to carry some portion of our thoughts.

The mice which haunted my house were not the common ones, which are said to have been introduced into the country, but a wild native kind not found in the village. I sent one to a distinguished naturalist, and it interested him much. When I was building, one of these had its nest underneath the house, and before I had laid the second floor, and swept out the shavings, would come out regularly at lunch time and pick up the crumbs at my feet. It probably had never seen a man before; and it soon became quite familiar, and would run over my shoes and up my clothes. It could readily ascend the sides of the room by short impulses, like a squirrel, which it resembled in its motions. At length, as I leaned with my elbow on the bench one day, it ran up my clothes, and along my sleeve, and round and round the paper which held my dinner, while I kept the latter close, and dodged and played at bopeep with it; and when at last I held still a piece of cheese between my thumb and finger, it came and nibbled it, sitting in my hand, and afterward cleaned its face and paws, like a fly, and walked away.

A phœbe soon built in my shed, and a robin for protection in a pine which grew against the house. In June the partridge (*Tetrao umbellus*), which is so shy a bird, led her brood past my windows, from the woods in the rear to the front of my house, clucking and calling to them like a hen, and in all her behavior proving herself the hen of the woods. The young suddenly disperse on your approach, at a signal from the mother, as if a whirlwind had swept them away, and they so exactly resemble the dried leaves and twigs that many a traveller has placed his foot in the midst of a brood, and heard the whir of the old bird as she flew off, and her anxious calls and mewing, or seen her trail her wings to attract his attention, without suspecting their neighborhood. The parent will sometimes roll and spin round before you in such a dishabille, that you cannot, for a few moments, detect what kind of creature it is. The young squat still and flat, often running their heads under a leaf, and mind only their mother's directions given from a distance, nor will your approach make them run again and betray themselves. You may even tread on them, or have your eyes on them for a minute, without discovering them. I have held them in my open hand at such a time, and still their only care, obedient to their mother and their instinct, was to squat there without fear or trembling. So perfect is this instinct, that once, when I had laid them on the leaves again, and one accidentally fell on its side, it was found with the rest in exactly the same position ten minutes afterward. They are not callow like the young of most birds, but more perfectly developed and precocious even than chickens. The remarkably adult yet innocent expression of their open and serene eyes is very memorable. All intelligence seems reflected in them. They suggest not merely the purity of infancy, but a wisdom clarified by experience. Such an eye was not born when the bird was, but is coeval with the sky it reflects. The woods do not yield another such a gem. The traveller does not often look into such a limpid well. The ignorant or reckless sportsman often shoots the parent at such a time, and leaves these innocents to fall a prey to some prowling beast or bird, or gradually mingle with the decaying leaves which they so much resemble. It is said that when hatched by a hen they will directly disperse on some alarm, and so are lost, for they never hear the mother's call which gathers them again. These were my hens and chickens.

It is remarkable how many creatures live wild and free though secret in the woods, and still sustain themselves in the neighborhood of towns, suspected by hunters only. How retired the otter manages to live here! He grows to be four feet long, as big as a small boy, perhaps without any human being getting a glimpse of him. I formerly saw the raccoon in the woods behind where my house is built, and probably still heard their whinnering at night. Commonly I rested an hour or two in the shade at noon, after planting, and ate my lunch, and read a little by a spring which was the source of a swamp and of a brook, oozing from under Brister's Hill, half a mile from my field. The approach to this was through a succession of descending grassy hollows, full of young pitch pines, into a larger wood about the swamp. There, in a very secluded and shaded spot, under a spreading white pine, there was yet a clean, firm sward to sit on. I had dug out the spring and made a well of clear gray water, where I could dip up a pailful without roiling it, and thither I went for this purpose almost every day in midsummer, when the pond was warmest. Thither, too, the woodcock led her brood, to probe the mud for worms, flying but a foot above them down the bank, while they ran in a troop beneath; but at last, spying me, she would leave her young and circle round and round me, nearer and nearer till within four or five feet, pretending broken wings and legs, to attract my attention, and get off her young, who would already have taken up their march, with faint, wiry peep, single file through the swamp, as she directed. Or I heard the peep of the young when I could not see the parent bird. There too the turtle doves sat over the spring, or fluttered from bough to bough of the soft white pines over my head; or the red squirrel, coursing down the nearest bough, was particularly familiar and inquisitive. You only need sit still long enough in some attractive spot in the woods that all its inhabitants may exhibit themselves to you by turns.

I was witness to events of a less peaceful character. One day when I went out to my wood-pile, or rather my pile of stumps, I observed two large ants, the one red, the other much larger, nearly half an inch long, and black, fiercely contending with one another. Having once got hold they never let go, but struggled and wrestled and rolled on the chips incessantly. Looking farther, I was surprised to find that the chips were covered with such combatants, that it was not a *duellum*, but a *bellum*, a war between two races of ants, the red always pitted against the black, and frequently two red ones to one black. The legions of these Myrmidons covered all the hills and vales in my wood-yard, and the ground was already strewn with the dead and dying, both red and black. It was the only battle which I have ever witnessed, the only battle-field I ever trod while the battle was raging; internecine war; the red republicans on the one hand, and the black imperialists on the other. On every side they were engaged in deadly combat, yet without any noise that I could hear, and human soldiers never fought so resolutely. I watched a couple that were fast locked in each other's embraces, in a little sunny valley amid the chips, now at noonday prepared to fight till the sun went down, or life went out. The smaller red champion had fastened himself like a vice to his adversary's front, and through all the tumblings on that field never for an instant ceased to gnaw at one of his feelers near the root, having already caused the other to go by the board; while the stronger black one dashed him from side to side, and, as I saw on looking nearer, had already divested him of several of his members. They fought with more pertinacity than bulldogs. Neither manifested the least disposition to retreat. It was evident that their battle-cry was 'Conquer or die.' In the meanwhile there came along a single red ant on the hillside of this valley, evidently full of excitement, who either had despatched his foe, or had not yet taken part in the battle; probably the latter, for he had lost none of his limbs; whose mother had charged him to return with his shield or upon it. Or perchance he was some Achilles, who had nourished his wrath apart, and had now come to avenge or rescue his Patroclus. He saw this unequal combat from afar — for the blacks were nearly twice the size of the red — he drew near with rapid pace till he stood on his guard within half an inch of the combatants; then, watching his opportunity, he sprang upon the black warrior, and commenced his operations near the root of his right fore leg, leaving the foe to select among his own members; and so there were three united for life, as if a new kind of attraction had been invented which put all other locks and cements to shame. I should not have wondered by this time to find that they had their respective musical bands stationed on some eminent chip, and playing their national airs the while, to excite the slow and cheer the dying combatants. I was myself excited somewhat even as if they had been men. The more you think of it, the less the difference. And certainly there is not the fight recorded in Concord history, at least, if in the history of America, that will bear a moment's comparison with this, whether for the numbers engaged in it, or for the patriotism and heroism displayed. For numbers and for carnage it was an Austerlitz or Dresden. Concord Fight! Two killed on the patriots' side, and Luther Blanchard wounded! Why here every ant was a Buttrick — 'Fire! for God's sake fire!' — and thousands shared the fate of Davis and Hosmer. There was not one hireling there. I have no doubt that it was a principle they fought for, as much as our ancestors, and not to avoid a three-penny tax on their tea; and the results of this battle will be as important and memorable to those whom it concerns as those of the battle of Bunker Hill, at least.

I took up the chip on which the three I have particularly described were struggling, carried it into my house, and placed it under a tumbler on my window-sill, in order to see the issue. Holding a microscope to the first-mentioned red ant, I saw that, though he was assiduously gnawing at the near fore leg of his enemy, having severed his remaining feeler, his own breast was all torn away, exposing what vitals he had there to the jaws of the black warrior, whose breastplate was apparently too thick for him to pierce; and the dark carbuncles of the sufferer's eyes shone with ferocity such as war only could excite. They struggled half an hour longer under the tumbler, and when I looked again the black soldier had severed the heads of his foes from their bodies, and the still living heads were hanging on either side of him like ghastly trophies at his saddle-bow, still apparently as firmly fastened as ever, and he was endeavoring with feeble struggles, being without feelers and with only the remnant of a leg, and I know not how many other wounds, to divest himself of them; which at length, after half an hour more, he accomplished. I raised the glass, and he went off over the window-sill in that crippled state. Whether he finally survived that combat, and spent the remainder of his days in some Hôtel des Invalides, I do not know; but I thought that his industry would not be worth much thereafter. I never learned which party was victorious, nor the cause of the war; but I felt for the rest of that day as if I had had my feelings excited and harrowed by witnessing the struggle, the ferocity and carnage, of a human battle before my door.

Kirby and Spence tell us that the battles of ants have long been celebrated and the date of them recorded, though they say that Huber is the only modern author who appears to have witnessed them. 'Æneas Sylvius,' say they, 'after giving a very circumstantial account of one contested with great obstinacy by a great and small species on the trunk of a pear tree,' adds that ' "this action was fought in the pontificate of Eugenius the Fourth, in the presence of Nicholas Pistoriensis, an eminent lawyer, who related the whole history of the battle with the greatest fidelity." A similar engagement between great and small ants is recorded by Olaus Magnus, in which the small ones, being victorious, are said to have buried the bodies of their own soldiers, but left those of their giant enemies a prey to the birds. This event happened previous to the expulsion of the tyrant Christiern the Second from Sweden.' The battle which I witnessed took place in the Presidency of Polk, five years before the passage of Webster's Fugitive-Slave Bill.

Many a village Bose, fit only to course a mud-turtle in a victualling cellar, sported his heavy quarters in the woods, without the knowledge of his master, and ineffectually smelled at old fox burrows and woodchucks' holes; led perchance by some slight cur which nimbly threaded the wood, and might still inspire a natural terror in its denizens; — now far behind his guide, barking like a canine bull toward some small squirrel which had treed itself for scrutiny, then, cantering off, bending the bushes with his weight, imagining that he is on the track of some stray member of the jerbilla family. Once I was surprised to see a cat walking along the stony shore of the pond, for they rarely wander so far from home. The surprise was mutual. Nevertheless the most domestic cat, which has lain on a rug all her days, appears quite at home in the woods, and, by her sly and stealthy behavior, proves herself more native there than the regular inhabitants. Once, when berrying, I met with a cat with young kittens in the woods, quite wild, and they all, like their mother, had their backs up and were fiercely spitting at me. A few years before I lived in the woods there was what was called a 'winged cat' in one of the farm-houses in Lincoln nearest the pond, Mr. Gilian Baker's. When I called to see her in June, 1842, she was gone a-hunting in the woods, as was her wont (I am not sure whether it was a male or female, and so use the more common pronoun), but her mistress told me that she came into the neighborhood a little more than a year before, in April, and was finally taken into their house; that she was of a dark brownish-gray color, with a white spot on her throat, and white feet, and had a large bushy tail like a fox; that in the winter the fur grew thick and flatted out along her sides, forming stripes ten or twelve inches long by two and a half wide, and under her chin like a muff, the upper side loose, the under matted like felt, and in the spring these appendages dropped off. They gave me a pair of her 'wings,' which I keep still. There is no appearance of a membrane about them. Some thought it was part flying squirrel or some other wild animal, which is not impossible, for, according to naturalists, prolific hybrids have been produced by the union of the marten and domestic cat. This would have been the right kind of cat for me to keep, if I had kept any; for why should not a poet's cat be winged as well as his horse?

In the fall the loon (*Colymbus glacialis*) came, as usual, to moult and bathe in the pond, making the woods ring with his wild laughter before I had risen. At rumor of his arrival all the Mill-dam sportsmen are on the alert, in gigs and on foot, two by two and three by three, with patent rifles and conical balls and spy-glasses. They come rustling through the woods like autumn leaves, at least ten men to one loon. Some station themselves on this side of the pond, some on that, for the poor bird cannot be omnipresent; if he dive here he must come up there. But now the kind October wind rises, rustling the leaves and rippling the surface of the water, so that no loon can be heard or seen, though his foes sweep the pond with spy-glasses, and make the woods resound with their discharges. The waves generously rise and dash angrily, taking sides with all water-fowl, and our sportsmen must beat a retreat to town and shop and unfinished jobs. But they were too often successful. When I went to get a pail of water early in the morning I frequently saw this stately bird sailing out of my cove within a few rods. If I endeavored to overtake him in a boat, in order to see how he would manœuvre, he would dive and be completely lost, so that I did not discover him again, sometimes, till the latter part of the day. But I was more than a match for him on the surface. He commonly went off in a rain.

As I was paddling along the north shore one very calm October afternoon, for such days especially they settle on to the lakes, like the milkweed down, having looked in vain over the pond for a loon, suddenly one, sailing out from the shore toward the middle a few rods in front of me, set up his wild laugh and betrayed himself. I pursued with a paddle and he dived, but when he came up I was nearer than before. He dived again, but I miscalculated the direction he would take, and we were fifty rods apart when he came to the surface this time, for I had helped to widen the interval; and again he laughed long and loud, and with more reason than before. He manœuvred so cunningly that I could not get within half a dozen rods of him. Each time, when he came to the surface, turning his head this way and that, he coolly surveyed the water and the land, and apparently chose his course so that he might come up where there was the widest expanse of water and at the greatest distance from the boat. It was surprising how quickly he made up his mind and put his resolve into execution. He led me at once to the widest part of the pond, and could not be driven from it. While he was thinking one thing in his brain, I was endeavoring to divine his thought in mine. It was a pretty game, played on the smooth surface of the pond, a man against a loon. Suddenly your adversary's checker disappears beneath the board, and the problem is to place yours nearest to where his will appear again. Sometimes he would come up unexpectedly on the opposite side of me, having apparently passed directly under the boat. So long-winded was he and so unweariable, that when he had swum farthest he would immediately plunge again, nevertheless; and then no wit could divine where in the deep pond, beneath the smooth surface, he might be speeding his way like a fish, for he had time and ability to visit the bottom of the pond in its deepest part. It is said that loons have been caught in the New York lakes eighty feet beneath the surface, with hooks set for trout — though Walden is deeper than that. How surprised must the fishes be to see this ungainly visitor from another sphere speeding his way amid their schools! Yet he appeared to know his course as surely under water as on the surface, and swam much faster there. Once or twice I saw a ripple where he approached the surface, just put his head out to reconnoitre, and instantly dived again. I found that it was as well for me to rest on my oars and wait his reappearing as to endeavor to calculate where he would rise; for again and again, when I was straining my eyes over the surface one way, I would suddenly be startled by his unearthly laugh behind me. But why, after displaying so much cunning, did he invariably betray himself the moment he came up by that loud laugh? Did not his white breast enough betray him? He was indeed a silly loon, I thought. I could commonly hear the plash of the water when he came up, and so also detected him. But after an hour he seemed as fresh as ever, dived as willingly, and swam yet farther than at first. It was surprising to see how serenely he sailed off with unruffled breast when he came to the surface, doing all the work with his webbed feet beneath. His usual note was this demoniac laughter, yet somewhat like that of a water-fowl; but occasionally, when he had balked me most successfully and come up a long way off, he uttered a long-drawn unearthly howl, probably more like that of a wolf than any bird; as when a beast puts his muzzle to the ground and deliberately howls. This was his looning — perhaps the wildest sound that is ever heard here, making the woods ring far and wide. I concluded that he laughed in derision of my efforts, confident of his own resources. Though the sky was by this time overcast, the pond was so smooth that I could see where he broke the surface when I did not hear him. His white breast, the stillness of the air, and the smoothness of the water were all against him. At length having come up fifty rods off, he uttered one of those prolonged howls, as if calling on the god of loons to aid him, and immediately there came a wind from the east and rippled the surface, and filled the whole air with misty rain, and I was impressed as if it were the prayer of the loon answered, and his god was angry with me; and so I left him disappearing far away on the tumultuous surface.

For hours, in fall days, I watched the ducks cunningly tack and veer and hold the middle of the pond, far from the sportsman; tricks which they will have less need to practise in Louisiana bayous. When compelled to rise they would sometimes circle round and round and over the pond at a considerable height, from which they could easily see to other ponds and the river, like black motes in the sky; and, when I thought they had gone off thither long since, they would settle down by a slanting flight of a quarter of a mile on to a distant part which was left free; but what beside safety they got by sailing in the middle of Walden I do not know, unless they love its water for the same reason that I do.

XIII. HOUSE-WARMING

In October I went a-graping to the river meadows, and loaded myself with clusters more precious for their beauty and fragrance than for food. There, too, I admired, though I did not gather, the cranberries, small waxen gems, pendants of the meadow grass, pearly and red, which the farmer plucks with an ugly rake, leaving the smooth meadow in a snarl, heedlessly measuring them by the bushel and the dollar only, and sells the spoils of the meads to Boston and New York; destined to be *jammed*, to satisfy the tastes of lovers of Nature there. So butchers rake the tongues of bison out of the prairie grass, regardless of the torn and drooping plant. The barberry's brilliant fruit was likewise food for my eyes merely; but I collected a small store of wild apples for coddling, which the proprietor and travellers had overlooked. When chestnuts were ripe I laid up half a bushel for winter. It was very exciting at that season to roam the then boundless chestnut woods of Lincoln — they now sleep their long sleep under the railroad — with a bag on my shoulder, and a stick to open burs with in my hand, for I did not always wait for the frost, amid the rustling of leaves and the loud reproofs of the red squirrels and the jays, whose half-consumed nuts I sometimes stole, for the burs which they had selected were sure to contain sound ones. Occasionally I climbed and shook the trees. They grew also behind my house, and one large tree, which almost overshadowed it, was, when in flower, a bouquet which scented the whole neighborhood, but the squirrels and the jays got most of its fruit; the last coming in flocks early in the morning and picking the nuts out of the burs before they fell. I relinquished these trees to them and visited the more distant woods composed wholly of chestnut. These nuts, as far as they went, were a good substitute for bread. Many other substitutes might, perhaps, be found. Digging one day for fishworms, I discovered the ground-nut (*Apios tuberosa*) on its string, the potato of the aborigines, a sort of fabulous fruit, which I had begun to doubt if I had ever dug and eaten in childhood, as I had told, and had not dreamed it. I had often since seen its crumpled red velvety blossom supported by the stems of other plants without knowing it to be the same. Cultivation has well-nigh exterminated it. It has a sweetish taste, much like that of a frost-bitten potato, and I found it better boiled than roasted. This tuber seemed like a faint promise of Nature to rear her own children and feed them simply here at some future period. In these days of fatted cattle and waving grain-fields this humble root, which was once the *totem* of an Indian tribe, is quite forgotten, or known only by its flowering vine; but let wild Nature reign here once more, and the tender and luxurious English grains will probably disappear before a myriad of foes, and without the care of man the crow may carry back even the last seed of corn to the great cornfield of the Indian's God in the southwest, whence he is said to have brought it; but the now almost exterminated ground-nut will perhaps revive and flourish in spite of frosts and wildness, prove itself indigenous, and resume its ancient importance and dignity as the diet of the hunter tribe. Some Indian Ceres or Minerva must have been the inventor and bestower of it; and when the reign of poetry commences here, its leaves and string of nuts may be represented on our works of art.

Already, by the first of September, I had seen two or three small maples turned scarlet across the pond, beneath where the white stems of three aspens diverged, at the point of a promontory, next the water. Ah, many a tale their color told! And gradually from week to week the character of each tree came out, and it admired itself reflected in the smooth mirror of the lake. Each morning the manager of this gallery substituted some new picture, distinguished by more brilliant or harmonious coloring, for the old upon the walls.

The wasps came by thousands to my lodge in October, as to winter quarters, and settled on my windows within and on the walls overhead, sometimes deterring visitors from entering. Each morning, when they were numbed with cold, I swept some of them out, but I did not trouble myself much to get rid of them; I even felt complimented by their regarding my house as a desirable shelter. They never molested me seriously, though they bedded with me; and they gradually disappeared, into what crevices I do not know, avoiding winter and unspeakable cold.

Like the wasps, before I finally went into winter quarters in November, I used to resort to the northeast side of Walden, which the sun, reflected from the pitch pine woods and the stony shore, made the fireside of the pond; it is so much pleasanter and wholesomer to be warmed by the sun while you can be, than by an artificial fire. I thus warmed myself by the still glowing embers which the summer, like a departed hunter, had left.

When I came to build my chimney I studied masonry. My bricks, being second-hand ones, required to be cleaned with a trowel, so that I learned more than usual of the qualities of bricks and trowels. The mortar on them was fifty years old, and was said to be still growing harder; but this is one of those sayings which men love to repeat whether they are true or not. Such sayings themselves grow harder and adhere more firmly with age, and it would take many blows with a trowel to clean an old wiseacre of them. Many of the villages of Mesopotamia are built of second-hand bricks of a very good quality, obtained from the ruins of Babylon, and the cement on them is older and probably harder still. However that may be, I was struck by the peculiar toughness of the steel which bore so many violent blows without being worn out. As my bricks had been in a chimney before, though I did not read the name of Nebuchadnezzar on them, I picked out as many fireplace bricks as I could find, to save work and waste, and I filled the spaces between the bricks about the fireplace with stones from the pond shore, and also made my mortar with the white sand from the same place. I lingered most about the fireplace, as the most vital part of the house. Indeed, I worked so deliberately, that though I commenced at the ground in the morning, a course of bricks raised a few inches above the floor served for my pillow at night; yet I did not get a stiff neck for it that I remember; my stiff neck is of older date. I took a poet to board for a fortnight about those times, which caused me to be put to it for room. He brought his own knife, though I had two, and we used to scour them by thrusting them into the earth. He shared with me the labors of cooking. I was pleased to see my work rising so square and solid by degrees, and reflected, that, if it proceeded slowly, it was calculated to endure a long time. The chimney is to some extent an independent structure, standing on the ground, and rising through the house to the heavens; even after the house is burned it still stands sometimes, and its importance and independence are apparent. This was toward the end of summer. It was now November.

The north wind had already begun to cool the pond, though it took many weeks of steady blowing to accomplish it, it is so deep. When I began to have a fire at evening, before I plastered my house, the chimney carried smoke particularly well, because of the numerous chinks between the boards. Yet I passed some cheerful evenings in that cool and airy apartment, surrounded by the rough brown boards full of knots, and rafters with the bark on high overhead. My house never pleased my eye so much after it was plastered, though I was obliged to confess that it was more comfortable. Should not every apartment in which man dwells be lofty enough to create some obscurity overhead, where flickering shadows may play at evening about the rafters? These forms are more agreeable to the fancy and imagination than fresco paintings or other the most expensive furniture. I now first began to inhabit my house, I may say, when I began to use it for warmth as well as shelter. I had got a couple of old fire-dogs to keep the wood from the hearth, and it did me good to see the soot form on the back of the chimney which I had built, and I poked the fire with more right and more satisfaction than usual. My dwelling was small, and I could hardly entertain an echo in it; but it seemed larger for being a single apartment and remote from neighbors. All the attractions of a house were concentrated in one room; it was kitchen, chamber, parlor, and keeping-room; and whatever satisfaction parent or child, master or servant, derive from living in a house, I enjoyed it all. Cato says, the master of a family (*patremfamilias*) must have in his rustic villa 'cellam oleariam, vinariam, dolia multa, uti lubeat caritatem expectare, et rei, et virtuti, et gloriae erit,' that is, 'an oil and wine cellar, many casks, so that it may be pleasant to expect hard times; it will be for his advantage, and virtue, and glory.' I had in my cellar a firkin of potatoes, about two quarts of peas with the weevil in them, and on my shelf a little rice, a jug of molasses, and of rye and Indian meal a peck each.

I sometimes dream of a larger and more populous house, standing in a golden age, of enduring materials, and without gingerbread work, which shall still consist of only one room, a vast, rude, substantial, primitive hall, without ceiling or plastering, with bare rafters and purlins supporting a sort of lower heaven over one's head — useful to keep off rain and snow, where the king and queen posts stand out to receive your homage, when you have done reverence to the prostrate Saturn of an older dynasty on stepping over the sill; a cavernous house, wherein you must reach up a torch upon a pole to see the roof; where some may live in the fireplace, some in the recess of a window, and some on settles, some at one end of the hall, some at another, and some aloft on rafters with the spiders, if they choose; a house which you have got into when you have opened the outside door, and the ceremony is over; where the weary traveller may wash, and eat, and converse, and sleep, without further journey; such a shelter as you would be glad to reach in a tempestuous night, containing all the essentials of a house, and nothing for house-keeping; where you can see all the treasures of the house at one view, and everything hangs upon its peg that a man should use; at once kitchen, pantry, parlor, chamber, storehouse, and garret; where you can see so necessary a thing as a barrel or a ladder, so convenient a thing as a cupboard, and hear the pot boil, and pay your respects to the fire that cooks your dinner, and the oven that bakes your bread, and the necessary furniture and utensils are the chief ornaments; where the washing is not put out, nor the fire, nor the mistress, and perhaps you are sometimes requested to move from off the trap-door, when the cook would descend into the cellar, and so learn whether the ground is solid or hollow beneath you without stamping. A house whose inside is as open and manifest as a bird's nest, and you cannot go in at the front door and out at the back without seeing some of its inhabitants; where to be a guest is to be presented with the freedom of the house, and not to be carefully excluded from seven eighths of it, shut up in a particular cell, and told to make yourself at home there — in solitary confinement. Nowadays the host does not admit you to *his* hearth, but has got the mason to build one for yourself somewhere in his alley, and hospitality is the art of *keeping* you at the greatest distance. There is as much secrecy about the cooking as if he had a design to poison you. I am aware that I have been on many a man's premises, and might have been legally ordered off, but I am not aware that I have been in many men's houses. I might visit in my old clothes a king and queen who lived simply in such a house as I have described, if I were going their way; but backing out of a modern palace will be all that I shall desire to learn, if ever I am caught in one.

It would seem as if the very language of our parlors would lose all its nerve and degenerate into *palaver* wholly, our lives pass at such remoteness from its symbols, and its metaphors and tropes are necessarily so far fetched, through slides and dumb-waiters, as it were; in other words, the parlor is so far from the kitchen and workshop. The dinner even is only the parable of a dinner, commonly. As if only the savage dwelt near enough to Nature and Truth to borrow a trope from them. How can the scholar, who dwells away in the North West Territory or the Isle of Man, tell what is parliamentary in the kitchen?

However, only one or two of my guests were ever bold enough to stay and eat a hasty-pudding with me; but when they saw that crisis approaching they beat a hasty retreat rather, as if it would shake the house to its foundations. Nevertheless, it stood through a great many hasty-puddings.

I did not plaster till it was freezing weather. I brought over some whiter and cleaner sand for this purpose from the opposite shore of the pond in a boat, a sort of conveyance which would have tempted me to go much farther if necessary. My house had in the meanwhile been shingled down to the ground on every side. In lathing I was pleased to be able to send home each nail with a single blow of the hammer, and it was my ambition to transfer the plaster from the board to the wall neatly and rapidly. I remembered the story of a conceited fellow, who, in fine clothes, was wont to lounge about the village once, giving advice to workmen. Venturing one day to substitute deeds for words, he turned up his cuffs, seized a plasterer's board, and having loaded his trowel without mishap, with a complacent look toward the lathing overhead, made a bold gesture thitherward; and straightway, to his complete discomfiture, received the whole contents in his ruffled bosom. I admired anew the economy and convenience of plastering, which so effectually shuts out the cold and takes a handsome finish, and I learned the various casualties to which the plasterer is liable. I was surprised to see how thirsty the bricks were which drank up all the moisture in my plaster before I had smoothed it, and how many pailfuls of water it takes to christen a new hearth. I had the previous winter made a small quantity of lime by burning the shells of the *Unio fluviatilis*, which our river affords, for the sake of the experiment; so that I knew where my materials came from. I might have got good limestone within a mile or two and burned it myself, if I had cared to do so.

The pond had in the meanwhile skimmed over in the shadiest and shallowest coves, some days or even weeks before the general freezing. The first ice is especially interesting and perfect, being hard, dark, and transparent, and affords the best opportunity that ever offers for examining the bottom where it is shallow; for you can lie at your length on ice only an inch thick, like a skater insect on the surface of the water, and study the bottom at your leisure, only two or three inches distant, like a picture behind a glass, and the water is necessarily always smooth then. There are many furrows in the sand where some creature has travelled about and doubled on its tracks; and, for wrecks, it is strewn with the cases of caddis-worms made of minute grains of white quartz. Perhaps these have creased it, for you find some of their cases in the furrows, though they are deep and broad for them to make. But the ice itself is the object of most interest, though you must improve the earliest opportunity to study it. If you examine it closely the morning after it freezes, you find that the greater part of the bubbles, which at first appeared to be within it, are against its under surface, and that more are continually rising from the bottom; while the ice is as yet comparatively solid and dark, that is, you see the water through it. These bubbles are from an eightieth to an eighth of an inch in diameter, very clear and beautiful, and you see your face reflected in them through the ice. There may be thirty or forty of them to a square inch. There are also already within the ice narrow oblong perpendicular bubbles about half an inch long, sharp cones with the apex upward; or oftener, if the ice is quite fresh, minute spherical bubbles one directly above another, like a string of beads. But these within the ice are not so numerous nor obvious as those beneath. I sometimes used to cast on stones to try the strength of the ice, and those which broke through carried in air with them, which formed very large and conspicuous white bubbles beneath. One day when I came to the same place forty-eight hours afterward, I found that those large bubbles were still perfect, though an inch more of ice had formed, as I could see distinctly by the seam in the edge of a cake. But as the last two days had been very warm, like an Indian summer, the ice was not now transparent, showing the dark green color of the water, and the bottom, but opaque and whitish or gray, and though twice as thick was hardly stronger than before, for the air bubbles had greatly expanded under this heat and run together, and lost their regularity; they were no longer one directly over another, but often like silvery coins poured from a bag, one overlapping another, or in thin flakes, as if occupying slight cleavages. The beauty of the ice was gone, and it was too late to study the bottom. Being curious to know what position my great bubbles occupied with regard to the new ice, I broke out a cake containing a middling sized one, and turned it bottom upward. The new ice had formed around and under the bubble, so that it was included between the two ices. It was wholly in the lower ice, but close against the upper, and was flattish, or perhaps slightly lenticular, with a rounded edge, a quarter of an inch deep by four inches in diameter; and I was surprised to find that directly under the bubble the ice was melted with great regularity in the form of a saucer reversed, to the height of five eighths of an inch in the middle, leaving a thin partition there between the water and the bubble, hardly an eighth of an inch thick; and in many places the small bubbles in this partition had burst out downward, and probably there was no ice at all under the largest bubbles, which were a foot in diameter. I inferred that the infinite number of minute bubbles which I had first seen against the under surface of the ice were now frozen in likewise, and that each, in its degree, had operated like a burning-glass on the ice beneath to melt and rot it. These are the little air-guns which contribute to make the ice crack and whoop.

At length the winter set in in good earnest, just as I had finished plastering, and the wind began to howl around the house as if it had not had permission to do so till then. Night after night the geese came lumbering in in the dark with a clangor and a whistling of wings, even after the ground was covered with snow, some to alight in Walden, and some flying low over the woods toward Fair Haven, bound for Mexico. Several times, when returning from the village at ten or eleven o'clock at night, I heard the tread of a flock of geese, or else ducks, on the dry leaves in the woods by a pond-hole behind my dwelling, where they had come up to feed, and the faint honk or quack of their leader as they hurried off. In 1845 Walden froze entirely over for the first time on the night of the 22d of December, Flint's and other shallower ponds and the river having been frozen ten days or more; in '46, the 16th; in '49, about the 31st; and in '50, about the 27th of December; in '52, the 5th of January; in '53, the 31st of December. The snow had already covered the ground since the 25th of November, and surrounded me suddenly with the scenery of winter. I withdrew yet farther into my shell, and endeavored to keep a bright fire both within my house and within my breast. My employment out of doors now was to collect the dead wood in the forest, bringing it in my hands or on my shoulders, or sometimes trailing a dead pine tree under each arm to my shed. An old forest fence which had seen its best days was a great haul for me. I sacrificed it to Vulcan, for it was past serving the god Terminus. How much more interesting an event is that man's supper who has just been forth in the snow to hunt, nay, you might say, steal, the fuel to cook it with! His bread and meat are sweet. There are enough fagots and waste wood of all kinds in the forests of most of our towns to support many fires, but which at present warm none, and, some think, hinder the growth of the young wood. There was also the driftwood of the pond. In the course of the summer I had discovered a raft of pitch pine logs with the bark on, pinned together by the Irish when the railroad was built. This I hauled up partly on the shore. After soaking two years and then lying high six months it was perfectly sound, though water-logged past drying. I amused myself one winter day with sliding this piecemeal across the pond, nearly half a mile, skating behind with one end of a log fifteen feet long on my shoulder, and the other on the ice; or I tied several logs together with a birch withe, and then, with a longer birch or alder which had a hook at the end, dragged them across. Though completely waterlogged and almost as heavy as lead, they not only burned long, but made a very hot fire; nay, I thought that they burned better for the soaking, as if the pitch, being confined by the water, burned longer, as in a lamp.

Gilpin, in his account of the forest borderers of England, says that 'the encroachments of trespassers, and the houses and fences thus raised on the borders of the forest,' were 'considered as great nuisances by the old forest law, and were severely punished under the name of *purprestures*, as tending *ad terrorem ferarum — ad nocumentum forestae*, etc.,' to the frightening of the game and the detriment of the forest. But I was interested in the preservation of the venison and the vert more than the hunters or woodchoppers, and as much as though I had been the Lord Warden himself; and if any part was burned, though I burned it myself by accident, I grieved with a grief that lasted longer and was more inconsolable than that of the proprietors; nay, I grieved when it was cut down by the proprietors themselves. I would that our farmers when they cut down a forest felt some of that awe which the old Romans did when they came to thin, or let in the light to, a consecrated grove (*lucum conlucare*), that is, would believe that it is sacred to some god. The Roman made an expiatory offering, and prayed, Whatever god or goddess thou art to whom this grove is sacred, be propitious to me, my family, and children, etc.

It is remarkable what a value is still put upon wood even in this age and in this new country, a value more permanent and universal than that of gold. After all our discoveries and inventions no man will go by a pile of wood. It is as precious to us as it was to our Saxon and Norman ancestors. If they made their bows of it, we make our gunstocks of it. Michaux, more than thirty years ago, says that the price of wood for fuel in New York and Philadelphia 'nearly equals, and sometimes exceeds, that of the best wood in Paris, though this immense capital annually requires more than three hundred thousand cords, and is surrounded to the distance of three hundred miles by cultivated plains.' In this town the price of wood rises almost steadily, and the only question is, how much higher it is to be this year than it was the last. Mechanics and tradesmen who come in person to the forest on no other errand, are sure to attend the wood auction, and even pay a high price for the privilege of gleaning after the woodchopper. It is now many years that men have resorted to the forest for fuel and the materials of the arts: the New Englander and the New Hollander, the Parisian and the Celt, the farmer and Robin Hood, Goody Blake and Harry Gill; in most parts of the world the prince and the peasant, the scholar and the savage, equally require still a few sticks from the forest to warm them and cook their food. Neither could I do without them.

Every man looks at his wood-pile with a kind of affection. I love to have mine before my window, and the more chips the better to remind me of my pleasing work. I had an old axe which nobody claimed, with which by spells in winter days, on the sunny side of the house, I played about the stumps which I had got out of my bean-field. As my driver prophesied when I was plowing, they warmed me twice — once while I was splitting them, and again when they were on the fire, so that no fuel could give out more heat. As for the axe, I was advised to get the village blacksmith to 'jump' it; but I jumped him, and, putting a hickory helve from the woods into it, made it do. If it was dull, it was at least hung true.

A few pieces of fat pine were a great treasure. It is interesting to remember how much of this food for fire is still concealed in the bowels of the earth. In previous years I had often gone 'prospecting' over some bare hillside, where a pitch pine wood had formerly stood, and got out the fat pine roots. They are almost indestructible. Stumps thirty or forty years old, at least, will still be sound at the core, though the sap-wood has all become vegetable mould, as appears by the scales of the thick bark forming a ring level with the earth four or five inches distant from the heart. With axe and shovel you explore this mine, and follow the marrowy store, yellow as beef tallow, or as if you had struck on a vein of gold, deep into the earth. But commonly I kindled my fire with the dry leaves of the forest, which I had stored up in my shed before the snow came. Green hickory finely split makes the wood-chopper's kindlings, when he has a camp in the woods. Once in a while I got a little of this. When the villagers were lighting their fires beyond the horizon, I too gave notice to the various wild inhabitants of Walden vale, by a smoky streamer from my chimney, that I was awake.

> Light-winged Smoke, Icarian bird,
> Melting thy pinions in thy upward flight,
> Lark without song, and messenger of dawn,
> Circling above the hamlets as thy nest;
> Or else, departing dream, and shadowy form
> Of midnight vision, gathering up thy skirts;
> By night star-veiling, and by day
> Darkening the light and blotting out the sun;
> Go thou my incense upward from this hearth,
> And ask the gods to pardon this clear flame.

Hard green wood just cut, though I used but little of that, answered my purpose better than any other. I sometimes left a good fire when I went to take a walk in a winter afternoon; and when I returned, three or four hours afterward, it would be still alive and glowing. My house was not empty though I was gone. It was as if I had left a cheerful housekeeper behind. It was I and Fire that lived there; and commonly my housekeeper proved trustworthy. One day, however, as I was splitting wood, I thought that I would just look in at the window and see if the house was not on fire; it was the only time I remember to have been particularly anxious on this score; so I looked and saw that a spark had caught my bed, and I went in and extinguished it when it had burned a place as big as my hand. But my house occupied so sunny and sheltered a position, and its roof was so low, that I could afford to let the fire go out in the middle of almost any winter day.

The moles nested in my cellar, nibbling every third potato, and making a snug bed even there of some hair left after plastering and of brown paper; for even the wildest animals love comfort and warmth as well as man, and they survive the winter only because they are so careful to secure them. Some of my friends spoke as if I was coming to the woods on purpose to freeze myself. The animal merely makes a bed, which he warms with his body, in a sheltered place; but man, having discovered fire, boxes up some air in a spacious apartment, and warms that, instead of robbing himself, makes that his bed, in which he can move about divested of more cumbrous clothing, maintain a kind of summer in the midst of winter, and by means of windows even admit the light, and with a lamp lengthen out the day. Thus he goes a step or two beyond instinct, and saves a little time for the fine arts. Though, when I had been exposed to the rudest blasts a long time, my whole body began to grow torpid, when I reached the genial atmosphere of my house I soon recovered my faculties and prolonged my life. But the most luxuriously housed has little to boast of in this respect, nor need we trouble ourselves to speculate how the human race may be at last destroyed. It would be easy to cut their threads any time with a little sharper blast from the north. We go on dating from Cold Fridays and Great Snows; but a little colder Friday, or greater snow would put a period to man's existence on the globe.

The next winter I used a small cooking-stove for economy, since I did not own the forest; but it did not keep fire so well as the open fire-place. Cooking was then, for the most part, no longer a poetic, but merely a chemic process. It will soon be forgotten, in these days of stoves, that we used to roast potatoes in the ashes, after the Indian fashion. The stove not only took up room and scented the house, but it concealed the fire, and I felt as if I had lost a companion. You can always see a face in the fire. The laborer, looking into it at evening, purifies his thoughts of the dross and earthiness which they have ac-cumulated during the day. But I could no longer sit and look into the fire, and the pertinent words of a poet recurred to me with new force.

> 'Never, bright flame, may be denied to me
> Thy dear, life imaging, close sympathy.
> What but my hopes shot upward e'er so bright?
> What but my fortunes sunk so low in night?
> Why art thou banished from our hearth and hall,
> Thou who art welcomed and beloved by all?
> Was thy existence then too fanciful
> For our life's common light, who are so dull?
> Did thy bright gleam mysterious converse hold
> With our congenial souls? secrets too bold?
>
> 'Well, we are safe and strong, for now we sit
> Beside a hearth where no dim shadows flit,
> Where nothing cheers nor saddens, but a fire
> Warms feet and hands — nor does to more aspire;
> By whose compact utilitarian heap
> The present may sit down and go to sleep,
> Nor fear the ghosts who from the dim past walked,
> And with us by the unequal light of the old wood fire talked.'

XIV. FORMER INHABITANTS; AND WINTER VISITORS

I WEATHERED some merry snow-storms, and spent some cheerful winter evenings by my fireside, while the snow whirled wildly without, and even the hooting of the owl was hushed. For many weeks I met no one in my walks but those who came occasionally to cut wood and sled it to the village. The elements, however, abetted me in making a path through the deepest snow in the woods, for when I had once gone through the wind blew the oak leaves into my tracks, where they lodged, and by absorbing the rays of the sun melted the snow, and so not only made a dry bed for my feet, but in the night their dark line was my guide. For human society I was obliged to conjure up the former occupants of these woods. Within the memory of many of my townsmen the road near which my house stands resounded with the laugh and gossip of inhabitants, and the woods which border it were notched and dotted here and there with their little gardens and dwellings, though it was then much more shut in by the forest than now. In some places, within my own remembrance, the pines would scrape both sides of a chaise at once, and women and children who were compelled to go this way to Lincoln alone and on foot did it with fear, and often ran a good part of the distance. Though mainly but a humble route to neighboring villages, or for the woodman's team, it once amused the traveller more than now by its variety, and lingered longer in his memory. Where now firm open fields stretch from the village to the woods, it then ran through a maple swamp on a foundation of logs, the remnants of which, doubtless, still underlie the present dusty highway, from the Stratton, now the Alms-House, Farm, to Brister's Hill.

East of my bean-field, across the road, lived Cato Ingraham, slave of Duncan Ingraham, Esquire, gentleman, of Concord village, who built his slave a house, and gave him permission to live in Walden Woods; — Cato, not Uticensis, but Concordiensis. Some say that he was a Guinea Negro. There are a few who remember his little patch among the walnuts, which he let grow up till he should be old and need them; but a younger and whiter speculator got them at last. He too, however, occupies an equally narrow house at present. Cato's half-obliterated cellar-hole still remains, though known to few, being concealed from the traveller by a fringe of pines. It is now filled with the smooth sumach (*Rhus glabra*), and one of the earliest species of goldenrod (*Solidago stricta*) grows there luxuriantly.

Here, by the very corner of my field, still nearer to town, Zilpha, a colored woman, had her little house, where she spun linen for the townsfolk, making the Walden Woods ring with her shrill singing, for she had a loud and notable voice. At length, in the war of 1812, her dwelling was set on fire by English soldiers, prisoners on parole, when she was away, and her cat and dog and hens were all burned up together. She led a hard life, and somewhat inhumane. One old frequenter of these woods remembers, that as he passed her house one noon he heard her muttering to herself over her gurgling pot — 'Ye are all bones, bones!' I have seen bricks amid the oak copse there.

Down the road, on the right hand, on Brister's Hill, lived Brister Freeman, 'a handy Negro,' slave of Squire Cummings once — there where grow still the apple trees which Brister planted and tended; large old trees now, but their fruit still wild and ciderish to my taste. Not long since I read his epitaph in the old Lincoln burying-ground, a little on one side, near the unmarked graves of some British grenadiers who fell in the retreat from Concord — where he is styled 'Sippio Brister' —

Scipio Africanus he had some title to be called — 'a man of color,' as if he were discolored. It also told me, with staring emphasis, when he died; which was but an indirect way of informing me that he ever lived. With him dwelt Fenda, his hospitable wife, who told fortunes, yet pleasantly — large, round, and black, blacker than any of the children of night, such a dusky orb as never rose on Concord before or since.

Farther down the hill, on the left, on the old road in the woods, are marks of some homestead of the Stratton family; whose orchard once covered all the slope of Brister's Hill, but was long since killed out by pitch pines, excepting a few stumps, whose old roots furnish still the wild stocks of many a thrifty village tree.

Nearer yet to town, you come to Breed's location, on the other side of the way, just on the edge of the wood; ground famous for the pranks of a demon not distinctly named in old mythology, who has acted a prominent and astounding part in our New England life, and deserves, as much as any mythological character, to have his biography written one day; who first comes in the guise of a friend or hired man, and then robs and murders the whole family — New-England Rum. But history must not yet tell the tragedies enacted here; let time intervene in some measure to assuage and lend an azure tint to them. Here the most indistinct and dubious tradition says that once a tavern stood; the well the same, which tempered the traveller's beverage and refreshed his steed. Here then men saluted one another, and heard and told the news, and went their ways again.

Breed's hut was standing only a dozen years ago, though it had long been unoccupied. It was about the size of mine. It was set on fire by mischievous boys, one Election night, if I do not mistake. I lived on the edge of the village then, and had just lost myself over Davenant's 'Gondibert,' that winter that I labored with a lethargy — which, by the way, I never knew whether to regard as a family complaint, having an uncle who goes to sleep shaving himself, and is obliged to sprout potatoes in a cellar Sundays, in order to keep awake and keep the Sabbath, or as the consequence of my attempt to read Chalmers' collection of English poetry without skipping. It fairly overcame my Nervii. I had just sunk my head on this when the bells rung fire, and in hot haste the engines rolled that way, led by a straggling troop of men and boys, and I among the foremost, for I had leaped the brook. We thought it was far south over the woods — we who had run to fires before — barn, shop, or dwelling-house, or all together. 'It's Baker's barn,' cried one. 'It is the Codman place,' affirmed another. And then fresh sparks went up above the wood, as if the roof fell in, and we all shouted 'Concord to the rescue!' Wagons shot past with furious speed and crushing loads, bearing, perchance, among the rest, the agent of the Insurance Company, who was bound to go however far; and ever and anon the engine bell tinkled behind, more slow and sure; and rearmost of all, as it was afterward whispered, came they who set the fire and gave the alarm. Thus we kept on like true idealists, rejecting the evidence of our senses, until at a turn in the road we heard the crackling and actually felt the heat of the fire from over the wall, and realized, alas! that we were there. The very nearness of the fire but cooled our ardor. At first we thought to throw a frog-pond on to it; but concluded to let it burn, it was so far gone and so worthless. So we stood round our engine, jostled one another, expressed our sentiments through speaking-trumpets, or in lower tone referred to the great conflagrations which the world has witnessed, including Bascom's shop, and, between ourselves, we thought that, were we there in season with our 'tub,' and a full frog-pond by, we could turn that threatened last and universal one into another flood. We finally retreated without doing any mischief — returned to sleep and 'Gondibert.' But as for 'Gondibert,' I would except that passage in the preface about wit being the soul's powder — 'but most of mankind are strangers to wit, as Indians are to powder.'

It chanced that I walked that way across the fields the following night, about the same hour, and hearing a low moaning at this spot, I drew near in the dark, and discovered the only survivor of the family that I know, the heir of both its virtues and its vices, who alone was interested in this burning, lying on his stomach and looking over the cellar wall at the still smouldering cinders beneath, muttering to himself, as is his wont. He had been working far off in the river meadows all day, and had improved the first moments that he could call his own to visit the home of his fathers and his youth. He gazed into the cellar from all sides and points of view by turns, always lying down to it, as if there was some treasure, which he remembered, concealed between the stones, where there was absolutely nothing but a heap of bricks and ashes. The house being gone, he looked at what there was left. He was soothed by the sympathy which my mere presence implied, and showed me, as well as the darkness permitted, where the well was covered up; which, thank Heaven, could never be burned; and he groped long about the wall to find the well-sweep which his father had cut and mounted, feeling for the iron hook or staple by which a burden had been fastened to the heavy end — all that he could now cling to — to convince me that it was no common 'rider.' I felt it, and still remark it almost daily in my walks, for by it hangs the history of a family.

Once more, on the left, where are seen the well and lilac bushes by the wall, in the now open field, lived Nutting and Le Grosse. But to return toward Lincoln.

Farther in the woods than any of these, where the road approaches nearest to the pond, Wyman the potter squatted, and furnished his townsmen with earthenware, and left descendants to succeed him. Neither were they rich in worldly goods, holding the land by sufferance while they lived; and there often the sheriff came in vain to collect the taxes, and 'attached a chip,' for form's sake, as I have read in his accounts, there being nothing else that he could lay his hands on. One day in midsummer, when I was hoeing, a man who was carrying a load of pottery to market stopped his horse against my field and inquired concerning Wyman the younger. He had long ago bought a potter's wheel of him, and wished to know what had become of him. I had read of the potter's clay and wheel in Scripture, but it had never occurred to me that the pots we use were not such as had come down unbroken from those days, or grown on trees like gourds somewhere, and I was pleased to hear that so fictile an art was ever practiced in my neighborhood.

The last inhabitant of these woods before me was an Irishman, Hugh Quoil (if I have spelt his name with coil enough), who occupied Wyman's tenement — Col. Quoil, he was called. Rumor said that he had been a soldier at Waterloo. If he had lived I should have made him fight his battles over again. His trade here was that of a ditcher. Napoleon went to St. Helena; Quoil came to Walden Woods. All I know of him is tragic. He was a man of manners, like one who had seen the world, and was capable of more civil speech than you could well attend to. He wore a greatcoat in midsummer, being affected with the trembling delirium, and his face was the color of carmine. He died in the road at the foot of Brister's Hill shortly after I came to the woods, so that I have not remembered him as a neighbor. Before his house was pulled down, when his comrades avoided it as 'an unlucky castle,' I visited it. There lay his old clothes curled up by use, as if they were himself, upon his raised plank bed. His pipe lay broken on the hearth, instead of a bowl broken at the fountain. The last could never have been the symbol of his death, for he confessed to me that, though he had heard of Brister's Spring, he had never seen it; and soiled cards, kings of diamonds, spades, and hearts, were scattered over the floor.

One black chicken which the administrator could not catch, black as night and as silent, not even croaking, awaiting Reynard, still went to roost in the next apartment. In the rear there was the dim outline of a garden, which had been planted but had never received its first hoeing, owing to those terrible shaking fits, though it was now harvest time. It was overrun with Roman wormwood and beggar-ticks, which last stuck to my clothes for all fruit. The skin of a woodchuck was freshly stretched upon the back of the house, a trophy of his last Waterloo; but no warm cap or mittens would he want more.

Now only a dent in the earth marks the site of these dwellings, with buried cellar stones, and strawberries, raspberries, thimble-berries, hazel-bushes, and sumachs growing in the sunny sward there; some pitch pine or gnarled oak occupies what was the chimney nook, and a sweet-scented black birch, perhaps, waves where the door-stone was. Sometimes the well dent is visible, where once a spring oozed; now dry and tearless grass; or it was covered deep — not to be discovered till some late day — with a flat stone under the sod, when the last of the race departed. What a sorrowful act must that be — the covering up of wells! coincident with the opening of wells of tears. These cellar dents, like deserted fox burrows, old holes, are all that is left where once were the stir and bustle of human life, and 'fate, free will, foreknowledge absolute,' in some form and dialect or other were by turns discussed. But all I can learn of their conclusions amounts to just this, that 'Cato and Brister pulled wool;' which is about as edifying as the history of more famous schools of philosophy.

Still grows the vivacious lilac a generation after the door and lintel and the sill are gone, unfolding its sweet-scented flowers each spring, to be plucked by the musing traveller; planted and tended once by children's hands, in front-yard plots — now standing by wallsides in retired pastures, and giving place to new-rising forests; — the last of that stirp, sole survivor of that family. Little did the dusky children think that the puny slip with its two eyes only, which they stuck in the ground in the shadow of the house and daily watered, would root itself so, and outlive them, and house itself in the rear that shaded it, and grown man's garden and orchard, and tell their story faintly to the lone wanderer a half-century after they had grown up and died — blossoming as fair, and smelling as sweet, as in that first spring. I mark its still tender, civil, cheerful lilac colors.

But this small village, germ of something more, why did it fail while Concord keeps its ground? Were there no natural advantages — no water privileges, forsooth? Ay, the deep Walden Pond and cool Brister's Spring — privilege to drink long and healthy draughts at these, all unimproved by these men but to dilute their glass. They were universally a thirsty race. Might not the basket, stable-broom, mat-making, corn-parching, linen-spinning, and pottery business have thrived here, making the wilderness to blossom like the rose, and a numerous posterity have inherited the land of their fathers? The sterile soil would at least have been proof against a lowland degeneracy. Alas! how little does the memory of these human inhabitants enhance the beauty of the landscape! Again, perhaps, Nature will try, with me for a first settler, and my house raised last spring to be the oldest in the hamlet.

I am not aware that any man has ever built on the spot which I occupy. Deliver me from a city built on the site of a more ancient city, whose materials are ruins, whose gardens cemeteries. The soil is blanched and accursed there, and before that becomes necessary the earth itself will be destroyed. With such reminiscences I repeopled the woods and lulled myself asleep.

At this season I seldom had a visitor. When the snow lay deepest no wanderer ventured near my house for a week or fortnight at a time, but there I lived as snug as a meadow mouse, or as cattle and poultry which are said to have survived for a long time buried in drifts, even without food; or like that early settler's family in the town of Sutton, in this State, whose cottage was completely covered by the great snow of 1717 when he was absent, and an Indian found it only by the hole which the chimney's breath made in the drift, and so relieved the family. But no friendly Indian concerned himself about me; nor needed he, for the master of the house was at home The Great Snow! How cheerful it is to hear of! When the farmers could not get to the woods and swamps with their teams, and were obliged to cut down the shade trees before their houses, and, when the crust was harder, cut off the trees in the swamps, ten feet from the ground, as it appeared the next spring.

In the deepest snows, the path which I used from the highway to my house, about half a mile long, might have been represented by a meandering dotted line, with wide intervals between the dots. For a week of even weather I took exactly the same number of steps, and of the same length, coming and going, stepping deliberately and with the precision of a pair of dividers in my own deep tracks — to such routine the winter reduces us — yet often they were filled with heaven's own blue. But no weather interfered fatally with my walks, or rather my going abroad, for I frequently tramped eight or ten miles through the deepest snow to keep an appointment with a beech tree, or a yellow birch, or an old acquaintance among the pines; when the ice and snow causing their limbs to droop, and so sharpening their tops, had changed the pines into fir trees; wading to the tops of the highest hills when the snow was nearly two feet deep on a level, and shaking down another snow-storm on my head at every step; or sometimes creeping and floundering thither on my hands and knees, when the hunters had gone into winter quarters. One afternoon I amused myself by watching a barred owl (*Strix nebulosa*) sitting on one of the lower dead limbs of a white pine, close to the trunk, in broad daylight, I standing within a rod of him. He could hear me when I moved and cronched the snow with my feet, but could not plainly see me. When I made most noise he would stretch out his neck, and erect his neck feathers, and open his eyes wide; but their lids soon fell again, and he began to nod. I too felt a slumberous influence after watching him half an hour, as he sat thus with his eyes half open, like a cat, winged brother of the cat. There was only a narrow slit left between their lids, by which he preserved a peninsular relation to me; thus, with half-shut eyes, looking out from the land of dreams, and endeavoring to realize me, vague object or mote that interrupted his visions. At length, on some louder noise or my nearer approach, he would grow uneasy and sluggishly turn about on his perch, as if impatient at having his dreams disturbed; and when he launched himself off and flapped through the pines, spreading his wings to unexpected breadth, I could not hear the slightest sound from them. Thus, guided amid the pine boughs rather by a delicate sense of their neighborhood than by sight, feeling his twilight way, as it were, with his sensitive pinions, he found a new perch, where he might in peace await the dawning of his day.

As I walked over the long causeway made for the railroad through the meadows, I encountered many a blustering and nipping wind, for nowhere has it freer play; and when the frost had smitten me on one cheek, heathen as I was, I turned to it the other also. Nor was it much better by the carriage road from Brister's Hill. For I came to town still, like a friendly Indian, when the contents of the broad open fields were all piled up between the walls of the Walden road, and half an hour sufficed to obliterate the tracks of the last traveller. And when I returned new drifts would have formed, through which I floundered, where the busy northwest wind had been depositing the powdery snow

round a sharp angle in the road, and not a rabbit's track, nor even the
fine print, the small type, of a meadow mouse was to be seen. Yet
I rarely failed to find, even in midwinter, some warm and springy
swamp where the grass and the skunk-cabbage still put forth with
perennial verdure, and some hardier bird occasionally awaited the
return of spring.

Sometimes, notwithstanding the snow, when I returned from my walk
at evening I crossed the deep tracks of a woodchopper leading from my
door, and found his pile of whittlings on the hearth, and my house filled
with the odor of his pipe. Or on a Sunday afternoon, if I chanced to
be at home, I heard the cronching of the snow made by the step of
a long-headed farmer, who from far through the woods sought my
house, to have a social 'crack;' one of the few of his vocation who are
'men on their farms;' who donned a frock instead of a professor's gown,
and is as ready to extract the moral out of church or state as to haul
a load of manure from his barn-yard. We talked of rude and simple
times, when men sat about large fires in cold, bracing weather, with
clear heads; and when other dessert failed, we tried our teeth on many
a nut which wise squirrels have long since abandoned, for those which
have the thickest shells are commonly empty.

The one who came from farthest to my lodge, through deepest snows
and most dismal tempests, was a poet. A farmer, a hunter, a soldier,
a reporter, even a philosopher, may be daunted; but nothing can deter
a poet, for he is actuated by pure love. Who can predict his comings
and goings? His business calls him out at all hours, even when doctors
sleep. We made that small house ring with boisterous mirth and resound with the murmur of much sober talk, making amends then to
Walden vale for the long silences. Broadway was still and deserted in
comparison. At suitable intervals there were regular salutes of laughter,
which might have been referred indifferently to the last-uttered or the
forth-coming jest. We made many a 'bran new' theory of life over a thin
dish of gruel, which combined the advantages of conviviality with the
clear-headedness which philosophy requires.

I should not forget that during my last winter at the pond there was
another welcome visitor, who at one time came through the village,
through snow and rain and darkness, till he saw my lamp through the
trees, and shared with me some long winter evenings. One of the
last of the philosophers — Connecticut gave him to the world — he
peddled first her wares, afterwards, as he declares, his brains. These
he peddles still, prompting God and disgracing man, bearing for fruit

his brain only, like the nut its kernel. I think that he must be the man of the most faith of any alive. His words and attitude always suppose a better state of things than other men **are** acquainted with, and he will be the last man to be disappointed as the ages revolve. He has no venture in the present. But though comparatively disregarded now, when his day comes, laws unsuspected by most will take effect, and masters of families and rulers will come to him for advice.

'How blind that cannot see serenity!'

A true friend of man; almost the only friend of human progress. An Old Mortality, say rather an Immortality, with unwearied patience and faith making plain the image engraven in men's bodies, the God of whom they are but defaced and leaning monuments. With his hospitable intellect he embraces children, beggars, insane, and scholars, and entertains the thought of all, adding to it commonly some breadth and elegance. I think that he should keep a caravansary on the world's highway, where philosophers of all nations might put up, and on his sign should be printed, 'Entertainment for man, but not for his beast. Enter ye that have leisure and a quiet mind, who earnestly seek the right road.' He is perhaps the sanest man and has the fewest crotchets of any I chance to know; the same yesterday and tomorrow. Of yore we had sauntered and talked, and effectually put the world behind us; for he was pledged to no institution in it, freeborn, *ingenuus*. Whichever way we turned, it seemed that the heavens and the earth had met together, since he enhanced the beauty of the landscape. A blue-robed man, whose fittest roof is the overarching sky which reflects his serenity. I do not see how he can ever die; Nature cannot spare him.

Having each some shingles of thought well dried, we sat and whittled them, trying our knives, and admiring the clear yellowish grain of the pumpkin pine. We waded so gently and reverently, or we pulled together so smoothly, that the fishes of thought were not scared from the stream, nor feared any angler on the bank, but came and went grandly, like the clouds which float through the western sky, and the mother-o'-pearl flocks which sometimes form and dissolve there. There we worked, revising mythology, rounding a fable here and there, and building castles in the air for which earth offered no worthy foundation. Great Looker! Great Expecter! to converse with whom was a New England Night's Entertainment. Ah! such discourse we had, hermit and philosopher, and the old settler I have spoken of — we three — it expanded and racked my little house; I should not dare to say how many pounds' weight there was above the atmospheric pressure on every circular inch; it opened its seams so that they had to be calked with much dulness thereafter to stop the consequent leak; — but I had enough of that kind of oakum already picked.

There was one other with whom I had 'solid seasons,' long to be remembered, at his house in the village, and who looked in upon me from time to time; but I had no more for society there.

There too, as everywhere, I sometimes expected the Visitor who never comes. The Vishnu Purana says, 'The house-holder is to remain at eventide in his courtyard as long as it takes to milk a cow, or longer if he pleases, to await the arrival of a guest.' I often performed this duty of hospitality, waited long enough to milk a whole herd of cows, but did not see the man approaching from the town.

XV. WINTER ANIMALS

WHEN the ponds were firmly frozen, they afforded not only new and shorter routes to many points, but new views from their surfaces of the familiar landscape around them. When I crossed Flint's Pond, after it was covered with snow, though I had often paddled about and skated over it, it was so unexpectedly wide and so strange that I could think of nothing but Baffin's Bay. The Lincoln hills rose up around me at the extremity of a snowy plain, in which I did not remember to have stood before; and the fishermen, at an indeterminable distance over the ice, moving slowly about with their wolfish dogs, passed for sealers or Esquimaux, or in misty weather loomed like fabulous creatures, and I did not know whether they were giants or pygmies. I took this course when I went to lecture in Lincoln in the evening, travelling in no road and passing no house between my own hut and the lecture room. In Goose Pond, which lay in my way, a colony of muskrats dwelt, and raised their cabins high above the ice, though none could be seen abroad when I crossed it. Walden, being like the rest usually bare of snow, or with only shallow and interrupted drifts on it, was my yard where I could walk freely when the snow was nearly two feet deep on a level elsewhere and the villagers were confined to their streets. There, far from the village street, and except at very long intervals, from the jingle of sleigh-bells, I slid and skated, as in a vast moose-yard well trodden, overhung by oak woods and solemn pines bent down with snow or bristling with icicles.

For sounds in winter nights, and often in winter days, I heard the forlorn but melodious note of a hooting owl indefinitely far; such a sound as the frozen earth would yield if struck with a suitable plectrum, the very *lingua vernacula* of Walden Wood, and quite familiar to me at last, though I never saw the bird while it was making it. I seldom opened my door in a winter evening without hearing it; *Hoo hoo hoo, hoorer hoo*, sounded sonorously, and the first three syllables accented somewhat like *how der do;* or sometimes *hoo hoo* only. One night in the beginning of winter, before the pond froze over, about nine o'clock, I was startled by the loud honking of a goose, and, stepping to the door, heard the sound of their wings like a tempest in the woods as they flew low over my house. They passed over the pond toward Fair Haven, seemingly deterred from settling by my light, their commodore honking all the while with a regular beat. Suddenly an unmistakable cat owl from very near me, with the most harsh and tremendous voice I ever heard from any inhabitant of the woods, responded at regular intervals to the goose, as if determined to expose and disgrace this intruder from Hudson's Bay by exhibiting a greater compass and volume of voice in a native, and *boo-hoo* him out of Concord horizon. What do you mean by alarming the citadel at this time of night consecrated to me? Do you think I am ever caught napping at such an hour, and that I have not got lungs and a larynx as well as yourself? *Boo-hoo, boo-hoo, boo-hoo!* It was one of the most thrilling discords I ever heard. And yet, if you had a discriminating ear, there were in it the elements of a concord such as these plains never saw nor heard.

I also heard the whooping of the ice in the pond, my great bed-fellow in that part of Concord, as if it were restless in its bed and would fain turn over, were troubled with flatulency and bad dreams; or I was waked by the cracking of the ground by the frost, as if some one had driven a team against my door, and in the morning would find a crack in the earth a quarter of a mile long and a third of an inch wide.

Sometimes I heard the foxes as they ranged over the snow-crust, in moonlight nights, in search of a partridge or other game, barking raggedly and demoniacally like forest dogs, as if laboring with some anxiety, or seeking expression, struggling for light and to be dogs out-right and run freely in the streets; for if we take the ages into our account, may there not be a civilization going on among brutes as well as men? They seemed to me to be rudimental, burrowing men, still standing on their defence, awaiting their transformation. Sometimes one came near to my window, attracted by my light, barked a vulpine curse at me, and then retreated.

Usually the red squirrel (*Sciurus Hudsonius*) waked me in the dawn, coursing over the roof and up and down the sides of the house, as if sent out of the woods for this purpose. In the course of the winter I threw out half a bushel of ears of sweet corn, which had not got ripe, on to the snow-crust by my door, and was amused by watching the motions of the various animals which were baited by it. In the twilight and the night the rabbits came regularly and made a hearty meal. All day long the red squirrels came and went, and afforded me much entertainment by their manœuvres. One would approach at first warily through the shrub oaks, running over the snow-crust by fits and starts like a leaf blown by the wind, now a few paces this way, with wonderful speed and waste of energy, making inconceivable haste with his 'trotters,' as if it were for a wager, and now as many paces that way, but never getting on more than half a rod at a time; and then suddenly pausing with a ludicrous expression and a gratuitous somerset, as if all the eyes in the universe were fixed on him — for all the motions of a squirrel, even in the most solitary recesses of the forest, imply spectators as much as those of a dancing girl — wasting more time in delay and circumspection than would have sufficed to walk the whole distance — I never saw one walk — and then suddenly, before you could say Jack Robinson, he would be in the top of a young pitch pine, winding up his clock and chiding all imaginary spectators, soliloquizing and talking to all the universe at the same time — for no reason that I could ever detect, or he himself was aware of, I suspect. At length he would reach the corn, and selecting a suitable ear, frisk about in the same uncertain trigonometrical way to the topmost stick of my wood-pile, before my window, where he looked me in the face, and there sit for hours, supplying himself with a new ear from time to time, nibbling at first voraciously and throwing the half-naked cobs about; till at length he grew more dainty still and played with his food, tasting only the inside of the kernel, and the ear, which was held balanced over the stick by one paw, slipped from his careless grasp and fell to the ground, when he would look over at it with a ludicrous expression of uncertainty, as if suspecting that it had life, with a mind not made up whether to get it again, or a new one, or be off; now thinking of corn, then listening to hear what was in the wind. So the little impudent fellow would waste many an ear in a forenoon; till at last, seizing some longer and plumper one, considerably bigger than himself, and skilfully balancing it, he would set out with it to the woods, like a tiger with a buffalo, by the same zigzag course and frequent pauses, scratching along with it as if it were too heavy for him and falling all the while, making its fall a diagonal between a perpendicular and horizontal, being determined to put it through at any rate; — a singularly frivolous and whimsical fellow; — and so he would get off with it to where he lived, perhaps carry it to the top of a pine tree forty or fifty rods distant, and I would afterwards find the cobs strewn about the woods in various directions.

At length the jays arrive, whose discordant screams were heard long before, as they were warily making their approach an eighth of a mile off, and in a stealthy and sneaking manner they flit from tree to tree, nearer and nearer, and pick up the kernels which the squirrels have dropped. Then, sitting on a pitch pine bough, they attempt to swallow in their haste a kernel which is too big for their throats and chokes them; and after great labor they disgorge it, and spend an hour in the endeavor to crack it by repeated blows with their bills. They were manifestly thieves, and I had not much respect for them; but the squirrels, though at first shy, went to work as if they were taking what was their own.

Meanwhile also came the chickadees in flocks, which, picking up the crumbs the squirrels had dropped, flew to the nearest twig, and, placing them under their claws, hammered away at them with their little bills, as if it were an insect in the bark, till they were sufficiently reduced for their slender throats. A little flock of these titmice came daily to pick a dinner out of my wood-pile, or the crumbs at my door, with faint flitting lisping notes, like the tinkling of icicles in the grass, or else with sprightly *day day day*, or more rarely, in springlike days, a wiry summery *phe-be* from the woodside. They were so familiar that at length one alighted on an armful of wood which I was carrying in, and pecked at the sticks without fear. I once had a sparrow alight upon my shoulder for a moment while I was hoeing in a village garden, and I felt that I was more distinguished by that circumstance than I should have been by any epaulet I could have worn. The squirrels also grew at last to be quite familiar, and occasionally stepped upon my shoe, when that was the nearest way.

When the ground was not yet quite covered, and again near the end of winter, when the snow was melted on my south hillside and about my wood-pile, the partridges came out of the woods morning and evening to feed there. Whichever side you walk in the woods the partridge bursts away on whirring wings, jarring the snow from the dry leaves and twigs on high, which comes sifting down in the sunbeams like golden dust, for this brave bird is not to be scared by winter. It is frequently covered up by drifts, and, it is said, 'sometimes plunges from on wing into the soft snow, where it remains concealed for a day or two.' I used to start them in the open land also, where they had come out of the woods at sunset to 'bud' the wild apple trees. They will come regularly every evening to particular trees, where the cunning sportsman lies in wait for them, and the distant orchards next the woods suffer thus not a little. I am glad that the partridge gets fed, at any rate. It is Nature's own bird which lives on buds and diet-drink.

In dark winter mornings, or in short winter afternoons, I sometimes heard a pack of hounds threading all the woods with hounding cry and yelp, unable to resist the instinct of the chase, and the note of the hunting-horn at intervals, proving that man was in the rear. The woods ring again, and yet no fox bursts forth on to the open level of the pond, nor following pack pursuing their Actæon. And perhaps at evening I see the hunters returning with a single brush trailing from their sleigh for a trophy, seeking their inn. They tell me that if the fox would remain in the bosom of the frozen earth he would be safe, or if he would run in a straight line away no foxhound could overtake him; but, having left his pursuers far behind, he stops to rest and listen till they come up, and when he runs he circles round to his old haunts, where the hunters await him. Sometimes, however, he will run upon a wall many rods, and then leap off far to one side, and he appears to know that water will not retain his scent. A hunter told me that he once saw a fox pursued by hounds burst out on to Walden when the ice was covered with shallow puddles, run part way across, and then return to the same shore. Ere long the hounds arrived, but here they lost the scent. Sometimes a pack hunting by themselves would pass my door, and circle round my house, and yelp and hound without regarding me, as if afflicted by a species of madness, so that nothing could divert them from the pursuit. Thus they circle until they fall upon the recent trail of a fox, for a wise hound will forsake everything else for this. One day a man came to my hut from Lexington to inquire after his hound that made a large track, and had been hunting for a week by himself. But I fear that he was not the wiser for all I told him, for every time I attempted to answer his questions he interrupted me by asking, 'What do you do here?' He had lost a dog, but found a man.

One old hunter who has a dry tongue, who used to come to bathe in Walden once every year when the water was warmest, and at such times looked in upon me, told me that many years ago he took his gun one afternoon and went out for a cruise in Walden Wood; and as he walked the Wayland road he heard the cry of hounds approaching, and ere long a fox leaped the wall into the road, and as quick as thought leaped the other wall out of the road, and his swift bullet had not touched him. Some way behind came an old hound and her three pups in full pursuit, hunting on their own account, and disappeared again in the woods. Late in the afternoon, as he was resting in the thick woods south of Walden, he heard the voice of the hounds far over toward Fair Haven still pursuing the fox; and on they came, their hounding cry which made all the woods ring sounding nearer and nearer, now from Well Meadow, now from the Baker Farm. For a long time he stood still and listened to their music, so sweet to a hunter's ear, when suddenly the fox appeared, threading the solemn aisles with an easy coursing pace, whose sound was concealed by a sympathetic rustle of the leaves, swift and still, keeping the ground, leaving his pursuers far behind; and, leaping upon a rock amid the woods, he sat erect and listening, with his back to the hunter. For a moment compassion restrained the latter's arm; but that was a short-lived mood, and as quick as thought can follow thought his piece was levelled, and *whang!* — the fox, rolling over the rock, lay dead on the ground. The hunter still kept his place and listened to the hounds. Still on they came, and now the near woods resounded through all their aisles with their demoniac cry. At length the old hound burst into view with muzzle to the ground, and snapping the air as if possessed, and ran directly to the rock; but, spying the dead fox, she suddenly ceased her hounding, as if struck dumb with amazement, and walked round and round him in silence; and one by one her pups arrived, and, like their mother, were sobered into silence by the mystery. Then the hunter came forward and stood in their midst, and the mystery was solved. They waited in silence while he skinned the fox, then followed the brush a while, and at length turned off into the woods again. That evening a Weston squire came to the Concord hunter's cottage to inquire for his hounds, and told how for a week they had been hunting on their own account from Weston woods. The Concord hunter told him what he knew and offered him the skin; but the other declined it and departed. He did not find his hounds that night, but the next day learned that they had crossed the river and put up at a farmhouse for the night, whence, having been well fed, they took their departure early in the morning.

The hunter who told me this could remember one Sam Nutting, who used to hunt bears on Fair Haven Ledges, and exchange their skins for rum in Concord village; who told him, even, that he had seen a moose there. Nutting had a famous foxhound named Burgoyne — he pronounced it Bugine — which my informant used to borrow. In the 'Wast Book' of an old trader of this town, who was also a captain, town-clerk, and representative, I find the following entry. Jan. 18th, 1742–3, 'John Melven Cr. by 1 Grey Fox 0 — 2 — 3;' they are not now found here; and in his ledger, Feb. 7th, 1743, Hezekiah Stratton has credit 'by ½ a Catt skin 0 — 1 — 4½;' of course, a wild-cat, for Stratton was a sergeant in the old French war, and would not have got credit for hunting less noble game. Credit is given for deerskins also, and they were daily sold. One man still preserves the horns of the last deer that was killed in this vicinity, and another has told me the particulars of the hunt in which his uncle was engaged. The hunters were formerly a numerous and merry crew here. I remember well one gaunt Nimrod who would catch up a leaf by the roadside and play a strain on it wilder and more melodious, if my memory serves me, than any hunting-horn.

At midnight, when there was a moon, I sometimes met with hounds in my path prowling about the woods, which would skulk out of my way, as if afraid, and stand silent amid the bushes till I had passed.

Squirrels and wild mice disputed for my store of nuts. There were scores of pitch pines around my house, from one to four inches in diameter, which had been gnawed by mice the previous winter — a Norwegian winter for them, for the snow lay long and deep, and they were obliged to mix a large proportion of pine bark with their other diet. These trees were alive and apparently flourishing at midsummer, and many of them had grown a foot, though completely girdled; but after another winter such were without exception dead. It is remarkable that a single mouse should thus be allowed a whole pine tree for its dinner, gnawing round instead of up and down it; but perhaps it is necessary in order to thin these trees, which are wont to grow up densely.

The hares (*Lepus Americanus*) were very familiar. One had her form under my house all winter, separated from me only by the flooring, and she startled me each morning by her hasty departure when I began to stir — thump, thump, thump, striking her head against the floor timbers in her hurry. They used to come round my door at dusk to nibble the potato parings which I had thrown out, and were so nearly the color of the ground that they could hardly be distinguished when still. Sometimes in the twilight I alternately lost and recovered sight of one sitting motionless under my window. When I opened my door in the evening, off they would go with a squeak and a bounce. Near at hand they only excited my pity. One evening one sat by my door two paces from me, at first trembling with fear, yet unwilling to move; a poor wee thing, lean and bony, with ragged ears and sharp nose, scant tail and slender paws. It looked as if Nature no longer contained the breed of nobler bloods, but stood on her last toes. Its large eyes appeared young and unhealthy, almost dropsical. I took a step, and lo, away it scud with an elastic spring over the snow-crust, straightening its body and its limbs into graceful length, and soon put the forest between me and itself — the wild free venison, asserting its vigor and the dignity of Nature. Not without reason was its slenderness. Such then was its nature. (*Lepus, levipes,* light-foot, some think.)

What is a country without rabbits and partridges? They are among the most simple and indigenous animal products; ancient and venerable families known to antiquity as to modern times; of the very hue and substance of Nature, nearest allied to leaves and to the ground — and to one another; it is either winged or it is legged. It is hardly as if you had seen a wild creature when a rabbit or a partridge bursts away, only a natural one, as much to be expected as rustling leaves. The partridge and the rabbit are still sure to thrive, like true natives of the soil, whatever revolutions occur. If the forest is cut off, the sprouts and bushes which spring up afford them concealment, and they become more numerous than ever. That must be a poor country indeed that does not support a hare. Our woods teem with them both, and around every swamp may be seen the partridge or rabbit walk, beset with twiggy fences and horse-hair snares, which some cow-boy tends.

XVI. THE POND IN WINTER

AFTER a still winter night I awoke with the impression that some question had been put to me, which I had been endeavoring in vain to answer in my sleep, as what — how — when — where? But there was dawning Nature, in whom all creatures live, looking in at my broad windows with serene and satisfied face, and no question on *her* lips. I awoke to an answered question, to Nature and daylight. The snow lying deep on the earth dotted with young pines, and the very slope of the hill on which my house is placed, seemed to say, Forward! Nature puts no question and answers none which we mortals ask. She has long ago taken her resolution. 'O Prince, our eyes contemplate with admiration and transmit to the soul the wonderful and varied spectacle of this universe. The night veils without doubt a part of this glorious creation; but day comes to reveal to us this great work, which extends from earth even into the plains of the ether.'

Then to my morning work. First I take an axe and pail and go in search of water, if that be not a dream. After a cold and snowy night it needed a divining-rod to find it. Every winter the liquid and trembling surface of the pond, which was so sensitive to every breath, and reflected every light and shadow, becomes solid to the depth of a foot or a foot and a half, so that it will support the heaviest teams, and perchance the snow covers it to an equal depth, and it is not to be distinguished from any level field. Like the marmots in the surrounding hills, it closes its eyelids and becomes dormant for three months or more. Standing on the snow-covered plain, as if in a pasture amid the hills, I cut my way first through a foot of snow, and then a foot of ice, and open a window under my feet, where, kneeling to drink, I look down into the quiet parlor of the fishes, pervaded by a softened light as through a window of ground glass, with its bright sanded floor the same as in summer; there a perennial waveless serenity reigns as in the amber twilight sky, corresponding to the cool and even temperament of the inhabitants. Heaven is under our feet as well as over our heads.

Early in the morning, while all things are crisp with frost, men come with fishing-reels and slender lunch, and let down their fine lines through the snowy field to take pickerel and perch; wild men, who instinctively follow other fashions and trust other authorities than their townsmen, and by their goings and comings stitch towns together in parts where else they would be ripped. They sit and eat their luncheon in stout fear-naughts on the dry oak leaves on the shore, as wise in natural lore as the citizen is in artificial. They never consulted with books, and know and can tell much less than they have done. The things which they practice are said not yet to be known. Here is one fishing for pickerel with grown perch for bait. You look into his pail with wonder as into a summer pond, as if he kept summer locked up at home, or knew where she had retreated. How, pray, did he get these in midwinter? Oh, he got worms out of rotten logs since the ground froze, and so he caught them. His life itself passes deeper in nature than the studies of the naturalist penetrate; himself a subject for the naturalist. The latter raises the moss and bark gently with his knife in search of insects; the former lays open logs to their core with his axe, and moss and bark fly far and wide. He gets his living by barking trees. Such a man has some right to fish, and I love to see nature carried out in him. The perch swallows the grub-worm, the pickerel swallows the perch, and the fisherman swallows the pickerel; and so all the chinks in the scale of being are filled.

When I strolled around the pond in misty weather I was sometimes amused by the primitive mode which some ruder fisherman had adopted. He would perhaps have placed alder branches over the narrow holes in the ice, which were four or five rods apart and an equal distance from the shore, and having fastened the end of the line to a stick to prevent its being pulled through, have passed the slack line over a twig of the alder, a foot or more above the ice, and tied a dry oak leaf to it, which, being pulled down, would show when he had a bite. These alders loomed through the mist at regular intervals as you walked half way round the pond.

Ah, the pickerel of Walden! when I see them lying on the ice, or in the well which the fisherman cuts in the ice, making a little hole to admit the water, I am always surprised by their rare beauty, as if they were fabulous fishes, they are so foreign to the streets, even to the woods, foreign as Arabia to our Concord life. They possess a quite dazzling and transcendent beauty which separates them by a wide interval from the cadaverous cod and haddock whose fame is trumpeted in our streets. They are not green like the pines, nor gray like the stones, nor blue like the sky; but they have, to my eyes, if possible, yet rarer colors, like flowers and precious stones, as if they were the pearls, the animalized *nuclei* or crystals of the Walden water. They, of course, are Walden all over and all through; are themselves small Waldens in the animal kingdom, Waldenses. It is surprising that they are caught here — that in this deep and capacious spring, far beneath the rattling teams and chaises and tinkling sleighs that travel the Walden road, this great gold and emerald fish swims. I never chanced to see its kind in any market; it would be the cynosure of all eyes there. Easily, with a few convulsive quirks, they give up their watery ghosts, like a mortal translated before his time to the thin air of heaven.

As I was desirous to recover the long lost bottom of Walden Pond, I surveyed it carefully, before the ice broke up, early in '46, with compass and chain and sounding line. There have been many stories told about the bottom, or rather no bottom, of this pond, which certainly had no foundation for themselves. It is remarkable how long men will believe in the bottomlessness of a pond without taking the trouble to sound it. I have visited two such Bottomless Ponds in one walk in this neighborhood. Many have believed that Walden reached quite through to the other side of the globe. Some who have lain flat on the ice for a long time, looking down through the illusive medium, perchance with watery eyes into the bargain, and driven to hasty conclusions by the fear of catching cold in their breasts, have seen vast holes 'into which a load of hay might be driven,' if there were anybody to drive it, the undoubted source of the Styx and entrance to the Infernal Regions from these parts. Others have gone down from the village with a 'fifty-six' and a wagon load of inch rope, but yet have failed to find any bottom; for while the 'fifty-six' was resting by the way, they were paying out the rope in the vain attempt to fathom their truly immeasurable capacity for marvellousness. But I can assure my readers that Walden has a reasonably tight bottom at a not unreasonable, though at an unusual, depth. I fathomed it easily with a cod-line and a stone weighing about a pound and a half, and could tell accurately when the stone left the bottom, by having to pull so much harder before the water got underneath to help me. The greatest depth was exactly one hundred and two feet; to which may be added the five feet which it has risen since, making one hundred and seven. This is a remarkable depth for so small an area; yet not an inch of it can be spared by the imagination. What if all ponds were shallow? Would it not react on the minds of men? I am thankful that this pond was made deep and pure for a symbol. While men believe in the infinite some ponds will be thought to be bottomless.

A factory-owner, hearing what depth I had found, thought that it could not be true, for, judging from his acquaintance with dams, sand would not lie at so steep an angle. But the deepest ponds are not so deep in proportion to their area as most suppose, and, if drained, would not leave very remarkable valleys. They are not like cups between the hills; for this one, which is so unusually deep for its area, appears in a vertical section through its centre not deeper than a shallow plate. Most ponds, emptied, would leave a meadow no more hollow than we frequently see. William Gilpin, who is so admirable in all that relates to landscapes, and usually so correct, standing at the head of Loch Fyne, in Scotland, which he describes as 'a bay of salt water, sixty or seventy fathoms deep, four miles in breadth,' and about fifty miles long, surrounded by mountains, observes, 'If we could have seen it immediately after the diluvian crash, or whatever convulsion of nature occasioned it, before the waters gushed in, what a horrid chasm must it have appeared!

> 'So high as heaved the tumid hills, so low
> Down sunk a hollow bottom broad and deep,
> Capacious bed of waters.'

But if, using the shortest diameter of Loch Fyne, we apply these proportions to Walden, which, as we have seen, appears already in a vertical section only like a shallow plate, it will appear four times as shallow. So much for the *increased* horrors of the chasm of Loch Fyne when emptied. No doubt many a smiling valley with its stretching cornfields occupies exactly such a 'horrid chasm,' from which the waters have receded, though it requires the insight and the far sight of the geologist to convince the unsuspecting inhabitants of this fact. Often an inquisitive eye may detect the shores of a primitive lake in the low horizon hills, and no subsequent elevation of the plain have been necessary to conceal their history. But it is easiest, as they who work on the highways know, to find the hollows by the puddles after a shower. The amount of it is, the imagination, give it the least license, dives deeper and soars higher than Nature goes. So, probably, the depth of the ocean will be found to be very inconsiderable compared with its breadth.

As I sounded through the ice I could determine the shape of the bottom with greater accuracy than is possible in surveying harbors which do not freeze over, and I was surprised at its general regularity. In the deepest part there are several acres more level than almost any field which is exposed to the sun, wind, and plow. In one instance, on a line arbitrarily chosen, the depth did not vary more than one foot in thirty rods; and generally, near the middle, I could calculate the variation for each one hundred feet in any direction beforehand within three or four inches. Some are accustomed to speak of deep and dangerous holes even in quiet sandy ponds like this, but the effect of water under these circumstances is to level all inequalities. The regularity of the bottom and its conformity to the shores and the range of the neighboring hills were so perfect that a distant promontory betrayed itself in the soundings quite across the pond, and its direction could be determined by observing the opposite shore. Cape becomes bar, and plain shoal, and valley and gorge deep water and channel.

When I had mapped the pond by the scale of ten rods to an inch, and put down the soundings, more than a hundred in all, I observed this remarkable coincidence. Having noticed that the number indicating the greatest depth was apparently in the centre of the map, I laid a rule on the map lengthwise, and then breadthwise, and found, to my surprise, that the line of greatest length intersected the line of greatest breadth *exactly* at the point of greatest depth, notwithstanding that the middle is so nearly level, the outline of the pond far from regular, and the extreme length and breadth were got by measuring into the coves; and I said to myself, Who knows but this hint would conduct to the deepest part of the ocean as well as of a pond or puddle? Is not this the rule also for the height of mountains, regarded as the opposite of valleys? We know that a hill is not highest at its narrowest part.

Of five coves, three, or all which had been sounded, were observed to have a bar quite across their mouths and deeper water within, so that the bay tended to be an expansion of water within the land not only horizontally but vertically, and to form a basin or independent pond, the direction of the two capes showing the course of the bar. Every harbor on the sea-coast, also, has its bar at its entrance. In proportion as the mouth of the cove was wider compared with its length, the water over the bar was deeper compared with that in the basin. Given, then, the length and breadth of the cove, and the character of the surrounding shore, and you have almost elements enough to make out a formula for all cases.

In order to see how nearly I could guess, with this experience, at the deepest point in a pond, by observing the outlines of a surface and the character of its shores alone, I made a plan of White Pond, which contains about forty-one acres, and, like this, has no island in it, nor any visible inlet or outlet; and as the line of greatest breadth fell very near the line of least breadth, where two opposite capes approached each other and two opposite bays receded, I ventured to mark a point a short distance from the latter line, but still on the line of greatest length, as the deepest. The deepest part was found to be within one hundred feet of this, still farther in the direction to which I had inclined, and was only one foot deeper, namely, sixty feet. Of course, a stream running through, or an island in the pond, would make the problem much more complicated.

If we knew all the laws of Nature, we should need only one fact, or the description of one actual phenomenon, to infer all the particular results at that point. Now we know only a few laws, and our result is vitiated, not, of course, by any confusion or irregularity in Nature, but by our ignorance of essential elements in the calculation. Our notions of law and harmony are commonly confined to those instances which we detect; but the harmony which results from a far greater number of seemingly conflicting, but really concurring, laws, which we have not detected, is still more wonderful. The particular laws are as our points of view, as, to the traveller, a mountain outline varies with every step, and it has an infinite number of profiles, though absolutely but one form. Even when cleft or bored through it is not comprehended in its entireness.

What I have observed of the pond is no less true in ethics. It is the law of average. Such a rule of the two diameters not only guides us toward the sun in the system and the heart in man, but draw lines through the length and breadth of the aggregate of a man's particular daily behaviors and waves of life into his coves and inlets, and where they intersect will be the height or depth of his character. Perhaps we need only to know how his shores trend and his adjacent country or circumstances, to infer his depth and concealed bottom. If he is surrounded by mountainous circumstances, an Achillean shore, whose peaks overshadow and are reflected in his bosom, they suggest a corresponding depth in him. But a low and smooth shore proves him shallow on that side. In our bodies, a bold projecting brow falls off to and indicates a corresponding depth of thought. Also there is a bar across the entrance of our every cove, or particular inclination; each is our harbor for a season, in which we are detained and partially land-locked. These inclinations are not whimsical usually, but their form, size, and direction are determined by the promontories of the shore, the ancient axes of elevation. When this bar is gradually increased by storms, tides, or currents, or there is a subsidence of the waters, so that it reaches to the surface, that which was at first but an inclination in the shore in which a thought was harbored becomes an individual lake, cut off from the ocean, wherein the thought secures its own conditions — changes, perhaps, from salt to fresh, becomes a sweet sea, dead sea, or a marsh. At the advent of each individual into this life, may we not suppose that such a bar has risen to the surface somewhere? It is true, we are such poor navigators that our thoughts, for the most part, stand off and on upon a harborless coast, are conversant only with the bights of the bays of poesy, or steer for the public ports of entry, and go into the dry docks of science, where they merely refit for this world, and no natural currents concur to individualize them.

As for the inlet or outlet of Walden, I have not discovered any but rain and snow and evaporation, though perhaps, with a thermometer and a line, such places may be found, for where the water flows into the pond it will probably be coldest in summer and warmest in winter. When the ice-men were at work here in '46–7, the cakes sent to the shore were one day rejected by those who were stacking them up there, not being thick enough to lie side by side with the rest; and the cutters thus discovered that the ice over a small space was two or three inches thinner than elsewhere, which made them think that there was an inlet there. They also showed me in another place what they thought was a 'leach-hole,' through which the pond leaked out under a hill into a neighboring meadow, pushing me out on a cake of ice to see it. It was a small cavity under ten feet of water; but I think that I can warrant the pond not to need soldering till they find a worse leak than that. One has suggested, that if such a 'leach-hole' should be found, its connection with the meadow, if any existed, might be proved by conveying some colored powder or sawdust to the mouth of the hole, and then putting a strainer over the spring in the meadow, which would catch some of the particles carried through by the current.

While I was surveying, the ice, which was sixteen inches thick, undulated under a slight wind like water. It is well known that a level cannot be used on ice. At one rod from the shore its greatest fluctuation, when observed by means of a level on land directed toward a graduated staff on the ice, was three quarters of an inch, though the ice appeared firmly attached to the shore. It was probably greater in the middle. Who knows but if our instruments were delicate enough we might detect an undulation in the crust of the earth? When two legs of my level were on the shore and the third on the ice, and the sights were directed over the latter, a rise or fall of the ice of an almost infinitesimal amount made a difference of several feet on a tree across the pond. When I began to cut holes for sounding there were three or four inches of water on the ice under a deep snow which had sunk it thus far; but the water began immediately to run into these holes, and continued to run for two days in deep streams, which wore away the ice on every side, and contributed essentially, if not mainly, to dry the surface of the pond; for, as the water ran in, it raised and floated the ice. This was somewhat like cutting a hole in the bottom of a ship to let the water out. When such holes freeze, and a rain succeeds, and finally a new freezing forms a fresh smooth ice over all, it is beautifully mottled internally by dark figures, shaped somewhat like a spider's web, what you may call ice rosettes, produced by the channels worn by the water flowing from all sides to a centre. Sometimes, also, when the ice was covered with shallow puddles, I saw a double shadow of myself, one standing on the head of the other, one on the ice, the other on the trees or hillside.

While yet it is cold January, and snow and ice are thick and solid, the prudent landlord comes from the village to get ice to cool his summer drink; impressively, even pathetically, wise, to foresee the heat and thirst of July now in January — wearing a thick coat and mittens! when so many things are not provided for. It may be that he lays up no treasures in this world which will cool his summer drink in the next. He cuts and saws the solid pond, unroofs the house of fishes, and carts off their very element and air, held fast by chains and stakes like corded wood, through the favoring winter air, to wintry cellars, to underlie the summer there. It looks like solidified azure, as, far off, it is drawn through the streets. These ice-cutters are a merry race, full of jest and sport, and when I went among them they were wont to invite me to saw pit-fashion with them, I standing underneath.

In the winter of '46–7 there came a hundred men of Hyperborean extraction swoop down on to our pond one morning, with many car-loads of ungainly-looking farming tools — sleds, plows, drill-barrows, turf-knives, spades, saws, rakes, and each man was armed with a double-pointed pike-staff, such as is not described in the New-England Farmer or the Cultivator. I did not know whether they had come to sow a crop of winter rye, or some other kind of grain recently introduced from Iceland. As I saw no manure, I judged that they meant to skim the land, as I had done, thinking the soil was deep and had lain fallow long enough. They said that a gentleman farmer, who was behind the scenes, wanted to double his money, which, as I understood, amounted to half a million already; but in order to cover each one of his dollars with another, he took off the only coat, ay, the skin itself, of Walden Pond in the midst of a hard winter. They went to work at once, plowing, harrowing, rolling, furrowing, in admirable order, as if they were bent on making this a model farm; but when I was looking sharp to see what kind of seed they dropped into the furrow, a gang of fellows by my side suddenly began to hook up the virgin mould itself, with a peculiar jerk, clean down to the sand, or rather the water — for it was a very springy soil — indeed all the *terra firma* there was — and haul it away on sleds, and then I guessed that they must be cutting peat in a bog. So they came and went every day, with a peculiar shriek from the locomotive, from and to some point of the polar regions, as it seemed to me, like a flock of arctic snowbirds. But sometimes Squaw Walden had her revenge, and a hired man, walking behind his team, slipped through a crack in the ground down toward Tartarus, and he who was so brave before suddenly became but the ninth part of a man, almost gave up his animal heat, and was glad to take refuge in my house, and acknowledged that there was some virtue in a stove; or sometimes the frozen soil took a piece of steel out of a plowshare, or a plow got set in the furrow and had to be cut out.

To speak literally, a hundred Irishmen, with Yankee overseers, came from Cambridge every day to get out the ice. They divided it into cakes by methods too well known to require description, and these, being sledded to the shore, were rapidly hauled off on to an ice platform, and raised by grappling irons and block and tackle, worked by horses, on to a stack, as surely as so many barrels of flour, and there placed evenly side by side, and row upon row, as if they formed the solid base of an obelisk designed to pierce the clouds. They told me that in a good day they could get out a thousand tons, which was the yield of about one acre. Deep ruts and 'cradle-holes' were worn in the ice, as on *terra firma*, by the passage of the sleds over the same track, and the horses invariably ate their oats out of cakes of ice hollowed out like buckets. They stacked up the cakes thus in the open air in a pile thirty-five feet high on one side and six or seven rods square, putting hay between the outside layers to exclude the air; for when the wind, though never so cold, finds a passage through, it will wear large cavities, leaving slight supports or studs only here and there, and finally topple it down. At first it looked like a vast blue fort or Valhalla; but when they began to tuck the coarse meadow hay into the crevices, and this became covered with rime and icicles, it looked like a venerable moss-grown and hoary ruin, built of azure-tinted marble, the abode of Winter, that old man we see in the almanac — his shanty, as if he had a design to estivate with us. They calculated that not twenty-five per cent of this would reach its destination, and that two or three per cent would be wasted in the cars. However, a still greater part of this heap had a different destiny from what was intended; for, either because the ice was found not to keep so well as was expected, containing more air than usual, or for some other reason, it never got to market. This heap, made in the winter of '46–7 and estimated to contain ten thousand tons, was finally covered with hay and boards; and though it was unroofed the following July, and a part of it carried off, the rest remaining exposed to the sun, it stood over that summer and the next winter, and was not quite melted till September, 1848. Thus the pond recovered the greater part.

Like the water, the Walden ice, seen near at hand, has a green tint, but at a distance is beautifully blue, and you can easily tell it from the white ice of the river, or the merely greenish ice of some ponds, a quarter of a mile off. Sometimes one of those great cakes slips from the ice-man's sled into the village street, and lies there for a week like a great emerald, an object of interest to all passers. I have noticed that a portion of Walden which in the state of water was green will often, when frozen, appear from the same point of view blue. So the hollows about this pond will, sometimes, in the winter, be filled with a greenish water somewhat like its own, but the next day will have frozen blue. Perhaps the blue color of water and ice is due to the light and air they contain, and the most transparent is the bluest. Ice is an interesting subject for contemplation. They told me that they had some in the ice-houses at Fresh Pond five years old which was as good as ever. Why is it that a bucket of water soon becomes putrid, but frozen remains sweet forever? It is commonly said that this is the difference between the affections and the intellect.

Thus for sixteen days I saw from my window a hundred men at work like busy husbandmen, with teams and horses and apparently all the implements of farming, such a picture as we see on the first page of the almanac; and as often as I looked out I was reminded of the fable of the lark and the reapers, or the parable of the sower, and the like; and now they are all gone, and in thirty days more, probably, I shall look from the same window on the pure sea-green Walden water there, reflecting the clouds and the trees, and sending up its evaporations in solitude, and no traces will appear that a man has ever stood there. Perhaps I shall hear a solitary loon laugh as he dives and plumes himself, or shall see a lonely fisher in his boat, like a floating leaf, beholding his form reflected in the waves, where lately a hundred men securely labored.

Thus it appears that the sweltering inhabitants of Charleston and New Orleans, of Madras and Bombay and Calcutta, drink at my well. In the morning I bathe my intellect in the stupendous and cosmogonal philosophy of the Bhagvat-Geeta, since whose composition years of the gods have elapsed, and in comparison with which our modern world and its literature seem puny and trivial; and I doubt if that philosophy is not to be referred to a previous state of existence, so remote is its sublimity from our conceptions. I lay down the book and go to my well for water, and lo! there I meet the servant of the Bramin, priest of Brahma and Vishnu and Indra, who still sits in his temple on the Ganges reading the Vedas, or dwells at the root of a tree with his crust and water jug. I meet his servant come to draw water for his master, and our buckets as it were grate together in the same well. The pure Walden water is mingled with the sacred water of the Ganges. With favoring winds it is wafted past the site of the fabulous islands of Atlantis and the Hesperides, makes the periplus of Hanno, and, floating by Ternate and Tidore and the mouth of the Persian Gulf, melts in the tropic gales of the Indian seas, and is landed in ports of which Alexander only heard the names.

XVII. SPRING

THE opening of large tracts by the ice-cutters commonly causes a pond to break up earlier; for the water, agitated by the wind, even in cold weather, wears away the surrounding ice. But such was not the effect on Walden that year, for she had soon got a thick new garment to take the place of the old. This pond never breaks up so soon as the others in this neighborhood, on account both of its greater depth and its having no stream passing through it to melt or wear away the ice. I never knew it to open in the course of a winter, not excepting that of '52–3, which gave the ponds so severe a trial. It commonly opens about the first of April, a week or ten days later than Flint's Pond and Fair Haven, beginning to melt on the north side and in the shallower parts where it began to freeze. It indicates better than any water hereabouts the absolute progress of the season, being least affected by transient changes of temperature. A severe cold of a few days' duration in March may very much retard the opening of the former ponds, while the temperature of Walden increases almost uninterruptedly. A thermometer thrust into the middle of Walden on the 6th of March, 1847, stood at $32°$, or freezing point; near the shore at $33°$; in the middle of Flint's Pond, the same day, at $32\frac{1}{2}°$; at a dozen rods from the shore, in shallow water, under ice a foot thick, at $36°$. This difference of three and a half degrees between the temperature of the deep water and the shallow in the latter pond, and the fact that a great proportion of it is comparatively shallow, show why it should break up so much sooner than Walden. The ice in the shallowest part was at this time several inches thinner than in the middle. In midwinter the middle had been the warmest and the ice thinnest there. So, also, every one who has waded about the shores of a pond in summer must have perceived how much warmer the water is close to the shore, where only three or four inches deep, than a little distance out, and on the surface where it is deep, than near the bottom. In spring the sun not only exerts an influence through the increased temperature of the air and earth, but its heat passes through ice a foot or more thick, and is reflected from the bottom in shallow water, and so also warms the water and melts the under side of the ice, at the same time that it is melting it more directly above, making it uneven, and causing the air bubbles which it contains to extend themselves upward and downward until it is completely honeycombed, and at last disappears suddenly in a single spring rain. Ice has its grain as well as wood, and when a cake begins to rot or 'comb,' that is, assume the appearance of honeycomb, whatever may be its position, the air cells are at right angles with what was the water surface. Where there is a rock or a log rising near to the surface the ice over it is much thinner, and is frequently quite dissolved by this reflected heat; and I have been told that in the experiment at Cambridge to freeze water in a shallow wooden pond, though the cold air circulated underneath, and so had access to both sides, the reflection of the sun from the bottom more than counterbalanced this advantage. When a warm rain in the middle of

the winter melts off the snow ice from Walden, and leaves a hard dark
or transparent ice on the middle, there will be a strip of rotten though
thicker white ice, a rod or more wide, about the shores, created by this
reflected heat. Also, as I have said, the bubbles themselves within the
ice operate as burning-glasses to melt the ice beneath.

The phenomena of the year take place every day in a pond on a small
scale. Every morning, generally speaking, the shallow water is being
warmed more rapidly than the deep, though it may not be made so
warm after all, and every evening it is being cooled more rapidly until
the morning. The day is an epitome of the year. The night is the
winter, the morning and evening are the spring and fall, and the noon
is the summer. The cracking and booming of the ice indicate a change
of temperature. One pleasant morning after a cold night, February
24th, 1850, having gone to Flint's Pond to spend the day, I noticed with
surprise, that when I struck the ice with the head of my axe, it resounded like a gong for many rods around, or as if I had struck on a
tight drum-head. The pond began to boom about an hour after sunrise,
when it felt the influence of the sun's rays slanted upon it from over the
hills; it stretched itself and yawned like a waking man with a gradually
increasing tumult, which was kept up three or four hours. It took
a short siesta at noon, and boomed once more toward night, as the sun
was withdrawing his influence. In the right stage of the weather a pond
fires its evening gun with great regularity. But in the middle of the day,
being full of cracks, and the air also being less elastic, it had completely
lost its resonance, and probably fishes and muskrats could not then have
been stunned by a blow on it. The fishermen say that the 'thundering
of the pond' scares the fishes and prevents their biting. The pond does
not thunder every evening, and I cannot tell surely when to expect its
thundering; but though I may perceive no difference in the weather, it
does. Who would have suspected so large and cold and thick-skinned
a thing to be so sensitive? Yet it has its law to which it thunders
obedience when it should as surely as the buds expand in the spring.
The earth is all alive and covered with papillæ. The largest pond is as
sensitive to atmospheric changes as the globule of mercury in its tube.

One attraction in coming to the woods to live was that I should have
leisure and opportunity to see the Spring come in. The ice in the pond
at length begins to be honeycombed, and I can set my heel in it as I
walk. Fogs and rains and warmer suns are gradually melting the snow;
the days have grown sensibly longer; and I see how I shall get through
the winter without adding to my wood-pile, for large fires are no longer

necessary. I am on the alert for the first signs of spring, to hear the chance note of some arriving bird, or the striped squirrel's chirp, for his stores must be now nearly exhausted, or see the woodchuck venture out of his winter quarters. On the 13th of March, after I had heard the bluebird, song sparrow, and red-wing, the ice was still nearly a foot thick. As the weather grew warmer it was not sensibly worn away by the water, nor broken up and floated off as in rivers, but, though it was completely melted for half a rod in width about the shore, the middle was merely honeycombed and saturated with water, so that you could put your foot through it when six inches thick; but by the next day evening, perhaps, after a warm rain followed by fog, it would have wholly disappeared, all gone off with the fog, spirited away. One year I went across the middle only five days before it disappeared entirely. In 1845 Walden was first completely open on the 1st of April; in '46, the 25th of March; in '47, the 8th of April; in '51, the 28th of March; in '52, the 18th of April; in '53, the 23d of March; in '54, about the 7th of April.

Every incident connected with the breaking up of the rivers and ponds and the settling of the weather is particularly interesting to us who live in a climate of so great extremes. When the warmer days come, they who dwell near the river hear the ice crack at night with a startling whoop as loud as artillery, as if its icy fetters were rent from end to end, and within a few days see it rapidly going out. So the alligator comes out of the mud with quakings of the earth. One old man, who has been a close observer of Nature, and seems as thoroughly wise in regard to all her operations as if she had been put upon the stocks when he was a boy, and he had helped to lay her keel — who has come to his growth, and can hardly acquire more of natural lore if he should live to the age of Methuselah — told me — and I was surprised to hear him express wonder at any of Nature's operations, for I thought that there were no secrets between them — that one spring day he took his gun and boat, and thought that he would have a little sport with the ducks. There was ice still on the meadows, but it was all gone out of the river, and he dropped down without obstruction from Sudbury, where he lived, to Fair Haven Pond, which he found, unexpectedly, covered for the most part with a firm field of ice. It was a warm day, and he was surprised to see so great a body of ice remaining. Not seeing any ducks, he hid his boat on the north or back side of an island in the pond, and then concealed himself in the bushes on the south side, to await them. The ice was melted for three or four rods from the shore, and there was a

smooth and warm sheet of water, with a muddy bottom, such as the
ducks love, within, and he thought it likely that some would be along
pretty soon. After he had lain still there about an hour he heard a low
and seemingly very distant sound, but singularly grand and impressive,
unlike anything he had ever heard, gradually swelling and increasing
as if it would have a universal and memorable ending, a sullen rush and
roar, which seemed to him all at once like the sound of a vast body of
fowl coming in to settle there, and, seizing his gun, he started up in
haste and excited; but he found, to his surprise, that the whole body of
the ice had started while he lay there, and drifted in to the shore, and
the sound he had heard was made by its edge grating on the shore —
at first gently nibbled and crumbled off, but at length heaving up and
scattering its wrecks along the island to a considerable height before it
came to a standstill.

At length the sun's rays have attained the right angle, and warm
winds blow up mist and rain and melt the snowbanks, and the sun,
dispersing the mist, smiles on a checkered landscape of russet and white
smoking with incense, through which the traveller picks his way from
islet to islet, cheered by the music of a thousand tinkling rills and
rivulets whose veins are filled with the blood of winter which they are
bearing off.

Few phenomena gave me more delight than to observe the forms
which thawing sand and clay assume in flowing down the sides of
a deep cut on the railroad through which I passed on my way to the
village, a phenomenon not very common on so large a scale, though the
number of freshly exposed banks of the right material must have been
greatly multiplied since railroads were invented. The material was
sand of every degree of fineness and of various rich colors, commonly
mixed with a little clay. When the frost comes out in the spring, and
even in a thawing day in the winter, the sand begins to flow down the
slopes like lava, sometimes bursting out through the snow and overflowing it where no sand was to be seen before. Innumerable little
streams overlap and interlace one with another, exhibiting a sort of
hybrid product, which obeys half way the law of currents, and half way
that of vegetation. As it flows it takes the forms of sappy leaves or
vines, making heaps of pulpy sprays a foot or more in depth, and resembling, as you look down on them, the laciniated, lobed, and im-
bricated thalluses of some lichens; or you are reminded of coral, of
leopard's paws or birds' feet, of brains or lungs or bowels, and excre-
ments of all kinds. It is a truly *grotesque* vegetation, whose forms and

color we see imitated in bronze, a sort of architectural foliage more ancient and typical than acanthus, chiccory, ivy, vine, or any vegetable leaves; destined perhaps, under some circumstances, to become a puzzle to future geologists. The whole cut impressed me as if it were a cave with its stalactites laid open to the light. The various shades of the sand are singularly rich and agreeable, embracing the different iron colors, brown, gray, yellowish, and reddish. When the flowing mass reaches the drain at the foot of the bank it spreads out flatter into *strands*, the separate streams losing their semicylindrical form and gradually becoming more flat and broad, running together as they are more moist, till they form an almost flat *sand*, still variously and beautifully shaded, but in which you can trace the original forms of vegetation; till at length, in the water itself, they are converted into *banks*, like those formed off the mouths of rivers, and the forms of vegetation are lost in the ripple-marks on the bottom.

The whole bank, which is from twenty to forty feet high, is sometimes overlaid with a mass of this kind of foliage, or sandy rupture, for a quarter of a mile on one or both sides, the produce of one spring day. What makes this sand foliage remarkable is its springing into existence thus suddenly. When I see on the one side the inert bank — for the sun acts on one side first — and on the other this luxuriant foliage, the creation of an hour, I am affected as if in a peculiar sense I stood in the laboratory of the Artist who made the world and me — had come to where he was still at work, sporting on this bank, and with excess of energy strewing his fresh designs about. I feel as if I were nearer to the vitals of the globe, for this sandy overflow is something such a foliaceous mass as the vitals of the animal body. You find thus in the very sands an anticipation of the vegetable leaf. No wonder that the earth expresses itself outwardly in leaves, it so labors with the idea inwardly. The atoms have already learned this law, and are pregnant by it. The overhanging leaf sees here its prototype. *Internally*, whether in the globe or animal body, it is a moist thick *lobe*, a word especially applicable to the liver and lungs and the *leaves* of fat ($\lambda\epsilon\iota\beta\omega$, *labor*, *lapsus*, to flow or slip downward, a lapsing; $\lambda o\beta\acute{o}s$, *globus*, lobe, globe; also lap, flap, and many other words); *externally* a dry thin leaf, even as the *f* and *v* are a pressed and dried *b*. The radicals of *lobe* are *lb*, the soft mass of the *b* (single-lobed, or B, double-lobed), with the liquid *l* behind it pressing it forward. In globe, *glb*, the guttural *g* adds to the meaning the capacity of the throat. The feathers and wings of birds are still drier and thinner leaves. Thus, also, you pass from the lumpish grub in the earth to the airy and fluttering butterfly. The very globe continually transcends and translates itself, and becomes winged in its orbit. Even ice begins with delicate crystal leaves, as if it had flowed into moulds which the fronds of water-plants have impressed on the watery mirror. The whole tree itself is but one leaf, and rivers are still vaster leaves whose pulp is intervening earth, and towns and cities are the ova of insects in their axils.

When the sun withdraws the sand ceases to flow, but in the morning the streams will start once more and branch and branch again into a myriad of others. You here see perchance how blood-vessels are formed. If you look closely you observe that first there pushes forward from the thawing mass a stream of softened sand with a drop-like point, like the ball of the finger, feeling its way slowly and blindly downward, until at last with more heat and moisture, as the sun gets higher, the most fluid portion, in its effort to obey the law to which the most inert also yields, separates from the latter and forms for itself a meandering channel or artery within that, in which is seen a little silvery stream glancing like lightning from one stage of pulpy leaves or branches to another, and ever and anon swallowed up in the sand. It is wonderful how rapidly yet perfectly the sand organizes itself as it flows, using the best material its mass affords to form the sharp edges of its channel. Such are the sources of rivers. In the silicious matter which the water deposits is perhaps the bony system, and in the still finer soil and organic matter the fleshy fibre or cellular tissue. What is man but a mass of thawing clay? The ball of the human finger is but a drop congealed. The fingers and toes flow to their extent from the thawing mass of the body. Who knows what the human body would expand and flow out to under a more genial heaven? Is not the hand a spreading *palm* leaf with its lobes and veins? The ear may be regarded, fancifully, as a lichen, *Umbilicaria*, on the side of the head, with its lobe or drop. The lip — *labium*, from *labor* (?) — laps or lapses from the sides of the cavernous mouth. The nose is a manifest congealed drop or stalactite. The chin is a still larger drop, the confluent dripping of the face. The cheeks are a slide from the brows into the valley of the face, opposed and diffused by the cheek bones. Each rounded lobe of the vegetable leaf, too, is a thick and now loitering drop, larger or smaller; the lobes are the fingers of the leaf; and as many lobes as it has, in so many directions it tends to flow, and more heat or other genial influences would have caused it to flow yet farther.

Thus it seemed that this one hillside illustrated the principle of all the operations of Nature. The Maker of this earth but patented a leaf. What Champollion will decipher this hieroglyphic for us, that we may turn over a new leaf at last? This phenomenon is more exhilarating to me than the luxuriance and fertility of vineyards. True, it is somewhat excrementitious in its character, and there is no end to the heaps of liver, lights, and bowels, as if the globe were turned wrong side outward; but this suggests at least that Nature has some bowels, and there again is mother of humanity. This is the frost coming out of the ground; this is Spring. It precedes the green and flowery spring, as mythology precedes regular poetry. I know of nothing more purgative of winter fumes and indigestions. It convinces me that Earth is still in her swaddling-clothes, and stretches forth baby fingers on every side. Fresh curls spring from the baldest brow. There is nothing inorganic. These foliaceous heaps lie along the bank like the slag of a furnace, showing that Nature is 'in full blast' within. The earth is not a mere fragment of dead history, stratum upon stratum like the leaves of a book, to be studied by geologists and antiquaries chiefly, but living poetry like the leaves of a tree, which precede flowers and fruit — not a fossil earth, but a living earth; compared with whose great central life all animal and vegetable life is merely parasitic. Its throes will heave our exuviæ from their graves. You may melt your metals and cast them into the most beautiful moulds you can; they will never excite me like the forms which this molten earth flows out into. And not only it, but the institutions upon it are plastic like clay in the hands of the potter.

Ere long, not only on these banks, but on every hill and plain and in every hollow, the frost comes out of the ground like a dormant quadruped from its burrow, and seeks the sea with music, or migrates to other climes in clouds. Thaw with his gentle persuasion is more powerful than Thor with his hammer. The one melts, the other but breaks in pieces.

When the ground was partially bare of snow, and a few warm days had dried its surface somewhat, it was pleasant to compare the first tender signs of the infant year just peeping forth with the stately beauty of the withered vegetation which had withstood the winter — life-everlasting, goldenrods, pinweeds, and graceful wild grasses, more obvious and interesting frequently than in summer even, as if their beauty was not ripe till then; even cotton-grass, cat-tails, mulleins, johnswort, hardhack, meadow-sweet, and other strong-stemmed plants, those unexhausted granaries which entertain the earliest birds —

decent weeds, at least, which widowed Nature wears. I am particularly attracted by the arching and sheaf-like top of the wool-grass; it brings back the summer to our winter memories, and is among the forms which art loves to copy, and which, in the vegetable kingdom, have the same relation to types already in the mind of man that astronomy has. It is an antique style, older than Greek or Egyptian. Many of the phenomena of Winter are suggestive of an inexpressible tenderness and fragile delicacy. We are accustomed to hear this king described as a rude and boisterous tyrant; but with the gentleness of a lover he adorns the tresses of Summer.

At the approach of spring the red squirrels got under my house, two at a time, directly under my feet as I sat reading or writing, and kept up the queerest chuckling and chirruping and vocal pirouetting and gurgling sounds that ever were heard; and when I stamped they only chirruped the louder, as if past all fear and respect in their mad pranks, defying humanity to stop them. No, you don't — chickaree — chickaree. They were wholly deaf to my arguments, or failed to perceive their force, and fell into a strain of invective that was irresistible.

The first sparrow of spring! The year beginning with younger hope than ever! The faint silvery warblings heard over the partially bare and moist fields from the bluebird, the song sparrow, and the red-wing, as if the last flakes of winter tinkled as they fell! What at such a time are histories, chronologies, traditions, and all written revelations? The brooks sing carols and glees to the spring. The marsh hawk, sailing low over the meadow, is already seeking the first slimy life that awakes. The sinking sound of melting snow is heard in all dells, and the ice dissolves apace in the ponds. The grass flames up on the hillsides like a spring fire — 'et primitus oritur herba imbribus primoribus evocata' — as if the earth sent forth an inward heat to greet the returning sun; not yellow but green is the color of its flame; — the symbol of perpetual youth, the grass-blade, like a long green ribbon, streams from the sod into the summer, checked indeed by the frost, but anon pushing on again, lifting its spear of last year's hay with the fresh life below. It grows as steadily as the rill oozes out of the ground. It is almost identical with that, for in the growing days of June, when the rills are dry, the grass-blades are their channels, and from year to year the herds drink at this perennial green stream, and the mower draws from it betimes their winter supply. So our human life but dies down to its root, and still puts forth its green blade to eternity.

Walden is melting apace. There is a canal two rods wide along the northerly and westerly sides, and wider still at the east end. A great field of ice has cracked off from the main body. I hear a song sparrow singing from the bushes on the shore — *olit, olit, olit* — *chip, chip, chip, che char* — *che wiss, wiss, wiss*. He too is helping to crack it. How handsome the great sweeping curves in the edge of the ice, answering somewhat to those of the shore, but more regular! It is unusually hard, owing to the recent severe but transient cold, and all watered or waved like a palace floor. But the wind slides eastward over its opaque surface in vain, till it reaches the living surface beyond. It is glorious to behold this ribbon of water sparkling in the sun, the bare face of the pond full of glee and youth, as if it spoke the joy of the fishes within it, and of the sands on its shore — a silvery sheen as from the scales of a leuciscus, as it were all one active fish. Such is the contrast between winter and spring. Walden was dead and is alive again. But this spring it broke up more steadily, as I have said.

The change from storm and winter to serene and mild weather, from dark and sluggish hours to bright and elastic ones, is a memorable crisis which all things proclaim. It is seemingly instantaneous at last. Suddenly an influx of light filled my house, though the evening was at hand, and the clouds of winter still overhung it, and the eaves were dripping with sleety rain. I looked out the window, and lo! where yesterday was cold gray ice there lay the transparent pond already calm and full of hope as in a summer evening, reflecting a summer evening sky in its bosom, though none was visible overhead, as if it had intelligence with some remote horizon. I heard a robin in the distance, the first I had heard for many a thousand years, methought, whose note I shall not forget for many a thousand more — the same sweet and powerful song as of yore. O the evening robin, at the end of a New England summer day! If I could ever find the twig he sits upon! I mean *he*; I mean *the twig*. This at least is not the *Turdus migratorius*. The pitch pines and shrub oaks about my house, which had so long drooped, suddenly resumed their several characters, looked brighter, greener, and more erect and alive, as if effectually cleansed and restored by the rain. I knew that it would not rain any more. You may tell by looking at any twig of the forest, ay, at your very wood-pile, whether its winter is past or not. As it grew darker, I was startled by the honking of geese flying low over the woods, like weary travellers getting in late from Southern lakes, and indulging at last in unrestrained complaint and mutual consolation. Standing at my door, I could hear the rush of their wings; when, driving toward my house, they suddenly spied my light, and with hushed clamor wheeled and settled in the pond. So I came in, and shut the door, and passed my first spring night in the woods.

In the morning I watched the geese from the door through the mist, sailing in the middle of the pond, fifty rods off, so large and tumultuous that Walden appeared like an artificial pond for their amusement. But when I stood on the shore they at once rose up with a great flapping of wings at the signal of their commander, and when they had got into rank circled about over my head, twenty-nine of them, and then steered straight to Canada, with a regular *honk* from the leader at intervals, trusting to break their fast in muddier pools. A 'plump' of ducks rose at the same time and took the route to the north in the wake of their noisier cousins.

For a week I heard the circling, groping clangor of some solitary goose in the foggy mornings, seeking its companion, and still peopling the woods with the sound of a larger life than they could sustain. In April the pigeons were seen again flying express in small flocks, and in due time I heard the martins twittering over my clearing, though it had not seemed that the township contained so many that it could afford me any, and I fancied that they were peculiarly of the ancient race that dwelt in hollow trees ere white men came. In almost all climes the tortoise and the frog are among the precursors and heralds of this season, and birds fly with song and glancing plumage, and plants spring and bloom, and winds blow, to correct this slight oscillation of the poles and preserve the equilibrium of nature.

As every season seems best to us in its turn, so the coming in of spring is like the creation of Cosmos out of Chaos and the realization of the Golden Age.

> 'Eurus ad Auroram Nabathaeaque regna recessit,
> Persidaque, et radiis juga subdita matutinis.'

> 'The East-Wind withdrew to Aurora and the Nabathæan kingdom,
> And the Persian, and the ridges placed under the morning rays.
> . . . .
> Man was born. Whether that Artificer of things,
> The origin of a better world, made him from the divine seed;
> Or the earth, being recent and lately sundered from the high
> Ether, retained some seeds of cognate heaven.'

A single gentle rain makes the grass many shades greener. So our prospects brighten on the influx of better thoughts. We should be blessed if we lived in the present always, and took advantage of every accident that befell us, like the grass which confesses the influence of the slightest dew that falls on it; and did not spend our time in atoning for the neglect of past opportunities, which we call doing our duty. We loiter in winter while it is already spring. In a pleasant spring morning all men's sins are forgiven. Such a day is a truce to vice. While such a sun holds out to burn, the vilest sinner may return. Through our own recovered innocence we discern the innocence of our neighbors. You may have known your neighbor yesterday for a thief, a drunkard, or a sensualist, and merely pitied or despised him, and despaired of the world; but the sun shines bright and warm this first spring morning, re-creating the world, and you meet him at some serene work, and see how his exhausted and debauched veins expand with still joy and bless the new day, feel the spring influence with the innocence of infancy, and all his faults are forgotten. There is not only an atmosphere of good will about him, but even a savor of holiness groping for expression, blindly and ineffectually perhaps, like a new-born instinct, and for a short hour the south hillside echoes to no vulgar jest. You see some innocent fair shoots preparing to burst from his gnarled rind and try another year's life, tender and fresh as the youngest plant. Even he has entered into the joy of his Lord. Why the jailer does not leave open his prison doors — why the judge does not dismiss his case — why the preacher does not dismiss his congregation! It is because they do not obey the hint which God gives them, nor accept the pardon which he freely offers to all.

'A return to goodness produced each day in the tranquil and beneficent breath of the morning, causes that in respect to the love of virtue and the hatred of vice, one approaches a little the primitive nature of man, as the sprouts of the forest which has been felled. In like manner the evil which one does in the interval of a day prevents the germs of virtues which began to spring up again from developing themselves and destroys them.

'After the germs of virtue have thus been prevented many times from developing themselves, then the beneficent breath of evening does not suffice to preserve them. As soon as the breath of evening does not suffice longer to preserve them, then the nature of man does not differ much from that of the brute. Men seeing the nature of this man like that of the brute, think that he has never possessed the innate faculty of reason. Are those the true and natural sentiments of man?'

> 'The Golden Age was first created, which without any avenger
> Spontaneously without law cherished fidelity and rectitude.

> Punishment and fear were not; nor were threatening words read
> On suspended brass; nor did the suppliant crowd fear
> The words of their judge; but were safe without an avenger.
> Not yet the pine felled on its mountains had descended
> To the liquid waves that it might see a foreign world,
> And mortals knew no shores but their own.
>
> . . . .
>
> There was eternal spring, and placid zephyrs with warm
> Blasts soothed the flowers born without seed.'

On the 29th of April, as I was fishing from the bank of the river near the Nine-Acre-Corner bridge, standing on the quaking grass and willow roots, where the muskrats lurk, I heard a singular rattling sound, somewhat like that of the sticks which boys play with their fingers, when, looking up, I observed a very slight and graceful hawk, like a nighthawk, alternately soaring like a ripple and tumbling a rod or two over and over, showing the under side of its wings, which gleamed like a satin ribbon in the sun, or like the pearly inside of a shell. This sight reminded me of falconry and what nobleness and poetry are associated with that sport. The merlin it seemed to me it might be called: but I care not for its name. It was the most ethereal flight I had ever witnessed. It did not simply flutter like a butterfly, nor soar like the larger hawks, but it sported with proud reliance in the fields of air; mounting again and again with its strange chuckle, it repeated its free and beautiful fall, turning over and over like a kite, and then recovering from its lofty tumbling, as if it had never set its foot on *terra firma*. It appeared to have no companion in the universe — sporting there alone — and to need none but the morning and the ether with which it played. It was not lonely, but made all the earth lonely beneath it. Where was the parent which hatched it, its kindred, and its father in the heavens? The tenant of the air, it seemed related to the earth but by an egg hatched some time in the crevice of a crag; — or was its native nest made in the angle of a cloud, woven of the rainbow's trimmings and the sunset sky, and lined with some soft midsummer haze caught up from earth? Its eyry now some cliffy cloud.

Beside this I got a rare mess of golden and silver and bright cupreous fishes, which looked like a string of jewels. Ah! I have penetrated to those meadows on the morning of many a first spring day, jumping from hummock to hummock, from willow root to willow root, when the wild river valley and the woods were bathed in so pure and bright a light as would have waked the dead, if they had been slumbering in their graves, as some suppose. There needs no stronger proof of immortality. All things must live in such a light. O Death, where was thy sting? O Grave, where was thy victory, then?

Our village life would stagnate if it were not for the unexplored forests and meadows which surround it. We need the tonic of wildness — to wade sometimes in marshes where the bittern and the meadow-hen lurk, and hear the booming of the snipe; to smell the whispering sedge where only some wilder and more solitary fowl builds her nest, and the mink crawls with its belly close to the ground. At the same time that we are earnest to explore and learn all things, we require that all things be mysterious and unexplorable, that land and sea be infinitely wild, unsurveyed and unfathomed by us because unfathomable. We can never have enough of nature. We must be refreshed by the sight of inexhaustible vigor, vast and titanic features, the sea-coast with its wrecks, the wilderness with its living and its decaying trees, the thunder-cloud, and the rain which lasts three weeks and produces freshets. We need to witness our own limits transgressed, and some life pasturing freely where we never wander. We are cheered when we observe the vulture feeding on the carrion which disgusts and disheartens us, and deriving health and strength from the repast. There was a dead horse in the hollow by the path to my house, which compelled me sometimes to go out of my way, especially in the night when the air was heavy, but the assurance it gave me of the strong appetite and inviolable health of Nature was my compensation for this. I love to see that Nature is so rife with life that myriads can be afforded to be sacrificed and suffered to prey on one another; that tender organizations can be so serenely squashed out of existence like pulp — tadpoles which herons gobble up, and tortoises and toads run over in the road; and that sometimes it has rained flesh and blood! With the liability to accident, we must see how little account is to be made of it. The impression made on a wise man is that of universal innocence. Poison is not poisonous after all, nor are any wounds fatal. Compassion is a very untenable ground. It must be expeditious. Its pleadings will not bear to be stereotyped.

Early in May, the oaks, hickories, maples, and other trees, just putting out amidst the pine woods around the pond, imparted a brightness like sunshine to the landscape, especially in cloudy days, as if the sun were breaking through mists and shining faintly on the hillsides here and there. On the third or fourth of May I saw a loon in the pond, and during the first week of the month I heard the whip-poor-will, the brown thrasher, the veery, the wood pewee, the chewink, and other birds. I had heard the wood thrush long before. The phœbe had already come once more and looked in at my door and window, to see if my house was cavern-like enough for her, sustaining herself on humming winds with clinched talons, as if she held by the air, while she surveyed the premises. The sulphur-like pollen of the pitch pine soon covered the pond and the stones and rotten wood along the shore, so that you could have collected a barrelful. This is the 'sulphur showers' we hear of. Even in Calidas' drama of Sacontala, we read of 'rills dyed yellow with the golden dust of the lotus.' And so the seasons went rolling on into summer, as one rambles into higher and higher grass.

Thus was my first year's life in the woods completed; and the second year was similar to it. I finally left Walden September 6th, 1847.

XVIII. CONCLUSION

To the sick the doctors wisely recommend a change of air and scenery. Thank Heaven, here is not all the world. The buckeye does not grow in New England, and the mockingbird is rarely heard here. The wild goose is more of a cosmopolite than we; he breaks his fast in Canada, takes a luncheon in the Ohio, and plumes himself for the night in a southern bayou. Even the bison, to some extent, keeps pace with the seasons, cropping the pastures of the Colorado only till a greener and sweeter grass awaits him by the Yellowstone. Yet we think that if rail fences are pulled down, and stone walls piled up on our farms, bounds are henceforth set to our lives and our fates decided. If you are chosen town clerk, forsooth, you cannot go to Tierra del Fuego this summer: but you may go to the land of infernal fire nevertheless. The universe is wider than our views of it.

Yet we should oftener look over the tafferel of our craft, like curious passengers, and not make the voyage like stupid sailors picking oakum. The other side of the globe is but the home of our correspondent. Our voyaging is only great-circle sailing, and the doctors prescribe for diseases of the skin merely. One hastens to southern Africa to chase the giraffe; but surely that is not the game he would be after. How long, pray, would a man hunt giraffes if he could? Snipes and woodcocks also may afford rare sport; but I trust it would be nobler game to shoot one's self.

> 'Direct your eye right inward, and you'll find
> A thousand regions in your mind
> Yet undiscovered. Travel them, and be
> Expert in home-cosmography.'

What does Africa — what does the West stand for? Is not our own interior white on the chart? black though it may prove, like the coast, when discovered. Is it the source of the Nile, or the Niger, or the Mississippi, or a Northwest Passage around this continent, that we would find? Are these the problems which most concern mankind? Is Franklin the only man who is lost, that his wife should be so earnest to find him? Does Mr. Grinnell know where he himself is? Be rather the Mungo Park, the Lewis and Clark and Frobisher, of your own streams and oceans; explore your own higher latitudes — with ship-loads of preserved meats to support you, if they be necessary; and pile the empty cans sky-high for a sign. Were preserved meats invented to preserve meat merely? Nay, be a Columbus to whole new continents and worlds within you, opening new channels, not of trade, but of thought. Every man is the lord of a realm beside which the earthly empire of the Czar is but a petty state, a hummock left by the ice. Yet some can be patriotic who have no *self*-respect, and sacrifice the greater to the less. They love the soil which makes their graves, but have no sympathy with the spirit which may still animate their clay. Patriotism is a maggot in their heads. What was the meaning of that South-Sea Exploring Expedition, with all its parade and expense, but an indirect recognition of the fact that there are continents and seas in the moral world to which every man is an isthmus or an inlet, yet unexplored by him, but that it is easier to sail many thousand miles through cold and storm and cannibals, in a government ship, with five hundred men and boys to assist one, than it is to explore the private sea, the Atlantic and Pacific Ocean of one's being alone.

> 'Erret, et extremos alter scrutetur Iberos.
> Plus habet hic vitae, plus habet ille viae.'

> Let them wander and scrutinize the outlandish Australians.
> I have more of God, they more of the road.

It is not worth the while to go round the world to count the cats in Zanzibar. Yet do this even till you can do better, and you may perhaps find some 'Symmes' Hole' by which to get at the inside at last.

England and France, Spain and Portugal, Gold Coast and Slave Coast, all front on this private sea; but no bark from them has ventured out of sight of land, though it is without doubt the direct way to India. If you would learn to speak all tongues and conform to the customs of all nations, if you would travel farther than all travellers, be naturalized in all climes, and cause the Sphinx to dash her head against a stone, even obey the precept of the old philosopher, and Explore thyself. Herein are demanded the eye and the nerve. Only the defeated and deserters go to the wars, cowards that run away and enlist. Start now on that farthest western way, which does not pause at the Mississippi or the Pacific, nor conduct toward a wornout China or Japan, but leads on direct, a tangent to this sphere, summer and winter, day and night, sun down, moon down, and at last earth down too.

It is said that Mirabeau took to highway robbery 'to ascertain what degree of resolution was necessary in order to place one's self in formal opposition to the most sacred laws of society.' He declared that 'a soldier who fights in the ranks does not require half so much courage as a foot-pad' — 'that honor and religion have never stood in the way of a well-considered and a firm resolve.' This was manly, as the world goes; and yet it was idle, if not desperate. A saner man would have found himself often enough 'in formal opposition' to what are deemed 'the most sacred laws of society,' through obedience to yet more sacred laws, and so have tested his resolution without going out of his way. It is not for a man to put himself in such an attitude to society, but to maintain himself in whatever attitude he find himself through obedience to the laws of his being, which will never be one of opposition to a just government, if he should chance to meet with such.

I left the woods for as good a reason as I went there. Perhaps it seemed to me that I had several more lives to live, and could not spare any more time for that one. It is remarkable how easily and insensibly we fall into a particular route, and make a beaten track for ourselves. I had not lived there a week before my feet wore a path from my door to the pond-side; and though it is five or six years since I trod it, it is still quite distinct. It is true, I fear, that others may have fallen into it, and so helped to keep it open. The surface of the earth is soft and impressible by the feet of men; and so with the paths which the mind travels. How worn and dusty, then, must be the highways of the world, how deep the ruts of tradition and conformity! I did not wish to take a cabin passage, but rather to go before the mast and on the deck of the world, for there I could best see the moonlight amid the mountains. I do not wish to go below now.

I learned this, at least, by my experiment: that if one advances confidently in the direction of his dreams, and endeavors to live the life which he has imagined, he will meet with a success unexpected in common hours. He will put some things behind, will pass an invisible boundary; new, universal, and more liberal laws will begin to establish themselves around and within him; or the old laws be expanded, and interpreted in his favor in a more liberal sense, and he will live with the license of a higher order of beings. In proportion as he simplifies his life, the laws of the universe will appear less complex, and solitude will not be solitude, nor poverty poverty, nor weakness weakness. If you have built castles in the air, your work need not be lost; that is where they should be. Now put the foundations under them.

It is a ridiculous demand which England and America make, that you shall speak so that they can understand you. Neither men nor toadstools grow so. As if that were important, and there were not enough to understand you without them. As if Nature could support but one order of understandings, could not sustain birds as well as quadrupeds, flying as well as creeping things, and *hush* and *whoa*, which Bright can understand, were the best English. As if there were safety in stupidity alone. I fear chiefly lest my expression may not be *extra-vagant* enough, may not wander far enough beyond the narrow limits of my daily experience, so as to be adequate to the truth of which I have been convinced. *Extra vagance!* it depends on how you are yarded. The migrating buffalo, which seeks new pastures in another latitude, is not extravagant like the cow which kicks over the pail, leaps the cowyard fence, and runs after her calf, in milking time. I desire to speak somewhere *without* bounds; like a man in a waking moment, to men in their waking moments; for I am convinced that I cannot exaggerate enough even to lay the foundation of a true expression. Who that has heard a strain of music feared then lest he should speak extravagantly any more forever? In view of the future or possible, we should live quite laxly and undefined in front, our outlines dim and misty on that side; as our shadows reveal an insensible perspiration toward the sun. The volatile truth of our words should continually betray the inadequacy of the residual statement. Their truth is instantly *translated;* its literal monument alone remains. The words which express our faith and piety are not definite; yet they are significant and fragrant like frankincense to superior natures.

Why level downward to our dullest perception always, and praise that as common sense? The commonest sense is the sense of men asleep, which they express by snoring. Sometimes we are inclined to class those who are once-and-a-half-witted with the half-witted, because we appreciate only a third part of their wit. Some would find fault with the morning red, if they ever got up early enough. 'They pretend,' as I hear, 'that the verses of Kabir have four different senses; illusion, spirit, intellect, and the exoteric doctrine of the Vedas;' but in this part of the world it is considered a ground for complaint if a man's writings admit of more than one interpretation. While England endeavors to cure the potato-rot, will not any endeavor to cure the brain-rot, which prevails so much more widely and fatally?

I do not suppose that I have attained to obscurity, but I should be proud if no more fatal fault were found with my pages on this score than was found with the Walden ice. Southern customers objected to its blue color, which is the evidence of its purity, as if it were muddy, and preferred the Cambridge ice, which is white, but tastes of weeds. The purity men love is like the mists which envelop the earth, and not like the azure ether beyond.

Some are dinning in our ears that we Americans, and moderns generally, are intellectual dwarfs compared with the ancients, or even the Elizabethan men. But what is that to the purpose? A living dog is better than a dead lion. Shall a man go and hang himself because he belongs to the race of pygmies, and not be the biggest pygmy that he can? Let every one mind his own business, and endeavor to be what he was made.

Why should we be in such desperate haste to succeed and in such desperate enterprises? If a man does not keep pace with his companions, perhaps it is because he hears a different drummer. Let him step to the music which he hears, however measured or far away. It is not important that he should mature as soon as an apple tree or an oak. Shall he turn his spring into summer? If the condition of things which we were made for is not yet, what were any reality which we can substitute? We will not be shipwrecked on a vain reality. Shall we with pains erect a heaven of blue glass over ourselves, though when it is done we shall be sure to gaze still at the true ethereal heaven far above, as if the former were not?

There was an artist in the city of Kouroo who was disposed to strive after perfection. One day it came into his mind to make a staff. Having considered that in an imperfect work time is an ingredient, but into a perfect work time does not enter, he said to himself, It shall be perfect in all respects, though I should do nothing else in my life.

He proceeded instantly to the forest for wood, being resolved that it should not be made of unsuitable material; and as he searched for and rejected stick after stick, his friends gradually deserted him, for they grew old in their works and died, but he grew not older by a moment. His singleness of purpose and resolution, and his elevated piety, endowed him, without his knowledge, with perennial youth. As he made no compromise with Time, Time kept out of his way, and only sighed at a distance because he could not overcome him. Before he had found a stock in all respects suitable the city of Kouroo was a hoary ruin, and he sat on one of its mounds to peel the stick. Before he had given it the proper shape the dynasty of the Candahars was at an end, and with the point of the stick he wrote the name of the last of that race in the sand, and then resumed his work. By the time he had smoothed and polished the staff Kalpa was no longer the pole-star; and ere he had put on the ferule and the head adorned with precious stones, Brahma had awoke and slumbered many times. But why do I stay to mention these things? When the finishing stroke was put to his work, it suddenly expanded before the eyes of the astonished artist into the fairest of all the creations of Brahma. He had made a new system in making a staff, a world with full and fair proportions; in which, though the old cities and dynasties had passed away, fairer and more glorious ones had taken their places. And now he saw by the heap of shavings still fresh at his feet, that, for him and his work, the former lapse of time had been an illusion, and that no more time had elapsed than is required for a single scintillation from the brain of Brahma to fall on and inflame the tinder of a mortal brain. The material was pure, and his art was pure; how could the result be other than wonderful?

No face which we can give to a matter will stead us so well at last as the truth. This alone wears well. For the most part, we are not where we are, but in a false position. Through an infirmity of our natures, we suppose a case, and put ourselves into it, and hence are in two cases at the same time, and it is doubly difficult to get out. In sane moments we regard only the facts, the case that is. Say what you have to say, not what you ought. Any truth is better than make-believe. Tom Hyde, the tinker, standing on the gallows, was asked if he had anything to say. 'Tell the tailors,' said he, 'to remember to make a knot in their thread before they take the first stitch.' His companion's prayer is forgotten.

However mean your life is, meet it and live it; do not shun it and call it hard names. It is not so bad as you are. It looks poorest when you are richest. The faultfinder will find faults even in paradise. Love your life, poor as it is. You may perhaps have some pleasant, thrilling, glorious hours, even in a poor-house. The setting sun is reflected from the windows of the almshouse as brightly as from the rich man's abode; the snow melts before its door as early in the spring. I do not see but a quiet mind may live as contentedly there, and have as cheering thoughts, as in a palace. The town's poor seem to me often to live the most independent lives of any. Maybe they are simply great enough to receive without misgiving. Most think that they are above being supported by the town; but it oftener happens that they are not above supporting themselves by dishonest means, which should be more disreputable. Cultivate poverty like a garden herb, like sage. Do not trouble yourself much to get new things, whether clothes or friends. Turn the old; return to them. Things do not change; we change. Sell your clothes and keep your thoughts. God will see that you do not want society. If I were confined to a corner of a garret all my days, like a spider, the world would be just as large to me while I had my thoughts about me. The philosopher said: 'From an army of three divisions one can take away its general, and put it in disorder; from the man the most abject and vulgar one cannot take away his thought.' Do not seek so anxiously to be developed, to subject yourself to many influences to be played on; it is all dissipation. Humility like darkness reveals the heavenly lights. The shadows of poverty and meanness gather around us, 'and lo! creation widens to our view.' We are often reminded that if there were bestowed on us the wealth of Crœsus, our aims must still be the same, and our means essentially the same. Moreover, if you are restricted in your range by poverty, if you cannot buy books and newspapers, for instance, you are but confined to the most significant and vital experiences; you are compelled to deal with the material which yields the most sugar and the most starch. It is life near the bone where it is sweetest. You are defended from being a trifler. No man loses ever on a lower level by magnanimity on a higher. Superfluous wealth can buy superfluities only. Money is not required to buy one necessary of the soul.

I live in the angle of a leaden wall, into whose composition was poured a little alloy of bell-metal. Often, in the repose of my mid-day, there reaches my ears a confused *tintinnabulum* from without. It is the noise of my contemporaries. My neighbors tell me of their adventures with famous gentlemen and ladies, what notabilities they met at the dinner-table; but I am no more interested in such things than in the contents of the Daily Times. The interest and the conversation are about costume and manners chiefly; but a goose is a goose still, dress it as you will. They tell me of California and Texas, of England and the Indies, of the Hon. Mr. —— of Georgia or of Massachusetts, all transient and fleeting phenomena, till I am ready to leap from their court-yard like the Mameluke bey. I delight to come to my bearings — not walk in procession with pomp and parade, in a conspicuous place, but to walk even with the Builder of the universe, if I may — not to live in this restless, nervous, bustling, trivial Nineteenth Century, but stand or sit thoughtfully while it goes by. What are men celebrating? They are all on a committee of arrangements, and hourly expect a speech from somebody. God is only the president of the day, and Webster is his orator. I love to weigh, to settle, to gravitate toward that which most strongly and rightfully attracts me; — not hang by the beam of the scale and try to weigh less — not suppose a case, but take the case that is; to travel the only path I can, and that on which no power can resist me. It affords me no satisfaction to commerce to spring an arch before I have got a solid foundation. Let us not play at kittly-benders. There is a solid bottom everywhere. We read that the traveller asked the boy if the swamp before him had a hard bottom. The boy replied that it had. But presently the traveller's horse sank in up to the girths, and he observed to the boy, 'I thought you said that this bog had a hard bottom.' 'So it has,' answered the latter, 'but you have not got half way to it yet.' So it is with the bogs and quicksands of society; but he is an old boy that knows it. Only what is thought, said, or done at a certain rare coincidence is good. I would not be one of those who will foolishly drive a nail into mere lath and plastering; such a deed would keep me awake nights. Give me a hammer, and let me feel for the furring. Do not depend on the putty. Drive a nail home and clinch it so faithfully that you can wake up in the night and think of your work with satisfaction — a work at which you would not be ashamed to invoke the Muse. So will help you God, and so only. Every nail driven should be as another rivet in the machine of the universe, you carrying on the work.

Rather than love, than money, than fame, give me truth. I sat at a table where were rich food and wine in abundance, and obsequious attendance, but sincerity and truth were not; and I went away hungry from the inhospitable board. The hospitality was as cold as the ices. I thought that there was no need of ice to freeze them. They talked to me of the age of the wine and the fame of the vintage; but I thought of an older, a newer, and purer wine, of a more glorious vintage, which

they had not got, and could not buy. The style, the house and grounds
and 'entertainment' pass for nothing with me. I called on the king, but
he made me wait in his hall, and conducted like a man incapacitated
for hospitality. There was a man in my neighborhood who lived in
a hollow tree. His manners were truly regal. I should have done better
had I called on him.

How long shall we sit in our porticoes practising idle and musty
virtues, which any work would make impertinent? As if one were to
begin the day with long-suffering, and hire a man to hoe his potatoes;
and in the afternoon go forth to practise Christian meekness and charity
with goodness aforethought! Consider the China pride and stagnant
self-complacency of mankind. This generation inclines a little to congratulate itself on being the last of an illustrious line; and in Boston
and London and Paris and Rome, thinking of its long descent, it speaks
of its progress in art and science and literature with satisfaction. There
are the Records of the Philosophical Societies, and the public Eulogies
of *Great Men!* It is the good Adam contemplating his own virtue. 'Yes,
we have done great deeds, and sung divine songs, which shall never die'
— that is, as long as *we* can remember them. The learned societies and
great men of Assyria — where are they? What youthful philosophers
and experimentalists we are! There is not one of my readers who has
yet lived a whole human life. These may be but the spring months in
the life of the race. If we have had the seven-years' itch, we have not
seen the seventeen-year locust yet in Concord. We are acquainted with
a mere pellicle of the globe on which we live. Most have not delved six
feet beneath the surface, nor leaped as many above it. We know not
where we are. Beside, we are sound asleep nearly half our time. Yet
we esteem ourselves wise, and have an established order on the surface.
Truly, we are deep thinkers, we are ambitious spirits! As I stand over
the insect crawling amid the pine needles on the forest floor, and endeavoring to conceal itself from my sight, and ask myself why it will
cherish those humble thoughts, and hide its head from me who might,
perhaps, be its benefactor, and impart to its race some cheering information, I am reminded of the greater Benefactor and Intelligence that
stands over me the human insect.

There is an incessant influx of novelty into the world, and yet we
tolerate incredible dulness. I need only suggest what kind of sermons are
still listened to in the most enlightened countries. There are such words
as joy and sorrow, but they are only the burden of a psalm, sung with
a nasal twang, while we believe in the ordinary and mean. We think

that we can change our clothes only. It is said that the British Empire is very large and respectable, and that the United States are a first-rate power. We do not believe that a tide rises and falls behind every man which can float the British Empire like a chip, if he should ever harbor it in his mind. Who knows what sort of seventeen-year locust will next come out of the ground? The government of the world I live in was not framed, like that of Britain, in after-dinner conversations over the wine.

The life in us is like the water in the river. It may rise this year higher than man has ever known it, and flood the parched uplands; even this may be the eventful year, which will drown out all our muskrats. It was not always dry land where we dwell. I see far inland the banks which the stream anciently washed, before science began to record its freshets. Every one has heard the story which has gone the rounds of New England, of a strong and beautiful bug which came out of the dry leaf of an old table of apple-tree wood, which had stood in a farmer's kitchen for sixty years, first in Connecticut, and afterward in Massachusetts — from an egg deposited in the living tree many years earlier still, as appeared by counting the annual layers beyond it; which was heard gnawing out for several weeks, hatched perchance by the heat of an urn. Who does not feel his faith in a resurrection and immortality strengthened by hearing of this? Who knows what beautiful and winged life, whose egg has been buried for ages under many concentric layers of woodenness in the dead dry life of society, deposited at first in the alburnum of the green and living tree, which has been gradually converted into the semblance of its well-seasoned tomb — heard perchance gnawing out now for years by the astonished family of man, as they sat round the festive board — may unexpectedly come forth from amidst society's most trivial and handselled furniture, to enjoy its perfect summer life at last!

I do not say that John or Jonathan will realize all this; but such is the character of that morrow which mere lapse of time can never make to dawn. The light which puts out our eyes is darkness to us. Only that day dawns to which we are awake. There is more day to dawn. The sun is but a morning star.

4. POEMS

ALTHOUGH when Thoreau first launched himself on a literary career he thought of himself primarily as a poet, he was never really successful in the field. It is true that he wrote more than two hundred poems, but few of them have proved worthy of anthologizing. Those few that are widely read today are read more for their content, for the ideas they express, than for their poetic form. Part of Thoreau's problem can be assigned to the fact that he was a transition poet, falling between the more "formal" work of his predecessors such as Bryant and the free verse of Walt Whitman whose *Leaves of Grass* postdated virtually all of Thoreau's work. His poetry was too rough hewn to be considered formal and too regular to be free verse. Another cause of failure lies in the fact that as a Transcendentalist he believed his poetry should be "inspired" and so he preferred not to rework it. A little polishing would have helped a great deal.

Although Thoreau was bitterly disappointed when even his mentor Ralph Waldo Emerson pointed out the weaknesses of his poetry, he finally came to realize it was not his true metier, destroyed many of his manuscript poems, and began to concentrate almost entirely on prose. (Only a tiny fraction of his extant poems can be dated later than the mid-1840's.) He stopped attempting to publish his poetry by itself and instead began to work those few in his portfolio he thought superior into the texts of his prose. Thus some of his best poems will not be found in this brief selection but imbedded in his prose works such as "Smoke" in *Walden* (See page 412), "Sic Vita" (which, incidentally, is not always recognized as the "shape poem" it is; turn it on its side and you will see it resembles the "bunch of violets . . . tied loosely with straw": see pages 235–236), and "Fog" (See page 146) in *A Week*.

But his early poetic efforts were not in vain. His apprentice work there gave him a better command of his talents. It was not long after he abandoned poetry that his prose began to take on new qualities. It became sturdier and, almost paradoxically, more poetic. His word choices became more vivid and his sentences more rhythmical. He taught himself to write some of the most poetic prose in our language, such as that we find in *Walden*.

Of the poems printed here, the lines from "Inspiration" are scattered through *A Week* (Walden edition: pp. 181, 182, 351, 372). It was a built-up poem, and the version here reprinted omits the first and the last nine stanzas of the whole poem. It gives us one of the clearest expositions of the Transcendental — or we might even say, mystical experience that we have. "The Soul's Season" was published in the *Boston Commonwealth* in 1863. It appears in the Walden edition (V, 407–409) under the title, "The Fall of the Leaf," with twelve more stanzas. "Pilgrims" appears in the *Journal* (I, 403–407) in a very different version. "The Departure" probably refers to Thoreau's parting from the Emerson family after his stay there. "Mission" was first printed by Mr. Sanborn in *The Critic* for March, 1881. "Prayer" appeared in an essay entitled "Prayers" by R. W. Emerson, in the *Dial* for July, 1842. "I Make Ye An Offer" is from a portion of *A Week* omitted in this edition (Walden edition: I, 69–70). The same is true of "Sympathy" (Walden edition: I, 276–277). It was first published in the *Dial*, July, 1840. The last two stanzas are omitted. The "Gentle Boy" was Edmund Sewall, a pupil in Thoreau's school and the younger brother of the Ellen Sewall to whom Thoreau later proposed marriage. "Not Unconcerned" is from "A Walk to Wachusett," (Walden edition: V, p. 144). "My Friends" will be found in the "Journal" (I, 447). "Yet Let Us Thank" is also in the "Journal" (I, 477). It was printed in the *Dial*, July, 1842.

I. INSPIRATION

If with light head erect I sing,
  Though all the Muses lend their force,
From my poor love of anything,
  The verse is weak and shallow as its source.

But if with bended neck I grope,
  Listening behind me for my wit,
With faith superior to hope,
  More anxious to keep back than forward it,

Making my soul accomplice there
  Unto the flame my heart hath lit,
Then will the verse forever wear —
  Time cannot bend the line which God hath writ.

Always the general show of things
  Floats in review before my mind,
And such true love and reverence brings,
  That sometimes I forget that I am blind.

But now there comes unsought, unseen,
  Some clear divine electuary,
And I, who had but sensual been,
  Grow sensible, and as God is, am wary.

I hearing get, who had but ears,
  And sight, who had but eyes before;
I moments live, who lived but years,
  And truth discern, who knew but learning's lore.

I hear beyond the range of sound,
  I see beyond the range of sight,

New earths and skies and seas around,
   And in my day the sun doth pale his light.

A clear and ancient harmony
   Pierces my soul through all its din,
As through its utmost melody —
   Farther behind than they, farther within.

More swift its bolt than lightning is,
   Its voice than thunder is more loud,
It doth expand my privacies
   To all, and leave me single in the crowd.

It speaks with such authority,
   With so serene and lofty tone,
That idle Time runs gadding by,
   And leaves me with Eternity alone.

Then chiefly is my natal hour,
   And only then my prime of life;
Of manhood's strength it is the flower,
   'Tis peace's end, and war's beginning strife.

II. THE SOUL'S SEASON

THANK God who seasons thus the year,
   And sometimes kindly slants his rays;
For in his winter he's most near
   And plainest seen upon the shortest days.

Who gently tempers now his heats,
   And then his harsher cold, lest we
Should surfeit on the summer's sweets,
   Or pine upon the winter's crudity.

A sober mind will walk alone,
  Apart from nature, if need be,
And only its own seasons own;
  For nature leaving its humanity.

Sometimes a late autumnal thought
  Has crossed my mind in green July,
And to its early freshness brought
  Late ripened fruits, and an autumnal sky.

III. PILGRIMS

'HAVE you not seen,
In ancient times,
Pilgrims pass by
Toward other climes,
With shining faces,
Youthful and strong,
Mounting this hill
With speech and with song?'

'Ah, my good sir,
I know not those ways;
Little my knowledge,
Tho' many my days.
When I have slumbered,
I have heard sounds
As of travelers passing
These my grounds.

''Twas a sweet music
Wafted them by,
I could not tell
If afar off or nigh.
Unless I dreamed it,

This was of yore:
I never told it
To mortal before,
Never remembered
But in my dreams
What to me waking
A miracle seems.'

IV. THE DEPARTURE

IN THIS roadstead I have ridden,
In this covert I have hidden;
Friendly thoughts were cliffs to me,
And I hid beneath their lee.

This true people took the stranger,
And warm-hearted housed the ranger;
They received their roving guest,
And have fed him with the best;

Whatsoe'er the land afforded
To the stranger's wish accorded;
Shook the olive, stripped the vine,
And expressed the strengthening wine.

And by night they did spread o'er him
What by day they spread before him;
That good-will which was repast
Was his covering at last.

The stranger moored him to their pier
Without anxiety or fear;
By day he walked the sloping land,
By night the gentle heavens he scanned.

When first his bark stood inland
To the coast of that far Finland,
Sweet-watered brooks came tumbling to the shore
The weary mariner to restore.

And still he stayed from day to day
If he their kindness might repay;
    But more and more
The sullen waves came rolling toward the shore.

And still the more the stranger waited,
The less his argosy was freighted,
And still the more he stayed,
The less his debt was paid.

So he unfurled his shrouded mast
To receive the fragrant blast;
And that sane refreshing gale
Which had wooed him to remain
    Again and again,
It was that filled his sail
    And drove him to the main.

All day the low-hung clouds
    Dropt tears into the sea;
And the wind amid the shrouds
    Sighed plaintively.

V. MISSION

I'VE searched my faculties around,
To learn why life to me was lent:
I will attend the faintest sound,
And then declare to man what God hath meant.

VI. PRAYER

GREAT God! I ask thee for no meaner pelf
Than that I may not disappoint myself;
That in my action I may soar as high
As I can now discern with this clear eye;

And next in value, which thy kindness lends,
That I may greatly disappoint my friends,
Howe'er they think or hope that it may be,
They may not dream how thou'st distinguished me;

That my weak hand may equal my firm faith,
And my life practice more than my tongue saith;
   That my low conduct may not show,
   Nor my relenting lines,
   That I thy purpose did not know,
   Or overrated thy designs.

VII. I MAKE YE AN OFFER

   I MAKE ye an offer,
   Ye gods, hear the scoffer,
   The scheme will not hurt you,
   If ye will find goodness, I will find virtue.
   Though I am your creature,
   And child of your nature,
   I have pride still unbended,
   And blood undescended,

Some free independence,
And my own descendants.

I cannot toil blindly,
Though ye behave kindly,
And I swear by the rood,
I'll be slave to no God.
If ye will deal plainly,
I will strive mainly,
If ye will discover,
Great plans to your lover,
And give him a sphere
Somewhat larger than here.

VIII. SYMPATHY

Lately, alas, I knew a gentle boy,
  Whose features all were cast in Virtue's mould,
As one she had designed for Beauty's toy,
  But after manned him for her own stronghold.

On every side he open was as day,
  That you might see no lack of strength within,
For walls and ports do only serve alway
  For a pretense to feebleness and sin.

Say not that Caesar was victorious,
  With toil and strife who stormed the House of Fame,
In other sense this youth was glorious,
  Himself a kingdom whereso'er he came.

No strength went out to get him victory,
  When all was income of its own accord;
For where he went none other was to see,
  But all were parcel of their noble lord.

He forayed like the subtile haze of summer,
  That stilly shows fresh landscapes to our eyes,
And revolutions works without a murmur,
  Or rustling of a leaf beneath the skies.

So was I taken unawares by this,
  I quite forgot my homage to confess;
Yet now am forced to know, though hard it is,
  I might have loved him had I loved him less.

Each moment as we nearer drew to each,
  A stern respect withheld us farther yet,
So that we seemed beyond each other's reach,
  And less acquainted than when first we met.

We two were one while we did sympathize,
  So could we not the simplest bargain drive;
And what avails it now that we are wise,
  If absence doth this doubleness contrive?

Eternity may not the chance repeat,
  But I must tread my single way alone,
In sad remembrance that we once did meet,
  And know that bliss irrevocably gone.

The spheres henceforth my elegy shall sing,
  For elegy has other subject none;
Each strain of music in my ears shall ring
  Knell of departure from that other one.

Make haste and celebrate my tragedy;
  With fitting strain resound ye woods and fields;
Sorrow is dearer in such case to me
  Than all the joys other occasion yields.

IX. NOT UNCONCERNED

NOT unconcerned Wachusett rears his head
   Above the field, so late from nature won,
With patient brow reserved, as one who read
   New annals in the history of man.

X. MY FRIENDS

MY FRIENDS, why should we live?
   Life is an idle war, a toilsome peace;
Today I would not give
   One small consent for its securest ease.

Shall we outwear the year
   In our pavilions on its dusty plain,
And yet no signal hear
   To strike our tents and take the road again?

Or else drag up the slope
   The heavy ordnance of religion's train?
Useless, but in the hope
   Some far remote and heavenward hill to gain.

XI. YET LET US THANK

YET let us thank the purblind **race**
Who still have thought it good
With lasting stone to mark the place
Where braver men have stood.

5. TRAVEL BOOKS

PREFATORY NOTE

THE THOREAU of the travel books or "excursions," as he liked to call them, is a very different Thoreau from that of *Walden* or "Civil Disobedience." The thoughtful, vigorous critic and dissenter is here replaced by a lighthearted commentator; the caustic, satiric humor by jovial puns and slapstick. Here and there in the travel essays social criticism surfaces momentarily, but for the most part they were written to amuse rather than to teach. They lack the deep seriousness of his major works, but they nonetheless have a charm of their own. Despite hundreds of attempts, no other author has so well caught the salty flavor of Cape Cod or the pine-scented wildness of the Maine woods.

The travel books and essays are among the few works that Thoreau wrote consciously for a popular market. Most of his writings he offered on an almost take-it-or-leave-it basis, making few concessions to contemporary taste. He said what he had to say, and that was that. But in the travel essays he very deliberately adopted a lighthearted tone and sweetened his style with jokes and witticisms. I do not wish to imply any lack of sincerity here on Thoreau's part, for three different times when magazine editors attempted to tone down some of the few caustic comments in his "excursions," Thoreau withdrew his manuscripts rather than accede. But in general in his travel essays he was writing to please.

As lighthearted as his "excursions" are, Thoreau sloughed off none of his responsibilities as a craftsman in writing them. Long before he started out on one of his journeys he gathered up and studied the local history, explorations, travel books, and natural history field books and took copious notes. (For a trip to Canada, for example, he consulted forty-five different works and filled an entire notebook with extracts.) Thus before he embarked he knew exactly what he wanted to see and where to look for it. He unfailingly carried a gazeteer with him and the best maps of the region he could obtain, often tracing them out of books or from wall maps when he could not buy them. And he never went anywhere without a notebook to jot down impressions while they were still fresh. Upon his return to Concord he expanded his notes into a much fuller account in his journal, and then embarked on a second round of reading to fill in gaps in his knowledge. Next the journal account was revised and tried out on the lecture platform. Then the lecture was reworked for periodical publication. A final intent was to meld the periodical essays into a book, but in the case of Thoreau's two book-length excursions, *Cape Cod* and *The Maine Woods*, his early death prevented his carrying this last step out. Both received their final editing after his death, and since his editors both worked hastily and lacked his creativity, the books are marred by rough edges that he would have polished had he had the opportunity.

The first of the excursions given here, "Ktaadn," is the account of a trip taken by Thoreau in the late summer of 1846, while he was living at Walden Pond. It is the first of the three essays that make up *The Maine Woods* and recounts Thoreau's first contact with the primeval wilderness. Although Indians and lumbermen had preceded him on the rivers and lakes, he was one of the very earliest to visit the top of Ktaadn (or Katahdin, as it is more commonly spelled today), Maine's highest mountain. Although he obviously reveled in the abundant flora and fauna of this primitive region, it will come as a surprise to those who think of Thoreau as a primitivist, that he was not always completely at ease in the wild. The chaotic violence of the mountain top was almost a traumatic experience for him. He returned to Concord a soberer man and with a fuller realization that what he wanted at heart was not an escape from civilization but an accord between man and nature, a blend of civilization and of wildness. As he said at the end of a later excursion to Maine, "It was a relief to get back to our smooth, but still varied landscape. For a permanent residence, it seemed to me that there could be no comparison between this and the wilderness." Wilderness is needed as an antidote to society, as a place to restore one's soul and spirit. But it is not a place for permanent residence — for Thoreau at least.

"Ktaadn" was first published in *Sartain's Union Magazine* for July through November, 1848, as "Ktaadn and the Maine Woods" and was first published in book form in *The Maine Woods* by Ticknor & Fields in 1864.

I. KTAADN[1]

ON THE 31st of August, 1846, I left Concord in Massachusetts for Bangor and the backwoods of Maine, by way of the railroad and steamboat, intending to accompany a relative of mine, engaged in the lumber trade in Bangor, as far as a dam on the West Branch of the Penobscot, in which property he was interested. From this place, which is about one hundred miles by the river above Bangor, thirty miles from the Houlton military road, and five miles beyond the last log hut, I proposed to make excursions to Mount Ktaadn, the second highest mountain in New England, about thirty miles distant, and to some of the lakes of the Penobscot, either alone or with such company as I might pick up there. It is unusual to find a camp so far in the woods at that season, when lumbering operations have ceased, and I was glad to avail myself of the circumstance of a gang of men being employed there at that time in repairing the injuries caused by the great freshet in the spring. The mountain may be approached more easily and directly on horseback and on foot from the northeast side, by the Aroostook road, and the Wassataquoik River; but in that case you see much less of the wilderness, none of the glorious river and lake scenery, and have no experience of the batteau and the boatman's life. I was fortunate also in the season of the year, for in the summer myriads of black flies, mosquitoes, and midges, or, as the Indians call them, 'no-see-ems,' make traveling in the woods almost impossible; but now their reign was nearly over.

Ktaadn, whose name is an Indian word signifying highest land, was

[1] From 'The Maine Woods.'

first ascended by white men in 1804. It was visited by Professor J. W. Bailey of West Point in 1836; by Dr. Charles T. Jackson, the State Geologist, in 1837; and by two young men from Boston in 1845. All these have given accounts of their expeditions. Since I was there, two or three other parties have made the excursion, and told their stories. Besides these, very few, even among backwoodsmen and hunters, have ever climbed it, and it will be a long time before the tide of fashionable travel sets that way. The mountainous region of the State of Maine stretches from near the White Mountains, northeasterly one hundred and sixty miles, to the head of the Aroostook River, and is about sixty miles wide. The wild or unsettled portion is far more extensive. So that some hours only of travel in this direction will carry the curious to the verge of a primitive forest, more interesting, perhaps, on all accounts, than they would reach by going a thousand miles westward.

The next forenoon, Tuesday, September 1, I started with my companion in a buggy from Bangor for 'up river,' expecting to be overtaken the next day night at Mattawamkeag Point, some sixty miles off, by two more Bangoreans, who had decided to join us in a trip to the mountain. We had each a knapsack or bag filled with such clothing and articles as were indispensable, and my companion carried his gun.

Within a dozen miles of Bangor we passed through the villages of Stillwater and Oldtown, built at the falls of the Penobscot, which furnish the principal power by which the Maine woods are converted into lumber. The mills are built directly over and across the river. Here is a close jam, a hard rub, at all seasons; and then the once green tree, long since white, I need not say as the driven snow, but as a driven log, becomes lumber merely. Here your inch, your two and your three inch stuff begins to be, and Mr. Sawyer marks off those spaces which decide the destiny of so many prostrate forests. Through this steel riddle, more or less coarse, is the arrowy Maine forest, from Ktaadn and Chesuncook, and the head-waters of the St. John, relentlessly sifted, till it comes out boards, clapboards, laths, and shingles such as the wind can take, still, perchance, to be slit and slit again, till men get a size that will suit. Think how stood the white pine tree on the shore of Chesuncook, its branches soughing with the four winds, and every individual needle trembling in the sunlight — think how it stands with it now — sold, perchance, to the New England Friction-Match Company! There were in 1837, as I read, two hundred and fifty sawmills on the Penobscot and its tributaries above Bangor, the greater part of them in this immediate neighborhood, and they sawed two hundred millions of feet of boards annually. To this is to be added the lumber of the Kennebec, Androscoggin, Saco, Passamaquoddy, and other streams. No wonder that we hear so often of vessels which are becalmed off our coast being surrounded a week at a time by floating lumber from the Maine woods. The mission of men there seems to be, like so many busy demons, to drive the forest all out of the country, from every solitary beaver swamp and mountain-side, as soon as possible.

At Oldtown, we walked into a batteau-manufactory. The making of batteaux is quite a business here for the supply of the Penobscot River. We examined some on the stocks. They are light and shapely vessels, calculated for rapid and rocky streams, and to be carried over long portages on men's shoulders, from twenty to thirty feet long, and only four or four and a half wide, sharp at both ends like a canoe, though broadest forward on the bottom, and reaching seven or eight feet over the water, in order that they may slip over rocks as gently as possible. They are made very slight, only two boards to a side, commonly secured to a few light maple or other hard-wood knees, but inward are of the clearest and widest white pine stuff, of which there is a great waste on account of their form, for the bottom is left perfectly flat, not only from side to side, but from end to end. Sometimes they become 'hogging' even, after long use, and the boatmen then turn them over and straighten them by a weight at each end. They told us that one wore out in two years, or often in a single trip, on the rocks, and sold for from fourteen to sixteen dollars. There was something refreshing and wildly musical to my ears in the very name of the white man's canoe, reminding me of Charlevoix and Canadian Voyageurs. The batteau is a sort of mongrel between the canoe and the boat, a fur-trader's boat.

The ferry here took us past the Indian island. As we left the shore, I observed a short, shabby, washerwoman-looking Indian — they commonly have the woebegone look of the girl that cried for spilt milk — just from 'up river,' land on the Oldtown side near a grocery, and, drawing up his canoe, take out a bundle of skins in one hand, and an empty keg or half-barrel in the other, and scramble up the bank with them. This picture will do to put before the Indian's history, that is, the history of his extinction. In 1837 there were three hundred and sixty-two souls left of this tribe. The island seemed deserted today, yet I observed some new houses among the weather-stained ones, as if the tribe had still a design upon life; but generally they have a very shabby, forlorn, and cheerless look, being all back side and woodshed, not homesteads, even Indian homesteads, but instead of home or abroadsteads, for their life is *domi aut militiæ*, at home or at war, or now rather *venatus*, that is, a hunting, and most of the latter. The church is the only trim-looking building, but that is not Abenaki, that was Rome's doings. Good Canadian it may be, but it is poor Indian. These were once a powerful tribe. Politics are all the rage with them now. I even thought that a row of wigwams, with a dance of powwows, and a prisoner tortured at the stake, would be more respectable than this.

We landed in Milford, and rode along on the east side of the Penobscot, having a more or less constant view of the river, and the Indian islands in it, for they retain all the islands as far up as Nicketow, at the mouth of the East Branch. They are generally well-timbered, and are said to be better soil than the neighboring shores. The river seemed shallow and rocky, and interrupted by rapids, rippling and gleaming in the sun. We paused a moment to see a fish hawk dive for a fish down straight as an arrow, from a great height, but he missed his prey this time. It was the Houlton road on which we were now traveling, over which some troops were marched once towards Mars' Hill, though not to Mars' *field*, as it proved. It is the main, almost the only, road in these parts, as straight and well made, and kept in as good repair as almost any you will find anywhere. Everywhere we saw signs of the great freshet — this house standing awry, and that where it was not founded, but where it was found, at any rate, the next day; and that other with a waterlogged look, as if it were still airing and drying its basement, and logs with everybody's marks upon them, and sometimes the marks of their having served as bridges, strewn along the road. We crossed the Sunkhaze, a summery Indian name, the Olemmon, Passadumkeag, and other streams, which make a greater show on the map than they now did on the road. At Passadumkeag we found anything but what the name implies — earnest politicians, to wit — white ones, I mean — on the alert to know how the election was likely to go; men who talked rapidly, with subdued voice, and a sort of factitious earnestness you could not help believing, hardly waiting for an introduction, one on each side of your buggy, endeavoring to say much in little, for they see you hold the whip impatiently, but always saying little in much. Caucuses they have had, it seems, and caucuses they are to have again — victory and defeat. Somebody may be elected, somebody may not. One man, a total stranger, who stood by our carriage in the dusk, actually frightened the horse with his asseverations, growing more solemnly positive as there was less in him to be positive about. So Passadumkeag did not look on the map. At sundown, leaving the river road awhile for shortness, we went by way of Enfield, where we stopped for the night. This, like most of the localities bearing names on this road, was a place to name which, in the midst of the unnamed and unincorporated wilderness, was to make a distinction without a difference, it seemed to me. Here, however, I noticed quite an orchard of healthy and well-grown apple trees, in a bearing state, it being the oldest settler's house in this region, but all natural fruit and comparatively worthless for want of a grafter. And so it is generally, lower down the river. It would be a good speculation, as well as a favor conferred on the settlers, for a Massachusetts boy to go down there with a trunk full of choice scions, and his grafting apparatus, in the spring.

The next morning we drove along through a high and hilly country, in view of Cold-Stream Pond, a beautiful lake four or five miles long, and came into the Houlton road again, here called the military road, at Lincoln, forty-five miles from Bangor, where there is quite a village for this country — the principal one above Oldtown. Learning that there were several wigwams here, on one of the Indian islands, we left our horse and wagon and walked through the forest half a mile to the river, to procure a guide to the mountain. It was not till after considerable search that we discovered their habitations — small huts, in a retired place, where the scenery was unusually soft and beautiful, and the shore skirted with pleasant meadows and graceful elms. We paddled ourselves across to the island side in a canoe, which we found on the shore. Near where we landed sat an Indian girl, ten or twelve years old, on a rock in the water, in the sun, washing, and humming or moaning a song meanwhile. It was an aboriginal strain. A salmon-spear, made wholly of wood, lay on the shore, such as they might have used before white men came. It had an elastic piece of wood fastened to one side of its point, which slipped over and closed upon the fish, somewhat like the contrivance for holding a bucket at the end of a well-pole. As we walked up to the nearest house, we were met by a sally of a dozen wolfish-looking dogs, which may have been lineal descendants from the ancient Indian dogs, which the first voyageurs describe as 'their wolves.' I suppose they were. The occupant soon appeared, with a long pole in his hand, with which he beat off the dogs, while he parleyed with us — a stalwart, but dull and greasy-looking fellow, who told us, in his sluggish way, in answer to our questions, as if it were the first serious business he had to do that day, that there *were* Indians going 'up river' — he and one other — today, before noon. And who was the other? Louis Neptune, who lives in the next house. Well, let us go over and see Louis together. The same doggish reception, and Louis Neptune makes his appearance — a small, wiry man, with puckered and wrinkled face, yet he seemed the chief man of the two; the same, as I remembered, who had accompanied Jackson to the mountain in '37. The same questions were put to Louis, and the same information obtained, while the other Indian stood by. It appeared that they were going to start by noon, with two canoes, to go up to Chesuncook to hunt moose — to be gone a month. 'Well, Louis, suppose you get to the Point (to the Five Islands, just below Mattawamkeag) to camp, we walk on up the West Branch tomorrow — four of us — and wait for you at the dam, or this side. You overtake us tomorrow or next day, and take us into your canoes. We stop for you, you stop for us. We pay you for your trouble.' 'Ye',' replied Louis, 'may be you carry some provision for all — some pork — some bread — and so pay.' He said, 'Me sure get some moose;' and when I asked if he thought Pomola would let us go up, he answered that we must plant one bottle of rum on the top; he had planted good many; and when he looked again, the rum was all gone. He had been up two or three times; he had planted letter — English, German, French, etc. These men were slightly clad in shirt and pantaloons, like laborers with us in warm weather. They did not invite us into their houses, but met us outside. So we left the Indians, thinking ourselves lucky to have secured such guides and companions.

There were very few houses along the road, yet they did not altogether fail, as if the law by which men are dispersed over the globe were a very stringent one, and not to be resisted with impunity or for slight reasons. There were even the germs of one or two villages just beginning to expand. The beauty of the road itself was remarkable. The various evergreens, many of which are rare with us — delicate and beautiful specimens of the larch, arbor-vitæ, ball-spruce, and fir-balsam, from a few inches to many feet in height — lined its sides, in some places like a long front yard, springing up from the smooth grass-plots which uninterruptedly border it, and are made fertile by its wash; while it was but a step on either hand to the grim, untrodden wilderness, whose tangled labyrinth of living, fallen, and decaying trees only the deer and moose, the bear and wolf can easily penetrate. More perfect specimens than any front-yard plot can show grew there to grace the passage of the Houlton teams.

About noon we reached the Mattawamkeag, fifty-six miles from Bangor by the way we had come, and put up at a frequented house still on the Houlton road, where the Houlton stage stops. Here was a substantial covered bridge over the Mattawamkeag, built, I think they said, some seventeen years before. We had dinner — where, by the way, and even at breakfast, as well as supper, at the public-houses on this road, the front rank is composed of various kinds of 'sweet cakes,' in a continuous line from one end of the table to the other. I think I may safely say that there was a row of ten or a dozen plates of this kind set before us two here. To account for which, they say that, when the lumberers come out of the woods, they have a craving for cakes and pies, and such sweet things, which there are almost unknown, and this is the *supply* to satisfy that *demand*. The supply is always equal to the demand, and these hungry men think a good deal of getting their money's worth. No doubt the balance of victuals is restored by the time they reach Bangor — Mattawamkeag takes off the raw edge. Well, over this front rank, I say, you, coming from the 'sweet cake' side, with a cheap philosophic indifference though it may be, have to assault what there is behind, which I do not by any means mean to insinuate is insufficient in quantity or quality to supply that other demand, of men, not from the woods but from the towns, for venison and strong country fare. After dinner we strolled down to the 'Point,' formed by the junction of the two rivers, which is said to be the scene of an ancient battle between the Eastern Indians and the Mohawks, and searched there carefully for relics, though the men at the bar-room had never heard of such things; but we found only some flakes of arrowhead stone, some points of arrowheads, one small leaden bullet, and some colored beads, the last to be referred, perhaps, to early fur-trader days. The Mattawamkeag, though wide, was a mere river's bed, full of rocks and shallows at this time, so that you could cross it almost dry-shod in boots; and I could hardly believe my companion, when he told me that he had been fifty or sixty miles up it in a batteau, through distant and still uncut forests. A batteau could hardly find a harbor now at its mouth. Deer and caribou, or reindeer, are taken here in the winter, in sight of the house.

Before our companions arrived, we rode on up the Houlton road seven miles to Molunkus, where the Aroostook road comes into it, and where there is a spacious public house in the woods, called the 'Molunkus House,' kept by one Libbey, which looked as if it had its hall for dancing and for military drills. There was no other evidence of man but this huge shingle palace in this part of the world; but sometimes even this is filled with travelers. I looked off the piazza round the

corner of the house up the Aroostook road, on which there was no
clearing in sight. There was a man just adventuring upon it this evening
in a rude, original, what you may call Aroostook wagon — a mere seat,
with a wagon swung under it, a few bags on it, and a dog asleep to
watch them. He offered to carry a message for us to anybody in that
country, cheerfully. I suspect that, if you should go to the end of the
world, you would find somebody there going farther, as if just starting
for home at sundown, and having a last word before he drove off.
Here, too, *was* a small trader, whom I did not see at first, who kept a
store — but no great store, certainly — in a small box over the way,
behind the Molunkus sign-post. It looked like the balance-box of
a patent hay-scales. As for his house, we could only conjecture where
that was; he may have been a boarder in the Molunkus House. I saw
him standing in his shop door — his shop was so small, that, if a traveler
should make demonstrations of entering in, *he* would have to go out by
the back way, and confer with his customer through a window, about
his goods in the cellar, or, more probably, bespoken, and yet on the
way. I should have gone in, for I felt a real impulse to trade, if I had
not stopped to consider what would become of him. The day before,
we had walked into a shop, over against an inn where we stopped, the
puny beginning of trade, which would grow at last into a firm copartnership in the future town or city — indeed, it was already 'Somebody
& Co.,' I forget who. The woman came forward from the penetralia
of the attached house, for 'Somebody & Co.' was in the burning, and
she sold us percussion-caps, canalés and smooth, and knew their prices
and qualities, and which the hunters preferred. Here was a little of
everything in a small compass to satisfy the wants and the ambition of
the woods — a stock selected with what pains and care, and brought
home in the wagon-box, or a corner of the Houlton team; but there
seemed to me, as usual, a preponderance of children's toys — dogs to
bark, and cats to mew, and trumpets to blow, where natives there
hardly are yet. As if a child born into the Maine woods, among the
pine cones and cedar berries, could not do without such a sugar-man
or skipping-jack as the young Rothschild has.

I think that there was not more than one house on the road to
Molunkus, or for seven miles. At that place we got over the fence into
a new field, planted with potatoes, where the logs were still burning
between the hills; and, pulling up the vines, found good-sized potatoes,
nearly ripe, growing like weeds, and turnips mixed with them. The
mode of clearing and planting is to fell the trees, and burn once what

will burn, then cut them up into suitable lengths, roll into heaps, and burn again; then, with a hoe, plant potatoes where you can come at the ground between the stumps and charred logs; for a first crop the ashes sufficing for manure, and no hoeing being necessary the first year. In the fall, cut, roll, and burn again, and so on, till the land is cleared; and soon it is ready for grain, and to be laid down. Let those talk of poverty and hard times who will in the towns and cities; cannot the emigrant who can pay his fare to New York or Boston pay five dollars more to get here — I paid three, all told, for my passage from Boston to Bangor, two hundred and fifty miles — and be as rich as he pleases, where land virtually costs nothing, and houses only the labor of building, and he may begin life as Adam did? If he will still remember the distinction of poor and rich, let him bespeak him a narrower house forthwith.

When we returned to the Mattawamkeag, the Houlton stage had already put up there; and a Province man was betraying his greenness to the Yankees by his questions. Why Province money won't pass here at par, when States' money is good at Fredericton — though this, perhaps, was sensible enough. From what I saw then, it appears that the Province man was now the only real Jonathan, or raw country bumpkin, left so far behind by his enterprising neighbors that he didn't know enough to put a question to them. No people can long continue provincial in character who have the propensity for politics and whittling, and rapid traveling, which the Yankees have, and who are leaving the mother country behind in the variety of their notions and inventions. The possession and exercise of practical talent merely are a sure and rapid means of intellectual culture and independence.

The last edition of Greenleaf's Map of Maine hung on the wall here, and, as we had no pocket-map, we resolved to trace a map of the lake country. So, dipping a wad of tow into the lamp, we oiled a sheet of paper on the oiled table-cloth, and, in good faith, traced what we afterwards ascertained to be a labyrinth of errors, carefully following the outlines of the imaginary lakes which the map contains. The Map of the Public Lands of Maine and Massachusetts is the only one I have seen that at all deserves the name. It was while we were engaged in this operation that our companions arrived. They had seen the Indians' fire on the Five Islands, and so we concluded that all was right.

Early the next morning we had mounted our packs, and prepared for a tramp up the West Branch, my companion having turned his horse out to pasture for a week or ten days, thinking that a bite of fresh grass and a taste of running water would do him as much good as backwoods fare and new country influences his master. Leaping over a fence, we began to follow an obscure trail up the northern bank of the Penobscot. There was now no road further, the river being the only highway, and but half a dozen log huts, confined to its banks, to be met with for thirty miles. On either hand, and beyond, was a wholly un-inhabited wilderness, stretching to Canada. Neither horse nor cow, nor vehicle of any kind, had ever passed over this ground; the cattle, and the few bulky articles which the loggers use, being got up in the winter on the ice, and down again before it breaks up. The evergreen woods had a decidedly sweet and bracing fragrance; the air was a sort of diet-drink, and we walked on buoyantly in Indian file, stretching our legs. Occasionally there was a small opening on the bank, made for the purpose of log-rolling, where we got a sight of the river — always a rocky and rippling stream. The roar of the rapids, the note of a whistler duck on the river, of the jay and chickadee around us, and of the pigeon woodpecker in the openings, were the sounds that we heard. This was what you might call a bran-new country; the only roads were of Nature's making, and the few houses were camps. Here, then, one could no longer accuse institutions and society, but must front the true source of evil.

There are three classes of inhabitants who either frequent or inhabit the country which we had now entered: first, the loggers, who, for a part of the year, the winter and spring, are far the most numerous, but in the summer, except a few explorers for timber, completely desert it; second, the few settlers I have named, the only permanent inhabit-ants, who live on the verge of it, and help raise supplies for the former; third, the hunters, mostly Indians, who range over it in their season.

At the end of three miles we came to the Mattaseunk stream and mill, where there was even a rude wooden railroad running down to the Penobscot, the last railroad we were to see. We crossed one tract, on the bank of the river, of more than a hundred acres of heavy timber, which had just been felled and burnt over, and was still smoking. Our trail lay through the midst of it, and was well-nigh blotted out. The trees lay at full length, four or five feet deep, and crossing each other in all directions, all black as charcoal, but perfectly sound within, still good for fuel or for timber; soon they would be cut into lengths and burnt again. Here were thousands of cords, enough to keep the poor of Boston and New York amply warm for a winter, which only cumbered the ground and were in the settler's way. And the whole of that solid and interminable forest is doomed to be gradually devoured thus by fire, like shavings, and no man be warmed by it. At Crocker's log hut, at the mouth of Salmon River, seven miles from the Point, one of the party commenced distributing a store of small, cent picture-books among the children, to teach them to read, and also newspapers, more or less recent, among the parents, than which nothing can be more acceptable to a backwoods people. It was really an important item in our outfit, and, at times, the only currency that would circulate. I walked through Salmon River with my shoes on, it being low water, but not without wetting my feet. A few miles farther we came to 'Marm Howard's,' at the end of an extensive clearing, where there were two or three log huts in sight at once, one on the opposite side of the river, and a few graves even, surrounded by a wooden paling, where already the rude forefathers of *a* hamlet lie, and a thousand years hence, perchance, some poet will write his 'Elegy in a Country Churchyard.' The 'Village Hampdens,' the 'mute, inglorious Miltons,' and Cromwells, 'guiltless of' their 'country's blood,' were yet unborn.

> 'Perchance in this *wild* spot *there will be* laid
>   Some heart once pregnant with celestial fire;
> Hands that the rod of empire might have swayed,
>   Or waked to ecstasy the living lyre.'

The next house was Fisk's, ten miles from the Point at the mouth of the East Branch, opposite to the island Nicketow, or the Forks, the last of the Indian islands. I am particular to give the names of the settlers and the distances, since every log hut in these woods is a public house, and such information is of no little consequence to those who may have occasion to travel this way. Our course here crossed the Penobscot, and followed the southern bank. One of the party, who entered the house in search of some one to set us over, reported a very neat dwelling, with plenty of books, and a new wife, just imported from Boston, wholly new to the woods. We found the East Branch a large and rapid stream at its mouth and much deeper than it appeared. Having with some difficulty discovered the trail again, we kept up the south side of the West Branch, or main river, passing by some rapids called Rock-Ebeeme, the roar of which we heard through the woods, and, shortly after, in the thickest of the wood, some empty loggers' camps, still new, which were occupied the previous winter. Though we saw a few more afterwards, I will make one account serve for all. These were such houses as the lumberers of Maine spend the winter in, in the wilderness. There were the camps and the hovels for the cattle, hardly distinguishable, except that the latter had no chimney. These camps were about twenty feet long by fifteen wide, built of logs — hemlock, cedar, spruce, or yellow birch — one kind alone, or all together, with the bark on; two or three large ones first, one directly above another, and notched together at the ends, to the height of three or four feet, then of smaller logs resting upon transverse ones at the ends, each of the last successively shorter than the other, to form the roof. The chimney was an oblong square hole in the middle, three or four feet in diameter, with a fence of logs as high as the ridge. The interstices were filled with moss, and the roof was shingled with long and handsome splints of cedar, or spruce, or pine, rifted with a sledge and cleaver. The fireplace, the most important place of all, was in shape and size like the chimney, and directly under it, defined by a log fence or fender on the ground, and a heap of ashes, a foot or two deep within, with solid benches of split logs running round it. Here the fire usually melts the snow, and dries the rain before it can descend to quench it. The faded beds of arbor-vitæ leaves extended under the eaves on either hand. There was the place for the water-pail, pork-barrel, and wash-basin, and generally a dingy pack of cards left on a log. Usually a good deal of whittling was expended on the latch, which was made of wood, in the form of an iron one. These houses are made comfortable by the huge fires, which can be afforded night and day. Usually the scenery about them is drear and savage enough; and the logger's camp is as completely in the woods as a fungus at the foot of a pine in a swamp; no outlook but to the sky overhead; no more clearing than is made by cutting down the trees of which it is built, and those which are necessary for fuel. If only it be well sheltered and convenient to his work, and near a spring, he wastes no thought on the prospect. They are very proper forest houses, the stems of the trees collected together and piled up around a man to keep out wind and rain — made of living green logs, hanging with moss and lichen, and with the curls and fringes of the yellow birch bark, and dripping with resin, fresh and moist, and redolent of swampy odors, with that sort of vigor and perennialness even about them that toad-stools suggest.[1] The logger's fare consists of tea, molasses, flour, pork

[1] Springer, in his *Forest Life* (1851) says that they first remove the leaves and turf, from the spot where they intend to build a camp, for fear of fire; also, that 'the spruce-tree is generally selected for camp-building, it being light, straight, and quite free from sap;' that 'the roof is finally covered with the boughs of the fir, spruce, and hemlock, so that when the snow falls upon the whole, the warmth of the camp is preserved in the coldest weather;' and that they make the log seat before the fire, called the 'Deacon's Seat,' of a spruce or fir split in halves, with three or four stout limbs left on one side for legs, which are not likely to get loose.

(sometimes beef), and beans. A great proportion of the beans raised in Massachusetts find their market here. On expeditions it is only hard bread and pork, often raw, slice upon slice, with tea or water, as the case may be.

The primitive wood is always and everywhere damp and mossy, so that I traveled constantly with the impression that I was in a swamp; and only when it was remarked that this or that tract, judging from the quality of the timber on it, would make a profitable clearing, was I reminded, that if the sun were let in it would make a dry field, like the few I had seen, at once. The best shod for the most part travel with wet feet. If the ground was so wet and spongy at this, the dryest part of a dry season, what must it be in the spring? The woods hereabouts abounded in beech and yellow birch, of which last there were some very large specimens; also spruce, cedar, fir, and hemlock; but we saw only the stumps of the white pine here, some of them of great size, these having been already culled out, being the only tree much sought after, even as low down as this. Only a little spruce and hemlock beside had been logged here. The Eastern wood which is sold for fuel in Massachusetts all comes from below Bangor. It was the pine alone, chiefly the white pine, that had tempted any but the hunter to precede us on this route.

Waite's farm, thirteen miles from the Point, is an extensive and elevated clearing, from which we got a fine view of the river, rippling and gleaming far beneath us. My companions had formerly had a good view of Ktaadn and the other mountains here, but today it was so smoky that we could see nothing of them. We could overlook an immense country of uninterrupted forest, stretching away up the East Branch toward Canada on the north and northwest, and toward the Aroostook valley on the northeast; and imagine what wild life was stirring in its midst. Here was quite a field of corn for this region, whose peculiar dry scent we perceived a third of a mile off, before we saw it.

Eighteen miles from the Point brought us in sight of McCauslin's, or 'Uncle George's,' as he was familiarly called by my companions, to whom he was well known, where we intended to break our long fast. His house was in the midst of an extensive clearing or intervale, at the mouth of the Little Schoodic River, on the opposite or north bank of the Penobscot. So we collected on a point of the shore, that we might be seen, and fired our gun as a signal, which brought out his dogs forthwith, and thereafter their master, who in due time took us across in his batteau. This clearing was bounded abruptly, on all sides but the river, by the naked stems of the forest, as if you were to cut only a few feet square in the midst of a thousand acres of mowing, and set down a thimble therein. He had a whole heaven and horizon to himself, and the sun seemed to be journeying over his clearing only the livelong day. Here we concluded to spend the night, and wait for the Indians, as there was no stopping-place so convenient above. He had seen no Indians pass, and this did not often happen without his knowledge. He thought that his dogs sometimes gave notice of the approach of Indians half an hour before they arrived.

McCauslin was a Kennebec man, of Scotch descent, who had been a waterman twenty-two years, and had driven on the lakes and head-waters of the Penobscot five or six springs in succession, but was now settled here to raise supplies for the lumberers and for himself. He entertained us a day or two with true Scotch hospitality, and would accept no recompense for it. A man of a dry wit and shrewdness, and a general intelligence which I had not looked for in the back woods. In fact, the deeper you penetrate into the woods, the more intelligent, and, in one sense, less countrified do you find the inhabitants; for always the pioneer has been a traveler, and, to some extent, a man of the world; and, as the distances with which he is familiar are greater, so is his information more general and far reaching than the villager's. If I were to look for a narrow, uninformed, and countrified mind, as opposed to the intelligence and refinement which are thought to emanate from cities, it would be among the rusty inhabitants of an old-settled country, on farms all run out and gone to seed with life-ever-lasting, in the towns about Boston, even on the high-road in Concord, and not in the back woods of Maine.

Supper was got before our eyes in the ample kitchen, by a fire which would have roasted an ox; many whole logs, four feet long, were con-sumed to boil our tea-kettle — birch, or beech, or maple, the same summer and winter; and the dishes were soon smoking on the table, late the arm-chair, against the wall, from which one of the party was expelled. The arms of the chair formed the frame on which the table rested; and, when the round top was turned up against the wall, it formed the back of the chair, and was no more in the way than the wall itself. This, we noticed, was the prevailing fashion in these log houses, in order to economize in room. There were piping-hot wheaten cakes, the flour having been brought up the river in batteaux — no Indian bread, for the upper part of Maine, it will be remembered, is a wheat country — and ham, eggs, and potatoes, and milk and cheese.

the produce of the farm; and also shad and salmon, tea sweetened with molasses, and sweet cakes, in contradistinction to the hot cakes not sweetened, the one white, the other yellow, to wind up with. Such we found was the prevailing fare, ordinary and extraordinary, along this river. Mountain cranberries (*Vaccinium Vitis-Idæa*), stewed and sweetened, were the common dessert. Everything here was in profusion, and the best of its kind. Butter was in such plenty that it was commonly used, before it was salted, to grease boots with.

In the night we were entertained by the sound of rain-drops on the cedar splints which covered the roof, and awaked the next morning with a drop or two in our eyes. It had set in for a storm, and we made up our minds not to forsake such comfortable quarters with this prospect, but wait for Indians and fair weather. It rained and drizzled and gleamed by turns, the livelong day. What we did there, how we killed the time would perhaps be idle to tell; how many times we buttered our boots, and how often a drowsy one was seen to sidle off to the bedroom. When it held up, I strolled up and down the bank, and gathered the harebell and cedar berries, which grew there; or else we tried by turns the long-handled axe on the logs before the door. The axe-helves here were made to chop standing on the log — a primitive log of course — and were, therefore, nearly a foot longer than with us. One while we walked over the farm and visited his well-filled barns with McCauslin. There were one other man and two women only here. He kept horses, cows, oxen, and sheep. I think he said that he was the first to bring a plow and a cow so far; and he might have added the last, with only two exceptions. The potato-rot had found him out here, too, the previous year, and got half or two thirds of his crop, though the seed was of his own raising. Oats, grass, and potatoes were his staples; but he raised, also, a few carrots and turnips, and 'a little corn for the hens,' for this was all that he dared risk, for fear that it would not ripen. Melons, squashes, sweet corn, beans, tomatoes, and many other vegetables, could not be ripened there.

The very few settlers along this stream were obviously tempted by the cheapness of the land mainly. When I asked McCauslin why more settlers did not come in, he answered, that one reason was, they could not buy the land, it belonged to individuals or companies who were afraid that their wild lands would be settled, and so incorporated into towns, and they be taxed for them; but to settling on the State's land there was no such hindrance. For his own part, he wanted no neighbors — he didn't wish to see any road by his house. Neighbors, even the best, were a trouble and expense, especially on the score of cattle and fences. They might live across the river, perhaps, but not on the same side.

The chickens here were protected by the dogs. As McCauslin said, 'The old one took it up first, and she taught the pup, and now they had got it into their heads that it wouldn't do to have anything of the bird kind on the premises.' A hawk hovering over was not allowed to alight, but barked off by the dogs circling underneath; and a pigeon, or a 'yellow-hammer,' as they called the pigeon woodpecker, on a dead limb or stump, was instantly expelled. It was the main business of their day, and kept them constantly coming and going. One would rush out of the house on the least alarm given by the other.

When it rained hardest, we returned to the house, and took down a tract from the shelf. There was the 'Wandering Jew,' cheap edition, and fine print, the 'Criminal Calendar,' and 'Parish's Geography,' and flash novels two or three. Under the pressure of circumstances, we read a little in these. With such aid, the press is not so feeble an engine, after all. This house, which was a fair specimen of those on this river, was built of huge logs, which peeped out everywhere, and were chinked with clay and moss. It contained four or five rooms. There were no sawed boards, or shingles, or clapboards, about it; and scarcely any tool but the axe had been used in its construction. The partitions were made of long clapboard-like splints, of spruce or cedar, turned to a delicate salmon-color by the smoke. The roof and sides were covered with the same, instead of shingles and clapboards, and some of a much thicker and larger size were used for the floor. These were all so straight and smooth, that they answered the purpose admirably, and a careless observer would not have suspected that they were not sawed and planed. The chimney and hearth were of vast size, and made of stone. The broom was a few twigs of arbor-vitæ tied to a stick; and a pole was suspended over the hearth, close to the ceiling, to dry stockings and clothes on. I noticed that the floor was full of small, dingy holes, as if made with a gimlet, but which were, in fact, made by the spikes, nearly an inch long, which the lumberers wear in their boots to prevent their slipping on wet logs. Just above McCauslin's, there is a rocky rapid, where logs jam in the spring; and many 'drivers' are there collected, who frequent his house for supplies; these were their tracks which I saw.

At sundown McCauslin pointed away over the forest, across the river, to signs of fair weather amid the clouds — some evening redness there. For even there the points of compass held; and there was a quarter of the heavens appropriated to sunrise and another to sunset.

The next morning, the weather proving fair enough for our purpose, we prepared to start, and, the Indians having failed us, persuaded McCauslin, who was not unwilling to revisit the scenes of his driving, to accompany us in their stead, intending to engage one other boatman on the way. A strip of cotton cloth for a tent, a couple of blankets, which would suffice for the whole party, fifteen pounds of hard bread, ten pounds of 'clear' pork, and a little tea, made up 'Uncle George's' pack. The last three articles were calculated to be provision enough for six men for a week, with what we might pick up. A tea-kettle, a frying-pan, and an axe, to be obtained at the last house, would complete our outfit.

We were soon out of McCauslin's clearing, and in the evergreen woods again. The obscure trail made by the two settlers above, which even the woodman is sometimes puzzled to discern, ere long crossed a narrow, open strip in the woods overrun with weeds, called the Burnt Land, where a fire had raged formerly, stretching northward nine or ten miles, to Millinocket Lake. At the end of three miles, we reached Shad Pond, or Noliseemack, an expansion of the river. Hodge, the Assistant State Geologist, who passed through this on the 25th of June, 1837, says, 'We pushed our boat through an acre or more of buck-beans, which had taken root at the bottom, and bloomed above the surface in the greatest profusion and beauty.' Thomas Fowler's house is four miles from McCauslin's, on the shore of the pond, at the mouth of the Millinocket River, and eight miles from the lake of the same name, on the latter stream. This lake affords a more direct course to Ktaadn, but we preferred to follow the Penobscot and the Pamadumcook lakes. Fowler was just completing a new log hut, and was sawing out a window through the logs, nearly two feet thick, when we arrived. He had begun to paper his house with spruce bark, turned inside out, which had a good effect, and was in keeping with the circumstances. Instead of water we got here a draught of beer, which, it was allowed, would be better; clear and thin, but strong and stringent as the cedar sap. It was as if we sucked at the very teats of Nature's pine-clad bosom in these parts — the sap of all Millinocket botany commingled — the topmost, most fantastic, and spiciest sprays of the primitive wood, and whatever invigorating and stringent gum or essence it afforded steeped and dissolved in it — a lumberer's drink, which would acclimate and naturalize a man at once — which would make him see green, and, if he slept, dream that he heard the wind sough among the pines. Here was a fife, praying to be played on, through which we breathed a few tuneful strains — brought hither to tame wild beasts. As we stood upon the pile of chips by the door, fish hawks were sailing overhead; and here, over Shad Pond, might daily be witnessed the tyranny of the bald eagle over that bird. Tom pointed away over the lake to a bald eagle's nest, which was plainly visible more than a mile off, on a pine, high above the surrounding forest, and was frequented from year to year by the same pair, and held sacred by him. There were these two houses only there, his low hut and the eagles' airy cart-load of fagots. Thomas Fowler, too, was persuaded to join us, for two men were necessary to manage the batteau, which was soon to be our carriage, and these men needed to be cool and skillful for the navigation of the Penobscot. Tom's pack was soon made, for he had not far to look for his waterman's boots, and a red flannel shirt. This is the favorite color with lumbermen; and red flannel is reputed to possess some mysterious virtues, to be most healthful and convenient in respect to perspiration. In every gang there will be a large proportion of red birds. We took here a poor and leaky batteau, and began to pole up the Millinocket two miles, to the elder Fowler's, in order to avoid the Grand Falls of the Penobscot, intending to exchange our batteau there for a better. The Millinocket is a small, shallow, and sandy stream, full of what I took to be lamprey-eels' or suckers' nests, and lined with musquash-cabins, but free from rapids, according to Fowler, excepting at its outlet from the lake. He was at this time engaged in cutting the native grass — rush-grass and meadow-clover, as he called it — on the meadows and small, low islands of this stream. We noticed flattened places in the grass on either side, where, he said, a moose had laid down the night before, adding, that there were thousands in these meadows.

Old Fowler's, on the Millinocket, six miles from McCauslin's, and twenty-four from the Point, is the last house. Gibson's, on the Sowadnehunk, is the only clearing above, but that had proved a failure, and was long since deserted. Fowler is the oldest inhabitant of these woods. He formerly lived a few miles from here, on the south side of the West Branch, where he built his house sixteen years ago, the first house built above the Five Islands. Here our new batteau was to be carried over the first portage of two miles, round the Grand Falls of the Penobscot, on a horse-sled made of saplings, to jump the numerous rocks in the way; but we had to wait a couple of hours for them to catch the horses, which were pastured at a distance, amid the stumps, and had wandered still farther off. The last of the salmon for this season had just been caught, and were still fresh in pickle, from which enough was extracted to fill our empty kettle, and so graduate our introduction to simpler forest fare. The week before they had lost nine sheep here out of their first flock, by the wolves. The surviving sheep came round the house, and seemed frightened, which induced them to go and look for the rest, when they found seven dead and lacerated, and two still alive. These last they carried to the house, and, as Mrs. Fowler said, they were merely scratched in the throat, and had no more visible wound than would be produced by the prick of a pin. She sheared off the wool from their throats, and washed them, and put on some salve, and turned them out, but in a few moments they were missing, and had not been found since. In fact, they were all poisoned, and those that were found swelled up at once, so that they saved neither skin nor wool. This realized the old fables of the wolves and the sheep, and convinced me that that ancient hostility still existed. Verily, the shepherd-boy did not need to sound a false alarm this time. There were steel traps by the door, of various sizes, for wolves, otter, and bears, with large claws instead of teeth, to catch in their sinews. Wolves are frequently killed with poisoned bait.

At length, after we had dined here on the usual backwoods fare, the horses arrived, and we hauled our batteau out of the water, and lashed it to its wicker carriage, and, throwing in our packs, walked on before, leaving the boatmen and driver, who was Tom's brother, to manage the concern. The route, which led through the wild pasture where the sheep were killed, was in some places the roughest ever traveled by horses, over rocky hills, where the sled bounced and slid along, like a vessel pitching in a storm; and one man was as necessary to stand at the stern, to prevent the boat from being wrecked, as a helmsman in the roughest sea. The philosophy of our progress was something like this: when the runner struck a rock three or four feet high, the sled bounced back and upwards at the same time; but, as the horses never ceased pulling, it came down on the top of the rock, and so we got over. This portage probably followed the trail of an ancient Indian carry round these falls. By two o'clock we, who had walked on before, reached the river above the falls, not far from the outlet of Quakish Lake, and waited for the batteau to come up. We had been here but a short time, when a thunder-shower was seen coming up from the west, over the still invisible lakes, and that pleasant wilderness which we were so eager to become acquainted with; and soon the heavy drops began to patter on the leaves around us. I had just selected the prostrate trunk of a huge pine, five or six feet in diameter, and was crawling under it, when, luckily, the boat arrived. It would have amused a sheltered man to witness the manner in which it was unlashed, and whirled over, while the first waterspout burst upon us. It was no sooner in the hands of the eager company than it was abandoned to the first revolutionary impulse, and to gravity, to adjust it; and they might have been seen all stooping to its shelter, and wriggling under like so many eels, before it was fairly deposited on the ground. When all were under, we propped up the lee side, and busied ourselves there whittling thole-pins for rowing, when we should reach the lakes; and made the woods ring, between the claps of thunder, with such boat-songs as we could remember. The horses stood sleek and shining with the rain, all drooping and crestfallen, while deluge after deluge washed over us; but the bottom of a boat may be relied on for a tight roof. At length, after two hours' delay at this place, a streak of fair weather appeared in the northwest, whither our course now lay, promising a serene evening for our voyage; and the driver returned with his horses, while we made haste to launch our boat, and commence our voyage in good earnest.

There were six of us, including the two boatmen. With our packs heaped up near the bows, and ourselves disposed as baggage to trim the boat, with instructions not to move in case we should strike a rock, more than so many barrels of pork, we pushed out into the first rapid, a slight specimen of the stream we had to navigate. With Uncle George in the stern, and Tom in the bows, each using a spruce pole about twelve feet long, pointed with iron,[1] and poling on the same side, we shot up the rapids like a salmon, the water rushing and roaring around, so that only a practiced eye could distinguish a safe course, or tell what was deep water and what rocks, frequently grazing the latter on one or both sides, with a hundred as narrow escapes as ever the Argo had in passing through the Symplegades. I, who had had some experience in boating, had never experienced any half so exhilarating before. We were lucky to have exchanged our Indians, whom we did not know, for these men, who, together with Tom's brother, were reputed the best boatmen on the river, and were at once indispensable pilots and pleasant companions. The canoe is smaller, more easily upset, and sooner worn out; and the Indian is said not to be so skillful in the management of the batteau. He is, for the most part, less to be relied on, and more disposed to sulks and whims. The utmost familiarity with dead streams, or with

---

[1] The Canadians call it *picquer de fond*.

the ocean, would not prepare a man for this peculiar navigation; and the most skillful boatman anywhere else would here be obliged to take out his boat and carry round a hundred times, still with great risk, as well as delay, where the practiced batteau-man poles up with comparative ease and safety. The hardy 'voyageur' pushes with incredible perseverance and success quite up to the foot of the falls, and then only carries round some perpendicular ledge, and launches again in

'The torrent's smoothness, ere it dash below,'

to struggle with the boiling rapids above. The Indians say that the river once ran both ways, one half up and the other down, but that, since the white man came, it all runs down, and now they must laboriously pole their canoes against the stream, and carry them over numerous portages. In the summer, all stores — the grindstone and the plow of the pioneer, flour, pork, and utensils for the explorer — must be conveyed up the river in batteaux; and many a cargo and many a boatman is lost in these waters. In the winter, however, which is very equable and long, the ice is the great highway, and the loggers' team penetrates to Chesuncook Lake, and still higher up, even two hundred miles above Bangor. Imagine the solitary sled-track running far up into the snowy and evergreen wilderness, hemmed in closely for a hundred miles by the forest, and again stretching straight across the broad surfaces of concealed lakes!

We were soon in the smooth water of the Quakish Lake, and took our turns at rowing and paddling across it. It is a small, irregular, but handsome lake, shut in on all sides by the forest, and showing no traces of man but some low boom in a distant cove, reserved for spring use. The spruce and cedar on its shores, hung with gray lichens, looked at a distance like the ghosts of trees. Ducks were sailing here and there on its surface, and a solitary loon, like a more living wave — a vital spot on the lake's surface — laughed and frolicked, and showed its straight leg, for our amusement. Joe Merry Mountain appeared in the northwest, as if it were looking down on this lake especially; and we had our first, but a partial view of Ktaadn, its summit veiled in clouds, like a dark isthmus in that quarter, connecting the heavens with the earth. After two miles of smooth rowing across this lake, we found ourselves in the river again, which was a continuous rapid for one mile, to the dam, requiring all the strength and skill of our boatmen to pole up it.

This dam is a quite important and expensive work for this country, whither cattle and horses cannot penetrate in the summer, raising the whole river ten feet, and flooding, as they said, some sixty square miles by means of the innumerable lakes with which the river connects. It is a lofty and solid structure, with sloping piers, some distance above, made of frames of logs filled with stones, to break the ice.[1] Here every log pays toll as it passes through the sluices.

We filed into the rude loggers' camp at this place, such as I have described, without ceremony, and the cook, at that moment the sole occupant, at once set about preparing tea for his visitors. His fireplace, which the rain had converted into a mud-puddle, was soon blazing again, and we sat down on the log benches around it to dry us. On the well-flattened and somewhat faded beds of arbor-vitæ leaves, which stretched on either hand under the eaves behind us, lay an odd leaf of the Bible, some genealogical chapter out of the Old Testament; and, half buried by the leaves, we found Emerson's Address on West India Emancipation, which had been left here formerly by one of our company, and *had made two converts to the Liberty party here*, as I was told; also, an odd number of the *Westminster Review*, for 1834, and a pamphlet entitled 'History of the Erection of the Monument on the Grave of Myron Holly.' This was the readable or reading matter in a lumberer's camp in the Maine woods, thirty miles from a road, which would be given up to the bears in a fortnight. These things were well thumbed and soiled. This gang was headed by one John Morrison, a good specimen of a Yankee; and was necessarily composed of men not bred to the business of dam-building, but who were jacks-at-all-trades, handy with the axe, and other simple implements, and well skilled in wood and water craft. We had hot cakes for our supper even here, white as snow-balls, but without butter, and the never-failing sweet cakes, with which we filled our pockets, foreseeing that we should not soon meet with the like again. Such delicate puffballs seemed a singular diet for back-woodsmen. There was also tea without milk, sweetened with molasses. And so, exchanging a word with John Morrison and his gang when we had returned to the shore, and also exchanging our batteau for a better still, we made haste to improve the little daylight that remained. This camp, exactly twenty-nine miles from Mattawamkeag Point by the way we had come, and about one hundred from Bangor by the river, was the last human habitation of any kind in this direction. Beyond, there was no trail, and the river and lakes, by batteaux and canoes, was

---

[1] Even the Jesuit missionaries, accustomed to the St. Lawrence and other rivers of Canada, in their first expeditions to the Abenaquinois, speak of rivers *ferrées de rochers*, shod with rocks. See also No. 10 *Relations,* for 1647, p. 185.

considered the only practicable route. We were about thirty miles by the river from the summit of Ktaadn, which was in sight, though not more than twenty, perhaps, in a straight line.

It being about the full of the moon, and a warm and pleasant evening, we decided to row five miles by moonlight to the head of the North Twin Lake, lest the wind should rise on the morrow. After one mile of river, or what the boatmen call 'thoroughfare' — for the river becomes at length only the connecting link between the lakes — and some slight rapid which had been mostly made smooth water by the dam, we entered the North Twin Lake just after sundown, and steered across for the river 'thoroughfare,' four miles distant. This is a noble sheet of water, where one may get the impression which a new country and a 'lake of the woods' are fitted to create. There was the smoke of no log hut nor camp of any kind to greet us, still less was any lover of nature or musing traveler watching our batteau from the distant hills; not even the Indian hunter was there, for he rarely climbs them, but hugs the river like ourselves. No face welcomed us but the fine fantastic sprays of free and happy evergreen trees, waving one above another in their ancient home. At first the red clouds hung over the western shore as gorgeously as if over a city, and the lake lay open to the light with even a civilized aspect, as if expecting trade and commerce, and towns and villas. We could distinguish the inlet to the South Twin, which is said to be the larger, where the shore was misty and blue, and it was worth the while to look thus through a narrow opening across the entire expanse of a concealed lake to its own yet more dim and distant shore. The shores rose gently to ranges of low hills covered with forests; and though, in fact, the most valuable white-pine timber, even about this lake, had been culled out, this would never have been suspected by the voyager. The impression, which indeed corresponded with the fact, was, as if we were upon a high table-land between the States and Canada, the northern side of which is drained by the St. John and Chaudière, the southern by the Penobscot and Kennebec. There was no bold, mountainous shore, as we might have expected, but only isolated hills and mountains rising here and there from the plateau. The country is an archipelago of lakes — the lake-country of New England. Their levels vary but a few feet, and the boatmen, by short portages, or by none at all, pass easily from one to another. They say that at very high water the Penobscot and the Kennebec flow into each other, or at any rate, that you may lie with your face in the one and your toes in the other. Even the Penobscot and St. John have been connected by a canal, so that the lumber of the Allegash, instead of going down the St. John, comes down the Penobscot; and the Indian's tradition, that the Penobscot once ran both ways for his convenience, is, in one sense, partially realized today.

None of our party but McCauslin had been above this lake, so we trusted to him to pilot us, and we could not but confess the importance of a pilot on these waters. While it is river, you will not easily forget which way is up-stream; but when you enter a lake, the river is completely lost, and you scan the distant shores in vain to find where it comes in. A stranger is, for the time at least, lost, and must set about a voyage of discovery first of all to find the river. To follow the windings of the shore when the lake is ten miles, or even more, in length, and of an irregularity which will not soon be mapped, is a wearisome voyage, and will spend his time and his provisions. They tell a story of a gang of experienced woodmen sent to a location on this stream, who were thus lost in the wilderness of lakes. They cut their way through thickets, and carried their baggage and their boats over from lake to lake, sometimes several miles. They carried into Millinocket Lake, which is on another stream, and is ten miles square, and contains a hundred islands. They explored its shores thoroughly, and then carried into another, and another, and it was a week of toil and anxiety before they found the Penobscot River again, and then their provisions were exhausted, and they were obliged to return.

While Uncle George steered for a small island near the head of the lake, now just visible, like a speck on the water, we rowed by turns swiftly over its surface, singing such boat songs as we could remember. The shores seemed at an indefinite distance in the moonlight. Occasionally we paused in our singing and rested on our oars, while we listened to hear if the wolves howled, for this is a common serenade, and my companions affirmed that it was the most dismal and unearthly of sounds; but we heard none this time. If we did not *hear*, however, we did *listen*, not without a reasonable expectation; that at least I have to tell — only some utterly uncivilized, big-throated owl hooted loud and dismally in the drear and boughy wilderness, plainly not nervous about his solitary life, nor afraid to hear the echoes of his voice there. We remembered also that possibly moose were silently watching us from the distant coves, or some surly bear or timid caribou had been startled by our singing. It was with new emphasis that we sang there the Canadian boat song —

> 'Row, brothers, row, the stream runs fast,
> The rapids are near and the daylight's past!'

which describes precisely our own adventure, and was inspired by the experience of a similar kind of life — for the rapids were ever near, and the daylight long past; the woods on shore looked dim, and many an Utawas' tide here emptied into the lake.

> 'Why should we yet our sail unfurl?
> There is not a breath the blue wave to curl!
> But, when the wind blows off the shore,
> Oh, sweetly we'll rest our weary oar.'

> 'Utawas' tide! this trembling moon
> Shall see us float o'er thy surges soon.'

At last we glided past the 'green isle,' which had been our landmark, all joining in the chorus; as if by the watery links of rivers and of lakes we were about to float over unmeasured zones of earth, bound on unimaginable adventures —

> 'Saint of this green isle! hear our prayers,
> 'Oh, grant us cool heavens and favoring airs!'

About nine o'clock we reached the river, and ran our boat into a natural haven between some rocks, and drew her out on the sand. This camping-ground McCauslin had been familiar with in his lumbering days, and he now struck it unerringly in the moonlight, and we heard the sound of the rill which would supply us with cool water emptying into the lake. The first business was to make a fire, an operation which was a little delayed by the wetness of the fuel and the ground, owing to the heavy showers of the afternoon. The fire is the main comfort of the camp, whether in summer or winter, and is about as ample at one season as at another. It is as well for cheerfulness as for warmth and dryness. It forms one side of the camp; one bright side at any rate. Some were dispersed to fetch in dead trees and boughs, while Uncle George felled the birches and beeches which stood convenient, and soon we had a fire some ten feet long by three or four high, which rapidly dried the sand before it. This was calculated to burn all night. We next proceeded to pitch our tent; which operation was performed by sticking our two spike-poles into the ground in a slanting direction, about ten feet apart, for rafters, and then drawing our cotton cloth over them, and tying it down at the ends, leaving it open in front, shed-fashion. But this evening the wind carried the sparks on to the tent and burned it. So we hastily drew up the batteau just within the edge of the woods before the fire, and propping up one side three or four feet high, spread the tent on the ground to lie on; and with the corner of a blanket, or what more or less we could get to put over us, lay down with our heads and bodies under the boat, and our feet and legs on the sand toward the fire. At first we lay awake, talking of our course, and finding ourselves in so convenient a posture for studying the heavens, with the moon and stars shining in our faces, our conversation naturally turned upon astronomy, and we recounted by turns the most interesting discoveries in that science. But at length we composed ourselves seriously to sleep. It was interesting, when awakened at midnight, to watch the grotesque and fiend-like forms and motions of some one of the party, who, not being able to sleep, had got up silently to arouse the fire, and add fresh fuel, for a change; now stealthily lugging a dead tree from out the dark, and heaving it on, now stirring up the embers with his fork, or tiptoeing about to observe the stars, watched, perchance, by half the prostrate party in breathless silence; so much the more intense because they were awake, while each supposed his neighbor sound asleep. Thus aroused, I, too, brought fresh fuel to the fire, and then rambled along the sandy shore in the moonlight, hoping to meet a moose come down to drink, or else a wolf. The little rill tinkled the louder, and peopled all the wilderness for me; and the glassy smoothness of the sleeping lake, laving the shores of a new world, with the dark, fantastic rocks rising here and there from its surface, made a scene not easily described. It has left such an impression of stern, yet gentle, wildness on my memory as will not soon be effaced. Not far from midnight we were one after another awakened by rain falling on our extremities; and as each was made aware of the fact by cold or wet, he drew a long sigh and then drew up his legs, until gradually we had all sidled round from lying at right angles with the boat, till our bodies formed an acute angle with it, and were wholly protected. When next we awoke, the moon and stars were shining again, and there were signs of dawn in the east. I have been thus particular in order to convey some idea of a night in the woods.

We had soon launched and loaded our boat, and, leaving our fire blazing, were off again before breakfast. The lumberers rarely trouble themselves to put out their fires, such is the dampness of the primitive forest; and this is one cause, no doubt, of the frequent fires in Maine, of which we hear so much on smoky days in Massachusetts. The forests are held cheap after the white pine has been culled out; and the explorers and hunters pray for rain only to clear the atmosphere of smoke. The woods were so wet today, however, that there was no danger of our fire spreading. After poling up half a mile of river, or thoroughfare, we rowed a mile across the foot of Pamadumcook Lake, which is the name given on the map to this whole chain of lakes, as if there was but one, though they are, in each instance, distinctly separated by a reach of the river, with its narrow and rocky channel and its rapids. This lake, which is one of the largest, stretched northwest ten miles, to hills and mountains in the distance. McCauslin pointed to some distant, and as yet inaccessible, forests of white pine, on the sides of a mountain in that direction. The Joe Merry Lakes, which lay between us and Moose-head, on the west, were recently, if they are not still, 'surrounded by some of the best timbered land in the State.' By another thoroughfare we passed into Deep Cove, a part of the same lake, which makes up two miles, toward the northeast, and rowing two miles across this, by another short thoroughfare, entered Ambejijis Lake.

At the entrance to a lake we sometimes observed what is technically called 'fencing-stuff,' or the unhewn timbers of which booms are formed, either secured together in the water, or laid up on the rocks and lashed to trees, for spring use. But it was always startling to discover so plain a trail of civilized man there. I remember that I was strangely affected, when we were returning, by the sight of a ring-bolt well drilled into a rock, and fastened with lead, at the head of this solitary Ambejijis Lake.

It was easy to see that driving logs must be an exciting as well as arduous and dangerous business. All winter long the logger goes on piling up the trees which he has trimmed and hauled in some dry ravine at the head of a stream, and then in the spring he stands on the bank and whistles for Rain and Thaw, ready to wring the perspiration out of his shirt to swell the tide, till suddenly, with a whoop and halloo from him, shutting his eyes, as if to bid farewell to the existing state of things, a fair proportion of his winter's work goes scrambling down the country, followed by his faithful dogs, Thaw and Rain and Freshet and Wind, the whole pack in full cry, toward the Orono Mills. Every log is marked with the owner's name, cut in the sapwood with an axe or bored with an auger, so deep as not to be worn off in the driving, and yet not so as to injure the timber; and it requires considerable ingenuity to invent new and simple marks where there are so many owners. They have quite an alphabet of their own, which only the practiced can read. One of my companions read off from his memorandum book some marks of his own logs, among which there were crosses, belts, crow's feet, girdles, etc., as, 'Y — girdle — crow-foot,' and various other devices. When the logs have run the gauntlet of innumerable

rapids and falls, each on its own account, with more or less jamming and
bruising, those bearing various owners' marks being mixed up together
— since all must take advantage of the same freshet — they are collected together at the heads of the lakes, and surrounded by a boom
fence of floating logs, to prevent their being dispersed by the wind, and
are thus towed all together, like a flock of sheep, across the lake, where
there is no current, by a windlass, or boom-head, such as we sometimes
saw standing on an island or headland, and, if circumstances permit,
with the aid of sails and oars. Sometimes, notwithstanding, the logs
are dispersed over many miles of lake surface in a few hours by winds
and freshets, and thrown up on distant shores, where the driver can
pick up only one or two at a time, and return with them to the thoroughfare; and before he gets his flock well through Ambejijis or Pamadumcook, he makes many a wet and uncomfortable camp on the shore. He
must be able to navigate a log as if it were a canoe, and be as indifferent
to cold and wet as a muskrat. He uses a few efficient tools — a lever
commonly of rock maple, six or seven feet long, with a stout spike in it,
strongly ferruled on, and a long spike-pole, with a screw at the end of
the spike to make it hold. The boys along shore learn to walk on floating logs as city boys on sidewalks. Sometimes the logs are thrown up
on rocks in such positions as to be irrecoverable but by another freshet
as high, or they jam together at rapids and falls, and accumulate in vast
piles, which the driver must start at the risk of his life. Such is the
lumber business, which depends on many accidents, as the early freezing of the rivers, that the teams may get up in season, a sufficient freshet
in the spring, to fetch the logs down, and many others.[1] I quote
Michaux on Lumbering on the Kennebec, then the source of the best
white pine lumber carried to England. 'The persons engaged in this
branch of industry are generally emigrants from New Hampshire....
In the summer they unite in small companies, and traverse these vast
solitudes in every direction, to ascertain the places in which the pines
abound. After cutting the grass and converting it into hay for the
nourishment of the cattle to be employed in their labor, they return
home. In the beginning of the winter they enter the forests again, establish themselves in huts covered with the bark of the canoe-birch,
or the arbor-vitæ; and, though the cold is so intense that the mercury

---

[1] 'A steady current or pitch of water is preferable to one either rising or diminishing;
as, when rising rapidly, the water at the middle of the river is considerably higher than
at the shores — so much so as to be distinctly perceived by the eye of a spectator on the
banks, presenting an appearance like a turnpike road. The lumber, therefore, is
always sure to incline from the centre of the channel toward either shore.' — Springer.

sometimes remains for several weeks from 40° to 50° [Fahr.] below the point of congelation, they persevere, with unabated courage, in their work.' According to Springer, the company consists of choppers, swampers — who make roads — barker and loader, teamster, and cook. 'When the trees are felled, they cut them into logs from fourteen to eighteen feet long, and, by means of their cattle, which they employ with great dexterity, drag them to the river, and, after stamping on them a mark of property, roll them on its frozen bosom. At the breaking of the ice, in the spring, they float down with the current.... The logs that are not drawn the first year,' adds Michaux, 'are attacked by large worms, which form holes about two lines in diameter, in every direction; but, if stripped of their bark, they will remain uninjured for thirty years.'

Ambejijis, this quiet Sunday morning, struck me as the most beautiful lake we had seen. It is said to be one of the deepest. We had the fairest view of Joe Merry, Double Top, and Ktaadn, from its surface. The summit of the latter had a singularly flat, table-land appearance, like a short highway, where a demigod might be let down to take a turn or two in an afternoon, to settle his dinner. We rowed a mile and a half to near the head of the lake, and, pushing through a field of lily-pads, landed, to cook our breakfast, by the side of a large rock, known to McCauslin. Our breakfast consisted of tea, with hard-bread and pork and fried salmon, which we ate with forks neatly whittled from alder twigs, which grew there, off strips of birch-bark for plates. The tea was black tea, without milk to color or sugar to sweeten it, and two tin dippers were our tea-cups. This beverage is as indispensable to the loggers as to any gossiping old women in the land, and they, no doubt, derive great comfort from it. Here was the site of an old logger's camp, remembered by McCauslin, now overgrown with weeds and bushes. In the midst of a dense underwood we noticed a whole brick, on a rock, in a small run, clean and red and square as in a brick-yard, which had been brought thus far formerly for tamping. Some of us afterward regretted that we had not carried this on with us to the top of the mountain, to be left there for our mark. It would certainly have been a simple evidence of civilized man. McCauslin said that large wooden crosses, made of oak, still sound, were sometimes found standing in this wilderness, which were set up by the first Catholic missionaries who came through to the Kennebec.

In the next nine miles, which were the extent of our voyage, and which it took us the rest of the day to get over, we rowed across several small lakes, poled up numerous rapids and thoroughfares, and carried over four portages. I will give the names and distances, for the benefit of future tourists. First, after leaving Ambejijis Lake, we had a quarter of a mile of rapids to the portage, or carry of ninety rods around Ambejijis Falls; then a mile and a half through Passamagamet Lake, which is narrow and river-like, to the falls of the same name — Ambejijis stream coming in on the right; then two miles through Katepskonegan Lake to the portage of ninety rods around Katepskonegan Falls, which name signifies 'carrying-place' — Passamagamet stream coming in on the left; then three miles through Pockwockomus Lake, a slight expansion of the river, to the portage of forty rods around the falls of the same name — Katepskonegan stream coming in on the left; then three quarters of a mile through Aboljacarmegus Lake, similar to the last, to the portage of forty rods around the falls of the same name; then half a mile of rapid water to the Sowadnehunk deadwater, and the Aboljacknagesic stream.

This is generally the order of names as you ascend the river: First, the lake, or, if there is no expansion, the deadwater; then the falls; then the stream emptying into the lake, or river above, all of the same name. First we came to Passamagamet Lake, then to Passamagamet Falls, then to Passamagamet Stream, emptying in. This order and identity of names, it will be perceived, is quite philosophical, since the deadwater or lake is always at least partially produced by the stream emptying in above; and the first fall below, which is the outlet of that lake, and where that tributary water makes its first plunge, also naturally bears the same name.

At the portage around Ambejijis Falls I observed a pork-barrel on the shore, with a hole eight or nine inches square cut in one side, which was set against an upright rock; but the bears, without turning or upsetting the barrel, had gnawed a hole in the opposite side, which looked exactly like an enormous rat-hole, big enough to put their heads in; and at the bottom of the barrel were still left a few mangled and slabbered slices of pork. It is usual for the lumberers to leave such supplies as they cannot conveniently carry along with them at carries or camps, to which the next comers do not scruple to help themselves, they being the property, commonly, not of an individual, but a company, who can afford to deal liberally.

I will describe particularly how we got over some of these portages and rapids, in order that the reader may get an idea of the boatman's life. At Ambejijis Falls, for instance, there was the roughest path imaginable cut through the woods; at first up hill, at an angle of nearly forty-five degrees, over rocks and logs without end. This was the manner of the portage. We first carried over our baggage, and deposited it on the shore at the other end; then, returning to the batteau, we dragged it up the hill by the painter, and onward, with frequent pauses, over half the portage. But this was a bungling way, and would soon have worn out the boat. Commonly, three men walk over with a batteau weighing from three to five or six hundred pounds on their heads and shoulders, the tallest standing under the middle of the boat, which is turned over, and one at each end, or else there are two at the bows. More cannot well take hold at once. But this requires some practice, as well as strength, and is in any case extremely laborious, and wearing to the constitution, to follow. We were, on the whole, rather an invalid party, and could render our boatmen but little assistance. Our two men at length took the batteau upon their shoulders, and, while two of us steadied it, to prevent it from rocking and wearing into their shoulders, on which they placed their hats folded, walked bravely over the remaining distance, with two or three pauses. In the same manner they accomplished the other portages. With this crushing weight they must climb and stumble along over fallen trees and slippery rocks of all sizes, where those who walked by the sides were continually brushed off, such was the narrowness of the path. But we were fortunate not to have to cut our path in the first place. Before we launched our boat, we scraped the bottom smooth again, with our knives, where it had rubbed on the rocks, to save friction.

To avoid the difficulties of the portage, our men determined to 'warp up' the Passamagamet Falls; so while the rest walked over the portage with the baggage, I remained in the batteau, to assist in warping up. We were soon in the midst of the rapids, which were more swift and tumultuous than any we had poled up, and had turned to the side of the stream for the purpose of warping, when the boatmen, who felt some pride in their skill, and were ambitious to do something more than usual, for my benefit, as I surmised, took one more view of the rapids, or rather the falls; and, in answer to our question, whether we couldn't get up there, the other answered that he guessed he'd try it. So we pushed again into the midst of the stream, and began to struggle with the current. I sat in the middle of the boat to trim it, moving slightly to the right or left as it grazed a rock. With an uncertain and wavering motion we wound and bolted our way up, until the bow was actually raised two feet above the stern at the steepest pitch; and then, when everything depended upon his exertions, the bowman's pole snapped in two; but before he had time to take the spare one, which I reached him, he had saved himself with the fragment upon a rock; and so we got up by a hair's breadth; and Uncle George exclaimed that that was never done before, and he had not tried it if he had not known whom he had got in the bow, nor he in the bow, if he had not known him in the stern. At this place there was a regular portage cut through the woods, and our boatmen had never known a batteau to ascend the falls. As near as I can remember, there was a perpendicular fall here, at the worst place of the whole Penobscot River, two or three feet at least. I could not sufficiently admire the skill and coolness with which they performed this feat, never speaking to each other. The bowman, not looking behind, but knowing exactly what the other is about, works as if he worked alone. Now sounding in vain for a bottom in fifteen feet of water, while the boat falls back several rods, held straight only with the greatest skill and exertion; or, while the sternman obstinately holds his ground, like a turtle, the bowman springs from side to side with wonderful suppleness and dexterity, scanning the rapids and the rocks with a thousand eyes; and now, having got a bite at last, with a lusty shove, which makes his pole bend and quiver, and the whole boat tremble, he gains a few feet upon the river. To add to the danger, the poles are liable at any time to be caught between the rocks, and wrenched out of their hands, leaving them at the mercy of the rapids — the rocks, as it were, lying in wait, like so many alligators, to catch them in their teeth, and jerk them from your hands, before you have stolen an effectual shove against their palates. The pole is set close to the boat, and the prow is made to overshoot, and just turn the corners of the rocks, in the very teeth of the rapids. Nothing but the length and lightness, and the slight draught of the batteau, enables them to make any headway. The bowman must quickly choose his course; there is no time to deliberate. Frequently the boat is shoved between rocks where both sides touch, and the waters on either hand are a perfect maelstrom.

Half a mile above this two of us tried our hands at poling up a slight rapid; and we were just surmounting the last difficulty, when an unlucky rock confounded our calculations; and while the batteau was sweeping round irrecoverably amid the whirlpool, we were obliged to resign the poles to more skillful hands.

Katepskonegan is one of the shallowest and weediest of the lakes, and looked as if it might abound in pickerel. The falls of the same name, where we stopped to dine, are considerable and quite picturesque. Here Uncle George had seen trout caught by the barrelful; but they would not rise to our bait at this hour. Halfway over this carry, thus far in the Maine wilderness on its way to the Provinces, we noticed a large, flaming, Oak Hall handbill, about two feet long, wrapped round the trunk of a pine, from which the bark had been stripped, and to which it was fast glued by the pitch. This should be recorded among the advantages of this mode of advertising, that so, possibly, even the bears and wolves, moose, deer, otter, and beaver, not to mention the Indian, may learn where they can fit themselves according to the latest fashion, or, at least, recover some of their own lost garments. We christened this the Oak Hall carry.

The forenoon was as serene and placid on this wild stream in the woods, as we are apt to imagine that Sunday in summer usually is in Massachusetts. We were occasionally startled by the scream of a bald eagle, sailing over the stream in front of our batteau; or of the fish hawks on whom he levies his contributions. There were, at intervals, small meadows of a few acres on the sides of the stream, waving with uncut grass, which attracted the attention of our boatmen, who regretted that they were not nearer to their clearings, and calculated how many stacks they might cut. Two or three men sometimes spend the summer by themselves, cutting the grass in these meadows, to sell to the loggers in the winter, since it will fetch a higher price on the spot than in any market in the State. On a small isle, covered with this kind of rush, or cut-grass, on which we landed to consult about our further course, we noticed the recent track of a moose, a large, roundish hole in the soft, wet ground, evincing the great size and weight of the animal that made it. They are fond of the water, and visit all these island meadows, swimming as easily from island to island as they make their way through the thickets on land. Now and then we passed what McCauslin called a pokelogan, an Indian term for what the drivers might have reason to call a poke-logs-in, an inlet that leads nowhere. If you get in, you have got to get out again the same way. These, and the frequent 'runrounds' which come into the river again, would embarrass an inexperienced voyager not a little.

The carry around Pockwockomus Falls was exceedingly rough and rocky, the batteau having to be lifted directly from the water up four or five feet on to a rock, and launched again down a similar bank. The rocks on this portage were covered with the *dents* made by the spikes in the lumberers' boots while staggering over under the weight of their batteaux; and you could see where the surface of some large rocks on which they had rested their batteaux was worn quite smooth with use. As it was, we had carried over but half the usual portage at this place for this stage of the water, and launched our boat in the smooth wave just curving to the fall, prepared to struggle with the most violent rapid we had to encounter. The rest of the party walked over the remainder of the portage, while I remained with the boatmen to assist in warping up. One had to hold the boat while the others got in to prevent it from going over the falls. When we had pushed up the rapids as far as possible, keeping close to the shore, Tom seized the painter and leaped out upon a rock just visible in the water, but he lost his footing, notwithstanding his spiked boots, and was instantly amid the rapids; but recovering himself by good luck, and reaching another rock, he passed the painter to me, who had followed him, and took his place again in the bows. Leaping from rock to rock in the shoal water, close to the shore, and now and then getting a bite with the rope round an upright one, I held the boat while one reset his pole, and then all three forced it upward against any rapid. This was 'warping up.' When a part of us walked round at such a place, we generally took the precaution to take out the most valuable part of the baggage for fear of being swamped.

As we poled up a swift rapid for half a mile above Aboljacarmegus Falls, some of the party read their own marks on the huge logs which lay piled up high and dry on the rocks on either hand, the relics probably of a jam which had taken place here in the Great Freshet in the spring. Many of these would have to wait for another great freshet, perchance, if they lasted so long, before they could be got off. It was singular enough to meet with property of theirs which they had never seen, and where they had never been before, thus detained by freshets and rocks when on its way to them. Methinks that must be where all my property lies, cast up on the rocks on some distant and unexplored stream, and waiting for an unheard-of freshet to fetch it down. O make haste, ye gods, with your winds and rains, and start the jam before it rots!

The last half mile carried us to the Sowadnehunk Deadwater, so called from the stream of the same name, signifying 'running between mountains,' an important tributary which comes in a mile above. Here we decided to camp, about twenty miles from the Dam, at the mouth of Murch Brook and the Aboljacknagesic, mountain streams, broad off from Ktaadn, and about a dozen miles from its summit, having made fifteen miles this day.

We had been told by McCauslin that we should here find trout enough; so, while some prepared the camp, the rest fell to fishing. Seizing the birch poles which some party of Indians, or white hunters, had left on the shore, and baiting our hooks with pork, and with trout, as soon as they were caught, we cast our lines into the mouth of the Aboljacknagesic, a clear, swift, shallow stream, which came in from Ktaadn. Instantly a shoal of white chivin (*Leuciscus pulchellus*), silvery roaches, cousin-trout, or what not, large and small, prowling thereabouts, fell upon our bait, and one after another were landed amidst the bushes. Anon their cousins, the true trout, took their turn, and alternately the speckled trout, and the silvery roaches, swallowed the bait as fast as we could throw in; and the finest specimens of both that I have ever seen, the largest one weighing three pounds, were heaved upon the shore, though at first in vain, to wriggle down into the water again, for we stood in the boat; but soon we learned to remedy this evil; for one, who had lost his hook, stood on shore to catch them as they fell in a perfect shower around him — sometimes, wet and slippery, full in his face and bosom, as his arms were outstretched to receive them. While yet alive, before their tints had faded, they glistened like the fairest flowers, the product of primitive rivers; and he could hardly trust his senses, as he stood over them, that these jewels should have swam away in that Aboljacknagesic water for so long, so many dark ages; — these bright fluviatile flowers, seen of Indians only, made beautiful, the Lord only knows why, to swim there! I could understand better for this, the truth of mythology, the fables of Proteus, and all those beautiful sea-monsters — how all history, indeed, put to a terrestrial use, is mere history; but put to a celestial, is mythology always.

But there is the rough voice of Uncle George, who commands at the frying-pan, to send over what you've got, and then you may stay till morning. The pork sizzles and cries for fish. Luckily for the foolish race, and this particularly foolish generation of trout, the night shut down at last, not a little deepened by the dark side of Ktaadn, which, like a permanent shadow, reared itself from the eastern bank. Lescarbot, writing in 1609, tells us that the Sieur Champdoré, who, with one of the people of the Sieur de Monts, ascended some fifty leagues up the St. John in 1608, found the fish so plenty, 'qu'en mettant la chaudière sur le feu ils en avoient pris suffisamment pour eux disner avant que l'eau fust chaude.' Their descendants here are no less numerous. So we accompanied Tom into the woods to cut cedar twigs for our bed. While he went ahead with the axe and lopped off the smallest twigs of the flat-leaved cedar, the arbor-vitæ of the gardens, we gathered them up, and returned with them to the boat, until it was loaded. Our bed was made with as much care and skill as a roof is shingled; beginning at the foot, and laying the twig end of the cedar upward, we advanced to the head, a course at a time, thus successively covering the stub-ends, and producing a soft and level bed. For us six it was about ten feet long by six in breadth. This time we lay under our tent, having pitched it more prudently with reference to the wind and the flame, and the usual huge fire blazed in front. Supper was eaten off a large log, which some freshet had thrown up. This night we had a dish of arbor-vitæ or cedar tea, which the lumberer sometimes uses when other herbs fail,

> 'A quart of arbor-vitæ,
> To make him strong and mighty' —

but I had no wish to repeat the experiment. It had too medicinal a taste for my palate. There was the skeleton of a moose here, whose bones some Indian hunters had picked on this very spot.

In the night I dreamed of trout-fishing; and, when at length I awoke, it seemed a fable that this painted fish swam there so near my couch, and rose to our hooks the last evening, and I doubted if I had not dreamed it all. So I arose before dawn to test its truth, while my companions were still sleeping. There stood Ktaadn with distinct and cloudless outline in the moonlight; and the rippling of the rapids was the only sound to break the stillness. Standing on the shore, I once more cast my line into the stream, and found the dream to be real and the fable true. The speckled trout and silvery roach, like flying-fish, sped swiftly through the moonlight air, describing bright arcs on the dark side of Ktaadn, until moonlight, now fading into daylight, brought satiety to my mind, and the minds of my companions, who had joined me.

By six o'clock, having mounted our packs and a good blanketful of trout, ready dressed, and swung up such baggage and provision as we wished to leave behind upon the tops of saplings, to be out of the reach of bears, we started for the summit of the mountain, distant, as Uncle George said the boatmen called it, about four miles, but as I judged, and as it proved, nearer fourteen. He had never been any nearer the mountain than this, and there was not the slightest trace of man to guide us farther in this direction. At first, pushing a few rods up the Aboljacknagesic, or 'open-land stream,' we fastened our batteau to a tree, and traveled up the north side, through burnt lands, now partially overgrown with young aspens and other shrubbery; but soon, recrossing this stream, where it was about fifty or sixty feet wide, upon a jam of logs and rocks — and you could cross it by this means almost anywhere — we struck at once for the highest peak, over a mile or more of comparatively open land, still very gradually ascending the while. Here it fell to my lot, as the oldest mountain-climber, to take the lead. So, scanning the woody side of the mountain, which lay still at an indefinite distance, stretched out some seven or eight miles in length before us, we determined to steer directly for the base of the highest peak, leaving a large slide, by which, as I have since learned, some of our predecessors ascended, on our left. This course would lead us parallel to a dark seam in the forest, which marked the bed of a torrent, and over a slight spur, which extended southward from the main mountain, from whose bare summit we could get an outlook over the country, and climb directly up the peak, which would then be close at hand. Seen from this point, a bare ridge at the extremity of the open land, Ktaadn presented a different aspect from any mountain I have seen, there being a greater proportion of naked rock rising abruptly from the forest; and we looked up at this blue barrier as if it were some fragment of a wall which anciently bounded the earth in that direction. Setting the compass for a northeast course, which was the bearing of the southern base of the highest peak, we were soon buried in the woods.

We soon began to meet with traces of bears and moose, and those of rabbits were everywhere visible. The tracks of moose, more or less recent, to speak literally, covered every square rod on the sides of the mountain; and these animals are probably more numerous there now than ever before, being driven into this wilderness, from all sides, by the settlements. The track of a full-grown moose is like that of a cow, or larger, and of the young, like that of a calf. Sometimes we found ourselves travelling in faint paths, which they had made, like cow-paths in the woods, only far more indistinct, being rather openings, affording imperfect vistas through the dense underwood, than trodden paths; and everywhere the twigs had been browsed by them, clipped as smoothly as if by a knife. The bark of trees was stripped up by them to the height of eight or nine feet, in long, narrow strips, an inch wide, still showing the distinct marks of their teeth. We expected nothing less than to meet a herd of them every moment, and our Nimrod held his shooting-iron in readiness; but we did not go out of our way to look for them, and, though numerous, they are so wary that the un-skillful hunter might range the forest a long time before he could get sight of one. They are sometimes dangerous to encounter, and will not turn out for the hunter, but furiously rush upon him and trample him to death, unless he is lucky enough to avoid them by dodging round a tree. The largest are nearly as large as a horse, and weigh sometimes one thousand pounds; and it is said that they can step over a five-foot gate in their ordinary walk. They are described as exceedingly awkward-looking animals, with their long legs and short bodies, making a ludicrous figure when in full run, but making great headway, nevertheless. It seemed a mystery to us how they could thread these woods, which it required all our suppleness to accomplish — climbing, stooping, and winding, alternately. They are said to drop their long and branching horns, which usually spread five or six feet, on their backs, and make their way easily by the weight of their bodies. Our boatmen said, but I know not with how much truth, that their horns are apt to be gnawed away by vermin while they sleep. Their flesh, which is more like beef than venison, is common in Bangor market.

We had proceeded on thus seven or eight miles, till about noon, with frequent pauses to refresh the weary ones, crossing a considerable mountain stream, which we conjectured to be Murch Brook, at whose mouth we had camped, all the time in woods, without having once seen the summit, and rising very gradually, when the boatmen beginning to despair a little, and fearing that we were leaving the mountain on one side of us, for they had not entire faith in the compass, McCauslin climbed a tree, from the top of which he could see the peak, when it appeared that we had not swerved from a right line, the compass down below still ranging with his arm, which pointed to the summit. By the side of a cool mountain rill, amid the woods, where the water began to partake of the purity and transparency of the air, we stopped to cook some of our fishes, which we had brought thus far in order to save our hard-bread and pork, in the use of which we had put ourselves on short allowance. We soon had a fire blazing, and stood around it, under the damp and sombre forest of firs and birches, each with a sharpened stick, three or four feet in length, upon which he had spitted his trout, or roach, previously well gashed and salted, our sticks radiating like the spokes of a wheel from one centre, and each crowding his particular fish into the most desirable exposure, not with the truest regard always to his neighbor's rights. Thus we regaled our, selves, drinking meanwhile at the spring, till one man's pack, at least, was considerably lightened, when we again took up our line of march.

At length we reached an elevation sufficiently bare to afford a view of the summit, still distant and blue, almost as if retreating from us. A torrent, which proved to be the same we had crossed, was seen tumbling down in front, literally from out of the clouds. But this glimpse at our whereabouts was soon lost, and we were buried in the woods again. The wood was chiefly yellow birch, spruce, fir, mountain-ash, or round-wood, as the Maine people call it, and moose-wood. It was the worst kind of travelling; sometimes like the densest scrub oak patches with us. The cornel, or bunch-berries, were very abundant, as well as Solomon's-seal and moose-berries. Blueberries were distributed along our whole route; and in one place the bushes were drooping with the weight of the fruit, still as fresh as ever. It was the 7th of September. Such patches afforded a grateful repast, and served to bait the tired party forward. When any lagged behind, the cry of 'blueberries' was most effectual to bring them up. Even at this elevation we passed through a moose-yard, formed by a large flat rock, four or five rods square, where they tread down the snow in winter. At length, fearing that if we held the direct course to the summit, we should not find any water near our camping-ground, we gradually swerved to the west, till, at four o'clock, we struck again the torrent which I have mentioned, and here, in view of the summit, the weary party decided to camp that night.

While my companions were seeking a suitable spot for this purpose, I improved the little daylight that was left in climbing the mountain alone. We were in a deep and narrow ravine, sloping up to the clouds, at an angle of nearly forty-five degrees, and hemmed in by walls of rock, which were at first covered with low trees, then with impenetrable thickets of scraggy birches and spruce trees, and with moss, but at last bare of all vegetation but lichens, and almost continually draped in clouds. Following up the course of the torrent which occupied this — and I mean to lay some emphasis on this word *up* — pulling myself up by the side of perpendicular falls of twenty or thirty feet, by the roots of firs and birches, and then, perhaps, walking a level rod or two in the thin stream, for it took up the whole road, ascending by huge steps, as it were, a giant's stairway, down which a river flowed, I had soon cleared the trees, and paused on the successive shelves, to look back over the country. The torrent was from fifteen to thirty feet wide, without a tributary, and seemingly not diminishing in breadth as I advanced; but still it came rushing and roaring down, with a copious tide, over and amidst masses of bare rock, from

the very clouds, as though a waterspout had just burst over the mountain. Leaving this at last, I began to work my way, scarcely less arduous than Satan's anciently through Chaos, up the nearest though not
the highest peak, at first scrambling on all fours over the tops of ancient black spruce trees (*Abies nigra*), old as the flood, from two to ten
or twelve feet in height, their tops flat and spreading, and their foliage blue, and nipped with cold, as if for centuries they had ceased growing upward against the bleak sky, the solid cold. I walked some good
rods erect upon the tops of these trees, which were overgrown with
moss and mountain cranberries. It seemed that in the course of time
they had filled up the intervals between the huge rocks, and the cold
wind had uniformly levelled all over. Here the principle of vegetation
was hard put to it. There was apparently a belt of this kind running
quite round the mountain, though, perhaps, nowhere so remarkable
as here. Once, slumping through, I looked down ten feet, into a dark and
cavernous region, and saw the stem of a spruce, on whose top I stood,
as on a mass of coarse basket-work, fully nine inches in diameter at the
ground. These holes were bears' dens, and the bears were even then
at home. This was the sort of garden I made my way *over*, for an
eighth of a mile, at the risk, it is true, of treading on some of the plants,
not seeing any path *through* it — certainly the most treacherous and
porous country I ever travelled.

> 'Nigh foundered on he fares,
> Treading the crude consistence, half on foot,
> Half flying.'

But nothing could exceed the toughness of the twigs — not one snapped
under my weight, for they had slowly grown. Having slumped, scrambled, rolled, bounced, and walked, by turns, over this scraggy country, I arrived upon a side-hill, or rather side-mountain, where rocks,
gray, silent rocks, were the flocks and herds that pastured, chewing a
rocky cud at sunset. They looked at me with hard gray eyes, without
a bleat or a low. This brought me to the skirt of a cloud, and bounded
my walk that night. But I had already seen that Maine country when
I turned about, waving, flowing, rippling, down below.

When I returned to my companions, they had selected a camping-
ground on the torrent's edge, and were resting on the ground; one was
on the sick list, rolled in a blanket, on a damp shelf of rock. It was a
savage and dreary scenery enough, so wildly rough, that they looked
long to find a level and open space for the tent. We could not well

camp higher, for want of fuel; and the trees here seemed so evergreen and sappy, that we almost doubted if they would acknowledge the influence of fire; but fire prevailed at last, and blazed here, too, like a good citizen of the world. Even at this height we met with frequent traces of moose, as well as of bears. As here was no cedar, we made our bed of coarser feathered spruce; but at any rate the feathers were plucked from the live tree. It was, perhaps, even a more grand and desolate place for a night's lodging than the summit would have been, being in the neighborhood of those wild trees, and of the torrent. Some more aërial and finer-spirited winds rushed and roared through the ravine all night, from time to time arousing our fire, and dispersing the embers about. It was as if we lay in the very nest of a young whirl-wind. At midnight, one of my bed-fellows, being startled in his dreams by the sudden blazing up to its top of a fir tree, whose green boughs were dried by the heat, sprang up, with a cry, from his bed, thinking the world on fire, and drew the whole camp after him.

In the morning, after whetting our appetite on some raw pork, a wafer of hard-bread, and a dipper of condensed cloud or waterspout, we all together began to make our way up the falls, which I have described; this time choosing the right hand, or highest peak, which was not the one I had approached before. But soon my companions were lost to my sight behind the mountain ridge in my rear, which still seemed ever retreating before me, and I climbed alone over huge rocks, loosely poised, a mile or more, still edging toward the clouds; for though the day was clear elsewhere, the summit was concealed by mist. The mountain seemed a vast aggregation of loose rocks, as if some time it had rained rocks, and they lay as they fell on the mountain sides, nowhere fairly at rest, but leaning on each other, all rocking stones, with cavities between, but scarcely any soil or smoother shelf. They were the raw materials of a planet dropped from an unseen quarry, which the vast chemistry of nature would anon work up, or work down, into the smiling and verdant plains and valleys of earth. This was an undone extremity of the globe; as in lignite we see coal in the process of formation.

At length I entered within the skirts of the cloud which seemed for-ever drifting over the summit, and yet would never be gone, but was generated out of that pure air as fast as it flowed away; and when, a quarter of a mile farther, I reached the summit of the ridge, which those who have seen it in clearer weather say is about five miles long, and contains a thousand acres of table-land, I was deep within the hostile ranks of clouds, and all objects were obscured by them. Now the wind would blow me out a yard of clear sunlight, wherein I stood; then a gray, dawning light was all it could accomplish, the cloud-line ever rising and falling with the wind's intensity. Sometimes it seemed as if the summit would be cleared in a few moments, and smile in sunshine; but what was gained on one side was lost on another. It was like sitting in a chimney and waiting for the smoke to blow away. It was, in fact, a cloud-factory — these were the cloud-works, and the wind turned them off done from the cool, bare rocks. Occasionally, when the windy columns broke in to me, I caught sight of a dark, damp crag to the right or left; the mist driving ceaselessly between it and me. It reminded me of the creations of the old epic and dramatic poets, of Atlas, Vulcan, the Cyclops, and Prometheus. Such was Caucasus and the rock where Prometheus was bound. Æschylus had no doubt visited such scenery as this. It was vast, Titanic, and such as man never inhabits. Some part of the beholder, even some vital part, seems to escape through the loose grating of his ribs as he ascends. He is more lone than you can imagine. There is less of substantial thought and fair understanding in him than in the plains where men inhabit. His reason is dispersed and shadowy, more thin and subtile, like the air. Vast, Titanic, inhuman Nature has got him at disadvantage, caught him alone, and pilfers him of some of his divine faculty. She does not smile on him as in the plains. She seems to say sternly, Why came ye here before your time. This ground is not prepared for you. Is it not enough that I smile in the valleys? I have never made this soil for thy feet, this air for thy breathing, these rocks for thy neighbors. I cannot pity nor fondle thee here, but forever relentlessly drive thee hence to where I *am* kind. Why seek me where I have not called thee, and then complain because you find me but a stepmother? Shouldst thou freeze or starve, or shudder thy life away, here is no shrine, nor altar, nor any access to my ear.

> 'Chaos and ancient Night, I come no spy
> With purpose to explore or to disturb
> The secrets of your realm, but...
> .   .   .   .   .   .   as my way
> Lies through your spacious empire up to light.'

The tops of mountains are among the unfinished parts of the globe, whither it is a slight insult to the gods to climb and pry into their secrets, and try their effect on our humanity. Only daring and insolent men, perchance, go there. Simple races, as savages, do not climb mountains — their tops are sacred and mysterious tracts never visited by them. Pomola is always angry with those who climb to the summit of Ktaadn.

According to Jackson, who, in his capacity of geological surveyor of the State, has accurately measured it, the altitude of Ktaadn is 5300 feet, or a little more than one mile above the level of the sea, and he adds, 'It is then evidently the highest point in the State of Maine, and is the most abrupt granite mountain in New England.' The peculiarities of that spacious table-land on which I was standing, as well as the remarkable semicircular precipice or basin on the eastern side, were all concealed by the mist. I had brought my whole pack to the top, not knowing but I should have to make my descent to the river, and possibly to the settled portion of the State alone, and by some other route, and wishing to have a complete outfit with me. But at length fearing that my companions would be anxious to reach the river before night, and knowing that the clouds might rest on the mountain for days, I was compelled to descend. Occasionally, as I came down, the wind would blow me a vista open, through which I could see the country eastward, boundless forests, and lakes, and streams, gleaming in the sun, some of them emptying into the East Branch. There were also new mountains in sight in that direction. Now and then some small bird of the sparrow family would flit away before me, unable to command its course, like a fragment of the gray rock blown off by the wind.

I found my companions where I had left them, on the side of the peak, gathering the mountain cranberries, which filled every crevice between the rocks, together with blueberries, which had a spicier flavor the higher up they grew, but were not the less agreeable to our palates. When the country is settled, and roads are made, these cranberries will perhaps become an article of commerce. From this elevation, just on the skirts of the clouds, we could overlook the country, west and south, for a hundred miles. There it was, the State of Maine, which we had seen on the map, but not much like that — immeasurable forest for the sun to shine on, that eastern *stuff* we hear of in Massachusetts. No clearing, no house. It did not look as if a solitary traveller had cut so much as a walking-stick there. Countless lakes — Moosehead in the southwest, forty miles long by ten wide, like a gleaming silver platter at the end of the table; Chesuncook, eighteen long by three wide, without an island; Millinocket, on the south, with its hundred islands; and a hundred others without a name; and mountains, also, whose names, for the most part, are known only to the Indians. The forest looked like a firm grass sward, and the effect of these lakes in its midst has been well compared, by one who has since visited this same spot, to that of a 'mirror broken into a thousand fragments, and wildly scattered over the grass, reflecting the full blaze of the sun.' It was a large farm for somebody, when cleared. According to the Gazetteer, which was printed before the boundary question was settled, this single Penobscot County, in which we were, was larger than the whole State of Vermont, with its fourteen counties; and this was only a part of the wild lands of Maine. We are concerned now, however, about natural, not political limits. We were about eighty miles, as the bird flies, from Bangor, or one hundred and fifteen, as we had ridden, and walked, and paddled. We had to console ourselves with the reflection that this view was probably as good as that from the peak, as far as it went; and what were a mountain without its attendant clouds and mists? Like ourselves, neither Bailey nor Jackson had obtained a clear view from the summit.

Setting out on our return to the river, still at an early hour in the day, we decided to follow the course of the torrent, which we supposed to be Murch Brook, as long as it would not lead us too far out of our way. We thus travelled about four miles in the very torrent itself, continually crossing and recrossing it, leaping from rock to rock, and jumping with the stream down falls of seven or eight feet, or sometimes sliding down on our backs in a thin sheet of water. This ravine had been the scene of an extraordinary freshet in the spring, apparently accompanied by a slide from the mountain. It must have been filled with a stream of stones and water, at least twenty feet above the present level of the torrent. For a rod or two, on either side of its channel, the trees were barked and splintered up to their tops, the birches bent over, twisted, and sometimes finely split, like a stable-broom; some, a foot in diameter, snapped off, and whole clumps of trees bent over with the weight of rocks piled on them. In one place we noticed a rock, two or three feet in diameter, lodged nearly twenty feet high in the crotch of a tree. For the whole four miles we saw but one rill emptying in, and the volume of water did not seem to be increased from the first. We travelled thus very rapidly with a downward impetus, and grew remarkably expert at leaping from rock to rock, for leap we must, and leap we did, whether there was any rock at the right distance or not. It was a pleasant picture when the foremost turned about and looked up the winding ravine, walled in with rocks and the green forest, to see, at intervals of a rod or two, a red-shirted or green-jacketed mountaineer against the white torrent, leaping down the channel with his pack on his back, or pausing upon a convenient rock in the midst of the torrent to mend a rent in his clothes, or unstrap the dipper at his belt to take a draught of the water. At one place we were startled by seeing, on a little sandy shelf by the side of the stream, the fresh print of a man's foot, and for a moment realized how Robinson Crusoe felt in a similar case; but at last we remembered that we had struck this stream on our way up, though we could not have told where, and one had descended into the ravine for a drink. The cool air above and the continual bathing of our bodies in mountain water, alternate foot, sitz, douche, and plunge baths, made this walk exceedingly refreshing, and we had travelled only a mile or two, after leaving the torrent, before every thread of our clothes was as dry as usual, owing perhaps to a peculiar quality in the atmosphere.

After leaving the torrent, being in doubt about our course, Tom threw down his pack at the foot of the loftiest spruce tree at hand, and shinned up the bare trunk some twenty feet, and then climbed through the green tower, lost to our sight, until he held the topmost spray in his hand.[1] McCauslin, in his younger days, had marched through the wilderness with a body of troops, under General Somebody, and with one other man did all the scouting and spying service. The General's word was, 'Throw down the top of that tree,' and there was no tree in the Maine woods so high that it did not lose its top in such a case. I have heard a story of two men being lost once in these woods, nearer to the settlements than this, who climbed the loftiest pine they could find, some six feet in diameter at the ground, from whose top they discovered a solitary clearing and its smoke. When at this height, some two hundred feet from the ground, one of them became dizzy, and fainted in his companion's arms, and the latter had to accomplish the descent with him, alternately fainting and reviving, as best he could. To Tom we cried, 'Where away does the summit bear? where the burnt lands?' The last he could only conjecture; he descried, however,

---

[1] 'The spruce tree,' says Springer in '51, 'is generally selected, principally for the superior facilities which its numerous limbs afford the climber. To gain the first limbs of this tree, which are from twenty to forty feet from the ground, a smaller tree is undercut and lodged against it, clambering up which the top of the spruce is reached. In some cases, when a very elevated position is desired, the spruce tree is lodged against the trunk of some lofty pine, up which we ascend to a height twice that of the surrounding forest.'
To indicate the direction of pines, one throws down a branch, and a man on the ground takes the bearing.

a little meadow and pond, lying probably in our course, which we concluded to steer for. On reaching this secluded meadow, we found fresh tracks of moose on the shore of the pond, and the water was still unsettled as if they had fled before us. A little farther, in a dense thicket, we seemed to be still on their trail. It was a small meadow, of a few acres, on the mountain-side, concealed by the forest, and perhaps never seen by a white man before, where one would think that the moose might browse and bathe, and rest in peace. Pursuing this course, we soon reached the open land, which went sloping down some miles toward the Penobscot.

Perhaps I most fully realized that this was primeval, untamed, and forever untamable *Nature*, or whatever else men call it, while coming down this part of the mountain. We were passing over 'Burnt Lands,' burnt by lightning, perchance, though they showed no recent marks of fire, hardly so much as a charred stump, but looked rather like a natural pasture for the moose and deer, exceedingly wild and desolate, with occasional strips of timber crossing them, and low poplars springing up, and patches of blueberries here and there. I found myself traversing them familiarly, like some pasture run to waste, or partially reclaimed by man; but when I reflected what man, what brother or sister or kinsman of our race made it and claimed it, I expected the proprietor to rise up and dispute my passage. It is difficult to conceive of a region uninhabited by man. We habitually presume his presence and influence everywhere. And yet we have not seen pure Nature, unless we have seen her thus vast and drear and unhuman, though in the midst of cities. Nature was here something savage and awful, though beautiful. I looked with awe at the ground I trod on, to see what the Powers had made there, the form and fashion and material of their work. This was that Earth of which we have heard, made out of Chaos and Old Night. Here was no man's garden, but the unhandselled globe. It was not lawn, nor pasture, nor mead, nor woodland, nor lea, nor arable, nor waste land. It was the fresh and natural surface of the planet Earth, as it was made forever and ever — to be the dwelling of man, we say — so Nature made it, and man may use it if he can. Man was not to be associated with it. It was Matter, vast, terrific — not his Mother Earth that we have heard of, not for him to tread on, or be buried in — no, it were being too familiar even to let his bones lie there — the home, this, of Necessity and Fate. There was clearly felt the presence of a force not bound to be kind to man. It was a place for heathenism and superstitious rites — to be inhabited by men nearer of kin to the rocks and to wild animals than we. We walked over it with a certain awe, stopping, from time to time, to pick the blueberries which grew there, and had a smart and spicy taste. Perchance where *our* wild pines stand, and leaves lie on their forest floor, in Concord, there were once reapers, and husbandmen planted grain; but here not even the surface had been scarred by man, but it was a specimen of what God saw fit to make this world. What is it to be admitted to a museum, to see a myriad of particular things, compared with being shown some star's surface, some hard matter in its home! I stand in awe of my body, this matter to which I am bound has become so strange to me. I fear not spirits, ghosts, of which I am one — *that* my body might — but I fear bodies, I tremble to meet them. What is this Titan that has possession of me? Talk of mysteries! Think of our life in nature — daily to be shown matter, to come in contact with it — rocks, trees, wind on our cheeks! the *solid* earth! the *actual* world! the *common sense! Contact! Contact! Who* are we? *where* are we?

Erelong we recognized some rocks and other features in the landscape which we had purposely impressed on our memories, and, quickening our pace, by two o'clock we reached the batteau.[1] Here we had expected to dine on trout, but in this glaring sunlight they were slow to take the bait, so we were compelled to make the most of the crumbs of our hard-bread and our pork, which were both nearly exhausted. Meanwhile we deliberated whether we should go up the river a mile farther, to Gibson's clearing, on the Sowadnehunk, where there was a deserted log hut, in order to get a half-inch auger, to mend one of our spike-poles with. There were young spruce trees enough around us, and we had a spare spike, but nothing to make a hole with. But as it was uncertain whether we should find any tools left there, we patched up the broken pole, as well as we could, for the downward voyage, in which there would be but little use for it. Moreover, we were unwilling to lose any time in this expedition, lest the wind should rise before we reached the larger lakes, and detain us; for a moderate wind produces quite a sea on these waters, in which a batteau will not live for a moment; and on one occasion McCauslin had been delayed a week at the head of the North Twin, which is only four miles across. We were nearly out of provisions, and ill prepared in this respect for what might possibly prove a week's journey round by the shore, fording innumerable streams, and threading a trackless forest, should any accident happen to our boat.

[1] The bears had not touched things on our possessions. They sometimes tear a batteau to pieces for the sake of the tar with which it is besmeared.

It was with regret that we turned our backs on Chesuncook, which McCauslin had formerly logged on, and the Allegash lakes. There were still longer rapids and portages above; among the last the Ripogenus Portage, which he described as the most difficult on the river, and three miles long. The whole length of the Penobscot is two hundred and seventy-five miles, and we are still nearly one hundred miles from its source. Hodge, the Assistant State Geologist, passed up this river in 1837, and by a portage of only one mile and three quarters crossed over into the Allegash, and so went down that into the St. John, and up the Madawaska to the Grand Portage across to the St. Lawrence. His is the only account that I know of an expedition through to Canada in this direction. He thus describes his first sight of the latter river, which, to compare small things with great, is like Balboa's first sight of the Pacific from the mountains of the Isthmus of Darien. 'When we first came in sight of the St. Lawrence,' he says, 'from the top of a high hill, the view was most striking, and much more interesting to me from having been shut up in the woods for the two previous months. Directly before us lay the broad river, extending across nine or ten miles, its surface broken by a few islands and reefs, and two ships riding at anchor near the shore. Beyond, extended ranges of uncultivated hills, parallel with the river. The sun was just going down behind them, and gilding the whole scene with its parting rays.'

About four o'clock, the same afternoon, we commenced our return voyage, which would require but little if any poling. In shooting rapids the boatmen use large and broad paddles, instead of poles, to guide the boat with. Though we glided so swiftly, and often smoothly, down, where it had cost us no slight effort to get up, our present voyage was attended with far more danger; for if we once fairly struck one of the thousand rocks by which we were surrounded, the boat would be swamped in an instant. When a boat is swamped under these circumstances, the boatmen commonly find no difficulty in keeping afloat at first, for the current keeps both them and their cargo up for a long way down the stream; and if they can swim, they have only to work their way gradually to the shore. The greatest danger is of being caught in an eddy behind some larger rock, where the water rushes up stream faster than elsewhere it does down, and being carried round and round under the surface till they are drowned. McCauslin pointed out some rocks which had been the scene of a fatal accident of this kind. Sometimes the body is not thrown out for several hours. He himself had performed such a circuit once, only his legs being visible to his companions; but he was fortunately thrown out in season to recover his breath.[1] In shooting the rapids, the boatman has this problem to solve: to choose a circuitous and safe course amid a thousand sunken rocks, scattered over a quarter or half a mile, at the same time that he is moving steadily on at the rate of fifteen miles an hour. Stop he cannot; the only question is, where will he go? The bowman chooses the course with all his eyes about him, striking broad off with his paddle, and drawing the boat by main force into her course. The sternman faithfully follows the bow.

We were soon at the Aboljacarmegus Falls. Anxious to avoid the delay, as well as the labor, of the portage here, our boatmen went forward first to reconnoitre, and concluded to let the batteau down the falls, carrying the baggage only over the portage. Jumping from rock to rock until nearly in the middle of the stream, we were ready to receive the boat and let her down over the first fall, some six or seven feet perpendicular. The boatmen stand upon the edge of a shelf of rock, where the fall is perhaps nine or ten feet perpendicular, in from one to two feet of rapid water, one on each side of the boat, and let it slide gently over, till the bow is run out ten or twelve feet in the air; then, letting it drop squarely, while one holds the painter, the other leaps in, and his companion following, they are whirled down the rapids to a new fall or to smooth water. In a very few minutes they had accomplished a passage in safety, which would be as foolhardy for the unskillful to attempt as the descent of Niagara itself. It seemed as if it needed only a little familiarity, and a little more skill, to navigate down such falls as Niagara itself with safety. At any rate, I should not despair of such men in the rapids above Table Rock, until I saw them actually go over the falls, so cool, so collected, so fertile in resources are they. One might have thought that these were falls, and that falls were not to be waded through with impunity, like a mud-puddle. There was really danger of their losing their sublimity in losing their power to harm us. Familiarity breeds contempt. The boatman pauses, perchance, on some shelf beneath a table-rock under the fall, standing in some cove of backwater two feet deep, and you hear his rough voice come up through the spray, coolly giving directions how to launch the boat this time.

Having carried round Pockwockomus Falls, our oars soon brought us to the Katepskonegan, or Oak Hall carry, where we decided to camp

---

[1] I cut this from a newspaper: 'On the 11th (instant?) [May, '49,] on Rappogenes Falls, Mr. John Delantee, of Orono, Me., was drowned while running logs. He was a citizen of Orono, and was twenty-six years of age. His companions found his body, enclosed it in bark, and buried it in the solemn woods.'

half-way over, leaving our batteau to be carried over in the morning on fresh shoulders. One shoulder of each of the boatmen showed a red spot as large as one's hand, worn by the batteau on this expedition; and this shoulder, as it did all the work, was perceptibly lower than its fellow, from long service. Such toil soon wears out the strongest constitution. The drivers are accustomed to work in the cold water in the spring, rarely ever dry; and if one falls in all over he rarely changes his clothes till night, if then, even. One who takes this precaution is called by a particular nickname, or is turned off. None can lead this life who are not almost amphibious. McCauslin said soberly, what is at any rate a good story to tell, that he had seen where six men were wholly under water at once, at a jam, with their shoulders to handspikes. If the log did not start, then they had to put out their heads to breathe. The driver works as long as he can see, from dark to dark, and at night has not time to eat his supper and dry his clothes fairly, before he is asleep on his cedar bed. We lay that night on the very bed made by such a party, stretching our tent over the poles which were still standing, but re-shingling the damp and faded bed with fresh leaves.

In the morning we carried our boat over and launched it, making haste lest the wind should rise. The boatmen ran down Passamagamet, and soon after Ambejijis Falls, while we walked round with the baggage. We made a hasty breakfast at the head of Ambejijis Lake on the remainder of our pork, and were soon rowing across its smooth surface again, under a pleasant sky, the mountain being now clear of clouds in the northeast. Taking turns at the oars, we shot rapidly across Deep Cove, the foot of Pamadumcook, and the North Twin, at the rate of six miles an hour, the wind not being high enough to disturb us, and reached the Dam at noon. The boatmen went through one of the log sluices in the batteau, where the fall was ten feet at the bottom, and took us in below. Here was the longest rapid in our voyage, and perhaps the running this was as dangerous and arduous a task as any. Shooting down sometimes at the rate, as we judged, of fifteen miles an hour, if we struck a rock we were split from end to end in an instant. Now like a bait bobbing for some river monster, amid the eddies, now darting to this side of the stream, now to that, gliding swift and smooth near to our destruction, or striking broad off with the paddle and drawing the boat to right or left with all our might, in order to avoid a rock. I suppose that it was like running the rapids of the Sault Sainte Marie, at the outlet of Lake Superior, and our boatmen probably displayed no less dexterity than the Indians there do. We soon ran through this mile, and floated in Quakish Lake.

After such a voyage, the troubled and angry waters, which once had seemed terrible and not to be trifled with, appeared tamed and subdued; they had been bearded and worried in their channels, pricked and whipped into submission with the spike-pole and paddle, gone through and through with impunity, and all their spirit and their danger taken out of them, and the most swollen and impetuous rivers seemed but playthings henceforth. I began, at length, to understand the boatman's familiarity with, and contempt for, the rapids. 'Those Fowler boys,' said Mrs. McCauslin, 'are perfect ducks for the water.' They had run down to Lincoln, according to her, thirty or forty miles, in a batteau, in the night, for a doctor, when it was so dark that they could not see a rod before them, and the river was swollen so as to be almost a continuous rapid, so that the doctor *cried*, when they brought him up by daylight, 'Why, Tom, how did you see to steer?' 'We didn't steer much — only kept her straight.' And yet they met with no accident. It is true, the more difficult rapids are higher up than this.

When we reached the Millinocket opposite to Tom's house, and were waiting for his folks to set us over — for we had left our batteau above the Grand Falls — we discovered two canoes, with two men in each, turning up this stream from Shad Pond, one keeping the opposite side of a small island before us, while the other approached the side where we were standing, examining the banks carefully for muskrats as they came along. The last proved to be Louis Neptune and his companion, now, at last, on their way up to Chesuncook after moose, but they were so disguised that we hardly knew them. At a little distance they might have been taken for Quakers, with their broad-brimmed hats and overcoats with broad capes, the spoils of Bangor, seeking a settlement in this Sylvania — or, nearer at hand, for fashionable gentlemen the morning after a spree. Met face to face, these Indians in their native woods looked like the sinister and slouching fellows whom you meet picking up strings and paper in the streets of a city. There is, in fact, a remarkable and unexpected resemblance between the degraded savage and the lowest classes in a great city. The one is no more a child of nature than the other. In the progress of degradation the distinction of races is soon lost. Neptune at first was only anxious to know what we 'kill,' seeing some partridges in the hands of one of the party, but we had assumed too much anger to permit of a reply. We thought Indians had some honor before. But — 'Me been sick. Oh, me unwell now. You make bargain, then me go.' They had in fact been delayed so long by a drunken frolic at the Five Islands, and they had not yet recovered from its effects. They had some young musquash in their canoes, which they dug out of the banks with a hoe, for food, not for their skins, for musquash are their principal food on these expeditions. So they went on up the Millinocket, and we kept down the bank of the Penobscot, after recruiting ourselves with a draught of Tom's beer, leaving Tom at his home.

Thus a man shall lead his life away here on the edge of the wilderness, on Indian Millinocket Stream, in a new world, far in the dark of a continent, and have a flute to play at evening here, while his strains echo to the stars, amid the howling of wolves; shall live, as it were, in the primitive age of the world, a primitive man. Yet he shall spend a sunny day, and in this century be my contemporary; perchance shall read some scattered leaves of literature, and sometimes talk with me. Why read history, then, if the ages and the generations are now! He lives three thousand years deep into time, an age not yet described by poets. Can you well go further back in history than this? Ay! ay! — for there turns up but now into the mouth of Millinocket Stream a still more ancient and primitive man, whose history is not brought down even to the former. In a bark vessel sewn with the roots of the spruce, with hornbeam paddles, he dips his way along. He is but dim and misty to me, obscured by the æons that lie between the bark canoe and the batteau. He builds no house of logs, but a wigwam of skins. He eats no hot bread and sweet cake, but musquash and moose meat and the fat of bears. He glides up the Millinocket and is lost to my sight, as a more distant and misty cloud is seen flitting by behind a nearer, and is lost in space. So he goes about his destiny, the red face of man.

After having passed the night, and buttered our boots for the last time, at Uncle George's, whose dogs almost devoured him for joy at his return, we kept on down the river the next day, about eight miles on foot, and then took a batteau, with a man to pole it, to Mattawamkeag, ten more. At the middle of that very night, to make a swift conclusion to a long story, we dropped our buggy over the half-finished bridge at Oldtown, where we heard the confused din and clink of a hundred saws, which never rest, and at six o'clock the next morning one of the party was steaming his way to Massachusetts.

What is most striking in the Maine wilderness is the continuousness of the forest, with fewer open intervals or glades than you had imagined. Except the few burnt lands, the narrow intervals on the rivers, the bare tops of the high mountains, and the lakes and streams, the forest is uninterrupted. It is even more grim and wild than you had antic-ipated, a damp and intricate wilderness, in the spring everywhere wet and miry. The aspect of the country, indeed, is universally stern and savage, excepting the distant views of the forest from hills, and the lake prospects, which are mild and civilizing in a degree. The lakes are something which you are unprepared for; they lie up so high, ex-posed to the light, and the forest is diminished to a fine fringe on their edges, with here and there a blue mountain, like amethyst jewels set around some jewel of the first water — so anterior, so superior, to all the changes that are to take place on their shores, even now civil and refined, and fair as they can ever be. These are not the artificial for-ests of an English king — a royal preserve merely. Here prevail no forest laws but those of nature. The aborigines have never been dis-possessed, nor nature disforested.

It is a country full of evergreen trees, of mossy silver birches and watery maples, the ground dotted with insipid small, red berries, and strewn with damp and moss-grown rocks — a country diversified with innumerable lakes and rapid streams, peopled with trout and various species of *leucisci*, with salmon, shad, and pickerel, and other fishes; the forest resounding at rare intervals with the note of the chickadee, the blue jay, and the woodpecker, the scream of the fish hawk and the eagle, the laugh of the loon, and the whistle of ducks along the solitary streams; at night, with the hooting of owls and howling of wolves; in summer, swarming with myriads of black flies and mosquitoes, more formidable than wolves to the white man. Such is the home of the moose, the bear, the caribou, the wolf, the beaver, and the Indian. Who shall describe the inexpressible tenderness and immortal life of the grim forest, where Nature, though it be midwinter, is ever in her spring, where the moss-grown and decaying trees are not old, but seem to enjoy a perpetual youth; and blissful, innocent Nature, like a serene infant, is too happy to make a noise, except by a few tinkling, lisping birds and trickling rills?

What a place to live, what a place to die and be buried in! There certainly men would live forever, and laugh at death and the grave. There they could have no such thoughts as are associated with the vil-lage graveyard — that make a grave out of one of those moist evergreen hummocks!

> Die and be buried who will,
> I mean to live here still;
> My nature grows ever more young
> The primitive pines among.

I am reminded by my journey how exceedingly new this country still is. You have only to travel for a few days into the interior and back parts even of many of the old States, to come to that very America which the Northmen, and Cabot, and Gosnold, and Smith, and Raleigh visited. If Columbus was the first to discover the islands, Americus Vespucius and Cabot, and the Puritans, and we their descendants, have discovered only the shores of America. While the Republic has already acquired a history world-wide, America is still unsettled and unexplored. Like the English in New Holland, we live only on the shores of a continent even yet, and hardly know where the rivers come from which float our navy. The very timber and boards and shingles of which our houses are made grew but yesterday in a wilderness where the Indian still hunts and the moose runs wild. New York has her wilderness within her own borders; and though the sailors of Europe are familiar with the soundings of her Hudson, and Fulton long since invented the steamboat on its waters, an Indian is still necessary to guide her scientific men to its headwaters in the Adirondack country.

Have we even so much as discovered and settled the shores? Let a man travel on foot along the coast, from the Passamaquoddy to the Sabine, or to the Rio Bravo, or to wherever the end is now, if he is swift enough to overtake it, faithfully following the windings of every inlet and of every cape, and stepping to the music of the surf — with a desolate fishing town once a week, and a city's port once a month to cheer him, and putting up at the lighthouses, when there are any — and tell me if it looks like a discovered and settled country, and not rather, for the most part, like a desolate island, and No-Man's Land.

We have advanced by leaps to the Pacific, and left many a lesser Oregon and California unexplored behind us. Though the railroad and the telegraph have been established on the shores of Maine, the Indian still looks out from her interior mountains over all these to the sea. There stands the city of Bangor, fifty miles up the Penobscot, at the head of navigation for vessels of the largest class, the principal lumber depot on this continent, with a population of twelve thousand, like a star on the edge of night, still hewing at the forests of which it is built, already overflowing with the luxuries and refinement of Europe, and sending its vessels to Spain, to England, and to the West Indies for its groceries — and yet only a few axemen have gone 'up river,' into the howling wilderness which feeds it. The bear and deer are still found within its limits; and the moose, as he swims the Penobscot, is entangled amid its shipping, and taken by foreign sailors in its harbor.

Twelve miles in the rear, twelve miles of railroad, are Orono and the Indian Island, the home of the Penobscot tribe, and then commence the batteau and the canoe, and the military road; and sixty miles above, the country is virtually unmapped and unexplored, and there still waves the virgin forest of the New World.

II. CAPE COD

PREFATORY NOTE

THOREAU was able to give the manuscript of *Cape Cod* more attention than that of *Maine Woods*. Nonetheless *Cape Cod* did not receive the final polishing he was wont to give his books and thus it still has some rough edges. It is based on three separate excursions he made to that sandy peninsula — in October of 1849, in June of 1850, and in July of 1855 — the first and last trips with his friend Ellery Channing, the second alone. (He made still another excursion to the Cape in 1857, but did not incorporate that into the text of this book.) To give the book a unity (a unity incidentally that *Maine Woods* lacks), he melded the accounts of the three excursions into one, tracing a single route from Concord, via Boston, Cohasset, and Bridgewater to Sandwich, where the Cape geographically begins, and thence out to Provincetown. Portions of the book were originally published as travel essays in *Putnam's Monthly* in 1855. At that time he indicated to George William Curtis, the editor, that he had doubts about the lengthy historical extracts he had inserted into the text, and suggested they be deleted, a suggestion that is followed in this edition. Several other deletions have been made for reasons of space, but I believe the essential flavor of the original narrative has been retained.

Cape Cod is the sunniest of all of Thoreau's books. It is lighthearted, whimsical, witty and at times even slapstick. His audiences are reported to have "laughed until they cried" when he read portions of it from the lecture platform. Yet, for all its humor, it is the most vivid and accurate portrait we have of the Cape and of its then inhabitants. We catch the sun glancing off the sand dunes, the turbulent waves rolling in against the cliffs, the harsh beauty of the landscape, the sturdy eccentricity of the natives. One can almost taste the salt and feel the sand as he reads its pages. And the sketch of the Wellfleet Oysterman is one of the great character portraits of American literature.

Cape Cod was first published in book form by Ticknor & Fields in 1865.

I. THE START[1]

WISHING to get a better view than I had yet had of the ocean, which, we are told, covers more than two thirds of the globe, but of which a man who lives a few miles inland may never see any trace, more than of another world, I made a visit to Cape Cod in October, 1849, another the succeeding June, and another to Truro in July, 1855; the first and last time with a single companion, the second time alone. I

[1] From Chapter I, the Shipwreck.

have spent, in all, about three weeks on the Cape; walked from Eastham to Provincetown twice on the Atlantic side, and once on the Bay side also, excepting four or five miles, and crossed the Cape half a dozen times on my way; but having come so fresh to the sea, I have got but little salted. My readers must expect only so much saltness as the land breeze acquires from blowing over an arm of the sea, or is tasted on the windows and the bark of trees twenty miles inland, after September gales. I have been accustomed to make excursions to the ponds within ten miles of Concord, but latterly I have extended my excursions to the seashore.

I did not see why I might not make a book on Cape Cod, as well as my neighbor on 'Human Culture.' It is but another name for the same thing, and hardly a sandier phase of it. As for my title, I suppose that the word Cape is from the French *cap;* which is from the Latin *caput*, a head; which is, perhaps, from the verb *capere*, to take — that being the part by which we take hold of a thing: — Take Time by the forelock. It is also the safest part to take a serpent by. And as for Cod, that was derived directly from that 'great store of cod-fish' which Captain Bartholomew Gosnold caught there in 1602; which fish appears to have been so called from the Saxon word *codde*, 'a case in which seeds are lodged,' either from the form of the fish, or the quantity of spawn it contains; whence also, perhaps, codling (*'pomum coctile'?*) and coddle — to cook green like peas. (V. Dic.)

Cape Cod is the bared and bended arm of Massachusetts: the shoulder is at Buzzard's Bay; the elbow, or crazy-bone, at Cape Mallebarre; the wrist at Truro; and the sandy fist at Provincetown — behind which the State stands on her guard, with her back to the Green Mountains, and her feet planted on the floor of the ocean, like an athlete protecting her Bay — boxing with northeast storms, and, ever and anon, heaving up her Atlantic adversary from the lap of earth — ready to thrust forward her other fist, which keeps guard the while upon her breast at Cape Ann.

On studying the map, I saw that there must be an uninterrupted beach on the east or outside of the forearm of the Cape, more than thirty miles from the general line of the coast, which would afford a good sea view, but that, on account of an opening in the beach, forming the entrance to Nauset Harbor, in Orleans, I must strike it in Eastham, if I approached it by land, and probably I could walk thence straight to Race Point, about twenty-eight miles, and not meet with any obstruction. . . .[1]

[1] Pages 5–19 (Walden edition), an account of a shipwreck at Cohasset, omitted.

II. STAGE-COACH VIEWS

AFTER spending the night in Bridgewater, and picking up a few arrow-heads there in the morning, we took the cars for Sandwich, where we arrived before noon. This was the terminus of the 'Cape Cod Railroad,' though it is but the beginning of the Cape. As it rained hard, with driving mists, and there was no sign of its holding up, we here took that almost obsolete conveyance, the stage, for 'as far as it went that day,' as we told the driver. We had forgotten how far a stage could go in a day, but we were told that the Cape roads were very 'heavy,' though they added that being of sand, the rain would improve them. This coach was an exceedingly narrow one, but as there was a slight spherical excess over two on a seat, the driver waited till nine passengers had got in, without taking the measure of any of them, and then shut the door after two or three ineffectual slams, as if the fault were all in the hinges or the latch — while we timed our inspirations and expirations so as to assist him.

We were now fairly on the Cape, which extends from Sandwich eastward thirty-five miles, and thence north and northwest thirty more, in all sixty-five, and has an average breadth of about five miles. In the interior it rises to the height of two hundred, and sometimes perhaps three hundred feet above the level of the sea. According to Hitchcock, the geologist of the State, it is composed almost entirely of sand, even to the depth of three hundred feet in some places, though there is probably a concealed core of rock a little beneath the surface, and it is of diluvian origin, excepting a small portion at the extremity and elsewhere along the shores, which is alluvial. For the first half of the Cape large blocks of stone are found, here and there, mixed with the sand, but for the last thirty miles boulders, or even gravel, are rarely met with.

Hitchcock conjectures that the ocean has, in course of time, eaten out Boston Harbor and other bays in the mainland, and that the minute fragments have been deposited by the currents at a distance from the shore, and formed this sand-bank. Above the sand, if the surface is subjected to agricultural tests, there is found to be a thin layer of soil gradually diminishing from Barnstable to Truro, where it ceases; but there are many holes and rents in this weather-beaten garment not likely to be stitched in time, which reveal the naked flesh of the Cape, and its extremity is completely bare.

I at once got out my book, the eighth volume of the Collections of the Massachusetts Historical Society, printed in 1802, which contains some short notices of the Cape towns, and began to read up to where I was, for in the cars I could not read as fast as I traveled. To those who came from the side of Plymouth, it said, 'After riding through a body of woods, twelve miles in extent, interspersed with but few houses, the settlement of Sandwich appears, with a more agreeable effect, to the eye of the traveler.' Another writer speaks of this as a beautiful village. But I think that our villages will bear to be contrasted only with one another, not with nature. I have no great respect for the writer's taste, who talks easily about *beautiful* villages, embellished, per-chance, with a 'fulling-mill,' 'a handsome academy,' or a meeting-house, and 'a number of shops for the different mechanic arts;' where the green and white houses of the gentry, drawn up in rows, front on a street of which it would be difficult to tell whether it is most like a desert or a long stable-yard. Such spots can be beautiful only to the weary traveler, or the returning native — or, perchance, the repentant misanthrope; not to him who, with unprejudiced senses, has just come out of the woods, and approaches one of them, by a bare road, through a succession of straggling homesteads where he cannot tell which is the almshouse. However, as for Sandwich, I cannot speak particularly. Ours was but half a Sandwich at most, and that must have fallen on the buttered side some time. I only saw that it was a closely built town for a small one, with glass-works to improve its sand, and narrow streets in which we turned round and round till we could not tell which way we were going, and the rain came in, first on this side and then on that, and I saw that they in the houses were more comfortable than we in the coach. My book also said of this town, 'The inhabitants, in general, are substantial livers' — that is, I suppose, they do not live like philosophers; but, as the stage did not stop long enough for us to dine, we had no opportunity to test the truth of this statement. It may have referred, however, to the quantity 'of oil they would yield.' It further said, 'The inhabitants of Sandwich generally manifest a fond and steady adherence to the manners, employments and modes of living which characterized their fathers,' which made me think that they were, after all, very much like all the rest of the world; — and it added that this was 'a resemblance, which, at this day, will constitute no impeachment of either their virtue or taste;' which remark proves to me that the writer was one with the rest of them. No people ever lived by cursing their fathers, however great a curse their fathers might have been to them. But it must be confessed that ours was old authority, and probably they have changed all that now.

Our route was along the Bay side, through Barnstable, Yarmouth, Dennis, and Brewster, to Orleans, with a range of low hills on our right, running down the Cape. The weather was not favorable for wayside views, but we made the most of such glimpses of land and water as we could get through the rain. The country was, for the most part, bare, or with only a little scrubby wood left on the hills. We noticed in Yarmouth — and, if I do not mistake, in Dennis — large tracts where pitch pines were planted four or five years before. They were in rows, as they appeared when we were abreast of them, and, excepting that there were extensive vacant spaces, seemed to be doing remarkably well. This, we were told, was the only use to which such tracts could be profitably put. Every higher eminence had a pole set up on it, with an old storm-coat or sail tied to it, for a signal, that those on the south side of the Cape, for instance, might know when the Boston packets had arrived on the north. It appeared as if this use must absorb the greater part of the old clothes of the Cape, leaving but few rags for the peddlers. The windmills on the hills — large weather-stained octagonal structures — and the salt-works scattered all along the shore, with their long rows of vats resting on piles driven into the marsh, their low, turtle-like roofs, and their slighter windmills, were novel and interesting objects to an inlander. The sand by the roadside was partially covered with bunches of a moss-like plant, *Hudsonia tomentosa*, which a woman in the stage told us was called 'poverty-grass,' because it grew where nothing else would.

I was struck by the pleasant equality which reigned among the stage company, and their broad and invulnerable good humor. They were what is called free and easy, and met one another to advantage, as men who had, at length, learned how to live. They appeared to know each other when they were strangers, they were so simple and downright. They were well met, in an unusual sense, that is, they met as well as they could meet, and did not seem to be troubled with any impediment. They were not afraid nor ashamed of one another, but were contented to make just such a company as the ingredients allowed. It was evident that the same foolish respect was not here claimed for mere wealth and station that is in many parts of New England; yet some of them were the 'first people,' as they are called, of the various towns through which we passed. Retired sea-captains, in easy circumstances, who talked of farming as sea-captains are wont; an erect, respectable, and trust-worthy-looking man, in his wrapper, some of the salt of the earth, who had formerly been the salt of the sea; or a more courtly gentleman, who, perchance, had been a representative to the General Court in his day; or a broad, red-faced Cape Cod man, who had seen too many storms to be easily irritated; or a fisherman's wife, who had been waiting a week for a coaster to leave Boston, and had at length come by the cars.

A strict regard for truth obliges us to say, that the few women whom we saw that day looked exceedingly pinched up. They had prominent chins and noses, having lost all their teeth, and a sharp *W* would repre-sent their profile. They were not so well preserved as their husbands; or perchance they were well preserved as dried specimens. (Their hus-bands, however, were pickled.) But we respect them not the less for all that; our own dental system is far from perfect. . . .[1]

III. THE PLAINS OF NAUSET

THE next morning, Thursday, October 11, it rained as hard as ever; but we were determined to proceed on foot, nevertheless. We first made some inquiries, with regard to the practicability of walking up the shore on the Atlantic side to Provincetown, whether we should meet with any creeks or marshes to trouble us. Higgins said that there was no obstruction, and that it was not much farther than by the road, but he thought that we should find it very 'heavy' walking in the sand; it was bad enough in the road, a horse would sink in up to the fetlocks there. But there was one man at the tavern who had walked it, and he said that we could go very well, though it was sometimes inconvenient and even dangerous walking under the bank, when there was a great tide, with an easterly wind, which caused the sand to cave. For the first four or five miles we followed the road, which here turns to the north on the elbow — the narrowest part of the Cape — that we might clear

[1] Pages 24–31 (Walden edition), omitted.

an inlet from the ocean, a part of Nauset Harbor, in Orleans, on our right. We found the traveling good enough for walkers on the sides of the roads, though it was 'heavy' for horses in the middle. We walked with our umbrellas behind us since it blowed hard as well as rained, with driving mists, as the day before, and the wind helped us over the sand at a rapid rate. Everything indicated that we had reached a strange shore. The road was a mere lane, winding over bare swells of bleak and barren-looking land. The houses were few and far between, besides being small and rusty, though they appeared to be kept in good repair, and their door-yards, which were the unfenced Cape, were tidy; or, rather, they looked as if the ground around them was blown clean by the wind. Perhaps the scarcity of wood here, and the consequent absence of the wood-pile and other wooden traps, had something to do with this appearance. They seemed, like mariners ashore, to have sat right down to enjoy the firmness of the land, without studying their postures or habiliments. To them it was merely *terra firma* and *cognita*, not yet *fertilis* and *jucunda*. Every landscape which is dreary enough has a certain beauty to my eyes, and in this instance its permanent qualities were enhanced by the weather. Everything told of the sea, even when we did not see its waste or hear its roar. For birds there were gulls, and for carts in the fields, boats turned bottom upward against the houses, and sometimes the rib of a whale was woven into the fence by the road-side. The trees were, if possible, rarer than the houses, excepting apple trees, of which there were a few small orchards in the hollows. These were either narrow and high, with flat tops, having lost their side branches, like huge plum bushes growing in exposed situations, or else dwarfed and branching immediately at the ground, like quince bushes. They suggested that, under like circumstances, all trees would at last acquire like habits of growth. I afterward saw on the Cape many full-grown apple trees not higher than a man's head; one whole orchard, indeed, where all the fruit could have been gathered by a man standing on the ground; but you could hardly creep beneath the trees. Some, which the owners told me were twenty years old, were only three and a half feet high, spreading at six inches from the ground five feet each way, and, being withal surrounded with boxes of tar to catch the canker-worms, they looked like plants in flower-pots, and as if they might be taken into the house in the winter. In another place, I saw some not much larger than currant bushes; yet the owner told me that they had borne a barrel and a half of apples that fall. If they had been placed close together, I could have cleared them all at a jump. I measured some near the Highland Light in Truro, which had been taken from the shrubby woods thereabouts when young, and grafted. One, which had been set ten years, was on an average eighteen inches high, and spread nine feet, with a flat top. It had borne one bushel of apples two years before. Another, probably twenty years old from the seed, was five feet high, and spread eighteen feet, branching, as usual, at the ground, so that you could not creep under it. This bore a barrel of apples two years before. The owner of these trees invariably used the personal pronoun in speaking of them; as, 'I got *him* out of the woods, but *he* doesn't bear.' The largest that I saw in that neighborhood was nine feet high to the topmost leaf, and spread thirty-three feet, branching at the ground five ways.

In one yard I observed a single very healthy-looking tree, while all the rest were dead or dying. The occupant said that his father had manured all but that one with blackfish.

This habit of growth should, no doubt, be encouraged, and they should not be trimmed up, as some traveling practitioners have advised. In 1802 there was not a single fruit tree in Chatham, the next town to Orleans, on the south; and the old account of Orleans says: 'Fruit trees cannot be made to grow within a mile of the ocean. Even those which are placed at a greater distance are injured by the east winds; and after violent storms in the spring, a saltish taste is perceptible on their bark.' We noticed that they were often covered with a yellow lichen like rust, the *Parmelia parietina.*

The most foreign and picturesque structures on the Cape, to an inlander, not excepting the salt-works, are the windmills — gray-looking, octagonal towers, with long timbers slanting to the ground in the rear, and there resting on a cart-wheel, by which their fans are turned round to face the wind. These appeared also to serve in some measure for props against its force. A great circular rut was worn around the building by the wheel. The neighbors who assemble to turn the mill to the wind are likely to know which way it blows, without a weather-cock. They looked loose and slightly locomotive, like huge wounded birds, trailing a wing or a leg, and reminded one of pictures of the Netherlands. Being on elevated ground, and high in themselves, they serve as landmarks — for there are no tall trees, or other objects commonly, which can be seen at a distance in the horizon; though the outline of the land itself is so firm and distinct, that an insignificant cone, or even precipice of sand, is visible at a great distance from over the sea. Sailors making the land commonly steer either by the windmills, or the meeting-houses. In the country, we are obliged to steer by the meeting-houses alone. Yet the meeting-house is a kind of windmill, which runs one day in seven, turned either by the winds of doctrine or public opinion, or more rarely by the winds of Heaven, where another sort of grist is ground, of which, if it be not all bran or musty, if it be not *plaster*, we trust to make bread of life.

There were, here and there, heaps of shells in the fields, where clams had been opened for bait; for Orleans is famous for its shell-fish, especially clams, or, as our author says, 'to speak more properly, worms.' The shores are more fertile than the dry land. The inhabitants measure their crops, not only by bushels of corn, but by barrels of clams. A thousand barrels of clam-bait are counted as equal in value to six or eight thousand bushels of Indian corn, and once they were procured without more labor or expense, and the supply was thought to be inexhaustible. 'For,' runs the history, 'after a portion of the shore has been dug over, and almost all the clams taken up, at the end of two years, it is said, they are as plenty there as ever. It is even affirmed by many persons, that it is as necessary to stir the clam ground frequently, as it is to hoe a field of potatoes; because if this labor is omitted, the clams will be crowded too closely together, and will be prevented from increasing in size.' But we were told that the small clam, *Mya arenaria*, was not so plenty here as formerly. Probably the clam-ground has been stirred too frequently, after all. Nevertheless, one man, who complained that they fed pigs with them and so made them scarce, told me that he dug and opened one hundred and twenty-six dollars' worth in one winter, in Truro.

We crossed a brook, not more than fourteen rods long, between Orleans and Eastham called Jeremiah's Gutter. The Atlantic is said sometimes to meet the Bay here, and isolate the northern part of the Cape. The streams of the Cape are necessarily formed on a minute scale since there is no room for them to run, without tumbling immediately into the sea; and beside, we found it difficult to run ourselves in that sand, when there was no want of room. Hence, the least channel where water runs, or may run, is important, and is dignified with a name. We read that there is no running water in Chatham, which is the next town. The barren aspect of the land would hardly be believed if described. It was such soil, or rather land, as, to judge from appearances, no farmer in the interior would think of cultivating, or even fencing. Generally, the plowed fields of the Cape look white and yellow, like a mixture of salt and Indian meal. This is called soil. All an inlander's notions of soil and fertility will be confounded by a visit to these parts, and he will not be able, for some time afterward, to distinguish soil from sand. The historian of Chatham says of a part of that town, which has been gained from the sea: 'There is a doubtful appearance of a soil's beginning to be formed. It is styled *doubtful*, because it would not be observed by every eye, and perhaps not acknowledged by many.' We thought that this would not be a bad description of the greater part of the Cape. There is a 'beach' on the west side of Eastham, which we crossed the next summer, half a mile wide, and stretching across the township, containing seventeen hundred acres, on which there is not now a particle of vegetable mould, though it formerly produced wheat. All sands are here called 'beaches,' whether they are waves of water or of air that dash against them, since they commonly have their origin on the shore. 'The sand in some places,' says the historian of Eastham, 'lodging against the beach grass, has been raised into hills fifty feet high, where twenty-five years ago no hills existed. In others it has filled up small valleys and swamps. Where a strong-rooted bush stood, the appearance is singular: a mass of earth and sand adheres to it, resembling a small tower. In several places rocks, which were formerly covered with soil, are disclosed; and being lashed by the sand, driven against them by the wind, look as if they were recently dug from a quarry.'

We were surprised to hear of the great crops of corn which are still raised in Eastham, notwithstanding the real and apparent barrenness. Our landlord in Orleans had told us that he raised three or four hundred bushels of corn annually, and also of the great number of pigs which he fattened. In Champlain's 'Voyages,' there is a plate representing the Indian corn-fields hereabouts, with their wigwams in the midst, as they appeared in 1605, and it was here that the Pilgrims, to quote their own words, 'bought eight or ten hogsheads of corn and beans' of the Nauset Indians, in 1622, to keep themselves from starving.[1] 'In 1667 the town [of Eastham] voted that every housekeeper should kill twelve blackbirds, or three crows, which did great damage to the

---

[1] They touched after this at a place called Mattachiest, where they got more corn; but their shallop being cast away in a storm, the Governor was obliged to return to Plymouth on foot, fifty miles through the woods. According to Mourt's Relation, 'he came safely home, though weary and *surbated*,' that is, foot-sore. (Ital. *sobattere*, Lat. *sub* or *solea battere*, to bruise the soles of the feet; v. Dic. Not 'from *acerbatus*, embittered or aggrieved,' as one commentator on this passage supposes.) This word is of very rare occurrence, being applied only to governors and persons of like description, who are in that predicament; though such generally have considerable mileage allowed them, and might save their soles if they cared.

corn, and this vote was repeated for many years.' In 1695 an additional order was passed, namely, that 'every unmarried man in the township shall kill six blackbirds, or three crows, while he remains single; as a penalty for not doing it, shall not be married until he obey this order.' The blackbirds, however, still molest the corn. I saw them at it the next summer, and there were many scarecrows, if not scare-blackbirds, in the fields, which I often mistook for men. From which I concluded, that either many men were not married, or many blackbirds were. Yet they put but three or four kernels in a hill, and let fewer plants remain than we do. In the account of Eastham, in the 'Historical Collections,' printed in 1802, it is said that 'more corn is produced than the inhabitants consume, and above a thousand bushels are annually sent to market. The soil being free from stones, a plough passes through it speedily; and after the corn has come up, a small Cape horse, somewhat larger than a goat, will, with the assistance of two boys, easily hoe three or four acres in a day. Several farmers are accustomed to produce five hundred bushels of grain annually, and not long since one raised eight hundred bushels on sixty acres.' Similar accounts are given today; indeed, the recent accounts are in some instances suspectable repetitions of the old, and I have no doubt that their statements are as often founded on the exception as the rule, and that by far the greater number of acres are as barren as they appear to be. It is sufficiently remarkable that any crops can be raised here, and it may be owing, as others have suggested, to the amount of moisture in the atmosphere, the warmth of the sand, and the rareness of frosts. A miller, who was sharpening his stones, told me that, forty years ago, he had been to a husking here, where five hundred bushels were husked in one evening, and the corn was piled six feet high or more, in the midst, but now fifteen or eighteen bushels to an acre were an average yield. I never saw fields of such puny and unpromising-looking corn, as in this town. Probably the inhabitants are contented with small crops from a great surface easily cultivated. It is not always the most fertile land that is the most profitable, and this sand may repay cultivation as well as the fertile bottoms of the West. It is said, moreover, that the vegetables raised in the sand, without manure, are remarkably sweet, the pumpkins especially, though when their seed is planted in the interior they soon degenerate. I can testify that the vegetables here, when they succeed at all, look remarkably green and healthy, though perhaps it is partly by contrast with the sand. Yet the inhabitants of the Cape towns, generally, do not raise their own meal or pork. Their gardens are commonly little patches that have been redeemed from the edges of the marshes and swamps.

All the morning we had heard the sea roar on the eastern shore, which was several miles distant; for it still felt the effects of the storm in which the St. John was wrecked — though a school-boy, whom we overtook, hardly knew what we meant, his ears were so used to it. He would have more plainly heard the same sound in a shell. It was a very inspiriting sound to walk by, filling the whole air, that of the sea dashing against the land, heard several miles inland. Instead of having a dog to growl before your door, to have an Atlantic Ocean to growl for a whole Cape! On the whole, we were glad of the storm, which would show us the ocean in its angriest mood. Charles Darwin was assured that the roar of the surf on the coast of Chiloe, after a heavy gale, could be heard at night a distance of '21 sea miles across a hilly and wooded country.' We conversed with the boy we have mentioned, who might have been eight years old, making him walk the while under the lee of our umbrella; for we thought it as important to know what was life on the Cape to a boy as to a man. We learned from him where the best grapes were to be found in that neighborhood. He was carrying his dinner in a pail; and, without any impertinent questions being put by us, it did at length appear of what it consisted. The homeliest facts are always the most acceptable to an inquiring mind. At length, before we got to Eastham meeting-house, we left the road and struck across the country for the eastern shore at Nauset Lights — three lights close together, two or three miles distant from us. They were so many that they might be distinguished from others; but this seemed a shiftless and costly way of accomplishing that object. We found ourselves at once on an apparently boundless plain, without a tree or a fence or, with one or two exceptions, a house in sight. Instead of fences, the earth was sometimes thrown up into a slight ridge. My companion compared it to the rolling prairies of Illinois. In the storm of wind and rain which raged when we traversed it, it no doubt appeared more vast and desolate than it really is. As there were no hills, but only here and there a dry hollow in the midst of the waste, and the distant horizon was concealed by mist, we did not know whether it was high or low. A solitary traveler whom we saw perambulating in the distance loomed like a giant. He appeared to walk slouchingly, as if held up from above by straps under his shoulders, as much as supported by the plain below. Men and boys would have appeared alike at a little distance, there being no object by which to measure them. Indeed, to an inlander, the Cape landscape

is a constant mirage. This kind of country extended a mile or two each
way. These were the 'Plains of Nauset,' once covered with wood, where
in winter the winds howl and the snow blows right merrily in the face
of the traveller. I was glad to have got out of the towns, where I am
wont to feel unspeakably mean and disgraced — to have left behind
me for a season the bar-rooms of Massachusetts, where the full-grown
are not weaned from savage and filthy habits — still sucking a cigar.
My spirits rose in proportion to the outward dreariness. The towns
need to be ventilated. The gods would be pleased to see some pure
flames from their altars. They are not to be appeased with cigar-
smoke. . . .[1]

IV. THE BEACH

AT LENGTH we reached the seemingly retreating boundary of the plain,
and entered what had appeared at a distance an upland marsh, but
proved to be dry sand covered with beach grass, the bearberry, bayberry, shrub oaks, and beach plum, slightly ascending as we approached
the shore; then, crossing over a belt of sand on which nothing grew,
though the roar of the sea sounded scarcely louder than before, and we
were prepared to go half a mile farther, we suddenly stood on the edge
of a bluff overlooking the Atlantic. Far below us was the beach, from
half a dozen to a dozen rods in width, with a long line of breakers
rushing to the strand. The sea was exceedingly dark and stormy, the
sky completely overcast, the clouds still dropping rain, and the wind
seemed to blow not so much as the exciting cause, as from sympathy
with the already agitated ocean. The waves broke on the bars at some
distance from the shore, and curving green or yellow as if over so many
unseen dams, ten or twelve feet high, like a thousand waterfalls, rolled
in foam to the sand. There was nothing but that savage ocean between
us and Europe.

Having got down the bank, and as close to the water as we could,
where the sand was the hardest, leaving the Nauset Lights behind us,
we began to walk leisurely up the beach, in a northwest direction,

---

[1] Pages 42–57 (Walden edition), omitted.

toward Provincetown, which was about twenty-five miles distant, still sailing under our umbrellas with a strong aft wind, admiring in silence, as we walked, the great force of the ocean stream —

$$\pi o \tau \alpha \mu o \hat{\imath} o\ \mu \acute{\epsilon} \gamma \alpha\ \sigma \theta \acute{\epsilon} \nu o \varsigma\ \text{'}\Omega \kappa \epsilon \alpha \nu o \hat{\imath} o.$$

The white breakers were rushing to the shore; the foam ran up the sand, and then ran back, as far as we could see (and we imagined how much farther along the Atlantic coast, before and behind us), as regularly, to compare great things with small, as the master of a choir beats time with his white wand; and ever and anon a higher wave caused us hastily to deviate from our path, and we looked back on our tracks filled with water and foam. The breakers looked like droves of a thousand wild horses of Neptune, rushing to the shore, with their white manes streaming far behind; and when, at length, the sun shone for a moment, their manes were rainbow-tinted. Also, the long kelp-weed was tossed up from time to time, like the tails of sea-cows sporting in the brine.

There was not a sail in sight, and we saw none that day, for they had all sought harbors in the late storm, and had not been able to get out again; and the only human beings whom we saw on the beach for several days were one or two wreckers looking for driftwood and fragments of wrecked vessels. After an easterly storm in the spring, this beach is sometimes strewn with Eastern wood from one end to the other, which, as it belongs to him who saves it, and the Cape is nearly destitute of wood, is a godsend to the inhabitants. We soon met one of these wreckers — a regular Cape Cod man, with whom we parleyed, with a bleached and weather-beaten face, within whose wrinkles I distinguished no particular feature. It was like an old sail endowed with life — a hanging-cliff of weather-beaten flesh — like one of the clay boulders which occurred in that sand-bank. He had on a hat which had seen salt water, and a coat of many pieces and colors, though it was mainly the color of the beach, as if it had been sanded. His variegated back — for his coat had many patches, even between the shoulders — was a rich study to us when we had passed him and looked round. It might have been dishonorable for him to have so many scars behind, it is true, if he had not had many more and more serious ones in front. He looked as if he sometimes saw a doughnut, but never descended to comfort; too grave to laugh, too tough to cry; as indifferent as a clam — like a sea-clam with hat on and legs, that was out walking the strand. He may have been one of the Pilgrims — Peregrine White, at least — who has kept on the back side of the Cape, and let the centuries go by. He was looking for wrecks, old logs, water-logged and covered with barnacles, or bits of boards and joists, even chips which he drew out of the reach of the tide, and stacked up to dry. When the log was too large to carry far, he cut it up where the last wave had left it, or rolling it a few feet, appropriated it by sticking two sticks into the ground crosswise above it. Some rotten trunk, which in Maine cumbers the ground, and is, perchance, thrown into the water on purpose, is here thus carefully picked up, split and dried, and husbanded. Before winter the wrecker painfully carries these things up the bank on his shoulders by a long diagonal slanting path made with a hoe in the sand, if there is no hollow at hand. You may see his hooked pike-staff always lying on the bank, ready for use. He is the true monarch of the beach, whose 'right there is none to dispute,' and he is as much identified with it as a beach-bird.

Crantz, in his account of Greenland, quotes Dalagen's relation of the ways and usages of the Greenlanders, and says, 'Whoever finds drift-wood, or the spoils of a shipwreck on the strand, enjoys it as his own, though he does not live there. But he must haul it ashore and lay a stone upon it, as a token that some one has taken possession of it, and this stone is the deed of security, for no other Greenlander will offer to meddle with it afterwards.' Such is the instinctive law of nations. We have also this account of driftwood in Crantz: 'As he (the Founder of Nature) has denied this frigid rocky region the growth of trees, he has bid the streams of the Ocean to convey to its shores a great deal of wood, which accordingly comes floating thither, part without ice, but the most part along with it, and lodges itself between the islands. Were it not for this, we Europeans should have no wood to burn there, and the poor Greenlanders (who, it is true, do not use wood, but train, for burning) would, however, have no wood to roof their houses, to erect their tents, as also to build their boats, and to shaft their arrows, (yet there *grew* some small but crooked alders, etc.,) by which they must procure their maintenance, clothing and train for warmth, light, and cooking. Among this wood are great trees torn up by the roots, which, by driving up and down for many years and rubbing on the ice, are quite bare of branches and bark, and corroded with great wood-worms. A small part of this drift-wood are willows, alder and birch trees, which come out of the bays in the south (*i.e.*, of Greenland); also large trunks of aspen-trees, which must come from a greater distance; but the greatest part is pine and fir. We find also a good deal of a sort of wood finely veined, with few branches; this I fancy is larch-wood, which likes to decorate the sides of lofty, stony mountains. There is also a solid, reddish wood, of a more agreeable fragrance than the common fir, with visible cross-veins; which I take to be the same species as the beautiful silver-firs, or *zirbel*, that have the smell of cedar, and grow on the high Grison hills, and the Switzers wainscot their rooms with them.' The wrecker directed us to a slight depression, called Snow's Hollow, by which we ascended the bank, for elsewhere, if not difficult, it was inconvenient to climb it on account of the sliding sand which filled our shoes.

This sand-bank -- the backbone of the Cape — rose directly from the beach to the height of a hundred feet or more above the ocean. It was with singular emotions that we first stood upon it and discovered what a place we had chosen to·walk on. On our right, beneath us, was the beach of smooth and gently-sloping sand, a dozen rods in width; next, the endless series of white breakers; further still, the light green water over the bar, which runs the whole length of the forearm of the Cape, and beyond this stretched the unwearied and illimitable ocean. On our left, extending back from the very edge of the bank, was a perfect desert of shining sand, from thirty to eighty rods in width, skirted in the distance by small sand-hills fifteen or twenty feet high; between which, however, in some places, the sand penetrated as much farther. Next commenced the region of vegetation — a succession of small hills and valleys covered with shrubbery, now glowing with the brightest imaginable autumnal tints; and beyond this were seen, here and there, the waters of the bay. Here, in Wellfleet, this pure sand plateau, known to sailors as the Table-Lands of Eastham, on account of its appearance, as seen from the ocean, and because it once made a part of that town — full fifty rods in width, and in many places much more, and sometimes full one hundred and fifty feet above the ocean — stretched away north-ward from the southern boundary of the town, without a particle of vegetation — as level almost as a table — for two and a half or three miles, or as far as the eye could reach; slightly rising towards the ocean, then stooping to the beach, by as steep a slope as sand could lie on, and as regular as a military engineer could desire. It was like the escarped rampart of a stupendous fortress, whose glacis was the beach, and whose champaign the ocean. From its surface we overlooked the greater part of the Cape. In short, we were traversing a desert, with the view of an autumnal landscape of extraordinary brilliancy, a sort of Promised Land, on the one hand, and the ocean on the other. Yet, though the prospect was so extensive, and the country for the most part destitute of trees, a house was rarely visible — we never saw one from the beach — and the solitude was that of the ocean and the desert combined. A thousand men could not have seriously interrupted it, but would have been lost in the vastness of the scenery as their footsteps in the sand.

The whole coast is so free from rocks, that we saw but one or two for more than twenty miles. The sand was soft like the beach, and trying to the eyes when the sun shone. A few piles of driftwood, which some wreckers had painfully brought up the bank and stacked up there to dry, being the only objects in the desert, looked indefinitely large and distant, even like wigwams, though, when we stood near them, they proved to be insignificant little 'jags' of wood.

For sixteen miles, commencing at the Nauset Lights, the bank held its height, though farther north it was not so level as here, but interrupted by slight hollows, and the patches of beach-grass and bayberry frequently crept into the sand to its edge. There are some pages entitled 'A Description of the Eastern Coast of the County of Barnstable,' printed in 1802, pointing out the spots on which the Trustees of the Humane Society have erected huts called Charity or Humane Houses, 'and other places where shipwrecked seamen may look for shelter.' Two thousand copies of this were dispersed, that every vessel which frequented this coast might be provided with one. I have read this Shipwrecked Seaman's Manual with a melancholy kind of interest, for the sound of the surf, or, you might say, the moaning of the sea, is heard all through it, as if its author were the sole survivor of a shipwreck himself. Of this part of the coast he says: 'This highland approaches the ocean with steep and lofty banks, which it is extremely difficult to climb, especially in a storm. In violent tempests, during very high tides, the sea breaks against the foot of them, rendering it then unsafe to walk on the strand which lies between them and the ocean. Should the seaman succeed in his attempt to ascend them, he must forbear to penetrate into the country, as houses are generally so remote that they would escape his research during the night; he must pass on to the valleys by which the banks are intersected. These valleys, which the inhabitants call Hollows, run at right angles with the shore, and in the middle or lowest part of them a road leads from the dwelling-houses to the sea.' By the word *road* must not always be understood a visible cart-track.

There were these two roads for us — an upper and a lower one — the bank and the beach; both stretching twenty-eight miles northwest, from Nauset Harbor to Race Point, without a single opening into the beach, and with hardly a serious interruption of the desert. If you were to ford the narrow and shallow inlet at Nauset Harbor, where there is not more than eight feet of water on the bar at full sea, you might walk ten or twelve miles farther, which would make a beach forty miles long — and the bank and beach, on the east side of Nantucket, are but a continuation of these. I was comparatively satisfied. There I had got the Cape under me, as much as if I were riding it barebacked. It was not as on the map, or seen from the stage-coach; but there I found it all out of doors, huge and real, Cape Cod! as it cannot be represented on a map, color it as you will; the thing itself, than which there is nothing more like it, no truer picture or account; which you cannot go farther and see. I cannot remember what I thought before that it was. They commonly celebrate those beaches only which have a hotel on them, not those which have a humane house alone. But I wished to see that seashore where man's works are wrecks; to put up at the true Atlantic House, where the ocean is land-lord as well as sea-lord, and comes ashore without a wharf for the landing; where the crumbling land is the only invalid, or at best is but dry land, and that is all you can say of it.

We walked on quite at our leisure, now on the beach, now on the bank, sitting from time to time on some damp log, maple or yellow birch, which had long followed the seas, but had now at last settled on land; or under the lee of a sand-hill, on the bank, that we might gaze steadily on the ocean. The bank was so steep, that, where there was no danger of its caving, we sat on its edge as on a bench. It was difficult for us landsmen to look out over the ocean without imagining land in the horizon; yet the clouds appeared to hang low over it, and rest on the water as they never do on the land, perhaps on account of the great distance to which we saw. The sand was not without advantage, for, though it was 'heavy' walking in it, it was soft to the feet; and, notwithstanding that it had been raining nearly two days, when it held up for half an hour, the sides of the sand-hills, which were porous and sliding, afforded a dry seat. All the aspects of this desert are beautiful, whether you behold it in fair weather or foul, or when the sun is just breaking out after a storm, and shining on its moist surface in the distance, it is so white, and pure, and level, and each slight inequality and track is so distinctly revealed; and when your eyes slide off this, they fall on the ocean. In summer the mackerel gulls — which here have their nests among the neighboring sand-hills — pursue the traveler anxiously, now and then diving close to his head with a squeak, and he may see them, like swallows, chase some crow which has been feeding on the beach, almost across the Cape.

Though for some time I have not spoken of the roaring of the breakers, and the ceaseless flux and reflux of the waves, yet they did not for a moment cease to dash and roar, with such a tumult that, if you had been there, you could scarcely have heard my voice the while; and they are dashing and roaring this very moment — though it may be with less din and violence — for there the sea never rests. We were wholly absorbed by this spectacle and tumult, and like Chryses, though in a different mood from him, we walked silent along the shore of the resounding sea.

$$\text{Βῆ δ' ἀκέων παρὰ θῖνα πολυφλοίσβοιο θαλάσσης.}^{1}$$

I put in a little Greek now and then, partly because it sounds so much like the ocean — though I doubt if Homer's *Mediterranean* Sea ever sounded so loud as this.

The attention of those who frequent the camp-meetings at Eastham is said to be divided between the preaching of the Methodists and the preaching of the billows on the back side of the Cape, for they all stream over here in the course of their stay. I trust that in this case the loudest voice carries it. With what effect may we suppose the ocean to say, 'My hearers!' to the multitude on the bank! On that side some John N. Maffit; on this, the Reverend Poluphloisboios Thalassa.

There was but little weed cast up here, and that kelp chiefly, there being scarcely a rock for rockweed to adhere to. Who has not had a vision from some vessel's deck, when he had still his land legs on, of this great brown apron, drifting half upright, and quite submerged through the green water, clasping a stone or a deep-sea mussel in its unearthly fingers? I have seen it carrying a stone half as large as my head. We sometimes watched a mass of this cable-like weed, as it was tossed up on the crest of a breaker, waiting with interest to see it come in, as if there was some treasure buoyed up by it; but we were always surprised and disappointed at the insignificance of the mass which had attracted us. As we looked out over the water, the smallest objects floating on it appeared indefinitely large, we were so impressed by the vastness of the ocean, and each one bore so large a proportion to the whole ocean, which we saw. We were so often disappointed in the size

<hr>

[1] We have no word in English to express the sound of many waves dashing at once, whether gently or violently πολυφλοίσβοιος to the ear, and, in the ocean's gentle moods, an ἀνάριθμον γέλασμα to the eye.

of such things as came ashore, the ridiculous bits of wood or weed with which the ocean labored, that we began to doubt whether the Atlantic itself would bear a still closer inspection, and would not turn out to be but a small pond, if it should come ashore to us. This kelp, oar-weed, tangle, devil's-apron, sole-leather, or ribbon-weed — as various species are called — appeared to us a singularly marine and fabulous product, a fit invention for Neptune to adorn his car with, or a freak of Proteus. All that is told of the sea has a fabulous sound to an inhabitant of the land, and all its products have a certain fabulous quality, as if they belonged to another planet, from seaweed to a sailor's yarn, or a fish story. In this element the animal and vegetable kingdoms meet and are strangely mingled. One species of kelp, according to Bory St. Vincent, has a stem fifteen hundred feet long, and hence is the longest vegetable known, and a brig's crew spent two days to no purpose collecting the trunks of another kind cast ashore on the Falkland Islands, mistaking it for driftwood.[1] This species looked almost edible; at least, I thought that if I were starving, I would try it. One sailor told me that the cows ate it. It cut like cheese; for I took the earliest opportunity to sit down and deliberately whittle up a fathom or two of it, that I might become more intimately acquainted with it, see how it cut, and if it were hollow all the way through. The blade looked like a broad belt, whose edges had been quilled, or as if stretched by hammering, and it was also twisted spirally. The extremity was generally worn and ragged from the lashing of the waves. A piece of the stem which I carried home shrunk to one quarter of its size a week afterward, and was completely covered with crystals of salt like frost. The reader will excuse my greenness — though it is not sea-greenness, like his, perchance — for I live by a river shore, where this weed does not wash up. When we consider in what meadows it grew, and how it was raked, and in what kind of hay weather got in or out, we may well be curious about it. One who **is** weather-wise has given the following account of the matter:

> 'When descends on the Atlantic
>> The gigantic
> Storm-wind of the equinox,
> Landward in his wrath he scourges
>> The toiling surges,
> Laden with seaweed from the rocks:
>
> From Bermuda's reefs; from edges
>> Of sunken ledges,

[1] See Harvey on *Algæ*.

In some far-off, bright Azore;
From Bahama, and the dashing,
        Silver-flashing
Surges of San Salvador;

'From the tumbling surf, that buries
        The Orkneyan Skerries,
Answering the hoarse Hebrides;
And from wrecks of ships, and drifting
        Spars, uplifting
On the desolate rainy seas; —

'Ever drifting, drifting, drifting
        On the shifting
Currents of the restless main.'

But he was not thinking of this shore, when he added —

Till in sheltered coves, and reaches
        Of sandy beaches,
All have found repose again.'

These weeds were the symbols of those grotesque and fabulous thoughts which have not yet got into the sheltered coves of literature.

'Ever drifting, drifting, drifting
        On the shifting
Currents of the restless heart;'
And not yet 'in books recorded,
        They, like hoarded
Household words, no more depart.'

The beach was also strewn with beautiful sea-jellies, which the wreckers called sun-squall, one of the lowest forms of animal life, some white, some wine-colored, and a foot in diameter. I at first thought that they were a tender part of some marine monster, which the storm or some other foe had mangled. What right has the sea to bear in its bosom such tender things as sea-jellies and mosses, when it has such a boisterous shore, that the stoutest fabrics are wrecked against it? Strange that it should undertake to dandle such delicate children in its arm. I did not at first recognize these for the same which I had formerly seen in myriads in Boston Harbor, rising, with a waving motion, to the surface, as if to meet the sun, and discoloring the waters far and wide, so that I seemed to be sailing through a mere sun-fish soup. They say that when you endeavor to take one up, it will spill out the other side of your hand like quicksilver. Before the land rose out of the ocean, and became *dry* land, chaos reigned; and between high and low water mark, where she is partially disrobed and rising, a sort of chaos reigns still, which only anomalous creatures can inhabit. Mackerel gulls were all the while flying over our heads and amid the breakers, sometimes two white ones pursuing a black one; quite at home in the storm, though they are as delicate organizations as sea-jellies and mosses; and we saw that they were adapted to their circumstances rather by their spirits than their bodies. Theirs must be an essentially wilder, that is, less human, nature, than that of larks and robins. Their note was like the sound of some vibrating metal, and harmonized well with the scenery and the roar of the surf, as if one had rudely touched the strings of the lyre, which ever lies on the shore; a ragged shred of ocean music tossed aloft on the spray. But if I were required to name a sound the remembrance of which most perfectly revives the impression which the beach has made, it would be the dreary peep of the piping plover (*Charadrius melodus*) which haunts there. Their voices, too, are heard as a fugacious part in the dirge which is ever played along the shore for those mariners who have been lost in the deep since first it was created. But through all this dreariness we seemed to have a pure and unqualified strain of eternal melody, for always the same strain which is a dirge to one household is a morning song of rejoicing to another.

A remarkable method of catching gulls, derived from the Indians, was practised in Wellfleet in 1794. 'The Gull House,' it is said, 'is built with crotches, fixed in the ground on the beach,' poles being stretched across for the top, and the sides made close with stakes and seaweed. 'The poles on the top [are] covered with lean whale. The man, being placed within, is not discovered by the fowls, and, while they are contending for and eating the flesh, he draws them in, one by one, between the poles, until he has collected forty or fifty.' Hence, perchance, a man is said to be *gulled*, when he is *taken in*. We read that one 'sort of gulls is called by the Dutch *mallemucke*, i.e., the foolish fly, because they fall upon a whale as eagerly as a fly, and, indeed, all gulls are foolishly bold and easy to be shot. The Norwegians call this bird *havhest*, sea-horse (and the English translator says, it is probably what we call boobies). If they have eaten too much, they throw it up, and eat it again till they are tired. It is this habit in the gulls of parting with their property [disgorging the contents of their stomachs to the skuas], which has given rise to the terms gull, guller, and gulling, among men.' We also read that they used to kill small birds which roosted on the beach at night, by making a fire with hog's lard in a frying-pan. The Indians probably used pine torches; the birds flocked to the light, and were knocked down with a stick. We noticed holes dug near the edge of the bank, where gunners conceal themselves to shoot the large gulls which coast up and down a-fishing, for these are considered good to eat.

We found some large clams, of the species *Mactra solidissima,* which the storm had torn up from the bottom, and cast ashore. I selected one of the largest, about six inches in length, and carried it along, thinking to try an experiment on it. We soon after met a wrecker, with a grapple and a rope, who said that he was looking for tow cloth, which had made part of the cargo of the ship Franklin, which was wrecked here in the spring, at which time nine or ten lives were lost. The reader may remember this wreck, from the circumstance that a letter was found in the captain's valise, which washed ashore, directing him to wreck the vessel before he got to America, and from the trial which took place in consequence. The wrecker said that tow cloth was still cast up in such storms as this. He also told us that the clam which I had was the sea-clam, or hen, and was good to eat. We took our nooning under a sand-hill, covered with beach-grass, in a dreary little hollow, on the top of the bank, while it alternately rained and shined. There, having reduced some damp driftwood, which I had picked up on the shore, to shavings with my knife, I kindled a fire with a match and some paper, and cooked my clam on the embers for my dinner; for breakfast was commonly the only meal which I took in a house on this excursion. When the clam was done, one valve held the meat, and the other the liquor. Though it was very tough, I found it sweet and savory, and ate *the whole* with a relish. Indeed, with the addition of a cracker or two, it would have been a bountiful dinner. I noticed that the shells were such as I had seen in the sugar-kit at home. Tied to a stick, they formerly made the Indian's hoe hereabouts.

At length, by mid-afternoon, after we had had two or three rainbows over the sea, the showers ceased, and the heavens gradually cleared up, though the wind still blowed as hard and the breakers ran as high as before. Keeping on, we soon after came to a charity-house, which we looked into to see how the shipwrecked mariner might fare. Far away in some desolate hollow by the seaside, just within the bank, stands a lonely building on piles driven into the sand, with a slight nail put through the staple, which a freezing man can bend, with some straw, perchance, on the floor on which he may lie, or which he may burn in the fireplace to keep him alive. Perhaps this hut has never been required to shelter a shipwrecked man, and the benevolent person who promised to inspect it annually, to see that the straw and matches are here, and that the boards will keep off the wind, has grown remiss and thinks that storms and shipwrecks are over; and this very night a perishing crew may pry open its door with their numbed fingers and leave half their number dead here by morning. When I thought what must be the condition of the families which alone would ever occupy or had occupied them, what must have been the tragedy of the winter evenings spent by human beings around their hearths, these houses, though they were meant for human dwellings, did not look cheerful to me. They appeared but a stage to the grave. The gulls flew around and screamed over them; the roar of the ocean in storms, and the lapse of its waves in calms, alone resounds through them, all dark and empty within, year in, year out, except, perchance, on one memorable night. Houses of entertainment for shipwrecked men! What kind of sailor's homes were they?

'Each hut,' says the author of the 'Description of the Eastern Coast of the County of Barnstable,' 'stands on piles, is eight feet long, eight feet wide, and seven feet high; a sliding door is on the south, a sliding shutter on the west, and a pole, rising fifteen feet above the top of the building, on the east. Within, it is supplied either with straw or hay; and is farther accommodated with a bench.' They have varied little from this model now. There are similar huts at the Isle of Sable and Anticosti, on the north, and how far south along the coast I know not. It is pathetic to read the minute and faithful directions which he gives to seamen who may be wrecked on this coast, to guide them to the nearest charity-house, or other shelter, for, as is said of Eastham, though there are a few houses within a mile of the shore, yet 'in a snow storm, which rages here with excessive fury, it would be almost impossible to discover them either by night or by day.' You hear their imaginary guide thus marshalling, cheering, directing the dripping, shivering, freezing troop along: 'At the entrance of this valley, the sand has gathered; so that at present a little climbing is necessary. Passing over several fences, and taking heed not to enter the wood on the right hand, at the distance of three quarters of a mile, a house is to be found. This house stands on the south side of the road; and not far from it, on the south, is Pamet River, which runs from east to west through a body of salt marsh.' To him cast ashore in Eastham, he says, 'The meeting house is without a steeple; but it may be distinguished from the dwelling houses near it by its situation, which is between two small groves of locusts, one on the south, and one on the north, that on the south being three times as long as the other. About a mile and a quarter from the hut, west by north, appear the top and arms of a windmill.' And so on for many pages.

We did not learn whether these houses had been the means of saving any lives, though this writer says, of one erected at the head of Stout's Creek, in Truro, that 'it was built in an improper manner, having a chimney in it; and was placed on a spot where no beach grass grew. The strong winds blew the sand from its foundation, and the weight of the chimney brought it to the ground; so that in January of the present year [1802] it was entirely demolished. This event took place about six weeks before the Brutus was cast away. If it had remained, it is probable that the whole of the unfortunate crew of that ship would have been saved, as they gained the shore a few rods only from the spot where the hut had stood.'

This 'charity-house,' as the wrecker called it, this 'Humane house,' as some call it, that is, the one to which we first came, had neither window nor sliding shutter, nor clapboards, nor paint. As we have said, there was a rusty nail put through the staple. However, as we wished to get an idea of a Humane house, and we hoped that we should never have a better opportunity, we put our eyes, by turns, to a knot-hole in the door, and, after long looking, without seeing, into the dark — not knowing how many shipwrecked men's bones we might see at last, looking with the eye of faith, knowing that, though to him that knocketh it may not always be opened, yet to him that looketh long enough through a knot-hole the inside shall be visible — for we had had some practice at looking inward — by steadily keeping our other ball covered from the light meanwhile, putting the outward world behind us, ocean and land, and the beach — till the pupil became enlarged and collected the rays of light that were wandering in that dark (for the pupil shall be enlarged by looking; there never was so dark a night but a faithful and patient eye, however small, might at last prevail over it) — after all this, I say, things began to take shape to our vision — if we may use this expression where there was nothing but emptiness — and we obtained the long-wished-for insight. Though we thought at first that it was a hopeless case, after several minutes' steady exercise of the divine faculty, our prospects began decidedly to brighten, and we were ready to exclaim with the blind bard of 'Paradise Lost and Regained,'

> 'Hail, holy Light! offspring of Heaven first-born,
> Or of the Eternal coeternal beam
> May I express thee unblamed?'

A little longer, and a chimney rushed red on our sight. In short, when our vision had grown familiar with the darkness, we discovered that there were some stones and some loose wads of wool on the floor, and an empty fireplace at the further end; but it *was not* supplied with matches, or straw, or hay, that we could see, nor 'accommodated with a bench.' Indeed, it was the wreck of all cosmical beauty there within.

Turning our backs on the outward world, we thus looked through the knot-hole into the Humane house, into the very bowels of mercy; and for bread we found a stone. It was literally a great cry (of sea-mews outside), and a little wool. However, we were glad to sit outside, under the lee of the Humane house, to escape the piercing wind; and there we thought how cold is charity! how inhumane humanity! This, then, is what charity hides! Virtues antique and far away, with ever a rusty nail over the latch; and very difficult to keep in repair, withal, it is so uncertain whether any will ever gain the beach near you. So we shivered round about, not being able to get into it, ever and anon looking through the knot-hole into that night without a star, until we concluded that it was not a *humane* house at all, but a seaside box, now shut up, belonging to some of the family of Night or Chaos, where they spent their summers by the sea, for the sake of the sea-breeze, and that it was not proper for us to be prying into their concerns.

My companion had declared before this that I had not a particle of sentiment, in rather absolute terms, to my astonishment; but I suspect he meant that my legs did not ache just then, though I am not wholly a stranger to that sentiment. But I did not intend this for a sentimental journey.

V. THE WELLFLEET OYSTERMAN

HAVING walked about eight miles since we struck the beach, and passed the boundary between Wellfleet and Truro, a stone post in the sand — for even this sand comes under the jurisdiction of one town or another — we turned inland over barren hills and valleys, whither the sea, for some reason, did not follow us, and, tracing up a Hollow, discovered two or three sober-looking houses within half a mile, uncommonly near the eastern coast. Their garrets were apparently so full of chambers, that their roofs could hardly lie down straight, and we did not doubt that there was room for us there. Houses near the sea are generally low and broad. These were a story and a half high; but if you merely counted the windows in their gable ends, you would think that there were many stories more, or, at any rate, that the half-story was the only one thought worthy of being illustrated. The great number of windows in the ends of the houses, and their irregularity in size and position, here and elsewhere on the Cape, struck us agreeably — as if each of the various occupants who had their *cunabula* behind had punched a hole where his necessities required it, and according to his size and stature, without regard to outside effect. There were windows for the grown folks, and windows for the children — three or four apiece; as a certain man had a large hole cut in his barn-door for the cat, and another smaller one for the kitten. Sometimes they were so low under the eaves that I thought they must have perforated the plate beam for another apartment, and I noticed some which were triangular, to fit that part more exactly. The ends of the houses had thus as many muzzles as a revolver, and, if the inhabitants have the same habit of staring out the windows that some of our neighbors have, a traveller must stand a small chance with them.

Generally, the old-fashioned and unpainted houses on the Cape looked more comfortable, as well as picturesque, than the modern and more pretending ones, which were less in harmony with the scenery, and less firmly planted.

These houses were on the shores of a chain of ponds, seven in number, the source of a small stream called Herring River, which empties into the Bay. There are many Herring Rivers on the Cape; they will, perhaps, be more numerous than herrings soon. We knocked at the door of the first house, but its inhabitants were all gone away. In the meanwhile, we saw the occupants of the next one looking out the window at us, and before we reached it an old woman came out and fastened the door of her bulkhead, and went in again. Nevertheless, we did not hesitate to knock at her door, when a grizzly-looking man appeared, whom we took to be sixty or seventy years old. He asked us, at first, suspiciously, where we were from, and what our business was; to which we returned plain answers.

'How far is Concord from Boston?' he inquired.

'Twenty miles by railroad.'

'Twenty miles by railroad,' he repeated.

'Didn't you ever hear of Concord of Revolutionary fame?'

'Didn't I ever hear of Concord? Why, I heard guns fire at the battle of Bunker Hill. [They heard the sound of heavy cannon across the Bay.] I am almost ninety; I am eighty-eight year old. I was fourteen year old at the time of Concord Fight — and where were you then?'

We were obliged to confess that we were not in the fight.

'Well, walk in, we'll leave it to the women,' said he.

So we walked in, surprised, and sat down, an old woman taking our hats and bundles, and the old man continued, drawing up to the large, old-fashioned fireplace —

'I am a poor, good-for-nothing crittur, as Isaiah says; I am all broken down this year. I am under petticoat government here.'

The family consisted of the old man, his wife, and his daughter, who appeared nearly as old as her mother, a fool, her son (a brutish-looking, middle-aged man, with a prominent lower face, who was standing by the hearth when we entered, but immediately went out), and a little boy of ten.

While my companion talked with the women, I talked with the old man. They said that he was old and foolish, but he was evidently too knowing for them.

'These women,' said he to me, 'are both of them poor good-for-nothing critturs. This one is my wife. I married her sixty-four years ago. She is eighty-four years old, and as deaf as an adder, and the other is not much better.'

He thought well of the Bible, or at least he *spoke* well, and did not *think* ill, of it, for that would not have been prudent for a man of his age. He said that he had read it attentively for many years, and he had much of it at his tongue's end. He seemed deeply impressed with a sense of his own nothingness, and would repeatedly exclaim —

'I am a nothing. What I gather from my Bible is just this; that man is a poor good-for-nothing crittur, and everything is just as God sees fit and disposes.'

'May I ask your name?' I said.

'Yes,' he answered, 'I am not ashamed to tell my name. My name is ——. My great-grandfather came over from England and settled here.'

He was an old Wellfleet oysterman, who had acquired a competency in that business, and had sons still engaged in it.

Nearly all the oyster shops and stands in Massachusetts, I am told, are supplied and kept by natives of Wellfleet, and a part of this town is still called Billingsgate from the oysters having been formerly planted there; but the native oysters are said to have died in 1770. Various causes are assigned for this, such as a ground frost, the carcasses of blackfish, kept to rot in the harbor, and the like, but the most common account of the matter is — and I find that a similar superstition with regard to the disappearance of fishes exists almost everywhere — that when Wellfleet began to quarrel with the neighboring towns about the right to gather them, yellow specks appeared in them, and Providence caused them to disappear. A few years ago sixty thousand bushels were annually brought from the South and planted in the harbor of Wellfleet till they attained 'the proper relish of Billingsgate;' but now they are imported commonly full-grown, and laid down near their markets, at Boston and elsewhere, where the water, being a mixture of salt and fresh, suits them better. The business was said to be still good and improving.

The old man said that the oysters were liable to freeze in the winter, if planted too high; but if it were not 'so cold as to strain their eyes' they were not injured. The inhabitants of New Brunswick have noticed that 'ice will not form over an oyster-bed, unless the cold is very intense indeed, and when the bays are frozen over the oyster-beds are easily discovered by the water above them remaining unfrozen, or as the French residents say, *dégelée*.' Our host said that they kept them in cellars all winter.

'Without anything to eat or drink?' I asked.

'Without anything to eat or drink,' he answered.

'Can the oysters move?'

'Just as much as my shoe.'

But when I caught him saying that they 'bedded themselves down in the sand, flat side up, round side down,' I told him that my shoe could not do that, without the aid of my foot in it; at which he said that they merely settled down as they grew; if put down in a square they would be found so; but the clam could move quite fast. I have since been told by oystermen of Long Island, where the oyster is still indigenous and abundant, that they are found in large masses attached to the parent in their midst, and are so taken up with their tongs; in which case, they say, the age of the young proves that there could have been no motion for five or six years at least. And Buckland in his 'Curiosities of Natural History' (page 50) says: 'An oyster, who has once taken up his position and fixed himself when quite young, can never make a change. Oysters, nevertheless, that have not fixed themselves, but remain loose at the bottom of the sea, have the power of locomotion; they open their shells to their fullest extent, and then suddenly contracting them, the expulsion of the water forwards gives a motion backwards. A fisherman at Guernsey told me that he had frequently seen oysters moving in this way.'

Some still entertain the question 'whether the oyster was indigenous in Massachusetts Bay,' and whether Wellfleet Harbor was a 'natural habitat' of this fish; but, to say nothing of the testimony of old oyster-men, which, I think, is quite conclusive, though the native oyster may now be extinct there, I saw that their shells, opened by the Indians, were strewn all over the Cape. Indeed, the Cape was at first thickly settled by Indians on account of the abundance of these and other fish. We saw many traces of their occupancy after this, in Truro, near Great Hollow, and at High Head, near East Harbor River — oysters, clams, cockles, and other shells, mingled with ashes and the bones of deer and other quadrupeds. I picked up half a dozen arrowheads, and in an hour or two could have filled my pockets with them. The Indians lived about the edges of the swamps, then probably in some instances ponds, for shelter and water. Moreover, Champlain, in the edition of his 'Voyages' printed in 1613, says that in the year 1606 he and Poitrin-court explored a harbor (Barnstable Harbor?) in the southerly part of what is now called Massachusetts Bay, in latitude 42°, about five leagues south, one point west of *Cap Blanc* (Cape Cod), and there they found many good oysters, and they named it '*le Port aux Huistres*' [sic] (Oyster Harbor). In one edition of his map (1632), the '*R. aux Escailles*' is drawn emptying into the same part of the bay, and on the map '*Novi Belgii*,' in Ogilby's America (1670), the words '*Port aux Huistres*' are placed against the same place. Also William Wood, who left New England in 1633, speaks, in his 'New England's Prospect,' published in 1634, of 'a great oyster-bank' in Charles River, and of another in the Mistick, each of which obstructed the navigation of its river. 'The oysters,' says he, 'be great ones in form of a shoe-horn; some be a foot long; these breed on certain banks that are bare every spring tide. This fish without the shell is so big, that it must admit of a division before you can well get it into your mouth.' Oysters are still found there.[1]

Our host told us that the sea-clam, or hen, was not easily obtained; it was raked up, but never on the Atlantic side, only cast ashore there in small quantities in storms. The fisherman sometimes wades in water several feet deep, and thrusts a pointed stick into the sand before him.

[1] Also, see Thomas Morton's 'New English Canaan,' p. 90.

When this enters between the valves of a clam, he closes them on it, and is drawn out. It has been known to catch and hold coot and teal which were preying on it. I chanced to be on the bank of the Acushnet at New Bedford one day since this, watching some ducks, when a man informed me that, having let out his young ducks to seek their food amid the samphire (*Salicornia*) and other weeds along the riverside at low tide that morning, at length he noticed that one remained stationary, amid the weeds, something preventing it from following the others, and going to it he found its foot tightly shut in a quahog's shell. He took up both together, carried them to his home, and his wife opening the shell with a knife released the duck and cooked the quahog. The old man said that the great clams were good to eat, but that they always took out a certain part which was poisonous, before they cooked them. 'People said it would kill a cat.' I did not tell him that I had eaten a large one entire that afternoon, but began to think that I was tougher than a cat. He stated that pedlers came round there, and sometimes tried to sell the women folks a skimmer, but he told them that their women had got a better skimmer than *they* could make, in the shell of their clams; it was shaped just right for this purpose. — They call them 'skim-alls' in some places. He also said that the sun-squall was poisonous to handle, and when the sailors came across it, they did not meddle with it, but heaved it out of their way. I told him that I had handled it that afternoon, and had felt no ill effects as yet. But he said it made the hands itch, especially if they had previously been scratched, or if I put it into my bosom, I should find out what it was.

He informed us that no ice ever formed on the back side of the Cape, or not more than once in a century, and but little snow lay there, it being either absorbed or blown or washed away. Sometimes in winter, when the tide was down, the beach was frozen, and afforded a hard road up the back side for some thirty miles, as smooth as a floor. One winter when he was a boy, he and his father 'took right out into the Back Side before daylight, and walked to Provincetown and back to dinner.'

When I asked what they did with all that barren-looking land, where I saw so few cultivated fields — 'Nothing,' he said.

'Then why fence your fields?'

'To keep the sand from blowing and covering up the whole.'

'The yellow sand,' said he, 'has some life in it, but the white little or none.'

When, in answer to his questions, I told him that I was a surveyor, he said that they who surveyed his farm were accustomed, where the ground was uneven, to loop up each chain as high as their elbows; that was the allowance they made, and he wished to know if I could tell him why they did not come out according to his deed, or twice alike. He seemed to have more respect for surveyors of the old school, which I did not wonder at. 'King George the Third,' said he, 'laid out a road four rods wide and straight, the whole length of the Cape,' but where it was now he could not tell.

This story of the surveyors reminded me of a Long-Islander, who once, when I had made ready to jump from the bow of his boat to the shore, and he thought that I underrated the distance and would fall short — though I found afterward that he judged of the elasticity of my joints by his own — told me that when he came to a brook which he wanted to get over, he held up one leg, and then, if his foot appeared to cover any part of the opposite bank, he knew that he could jump it. 'Why,' I told him, 'to say nothing of the Mississippi, and other small watery streams, I could blot out a star with my foot, but I would not engage to jump that distance,' and asked how he knew when he had got his leg at the right elevation. But he regarded his legs as no less accurate than a pair of screw dividers or an ordinary quadrant, and appeared to have a painful recollection of every degree and minute in the arc which they described; and he would have had me believe that there was a kind of hitch in his hip-joint which answered the purpose. I suggested that he should connect his two ankles by a string of the proper length, which should be the chord of an arc, measuring his jumping ability on horizontal surfaces — assuming one leg to be a perpendicular to the plane of the horizon, which, however, may have been too bold an assumption in this case. Nevertheless, this was a kind of geometry in the legs which it interested me to hear of.

Our host took pleasure in telling us the names of the ponds, most of which we could see from his windows, and making us repeat them after him, to see if we had got them right. They were Gull Pond, the largest and a very handsome one, clear and deep, and more than a mile in circumference, Newcomb's, Swett's, Slough, Horse-Leech, Round, and Herring Ponds, all connected at high water, if I do not mistake. The coast-surveyors had come to him for their names, and he told them of one which they had not detected. He said that they were not so high as formerly. There was an earthquake about four years before he was born, which cracked the pans of the ponds, which were of iron, and caused them to settle. I did not remember to have read of this. Innumerable gulls used to resort to them; but the large gulls were now very scarce, for, as he said, the English robbed their nests far in the north, where they breed. He remembered well when gulls were taken in the gull-house, and when small birds were killed by means of a frying-pan and fire at night. His father once lost a valuable horse from this cause. A party from Wellfleet having lighted their fire for this purpose, one dark night, on Billingsgate Island, twenty horses which were pastured there, and this colt among them, being frightened by it, and endeavoring in the dark to cross the passage which separated them from the neighboring beach, and which was then fordable at low tide, were all swept out to sea and drowned. I observed that many horses were still turned out to pasture all summer on the islands and beaches in Wellfleet, Eastham, and Orleans, as a kind of common. He also 'described the killing of what he called 'wild hens,' here, after they had gone to roost in the woods, when he was a boy. Perhaps they were 'prairie hens' (pinnated grouse).

He liked the beach pea (*Lathyrus maritimus*), cooked green, as well as the cultivated. He had seen it growing very abundantly in Newfoundland, where also the inhabitants ate them, but he had never been able to obtain any ripe for seed. We read, under the head of Chatham, that 'in 1555, during a time of great scarcity, the people about Orford, in Sussex [England] were preserved from perishing by eating the seeds of this plant, which grew there in great abundance upon the sea coast. Cows, horses, sheep, and goats eat it.' But the writer who quoted this could not learn that they had ever been used in Barnstable County.

He had been a voyager, then? Oh, he had been about the world in his day. He once considered himself a pilot for all our coast; but now they had changed the names so he might be bothered.

He gave us to taste what he called the Summer Sweeting, a pleasant apple which he raised, and frequently grafted from, but had never seen growing elsewhere, except once — three trees on Newfoundland, or at the Bay of Chaleur, I forget which, as he was sailing by. He was sure that he could tell the tree at a distance.

At length the fool, whom my companion called the wizard, came in, muttering between his teeth, 'Damn book-pedlers — all the time talking about books. Better do something. Damn 'em. I'll shoot 'em. Got a doctor down here. Damn him, I'll get a gun and shoot him;' never once holding up his head. Whereat the old man stood up and said in a loud voice, as if he was accustomed to command, and this was not the first time he had been obliged to exert his authority there: 'John, go sit down, mind your business — we've heard you talk before — precious little you'll do — your bark is worse than your bite.' But, without minding, John muttered the same gibberish over again, and then sat down at the table which the old folks had left. He ate all there was on it, and then turned to the apples, which his aged mother was paring, that she might give her guests some apple-sauce for breakfast, but she drew them away and sent him off.

When I approached this house the next summer, over the desolate hills between it and the shore, which are worthy to have been the birth-place of Ossian, I saw the wizard in the midst of a corn-field on the hill-side, but, as usual, he loomed so strangely, that I mistook him for a scarecrow.

This was the merriest old man that we had ever seen, and one of the best preserved. His style of conversation was coarse and plain enough to have suited Rabelais. He would have made a good Panurge. Or rather he was a sober Silenus, and we were the boys Chromis and Mnasilus, who listened to his story.

> 'Not by Hæmonian hills the Thracian bard,
> Nor awful Phœbus was on Pindus heard
> With deeper silence or with more regard.'

There was a strange mingling of past and present in his conversation, for he had lived under King George, and might have remembered when Napoleon and the moderns generally were born. He said that one day, when the troubles between the Colonies and the mother country first broke out, as he, a boy of fifteen, was pitching hay out of a cart, one Donne, an old Tory, who was talking with his father, a good Whig, said to him, 'Why, Uncle Bill, you might as well undertake to pitch that pond into the ocean with a pitchfork, as for the Colonies to undertake to gain their independence.' He remembered well General Washington, and how he rode his horse along the streets of Boston, and he stood up to show us how he looked.

'He was a r—a—ther large and portly-looking man, a manly and resolute-looking officer, with a pretty good leg as he sat on his horse.' — 'There, I'll tell you, this was the way with Washington.' Then he jumped up again, and bowed gracefully to right and left, making show as if he were waving his hat. Said he, '*That* was Washington.'

He told us many anecdotes of the Revolution, and was much pleased when we told him that we had read the same in history, and that his account agreed with the written.

'Oh,' he said, 'I know, I know! I was a young fellow of sixteen, with my ears wide open; and a fellow of that age, you know, is pretty wide awake, and likes to know everything that's going on. Oh, I know!'

He told us the story of the wreck of the Franklin, which took place there the previous spring; how a boy came to his house early in the morning to know whose boat that was by the shore, for there was a vessel in distress, and he, being an old man, first ate his breakfast, and then walked over to the top of the hill by the shore, and sat down there, having found a comfortable seat, to see the ship wrecked. She was on the bar, only a quarter of a mile from him, and still nearer to the men on the beach, who had got a boat ready, but could render no assistance on account of the breakers, for there was a pretty high sea running. There were the passengers all crowded together in the forward part of the ship, and some were getting out of the cabin windows and were drawn on deck by the others.

'I saw the captain get out his boat,' said he; 'he had one little one; and then they jumped into it one after another, down as straight as an arrow. I counted them. There were nine. One was a woman, and she jumped as straight as any of them. Then they shoved off. The sea took them back, one wave went over them, and when they came up there were six still clinging to the boat; I counted them. The next waves turned the boat bottom upward, and emptied them all out. None of them ever came ashore alive. There were the rest of them all crowded together on the forecastle, the other parts of the ship being under water. They had seen all that happened to the boat. At length a heavy sea separated the forecastle from the rest of the wreck, and set it inside of the worst breaker, and the boat was able to reach them, and it saved all that were left, but one woman.'

He also told us of the steamer Cambria's getting aground on this shore a few months before we were there, and of her English passengers who roamed over his grounds, and who, he said, thought the prospect from the high hill by the shore, 'the most delightsome they had ever seen,' and also of the pranks which the ladies played with his scoop-net in the ponds. He spoke of these travellers with their purses full of guineas, just as our provincial fathers used to speak of British bloods in the time of King George the Third.

Quid loquar? Why repeat what he told us?

> 'Aut Scyllam Nisi, quam fama secuta est,
> Candida succinctam latrantibus inguina monstris,
> Dulichias vexâsse rates, et gurgite in alto
> Ah! timidos nautas canibus lacerâsse marinis?'

In the course of the evening I began to feel the potency of the clam which I had eaten, and I was obliged to confess to our host that I was no tougher than the cat he told of; but he answered, that he was a plain-spoken man, and he could tell me that it was all imagination. At any rate, it proved an emetic in my case, and I was made quite sick by it for a short time, while he laughed at my expense. I was pleased to read afterward, in Mourt's Relation of the landing of the Pilgrims in Provincetown Harbor these words: 'We found great muscles [the old editor says that they were undoubtedly sea-clams] and very fat and full of sea-pearl; but we could not eat them, for they made us all sick that did eat, as well sailors as passengers, . . . but they were soon well again.' It brought me nearer to the Pilgrims to be thus reminded by a similar experience that I was so like them. Moreover, it was a valuable con-firmation of their story, and I am prepared now to believe every word of Mourt's Relation. I was also pleased to find that man and the clam lay still at the same angle to one another. But I did not notice sea-pearl. Like Cleopatra, I must have swallowed it. I have since dug these clams on a flat in the Bay and observed them. They could squirt full ten feet before the wind, as appeared by the marks of the drops on the sand.

'Now I am going to ask you a question,' said the old man, 'and I don't know as you can tell me; but you are a learned man, and I never had any learning, only what I got by natur.' — It was in vain that we re-minded him that he could quote Josephus to our confusion. — 'I've thought, if I ever met a learned man I should like to ask him this ques-tion. Can you tell me how *Axy* is spelt, and what it means? *Axy*,' says he; 'there's a girl over here is named *Axy*. Now what is it? What does it mean? Is it Scripture? I've read my Bible twenty-five years over and over, and I never came across it.'

'Did you read it twenty-five years for this object?' I asked.

'Well, *how* is it spelt? Wife, how is it spelt?'

She said, 'It is in the Bible; I've seen it.'

'Well, how do you spell it?'

'I don't know. A c h, ach, s e h, seh — Achseh.'

'Does that spell Axy? Well, do *you* know what it means?' asked he, turning to me.

'No,' I replied, 'I never heard the sound before.'

'There was a schoolmaster down here once, and they asked him what it meant, and he said it had no more meaning than a bean-pole.'

I told him that I held the same opinion with the schoolmaster. I had been a schoolmaster myself, and had had strange names to deal with. I also heard of such names as Zoheth, Beriah, Amaziah, Bethuel, and Shearjashub, hereabouts.

At length the little boy, who had a seat quite in the chimney-corner, took off his stockings and shoes, warmed his feet, and having had his sore leg freshly salved, went off to bed; then the fool made bare his knotty-looking feet and legs, and followed him; and finally the old man exposed his calves also to our gaze. We had never had the good fortune to see an old man's legs before, and were surprised to find them fair and plump as an infant's, and we thought that he took a pride in exhibiting them. He then proceeded to make preparations for retiring, discoursing meanwhile with Panurgic plainness of speech on the ills to which old humanity is subject. We were a rare haul for him. He could commonly get none but ministers to talk to, though sometimes ten of them at once, and he was glad to meet some of the laity at leisure. The evening was not long enough for him. As I had been sick, the old lady asked if I would not go to bed — it was getting late for old people; but the old man, who had not yet done his stories, said, 'You ain't particular, are you?'

'Oh, no,' said I, 'I am in no hurry. I believe I have weathered the Clam cape.'

'They are good,' said he; 'I wish I had some of them now.'

'They never hurt me,' said the old lady.

'But then you took out the part that killed a cat,' said I.

At last we cut him short in the midst of his stories, which he promised to resume in the morning. Yet, after all, one of the old ladies who came into our room in the night to fasten the fire-board, which rattled, as she went out took the precaution to fasten us in. Old women are by nature more suspicious than old men. However, the winds howled around the house, and made the fire-boards as well as the casements rattle well that night. It was probably a windy night for any locality, but we could not distinguish the roar which was proper to the ocean from that which was due to the wind alone.

The sounds which the ocean makes must be very significant and interesting to those who live near it. When I was leaving the shore at this place the next summer, and had got a quarter of a mile distant, ascending a hill, I was startled by a sudden, loud sound from the sea, as if a large steamer were letting off steam by the shore, so that I caught my breath and felt my blood run cold for an instant, and I turned about, expecting to see one of the Atlantic steamers thus far out of her course, but there was nothing unusual to be seen. There was a low bank at the entrance of the Hollow, between me and the ocean, and suspecting that I might have risen into another stratum of air in ascending the hill — which had wafted to me only the ordinary roar of the sea — I immediately descended again, to see if I lost hearing of it; but, without regard to my ascending or descending, it died away in a minute or two, and yet there was scarcely any wind all the while. The old man said that this was what they called the 'rut,' a peculiar roar of the sea before the wind changes, which, however, he could not account for. He thought that he could tell all about the weather from the sounds which the sea made.

Old Josselyn, who came to New England in 1638, has it among his weather-signs, that 'the resounding of the sea from the shore, and murmuring of the winds in the woods, without apparent wind, sheweth wind to follow.'

Being on another part of the coast one night since this, I heard the roar of the surf a mile distant, and the inhabitants said it was a sign that the wind would work round east, and we should have rainy weather. The ocean was heaped up somewhere at the eastward, and this roar was occasioned by its effort to preserve its equilibrium, the wave reaching the shore before the wind. Also the captain of a packet between this country and England told me that he sometimes met with a wave on the Atlantic coming against the wind, perhaps in a calm sea, which indicated that at a distance the wind was blowing from an opposite quarter, but the undulation had travelled faster than it. Sailors tell of 'tide-rips' and 'ground-swells,' which they suppose to have been occasioned by hurricanes and earthquakes, and to have travelled many hundred, and sometimes even two or three thousand miles.

Before sunrise the next morning they let us out again, and I ran over to the beach to see the sun come out of the ocean. The old woman of eighty-four winters was already out in the cold morning wind, bareheaded, tripping about like a young girl, and driving up the cow to milk. She got the breakfast with dispatch, and without noise or bustle; and meanwhile the old man resumed his stories, standing before us, who were sitting, with his back to the chimney, and ejecting his tobacco-juice right and left into the fire behind him, without regard to the various dishes which were there preparing. At breakfast we had eels, buttermilk cake, cold bread, green beans, doughnuts, and tea. The old man talked a steady stream; and when his wife told him he had better eat his breakfast, he said, 'Don't hurry me; I have lived too long to be hurried.' I ate of the apple-sauce and the doughnuts, which I thought had sustained the least detriment from the old man's shots, but my companion refused the apple-sauce, and ate of the hot cake and green beans, which had appeared to him to occupy the safest part of the hearth. But on comparing notes afterward, I told him that the butter-milk cake was particularly exposed, and I saw how it suffered repeat-edly, and therefore I avoided it; but he declared that, however that might be, he witnessed that the apple-sauce was seriously injured, and had therefore declined that. After breakfast we looked at his clock, which was out of order, and oiled it with some 'hen's grease,' for want of sweet oil, for he scarcely could believe that we were not tinkers or pedlers; meanwhile, he told a story about visions, which had reference to a crack in the clock-case made by frost one night. He was curious to know to what religious sect we belonged. He said that he had been to hear thirteen kinds of preaching in one month, when he was young, but he did not join any of them — he stuck to his Bible. There was nothing like any of them in his Bible. While I was shaving in the next room, I heard him ask my companion to what sect he belonged, to which he answered —

'Oh, I belong to the Universal Brotherhood.'

'What's that?' he asked, 'Sons o' Temperance?'

Finally, filling our pockets with doughnuts, which he was pleased to find that we called by the same name that he did, and paying for our entertainment, we took our departure; but he followed us out of doors, and made us tell him the names of the vegetables which he had raised from seeds that came out of the Franklin. They were cabbage, broccoli, and parsley. As I had asked him the names of so many things, he tried me in turn with all the plants which grew in his garden, both wild and cultivated. It was about half an acre, which he cultivated wholly himself. Besides the common garden vegetables, there were yellow dock, lemon balm, hyssop, gill-go-over-the-ground, mouse-ear, chick-weed, Roman wormwood, elecampane, and other plants. As we stood there, I saw a fish hawk stoop to pick a fish out of his pond.

'There,' said I, 'he has got a fish.'

'Well,' said the old man, who was looking all the while, but could see nothing, 'he didn't dive, he just wet his claws.'

And, sure enough, he did not this time, though it is said that they often do, but he merely stooped low enough to pick him out with his talons; but as he bore his shining prey over the bushes, it fell to the ground, and we did not see that he recovered it. That is not their practice.

Thus, having had another crack with the old man, he standing bare-headed under the eaves, he directed us 'athwart the fields,' and we took to the beach again for another day, it being now late in the morning.

It was but a day or two after this that the safe of the Provincetown Bank was broken open and robbed by two men from the interior, and we learned that our hospitable entertainers did at least transiently harbor the suspicion that we were the men.

VI. THE BEACH AGAIN

OUR way to the high sand-bank which I have described as extending all along the coast led, as usual, through patches of bayberry bushes, which straggled into the sand. This, next to the shrub oak, was perhaps the most common shrub thereabouts. I was much attracted by its odoriferous leaves and small gray berries which are clustered about the short twigs, just below the last year's growth. I know of but two bushes in Concord, and they, being staminate plants, do not bear fruit. The berries gave it a venerable appearance, and they smelled quite spicy, like small confectionery. Robert Beverley, in his 'History of Virginia,' published in 1705, states that 'at the mouth of their rivers, and all along upon the sea and bay, and near many of their creeks and swamps, grows the myrtle, bearing a berry, of which they make a hard, brittle wax, of a curious green color, which by refining becomes almost transparent. Of this they make candles, which are never greasy to the touch nor melt with lying in the hottest weather; neither does the snuff of these ever offend the smell, like that of a tallow candle; but, instead of being disagreeable, if an accident puts a candle out, it yields a pleasant fragrancy to all that are in the room; insomuch that nice people often put them out on purpose to have the incense of the expiring snuff. The melting of these berries is said to have been first found out bv a surgeon in New England, who performed wonderful things with a salve made of them.' From the abundance of berries still hanging on the bushes, we judged that the inhabitants did not generally collect them for tallow, though we had seen a piece in the house we had just left. I have since made some tallow myself. Holding a basket beneath the bare twigs in

April, I rubbed them together between my hands and thus gathered about a quart in twenty minutes, to which were added enough to make three pints, and I might have gathered them much faster with a suitable rake and a large shallow basket. They have little prominences like those of an orange all creased in tallow, which also fills the interstices down to the stone. The oily part rose to the top, making it look like a savory black broth, which smelled much like balm or other herb tea. You let it cool, then skim off the tallow from the surface, melt this again, and strain it. I got about a quarter of a pound weight from my three pints, and more yet remained within the berries. A small portion cooled in the form of small flattish hemispheres, like crystallizations, the size of a kernel of corn (nuggets I called them as I picked them out from amid the berries). Loudon says, that 'cultivated trees are said to yield more wax than those that are found wild.' [1] If you get any pitch on your hands in the pine woods you have only to rub some of these berries between your hands to start it off. But the ocean was the grand fact there, which made us forget both bayberries and men.

Today the air was beautifully clear, and the sea no longer dark and stormy, though the waves still broke with foam along the beach, but sparkling and full of life. Already that morning I had seen the day break over the sea as if it came out of its bosom:

> 'The saffron-robed Dawn rose in haste from the streams
> Of Ocean, that she might bring light to immortals and to mortals.'

The sun rose visibly at such a distance over the sea, that the cloud-bank in the horizon, which at first concealed him, was not perceptible until he had risen high behind it, and plainly broke and dispersed it, like an arrow. But as yet I looked at him as rising over land, and could not, without an effort, realize that he was rising over the sea. Already I saw some vessels on the horizon, which had rounded the Cape in the night, and were now well on their watery way to other lands.

We struck the beach again in the south part of Truro. In the early part of the day, while it was flood tide, and the beach was narrow and soft, we walked on the bank, which was very high here, but not so level as the day before, being more interrupted by slight hollows. The author of the 'Description of the Eastern Coast' says of this part, that 'the bank is very high and steep. From the edge of it, west, there is a strip of sand, a hundred yards in breadth. Then succeeds low brushwood, a quarter of a mile wide, and almost impassable. After which

---

[1] See Duplessy, *Végétaux Résineux*, vol. II, p. 60.

comes a thick, perplexing forest in which not a house is to be discovered. Seamen, therefore, though the distance between these two vallies [Newcomb's and Brush Hollows] is great, must not attempt to enter the wood, as in a snow storm they must undoubtedly perish.' This is still a true description of the country, except that there is not much high wood left.

There were many vessels, like gulls, skimming over the surface of the sea, now half concealed in its troughs, their dolphin-strikers plowing the water, now tossed on the top of the billows. One, a barque standing down parallel with the coast, suddenly furled her sails, came to anchor, and swung round in the wind, near us, only half a mile from the shore. At first we thought that her captain wished to communicate with us, and perhaps we did not regard the signal of distress, which a mariner would have understood, and he cursed us for cold-hearted wreckers who turned our backs on him. For hours we could still see her anchored there behind us, and we wondered how she could afford to loiter so long in her course. Or was she a smuggler who had chosen that wild beach to land her cargo on? Or did they wish to catch fish, or paint their vessel? Ere long other barques, and brigs, and schooners, which had in the meanwhile doubled the Cape, sailed by her in the smacking breeze, and our consciences were relieved. Some of these vessels lagged behind, while others steadily went ahead. We narrowly watched their rig and the cut of their jibs, and how they walked the water, for there was all the difference between them that there is between living creatures. But we wondered that they should be remembering Boston and New York and Liverpool, steering for them, out there; as if the sailor might forget his peddling business on such a grand highway. They had perchance brought oranges from the Western Isles; and were they carrying back the peel? We might as well transport our old traps across the ocean of eternity. Is *that* but another 'trading flood,' with its blessed isles? Is Heaven such a harbor as the Liverpool docks?

Still held on without a break the inland barrens and shrubbery, the desert and the high sand-bank with its even slope, the broad white beach, the breakers, the green water on the bar, and the Atlantic Ocean; and we traversed with delight new reaches of the shore; we took another lesson in sea-horses' manes and sea-cows' tails, in sea-jellies and sea-clams, with our new-gained experience. The sea ran hardly less than the day before. It seemed with every wave to be subsiding, because such was our expectation, and yet when hours had elapsed we could see no difference. But there it was, balancing itself, the restless ocean by our side, lurching in its gait. Each wave left the sand all braided or woven, as it were with a coarse woof and warp, and a distinct raised edge to its rapid work. We made no haste, since we wished to see the ocean at our leisure, and indeed that soft sand was no place in which to be in a hurry, for one mile there was as good as two elsewhere. Besides, we were obliged frequently to empty our shoes of the sand which one took in in climbing or descending the bank.

As we were walking close to the water's edge this morning, we turned round, by chance, and saw a large black object which the waves had just cast up on the beach behind us, yet too far off for us to distinguish what it was; and when we were about to return to it, two men came running from the bank, where no human beings had appeared before, as if they had come out of the sand, in order to save it before another wave took it. As we approached, it took successively the form of a huge fish, a drowned man, a sail or a net, and finally of a mass of tow-cloth, part of the cargo of the Franklin, which the men loaded into a cart.

Objects on the beach, whether men or inanimate things, look not only exceedingly grotesque, but much larger and more wonderful than they actually are. Lately, when approaching the seashore several degrees south of this, I saw before me, seemingly half a mile distant, what appeared like bold and rugged cliffs on the beach, fifteen feet high, and whitened by the sun and waves; but after a few steps it proved to be low heaps of rags — part of the cargo of a wrecked vessel — scarcely more than a foot in height. Once also it was my business to go in search of the relics of a human body, mangled by sharks, which had just been cast up, a week after a wreck, having got the direction from a lighthouse: I should find it a mile or two distant over the sand, a dozen rods from the water, covered with a cloth, by a stick stuck up. I expected that I must look very narrowly to find so small an object, but the sandy beach, half a mile wide, and stretching farther than the eye could reach, was so perfectly smooth and bare, and the mirage toward the sea so magnifying, that when I was half a mile distant the insignificant sliver which marked the spot looked like a bleached spar, and the relics were as conspicuous as if they lay in state on that sandy plain, or a generation had labored to pile up their cairn there. Close at hand they were simply some bones with a little flesh adhering to them, in fact only a slight inequality in the sweep of the shore. There was nothing at all remarkable about them, and they were singularly inoffensive both to the senses and the imagination. But as I stood there they grew more and more imposing. They were alone with the beach and the sea, whose hollow roar seemed addressed to them, and I was impressed as if there was an understanding between them and the ocean which necessarily left me out, with my snivelling sympathies. That dead body had taken possession of the shore, and reigned over it as no living one could, in the name of a certain majesty which belonged to it. . . . [1]

Sometimes we helped a wrecker turn over a larger log than usual, or we amused ourselves with rolling stones down the bank, but we rarely could make one reach the water, the beach was so soft and wide; or we bathed in some shallow within a bar, where the sea covered us with sand at every flux, though it was quite cold and windy. The ocean there is commonly but a tantalizing prospect in hot weather, for with all that water before you, there is, as we were afterward told, no bathing on the Atlantic side, on account of the undertow and the rumor of sharks. At the lighthouse, both in Eastham and Truro, the only houses quite on the shore, they declared, the next year, that they would not bathe there 'for any sum,' for they sometimes saw the sharks tossed up and quiver for a moment on the sand. Others laughed at these stories, but perhaps they could afford to because they never bathed anywhere. One old wrecker told us that he killed a regular man-eating shark fourteen feet long, and hauled him out with his oxen, where we had bathed; and another, that his father caught a smaller one of the same kind that was stranded there, by standing him up on his snout so that the waves could not take him. They will tell you tough stories of sharks all over the Cape, which I do not presume to doubt utterly — how they will sometimes upset a boat, or tear it in pieces, to get at the man in it. I can easily believe in the undertow, but I have no doubt that one shark in a dozen years is enough to keep up the reputation of a beach a hundred miles long. I should add, however, that in July we walked on the bank here a quarter of a mile parallel with a fish about six feet in length, possibly a shark, which was prowling slowly along within two rods of the shore. It was of a pale brown color, singularly film-like and indistinct in the water, as if all nature abetted this child of ocean, and showed many darker transverse bars or rings whenever it came to the surface. It is well known that different fishes even of the same species are colored by the water they inhabit. We saw it go into a little cove or bathing-tub, where we had just been bathing, where the water was only four or five feet deep at that time, and after exploring it go slowly out again; but

[1] Pages 108–111 (Walden edition), omitted.

we continued to bathe there, only observing first from the bank if the cove was preoccupied. We thought that the water was fuller of life, more aerated perhaps than that of the Bay, like soda-water, for we were as particular as young salmon, and the expectation of encountering a shark did not subtract anything from its life-giving qualities.

Sometimes we sat on the wet beach and watched the beach-birds, sandpipers, and others, trotting along close to each wave, and waiting for the sea to cast up their breakfast. The former (*Charadrius melodus*) ran with great rapidity, and then stood stock-still, remarkably erect, and hardly to be distinguished from the beach. The wet sand was covered with small skipping sea-fleas, which apparently made a part of their food. These last are the little scavengers of the beach, and are so numerous that they will devour large fishes which have been cast up, in a very short time. One little bird not larger than a sparrow — it may have been a phalarope — would alight on the turbulent surface where the breakers were five or six feet high, and float buoyantly there like a duck, cunningly taking to its wings and lifting itself a few feet through the air over the foaming crest of each breaker, but sometimes out-riding safely a considerable billow which hid it some seconds, when its instinct told it that it would not break. It was a little creature thus to sport with the ocean, but it was as perfect a success in its way as the breakers in theirs. There was also an almost uninterrupted line of coots rising and falling with the waves, a few rods from the shore, the whole length of the Cape. They made as constant a part of the ocean's border as the pads or pickerel-weed do of that of a pond. We read the following as to the storm petrel (*Thalassidroma Wilsonii*), which is seen in the Bay as well as on the outside. 'The feathers on the breast of the Storm Petrel are, like those of all swimming birds, water-proof; but substances not susceptible of being wetted with water are, for that very reason, the best fitted for collecting oil from its surface. That function is performed by the feathers on the breast of the Storm Petrels as they touch on the surface; and though that may not be the only way in which they procure their food, it is certainly that in which they obtain great part of it. They dash along till they have loaded their feathers and then they pause upon the waves and remove the oil with their bills.'

Thus we kept on along the gently curving shore, seeing two or three miles ahead at once — along this ocean sidewalk, where there was none to turn out for, with the middle of the road, the highway of nations, on our right, and the sand cliffs of the Cape on our left. We saw this forenoon a part of the wreck of a vessel, probably the Franklin, a large piece fifteen feet square, and still freshly painted. With a grapple and a line we could have saved it, for the waves repeatedly washed it within cast, but they as often took it back. It would have been a lucky haul for some poor wrecker, for I have been told that one man who paid three or four dollars for a part of the wreck of that vessel, sold fifty or sixty dollars' worth of iron out of it. Another, the same who picked up the captain's valise with the memorable letter in it, showed me, growing in his garden, many pear and plum trees which washed ashore from her, all nicely tied up and labelled, and he said that he might have got five hundred dollars' worth; for a Mr. Bell was importing the nucleus of a nursery to be established near Boston. His turnip-seed came from the same source. Also valuable spars from the same vessel and from the Cactus lay in his yard. In short the inhabitants visit the beach to see what they have caught as regularly as a fisherman his weir or a lumberer his boom; the Cape is their boom. I heard of one who had recently picked up twenty barrels of apples in good condition, probably a part of a deck load thrown over in a storm.

Though there are wreck-masters appointed to look after valuable property which must be advertised, yet undoubtedly a great deal of value is secretly carried off. But are we not all wreckers contriving that some treasure may be washed up on our beach, that we may secure it, and do we not infer the habits of these Nauset and Barnegat wreckers, from the common modes of getting a living?

The sea, vast and wild as it is, bears thus the waste and wrecks of human art to its remotest shore. There is no telling what it may not vomit up. It lets nothing lie; not even the giant clams which cling to its bottom. It is still heaving up the tow-cloth of the Franklin, and perhaps a piece of some old pirate's ship, wrecked more than a hundred years ago, comes ashore today. Some years since, when a vessel was wrecked here which had nutmegs in her cargo, they were strewn all along the beach, and for a considerable time were not spoiled by the salt water. Soon afterward, a fisherman caught a cod which was full of them. Why, then, might not the Spice-Islanders shake their nutmeg trees into the ocean, and let all nations who stand in need of them pick them up? However, after a year, I found that the nutmegs from the Franklin had become soft.

You might make a curious list of articles which fishes have swallowed — sailors' open clasp-knives, and bright tin snuff-boxes — not knowing what was in them — and jugs, and jewels, and Jonah. The other day I came across the following scrap in a newspaper:

A Religious Fish. — A short time ago, mine host Steward, of the Denton Hotel, purchased a rock-fish, weighing about sixty pounds. On opening it he found in it a certificate of membership of the M. E. Church, which we read as follows:

Member

Methodist E. Church,
    Founded A. D. 1784.
Quarterly Ticket.   18

Minister.

'For our light affliction, which is but for a moment, worketh for us a far more exceeding *and* eternal weight of glory.' — 2 Cor. iv. 17.

'O what are all my sufferings here,
    If, Lord, thou count me meet
With that enraptured host t'appear,
    And worship at thy feet.'

The paper was, of course, in a crumpled and wet condition, but on exposing it to the sun, and ironing the kinks out of it, it became quite legible. — Denton (Md.) *Journal*.

From time to time we saved a wreck ourselves, a box or barrel, and set it on its end, and appropriated it with crossed sticks; and it will lie there perhaps, respected by brother wreckers, until some more violent storm shall take it, really lost to man until wrecked again. We also saved, at the cost of wet feet only, a valuable cord and buoy, part of a seine, with which the sea was playing, for it seemed ungracious to refuse the least gift which so great a personage offered you. We brought this home and still use it for a garden line. I picked up a bottle half buried in the wet sand, covered with barnacles, but stoppled tight, and half full of red ale, which still smacked of juniper — all that remained I fancied from the wreck of a rowdy world — that great salt sea on the one hand, and this little sea of ale on the other, preserving their separate characters. What if it could tell us its adventures over countless ocean waves! Man would not be man through such ordeals as it had passed. But as I poured it slowly out on to the sand, it seemed to me that man himself was like a half-emptied bottle of pale ale, which Time had drunk so far, yet stoppled tight for a while, and drifting about in the ocean of circumstances, but destined ere long to mingle with the surrounding waves, or be spilled amid the sands of a distant shore.

In the summer I saw two men fishing for bass hereabouts. Their bait was a bullfrog, or several small frogs in a bunch, for want of squid. They followed a retiring wave, and whirling their lines round and round their heads with increasing rapidity, threw them as far as they could into the sea; then retreating, sat down flat on the sand, and waited for a bite. It was literally (or *littorally*) walking down to the shore, and throwing your line into the Atlantic. I should not have known what might take hold of the other end, whether Proteus or another. At any rate, if you could not pull him in, why, you might let him go without being pulled in yourself. And *they* knew by experience that it would be a striped bass, or perhaps a cod, for these fishes play along near the shore.

From time to time we sat under the lee of a sandhill on the bank, thinly covered with coarse beach-grass, and steadily gazed on the sea, or watched the vessels going south, all Blessings of the Bay of course. We could see a little more than half a circle of ocean, besides the glimpses of the Bay which we got behind us; the sea there was not wild and dreary in all respects, for there were frequently a hundred sail in sight at once on the Atlantic. You can commonly count about eighty in a favorable summer day, and pilots sometimes land and ascend the bank to look out for those which require their services. These had been waiting for fair weather, and had come out of Boston Harbor together. The same is the case when they have been assembled in the Vineyard Sound, so that you may see but few one day, and a large fleet the next. Schooners with many jibs and staysails crowded all the sea road; square-rigged vessels with their great height and breadth of canvas were ever and anon appearing out of the far horizon, or disappearing and sinking into it; here and there a pilot-boat was towing its little boat astern toward some distant foreigner who had just fired a gun, the echo of which along the shore sounded like the caving of the bank. We could see the pilot looking through his glass toward the distant ship which was putting back to speak with him. He sails many a mile to meet her; and now she puts her sails aback, and communicates with him alongside — sends some important message to the owners, and then bids farewell to these shores for good and all; or, perchance a propeller passed and made fast to some disabled craft, or one that had been becalmed, whose cargo of fruit might spoil. Though silently, and for the most part incommunicatively, going about their business, they were, no doubt, a source of cheerfulness and a kind of society to one another.

Today it was the Purple Sea, an epithet which I should not before have accepted. There were distinct patches of the color of a purple grape with the bloom rubbed off. But first and last the sea is of all colors. Well writes Gilpin concerning 'the brilliant hues which are continually playing on the surface of a quiet ocean,' and this was not too turbulent at a distance from the shore. 'Beautiful,' says he, 'no doubt in a high degree are those glimmering tints which often invest the tops of mountains; but they are mere coruscations compared with these marine colors, which are continually varying and shifting into each other in all the vivid splendor of the rainbow, through the space often of several leagues.' Commonly, in calm weather, for half a mile from the shore, where the bottom tinges it, the sea is green, or greenish, as are some ponds; then blue for many miles, often with purple tinges, bounded in the distance by a light, almost silvery stripe; beyond which there is generally a dark-blue rim, like a mountain ridge in the horizon, as if, like that, it owed its color to the intervening atmosphere. On another day, it will be marked with long streaks, alternately smooth and rippled, light-colored and dark, even like our inland meadows in a freshet, and showing which way the wind sets.

Thus we sat on the foaming shore, looking on the wine-colored ocean,

Θίν' ἐφ' ἁλὸς πολιῆς, ὁρόων ἐπὶ οἴνοπα πόντον.

Here and there was a darker spot on its surface, the shadow of a cloud, though the sky was so clear that no cloud would have been noticed otherwise, and no shadow would have been seen on the land, where a much smaller surface is visible at once. So, distant clouds and showers may be seen on all sides by a sailor in the course of a day, which do not necessarily portend rain where he is. In July we saw similar dark-blue patches where schools of menhaden rippled the surface, scarcely to be distinguished from the shadows of clouds. Sometimes the sea was spotted with them far and wide, such is its inexhaustible fertility. Close at hand you see their back fin, which is very long and sharp, projecting two or three inches above water. From time to time also we saw the white bellies of the bass playing along the shore.

It was a poetic recreation to watch those distant sails steering for half-fabulous ports, whose very names are a mysterious music to our ears; Fayal, and Bab-el-Mandeb, ay, and Chagres, and Panama — bound to the famous Bay of San Francisco, and the golden streams of Sacramento and San Joaquin, to Feather River and the American Fork, where Sutter's Fort presides, and inland stands the City de los Angeles. It is remarkable that men do not sail the sea with more expectation. Nothing remarkable was ever accomplished in a prosaic mood. The heroes and discoverers have found true more than was previously believed, only when they were expecting and dreaming of something more than their contemporaries dreamed of, or even themselves discovered, that is, when they were in a frame of mind fitted to behold the truth. Referred to the world's standard, they are always insane. Even savages have indirectly surmised as much. Humboldt, speaking of Columbus approaching the New World, says: 'The grateful coolness of the evening air, the ethereal purity of the starry firmament, the balmy fragrance of flowers, wafted to him by the land breeze, all led him to suppose (as we are told by Herrera, in the Decades) that he was approaching the garden of Eden, the sacred abode of our first parents. The Orinoco seemed to him one of the four rivers which, according to the venerable tradition of the ancient world, flowed from Paradise, to water and divide the surface of the earth, newly adorned with plants.' So even the expeditions for the discovery of El Dorado, and of the Fountain of Youth, led to real, if not compensatory discoveries.

We discerned vessels so far off, when once we began to look, that only the tops of their masts in the horizon were visible, and it took a strong intention of the eye, and its most favorable side, to see them at all, and sometimes we doubted if we were not counting our eyelashes. Charles Darwin states that he saw, from the base of the Andes, 'the masts of the vessels at anchor in the bay of Valparaiso, although not less than twenty-six geographical miles distant,' and that Anson had been surprised at the distance at which his vessels were discovered from the coast, without knowing the reason, namely, the great height of the land and the transparency of the air. Steamers may be detected much farther than sailing vessels, for, as one says, when their hulls and masts of wood and iron are down, their smoky masts and streamers still betray them; and the same writer, speaking of the comparative advantages of bituminous and anthracite coal for war-steamers, states that 'from the ascent of the columns of smoke above the horizon, the motions of the steamers in Calais Harbor [on the coast of France] are at all times observable at Ramsgate [on the English coast], from the first lighting of the fires to the putting out at sea; and that in America the steamers burning the fat bituminous coal can be tracked at sea at least seventy miles before the hulls become visible, by the dense columns of black smoke pouring out of their chimneys, and trailing along the horizon.'

Though there were numerous vessels at this great distance in the horizon on every side, yet the vast spaces between them, like the spaces between the stars — far as they were distant from us, so were they from one another — nay, some were twice as far from each other as from us — impressed us with a sense of the immensity of the ocean, the 'unfruitful ocean,' as it has been called, and we could see what proportion man and his works bear to the globe. As we looked off, and saw the water growing darker and darker and deeper and deeper the farther we looked, till it was awful to consider, and it appeared to have no relation to the friendly land, either as shore or bottom — of what use is a bottom if it is out of sight, if it is two or three miles from the surface, and you are to be drowned so long before you get to it, though it were made of the same stuff with your native soil? — over that ocean where, as the Veda says, 'there is nothing to give support, nothing to rest upon, nothing to cling to,' I felt that I was a land animal. The man in a balloon even may commonly alight on the earth in a few moments, but the sailor's only hope is that he may reach the distant shore. I could then appreciate the heroism of the old navigator, Sir Humphrey Gilbert, of whom it is related, that being overtaken by a storm when on his return from America, in the year 1583, far northeastward from where we were, sitting abaft with a book in his hand, just before he was swallowed up in the deep, he cried out to his comrades in the Hind, as they came within hearing, 'We are as near to Heaven by sea as by land.' I saw that it would not be easy to realize.

On Cape Cod the next most eastern land you hear of is St. George's Bank (the fishermen tell of 'Georges,' 'Cashus,' and other sunken lands which they frequent). Every Cape man has a theory about George's Bank having been an island once, and in their accounts they gradually reduce the shallowness from six, five, four, two fathoms, to somebody's confident assertion that he has seen a mackerel gull sitting on a piece of dry land there. It reminded me, when I thought of the shipwrecks which had taken place there, of the Isle of Demons, laid down off this coast in old charts of the New World. There must be something monstrous, methinks, in a vision of the sea bottom from over some bank a thousand miles from the shore, more awful than its imagined bottomlessness; a drowned continent, all livid and frothing at the nostrils, like the body of a drowned man, which is better sunk deep than near the surface.

I have been surprised to discover from a steamer the shallowness of Massachusetts Bay itself. Off Billingsgate Point I could have touched the bottom with a pole, and I plainly saw it variously shaded with seaweed, at five or six miles from the shore. This is 'the Shoalground of the Cape,' it is true, but elsewhere the Bay is not much deeper than a country pond. We are told that the deepest water in the English Channel between Shakespeare's Cliff and Cape Gris-Nez, in France, is one hundred and eighty feet; and Guyot says that 'the Baltic Sea has a depth of only one hundred and twenty feet between the coasts of Germany and those of Sweden,' and 'the Adriatic between Venice and Trieste has a depth of only one hundred and thirty feet.' A pond in my native town, only half a mile long, is more than one hundred feet deep.

The ocean is but a larger lake. At midsummer you may sometimes see a strip of glassy smoothness on it, a few rods in width and many miles long, as if the surface there were covered with a thin pellicle of oil, just as on a country pond; a sort of standstill, you would say, at the meeting or parting of two currents of air (if it does not rather mark the unrippled steadiness of a current of water beneath), for sailors tell of the ocean and land breeze meeting between the fore and aft sails of a vessel, while the latter are full, the former being suddenly taken aback. Daniel Webster, in one of his letters describing blue-fishing off Martha's Vineyard, referring to those smooth places, which fishermen and sailors call 'slicks,' says: 'We met with them yesterday, and our boatman made for them, whenever discovered. He said they were caused by the blue-fish chopping up their prey. That is to say, those voracious fellows get into a school of menhaden, which are too large to swallow whole, and they bite them into pieces to suit their tastes. And the oil from this butchery, rising to the surface, makes the "slick." '

Yet this same placid ocean, as civil now as a city's harbor, a place for ships and commerce, will ere long be lashed into sudden fury, and all its caves and cliffs will resound with tumult. It will ruthlessly heave these vessels to and fro, break them in pieces in its sandy or stony jaws, and deliver their crews to sea-monsters. It will play with them like seaweed, distend them like dead frogs, and carry them about, now high, now low, to show to the fishes, giving them a nibble. This gentle ocean will toss and tear the rag of a man's body like the father of mad bulls, and his relatives may be seen seeking the remnants for weeks along the strand. From some quiet inland hamlet they have rushed weeping to the unheard-of shore, and now stand uncertain where a sailor has recently been buried amid the sand-hills.

It is generally supposed that they who have long been conversant with the ocean can foretell, by certain indications, such as its roar and the notes of sea-fowl, when it will change from calm to storm; but probably no such ancient mariner as we dream of exists; they know no more, at least, than the older sailors do about this voyage of life on which we are all embarked. Nevertheless, we love to hear the sayings of old sailors, and their accounts of natural phenomena which totally

ignore, and are ignored by, science; and possibly they have not always
looked over the gunwale so long in vain. Kalm repeats a story which
was told him in Philadelphia by a Mr. Cock, who was one day sailing
to the West Indies in a small yacht, with an old man on board who was
well acquainted with those seas. 'The old man sounding the depth,
called to the mate to tell Mr. Cock to launch the boats immediately,
and to put a sufficient number of men into them, in order to tow the
yacht during the calm, that they might reach the island before them as
soon as possible, as within twenty-four hours there would be a strong
hurricane. Mr. Cock asked him what reasons he had to think so; the
old man replied, that on sounding, he saw the lead in the water at a
distance of many fathoms more than he had seen it before; that therefore the water was become clear all of a sudden, which he looked upon
as a certain sign of an impending hurricane in the sea.' The sequel of
the story is that by good fortune, and by dint of rowing, they managed
to gain a safe harbor before the hurricane had reached its height; but
it finally raged with so much violence, that not only many ships were lost
and houses unroofed, but even their own vessel in harbor was washed so
far on shore that several weeks elapsed before it could be got off.

The Greeks would not have called the ocean ἀτρύγετος, or unfruitful, though it does not produce wheat, if they had viewed it by the
light of modern science, for naturalists now assert that 'the sea, and
not the land, is the principal seat of life' — though not of vegetable life.
Darwin affirms that 'our most thickly inhabited forests appear almost as
deserts when we come to compare them with the corresponding regions
of the ocean.' Agassiz and Gould tell us that 'the sea teems with animals
of all classes, far beyond the extreme point of flowering plants;' but
they add that 'experiments of dredging in very deep water have also
taught us that the abyss of the ocean is nearly a desert;' — 'so that
modern investigations,' to quote the words of Desor, 'merely go to confirm the great idea which was vaguely anticipated by the ancient poets
and philosophers, that the Ocean is the origin of all things.' Yet
marine animals and plants hold a lower rank in the scale of being than
land animals and plants. 'There is no instance known,' says Desor, 'of
an animal becoming aquatic in its perfect state, after having lived in its
lower stage on dry land,' but as in the case of the tadpole, 'the progress
invariably points towards the dry land.' In short, the dry land itself
came through and out of the water in its way to the heavens, for, 'in
going back through the geological ages, we come to an epoch when,
according to all appearances, the dry land did not exist, and when the

surface of our globe was entirely covered with water.' We looked on the sea, then, once more, not as ἀτρύγετος, or unfruitful, but as it has been more truly called, the 'laboratory of continents.'

Though we have indulged in some placid reflections of late, the reader must not forget that the dash and roar of the waves were incessant. Indeed, it would be well if he were to read with a large conchshell at his ear. But notwithstanding that it was very cold and windy today, it was such cold as we thought would not cause one to take cold who was exposed to it, owing to the saltness of the air and the dryness of the soil. Yet the author of the old 'Description of Wellfleet' says, 'The atmosphere is very much impregnated with saline particles, which, perhaps, with the great use of fish, and the neglect of cider and spruce-beer, may be a reason why the people are more subject to sore mouths and throats than in other places.' . . . [1]

IX. THE SEA AND THE DESERT

THE lighthouse lamps were still burning, though now with a silvery lustre, when I rose to see the sun come out of the ocean; for he still rose eastward of us; but I was convinced that he must have come out of a dry bed beyond that stream, though he seemed to come out of the water.

> 'The sun once more touched the fields,
>   Mounting to heaven from the fair flowing
>   Deep-running Ocean.'

Now we saw countless sails of mackerel-fishers abroad on the deep, one fleet in the north just pouring round the Cape, another standing down toward Chatham, and our host's son went off to join some lagging member of the first which had not yet left the Bay.

Before we left the lighthouse we were obliged to anoint our shoes faithfully with tallow, for walking on the beach, in the salt water and the sand, had turned them red and crisp. To counterbalance this, I have remarked that the seashore, even where muddy, as it is not here, is singularly clean; for, notwithstanding the spattering of the water and

[1] Pages 129–175 (Walden edition), including Chapters VII and VIII, omitted.

mud and squirting of the clams, while walking to and from the boat, your best black pants retain no stain nor dirt, such as they would acquire from walking in the country.

We have heard that a few days after this, when the Provincetown Bank was robbed, speedy emissaries from Provincetown made particular inquiries concerning us at this lighthouse. Indeed, they traced us all the way down the Cape, and concluded that we came by this unusual route down the back side and on foot in order that we might discover a way to get off with our booty when we had committed the robbery. The Cape is so long and narrow, and so bare withal, that it is well-nigh impossible for a stranger to visit it without the knowledge of its inhabitants generally, unless he is wrecked on to it in the night. So, when this robbery occurred, all their suspicions seem to have at once centred on us two travellers who had just passed down it. If we had not chanced to leave the Cape so soon, we should probably have been arrested. The real robbers were two young men from Worcester County who travelled with a centre-bit, and are said to have done their work very neatly. But the only bank that we pried into was the great Cape Cod sand-bank, and we robbed it only of an old French crown piece, some shells and pebbles, and the materials of this story.

Again we took to the beach for another day (October 13), walking along the shore of the resounding sea, determined to get it into us. We wished to associate with the ocean until it lost the pond-like look which it wears to a countryman. We still thought that we could see the other side. Its surface was still more sparkling than the day before, and we beheld 'the countless smilings of the ocean waves;' though some of them were pretty broad grins, for still the wind blew and the billows broke in foam along the beach. The nearest beach to us on the other side, whither we looked, due east, was on the coast of Galicia, in Spain, whose capital is Santiago, though by old poets' reckoning it should have been Atlantis or the Hesperides; but heaven is found to be farther west now. At first we were abreast of that part of Portugal *entre Douro e Miño*, and then Galicia and the port of Pontevedra opened to us as we walked along; but we did not enter, the breakers ran so high. The bold headland of Cape Finisterre, a little north of east, jutted toward us next, with its vain brag, for we flung back — 'Here is Cape Cod — Cape Land's-Beginning.' A little indentation toward the north — for the land loomed to our imaginations by a common mirage — we knew was the Bay of Biscay, and we sang:

'There we lay, till next day,
In the Bay of Biscay O!'

A little south of east was Palos, where Columbus weighed anchor, and farther yet the pillars which Hercules set up; concerning which when we inquired at the top of our voices what was written on them — for we had the morning sun in our faces, and could not see distinctly — the inhabitants shouted *Ne plus ultra* (no more beyond), but the wind bore to us the truth only, *plus ultra* (more beyond), and over the Bay westward was echoed *ultra* (beyond). We spoke to them through the surf about the Far West, the true Hesperia, ἕως πέρας or end of the day, the This Side Sundown, where the sun was extinguished in the *Pacific*, and we advised them to pull up stakes and plant those pillars of theirs on the shore of California, whither all our folks were gone — the only *ne plus ultra* now. Whereat they looked crestfallen on their cliffs, for we had taken the wind out of all their sails.

We could not perceive that any of their leavings washed up here, though we picked up a child's toy, a small dismantled boat, which may have been lost at Pontevedra.

The Cape became narrower and narrower as we approached its wrist between Truro and Provincetown, and the shore inclined more decidedly to the west. At the head of East Harbor Creek, the Atlantic is separated but by half a dozen rods of sand from the tidewaters of the Bay. From the Clay Pounds the bank flatted off for the last ten miles to the extremity at Race Point, though the highest parts, which are called 'islands' from their appearance at a distance on the sea, were still seventy or eighty feet above the Atlantic, and afforded a good view of the latter, as well as a constant view of the Bay, there being no trees nor a hill sufficient to interrupt it. Also the sands began to invade the land more and more, until finally they had entire possession from sea to sea, at the narrowest part. For three or four miles between Truro and Provincetown there were no inhabitants from shore to shore, and there were but three or four houses for twice that distance.

As we plodded along, either by the edge of the ocean, where the sand was rapidly drinking up the last wave that wet it, or over the sand-hills of the bank, the mackerel fleet continued to pour round the Cape north of us, ten or fifteen miles distant, in countless numbers, schooner after schooner, till they made a city on the water. They were so thick that many appeared to be afoul of one another; now all standing on this tack, now on that. We saw how well the New-Englanders had followed up Captain John Smith's suggestions with regard to the fisheries, made in 1616 — to what a pitch they had carried 'this contemptible trade of fish,' as he significantly styles it, and were now equal to the Hollanders whose example he holds up for the English to emulate; notwithstanding that 'in this faculty,' as he says, 'the former are so naturalized, and of their vents so certainly acquainted, as there is no likelihood they will ever be paralleled, having two or three thousand busses, flat-bottoms, sword-pinks, todes, and such like, that breeds them sailors, mariners, soldiers, and merchants, never to be wrought out of that trade and fit for any other.' We thought that it would take all these names and more to describe the numerous craft which we saw. Even then, some years before our 'renowned sires' with their 'peerless dames' stepped on Plymouth Rock, he wrote 'Newfoundland doth yearly fraught near eight hundred sail of ships with a silly, lean, skinny poor-john, and cor-fish,' though all their supplies must be annually transported from Europe. Why not plant a colony here then, and raise those supplies on the spot? 'Of all the four parts of the world,' says he, 'that I have yet seen, not inhabited, could I have but means to transport a colony, I would rather live here than anywhere. And if it did not maintain itself, were we but once indifferently well fitted, let us starve.' Then 'fishing before your doors,' you 'may every night sleep quietly ashore, with good cheer and what fires you will, or, when you please, with your wives and family.' Already he anticipates 'the new towns in New England in memory of their old' — and who knows what may be discovered in the 'heart and entrails' of the land, 'seeing even the very edges,' etc., etc.

All this has been accomplished, and more, and where is Holland now? Verily the Dutch have taken it. There was no long interval between the suggestion of Smith and the eulogy of Burke.

Still one after another the mackerel schooners hove in sight round the head of the Cape, 'whitening all the sea road,' and we watched each one for a moment with an undivided interest. It seemed a pretty sport. Here in the country it is only a few idle boys or loafers that go a-fishing on a rainy day; but there it appeared as if every able-bodied man and helpful boy in the Bay had gone out on a pleasure excursion in their yachts, and all would at last land and have a chowder on the Cape. The gazetteer tells you gravely how many of the men and boys of these towns are engaged in the whale, cod, and mackerel fishery, how many go to the banks of Newfoundland, or the coast of Labrador, the Straits of Belle Isle or the Bay of Chaleurs (Shalore, the sailors call it); as if I were to reckon up the number of boys in Concord who are engaged during the summer in the perch, pickerel, bream, horn-pout, and shiner fishery, of which no one keeps the statistics — though I think that it is pursued with as much profit to the moral and intellectual man (or boy), and certainly with less danger to the physical one.

One of my playmates, who was apprenticed to a printer, and was somewhat of a wag, asked his master one afternoon if he might go a-fishing, and his master consented. He was gone three months. When he came back, he said that he had been to the Grand Banks, and went to setting type again as if only an afternoon had intervened.

I confess I was surprised to find that so many men spent their whole day, ay, their whole lives almost, a-fishing. It is remarkable what a serious business men make of getting their dinners, and how universally shiftlessness and a grovelling taste take refuge in a merely ant-like industry. Better go without your dinner, I thought, than be thus everlastingly fishing for it like a cormorant. Of course, *viewed from the shore*, our pursuits in the country appear not a whit less frivolous.

I once sailed three miles on a mackerel cruise myself. It was a Sunday evening after a very warm day in which there had been frequent thunder-showers, and I had walked along the shore from Cohasset to Duxbury. I wished to get over from the last place to Clark's Island, but no boat could stir, they said, at that stage of the tide, they being left high on the mud. At length I learned that the tavern-keeper, Winsor, was going out mackerelling with seven men that evening, and would take me. When there had been due delay, we one after another straggled down to the shore in a leisurely manner, as if waiting for the tide still, and in india-rubber boots, or carrying our shoes in our hands, waded to the boats, each of the crew bearing an armful of wood, and one a bucket of new potatoes besides. Then they resolved that each should bring one more armful of wood, and that would be enough. They had already got a barrel of water, and had some more in the schooner. We shoved the boats a dozen rods over the mud and water till they floated, then, rowing half a mile to the vessel, climbed aboard, and there we were in a mackerel schooner, a fine stout vessel of forty-three tons, whose name I forget. The baits were not dry on the hooks. There was the mill in which they ground the mackerel, and the trough to hold it, and the long-handled dipper to cast it overboard with; and already in the harbor we saw the surface rippled with schools of small mackerel, the real *Scomber vernalis*. The crew proceeded leisurely to weigh anchor and raise their two sails, there being a fair but very slight wind; — and the sun now setting clear and shining on the vessel after the thunder-showers, I thought that I could not have commenced the voyage under more favorable auspices. They had four dories and commonly fished in them, else they fished on the starboard side aft where their lines hung ready, two to a man. The boom swung round once or twice, and Winsor cast overboard the foul juice of mackerel mixed with rain-water which remained in his trough, and then we gathered about the helmsman and told stories. I remember that the compass was affected by iron in its neighborhood and varied a few degrees. There was one among us just returned from California, who was now going as passenger for his health and amusement. They expected to be gone about a week, to begin fishing the next morning, and to carry their fish fresh to Boston. They landed me at Clark's Island, where the Pilgrims landed, for my companions wished to get some milk for the voyage. But I had seen the whole of it. The rest was only going to sea and catching the mackerel. Moreover, it was as well that I did not remain with them, considering the small quantity of supplies they had taken.

Now I saw the mackerel fleet *on its fishing-ground*, though I was not at first aware of it. So my experience was complete.

It was even more cold and windy today than before, and we were frequently glad to take shelter behind a sand-hill. None of the elements were resting. On the beach there is a ceaseless activity, always something going on, in storm and in calm, winter and summer, night and day. Even the sedentary man here enjoys a breadth of view which is almost equivalent to motion. In clear weather the laziest may look across the Bay as far as Plymouth at a glance, or over the Atlantic as far as human vision reaches, merely raising his eyelids; or if he is too lazy to look after all, he can hardly help *hearing* the ceaseless dash and roar of the breakers. The restless ocean may at any moment cast up a whale or a wrecked vessel at your feet. All the reporters in the world, the most rapid stenographers, could not report the news it brings. No creature could move slowly where there was so much life around. The few wreckers were either going or coming, and the ships and the sand-pipers, and the screaming gulls overhead; nothing stood still but the shore. The little beach-birds trotted past close to the water's edge, or paused but an instant to swallow their food, keeping time with the elements. I wondered how they ever got used to the sea, that they ventured so near the waves. Such tiny inhabitants the land brought forth! except one fox. And what could a fox do, looking on the Atlantic from that high bank? What is the sea to a fox? Sometimes we met a wrecker with his cart and dog — and his dog's faint bark at us wayfarers, heard through the roaring of the surf, sounded ridiculously faint. To see a little trembling dainty-footed cur stand on the margin of the ocean, and ineffectually bark at a beach-bird, amid the roar of the Atlantic! Come with design to bark at a whale, perchance! That sound will do for farmyards. All the dogs looked out of place there, naked and as if shuddering at the vastness; and I thought that they would not have been there had it not been for the countenance of their masters. Still less could you think of a cat bending her steps that way, and shaking her wet foot over the Atlantic; yet even this happens sometimes, they tell me. In summer I saw the tender young of the piping plover, like chickens just hatched, mere pinches of down on two legs, running in troops, with a faint peep, along the edge of the waves. I used to see packs of half-wild dogs haunting the lonely beach on the south shore of Staten Island, in New York Bay, for the sake of the carrion there cast up; and I remember that once, when for a long time I had heard a furious barking in the tall grass of the marsh, a pack of half a dozen large dogs burst forth on to the beach, pursuing a little one which ran straight to me for protection, and I afforded it with some stones, though at some risk to myself; but the next day the little one was the first to bark at me. Under these circumstances I could not but remember the words of the poet:

> 'Blow, blow, thou winter wind,
> Thou art not so unkind
> As *his* ingratitude;
> Thy tooth is not so keen,
> Because thou art not seen,
> Although thy breath be rude.
>
> 'Freeze, freeze, thou bitter sky,
> Thou dost not bite so nigh
> As benefits forgot;
> Though thou the waters warp,
> Thy sting is not so sharp
> As friend remembered not.'

Sometimes, when I was approaching the carcass of a horse or ox which lay on the beach there, where there was no living creature in sight, a dog would unexpectedly emerge from it and slink away with a mouthful of offal.

The seashore is a sort of neutral ground, a most advantageous point from which to contemplate this world. It is even a trivial place. The waves forever rolling to the land are too far-travelled and untamable to be familiar. Creeping along the endless beach amid the sun-squall and the foam, it occurs to us that we, too, are the product of sea-slime.

It is a wild, rank place, and there is no flattery in it. Strewn with crabs, horseshoes, and razor clams, and whatever the sea casts up — a vast *morgue*, where famished dogs may range in packs, and crows come daily to glean the pittance which the tide leaves them. The carcasses of men and beasts together lie stately up upon its shelf, rotting and bleaching in the sun and waves, and each tide turns them in their beds, and tucks fresh sand under them. There is naked Nature — inhumanly sincere, wasting no thought on man, nibbling at the cliffy shore where gulls wheel amid the spray. . . . [1]

---

6. SELECTIONS FROM THE 'JOURNAL' [2]

I. NATURE

[1837–47.] Yesterday I skated after a fox over the ice. Occasionally he sat on his haunches and barked at me like a young wolf. It made me think of the bear and her cubs mentioned by Captain Parry, I think. All brutes seem to have a genius for mystery, an Oriental aptitude for symbols and the language of signs; and this is the origin of Pilpay and Æsop. The fox manifested an almost human suspicion of mystery in my actions. While I skated directly after him, he cantered at the top of his speed; but when I stood still, though his fear was not abated, some strange but inflexible law of his nature caused him to stop also, and sit again on his haunches. While I still stood motionless, he would go

[1] Pages 187 to end (Walden edition), omitted.
[2] For Prefatory Note see page 3.

slowly a rod to one side, then sit and bark, then a rod to the other side, and sit and bark again, but did not retreat, as if spellbound. When, however, I commenced the pursuit again, he found himself released from his durance.

Plainly the fox belongs to a different order of things from that which reigns in the village. Our courts, though they offer a bounty for his hide, and our pulpits, though they draw many a moral from his cunning, are in few senses contemporary with his free forest life.

Aug. 24, 1845. Again I remember that as I was leaving the Irish man's roof after the rain and bending my steps again to the shore of the lake — my haste to catch pickerel wading in retired meadows in sloughs & bog holes in forlorn and wild savage places — seemed for an instant trivial to me who had been sent to school and college — but then in an instant as I ran down the hill with the rainbow over my shoulder and some faint tinkling sounds borne to my ear thro the cleansed air from I know not what quarter my genius said from the western heaven — go fish & hunt far & wide day by day — and rest thee by many hearth-sides without misgiving.[1] Rise free from care before the dawn, and seek adventures. Let the noon find thee by other brooks — and the night over take thee every-where at home. Lead such a life as the children that chase butterflies in a meadow. There are no larger fields than these — no nobler games — no more extended earth. With thy life uninsured live free and forever as you were planted. Grow wild according to thy nature like these ferns and brakes which study not morals nor philosophy nor strive to become cultivated grass for cattle to eat — these bull rushes behind which you [see? [2]] the red evening sky over the lake — as if they were the masts of vessels in a crowded venice harbor. Let the thunder rumble in thy own tongue — what if it brings rain to farmer's crops that is not its errand to thee — take shelter under the cloud — while others fly to carts and sheds.

Enjoy thy dominion — and name anew the fowl and the quadruped and all creeping things. Seek without toil thy daily food. Thy sustenance — is it not in nature?

Through want of confidence in the Gods men are where they are — buying and selling — *owning* land — following trades — and spending their lives ignobly.

By usurer's craft we strive to retain & increase the divinity in us; when the infinitely greater part of divinity is out of us.

[1] [A paragraph indicated, but the sign is incomplete.]
[2] [Thoreau omits a word here.]

[NOTE. These passages are from two pages torn from the 'Journal' and now in the Huntington Library collection of Thoreau's working sheets for 'Walden.' They were copied by Professor Odell Shepard and are used by his permission and the Library's. In their first quite different version they appear in the 'Journal,' I, 385, dated August 23, 1845. They were revised the next day in the form which appears here. The third revision in briefer statement will be found in 'Walden' in the chapter called Baker Farm. (See pages 378–84.) I print the library version here not only because of its particular excellence, but also because it illustrates Thoreau's peculiar punctuation, which has been made orthodox in the published 'Journal' from which all the other excerpts are made.]

1850. Again and again I heard and saw the commotion, but could not guess the cause of it — what kind of life had its residence in that insignificant pool. We sat down on the hillside. Ere long a muskrat came swimming by as if attracted by the same disturbance, and then another and another, till three had passed, and I began to suspect that they were at the bottom of it. Still ever and anon I observed the same commotion in the waters over the same spot, and at length I observed the snout of some creature slyly raised above the surface after each commotion, as if to see if it were observed by foes, and then but a few rods distant I saw another snout above the water and began to divine the cause of the disturbance. Putting off my shoes and stockings, I crept stealthily down the hill and waded out slowly and noiselessly about a rod from the firm land, keeping behind the tussocks, till I stood behind the tussock near which I had observed the splashing. Then, suddenly stooping over it, I saw through the shallow but muddy water that there was a mud turtle there, and thrusting in my hand at once caught him by the claw, and, quicker than I can tell it, heaved him high and dry ashore; and there came out with him a large pout just dead and partly devoured, which he held in his jaws. It was the pout in his flurry and the turtle in his struggles to hold him fast which had created the commotion. There he had lain, probably buried in the mud at the bottom up to his eyes, till the pout came sailing over, and then this musky lagune had put forth in the direction of his ventral fins, expanding suddenly under the influence of a more than vernal heat — there are sermons in stones, aye and mud turtles at the bottoms of the pools — in the direction of his ventral fins, his tender white belly, where he kept no eye; and the minister squeaked his last. Oh, what an eye was there, my countrymen! buried in mud up to the lids, meditating on what? sleepless at the bottom of the pool, at the top of the bottom, directed heavenward, in no danger from motes. Pouts expect their foes not from below. Suddenly a mud volcano swallowed him up, seized his midriff; he fell into those relentless jaws from which there is no escape, which relax not their hold even in death. There the pout might calculate on remaining until nine days after the head was cut off. Sculled through Heywood's shallow meadow, not thinking of foes, looking through the water up into the sky. I saw his [the turtle's] brother sunning and airing his broad back like a ship bottom up which had been scuttled — foundered at sea. I had no idea that there was so much going on in Heywood's meadow.

June, 1850. I observe tonight, June 15th, the air over the river by the Leaning Hemlocks filled with myriads of newly fledged insects drifting and falling as it were like snowflakes from the maples, only not so white. Now they drift up the stream, now down, while the river below is dimpled with the fishes rising to swallow the innumerable insects which have fallen [into] it and are struggling with it. I saw how He fed his fish. They, swimming in the dark nether atmosphere of the river, rose lazily to its surface to swallow such swimmers of the light upper atmosphere as sank to its bottom.

Sept. 1850. And as I sat amid the hickory trees
And the young sumachs, enjoying the prospect, a neat herd of cows approached, of unusually fair proportions and smooth, clean skins, evidently petted by their owner, who must have carefully selected them. One more confiding heifer, the fairest of the herd, did by degrees approach as if to take some morsel from our hands, while our hearts leaped to our mouths with expectation and delight. She by degrees drew near with her fair limbs progressive, making pretence of browsing; nearer and nearer, till there was wafted toward us the bovine fragrance — cream of all the dairies that ever were or will be — and then she raised her gentle muzzle toward us, and snuffed an honest recognition within hand's reach. I saw 'twas possible for his herd to inspire with love the herdsman. She was as delicately featured as a hind. Her hide was mingled white and fawn-color, and on her muzzle's tip there was a white spot not bigger than a daisy, and on her side toward me the map of Asia plain to see.

Farewell, dear heifer! Though thou forgettest me, my prayer to heaven shall be that thou may'st not forget thyself. There was a whole bucolic in her snuff. I saw her name was Sumach. And by the kindred spots I knew her mother, more sedate and matronly, with full-grown bag; and on her sides was Asia, great and small, the plains of Tartary, even to the pole, while on her daughter it was Asia Minor. She not disposed to wanton with the herdsman.

And as I walked, she followed me, and took an apple from my hand, and seemed to care more for the hand than apple. So innocent a face as I have rarely seen on any creature, and I have looked in face of many heifers. And as she took the apple from my hand, I caught the apple of her eye. She smelled as sweet as the clethra blossom. There was no sinister expression. And for horns, though she had them, they were so well disposed in the right place, bent neither up nor down, I do not now remember she had any. No horn was held toward me.

Nov. 25, 1850. I saw a muskrat come out of a hole in the ice. He is a man wilder than Ray or Melvin. While I am looking at him, I am thinking what he is thinking of me. He is a different sort of a man, that is all. He would dive when I went nearer, then reappear again, and had kept open a place five or six feet square so that it had not frozen, by swimming about in it. Then he would sit on the edge of the ice and busy himself about something, I could not see whether it was a clam or not. What a cold-blooded fellow! thoughts at a low temperature, sitting perfectly still so long on ice covered with water, mumbling a cold, wet clam in its shell. What safe, low, moderate thoughts it must have! It does not get on to stilts. The generations of muskrats do not fail. They are not preserved by the legislature of Massachusetts.

July 21, 1851. The forenoon is fuller of light. The butterflies on the flowers look like other and frequently larger flowers themselves. Now I yearn for one of those old, meandering, dry, uninhabited roads, which lead away from towns, which lead us away from temptation, which conduct to the outside of earth, over its uppermost crust; where you may forget in what country you·are travelling; where no farmer can complain that you are treading down his grass, no gentleman who has recently constructed a seat in the country that you are trespassing; on which you can go off at half-cock and wave adieu to the village; along which you may travel like a pilgrim, going nowhither; where travellers are not too often to be met; where my spirit is free; where the walls and fences are not cared for; where your head is more in heaven than your feet are on earth; which have long reaches where you can see the approaching traveller half a mile off and be prepared for him; not so luxuriant a soil as to attract men; some root and stump fences which do not need attention; where travellers have no occasion to stop, but pass along and leave you to your thoughts; where it makes no odds which way you face, whether you are going or coming, whether it is morning or evening, mid-noon or midnight; where earth is cheap enough by being public; where you can walk and think with least obstruction, there being nothing to measure progress by; where you can pace when your breast is full, and cherish your moodiness; where you are not in false relations with men, are not dining nor conversing with them; by which you may go to the uttermost parts of the earth. It is wide enough, wide as the thoughts it allows to visit you. Sometimes it is some particular half-dozen rods which I wish to find myself pacing over, as where certain airs blow; then my life will come to me, methinks; like a hunter I walk in wait for it. When I am against this bare promontory of a huckleberry hill, then forsooth my thoughts will expand. Is it some influence, as a vapor which exhales from the ground, or something in the gales which blow there, or in all things there brought together agreeably to my spirit? The walls must not be too high, imprisoning me, but low, with numerous gaps. The trees must not be too numerous, nor the hills too near, bounding the view, nor the soil too rich, attracting the attention to the earth. It must simply be the way and the life — a way that was never known to be repaired, nor to need repair, within the memory of the oldest inhabitant. I cannot walk habitually in those ways that are liable to be mended; for sure it was the devil only that wore them. Never by the heel of thinkers (of thought) were they worn; the zephyrs could repair that damage. The saunterer wears out no road, even though he travel on it, and therefore should pay no highway, or rather *low* way, tax. He may be taxed to construct a higher way than men travel. A way which no geese defile, nor hiss along it, but only sometimes their wild brethren fly far overhead; which the kingbird and the swallow twitter over, and the song sparrow sings on its rails; where the small red butterfly is at home on the yarrow, and no boys threaten it with imprisoning hat. There I can walk and stalk and pace and plod. Which nobody but Jonas Potter travels beside me; where no cow but his is tempted to linger for the herbage by its side; where the guideboard is fallen, and now the hand points to heaven significantly — to a Sudbury and Marlborough in the skies. That's a road I can travel, that the particular Sudbury I am bound for, six miles an hour, or two, as you please; and few there be that enter thereon. There I can walk, and recover the lost child that I am without any ringing of a bell; where there was nothing ever discovered to detain a traveller, but all went through about their business; where I never passed the time of day with any — indifferent to me were the arbitrary divisions of time; where

Tullus Hostilius might have disappeared — at any rate has never been seen. The road to the Corner! the ninety and nine acres that you go through to get there! I would rather see it again, though I saw it this morning, than Gray's churchyard. The road whence you may hear a stake-driver, a whip-poor-will, a quail in a midsummer day, a — yes, a quail comes nearest to the *gum-c* [1] bird heard there; where it would not be sport for a sportsman to go. And the mayweed looks up in my face — not there; the pale lobelia, the Canada snapdragon, rather. A little hardhack and meadowsweet peep over the fence — nothing more serious to obstruct the view — and thimble-berries are the food of thought, before the drought, along by the walls.

It is they who go to Brighton and to market that wear out the roads, and they should pay all the tax. The deliberate pace of a thinker never made a road the worse for travelling on.

Aug. 20, 1851. What a faculty must that be which can paint the most barren landscape and humblest life in glorious colors! It is pure and invigorated senses reacting on a sound and strong imagination. Is not that the poet's case? The intellect of most men is barren. They neither fertilize nor are fertilized. It is the marriage of the soul with Nature that makes the intellect fruitful, that gives birth to imagination. When we were dead and dry as the highway, some sense which has been healthily fed will put us in relation with Nature, in sympathy with her; some grains of fertilizing pollen, floating in the air, fall on us, and suddenly the sky is all one rainbow, is full of music and fragrance and flavor. The man of intellect only, the prosaic man, is a barren, staminiferous flower; the poet is a fertile and perfect flower. Men are such confirmed arithmeticians and slaves of business that I cannot easily find a blank-book that has not a red line or a blue one for the dollars and cents, or some such purpose.

Sept. 3, 1851. Why was there never a poem on the cricket? When I sat on Lee's Cliff the other day (August 29th), I saw a man working with a horse in a field by the river, carting dirt; and the horse and his relation to him struck me as very remarkable. There was the horse, a mere animated machine — though his tail was brushing off the flies — his whole existence subordinated to the man's, with no tradition, perhaps no instinct, in him of independence and freedom, of a time when he was wild and free — completely humanized. No compact made with him that he should have the Saturday afternoons, or the Sundays, or

---

[1] [So Channing (p. 128), who calls it 'one of Thoreau's names for some bird, so named by the farmers.' The word as written is far from clear.]

any holidays. His independence never recognized, it being now quite forgotten both by men and by horses that the horse was ever free. For I am not aware that there are any wild horses known surely not to be descended from tame ones. Assisting that man to pull down that bank and spread it over the meadow; only keeping off the flies with his tail, and stamping, and catching a mouthful of grass or leaves from time to time, on his own account — all the rest for man. It seemed hardly worth while that he should be *animated* for this. It was plain that the man was not educating the horse; not trying to develop his nature, but merely getting work out of him. That mass of animated matter seemed more completely the servant of man than any inanimate. For slaves have their holidays; a heaven is conceded to them, but to the horse none. Now and forever he is man's slave. The more I considered, the more the man seemed akin to the horse; only his was the stronger will of the two. For a little further on I saw an Irishman shovelling, who evidently was as much tamed as the horse. He had stipulated that to a certain extent his independence be recognized, and yet really he was but little more independent. I had always instinctively regarded the horse as a free people somewhere, living wild. Whatever has not come under the sway of man is wild. In this sense original and independent men are wild — not tamed and broken by society. Now for my part I have such a respect for the horse's nature as would tempt me to let him alone; not to interfere with him — his walks, his diet, his loves. But by mankind he is treated simply as if he were an engine which must have rest and is sensible of pain. Suppose that every squirrel were made to turn a coffee-mill! Suppose that the gazelles were made to draw milk-carts!

There he was with his tail cut off, because it was in the way, or to suit the taste of his owner; his mane trimmed, and his feet shod with iron that he might wear longer. What is a horse but an animal that has lost its liberty? What is it but a system of slavery? and do you not thus by *insensible* and unimportant degrees come to human slavery? Has lost its liberty! — and has man got any more liberty himself for having robbed the horse, or has he lost just as much of his own, and become more like the horse he has robbed? Is not the other end of the bridle in this case, too, coiled round his own neck? Hence stable-boys, jockeys, all that class that is daily transported by fast horses. There he stood with his oblong square figure (his tail being cut off) seen against the water, brushing off the flies with his tail and stamping, braced back while the man was filling the cart.

Sept. 22, 1851. Standing on Bear Hill in Lincoln. The black birches (I think they are), now yellow, on the south side of Flint's Pond, on the hillside, look like flames. The chestnut trees are brownish-yellow as well as green. It is a beautifully clear and bracing air, with just enough coolness, full of the memory of frosty mornings, through which all things are distinctly seen and the fields look as smooth as velvet. The fragrance of grapes is on the breeze and the red drooping barberries sparkle amid the leaves. From the hill on the south side of the pond, the forests have a singularly rounded and bowery look, clothing the hills quite down to the water's edge and leaving no shore; the ponds are like drops of dew amid and partly covering the leaves. So the great globe is luxuriously crowded without margin.

Nov. 13, 1851. To Fair Haven Hill.

A cold and dark afternoon, the sun being behind clouds in the west. The landscape is barren of objects, the trees being leafless, and so little light in the sky for variety. Such a day as will almost oblige a man to eat his own heart. A day in which you must hold on to life by your teeth. You can hardly ruck up any skin on Nature's bones. The sap is down; she won't peel. Now is the time to cut timber for yokes and ox-bows, leaving the tough bark on — yokes for your own neck. Finding yourself yoked to Matter and to Time. Truly a hard day, hard times these! Not a mosquito left. Not an insect to hum. Crickets gone into winter quarters. Friends long since gone there, and you left to walk on frozen ground, with your hands in your pockets. Ah, but is not this a glorious time for your deep inward fires? And will not your green hickory and white oak burn clear in this frosty air? Now is not your manhood taxed by the great Assessor? Taxed for having a soul, a ratable soul. A day when you cannot pluck a flower, cannot dig a parsnip, nor pull a turnip, for the frozen ground! What do the thoughts find to live on? What avails you now the fire you stole from heaven? Does not each thought become a vulture to gnaw your vitals? No Indian summer have we had this November. I see but few traces of the perennial spring. Now is there nothing, not even the cold beauty of ice crystals and snowy architecture, nothing but the echo of your steps over the frozen ground, no voice of birds nor frogs. You are dry as a farrow cow. The earth will not admit a spade. All fields lie fallow. Shall not your mind? True, the freezing ground is being prepared for immeasurable snows, but there are brave thoughts within you that shall remain to rustle the winter through like white oak leaves upon your boughs, or like scrub oaks that remind the traveller of a fire upon the hillsides; or evergreen thoughts, cold even in mid-summer, by their nature shall contrast the more fairly with the snow. Some warm springs shall still tinkle and fume, and send their column of vapor to the skies.

April 16, 1852. As I turned round the corner of Hubbard's Grove, saw a woodchuck, the first of the season, in the middle of the field, six or seven rods from the fence which bounds the wood, and twenty rods distant. I ran along the fence and cut him off, or rather overtook him, though he started at the same time. When I was only a rod and a half off, he stopped, and I did the same; then he ran again, and I ran up within three feet of him, when he stopped again, the fence being between us. I squatted down and surveyed him at my leisure. His eyes were dull black and rather inobvious, with a faint chestnut (?) iris, with but little expression and that more of resignation than of anger. The general aspect was a coarse grayish brown, a sort of grisel (?). A lighter brown next the skin, then black or very dark brown and tipped with whitish rather loosely. The head between a squirrel and a bear, flat on the top and dark brown, and darker still or black on the tip of the nose. The whiskers black, two inches long. The ears very small and roundish, set far back and nearly buried in the fur. Black feet, with long and slender claws for digging. It appeared to tremble, or perchance shivered with cold. When I moved, it gritted its teeth quite loud, sometimes striking the under jaw against the other chatter-ingly, sometimes grinding one jaw on the other, yet as if more from instinct than anger. Whichever way I turned, that way it headed. I took a twig a foot long and touched its snout, at which it started forward and bit the stick, lessening the distance between us to two feet, and still it held all the ground it gained. I played with it tenderly awhile with the stick, trying to open its gritting jaws. Ever its long incisors, two above and two below, were presented. But I thought it would go to sleep if I stayed long enough. It did not sit upright as sometimes, but *standing* on its fore feet with its head down, *i.e.* half sitting, half standing. We sat looking at one another about half an hour, till we began to feel mesmeric influences. When I was tired, I moved away, wishing to see him run, but I could not start him. He would not stir as long as I was looking at him or could see him. I walked round him; he turned as fast and fronted me still. I sat down by his side within a foot. I talked to him *quasi* forest lingo, baby-talk, at any rate in a conciliatory tone, and thought that I had some influence on him. He gritted his teeth less. I chewed checkerberry leaves and presented them to his nose at last without a grit; though I saw that by so much gritting of the teeth he had worn them rapidly and they were covered with a fine white powder, which, if you measured it thus, would have made his anger terrible. He did not mind any noise I might make. With a little stick I lifted one of his paws to examine it, and held it up at pleasure. I turned him over to see what color he was beneath (darker or more purely brown), though he turned himself back again sooner than I could have wished. His tail was also all brown, though not very dark, rat-tail like, with loose hairs standing out on all sides like a caterpillar brush. He had a rather mild look. I spoke kindly to him. I reached checkerberry leaves to his mouth. I stretched my hands over him, though he turned up his head and still gritted a little. I laid my hand on him, but immediately took it off again, instinct not being wholly overcome. If I had had a few fresh bean leaves, thus in advance of the season, I am sure I should have tamed him completely. It was a frizzly tail. His is a humble, terrestrial color like the partridge's, well concealed where dead wiry grass rises above darker brown or chestnut dead leaves — a modest color. If I had had some food, I should have ended with stroking him at my leisure. Could easily have wrapped him in my handkerchief. He was not fat nor particularly lean. I finally had to leave him without seeing him move from the place. A large, clumsy, burrowing squirrel. *Arctomys*, bear-mouse. I respect him as one of the natives. He lies there, by his color and habits so naturalized amid the dry leaves, the withered grass, and the bushes. A sound nap, too, he has enjoyed in his native fields, the past winter. I think I might learn some wisdom of him. His ancestors have lived here longer than mine. He is more thoroughly acclimated and naturalized than I. Bean leaves the red man raised for him, but he can do without them.

June 15, 1852. I hear the scream of a great hawk, sailing with a ragged wing against the high wood-side, apparently to scare his prey and so detect it — shrill, harsh, fitted to excite terror in sparrows and to issue from his split and curved bill. I see his open bill the while against the sky. Spit with force from his mouth with an undulatory quaver imparted to it from his wings or motion as he flies. A hawk's ragged wing will grow whole again, but so will not a poet's.

June 19, 1852. It requires considerable skill in crossing a country to avoid the houses and too cultivated parts — somewhat of the engineer's or gunner's skill — so to pass a house, if you must go near it through high grass — pass the enemy's lines where houses are thick — as to make a hill or wood screen you — to shut every window with an apple tree. For that route which most avoids the houses is not only the one in which you will be least molested, but it is by far the most agreeable. Saw the handsomest large maple west of this hill that I ever saw. We crawled through the end of a swamp on our bellies, the bushes were so thick, to screen us from a house forty rods off whose windows completely commanded the open ground, leaping some broad ditches, and when we emerged into the grass ground, some apple trees near the house beautifully screened us. It is rare that you cannot avoid a grain-field or piece of English mowing by skirting a corn-field or nursery near by, but if you must go through high grass, then step lightly and in each other's tracks.

June 20, 1852. Lying with my window open, these warm, even sultry nights, I hear the sonorously musical trump of the bullfrogs from time to time, from some distant shore of the river, as if the world were given up to them. By those villagers who live on the street they are never seen and rarely heard by day, but in the quiet sultry nights their notes ring from one end of the town to another. It is as if you had waked up in the infernal regions. I do not know for a time in what world I am. It affects my morals, and all questions take a new aspect from this sound. At night bullfrogs lie on the pads and answer to one another all over North America; undoubtedly there is an incessant and uninterrupted chain of sound, *troomp, troomp, troomp,* from the Atlantic to the Pacific (*vide* if they reach so far west), further than Britain's morning gun. It is the snoring music of nature at night. When you wake thus at midnight and hear this sonorous trump from far in the horizon, you need not go to Dante for an idea of the infernal regions. It requires the night air, this sound. How allied to a pad in place, in color — for his greenish back is the leaf and his yellow throat the flower — even in form, with his sesquipedality of belly! (And other, white-bellied frogs are white lilies.) Through the summer he lies on the pads, or with his head out, and in the winter buries himself at their roots (?). The bull-paddock! His eyes like the buds of the *Nuphar Kalmiana.* Methinks his skin would stand water without shrinking forever. Gloves made of it for rainy weather, for trout-fishers!! Frogs appear slow to make up their minds, but then they act precipitately. As long as they are here, they are here, and express no intention of removing; but the idea of removing fills them instantaneously, as nature, abhorring, fills a vacuum. Now they are fixed and imperturbable like the Sphinx, and now they go off with short, squatty leaps over the spatter-dock, on the irruption of the least idea.

July 5, 1852. The wood thrush's is no opera music; it is not so much the composition as the strain, the tone — cool bars of melody from the atmosphere of everlasting morning or evening. It is the quality of the song, not the sequence. In the peawai's note there is some sultriness, but in the thrush's, though heard at noon, there is the liquid coolness of things that are just drawn from the bottom of springs. The thrush alone declares the immortal wealth and vigor that is in the forest. Here is a bird in whose strain the story is told, though Nature waited for the science of æsthetics to discover it to man. Whenever a man hears it, he is young, and Nature is in her spring. Wherever he hears it, it is a new world and a free country, and the gates of heaven are not shut against him. Most other birds sing from the level of my ordinary cheerful hours — a carol; but this bird never fails to speak to me out of an ether purer than that I breathe, of immortal beauty and vigor. He deepens the significance of all things seen in the light of his strain. He sings to make men take higher and truer views of things. He sings to amend their institutions; to relieve the slave on the plantation and the prisoner in his dungeon, the slave in the house of luxury and the prisoner of his own low thoughts.

July 10, 1852. There are but few fishes to be seen. They have, no doubt, retreated to the deepest water. In one somewhat muddier place close to the shore I came upon an old pout cruising with her young. She dashed away at my approach, but the fry remained. They were of various sizes, from one third of an inch to one and a half inches, quite black and pout-shaped, except that the head was most developed in the smallest. They were constantly moving about in a somewhat circular or rather lenticular school, about fifteen or eighteen inches in diameter, and I estimated that there were at least one thousand of them. Presently the old pout came back and took the lead of her brood, which followed her, or rather gathered about her, like chickens about a hen; but this mother had so many children she didn't know what to do. Her maternal yearnings must be on a great scale. When one half of the divided school found her out they came down upon her and completely invested her like a small cloud. She was soon joined by another smaller pout, apparently her mate, and all, both old and young, began to be very familiar with me. They came round my legs and felt them with their feelers, and the old pouts nibbled my toes, while the fry half concealed my feet. Probably if I had been standing on the bank, with my clothes on, they would have been more shy. Ever and anon the old pouts dashed aside to drive away a passing bream or perch. The larger one kept circling about her charge as if to keep them together within a certain compass. If any of her flock were lost or drowned she would hardly have missed them. I wondered if there was any calling of the roll at night; whether she, like a faithful shepherdess, ever told her tale under some hawthorn in the river dales. Ever ready to do battle with the wolves that might break into her fold.

Aug. 31, 1852. Looking westward, the surface of the water on the meadows in the sun has a slight dusty appearance, with clear black lines, as if some water nymph had written 'slut' with her finger there.

June 7, 1853. Visited my nighthawk on her nest. Could hardly believe my eyes when I stood within seven feet and beheld her sitting on her eggs, her head to me. She looked so Saturnian, so one with the earth, so sphinx-like, a relic of the reign of Saturn which Jupiter did not destroy, a riddle that might well cause a man to go dash his head against a stone. It was not an actual living creature, far less a winged creature of the air, but a figure in stone or bronze, a fanciful production of art, like the gryphon or phœnix. In fact, with its breast toward me, and owing to its color or size no bill perceptible, it looked like the end [of] a brand, such as are common in a clearing, its breast mottled or alternately waved with dark brown and gray, its flat, grayish, weather-beaten crown, its eyes nearly closed, purposely, lest those bright beads should betray it, with the stony cunning of the sphinx. A fanciful work in bronze to ornament a mantel. It was enough to fill one with awe. The sight of this creature sitting on its eggs impressed me with the venerableness of the globe. There was nothing novel about it. All the while, this seemingly sleeping bronze sphinx, as motionless as the earth, was watching me with intense anxiety through those narrow slits in its eyelids. Another step, and it fluttered down the hill close to the ground, with a wabbling motion, as if touching the ground now with the tip of one wing, now with the other, so ten rods to the water, which [it] skimmed close over a few rods, then rose and soared in the air above me. Wonderful creature, which sits motionless on its eggs on the barest, most exposed hills, through pelting storms of rain or hail, as if it were a rock or a part of the earth itself, the outside of the globe, with its eyes shut and its wings folded, and, after the two days' storm, when you think it has become a fit symbol of the rheumatism, it suddenly rises into the air a bird, one of the most aerial, supple, and graceful of creatures, without stiffness in its wings or joints! It was a fit prelude to meeting Prometheus bound to his rock on Caucasus.

July 24, 1853. The smaller purple fringed orchis has not quite filled out its spike. What a surprise to detect under the dark, damp, cavernous copse, where some wild beast might fitly prowl, this splendid flower, silently standing with all its eyes on you!

July 30, 1853. Saw some green galls on a goldenrod (?) three quarters of an inch in diameter, shaped like a fruit or an Eastern temple, with two or three little worms inside, completely changing the destiny of the plant, showing the intimate relation between animal and vegetable life. The animal signifies its wishes by a touch, and the plant, instead of going on to blossom and bear its normal fruit, devotes itself to the service of the insect and becomes its cradle and food. It suggests that Nature is a kind of gall, that the Creator stung her and man is the grub she is destined to house and feed. The plant rounds off and paints the gall with as much care and love as its own flower and fruit, admiring it perchance even more.

Feb. 5, 1854. Shall we not have sympathy with the muskrat which gnaws its third leg off, not as pitying its sufferings, but, through our kindred mortality, appreciating its majestic pains and its heroic virtue? Are we not made its brothers by fate? For whom are psalms sung and mass said, if not for such worthies as these? When I hear the church organ peal, or feel the trembling tones of the bass viol, I see in imagination the musquash gnawing off his leg, I offer up a note that his affliction may be sanctified to each and all of us. Prayer and praise fitly follow such exploits. I look round for majestic pains and pleasures. They have our sympathy, both in their joys and in their pains. When I think of the tragedies which are constantly permitted in the course of all animal life, they make the plaintive strain of the universal harp which elevates us above the trivial. When I think of the muskrat gnawing off his leg, it is as the plectrum on the harp or the bow upon the viol, drawing forth a majestic strain or psalm, which immeasurably dignifies our common fate. Even as the worthies of mankind are said to recommend human life by having lived it, so I could not spare the example of the muskrat.

March 2, 1854. On the outside all the life of the earth is expressed in the animal or vegetable, but make a deep cut in it and you find it vital; you find in the very sands an anticipation of the vegetable leaf. No wonder, then, that plants grow and spring in it. The atoms have already learned the law. Let a vegetable sap convey it upwards and you have a vegetable leaf. No wonder that the earth expresses itself outwardly in leaves, which labors with the idea thus inwardly. The overhanging leaf sees here its prototype. The earth is pregnant with law.

April 13, 1854. On the evening of the 5th the body of a man was found in the river between Fair Haven Pond and Lee's, much wasted. How these events disturb our associations and tarnish the landscape! It is a serious injury done to a stream.

April 26, 1854. The wood thrush afar — so superior a strain to that of other birds. I was doubting if it would affect me as of yore, but it did measurably. I did not believe there could be such differences. This is the gospel according to the wood thrush. He makes a sabbath out of a week-day. I could go to hear him, could buy a pew in his church. Did he ever practise pulpit eloquence? He is right on the slavery question.

Sept. 8, 1854. Many green-briar leaves are very agreeably thickly spotted now with reddish brown, or fine green on a yellow or green ground, producing a wildly variegated leaf. I have seen nothing more rich. Some of these curled leaves are five inches wide with a short point. It is a leaf now for poets to sing about, a leaf to inspire poets. Now, while I am gathering grapes, I see them. It excites me to a sort of autumnal madness. They are leaves for Satyrus and Faunus to make their garlands of. My thoughts break out like them, spotted all over, yellow and green and brown. The freckled leaf. Perhaps they should be poison, to be thus spotted. I fancied these brown were blood-red spots, by contrast, but they are not. Now for the ripening year! Even leaves are *beginning* to be ripe.

Jan. 12, 1855. Perhaps what most moves us in winter is some reminiscence of far-off summer. How we leap by the side of the open brooks! What beauty in the running brooks! What life! What society! The cold is merely superficial; it is summer still at the core, far, far within. It is in the cawing of the crow, the crowing of the cock, the warmth of the sun on our backs. I hear faintly the cawing of a crow far, far away, echoing from some unseen wood-side, as if deadened by the springlike vapor which the sun is drawing from the ground. It mingles with the slight murmur of the village, the sound of children at play, as one stream empties gently into another, and the wild and tame are one. What a delicious sound! It is not merely crow calling to crow, for it speaks to me too. I am part of one great creature with him; if he has voice, I have ears. I can hear what he calls, and have engaged not to shoot nor stone him if he will caw to me each spring. On the one hand, it may be, is the sound of children at school saying their a, b, ab's, on the other, far in the wood-fringed horizon, the cawing of crows from their blessed eternal vacation, out at their long recess, children who have got dismissed! While the vaporous incense goes up from all the fields of the spring — if it were spring. Ah, bless the Lord, O my soul! bless him for wildness, for crows that will not alight within gunshot! and bless him for hens, too, that croak and cackle in the yard!

March 24, 1855. Passing up the Assabet, by the Hemlocks, where there has been a slide and some rocks have slid down into the river, I think I see how rocks come to be found in the midst of rivers. Rivers are continually changing their channels — eating into one bank and adding their sediment to the other — so that frequently where there is a great bend you see a high and steep bank or hill on one side, which the river washes, and a broad meadow on the other. As the river eats into the hill, especially in freshets, it undermines the rocks, large and small, and they slide down, alone or with the sand and soil, to the water's edge. The river continues to eat into the hill, carrying away all the lighter parts [of] the sand and soil, to add to its meadows or islands somewhere, but leaves the rocks where they rested, and thus in course of time they occupy the middle of the stream and, later still, the middle of the meadow, perchance, though it may be buried under the mud. But this does not explain how so many rocks lying in streams have been split in the direction of the current. Again, rivers appear to have travelled back and worn into the meadows of their creating, and then they become more meandering than ever. Thus in the course of ages the rivers wriggle in their beds, till it feels comfortable under them. Time is cheap and rather insignificant. It matters not whether it is a river which changes from side to side in a geological period or an eel that wriggles past in an instant.

April 13, 1855. The common hazel just out. It is perhaps the prettiest flower of the *shrubs* that have opened. A little bunch of (in this case) half a dozen catkins, one and three quarters inches long, trembling in the wind, shedding golden pollen on the hand, and, close by, as many minute, but clear crystalline crimson stars at the end of a bare and seemingly dead twig. For two or three days in my walks, I had given the hazel catkins a fillip with my finger under their chins to see if they were in bloom, but in vain; but here, on the warm south side of a wood, I find one bunch fully out and completely relaxed. They know when to trust themselves to the weather.

April 6, 1856. Just beyond Wood's Bridge, I hear the pewee. With what confidence after the lapse of many months, I come out to this waterside, some warm and pleasant spring morning, and, listening, hear, from farther or nearer, through the still concave of the air, the note of the first pewee! If there is one within half a mile, it will be here, and I shall be sure to hear its simple notes from those trees, borne over the water. It is remarkable how large a mansion of the air you can explore with your ears in the still morning by the waterside.

May 18, 1856. *Sailed* back on Hubbard's redstart path, and there saw a mud turtle draw in his head, of which I saw the half, about eight rods off. Pushed to the spot, where the water was about a foot deep, and at length detected him spread out on the bottom, his monstrous head and tail and legs outspread, probably directly under where he had appeared. At first, I suspect, I mistook him for a rock, for he was thickly covered with a short green moss-like conferva (?) — a venerable object, a true son of the meadow, suggesting what vigor! what naturalness! Perchance to make the moss grow on your back without injuring your health! How many things can he sustain on his shell where the mosses grow? He looked like an antediluvian under that green, shaggy shell, tougher than the rock you mistake it for. No wonder the Indian reverenced him as a god. Think of the time when he was an infant. There is your native American, who was before Columbus, perchance. Grown, not gray, but green with the lapse of ages. Living with the life of the meadow. I took off my coat, stripped up my shirt-sleeve, and caught him by his great rough tail. He snapped at me and my paddle, striking his snout against the side of the boat till he made it bleed. Though I held him down with an oar for a lever and my foot on it, he would suddenly lift all together, or run out his head and knock the oar and my leg aside. He held up his head to me and, with his mouth wide open, hissed in his breathing like a locomotive for a quarter of an hour, and I could look straight down his monstrous gullet ten inches.

Aug. 30, 1856. I see that all is not garden and cultivated field and crops, that there are square rods in Middlesex County as purely primitive and wild as they were a thousand years ago, which have escaped the plow and the axe and the scythe and the cranberry-rake, little oases of wildness in the desert of our civilization, wild as a square rod on the moon, supposing it to be uninhabited. I believe almost in the personality of such planetary matter, feel something akin to reverence for it, can even worship it as terrene, titanic matter extant in my day. We are so different we admire each other, we healthily attract one another. I love it as a maiden. These spots are meteoric, aerolitic, and such matter has in all ages been worshipped. Aye, when we are lifted out of the slime and film of our habitual life, we see the whole globe to be an aerolite, and reverence it as such, and make pilgrimages to it, far off as it is. How happens it that we reverence the stones which fall from another planet, and not the stones which belong to this — another globe, not this — heaven, and not earth? Are not the stones in Hodge's wall as good as the aerolite at Mecca? Is not our broad back-door-stone as good as any corner-stone in heaven?

It would imply the regeneration of mankind, if they were to become elevated enough to truly worship stocks and stones. It is the sentiment of fear and slavery and habit which makes a heathenish idolatry. Such idolaters abound in all countries, and heathen cross the seas to reform heathen, dead to bury the dead, and all go down to the pit together. If I could, I would worship the parings of my nails. If he who makes two blades of grass grow where one grew before is a benefactor, he who discovers two gods where there was only known the one (and such a one!) before is a still greater benefactor. I would fain improve every opportunity to wonder and worship, as a sunflower welcomes the light! The more thrilling, wonderful, divine objects I behold in a day, the more expanded and immortal I become. If a stone appeals to me and elevates me, tells me how many miles I have ccme, how many remain to travel — and the more, the better — reveals the future to me in some measure, it is a matter of private rejoicing. If it did the same service to all, it might well be a matter of public rejoicing.

Dec. 1, 1856. The dear wholesome color of shrub oak leaves, so clean and firm, not decaying, but which have put on a kind of immortality, nòt wrinkled and thin like the white oak leaves, but full-veined and plump, as nearer earth. Well-tanned leather on the one side, sun-tanned, color of colors, color of the cow and the deer, silver-downy beneath, turned toward the late bleached and russet fields. What are acanthus leaves and the rest to this? Emblem of my winter condition. I love and could embrace the shrub oak with its scanty garment of leaves rising above the snow, lowly whispering to me, akin to winter thoughts, and sunsets, and to all virtue. Covert which the hare and the partridge seek, and I too seek. What cousin of mine is the shrub oak? How can any man suffer long? For a sense of want is a prayer, and all prayers are answered. Rigid as iron, clean as the atmosphere, hardy as virtue, innocent and sweet as a maiden is the shrub oak. In proportion as I know and love it, I am natural and sound as a partridge. I felt a positive yearning toward one bush this afternoon. There was a match found for me at last. I fell in love with a shrub oak. Tenacious of its leaves, which shrivel not but retain a certain wintry life in them, firm shields, painted in fast colors a rich brown. The deer mouse, too, knows the shrub oak and has its hole in the snow by the shrub oak's stem. . . .

Well named *shrub oak*. Low, robust, hardy, indigenous. Well known to the striped squirrel and the partridge and rabbit. The squirrel nibbles its nuts sitting upon an old stump of its larger cousins. What is Peruvian bark to your bark? How many rents I owe to you! how many eyes put out! how many bleeding fingers! How many shrub oak patches I have been through, stooping, winding my way, bending the twigs aside, guiding myself by the sun, over hills and valleys and plains, resting in clear grassy spaces! I love to go through a patch of shrub oak in a bee-line, where you tear your clothes and put your eyes out.

Dec. 6, 1856. On all sides, in swamps and about their edges and in the woods, the bare shrubs are sprinkled with buds, more or less noticeable and pretty, their little gemmæ or gems, their most vital and attractive parts now, almost all the greenness and color left, greens and salads for the birds and rabbits. Our eyes go searching along the stems for what is most vivacious and characteristic, the concentrated summer gone into winter quarters. For we are hunters pursuing the summer on snow-shoes and skates, all winter long. There is really but one season in our hearts.

Jan. 27, 1858. To Hill and beyond. It is so mild and moist as I saunter along by the wall and east of the Hill that I remember, or anticipate, one of those warm rain-storms in the spring, when the earth is just laid bare, the wind is south, and the cladonia lichens are swollen and lusty with moisture, your foot sinking into them and pressing the water out as from a sponge, and the sandy places also are drinking it in. You wander indefinitely in a beaded coat, wet to the skin of your legs, sit on moss-clad rocks and stumps, and hear the lisping of migrating sparrows flitting amid the shrub oaks, sit long at a time, still, and have your thoughts. A rain which is as serene as fair weather, suggesting fairer weather than was ever seen. You could hug the clods that defile you. You feel the fertilizing influence of the rain in your mind. The part of you that is wettest is fullest of life, like the lichens. You discover evidences of immortality not known to divines. You cease to die. You detect some buds and sprouts of life. Every step in the old rye field is on virgin soil.

And then the rain comes thicker and faster than before, thawing the remaining frost in the ground, detaining the migrating bird; and you turn your back to it, full of serene, contented thoughts, soothed by the steady dropping on the withered leaves, more at home for being abroad, more comfortable for being wet, sinking at each step deep into the thawing earth, gladly breaking through the gray rotting ice. The dullest sounds seem sweetly modulated by the air. You leave your tracks in fields of spring rye, scaring the fox-colored sparrows along the wood-sides. You cannot go home yet; you stay and sit in the rain.

May 10, 1858. I hear in several places the low dumping notes of awakened bullfrogs, what I call their *pebbly* notes, as if they were cracking pebbles in their mouths; not the plump *dont dont* or *ker dont*, but *kerdle dont dont*. As if they sat round mumbling pebbles. At length, near Ball's Hill, I hear the first regular bullfrog's trump. Some fainter ones far off are very like the looing [*sic*] of cows. This sound, heard low and far off over meadows when the warmer hours have come, grandly inaugurates the summer. I perspire with rowing in my thick coat and wish I had worn a thin one. This trumpeter, marching or leaping in the van of advancing summer, whom I now hear coming on over the green meadows, seems to say, '*Take off your coat, take off your coat, take off your coat!*' He says, 'Here comes a gale that I can breathe. This is something like; this is what I call summer.' I see three or four of them sitting silent in one warm meadow bay. Evidently their breeding-season now begins. But they are soon silent as yet, and it is only an occasional and transient trump that you hear. That season which is bounded on the north, on the spring side at least, by the trump of the bullfrog. This note is like the first colored petals within the calyx of a flower. It conducts us toward the germ of the flower summer. He knows no winter. I hear in his tone the rumors of summer heats. By this note he reassures the season. Not till the air is of that quality that it can support this sound does he emit it. It requires a certain sonorousness. The van is led by the croaking wood frog and the little peeping hylodes, and at last comes this pursy trumpeter, the air growing more and more genial, and even sultry, as well as sonorous. As soon as Nature is ready for him to play his part, she awakens him with a warmer, perchance a sultry, breath and excites him to sound his trombone. It reminds me at once of tepid waters and of bathing. His trump is to the ear what the yellow lily or spatter-dock is to the eye. He swears by the powers of mud. It is enough for the day to have heard only the first half-trump of an early awakened one from far in some warm meadow bay. It is a certain revelation and anticipation of the livelong summer to come. It gives leave to the corn to grow and to the heavens to thunder and lighten. It gives leave to the invalid to take the air. Our climate is now as tropical as any. It says, Put out your fires and sit in the fire which the sun has kindled.

Nov. 7, 1858. It cleared up this forenoon. I leave my boat opposite the Hemlocks. I see the cold sunlight from some glade between the clouds falling on distant oak woods, now nearly bare, and as I glance up the hill between them, seeing the bare but bright hillside beyond, I think, Now we are left to the hemlocks and pines with their silvery light, to the bare trees and withered grass. The very rocks and stones in the rocky roads (that beyond Farmer's) look white in the clear November light, especially after the rain. We are left to the chickadee's familiar notes, and the jay for trumpeter. What struck me was a certain emptiness beyond, between the hemlocks and the hill, in the cool, washed air, as if I appreciated even here the absence of insects from it. It suggested agreeably to me a mere space in which to walk briskly. The fields are bleak, and they are, as it were, vacated. The very earth is like a house shut up for the winter, and I go knocking about it in vain. But just then I heard a chickadee on a hemlock, and was inexpressibly cheered to find that an old acquaintance was yet stirring about the premises, and was, I was assured, to be there all winter. All that was evergreen in me revived at once.

Nov. 30, 1858. I cannot but see still in my mind's eye those little striped breams poised in Walden's glaucous water. They balance all the rest of the world in my estimation at present, for this is the bream that I have just found, and for the time I neglect all its brethren and am ready to kill the fatted calf on its account. For more than two centuries have men fished here and have not distinguished this permanent settler of the township. It is not like a new bird, a transient visitor that may not be seen again for years, but there it dwells and has dwelt permanently, who can tell how long? When my eyes first rested on Walden the striped bream was poised in it, though I did not see it, and when Tahatawan paddled his canoe there. How wild it makes the pond and the township to find a new fish in it! America renews her youth here. But in my account of this bream I cannot go a hair's breadth beyond the mere statement that it exists — the miracle of its existence, my contemporary and neighbor, yet so different from me! I can only poise my thought there by its side and try to think like a bream for a moment. I can only think of precious jewels, of music, poetry, beauty, and the mystery of life. I only see the bream in its orbit, as I see a star, but I care not to measure its distance or weight. The bream, appreciated, floats in the pond as the centre of the system, another image of God. Its life no man can explain more than he can his own. I want you to perceive the mystery of the bream. I have a contemporary in Walden. It has fins where I have legs and arms. I have a friend among the fishes, at least a new acquaintance. Its character will interest me, I trust, not its clothes and anatomy. I do not want it to eat. Acquaintance with it is to make my life more rich and eventful. It is as if a poet or an anchorite had moved into the town, whom I can see from time to time and think of yet oftener. Perhaps there are a thousand of these striped bream which no one had thought of in that pond — not their mere impressions in stone, but in the full tide of the bream life.

Feb. 16, 1859. The hen-hawk and the pine are friends. The same thing which keeps the hen-hawk in the woods, away from the cities, keeps me here. That bird settles with confidence on a white pine top and not upon your weathercock. That bird will not be poultry of yours, lays no eggs for you, forever hides its nest. Though willed, or *wild*, it is not willful in its wildness. The unsympathizing man regards the wildness of some animals, their strangeness to him, as a sin; as if all their virtue consisted in their tamableness. He has always a charge in his gun ready for their extermination. What we call wildness is a civilization other than our own. The hen-hawk shuns the farmer, but it seeks the friendly shelter and support of the pine. It will not consent to walk in the barn-yard, but it loves to soar above the clouds. It has its own way and is beautiful, when we would fain subject it to our will. So any surpassing work of art is strange and wild to the mass of men, as is genius itself. No hawk that soars and steals our poultry is wilder than genius, and none is more persecuted or above persecution. It can never be poet laureate, to say 'Pretty Poll' and 'Polly want a cracker.'

March 28, 1859. P.M. It is now high time to look for arrowheads, etc. I spend many hours every spring gathering the crop which the melting snow and rain have washed bare. When, at length, some island in the meadow or some sandy field elsewhere has been plowed, perhaps for rye, in the fall, I take note of it, and do not fail to repair thither as soon as the earth begins to be dry in the spring. If the spot chances never to have been cultivated before, I am the first to gather a crop from it. The farmer little thinks that another reaps a harvest which is the fruit of his toil. As much ground is turned up in a day by the plow as Indian implements could not have turned over in a month, and my eyes rest on the evidences of an aboriginal life which passed here a thousand years ago perchance. Especially if the knolls in the meadows are washed by a freshet where they have been plowed the previous fall, the soil will be taken away lower down and the stones left — the arrowheads, etc., and soapstone pottery amid them — somewhat as gold is washed in a dish or tom. I landed on two spots this afternoon and picked up a dozen arrowheads. It is one of the regular pursuits of the spring. As much as sportsmen go in pursuit of ducks, and gunners of musquash, and scholars of rare books, and travellers of adventures, and poets of ideas, and all men of money, I go in search of arrowheads when the proper season comes round again. So I help myself to live worthily, and loving my life as I should. . . .

I have not decided whether I had better publish my experience in searching for arrowheads in three volumes, with plates and an index, or try to compress it into one. These durable implements seem to have been suggested to the Indian mechanic with a view to my entertainment in a succeeding period. After all the labor expended on it, the bolt may have been shot but once perchance, and the shaft which was devoted to it decayed, and there lay the arrowhead, sinking into the ground, awaiting me. They lie all over the hills with like expectation, and in due time the husbandman is sent, and, tempted by the promise of corn or rye, he plows the land and turns them up to my view. Many as I have found, methinks the last one gives me about the same delight that the first did. Some time or other, you would say, it had rained arrowheads, for they lie all over the surface of America. You may have your peculiar tastes. Certain localities in your town may seem from association unattractive and uninhabitable to you. You may wonder that the land bears any money value there, and pity some poor fellow who is said to survive in that neighborhood. But plow up a new field there, and you will find the omnipresent arrow-points strewn over it, and it will appear that the red man, with other tastes and associations, lived there too. No matter how far from the modern road or meeting-house, no matter how near. They lie in the meeting-house cellar, and they lie in the distant cow-pasture. And some collections which were made a century ago by the curious like myself have been dispersed again, and they are still as good as new. You cannot tell the third-hand ones (for they are all second-hand) from the others, such is their persistent out-of-door durability; for they were chiefly made to be lost. They are sown, like a grain that is slow to germinate, broadcast over the earth. Like the dragon's teeth which bore a crop of soldiers, these bear crops of philosophers and poets, and the same seed is just as good to plant again. It is a stone fruit. Each one yields me a thought. I come nearer to the maker of it than if I found his bones. His bones would not prove any wit that wielded them, such as this work of his bones does. It is humanity inscribed on the face of the earth, patent to my eyes as soon as the snow goes off, not hidden away in some crypt or grave or under a pyramid. No disgusting mummy, but a clean stone, the best symbol or letter that could have been transmitted to me.

The Red Man, his mark 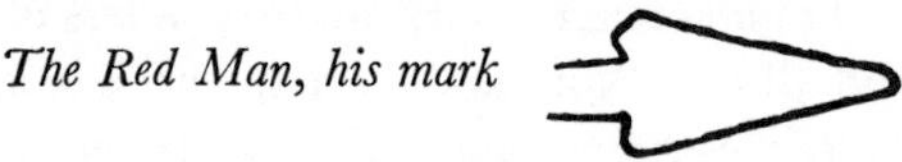

At every step I see it, and I can easily supply the 'Tahatawan' or 'Man-tatuket' that might have been written if he had had a clerk. It is no single inscription on a particular rock, but a footprint — rather a mind-print — left everywhere, and altogether illegible. No vandals, however vandalic in their disposition, can be so industrious as to destroy them.

Time will soon destroy the works of famous painters and sculptors, but the Indian arrowhead will balk his efforts and Eternity will have to come to his aid. They are not fossil bones, but, as it were, fossil thoughts, forever reminding me of the mind that shaped them. I would fain know that I am treading in the tracks of human game — that I am on the trail of mind — and these little reminders never fail to set me right. When I see these signs I know that the subtle spirits that made them are not far off, into whatever form transmuted. What if you do plow and hoe amid them, and swear that not one stone shall be left upon another? They are only the less like to break in that case. When you turn up one layer you bury another so much the more securely. They are at peace with rust. This arrow-headed character promises to outlast all others. The larger pestles and axes may, perchance, grow scarce and be broken, but the arrowhead shall, perhaps, never cease to wing its way through the ages to eternity. It was originally winged for but a short flight, but it still, to my mind's eye, wings its way through the ages, bearing a message from the hand that shot it. Myriads of arrow-points lie sleeping in the skin of the revolving earth, while meteors revolve in space. The footprint, the mind-print of the oldest men. When some Vandal chieftain has razed to the earth the British Museum, and, perchance, the winged bulls from Nineveh shall have lost most if not all of their features, the arrowheads which the museum contains will, perhaps, find themselves at home again in familiar dust, and resume their shining in new springs upon the bared surface of the earth then, to be picked up for the thousandth time by the shepherd or savage that may be wandering there, and once more suggest their story to him. Indifferent they to British Museums, and, no doubt, Nineveh bulls are old acquaintances of theirs, for they have camped on the plains of Mesopotamia, too, and were buried *with* the winged bulls.

They cannot be said to be lost nor found. Surely their use was not so much to bear its fate to some bird or quadruped, or man, as it was to lie here near the surface of the earth for a perpetual reminder to the generations that come after. As for museums, I think it is better to let Nature take care of our antiquities. These are our antiquities, and they are cleaner to think of than the rubbish of the Tower of London, and they are a more ancient armor than is there. It is a recommendation that they are so inobvious — that they occur only to the eye and thought that chances to be directed toward them. When you pick up an arrow-head and put it in your pocket, it may say: 'Eh, you think you have got me, do you? But I shall wear a hole in your pocket at last, or if you put me in your cabinet, your heir or great-grandson will forget me or throw me out the window directly, or when the house falls I shall drop into the cellar, and there I shall lie quite at home again. Ready to be *found* again, eh? Perhaps some new red man that is to come will fit me to a shaft and make me do his bidding for a bow-shot. What reck I?'

Sept. 29, 1859. Going along this old Carlisle road — road for walkers, for berry-pickers, and no more worldly travellers; road for Melvin and Clark, not for the sheriff nor butcher nor the baker's jingling cart; road where all wild things and fruits abound, where there are countless rocks to jar those who venture there in wagons; which no jockey, no wheelwright in his right mind, drives over, no little spidery gigs and Flying Childers; road which leads to and through a great but not famous garden, zoölogical and botanical garden, at whose *gate* you never arrive — as I was going along there, I perceived the grateful scent of the dicksonia fern, now partly decayed, and it reminds me of all up-country with its springy mountainsides and unexhausted vigor. Is there any essence of dicksonia fern, I wonder? Surely that giant who, my neighbor expects, is to bound up the Alleghanies will have his handkerchief scented with that. In the lowest part of the road the dicksonia by the wall-sides is more than half frost-bitten and withered — a sober Quaker-color, brown crape! — though not so tender or early [?] as the cinnamon fern; but soon I rise to where they are more yellow and green, and so my route is varied. On the higher places there are very handsome tufts of it, all yellowish outside and green within. The sweet fragrance of decay! When I wade through by narrow cow-paths, it is as if I had strayed into an ancient and decayed herb-garden. Proper for old ladies to scent their handkerchiefs with. Nature perfumes her garments with this essence now especially. She gives it to those who go a-barberrying and on dank autumnal walks. The essence of this as well as of new-mown hay, surely! The very scent of it, if you have a decayed frond in your chamber, will take you far up country in a twinkling. You would think you had gone after the cows there, or were lost on the mountains. It will make you as cool and well as a frog — a wood frog, *Rana sylvatica*. It is the scent the earth yielded in the saurian period, before man was created and fell, before milk and water were invented, and the mints. Far wilder than they. *Rana sylvatica* passed judgment on it, or rather that peculiar-scented *Rana palustris*. It was in his reign it was introduced. That is the scent of the Silurian Period precisely, and a modern beau may scent his handkerchief with it. Before man had come and the plants that chiefly serve him. There were no *Rosaceæ* nor mints then. So the earth smelled in the Silurian (?) Period, before man was created and any soil had been debauched with manure. The saurians had their handkerchiefs scented with it. For all the ages are represented still and you can smell them out. . . .

Road — that old Carlisle one — that leaves towns behind; where you put off worldly thoughts; where you do not carry a watch, nor remember the proprietor; where the proprietor is the only trespasser — looking after *his* apples! — the only one who mistakes his calling there, whose title is not good; where fifty may be a-barberrying and you do not see one. It is an endless succession of glades where the barberries grow thickest, successive yards amid the barberry bushes where you do not see out. There I see Melvin and the robins, and many a nut-brown maid *sashé*-ing [*sic*] to the barberry bushes in hoops and crinoline, and none of them see me. The world-surrounding hoop! faery rings! Oh, the jolly cooper's trade it is the best of any! Carried to the furthest isles where civilized man penetrates. This the girdle they've put round the world! Saturn or Satan set the example. Large and small hogsheads, barrels, kegs, worn by the misses that go to that lone schoolhouse in the Pinkham notch. The lonely horse in its pasture is glad to see company, comes forward to be noticed and takes an apple from your hand. Others are called *great* roads, but this is greater than they all. The road is only laid out, offered to walkers, not *accepted* by the town and the travelling world. To be represented by a dotted line on charts, or drawn in lime-juice, undiscoverable to the uninitiated, to be held to a warm imagination. No guide-boards indicate it. No odometer would indicate the miles a wagon had run there. Rocks which the druids *might* have raised — if they could. There I go searching for malic acid of the right quality, with my tests. The process is simple. Place the fruit between your jaws and then endeavor to make your teeth meet. The very earth contains it. The Easterbrooks Country contains malic acid.

Aug. 22, 1860. It is true, as is said, that we have as good a right to make berries private property as to make grass and trees such; but what I chiefly regret is the, in effect, dog-in-the-manger result, for at the same time that we exclude mankind from gathering berries in our field, we exclude them from gathering health and happiness and inspiration and a hundred other far finer and nobler fruits than berries, which yet we shall not gather ourselves there, nor even carry to market. We strike only one more blow at a simple and wholesome relation to nature. As long as the berries are free to all comers they are beautiful, though they may be few and small, but tell me that is a blueberry swamp which somebody has hired, and I shall not want even to look at it. In laying claim for the first time to the spontaneous fruit of our pastures we are, accordingly, aware of a little meanness inevitably, and the gay berry party whom we turn away naturally look down on and despise us. If it were left to the berries to say who should have them, is it not likely that they would prefer to be gathered by the party of children in the hay-rigging, who have come to have a good time merely?

I do not see clearly that these successive losses are ever quite made up to us. This is one of the taxes which we pay for having a railroad. Almost all our improvements, so called, tend to convert the country into the town.

This suggests what origin and foundation many of our laws and institutions have, and I do not say this by way of complaining of this particular custom. Not that I love Cæsar less, but Rome more.

Jan. 3, 1861. What are the natural features which make a township handsome? A river, with its waterfalls and meadows, a lake, a hill, a cliff or individual rocks, a forest, and ancient trees standing singly. Such things are beautiful; they have a high use which dollars and cents never represent. If the inhabitants of a town were wise, they would seek to preserve these things, though at a considerable expense; for such things educate far more than any hired teachers or preachers, or any at present recognized system of school education. I do not think him fit to be the founder of a state or even of a town who does not foresee the use of these things, but legislates chiefly for oxen, as it were.

Far the handsomest thing I saw in Boxboro was its noble oak wood. I doubt if there is a finer one in Massachusetts. Let her keep it a century longer, and men will make pilgrimages to it from all parts of the

country; and yet it would be very like the rest of New England if Boxboro were ashamed of that woodland. . . .

It would be worth the while if in each town there were a committee
appointed to see that the beauty of the town received no detriment. If
we have the largest boulder in the county, then it should not belong to
an individual, nor be made into door-steps.

As in many countries precious metals belong to the crown, so here
more precious natural objects of rare beauty should belong to the
public.

Not only the channel but one or both banks of every river should be
a public highway. The only use of a river is not to float on it.

Think of a mountain-top in the township — even to the minds of the
Indians a sacred place — only accessible through private grounds!
a temple, as it were, which you cannot enter except by trespassing and
at the risk of letting out or letting in somebody's cattle! in fact the temple
itself in this case private property and standing in a man's cow-yard —
for such is commonly the case! . . .

How few ever get beyond feeding, clothing, sheltering, and warming
themselves in this world, and begin to treat themselves as human beings
— as intellectual and moral beings! Most seem not to see any further —
not to see over the ridge-pole of their barns — or to be exhausted and
accomplish nothing more than a full barn, though it may be accompanied by an empty head. They venture a little, run some risks, when
it is a question of a larger crop of corn or potatoes; but they are commonly timid and count their coppers, when the question is whether
their children shall be educated. He who has the reputation of being
the thriftiest farmer and making the best bargains is really the most
thriftless and makes the worst. It is safest to invest in knowledge, for
the probability is that you can carry that with you wherever you go.

But most men, it seems to me, do not care for Nature and would sell
their share in all her beauty, as long as they may live, for a stated sum —
many for a glass of rum. Thank God, men cannot as yet fly, and lay
waste the sky as well as the earth! We are safe on that side for the
present. It is for the very reason that some do not care for those things
that we need to continue to protect all from the vandalism of a few.

March 18, 1861. When I pass by a twig of willow, though of the
slenderest kind, rising above the sedge in some dry hollow early in
December, or in midwinter above the snow, my spirits rise as if it were
an oasis in the desert. The very name 'sallow' (*salix*, from the Celtic
sal-lis, near water) suggests that there is some natural sap or blood

flowing there. It is a divining wand that has not failed, but stands with its root in the fountain. . . .

Ah, willow! willow! Would that I always possessed thy good spirits.

II. MY WORK

Feb. 8, 1841. My Journal is that of me which would else spill over and run to waste, gleanings from the field which in action I reap. I must not live for it, but in it for the gods. They are my correspondent, to whom daily I send off this sheet postpaid. I am clerk in their counting-room, and at evening transfer the account from day-book to ledger. It is as a leaf which hangs over my head in the path. I bend the twig and write my prayers on it; then letting it go, the bough springs up and shows the scrawl to heaven.

Aug. 4, 1841. *Wednesday.* My pen is a lever which, in proportion as the near end stirs me further within, the further end reaches to a greater depth in the reader.

Nov. 16, 1850. Somebody shut the cat's tail in the door just now, and she made such a caterwaul as has driven two whole worlds out of my thoughts. I saw unspeakable things in the sky and looming in the horizon of my mind, and now they are all reduced to a cat's tail. Vast films of thought floated through my brain, like clouds pregnant with rain enough to fertilize and restore a world, and now they are all dissipated.

July 23, 1851. You must walk so gently as to hear the finest sounds, the faculties being in repose. Your mind must not perspire. True, out of doors my thought is commonly drowned, as it were, and shrunken, pressed down by stupendous piles of light ethereal influences, for the pressure of the atmosphere is still fifteen pounds to a square inch. I can do little more than preserve the equilibrium and resist the pressure of the atmosphere. I can only nod like the rye-heads in the breeze. I expand more surely in my chamber, as far as expression goes, as if that pressure were taken off; but here outdoors is the place to store up influences. . . .

July 23, 1851. But this habit of close observation — in Humboldt, Darwin, and others. Is it to be kept up long, this science? Do not tread on the heels of your experience. Be impressed without making a minute of it. Poetry puts an interval between the impression and the expression — waits till the seed germinates naturally.

Aug. 28, 1851. I omit the unusual — the hurricanes and earthquakes — and describe the common. This has the greatest charm and is the true theme of poetry. You may have the extraordinary for your province, if you will let me have the ordinary. Give me the obscure life, the cottage of the poor and humble, the workdays of the world, the barren fields, the smallest share of all things but poetic perception. Give me but the eyes to see the things which you possess.

Sept. 2, 1851. We cannot write well or truly but what we write with gusto. The body, the senses, must conspire with the mind. Expression is the act of the whole man, that our speech may be vascular. The intellect is powerless to express thought without the aid of the heart and liver and of every member. Often I feel that my head stands out too dry, when it should be immersed. A writer, a man writing, is the scribe of all nature; he is the corn and the grass and the atmosphere writing. It is always essential that we love to do what we are doing, do it with a heart. The maturity of the mind, however, may perchance consist with a certain dryness.

Sept. 8, 1851. No fog this morning. Shall I not have words as fresh as my thoughts? Shall I use any other man's word? A genuine thought or feeling can find expression for itself, if it have to invent hieroglyphics. It has the universe for type-metal. It is for want of original thought that one man's style is like another's.

Nov. 9, 1851. I, too, would fain set down something beside facts. Facts should only be as the frame to my pictures; they should be material to the mythology which I am writing; not facts to assist men to make money, farmers to farm profitably, in any common sense; facts to tell who I am, and where I have been or what I have thought: as now the bell rings for evening meeting, and its volumes of sound, like smoke which rises from where a cannon is fired, make the tent in which I dwell. My facts shall be falsehoods to the common sense. I would so state facts that they shall be significant, shall be myths or mythologic. Facts which the mind perceived, thoughts which the body thought — with these I deal. I, too, cherish vague and misty forms, vaguest when the cloud at which I gaze is dissipated quite and naught but the skyey depths are seen.

Nov. 12, 1851. Write often, write upon a thousand themes, rather than long at a time, not trying to turn too many feeble somersets in the air — and so come down upon your head at last. Antæus-like, be not long absent from the ground. Those sentences are good and well discharged which are like so many little resiliencies from the spring floor of our life — a distinct fruit and kernel itself, springing from terra firma. Let there be as many distinct plants as the soil and the light can sustain. Take as many bounds in a day as possible. Sentences uttered with your back to the wall. Those are the admirable bounds when the performer has lately touched the springboard. A good bound into the air from the air [*sic*] is a good and wholesome experience, but what shall we say to a man's leaping off precipices in the attempt to fly? He comes down like lead. In the meanwhile, you have got your feet planted upon the rock, with the rock also at your back, and, as in the case of King James and Roderick Dhu, can say,

> 'Come one, come all! this rock shall fly
> From its firm base as soon as I.'

Such, uttered or not, is the strength of your sentence. Sentences in which there is no strain. A fluttering and inconstant and *quasi* inspiration, and ever memorable Icarian fall, in which your helpless wings are expanded merely by your swift descent into the *pelagos* beneath.

Dec. 12, 1851. I have been surveying for twenty or thirty days, living coarsely, even as respects my diet — for I find that that will always alter to suit my employment — indeed, leading a quite trivial life; and to-night, for the first time, had made a fire in my chamber and endeavored to return to myself. I wished to ally myself to the powers that rule the universe. I wished to dive into some deep stream of thoughtful and devoted life, which meandered through retired and fertile meadows far from towns. I wished to do again, or for once, things quite congenial to my highest inmost and most sacred nature, to lurk in crystalline thought like the trout under verdurous banks, where stray mankind should only see my bubble come to the surface. I wished to live, ah! as far away as a man can think. I wished for leisure and quiet to let my life flow in its proper channels, with its proper currents; when I might not waste the days, might establish daily prayer and thanksgiving in my family; might do my own work and not the work of Concord and Carlisle, which would yield me better than money. (How much forbearance, aye, sacrifice and loss, goes to every accomplishment! I am thinking by what long discipline and at what cost a man learns to speak simply at last.)

Jan. 26, 1852. Nature never indulges in exclamations, never says

Ah! or Alas! She is not of French descent. She is a plain writer, uses few gestures, does not add to her verbs, uses few adverbs, uses no expletives. I find that I use many words for the sake of emphasis which really add nothing to the force of my sentences, and they look relieved the moment I have cancelled these. Words by which I express my mood, my conviction, rather than the simple truth.

Jan. 30, 1852. Do nothing merely out of good resolutions. Discipline yourself only to yield to love; suffer yourself to be attracted. It is in vain to write on chosen themes. We must wait till they have kindled a flame in our minds. There must be the copulating and generating force of love behind every effort destined to be successful. The cold resolve gives birth to, begets, nothing. The theme that seeks me, not I it. The poet's relation to his theme is the relation of lovers. It is no more to be courted. Obey, report.

Sept. 13, 1852. I must walk more with free senses. It is as bad to *study* stars and clouds as flowers and stones. I must let my senses wander as my thoughts, my eyes see without looking. Carlyle said that how to observe was to look, but I say that it is rather to see, and the more you look the less you will observe. I have the habit of attention to such excess that my senses get no rest, but suffer from a constant strain. Be not preoccupied with looking. Go not to the object; let it come to you. When I have found myself ever looking down and confining my gaze to the flowers, I have thought it might be well to get into the habit of observing the clouds as a corrective; but no! that study would be just as bad. What I need is not to look at all, but a true sauntering of the eye.

Sept. 19, 1854. Thinking this afternoon of the prospect of my writing lectures and going abroad to read them the next winter, I realized how incomparably great the advantages of obscurity and poverty which I have enjoyed so long (and may still perhaps enjoy). I thought with what more than princely, with what poetical, leisure I had spent my years hitherto, without care or engagement, fancy-free. I have given myself up to nature; I have lived so many springs and summers and autumns and winters as if I had nothing else to do but *live* them, and imbibe whatever nutriment they had for me; I have spent a couple of years, for instance, with the flowers chiefly, having none other so binding engagement as to observe when they opened; I could have afforded to spend a whole fall observing the changing tints of the foliage. Ah, how I have thriven on solitude and poverty! I cannot overstate this advantage. I do not see how I could have enjoyed it, if the public had been expecting as much of me as there is danger now that they will. If I go abroad lecturing, how shall I ever recover the lost winter?

Dec. 6, 1854. After lecturing twice this winter I feel that I am in danger of cheapening myself by trying to become a successful lecturer, *i.e.*, to interest my audiences. I am disappointed to find that most that I am and value myself for is lost, or worse than lost, on my audience. I fail to get even the attention of the mass. I should suit them better if I suited myself less. I feel that the public demand an average man — average thoughts and manners — not originality, nor even absolute excellence. You cannot interest them except as you are like them and sympathize with them. I would rather that my audience come to me than that I should go to them, and so they be sifted; *i.e.*, I would rather write books than lectures. That is fine, this coarse. To read to a promiscuous audience who are at your mercy the fine thoughts you solaced yourself with far away is as violent as to fatten geese by cramming, and in this case they do not get fatter.

Dec. 4, 1856. My first botany, as I remember, was Bigelow's 'Plants of Boston and Vicinity,' which I began to use about twenty years ago, looking chiefly for the popular names and the short references to the localities of plants, even without any regard to the plant. I also learned the names of many, but without using any system, and forgot them soon. I was not inclined to pluck flowers; preferred to leave them where they were, liked them best there. I was never in the least interested in plants in the house. But from year to year we look at Nature with new eyes. About half a dozen years ago I found myself again attending to plants with more method, looking out the name of each one and remembering it. I began to bring them home in my hat, a straw one with a scaffold lining to it, which I called my botany-box. I never used any other, and when some whom I visited were evidently surprised at its dilapidated look, as I deposited it on their front entry table, I assured them it was not so much my hat as my botany-box. I remember gazing with interest at the swamps about those days and wondering if I could ever attain to such familiarity with plants that I should know the species of every twig and leaf in them, that I should be acquainted with every plant (excepting grasses and cryptogamous ones), summer and winter, that I saw. Though I knew most of the flowers, and there were not in any particular swamp more than half a dozen shrubs that I did not know, yet these made it seem like a maze to me, of a thousand strange species, and I even thought of commencing at one end and looking it faithfully and laboriously through till I knew it all. I little thought that in a year or two I should have attained to that knowledge without all that labor. Still I never studied botany, and do not today systematically, the most natural system is still so artificial. I wanted to know my neighbors, if possible — to get a little nearer to them. I soon found myself observing when plants first blossomed and leafed, and I followed it up early and late, far and near, several years in succession, running to different sides of the town and into the neighboring towns, often between twenty and thirty miles in a day. I often visited a particular plant four or five miles distant, half a dozen times within a fortnight, that I might know exactly when it opened, beside attending to a great many others in different directions and some of them equally distant, at the same time. At the same time I had an eye for birds and whatever else might offer.

April 1, 1860. The fruit a thinker bears is *sentences* — statements or opinions. He seeks to affirm something as true. I am surprised that my affirmations or utterances come to me ready-made — not fore-thought — so that I occasionally awake in the night simply to let fall ripe a statement which I had never consciously considered before, and as surprising and novel and agreeable to me as anything can be. As if we only thought by sympathy with the universal mind, which thought while we were asleep. There is such a necessity [to] make a definite statement that our minds at length do it without our consciousness, just as we carry our food to our mouths. This occurred to me last night, but I was so surprised by the fact which I have just endeavored to report that I have entirely forgotten what the particular observation was.

III. CRITICISM

Nov. 15, 1850. Suppose the muskrat or beaver were to turn his views [*sic*] to literature, what fresh views of nature would he present! The fault of our books and other deeds is that they are too humane, I want something speaking in some measure to the condition of muskrats and skunk-cabbage as well as of men — not merely to a pining and complaining coterie of philanthropists.

Aug. 22, 1851. It is the fault of some excellent writers — De Quincey's first impressions on seeing London suggest it to me — that they express themselves with too great fullness and detail. They give the most faithful, natural, and lifelike account of their sensations, mental and physical, but they lack moderation and sententiousness. They do not affect us by an ineffectual earnestness and a reserve of meaning, like a stutterer; they say all they mean. Their sentences are not concentrated and nutty. Sentences which suggest far more than they say, which have an atmosphere about them, which do not merely report an old, but make a new, impression; sentences which suggest as many things and are as durable as a Roman aqueduct; to frame these, that is the *art* of writing. Sentences which are expensive, towards which so many volumes, so much life, went; which lie like boulders on the page, up and down or across; which contain the seed of other sentences, not mere repetition, but creation; which a man might sell his grounds and castles to build. If De Quincey had suggested each of his pages in a sentence and passed on, it would have been far more excellent writing. His style is nowhere kinked and knotted up into something hard and significant, which you could swallow like a diamond, without digesting.

Sept. 2, 1851. Old Cato says well, '*Patremfamilias vendacem, non emacem, esse oportet.*' These Latin terminations express better than any English that I know the greediness, as it were, and tenacity of purpose with which the husbandman and householder is required to be a seller and not a buyer — with mastiff-like tenacity — these *lipped* words, which, like the lips of moose and browsing creatures, gather in the herbage and twigs with a certain greed. This termination *cious* adds force to a word, like the lips of browsing creatures, which greedily collect what the jaw holds; as in the word 'tenacious' the first half represents the kind of jaw which holds, the last the lips which collect. It can only be pronounced by a certain opening and protruding of the lips; so 'avaricious.' These words express the sense of their simple roots with the addition, as it were, of a certain lip greediness. Hence 'capacious' and 'capacity,' 'emacity.' When these expressive words are used, the hearer gets something to chew upon. To be a seller with the tenacity and firmness and steadiness of the jaws which hold and the greediness of the lips which collect. The audacious man not only dares, but he greedily collects more danger to dare. The avaricious man not only desires and satisfies his desire, but he collects ever new browse in anticipation of his ever-springing desires. What is *luscious* is especially enjoyed by the lips. The mastiff-mouthed are tenacious. To be a seller with mastiff-mouthed tenacity of purpose, with moose-lipped greediness

— ability to browse! To be edacious and voracious is to be not nibbling and swallowing merely, but eating and swallowing while the lips are greedily collecting more food.

Nov. 1, 1851. It is a rare qualification to be able to state a fact simply and adequately, to digest some experience cleanly, to say 'yes' and 'no' with authority, to make a square edge, to conceive and suffer the truth to pass through us living and intact, even as a waterfowl an eel, as it flies over the meadows, thus stocking new waters. First of all a man must see, before he can say. Statements are made but partially. Things are said with reference to certain conventions or existing institutions, not absolutely. A fact truly and absolutely stated is taken out of the region of common sense and acquires a mythologic or universal significance. Say it and have done with it. Express it without expressing yourself. See not with the eye of science, which is barren, nor of youthful poetry, which is impotent. But taste the world and digest it. It would seem as if things got said but rarely and by chance. As you *see*, so at length will you *say*. When facts are seen superficially, they are seen as they lie in relation to certain institutions, perchance. But I would have them expressed as more deeply seen, with deeper references; so that the hearer or reader cannot recognize them or apprehend their significance from the platform of common life, but it will be necessary that he be in a sense translated in order to understand them; when the truth respecting his things shall naturally exhale from a man like the odor of the muskrat from the coat of the trapper. At first blush a man is not capable of reporting truth; he must be drenched and saturated with it first. What was *enthusiasm* in the young man must become *temperament* in the mature man. Without excitement, heat, or passion, he will survey the world which excited the youth and threw him off his balance. As all things are significant, so all words should be significant. It is a fault which attaches to the speaker, to speak flippantly or superficially of anything. Of what use are words which do not move the hearer — are not oracular and fateful? A style in which the matter is all in all, and the manner nothing at all.

March 16, 1852. The Library a wilderness of books. Looking over books on Canada written within the last three hundred years, could see how one had been built upon another, each author consulting and referring to his predecessors. You could read most of them without changing your leg on the steps. It is necessary to find out exactly what books to read on a given subject. Though there may be a thousand books written upon it, it is only important to read three or four; they will contain all that is essential, and a few pages will show which they are. Books which are books are all that you want, and there are but half a dozen in any thousand. I saw that while we are clearing the forest in our westward progress, we are accumulating a forest of books in our rear, as wild and unexplored as any of nature's primitive wildernesses. The volumes of the Fifteenth, Sixteenth, and Seventeenth Centuries, which lie so near on the shelf, are rarely opened, are effectually forgotten and not implied by our literature and newspapers. When I looked into Purchas's Pilgrims, it affected me like looking into an impassable swamp, ten feet deep with sphagnum, where the monarchs of the forest, covered with mosses and stretched along the ground, were making haste to become peat. Those old books suggested a certain fertility, an Ohio soil, as if they were making a humus for new literatures to spring in. I heard the bellowing of bullfrogs and the hum of mosquitoes reverberating through the thick embossed covers when I had closed the book. Decayed literature makes the richest of all soils.

July 14, 1852. A writer who does not speak out of a full experience uses torpid words, wooden or lifeless words, such words as 'humanitary,' which have a paralysis in their tails.

The youth gets together his materials to build a bridge to the moon, or perchance a palace or temple on the earth, and at length the middle-aged man concludes to build a wood-shed with them.

March 23, 1853. Evelyn and others wrote when the language was in a tender, nascent state and could be moulded to express the shades of meaning; when sesquipedalian words, long since cut and apparently dried and drawn to mill — not yet to the dictionary lumber-yard — put forth a fringe of green sprouts here and there along in the angles of their rugged bark, their very bulk insuring some sap remaining; some florid suckers they sustain at least. Which words, split into shingles and laths, will supply poets for ages to come.

Sept. 4, 1854. In the wood-paths I find a great many of the Castile-soap galls, more or less fresh. Some are saddled on the twigs. They are now dropping from the shrub oaks. Is not Art itself a gall? Nature is stung by God and the seed of man planted in her. The artist changes the direction of Nature and makes her grow according to his idea. If the gall was anticipated when the oak was made, so was the canoe when the birch was made. Genius stings Nature, and she grows according to its idea.

Feb. 27, 1856. The papers are talking about the prospect of a war between England and America. Neither side sees how its country can avoid a long and fratricidal war without sacrificing its honor. Both nations are ready to take a desperate step, to forget the interests of civilization and Christianity and their commercial prosperity and fly at each other's throats. When I see an individual thus beside himself, thus desperate, ready to shoot or be shot, like a blackleg who has little to lose, no serene aims to accomplish, I think he is a candidate for bedlam. What asylum is there for nations to go to? Nations are thus ready to talk of wars and challenge one another, because they are made up to such an extent of poor, low-spirited, despairing men, in whose eyes the chance of shooting somebody else without being shot themselves exceeds their actual good fortune. Who, in fact, will be the first to enlist but the most desperate class, they who have lost all hope? And they may at last infect the rest.

Dec. 2, 1856. As for the sensuality in Whitman's 'Leaves of Grass,' I do not so much wish that it was not written, as that men and women were so pure that they could read it without harm.

April 2, 1858. It appears to me that the wisest philosophers that I know are as foolish as Sancho Panza dreaming of his Island. Considering the ends they propose and the obstructions in their paths, they are even. One philosopher is feeble enough alone, but observe how each multiplies his difficulties — by how many unnecessary links he allies himself to the existing state of things. He girds himself for his enterprise with fasting and prayer, and then, instead of pressing forward like a light-armed soldier, with the fewest possible hindrances, he at once hooks himself on to some immovable institution, as a family, the very rottenest of them all, and begins to sing and scratch gravel *towards* his objects. Why, it is as much as the strongest man can do decently to bury his friends and relations without making a new world of it. But if the philosopher is as foolish as Sancho Panza, he is also as wise, and nothing so truly makes a thing so or so as thinking it so.

May 6, 1858. What is all your building, if you do not build with thoughts? No exercise implies more real manhood and vigor than joining thought to thought. How few men can tell what they have thought! I hardly know half a dozen who are not too lazy for this. They cannot get over some difficulty, and therefore they are on the long way round. You conquer fate by thought. If you think the fatal thought of men and institutions, you need never pull the trigger. The consequences of thinking inevitably follow. There is no more Herculean task than to think a thought about this life and then get it expressed.

Oct. 19, 1858. They may make equally good pails, and cheaper as well as faster, at the pail-factory with the home-made ones, but that interests me less, because the man is turned partly into a machine there himself. In this case, the workman's relation to his work is more poetic, he also shows more dexterity and is more of a man. You come away from the great factory saddened, as if the chief end of man were to make pails; but, in the case of the countryman who makes a few by hand, rainy days, the relative importance of human life and of pails is preserved, and you come away thinking of the simple and helpful life of the man — you do not turn pale at the thought — and would fain go to making pails yourself. We admire more the man who can use an axe or adze skilfully than him who can merely tend a machine. When labor is reduced to turning a crank it is no longer amusing nor truly profitable; but let this business become very profitable in a pecuniary sense, and so be 'driven,' as the phrase is, and carried on on a large scale, and the man is sunk in it, while only the pail or tray floats; we are interested in it only in the same way as the proprietor or company is.

Nov. 9, 1858. It is of no use to plow deeper than the soil is, unless you mean to follow up that mode of cultivation persistently, manuring highly and carting on muck at each plowing — making a soil, in short. Yet many a man likes to tackle mighty themes, like immortality, but in his discourse he turns up nothing but yellow sand, under which what little fertile and available surface soil he may have is quite buried and lost. He should teach frugality rather — how to postpone the fatal hour — should plant a crop of beans. He might have raised enough of these to make a deacon of him, though never a preacher. Many a man runs his plow so deep in heavy or stony soil that it sticks fast in the furrow. It is a great art in the writer to improve from day to day just that soil and fertility which he has, to harvest that crop which his life yields, whatever it may be, not be straining as if to reach apples or oranges when he yields only ground-nuts. He should be digging, not soaring. Just as earnest as your life is, so deep is your soil. If strong and deep, you will sow wheat and raise bread of life in it.

Jan. 2, 1859. When I hear the hypercritical quarrelling about grammar and style, the position of the particles, etc., etc., stretching or contracting every speaker to certain rules of theirs — Mr. Webster, perhaps, not having spoken according to Mr. Kirkham's rule — I see that they forget that the first requisite and rule is that expression shall be vital and natural, as much as the voice of a brute or an interjection: first of all, mother tongue; and last of all, artificial or father tongue. Essentially your truest poetic sentence is as free and lawless as a lamb's bleat. The

grammarian is often one who can neither cry nor laugh, yet thinks that
he can express human emotions. So the posture-masters tell you how
you shall walk — turning your toes out, perhaps, excessively — but so
the beautiful walkers are not made.

Oct. 16, 1859. Talk about learning our *letters* and being *literate!* Why,
the roots of *letters* are *things*. Natural objects and phenomena are the
original symbols or types which express our thoughts and feelings, and
yet American scholars, having little or no root in the soil, commonly
strive with all their might to confine themselves to the imported symbols
alone. All the true growth and experience, the living speech, they would
fain reject as 'Americanisms.' It is the old error, which the church, the
state, the school ever commit, choosing darkness rather than light, holding fast to the old and to tradition. A more intimate knowledge, a
deeper experience, will surely originate a word. When I really know
that our river pursues a serpentine course to the Merrimack, shall I continue to describe it by referring to some other river no older than itself
which is like it, and call it a *meander?* It is no more *meandering* than the
Meander is *musketaquidding*. As well sing of the nightingale here as the
Meander. What if there were a tariff on words, on language, for the
encouragement of home manufactures? Have we not the genius to coin
our own? Let the schoolmaster distinguish the true from the counterfeit.

Feb. 13, 1860. Always you have to contend with the stupidity of men.
It is like a stiff soil, a hard-pan. If you go deeper than usual, you are
sure to meet with a pan made harder even by the superficial cultivation.
The stupid you have always with you. Men are more obedient at first to
words than ideas. They mind names more than things. Read to them
a lecture on 'Education,' naming that subject, and they will think that
they have heard something important, but call it 'Transcendentalism,'
and they will think it moonshine. Or halve your lecture, and put
a psalm at the beginning and a prayer at the end of it and read it from
a pulpit, and they will pronounce it good without thinking.

March 18, 1861. You can't read any genuine history — as that of
Herodotus or the Venerable Bede — without perceiving that our interest depends not on the subject but on the man — on the manner in
which he treats the subject and the importance he gives it. A feeble
writer and without genius must have what he thinks a great theme,
which we are already interested in through the accounts of others, but
a genius — a Shakespeare, for instance — would make the history of
his parish more interesting than another's history of the world.

IV. SAYINGS

June 4, 1839. The words of some men are thrown forcibly against you and adhere like burs.

July 25, 1839. There is no remedy for love but to love more.

July 2, 1840. They who are ready to go are already invited.

Jan. 30, 1841. The guilty never escape, for a steed stands ever ready saddled and bridled at God's door, and the sinner surrenders at last.

Feb. 2, 1841. There is always a single ear in the audience, to which we address ourselves.

April 26, 1841. It is a great art to saunter.

May 3, 1841. The man of principle gets never a holiday. Our true character silently underlies all our words and actions, as the granite underlies the other strata. Its steady pulse does not cease for any deed of ours, as the sap is still ascending in the stalk of the fairest flower.

Aug. 18, 1841. The best poets, after all, exhibit only a tame and civil side of nature. They have not seen the west side of any mountain.

1841. The love which is preached nowadays is an ocean of new milk for a man to swim in. I hear no surf nor surge, but the winds coo over it.

Jan. 7, 1842. The sudden revolutions of these times and this generation have acquired a very exaggerated importance. They do not interest me much, for they are not in harmony with the longer periods of nature. The present, in any aspect in which it can be presented to the smallest audience, is always mean. God does not sympathize with the popular movements.

Jan. 8, 1842. What offends me most in my compositions is the moral element in them. The repentant say never a brave word. Their resolves should be mumbled in silence. Strictly speaking, morality is not healthy. Those undeserved joys which come uncalled and make us more pleased than grateful are they that sing.

Feb. 19, 1842. I am amused to see from my window here how busily man has divided and staked off his domain. God must smile at his puny fences running hither and thither everywhere over the land.

Sept., 1850. Man has a million eyes, and the race knows infinitely more than the individual. Consent to be wise through your race.

Sept., 1850. The question is not whether you drink, but what liquor.

Sept., 1850. The imagination never forgives an insult.

Nov. 11, 1850. Some circumstantial evidence is very strong, as when you find a trout in the milk.

1851. Nature and man; some prefer the one, others the other; but that is all *de gustibus*. It makes no odds at what well you drink, provided it be a well-head.

May 1, 1851. Nations! What are nations? Tartars! and Huns! and Chinamen! Like insects they swarm. The historian strives in vain to make them memorable. It is for want of a man that there are so many men. It is individuals that populate the world.

Aug. 19, 1851. The way in which men cling to old institutions after the life has departed out of them, and out of themselves, reminds me of those monkeys which cling by their tails — aye, whose tails contract about the limbs, even the dead limbs, of the forest, and they hang suspended beyond the hunter's reach long after they are dead. It is of no use to argue with such men. They have not an apprehensive intellect, but merely, as it were, a prehensile tail. Their intellect possesses merely the quality of a prehensile tail. The tail itself contracts around the dead limb even after they themselves are dead, and not till sensible corruption takes place do they fall.

Aug. 19, 1851. How vain it is to sit down to write when you have not stood up to live!

Aug. 28, 1851. The poet is a man who lives at last by watching his moods. An old poet comes at last to watch his moods as narrowly as a cat does a mouse.

Sept. 7, 1851. Nothing is so much to be feared as fear. Atheism may comparatively be popular with God himself.

May 10, 1853. With Alcott almost alone is it possible to put all institutions behind us. Every other man owns some stock in this or that one, and will not forget it.

Feb. 2, 1854. Is not January the hardest month to get through? When you have weathered that, you get into the gulf-stream of winter, nearer the shores of spring.

Feb. 20, 1854. Dead trees love the fire.

March 2, 1854. A Corner man tells me that Witherell has seen a bluebird, and Martial Miles thought that he heard one. I doubt it. It may have been given to Witherell to see the first bluebird, so much has been withholden from him.

March 15, 1854. I am sorry to think that you do not get a man's most effective criticism until you provoke him. Severe truth is expressed with some bitterness.

April 19, 1854. I am not interested in mere phenomena, though it were the explosion of a planet, only as it may have lain in the experience of a human being.

April 27, 1854. Most men are engaged in business the greater part of their lives, because the soul abhors a vacuum, and they have not discovered any continuous employment for man's nobler faculties. Accordingly they do not pine, because they are not greatly disappointed.

Oct. 19, 1855. Talking with Bellew this evening about Fourierism and communities, I said that I suspected any enterprise in which two were engaged together. 'But,' said he, 'it is difficult to make a stick stand unless you slant two or more against it.' 'Oh, no,' answered I, 'you may split its lower end into three, or drive it single into the ground, which is the best way; but most men, when they start on a new enterprise, not only figuratively, but really, *pull up stakes.* When the sticks prop one another, none, or only one, stands erect.'

April 2, 1856. I cannot but think it nobler, as it is rarer, to appreciate some beauty than to feel much sympathy with misfortune. The Powers are kinder to me when they permit me to enjoy this beauty than if they were to express any amount of compassion for me. I could never excuse them that.

May 24, 1857. Heard one speak today of his sense of awe at the thought of God, and suggested to him that awe was the cause of the potato-rot. The same speaker dwelt on the sufferings of life, but my advice was to go about one's business, suggesting that no ecstasy was ever interrupted, nor its fruit blasted. As for completeness and roundness, to be sure, we are each like one of the laciniæ of a lichen, a torn fragment, but not the less cheerfully we expand in a moist day and assume unexpected colors. We want no completeness but intensity of life.

March 2, 1858. There is no need of a law to check the licence of the press. It is law enough, and more than enough, to itself. Virtually, the community have come together and agreed what things shall be uttered, have agreed on a platform and to excommunicate him who departs from it, and not one in a thousand dares utter anything else. There are plenty of journals brave enough to say what they think about the government, this being a free one; but I know of none, widely circulated or well conducted, that dares say what it thinks about the Sunday or the Bible. They have been bribed to keep dark. They are in the service of hypocrisy.

Feb. 14, 1859. As I walk over thin ice, settling it down, I see great bubbles under, three or four feet wide, go waddling or wobbling away like a scared lady impeded by her train. I have but little doubt that the musquash gets air from these bubbles, which are probably very conspicuous under the ice. They are its reservoirs.

Dec. 12, 1859. I am inclined to think of late that as much depends on the state of the bowels as of the stars. As are your bowels, so are the stars.

Jan. 27, 1860. When you think that your walk is profitless and a failure, and you can hardly persuade yourself not to return, it is on the point of being a success, for then you are in that subdued and knocking mood to which Nature never fails to open.

Feb. 3, 1860. When I read some of the rules for speaking and writing the English language correctly — as that a sentence must never end with a particle — and perceive how implicitly even the learned obey it, I think —

> Any fool can make a rule
> And every fool will mind it.

Feb. 12, 1860. Whatever aid is to be derived from the use of a scientific term, we can never begin to see anything as it is so long as we remember the scientific term which always our ignorance has imposed on it. Natural objects and phenomena are in this sense forever wild and unnamed by us.

Nov. 23, 1860. It was some compensation for Commodore Porter, who may have introduced some cannon-balls and bombshells into ports where they were not wanted, to have introduced the Valparaiso squash into the United States. I think that this eclipses his military glory.

7. NATURE ESSAYS

PREFATORY NOTE

UNTIL the comparatively recent upsurge of interest in Thoreau's political essays such as "Civil Disobedience" and his exposition of the idea of the simple life in *Walden*, he has been primarily known as a nature writer and many still think of him predominantly as that. He is unquestionably without peer as a nature essayist — his is the standard by which all other nature writers, be they American, European, or Oriental, are judged. Indeed, a very good case can be made that he was the inventor of the nature essay as a form of literature. He was the first to realize that in writing about nature he could do more than simply report on natural phenomena as had Gilbert White and Crevecoeur and Audubon, that he could weave and polish his findings into a truly belletristic form. Virtually all nature writers since his day have followed in his footsteps.

One of the unique charms of his nature writing is that he displays not the least condescension toward either his subject matter or his readers. It is very easy to fall into the sentimentalism of the pathetic fallacy, treating all fauna — and even the flora — as unrealized human beings, naming them Jimmy Skunk and Peter Rabbit as though if they would only become more human they would improve their station in life. Thoreau never once takes that misstep. He accepts them for exactly what they are and accepts both their strengths and weaknesses as essential parts of their nature. Thus he achieves an objectivity that few others have matched. On the other hand, neither does he condescend toward his reader, ostentatiously displaying a superior knowledge. Rather his whole attitude is to share the joys he finds in the world around him with those who like him find unremitting joy in nature and to lead others to that joy.

"The Natural History of Massachusetts" was written at Ralph Waldo Emerson's request as a review of a series of documents published by the Commonwealth of Massachusetts on the natural history of the area. Actually he gets around to reviewing the documents only in the closing paragraphs of the essay. The great majority of it is a paean to the beauties of the world in which he lived, most of it culled from the early years of his journal. It was one of his earliest pieces to reach print — in the July, 1842 issue of the Transcendentalist *Dial* and the first one to more than hint of the poetical beauty of style that he was later to achieve in his masterpieces such as *Walden.*

"Walking" was originally written in the early 1850's as a lecture and he delivered it a number of times from the public platform, revising and expanding it each time until it grew so large he had to divide it in two, entitling the latter section "The Wild." Then later when he prepared the whole for publication — in the June, 1862 *Atlantic Monthly* — he stitched the two parts back together again — though the seam (in this edition on page 672) is still obvious to the observant reader. Toward the end the essay tends to peter out as though Thoreau had tired from his long walk. Despite these technical flaws, it has long been one of his most popular and most frequently anthologized essays. It is one of the fullest expositions of one of Thoreau's favorite themes — man's need of wilderness as a panacea for the ills of civilization. As he says, "In wildness is the preservation of the world."

"Autumnal Tints" and "Wild Apples" are both lighthearted, familiar essays, written originally for the lecture platform and not published until after his death. Of the former, one of his contemporaries complained that Thoreau spoke as though his audience had never seen autumn foliage, but it is doubtful that any had ever seen it and appreciated it as fully as he. "Wild Apples" is one of Thoreau's few writings that could be called whimsical. It has a lighter touch that titillated his lecture audiences. His tales of the hedgehog gathering apples on his quills and of the apple trees' battles with the cows have become part of our American folklore. Nursery catalog compilers, if they have a sense of humor, should try adopting some of Thoreau's names for their new species. They were first published in the *Atlantic Monthly* in October, 1862, and November, 1862, respectively.

"The Succession of Forest Trees" is Thoreau's most significant direct contribution to science. (I say "direct" for indirectly his journals have proved an invaluable source book for historical studies of the flora, fauna, ecology, and meterology of the area.) Puzzled by the fact that when oak groves in the Concord area were cut down, pine trees grew in their place, and vice versa, and refusing to accept the local farmers' belief in spontaneous generation of the new trees, he made an extensive study of the phenomenon and presented his findings before the 1860 meeting of the Middlesex Agricultural Society. It was first published in the *New York Tribune* for October 6, 1860, and also incorporated into the 1860 annual reports of the Middlesex Agricultural Society and the Massachusetts Board of Agriculture. (Although two other men were to stumble upon the same explanation almost simultaneously, Thoreau's was an independent discovery.) His findings were a great source of satisfaction to him. For many years he had earned a large part of his living through the surveying of Concord woodlots and it bothered his conscience that such surveys were usually a preliminary to the cutting of the wood by the owners, thus he himself was indirectly bringing about the destruction of the woods of Concord that he loved so deeply. Through his studies of succession he was able to propose a vastly more efficient method of reforesting the harvested areas and thus preserving the woods. So intrigued did Thoreau become with his studies of tree growth that in the year before his death he embarked on a far more detailed study of the subject. Unfortunately his death in 1862 cut that project short and he left behind a huge welter of unassimilated notes most of which are still unpublished, the manuscripts themselves being in the Berg Collection of the New York Public Library in New York City.

I. NATURAL HISTORY OF MASSACHUSETTS[1]

BOOKS of natural history make the most cheerful winter reading. I read in Audubon with a thrill of delight, when the snow covers the ground, of the magnolia, and the Florida keys, and their warm sea-breezes; of the fence-rail, and the cotton-tree, and the migrations of the rice-bird; of the breaking up of winter in Labrador, and the melting of the snow on the forks of the Missouri; and owe an accession of health to these reminiscences of luxuriant nature.

> Within the circuit of this plodding life,
> There enter moments of an azure hue,
> Untarnished fair as is the violet
> Or anemone, when the spring strews them
> By some meandering rivulet, which make
> The best philosophy untrue that aims
> But to console man for his grievances.
> I have remembered, when the winter came,
> High in my chamber in the frosty nights,
> When in the still light of the cheerful moon,
> On every twig and rail and jutting spout,
> The icy spears were adding to their length

---

[1] *Reports — on the Fishes, Reptiles, and Birds; the Herbaceous Plants and Quadrupeds; the Insects Injurious to Vegetation; and the Invertebrate Animals of Massachusetts.* Published agreeably to an Order of the Legislature, by the Commissioners on the Zoological and Botanical Survey of the State.

> Against the arrows of the coming sun,
> How in the shimmering noon of summer past
> Some unrecorded beam slanted across
> The upland pastures where the Johnswort grew;
> Or heard, amid the verdure of my mind,
> The bee's long smothered hum, on the blue flag
> Loitering amidst the mead; or busy rill,
> Which now through all its course stands still and dumb,
> Its own memorial — purling at its play
> Along the slopes, and through the meadows next,
> Until its youthful sound was hushed at last
> In the staid current of the lowland stream;
> Or seen the furrows shine but late upturned,
> And where the fieldfare followed in the rear,
> When all the fields around lay bound and hoar
> Beneath a thick integument of snow.
> So by God's cheap economy made rich
> To go upon my winter's task again.

I am singularly refreshed in winter when I hear of service-berries, poke-weed, juniper. Is not heaven made up of these cheap summer glories? There is a singular health in those words, Labrador and East Main, which no desponding creed recognizes. How much more than Federal are these States! If there were no other vicissitudes than the seasons, our interest would never tire. Much more is adoing than Congress wots of. What journal do the persimmon and the buckeye keep, and the sharp-shinned hawk? What is transpiring from summer to winter in the Carolinas, and the Great Pine Forest, and the Valley of the Mohawk? The merely political aspect of the land is never very cheering; men are degraded when considered as the members of a political organization. On this side all lands present only the symptoms of decay. I see but Bunker Hill and Sing-Sing, the District of Columbia and Sullivan's Island, with a few avenues connecting them. But paltry are they all beside one blast of the east or the south wind which blows over them.

In society you will not find health, but in nature. Unless our feet at least stood in the midst of nature, all our faces would be pale and livid. Society is always diseased, and the best is the most so. There is no scent in it so wholesome as that of the pines, nor any fragrance so penetrating and restorative as the life-everlasting in high pastures. I would keep some book of natural history always by me as a sort of elixir, the reading of which should restore the tone of the system. To the sick, indeed, nature is sick, but to the well, a fountain of health. To him who contemplates a trait of natural beauty no harm nor disappointment can come. The doctrines of despair, of spiritual or political tyranny or servitude, were never taught by such as shared the serenity of nature. Surely good courage will not flag here on the Atlantic border, as long as we are flanked by the Fur Countries. There is enough in that sound to cheer one under any circumstances. The spruce, the hemlock, and the pine will not countenance despair. Methinks some creeds in vestries and churches do forget the hunter wrapped in furs by the Great Slave Lake, and that the Esquimaux sledges are drawn by dogs, and in the twilight of the northern night the hunter does not give over to follow the seal and walrus on the ice. They are of sick and diseased imaginations who would toll the world's knell so soon. Cannot these sedentary sects do better than prepare the shrouds and write the epitaphs of those other busy living men? The practical faith of all men belies the preacher's consolation. What is any man's discourse to me, if I am not sensible of something in it as steady and cheery as the creak of crickets? In it the woods must be relieved against the sky. Men tire me when I am not constantly greeted and refreshed as by the flux of sparkling streams. Surely joy is the condition of life. Think of the young fry that leap in ponds, the myriads of insects ushered into being on a summer evening, the incessant note of the hyla with which the woods ring in the spring, the nonchalance of the butterfly carrying accident and change painted in a thousand hues upon its wings, or the brook minnow stoutly stemming the current, the lustre of whose scales, worn bright by the attrition, is reflected upon the bank!

We fancy that this din of religion, literature, and philosophy, which is heard in pulpits, lyceums, and parlors, vibrates through the universe, and is as catholic a sound as the creaking of the earth's axle; but if a man sleep soundly, he will forget it all between sunset and dawn. It is the three-inch swing of a pendulum in a cupboard, which the great pulse of nature vibrates by and through each instant. When we lift our eyelids and open our ears, it disappears with smoke and rattle like the cars on a railroad. When I detect a beauty in any of the recesses of nature, I am reminded, by the serene and retired spirit in which it requires to be contemplated, of the inexpressible privacy of a life — how silent and unambitious it is. The beauty there is in mosses must be considered from the holiest, quietest nook. What an admirable training is science for the more active warfare of life! Indeed, the unchallenged bravery which these studies imply, is far more impressive than the trumpeted valor of the warrior. I am pleased to learn that Thales was up and stirring by night not unfrequently, as his astronomical discoveries prove. Linnæus, setting out for Lapland, surveys his 'comb' and 'spare shirt,' 'leathern breeches' and 'gauze cap to keep off gnats,' with as much complacency as Bonaparte a park of artillery for the Russian campaign. The quiet bravery of the man is admirable. His eye is to take in fish, flower, and bird, quadruped and biped. Science is always brave; for to know is to know good; doubt and danger quail before her eye. What the coward overlooks in his hurry, she calmly scrutinizes, breaking ground like a pioneer for the array of arts that follow in her train. But cowardice is unscientific; for there cannot be a science of ignorance. There may be a science of bravery, for that advances; but a retreat is rarely well conducted; if it is, then is it an orderly advance in the face of circumstances.

But to draw a little nearer to our promised topics. Entomology extends the limits of being in a new direction, so that I walk in nature with a sense of greater space and freedom. It suggests besides, that the universe is not rough-hewn, but perfect in its details. Nature will bear the closest inspection; she invites us to lay our eye level with the smallest leaf, and take an insect view of its plain. She has no interstices; every part is full of life. I explore, too, with pleasure, the sources of the myriad sounds which crowd the summer noon, and which seem the very grain and stuff of which eternity is made. Who does not remember the shrill roll-call of the harvest-fly? There were ears for these sounds in Greece long ago, as Anacreon's ode will show.

> 'We pronounce thee happy, Cicada,
> For on the tops of the trees,
> Drinking a little dew,
> Like any king thou singest,
> For thine are they all,
> Whatever thou seest in the fields,
> And whatever the woods bear.
> Thou art the friend of the husbandmen,
> In no respect injuring any one;
> And thou art honored among men,
> Sweet prophet of summer.
> The Muses love thee,
> And Phœbus himself loves thee,
> And has given thee a shrill song;
> Age does not wrack thee,
> Thou skillful, earthborn, song-loving,
> Unsuffering, bloodless one;
> Almost thou art like the gods.'

In the autumn days, the creaking of crickets is heard at noon over all the land, and as in summer they are heard chiefly at nightfall, so then by their incessant chirp they usher in the evening of the year. Nor can all the vanities that vex the world alter one whit the measure that night has chosen. Every pulse-beat is in exact time with the cricket's chant and the tickings of the death-watch in the wall. Alternate with these if you can.

About two hundred and eighty birds either reside permanently in the State, or spend the summer only, or make us a passing visit. Those which spend the winter with us have obtained our warmest sympathy. The nut-hatch and chickadee flitting in company through the dells of the wood, the one harshly scolding at the intruder, the other with a faint lisping note enticing him on; the jay screaming in the orchard; the crow cawing in unison with the storm; the partridge, like a russet link extended over from autumn to spring, preserving unbroken the chain of summers; the hawk with warrior-like firmness abiding the blasts of winter; the robin [1] and lark lurking by warm springs in the woods; the familiar snowbird culling a few seeds in the garden or a few crumbs in the yard; and occasionally the shrike, with heedless and unfrozen melody bringing back summer again:

> His steady sails he never furls
> At any time o' year,
> And perching now on Winter's curls,
> He whistles in his ear.

As the spring advances, and the ice is melting in the river, our earliest and straggling visitors make their appearance. Again does the old Teian poet sing as well for New England as for Greece, in the

RETURN OF SPRING

> Behold, how, Spring appearing,
> The Graces send forth roses;
> Behold, how the wave of the sea
> Is made smooth by the calm;
> Behold, how the duck dives;
> Behold, how the crane travels;

---

[1] A white robin and a white quail have occasionally been seen. It is mentioned in Audubon as remarkable that the nest of a robin should be found on the ground; but this bird seems to be less particular than most in the choice of a building-spot. I have seen its nest placed under the thatched roof of a deserted barn, and in one instance, where the adjacent country was nearly destitute of trees, together with two of the phœbe, upon the end of a board in the loft of a sawmill, but a few feet from the saw, which vibrated several inches with the motion of the machinery.

> And Titan shines constantly bright.
> The shadows of the clouds are moving;
> The works of man shine;
> The earth puts forth fruits;
> The fruit of the olive puts forth.
> The cup of Bacchus is crowned,
> Along the leaves, along the branches,
> The fruit, bending them down, flourishes.

The ducks alight at this season in the still water, in company with the gulls, which do not fail to improve an east wind to visit our meadows, and swim about by twos and threes, pluming themselves, and diving to peck at the root of the lily, and the cranberries which the frost has not loosened. The first flock of geese is seen beating to north, in long harrows and waving lines; the jingle of the song sparrow salutes us from the shrubs and fences; the plaintive note of the lark comes clear and sweet from the meadow; and the bluebird, like an azure ray, glances past us in our walk. The fish hawk, too, is occasionally seen at this season sailing majestically over the water, and he who has once observed it will not soon forget the majesty of its flight. It sails the air like a ship of the line, worthy to struggle with the elements, falling back from time to time like a ship on its beam ends, and holding its talons up as if ready for the arrows, in the attitude of the national bird. It is a great presence, as of the master of river and forest. Its eye would not quail before the owner of the soil, but make him feel like an intruder on its domains. And then its retreat, sailing so steadily away, is a kind of advance. I have by me one of a pair of ospreys, which have for some years fished in this vicinity, shot by a neighboring pond, measuring more than two feet in length, and six in the stretch of its wings. Nuttall mentions that 'the ancients, particularly Aristotle, pretended that the ospreys taught their young to gaze at the sun, and those who were unable to do so were destroyed. Linnæus even believed, on ancient authority, that one of the feet of this bird had all the toes divided, while the other was partly webbed, so that it could swim with one foot, and grasp a fish with the other.' But that educated eye is now dim, and those talons are nerveless. Its shrill scream seems yet to linger in its throat, and the roar of the sea in its wings. There is the tyranny of Jove in its claws, and his wrath in the erectile feathers of the head and neck. It reminds me of the Argonautic expedition, and would inspire the dullest to take flight over Parnassus.

The booming of the bittern, described by Goldsmith and Nuttall, is frequently heard in our fens, in the morning and evening, sounding like a pump, or the chopping of wood in a frosty morning in some distant farm-yard. The manner in which this sound is produced I have not seen anywhere described. On one occasion, the bird has been seen by one of my neighbors to thrust its bill into the water, and suck up as much as it could hold, then, raising its head, it pumped it out again with four or five heaves of the neck, throwing it two or three feet, and making the sound each time.

At length the summer's eternity is ushered in by the cackle of the flicker among the oaks on the hillside, and a new dynasty begins with calm security.

In May and June the woodland quire is in full tune, and, given the immense spaces of hollow air, and this curious human ear, one does not see how the void could be better filled.

> Each summer sound
> Is a summer round.

As the season advances, and those birds which make us but a passing visit depart, the woods become silent again, and but few feathers ruffle the drowsy air. But the solitary rambler may still find a response and expression for every mood in the depths of the wood.

> Sometimes I hear the veery's [1] clarion,
> Or brazen trump of the impatient jay,
> And in secluded woods the chickadee
> Doles out her scanty notes, which sing the praise
> Of heroes, and set forth the loveliness
> Of virtue evermore.

The phœbe still sings in harmony with the sultry weather by the brink of the pond, nor are the desultory hours of noon in the midst of the village without their minstrel.

> Upon the lofty elm-tree sprays
> The vireo rings the changes sweet,
> During the trivial summer days,
> Striving to lift our thoughts above the street.

With the autumn begins in some measure a new spring. The plover is heard whistling high in the air over the dry pastures, the finches flit from tree to tree, the bobolinks and flickers fly in flocks, and the gold-

---

[1] This bird, which is so well described by Nuttall, but is apparently unknown by the author of the Report, is one of the most common in the woods in this vicinity, and in Cambridge I have heard the college yard ring with its trill. The boys call it 'yorrick,' from the sound of its querulous and chiding note, as it flits near the traveller through the underwood. The cowbird's egg is occasionally found in its nest, as mentioned by Audubon.

finch rides on the earliest blast, like a winged hyla peeping amid the rustle of the leaves. The crows, too, begin now to congregate; you may stand and count them as they fly low and straggling over the landscape, singly or by twos and threes, at intervals of half a mile, until a hundred have passed.

I have seen it suggested somewhere that the crow was brought to this country by the white man; but I shall as soon believe that the white man planted these pines and hemlocks. He is no spaniel to follow our steps; but rather flits about the clearings like the dusky spirit of the Indian, reminding me oftener of Philip and Powhatan than of Winthrop and Smith. He is a relic of the dark ages. By just so slight, by just so lasting a tenure does superstition hold the world ever; there is the rook in England, and the crow in New England.

> Thou dusky spirit of the wood,
> Bird of an ancient brood,
> Flitting thy lonely way,
> A meteor in the summer's day,
> From wood to wood, from hill to hill,
> Low over forest, field, and rill,
> What wouldst thou say?
> Why shouldst thou haunt the day?
> What makes thy melancholy float?
> What bravery inspires thy throat,
> And bears thee up above the clouds,
> Over desponding human crowds,
> Which far below
> Lay thy haunts low?

The late walker or sailor, in the October evenings, may hear the murmurings of the snipe, circling over the meadows, the most spirit-like sound in nature; and still later in the autumn, when the frosts have tinged the leaves, a solitary loon pays a visit to our retired ponds, where he may lurk undisturbed till the season of moulting is passed, making the woods ring with his wild laughter. This bird, the Great Northern Diver, well deserves its name; for when pursued with a boat, it will dive, and swim like a fish under water, for sixty rods or more, as fast as a boat can be paddled, and its pursuer, if he would discover his game again, must put his ear to the surface to hear where it comes up. When it comes to the surface, it throws the water off with one shake of its wings, and calmly swims about until again disturbed.

These are the sights and sounds which reach our senses oftenest during the year. But sometimes one hears a quite new note, which has for background other Carolinas and Mexicos than the books describe, and learns that his ornithology has done him no service.

It appears from the Report that there are about forty quadrupeds belonging to the State, and among these one is glad to hear of a few bears, wolves, lynxes, and wildcats.

When our river overflows its banks in the spring, the wind from the meadows is laden with a strong scent of musk, and by its freshness advertises me of an unexplored wildness. Those backwoods are not far off then. I am affected by the sight of the cabins of the muskrat, made of mud and grass, and raised three or four feet along the river, as when I read of the barrows of Asia. The muskrat is the beaver of the settled States. Their number has even increased within a few years in this vicinity. Among the rivers which empty into the Merrimack, the Concord is known to the boatmen as a dead stream. The Indians are said to have called it Musketaquid, or Prairie River. Its current being much more sluggish and its water more muddy than the rest, it abounds more in fish and game of every kind. According to the History of the town, 'The fur-trade was here once very important. As early as 1641, a company was formed in the colony, of which Major Willard of Concord was superintendent, and had the exclusive right to trade with the Indians in furs and other articles; and for this right they were obliged to pay into the public treasury one twentieth of all the furs they obtained.' There are trappers in our midst still, as well as on the streams of the far West, who night and morning go the round of their traps, without fear of the Indian. One of these takes from one hundred and fifty to two hundred muskrats in a year, and even thirty-six have been shot by one man in a day. Their fur, which is not nearly as valuable as formerly, is in good condition in the winter and spring only; and upon the breaking up of the ice, when they are driven out of their holes by the water, the greatest number is shot from boats, either swimming or resting on their stools, or slight supports of grass and reeds, by the side of the stream. Though they exhibit considerable cunning at other times, they are easily taken in a trap, which has only to be placed in their holes, or wherever they frequent, without any bait being used, though it is sometimes rubbed with their musk. In the winter the hunter cuts holes in the ice, and shoots them when they come to the surface. Their burrows are usually in the high banks of the river, with the entrance under water, and rising within to above the level of high water. Sometimes their nests, composed of dried meadow-grass and flags, may be discovered where the bank is low and spongy, by the yielding of the ground under the feet. They have from three to seven or eight young in the spring.

Frequently, in the morning or evening, a long ripple is seen in the still water, where a muskrat is crossing the stream, with only its nose above the surface, and sometimes a green bough in its mouth to build its house with. When it finds itself observed, it will dive and swim five or six rods under water, and at length conceal itself in its hole, or the weeds. It will remain under water for ten minutes at a time, and on one occasion has been seen, when undisturbed, to form an air-bubble under the ice, which contracted and expanded as it breathed at leisure. When it suspects danger on shore, it will stand erect like a squirrel, and survey its neighborhood for several minutes, without moving.

In the fall, if a meadow intervene between their burrows and the stream, they erect cabins of mud and grass, three or four feet high, near its edge. These are not their breeding-places, though young are some-times found in them in late freshets, but rather their hunting-lodges, to which they resort in the winter with their food, and for shelter. Their food consists chiefly of flags and fresh-water mussels, the shells of the latter being left in large quantities around their lodges in the spring.

The Penobscot Indian wears the entire skin of a muskrat, with the legs and tail dangling, and the head caught under his girdle, for a pouch, into which he puts his fishing-tackle, and essences to scent his traps with.

The bear, wolf, lynx, wildcat, deer, beaver, and marten have dis-appeared; the otter is rarely if ever seen here at present; and the mink is less common than formerly.

Perhaps of all our untamed quadrupeds, the fox has obtained the widest and most familiar reputation, from the time of Pilpay and Æsop to the present day. His recent tracks still give variety to a winter's walk. I tread in the steps of the fox that has gone before me by some hours, or which perhaps I have started, with such a tiptoe of expectation as if I were on the trail of the Spirit itself which resides in the wood, and expected soon to catch it in its lair. I am curious to know what has determined its graceful curvatures, and how surely they were coincident with the fluctuations of some mind. I know which way a mind wended, what horizon it faced, by the setting of these tracks, and whether it moved slowly or rapidly, by their greater or less intervals and distinct-ness; for the swiftest step leaves yet a lasting trace. Sometimes you will see the trails of many together, and where they have gambolled and gone through a hundred evolutions, which testify to a singular listlessness and leisure in nature.

When I see a fox run across the pond on the snow, with the carelessness of freedom, or at intervals trace his course in the sunshine along the ridge of a hill, I give up to him sun and earth as to their true proprietor. He does not go in the sun, but it seems to follow him, and there is a visible sympathy between him and it. Sometimes, when the snow lies light and but five or six inches deep, you may give chase and come up with one on foot. In such a case he will show a remarkable presence of mind, choosing only the safest direction, though he may lose ground by it. Notwithstanding his fright, he will take no step which is not beautiful. His pace is a sort of leopard canter, as if he were in no wise impeded by the snow, but were husbanding his strength all the while. When the ground is uneven, the course is a series of graceful curves, conforming to the shape of the surface. He runs as though there were not a bone in his back. Occasionally dropping his muzzle to the ground for a rod or two, and then tossing his head aloft, when satisfied of his course. When he comes to a declivity, he will put his fore feet together, and slide swiftly down it, shoving the snow before him. He treads so softly that you would hardly hear it from any nearness, and yet with such expression that it would not be quite inaudible at any distance.

Of fishes, seventy-five genera and one hundred and seven species are described in the Report. The fisherman will be startled to learn that there are but about a dozen kinds in the ponds and streams of any inland town; and almost nothing is known of their habits. Only their names and residence make one love fishes. I would know even the number of their fin-rays, and how many scales compose the lateral line. I am the wiser in respect to all knowledges, and the better qualified for all fortunes, for knowing that there is a minnow in the brook. Methinks I have need even of his sympathy, and to be his fellow in a degree.

I have experienced such simple delight in the trivial matters of fishing and sporting, formerly, as might have inspired the muse of Homer or Shakespeare; and now, when I turn the pages and ponder the plates of the Angler's Souvenir, I am fain to exclaim —

'Can such things be,
And overcome us like a summer's cloud?'

Next to nature, it seems as if man's actions were the most natural, they so gently accord with her. The small seines of flax stretched across the shallow and transparent parts of our river are no more intrusion than the cobweb in the sun. I stay my boat in mid-current, and look down in the sunny water to see the civil meshes of his nets, and wonder how the blustering people of the town could have done this elvish work. The twine looks like a new river-weed, and is to the river as a beautiful memento of man's presence in nature, discovered as silently and delicately as a footprint in the sand.

When the ice is covered with snow, I do not suspect the wealth under my feet; that there is as good as a mine under me wherever I go. How many pickerel are poised on easy fin fathoms below the loaded wain! The revolution of the seasons must be a curious phenomenon to them. At length the sun and wind brush aside their curtain, and they see the heavens again.

Early in the spring, after the ice has melted, is the time for spearing fish. Suddenly the wind shifts from northeast and east to west and south, and every icicle, which has tinkled on the meadow grass so long, trickles down its stem, and seeks its level unerringly with a million comrades. The steam curls up from every roof and fence.

> I see the civil sun drying earth's tears,
> Her tears of joy, which only faster flow.

In the brooks is heard the slight grating sound of small cakes of ice, floating with various speed, full of content and promise, and where the water gurgles under a natural bridge, you may hear these hasty rafts hold conversation in an undertone. Every rill is a channel for the juices of the meadow. In the ponds the ice cracks with a merry and inspiriting din, and down the larger streams is whirled grating hoarsely, and crashing its way along, which was so lately a highway for the woodman's team and the fox, sometimes with the tracks of the skaters still fresh upon it, and the holes cut for pickerel. Town committees anxiously inspect the bridges and causeways, as if by mere eye-force to intercede with the ice and save the treasury.

> The river swelleth more and more,
> Like some sweet influence stealing o'er
> The passive town; and for a while
> Each tussock makes a tiny isle,
> Where, on some friendly Ararat,
> Resteth the weary water-rat.
>
> No ripple shows Musketaquid,
> Her very current e'en is hid,
> As deepest souls do calmest rest
> When thoughts are swelling in the breast,

And she that in the summer's drought
Doth make a rippling and a rout,
Sleeps from Nahshawtuck to the Cliff,
Unruffled by a single skiff.
But by a thousand distant hills
The louder roar a thousand rills,
And many a spring which now is dumb,
And many a stream with smothered hum,
Doth swifter well and faster glide,
Though buried deep beneath the tide.
Our village shows a rural Venice,
Its broad lagoons where yonder fen is;
As lovely as the Bay of Naples
Yon placid cove amid the maples;
And in my neighbor's field of corn
I recognize the Golden Horn.

Here Nature taught from year to year,
When only red men came to hear —
Methinks 'twas in this school of art
Venice and Naples learned their part;
But still their mistress, to my mind,
Her young disciples leaves behind.

The fisherman now repairs and launches his boat. The best time for spearing is at this season, before the weeds have begun to grow, and while the fishes lie in the shallow water, for in summer they prefer the cool depths, and in the autumn they are still more or less concealed by the grass. The first requisite is fuel for your crate; and for this purpose the roots of the pitch pine are commonly used, found under decayed stumps, where the trees have been felled eight or ten years.

With a crate, or jack, made of iron hoops, to contain your fire, and attached to the bow of your boat about three feet from the water, a fish-spear with seven tines and fourteen feet long, a large basket or barrow to carry your fuel and bring back your fish, and a thick outer garment, you are equipped for a cruise. It should be a warm and still evening; and then, with a fire crackling merrily at the prow, you may launch forth like a cucullo into the night. The dullest soul cannot go upon such an expedition without some of the spirit of adventure; as if he had stolen the boat of Charon and gone down the Styx on a midnight expedition into the realms of Pluto. And much speculation does this wandering star afford to the musing night-walker, leading him on and on, jack-o'-lantern-like, over the meadows; or, if he is wiser, he amuses himself with imagining what of human life, far in the silent night, is flitting moth-like round its candle. The silent navigator shoves his craft gently over the water, with a smothered pride and sense of benefaction, as if he were the phosphor, or light-bringer, to these dusky realms, or some sister moon, blessing the spaces with her light. The waters, for a rod or two on either hand and several feet in depth, are lit up with more than noonday distinctness, and he enjoys the opportunity which so many have desired, for the roofs of a city are indeed raised, and he surveys the midnight economy of the fishes. There they lie in every variety of posture; some on their backs, with their white bellies uppermost, some suspended in mid-water, some sculling gently along with a dreamy motion of the fins, and others quite active and wide awake — a scene not unlike what the human city would present. Occasionally he will encounter a turtle selecting the choicest morsels, or a muskrat resting on a tussock. He may exercise his dexterity, if he sees fit, on the more distant and active fish, or fork the nearer into his boat, as potatoes out of a pot, or even take the sound sleepers with his hands. But these last accomplishments he will soon learn to dispense with, distinguishing the real object of his pursuit, and find compensation in the beauty and never-ending novelty of his position. The pines growing down to the water's edge will show newly as in the glare of a conflagration; and as he floats under the willows with his light, the song sparrow will often wake on her perch, and sing that strain at midnight which she had meditated for the morning. And when he has done, he may have to steer his way home through the dark by the north star, and he will feel himself some degrees nearer to it for having lost his way on the earth.

The fishes commonly taken in this way are pickerel, suckers, perch, eels, pouts, breams, and shiners — from thirty to sixty weight in a night. Some are hard to be recognized in the unnatural light, especially the perch, which, his dark bands being exaggerated, acquires a ferocious aspect. The number of these transverse bands, which the Report states to be seven, is, however, very variable, for in some of our ponds they have nine and ten even.

It appears that we have eight kinds of tortoises, twelve snakes — but one of which is venomous — nine frogs and toads, nine salamanders, and one lizard, for our neighbors.

I am particularly attracted by the motions of the serpent tribe. They make our hands and feet, the wings of the bird, and the fins of the fish seem very superfluous, as if Nature had only indulged her fancy in making them. The black snake will dart into a bush when pursued, and circle round and round with an easy and graceful motion, amid the thin and bare twigs, five or six feet from the ground, as a bird flits from bough to bough, or hang in festoons between the forks. Elasticity and flexibleness in the simpler forms of animal life are equivalent to a complex system of limbs in the higher; and we have only to be as wise and wily as the serpent, to perform as difficult feats without the vulgar assistance of hands and feet.

In May, the snapping turtle (*Emysaurus serpentina*) is frequently taken on the meadows and in the river. The fisherman, taking sight over the calm surface, discovers its snout projecting above the water, at the distance of many rods, and easily secures his prey through its unwillingness to disturb the water by swimming hastily away, for, gradually drawing its head under, it remains resting on some limb or clump of grass. Its eggs, which are buried at a distance from the water, in some soft place, as a pigeon-bed, are frequently devoured by the skunk. It will catch fish by daylight, as a toad catches flies, and is said to emit a transparent fluid from its mouth to attract them.

Nature has taken more care than the fondest parent for the education and refinement of her children. Consider the silent influence which flowers exert, no less upon the ditcher in the meadow than the lady in the bower. When I walk in the woods, I am reminded that a wise purveyor has been there before me; my most delicate experience is typified there. I am struck with the pleasing friendships and unanimities of nature, as when the lichen on the trees takes the form of their leaves. In the most stupendous scenes you will see delicate and fragile features, as slight wreaths of vapor, dew-lines, feathery sprays, which suggest a high refinement, a noble blood and breeding, as it were. It is not hard to account for elves and fairies; they represent this light grace, this ethereal gentility. Bring a spray from the wood, or a crystal from the brook, and place it on your mantel, and your household ornaments will seem plebeian beside its nobler fashion and bearing. It will wave superior there, as if used to a more refined and polished circle. It has a salute and a response to all your enthusiasm and heroism.

In the winter, I stop short in the path to admire how the trees grow up without forethought, regardless of the time and circumstances. They do not wait as man does, but now is the golden age of the sapling. Earth, air, sun, and rain are occasion enough; they were no better in primeval centuries. The 'winter of *their* discontent' never comes. Witness the buds of the native poplar standing gayly out to the frost on the sides of its bare switches. They express a naked confidence. With cheerful heart one could be a sojourner in the wilderness, if he were sure to find there the catkins of the willow or the alder. When I read of them in the accounts of northern adventurers, by Baffin's Bay or Mackenzie's River, I see how even there, too, I could dwell. They are our little vegetable redeemers. Methinks our virtue will hold out till they come again. They are worthy to have had a greater than Minerva or Ceres for their inventor. Who was the benignant goddess that bestowed them on mankind?

Nature is mythical and mystical always, and works with the license and extravagance of genius. She has her luxurious and florid style as well as art. Having a pilgrim's cup to make, she gives to the whole — stem, bowl, handle, and nose — some fantastic shape, as if it were to be the car of some fabulous marine deity, a Nereus or Triton.

In the winter, the botanist need not confine himself to his books and herbarium, and give over his outdoor pursuits, but may study a new department of vegetable physiology, what may be called crystalline botany, then. The winter of 1837 was unusually favorable for this. In December of that year, the Genius of vegetation seemed to hover by night over its summer haunts with unusual persistency. Such a hoar-frost as is very uncommon here or anywhere, and whose full effects can never be witnessed after sunrise, occurred several times. As I went forth early on a still and frosty morning, the trees looked like airy creatures of darkness caught napping; on this side huddled together, with their gray hairs streaming, in a secluded valley which the sun had not penetrated; on that, hurrying off in Indian file along some watercourse, while the shrubs and grasses, like elves and fairies of the night, sought to hide their diminished heads in the snow. The river, viewed from the high bank, appeared of a yellowish-green color, though all the land-scape was white. Every tree, shrub, and spire of grass, that could raise its head above the snow, was covered with a dense ice-foliage, answer-ing, as it were, leaf for leaf to its summer dress. Even the fences had put forth leaves in the night. The centre, diverging, and more minute fibres were perfectly distinct, and the edges regularly indented. These leaves were on the side of the twig or stubble opposite to the sun, meeting it for the most part at right angles, and there were others standing out at all possible angles upon these and upon one another, with no twig or stubble supporting them. When the first rays of the sun slanted over the scene, the grasses seemed hung with innumerable jewels, which jingled merrily as they were brushed by the foot of the traveller, and reflected all the hues of the rainbow, as he moved from side to side. It struck me that these ghost leaves, and the green ones whose forms they assume, were the creatures of but one law; that in obedience to the same law the vegetable juices swell gradually into the perfect leaf, on the one hand, and the crystalline particles troop to their standard in the same order, on the other. As if the material were indifferent, but the law one and invariable, and every plant in the spring but pushed up into and filled a permanent and eternal mould, which, summer and winter forever, is waiting to be filled.

This foliate structure is common to the coral and the plumage of birds, and to how large a part of animate and inanimate nature. The same independence of law on matter is observable in many other instances, as in the natural rhymes, when some animal form, color, or odor has its counterpart in some vegetable. As, indeed, all rhymes imply an eternal melody, independent of any particular sense.

As confirmation of the fact that vegetation is but a kind of crystallization, every one may observe how, upon the edge of the melting frost on the window, the needle-shaped particles are bundled together so as to resemble fields waving with grain, or shocks rising here and there from the stubble; on one side the vegetation of the torrid zone, high-towering palms and wide-spread banyans, such as are seen in pictures of oriental scenery; on the other, arctic pines stiff frozen, with downcast branches.

Vegetation has been made the type of all growth; but as in crystals the law is more obvious, their material being more simple, and for the most part more transient and fleeting, would it not be as philosophical as convenient to consider all growth, all filling up within the limits of nature, but a crystallization more or less rapid?

On this occasion, in the side of the high bank of the river, wherever the water or other cause had formed a cavity, its throat and outer edge, like the entrance to a citadel, bristled with a glistening ice-armor. In one place you might see minute ostrich-feathers, which seemed the waving plumes of the warriors filing into the fortress; in another, the glancing, fan-shaped banners of the Lilliputian host; and in another, the needle-shaped particles collected into bundles, resembling the plumes of the pine, might pass for a phalanx of spears. From the under side of the ice in the brooks, where there was a thicker ice below, depended a mass of crystallization, four or five inches deep, in the form of prisms, with their lower ends open, which, when the ice was laid on its smooth side, resembled the roofs and steeples of a Gothic city, or the vessels of a crowded haven under a press of canvas. The very mud in the road, where the ice had melted, was crystallized with deep rectilinear fissures, and the crystalline masses in the sides of the ruts resembled exactly asbestos in the disposition of their needles. Around the roots of the stubble and flower-stalks, the frost was gathered into the form of irregular conical shells, or fairy rings. In some places the ice-crystals were lying upon granite rocks, directly over crystals of quartz, the frostwork of a longer night, crystals of a longer period, but, to some eye unprejudiced by the short term of human life, melting as fast as the former.

In the Report on the Invertebrate Animals, this singular fact is recorded, which teaches us to put a new value on time and space: 'The distribution of the marine shells is well worthy of notice as a geological fact. Cape Cod, the right arm of the Commonwealth, reaches out into the ocean, some fifty or sixty miles. It is nowhere many miles wide, but this narrow point of land has hitherto proved a barrier to the migrations of many species of Mollusca. Several genera and numerous species, which are separated by the intervention of only a few miles of land, are effectually prevented from mingling by the Cape, and do not pass from one side to the other. . . . Of the one hundred and ninety-seven marine species, eighty-three do not pass to the south shore, and fifty are not found on the north shore of the Cape.'

That common mussel, the *Unio complanatus*, or more properly *fluviatilis*, left in the spring by the muskrat upon rocks and stumps, appears to have been an important article of food with the Indians. In one place, where they are said to have feasted, they are found in large quantities, at an elevation of thirty feet above the river, filling the soil to the depth of a foot, and mingled with ashes and Indian remains.

The works we have placed at the head of our chapter, with as much license as the preacher selects his text, are such as imply more labor than enthusiasm. The State wanted complete catalogues of its natural riches, with such additional facts merely as would be directly useful.

The reports on Fishes, Reptiles, Insects, and Invertebrate Animals, however, indicate labor and research, and have a value independent of the object of the legislature.

Those of Herbaceous Plants and Birds cannot be of much value, as long as Bigelow and Nuttall are accessible. They serve but to indicate, with more or less exactness, what species are found in the State. We detect several errors ourselves, and a more practised eye would no doubt expand the list.

The Quadrupeds deserved a more final and instructive report than they have obtained.

These volumes deal much in measurements and minute descriptions, not interesting to the general reader, with only here and there a colored sentence to allure him, like those plants growing in dark forests, which bear only leaves without blossoms. But the ground was comparatively unbroken, and we will not complain of the pioneer, if he raises no flowers with his first crop. Let us not underrate the value of a fact; it will one day flower in a truth. It is astonishing how few facts of importance are added in a century to the natural history of any animal. The natural history of man himself is still being gradually written. Men are knowing enough after their fashion. Every countryman and dairy-maid knows that the coats of the fourth stomach of the calf will curdle milk, and what particular mushroom is a safe and nutritious diet. You cannot go into any field or wood, but it will seem as if every stone had been turned, and the bark on every tree ripped up. But, after all, it is much easier to discover than to see when the cover is off. It has been well said that 'the attitude of inspection is prone.' Wisdom does not inspect, but behold. We must look a long time before we can see. Slow are the beginnings of philosophy. He has something demoniacal in him, who can discern a law or couple two facts. We can imagine a time when 'Water runs down hill' may have been taught in the schools. The true man of science will know nature better by his finer organization; he will smell, taste, see, hear, feel, better than other men. His will be a deeper and finer experience. We do not learn by inference and deduction and the application of mathematics to philosophy, but by direct intercourse and sympathy. It is with science as with ethics — we cannot know truth by contrivance and method; the Baconian is as false as any other, and with all the helps of machinery and the arts, the most scientific will still be the healthiest and friendliest man, and possess a more perfect Indian wisdom.

II. WALKING

I wish to speak a word for Nature, for absolute freedom and wildness, as contrasted with a freedom and culture merely civil — to regard man as an inhabitant, or a part and parcel of Nature, rather than a member of society. I wish to make an extreme statement, if so I may make an emphatic one, for there are enough champions of civilization: the minister and the school committee and every one of you will take care of that.

I have met with but one or two persons in the course of my life who understood the art of Walking, that is, of taking walks — who had a genius, so to speak, for *sauntering*, which word is beautifully derived 'from idle people who roved about the country, in the Middle Ages, and asked charity, under pretense of going *à la Sainte Terre*,' to the Holy Land, till the children exclaimed, 'There goes a *Sainte-Terrer*,' a Saunterer, a Holy-Lander. They who never go to the Holy Land in their walks, as they pretend, are indeed mere idlers and vagabonds; but they who do go there are saunterers in the good sense, such as I mean. Some, however, would derive the word from *sans terre*, without land or a home, which, therefore, in the good sense, will mean, having no particular home, but equally at home everywhere. For this is the secret of successful sauntering. He who sits still in a house all the time may be the greatest vagrant of all; but the saunterer, in the good sense, is no more vagrant than the meandering river, which is all the while sedulously seeking the shortest course to the sea. But I prefer the first, which, indeed, is the most probable derivation. For every walk is a sort of crusade, preached by some Peter the Hermit in us, to go forth and reconquer this Holy Land from the hands of the Infidels.

It is true, we are but faint-hearted crusaders, even the walkers, nowadays, who undertake no persevering, never-ending enterprises. Our expeditions are but tours, and come round again at evening to the old hearth-side from which we set out. Half the walk is but retracing our steps. We should go forth on the shortest walk, perchance, in the spirit of undying adventure, never to return — prepared to send back our embalmed hearts only as relics to our desolate kingdoms. If you are ready to leave father and mother, and brother and sister, and wife and child and friends, and never see them again — if you have paid your debts, and made your will, and settled all your affairs, and are a free man, then you are ready for a walk.

To come down to my own experience, my companion and I, for I sometimes have a companion, take pleasure in fancying ourselves knights of a new, or rather an old, order — not Equestrians or Chevaliers, not Ritters or Riders, but Walkers, a still more ancient and honorable class, I trust. The chivalric and heroic spirit which once belonged to the Rider seems now to reside in, or perchance to have subsided into, the Walker — not the Knight, but Walker, Errant. He is a sort of fourth estate, outside of Church and State and People.

We have felt that we almost alone hereabouts practised this noble art; though, to tell the truth, at least if their own assertions are to be received, most of my townsmen would fain walk sometimes, as I do, but they cannot. No wealth can buy the requisite leisure, freedom, and independence which are the capital in this profession. It comes only by the grace of God. It requires a direct dispensation from Heaven to become a walker. You must be born into the family of the Walkers. *Ambulator nascitur, non fit.* Some of my townsmen, it is true, can remember and have described to me some walks which they took ten years ago, in which they were so blessed as to lose themselves for half an hour in the woods; but I know very well that they have confined themselves to the highway ever since, whatever pretensions they may make to belong to this select class. No doubt they were elevated for a moment as by the reminiscence of a previous state of existence, when even they were foresters and outlaws.

> 'When he came to grene wode,
>   In a mery mornynge,
> There he herde the notes small
>   Of byrdes mery syngynge.
>
> 'It is ferre gone, sayd Robyn,
>   That I was last here;
> Me lyste a lytell for to shote
>   At the donne dere.'

I think that I cannot preserve my health and spirits, unless I spend four hours a day at least — and it is commonly more than that — sauntering through the woods and over the hills and fields, absolutely free from all worldly engagements. You may safely say, A penny for your thoughts, or a thousand pounds. When sometimes I am reminded that the mechanics and shopkeepers stay in their shops not only all the forenoon, but all the afternoon too, sitting with crossed legs, so many of them — as if the legs were made to sit upon, and not to stand or walk upon — I think that they deserve some credit for not having all committed suicide long ago.

I, who cannot stay in my chamber for a single day without acquiring some rust, and when sometimes I have stolen forth for a walk at the eleventh hour, or four o'clock in the afternoon, too late to redeem the day, when the shades of night were already beginning to be mingled with the daylight, have felt as if I had committed some sin to be atoned for — I confess that I am astonished at the power of endurance, to say nothing of the moral insensibility, of my neighbors who confine themselves to shops and offices the whole day for weeks and months, aye, and years almost together. I know not what manner of stuff they are of — sitting there now at three o'clock in the afternoon, as if it were three o'clock in the morning. Bonaparte may talk of the three-o'clock-in-the-morning courage, but it is nothing to the courage which can sit down cheerfully at this hour in the afternoon over against one's self whom you have known all the morning, to starve out a garrison to whom you are bound by such strong ties of sympathy. I wonder that about this time, or say between four and five o'clock in the afternoon, too late for the morning papers and too early for the evening ones, there is not a general explosion heard up and down the street, scattering a legion of antiquated and house-bred notions and whims to the four winds for an airing — and so the evil cure itself.

How womankind, who are confined to the house still more than men, stand it I do not know; but I have ground to suspect that most of them do not *stand* it at all. When, early in a summer afternoon, we have been shaking the dust of the village from the skirts of our garments, making haste past those houses with purely Doric or Gothic fronts, which have such an air of repose about them, my companion whispers that probably about these times their occupants are all gone to bed. Then it is that I appreciate the beauty and the glory of architecture, which itself never turns in, but forever stands out and erect, keeping watch over the slumberers.

No doubt temperament, and, above all, age, have a good deal to do with it. As a man grows older, his ability to sit still and follow indoor occupations increases. He grows vespertinal in his habits as the evening of life approaches, till at last he comes forth only just before sundown, and gets all the walk that he requires in half an hour.

But the walking of which I speak has nothing in it akin to taking exercise, as it is called, as the sick take medicine at stated hours — as the swinging of dumbbells or chairs; but is itself the enterprise and adventure of the day. If you would get exercise, go in search of the springs of life. Think of a man's swinging dumbbells for his health, when those springs are bubbling up in far-off pastures unsought by him!

Moreover, you must walk like a camel, which is said to be the only beast which ruminates when walking. When a traveller asked Wordsworth's servant to show him her master's study, she answered, 'Here is his library, but his study is out of doors.'

Living much out of doors, in the sun and wind, will no doubt produce a certain roughness of character — will cause a thicker cuticle to grow over some of the finer qualities of our nature, as on the face and hands, or as severe manual labor robs the hands of some of their delicacy of touch. So staying in the house, on the other hand, may produce a softness and smoothness, not to say thinness of skin, accompanied by an increased sensibility to certain impressions. Perhaps we should be more susceptible to some influences important to our intellectual and moral growth, if the sun had shone and the wind blown on us a little less; and no doubt it is a nice matter to proportion rightly the thick and thin skin. But methinks that is a scurf that will fall off fast enough — that the natural remedy is to be found in the proportion which the night bears to the day, the winter to the summer, thought to experience. There will be so much the more air and sunshine in our thoughts. The callous palms of the laborer are conversant with finer tissues of self-respect and heroism, whose touch thrills the heart, than the languid fingers of idleness. That is mere sentimentality that lies abed by day and thinks itself white, far from the tan and callus of experience.

When we walk, we naturally go to the fields and woods: what would become of us, if we walked only in a garden or a mall? Even some sects of philosophers have felt the necessity of importing the woods to themselves, since they did not go to the woods. 'They planted groves and walks of Platanes,' where they took *subdiales ambulationes* in porticos open to the air. Of course it is of no use to direct our steps to the woods, if they do not carry us thither. I am alarmed when it happens that I have walked a mile into the woods bodily, without getting there in spirit. In my afternoon walk I would fain forget all my morning occupations and my obligations to society. But it sometimes happens that I cannot easily shake off the village. The thought of some work will run in my head and I am not where my body is — I am out of my senses. In my walks I would fain return to my senses. What business have I in the woods, if I am thinking of something out of the woods? I suspect myself, and cannot help a shudder, when I find myself so implicated even in what are called good works — for this may sometimes happen.

My vicinity affords many good walks; and though for so many years I have walked almost every day, and sometimes for several days together, I have not yet exhausted them. An absolutely new prospect is a great happiness, and I can still get this any afternoon. Two or three hours' walking will carry me to as strange a country as I expect ever to see. A single farmhouse which I had not seen before is sometimes as good as the dominions of the King of Dahomey. There is in fact a sort of harmony discoverable between the capabilities of the landscape within a circle of ten miles' radius, or the limits of an afternoon walk, and the threescore years and ten of human life. It will never become quite familiar to you.

Nowadays almost all man's improvements, so called, as the building of houses and the cutting down of the forest and of all large trees, simply deform the landscape, and make it more and more tame and cheap. A people who would begin by burning the fences and let the forest stand! I saw the fences half consumed, their ends lost in the middle of the prairie, and some worldly miser with a surveyor looking after his bounds, while heaven had taken place around him, and he did not see the angels going to and fro, but was looking for an old post-hole in the midst of paradise. I looked again, and saw him standing in the middle of a boggy Stygian fen, surrounded by devils, and he had found his bounds without a doubt, three little stones, where a stake had been driven, and looking nearer, I saw that the Prince of Darkness was his surveyor.

I can easily walk ten, fifteen, twenty, any number of miles, commencing at my own door, without going by any house, without crossing a road except where the fox and the mink do: first along by the river, and then the brook, and then the meadow and the woodside. There are square miles in my vicinity which have no inhabitant. From many a hill I can see civilization and the abodes of man afar. The farmers and their works are scarcely more obvious than woodchucks and their burrows. Man and his affairs, church and state and school, trade and commerce, and manufactures and agriculture, even politics, the most alarming of them all — I am pleased to see how little space they occupy in the landscape. Politics is but a narrow field, and that still narrower highway yonder leads to it. I sometimes direct the traveller thither. If you would go to the political world, follow the great road — follow that market-man, keep his dust in your eyes, and it will lead you straight to it; for it, too, has its place merely, and does not occupy all space. I pass from it as from a bean-field into the forest, and it is forgotten. In one half-hour I can walk off to some portion of the earth's surface where a man does not stand from one year's end to another, and there, consequently, politics are not, for they are but as the cigar-smoke of a man.

The village is the place to which the roads tend, a sort of expansion of the highway, as a lake of a river. It is the body of which roads are the arms and legs — a trivial or quadrivial place, the thoroughfare and ordinary of travellers. The word is from the Latin *villa*, which together with *via*, a way, or more anciently *ved* and *vella*, Varro derives from *veho*, to carry, because the villa is the place to and from which things are carried. They who got their living by teaming were said *vellaturam facere*. Hence, too, the Latin word *vilis* and our vile, also *villain*. This suggests what kind of degeneracy villagers are liable to. They are way-worn by the travel that goes by and over them, without travelling themselves.

Some do not walk at all; others walk in the highways; a few walk across lots. Roads are made for horses and men of business. I do not travel in them much, comparatively, because I am not in a hurry to get to any tavern or grocery or livery-stable or depot to which they lead. I am a good horse to travel, but not from choice a roadster. The landscape-painter uses the figures of men to mark a road. He would not make that use of my figure. I walk out into a nature such as the old prophets and poets, Menu, Moses, Homer, Chaucer, walked in. You may name it America, but it is not America; neither Americus Vespucius, nor Columbus, nor the rest were the discoverers of it. There is a truer account of it in mythology than in any history of America, so called, that I have seen.

However, there are a few old roads that may be trodden with profit, as if they led somewhere now that they are nearly discontinued. There is the Old Marlborough Road, which does not go to Marlborough now, methinks, unless that is Marlborough where it carries me. I am the bolder to speak of it here, because I presume that there are one or two such roads in every town.

THE OLD MARLBOROUGH ROAD

Where they once dug for money,
But never found any;
Where sometimes Martial Miles
Singly files,
And Elijah Wood,
I fear for no good:
No other man,
Save Elisha Dugan —

O man of wild habits,
Partridges and rabbits,
Who hast no cares
Only to set snares,
Who liv'st all alone,
Close to the bone,
And where life is sweetest
Constantly eatest.
When the spring stirs my blood
With the instinct to travel,
I can get enough gravel
On the Old Marlborough Road.
Nobody repairs it,
For nobody wears it;
It is a living way,
As the Christians say.
Not many there be
Who enter therein,
Only the guests of the
Irishman Quin.
What is it, what is it,
But a direction out there,
And the bare possibility
Of going somewhere?
Great guide-boards of stone,
But travellers none;
Cenotaphs of the towns
Named on their crowns,
It is worth going to see
Where you *might* be.
What king
Did the thing,
I am still wondering;
Set up how or when,
By what selectmen,
Gourgas or Lee,
Clark or Darby?
They're a great endeavor
To be something forever;
Blank tablets of stone,
Where a traveller might groan,
And in one sentence
Grave all that is known;
Which another might read,
In his extreme need.
I know one or two
Lines that would do,
Literature that might stand

> All over the land,
>   Which a man could remember
>   Till next December,
>   And read again in the spring,
>   After the thawing.
> If with fancy unfurled
>   You leave your abode,
> You may go round the world
>   By the Old Marlborough Road.

At present, in this vicinity, the best part of the land is not private property; the landscape is not owned, and the walker enjoys comparative freedom. But possibly the day will come when it will be partitioned off into so-called pleasure-grounds, in which a few will take a narrow and exclusive pleasure only — when fences shall be multiplied, and man-traps and other engines invented to confine men to the *public* road, and walking over the surface of God's earth shall be construed to mean trespassing on some gentleman's grounds. To enjoy a thing exclusively is commonly to exclude yourself from the true enjoyment of it. Let us improve our opportunities, then, before the evil days come.

What is it that makes it so hard sometimes to determine whither we will walk? I believe that there is a subtle magnetism in Nature, which, if we unconsciously yield to it, will direct us aright. It is not indifferent to us which way we walk. There is a right way; but we are very liable from heedlessness and stupidity to take the wrong one. We would fain take that walk, never yet taken by us through this actual world, which is perfectly symbolical of the path which we love to travel in the interior and ideal world; and sometimes, no doubt, we find it difficult to choose our direction, because it does not yet exist distinctly in our idea.

When I go out of the house for a walk, uncertain as yet whither I will bend my steps, and submit myself to my instinct to decide for me, I find, strange and whimsical as it may seem, that I finally and inevitably settle southwest, toward some particular wood or meadow or deserted pasture or hill in that direction. My needle is slow to settle — varies a few degrees, and does not always point due southwest, it is true, and it has good authority for this variation, but it always settles between west and south-southwest. The future lies that way to me, and the earth seems more unexhausted and richer on that side. The outline which would bound my walks would be, not a circle, but a parabola, or rather like one of those cometary orbits which have been thought to be non-returning curves, in this case opening westward, in which my house

occupies the place of the sun. I turn round and round irresolute sometimes for a quarter of an hour, until I decide, for a thousandth time,
that I will walk into the southwest or west. Eastward I go only by
force; but westward I go free. Thither no business leads me. It is hard
for me to believe that I shall find fair landscapes or sufficient wildness
and freedom behind the eastern horizon. I am not excited by the
prospect of a walk thither; but I believe that the forest which I see in
the western horizon stretches uninterruptedly toward the setting sun,
and there are no towns nor cities in it of enough consequence to disturb
me. Let me live where I will, on this side is the city, on that the wilderness, and ever I am leaving the city more and more, and withdrawing
into the wilderness. I should not lay so much stress on this fact, if I did
not believe that something like this is the prevailing tendency of my
countrymen. I must walk toward Oregon, and not toward Europe.
And that way the nation is moving, and I may say that mankind progress from east to west. Within a few years we have witnessed the
phenomenon of a southeastward migration, in the settlement of Australia; but this affects us as a retrograde movement, and, judging from
the moral and physical character of the first generation of Australians,
has not yet proved a successful experiment. The eastern Tartars think
that there is nothing west beyond Thibet. 'The world ends there,' say
they; 'beyond there is nothing but a shoreless sea.' It is unmitigated
East where they live.

We go eastward to realize history and study the works of art and
literature, retracing the steps of the race; we go westward as into the
future, with a spirit of enterprise and adventure. The Atlantic is a
Lethean stream, in our passage over which we have had an opportunity
to forget the Old World and its institutions. If we do not succeed this
time, there is perhaps one more chance for the race left before it arrives
on the banks of the Styx; and that is in the Lethe of the Pacific, which
is three times as wide.

I know not how significant it is, or how far it is an evidence of
singularity, that an individual should thus consent in his pettiest walk
with the general movement of the race; but I know that something akin
to the migratory instinct in birds and quadrupeds — which, in some
instance, is known to have affected the squirrel tribe, impelling them
to a general and mysterious movement, in which they were seen, say
some, crossing the broadest rivers, each on its particular chip, with its
tail raised for a sail, and bridging narrower streams with their dead —
that something like the *furor* which affects the domestic cattle in the

spring, and which is referred to a worm in their tails, affects both nations and individuals, either perennially or from time to time. Not a flock of wild geese cackles over our town, but it to some extent unsettles the value of real estate here, and, if I were a broker, I should probably take that disturbance into account.

> 'Than longen folk to gon on pilgrimages,
> And palmeres for to seken strange strondes.'

Every sunset which I witness inspires me with the desire to go to a West as distant and as fair as that into which the sun goes down. He appears to migrate westward daily, and tempt us to follow him. He is the Great Western Pioneer whom the nations follow. We dream all night of those mountain-ridges in the horizon, though they may be of vapor only, which were last gilded by his rays. The island of Atlantis, and the islands and gardens of the Hesperides, a sort of terrestrial paradise, appear to have been the Great West of the ancients, enveloped in mystery and poetry. Who has not seen in imagination, when looking into the sunset sky, the gardens of the Hesperides, and the foundation of all those fables?

Columbus felt the westward tendency more strongly than any before. He obeyed it, and found a New World for Castile and Leon. The herd of men in those days scented fresh pastures from afar.

> 'And now the sun had stretched out all the hills,
> And now was dropped into the western bay;
> At last *he* rose, and twitched his mantle blue;
> Tomorrow to fresh woods and pastures new.'

Where on the globe can there be found an area of equal extent with that occupied by the bulk of our States, so fertile and so rich and varied in its productions, and at the same time so habitable by the European, as this is? Michaux, who knew but part of them, says that 'the species of large trees are much more numerous in North America than in Europe; in the United States there are more than one hundred and forty species that exceed thirty feet in height; in France there are but thirty that attain this size.' Later botanists more than confirm his observations. Humboldt came to America to realize his youthful dreams of a tropical vegetation, and he beheld it in its greatest perfection in the primitive forests of the Amazon, the most gigantic wilderness on the earth, which he has so eloquently described. The geographer Guyot, himself a European, goes farther — farther than I am ready to follow him; yet not when he says: 'As the plant is made for the animal, as the vegetable world is made for the animal world, America is made for the man of the Old World. . . . The man of the Old World sets out upon his way. Leaving the highlands of Asia, he descends from station to station towards Europe. Each of his steps is marked by a new civilization superior to the preceding, by a greater power of development. Arrived at the Atlantic, he pauses on the shore of this unknown ocean, the bounds of which he knows not, and turns upon his footprints for an instant.' When he has exhausted the rich soil of Europe, and reinvigorated himself, 'then recommences his adventurous career westward as in the earliest ages.' So far Guyot.

From this western impulse coming in contact with the barrier of the Atlantic sprang the commerce and enterprise of modern times. The younger Michaux, in his 'Travels West of the Alleghanies in 1802,' says that the common inquiry in the newly settled West was, ' "From what part of the world have you come?" As if these vast and fertile regions would naturally be the place of meeting and common country of all the inhabitants of the globe.'

To use an obsolete Latin word, I might say, *Ex Oriente lux; ex Occidente* FRUX. From the East light; from the West fruit.

Sir Francis Head, an English traveller and a Governor-General of Canada, tells us that 'in both the northern and southern hemispheres of the New World, Nature has not only outlined her works on a larger scale, but has painted the whole picture with brighter and more costly colors than she used in delineating and in beautifying the Old World. . . . The heavens of America appear infinitely higher, the sky is bluer, the air is fresher, the cold is intenser, the moon looks larger, the stars are brighter, the thunder is louder, the lightning is vivider, the wind is stronger, the rain is heavier, the mountains are higher, the rivers longer, the forests bigger, the plains broader.' This statement will do at least to set against Buffon's account of this part of the world and its productions.

Linnæus said long ago, 'Nescio quæe facies *laeta, glabra* plantis Americanis' (I know not what there is of joyous and smooth in the aspect of American plants); and I think that in this country there are no, or at most very few, *Africanae bestiae,* African beasts, as the Romans called them, and that in this respect also it is peculiarly fitted for the habitation of man. We are told that within three miles of the centre of the East-Indian city of Singapore, some of the inhabitants are annually carried off by tigers; but the traveller can lie down in the woods at night almost anywhere in North America without fear of wild beasts.

These are encouraging testimonies. If the moon looks larger here than in Europe, probably the sun looks larger also. If the heavens of America appear infinitely higher, and the stars brighter, I trust that these facts are symbolical of the height to which the philosophy and poetry and religion of her inhabitants may one day soar. At length, perchance, the immaterial heaven will appear as much higher to the American mind, and the intimations that star it as much brighter. For I believe that climate does thus react on man — as there is something in the mountain air that feeds the spirit and inspires. Will not man grow to greater perfection intellectually as well as physically under these influences? Or is it unimportant how many foggy days there are in his life? I trust that we shall be more imaginative, that our thoughts will be clearer, fresher, and more ethereal, as our sky — our understanding more comprehensive and broader, like our plains — our intellect generally on a grander scale, like our thunder and lightning, our rivers and mountains and forests — and our hearts shall even correspond in breadth and depth and grandeur to our inland seas. Perchance there will appear to the traveller something, he knows not what, of *laeta* and *glabra*, of joyous and serene, in our very faces. Else to what end does the world go on, and why was America discovered?

To Americans I hardly need to say,

'Westward the star of empire takes its way.'

As a true patriot, I should be ashamed to think that Adam in paradise was more favorably situated on the whole than the backwoodsman in this country.

Our sympathies in Massachusetts are not confined to New England; though we may be estranged from the South, we sympathize with the West. There is the home of the younger sons, as among the Scandinavians they took to the sea for their inheritance. It is too late to be studying Hebrew; it is more important to understand even the slang of today.

Some months ago I went to see a panorama of the Rhine. It was like a dream of the Middle Ages. I floated down its historic stream in something more than imagination, under bridges built by the Romans, and repaired by later heroes, past cities and castles whose very names were music to my ears, and each of which was the subject of a legend. There were Ehrenbreitstein and Rolandseck and Coblentz, which I knew only in history. They were ruins that interested me chiefly. There seemed to come up from its waters and its vine-clad hills and valleys a hushed music as of Crusaders departing for the Holy Land. I floated along under the spell of enchantment, as if I had been transported to an heroic age, and breathed an atmosphere of chivalry.

Soon after, I went to see a panorama of the Mississippi, and as I worked my way up the river in the light of today, and saw the steamboats wooding up, counted the rising cities, gazed on the fresh ruins of Nauvoo, beheld the Indians moving west across the stream, and, as before I had looked up the Moselle, now looked up the Ohio and the Missouri and heard the legends of Dubuque and of Wenona's Cliff — still thinking more of the future than of the past or present — I saw that this was a Rhine stream of a different kind; that the foundations of castles were yet to be laid, and the famous bridges were yet to be thrown over the river; and I felt that *this was the heroic age itself*, though we know it not, for the hero is commonly the simplest and obscurest of men.

The West of which I speak is but another name for the Wild; and what I have been preparing to say is, that in Wildness is the preservation of the World. Every tree sends its fibres forth in search of the Wild. The cities import it at any price. Men plow and sail for it. From the forest and wilderness come the tonics and barks which brace mankind. Our ancestors were savages. The story of Romulus and Remus being suckled by a wolf is not a meaningless fable. The founders of every state which has risen to eminence have drawn their nourishment and vigor from a similar wild source. It was because the children of the Empire were not suckled by the wolf that they were conquered and displaced by the children of the northern forests who were.

I believe in the forest, and in the meadow, and in the night in which the corn grows. We require an infusion of hemlock spruce or arborvitæ in our tea. There is a difference between eating and drinking for strength and from mere gluttony. The Hottentots eagerly devour the marrow of the koodoo and other antelopes raw, as a matter of course. Some of our northern Indians eat raw the marrow of the Arctic reindeer, as well as various other parts, including the summits of the antlers, as long as they are soft. And herein, perchance, they have stolen a march on the cooks of Paris. They get what usually goes to feed the fire. This is probably better than stall-fed beef and slaughter-house pork to make a man of. Give me a wildness whose glance no civilization can endure — as if we lived on the marrow of koodoos devoured raw.

There are some intervals which border the strain of the wood thrush, to which I would migrate — wild lands where no settler has squatted; to which, methinks, I am already acclimated.

The African hunter Cumming tells us that the skin of the eland, as well as that of most other antelopes just killed, emits the most delicious perfume of trees and grass. I would have every man so much like a wild antelope, so much a part and parcel of nature, that his very person should thus sweetly advertise our senses of his presence, and remind us of those parts of nature which he most haunts. I feel no disposition to be satirical, when the trapper's coat emits the odor of musquash even; it is a sweeter scent to me than that which commonly exhales from the merchant's or the scholar's garments. When I go into their wardrobes and handle their vestments, I am reminded of no grassy plains and flowery meads which they have frequented, but of dusty merchants' exchanges and libraries rather.

A tanned skin is something more than respectable, and perhaps olive is a fitter color than white for a man — a denizen of the woods. 'The pale white man!' I do not wonder that the African pitied him. Darwin the naturalist says, 'A white man bathing by the side of a Tahitian was like a plant bleached by the gardener's art, compared with a fine, dark green one, growing vigorously in the open fields.'

Ben Jonson exclaims —

'How near to good is what is fair!'

So I would say,

How near to good is what is *wild!*

Life consists with wildness. The most alive is the wildest. Not yet subdued to man, its presence refreshes him. One who pressed forward incessantly and never rested from his labors, who grew fast and made infinite demands on life, would always find himself in a new country or wilderness, and surrounded by the raw material of life. He would be climbing over the prostrate stems of primitive forest-trees.

Hope and the future for me are not in lawns and cultivated fields, not in towns and cities, but in the impervious and quaking swamps. When, formerly, I have analyzed my partiality for some farm which I had contemplated purchasing, I have frequently found that I was attracted solely by a few square rods of impermeable and unfathomable bog — a natural sink in one corner of it. That was the jewel which dazzled me. I derive more of my subsistence from the swamps which surround my native town than from the cultivated gardens in the village. There

are no richer parterres to my eyes than the dense beds of dwarf andromeda (*Cassandra calyculata*) which cover these tender places on the
earth's surface. Botany cannot go farther than tell me the names of the
shrubs which grow there — the high blueberry, panicled andromeda,
lambkill, azalea, and rhodora — all standing in the quaking sphagnum.
I often think that I should like to have my house front on this mass of
dull red bushes, omitting other flower plots and borders, transplanted
spruce and trim box, even gravelled walks — to have this fertile spot
under my windows, not a few imported barrowfuls of soil only to
cover the sand which was thrown out in digging the cellar. Why not
put my house, my parlor, behind this plot, instead of behind that meagre
assemblage of curiosities, that poor apology for a Nature and Art,
which I call my front yard? It is an effort to clear up and make a decent
appearance when the carpenter and mason have departed, though
done as much for the passer-by as the dweller within. The most taste-
ful front-yard fence was never an agreeable object of study to me; the
most elaborate ornaments, acorn tops, or what not, soon wearied and
disgusted me. Bring your sills up to the very edge of the swamp, then
(though it may not be the best place for a dry cellar), so that there be
no access on that side to citizens. Front yards are not made to walk in,
but, at most, through, and you could go in the back way.

Yes, though you may think me perverse, if it were proposed to me to
dwell in the neighborhood of the most beautiful garden that ever
human art contrived, or else of a Dismal Swamp, I should certainly
decide for the swamp. How vain, then, have been all your labors,
citizens, for me!

My spirits infallibly rise in proportion to the outward dreariness.
Give me the ocean, the desert, or the wilderness! In the desert, pure
air and solitude compensate for want of moisture and fertility. The
traveller Burton says of it: 'Your *morale* improves; you become frank and
cordial, hospitable and single-minded. . . . In the desert, spirituous
liquors excite only disgust. There is a keen enjoyment in a mere animal
existence.' They who had been travelling long on the steppes of Tartary
say, 'On reëntering cultivated lands, the agitation, perplexity, and
turmoil of civilization oppressed and suffocated us; the air seemed to fail
us, and we felt every moment as if about to die of asphyxia.' When
I would recreate myself, I seek the darkest wood, the thickest and most
interminable and, to the citizen, most dismal, swamp. I enter a swamp
as a sacred place, a *sanctum sanctorum*. There is the strength, the marrow, of Nature. The wildwood covers the virgin mould, and the same

soil is good for men and for trees. A man's health requires as many acres of meadow to his prospect as his farm does loads of muck. There are the strong meats on which he feeds. A town is saved, not more by the righteous men in it than by the woods and swamps that surround it. A township where one primitive forest waves above while another primitive forest rots below — such a town is fitted to raise not only corn and potatoes, but poets and philosophers for the coming ages. In such a soil grew Homer and Confucius and the rest, and out of such a wilderness comes the Reformer eating locusts and wild honey.

To preserve wild animals implies generally the creation of a forest for them to dwell in or resort to. So it is with man. A hundred years ago they sold bark in our streets peeled from our own woods. In the very aspect of those primitive and rugged trees there was, methinks, a tanning principle which hardened and consolidated the fibres of men's thoughts. Ah! already I shudder for these comparatively degenerate days of my native village, when you cannot collect a load of bark of good thickness, and we no longer produce tar and turpentine.

The civilized nations — Greece, Rome, England — have been sustained by the primitive forests which anciently rotted where they stand. They survive as long as the soil is not exhausted. Alas for human culture! little is to be expected of a nation, when the vegetable mould is exhausted, and it is compelled to make manure of the bones of its fathers. There the poet sustains himself merely by his own superfluous fat, and the philosopher comes down on his marrow-bones.

It is said to be the task of the American 'to work the virgin soil,' and that 'agriculture here already assumes proportions unknown everywhere else.' I think that the farmer displaces the Indian even because he redeems the meadow, and so makes himself stronger and in some respects more natural. I was surveying for a man the other day a single straight line one hundred and thirty-two rods long, through a swamp at whose entrance might have been written the words which Dante read over the entrance to the infernal regions, 'Leave all hope, ye that enter' — that is, of ever getting out again; where at one time I saw my employer actually up to his neck and swimming for his life in his property, though it was still winter. He had another similar swamp which I could not survey at all, because it was completely under water, and nevertheless, with regard to a third swamp, which I did *survey* from a distance, he remarked to me, true to his instincts, that he would not part with it for any consideration, on account of the mud which it contained. And that man intends to put a girdling ditch round the whole in the course of forty months, and so redeem it by the magic of his spade. I refer to him only as the type of a class.

The weapons with which we have gained our most important victories, which should be handed down as heirlooms from father to son, are not the sword and the lance, but the bushwhack, the turf-cutter, the spade, and the bog hoe, rusted with the blood of many a meadow, and begrimed with the dust of many a hard-fought field. The very winds blew the Indian's cornfield into the meadow, and pointed out the way which he had not the skill to follow. He had no better implement with which to intrench himself in the land than a clamshell. But the farmer is armed with plow and spade.

In literature it is only the wild that attracts us. Dullness is but another name for tameness. It is the uncivilized free and wild thinking in Hamlet and the Iliad, in all the scriptures and mythologies, not learned in the schools, that delights us. As the wild duck is more swift and beautiful than the tame, so is the wild — the mallard — thought, which 'mid falling dews wings its way above the fens. A truly good book is something as natural, and as unexpectedly and unaccountably fair and perfect, as a wild-flower discovered on the prairies of the West or in the jungles of the East. Genius is a light which makes the darkness visible, like the lightning's flash, which perchance shatters the temple of knowledge itself — and not a taper lighted at the hearth-stone of the race, which pales before the light of common day.

English literature, from the days of the minstrels to the Lake Poets — Chaucer and Spenser and Milton, and even Shakespeare, included — breathes no quite fresh and, in this sense, wild strain. It is an essentially tame and civilized literature, reflecting Greece and Rome. Her wilderness is a greenwood, her wild man a Robin Hood. There is plenty of genial love of Nature, but not so much of Nature herself. Her chronicles inform us when her wild animals, but not when the wild man in her, became extinct.

The science of Humboldt is one thing, poetry is another thing. The poet today, notwithstanding all the discoveries of science, and the accumulated learning of mankind, enjoys no advantage over Homer.

Where is the literature which gives expression to Nature? He would be a poet who could impress the winds and streams into his service, to speak for him; who nailed words to their primitive senses, as farmers drive down stakes in the spring, which the frost has heaved; who derived his words as often as he used them — transplanted them to his page with earth adhering to their roots; whose words were so true and fresh and natural that they would appear to expand like the buds at the approach of spring, though they lay half smothered between two musty leaves in a library — aye, to bloom and bear fruit there, after their kind, annually, for the faithful reader, in sympathy with surrounding Nature.

I do not know of any poetry to quote which adequately expresses this yearning for the Wild. Approached from this side, the best poetry is tame. I do not know where to find in any literature, ancient or modern, any account which contents me of that Nature with which even I am acquainted. You will perceive that I demand something which no Augustan nor Elizabethan age, which no *culture*, in short, can give. Mythology comes nearer to it than anything. How much more fertile a Nature, at least, has Grecian mythology its root in than English literature! Mythology is the crop which the Old World bore before its soil was exhausted, before the fancy and imagination were affected with blight; and which it still bears, wherever its pristine vigor is unabated. All other literatures endure only as the elms which overshadow our houses; but this is like the great dragon-tree of the Western Isles, as old as mankind, and, whether that does or not, will endure as long; for the decay of other literatures makes the soil in which it thrives.

The West is preparing to add its fables to those of the East. The valleys of the Ganges, the Nile, and the Rhine having yielded their crop, it remains to be seen what the valleys of the Amazon, the Plate, the Orinoco, the St. Lawrence, and the Mississippi will produce. Perchance, when, in the course of ages, American liberty has become a fiction of the past — as it is to some extent a fiction of the present — the poets of the world will be inspired by American mythology.

The wildest dreams of wild men, even, are not the less true, though they may not recommend themselves to the sense which is most common among Englishmen and Americans today. It is not every truth that recommends itself to the common sense. Nature has a place for the wild clematis as well as for the cabbage. Some expressions of truth are reminiscent — others merely *sensible*, as the phrase is — others prophetic. Some forms of disease, even, may prophesy forms of health. The geologist has discovered that the figures of serpents, griffins, flying dragons, and other fanciful embellishments of heraldry, have their prototypes in the forms of fossil species which were extinct before man was created, and hence 'indicate a faint and shadowy knowledge of a previous state of organic existence.' The Hindoos dreamed that the earth rested on an elephant, and the elephant on a tortoise, and the tortoise on a serpent; and though it may be an unimportant coincidence, it will not be out of place here to state, that a fossil tortoise has lately been discovered in Asia large enough to support an elephant. I confess that I am partial to these wild fancies, which transcend the order of time and development. They are the sublimest recreation of the intellect. The partridge loves peas, but not those that go with her into the pot.

In short, all good things are wild and free. There is something in a strain of music, whether produced by an instrument or by the human voice — take the sound of a bugle in a summer night, for instance — which by its wildness, to speak without satire, reminds me of the cries emitted by wild beasts in their native forests. It is so much of their wildness as I can understand. Give me for my friends and neighbors wild men, not tame ones. The wildness of the savage is but a faint symbol of the awful ferity with which good men and lovers meet.

I love even to see the domestic animals reassert their native rights — any evidence that they have not wholly lost their original wild habits and vigor; as when my neighbor's cow breaks out of her pasture early in the spring and boldly swims the river, a cold, gray tide, twenty-five or thirty rods wide, swollen by the melted snow. It is the buffalo crossing the Mississippi. This exploit confers some dignity on the herd in my eyes — already dignified. The seeds of instinct are preserved under the thick hides of cattle and horses, like seeds in the bowels of the earth, an indefinite period.

Any sportiveness in cattle is unexpected. I saw one day a herd of a dozen bullocks and cows running about and frisking in unwieldy sport, like huge rats, even like kittens. They shook their heads, raised their tails, and rushed up and down a hill, and I perceived by their horns, as well as by their activity, their relation to the deer tribe. But, alas! a sudden loud *Whoa!* would have damped their ardor at once, reduced them from venison to beef, and stiffened their sides and sinews like the locomotive. Who but the Evil One has cried 'Whoa!' to mankind? Indeed, the life of cattle, like that of many men, is but a sort of locomotiveness; they move a side at a time, and man, by his machinery, is meeting the horse and the ox half-way. Whatever part the whip has touched is thenceforth palsied. Who would ever think of **a** *side* of any of the supple cat tribe, as we speak of a *side* of beef?

I rejoice that horses and steers have to be broken before they can be made the slaves of men, and that men themselves have some wild oats still left to sow before they become submissive members of society.

Undoubtedly, all men are not equally fit subjects for civilization; and because the majority, like dogs and sheep, are tame by inherited disposition, this is no reason why the others **should** have their natures broken that they may be reduced to the same level. Men are in the main alike, but they were made several in order that they might be various. If a low use is to be served, one man will do nearly or quite as well as another; if a high one, individual excellence is to be regarded. Any man can stop a hole to keep the wind away, but no other man could serve so rare a use as the author of this illustration did. Confucius says, 'The skins of the tiger and the leopard, when they are tanned, are as the skins of the dog and the sheep tanned.' But it is not the part of a true culture to tame tigers, any more than it is to make sheep ferocious; and tanning their skins for shoes is not the best use to which they can be put.

When looking over a list of men's names in a foreign language, as of military officers, or of authors who have written on a particular subject, I am reminded once more that there is nothing in a name. The name Menschikoff, for instance, has nothing in it to my ears more human than a whisker, and it may belong to a rat. As the names of the Poles and Russians are to us, so are ours to them. It is as if they had been named by the child's rigmarole, *Iery, wiery ichery van, tittle-tol-tan.* I see in my mind a herd of wild creatures swarming over the earth, and to each the herdsman has affixed some barbarous sound in his own dialect. The names of men are, of course, as cheap and meaningless as *Bose* and *Tray*, the names of dogs.

Methinks it would be some advantage to philosophy if men were named merely in the gross, as they are known. It would be necessary only to know the genus and perhaps the race or variety, to know the individual. We are not prepared to believe that every private soldier in a Roman army had a name of his own — because we have not supposed that he had a character of his own.

At present our only true names are nicknames. I knew a boy who, from his peculiar energy, was called 'Buster' by his playmates, and this rightly supplanted his Christian name. Some travellers tell us that an Indian had no name given him at first, but earned it, and his name was his fame; and among some tribes he acquired a new name with every new exploit. It is pitiful when a man bears a name for convenience merely, who has earned neither name nor fame.

I will not allow mere names to make distinctions for me, but still see men in herds for all them. A familiar name cannot make a man less

strange to me. It may be given to a savage who retains in secret his own
wild title earned in the woods. We have a wild savage in us, and a
savage name is perchance somewhere recorded as ours. I see that my
neighbor, who bears the familiar epithet William or Edwin, takes it off
with his jacket. It does not adhere to him when asleep or in anger, or
aroused by any passion or inspiration. I seem to hear pronounced
by some of his kin at such a time his original wild name in some jaw-
breaking or else melodious tongue.

Here is this vast, savage, howling mother of ours, Nature, lying all
around, with such beauty, and such affection for her children, as the
leopard; and yet we are so early weaned from her breast to society, to
that culture which is exclusively an interaction of man on man — a sort
of breeding in and in, which produces at most a merely English nobility,
a civilization destined to have a speedy limit.

In society, in the best institutions of men, it is easy to detect a certain
precocity. When we should still be growing children, we are already
little men. Give me a culture which imports much muck from the
meadows, and deepens the soil — not that which trusts to heating
manures, and improved implements and modes of culture only!

Many a poor sore-eyed student that I have heard of would grow
faster, both intellectually and physically, if, instead of sitting up so very
late, he honestly slumbered a fool's allowance.

There may be an excess even of informing light. Niepce, a Frenchman, discovered 'actinism,' that power in the sun's rays which produces a chemical effect; that granite rocks, and stone structures, and
statues of metal 'are all alike destructively acted upon during the
hours of sunshine, and, but for provisions of Nature no less wonderful,
would soon perish under the delicate touch of the most subtile of the
agencies of the universe.' But he observed that 'those bodies which
underwent this change during the daylight possessed the power of
restoring themselves to their original conditions during the hours of
night, when this excitement was no longer influencing them.' Hence
it has been inferred that 'the hours of darkness are as necessary to the
inorganic creation as we know night and sleep are to the organic kingdom.' Not even does the moon shine every night, but gives place to
darkness.

I would not have every man nor every part of a man cultivated, any
more than I would have every acre of earth cultivated: part will be
tillage, but the greater part will be meadow and forest, not only serving

an immediate use, but preparing a mould against a distant future, by the annual decay of the vegetation which it supports.

There are other letters for the child to learn than those which Cadmus invented. The Spaniards have a good term to express this wild and dusky knowledge, *Gramatica parda*, tawny grammar, a kind of mother-wit derived from that same leopard to which I have referred.

We have heard of a Society for the Diffusion of Useful Knowledge. It is said that knowledge is power, and the like. Methinks there is equal need of a Society for the Diffusion of Useful Ignorance, what we will call Beautiful Knowledge, a knowledge useful in a higher sense: for what is most of our boasted so-called knowledge but a conceit that we know something, which robs us of the advantage of our actual ignorance? What we call knowledge is often our positive ignorance; ignorance our negative knowledge. By long years of patient industry and reading of the newspapers — for what are the libraries of science but files of newspapers? — a man accumulates a myriad facts, lays them up in his memory, and then when in some spring of his life he saunters abroad into the Great Fields of thought, he, as it were, goes to grass like a horse and leaves all his harness behind in the stable. I would say to the Society for the Diffusion of Useful Knowledge, sometimes — Go to grass. You have eaten hay long enough. The spring has come with its green crop. The very cows are driven to their country pastures before the end of May; though I have heard of one unnatural farmer who kept his cow in the barn and fed her on hay all the year round. So, frequently, the Society for the Diffusion of Useful Knowledge treats its cattle.

A man's ignorance sometimes is not only useful, but beautiful — while his knowledge, so called, is oftentimes worse than useless, besides being ugly. Which is the best man to deal with — he who knows nothing about a subject, and, what is extremely rare, knows that he knows nothing, or he who really knows something about it, but thinks that he knows all?

My desire for knowledge is intermittent, but my desire to bathe my head in atmospheres unknown to my feet is perennial and constant. The highest that we can attain to is not Knowledge, but Sympathy with Intelligence. I do not know that this higher knowledge amounts to anything more definite than a novel and grand surprise on a sudden revelation of the insufficiency of all that we called Knowledge before — a discovery that there are more things in heaven and earth than are dreamed of in our philosophy. It is the lighting up of the mist by the sun. Man cannot *know* in any higher sense than this, any more than he can look serenely and with impunity in the face of the sun: Ὥs τὶ νοῶν, οὐ κεῖνον νοήσεις, 'You will not perceive that, as perceiving a particular thing,' say the Chaldean Oracles.

There is something servile in the habit of seeking after a law which we may obey. We may study the laws of matter at and for our convenience, but a successful life knows no law. It is an unfortunate discovery certainly, that of a law which binds us where we did not know before that we were bound. Live free, child of the mist — and with respect to knowledge we are all children of the mist. The man who takes the liberty to live is superior to all the laws, by virtue of his relation to the lawmaker. 'That is active duty,' says the Vishnu Purana, 'which is not for our bondage; that is knowledge which is for our liberation: all other duty is good only unto weariness; all other knowledge is only the cleverness of an artist.'

It is remarkable how few events or crises there are in our histories, how little exercised we have been in our minds, how few experiences we have had. I would fain be assured that I am growing apace and rankly, though my very growth disturb this dull equanimity — though it be with struggle through long, dark muggy nights or seasons of gloom. It would be well if all our lives were a divine tragedy even, instead of this trivial comedy or farce. Dante, Bunyan, and others appear to have been exercised in their minds more than we: they were subjected to a kind of culture such as our district schools and colleges do not contemplate. Even Mahomet, though many may scream at his name, had a good deal more to live for, aye, and to die for, than they have commonly.

When, at rare intervals, some thought visits one, as perchance he is walking on a railroad, then, indeed, the cars go by without his hearing them. But soon, by some inexorable law, our life goes by and the cars return.

> 'Gentle breeze, that wanderest unseen,
> And bendest the thistles round Loira of storms,
> Traveller of the windy glens,
> Why hast thou left my ear so soon?'

While almost all men feel an attraction drawing them to society, few are attracted strongly to Nature. In their reaction to Nature men appear to me for the most part, notwithstanding their arts, lower than the animals. It is not often a beautiful relation, as in the case of the animals. How little appreciation of the beauty of the landscape there is among us! We have to be told that the Greeks called the world Κόσμος, Beauty, or Order, but we do not see clearly why they did so, and we esteem it at best only a curious philological fact.

For my part, I feel that with regard to Nature I live a sort of border life, on the confines of a world into which I make occasional and transient forays only, and my patriotism and allegiance to the state into whose territories I seem to retreat are those of a moss-trooper. Unto a life which I call natural I would gladly follow even a will-o'-the-wisp through bogs and sloughs unimaginable, but no moon nor firefly has shown me the causeway to it. Nature is a personality so vast and universal that we have never seen one of her features. The walker in the familiar fields which stretch around my native town sometimes finds himself in another land than is described in their owners' deeds, as it were in some faraway field on the confines of the actual Concord, where her jurisdiction ceases, and the idea which the word Concord suggests ceases to be suggested. These farms which I have myself surveyed, these bounds which I have set up, appear dimly still as through a mist; but they have no chemistry to fix them; they fade from the surface of the glass, and the picture which the painter painted stands out dimly from beneath. The world with which we are commonly acquainted leaves no trace, and it will have no anniversary.

I took a walk on Spaulding's Farm the other afternoon. I saw the setting sun lighting up the opposite side of a stately pine wood. Its golden rays straggled into the aisles of the wood as into some noble hall. I was impressed as if some ancient and altogether admirable and shining family had settled there in that part of the land called Concord, unknown to me — to whom the sun was servant — who had not gone into society in the village — who had not been called on. I saw their park, their pleasure-ground, beyond through the wood, in Spaulding's cranberry-meadow. The pines furnished them with gables as they grew. Their house was not obvious to vision; the trees grew through it. I do not know whether I heard the sounds of a suppressed hilarity or not. They seemed to recline on the sunbeams. They have sons and daughters. They are quite well. The farmer's cart-path, which leads directly through their hall, does not in the least put them out, as the muddy bottom of a pool is sometimes seen through the reflected skies. They never heard of Spaulding, and do not know that he is their neighbor — notwithstanding I heard him whistle as he drove his team through the house. Nothing can equal the serenity of their lives. Their coat-of-arms is simply a lichen. I saw it painted on the pines and oaks. Their attics were in the tops of the trees. They are of no politics. There was no noise of labor. I did not perceive that they were weaving or spinning. Yet I did detect, when the wind lulled and hearing was done away, the finest imaginable sweet musical hum — as of a distant hive in May — which perchance was the sound of their thinking. They had no idle thoughts, and no one without could see their work, for their industry was not as in knots and excrescences embayed.

But I find it difficult to remember them. They fade irrevocably out of my mind even now while I speak, and endeavor to recall them and recollect myself. It is only after a long and serious effort to recollect my best thoughts that I became again aware of their cohabitancy. If it were not for such families as this, I think I should move out of Concord.

We are accustomed to say in New England that few and fewer pigeons visit us every year. Our forests furnish no mast for them. So, it would seem, few and fewer thoughts visit each growing man from year to year, for the grove in our minds is laid waste — sold to feed unnecessary fires of ambition, or sent to mill — and there is scarcely a twig left for them to perch on. They no longer build nor breed with us. In some more genial season, perchance, a faint shadow flits across the landscape of the mind, cast by the *wings* of some thought in its vernal or autumnal migration, but, looking up, we are unable to detect the substance of the thought itself. Our winged thoughts are turned to poultry. They no longer soar, and they attain only to a Shanghai and Cochin-China grandeur. Those *gra-a-ate thoughts*, those *gra-a-ate* men you hear of!

We hug the earth — how rarely we mount! Methinks we might elevate ourselves a little more. We might climb a tree, at least. I found my account in climbing a tree once. It was a tall white pine, on the top of a hill; and though I got well pitched, I was well paid for it, for I discovered new mountains in the horizon which I had never seen before — so much more of the earth and the heavens. I might have walked about the foot of the tree for threescore years and ten, and yet I certainly should never have seen them. But, above all, I discovered around me — it was near the end of June — on the ends of the topmost branches only, a few minute and delicate red cone-like blossoms, the fertile flower of the white pine looking heavenward. I carried straightway to the village the topmost spire, and showed it to stranger jurymen who walked the streets — for it was court week — and to farmers and lumber-dealers and woodchoppers and hunters, and not one had ever seen the like before, but they wondered as at a star dropped down. Tell of ancient architects finishing their works on the tops of columns as perfectly as on the lower and more visible parts! Nature has from the first expanded the minute blossoms of the forest only toward the heavens, above men's heads and unobserved by them. We see only the flowers that are under our feet in the meadows. The pines have developed their delicate blossoms on the highest twigs of the wood every summer for ages, as well over the heads of Nature's red children as of her white ones; yet scarcely a farmer or hunter in the land has ever seen them.

Above all, we cannot afford not to live in the present. He is blessed over all mortals who loses no moment of the passing life in remembering the past. Unless our philosophy hears the cock crow in every barn-yard within our horizon, it is belated. That sound commonly reminds us that we are growing rusty and antique in our employments and habits of thought. His philosophy comes down to a more recent time than ours. There is something suggested by it that is a newer testament — the gospel according to this moment. He has not fallen astern; he has got up early and kept up early, and to be where he is to be in season, in the foremost rank of time. It is an expression of the health and sound-ness of Nature, a brag for all the world — healthiness as of a spring burst forth, a new fountain of the Muses, to celebrate this last instant of time. Where he lives no fugitive slave laws are passed. Who has not betrayed his master many times since last he heard that note?

The merit of this bird's strain is in its freedom from all plaintiveness. The singer can easily move us to tears or to laughter, but where is he who can excite in us a pure morning joy? When, in doleful dumps, breaking the awful stillness of our wooden sidewalk on a Sunday, or, perchance, a watcher in the house of mourning, I hear a cockerel crow far or near, I think to myself, 'There is one of us well, at any rate' — and with a sudden gush return to my senses.

We had a remarkable sunset one day last November. I was walking in a meadow, the source of a small brook, when the sun at last, just before setting, after a cold, gray day, reached a clear stratum in the horizon, and the softest, brightest morning sunlight fell on the dry grass and on the stems of the trees in the opposite horizon and on the leaves of the shrub oaks on the hillside, while our shadows stretched long over the meadow eastward, as if we were the only motes in its beams. It was such a light as we could not have imagined a moment before, and the air also was so warm and serene that nothing was wanting to make a paradise of that meadow. When we reflected that this was not a solitary phenomenon, never to happen again, but that it would happen forever and ever, an infinite number of evenings, and cheer and reassure the latest child that walked there, it was more glorious still.

The sun sets on some retired meadow, where no house is visible, with all the glory and splendor that it lavishes on cities, and perchance as it has never set before — where there is but a solitary marsh hawk to have his wings gilded by it, or only a musquash looks out from his cabin, and there is some little blackveined brook in the midst of the marsh, just beginning to meander, winding slowly round a decaying stump. We walked in so pure and bright a light, gilding the withered grass and leaves, so softly and serenely bright, I thought I had never bathed in such a golden flood, without a ripple or a murmur to it. The west side of every wood and rising ground gleamed like the boundary of Elysium, and the sun on our backs seemed like a gentle herdsman driving us home at evening.

So we saunter toward the Holy Land, till one day the sun shall shine more brightly than ever he has done, shall perchance shine into our minds and hearts, and light up our whole lives with a great awakening light, as warm and serene and golden as on a bankside in autumn.

III. AUTUMNAL TINTS

EUROPEANS coming to America are surprised by the brilliancy of our autumnal foliage. There is no account of such a phenomenon in English poetry, because the trees acquire but few bright colors there. The most that Thomson says on this subject in his 'Autumn' is contained in the lines,

> 'But see the fading many-colored woods
> Shade deepening over shade, the country round
> Imbrown; a crowded umbrage, dusk and dun,

> Of every hue, from wan declining green
> To sooty dark;'

and in the line in which he speaks of

> 'Autumn beaming o'er the yellow woods.'

The autumnal change of our woods has not made a deep impression on our own literature yet. October has hardly tinged our poetry.

A great many, who have spent their lives in cities, and have never chanced to come into the country at this season, have never seen this, the flower, or rather the ripe fruit, of the year. I remember riding with one such citizen, who, though a fortnight too late for the most brilliant tints, was taken by surprise, and would not believe that there had been any brighter. He had never heard of this phenomenon before. Not only many in our towns have never witnessed it, but it is scarcely remembered by the majority from year to year.

Most appear to confound changed leaves with withered ones, as if they were to confound ripe apples with rotten ones. I think that the change to some higher color in a leaf is an evidence that it has arrived at a late and perfect maturity, answering to the maturity of fruits. It is generally the lowest and oldest leaves which change first. But as the perfect-winged and usually bright-colored insect is short-lived, so the leaves ripen but to fall.

Generally, every fruit, on ripening, and just before it falls, when it commences a more independent and individual existence, requiring less nourishment from any source, and that not so much from the earth through its stem as from the sun and air, acquires a bright tint. So do leaves. The physiologist says it is 'due to an increased absorption of oxygen.' That is the scientific account of the matter — only a reassertion of the fact. But I am more interested in the rosy cheek than I am to know what particular diet the maiden fed on. The very forest and herbage, the pellicle of the earth, must acquire a bright color, an evidence of its ripeness — as if the globe itself were a fruit on its stem, with ever a cheek toward the sun.

Flowers are but colored leaves, fruits but ripe ones. The edible part of most fruits is, as the physiologist says, 'the parenchyma or fleshy tissue of the leaf,' of which they are formed.

Our appetites have commonly confined our views of ripeness and its phenomena, color, mellowness, and perfectness, to the fruits which we eat, and we are wont to forget that an immense harvest which we do not eat, hardly use at all, is annually ripened by Nature. At our annual cattle-shows and horticultural exhibitions, we make, as we think, a great show of fair fruits, destined, however, to a rather ignoble end, fruits not valued for their beauty chiefly. But round about and within our towns there is annually another show of fruits, on an infinitely grander scale, fruits which address our taste for beauty alone.

October is the month for painted leaves. Their rich glow now flashes round the world. As fruits and leaves and the day itself acquire a bright tint just before they fall, so the year near its setting. October is its sunset sky; November the later twilight.

I formerly thought that it would be worth the while to get a specimen leaf from each changing tree, shrub, and herbaceous plant, when it had acquired its brightest characteristic color, in its transition from the green to the brown state, outline it, and copy its color exactly, with paint, in a book, which should be entitled 'October, or Autumnal Tints' — beginning with the earliest reddening woodbine and the lake of radical leaves, and coming down through the maples, hickories, and sumachs, and many beautifully freckled leaves less generally known, to the latest oaks and aspens. What a memento such a book would be! You would need only to turn over its leaves to take a ramble through the autumn woods whenever you pleased. Or if I could preserve the leaves themselves, unfaded, it would be better still. I have made but little progress toward such a book, but I have endeavored, instead, to describe all these bright tints in the order in which they present themselves. The following are some extracts from my notes.

THE PURPLE GRASSES

By the twentieth of August, everywhere in woods and swamps we are reminded of the fall, both by the richly spotted sarsaparilla leaves and brakes, and the withering and blackened skunk-cabbage and hellebore, and, by the riverside, the already blackening pontederia.

The purple grass (*Eragrostis pectinacea*) is now in the height of its beauty. I remember still when I first noticed this grass particularly. Standing on a hillside near our river, I saw, thirty or forty rods off, a stripe of purple half a dozen rods long, under the edge of a wood, where the ground sloped toward a meadow. It was as high-colored and interesting, though not quite so bright, as the patches of rhexia, being a darker purple, like a berry's stain laid on close and thick. On going to and examining it, I found it to be a kind of grass in bloom, hardly a foot high, with but few green blades, and a fine spreading panicle of purple flowers, a shallow, purplish mist trembling around me. Close at hand it appeared but a dull purple, and made little impression on the eye; it was even difficult to detect; and if you plucked a single plant, you were surprised to find how thin it was, and how little color it had. But viewed at a distance in a favorable light, it was of a fine lively purple, flower-like, enriching the earth. Such puny causes combine to produce these decided effects. I was the more surprised and charmed because grass is commonly of a sober and humble color.

With its beautiful purple blush it reminds me, and supplies the place, of the rhexia, which is now leaving off, and it is one of the most interesting phenomena of August. The finest patches of it grow on waste strips or selvages of land at the base of dry hills, just above the edge of the meadows, where the greedy mower does not deign to swing his scythe; for this is a thin and poor grass, beneath his notice. Or, it may be, because it is so beautiful he does not know that it exists; for the same eye does not see this and timothy. He carefully gets the meadow-hay and the more nutritious grasses which grow next to that, but he leaves this fine purple mist for the walker's harvest — fodder for his fancy stock. Higher up the hill, perchance, grow also blackberries, John's-wort, and neglected, withered, and wiry June-grass. How fortunate that it grows in such places, and not in the midst of the rank grasses which are annually cut! Nature thus keeps use and beauty distinct. I know many such localities, where it does not fail to present itself annually, and paint the earth with its blush. It grows on the gentle slopes, either in a continuous patch or in scattered and rounded tufts a foot in diameter, and it lasts till it is killed by the first smart frosts.

In most plants the corolla or calyx is the part which attains the highest color, and is the most attractive; in many it is the seed-vessel or fruit; in others, as the red maple, the leaves; and in others still it is the very culm itself which is the principal flower or blooming part.

The last is especially the case with the poke or garget (*Phytolacca decandra*). Some which stand under our cliffs quite dazzle me with their purple stems now and early in September. They are as interesting to me as most flowers, and one of the most important fruits of our autumn. Every part is flower (or fruit), such is its superfluity of color — stem, branch, peduncle, pedicel, petiole, and even the at length yellowish, purple-veined leaves. Its cylindrical racemes of berries of various hues, from green to dark purple, six or seven inches long, are gracefully drooping on all sides, offering repasts to the birds; and even the sepals from which the birds have picked the berries are a brilliant lake red, with crimson flame-like reflections, equal to anything of the kind — all on fire with ripeness. Hence the *lacca*, from *lac*, lake. There are at the same time flower-buds, flowers, green berries, dark-purple or ripe ones, and these flower-like sepals, all on the same plant.

We love to see any redness in the vegetation of the temperate zone. It is the color of colors. This plant speaks to our blood. It asks a bright sun on it to make it show to best advantage, and it must be seen at this season of the year. On warm hillsides its stems are ripe by the twenty-third of August. At that date I walked through a beautiful grove of them, six or seven feet high, on the side of one of our cliffs, where they ripen early. Quite to the ground they were a deep, brilliant purple, with a bloom contrasting with the still clear green leaves. It appears a rare triumph of Nature to have produced and perfected such a plant, as if this were enough for a summer. What a perfect maturity it arrives at! It is the emblem of a successful life concluded by a death not premature, which is an ornament to Nature. What if we were to mature as perfectly, root and branch, glowing in the midst of our decay, like the poke! I confess that it excites me to behold them. I cut one for a cane, for I would fain handle and lean on it. I love to press the berries between my fingers, and see their juice staining my hand. To walk amid these upright, branching casks of purple wine, which retain and diffuse a sunset glow, tasting each one with your eye, instead of counting the pipes on a London dock, what a privilege! For Nature's vintage is not confined to the vine. Our poets have sung of wine, the product of a foreign plant which commonly they never saw, as if our own plants had no juice in them more than the singers. Indeed, this has been called by some the American grape, and, though a native of America, its juices are used in some foreign countries to improve the color of the wine; so that the poetaster may be celebrating the virtues of the poke without knowing it. Here are berries enough to paint afresh the western sky, and play the bacchanal with, if you will. And what flutes its ensanguined stems would make, to be used in such a dance! It is truly a royal plant. I could spend the evening of the year musing amid the poke stems. And perchance amid these groves might arise at last a new school of philosophy or poetry. It lasts all through September.

At the same time with this, or near the end of August, a to me very interesting genus of grasses, andropogons, or beard-grasses, is in its prime: *Andropogon furcatus*, forked beard-grass, or call it purple-fingered grass; *Andropogon scoparius*, purple wood-grass; and *Andropogon* (now called *Sorghum) nutans*, Indian-grass. The first is a very tall and slender-culmed grass, three to seven feet high, with four or five purple finger-like spikes raying upward from the top. The second is also quite slender, growing in tufts two feet high by one wide, with culms often somewhat curving, which, as the spikes go out of bloom, have a whitish, fuzzy look. These two are prevailing grasses at this season on dry and sandy fields and hillsides. The culms of both, not to mention their pretty flowers, reflect a purple tinge, and help to declare the ripeness of the year. Perhaps I have the more sympathy with them because they are despised by the farmer, and occupy sterile and neglected soil. They are high-colored, like ripe grapes, and express a maturity which the spring did not suggest. Only the August sun could have thus burnished these culms and leaves. The farmer has long since done his upland haying, and he will not condescend to bring his scythe to where these slender wild grasses have at length flowered thinly; you often see spaces of bare sand amid them. But I walk encouraged between the tufts of purple wood-grass over the sandy fields, and along the edge of the shrub oaks, glad to recognize these simple contemporaries. With thoughts cutting a broad swathe I 'get' them, with horse-raking thoughts I gather them into windrows. The fine-eared poet may hear the whetting of my scythe. These two were almost the first grasses that I learned to distinguish, for I had not known by how many friends I was surrounded; I had seen them simply as grasses standing. The purple of their culms also excites me like that of the poke-weed stems.

Think what refuge there is for one, before August is over, from college commencements and society that isolates! I can skulk amid the tufts of purple wood-grass on the borders of the 'Great Fields.' Wherever I walk these afternoons, the purple-fingered grass also stands like a guide-board, and points my thoughts to more poetic paths than they have lately travelled.

A man shall perhaps rush by and trample down plants as high as his head, and cannot be said to know that they exist, though he may have cut many tons of them, littered his stables with them, and fed them to his cattle for years. Yet, if he ever favorably attends to them, he may be overcome by their beauty. Each humblest plant, or weed, as we call it, stands there to express some thought or mood of ours; and yet how long it stands in vain! I had walked over those Great Fields so many Augusts, and never yet distinctly recognized these purple companions that I had there. I had brushed against them and trodden on them, forsooth; and now, at last, they, as it were, rose up and blessed me. Beauty and true wealth are always thus cheap and despised. Heaven might be defined as the place which men avoid. Who can doubt that these grasses, which the farmer says are of no account to him, find some compensation in your appreciation of them? I may say that I never saw them before; though, when I came to look them face to face, there did come down to me a purple gleam from previous years; and now, wherever I go, I see hardly anything else. It is the reign and presidency of the andropogons.

Almost the very sands confess the ripening influence of the August sun, and methinks, together with the slender grasses waving over them, reflect a purple tinge. The impurpled sands! Such is the consequence of all this sunshine absorbed into the pores of plants and of the earth. All sap or blood is now wine-colored. At last we have not only the purple sea, but the purple land.

The chestnut beard-grass, Indian-grass, or wood-grass, growing here and there in waste places, but more rare than the former (from two to four or five feet high), is still handsomer and of more vivid colors than its congeners, and might well have caught the Indian's eye. It has a long, narrow, one-sided, and slightly nodding panicle of bright purple and yellow flowers, like a banner raised above its reedy leaves. These bright standards are now advanced on the distant hillsides, not in large armies, but in scattered troops or single file, like the red men. They stand thus fair and bright, representative of the race which they are named after, but for the most part unobserved as they. The expression of this grass haunted me for a week, after I first passed and noticed it, like the glance of an eye. It stands like an Indian chief taking a last look at his favorite hunting-grounds.

THE RED MAPLE

By the twenty-fifth of September, the red maples generally are beginning to be ripe. Some large ones have been conspicuously changing for a week, and some single trees are now very brilliant. I notice a small one, half a mile off across a meadow, against the green woodside there, a far brighter red than the blossoms of any tree in summer, and more conspicuous. I have observed this tree for several autumns invariably changing earlier than its fellows, just as one tree ripens its fruit earlier than another. It might serve to mark the season, perhaps. I should be sorry if it were cut down. I know of two or three such trees in different parts of our town, which might, perhaps, be propagated from, as early ripeners or September trees, and their seed be advertised in the market, as well as that of radishes, if we cared as much about them.

At present these burning bushes stand chiefly along the edge of the meadows, or I distinguish them afar on the hillsides here and there. Sometimes you will see many small ones in a swamp turned quite crimson when all other trees around are still perfectly green, and the former appear so much the brighter for it. They take you by surprise, as you are going by on one side, across the fields, thus early in the season, as if it were some gay encampment of the red men, or other foresters, of whose arrival you had not heard.

Some single trees, wholly bright scarlet, seen against others of their kind still freshly green, or against evergreens, are more memorable than whole groves will be by and by. How beautiful, when a whole tree is like one great scarlet fruit full of ripe juices, every leaf, from lowest limb to topmost spire, all aglow, especially if you look toward the sun! What more remarkable object can there be in the landscape? Visible for miles, too fair to be believed. If such a phenomenon occurred but once, it would be handed down by tradition to posterity, and get into the mythology at last.

The whole tree thus ripening in advance of its fellows attains a singular preëminence, and sometimes maintains it for a week or two. I am thrilled at the sight of it, bearing aloft its scarlet standard for the regiment of green-clad foresters around, and I go half a mile out of my way to examine it. A single tree becomes thus the crowning beauty of some meadowy vale, and the expression of the whole surrounding forest is at once more spirited for it.

A small red maple has grown, perchance, far away at the head of some retired valley, a mile from any road, unobserved. It has faithfully discharged the duties of a maple there, all winter and summer, neglected none of its economies, but added to its stature in the virtue which belongs to a maple, by a steady growth for so many months, never having gone gadding abroad, and is nearer heaven than it was in the spring. It has faithfully husbanded its sap, and afforded a shelter to the wandering bird, has long since ripened its seeds and committed them to the winds, and has the satisfaction of knowing, perhaps, that a thousand little well-behaved maples are already settled in life somewhere. It deserves well of Mapledom. Its leaves have been asking it from time to time, in a whisper, 'When shall we redden?' And now, in this month of September, this month of travelling, when men are hastening to the seaside, or the mountains, or the lakes, this modest maple, still without budging an inch, travels in its reputation — runs up its scarlet flag on that hillside, which shows that it has finished its summer's work before all other trees, and withdraws from the contest. At the eleventh hour of the year, the tree which no scrutiny could have detected here when it was most industrious is thus, by the tint of its maturity, by its very blushes, revealed at last to the careless and distant traveller, and leads his thoughts away from the dusty road into those brave solitudes which it inhabits. It flashes out conspicuous with all the virtue and beauty of a maple — *Acer rubrum*. We may now read its title, or *rubric*, clear. Its *virtues*, not its sins, are as scarlet.

Notwithstanding the red maple is the most intense scarlet of any of our trees, the sugar maple has been the most celebrated, and Michaux in his 'Sylva' does not speak of the autumnal color of the former. About the second of October, these trees, both large and small, are most brilliant, though many are still green. In 'sprout-lands' they seem to vie with one another, and ever some particular one in the midst of the crowd will be of a peculiarly pure scarlet, and by its more intense color attract our eye even at a distance, and carry off the palm. A large red maple swamp, when at the height of its change, is the most obviously brilliant of all tangible things, where I dwell, so abundant is this tree with us. It varies much both in form and color. A great many are merely yellow; more, scarlet; others, scarlet deepening into crimson, more red than common. Look at yonder swamp of maples mixed with pines, at the base of a pine-clad hill, a quarter of a mile off, so that you get the full effect of the bright colors, without detecting the imperfections of the leaves, and see their yellow, scarlet, and crimson fires, of all tints, mingled and contrasted with the green. Some maples are yet green, only yellow or crimson-tipped on the edges of their flakes, like the edges of a hazelnut bur; some are wholly brilliant scarlet, raying out regularly and finely every way, bilaterally, like the veins of a leaf; others, of more irregular form, when I turn my head slightly, emptying out some of its earthiness and concealing the trunk of the tree, seem to rest heavily flake on flake, like yellow and scarlet clouds, wreath upon wreath, or like snow-drifts driving through the air, stratified by the wind. It adds greatly to the beauty of such a swamp at this season, that, even though there may be no other trees interspersed, it is not seen as a simple mass of color, but, different trees being of different colors and hues, the outline of each crescent treetop is distinct, and where one laps on to another. Yet a painter would hardly venture to make them thus distinct a quarter of a mile off.

As I go across a meadow directly toward a low rising ground this bright afternoon, I see, some fifty rods off toward the sun, the top of a maple swamp just appearing over the sheeny russet edge of the hill, a stripe apparently twenty rods long by ten feet deep, of the most intensely brilliant scarlet, orange, and yellow, equal to any flowers or fruits, or any tints ever painted. As I advance, lowering the edge of the hill which makes the firm foreground or lower frame of the picture, the depth of the brilliant grove revealed steadily increases, suggesting that the whole of the inclosed valley is filled with such color. One wonders that the tithing-men and fathers of the town are not out to see what the trees mean by their high colors and exuberance of spirits, fearing that some mischief is brewing. I do not see what the Puritans did at this season, when the maples blaze out in scarlet. They certainly could not have worshipped in groves then. Perhaps that is what they built meeting-houses and fenced them round with horse-sheds for.

THE ELM

Now too, the first of October, or later, the elms are at the height of their autumnal beauty — great brownish-yellow masses, warm from their September oven, hanging over the highway. Their leaves are perfectly ripe. I wonder if there is any answering ripeness in the lives of the men who live beneath them. As I look down our street, which is lined with them, they remind me both by their form and color of yellowing sheaves of grain, as if the harvest had indeed come to the village itself, and we might expect to find some maturity and *flavor* in the thoughts of the villagers at last. Under those bright rustling yellow piles just ready to fall on the heads of the walkers, how can any crudity or greenness of thought or act prevail? When I stand where half a dozen large elms droop over a house, it is as if I stood within a ripe pumpkin-rind, and I feel as mellow as if I were the pulp, though I may be somewhat stringy and seedy withal. What is the late greenness of the English elm, like a cucumber out of season, which does not know when to have done, compared with the early and golden maturity of the American tree? The street is the scene of a great harvest-home. It would be worth the while to set out these trees, if only for their autumnal value. Think of these great yellow canopies or parasols held over our heads and houses by the mile together, making the village all one and compact — an *ulmarium*, which is at the same time a nursery of men! And then how gently and unobserved they drop their burden and let in the

sun when it is wanted, their leaves not heard when they fall on our roofs
and in our streets; and thus the village parasol is shut up and put away!
I see the market-man driving into the village, and disappearing under
its canopy of elm-tops, with *his* crop, as into a great granary or barn-
yard. I am tempted to go thither as to a husking of thoughts, now dry
and ripe, and ready to be separated from their integuments; but, alas!
I foresee that it will be chiefly husks and little thought, blasted pig-corn,
fit only for cob-meal — for, as you sow, so shall you reap.

FALLEN LEAVES

By the sixth of October the leaves generally begin to fall, in successive
showers, after frost or rain; but the principal leaf-harvest, the acme of
the *Fall*, is commonly about the sixteenth. Some morning at that date
there is perhaps a harder frost than we have seen, and ice formed under
the pump, and now, when the morning wind rises, the leaves come down
in denser showers than ever. They suddenly form thick beds or carpets
on the ground, in this gentle air, or even without wind, just the size
and form of the tree above. Some trees, as small hickories, appear to
have dropped their leaves instantaneously, as a soldier grounds arms at
a signal; and those of the hickory, being bright yellow still, though
withered, reflect a blaze of light from the ground where they lie. Down
they have come on all sides, at the first earnest touch of autumn's
wand, making a sound like rain.

Or else it is after moist and rainy weather that we notice how great
a fall of leaves there has been in the night, though it may not yet be the
touch that loosens the rock maple leaf. The streets are thickly strewn
with the trophies, and fallen elm leaves make a dark brown pavement
under our feet. After some remarkably warm Indian-summer day or
days, I perceive that it is the unusual heat which, more than anything,
causes the leaves to fall, there having been, perhaps, no frost nor rain
for some time. The intense heat suddenly ripens and wilts them, just
as it softens and ripens peaches and other fruits, and causes them to drop.

The leaves of late red maples, still bright, strew the earth, often
crimson-spotted on a yellow ground, like some wild apples — though
they preserve these bright colors on the ground but a day or two,
especially if it rains. On causeways I go by trees here and there all bare
and smoke-like, having lost their brilliant clothing; but there it lies,
nearly as bright as ever, on the ground on one side, and making nearly
as regular a figure as lately on the tree. I would rather say that I first

observe the trees thus flat on the ground like a permanent colored shadow, and they suggest to look for the boughs that bore them. A queen might be proud to walk where these gallant trees have spread their bright cloaks in the mud. I see wagons roll over them as a shadow or a reflection, and the drivers heed them just as little as they did their shadows before.

Birds' nests, in the huckleberry and other shrubs, and in trees, are already being filled with the withered leaves. So many have fallen in the woods that a squirrel cannot run after a falling nut without being heard. Boys are raking them in the streets, if only for the pleasure of dealing with such clean, crisp substances. Some sweep the paths scrupulously neat, and then stand to see the next breath strew them with new trophies. The swamp floor is thickly covered, and the *Lycopodium lucidulum* looks suddenly greener amid them. In dense woods they half cover pools that are three or four rods long. The other day I could hardly find a well-known spring, and even suspected that it had dried up, for it was completely concealed by freshly fallen leaves; and when I swept them aside and revealed it, it was like striking the earth, with Aaron's rod, for a new spring. Wet grounds about the edges of swamps look dry with them. At one swamp, where I was surveying, thinking to step on a leafy shore from a rail, I got into the water more than a foot deep.

When I go to the river the day after the principal fall of leaves, the sixteenth, I find my boat all covered, bottom and seats, with the leaves of the golden willow under which it is moored, and I set sail with a cargo of them rustling under my feet. If I empty it, it will be full again tomorrow. I do not regard them as litter, to be swept out, but accept them as suitable straw or matting for the bottom of my carriage. When I turn up into the mouth of the Assabet, which is wooded, large fleets of leaves are floating on its surface, as it were getting out to sea, with room to tack; but next the shore, a little farther up, they are thicker than foam, quite concealing the water for a rod in width, under and amid the alders, button-bushes, and maples, still perfectly light and dry, with fibre unrelaxed; and at a rocky bend where they are met and stopped by the morning wind, they sometimes form a broad and dense crescent quite across the river. When I turn my prow that way, and the wave which it makes strikes them, list what a pleasant rustling from these dry substances getting on one another! Often it is their undulation only which reveals the water beneath them. Also every motion of the wood turtle on the shore is betrayed by their rustling there. Or even in mid-channel, when the wind rises, I hear them blown with a rustling sound. Higher up they are slowly moving round and round in some great eddy which the river makes, as that at the 'Leaning Hemlocks,' where the water is deep, and the current is wearing into the bank.

Perchance, in the afternoon of such a day, when the water is perfectly calm and full of reflections, I paddle gently down the main stream, and turning up the Assabet, reach a quiet cove, where I unexpectedly find myself surrounded by myriads of leaves, like fellow-voyagers, which seem to have the same purpose, or want of purpose, with myself. See this great fleet of scattered leaf-boats which we paddle amid, in this smooth river-bay, each one curled up on every side by the sun's skill, each nerve a stiff spruce knee — like boats of hide, and of all patterns — Charon's boat probably among the rest — and some with lofty prows and poops, like the stately vessels of the ancients, scarcely moving in the sluggish current — like the great fleets, the dense Chinese cities of boats, with which you mingle on entering some great mart, some New York or Canton, which we are all steadily approaching together. How gently each has been deposited on the water! No violence has been used towards them yet, though, perchance, palpitating hearts were present at the launching. And painted ducks, too, the splendid wood duck among the rest, often come to sail and float amid the painted leaves — barks of a nobler model still!

What wholesome herb drinks are to be had in the swamps now! What strong medicinal but rich scents from the decaying leaves! The rain falling on the freshly dried herbs and leaves, and filling the pools and ditches into which they have dropped thus clean and rigid, will soon convert them into tea — green, black, brown, and yellow teas, of all degrees of strength, enough to set all Nature a-gossiping. Whether we drink them or not, as yet, before their strength is drawn, these leaves, dried on great Nature's coppers, are of such various pure and delicate tints as might make the fame of Oriental teas.

How they are mixed up, of all species, oak and maple and chestnut and birch! But Nature is not cluttered with them; she is a perfect husbandman; she stores them all. Consider what a vast crop is thus annually shed on the earth! This, more than any mere grain or seed, is the great harvest of the year. The trees are now repaying the earth with interest what they have taken from it. They are discounting. They are about to add a leaf's thickness to the depth of the soil. This is the beautiful way in which Nature gets her muck, while I chaffer with this man and that, who talks to me about sulphur and the cost of carting. We are all the richer for their decay. I am more interested in this crop than in the English grass alone or in the corn. It prepares the virgin mould for future corn-fields and forests, on which the earth fattens. It keeps our homestead in good heart.

For beautiful variety no crop can be compared with this. Here is not merely the plain yellow of the grains, but nearly all the colors that we know, the brightest blue not excepted: the early blushing maple, the poison sumach blazing its sins as scarlet, the mulberry ash, the rich chrome yellow of the poplars, the brilliant red huckleberry, with which the hills' backs are painted, like those of sheep. The frost touches them, and, with the slightest breath of returning day or jarring of earth's axle, see in what showers they come floating down! The ground is all parti-colored with them. But they still live in the soil, whose fertility and bulk they increase, and in the forests that spring from it. They stoop to rise, to mount higher in coming years, by subtle chemistry, climbing by the sap in the trees; and the sapling's first fruits thus shed, transmuted at last, may adorn its crown, when, in after years, it has become the monarch of the forest.

It is pleasant to walk over the beds of these fresh, crisp, and rustling leaves. How beautifully they go to their graves! how gently lay themselves down and turn to mould! — painted of a thousand hues, and fit to make the beds of us living. So they troop to their last resting-place, light and frisky. They put on no weeds, but merrily they go scampering over the earth, selecting the spot, choosing a lot, ordering no iron fence, whispering all through the woods about it — some choosing the spot where the bodies of men are mouldering beneath, and meeting them half-way. How many flutterings before they rest quietly in their graves! They that soared so loftily, how contentedly they return to dust again, and are laid low, resigned to lie and decay at the foot of the tree, and afford nourishment to new generations of their kind, as well as to flutter on high! They teach us how to die. One wonders if the time will ever come when men, with their boasted faith in immortality, will lie down as gracefully and as ripe — with such an Indian-summer serenity will shed their bodies, as they do their hair and nails.

When the leaves fall, the whole earth is a cemetery pleasant to walk in. I love to wander and muse over them in their graves. Here are no lying nor vain epitaphs. What though you own no lot at Mount Auburn? Your lot is surely cast somewhere in this vast cemetery, which has been consecrated from of old. You need attend no auction to secure a place. There is room enough here. The loosestrife shall bloom and the huckleberry-bird sing over your bones. The woodman and hunter shall be your sextons, and the children shall tread upon the borders as much as they will. Let us walk in the cemetery of the leaves; this is your true Greenwood Cemetery.

THE SUGAR MAPLE

But think not that the splendor of the year is over; for as one leaf does not make a summer, neither does one falling leaf make an autumn. The smallest sugar maples in our streets make a great show as early as the fifth of October, more than any other trees there. As I look up the main street, they appear like painted screens standing before the houses; yet many are green. But now, or generally by the seventeenth of October, when almost all red maples and some white maples are bare, the large sugar maples also are in their glory, glowing with yellow and red, and show unexpectedly bright and delicate tints. They are remarkable for the contrast they often afford of deep blushing red on one half and green on the other. They become at length dense masses of rich yellow with a deep scarlet blush, or more than blush, on the exposed surfaces. They are the brightest trees now in the street.

The large ones on our Common are particularly beautiful. A delicate but warmer than golden yellow is now the prevailing color, with scarlet cheeks. Yet, standing on the east side of the Common just before sundown, when the western light is transmitted through them, I see that their yellow even, compared with the pale lemon yellow of an elm close by, amounts to a scarlet, without noticing the bright scarlet portions. Generally, they are great regular oval masses of yellow and scarlet. All the sunny warmth of the season, the Indian summer, seems to be absorbed in their leaves. The lowest and inmost leaves next the bole are, as usual, of the most delicate yellow and green, like the complexion of young men brought up in the house. There is an auction on the Common today, but its red flag is hard to be discerned amid this blaze of color.

Little did the fathers of the town anticipate this brilliant success, when they caused to be imported from farther in the country some straight poles with their tops cut off, which they called sugar maples; and, as I remember, after they were set out, a neighboring merchant's clerk, by way of jest, planted beans about them. Those which were then jestingly called bean-poles are today far the most beautiful objects noticeable in our streets. They are worth all and more than they have cost — though one of the selectmen, while setting them out, took the cold which occasioned his death — if only because they have filled the open eyes of children with their rich color unstintedly so many Octobers. We will not ask them to yield us sugar in the spring, while they afford us so fair a prospect in the autumn. Wealth indoors may be the inheritance of few, but it is equally distributed on the Common. All children alike can revel in this golden harvest.

Surely trees should be set in our streets with a view to their October splendor, though I doubt whether this is ever considered by the 'Tree Society.' Do you not think it will make some odds to these children that they were brought up under the maples? Hundreds of eyes are steadily drinking in this color, and by these teachers even the truants are caught and educated the moment they step abroad. Indeed, neither the truant nor the studious is at present taught color in the schools. These are instead of the bright colors in apothecaries' shops and city windows. It is a pity that we have no more *red* maples, and some hickories, in our streets as well. Our paint-box is very imperfectly filled. Instead of, or beside, supplying such paint-boxes as we do, we might supply these natural colors to the young. Where else will they study color under greater advantages? What School of Design can vie with this? Think how much the eyes of painters of all kinds, and of manufacturers of cloth and paper, and paper-stainers, and countless others, are to be educated by these autumnal colors. The stationer's envelopes may be of very various tints, yet not so various as those of the leaves of a single tree. If you want a different shade or tint of a particular color, you have only to look farther within or without the tree or the wood. These leaves are not many dipped in one dye, as at the dye-house, but they are dyed in light of infinitely various degrees of strength and left to set and dry there.

Shall the names of so many of our colors continue to be derived from those of obscure foreign localities, as Naples yellow, Prussian blue, raw Sienna, burnt Umber, Gamboge? (surely the Tyrian purple must have faded by this time), or from comparatively trivial articles of commerce — chocolate, lemon, coffee, cinnamon, claret? (shall we compare our hickory to a lemon, or a lemon to a hickory?) or from ores and oxides which few ever see? Shall we so often, when describing to our neighbors the color of something we have seen, refer them, not to some natural object in our neighborhood, but perchance to a bit of earth fetched from the other side of the planet, which possibly they may find at the apothecary's, but which probably neither they nor we ever saw? Have we not an *earth* under our feet — aye, and a sky over our heads? Or is the last *all* ultramarine? What do we know of sapphire, amethyst, emerald, ruby, amber, and the like — most of us who take these names in vain? Leave these precious words to cabinet-keepers, virtuosos, and maids-of-honor — to the Nabobs, Begums, and Chobdars of Hindostan, or wherever else. I do not see why, since America and her autumn woods have been discovered, our leaves should not compete with the precious stones in giving names to colors; and, indeed, I believe that in course of time the names of some of our trees and shrubs, as well as flowers, will get into our popular chromatic nomenclature.

But of much more importance than a knowledge of the names and distinctions of color is the joy and exhilaration which these colored leaves excite. Already these brilliant trees throughout the street, without any more variety, are at least equal to an annual festival and holiday, or a week of such. These are cheap and innocent gala-days, celebrated by one and all without the aid of committees or marshals, such a show as may safely be licensed, not attracting gamblers or rum-sellers, not requiring any special police to keep the peace. And poor indeed must be that New England village's October which has not the maple in its streets. This October festival costs no powder, nor ringing of bells, but every tree is a living liberty-pole on which a thousand bright flags are waving.

No wonder that we must have our annual cattle-show, and fall training, and perhaps cornwallis, our September courts, and the like. Nature herself holds her annual fair in October, not only in the streets, but in every hollow and on every hillside. When lately we looked into that red maple swamp all ablaze, where the trees were clothed in their vestures of most dazzling tints, did it not suggest a thousand gypsies beneath — a race capable of wild delight — or even the fabled fauns, satyrs, and wood-nymphs come back to earth? Or was it only a congregation of wearied woodchoppers, or of proprietors come to inspect their lots, that we thought of? Or, earlier still, when we paddled on the river through that fine-grained September air, did there not appear to be something new going on under the sparkling surface of the stream, a shaking of props, at least, so that we made haste in order to be up in time? Did not the rows of yellowing willows and button-bushes on each side seem like rows of booths, under which, perhaps, some fluviatile egg-pop equally yellow was effervescing? Did not all these suggest that man's spirits should rise as high as Nature's — should hang out their flag, and the routine of his life be interrupted by an analogous expression of joy and hilarity?

No annual teaching or muster of solidery, no celebration with its scarfs and banners, could import into the town a hundredth part of the annual splendor of our October. We have only to set the trees, or let them stand, and Nature will find the colored drapery — flags of all her nations, some of whose private signals hardly the botanist can read — while we walk under the triumphal arches of the elms. Leave it to Nature to appoint the days, whether the same as in neighboring States or not, and let the clergy read her proclamations, if they can understand them. Behold what a brilliant drapery is her woodbine flag! What public-spirited merchant, think you, has contributed this part of the show? There is no handsomer shingling and paint than this vine, at present covering a whole side of some houses. I do not believe that the ivy *never sere* is comparable to it. No wonder it has been extensively introduced into London. Let us have a good many maples and hickories and scarlet oaks, then, I say. Blaze away! Shall that dirty roll of bunting in the gun-house be all the colors a village can display? A village is not complete, unless it have these trees to mark the season in it. They are important, like the town clock. A village that has them not will not be found to work well. It has a screw loose, an essential part is wanting. Let us have willows for spring, elms for summer, maples and walnuts and tupeloes for autumn, evergreens for winter, and oaks for all seasons. What is a gallery in a house to a gallery in the streets, which every market-man rides through, whether he will or not? Of course, there is not a picture-gallery in the country which would be worth so much to us as is the western view at sunset under the elms of our main street. They are the frame to a picture which is daily painted behind them. An avenue of elms as large as our largest and three miles long would seem to lead to some admirable place, though only C—— were at the end of it.

A village needs these innocent stimulants of bright and cheering prospects to keep off melancholy and superstition. Show me two villages, one embowered in trees and blazing with all the glories of October, the other a merely trivial and treeless waste, or with only a single tree or two for suicides, and I shall be sure that in the latter will be found the most starved and bigoted religionists and the most desperate drinkers. Every wash-tub and milk-can and gravestone will be exposed. The inhabitants will disappear abruptly behind their barns and houses, like desert Arabs amid their rocks, and I shall look to see spears in their hands. They will be ready to accept the most barren and forlorn doctrine — as that the world is speedily coming to an end, or has already got to it, or that they themselves are turned wrong side outward. They will perchance crack their dry joints at one another and call it a spiritual communication.

But to confine ourselves to the maples. What if we were to take half as much pains in protecting them as we do in setting them out — not stupidly tie our horses to our dahlia stems?

What meant the fathers by establishing this *perfectly living* institution before the church — this institution which needs no repairing nor repainting, which is continually enlarged and repaired by its growth? Surely they

> 'Wrought in sad sincerity;
>   Themselves from God they could not free;
>   They *planted* better than they knew; —
>   The conscious *trees* to beauty grew.'

Verily these maples are cheap preachers, permanently settled, which preach their half-century, and century, aye, and century-and-a-half sermons, with constantly increasing unction and influence, ministering to many generations of men; and the least we can do is to supply them with suitable colleagues as they grow infirm.

THE SCARLET OAK

Belonging to a genus which is remarkable for the beautiful form of its leaves, I suspect that some scarlet oak leaves surpass those of all other oaks in the rich and wild beauty of their outlines. I judge from an acquaintance with twelve species, and from drawings which I have seen of many others.

Stand under this tree and see how finely its leaves are cut against the sky — as it were, only a few sharp points extending from a midrib. They look like double, treble, or quadruple crosses. They are far more ethereal than the less deeply scalloped oak leaves. They have so little leafy *terra firma* that they appear melting away in the light, and scarcely obstruct our view. The leaves of very young plants are, like those of full-grown oaks of other species, more entire, simple, and lumpish in their outlines, but these, raised high on old trees, have solved the leafy problem. Lifted higher and higher, and sublimated more and more, putting off some earthiness and cultivating more intimacy with the light each year, they have at length the least possible amount of earthy matter, and the greatest spread and grasp of skyey influences. There they dance, arm in arm with the light — tripping it on fantastic points, fit partners in those aerial halls. So intimately mingled are they with it, that, what with their slenderness and their glossy surfaces, you can hardly tell at last what in the dance is leaf and what is light. And when no zephyr stirs, they are at most but a rich tracery to the forest windows.

I am again struck with their beauty, when, a month later, they thickly strew the ground in the woods, piled one upon another under my feet. They are then brown above, but purple beneath. With their narrow lobes and their bold, deep scallops reaching almost to the middle, they suggest that the material must be cheap, or else there has been a lavish expense in their creation, as if so much had been cut out. Or else they seem to us the remnants of the stuff out of which leaves have been cut with a die. Indeed, when they lie thus one upon another, they remind me of a pile of scrap-tin.

Or bring one home, and study it closely at your leisure, by the fireside. It is a type, not from any Oxford font, not in the Basque nor the arrow-headed character, not found on the Rosetta Stone, but destined to be copied in sculpture one day, if they ever get to whittling stone here. What a wild and pleasing outline, a combination of graceful curves and angles! The eye rests with equal delight on what is not leaf and on what is leaf — on the broad, free, open sinuses, and on the long, sharp, bristle-pointed lobes. A simple oval outline would include it all, if you connected the points of the leaf; but how much richer is it than that, with its half-dozen deep scallops, in which the eye and thought of the beholder are embayed! If I were a drawing-master, I would set my pupils to copying these leaves, that they might learn to draw firmly and gracefully.

Regarded as water, it is like a pond with half a dozen broad rounded promontories extending nearly to its middle, half from each side, while its watery bays extend far inland, like sharp friths, at each of whose heads several fine streams empty in — almost a leafy archipelago.

But it oftener suggests land, and, as Dionysius and Pliny compared the form of the Morea to that of the leaf of the Oriental plane tree, so this leaf reminds me of some fair wild island in the ocean, whose extensive coast, alternate rounded bays with smooth strands, and sharp-pointed rocky capes, mark it as fitted for the habitation of man, and destined to become a centre of civilization at last. To the sailor's eye, it is a much indented shore. Is it not, in fact, a shore to the aerial ocean, on which the windy surf beats? At sight of this leaf we are all mariners — if not vikings, buccaneers, and filibusters. Both our love of repose and our spirit of adventure are addressed. In our most casual glance, perchance, we think that if we succeed in doubling those sharp capes we shall find deep, smooth, and secure havens in the ample bays. How different from the white oak leaf, with its rounded headlands, on which no lighthouse need be placed! That is an England, with its long civil history, that may be read. This is some still unsettled New-found Island or Celebes. Shall we go and be rajahs there?

By the twenty-sixth of October the large scarlet oaks are in their prime, when other oaks are usually withered. They have been kindling their fires for a week past, and now generally burst into a blaze. This alone of *our* indigenous deciduous trees (excepting the dogwood, of which I do not know half a dozen, and they are but large bushes) is now in its glory. The two aspens and the sugar maple come nearest to it in date, but they have lost the greater part of their leaves. Of evergreens, only the pitch pine is still commonly bright.

But it requires a particular alertness, if not devotion to these phenomena, to appreciate the wide-spread, but late and unexpected glory of the scarlet oaks. I do not speak here of the small trees and shrubs, which are commonly observed, and which are now withered, but of the large trees. Most go in and shut their doors, thinking that bleak and colorless November has already come, when some of the most brilliant and memorable colors are not yet lit.

This very perfect and vigorous one, about forty feet high, standing in an open pasture, which was quite glossy green on the twelfth, is now, the twenty-sixth, completely changed to bright dark-scarlet — every leaf, between you and the sun, as if it had been dipped into a scarlet dye. The whole tree is much like a heart in form, as well as color. Was not this worth waiting for? Little did you think, ten days ago, that that cold green tree would assume such color as this. Its leaves are still firmly attached, while those of other trees are falling around it. It seems to say: 'I am the last to blush, but I blush deeper than any of ye. I bring up the rear in my red coat. We scarlet ones, alone of oaks, have not given up the fight.'

The sap is now, and even far into November, frequently flowing fast in these trees, as in maples in the spring; and apparently their bright tints, now that most other oaks are withered, are connected with this phenomenon. They are full of life. It has a pleasantly astringent, acorn-like taste, this strong oak wine, as I find on tapping them with my knife.

Looking across this woodland valley, a quarter of a mile wide, how rich those scarlet oaks embosomed in pines, their bright red branches intimately intermingled with them! They have their full effect there. The pine boughs are the green calyx to their red petals. Or, as we go along a road in the woods, the sun striking endwise through it, and lighting up the red tents of the oaks, which on each side are mingled with the liquid green of the pines, makes a very gorgeous scene. Indeed, without the evergreens for contrast, the autumnal tints would lose much of their effect.

The scarlet oak asks a clear sky and the brightness of late October days. These bring out its colors. If the sun goes into a cloud they become comparatively indistinct. As I sit on a cliff in the southwest part of our town, the sun is now getting low, and the woods in Lincoln, south and east of me, are lit up by its more level rays; and in the scarlet oaks, scattered so equally over the forest, there is brought out a more brilliant redness than I had believed was in them. Every tree of this species which is visible in those directions, even to the horizon, now stands out distinctly red. Some great ones lift their red backs high above the woods, in the next town, like huge roses with a myriad of fine petals; and some more slender ones, in a small grove of white pines on Pine Hill in the east, on the very verge of the horizon, alternating with the pines on the edge of the grove, and shouldering them with their red coats, look like soldiers in red amid hunters in green. This time it is Lincoln green, too. Till the sun got low, I did not believe that there were so many red-coats in the forest army. Theirs is an intense, burning red, which would lose some of its strength, methinks, with every step you might take toward them; for the shade that lurks amid their foliage does not report itself at this distance, and they are unanimously red. The focus of their reflected color is in the atmosphere far on this side. Every such tree becomes a nucleus of red, as it were, where, with the declining sun, that color grows and glows. It is partly borrowed fire, gathering strength from the sun on its way to your eye. It has only some comparatively dull red leaves for a rallying-point, or kindling-stuff, to start it, and it becomes an intense scarlet or red mist, or fire, which finds fuel for itself in the very atmosphere. So vivacious is redness. The very rails reflect a rosy light at this hour and season. You see a redder tree than exists.

If you wish to count the scarlet oaks, do it now. In a clear day stand thus on a hilltop in the woods, when the sun is an hour high, and every one within range of your vision, excepting in the west, will be revealed. You might live to the age of Methuselah and never find a tithe of them, otherwise. Yet sometimes even in a dark day I have thought them as bright as I ever saw them. Looking westward, their colors are lost in a blaze of light; but in other directions the whole forest is a flower-garden, in which these late roses burn, alternating with green, while the so-called 'gardeners,' walking here and there, perchance, beneath, with spade and water-pot, see only a few little asters amid withered leaves.

These are *my* China-asters, *my* late garden-flowers. It costs me nothing for a gardener. The falling leaves, all over the forest, are protecting the roots of my plants. Only look at what is to be seen, and you will have garden enough, without deepening the soil in your yard. We have only to elevate our view a little, to see the whole forest as a garden. The blossoming of the scarlet oak — the forest-flower, surpassing all in splendor (at least since the maple)! I do not know but they interest me more than the maples, they are so widely and equally dispersed through-out the forest; they are so hardy, a nobler tree on the whole; our chief November flower, abiding the approach of winter with us, imparting warmth to early November prospects. It is remarkable that the latest bright color that is general should be this deep, dark scarlet and red, the intensest of colors. The ripest fruit of the year; like the cheek of a hard, glossy red apple, from the cold Isle of Orleans, which will not be mellow for eating till next spring! When I rise to a hilltop, a thousand of these great oak roses, distributed on every side, as far as the horizon! I admire them four or five miles off! This my unfailing prospect for a fortnight past! This late forest-flower surpasses all that spring or summer could do. Their colors were but rare and dainty specks comparatively (created for the nearsighted, who walk amid the humblest herbs and underwoods), and made no impression on a distant eye. Now it is an extended forest or a mountain-side, through or along which we journey from day to day, that bursts into bloom. Comparatively, our gardening is on a petty scale — the gardener still nursing a few asters amid dead weeds, ignorant of the gigantic asters and roses which, as it were, over-shadow him, and ask for none of his care. It is like a little red paint ground on a saucer, and held up against the sunset sky. Why not take more elevated and broader views, walk in the great garden; not skulk in a little 'debauched' nook of it? consider the beauty of the forest, and not merely of a few impounded herbs?

Let your walks now be a little more adventurous; ascend the hills. If, about the last of October, you ascend any hill in the outskirts of our town, and probably of yours, and look over the forest, you may see — well, what I have endeavored to describe. All this you surely *will* see, and much more, if you are prepared to see it — if you *look* for it. Otherwise, regular and universal as this phenomenon is, whether you stand on the hilltop or in the hollow, you will think for threescore years and ten that all the wood is, at this season, sere and brown. Objects are concealed from our view, not so much because they are out of the course of our visual ray as because we do not bring our minds and eyes to bear on them; for there is no power to see in the eye itself, any more than in any other jelly. We do not realize how far and widely, or how near and narrowly, we are to look. The greater part of the phenomena of Nature are for this reason concealed from us all our lives. The gardener sees only the gardener's garden. Here, too, as in political economy, the supply answers to the demand. Nature does not cast pearls before swine. There is just as much beauty visible to us in the landscape as we are prepared to appreciate — not a grain more. The actual objects which one man will see from a particular hilltop are just as different from those which another will see as the beholders are different. The scarlet oak must, in a sense, be in your eye when you go forth. We cannot see anything until we are possessed with the idea of it, take it into our heads — and then we can hardly see anything else. In my botanical rambles I find that, first, the idea, or image, of a plant occupies my thoughts, though it may seem very foreign to this locality — no nearer than Hudson's Bay — and for some weeks or months I go thinking of it, and expecting it, unconsciously, and at length I surely see it. This is the history of my finding a score or more of rare plants which I could name. A man sees only what concerns him. A botanist absorbed in the study of grasses does not distinguish the grandest pasture oaks. He, as it were, tramples down oaks unwittingly in his walk, or at most sees only their shadows. I have found that it required a different intention of the eye, in the same locality, to see different plants, even when they were closely allied, as *Juncaceae* and *Gramineae:* when I was looking for the former, I did not see the latter in the midst of them. How much more, then, it requires different intentions of the eye and of the mind to attend to different departments of knowledge! How differently the poet and the naturalist look at objects!

Take a New England selectman, and set him on the highest of our hills, and tell him to look — sharpening his sight to the utmost, and putting on the glasses that suit him best (aye, using a spy-glass, if he likes) — and make a full report. What, probably, will he *spy?* — what will he *select* to look at? Of course, he will see a Brocken spectre of himself. He will see several meeting-houses, at least, and, perhaps, that somebody ought to be assessed higher than he is, since he has so handsome a wood-lot. Now take Julius Cæsar, or Emanuel Swedenborg, or a Fiji-Islander, and set him up there. Or suppose all together, and let them compare notes afterward. Will it appear that they have enjoyed the same prospect? What they will see will be as different as Rome was from heaven or hell, or the last from the Fiji Islands. For aught we know, as strange a man as any of these is always at our elbow.

Why, it takes a sharpshooter to bring down even such trivial game as snipes and woodcocks; he must take very particular aim, and know what he is aiming at. He would stand a very small chance, if he fired at random into the sky, being told that snipes were flying there. And so is it with him that shoots at beauty; though he wait till the sky falls, he will not bag any, if he does not already know its seasons and haunts, and the color of its wing — if he has not dreamed of it, so that he can *anticipate* it; then, indeed, he flushes it at every step, shoots double and on the wing, with both barrels, even in corn-fields. The sportsman trains himself, dresses, and watches unweariedly, and loads and primes for his particular game. He prays for it, and offers sacrifices, and so he gets it. After due and long preparation, schooling his eye and hand, dreaming awake and asleep, with gun and paddle and boat, he goes out after meadow-hens, which most of his townsmen never saw nor dreamed of, and paddles for miles against a head wind, and wades in water up to his knees, being out all day without his dinner, and *therefore* he gets them. He had them half-way into his bag when he started, and has only to shove them down. The true sportsman can shoot you almost any of his game from his windows: what else has he windows or eyes for? It comes and perches at last on the barrel of his gun; but the rest of the world never see it *with the feathers on.* The geese fly exactly under his zenith, and honk when they get there, and he will keep himself supplied by firing up his chimney; twenty musquash have the refusal of each one of his traps before it is empty. If he lives, and his game spirit increases, heaven and earth shall fail him sooner than game; and when he dies, he will go to more extensive and, perchance, happier hunting-grounds. The fisherman, too, dreams of fish, sees a bobbing cork in his dreams, till he can almost catch them in his sink-spout. I knew a girl who, being sent to pick huckleberries, picked wild gooseberries by the quart, where no one else knew that there were any, because she was accustomed to pick them up-country where she came from. The astronomer knows where to go star-gathering, and sees one clearly in his mind before any have seen it with a glass. The hen scratches and finds her food right under where she stands; but such is not the way with the hawk.

These bright leaves which I have mentioned are not the exception, but the rule; for I believe that all leaves, even grasses and mosses, acquire brighter colors just before their fall. When you come to observe faithfully the changes of each humblest plant, you find that each has, sooner or later, its peculiar autumnal tint; and if you undertake to make a complete list of the bright tints, it will be nearly as long as a catalogue of the plants in your vicinity.

IV. WILD APPLES

THE HISTORY OF THE APPLE TREE

It is remarkable how closely the history of the apple tree is connected with that of man. The geologist tells us that the order of the *Rosaceae* which includes the apple, also the true grasses, and the *Labiatae*, or mints, were introduced only a short time previous to the appearance of man on the globe.

It appears that apples made a part of the food of that unknown primitive people whose traces have lately been found at the bottom of the Swiss lakes, supposed to be older than the foundation of Rome, so old that they had no metallic implements. An entire black and shrivelled crab-apple has been recovered from their stores.

Tacitus says of the ancient Germans that they satisfied their hunger with wild apples (*agrestia poma*), among other things.

Niebuhr observes that 'the words for a house, a field, a plow, plowing, wine, oil, milk, sheep, apples, and others relating to agriculture and the gentler way of life, agree in Latin and Greek, while the Latin words for all objects pertaining to war or the chase are utterly alien from the

Greek.' Thus the apple tree may be considered a symbol of peace no less than the olive.

The apple was early so important, and generally distributed, that its name traced to its root in many languages signifies fruit in general. Μῆλον, in Greek, means an apple, also the fruit of other trees, also a sheep and any cattle, and finally riches in general.

The apple tree has been celebrated by the Hebrews, Greeks, Romans, and Scandinavians. Some have thought that the first human pair were tempted by its fruit. Goddesses are fabled to have contended for it, dragons were set to watch it, and heroes were employed to pluck it.

The tree is mentioned in at least three places in the Old Testament, and its fruit in two or three more. Solomon sings, 'As the apple-tree among the trees of the wood, so is my beloved among the sons.' And again, 'Stay me with flagons, comfort me with apples.' The noblest part of man's noblest feature is named from this fruit, 'the apple of the eye.'

The apple tree is also mentioned by Homer and Herodotus. Ulysses saw in the glorious garden of Alcinoüs 'pears and pomegranates, and apple trees bearing beautiful fruit' (καὶ μηλέαι ἀγλαόκαρποι). And according to Homer, apples were among the fruits which Tantalus could not pluck, the wind ever blowing their boughs away from him. Theophrastus knew and described the apple tree as a botanist.

According to the Prose Edda, 'Iduna keeps in a box the apples which the gods, when they feel old age approaching, have only to taste of to become young again. It is in this manner that they will be kept in renovated youth until Ragnarök' (or the destruction of the gods).

I learn from Loudon that 'the ancient Welsh bards were rewarded for excelling in song by the token of the apple-spray;' and 'in the Highlands of Scotland the apple-tree is the badge of the clan Lamont.'

The apple tree (*Pyrus malus*) belongs chiefly to the northern temperate zone. Loudon says that 'it grows spontaneously in every part of Europe except the frigid zone, and throughout Western Asia, China, and Japan.' We have also two or three varieties of the apple indigenous in North America. The cultivated apple tree was first introduced into this country by the earliest settlers, and is thought to do as well or better here than anywhere else. Probably some of the varieties which are now cultivated were first introduced into Britain by the Romans.

Pliny, adopting the distinction of Theophrastus, says, 'Of trees there are some which are altogether wild (*sylvestres*), some more civilized (*urbaniores*).' Theophrastus includes the apple among the last; and, indeed, it is in this sense the most civilized of all trees. It is as harmless as a dove, as beautiful as a rose, and as valuable as flocks and herbs. It has been longer cultivated than any other, and so is more humanized; and who knows but, like the dog, it will at length be no longer traceable to its wild original? It migrates with man, like the dog and horse and cow: first, perchance, from Greece to Italy, thence to England, thence to America; and our Western emigrant is still marching steadily toward the setting sun with the seeds of the apple in his pocket, or perhaps a few young trees strapped to his load. At least a million apple trees are thus set farther westward this year than any cultivated ones grew last year. Consider how the Blossom Week, like the Sabbath, is thus annually spreading over the prairies; for when man migrates, he carries with him not only his birds, quadrupeds, insects, vegetables, and his very sward, but his orchard also.

The leaves and tender twigs are an agreeable food to many domestic animals, as the cow, horse, sheep, and goat; and the fruit is sought after by the first, as well as by the hog. Thus there appears to have existed a natural alliance between these animals and this tree from the first. 'The fruit of the crab in the forests of France' is said to be 'a great resource for the wild boar.'

Not only the Indian, but many indigenous insects, birds, and quadrupeds, welcomed the apple tree to these shores. The tent caterpillar saddled her eggs on the very first twig that was formed, and it has since shared her affections with the wild cherry; and the canker-worm also in a measure abandoned the elm to feed on it. As it grew apace, the bluebird, robin, cherrybird, kingbird, and many more came with haste and built their nests and warbled in its boughs, and so became orchard-birds, and multiplied more than ever. It was an era in the history of their race. The downy woodpecker found such a savory morsel under its bark that he perforated it in a ring quite round the tree, before he left it — a thing which he had never done before, to my knowledge. It did not take the partridge long to find out how sweet its buds were, and every winter eve she flew, and still flies, from the wood, to pluck them, much to the farmer's sorrow. The rabbit, too, was not slow to learn the taste of its twigs and bark; and when the fruit was ripe, the squirrel half rolled, half carried it to his hole; and even the musquash crept up the bank from the brook at evening, and greedily devoured it, until he had worn a path in the grass there; and when it was frozen and thawed, the crow and the jay were glad to taste it occasionally. The owl crept into the first apple tree that became hollow, and fairly hooted with delight, finding it just the place for him; so, settling down into it, he has remained there ever since.

My theme being the Wild Apple, I will merely glance at some of the seasons in the annual growth of the cultivated apple, and pass on to my special province.

The flowers of the apple are perhaps the most beautiful of any tree's, so copious and so delicious to both sight and scent. The walker is frequently tempted to turn and linger near some more than usually handsome one, whose blossoms are two-thirds expanded. How superior it is in these respects to the pear, whose blossoms are neither colored nor fragrant!

By the middle of July, green apples are so large as to remind us of coddling, and of the autumn. The sward is commonly strewed with little ones which fall stillborn, as it were — Nature thus thinning them for us. The Roman writer Palladius said, 'If apples are inclined to fall before their time, a stone placed in a split root will retain them.' Some such notion, still surviving, may account for some of the stones which we see placed, to be overgrown, in the forks of trees. They have a saying, in Suffolk, England.

> 'At Michaelmas time, or a little before,
> Half an apple goes to the core.'

Early apples begin to be ripe about the first of August; but I think that none of them are so good to eat as some to smell. One is worth more to scent your handkerchief with than any perfume which they sell in the shops. The fragrance of some fruits is not to be forgotten, along with that of flowers. Some gnarly apple which I pick up in the road reminds me by its fragrance of all the wealth of Pomona — carrying me forward to those days when they will be collected in golden and ruddy heaps in the orchards and about the cider-mills.

A week or two later, as you are going by orchards or gardens, especially in the evenings, you pass through a little region possessed by the fragrance of ripe apples, and thus enjoy them without price, and without robbing anybody.

There is thus about all natural products a certain volatile and ethereal quality which represents their highest value, and which cannot be vulgarized, or bought and sold. No mortal has ever enjoyed the perfect flavor of any fruit, and only the godlike among men begin to taste its ambrosial qualities. For nectar and ambrosia are only those fine flavors of every earthly fruit which our coarse palates fail to perceive —

just as we occupy the heaven of the gods without knowing it. When I see a particularly mean man carrying a load of fair and fragrant early apples to market, I seem to see a contest going on between him and his horse, on the one side, and the apples on the other, and, to my mind, the apples always gain it. Pliny says that apples are the heaviest of all things, and that the oxen begin to sweat at the mere sight of a load of them. Our driver begins to lose his load the moment he tries to transport them to where they do not belong, that is, to any but the most beautiful. Though he gets out from time to time, and feels of them, and thinks they are all there, I see the stream of their evanescent and celestial qualities going to heaven from his cart, while the pulp and skin and core only are going to market. They are not apples, but pomace. Are not these still Iduna's apples, the taste of which keeps the gods forever young? and think you that they will let Loki or Thjassi carry them off to Jötunheim, while they grow wrinkled and gray? No, for Ragnarök, or the destruction of the gods, is not yet.

There is another thinning of the fruit, commonly near the end of August or in September, when the ground is strewn with windfalls; and this happens especially when high winds occur after rain. In some orchards you may see fully three quarters of the whole crop on the ground, lying in a circular form beneath the trees, yet hard and green, or, if it is a hillside, rolled far down the hill. However, it is an ill wind that blows nobody any good. All the country over, people are busy picking up the windfalls, and this will make them cheap for early apple pies.

In October, the leaves falling, the apples are more distinct on the trees. I saw one year in a neighboring town some trees fuller of fruit than I remember to have ever seen before, small yellow apples hanging over the road. The branches were gracefully drooping with their weight, like a barberry bush, so that the whole tree acquired a new character. Even the topmost branches, instead of standing erect, spread and drooped in all directions; and there were so many poles supporting the lower ones that they looked like pictures of banyan trees. As an old English manuscript says, 'The mo appelen the tree bereth the more sche boweth to the folk.'

Surely the apple is the noblest of fruits. Let the most beautiful or the swiftest have it. That should be the 'going' price of apples.

Between the 5th and 20th of October I see the barrels lie under the trees. And perhaps I talk with one who is selecting some choice barrels to fulfill an order. He turns a specked one over many times before he

leaves it out. If I were to tell what is passing in my mind, I should say
that every one was specked which he had handled; for he rubs off all
the bloom, and those fugacious ethereal qualities leave it. Cool evenings
prompt the farmers to make haste, and at length I see only the ladders
here and there left leaning against the trees.

It would be well, if we accepted these gifts with more joy and gratitude, and did not think it enough simply to put a fresh load of compost
about the tree. Some old English customs are suggestive at least. I find
them described chiefly in Brand's 'Popular Antiquities.' It appears
that 'on Christmas Eve the farmers and their men in Devonshire take
a large bowl of cider, with a toast in it, and carrying it in state to the
orchard, they salute the apple-trees with much ceremony, in order to
make them bear well the next season.' This salutation consists in
'throwing some of the cider about the roots of the tree, placing bits of
the toast on the branches,' and then, 'encircling one of the best bearing
trees in the orchard, they drink the following toast three several times:

> 'Here's to thee, old apple tree,
> Whence thou mayst bud, and whence thou mayst blow,
> And whence thou mayst bear apples enow!
> Hats-full! caps-full!
> Bushel, bushel, sacks-full!
> And my pockets full, too! Hurra!'

Also what was called 'apple-howling' used to be practised in various
counties of England on New Year's Eve. A troop of boys visited the
different orchards, and, encircling the apple trees, repeated the following words:

> 'Stand fast, root! bear well, top!
> Pray God send us a good howling crop:
> Every twig, apples big;
> Every bough, apples enow!'

'They then shout in chorus, one of the boys accompanying them on
a cow's horn. During this ceremony they rap the trees with their sticks.'
This is called 'wassailing' the trees, and is thought by some to be 'a relic
of the heathen sacrifice to Pomona.'

Herrick sings —

> 'Wassaile the trees that they may beare
> You many a plum and many a peare;
> For more or less fruits they will bring
> As you so give them wassailing.'

Our poets have as yet a better right to sing of cider than of wine; but it behooves them to sing better than English Phillips did, else they will do no credit to their Muse.

THE WILD APPLE

So much for the more civilized apple trees (*urbaniores,* as Pliny calls them). I love better to go through the old orchards of ungrafted apple-trees, at what ever season of the year — so irregularly planted: sometimes two trees standing close together; and the rows so devious that you would think that they not only had grown while the owner was sleeping, but had been set out by him in a somnambulic state. The rows of grafted fruit will never tempt me to wander amid them like these. But I now, alas, speak rather from memory than from any recent experience, such ravages have been made!

Some soils, like a rocky tract called the Easterbrooks Country in my neighborhood, are so suited to the apple, that it will grow faster in them without any care, or if only the ground is broken up once a year, than it will in many places with any amount of care. The owners of this tract allow that the soil is excellent for fruit, but they say that it is so rocky that they have not patience to plough it, and that, together with the distance, is the reason why it is not cultivated. There are, or were recently, extensive orchards there standing without order. Nay, they spring up wild and bear well there in the midst of pines, birches, maples, and oaks. I am often surprised to see rising amid these trees the rounded tops of apple trees glowing with red or yellow fruit, in harmony with the autumnal tints of the forest.

Going up the side of a cliff about the first of November, I saw a vigorous young apple tree, which, planted by birds or cows, had shot up amid the rocks and open woods there, and had now much fruit on it, uninjured by the frosts, when all cultivated apples were gathered. It was a rank, wild growth, with many green leaves on it still, and made an impression of thorniness. The fruit was hard and green, but looked as if it would be palatable in the winter. Some was dangling on the twigs, but more half buried in the wet leaves under the tree, or rolled far down the hill amid the rocks. The owner knows nothing of it. The day was not observed when it first blossomed, nor when it first bore fruit, unless by the chickadee. There was no dancing on the green beneath it in its honor, and now there is no hand to pluck its fruit — which is only gnawed by squirrels, as I perceive. It has done double duty — not only borne this crop, but each twig has grown a foot into the air. And this is *such* fruit! bigger than many berries, we must admit, and carried home will be sound and palatable next spring. What care I for Iduna's apples so long as I can get these?

When I go by this shrub thus late and hardy, and see its dangling fruit, I respect the tree, and I am grateful for Nature's bounty, even though I cannot eat it. Here on this rugged and woody hillside has grown an apple tree, not planted by man, no relic of a former orchard, but a natural growth, like the pines and oaks. Most fruits which we prize and use depend entirely on our care. Corn and grain, potatoes, peaches, melons, etc., depend altogether on our planting; but the apple emulates man's independence and enterprise. It is not simply carried, as I have said, but, like him, to some extent, it has migrated to this New World, and is even, here and there, making its way amid the aboriginal trees; just as the ox and dog and horse sometimes run wild and maintain themselves.

Even the sourest and crabbedest apple, growing in the most unfavorable position, suggests such thoughts as these, it is so noble a fruit.

THE CRAB

Nevertheless, *our* wild apple is wild only like myself, perchance, who belong not to the aboriginal race here, but have strayed into the woods from the cultivated stock. Wilder still, as I have said, there grows elsewhere in this country a native and aboriginal crab-apple, *Malus coronaria*, 'whose nature has not yet been modified by cultivation.' It is found from western New York to Minnesota, and southward. Michaux says that its ordinary height 'is fifteen or eighteen feet, but it is sometimes found twenty-five or thirty feet high,' and that the large ones 'exactly resemble the common apple tree.' 'The flowers are white mingled with rose color, and are collected in corymbs.' They are remarkable for their delicious odor. The fruit, according to him, is about an inch and a half in diameter, and is intensely acid. Yet they make fine sweetmeats and also cider of them. He concludes that 'if, on being cultivated, it does not yield new and palatable varieties, it will at least be celebrated for the beauty of its flowers, and for the sweetness of its perfume.'

I never saw the crab-apple till May, 1861. I had heard of it through Michaux, but more modern botanists, so far as I know, have not treated it as of any peculiar importance. Thus it was a half-fabulous tree to me

I contemplated a pilgrimage to the 'Glades,' a portion of Pennsylvania where it was said to grow to perfection. I thought of sending to a nursery for it, but doubted if they had it, or would distinguish it from European varieties. At last I had occasion to go to Minnesota, and on entering Michigan I began to notice from the cars a tree with handsome rose-colored flowers. At first I thought it some variety of thorn; but it was not long before the truth flashed on me, that this was my long-sought crab-apple. It was the prevailing flowering shrub or tree to be seen from the cars at that season of the year — about the middle of May. But the cars never stopped before one, and so I was launched on the bosom of the Mississippi without having touched one, experiencing the fate of Tantalus. On arriving at St. Anthony's Falls, I was sorry to be told that I was too far north for the crab-apple. Nevertheless I succeeded in finding it about eight miles west of the Falls; touched it and smelled it, and secured a lingering corymb of flowers for my herbarium. This must have been near its northern limit.

HOW THE WILD APPLE GROWS

But though these are indigenous, like the Indians, I doubt whether they are any hardier than those backwoodsmen among the apple trees, which, though descended from cultivated stocks, plant themselves in distant fields and forests, where the soil is favorable to them. I know of no trees which have more difficulties to contend with, and which more sturdily resist their foes. These are the ones whose story we have to tell. It oftentimes reads thus:

Near the beginning of May, we notice little thickets of apple trees just springing up in the pastures where cattle have been — as the rocky ones of our Easterbrooks Country, or the top of Nobscot Hill, in Sudbury. One or two of these, perhaps, survive the drought and other accidents — their very birthplace defending them against the encroaching grass and some other dangers, at first.

> In two years' time 't had thus
>   Reached the level of the rocks,
> Admired the stretching world,
>   Nor feared the wandering flocks.

> But at this tender age
>   Its sufferings began:
> There came a browsing ox
>   And cut it down a span.

This time, perhaps, the ox does not notice it amid the grass; but the next year, when it has grown more stout, he recognizes it for a fellow-emigrant from the old country, the flavor of whose leaves and twigs he well knows; and though at first he pauses to welcome it, and express his surprise, and gets for answer, 'The same cause that brought you here brought me,' he nevertheless browses it again, reflecting, it may be, that he has some title to it.

Thus cut down annually, it does not despair; but, putting forth two short twigs for every one cut off, it spreads out low along the ground in the hollows or between the rocks, growing more stout and scrubby, until it forms, not a tree as yet, but a little pyramidal, stiff, twiggy mass, almost as solid and impenetrable as a rock. Some of the densest and most impenetrable clumps of bushes that I have ever seen, as well on account of the closeness and stubbornness of their branches as of their thorns, have been these wild apple scrubs. They are more like the scrubby fir and black spruce on which you stand, and sometimes walk, on the tops of mountains, where cold is the demon they contend with, than anything else. No wonder they are prompted to grow thorns at last, to defend themselves against such foes. In their thorniness, however, there is no malice, only some malic acid.

The rocky pastures of the tract I have referred to — for they maintain their ground best in a rocky field — are thickly sprinkled with these little tufts, reminding you often of some rigid gray mosses or lichens, and you see thousands of little trees just springing up between them, with the seed still attached to them.

Being regularly clipped all around each year by the cows, as a hedge with shears, they are often of a perfect conical or pyramidal form, from one to four feet high, and more or less sharp, as if trimmed by the gardener's art. In the pastures on Nobscot Hill and its spurs, they make fine dark shadows when the sun is low. They are also an excellent covert from hawks for many small birds that roost and build in them. Whole flocks perch in them at night, and I have seen three robins' nests in one which was six feet in diameter.

No doubt many of these are already old trees, if you reckon from the day they were planted, but infants still when you consider their development and the long life before them. I counted the annual rings of some which were just one foot high, and as wide as high, and found that they were about twelve years old, but quite sound and thrifty! They were so low that they were unnoticed by the walker, while many of their contemporaries from the nurseries were already bearing considerable crops. But what you gain in time is perhaps in this case, too, lost in power — that is, in the vigor of the tree. This is their pyramidal state.

The cows continue to browse them thus for twenty years or more, keeping them down and compelling them to spread, until at last they are so broad that they become their own fence, when some interior shoot, which their foes cannot reach, darts upward with joy: for it has not forgotten its high calling, and bears its own peculiar fruit in triumph.

Such are the tactics by which it finally defeats its bovine foes. Now, if you have watched the progress of a particular shrub, you will see that it is no longer a simple pyramid or cone, but that out of its apex there rises a sprig or two, growing more lustily perchance than an orchard-tree, since the plant now devotes the whole of its repressed energy to these upright parts. In a short time these become a small tree, an inverted pyramid resting on the apex of the other, so that the whole has now the form of a vast hour-glass. The spreading bottom, having served its purpose, finally disappears, and the generous tree permits the now harmless cows to come in and stand in its shade, and rub against and redden its trunk, which has grown in spite of them, and even to taste a part of its fruit, and so disperse the seed.

Thus the cows create their own shade and food; and the tree, its hour-glass being inverted, lives a second life, as it were.

It is an important question with some nowadays, whether you should trim young apple trees as high as your nose or as high as your eyes. The ox trims them up as high as he can reach, and that is about the right height, I think.

In spite of wandering kine, and other adverse circumstances, that despised shrub, valued only by small birds as a covert and shelter from hawks, has its blossom week at last, and in course of time its harvest, sincere, though small.

By the end of some October, when its leaves have fallen, I frequently see such a central sprig, whose progress I have watched, when I thought it had forgotten its destiny, as I had, bearing its first crop of small green or yellow or rosy fruit, which the cows cannot get at over the bushy and thorny hedge which surrounds it, and I make haste to taste the new and undescribed variety. We have all heard of the numerous varieties of fruit invented by Van Mons and Knight. This is the system of Van Cow, and she has invented far more and more memorable varieties than both of them.

Through what hardships it may attain to bear a sweet fruit! Though somewhat small, it may prove equal, if not superior, in flavor to that which has grown in a garden — will perchance be all the sweeter and more palatable for the very difficulties it has had to contend with. Who knows but this chance wild fruit, planted by a cow or a bird on some remote and rocky hillside, where it is as yet unobserved by man, may be the choicest of all its kind, and foreign potentates shall hear of it, and royal societies seek to propagate it, though the virtues of the perhaps truly crabbed owner of the soil may never be heard of — at least, beyond the limits of his village? It was thus the Porter and the Baldwin grew.

Every wild apple shrub excites our expectation thus, somewhat as every wild child. It is, perhaps, a prince in disguise. What a lesson to man! So are human beings, referred to the highest standard, the celestial fruit which they suggest and aspire to bear, browsed on by fate; and only the most persistent and strongest genius defends itself and prevails, sends a tender scion upward at last, and drops its perfect fruit on the ungrateful earth. Poets and philosophers and statesmen thus spring up in the country pastures, and outlast the hosts of unoriginal men.

Such is always the pursuit of knowledge. The celestial fruits, the golden apples of the Hesperides, are ever guarded by a hundred-headed dragon which never sleeps, so that it is an Herculean labor to pluck them.

This is one, and the most remarkable way in which the wild apple is propagated; but commonly it springs up at wide intervals in woods and swamp, and by the sides of roads, as the soil may suit it, and grows with comparative rapidity. Those which grow in dense woods are very tall and slender. I frequently pluck from these trees a perfectly mild and tamed fruit. As Palladius says, '*Et injussu consternitur ubere mali:*' And the ground is strewn with the fruit of an unbidden apple tree.

It is an old notion that, if these wild trees do not bear a valuable fruit of their own, they are the best stocks by which to transmit to posterity the most highly prized qualities of others. However, I am not in search of stocks, but the wild fruit itself, whose fierce gust has suffered no 'inteneration.' It is not my

'highest plot
To plant the Bergamot.'

THE FRUIT, AND ITS FLAVOR

The time for wild apples is the last of October and the first of November. They then get to be palatable, for they ripen late, and they are still perhaps as beautiful as ever. I make a great account of these fruits, which the farmers do not think it worth the while to gather — wild flavors of the Muse, vivacious and inspiriting. The farmer thinks that he has better in his barrels, but he is mistaken, unless he has a walker's appetite and imagination, neither of which can he have.

Such as grow quite wild, and are left out till the first of November, I presume that the owner does not mean to gather. They belong to children as wild as themselves — to certain active boys that I know — to the wild-eyed woman of the fields, to whom nothing comes amiss, who gleans after all the world, and, moreover, to us walkers. We have met with them, and they are ours. These rights, long enough insisted upon, have come to be an institution in some old countries, where they have learned how to live. I hear that 'the custom of grippling, which may be called apple-gleaning, is, or was formerly, practised in Herefordshire. It consists in leaving a few apples, which are called the gripples, on every tree, after the general gathering, for the boys, who go with climbing-poles and bags to collect them.'

As for those I speak of, I pluck them as a wild fruit, native to this quarter of the earth — fruit of old trees that have been dying ever since I was a boy and are not yet dead, frequented only by the woodpecker and the squirrel, deserted now by the owner, who has not faith enough to look under their boughs. From the appearance of the tree-top, at a little distance, you would expect nothing but lichens to drop from it, but your faith is rewarded by finding the ground strewn with spirited fruit — some of it, perhaps, collected at squirrel-holes, with the marks of their teeth by which they carried them — some containing a cricket or two silently feeding within, and some, especially in damp days, a shell-less snail. The very sticks and stones lodged in the tree-top might have convinced you of the savoriness of the fruit which has been so eagerly sought after in past years.

I have seen no account of these among the 'Fruits and Fruit-Trees of America,' though they are more memorable to my taste than the grafted kinds; more racy and wild American flavors do they possess when October and November, when December and January, and perhaps February and March even, have assuaged them somewhat. An old farmer in my neighborhood, who always selects the right word, says that 'they have a kind of bow-arrow tang.'

Apples for grafting appear to have been selected commonly, not so much for their spirited flavor, as for their mildness, their size, and bearing qualities — not so much for their beauty, as for their fairness and soundness. Indeed, I have no faith in the selected lists of pomological gentlemen. Their 'Favorites' and 'None-suches' and 'Seek-no-farthers,' when I have fruited them, commonly turn out very tame and forgettable. They are eaten with comparatively little zest, and have no real *tang* nor *smack* to them.

What if some of these wildings are acrid and puckery, genuine *verjuice*, do they not still belong to the *Pomaceæ*, which are uniformly innocent and kind to our race? I still begrudge them to the cider-mill. Perhaps they are not fairly ripe yet.

No wonder that these small and high-colored apples are thought to make the best cider. Loudon quotes from the 'Herefordshire Report,' that 'apples of a small size are always, if equal in quality, to be preferred to those of a larger size, in order that the rind and kernel may bear the greatest proportion to the pulp, which affords the weakest and most watery juice.' And he says that, 'to prove this, Dr. Symonds, of Hereford, about the year 1800, made one hogshead of cider entirely from the rinds and cores of apples, and another from the pulp only, when the first was found of extraordinary strength and flavor, while the latter was sweet and insipid.'

Evelyn says that the 'Red-strake' was the favorite cider-apple in his day; and he quotes one Dr. Newburg as saying, 'In Jersey 'tis a general observation, as I hear, that the more of red any apple has in its rind, the more proper it is for this use. Pale-faced apples they exclude as much as may be from their cider-vat.' This opinion still prevails.

All apples are good in November. Those which the farmer leaves out as unsalable and unpalatable to those who frequent the markets are choicest fruit to the walker. But it is remarkable that the wild apple, which I praise as so spirited and racy when eaten in the fields or woods, being brought into the house has frequently a harsh and crabbed taste. The Saunterer's Apple not even the saunterer can eat in the house. The palate rejects it there, as it does haws and acorns, and demands a tamed one; for there you miss the November air, which is the sauce it is to be eaten with. Accordingly, when Tityrus, seeing the lengthening shadows, invites Melibœus to go home and pass the night with him, he promises him *mild* apples and soft chestnuts — *mitia poma, castaneæ molles*. I frequently pluck wild apples of so rich and spicy a flavor that I wonder all orchardists do not get a scion from that tree, and I fail not to bring home my pockets full. But perchance, when I take one out of my desk and taste it in my chamber, I find it unexpectedly crude — sour enough to set a squirrel's teeth on edge and make a jay scream.

These apples have hung in the wind and frost and rain till they have absorbed the qualities of the weather or season, and thus are highly *seasoned*, and they *pierce* and *sting* and *permeate* us with their spirit. They must be eaten in *season*, accordingly — that is, out-of-doors.

To appreciate the wild and sharp flavors of these October fruits, it is necessary that you be breathing the sharp October or November air. The outdoor air and exercise which the walker gets give a different tone to his palate, and he craves a fruit which the sedentary would call harsh and crabbed. They must be eaten in the fields, when your system is all aglow with exercise, when the frosty weather nips your fingers, the wind rattles the bare boughs or rustles the few remaining leaves, and the jay is heard screaming around. What is sour in the house a bracing walk makes sweet. Some of these apples might be labelled, 'To be eaten in the wind.'

Of course no flavors are thrown away; they are intended for the taste that is up to them. Some apples have two distinct flavors, and perhaps one half of them must be eaten in the house, the other outdoors. One Peter Whitney wrote from Northborough in 1782, for the Proceedings of the Boston Academy, describing an apple tree in that town 'producing fruit of opposite qualities, part of the same apple being frequently sour and the other sweet;' also some all sour, and others all sweet, and this diversity on all parts of the tree.

There is a wild apple on Nawshawtuct Hill in my town which has to me a peculiarly pleasant bitter tang, not perceived till it is three-quarters tasted. It remains on the tongue. As you eat it, it smells exactly like a squash-bug. It is a sort of triumph to eat and relish it.

I hear that the fruit of a kind of plum tree in Provence is 'called *Prunes sibarelles*, because it is impossible to whistle after having eaten them, from their sourness.' But perhaps they were only eaten in the house and in summer, and if tried out-of-doors in a stinging atmosphere, who knows but you could whistle an octave higher and clearer?

In the fields only are the sours and bitters of Nature appreciated; just as the woodchopper eats his meal in a sunny glade, in the middle of a winter day, with content, basks in a sunny ray there, and dreams of summer in a degree of cold which, experienced in a chamber, would make a student miserable. They who are at work abroad are not cold, but rather it is they who sit shivering in houses. As with temperatures, so with flavors; as with cold and heat, so with sour and sweet. This natural raciness, the sours and bitters which the diseased palate refuses, are the true condiments.

Let your condiments be in the condition of your senses. To appreciate the flavor of these wild apples requires vigorous and healthy senses, *papillæ* firm and erect on the tongue and palate, not easily flattened and tamed.

From my experience with wild apples, I can understand that there may be reasons for a savage's preferring many kinds of food which the civilized man rejects. The former has the palate of an outdoor man. It takes a savage or wild taste to appreciate a wild fruit.

What a healthy out-of-door appetite it takes to relish the apple of life, the apple of the world, then!

> 'Nor is it every apple I desire,
>   Nor that which pleases every palate best;
> 'Tis not the lasting Deuxan I require,
>   Nor yet the red-cheeked Greening I request,
> Nor that which first beshrewed the name of wife,
> Nor that whose beauty caused the golden strife:
> No, no! bring me an apple from the tree of life.'

So there is one *thought* for the field, another for the house. I would have my thoughts, like wild apples, to be food for walkers, and will not warrant them to be palatable if tasted in the house.

THEIR BEAUTY

Almost all wild apples are handsome. They cannot be too gnarly and crabbed and rusty to look at. The gnarliest will have some redeeming traits even to the eye. You will discover some evening redness dashed or sprinkled on some protuberance or in some cavity. It is rare that the summer lets an apple go without streaking or spotting it on some part of its sphere. It will have some red stains, commemorating the mornings and evenings it has witnessed; some dark and rusty blotches, in memory of the clouds and foggy, mildewy days that have passed over it; and a spacious field of green reflecting the general face of nature — green even as the fields; or a yellow ground, which implies a milder flavor — yellow as the harvest, or russet as the hills.

Apples, these I mean, unspeakably fair — apples not of Discord, but of Concord! Yet not so rare but that the homelist may have a share. Painted by the frosts, some a uniform clear bright yellow, or red, or crimson, as if their spheres had regularly revolved, and enjoyed the influence of the sun on all sides alike — some with the faintest pink blush imaginable — some brindled with deep red streaks like a cow, or with hundreds of fine blood-red rays running regularly from the stem-dimple to the blossom end, like meridional lines, on a straw-colored ground — some touched with a greenish rust, like a fine lichen, here and there, with crimson blotches or eyes more or less confluent and fiery when wet — and others gnarly, and freckled or peppered all over on the stem side with fine crimson spots on a white ground, as if accidentally sprinkled from the brush of Him who paints the autumn leaves. Others, again, are sometimes red inside, perfused with a beautiful blush, fairy food, too beautiful to eat — apple of the Hesperides, apple of the evening sky! But like shells and pebbles on the seashore, they must be seen as they sparkle amid the withering leaves in some dell in the woods, in the autumnal air, or as they lie in the wet grass, and not when they have wilted and faded in the house.

THE NAMING OF THEM

It would be a pleasant pastime to find suitable names for the hundred varieties which go to a single heap at the cider-mill. Would it not tax a man's invention — no one to be named after a man, and all in the *lingua vernacula?* Who shall stand godfather at the christening of the wild apples? It would exhaust the Latin and Greek languages, if they were used, and make the *lingua vernacula* flag. We should have to call in the sunrise and the sunset, the rainbow and the autumn woods and the wild-flowers, and the woodpecker and the purple finch and the squirrel and the jay and the butterfly, the November traveller and the truant boy, to our aid.

In 1836 there were in the garden of the London Horticultural Society more than fourteen hundred distinct sorts. But here are species which they have not in their catalogue, not to mention the varieties which our crab might yield to cultivation.

Let us enumerate a few of these. I find myself compelled, after all, to give the Latin names of some for the benefit of those who live where English is not spoken — for they are likely to have a world-wide reputation.

There is, first of all, the Wood Apple (*Malus sylvatica*); the Blue-Jay Apple; the Apple which grows in Dells in the Woods (*sylvestrivallis*), also in Hollows in Pastures (*campestrivallis*); the Apple that grows in an old

Cellar-Hole (*Malus cellaris*); the Meadow Apple; the Partridge Apple;
the Truant's Apple (*cessatoris*), which no boy will ever go by without
knocking off some, however *late* it may be; the Saunterer's Apple — you
must lose yourself before you can find the way to that; the Beauty of
the Air (*decus aëris*); December-Eating; the Frozen-Thawed (*gelato-
soluta*), good only in that state; the Concord Apple, possibly the same
with the *Musketaquidensis;* the Assabet Apple; the Brindled Apple; Wine
of New England; the Chickaree Apple; the Green Apple (*Malus viridis*)
— this has many synonyms: in an imperfect state, it is the *choleramor-
bifera aut dysenterifera, puerulis dilectissima;* the Apple which Atalanta
stopped to pick up; the Hedge Apple (*Malus sepium*); the Slug Apple
(*limacea*); the Railroad Apple, which perhaps came from a core thrown
out of the cars; the Apple whose Fruit we tasted in our Youth; our
Particular Apple, not to be found in any catalogue; *pedestrium solatium;*
also the Apple where hangs the Forgotten Scythe; Iduna's Apples, and
the Apples which Loki found in the Wood; and a great many more
I have on my list, too numerous to mention — all of them good. As
Bodæus exclaims, referring to the cultivated kinds, and adapting Virgil
to his case, so I, adapting Bodæus,

> 'Not if I had a hundred tongues, a hundred mouths,
> An iron voice, could I describe all the forms
> And reckon up all the names of these *wild apples.*'

THE LAST GLEANING

By the middle of November the wild apples have lost some of their
brilliancy, and have chiefly fallen. A great part are decayed on the
ground, and the sound ones are more palatable than before. The note
of the chickadee sounds now more distinct, as you wander amid the old
trees, and the autumnal dandelion is half closed and tearful. But still,
if you are a skilful gleaner, you may get many a pocketful even of
grafted fruit, long after apples are supposed to be gone out-of-doors.
I know a Blue Pearmain tree, growing within the edge of a swamp,
almost as good as wild. You would not suppose that there was any
fruit left there, on the first survey, but you must look according to
system. Those which lie exposed are quite brown and rotten now, or
perchance a few still show one blooming cheek here and there amid the
wet leaves. Nevertheless, with experienced eyes, I explore amid the
bare alders and the huckleberry bushes and the withered sedge, and in
the crevices of the rocks, which are full of leaves, and pry under the

fallen and decaying ferns, which, with apple and alder leaves, thickly strew the ground. For I know that they lie concealed, fallen into hollows long since and covered up by the leaves of the tree itself — a proper kind of packing. From these lurking-places, anywhere within the circumference of the tree, I draw forth the fruit, all wet and glossy, maybe nibbled by rabbits and hollowed out by crickets, and perhaps with a leaf or two cemented to it (as Curzon an old manuscript from a monastery's mouldy cellar), but still with a rich bloom on it, and at least as ripe and well-kept, if not better than those in barrels, more crisp and lively than they. If these resources fail to yield anything, I have learned to look between the bases of the suckers which spring thickly from some horizontal limb, for now and then one lodges there, or in the very midst of an alder-clump, where they are covered by leaves, safe from cows which may have smelled them out. If I am sharp-set, for I do not refuse the Blue Pearmain, I fill my pockets on each side; and as I retrace my steps in the frosty eve, being perhaps four or five miles from home, I eat one first from this side, and then from that, to keep my balance.

I learn from Topsell's Gesner, whose authority appears to be Albertus, that the following is the way in which the hedgehog collects and carries home his apples. He says — 'His meat is apples, worms, or grapes: when he findeth apples or grapes on the earth, he rolleth himself upon them, until he have filled all his prickles, and then carrieth them home to his den, never bearing above one in his mouth; and if it fortune that one of them fall off by the way, he likewise shaketh off all the residue, and walloweth upon them afresh, until they be all settled upon his back again. So, forth he goeth, making a noise like a cart-wheel; and if he have any young ones in his nest, they pull off his load wherewithal he is loaded, eating thereof what they please, and laying up the residue for the time to come.'

THE 'FROZEN-THAWED' APPLE

Toward the end of November, though some of the sound ones are yet more mellow and perhaps more edible, they have generally, like the leaves, lost their beauty, and are beginning to freeze. It is finger-cold, and prudent farmers get in their barrelled apples, and bring you the apples and cider which they have engaged; for it is time to put them into the cellar. Perhaps a few on the ground show their red cheeks above the early snow, and occasionally some even preserve their color and soundness under the snow throughout the winter. But generally at the beginning of the winter they freeze hard, and soon, though undecayed, acquire the color of a baked apple.

Before the end of December, generally, they experience their first thawing. Those which a month ago were sour, crabbed, and quite unpalatable to the civilized taste, such at least as were frozen while sound, let a warmer sun come to thaw them — for they are extremely sensitive to its rays — are found to be filled with a rich, sweet cider, better than any bottled cider that I know of, and with which I am better acquainted than with wine. All apples are good in this state, and your jaws are the cider-press. Others, which have more substance, are a sweet and luscious food — in my opinion of more worth than the pineapples which are imported from the West Indies. Those which lately even I tasted only to repent of it — for I am semicivilized — which the farmer willingly left on the tree, I am now glad to find have the property of hanging on like the leaves of the young oaks. It is a way to keep cider sweet without boiling. Let the frost come to freeze them first, solid as stones, and then the rain or a warm winter day to thaw them, and they will seem to have borrowed a flavor from heaven through the medium of the air in which they hang. Or perchance you find, when you get home, that those which rattled in your pocket have thawed, and the ice is turned to cider. But after the third or fourth freezing and thawing they will not be found so good.

What are the imported half-ripe fruits of the torrid south, to this fruit matured by the cold of the frigid north? These are those crabbed apples with which I cheated my companion, and kept a smooth face that I might tempt him to eat. Now we both greedily fill our pockets with them — bending to drink the cup and save our lappets from the overflowing juice — and grow more social with their wine. Was there one that hung so high and sheltered by the tangled branches that our sticks could not dislodge it?

It is a fruit never carried to market, that I am aware of — quite distinct from the apple of the markets, as from dried apple and cider — and it is not every winter that produces it in perfection.

The era of the Wild Apple will soon be past. It is a fruit which will probably become extinct in New England. You may still wander through old orchards of native fruit of great extent, which for the most part went to the cider-mill, now all gone to decay. I have heard of an orchard in a distant town, on the side of a hill, where the apples rolled down and lay four feet deep against a wall on the lower side, and this the owner cut down for fear they should be made into cider. Since the temperance reform and the general introduction of grafted fruit, no native apple trees, such as I see everywhere in deserted pastures, and where the woods have grown up around them, are set out. I fear that he who walks over these fields a century hence will not know the pleasure of knocking off wild apples. Ah, poor man, there are many pleasures which he will not know! Notwithstanding the prevalence of the Baldwin and the Porter, I doubt if so extensive orchards are set out today in my town as there were a century ago, when those vast straggling cider-orchards were planted, when men both ate and drank apples, when the pomace-heap was the only nursery, and trees cost nothing but the trouble of setting them out. Men could afford then to stick a tree by every wall-side and let it take its chance. I see nobody planting trees today in such out of the way places, along the lonely roads and lanes, and at the bottom of dells in the wood. Now that they have grafted trees, and pay a price for them, they collect them into a plat by their houses, and fence them in — and the end of it all will be that we shall be compelled to look for our apples in a barrel.

This is 'The word of the Lord that came to Joel the son of Pethuel.

'Here this, ye old men, and give ear, all ye inhabitants of the land! Hath this been in your days, or even in the days of your fathers? . . .

'That which the palmerworm hath left hath the locust eaten; and that which the locust hath left hath the cankerworm eaten; and that which the cankerworm hath left hath the caterpillar eaten.

'Awake, ye drunkards, and weep; and howl, all ye drinkers of wine, because of the new wine; for it is cut off from your mouth.

'For a nation is come up upon my land, strong, and without number, whose teeth are the teeth of a lion, and he hath the cheek teeth of a great lion.

'He hath laid my vine waste, and barked my fig tree: he hath made it clean bare, and cast it away; the branches thereof are made white. . . .

'Be ye ashamed, O yet husbandmen; howl, O ye vinedressers. . . .

'The vine is dried up, and the fig tree languisheth; the pomegranate tree, the palm tree also, and the apple tree, even all the trees of the field, are withered: because joy is withered away from the sons of men.'

V. THE SUCCESSION OF FOREST TREES [1]

EVERY man is entitled to come to Cattle-Show, even a transcendentalist; and for my part I am more interested in the men than in the cattle. I wish to see once more those old familiar faces, whose names I do not know, which for me represent the Middlesex country, and come as near being indigenous to the soil as a white man can; the men who are not above their business, whose coats are not too black, whose shoes do not shine very much, who never wear gloves to conceal their hands. It is true, there are some queer specimens of humanity attracted to our festival, but all are welcome. I am pretty sure to meet once more that weak-minded and whimsical fellow, generally weak-bodied too, who prefers a crooked stick for a cane; perfectly useless, you would say, only *bizarre*, fit for a cabinet, like a petrified snake. A ram's horn would be as convenient, and is yet more curiously twisted. He brings that much indulged bit of the country with him, from some town's end or other, and introduces it to Concord groves, as if he had promised it so much sometimes. So some, it seems to me, elect their rulers for their crooked-ness. But I think that a straight stick makes the best cane, and an up-right man the best ruler. Or why choose a man to do plain work who is distinguished for his oddity? However, I do not know but you will think that they have committed this mistake who invited me to speak to you today.

In my capacity of surveyor, I have often talked with some of you, my employers, at your dinner-tables, after having gone round and round and behind your farming, and ascertained exactly what its limits were. Moreover, taking a surveyor's and a naturalist's liberty, I have been in the habit of going across your lots much oftener than is usual, as many of you, perhaps to your sorrow, are aware. Yet many of you, to my relief, have seemed not to be aware of it; and, when I came across you in some out-of-the-way nook of your farms, have inquired, with an air of surprise, if I were not lost, since you had never seen me in that

[1] An Address read to the Middlesex Agricultural Society in Concord, September, 1860.

part of the town or county before; when, if the truth were known, and it had not been for betraying my secret, I might with more propriety have inquired if *you* were not lost, since I had never seen *you* there before. I have several times shown the proprietor the shortest way out of his wood-lot.

Therefore, it would seem that I have some title to speak to you today; and considering what that title is, and the occasion that has called us together, I need offer no apology if I invite your attention, for the few moments that are allotted me, to a purely scientific subject.

At those dinner-tables referred to, I have often been asked, as many of you have been, if I could tell how it happened, that when a pine wood was cut down an oak one commonly sprang up, and *vice versa*. To which I have answered, and now answer, that I can tell — that it is no mystery to me. As I am not aware that this has been clearly shown by any one, I shall lay the more stress on this point. Let me lead you back into your wood-lots again.

When, hereabouts, a single forest tree or a forest springs up naturally where none of its kind grew before, I do not hesitate to say, though in some quarters still it may sound paradoxical, that it came from a seed. Of the various ways by which trees are *known* to be propagated — by transplanting, cuttings, and the like — this is the only supposable one under these circumstances. No such tree has ever been known to spring from anything else. If any one asserts that it sprang from something else, or from nothing, the burden of proof lies with him.

It remains, then, only to show how the seed is transported from where it grows to where it is planted. This is done chiefly by the agency of the wind, water, and animals. The lighter seeds, as those of pines and maples, are transported chiefly by wind and water; the heavier, as acorns and nuts, by animals.

In all the pines, a very thin membrane, in appearance much like an insect's wing, grows over and around the seed, and independent of it, while the latter is being developed within its base. Indeed this is often perfectly developed, though the seed is abortive; nature being, you would say, more sure to provide the means of transporting the seed, than to provide the seed to be transported. In other words, a beautiful thin sack is woven around the seed, with a handle to it such as the wind can take hold of, and it is then committed to the wind, expressly that it may transport the seed and extend the range of the species; and this it does, as effectually as when seeds are sent by mail in a different kind of sack from the Patent Office. There is a patent office at the seat of government of the universe, whose managers are as much interested in the dispersion of seeds as anybody at Washington can be, and their operations are infinitely more extensive and regular.

There is, then, no necessity for supposing that the pines have sprung up from nothing, and I am aware that I am not at all peculiar in asserting that they come from seeds, though the mode of their propagation *by nature* has been but little attended to. They are very extensively raised from the seed in Europe, and are beginning to be here.

When you cut down an oak wood, a pine wood will not *at once* spring up there unless there are, or have been quite recently, seed-bearing pines near enough for the seeds to be blown from them. But, adjacent to a forest of pines, if you prevent other crops from growing there, you will surely have an extension of your pine forest, provided the soil is suitable.

As for the heavy seeds and nuts which are not furnished with wings, the notion is still a very common one that, when the trees which bear these spring up where none of their kind were noticed before, they have come from seeds or other principles spontaneously generated there in an unusual manner, or which have lain dormant in the soil for centuries, or perhaps been called into activity by the heat of a burning. I do not believe these assertions, and I will state some of the ways in which, according to my observation, such forests are planted and raised.

Every one of these seeds, too, will be found to be winged or legged in another fashion. Surely it is not wonderful that cherry trees of all kinds are widely dispersed, since their fruit is well known to be the favorite food of various birds. Many kinds are called bird cherries, and they appropriate many more kinds, which are not so called. Eating cherries is a bird-like employment, and unless we disperse the seeds occasionally, as they do, I shall think that the birds have the best right to them. See how artfully the seed of a cherry is placed in order that a bird may be compelled to transport it — in the very midst of a tempting pericarp, so that the creature that would devour this must commonly take the stone also into its mouth or bill. If you ever ate a cherry, and did not make two bites of it, you must have perceived it — right in the centre of the luscious morsel, a large earthy residuum left on the tongue. We thus take into our mouths cherry-stones as big as peas, a dozen at once, for Nature can persuade us to do almost anything when she would compass her ends. Some wild men and children instinctively swallow these, as the birds do when in a hurry, it being the shortest way to get rid of them. Thus, though these seeds are not provided with vegetable wings,

Nature has impelled the thrush tribe to take them into their bills and fly away with them; and they are winged in another sense, and more effectually than the seeds of pines, for these are carried even against the wind. The consequence is, that cherry trees grow not only here but there. The same is true of a great many other seeds.

But to come to the observation which suggested these remarks. As I have said, I suspect that I can throw some light on the fact that when hereabouts a dense pine wood is cut down, oaks and other hard woods may at once take its place. I have got only to show that the acorns and nuts, provided they are grown in the neighborhood, are regularly planted in such woods; for I assert that if an oak tree has not grown within ten miles, and man has not carried acorns thither, then an oak wood will not spring up *at once*, when a pine wood is cut down.

Apparently, there were only pines there before. They are cut off, and after a year or two you see oaks and other hard woods springing up there, with scarcely a pine amid them, and the wonder commonly is, how the seed could have lain in the ground so long without decaying. But the truth is, that it has not lain in the ground so long, but is regularly planted each year by various quadrupeds and birds.

In this neighborhood, where oaks and pines are about equally dispersed, if you look through the thickest pine wood, even the seemingly unmixed pitch pine ones, you will commonly detect many little oaks, birches, and other hard woods, sprung from seeds carried into the thicket by squirrels and other animals, and also blown thither, but which are overshadowed and choked by the pines. The denser the evergreen wood, the more likely it is to be well planted with these seeds, because the planters incline to resort with their forage to the closest covert. They also carry it into birch and other woods. This planting is carried on annually, and the oldest seedlings annually die; but when the pines are cleared off, the oaks, having got just the start they want, and now secured favorable conditions, immediately spring up to trees.

The shade of a dense pine wood is more unfavorable to the springing up of pines of the same species than of oaks within it, though the former may come up abundantly when the pines are cut, if there chance to be sound seed in the ground.

But when you cut off a lot of hard wood, very often the little pines mixed with it have a similar start, for the squirrels have carried off the nuts to the pines, and not to the more open wood, and they commonly make pretty clean work of it; and moreover, if the wood was old, the sprouts will be feeble or entirely fail; to say nothing about the soil being, in a measure, exhausted for this kind of crop.

If a pine wood is surrounded by a white oak one chiefly, white oaks may be expected to succeed when the pines are cut. If it is surrounded instead by an edging of shrub oaks, then you will probably have a dense shrub oak thicket.

I have no time to go into details, but will say, in a word, that while the wind is conveying the seeds of pines into hard woods and open lands, the squirrels and other animals are conveying the seeds of oaks and walnuts into the pine woods, and thus a rotation of crops is kept up.

I affirmed this confidently many years ago, and an occasional examination of dense pine woods confirmed me in my opinion. It has long been known to observers that squirrels bury nuts in the ground, but I am not aware that any one has thus accounted for the regular succession of forests.

On the 24th of September, in 1857, as I was paddling down the Assabet, in this town, I saw a red squirrel run along the bank under some herbage, with something large in its mouth. It stopped near the foot of a hemlock, within a couple of rods of me, and, hastily pawing a hole with its fore feet, dropped its booty into it, covered it up, and retreated part way up the trunk of the tree. As I approached the shore to examine the deposit, the squirrel, descending part way, betrayed no little anxiety about its treasure, and made two or three motions to recover it before it finally retreated. Digging there, I found two green pignuts joined together, with the thick husks on, buried about an inch and a half under the reddish soil of decayed hemlock leaves — just the right depth to plant it. In short, this squirrel was then engaged in accomplishing two objects, to wit, laying up a store of winter food for itself, and planting a hickory wood for all creation. If the squirrel was killed, or neglected its deposit, a hickory would spring up. The nearest hickory tree was twenty rods distant. These nuts were there still just fourteen days later, but were gone when I looked again. November 21st, or six weeks later still.

I have since examined more carefully several dense woods, which are said to be, and are apparently, exclusively pine, and always with the same result. For instance, I walked the same day to a small but very dense and handsome white pine grove, about fifteen rods square, in the east part of this town. The trees are large for Concord, being from ten to twenty inches in diameter, and as exclusively pine as any wood that I know. Indeed, I selected this wood because I thought it the least likely to contain anything else. It stands on an open plain or pasture, except that it adjoins another small pine wood, which has a few little oaks in it, on the southeast side. On every other side, it was at least thirty rods from the nearest woods. Standing on the edge of this grove and looking through it, for it is quite level and free from underwood, for the most part bare, red-carpeted ground, you would have said that there was not a hardwood tree in it, young or old. But on looking carefully along over its floor I discovered, though it was not till my eye had got used to the search, that, alternating with thin ferns, and small blueberry bushes, there was, not merely here and there, but as often as every five feet and with a degree of regularity, a little oak, from three to twelve inches high, and in one place I found a green acorn dropped by the base of a pine.

I confess I was surprised to find my theory so perfectly proved in this case. One of the principal agents in this planting, the red squirrels, were all the while curiously inspecting me, while I was inspecting their plantation. Some of the little oaks had been browsed by cows, which resorted to this wood for shade.

After seven or eight years, the hard woods evidently find such a locality unfavorable to their growth, the pines being allowed to stand. As an evidence of this, I observed a diseased red maple twenty-five feet long, which had been recently prostrated, though it was still covered with green leaves, the only maple in any position in the wood.

But although these oaks almost invariably die if the pines are not cut down, it is probable that they do better for a few years under their shelter than they would anywhere else.

The very extensive and thorough experiments of the English have at length led them to adopt a method of raising oaks almost precisely like this which somewhat earlier had been adopted by Nature and her squirrels here; they have simply rediscovered the value of pines as nurses for oaks. The English experimenters seem, early and generally, to have found out the importance of using trees of some kind as nurse-plants for the young oaks. I quote from Loudon what he describes as 'the ultimatum on the subject of planting and sheltering oaks' — 'an abstract of the practice adopted by the government officers in the national forests' of England, prepared by Alexander Milne.

At first some oaks had been planted by themselves, and others mixed with Scotch pines; 'but in all cases,' says Mr. Milne, 'where oaks were planted actually among the pines and surrounded by them [though the soil might be inferior], the oaks were found to be much the best.' 'For several years past, the plan pursued has been to plant the inclosures with Scotch pines only [a tree very similar to our pitch pine], and when the pines have got to the height of five or six feet, then to put in good strong oak plants of about four or five years' growth among the pines — not cutting away any pines at first, unless they happen to be so strong and thick as to overshadow the oaks. In about two years it becomes necessary to shred the branches of the pines, to give light and air to the oaks, and in about two or three more years to begin gradually to remove the pines altogether, taking out a certain number each year, so that, at the end of twenty or twenty-five years, not a single Scotch pine shall be left; although, for the first ten or twelve years, the plantation may have appeared to contain nothing else but pine. The advantage of this mode of planting has been found to be that the pines dry and ameliorate the soil, destroying the coarse grass and brambles which frequently choke and injure oaks; and that no mending over is necessary, as scarcely an oak so planted is found to fail.'

Thus much the English planters have discovered by patient experiment, and, for aught I know, they have taken out a patent for it; but they appear not to have discovered that it was discovered before, and that they are merely adopting the method of Nature, which she long ago made patent to all. She is all the while planting the oaks amid the pines without our knowledge, and at last, instead of government officers, we send a party of woodchoppers to cut down the pines, and so rescue an oak forest, at which we wonder as if it had dropped from the skies.

As I walk amid hickories, even in August, I hear the sound of green pignuts falling from time to time, cut off by the chickaree over my head. In the fall, I notice on the ground, either within or in the neighborhood of oak woods, on all sides of the town, stout oak twigs three or four inches long, bearing half a dozen empty acorn-cups, which twigs have been gnawed off by squirrels, on both sides of the nuts, in order to make them more portable. The jays scream and the red squirrels scold while you are clubbing and shaking the chestnut trees, for they are there on the same errand, and two of a trade never agree. I frequently see a red or gray squirrel cast down a green chestnut bur, as I am going through the woods, and I used to think, sometimes, that they were cast at me. In fact, they are so busy about it, in the midst of the chestnut season, that you cannot stand long in the woods without hearing one fall. A sportsman told me that he had, the day before — that was in the middle of October — seen a green chestnut bur dropped on our great river meadow, fifty rods from the nearest wood, and much further from the nearest chestnut tree, and he could not tell how it came there. Occasionally, when chestnutting in midwinter, I find thirty or forty nuts in a pile, left in its gallery, just under the leaves, by the common wood mouse (*Mus leucopus*).

But especially, in the winter, the extent to which this transportation and planting of nuts is carried on is made apparent by the snow. In almost every wood, you will see where the red or gray squirrels have pawed down through the snow in a hundred places, sometimes two feet deep, and almost always directly to a nut or a pine cone, as directly as if they had started from it and bored upward — which you and I could not have done. It would be difficult for us to find one before the snow falls. Commonly, no doubt, they had deposited them there in the fall. You wonder if they remember the localities, or discover them by the scent. The red squirrel commonly has its winter abode in the earth under a thicket of evergreens, frequently under a small clump of evergreens in the midst of a deciduous wood. If there are any nut trees which still retain their nuts standing at a distance without the wood, their paths often lead directly to and from them. We therefore need not suppose an oak standing here and there *in* the wood in order to seed it, but if a few stand within twenty or thirty rods of it, it is sufficient.

I think that I may venture to say that every white pine cone that falls to the earth naturally in this town, before opening and losing its seeds, and almost every pitch pine one that falls at all, is cut off by a squirrel, and they begin to pluck them long before they are ripe, so that when the crop of white pine cones is a small one, as it commonly is, they cut off thus almost every one of these before it fairly ripens. I think, moreover, that their design, if I may so speak, in cutting them off green, is, partly, to prevent their opening and losing their seeds, for these are the ones for which they dig through the snow, and the only white pine cones which contain anything then. I have counted in one heap, within a diameter of four feet, the cores of 239 pitch pine cones which had been cut off and stripped by the red squirrel the previous winter.

The nuts thus left on the surface, or buried just beneath it, are placed in the most favorable circumstances for germinating. I have sometimes wondered how those which merely fell on the surface of the earth got planted; but, by the end of December, I find the chestnut of the same year partially mixed with the mould, as it were, under the decaying and mouldy leaves, where there is all the moisture and manure they want, for the nuts fall fast. In a plentiful year, a large proportion of the nuts are thus covered loosely an inch deep, and are, of course, somewhat concealed from squirrels. One winter, when the crop had been abundant, I got, with the aid of a rake, many quarts of these nuts as late as the tenth of January, and though some bought at the store the same day were more than half of them mouldy, I did not find a single mouldy one among these which I picked from under the wet and mouldy leaves, where they had been snowed on once or twice. Nature knows how to pack them best. They were still plump and tender. Apparently, they do not heat there, though wet. In the spring they were all sprouting.

Loudon says that 'when the nut [of the common walnut of Europe] is to be preserved through the winter for the purpose of planting in the following spring, it should be laid in a rot-heat, as soon as gathered, with the husk on, and the heap should be turned over frequently in the course of the winter.'

Here, again, he is stealing Nature's 'thunder.' How can a poor mortal do otherwise? for it is she that finds fingers to steal with, and the treasure to be stolen. In the planting of the seeds of most trees, the best gardeners do no more than follow Nature, though they may not know it. Generally, both large and small ones are most sure to germinate, and succeed best, when only beaten into the earth with the back of a spade, and then covered with leaves or straw. These results to which planters have arrived remind us of the experience of Kane and his companions at the north, who, when learning to live in that climate, were surprised to find themselves steadily adopting the customs of the natives, simply becoming Esquimaux. So, when we experiment in planting forests, we find ourselves at last doing as Nature does. Would it not be well to consult with Nature in the outset? for she is the most extensive and experienced planter of us all, not excepting the Dukes of Athol.

In short, they who have not attended particularly to this subject are but little aware to what an extent quadrupeds and birds are employed, especially in the fall, in collecting, and so disseminating and planting, the seeds of trees. It is the almost constant employment of the squirrels at that season, and you rarely meet with one that has not a nut in its mouth, or is not just going to get one. One squirrel-hunter of this town told me that he knew of a walnut tree which bore particularly good nuts, but that on going to gather them one fall, he found that he had been anticipated by a family of a dozen red squirrels. He took out of the tree, which was hollow, one bushel and three pecks by measurement, without the husks, and they supplied him and his family for the winter. It would be easy to multiply instances of this kind. How commonly in the fall you see the cheek-pouches of the striped squirrel distended by a quantity of nuts! This species gets its scientific name, *Tamias*, or the steward, from its habit of storing up nuts and other seeds. Look under a nut tree a month after the nuts have fallen, and see what proportion of sound nuts to the abortive ones and shells you will find ordinarily. They have been already eaten, or dispersed far and wide. The ground looks like a platform before a grocery, where the gossips of the village sit to crack nuts and less savory jokes. You have come, you would say, after the feast was over, and are presented with the shells only.

Occasionally, when threading the woods in the fall, you will hear a sound as if some one had broken a twig, and, looking up, see a jay pecking at an acorn, or you will see a flock of them at once about it, in the top of an oak, and hear them break them off. They then fly to a suitable limb, and placing the acorn under one foot, hammer away at it busily, making a sound like a woodpecker's tapping, looking round from time to time to see if any foe is approaching, and soon reach the meat, and nibble at it, holding up their heads to swallow, while they hold the remainder very firmly with their claws. Nevertheless it often drops to the ground before the bird has done with it. I can confirm what William Bartram wrote to Wilson, the ornithologist, that 'the jay is one of the most useful agents in the economy of nature, for disseminating forest trees and other nuciferous and hard-seeded vegetables on which they feed. Their chief employment during the autumnal season is foraging to supply their winter stores. In performing this necessary duty they drop abundance of seed in their flight over fields, hedges, and by fences, where they alight to deposit them in the postholes, etc. It is remarkable what numbers of young trees rise up in fields and pastures after a wet winter and spring. These birds alone are capable, in a few years' time, to replant all the cleared lands.'

I have noticed that squirrels also frequently drop their nuts in open land, which will still further account for the oaks and walnuts which spring up in pastures, for, depend on it, every new tree comes from a seed. When I examine the little oaks, one or two years old, in such places, I invariably find the empty acorn from which they sprung.

So far from the seed having lain dormant in the soil since oaks grew there before, as many believe, it is well known that it is difficult to preserve the vitality of acorns long enough to transport them to Europe; and it is recommended in Loudon's 'Arboretum,' as the safest course, to sprout them in pots on the voyage. The same authority states that 'very few acorns of any species will germinate after having been kept a year,' that beech mast 'only retains its vital properties one year,' and the black walnut 'seldom more than six months after it has ripened.' I have frequently found that in November almost every acorn left on the ground had sprouted or decayed. What with frost, drouth, moisture, and worms, the greater part are soon destroyed. Yet it is stated by one botanical writer that 'acorns that have lain for centuries, on being ploughed up, have soon vegetated.'

Mr. George B. Emerson, in his valuable Report on the Trees and Shrubs of this State, says of the pines: 'The tenacity of life of the seeds is remarkable. They will remain for many years unchanged in the ground, protected by the coolness and deep shade of the forest above them. But when the forest is removed, and the warmth of the sun admitted, they immediately vegetate.' Since he does not tell us on what observation his remark is founded, I must doubt its truth. Besides, the experience of nursery-men makes it the more questionable.

The stories of wheat raised from seed buried with an ancient Egyptian, and of raspberries raised from seed found in the stomach of a man in England, who is supposed to have died sixteen or seventeen hundred years ago, are generally discredited, simply because the evidence is not conclusive.

Several men of science, Dr. Carpenter among them, have used the statement that beach plums sprang up in sand which was dug up forty miles inland in Maine, to prove that the seed had lain there a very long time, and some have inferred that the coast has receded so far. But it seems to me necessary to their argument to show, first, that beach plums grow only on a beach. They are not uncommon here, which is about half that distance from the shore; and I remember a dense patch a few miles north of us, twenty-five miles inland, from which the fruit was annually carried to market. How much further inland they grow, I know not. Dr. Charles T. Jackson speaks of finding 'beach plums' (perhaps they were this kind) more than one hundred miles inland in Maine.

It chances that similar objections lie against all the more notorious instances of the kind on record.

Yet I am prepared to believe that some seeds, especially small ones, may retain their vitality for centuries under favorable circumstances. In the spring of 1859, the old Hunt house, so called, in this town, whose chimney bore the date 1703, was taken down. This stood on land which belonged to John Winthrop, the first governor of Massachusetts, and a part of the house was evidently much older than the above date, and belonged to the Winthrop family. For many years I have ransacked this neighborhood for plants, and I consider myself familiar with its productions. Thinking of the seeds which are said to be sometimes dug up at an unusual depth in the earth, and thus to reproduce long extinct plants, it occurred to me last fall that some new or rare plants might have sprung up in the cellar of this house, which had been covered from the light so long. Searching there on the 22d of September, I found, among other rank weeds, a species of nettle (*Urtica urens*) which I had not found before; dill, which I had not seen growing spontaneously; the Jerusalem oak (*Chenopodium Botrys*), which I had seen wild in but one place; black nightshade (*Solanum nigrum*), which is quite rare hereabouts, and common tobacco, which, though it was often cultivated here in the last century, has for fifty years been an unknown plant in this town, and a few months before this not even I had heard that one man, in the north part of the town, was cultivating a few plants for his own use. I have no doubt that some or all of these plants sprang from seeds which had long been buried under or about that house, and that that tobacco is an additional evidence that the plant was formerly cultivated here. The cellar has been filled up this year, and four of those plants, including the tobacco, are now again extinct in that locality.

It is true, I have shown that the animals consume a great part of the seeds of trees, and so, at least, effectually prevent their becoming trees; but in all these cases, as I have said, the consumer is compelled to be at the same time the disperser and planter, and this is the tax which he pays to Nature. I think it is Linnæus who says that while the swine is rooting for acorns he is planting acorns.

Though I do not believe that a plant will spring up where no seed has been, I have great faith in a seed — a, to me, equally mysterious origin for it. Convince me that you have a seed there, and I am prepared to expect wonders. I shall even believe that the millennium is at hand, and that the reign of justice is about to commence, when the Patent Office, or Government, begins to distribute, and the people to plant, the seeds of these things.

In the spring of 1857 I planted six seeds sent to me from the Patent Office, and labelled, I think, *Poitrine jaune grosse*, large yellow squash. Two came up, and one bore a squash which weighed 123½ pounds, the other bore four, weighing together 186¼ pounds. Who would have believed that there was 310 pounds of *poitrine jaune grosse* in that corner of my garden? These seeds were the bait I used to catch it, my ferrets which I sent into its burrow, my brace of terriers which unearthed it.

A little mysterious hoeing and manuring was all the *abracadabra presto-change* that I used, and lo! true to the label, they found for me 310 pounds of *poitrine jaune grosse* there, where it never was known to be, nor was before. These talismans had perchance sprung from America at first, and returned to it with unabated force. The big squash took a premium at your fair that fall, and I understood that the man who bought it, intended to sell the seeds for ten cents apiece. (Were they not cheap at that?) But I have more hounds of the same breed. I learn that one which I despatched to a distant town, true to its instincts, points to the large yellow squash there, too, where no hound ever found it before, as its ancestors did here and in France.

Other seeds I have which will find other things in that corner of my garden, in like fashion, almost any fruit you wish, every year for ages, until the crop more than fills the whole garden. You have but little more to do than throw up your cap for entertainment these American days. Perfect alchemists I keep who can transmute substances without end, and thus the corner of my garden is an inexhaustible treasure-chest. Here you can dig, not gold, but the value which gold merely represents; and there is no Signor Blitz about it. Yet farmers' sons will stare by the hour to see a juggler draw ribbons from his throat, though he tells them it is all deception. Surely, men love darkness rather than light

8. ON RELIGION AND FRIENDSHIP

PREFATORY NOTE

As I HAVE SAID ABOVE, when Thoreau wrote his first book, *A Week on the Concord and Merrimack Rivers*, he inserted into the narrative of the expedition many short pieces from his portfolio of published and unpublished writings including poems, translations, historical tales, and literary and philosophical essays, many if not most of which had precious little connection with the expedition narrative itself. In the condensed version of *A Week* given above, these insertions have been removed so that we may concentrate on the travel narrative. "Friendship" and "The Christian Fable" are two of the omitted inserts and, as will be seen, are really independent essays in themselves.

Thoreau was a deeply religious man in the sense at least that he was always greatly concerned with the moral and ethical problems facing mankind. But he was not at all conventional or orthodox in his beliefs. Raised as a Unitarian, he "signed off" from the church as soon as he reached legal maturity, as he tells us in his essay on "Civil Disobedience," and from then on virtually never attended church services; the religious hypocrisy of his neighbors who professed Christianity but failed to practice it was more than he could tolerate. The fact that the church as an institution was one of the centers of opposition to the antislavery movement confounded him. The narrow bigotry of New England orthodoxy toward every other religious tradition apalled him. As a result, since he was never one to hide his own unorthodox views, he did not hesitate to speak out against the church. One of the important factors in the publishing failure of *A Week* is that his outspokenness in this excerpt we have entitled "The Christian Fable" alienated the major reviewers who then denounced the book as a whole. He still irks the conventional today. It was only a few years ago, that each spring a certain Concord lady would place a bouquet of flowers on Emerson's grave, another on Hawthorne's and then turning to Thoreau's would shake her fist and shout, "None for you, you dirty little atheist." Yet for many, many people, Thoreau's writings are profoundly religious and a central part of their devotional reading.

"Friendship" is one of Thoreau's most popular pieces. It has been reprinted in almost innumerable "gift-book" editions. But oddly it is as unconventional in its own way as "The Christian Fable" is in its. It is no ordinary, everyday conception of friendship that he espouses, but rather a highly idealized Platonic relationship, so highly idealized in fact that he was never able to find such a friend in reality. He found himself constantly disappointed in those friendships he did form. Thoreau's emotional relationships with his fellow human beings have understandably been the subject of much speculation.[1] Why, almost everyone asks, did he never marry? Why was he so frequently attracted to older women? What about his idolization of young Edmund Sewall? Why, after the rejection of his marriage proposal by Ellen Sewall did he not turn to someone else? Unfortunately there is not the space here to attempt to answer those questions. But that there are such questions indicate that there were many tensions in Thoreau's personal life. What is remarkable is that he was able to engender out of these tensions not frustrations but a creative drive that produced some of the outstanding masterpieces of our literature.

[1] The sanest discussion of these problems is, I believe, an essay by James Armstrong on "Thoreau as Philosopher of Love," which may be found in my *Henry David Thoreau: A Profie* (New York, 1971, pp. 222–243).

I. THE CHRISTIAN FABLE [1]

MOST people with whom I talk, men and women even of some originality and genius, have their scheme of the universe all cut and dried — very *dry*, I assure you, to hear, dry enough to burn, dry-rotted and powder-post, methinks — which they set up between you and them in the shortest intercourse; an ancient and tottering frame with all its boards blown off. They do not walk without their bed. Some, to me, seemingly very unimportant and unsubstantial things and relations are for them everlastingly settled — as Father, Son, and Holy Ghost, and the like. These are like the everlasting hills to them. But in all my wanderings I never came across the least vestige of authority for these things. They have not left so distinct a trace as the delicate flower of a remote geological period on the coal in my grate. The wisest man preaches no doctrines; he has no scheme; he sees no rafter, not even a cobweb, against the heavens. It is clear sky. If I ever see more clearly at one time than at another, the medium through which I see is clearer. To see from earth to heaven, and see there standing, still a fixture, that old Jewish scheme! What right have you to hold up this obstacle to my understanding you, to your understanding me! You did not invent it; it was imposed on you. Examine your authority. Even Christ, we fear, had his scheme, his conformity to tradition, which slightly vitiates his teaching. He had not swallowed all formulas. He preached some mere doctrines. As for me, Abraham, Isaac, and Jacob are now only the subtilest imaginable essences, which would not stain the morning sky. Your scheme must be the framework of the universe; all other schemes will soon be ruins. The perfect God in his revelations of himself has never got to the length of one such proposition as you, his prophets, state. Have you learned the alphabet of heaven and can count three? Do you know the number of God's family? Can you put mysteries into words? Do you presume to fable of the ineffable? Pray, what geog-

---

[1] This essay is taken from 'A Week on the Concord and Merrimack Rivers,' p. 7 (Walden Edition), in which it is clearly an insert. A few pages of preparation are omitted.

rapher are you, that speak of heaven's topography? Whose friend are
you, that speak of God's personality? Do you, Miles Howard, think
that he has made you his confidant? Tell me of the height of the mountains of the moon, or of the diameter of space, and I may believe you,
but of the secret history of the Almighty, and I shall pronounce thee
mad. Yet we have a sort of family history of our God — so have the
Tahitians of theirs — and some old poet's grand imagination is imposed
on us as adamantine everlasting truth, and God's own word. Pythagoras says, truly enough, 'A true assertion respecting God is an assertion of God;' but we may well doubt if there is any example of this in
literature.

The New Testament is an invaluable book, though I confess to having
been slightly prejudiced against it in my very early days by the church
and the Sabbath-school, so that it seemed, before I read it, to be the
yellowest book in the catalogue. Yet I early escaped from their meshes.
It was hard to get the commentaries out of one's head and taste its true
flavor. I think that Pilgrim's Progress is the best sermon which has been
preached from this text; almost all other sermons that I have heard, or
heard of, have been but poor imitations of this. It would be a poor
story to be prejudiced against the Life of Christ because the book has
been edited by Christians. In fact, I love this book rarely, though it is
a sort of castle in the air to me, which I am permitted to dream. Having
come to it so recently and freshly, it has the greater charm, so that I cannot find any to talk with about it. I never read a novel, they have so
little real life and thought in them. The reading which I love best is the
scriptures of the several nations, though it happens that I am better
acquainted with those of the Hindoos, the Chinese, and the Persians,
than of the Hebrews, which I have come to last. Give me one of these
bibles, and you have silenced me for a while. When I recover the use
of my tongue, I am wont to worry my neighbors with the new sentences;
but commonly they cannot see that there is any wit in them. Such has
been my experience with the New Testament. I have not yet got to the
crucifixion, I have read it over so many times. I should love dearly to
read it aloud to my friends, some of whom are seriously inclined; it is so
good, and I am sure that they have never heard it, it fits their case
exactly, and we should enjoy it so much together — but I instinctively
despair of getting their ears. They soon show, by signs not to be mistaken, that it is inexpressibly wearisome to them. I do not mean to
imply that I am any better than my neighbors; for, alas! I know that
I am only as good, though I love better books than they.

It is remarkable that, notwithstanding the universal favor with which the New Testament is outwardly received, and even the bigotry with which it is defended, there is no hospitality shown to, there is no appreciation of, the order of truth with which it deals. I know of no book that has so few readers. There is none so truly strange, and heretical, and unpopular. To Christians, no less than Greeks and Jews, it is foolishness and a stumbling-block. There are, indeed, severe things in it which no man should read aloud more than once. 'Seek first the kingdom of heaven.' 'Lay not up for yourselves treasures on earth.' 'If thou wilt be perfect, go and sell that thou hast, and give to the poor, and thou shalt have treasure in heaven:' 'For what is a man profited, if he shall gain the whole world, and lose his own soul? Or what shall a man give in exchange for his soul?' Think of this, Yankees! 'Verily, I say unto you, if ye have faith as a grain of mustard seed, ye shall say unto this mountain, Remove hence to yonder place, and it shall remove; and nothing shall be impossible unto you.' Think of repeating these things to a New England audience! thirdly, fourthly, fifteenthly, till there are three barrels of sermons! who, without cant, can read them aloud? Who, without cant, can hear them, and not go out of the meeting-house? They never *were* read, they never *were* heard. Let but one of these sentences be rightly read, from any pulpit in the land, and there would not be left one stone of that meeting-house upon another.

Yet the New Testament treats of man and man's so-called spiritual affairs too exclusively, and is too constantly moral and personal, to alone content me, who am not interested solely in man's religious or moral nature, or in man even. I have not the most definite designs on the future. Absolutely speaking, Do unto others as you would that they should do unto you is by no means a golden rule, but the best of current silver. An honest man would have but little occasion for it. It is golden not to have any rule at all in such a case. The book has never been written which is to be accepted without any allowance. Christ was a sublime actor on the stage of the world. He knew what he was thinking of when he said, 'Heaven and earth shall pass away, but my words shall not pass away.' I draw near to him at such a time. Yet he taught mankind but imperfectly how to live; his thoughts were all directed toward another world. There is another kind of success than his. Even here we have a sort of living to get, and must buffet it somewhat longer. There are various tough problems yet to solve, and we must make shift to live, betwixt spirit and matter, such a human life as we can.

A healthy man, with steady employment, as wood-chopping at fifty cents a cord, and a camp in the woods, will not be a good subject for Christianity. The New Testament may be a choice book to him on some, but not on all or most of his days. He will rather go a-fishing in his leisure hours. The Apostles, though they were fishers too, were of the solemn race of sea-fishers, and never trolled for pickerel on inland streams.

Men have a singular desire to be good without being good for anything, because, perchance, they think vaguely that so it will be good for them in the end. The sort of morality which the priests inculcate is a very subtle policy, far finer than the politicians', and the world is very successfully ruled by them as the policemen. It is not worth the while to let our imperfections disturb us always. The conscience really does not, and ought not to monopolize the whole of our lives, any more than the heart or the head. It is as liable to disease as any other part. I have seen some whose consciences, owing undoubtedly to former indulgence, had grown to be as irritable as spoilt children, and at length gave them no peace. They did not know when to swallow their cud, and their lives of course yielded no milk.

> Conscience is instinct bred in the house;
> Feeling and Thinking propagate the sin
> By an unnatural breeding in and in.
> I say, Turn it outdoors,
> Into the moors.
> I love a life whose plot is simple,
> And does not thicken with every pimple,
> A soul so sound no sickly conscience binds it,
> That makes the universe no worse than 't finds it.
> I love an earnest soul,
> Whose mighty joy and sorrow
> Are not drowned in a bowl,
> And brought to life tomorrow;
> That lives one tragedy,
> And not seventy;
> A conscience worth keeping,
> Laughing not weeping;
> A conscience wise and steady,
> And forever ready;
> Not changing with events,
> Dealing in compliments;
> A conscience exercised about
> Large things, where one *may* doubt.
> I love a soul not all of wood,
> Predestinated to be good,

But true to the backbone
Unto itself alone,
And false to none;
Born to its own affairs,
Its own joys and own cares;
By whom the work which **God begun**
Is finished, and not undone;
Taken up where he left off,
Whether to worship or to scoff:
If not good, why then evil,
If not good god, good devil.
Goodness! — you hypocrite, come out of that,
Live your life, do your work, then take **your hat.**
I have no patience towards
Such conscientious cowards.
Give me simple laboring folk,
Who love their work,
Whose virtue is a song
To cheer God along.

I was once reproved by a minister who was driving a poor beast to some meeting-house horse-sheds among the hills of New Hampshire, because I was bending my steps to a mountain-top on the Sabbath, instead of a church, when I would have gone farther than he to hear a true word spoken on that or any day. He declared that I was 'breaking the Lord's fourth commandment,' and proceeded to enumerate, in a sepulchral tone, the disasters which had befallen him whenever he had done any ordinary work on the Sabbath. He really thought that a god was on the watch to trip up those men who followed any secular work on this day, and did not see that it was the evil conscience of the workers that did it. The country is full of this superstition, so that when one enters a village the church, not only really but from association, is the ugliest looking building in it, because it is the one in which human nature stoops the lowest and is most disgraced. Certainly, such temples as these shall ere long cease to deform the landscape. There are few things more disheartening and disgusting than when you are walking the streets of a strange village on the Sabbath, to hear a preacher shouting like a boatswain in a gale of wind, and thus harshly profaning the quiet atmosphere of the day. You fancy him to have taken off his coat, as when men are about to do hot and dirty work.

If I should ask the minister of Middlesex to let me speak in his pulpit on a Sunday, he would object because I do not pray as he does, or because I am not ordained. What under the sun are these things?

Really, there is no infidelity, nowadays, so great as that which prays, and keeps the Sabbath, and rebuilds the churches. The sealer of the South Pacific preaches a truer doctrine. The church is a sort of hospital for men's souls, and as full of quackery as the hospital for their bodies. Those who are taken into it live like pensioners in their Retreat or Sailor's Snug Harbor, where you may see a row of religious cripples sitting outside in sunny weather. Let not the apprehension that he may one day have to occupy a ward therein discourage the cheerful labors of the able-souled man. While he remembers the sick in their extremities, let him not look thither as to his goal. One is sick at heart of this pagoda worship. It is like the beating of gongs in a Hindoo subterranean temple. In dark places and dungeons the preacher's words might perhaps strike root and grow, but not in broad daylight in any part of the world that I know. The sound of the Sabbath bell far away, now breaking on these shores, does not awaken pleasing associations, but melancholy and sombre ones rather. One involuntarily rests on his oar, to humor his unusually meditative mood. It is as the sound of many catechisms and religious books twanging a canting peal round the earth, seeming to issue from some Egyptian temple and echo along the shore of the Nile, right opposite to Pharaoh's palace and Moses in the bulrushes, startling a multitude of storks and alligators basking in the sun.

Everywhere 'good men' sound a retreat, and the word has gone forth to fall back on innocence. Fall forward rather on to whatever there is there. Christianity only hopes. It has hung its harp on the willows, and cannot sing a song in a strange land. It has dreamed a sad dream, and does not yet welcome the morning with joy. The mother tells her falsehoods to her child, but, thank Heaven, the child does not grow up in its parent's shadow. Our mother's faith has not grown with her experience. Her experience has been too much for her. The lesson of life was too hard for her to learn.

It is remarkable that almost all speakers and writers feel it to be incumbent on them, sooner or later, to prove or to acknowledge the personality of God. Some Earl of Bridgewater, thinking it better late than never, has provided for it in his will. It is a sad mistake. In reading a work on agriculture, we have to skip the author's moral reflections, and the words 'Providence' and 'He' scattered along the page, to come at the profitable level of what he has to say. What he calls his religion is for the most part offensive to the nostrils. He should know better than expose himself, and keep his foul sores covered till they are quite healed. There is more religion in men's science than there is science in their religion. Let us make haste to the report of the committee on swine.

A man's real faith is never contained in his creed, nor is his creed an article of his faith. The last is never adopted. This it is that permits him to smile ever, and to live even as bravely as he does. And yet he clings anxiously to his creed, as to a straw, thinking that that does him good service because his sheet anchor does not drag.

In most men's religion, the ligature which should be its umbilical cord connecting them with divinity is rather like that thread which the accomplices of Cylon held in their hands when they went abroad from the temple of Minerva, the other end being attached to the statue of the goddess. But frequently, as in their case, the thread breaks, being stretched, and they are left without an asylum.

'A good and pious man reclined his head on the bosom of contemplation, and was absorbed in the ocean of a revery. At the instant when he awaked from his vision, one of his friends, by way of pleasantry, said, What rare gift have you brought us from that garden, where you have been recreating? He replied, I fancied to myself and said, when I can reach the rose-bower, I will fill my lap with the flowers, and bring them as a present to my friends; but when I got there, the fragrance of the roses so intoxicated me, that the skirt dropped from my hands.——"O bird of dawn! learn the warmth of affection from the moth; for that scorched creature gave up the ghost, and uttered not a groan: These vain pretenders are ignorant of him they seek after; for of him that knew him we never heard again: — O thou! who towerest above the flights of conjecture, opinion, and comprehension; whatever has been reported of thee we have heard and read; the congregation is dismissed, and life drawn to a close; and we still rest at our first encomium of thee!" ' [1]

[1] Sadi.

II. FRIENDSHIP[1]

One or two persons come to my house from time to time, there being proposed to them the faint possibility of intercourse. They are as full as they are silent, and wait for my plectrum to stir the strings of their lyre. If they could ever come to the length of a sentence, or hear one, on that ground they are dreaming of! They speak faintly, and do not obtrude themselves. They have heard some news, which none, not even they themselves, can impart. It is a wealth they can bear about them which can be expended in various ways. What came they out to seek?

No word is oftener on the lips of men than Friendship, and indeed no thought is more familiar to their aspirations. All men are dreaming of it, and its drama, which is always a tragedy, is enacted daily. It is the secret of the universe. You may thread the town, you may wander the country, and none shall ever speak of it, yet thought is everywhere busy about it, and the idea of what is possible in this respect affects our behavior toward all new men and women, and a great many old ones. Nevertheless, I can remember only two or three essays on this subject in all literature. No wonder that the Mythology, and Arabian Nights, and Shakespeare, and Scott's novels entertain us — we are poets and fablers and dramatists and novelists ourselves. We are continually acting a part in a more interesting drama than any written. We are dreaming that our Friends are our *Friends*, and that we are our Friends' *Friends*. Our actual Friends are but distant relations of those to whom we are pledged. We never exchange more than three words with a Friend in our lives on that level to which our thoughts and feelings almost habitually rise. One goes forth prepared to say, 'Sweet Friends!' and the salutation is, 'Damn your eyes!' But never mind; faint heart never won true Friend. O my Friend, may it come to pass once, that when you are my Friend I may be yours.

[1] This essay is taken from 'A Week on the Concord and Merrimack Rivers,' pp. 280–307 (Walden Edition), in which it was a late insert. A few pages of preparation are omitted.

Of what use the friendliest dispositions even, if there are no hours given to Friendship, if it is forever postponed to unimportant duties and relations? Friendship is first, Friendship last. But it is equally impossible to forget our Friends, and to make them answer to our ideal. When they say farewell, then indeed we begin to keep them company. How often we find ourselves turning our backs on our actual Friends, that we may go and meet their ideal cousins. I would that I were worthy to be any man's Friend.

What is commonly honored with the name of Friendship is no very profound or powerful instinct. Men do not, after all, *love* their Friends greatly. I do not often see the farmers made seers and wise to the verge of insanity by their friendship for one another. They are not often transfigured and translated by love in each other's presence. I do not observe them purified, refined, and elevated by the love of a man. If one abates a little the price of his wood, or gives a neighbor his vote at town-meeting, or a barrel of apples, or lends him his wagon frequently, it is esteemed a rare instance of Friendship. Nor do the farmers' wives lead lives consecrated to Friendship. I do not see the pair of farmer Friends of either sex prepared to stand against the world. There are only two or three couples in history. To say that a man is your Friend means commonly no more than this, that he is not your enemy. Most contemplate only what would be the accidental and trifling advantages of Friendship, so that the Friend can assist in time of need, by his substance, or his influence, or his counsel; but he who foresees such advantages in this relation proves himself blind to its real advantage, or indeed wholly inexperienced in the relation itself. Such services are particular and menial, compared with the perpetual and all-embracing service which it is. Even the utmost goodwill and harmony and practical kindness are not sufficient for Friendship, for Friends do not live in harmony merely, as some say, but in melody. We do not wish for Friends to feed and clothe our bodies — neighbors are kind enough for that — but to do the like office to our spirits. For this few are rich enough, however well disposed they may be. For the most part we stupidly confound one man with another. The dull distinguish only races or nations, or at most classes, but the wise man, individuals. To his Friend a man's peculiar character appears in every feature and in every action, and it is thus drawn out and improved by him.

Think of the importance of Friendship in the education of men.

> 'He that hath love and judgment too,
> Sees more than any other doe.'

It will make a man honest; it will make him a hero; it will make him a saint. It is the state of the just dealing with the just, the magnanimous with the magnanimous, the sincere with the sincere, man with man.

And it is well said by another poet —

> 'Why love among the virtues is not known,
> It is that love contracts them all in one.'

All the abuses which are the object of reform with the philanthropist, the statesman, and the housekeeper are unconsciously amended in the intercourse of Friends. A Friend is one who incessantly pays us the compliment of expecting from us all the virtues, and who can appreciate them in us. It takes two to speak the truth — one to speak, and another to hear. How can one treat with magnanimity mere wood and stone? If we dealt only with the false and dishonest, we should at last forget how to speak truth. Only lovers know the value and magnanimity of truth, while traders prize a cheap honesty, and neighbors and acquaintance a cheap civility. In our daily intercourse with men, our nobler faculties are dormant and suffered to rust. None will pay us the compliment to expect nobleness from us. Though we have gold to give, they demand only copper. We ask our neighbor to suffer himself to be dealt with truly, sincerely, nobly; but he answers no by his deafness. He does not even hear this prayer. He says practically, I will be content if you treat me as 'no better than I should be,' as deceitful, mean, dishonest, and selfish. For the most part, we are contented so to deal and to be dealt with, and we do not think that for the mass of men there is any truer and nobler relation possible. A man may have *good* neighbors, so called, and acquaintances, and even companions, wife, parents, brothers, sisters, children, who meet himself and one another on this ground only. The state does not demand justice of its members, but thinks that it succeeds very well with the least degree of it, hardly more than rogues practice; and so do the neighborhood and the family. What is commonly called Friendship even is only a little more honor among rogues.

But sometimes we are said to *love* another, that is, to stand in a true relation to him, so that we give the best to, and receive the best from, him. Between whom there is hearty truth, there is love; and in proportion to our truthfulness and confidence in one another, our lives are divine and miraculous, and answer to our ideal. There are passages of affection in our intercourse with mortal men and women, such as no prophecy had taught us to expect, which transcend our earthly life, and anticipate Heaven for us. What is this Love that may come right into the middle of a prosaic Goffstown day, equal to any of the gods? that discovers a new world, fair and fresh and eternal, occupying the place of the old one, when to the common eye a dust has settled on the universe? which world cannot else be reached, and does not exist. What other words, we may almost ask, are memorable and worthy to be repeated than those which love has inspired? It is wonderful that they were ever uttered. They are few and rare indeed, but, like a strain of music, they are incessantly repeated and modulated by the memory. All other words crumble off with the stucco which overlies the heart. We should not dare to repeat these now aloud. We are not competent to hear them at all times.

The books for young people say a great deal about the *selection* of Friends; it is because they really have nothing to say about *Friends*. They mean associates and confidants merely. 'Know that the contrariety of foe and Friend proceeds from God.' Friendship takes place between those who have an affinity for one another, and is a perfectly natural and inevitable result. No professions nor advances will avail. Even speech, at first, necessarily has nothing to do with it; but it follows after silence, as the buds in the graft do not put forth into leaves till long after the graft has taken. It is a drama in which the parties have no part to act. We are all Mussulmans and fatalists in this respect. Impatient and uncertain lovers think that they must say or do something kind whenever they meet; they must never be cold. But they who are Friends do not do what they *think* they must, but what they *must*. Even their Friendship is to some extent but a sublime phenomenon to them.

The true and not despairing Friend will address his Friend in some such terms as these.

'I never asked thy leave to let me love thee — I have a right. I love thee not as something private and personal, which is *your own*, but as something universal and worthy of love, *which I have found*. Oh, how I think of you! You are purely good — you are infinitely good. I can trust you forever. I did not think that humanity was so rich. Give me an opportunity to live.'

'You are the fact in a fiction — you are the truth more strange and admirable than fiction. Consent only to be what you are. I alone will never stand in your way.'

'This is what I would like — to be as intimate with you as our spirits are intimate — respecting you as I respect my ideal. Never to profane one another by word or action, even by a thought. Between us, if necessary, let there be no acquaintance.'

'I have discovered you; how can you be concealed from me?'

The Friend asks no return but that his Friend will religiously accept and wear and not disgrace his apotheosis of him. They cherish each other's hopes. They are kind to each other's dreams.

Though the poet says, "'Tis the preëminence of Friendship to impute excellence,' yet we can never praise our Friend, nor esteem him praiseworthy, nor let him think that he can please us by any *behavior*, or ever *treat* us well enough. That kindness which has so good a reputation elsewhere can least of all consist with this relation, and no such affront can be offered to a Friend as a conscious good-will, a friendliness which is not a necessity of the Friend's nature.

The sexes are naturally most strongly attracted to one another by constant constitutional differences, and are most commonly and surely the complements of each other. How natural and easy it is for man to secure the attention of woman to what interests himself! Men and women of equal culture, thrown together, are sure to be of a certain value to one another, more than men to men. There exists already a natural disinterestedness and liberality in such society, and I think that any man will more confidently carry his favorite books to read to some circle of intelligent women, than to one of his own sex. The visit of man to man is wont to be an interruption, but the sexes naturally expect one another. Yet Friendship is no respecter of sex; and perhaps it is more rare between the sexes than between two of the same sex.

Friendship is, at any rate, a relation of perfect equality. It cannot well spare any outward sign of equal obligation and advantage. The nobleman can never have a Friend among his retainers, nor the king among his subjects. Not that the parties to it are in all respects equal, but they are equal in all that respects or affects their Friendship. The one's love is exactly balanced and represented by the other's. Persons are only the vessels which contain the nectar, and the hydrostatic paradox is the symbol of love's law. It finds its level and rises to its fountain-head in all breasts, and its slenderest column balances the ocean.

> 'And love as well the shepherd can
> As can the mighty nobleman.'

The one sex is not, in this respect, more tender than the other. A hero's love is as delicate as a maiden's.

Confucius said, 'Never contract Friendship with a man who is not better than thyself.' It is the merit and preservation of Friendship, that it takes place on a level higher than the actual characters of the parties would seem to warrant. The rays of light come to us in such a curve that every man whom we meet appears to be taller than he actually is. Such foundation has civility. My Friend is that one whom I can associate with my choicest thought. I always assign to him a nobler employment in my absence than I ever find him engaged in; and I imagine that the hours which he devotes to me were snatched from a higher society. The sorest insult which I ever received from a Friend was when he behaved with the license which only long and cheap acquaintance allows to one's faults, in my presence, without shame, and still addressed me in friendly accents. Beware, lest thy Friend learn at last to tolerate one frailty of thine, and so an obstacle be raised to the progress of thy love. There are times when we have had enough even of our Friends, when we begin inevitably to profane one another, and must withdraw religiously into solitude and silence, the better to prepare ourselves for a loftier intimacy. Silence is the ambrosial night in the intercourse of Friends, in which their sincerity is recruited and takes deeper root.

Friendship is never established as an understood relation. Do you demand that I be less your Friend that you may know it? Yet what right have I to think that another cherishes so rare a sentiment for me? It is a miracle which requires constant proofs. It is an exercise of the purest imagination and the rarest faith. It says by a silent but eloquent behavior, 'I will be so related to thee as thou canst imagine; even so thou mayest believe. I will spend truth — all my wealth on thee' — and the Friend responds silently through his nature and life, and treats his Friend with the same divine courtesy. He knows us literally through thick and thin. He never asks for a sign of love, but can distinguish it by the features which it naturally wears. We never need to stand upon ceremony with him with regard to his visits. Wait not till I invite thee, but observe that I am glad to see thee when thou comest. It would be paying too dear for thy visit to ask for it. Where my Friend lives there are all riches and every attraction, and no slight obstacle can keep me from him. Let me never have to tell thee what I have not to tell. Let our intercourse be wholly above ourselves, and draw us up to it.

The language of Friendship is not words, but meanings. It is an intelligence above language. One imagines endless conversations with his Friend, in which the tongue shall be loosed, and thoughts be spoken without hesitancy or end; but the experience is commonly far otherwise. Acquaintances may come and go, and have a word ready for every occasion; but what puny word shall he utter whose very breath is thought and meaning? Suppose you go to bid farewell to your Friend who is setting out on a journey; what other outward sign do you know than to shake his hand? Have you any palaver ready for him then? any box of salve to commit to his pocket? any particular message to send by him? any statement which you had forgotten to make? — as if you could forget anything. No, it is much that you take his hand and say Farewell; that you could easily omit; so far custom has prevailed. It is even painful, if he is to go, that he should linger so long. If he must go, let him go quickly. Have you any *last* words? Alas, it is only the word of words, which you have so long sought and found not; *you* have not a *first* word yet. There are few even whom I should venture to call earnestly by their most proper names. A name pronounced is the recognition of the individual to whom it belongs. He who can pronounce my name aright, he can call me, and is entitled to my love and service. Yet reserve is the freedom and abandonment of lovers. It is the reserve of what is hostile or indifferent in their natures, to give place to what is kindred and harmonious.

The violence of love is as much to be dreaded as that of hate. When it is durable it is serene and equable. Even its famous pains begin only with the ebb of love, for few are indeed lovers, though all would fain be. It is one proof of a man's fitness for Friendship that he is able to do without that which is cheap and passionate. A true Friendship is as wise as it is tender. The parties to it yield implicitly to the guidance of their love, and know no other law nor kindness. It is not extravagant and insane, but what it says is something established henceforth, and will bear to be stereotyped. It is a truer truth, it is better and fairer news, and no time will ever shame it, or prove it false. This is a plant which thrives best in a temperate zone, where summer and winter alternate with one another. The Friend is a *necessarius*, and meets his Friend on homely ground; not on carpets and cushions, but on the ground and on rocks they will sit, obeying the natural and primitive laws. They will meet without any outcry, and part without loud sorrow. Their relation implies such qualities as the warrior prizes; for it takes a valor to open the hearts of men as well as the gates of castles. It is not an idle sympathy and mutual consolation merely, but a heroic sympathy of aspiration and endeavor.

> 'When manhood shall be matched so
> That fear can take no place,
> Then weary *works* make warriors
> Each other to embrace.'

The Friendship which Wawatam testified for Henry the fur-trader, as described in the latter's 'Adventures,' so almost bare and leafless, yet not blossomless nor fruitless, is remembered with satisfaction and security. The stern, imperturbable warrior, after fasting, solitude, and mortification of body, comes to the white man's lodge, and affirms that he is the white brother whom he saw in his dream, and adopts him henceforth. He buries the hatchet as it regards his friend, and they hunt and feast and make maple-sugar together. 'Metals unite from fluxility; birds and beasts from motives of convenience; fools from fear and stupidity; and just men at sight.' If Wawatam would taste the 'white man's milk' with his tribe, or take his bowl of human broth made of the trader's fellow-countrymen, he first finds a place of safety for his Friend, whom he has rescued from a similar fate. At length, after a long winter of undisturbed and happy intercourse in the family of the chieftain in the wilderness, hunting and fishing, they return in the spring to Michilimackinac to dispose of their furs; and it becomes necessary for Wawatam to take leave of his Friend at the Isle aux Outardes, when the latter, to avoid his enemies, proceeded to the Sault de Sainte Marie, supposing that they were to be separated for a short time only. 'We now exchanged farewells,' says Henry, 'with an emotion entirely reciprocal. I did not quit the lodge without the most grateful sense of the many acts of goodness which I had experienced in it, nor without the sincerest respect for the virtues which I had witnessed among its members. All the family accompanied me to the beach; and the canoe had no sooner put off than Wawatam commenced an address to the Kichi Manito, beseeching him to take care of me, his brother, till we should next meet. We had proceeded to too great a distance to allow of our hearing his voice, before Wawatam had ceased to offer up his prayers.' We never hear of him again.

Friendship is not so kind as is imagined; it has not much human blood in it, but consists with a certain disregard for men and their erections, the Christian duties and humanities, while it purifies the air like electricity. There may be the sternest tragedy in the relation of two more than usually innocent and true to their highest instincts. We may call it an essentially heathenish intercourse, free and irresponsible in its nature, and practising all the virtues gratuitously. It is not the highest sympathy merely, but a pure and lofty society, a fragmentary and god-like intercourse of ancient date, still kept up at intervals, which, remembering itself, does not hesitate to disregard the humbler rights and duties of humanity. It requires immaculate and godlike qualities full-grown, and exists at all only by condescension and anticipation of the remotest future. We love nothing which is merely good and not fair, if such a thing is possible. Nature puts some kind of blossom before every fruit, not simply a calyx behind it. When the Friend comes out of his heathenism and superstition, and breaks his idols, being converted by the precepts of a newer testament; when he forgets his mythology, and treats his Friend like a Christian, or as he can afford — then Friendship ceases to be Friendship, and becomes charity; that principle which established the almshouse is now beginning with its charity at home, and establishing an almshouse and pauper relations there.

As for the number which this society admits, it is at any rate to be begun with one, the noblest and greatest that we know, and whether the world will ever carry it further — whether, as Chaucer affirms,

> 'There be mo sterres in the skie than a pair,'

remains to be proved;

> 'And certaine he is well begone
> Among a thousand that findeth one.'

We shall not surrender ourselves heartily to any while we are conscious that another is more deserving of our love. Yet Friendship does not stand for numbers; the Friend does not count his Friends on his fingers; they are not numerable. The more there are included by this bond, if they are indeed included, the rarer and diviner the quality of the love that binds them. I am ready to believe that as private and intimate a relation may exist by which three are embraced, as between two. Indeed, we cannot have too many friends; the virtue which we appreciate we to some extent appropriate, so that thus we are made at last more fit for every relation of life. A base Friendship is of a narrowing and exclusive tendency, but a noble one is not exclusive; its very superfluity and dispersed love is the humanity which sweetens society, and sympathizes with foreign nations; for though its foundations are private, it is, in effect, a public affair and a public advantage, and the Friend, more than the father of a family, deserves well of the state.

The only danger in Friendship is that it will end. It is a delicate plant, though a native. The least unworthiness, even if it be unknown to one's self, vitiates it. Let the Friend know that those faults which he observes in his Friend his own faults attract. There is no rule more invariable than that we are paid for our suspicions by finding what we suspected. By our narrowness and prejudices we say, I will have so much and such of you, my Friend, no more. Perhaps there are none charitable, none disinterested, none wise, noble, and heroic enough, for a true and lasting Friendship.

I sometimes hear my Friends complain finely that I do not appreciate their fineness. I shall not tell them whether I do or not. As if they expected a vote of thanks for every fine thing which they uttered or did. Who knows but it was finely appreciated? It may be that your silence was the finest thing of the two. There are some things which a man never speaks of, which are much finer kept silent about. To the highest communications we only lend a silent ear. Our finest relations are not simply kept silent about, but buried under a positive depth of silence never to be revealed. It may be that we are not even yet acquainted. In human intercourse the tragedy begins, not when there is misunderstanding about words, but when silence is not understood. Then there can never be an explanation. What avails it that another loves you, if he does not understand you? Such love is a curse. What sort of companions are they who are presuming always that their silence is more expressive than yours? How foolish, and inconsiderate, and unjust, to conduct as if you were the only party aggrieved! Has not your Friend always equal ground of complaint? No doubt my Friends sometimes speak to me in vain, but they do not know what things I hear which they are not aware that they have spoken. I know that I have frequently disappointed them by not giving them words when they expected them, or such as they expected. Whenever I see my Friend I speak to him; but the expecter, the man with the ears, is not he. They will complain too that you are hard. O ye that would have the cocoanut wrong side outwards, when next I weep I will let you know. They ask for words and deeds, when a true relation is word and deed. If they know not of these things, how can they be informed? We often forbear to confess our feelings, not from pride, but for fear that we could not continue to love the one who required us to give such proof of our affection.

I know a woman who possesses a restless and intelligent mind, interested in her own culture, and earnest to enjoy the highest possible advantages, and I meet her with pleasure as a natural person who not a little provokes me, and I suppose is stimulated in turn by myself. Yet our acquaintance plainly does not attain to that degree of confidence and sentiment which women, which all, in fact, covet. I am glad to help her, as I am helped by her; I like very well to know her with a sort of stranger's privilege, and hesitate to visit her often, like her other Friends. My nature pauses here, I do not well know why. Perhaps she does not make the highest demand on me, a religious demand. Some, with whose prejudices or peculiar bias I have no sympathy, yet inspire me with confidence, and I trust that they confide in me also as a religious heathen at least — a good Greek. I, too, have principles as well founded as their own. If this person could conceive that, without wilfulness. I associate with her as far as our destinies are coincident, as far as our Good Geniuses permit, and still value such intercourse, it would be a grateful assurance to me. I feel as if I appeared careless, indifferent, and without principle to her, not expecting more and yet not content with less. If she could know that I make an infinite demand on myself, as well as on all others, she would see that this true though incomplete intercourse is infinitely better than a more unreserved but falsely grounded one, without the principle of growth in it. For a companion, I require one who will make an equal demand on me with my own genius. Such a one will always be rightly tolerant. It is suicide, and corrupts good manners, to welcome any less than this. I value and trust those who love and praise my aspiration rather than my performance. If you would not stop to look at me, but look whither I am looking, and farther, then my education could not dispense with your company.

> My love must be as free
> As is the eagle's wing,
> Hovering o'er land and sea
> And everything.

> I must not dim my eye
> In thy saloon,
> I must not leave my sky
> And nightly moon.

> Be not the fowler's net
> Which stays my flight,
> And craftily is set
> T' allure the sight.

> But be the favoring gale
>   That bears me on,
> And still doth fill my sail
>   When thou art gone.

> I cannot leave my sky
>   For thy caprice,
> True love would soar as high
>   As heaven is.

> The eagle would not brook
>   Her mate thus won,
> Who trained his eye to look
>   Beneath the sun.

Few things are more difficult than to help a Friend in matters which do not require the aid of Friendship, but only a cheap and trivial service, if your Friendship wants the basis of a thorough practical acquaintance. I stand in the friendliest relation, on social and spiritual grounds, to one who does not perceive what practical skill I have, but when he seeks my assistance in such matters, is wholly ignorant of that one with whom he deals; does not use my skill, which in such matters is much greater than his, but only my hands. I know another, who, on the contrary, is remarkable for his discrimination in this respect; who knows how to make use of the talents of others when he does not possess the same; knows when not to look after or oversee, and stops short at his man. It is a rare pleasure to serve him, which all laborers know. I am not a little pained by the other kind of treatment. It is as if, after the friendliest and most ennobling intercourse, your Friend should use you as a hammer, and drive a nail with your head, all in good faith; notwithstanding that you are a tolerable carpenter, as well as his good Friend, and would use a hammer cheerfully in his service. This want of perception is a defect which all the virtues of the heart cannot supply:

> The Good how can we trust
> Only the Wise are just.
> The Good we use,
> The Wise we cannot choose.
> These there are none above;
> The Good they know and love,
> But are not known again
> By those of lesser ken.

> They do not charm us with their eyes,
> But they transfix with their advice;
> No partial sympathy they feel,
> With private woe or private weal,
> But with the universe joy and sigh,
> Whose knowledge is their sympathy.

Confucius said: 'To contract ties of Friendship with any one is to contract Friendship with his virtue. There ought not to be any other motive in Friendship.' But men wish us to contract Friendship with their vice also. I have a Friend who wishes me to see that to be right which I know to be wrong. But if Friendship is to rob me of my eyes, if it is to darken the day, I will have none of it. It should be expansive and inconceivably liberalizing in its effects. True Friendship can afford true knowledge. It does not depend on darkness and ignorance. A want of discernment cannot be an ingredient in it. If I can see my Friend's virtues more distinctly than another's, his faults too are made more conspicuous by contrast. We have not so good a right to hate any as our Friend. Faults are not the less faults because they are invariably balanced by corresponding virtues, and for a fault there is no excuse, though it may appear greater than it is in many ways. I have never known one who could bear criticism, who could not be flattered, who would not bribe his judge, or was content that the truth should be loved always better than himself.

If two travellers would go their way harmoniously together, the one must take as true and just a view of things as the other, else their path will not be strewn with roses. Yet you can travel profitably and pleasantly even with a blind man, if he practises common courtesy, and when you converse about the scenery will remember that he is blind but that you can see; and you will not forget that his sense of hearing is probably quickened by his want of sight. Otherwise you will not long keep company. A blind man and a man in whose eyes there was no defect were walking together, when they came to the edge of a precipice. 'Take care, my friend,' said the latter, 'here is a steep precipice; go no farther this way.' 'I know better,' said the other, and stepped off.

It is impossible to say all that we think, even to our truest Friend. We may bid him farewell forever sooner than complain, for our complaint is too well grounded to be uttered. There is not so good an understanding between any two, but the exposure by the one of a serious fault in the other will produce a misunderstanding in proportion to its heinousness. The constitutional differences which always exist, and are obstacles to a perfect Friendship, are forever a forbidden theme to the lips of Friends. They advise by their whole behavior. Nothing can reconcile them but love. They are fatally late when they undertake to explain and treat with one another like foes. Who will take an apology for a Friend? They must apologize like dew and frost, which are off again with the sun, and which all men know in their hearts to be beneficent. The necessity itself for explanation — what explanation will atone for that?

True love does not quarrel for slight reasons, such mistakes as mutual acquaintances can explain away, but, alas, however slight the apparent cause, only for adequate and fatal and everlasting reasons, which can never be set aside. Its quarrel, if there is any, is ever recurring, notwithstanding the beams of affection which invariably come to gild its tears; as the rainbow, however beautiful and unerring a sign, does not promise fair weather forever, but only for a season. I have known two or three persons pretty well, and yet I have never known advice to be of use but in trivial and transient matters. One may know what another does not, but the utmost kindness cannot impart what is requisite to make the advice useful. We must accept or refuse one another as we are. I could tame a hyena more easily than my Friend. He is a material which no tool of mine will work. A naked savage will fell an oak with a firebrand, and wear a hatchet out of a rock by friction, but I cannot hew the smallest chip out of the character of my Friend, either to beautify or deform it.

The lover learns at last that there is no person quite transparent and trustworthy, but every one has a devil in him that is capable of any crime in the long run. Yet, as an Oriental philosopher has said, 'Although Friendship between good men is interrupted, their principles remain unaltered. The stalk of the lotus may be broken, and the fibres remain connected.'

Ignorance and bungling with love are better than wisdom and skill without. There may be courtesy, there may be even temper, and wit, and talent, and sparkling conversation, there may be good-will even — and yet the humanest and divinest faculties pine for exercise. Our life without love is like coke and ashes. Men may be pure as alabaster and Parian marble, elegant as a Tuscan villa, sublime as Niagara, and yet if there is no milk mingled with the wine at their entertainments, better is the hospitality of Goths and Vandals.

My Friend is not of some other race or family of men, but flesh of my flesh, bone of my bone. He is my real brother. I see his nature groping yonder so like mine. We do not live far apart. Have not the fates associated us in many ways? It says, in the Vishnu Purana, 'Seven paces together is sufficient for the friendship of the virtuous, but thou and I have dwelt together.' Is it of no significance that we have so long partaken of the same loaf, drank at the same fountain, breathed the same air summer and winter, felt the same heat and cold; that the same fruits have been pleased to refresh us both, and we have never had a thought of different fibre the one from the other?

> Nature doth have her dawn each day,
>   But mine are far between;
> Content, I cry, for, sooth to say,
>   Mine brightest are, I ween.
>
> For when my sun doth deign to rise,
>   Though it be her noontide,
> Her fairest field in shadow lies
>   Nor can my light abide.
>
> Sometimes I bask me in her day,
>   Conversing with my mate,
> But if we interchange one ray,
>   Forthwith her heats abate.
>
> Through his discourse I climb and see,
>   As from some eastern hill,
> A brighter morrow rise to me
>   Than lieth in her skill.
>
> As 't were two summer days in one,
>   Two Sundays come together,
> Our rays united make one sun,
>   With fairest summer weather.

As surely as the sunset in my latest November shall translate me to the ethereal world, and remind me of the ruddy morning of youth; as surely as the last strain of music which falls on my decaying ear shall make age to be forgotten, or, in short, the manifold influences of nature survive during the term of our natural life, so surely my Friend shall forever be my Friend, and reflect a ray of God to me, and time shall foster and adorn and consecrate our Friendship, no less than the ruins of temples. As I love nature, as I love singing birds, and gleaming stubble, and flowing rivers, and morning and evening, and summer and winter, I love thee, my Friend.

But all that can be said of Friendship is like botany to flowers. How can the understanding take account of its friendliness?

Even the death of Friends will inspire us as much as their lives. They will leave consolation to the mourners, as the rich leave money to defray the expenses of their funerals, and their memories will be incrusted over with sublime and pleasing thoughts, as monuments of other men are overgrown with moss; for our Friends have no place in the grave-yard.

This to our cis-Alpine and cis-Atlantic Friends.

Also this other word of entreaty and advice to the large and respectable nation of Acquaintances, beyond the mountains; — Greeting.

My most serene and irresponsible neighbors, let us see that we have the whole advantage of each other; we will be useful, at least, if not admirable, to one another. I know that the mountains which separate us are high, and covered with perpetual snow, but despair not. Improve the serene winter weather to scale them. If need be, soften the rocks with vinegar. For here lie the verdant plains of Italy ready to receive you. Nor shall I be slow on my side to penetrate to your Provence. Strike then boldly at head or heart or any vital part. Depend upon it, the timber is well seasoned and tough, and will bear rough usage; and if it should crack, there is plenty more where it came from. I am no piece of crockery that cannot be jostled against my neighbor without danger of being broken by the collision, and must needs ring false and jarringly to the end of my days, when once I am cracked; but rather one of the old-fashioned wooden trenchers, which one while stands at the head of the table, and at another is a milking-stool, and at another a seat for children, and finally goes down to its grave not unadorned with honorable scars, and does not die till it is worn out. Nothing can shock a brave man but dullness. Think how many rebuffs every man has experienced in his day; perhaps has fallen into a horse-pond, eaten fresh-water clams, or worn one shirt for a week without washing. Indeed, you cannot receive a shock unless you have an electric affinity for that which shocks you. Use me, then, for I am useful in my way, and stand as one of many petitioners, from toadstool and henbane up to dahlia and violet, supplicating to be put to my use, if by any means ye may find me serviceable: whether for a medicated drink or bath, as balm and lavender; or for fragrance, as verbena and geranium; or for sight, as cactus; or for thoughts, as pansy. These humbler, at least, if not those higher uses.

Ah, my dear Strangers and Enemies, I would not forget you. I can well afford to welcome you. Let me subscribe myself Yours ever and truly — your much obliged servant. We have nothing to fear from our foes; God keeps a standing army for that service; but we have no ally against our Friends, those ruthless Vandals.

Once more to one and all,

> 'Friends, Romans, Countrymen, and Lovers.'

> Let such pure hate still underprop
> Our love, that we may be
> Each other's conscience,
> And have our sympathy
> Mainly from thence.

> We'll one another treat like gods,
> And all the faith we have
> In virtue and in truth, bestow
> On either, and suspicion leave
> To gods below.

> Two solitary stars —
> Unmeasured systems far
> Between us roll,
> But by our conscious light we are
> Determined to one pole.

> What need confound the sphere? —
> Love can afford to wait.
> For it no hour's too late
> That witnesseth one duty's end,
> Or to another doth beginning lend.

> It will subserve no use,
> More than the tints of flowers,
> Only the independent guest
> Frequents its bowers,
> Inherits its bequest.

> No speech though kind has it,
> But kinder silence doles
> Unto its mates,
> By night consoles,
> By day congratulates.

What saith the tongue to tongue?
What heareth ear of ear?
By the decrees of fate
From year to year,
Does it communicate.

Pathless the gulf of feeling yawns —
No trivial bridge of words,
Or arch of boldest span,
Can leap the moat that girds
The sincere man.

No show of bolts and bars
Can keep the foeman out,
Or 'scape his secret mine
Who entered with the doubt
That drew the line.

No warder at the gate
Can let the friendly in,
But, like the sun, o'er all
He will the castle win,
And shine along the wall.

There's nothing in the world I know
That can escape from love,
For every depth it goes below,
And every height above.

It waits as waits the sky,
Until the clouds go by,
Yet shines serenely on
With an eternal day,
Alike when they are gone,
And when they stay.

Implacable is Love —
Foes may be bought or teased
From their hostile intent,
But he goes unappeased
Who is on kindness bent.

9. MAN AGAINST THE STATE

PREFATORY NOTE

THOREAU's importance as a political writer was not recognized until well into the twentieth century. Although he spoke out vociferously and cogently for the rights of the individual time and time again, he was completely ignored by his contemporaries. One searches in vain through their writings for any comment at all, negative or positive, on Thoreau's political theories. It was not until Leo Tolstoi in Russia in the last decade of the nineteenth century and Mahatma Gandhi in South Africa in the first decade of the twentieth realized the political effectiveness of Thoreau's theories of civil disobedience that people became aware of his importance. Since then "Civil Disobedience" has become one of the most influential political documents in the world rivaled only by the radically different "Communist Manifesto" of Karl Marx in its impact. Thoreau's essay through Gandhi's application, freed India from the British Empire; through its use by the resistance movement in Europe, helped bring about the overthrow of Hitler's facism; under the leadership of Martin Luther King, brought about the first major breakthroughs in the struggles of the American blacks for equality; in the student riots of the late 1960's, precipitated major changes in the structure and programs of colleges and universities around the world; and in 1968, was a factor in bringing the career of an American President to a close.

Thoreau wrote "Civil Disobedience" first as a lecture to explain to his fellow townsmen in Concord why he had refused to pay his poll tax as a protest against slavery and had thus ended up in jail one night late in July of 1846. That over his protest his Aunt Maria had paid his tax for him and he was literally thrown out of jail the next morning detracts not one whit from the strength of his position nor the validity of his philosophy. The lecture was first published in Elizabeth Peabody's periodical *Aesthetic Papers* in 1849 under the title "Resistance to Civil Government." It did not attain its present title until its first (posthumous) book publication in 1866.

Although Thoreau apparently coined the phrase "civil disobedience" — at least there has not yet been found an earlier usage of the term than his — he did not originate the idea. It can be found as early as in the writings of Sophocles, Mencius, and Boethius. Thoreau's contribution is that he so succinctly and effectively enunciated the doctrines that his essay has literally become a manual of arms for those minority groups who, believing their government to be acting immorally, wish to awaken the conscience of its people. It has aptly been called the Declaration of Independence for the individual conscience.

"Life without Principle" is the epitome of Thoreau's philosophy of life. It is perhaps too concentrated to be a good introduction to his work, but it is a superb summary. I have found it is almost invariably the favorite essay of the most ardent Thoreauvians. Thoreau worked on it for many years, using it on the lecture platform on many occasions and constantly honing it down toward its final sharpness. At various times he entitled it "Getting a Living," "Life Misspent," "Higher Laws," and, most appropriately perhaps, "What Shall It Profit," referring of course to the Biblical "What shall it profit a man if he gain the whole world but lose his own soul?" Like "Civil Disobedience" with its emphasis on individualism it is pure Transcendentalism. It was first published in the *Atlantic Monthly* for October, 1863.

"Paradise (to be) Regained" is Thoreau's reply to the communal movements so popular in his day (and ours). Although he was always glad to find anyone concerned deeply enough about the welfare of mankind to be involved in a reform movement, he believed most reformers went about their work back end to. They believed if one created the ideal society, the individual would reform himself. Thoreau, on the other hand, Transcendentalist that he was, believed that only if the individual reformed himself could we achieve the ideal society. Thus when George Ripley and his friends invited Thoreau to participate in Brook Farm, he replied (in his journal), "As for these communities, I think I had rather keep bachelor's hall in hell than go to board in heaven. Do you think your virtue will be boarded with you?" And when he found the opportunity to review Etzler's Utopian *Paradise within the Reach of All Men*, for O'Sullivan's *Democratic Review*, although acknowledging Etzler's noble aims, he rejected Etzler's proposed reforms so strongly that O'Sullivan for a time hesitated to print Thoreau's review in his magazine, fearing it would offend the then widespread and influential Fourierist socialists. It was finally published in the *Democratic Review* for November, 1843. "The chief fault of this book," Thoreau said, "is, that it aims to secure the greatest degree of gross comfort and pleasure merely . . . But a moral reform must take place first, and then the necessity of the other will be superseded, and we shall sail and plow by its force alone."

As much as some people shy away from the term because of its unfortunate popular connotations of violence, Thoreau was, pure and simple, an anarchist — a philosophic anarchist, a nonviolent anarchist, a gentle anarchist — but, nonetheless, an anarchist. He believed supremely in the individual. He believed that the government served the citizen and not the citizen the state. To some, such a philosophy appears to court utter chaos. They picture a world in which no one obeys any law, forgetting both that we obey most laws not because society forces us to, but because we recognize they are for our mutual convenience and that once a law becomes sufficiently unpopular (witness the 18th Amendment), no amount of governmental coercion can enforce it effectively. What we need is not a disciplined society, but disciplined individuals. And the very heart of Thoreau's anarchist philosophy is that the individual *must* discipline himself. Thoreau is the voice of conscientious individualism.

I. PARADISE (TO BE) REGAINED[1]

WE LEARN that Mr. Etzler is a native of Germany, and originally published his book in Pennsylvania, ten or twelve years ago; and now a second English edition, from the original American one, is demanded by his readers across the water, owing, we suppose, to the recent spread of Fourier's doctrines. It is one of the signs of the times. We confess that we have risen from reading this book with enlarged ideas, and grander conceptions of our duties in this world. It did expand us a little. It is worth attending to, if only that it entertains large questions. Consider what Mr. Etzler proposes:

'Fellow-men! I promise to show the means of creating a paradise within ten years, where everything desirable for human life may be had by every man in superabundance, without labor, and without pay; where the whole face of nature shall be changed into the most beautiful forms, and man may live in the most magnificent palaces, in all imaginable refinements of luxury, and in the most delightful gardens; where he may accomplish, without labor, in one year, more than hitherto could be done in thousands of years; may level mountains, sink valleys, create lakes, drain lakes and swamps, and intersect the land everywhere with beautiful canals, and roads for transporting heavy loads of many thousand tons, and for travelling one thousand miles in twenty-four hours; may cover the ocean with floating islands movable in any desired direction with immense power and celerity, in perfect security, and with all comforts and luxuries, bearing gardens and palaces, with thousands of families, and provided with rivulets of sweet water; may explore the interior of the globe, and travel from pole to pole in a fortnight; provide himself with means, unheard of yet, for increasing his knowledge of the world, and so his intelligence; lead

---

[1] *The Paradise within the Reach of all Men, without Labor, by Powers of Nature and Machinery. An Address to all intelligent Men.* In Two Parts. By J. A. Etzler. Part First. Second English Edition. London. 1842. Pp. 55.

a life of continual happiness, of enjoyments yet unknown; free himself from almost all the evils that afflict mankind, except death, and even put death far beyond the common period of human life, and finally render it less afflicting. Mankind may thus live in and enjoy a new world, far superior to the present, and raise themselves far higher in the scale of being.'

It would seem from this and various indications beside, that there is a transcendentalism in mechanics as well as in ethics. While the whole field of the one reformer lies beyond the boundaries of space, the other is pushing his schemes for the elevation of the race to its utmost limits. While one scours the heavens, the other sweeps the earth. One says he will reform himself, and then nature and circumstances will be right. Let us not obstruct ourselves, for that is the greatest friction. It is of little importance though a cloud obstruct the view of the astronomer compared with his own blindness. The other will reform nature and circumstances, and then man will be right. Talk no more vaguely, says he, of reforming the world — I will reform the globe itself. What matters it whether I remove this humor out of my flesh, or this pestilent humor from the fleshy part of the globe? Nay, is not the latter the more generous course? At present the globe goes with a shattered constitution in its orbit. Has it not asthma, and ague, and fever, and dropsy, and flatulence, and pleurisy, and is it not afflicted with vermin? Has it not its healthful laws counteracted, and its vital energy which will yet redeem it? No doubt the simple powers of nature, properly directed by man, would make it healthy and a paradise; as the laws of man's own constitution but wait to be obeyed, to restore him to health and happiness. Our panaceas cure but few ails, our general hospitals are private and exclusive. We must set up another Hygeia than is now worshipped. Do not the quacks even direct small doses for children, larger for adults, and larger still for oxen and horses? Let us remember that we are to prescribe for the globe itself.

This fair homestead has fallen to us, and how little have we done to improve it, how little have we cleared and hedged and ditched! We are too inclined to go hence to a 'better land,' without lifting a finger, as our farmers are moving to the Ohio soil; but would it not be more heroic and faithful to till and redeem this New England soil of the world? The still youthful energies of the globe have only to be directed in their proper channel. Every gazette brings accounts of the untutored freaks of the wind — shipwrecks and hurricanes which the mariner and planter accept as special or general providences; but they touch our consciences, they remind us of our sins. Another deluge would disgrace mankind. We confess we never had much respect for that antediluvian race. A thoroughbred business man cannot enter heartily upon the business of life without first looking into his accounts. How many things are now at loose ends! Who knows which way the wind will blow tomorrow? Let us not succumb to nature. We will marshal the clouds and restrain tempests; we will bottle up pestilent exhalations; we will probe for earthquakes, grub them up, and give vent to the dangerous gas; we will disembowel the volcano, and extract its poison, take its seed out. We will wash water, and warm fire, and cool ice, and underprop the earth. We will teach birds to fly, and fishes to swim, and ruminants to chew the cud. It is time we had looked into these things.

And it becomes the moralist, too, to inquire what man might do to improve and beautify the system; what to make the stars shine more brightly, the sun more cheery and joyous, the moon more placid and content. Could he not heighten the tints of flowers and the melody of birds? Does he perform his duty to the inferior races? Should he not be a god to them? What is the part of magnanimity to the whale and the beaver? Should we not fear to exchange places with them for a day, lest by their behavior they should shame us? Might we not treat with magnanimity the shark and the tiger, not descend to meet them on their own level, with spears of shark's teeth and bucklers of tiger's skin? We slander the hyena; man is the fiercest and cruelest animal. Ah! he is of little faith; even the erring comets and meteors would thank him, and return his kindness in their kind.

How meanly and grossly do we deal with nature! Could we not have a less gross labor? What else do these fine inventions suggest — magnetism, the daguerreotype, electricity? Can we not do more than cut and trim the forest? — can we not assist in its interior economy, in the circulation of the sap? Now we work superficially and violently. We do not suspect how much might be done to improve our relation to animated nature even; what kindness and refined courtesy there might be.

There are certain pursuits which, if not wholly poetic and true, do at least suggest a nobler and finer relation to nature than we know. The keeping of bees, for instance, is a very slight interference. It is like directing the sunbeams. All nations, from the remotest antiquity, have thus fingered nature. There are Hymettus and Hybla, and how many bee-renowed spots beside! There is nothing gross in the idea of these little herds — their hum like the faintest low of kine in the meads. A pleasant reviewer has lately reminded us that in some places they are led out to pasture where the flowers are most abundant. 'Columella tells us,' says he, 'that the inhabitants of Arabia sent their hives into Attica to benefit by the later-blowing flowers.' Annually are the hives, in immense pyramids, carried up the Nile in boats, and suffered to float slowly down the stream by night, resting by day, as the flowers put forth along the banks; and they determine the richness of any locality, and so the profitableness of delay, by the sinking of the boat in the water. We are told, by the same reviewer, of a man in Germany, whose bees yielded more honey than those of his neighbors, with no apparent advantage; but at length he informed them, that he had turned his hives one degree more to the east, and so his bees, having two hours the start in the morning, got the first sip of honey. True, there is treachery and selfishness behind all this, but these things suggest to the poetic mind what might be done.

Many examples there are of a grosser interference, yet not without their apology. We saw last summer, on the side of a mountain, a dog employed to churn for a farmer's family, travelling upon a horizontal wheel, and though he had sore eyes, an alarming cough, and withal a demure aspect, yet their bread did get buttered for all that. Undoubtedly, in the most brilliant successes, the first rank is always sacrificed. Much useless travelling of horses, *in extenso*, has of late years been improved for man's behoof, only two forces being taken advantage of — the gravity of the horse, which is the centripetal, and his centrifugal inclination to go ahead. Only these two elements in the calculation. And is not the creature's whole economy better economized thus? Are not all finite beings better pleased with motions relative than absolute? And what is the great globe itself but such a wheel — a larger treadmill — so that our horse's freest steps over prairies are oftentimes balked and rendered of no avail by the earth's motion on its axis? But here he is the central agent and motive-power; and, for variety of scenery, being provided with a window in front, do not the ever-varying activity and fluctuating energy of the creature himself work the effect of the most varied scenery on a country road? It must be confessed that horses at present work too exclusively for men, rarely men for horses; and the brute degenerates in man's society.

It will be seen that we contemplate a time when man's will shall be law to the physical world, and he shall no longer be deterred by such abstractions as time and space, height and depth, weight and hardness, but shall indeed be the lord of creation. 'Well,' says the faithless reader, ' "life is short, but art is long;" where is the power that will effect all these changes?' This it is the very object of Mr. Etzler's volume to show. At present, he would merely remind us that there are innumerable and immeasurable powers already existing in nature, unimproved on a large scale, or for generous and universal ends, amply sufficient for these purposes. He would only indicate their existence, as a surveyor makes known the existence of a water-power on any stream; but for their application he refers us to a sequel to this book, called the 'Mechanical System.' A few of the most obvious and familiar of these powers are the Wind, the Tide, the Waves, the Sunshine. Let us consider their value.

First, there is the power of the Wind, constantly exerted over the globe. It appears from observation of a sailing-vessel, and from scientific tables, that the average power of the wind is equal to that of one horse for every one hundred square feet. We do not attach much value to this statement of the comparative power of the wind and horse, for no common ground is mentioned on which they can be compared. Undoubtedly, each is incomparably excellent in its way, and every general comparison made for such practical purposes as are contemplated, which gives a preference to the one, must be made with some unfairness to the other. The scientific tables are, for the most part, true only in a tabular sense. We suspect that a loaded wagon, with a light sail, ten feet square, would not have been blown so far by the end of the year, under equal circumstances, as a common racer or dray horse would have drawn it. And how many crazy structures on our globe's surface, of the same dimensions, would wait for dry-rot if the traces of one horse were hitched to them, even to their windward side? Plainly this is not the principal of comparison. But even the steady and constant force of the horse may be rated as equal to his weight at least. Yet we should prefer to let the zephyrs and gales bear, with all their weight, upon our fences, than that Dobbin, with feet braced, should lean ominously against them for a season.

Nevertheless, here is an almost incalculable power at our disposal, yet how trifling the use we made of it! It only serves to turn a few mills, blow a few vessels across the ocean, and a few trivial ends besides. What a poor compliment do we pay to our indefatigable and energetic servant!

Men having discovered the power of falling water, which, after all, is comparatively slight, how eagerly do they seek out and improve these *privileges!* Let a difference of but a few feet in level be discovered on some stream near a populous town, some slight occasion for gravity to act, and the whole economy of the neighborhood is changed at once. Men do indeed speculate about and with this power as if it were the only privilege. But meanwhile this aerial stream is falling from far greater heights with more constant flow, never shrunk by drought, offering mill-sites wherever the wind blows; a Niagara in the air, with no Canada side; — only the application is hard.

There are the powers, too, of the Tide and Waves, constantly ebbing and flowing, lapsing and relapsing, but they serve man in but few ways. They turn a few tide-mills, and perform a few other insignificant and accidental services only. We all perceive the effect of the tide; how imperceptibly it creeps up into our harbors and rivers, and raises the heaviest navies as easily as the lightest chip. Everything that floats must yield to it. But man, slow to take nature's constant hint of assistance, makes slight and irregular use of this power, in careening ships and getting them afloat when aground.

This power may be applied in various ways. A large body, of the heaviest materials that will float, may first be raised by it, and being attached to the end of a balance reaching from the land, or from a stationary support fastened to the bottom, when the tide falls the whole weight will be brought to bear upon the end of the balance. Also, when the tide rises, it may be made to exert a nearly equal force in the opposite direction. It can be employed wherever a *point d'appui* can be obtained.

Verily, the land would wear a busy aspect at the spring and neap tide, and these island ships, these *terrae infirmae*, which realize the fables of antiquity, affect our imagination. We have often thought that the fittest locality for a human dwelling was on the edge of the land, that there the constant lesson and impression of the sea might sink deep into the life and character of the landsman, and perhaps impart a marine tint to his imagination. It is a noble word, that *mariner* — one who is conversant with the sea. There should be more of what it signifies in each of us. It is a worthy country to belong to — we look to see him not disgrace it. Perhaps we should be equally mariners and terreners, and even our Green Mountains need some of that sea-green to be mixed with them.

The computation of the power of the Waves is less satisfactory. While only the average power of the wind and the average height of the tide were taken before, now the extreme height of the waves is used, for they are made to rise ten feet above the level of the sea, to which, adding ten more for depression, we have twenty feet, or the extreme height of a wave. Indeed, the power of the waves, which is produced by the wind blowing obliquely and at disadvantage upon the water, is made to be, not only three thousand times greater than that of the tide, but one hundred times greater than that of the wind itself, meeting its object at right angles. Moreover, this power is measured by the area of the vessel, and not by its length mainly, and it seems to be forgotten that the motion of the waves is chiefly undulatory, and exerts a power only within the limits of a vibration, else the very continents, with their extensive coasts, would soon be set adrift.

Finally, there is the power to be derived from Sunshine, by the principle on which Archimedes contrived his burning-mirrors, a multiplication of mirrors reflecting the rays of the sun upon the same spot, till the requisite degree of heat is obtained. The principal application of this power will be to the boiling of water and production of steam. So much for these few and more obvious powers, already used to a trifling extent. But there are innumerable others in nature, not described nor discovered. These, however, will do for the present. This would be to make the sun and the moon equally our satellites. For, as the moon is the cause of the tides, and the sun the cause of the wind, which, in turn, is the cause of the waves, all the work of this planet would be performed by these far influences.

'We may store up water in some eminent pond, and take out of this store, at any time, as much water through the outlet as we want to employ, by which means the original power may react for many days after it has ceased. . . . Such reservoirs of moderate elevation or size need not be made artificially, but will be found made by nature very frequently, requiring but little aid for their completion. They require no regularity of form. Any valley, with lower grounds in its vicinity, would answer the purpose. Small crevices may be filled up. Such places may be eligible for the beginning of enterprises of this kind.'

The greater the height, of course, the less water required. But suppose a level and dry country; then hill and valley, and 'eminent pond,' are to be constructed by main force; or, if the springs are unusually low, then dirt and stones may be used, and the disadvantage arising from friction will be counterbalanced by their greater gravity. Nor shall a single rood of dry land be sunk in such artificial ponds as may be wanted, but their surfaces 'may be covered with rafts decked with fertile earth, and all kinds of vegetables which may grow there as well as any where else.'

And, finally, by the use of thick envelopes retaining the heat, and other contrivances, 'the power of steam caused by sunshine may react at will, and thus be rendered perpetual, no matter how often or how long the sunshine may be interrupted.'

Here is power enough, one would think, to accomplish somewhat. These are the Powers below. O ye millwrights, ye engineers, ye operatives and speculators of every class, never again complain of a want of power: it is the grossest form of infidelity. The question is, not how we shall execute, but what. Let us not use in a niggardly manner what is thus generously offered.

Consider what revolutions are to be effected in agriculture. First, in the new country a machine is to move along, taking out trees and stones to any required depth, and piling them up in convenient heaps; then the same machine, 'with a little alteration,' is to plane the ground perfectly, till there shall be no hills nor valleys, making the requisite canals, ditches, and roads as it goes along. The same machine, 'with some other little alterations,' is then to sift the ground thoroughly, supply fertile soil from other places if wanted, and plant it; and finally the same machine, 'with a little addition,' is to reap and gather in the crop, thresh and grind it, or press it to oil, or prepare it any way for final use. For the description of these machines we are referred to 'Etzler's Mechanical System,' pages 11 to 27. We should be pleased to see that 'Mechanical System.' We have great faith in it. But we cannot stop for applications now.

Who knows but by accumulating the power until the end of the present century, using meanwhile only the smallest allowance, reserving all that blows, all that shines, all that ebbs and flows, all that dashes, we may have got such a reserved accumulated power as to run the earth off its track into a new orbit, some summer, and so change the tedious vicissitude of the seasons? Or, perchance, coming generations will not abide the dissolution of the globe, but, availing themselves of future inventions in aerial locomotion, and the navigation of space, the entire race may migrate from the earth, to settle some vacant and more western planet, it may be still healthy, perchance unearthy, not composed of dirt and stones, whose primary strata only are strewn, and where no weeds are sown. It took but little art, a simple application of natural laws, a canoe, a paddle, and a sail of matting, to people the isles of the Pacific, and a little more will people the shining isles of space.

Do we not see in the firmament the lights carried along the shore by night, as Columbus did? Let us not despair nor mutiny.

'The dwellings also ought to be very different from what is known, if the full benefit of our means is to be enjoyed. They are to be of a structure for which we have no name yet. They are to be neither palaces, nor temples, nor cities, but a combination of all, superior to whatever is known.

'Earth may be baked into bricks, or even vitrified stone by heat — we may bake large masses of any size and form, into stone and vitrified substance of the greatest durability, lasting even thousands of years, out of clayey earth, or of stones ground to dust, by the application of burning-mirrors. This is to be done in the open air without other preparation than gathering the substance, grinding and mixing it with water and cement, moulding or casting it, and bringing the focus of the burning-mirrors of proper size upon the same.'

The character of the architecture is to be quite different from what it ever has been hitherto; large solid masses are to be baked or cast in one piece, ready shaped in any form that may be desired. The building may, therefore, consist of columns two hundred feet high and upwards, of proportionate thickness, and of one entire piece of vitrified substance; huge pieces are to be moulded so as to join and hook on to each other firmly, by proper joints and folds, and not to yield in any way without breaking.

'Foundries, of any description, are to be heated by burning-mirrors, and will require no labor, except the making of the first moulds and the superintendence for gathering the metal and taking the finished articles away.'

Alas! in the present state of science, we must take the finished articles away; but think not that man will always be the victim of circumstances.

The countryman who visited the city, and found the streets cluttered with bricks and lumber, reported that it was not yet finished; and one who considers the endless repairs and reforming of our houses might well wonder when they will be done. But why may not the dwellings of men on this earth be built, once for all, of some durable material, some Roman or Etruscan masonry, which will stand, so that time shall only adorn and beautify them? Why may we not finish the outward world for posterity, and leave them leisure to attend to the inner? Surely, all the gross necessities and economies might be cared for in a few years. All might be built and baked and stored up, during this, the term-time of the world, against the vacant eternity, and the globe go provisioned and furnished, like our public vessels, for its voyage through space, as through some Pacific Ocean, while we would 'tie up the rudder and sleep before the wind,' as those who sail from Lima to Manilla.

But, to go back a few years in imagination, think not that life in these crystal palaces is to bear any analogy to life in our present humble cottages. Far from it. Clothed, once for all, in some 'flexible stuff,' more durable than George Fox's suit of leather, composed of 'fibres of vegetables,' 'glutinated' together by some 'cohesive substances,' and made into sheets, like paper, of any size or form, man will put far from him corroding care and the whole host of ills.

'The twenty-five halls in the inside of the square are to be each two hundred feet square and high; the forty corridors, each one hundred feet long and twenty wide; the eighty galleries, each from 1,000 to 1,250 feet long; about 7,000 private rooms, the whole surrounded and intersected by the grandest and most splendid colonnades imaginable; floors, ceilings, columns, with their various beautiful and fanciful intervals, all shining, and reflecting to infinity all objects and persons, with splendid lustre of all beautiful colors, and fanciful shapes and pictures.

'All galleries, outside and within the halls, are to be provided with many thousand commodious and most elegant vehicles, in which persons may move up and down like birds, in perfect security, and without exertion. . . . Any member may procure himself all the common articles of his daily wants, by a short turn of some crank, without leaving his apartment.

'One or two persons are sufficient to direct the kitchen business. They have nothing else to do but to superintend the cookery, and to watch the time of the victuals being done, and then to remove them, with the table and vessels, into the dining-hall, or to the respective private apartments, by a slight motion of the hand at some crank. . . . *Any very extraordinary desire of any person may be satisfied by going to the place where the thing is to be had; and anything that requires a particular preparation in cooking or baking may be done by the person who desires it.'*

This is one of those instances in which the individual genius is found to consent, as indeed it always does, at last, with the universal. This last sentence has a certain sad and sober truth, which reminds us of the scripture of all nations. All expression of truth does at length take this deep ethical form. Here is hint of a place the most eligible of any in space, and of a servitor, in comparison with whom all other helps dwindle into insignificance. We hope to hear more of him anon, for even a Crystal Palace would be deficient without his invaluable services.

And as for the environs of the establishment: —

'There will be afforded the most enrapturing views to be fancied, out of the private apartments, from the galleries, from the roof, from its turrets and cupolas — gardens, as far as the eye can see, full of fruits and flowers, arranged in the most beautiful order, with walks, colonnades, aqueducts, canals, ponds, plains, amphitheatres, terraces, fountains, sculptural works, pavilions, gondolas, places for public amusement, etc., to delight the eye and fancy, the taste and smell. . . . The walks and roads are to be paved with hard vitrified large plates, so as to be always clean from all dirt in any weather or season. . . .

'The walks may be covered with porticoes adorned with magnificent columns, statues, and sculptural works; all of vitrified substance, and lasting forever. At night the roof and the inside and outside of the whole square are illuminated by gas-light, which, in the mazes of many-colored crystal-like colonnades and vaultings, is reflected with a brilliancy that gives to the whole a lustre of precious stones, as far as the eye can see. Such are the future abodes of men. . . . Such is the life reserved to true intelligence, but withheld from ignorance, prejudice, and stupid adherence to custom.'

Thus is Paradise to be Regained, and that old and stern decree at length reversed. Man shall no more earn his living by the sweat of his brow. All labor shall be reduced to 'a short turn of some crank,' and 'taking the finished articles away.' But there is a crank — oh, how hard to be turned! Could there not be a crank upon a crank — an infinitely small crank? — we would fain inquire. No — alas! not. But there is a certain divine energy in every man, but sparingly employed as yet, which may be called the crank within — the crank after all — the prime mover in all machinery — quite indispensable to all work. Would that we might get our hands on its handle! In fact, no work can be shirked. It may be postponed indefinitely, but not infinitely. Nor can any really important work be made easier by coöperation or machinery. Not one particle of labor now threatening any man can be routed without being performed. It cannot be hunted out of the vicinity like jackals and hyenas. It will not run. You may begin by sawing the little sticks, or you may saw the great sticks first, but sooner or later you must saw them both.

We will not be imposed upon by this vast application of forces. We believe that most things will have to be accomplished still by the application called Industry. We are rather pleased, after all, to consider the small private, but both constant and accumulated, force which stands behind every spade in the field. This it is that makes the valleys shine, and the deserts really bloom. Sometimes, we confess, we are so degenerate as to reflect with pleasure on the days when men were yoked like cattle, and drew a crooked stick for a plough. After all, the great interests and methods were the same.

It is a rather serious objection to Mr. Etzler's schemes, that they require time, men, and money, three very superfluous and inconvenient things for an honest and well-disposed man to deal with. 'The whole world,' he tells us, 'might therefore be really changed into a paradise, within less than ten years, commencing from the first year of an association for the purpose of constructing and applying the machinery.' We are sensible of a startling incongruity when time and money are mentioned in this connection. The ten years which are proposed would be a tedious while to wait, if every man were at his post and did his duty, but quite too short a period, if we are to take time for it. But this fault is by no means peculiar to Mr. Etzler's schemes. There is far too much hurry and bustle, and too little patience and privacy, in all our methods, as if something were to be accomplished in centuries. The true reformer does not want time, nor money, nor coöperation, nor advice. What is time but the stuff delay is made of? And depend upon it, our virtue will not live on the interest of our money. He expects no income, but outgoes; so soon as we begin to count the cost, the cost begins. And as for advice, the information floating in the atmosphere of society is as evanescent and unserviceable to him as gossamer for clubs of Hercules. There is absolutely no common sense; it is common nonsense. If we are to risk a cent or a drop of our blood, who then shall advise us? For ourselves, we are too young for experience. Who is old enough? We are older by faith than by experience. In the unbending of the arm to do the deed there is experience worth all the maxims in the world.

'It will now be plainly seen that the execution of the proposals is not proper for individuals. Whether it be proper for government at this time, before the subject has become popular, is a question to be decided; all that is to be done is to step forth, after mature reflection, to confess loudly one's conviction, and to constitute societies. Man is powerful but in union with many. Nothing great, for the improvement of his own condition, or that of his fellow-men, can ever be effected by individual enterprise.'

Alas! this is the crying sin of the age, this want of faith in the prevalence of a man. Nothing can be effected but by one man. He who wants help wants everything. True, this is the condition of our weakness, but it can never be the means of our recovery. We must first succeed alone, that we may enjoy our success together. We trust that the social movements which we witness indicate an aspiration not to be thus cheaply satisfied. In this matter of reforming the world, we have little faith in corporations; not thus was it first formed.

But our author is wise enough to say that the raw materials for the accomplishment of his purposes are 'iron, copper, wood, earth chiefly, and a union of men whose eyes and understanding are not shut up by preconceptions.' Ay, this last may be what we want mainly — a company of 'odd fellows' indeed.

'Small shares of twenty dollars will be sufficient' — in all, from '200,000 to 300,000' — 'to create the first establishment for a whole community of from 3,000 to 4,000 individuals'; at the end of five years we shall have a principal of 200 millions of dollars, and so paradise will be wholly regained at the end of the tenth year. But, alas! the ten years have already elapsed, and there are no signs of Eden yet, for want of the requisite funds to begin the enterprise in a hopeful manner. Yet it seems a safe investment. Perchance they could be hired at a low rate, the property being mortgaged for security, and, if necessary, it could be given up in any stage of the enterprise, without loss, with the fixtures.

But we see two main difficulties in the way: first, the successful application of the powers by machinery (we have not yet seen the 'Mechanical System'), and, secondly, which is infinitely harder, the application of man to the work by faith. This it is, we fear, which will prolong the ten years to ten thousand at least. It will take a power more than '80,000 times greater than all the men on earth could effect with their nerves' to persuade men to use that which is already offered them. Even a greater than this physical power must be brought to bear upon that moral power. Faith, indeed, is all the reform that is needed; it is itself a reform. Doubtless, we are as slow to conceive of Paradise as of Heaven, of a perfect natural as of a perfect spiritual world. We see how past ages have loitered and erred. 'Is perhaps our generation free from irrationality and error? Have we perhaps reached now the summit of human wisdom, and need no more to look out for mental or physical improvement?' Undoubtedly, we are never so visionary as to be prepared for what the next hour may bring forth.

Μέλλει τὸ θεῖον δ' ἔστι τοιοῦτον φύσει.

The Divine is about to be, and such is its nature. In our wisest moments we are secreting a matter, which, like the lime of the shell-fish, incrusts us quite over, and well for us if, like it, we cast our shells from time to time, though they be pearl and of fairest tint. Let us consider under what disadvantages Science has hitherto labored before we pronounce thus confidently on her progress.

Mr. Etzler is not one of the enlightened practical men, the pioneers of the actual, who move with the slow, deliberate tread of science, conserving the world; who execute the dreams of the last century, though they have no dreams of their own; yet he deals in the very raw but still solid material of all inventions. He has more of the practical than usually belongs to so bold a schemer, so resolute a dreamer. Yet his success is in theory, and not in practice, and he feeds our faith rather than contents our understanding. His book wants order, serenity, dignity, everything — but it does not fail to impart what only man can impart to man of much importance, his own faith. It is true his dreams are not thrilling nor bright enough, and he leaves off to dream where he who dreams just before the dawn begins. His castles in the air fall to the ground, because they are not built lofty enough; they should be secured to heaven's roof. After all, the theories and speculations of men concern us more than their puny accomplishment. It is with a certain coldness and languor that we loiter about the actual and so-called practical. How little do the most wonderful inventions of modern times detain us. They insult nature. Every machine, or particular application, seems a slight outrage against universal laws. How many fine inventions are there which do not clutter the ground? We think that those only succeed which minister to our sensible and animal wants, which bake or brew, wash or warm, or the like. But are those of no account which are patented by fancy and imagination, and succeed so admirably in our dreams that they give the tone still to our waking thoughts? Already nature is serving all those uses which science slowly derives on a much higher and grander scale to him that will be served by her. When the sunshine falls on the path of the poet, he enjoys all those pure benefits and pleasures which the arts slowly and partially realize from age to age. The winds which fan his cheek waft him the sum of that profit and happiness which their lagging inventions supply.

The chief fault of this book is, that it aims to secure the greatest degree of gross comfort and pleasure merely. It paints a Mahometan's heaven, and stops short with singular abruptness when we think it is drawing near to the precincts of the Christian's — and we trust we have not made here a distinction without a difference. Undoubtedly if we were to reform this outward life truly and thoroughly, we should find no duty of the inner omitted. It would be employment for our whole nature; and what we should do thereafter would be as vain a question as to ask the bird what it will do when its nest is built and its brood reared. But a moral reform must take place first, and then the necessity of the other will be superseded, and we shall sail and plow by its force alone. There is a speedier way than the 'Mechanical System' can show to fill up marshes, to drown the roar of the waves, to tame hyenas, secure agreeable environs, diversify the land, and refresh it with 'rivulets of sweet water,' and that is by the power of rectitude and true behavior. It is only for a little while, only occasionally, methinks, that we want a garden. Surely a good man need not be at the labor to level a hill for the sake of a prospect, or raise fruits and flowers, and construct floating islands, for the sake of a paradise. He enjoys better prospects than lie behind any hill. Where an angel travels it will be paradise all the way, but where Satan travels it will be burning marl and cinders. What says Veeshnoo Sarma? 'He whose mind is at ease is possessed of all riches. Is it not the same to one whose foot is inclosed in a shoe, as if the whole surface of the earth were covered with leather?'

He who is conversant with the supernal powers will not worship these inferior deities of the wind, waves, tide, and sunshine. But we would not disparage the importance of such calculations as we have described. They are truths in physics, because they are true in ethics. The moral powers no one would presume to calculate. Suppose we could compare the moral with the physical, and say how many horse-power the force of love, for instance, blowing on every square foot of a man's soul, would equal. No doubt we are well aware of this force; figures would not increase our respect for it; the sunshine is equal to but one ray of its heat. The light of the sun is but the shadow of love. 'The souls of men loving and fearing God,' says Raleigh, 'receive influence from that divine light itself, whereof the sun's clarity, and that of the stars, is by Plato called but a shadow. *Lumen est umbra Dei, Deus est Lumen Luminis.* Light is the shadow of God's brightness, who is the light of light,' and, we may add, the heat of heat. Love is the wind, the tide, the waves, the sunshine. Its power is incalculable; it is many horse-power. It never ceases, it never slacks; it can move the globe without a resting-place; it can warm without fire; it can feed without meat; it can clothe without garments; it can shelter without roof; it can make a paradise within which will dispense with a paradise without.

But though the wisest men in all ages have labored to publish this force, and every human heart is, sooner or later, more or less, made to feel it, yet how little is actually applied to social ends! True, it is the motive-power of all successful social machinery; but as in physics we have made the elements do only a little drudgery for us — steam to take the place of a few horses, wind of a few oars, water of a few cranks and handmills — as the mechanical forces have not yet been generously and largely applied to make the physical world answer to the ideal, so the power of love has been but meanly and sparingly applied, as yet. It has patented only such machines as the almshouse, the hospital, and the Bible Society, while its infinite wind is still blowing, and blowing down these very structures too, from time to time. Still less are we accumulating its power, and preparing to act with greater energy at a future time. Shall we not contribute our shares to this enterprise, then?

II. CIVIL DISOBEDIENCE

I HEARTILY accept the motto, 'That government is best which governs least;' and I should like to see it acted up to more rapidly and systematically. Carried out, it finally amounts to this, which also I believe — 'That government is best which governs not at all;' and when men are prepared for it, that will be the kind of government which they will have. Government is at best but an expedient; but most governments are usually, and all governments are sometimes, inexpedient. The objections which have been brought against a standing army, and they are many and weighty, and deserve to prevail, may also at last be brought against a standing government. The standing army is only an arm of the standing government. The government itself, which is only the mode which the people have chosen to execute their will, is equally liable to be abused and perverted before the people can act through it. Witness thé present Mexican war, the work of comparatively a few individuals using the standing government as their tool; for, in the outset, the people would not have consented to this measure.

This American government — what is it but a tradition, though a recent one, endeavoring to transmit itself unimpaired to posterity, but each instant losing some of its integrity? It has not the vitality and force of a single living man; for a single man can bend it to his will. It is a sort of wooden gun to the people themselves. But it is not the less necessary for this; for the people must have some complicated machinery or other, and hear its din, to satisfy that idea of government which they have. Governments show thus how successfully men can be imposed on, even impose on themselves, for their own advantage. It is excellent, we must all allow. Yet this government never of itself furthered any enterprise, but by the alacrity with which it got out of its way. *It* does not keep the country free. *It* does not settle the West. *It* does not educate. The character inherent in the American people has done all that has been accomplished; and it would have done somewhat more, if the government had not sometimes got in its way. For government is an expedient by which men would fain succeed in letting one another alone; and, as has been said, when it is most expedient, the governed are most let alone by it. Trade and commerce, if they were not made of india-rubber, would never manage to bounce over the obstacles which legislators are continually putting in their way; and, if one were to judge these men wholly by the effects of their actions and not partly by their intentions, they would deserve to be classed and punished with those mischievous persons who put obstructions on the rail-roads.

But, to speak practically and as a citizen, unlike those who call them-selves no-government men, I ask for, not at once no government, but *at once* a better government. Let every man make known what kind of government would command his respect, and that will be one step toward obtaining it.

After all, the practical reason why, when the power is once in the hands of the people, a majority are permitted, and for a long period continue, to rule is not because they are most likely to be in the right, nor because this seems fairest to the minority, but because they are physically the strongest. But a government in which the majority rule in all cases cannot be based on justice, even as far as men understand it. Can there not be a government in which majorities do not virtually decide right and wrong, but conscience? — in which majorities decide only those questions to which the rule of expediency is applicable? Must the citizen ever for a moment, or in the least degree, resign his conscience to the legislator? Why has every man a conscience, then? I think that we should be men first, and subjects afterward. It is not desirable to cultivate a respect for the law, so much as for the right. The only obligation which I have a right to assume is to do at any time what I think right. It is truly enough said that a corporation has no conscience; but a corporation of conscientious men is a corporation *with* a conscience. Law never made men a whit more just; and, by means of their respect for it, even the well-disposed are daily made the agents of injustice. A common and natural result of an undue respect for law is, that you may see a file of soldiers, colonel, captain, corporal, privates, powder-monkeys, and all, marching in admirable order over hill and dale to the wars, against their wills, ay, against their common sense and consciences, which makes it very steep marching indeed, and produces a palpitation of the heart. They have no doubt that it is a damnable business in which they are concerned; they are all peaceably inclined. Now, what are they? Men at all? or small movable forts and magazines, at the service of some unscrupulous man in power? Visit the Navy-Yard, and behold a marine, such a man as an American government can make, or such as it can make a man with its black arts — a mere shadow and reminiscence of humanity, a man laid out alive and standing, and already, as one may say, buried under arms with funeral accompaniments, though it may be,

> 'Not a drum was heard, not a funeral note,
>   As his corse to the rampart we hurried;
> Not a soldier discharged his farewell shot
>   O'er the grave where our hero we buried.'

The mass of men serve the state thus, not as men mainly, but as machines, with their bodies. They are the standing army, and the militia, jailers, constables, *posse comitatus*, etc. In most cases there is no free exercise whatever of the judgment or of the moral sense; but they put themselves on a level with wood and earth and stones; and wooden men can perhaps be manufactured that will serve the purpose as well. Such command no more respect than men of straw or a lump of dirt. They have the same sort of worth only as horses and dogs. Yet such as these even are commonly esteemed good citizens. Others — as most legislators, politicians, lawyers, ministers, and office-holders — serve the state chiefly with their heads; and, as they rarely make any moral distinctions, they are as likely to serve the devil, without *intending* it, as God. A very few — as heroes, patriots, martyrs, reformers in the great sense, and *men* — serve the state with their consciences also, and so necessarily resist it for the most part; and they are commonly treated as enemies by it. A wise man will only be useful as a man, and will not

submit to be 'clay,' and 'stop a hole to keep the wind away,' but leave
that office to his dust at least:

> 'I am too high-born to be propertied,
> To be a secondary at control,
> Or useful serving-man and instrument
> To any sovereign state throughout the world.'

He who gives himself entirely to his fellow-men appears to them useless and selfish; but he who gives himself partially to them is pronounced
a benefactor and philanthropist.

How does it become a man to behave toward this American government today? I answer, that he cannot without disgrace be associated
with it. I cannot for an instant recognize that political organization as
my government which is the *slave's* government also.

All men recognize the right of revolution; that is, the right to refuse
allegiance to, and to resist, the government, when its tyranny or its
inefficiency are great and unendurable. But almost all say that such is
not the case now. But such was the case, they think, in the Revolution
of '75. If one were to tell me that this was a bad government because it
taxed certain foreign commodities brought to its ports, it is most
probable that I should not make an ado about it, for I can do without
them. All machines have their friction; and possibly this does enough
good to counterbalance the evil. At any rate, it is a great evil to make
a stir about it. But when the friction comes to have its machine, and
oppression and robbery are organized, I say, let us not have such a
machine any longer. In other words, when a sixth of the population of
a nation which has undertaken to be the refuge of liberty are slaves, and
a whole country is unjustly overrun and conquered by a foreign army,
and subjected to military law, I think that it is not too soon for honest
men to rebel and revolutionize. What makes this duty the more urgent
is the fact that the country so overrun is not our own, but ours is the
invading army.

Paley, a common authority with many on moral questions, in his
chapter on the 'Duty of Submission to Civil Government,' resolves all
civil obligation into expediency; and he proceeds to say that 'so long as
the interest of the whole society requires it, that is, so long as the
established government cannot be resisted or changed without public
inconveniency, it is the will of God . . . that the established government
be obeyed — and no longer. This principle being admitted, the justice
of every particular case of resistance is reduced to a computation of the

quantity of the danger and grievance on the one side, and of the probability and expense of redressing it on the other.' Of this, he says, every
man shall judge for himself. But Paley appears never to have contemplated those cases to which the rule of expediency does not apply, in
which a people, as well as an individual, must do justice, cost what it
may. If I have unjustly wrested a plank from a drowning man, I must
restore it to him though I drown myself. This, according to Paley,
would be inconvenient. But he that would save his life, in such a case,
shall lose it. This people must cease to hold slaves, and to make war on
Mexico, though it cost them their existence as a people.

In their practice, nations agree with Paley; but does any one think
that Massachusetts does exactly what is right at the present crisis?

> 'A drab of state, a cloth-o'-silver slut,
> To have her train borne up, and her soul trail in the dirt.'

Practically speaking, the opponents to a reform in Massachusetts are
not a hundred thousand politicians at the South, but a hundred thous-
and merchants and farmers here, who are more interested in commerce
and agriculture than they are in humanity, and are not prepared to do
justice to the slave and to Mexico, *cost what it may*. I quarrel not with
far-off foes, but with those who, near at home, coöperate with, and do
the bidding of, those far away, and without whom the latter would be
harmless. We are accustomed to say, that the mass of men are unprepared; but improvement is slow, because the few are not materially
wiser or better than the many. It is not so important that many should
be as good as you, as that there be some absolute goodness somewhere;
for that will leaven the whole lump. There are thousands who are *in
opinion* opposed to slavery and to the war, who yet in effect do nothing
to put an end to them; who, esteeming themselves children of Washington and Franklin, sit down with their hands in their pockets, and say
that they know not what to do, and do nothing; who even postpone the
question of freedom to the question of free trade, and quietly read the
prices-current along with the latest advices from Mexico, after dinner,
and, it may be, fall asleep over them both. What is the price-current
of an honest man and patriot today? They hesitate, and they regret,
and sometimes they petition; but they do nothing in earnest and with
effect. They will wait, well disposed, for others to remedy the evil, that
they may no longer have it to regret. At most, they give only a cheap
vote, and a feeble countenance and God-speed, to the right, as it goes
by them. There are nine hundred and ninety-nine patrons of virtue to

one virtuous man. But it is easier to deal with the real possessor of a thing than with the temporary guardian of it.

All voting is a sort of gaming, like checkers or backgammon, with a slight moral tinge to it, a playing with right and wrong, with moral questions; and betting naturally accompanies it. The character of the voters is not staked. I cast my vote, perchance, as I think right; but I am not vitally concerned that that right should prevail. I am willing to leave it to the majority. Its obligation, therefore, never exceeds that of expediency. Even voting *for the right* is *doing* nothing for it. It is only expressing to men feebly your desire that it should prevail. A wise man will not leave the right to the mercy of chance, nor wish it to prevail through the power of the majority. There is but little virtue in the action of masses of men. When the majority shall at length vote for the abolition of slavery, it will be because they are indifferent to slavery, or because there is but little slavery left to be abolished by their vote. *They* will then be the only slaves. Only *his* vote can hasten the abolition of slavery who asserts his own freedom by his vote.

I hear of a convention to be held at Baltimore, or elsewhere, for the selection of a candidate for the Presidency, made up chiefly of editors, and men who are politicians by profession; but I think, what is it to any independent, intelligent, and respectable man what decision they may come to? Shall we not have the advantage of his wisdom and honesty, nevertheless? Can we not count upon some independent votes? Are there not many individuals in the country who do not attend conventions? But no: I find that the respectable man, so called, has immediately drifted from his position, and despairs of his country, when his country has more reason to despair of him. He forthwith adopts one of the candidates thus selected as the only *available* one, thus proving that he is himself *available* for any purposes of the demagogue. His vote is of no more worth than that of any unprincipled foreigner or hireling native, who may have been bought. O for a man who is a *man*, and, as my neighbor says, has a bone in his back which you cannot pass your hand through! Our statistics are at fault: the population has been returned too large. How many *men* are there to a square thousand miles in this country? Hardly one. Does not America offer any inducement for men to settle here? The American has dwindled into an Odd Fellow — one who may be known by the development of his organ of gregariousness, and a manifest lack of intellect and cheerful self-reliance; whose first and chief concern, on coming into the world, is to see that the almshouses are in good repair; and, before yet he has lawfully donned the virile garb, to collect a fund for the support of the widows and orphans that may be; who, in short, ventures to live only by the aid of the Mutual Insurance company, which has promised to bury him decently.

It is not a man's duty, as a matter of course, to devote himself to the eradication of any, even the most enormous, wrong; he may still properly have other concerns to engage him; but it is his duty, at least, to wash his hands of it, and, if he gives it no thought longer, not to give it practically his support. If I devote myself to other pursuits and contemplations, I must first see, at least, that I do not pursue them sitting upon another man's shoulders. I must get off him first, that he may pursue his contemplations too. See what gross inconsistency is tolerated. I have heard some of my townsmen say, 'I should like to have them order me out to help put down an insurrection of the slaves, or to march to Mexico; — see if I would go;' and yet these very men have each, directly by their allegiance, and so indirectly, at least, by their money, furnished a substitute. The soldier is applauded who refuses to serve in an unjust war by those who do not refuse to sustain the unjust government which makes the war; is applauded by those whose own act and authority he disregards and sets at naught; as if the state were penitent to that degree that it hired one to scourge it while it sinned, but not to that degree that it left off sinning for a moment. Thus, under the name of Order and Civil Government, we are all made at last to pay homage to and support our own meanness. After the first blush of sin comes its indifference; and from immoral it becomes, as it were, *un*moral, and not quite unnecessary to that life which we have made.

The broadest and most prevalent error requires the most disinterested virtue to sustain it. The slight reproach to which the virtue of patriotism is commonly liable, the noble are most likely to incur. Those who, while they disapprove of the character and measures of a government, yield to it their allegiance and support are undoubtedly its most conscientious supporters, and so frequently the most serious obstacles to reform. Some are petitioning the State to dissolve the Union, to disregard the requisitions of the President. Why do they not dissolve it themselves — the union between themselves and the State — and refuse to pay their quota into its treasury? Do not they stand in the same relation to the State that the State does to the Union? And have not the same reasons prevented the State from resisting the Union which have prevented them from resisting the State?

How can a man be satisfied to entertain an opinion merely, and enjoy *it?* Is there any enjoyment in it, if his opinion is that he is aggrieved? If you are cheated out of a single dollar by your neighbor, you do not rest satisfied with knowing that you are cheated, or with saying that you are cheated, or even with petitioning him to pay you your due; but you take effectual steps at once to obtain the full amount, and see that you are never cheated again. Action from principle, the perception and the performance of right, changes things and relations; it is essentially revolutionary, and does not consist wholly with anything which was. It not only divides States and churches, it divides families; ay, it divides the *individual*, separating the diabolical in him from the divine.

Unjust laws exist: shall we be content to obey them, or shall we endeavor to amend them, and obey them until we have succeeded, or shall we transgress them at once? Men generally, under such a government as this, think that they ought to wait until they have persuaded the majority to alter them. They think that, if they should resist, the remedy would be worse than the evil. But it is the fault of the government itself that the remedy *is* worse than the evil. *It* makes it worse. Why is it not more apt to anticipate and provide for reform? Why does it not cherish its wise minority? Why does it cry and resist before it is hurt? Why does it not encourage its citizens to be on the alert to point out its faults, and *do* better than it would have them? Why does it always crucify Christ, and excommunicate Copernicus and Luther, and pronounce Washington and Franklin rebels?

One would think, that a deliberate and practical denial of its authority was the only offence never contemplated by government; else, why has it not assigned its definite, its suitable and proportionate, penalty? If a man who has no property refuses but once to earn nine shillings for the State, he is put in prison for a period unlimited by any law that I know, and determined only by the discretion of those who placed him there; but if he should steal ninety times nine shillings from the State, he is soon permitted to go at large again.

If the injustice is part of the necessary friction of the machine of government, let it go, let it go: perchance it will wear smooth — certainly the machine will wear out. If the injustice has a spring, or a pulley, or a rope, or a crank, exclusively for itself, then perhaps you may consider whether the remedy will not be worse than the evil; but if it is of such a nature that it requires you to be the agent of injustice to another, then, I say, break the law. Let your life be a counter-friction to stop the machine. What I have to do is to see, at any rate, that I do not lend myself to the wrong which I condemn.

As for adopting the ways which the State has provided for remedying the evil, I know not of such ways. They take too much time, and a man's life will be gone. I have other affairs to attend to. I came into this world, not chiefly to make this a good place to live in, but to live in it, be it good or bad. A man has not everything to do, but something; and because he cannot do *everything*, it is not necessary that he should do *something* wrong. It is not my business to be petitioning the Governor or the Legislature any more than it is theirs to petition me; and if they should not hear my petition, what should I do then? But in this case the State has provided no way: its very Constitution is the evil. This may seem to be harsh and stubborn and unconciliatory; but it is to treat with the utmost kindness and consideration the only spirit that can appreciate or deserves it. So is all change for the better, like birth and death, which convulse the body.

I do not hesitate to say, that those who call themselves Abolitionists should at once effectually withdraw their support, both in person and property, from the government of Massachusetts, and not wait till they constitute a majority of one, before they suffer the right to prevail through them. I think that it is enough if they have God on their side, without waiting for that other one. Moreover, any man more right than his neighbors constitutes a majority of one already.

I meet this American government, or its representative, the State government, directly, and face to face, once a year — no more — in the person of its tax-gatherer; this is the only mode in which a man situated as I am necessarily meets it; and it then says distinctly, Recognize me; and the simplest, the most effectual, and, in the present posture of affairs, the indispensablest mode of treating with it on this head, of expressing your little satisfaction with and love for it, is to deny it then. My civil neighbor, the tax-gatherer, is the very man I have to deal with — for it is, after all, with men and not with parchment that I quarrel — and he has voluntarily chosen to be an agent of the government. How shall he ever know well what he is and does as an officer of the government, or as a man, until he is obliged to consider whether he shall treat me, his neighbor, for whom he has respect, as a neighbor and well-disposed man, or as a maniac and disturber of the peace, and see if he can get over this obstruction to his neighborliness without a ruder and more impetuous thought or speech corresponding with his action. I know this well, that if one thousand, if one hundred, if ten men whom

I could name — if ten *honest* men only — ay, if *one* HONEST man, in this State of Massachusetts, *ceasing to hold slaves,* were actually to withdraw from this copartnership, and be locked up in the county jail therefor, it would be the abolition of slavery in America. For it matters not how small the beginning may seem to be: what is once well done is done forever. But we love better to talk about it: that we say is our mission. Reform keeps many scores of newspapers in its service, but not one man. If my esteemed neighbor, the State's ambassador, who will devote his days to the settlement of the question of human rights in the Council Chamber, instead of being threatened with the prisons of Carolina, were to sit down the prisoner of Massachusetts, that State which is so anxious to foist the sin of slavery upon her sister — though at present she can discover only an act of inhospitality to be the ground of a quarrel with her — the Legislature would not wholly waive the subject the following winter.

Under a government which imprisons any unjustly, the true place for a just man is also a prison. The proper place today, the only place which Massachusetts has provided for her freer and less desponding spirits, is in her prisons, to be put out and locked out of the State by her own act, as they have already put themselves out by their principles. It is there that the fugitive slave, and the Mexican prisoner on parole, and the Indian come to plead the wrongs of his race should find them; on that separate, but more free and honorable, ground, where the State places those who are not *with* her, but *against* her — the only house in a slave State in which a free man can abide with honor. If any think that their influence would be lost there, and their voices no longer afflict the ear of the State, that they would not be as an enemy within its walls, they do not know by how much truth is stronger than error, nor how much more eloquently and effectively he can combat injustice who has experienced a little in his own person. Cast your whole vote, not a strip of paper merely, but your whole influence. A minority is powerless while it conforms to the majority; it is not even a minority then; but it is irresistible when it clogs by its whole weight. If the alternative is to keep all just men in prison, or give up war and slavery, the State will not hesitate which to choose. If a thousand men were not to pay their tax-bills this year, that would not be a violent and bloody measure, as it would be to pay them, and enable the State to commit violence and shed innocent blood. This is, in fact, the definition of a peaceable revolution, if any such is possible. If the tax-gatherer, or any other public officer, asks me, as one has done, 'But what shall I do?' my answer is, 'If you really wish to do anything, resign your office.' When the subject has refused allegiance, and the officer has resigned his office, then the revolution is accomplished. But even suppose blood should flow. Is there not a sort of blood shed when the conscience is wounded? Through this wound a man's real manhood and immortality flow out, and he bleeds to an everlasting death. I see this blood flowing now.

I have contemplated the imprisonment of the offender, rather than the seizure of his goods — though both will serve the same purpose — because they who assert the purest right, and consequently are most dangerous to a corrupt State, commonly have not spent much time in accumulating property. To such the State renders comparatively small service, and a slight tax is wont to appear exorbitant, particularly if they are obliged to earn it by special labor with their hands. If there were one who lived wholly without the use of money, the State itself would hesitate to demand it of him. But the rich man — not to make any invidious comparison — is always sold to the institution which makes him rich. Absolutely speaking, the more money, the less virtue; for money comes between a man and his objects, and obtains them for him; and it was certainly no great virtue to obtain it. It puts to rest many questions which he would otherwise be taxed to answer; while the only new question which it puts is the hard but superfluous one, how to spend it. Thus his moral ground is taken from under his feet. The opportunities of living are diminished in proportion as what are called the 'means' are increased. The best thing a man can do for his culture when he is rich is to endeavor to carry out those schemes which he entertained when he was poor. Christ answered the Herodians according to their condition. 'Show me the tribute-money,' said he; — and one took a penny out of his pocket; — if you use money which has the image of Cæsar on it, and which he has made current and valuable, that is, *if you are men of the State*, and gladly enjoy the advantages of Cæsar's government, then pay him back some of his own when he demands it. 'Render therefore to Cæsar that which is Cæsar's, and to God those things which are God's' — leaving them no wiser than before as to which was which; for they did not wish to know.

When I converse with the freest of my neighbors, I perceive that, whatever they may say about the magnitude and seriousness of the question, and their regard for the public tranquillity, the long and the short of the matter is, that they cannot spare the protection of the existing government, and they dread the consequences to their property and families of disobedience to it. For my own part, I should not like to think that I ever rely on the protection of the State. But, if I deny the authority of the State when it presents its tax-bill, it will soon take and waste all my property, and so harass me and my children without end. This is hard. This makes it impossible for a man to live honestly, and at the same time comfortably, in outward respects. It will not be worth the while to accumulate property; that would be sure to go again. You must hire or squat somewhere, and raise but a small crop, and eat that soon. You must live within yourself, and depend upon yourself always tucked up and ready for a start, and not have many affairs. A man may grow rich in Turkey even, if he will be in all respects a good subject of the Turkish government. Confucius said: 'If a state is governed by the principles of reason, poverty and misery are subjects of shame; if a state is not governed by the principles of reason, riches and honors are the subjects of shame.' No: until I want the protection of Massachusetts to be extended to me in some distant Southern port, where my liberty is endangered, or until I am bent solely on building up an estate at home by peaceful enterprise, I can afford to refuse allegiance to Massachusetts, and her right to my property and life. It costs me less in every sense to incur the penalty of disobedience to the State than it would to obey. I should feel as if I were worth less in that case.

Some years ago, the State met me in behalf of the Church, and commanded me to pay a certain sum toward the support of a clergyman whose preaching my father attended, but never I myself. 'Pay,' it said, 'or be locked up in the jail.' I declined to pay. But, unfortunately, another man saw fit to pay it. I did not see why the schoolmaster should be taxed to support the priest, and not the priest the schoolmaster; for I was not the State's schoolmaster, but I supported myself by voluntary subscription. I did not see why the lyceum should not present its tax-bill, and have the State to back its demand, as well as the Church. However, at the request of the selectmen, I condescended to make some such statement as this in writing: — 'Know all men by these presents, that I, Henry Thoreau, do not wish to be regarded as a member of any incorporated society which I have not joined.' This I gave to the town clerk; and he has it. The State, having thus learned that I did not wish to be regarded as a member of that church, has never made a like demand on me since; though it said that it must adhere to its original presumption that time. If I had known how to name them, I should then have signed off in detail from all the societies which I never signed on to; but I did not know where to find a complete list.

I have paid no poll-tax for six years. I was put into a jail once on this account, for one night; and, as I stood considering the walls of solid stone, two or three feet thick, the door of wood and iron, a foot thick, and the iron grating which strained the light, I could not help being struck with the foolishness of that institution which treated me as if I were mere flesh and blood and bones, to be locked up. I wondered that it should have concluded at length that this was the best use it could put me to, and had never thought to avail itself of my services in some way. I saw that, if there was a wall of stone between me and my towns-men, there was a still more difficult one to climb or break through before they could get to be as free as I was. I did not for a moment feel confined, and the walls seemed a great waste of stone and mortar. I felt as if I alone of all my townsmen had paid my tax. They plainly did not know how to treat me, but behaved like persons who are underbred. In every threat and in every compliment there was a blunder; for they thought that my chief desire was to stand the other side of that stone wall. I could not but smile to see how industriously they locked the door on my meditations, which followed them out again without let or hindrance, and *they* were really all that was dangerous. As they could not reach me, they had resolved to punish my body; just as boys, if they cannot come at some person against whom they have a spite, will abuse his dog. I saw that the State was half-witted, that it was timid as a lone woman with her silver spoons, and that it did not know its friends from its foes, and I lost all my remaining respect for it, and pitied it.

Thus the State never intentionally confronts a man's sense, intellectual or moral, but only his body, his senses. It is not armed with superior wit or honesty, but with superior physical strength. I was not born to be forced. I will breathe after my own fashion. Let us see who is the strongest. What force has a multitude? They only can force me who obey a higher law than I. They force me to become like themselves. I do not hear of *men* being *forced* to live this way or that by masses of men. What sort of life were that to live? When I meet a government which says to me, 'Your money or your life,' why should I be in haste to give it my money? It may be in a great strait, and not know what to do: I cannot help that. It must help itself; do as I do. It is not worth the while to snivel about it. I am not responsible for the successful working of the machinery of society. I am not the son of the engineer. I perceive that, when an acorn and a chestnut fall side by side, the one does not remain inert to make way for the other, but both obey their own laws, and spring and grow and flourish as best they can, till one, perchance, overshadows and destroys the other. If a plant cannot live according to its nature, it dies; and so a man.

The night in prison was novel and interesting enough. The prisoners in their shirt-sleeves were enjoying a chat and the evening air in the doorway, when I entered. But the jailer said, 'Come, boys, it is time to lock up;' and so they dispersed, and I heard the sound of their steps returning into the hollow apartments. My room-mate was introduced to me by the jailer as 'a first-rate fellow and a clever man.' When the door was locked, he showed me where to hang my hat, and how he managed matters there. The rooms were whitewashed once a month; and this one, at least, was the whitest, most simply furnished, and probably the neatest apartment in the town. He naturally wanted to know where I came from, and what brought me there; and, when I had told him, I asked him in my turn how he came there, presuming him to be an honest man, of course; and, as the world goes, I believe he was. 'Why,' said he, 'they accuse me of burning a barn; but I never did it.' As near as I could discover, he had probably gone to bed in a barn when drunk, and smoked his pipe there; and so a barn was burnt. He had the reputation of being a clever man, had been there some three months waiting for his trial to come on, and would have to wait as much longer; but he was quite domesticated and contented, since he got his board for nothing, and thought that he was well treated.

He occupied one window, and I the other; and I saw that if one stayed there long, his principal business would be to look out the window. I had soon read all the tracts that were left there, and examined where former prisoners had broken out, and where a grate had been sawed off, and heard the history of the various occupants of that room; for I found that even here there was a history and a gossip which never circulated beyond the walls of the jail. Probably this is the only house in the town where verses are composed, which are afterward printed in a circular form, but not published. I was shown quite a long list of verses which were composed by some young men who had been detected in an attempt to escape, who avenged themselves by singing them.

I pumped my fellow-prisoner as dry as I could, for fear I should never see him again; but at length he showed me which was my bed, and left me to blow out the lamp.

It was like travelling into a far country, such as I had never expected to behold, to lie there for one night. It seemed to me that I never had heard the town clock strike before, nor the evening sounds of the village;

for we slept with the windows open, which were inside the grating. It was to see my native village in the light of the Middle Ages, and our Concord was turned into a Rhine stream, and visions of knights and castles passed before me. They were the voices of old burghers that I heard in the streets. I was an involuntary spectator and auditor of whatever was done and said in the kitchen of the adjacent village inn — a wholly new and rare experience to me. It was a closer view of my native town. I was fairly inside of it. I never had seen its institutions before. This is one of its peculiar institutions; for it is a shire town. I began to comprehend what its inhabitants were about.

In the morning, our breakfasts were put through the hole in the door, in small oblong-square tin pans, made to fit, and holding a pint of chocolate, with brown bread, and an iron spoon. When they called for the vessels again, I was green enough to return what bread I had left; but my comrade seized it, and said that I should lay that up for lunch or dinner. Soon after he was let out to work at haying in a neighboring field, whither he went every day, and would not be back till noon; so he bade me good-day, saying that he doubted if he should see me again.

When I came out of prison — for some one interfered, and paid that tax — I did not perceive that great changes had taken place on the common, such as he observed who went in a youth and emerged a tottering and gray-headed man; and yet a change had to my eyes come over the scene — the town, and State, and country — greater than any that mere time could effect. I saw yet more distinctly the State in which I lived. I saw to what extent the people among whom I lived could be trusted as good neighbors and friends; that their friendship was for summer weather only; that they did not greatly propose to do right; that they were a distinct race from me by their prejudices and superstitions, as the Chinamen and Malays are; that in their sacrifices to humanity they ran no risks, not even to their property; that after all they were not so noble but they treated the thief as he had treated them, and hoped, by a certain outward observance and a few prayers, and by walking in a particular straight though useless path from time to time, to save their souls. This may be to judge my neighbors harshly; for I believe that many of them are not aware that they have such an institution as the jail in their village.

It was formerly the custom in our village, when a poor debtor came out of jail, for his acquaintances to salute him, looking through their fingers, which were crossed to represent the grating of a jail window, 'How do ye do?' My neighbors did not thus salute me, but first looked

at me, and then at one another, as if I had returned from a long journey.
I was put into jail as I was going to the shoemaker's to get a shoe which
was mended. When I was let out the next morning, I proceeded to
finish my errand, and, having put on my mended shoe, joined a huckleberry party, who were impatient to put themselves under my conduct;
and in half an hour — for the horse was soon tackled — was in the
midst of a huckleberry field, on one of our highest hills, two miles off,
and then the State was nowhere to be seen.

This is the whole history of 'My Prisons.'

I have never declined paying the highway tax, because I am as
desirous of being a good neighbor as I am of being a bad subject; and
as for supporting schools, I am doing my part to educate my fellow-
countrymen now. It is for no particular item in the tax-bill that I refuse
to pay it. I simply wish to refuse allegiance to the State, to withdraw
and stand aloof from it effectually. I do not care to trace the course
of my dollar, if I could, till it buys a man or a musket to shoot one with
— the dollar is innocent — but I am concerned to trace the effects of
my allegiance. In fact, I quietly declare war with the State, after my
fashion, though I will still make what use and get what advantage of
her I can, as is usual in such cases.

If others pay the tax which is demanded of me, from a sympathy with
the State, they do but what they have already done in their own case,
or rather they abet injustice to a greater extent than the State requires.
If they pay the tax from a mistaken interest in the individual taxed, to
save his property, or prevent his going to jail, it is because they have
not considered wisely how far they let their private feelings interfere
with the public good.

This, then, is my position at present. But one cannot be too much
on his guard in such a case, lest his action be biased by obstinacy or an
undue regard for the opinions of men. Let him see that he does only
what belongs to himself and to the hour.

I think sometimes, Why, this people mean well, they are only ignorant; they would do better if they knew how: why give your neighbors
this pain to treat you as they are not inclined to? But I think again,
This is no reason why I should do as they do, or permit others to suffer
much greater pain of a different kind. Again, I sometimes say to myself,
When many millions of men, without heat, without ill will, without
personal feeling of any kind, demand of you a few shillings only, without the possibility, such is their constitution, of retracting or altering

their present demand, and without the possibility, on your side, of appeal to any other millions, why expose yourself to this overwhelming brute force? You do not resist cold and hunger, the winds and the waves, thus obstinately; you quietly submit to a thousand similar necessities. You do not put your head into the fire. But just in proportion as I regard this as not wholly a brute force, but partly a human force, and consider that I have relations to those millions as to so many millions of men, and not of mere brute or inanimate things, I see that appeal is possible, first and instantaneously, from them to the Maker of them, and, secondly, from them to themselves. But if I put my head deliberately into the fire, there is no appeal to fire or to the Maker of fire, and I have only myself to blame. If I could convince myself that I have any right to be satisfied with men as they are, and to treat them accordingly, and not according, in some respects, to my requisitions and expectations of what they and I ought to be, then, like a good Mussulman and fatalist, I should endeavor to be satisfied with things as they are, and say it is the will of God. And, above all, there is this difference between resisting this and a purely brute or natural force, that I can resist this with some effect; but I cannot expect, like Orpheus, to change the nature of the rocks and trees and beasts.

I do not wish to quarrel with any man or nation. I do not wish to split hairs, to make fine distinctions, or set myself up as better than my neighbors. I seek rather, I may say, even an excuse for conforming to the laws of the land. I am but too ready to conform to them. Indeed, I have reason to suspect myself on this head; and each year, as the taxgatherer comes round, I find myself disposed to review the acts and position of the general and State governments, and the spirit of the people, to discover a pretext for conformity.

> 'We must affect our country as our parents,
> And if at any time we alienate
> Our love or industry from doing it honor,
> We must respect effects and teach the soul
> Matter of conscience and religion,
> And not desire of rule or benefit.'

I believe that the State will soon be able to take all my work of this sort out of my hands, and then I shall be no better a patriot than my fellow-countrymen. Seen from a lower point of view, the Constitution, with all its faults, is very good; the law and the courts are very respectable; even this State and this American government are, in many respects, very admirable, and rare things, to be thankful for, such as a great many have described them; but seen from a point of view a little higher, they are what I have described them; seen from a higher still, and the highest, who shall say what they are, or that they are worth looking at or thinking of at all?

However, the government does not concern me much, and I shall bestow the fewest possible thoughts on it. It is not many moments that I live under a government, even in this world. If a man is thought-free, fancy-free, imagination-free, that which *is not* never for a long time appearing *to be* to him, unwise rulers or reformers cannot fatally interrupt him.

I know that most men think differently from myself; but those whose lives are by profession devoted to the study of these or kindred subjects content me as little as any. Statesmen and legislators, standing so completely within the institution, never distinctly and nakedly behold it. They speak of moving society, but have no resting-place without it. They may be men of a certain experience and discrimination, and have no doubt invented ingenious and even useful systems, for which we sincerely thank them; but all their wit and usefulness lie within certain not very wide limits. They are wont to forget that the world is not governed by policy and expediency. Webster never goes behind government, and so cannot speak with authority about it. His words are wisdom to those legislators who contemplate no essential reform in the existing government; but for thinkers, and those who legislate for all time, he never once glances at the subject. I know of those whose serene and wise speculations on this theme would soon reveal the limits of his mind's range and hospitality. Yet, compared with the cheap professions of most reformers, and the still cheaper wisdom and elo-quence of politicians in general, his are almost the only sensible and valuable words, and we thank Heaven for him. Comparatively, he is always strong, original, and, above all, practical. Still, his quality is not wisdom, but prudence. The lawyer's truth is not Truth, but con-sistency or a consistent expediency. Truth is always in harmony with herself, and is not concerned chiefly to reveal the justice that may con-sist with wrong-doing. He well deserves to be called, as he has been called, the Defender of the Constitution. There are really no blows to be given by him but defensive ones. He is not a leader, but a follower. His leaders are the men of '87. 'I have never made an effort,' he says, 'and never propose to make an effort; I have never countenanced an effort, and never mean to countenance an effort, to disturb the arrange-ment as originally made, by which the various States came into the

Union.' Still thinking of the sanction which the Constitution gives to slavery, he says, 'Because it was a part of the original compact — let it stand.' Notwithstanding his special acuteness and ability, he is unable to take a fact out of its merely political relations, and behold it as it lies absolutely to be disposed of by the intellect — what, for instance, it behooves a man to do here in America today with regard to slavery — but ventures, or is driven, to make some such desperate answer as the following, while professing to speak absolutely, and as a private man — from which what new and singular code of social duties might be inferred? 'The manner,' says he, 'in which the governments of those States where slavery exists are to regulate it is for their own consideration, under their responsibility to their constituents, to the general laws of propriety, humanity, and justice, and to God. Associations formed elsewhere, springing from a feeling of humanity, or any other cause, have nothing whatever to do with it. They have never received any encouragement from me, and they never will.' [1]

They who know of no purer sources of truth, who have traced up its stream no higher, stand, and wisely stand, by the Bible and the Constitution, and drink at it there with reverence and humility; but they who behold where it comes trickling into this lake or that pool, gird up their loins once more, and continue their pilgrimage toward its fountain-head.

No man with a genius for legislation has appeared in America. They are rare in the history of the world. There are orators, politicians, and eloquent men, by the thousand; but the speaker has not yet opened his mouth to speak who is capable of settling the much-vexed questions of the day. . We love eloquence for its own sake, and not for any truth which it may utter, or any heroism it may inspire. Our legislators have not yet learned the comparative value of free trade and of freedom, of union, and of rectitude, to a nation. They have no genius or talent for comparatively humble questions of taxation and finance, commerce and manufactures and agriculture. If we were left solely to the wordy wit of legislators in Congress for our guidance, uncorrected by the seasonable experience and the effectual complaints of the people, America would not long retain her rank among the nations. For eighteen hundred years, though perchance I have no right to say it, the New Testament has been written; yet where is the legislator who has wisdom and practical talent enough to avail himself of the light which it sheds on the science of legislation?

[1] These extracts have been inserted since the lecture was read.

The authority of government, even such as I am willing to submit to — for I will cheerfully obey those who know and can do better than I, and in many things even those who neither know nor can do so well — is still an impure one: to be strictly just, it must have the sanction and consent of the governed. It can have no pure right over my person and property but what I concede to it. The progress from an absolute to a limited monarchy, from a limited monarchy to a democracy, is a progress toward a true respect for the individual. Even the Chinese philosopher was wise enough to regard the individual as the basis of the empire. Is a democracy, such as we know it, the last improvement possible in government? Is it not possible to take a step further towards recognizing and organizing the rights of man? There will never be a really free and enlightened State until the State comes to recognize the individual as a higher and independent power, from which all its own power and authority are derived, and treats him accordingly. I please myself with imagining a State at least which can afford to be just to all men, and to treat the individual with respect as a neighbor; which even would not think it inconsistent with its own repose if a few were to live aloof from it, not meddling with it, nor embraced by it, who fulfilled all the duties of neighbors and fellow-men. A State which bore this kind of fruit, and suffered it to drop off as fast as it ripened, would prepare the way for a still more perfect and glorious State, which also I have imagined, but not yet anywhere seen.

III. LIFE WITHOUT PRINCIPLE

At a lyceum, not long since, I felt that the lecturer had chosen a theme too foreign to himself, and so failed to interest me as much as he might have done. He described things not in or near to his heart, but toward his extremities and superficies. There was, in this sense, no truly central or centralizing thought in the lecture. I would have had him deal with his privatest experience, as the poet does. The greatest compliment that was ever paid me was when one asked me what *I thought*, and attended to my answer. I am surprised, as well as delighted, when this happens, it is such a rare use he would make of me, as if he were acquainted with the tool. Commonly, if men want anything of me, it is only to know how many acres I make of their land — since I am a surveyor — or, at most, what trivial news I have burdened myself with. They never will go to law for my meat; they prefer the shell. A man once came a considerable distance to ask me to lecture on Slavery; but on conversing with him, I found that he and his clique expected seven eighths of the lecture to be theirs, and only one eighth mine; so I declined. I take it for granted, when I am invited to lecture anywhere — for I have had a little experience in that business — that there is a desire to hear what *I think* on some subject, though I may be the greatest fool in the country — and not that I should say pleasant things merely, or such as the audience will assent to; and I resolve, accordingly, that I will give them a strong dose of myself. They have sent for me, and engaged to pay for me, and I am determined that they shall have me, though I bore them beyond all precedent.

So now I would say something similar to you, my readers. Since *you* are my readers, and I have not been much of a traveller, I will not talk about people a thousand miles off, but come as near home as I can. As the time is short, I will leave out all the flattery, and retain all the criticism.

Let us consider the way in which we spend our lives.

This world is a place of business. What an infinite bustle! I am awaked almost every night by the panting of the locomotive. It interrupts my dreams. There is no sabbath. It would be glorious to see mankind at leisure for once. It is nothing but work, work, work. I cannot easily buy a blank-book to write thoughts in; they are commonly ruled for dollars and cents. An Irishman, seeing me making a minute in the fields, took it for granted that I was calculating my wages. If a man was tossed out of a window when an infant, and so made a cripple for life, or scared out of his wits by the Indians, it is regretted chiefly because he was thus incapacitated for — business! I think that there is nothing, not even crime, more opposed to poetry, to philosophy, ay, to life itself, than this incessant business.

There is a coarse and boisterous money-making fellow in the outskirts of our town, who is going to build a bank-wall under the hill along the edge of his meadow. The powers have put this into his head to keep him out of mischief, and he wishes me to spend three weeks digging there with him. The result will be that he will perhaps get some more money to hoard, and leave for his heirs to spend foolishly. If I do this, most will commend me as an industrious and hard-working man; but if I choose to devote myself to certain labors which yield more real profit, though but little money, they may be inclined to look on me as an idler. Nevertheless, as I do not need the police of meaningless labor to regulate me, and do not see anything absolutely praiseworthy in this fellow's undertaking any more than in many an enterprise of our own or foreign governments, however amusing it may be to him or them, I prefer to finish my education at a different school.

If a man walk in the woods for love of them half of each day, he is in danger of being regarded as a loafer; but if he spends his whole day as a speculator, shearing off those woods and making earth bald before her time, he is esteemed an industrious and enterprising citizen. As if a town had no interest in its forests but to cut them down!

Most men would feel insulted if it were proposed to employ them in throwing stones over a wall, and then in throwing them back, merely that they might earn their wages. But many are no more worthily employed now. For instance: just after sunrise, one summer morning, I noticed one of my neighbors walking beside his team, which was slowly drawing a heavy hewn stone swung under the axle, surrounded by an atmosphere of industry — his day's work begun — his brow commenced to sweat — a reproach to all sluggards and idlers — pausing abreast the shoulders of his oxen, and half turning round with a flourish of his merciful whip, while they gained their length on him. And I thought, Such is the labor which the American Congress exists to protect — honest, manly toil — honest as the day is long — that makes his bread taste sweet, and keeps society sweet — which all men respect and have consecrated; one of the sacred band, doing the needful but irksome drudgery. Indeed, I felt a slight reproach, because I observed this from a window, and was not abroad and stirring about a similar business. The day went by, and at evening I passed the yard of another neighbor, who keeps many servants, and spends much money foolishly, while he adds nothing to the common stock, and there I saw the stone of the morning lying beside a whimsical structure intended to adorn this Lord Timothy Dexter's premises, and the dignity forthwith departed from the teamster's labor, in my eyes. In my opinion, the sun was made to light worthier toil than this. I may add that his employer has since run off, in debt to a good part of the town, and, after passing through Chancery, has settled somewhere else, there to become once more a patron of the arts.

The ways by which you may get money almost without exception lead downward. To have done anything by which you earned money *merely* is to have been truly idle or worse. If the laborer gets no more than the wages which his employer pays him, he is cheated, he cheats himself. If you would get money as a writer or lecturer, you must be popular, which is to go down perpendicularly. Those services which the community will most readily pay for, it is most disagreeable to render. You are paid for being something less than a man. The State does not commonly reward a genius any more wisely. Even the poet laureate would rather not have to celebrate the accidents of royalty. He must be bribed with a pipe of wine; and perhaps another poet is called away from his muse to gauge that very pipe. As for my own business, even that kind of surveying which I could do with most satisfaction my employers do not want. They would prefer that I should do my work coarsely and not too well, ay, not well enough. When I observe that there are different ways of surveying, my employer commonly asks which will give him the most land, not which is most correct. I once invented a rule for measuring cord-wood, and tried to introduce it in Boston; but the measurer there told me that the sellers did not wish to have their wood measured correctly — that he was already too accurate for them, and therefore they commonly got their wood measured in Charlestown before crossing the bridge.

The aim of the laborer should be, not to get his living, to get 'a good job,' but to perform well a certain work; and, even in a pecuniary sense, it would be economy for a town to pay its laborers so well that they would not feel that they were working for low ends, as for a livelihood merely, but for scientific, or even moral ends. Do not hire a man who does your work for money, but him who does it for love of it.

It is remarkable that there are few men so well employed, so much to their minds, but that a little money or fame would commonly buy them off from their present pursuit. I see advertisements for *active* young men, as if activity were the whole of a young man's capital. Yet I have been surprised when one has with confidence proposed to me, a grown man, to embark in some enterprise of his, as if I had absolutely nothing to do, my life having been a complete failure hitherto. What a doubtful compliment this to pay me! As if he had met me half-way across the ocean beating up against the wind, but bound nowhere, and proposed to me to go along with him! If I did, what do you think the underwriters would say? No, no! I am not without employment at this stage of the voyage. To tell the truth, I saw an advertisement for able-bodied seamen, when I was a boy, sauntering in my native port, and as soon as I came of age I embarked.

The community has no bribe that will tempt a wise man. You may raise money enough to tunnel a mountain, but you cannot raise money enough to hire a man who is minding *his own* business. An efficient and valuable man does what he can, whether the community pay him for it or not. The inefficient offer their inefficiency to the highest bidder, and are forever expecting to be put into office. One would suppose that they were rarely disappointed.

Perhaps I am more than usually jealous with respect to my freedom. I feel that my connection with and obligation to society are still very slight and transient. Those slight labors which afford me a livelihood, and by which it is allowed that I am to some extent serviceable to my contemporaries, are as yet commonly a pleasure to me, and I am not often reminded that they are a necessity. So far I am successful. But I foresee that if my wants should be much increased, the labor required to supply them would become a drudgery. If I should sell both my forenoons and afternoons to society, as most appear to do, I am sure that for me there would be nothing left worth living for. I trust that I shall never thus sell my birthright for a mess of pottage. I wish to suggest that a man may be very industrious, and yet not spend his time well. There is no more fatal blunderer than he who consumes the greater part of his life getting his living. All great enterprises are self-supporting. The poet, for instance, must sustain his body by his poetry, as a steam planing-mill feeds its boilers with the shavings it makes. You must get your living by loving. But as it is said of the merchants that ninety-seven in a hundred fail, so the life of men generally, tried by this standard, is a failure, and bankruptcy may be surely prophesied.

Merely to come into the world the heir of a fortune is not to be born, but to be still-born, rather. To be supported by the charity of friends, or a government pension — provided you continue to breathe — by whatever fine synonyms you describe these relations, is to go into the almshouse. On Sundays the poor debtor goes to church to take an account of stock, and finds, of course, that his outgoes have been greater than his income. In the Catholic Church, especially, they go into chancery, make a clean confession, give up all, and think to start again. Thus men will lie on their backs, talking about the fall of man, and never make an effort to get up.

As for the comparative demand which men make on life, it is an important difference between two, that the one is satisfied with a level success, that his marks can all be hit by point-blank shots, but the other, however low and unsuccessful his life may be, constantly elevates his aim, though at a very slight angle to the horizon. I should much rather be the last man — though, as the Orientals say, 'Greatness doth not approach him who is forever looking down; and all those who are looking high are growing poor.'

It is remarkable that there is little or nothing to be remembered written on the subject of getting a living; how to make getting a living not merely honest and honorable, but altogether inviting and glorious; for if *getting* a living is not so, then living is not. One would think, from looking at literature, that this question had never disturbed a solitary individual's musings. Is it that men are too much disgusted with their experience to speak of it? The lesson of value which money teaches, which the Author of the Universe has taken so much pains to teach us, we are inclined to skip altogether. As for the means of living, it is wonderful how indifferent men of all classes are about it, even reformers, so called — whether they inherit, or earn, or steal it. I think that Society has done nothing for us in this respect, or at least has undone what she has done. Cold and hunger seem more friendly to my nature than those methods which men have adopted and advise to ward them off.

The title *wise* is, for the most part, falsely applied. How can one be a wise man, if he does not know any better how to live than other men? — if he is only more cunning and intellectually subtle? Does Wisdom work in a tread-mill? or does she teach how to succeed *by her example?* Is there any such thing as wisdom not applied to life? Is she merely the miller who grinds the finest logic? It is pertinent to ask if Plato got his *living* in a better way or more successfully than his contemporaries — or did he succumb to the difficulties of life like other men? Did he seem to prevail over some of them merely by indifference, or by assuming grand airs? or find it easier to live, because his aunt remembered him in her will? The ways in which most men get their living, that is, live, are mere makeshifts, and a shirking of the real business of life — chiefly because they do not know, but partly because they do not mean, any better.

The rush to California, for instance, and the attitude, not merely of merchants, but of philosophers and prophets, so called, in relation to it, reflect the greatest disgrace on mankind. That so many are ready to live by luck, and so get the means of commanding the labor of others less lucky, without contributing any value to society! And that is called enterprise! I know of no more startling development of the immorality of trade, and all the common modes of getting a living.

The philosophy and poetry and religion of such a mankind are not worth the dust of a puffball. The hog that gets his living by rooting, stirring up the soil so, would be ashamed of such company. If I could command the wealth of all the worlds by lifting my finger, I would not pay *such* a price for it. Even Mahomet knew that God did not make this world in jest. It makes God to be a moneyed gentleman who scatters a handful of pennies in order to see mankind scramble for them. The world's raffle! A subsistence in the domains of Nature a thing to be raffled for! What a comment, what a satire, on our institutions! The conclusion will be, that mankind will hang itself upon a tree. And have all the precepts in all the Bibles taught men only this? and is the last and most admirable invention of the human race only an improved muck-rake? Is this the ground on which Orientals and Occidentals meet? Did God direct us so to get our living, digging where we never planted — and He would, perchance, reward us with lumps of gold?

God gave the righteous man a certificate entitling him to food and raiment, but the unrighteous man found a facsimile of the same in God's coffers, and appropriated it, and obtained food and raiment like the former. It is one of the most extensive systems of counterfeiting that the world has seen. I did not know that mankind was suffering for want of gold. I have seen a little of it. I know that it is very malleable, but not so malleable as wit. A grain of gold will gild a great surface, but not so much as a grain of wisdom.

The gold-digger in the ravines of the mountains is as much a gambler as his fellow in the saloons of San Francisco. What difference does it make whether you shake dirt or shake dice? If you win, society is the loser. The gold-digger is the enemy of the honest laborer, whatever checks and compensations there may be. It is not enough to tell me that you worked hard to get your gold. So does the Devil work hard. The way of transgressors may be hard in many respects. The humblest observer who goes to the mines sees and says that gold-digging is of the character of a lottery; the gold thus obtained is not the same thing with the wages of honest toil. But, practically, he forgets what he has seen, for he has seen only the fact, not the principle, and goes into trade there, that is, buys a ticket in what commonly proves another lottery, where the fact is not so obvious.

After reading Howitt's account of the Australian gold-diggings one evening, I had in my mind's eye, all night, the numerous valleys, with their streams, all cut up with foul pits, from ten to one hundred feet deep, and half a dozen feet across, as close as they can be dug, and partly filled with water — the locality to which men furiously rush to probe for their fortunes — uncertain where they shall break ground — not knowing but the gold is under their camp itself — sometimes digging one hundred and sixty feet before they strike the vein, or then missing it by a foot — turned into demons, and regardless of each others' rights, in their thirst for riches — whole valleys, for thirty miles, suddenly honeycombed by the pits of the miners, so that even hundreds are drowned in them — standing in water, and covered with mud and clay, they work night and day, dying of exposure and disease. Having read this, and partly forgotten it, I was thinking, accidentally, of my own unsatisfactory life, doing as others do; and with that vision of the diggings still before me, I asked myself why *I* might not be washing some gold daily, though it were only the finest particles — why *I* might not sink a shaft down to the gold within me, and work that mine. *There* is a Ballarat, a Bendigo for you — what though it were a sulky-gully? At any rate, I might pursue some path, however solitary and narrow and crooked, in which I could walk with love and reverence. Wherever a man separates from the multitude, and goes his own way in this mood, there indeed is a fork in the road, though ordinary travellers may see only a gap in the paling. His solitary path across lots will turn out the *higher way* of the two.

Men rush to California and Australia as if the true gold were to be found in that direction; but that is to go to the very opposite extreme to where it lies. They go prospecting farther and farther away from the true lead, and are most unfortunate when they think themselves most successful. Is not our *native* soil auriferous? Does not a stream from the golden mountains flow through our native valley? and has not this for more than geologic ages been bringing down the shining particles and forming the nuggets for us? Yet, strange to tell, if a digger steal away, prospecting for this true gold, into the unexplored solitudes around us, there is no danger that any will dog his steps, and endeavor to supplant him. He may claim and undermine the whole valley even, both the cultivated and the uncultivated portions, his whole life long in peace, for no one will ever dispute his claim. They will not mind his cradles or his toms. He is not confined to a claim twelve feet square, as at Ballarat, but may mine anywhere, and wash the whole wide world in his tom.

Howitt says of the man who found the great nugget which weighed twenty-eight pounds, at the Bendigo diggings in Australia: 'He soon began to drink; got a horse, and rode all about, generally at full gallop, and, when he met people, called out to inquire if they knew who he was, and then kindly informed them that he was "the bloody wretch that had found the nugget." At last he rode full speed against a tree, and nearly knocked his brains out.' I think, however, there was no danger of that, for he had already knocked his brains out against the nugget. Howitt adds, 'He is a hopelessly ruined man.' But he is a type of the class. They are all fast men. Hear some of the names of the places where they dig: 'Jackass Flat' — 'Sheep's-Head Gully' — 'Murderer's Bar,' etc. Is there no satire in these names? Let them carry their ill-gotten wealth where they will, I am thinking it will still be 'Jackass Flat,' if not 'Murderer's Bar,' where they live.

The last resource of our energy has been the robbing of graveyards on the Isthmus of Darien, an enterprise which appears to be but in its infancy; for, according to late accounts, an act has passed its second reading in the legislature of New Granada, regulating this kind of mining; and a correspondent of the 'Tribune' writes: 'In the dry season, when the weather will permit of the country being properly prospected, no doubt other rich *guacas* [that is, graveyards] will be found.' To emigrants he says: 'do not come before December; take the Isthmus route in preference to the Boca del Toro one; bring no useless baggage, and do not cumber yourself with a tent; but a good pair of blankets will be necessary; a pick, shovel, and axe of good material will be almost all that is required:' advice which might have been taken from the 'Burker's Guide.' And he concludes with this line in Italics and small capitals: '*If you are doing well at home*, STAY THERE,' which may fairly be interpreted to mean, 'If you are getting a good living by robbing grave-yards at home, stay there.'

But why go to California for a text? She is the child of New England, bred at her own school and church.

It is remarkable that among all the preachers there are so few moral teachers. The prophets are employed in excusing the ways of men. Most reverend seniors, the *illuminati* of the age, tell me, with a gracious, reminiscent smile, betwixt an aspiration and a shudder, not to be too tender about these things — to lump all that, that is, make a lump of gold of it. The highest advice I have heard on these subjects was grovelling. The burden of it was — It is not worth your while to under-take to reform the world in this particular. Do not ask how your bread is buttered; it will make you sick, if you do — and the like. A man had better starve at once than lose his innocence in the process of getting his bread. If within the sophisticated man there is not an unsophisticated one, then he is but one of the devil's angels. As we grow old, we live more coarsely, we relax a little in our disciplines, and, to some extent, cease to obey our finest instincts. But we should be fastidious to the extreme of sanity, disregarding the gibes of those who are more unfortunate than ourselves.

In our science and philosophy, even, there is commonly no true and absolute account of things. The spirit of sect and bigotry has planted its hoof amid the stars. You have only to discuss the problem, whether the stars are inhabited or not, in order to discover it. Why must we daub the heavens as well as the earth? It was an unfortunate discovery that Dr. Kane was a Mason, and that Sir John Franklin was another. But it was a more cruel suggestion that possibly that was the reason why the former went in search of the latter. There is not a popular magazine in this country that would dare to print a child's thought on important subjects without comment. It must be submitted to the D.D.'s. I would it were the chickadee-dees.

You come from attending the funeral of mankind to attend to a natural phenomenon. A little thought is sexton to all the world.

I hardly know an *intellectual* man, even, who is so broad and truly liberal that you can think aloud in his society. Most with whom you endeavor to talk soon come to a stand against some institution in which they appear to hold stock — that is, some particular, not universal, way of viewing things. They will continually thrust their own low roof, with its narrow skylight, between you and the sky, when it is the unobstructed heavens you would view. Get out of the way with your cobwebs; wash your windows, I say! In some lyceums they tell me that they have voted to exclude the subject of religion. But how do I know what their religion is, and when I am near to or far from it? I have walked into such an arena and done my best to make a clean breast of what religion I have experienced, and the audience never suspected what I was about. The lecture was as harmless as moonshine to them. Whereas, if I had read to them the biography of the greatest scamps in history, they might have thought that I had written the lives of the deacons of their church. Ordinarily, the inquiry is, Where did you come from? or, Where are you going? That was a more pertinent question which I overheard one of my auditors put to another one — 'What does he lecture for?' It made me quake in my shoes.

To speak impartially, the best men that I know are not serene, a world in themselves. For the most part, they dwell in forms, and flatter and study effect only more finely than the rest. We select granite for the underpinning of our houses and barns; we build fences of stone; but we do not ourselves rest on an underpinning of granitic truth, the lowest primitive rock. Our sills are rotten. What stuff is the man made of who is not coexistent in our thought with the purest and subtilest truth? I often accuse my finest acquaintances of an immense frivolity; for, while there are manners and compliments we do not meet, we do not teach one another the lessons of honesty and sincerity that the brutes do, or of steadiness and solidity that the rocks do. The fault is commonly mutual, however; for we do not habitually demand any more of each other.

That excitement about Kossuth, consider how characteristic, but superficial, it was! — only another kind of politics or dancing. Men were making speeches to him all over the country, but each expressed only the thought, or the want of thought, of the multitude. No man stood on truth. They were merely banded together, as usual one leaning on another, and all together on nothing; as the Hindoos made the world rest on an elephant, the elephant on a tortoise, and the tortoise on a serpent, and had nothing to put under the serpent. For all fruit of that stir we have the Kossuth hat.

Just so hollow and ineffectual, for the most part, is our ordinary conversation. Surface meets surface. When our life ceases to be inward and private, conversation degenerates into mere gossip. We rarely meet a man who can tell us any news which he has not read in a newspaper, or been told by his neighbor; and, for the most part, the only difference between us and our fellow is that he has seen the newspaper, or been out to tea, and we have not. In proportion as our inward life fails, we go more constantly and desperately to the post-office. You may depend on it, that the poor fellow who walks away with the greatest number of letters, proud of his extensive correspondence, has not heard from himself this long while.

I do not know but it is too much to read one newspaper a week. I have tried it recently, and for so long it seems to me that I have not dwelt in my native region. The sun, the clouds, the snow, the trees say not so much to me. You cannot serve two masters. It requires more than a day's devotion to know and to possess the wealth of a day.

We may well be ashamed to tell what things we have read or heard in our day. I did not know why my news should be so trivial — considering what one's dreams and expectations are, why the developments should be so paltry. The news we hear, for the most part, is not news to our genius. It is the stalest repetition. You are often tempted to ask why such stress is laid on a particular experience which you have had — that, after twenty-five years, you should meet Hobbins, Registrar of Deeds, again on the sidewalk. Have you not budged an inch, then? Such is the daily news. Its facts appear to float in the atmosphere, insignificant as the sporules of fungi, and impinge on some neglected *thallus*, or surface of our minds, which affords a basis for them, and hence a parasitic growth. We should wash ourselves clean of such news. Of what consequence, though our planet explode, if there is no character involved in the explosion? In health we have not the least curiosity about such events. We do not live for idle amusement. I would not run round a corner to see the world blow up.

All summer, and far into the autumn, perchance, you unconsciously went by the newspapers and the news, and now you find it was because the morning and the evening were full of news to you. Your walks were full of incidents. You attended, not to the affairs of Europe, but to your own affairs in Massachusetts fields. If you chance to live and move and have your being in that thin stratum in which the events that make the news transpire — thinner than the paper on which it is printed — then these things will fill the world for you; but if you soar above or dive below that plane, you cannot remember nor be reminded of them. Really to see the sun rise or go down every day, so to relate ourselves to a universal fact, would preserve us sane forever. Nations! What are nations? Tartars, and Huns, and Chinamen! Like insects, they swarm. The historian strives in vain to make them memorable. It is for want of a man that there are so many men. It is individuals that populate the world. Any man thinking may say with the Spirit of Lodin —

> 'I look down from my height on nations,
> And they become ashes before me; —
> Calm is my dwelling in the clouds;
> Pleasant are the great fields of my rest.'

Pray, let us live without being drawn by dogs, Esquimaux-fashion, tearing over hill and dale, and biting each other's ears.

Not without a slight shudder at the danger, I often perceive how near I had come to admitting into my mind the details of some trivial affair — the news of the street; and I am astonished to observe how willing men are to lumber their minds with such rubbish — to permit idle rumors and incidents of the most insignificant kind to intrude on ground which should be sacred to thought. Shall the mind be a public arena, where the affairs of the street and the gossip of the tea-table chiefly are discussed? Or shall it be a quarter of heaven itself — an hypæthral temple, consecrated to the service of the gods? I find it so difficult to dispose of the few facts which to me are significant, that I hesitate to burden my attention with those which are insignificant, which only a divine mind could illustrate. Such is, for the most part, the news in newspapers and conversation. It is important to preserve the mind's chastity in this respect. Think of admitting the details of a single case of the criminal court into our thoughts, to stalk profanely through their very *sanctum sanctorum* for an hour, ay, for many hours! to make a very barroom of the mind's inmost apartment, as if for so long the dust of the street had occupied us — the very street itself, with all its travel, its bustle, and filth, had passed through our thoughts' shrine! Would it not be an intellectual and moral suicide? When I have been compelled to sit spectator and auditor in a court-room for some hours, and have seen my neighbors, who were not compelled, stealing in from time to time, and tiptoeing about with washed hands and faces, it has appeared to my mind's eye, that, when they took off their hats, their ears suddenly expanded into vast hoppers for sound, between which even their narrow heads were crowded. Like the vanes of windmills, they caught the broad but shallow stream of sound, which, after a few titillating gyrations in their coggy brains, passed out the other side. I wondered if, when they got home, they were as careful to wash their ears as before their hands and faces. It has seemed to me, at such a time, that the auditors and the witnesses, the jury and the counsel, the judge and the criminal at the bar — if I may presume him guilty before he is convicted — were all equally criminal, and a thunderbolt might be expected to descend and consume them all together.

By all kinds of traps and signboards, threatening the extreme penalty of the divine law, exclude such trespassers from the only ground which can be sacred to you. It is so hard to forget what it is worse than useless to remember! If I am to be a thoroughfare, I prefer that it be of the mountain brooks, the Parnassian streams, and not the town sewers. There is inspiration, that gossip which comes to the ear of the attentive mind from the courts of heaven. There is the profane and stale revelation of the barroom and the police court. The same ear is fitted to receive both communications. Only the character of the hearer determines to which it shall be open, and to which closed. I believe that the mind can be permanently profaned by the habit of attending to trivial things, so that all our thoughts shall be tinged with triviality. Our very intellect shall be macadamized, as it were -— its foundation broken into fragments for the wheels of travel to roll over; and if you would know what will make the most durable pavement, surpassing rolled stones, spruce blocks, and asphaltum, you have only to look into some of our minds which have been subjected to this treatment so long.

If we have thus desecrated ourselves — as who has not? — the remedy will be by wariness and devotion to reconsecrate ourselves, and make once more a fane of the mind. We should treat our minds, that is, ourselves, as innocent and ingenuous children, whose guardians we are, and be careful what objects and what subjects we thrust on their attention. Read not the Times. Read the Eternities. Conventionalities are at length as bad as impurities. Even the facts of science may dust the mind by their dryness, unless they are in a sense effaced each morning, or rather rendered fertile by the dews of fresh and living truth. Knowledge does not come to us by details, but in flashes of light from heaven. Yes, every thought that passes through the mind helps to wear and tear it, and to deepen the ruts, which, as in the streets of Pompeii, evince how much it has been used. How many things there are concerning which we might well deliberate whether we had better know them — had better let their peddling-carts be driven, even at the slowest trot or walk, over that bridge of glorious span by which we trust to pass at last from the farthest brink of time to the nearest shore of eternity! Have we no culture, no refinement — but skill only to live coarsely and serve the Devil? — to acquire a little worldly wealth, or fame, or liberty, and make a false show with it, as if we were all husk and shell, with no tender and living kernel to us? Shall our institutions be like those chestnut burs which contain abortive nuts, perfect only to prick the fingers?

America is said to be the arena on which the battle of freedom is to be fought; but surely it cannot be freedom in a merely political sense that is meant. Even if we grant that the American has freed himself from a political tyrant, he is still the slave of an economical and moral tyrant. Now that the republic — the *res-publica* — has been settled, it is time to look after the *res-privata* — the private state — to see, as the Roman senate charged its consuls, '*ne quid res*-PRIVATA *detrimenti caperet,*' that the *private* state receive no detriment.

Do we call this the land of the free? What is it to be free from King George and continue the slaves of King Prejudice? What is it to be born free and not to live free? What is the value of any political freedom, but as a means to moral freedom? Is it a freedom to be slaves, or a freedom to be free, of which we boast? We are a nation of politicians, concerned about the outmost defences only of freedom. It is our children's children who may perchance be really free. We tax ourselves unjustly. There is a part of us which is not represented. It is taxation without representation. We quarter troops, we quarter fools and cattle of all sorts upon ourselves. We quarter our gross bodies on our poor souls, till the former eat up all the latter's substance.

With respect to a true culture and manhood, we are essentially provincial still, not metropolitan — mere Jonathans. We are provincial, because we do not find at home our standards; because we do not worship truth, but the reflection of truth; because we are warped and narrowed by an exclusive devotion to trade and commerce and manufactures and agriculture and the like, which are but means, and not the end.

So is the English Parliament provincial. Mere country bumpkins, they betray themselves, when any more important question arises for them to settle, the Irish question, for instance — the English question why did I not say? Their natures are subdued to what they work in. Their 'good breeding' respects only secondary objects. The finest manners in the world are awkwardness and fatuity when contrasted with a finer intelligence. They appear but as the fashions of past days — mere courtliness, knee-buckles and small-clothes, out of date. It is the vice, but not the excellence of manners, that they are continually being deserted by the character; they are cast-off-clothes or shells, claiming the respect which belonged to the living creature. You are presented with the shells instead of the meat, and it is no excuse generally, that, in the case of some fishes, the shells are of more worth than the meat. The man who thrusts his manners upon me does as if he were to insist on introducing me to his cabinet of curiosities, when I wished to see himself. It was not in this sense that the poet Decker called Christ 'the first true gentleman that ever breathed.' I repeat that in this sense the most splendid court in Christendom is provincial, having authority to consult about Transalpine interests only, and not the affairs of Rome. A prætor or proconsul would suffice to settle the questions which absorb the attention of the English Parliament and the American Congress.

Government and legislation! these I thought were respectable professions. We have heard of heaven-born Numas, Lycurguses, and Solons, in the history of the world, whose *names* at least may stand for ideal legislators; but think of legislating to *regulate* the breeding of slaves, or the exportation of tobacco! What have divine legislators to do with the exportation or the importation of tobacco? what humane ones with the breeding of slaves? Suppose you were to submit the question to any son of God — and has He no children in the Nineteenth Century? is it a family which is extinct? — in what condition would you get it again? What shall a State like Virginia say for itself at the last day, in which these have been the principal, the staple productions? What ground is there for patriotism in such a State? I derive my facts from statistical tables which the States themselves have published.

A commerce that whitens every sea in quest of nuts and raisins, and makes slaves of its sailors for this purpose! I saw, the other day, a vessel which had been wrecked, and many lives lost, and her cargo of rags, juniper berries, and bitter almonds were strewn along the shore. It seemed hardly worth the while to tempt the dangers of the sea between Leghorn and New York for the sake of a cargo of juniper berries and bitter almonds. America sending to the Old World for her bitters! Is not the sea-brine, is not shipwreck, bitter enough to make the cup of life go down here? Yet such, to a great extent, is our boasted commerce; and there are those who style themselves statesmen and philosophers who are so blind as to think that progress and civilization depend on precisely this kind of interchange and activity — the activity of flies about a molasses-hogshead. Very well, observes one, if men were oysters. And very well, answer I, if men were mosquitoes.

Lieutenant Herndon, whom our government sent to explore the Amazon, and, it is said, to extend the area of slavery, observed that there was wanting there 'an industrious and active population, who know what the comforts of life are, and who have artificial wants to draw out the great resources of the country.' But what are the 'artificial wants' to be encouraged? Not the love of luxuries, like the tobacco and slaves of, I believe, his native Virginia, nor the ice and granite and other material wealth of our native New England; nor are 'the great resources of a country' that fertility or barrenness of soil which produces these. The chief want, in every State that I have been into, was a high and earnest purpose in its inhabitants. This alone draws out 'the great resources' of Nature, and at last taxes her beyond her resources; for man naturally dies out of her. When we want culture more than potatoes, and illumination more than sugar-plums, then the great resources of a world are taxed and drawn out, and the result, or staple production, is, not slaves, nor operatives, but men — those rare fruits called heroes, saints, poets, philosophers, and redeemers.

In short, as a snow-drift is formed where there is a lull in the wind, so,

one would say, where there is a lull of truth, an institution springs up.
But the truth blows right on over it, nevertheless, and at length blows it
down.

What is called politics is comparatively something so superficial and
inhuman, that practically I have never fairly recognized that it concerns
me at all. The newspapers, I perceive, devote some of their columns
specially to politics or government without charge; and this, one would
say, is all that saves it; but as I love literature and to some extent the
truth also, I never read those columns at any rate. I do not wish to
blunt my sense of right so much. I have not got to answer for having
read a single President's Message. A strange age of the world this, when
empires, kingdoms, and republics come a-begging to a private man's
door, and utter their complaints at his elbow! I cannot take up a newspaper but I find that some wretched government or other, hard pushed
and on its last legs, is interceding with me, the reader, to vote for it —
more importunate than an Italian beggar; and if I have a mind to look
at its certificate, made, perchance, by some benevolent merchant's
clerk, or the skipper that brought it over, for it cannot speak a word of
English itself, I shall probably read of the eruption of some Vesuvius,
or the overflowing of some Po, true or forged, which brought it into this
condition. I do not hesitate, in such a case, to suggest work, or the
almshouse; or why not keep its castle in silence, as I do commonly?
The poor President, what with preserving his popularity and doing his
duty, is completely bewildered. The newspapers are the ruling power.
Any other government is reduced to a few marines at Fort Independence. If a man neglects to read the Daily Times, government will go
down on its knees to him, for this is the only treason in these days.

Those things which now most engage the attention of men, as politics
and the daily routine, are, it is true, vital functions of human society,
but should be unconsciously performed, like the corresponding functions of the physical body. They are *infra*-human, a kind of vegetation.
I sometimes awake to a half-consciousness of them going on about me,
as a man may become conscious of some of the processes of digestion
in a morbid state, and so have the dyspepsia, as it is called. It is as if
a thinker submitted himself to be rasped by the great gizzard of creation. Politics is, as it were, the gizzard of society, full of grit and gravel,
and the two political parties are its two opposite halves — sometimes
split into quarters, it may be, which grind on each other. Not only
individuals, but states, have thus a confirmed dyspepsia, which expresses itself, you can imagine by what sort of eloquence. Thus our life

is not altogether a forgetting, but also, alas! to a great extent, a remembering, of that which we should never have been conscious of,
certainly not in our waking hours. Why should we not meet, not always
as dyspeptics, to tell our bad dreams, but sometimes as *eupeptics*, to
congratulate each other on the ever-glorious morning? I do not make
an exorbitant demand, surely.

10. JOHN BROWN'S BODY

PREFATORY NOTE

No MAN had a greater impact on Thoreau's last years than John Brown.
The two men met only twice — and briefly each time at that — when Brown
surged through Massachusetts in 1857 and in 1859 in a search for funds for his
antislavery activities, but Thoreau immediately recognized his heroic stature.
(The Transcendentalists believed strongly in "heroes and hero-worship," but
it is significant that while his colleagues tended to worship heroes of the past,
Thoreau's heroes — John Brown, Walt Whitman, and Joe Polis, his Indian
guide, as Emerson once named them — were men of his own day.) When
John Brown struck out at Harpers Ferry, Thoreau's was the first voice in the
entire nation to be raised in his defense. He wrote out his "Plea for Captain
John Brown" at white heat, staying up most of a night to do it. Even the
most ardent Abolitionists shied away from approving Brown's action, fearing
that his violence had besmeared all antislavery activity. When Thoreau an-
nounced he was calling a meeting in the Concord Town Hall to read his
"Plea," local abolitionists pleaded that it was not expedient. His reply was
that he was not asking for advice, but announcing a meeting. Even two
members of his own family voiced their objection. The selectmen were obliged
by law to give him, a citizen of the town, use of the hall, but they demonstrated
their dissent by refusing to ring the town bell — so Thoreau rang it himself.
Most, according to Edward Emerson, came intending to scoff, but so intense

was his delivery — he read it as if it burned him, one observer commented — that they found themselves sympathizing almost against their will. A few days later when Frederick Douglass, the black orator, canceled a speaking engagement in Boston and fled the country because papers found in Brown's possession had incriminated him, Thoreau accepted an invitation to replace him and delivered the "Plea" in one of Boston's largest halls, filling every chair. Three days later he repeated it in Worcester with equal success. He then attempted to have it printed in pamphlet form, hoping to turn any profits over to Brown's defense fund. When James Redpath, another admirer of Brown, in the spring of 1860 gathered together a whole volume of essays on Brown entitled *Echoes of Harper's Ferry*, Thoreau instead turned the essay over to him for the same purpose and more than 33,000 copies were sold in less than a month.

When it became obvious to all that Brown was doomed, Thoreau gathered his friends together and arranged a memorial service in Concord's town hall the afternoon Brown was executed. Here he read a brief paper entitled "After the Death of John Brown" and the following summer when Brown was buried on his farm at North Elba, New York, Thoreau, unable to attend, sent along another brief paper entitled "The Last Days of John Brown" to be read for him. These latter two essays, since they primarily are devoted to reasserting his original position, are omitted here but can be found in his collected works. In the spring of 1860 Thoreau's friend and neighbor, Frank B. Sanborn, who had been Brown's chief fund-raiser, was seized by federal marshals to force him to testify before a Senate hearing. Thoreau was one of those who rushed out to hold the marshals at bay until a writ of habeas corpus could be obtained. When the next day the state supreme court discharged Sanborn from arrest, Thoreau spoke at a victory meeting in Concord. It was a brief and impromptu speech, but since it has a flavor all its own and has never been included in his collected works, it is worth including here — the text from a contemporary newspaper:

> Henry T. [sic] Thoreau, a genius and a philosopher, and reputed to be a man of practical sense and tact — his business a surveyor — said he heard the bells ringing last night, as he supposed for fire, but it proved to be the hottest fire he ever witnessed in Concord. He denounced what he termed the mean and sneaking method the United States officials took to accomplish their purpose. Early in the evening there appeared a poor boy, under a forged name, seeking aid. This is the course the Senate of the United States took to arrest one of their fellow citizens. The kidnappers, he said, should have been in their place. (Applause.) He thought somebody should have taken the responsibility to arrest them at the time of the arrest of Sanborn. That was a mistake. Many had been congratulated because the affair had been conducted in a lawful and orderly manner, and their friend was now free according to law. He did not agree with them. No. The Concord people didn't ring the fire alarm bells according to law — they didn't cheer according to law — they didn't groan according to law — (loud applause) — and as he didn't talk according to law, he thought he would stop and give way to some other speaker.

Many have thought Thoreau's John Brown essays a reversal of his earlier more pacifistic stand in "Civil Disobedience," that he was now endorsing the use of violence. A careful reader however will note that it is not Brown's violence Thoreau was endorsing, but rather the fact that Brown was willing to sacrifice his own life for a principle. That to Thoreau was the essence of heroism. As for Brown's cold-blooded Pottawatomie massacres, they did not become public knowledge until after Thoreau's death.

A PLEA FOR CAPTAIN JOHN BROWN

I TRUST that you will pardon me for being here. I do not wish to force my thoughts upon you, but I feel forced myself. Little as I know of Captain Brown, I would fain do my part to correct the tone and the statements of the newspapers, and of my countrymen generally, respecting his character and actions. It costs us nothing to be just. We can at least express our sympathy with, and admiration of, him and his companions, and that is what I now propose to do.

First, as to his history. I will endeavor to omit, as much as possible, what you have already read. I need not describe his person to you, for probably most of you have seen and will not soon forget him. I am told that his grandfather, John Brown, was an officer in the Revolution; that he himself was born in Connecticut about the beginning of this century, but early went with his father to Ohio. I heard him say that his father was a contractor who furnished beef to the army there, in the War of

1812; that he accompanied him to the camp, and assisted him in that employment, seeing a good deal of military life — more, perhaps, than if he had been a soldier; for he was often present at the councils of the officers. Especially, he learned by experience how armies are supplied and maintained in the field — a work which, he observed, requires at least as much experience and skill as to lead them in battle. He said that few persons had any conception of the cost, even the pecuniary cost, of firing a single bullet in war. He saw enough, at any rate, to disgust him with a military life; indeed, to excite in him a great abhorrence of it; so much so, that though he was tempted by the offer of some petty office in the army, when he was about eighteen, he not only declined that, but he also refused to train when warned, and was fined for it. He then resolved that he would never have anything to do with any war, unless it were a war for liberty.

When the troubles in Kansas began, he sent several of his sons thither to strengthen the party of the Free State men, fitting them out with such weapons as he had; telling them that if the troubles should increase, and there should be need of him, he would follow, to assist them with his hand and counsel. This, as you all know, he soon after did; and it was through his agency, far more than any other's, that Kansas was made free.

For a part of his life he was a surveyor, and at one time he was engaged in wool-growing, and he went to Europe as an agent about that business. There, as everywhere, he had his eyes about him, and made many original observations. He said, for instance, that he saw why the soil of England was so rich, and that of Germany (I think it was) so poor, and he thought of writing to some of the crowned heads about it. It was because in England the peasantry live on the soil which they cultivate, but in Germany they are gathered into villages at night. It is a pity that he did not make a book of his observations.

I should say that he was an old-fashioned man in his respect for the Constitution, and his faith in the permanence of this Union. Slavery he deemed to be wholly opposed to these, and he was its determined foe.

He was by descent and birth a New England farmer, a man of great common sense, deliberate and practical as that class is, and tenfold more so. He was like the best of those who stood at Concord Bridge once, on Lexington Common, and on Bunker Hill, only he was firmer and higher-principled than any that I have chanced to hear of as there. It was no abolition lecturer that converted him. Ethan Allen and Stark, with whom he may in some respects be compared, were rangers in a lower and less important field. They could bravely face their country's foes, but he had the courage to face his country herself when she was in the wrong. A Western writer says, to account for his escape from so many perils, that he was concealed under a 'rural exterior'; as if, in that prairie land, a hero should, by good rights, wear a citizen's dress only.

He did not go to the college called Harvard, good old Alma Mater as she is. He was not fed on the pap that is there furnished. As he phrased it, 'I know no more of grammar than one of your calves.' But he went to the great university of the West, where he sedulously pursued the study of Liberty, for which he had early betrayed a fondness, and having taken many degrees, he finally commenced the public practice of Humanity in Kansas, as you all know. Such were *his humanities*, and not any study of grammar. He would have left a Greek accent slanting the wrong way, and righted up a falling man.

He was one of that class of whom we hear a great deal, but, for the most part, see nothing at all — the Puritans. It would be in vain to kill him. He died lately in the time of Cromwell, but he reappeared here. Why should he not? Some of the Puritan stock are said to have come over and settled in New England. They were a class that did something else than celebrate their forefathers' day, and eat parched corn in remembrance of that time. They were neither Democrats nor Republicans, but men of simple habits, straightforward, prayerful; not thinking much of rulers who did not fear God, not making many compromises, nor seeking after available candidates.

'In his camp,' as one has recently written, and as I have myself heard him state, 'he permitted no profanity; no man of loose morals was suffered to remain there, unless, indeed, as a prisoner of war. "I would rather," said he, "have the small-pox, yellow fever, and cholera, all together in my camp, than a man without principle. . . . It is a mistake, sir, that our people make, when they think that bullies are the best fighters, or that they are the fit men to oppose these Southerners. Give me men of good principles — God-fearing men — men who respect themselves, and with a dozen of them I will oppose any hundred such men as these Buford ruffians."' He said that if one offered himself to be a soldier under him, who was forward to tell what he could or would do if he could only get sight of the enemy, he had but little confidence in him.

He was never able to find more than a score or so of recruits whom he would accept, and only about a dozen, among them his sons, in whom he had perfect faith. When he was here, some years ago, he showed to a few a little manuscript book — his 'orderly book' I think he called it — containing the names of his company in Kansas, and the rules by which they bound themselves; and he stated that several of them had already sealed the contract with their blood. When some one remarked that, with the addition of a chaplain, it would have been a perfect Cromwellian troop, he observed that he would have been glad to add a chaplain to the list, if he could have found one who could fill that office worthily. It is easy enough to find one for the United States Army. I believe that he had prayers in his camp morning and evening, nevertheless.

He was a man of Spartan habits, and at sixty was scrupulous about his diet at your table, excusing himself by saying that he must eat sparingly and fare hard, as became a soldier, or one who was fitting himself for difficult enterprises, a life of exposure.

A man of rare common sense and directness of speech, as of action; a transcendentalist above all, a man of ideas and principles — that was what distinguished him. Not yielding to a whim or transient impulse, but carrying out the purpose of a life. I noticed that he did not overstate anything, but spoke within bounds. I remember, particularly, how, in his speech here, he referred to what his family had suffered in Kansas, without ever giving the least vent to his pent-up fire. It was a volcano with an ordinary chimney-flue. Also referring to the deeds of certain Border Ruffians, he said, rapidly paring away his speech, like an experienced soldier, keeping a reserve of force and meaning, 'They had a perfect right to be hung.' He was not in the least a rhetorician, was not talking to Buncombe or his constituents anywhere, had no need to invent anything but to tell the simple truth, and communicate his own resolution; therefore he appeared incomparably strong, and eloquence in Congress and elsewhere seemed to me at a discount. It was like the speeches of Cromwell compared with those of an ordinary king.

As for his tact and prudence, I will merely say, that at a time when scarcely a man from the Free States was able to reach Kansas by any direct route, at least without having his arms taken from him, he, carrying what imperfect guns and other weapons he could collect, openly and slowly drove an ox-cart through Missouri, apparently in the capacity of a surveyor, with his surveying compass exposed in it, and so passed unsuspected, and had ample opportunity to learn the designs of the enemy. For some time after his arrival he still followed the same profession. When, for instance, he saw a knot of the ruffians on the prairie, discussing, of course, the single topic which then occupied their minds, he would, perhaps, take his compass and one of his sons, and proceed to run an imaginary line right through the very spot on which that conclave had assembled, and when he came up to them, he would naturally pause and have some talk with them, learning their news, and, at last, all their plans perfectly; and having thus completed his real survey he would resume his imaginary one, and run on his line till he was out of sight.

When I expressed surprise that he could live in Kansas at all, with a price set upon his head, and so large a number, including the authorities, exasperated against him, he accounted for it by saying, 'It is perfectly well understood that I will not be taken.' Much of the time for some years he has had to skulk in swamps, suffering from poverty, and from sickness which was the consequence of exposure, befriended only by Indians and a few whites. But though it might be known that he was lurking in a particular swamp, his foes commonly did not care to go in after him. He could even come out into a town where there were more Border Ruffians than Free State men, and transact some business, without delaying long, and yet not be molested; for, said he, 'no little handful of men were willing to undertake it, and a large body could not be got together in season.'

As for his recent failure, we do not know the facts about it. It was evidently far from being a wild and desperate attempt. His enemy Mr. Vallandigham is compelled to say that 'it was among the best planned and executed conspiracies that ever failed.'

Not to mention his other successes, was it a failure, or did it show a want of good management, to deliver from bondage a dozen human beings, and walk off with them by broad daylight, for weeks if not months, at a leisurely pace, through one State after another, for half the length of the North, conspicuous to all parties, with a price set upon his head, going into a court-room on his way and telling what he had done, thus convincing Missouri that it was not profitable to try to hold slaves in his neighborhood? — and this, not because the government menials were lenient, but because they were afraid of him.

Yet he did not attribute his success, foolishly, to 'his star,' or to any magic. He said, truly, that the reason why such greatly superior numbers quailed before him was, as one of his prisoners confessed, because they *lacked a cause* — a kind of armor which he and his party never lacked. When the time came, few men were found willing to lay down their lives in defence of what they knew to be wrong; they did not like that this should be their last act in this world.

But to make haste to *his* last act, and its effects.

The newspapers seem to ignore, or perhaps are really ignorant, of the fact that there are at least as many as two or three individuals to a town throughout the North who think much as the present speaker does about him and his enterprise. I do not hesitate to say that they are an important and growing party. We aspire to be something more than stupid and timid chattels, pretending to read history and our Bibles, but desecrating every house and every day we breathe in. Perhaps anxious politicians may prove that only seventeen white men and five negroes were concerned in the late enterprise; but their very anxiety to prove this might suggest to themselves that all is not told. Why do they still dodge the truth? They are so anxious because of a dim consciousness of the fact, which they did not distinctly face, that at least a million of the free inhabitants of the United States would have rejoiced if it had succeeded. They at most only criticise the tactics. Though we wear no crape, the thought of that man's position and probable fate is spoiling many a man's day here at the North for other thinking. If any one who has seen him here can pursue successfully any other train of thought, I do not know what he is made of. If there is any such who gets his usual allowance of sleep, I will warrant him to fatten easily under any circumstances which do not touch his body or purse. I put a piece of paper and a pencil under my pillow, and when I could not sleep I wrote in the dark.

On the whole, my respect for my fellow-men, except as one may outweigh a million, is not being increased these days. I have noticed the cold-blooded way in which newspaper writers and men generally speak of this event, as if an ordinary malefactor, though one of unusual 'pluck' — as the Governor of Virginia is reported to have said, using the language of the cock-pit, 'the gamest man he ever saw' — had been caught, and were about to be hung. He was not dreaming of his foes when the governor thought he looked so brave. It turns what sweetness I have to gall, to hear, or hear of, the remarks of some of my neighbors. When we heard at first that he was dead, one of my townsmen observed that 'he died as the fool dieth'; which, pardon me, for an instant suggested a likeness in him dying to my neighbor living. Others, craven-hearted, said disparagingly, that 'he threw his life away,' because he resisted the government. Which way have they thrown *their* lives, pray? — such as would praise a man for attacking singly an ordinary band of thieves or murderers. I hear another ask, Yankee-like, 'What will he gain by it?' as if he expected to fill his pockets by this enterprise. Such a one has no idea of gain but in this wordly sense. If it does not lead to a 'surprise' party, if he does not get a new pair of boots, or a vote of thanks, it must be a failure. 'But he won't gain anything by it.' Well, no, I don't suppose he could get four-and-sixpence a day for being hung, take the year round; but then he stands a chance to save a considerable part of his soul — and *such* a soul! — when *you* do not. No doubt you can get more in your market for a quart of milk than for a quart of blood, but that is not the market that heroes carry their blood to.

Such do not know that like the seed is the fruit, and that, in the moral world, when good seed is planted, good fruit is inevitable, and does not depend on our watering and cultivating; that when you plant, or bury, a hero in his field, a crop of heroes is sure to spring up. This is a seed of such force and vitality, that it does not ask our leave to germinate.

The momentary charge at Balaklava, in obedience to a blundering command, proving what a perfect machine the soldier is, has, properly enough, been celebrated by a poet laureate; but the steady, and for the most part successful, charge of this man, for some years, against the legions of Slavery, in obedience to an infinitely higher command, is as much more memorable than that as an intelligent and conscientious man is superior to a machine. Do you think that that will go unsung?

'Served him right' — 'A dangerous man' — 'He is undoubtedly insane.' So they proceed to live their sane, and wise, and altogether admirable lives, reading their Plutarch a little, but chiefly pausing at that feat of Putnam, who was let down into a wolf's den; and in this wise they nourish themselves for brave and patriotic deeds some time or other. The Tract Society could afford to print that story of Putnam. You might open the district schools with the reading of it, for there is nothing about Slavery or the Church in it; unless it occurs to the reader that some pastors are *wolves* in sheep's clothing. 'The American Board of Commissioners for Foreign Missions,' even, might dare to protest against *that* wolf. I have heard of boards, and of American boards, but it chances that I never heard of this particular lumber till lately. And yet I hear of Northern men, and women, and children, by families, buying a 'life-membership' in such societies as these. A life-membership in the grave! You can get buried cheaper than that.

Our foes are in our midst and all about us. There is hardly a house but is divided against itself, for our foe is the all but universal woodenness of both head and heart, the want of vitality in man, which is the effect of our vice; and hence are begotten fear, superstition, bigotry, persecution, and slavery of all kinds. We are mere figure-heads upon a hulk, with livers in the place of hearts. The curse is the worship of idols, which at length changes the worshipper into a stone image himself; and the New Englander is just as much an idolater as the Hindoo. This man was an exception, for he did not set up even a political graven image between him and his God.

A church that can never have done with excommunicating Christ while it exists! Away with your broad and flat churches, and your narrow and tall churches! Take a step forward, and invent a new style of out-houses. Invent a salt that will save you, and defend our nostrils.

The modern Christian is a man who has consented to say all the prayers in the liturgy, provided you will let him go straight to bed and sleep quietly afterward. All his prayers begin with 'Now I lay me down to sleep,' and he is forever looking forward to the time when he shall go to his '*long* rest.' He has consented to perform certain old-established charities, too, after a fashion, but he does not wish to hear of any new-fangled ones; he doesn't wish to have any supplementary articles added to the contract, to fit it to the present time. He shows the whites of his eyes on the Sabbath, and the blacks all the rest of the week. The evil is not merely a stagnation of blood, but a stagnation of spirit. Many, no doubt, are well disposed, but sluggish by constitution and by habit, and they cannot conceive of a man who is actuated by higher motives than they are. Accordingly they pronounce this man insane, for they know that *they* could never act as he does, as long as they are themselves.

We dream of foreign countries, of other times and races of men, placing them at a distance in history or space; but let some significant event like the present occur in our midst, and we discover, often, this distance and this strangeness between us and our nearest neighbors. *They* are our Austrias, and Chinas, and South Sea Islands. Our crowded society becomes well spaced all at once, clean and handsome to the eye — a city of magnificent distances. We discover why it was that we never got beyond compliments and surfaces with them before; we become aware of as many versts between us and them as there are between a wandering Tartar and a Chinese town. The thoughtful man becomes a hermit in the thoroughfares of the market-place. Impassable seas suddenly find their level between us, or dumb steppes stretch themselves out there. It is the difference of constitution, of intelligence, and faith, and not streams and mountains, that make the true and impassable boundaries between individuals and between states. None but the like-minded can come plenipotentiary to our court.

I read all the newspapers I could get within a week after this event, and I do not remember in them a single expression of sympathy for these men. I have since seen one noble statement, in a Boston paper, not editorial. Some voluminous sheets decided not to print the full report of Brown's words to the exclusion of other matter. It was as if a publisher should reject the manuscript of the New Testament, and print Wilson's last speech. The same journal which contained this pregnant news was chiefly filled, in parallel columns, with the reports of the political conventions that were being held. But the descent to them was too steep. They should have been spared this contrast — been printed in an extra, at least. To turn from the voices and deeds of earnest men to the *cackling* of political conventions! Office-seekers and speech-makers, who do not so much as lay an honest egg, but wear their breasts bare upon an egg of chalk! Their great game is the game of straws, or rather that universal aboriginal game of the platter, at which the Indians cried *hub, bub!* Exclude the reports of religious and political conventions, and publish the words of a living man.

But I object not so much to what they have omitted as to what they have inserted. Even the *Liberator* called it 'a misguided, wild, and apparently insane — effort.' As for the herd of newspapers and magazines, I do not chance to know an editor in the country who will deliberately print anything which he knows will ultimately and permanently reduce the number of his subscribers. They do not believe that it would be expedient. How then can they print truth? If we do not say pleasant things, they argue, nobody will attend to us. And so they do like some travelling auctioneers, who sing an obscene song, in order to draw a crowd around them. Republican editors, obliged to get their sentences ready for the morning edition, and accustomed to look at everything by the twilight of politics, express no admiration, nor true sorrow even, but call these men 'deluded fanatics' — 'mistaken men' — 'insane,' or 'crazed.' It suggests what a *sane* set of editors we are blessed with, *not* 'mistaken men'; who know very well on which side their bread is buttered, at least.

A man does a brave and humane deed, and at once, on all sides, we hear people and parties declaring, 'I didn't do it, nor countenance *him* to do it, in any conceivable way. It can't be fairly inferred from my past career.' I, for one, am not interested to hear you define your position. I don't know that I ever was or ever shall be. I think it is mere egotism, or impertinent at this time. Ye needn't take so much pains to wash your skirts of him. No intelligent man will ever be convinced that he was any creature of yours. He went and came, as he himself informs us, 'under the auspices of John Brown and nobody else.' The Republican Party does not perceive how many his *failure* will make to vote more correctly than they would have them. They have counted the votes of Pennsylvania & Co., but they have not correctly counted Captain Brown's vote. He has taken the wind out of their sails — the little wind they had — and they may as well lie to and repair.

What though he did not belong to your clique! Though you may not approve of his method or his principles, recognize his magnanimity. Would you not like to claim kindredship with him in that, though in no other thing he is like, or likely, to you? Do you think that you would lose your reputation so? What you lost at the spile, you would gain at the bung.

If they do not mean all this, then they do not speak the truth, and say what they mean. They are simply at their old tricks still.

'It was always conceded to him,' *says one who calls him crazy*, 'that he was a conscientious man, very modest in his demeanor, apparently inoffensive, until the subject of Slavery was introduced, when he would exhibit a feeling of indignation unparalleled. '

The slave-ship is on her way, crowded with its dying victims; new cargoes are being added in mid-ocean; a small crew of slaveholders, countenanced by a large body of passengers, is smothering four millions under the hatches, and yet the politician asserts that the only proper way by which deliverance is to be obtained is by 'the quiet diffusion of the sentiments of humanity,' without any 'outbreak.' As if the sentiments of humanity were ever found unaccompanied by its deeds, and you could disperse them, all finished to order, the pure article, as easily as water with a watering-pot, and so lay the dust. What is that that I hear cast overboard? The bodies of the dead that have found deliverance. That is the way we are 'diffusing' humanity, and its sentiments with it.

Prominent and influential editors, accustomed to deal with politicians, men of an infinitely lower grade, say, in their ignorance, that he acted 'on the principle of revenge.' They do not know the man. They must enlarge themselves to conceive of him. I have no doubt that the time will come when they will begin to see him as he was. They have got to conceive of a man of faith and of religious principle, and not a politician or an Indian; of a man who did not wait till he was personally interfered with or thwarted in some harmless business before he gave his life to the cause of the oppressed.

If Walker may be considered the representative of the South, I wish I could say that Brown was the representative of the North. He was a superior man. He did not value his bodily life in comparison with ideal things. He did not recognize unjust human laws, but resisted them as he was bid. For once we are lifted out of the trivialness and dust of politics into the region of truth and manhood. No man in America has ever stood up so persistently and effectively for the dignity of human nature, knowing himself for a man, and the equal of any and all governments. In that sense he was the most American of us all. He needed no babbling lawyer, making false issues, to defend him. He was more than a match for all the judges that American voters, or office-holders of whatever grade, can create. He could not have been tried by a jury of his peers, because his peers did not exist. When a man stands up serenely against the condemnation and vengeance of mankind, rising above them literally *by a whole body* — even though he were of late the vilest murderer, who has settled that matter with himself — the spectacle is a sublime one — didn't ye know it, ye *Liberators*, ye *Tribunes*, ye *Republicans?* — and we become criminal in comparison. Do yourselves the honor to recognize him. He needs none of your respect.

As for the Democratic journals, they are not human enough to affect me at all. I do not feel indignation at anything they may say.

I am aware that I anticipate a little — that he was still, at the last accounts, alive in the hands of his foes; but that being the case, I have all along found myself thinking and speaking of him as physically dead.

I do not believe in erecting statues to those who still live in our hearts, whose bones have not yet crumbled in the earth around us, but I would rather see the statue of Captain Brown in the Massachusetts State-House yard than that of any other man whom I know. I rejoice that I live in this age, that I am his contemporary.

What a contrast, when we turn to that political party which is so anxiously shuffling him and his plot out of its way, and looking around for some available slaveholder, perhaps, to be its candidate, at least for one who will execute the Fugitive Slave Law, and all those other unjust laws which he took up arms to annul!

Insane! A father and six sons, and one son-in-law, and several more men besides — as many at least as twelve disciples — all struck with insanity at once; while the same tyrant holds with a firmer gripe than ever his four millions of slaves, and a thousand sane editors, his abettors, are saving their country and their bacon! Just as insane were his efforts in Kansas. Ask the tyrant who is his most dangerous foe, the sane man or the insane? Do the thousands who know him best, who have rejoiced at his deeds in Kansas, and have afforded him material aid there, think him insane? Such a use of this word is a mere trope with most who persist in using it, and I have no doubt that many of the rest have already in silence retracted their words.

Read his admirable answers to Mason and others. How they are dwarfed and defeated by the contrast! On the one side, half-brutish, half-timid questioning; on the other, truth, clear as lightning, crashing into their obscene temples. They are made to stand with Pilate, and Gessler, and the Inquisition. How ineffectual their speech and action! and what a void their silence! They are but helpless tools in this great work. It was no human power that gathered them about this preacher.

What have Massachusetts and the North sent a few *sane* representatives to Congress for, of late years? — to declare with effect what kind of sentiments? All their speeches put together and boiled down — and probably they themselves will confess it — do not match for manly directness and force, and for simple truth, the few casual remarks of crazy John Brown on the floor of the Harper's Ferry engine-house — that man whom you are about to hang, to send to the other world, though not to represent *you* there. No, he was not our representative in any sense. He was too fair a specimen of a man to represent the like of us. Who, then, *were* his constituents? If you read his words understandingly you will find out. In his case there is no idle eloquence, no made, nor maiden speech, no compliments to the oppressor. Truth is his inspirer, and earnestness the polisher of his sentences. He could afford to lose his Sharp's rifles, while he retained his faculty of speech — a Sharp's rifle of infinitely surer and longer range.

And the New York *Herald* reports the conversation *verbatim!* It does not know of what undying words it is made the vehicle.

I have no respect for the penetration of any man who can read the report of that conversation and still call the principal in it insane. It has the ring of a saner sanity than an ordinary discipline and habits of life, than an ordinary organization, secure. Take any sentence of it — 'Any questions that I can honorably answer, I will; not otherwise. So far as I am myself concerned, I have told everything truthfully. I value my word, sir.' The few who talk about his vindictive spirit, while they really admire his heroism, have no test by which to detect a noble man, no amalgam to combine with his pure gold. They mix their own dross with it.

It is a relief to turn from these slanders to the testimony of his more truthful, but frightened jailers and hangmen. Governor Wise speaks far more justly and appreciatingly of him than any Northern editor, or politician, or public personage, that I chance to have heard from. I know that you can afford to hear him again on this subject. He says: 'They are themselves mistaken who take him to be a madman. . . . He is cool, collected, and indomitable, and it is but just to him to say that he was humane to his prisoners. . . . And he inspired me with great trust in his integrity as a man of truth. He is a fanatic, vain and garrulous' (I leave that part to Mr. Wise), 'but firm, truthful, and intelligent. His men, too, who survive, are like him. . . . Colonel Washington says that he was the coolest and firmest man he ever saw in defying danger and death. With one son dead by his side, and another shot through, he felt the pulse of his dying son with one hand, and held his rifle with the other, and commanded his men with the utmost composure, encouraging them to be firm, and to sell their lives as dear as they could. Of the three white prisoners, Brown, Stevens, and Coppoc, it was hard to say which was most firm.'

Almost the first Northern men whom the slaveholder has learned to respect!

The testimony of Mr. Vallandigham, though less valuable, is of the same purport, that 'it is vain to underrate either the man or his conspiracy. . . . He is the farthest possible removed from the ordinary ruffian, fanatic, or madman.'

'All is quiet at Harper's Ferry,' say the journals. What is the character of that calm which follows when the law and the slaveholder prevail? I regard this event as a touchstone designed to bring out, with glaring distinctness, the character of this government. We needed to be thus assisted to see it by the light of history. It needed to see itself. When a government puts forth its strength on the side of injustice, as ours to maintain slavery and kill the liberators of the slave, it reveals itself a merely brute force, or worse, a demoniacal force. It is the head of the Plug-Uglies. It is more manifest than ever that tyranny rules. I see this government to be effectually allied with France and Austria in oppressing mankind. There sits a tyrant holding fettered four millions of slaves; here comes their heroic liberator. This most hypocritical and diabolical government looks up from its seat on the gasping four millions, and inquires with an assumption of innocence: 'What do you assault me for? Am I not an honest man? Cease agitation on this subject, or I will make a slave of you, too, or else hang you.'

We talk about a *representative* government; but what a monster of a government is that where the noblest faculties of the mind, and the *whole* heart, are not *represented!* A semihuman tiger or ox, stalking over the earth, with its heart taken out and the top of its brain shot away. Heroes have fought well on their stumps when their legs were shot off, but I never heard of any good done by such a government as that.

The only government that I recognize — and it matters not how few are at the head of it, or how small its army — is that power that establishes justice in the land, never that which establishes injustice. What shall we think of a government to which all the truly brave and just men in the land are enemies, standing between it and those whom it oppresses? A government that pretends to be Christian and crucifies a million Christs every day!

Treason! Where does such treason take its rise? I cannot help thinking of you as you deserve, ye governments. Can you dry up the fountains of thought? High treason, when it is resistance to tyranny here below, has its origin in, and is first committed by, the power that makes and forever re-creates man. When you have caught and hung all these human rebels, you have accomplished nothing but your own guilt, for you have not struck at the fountain-head. You presume to contend with a foe against whom West Point cadets and rifled cannon *point* not. Can all the art of the cannon-founder tempt matter to turn against its maker? Is the form in which the founder thinks he casts it more essential than the constitution of it and of himself?

The United States have a coffle of four millions of slaves. They are determined to keep them in this condition; and Massachusetts is one of the confederated overseers to prevent their escape. Such are not all the inhabitants of Massachusetts, but such are they who rule and are obeyed here. It was Massachusetts, as well as Virginia, that put down this insurrection at Harper's Ferry. She sent the marines there, and she will have *to pay the penalty of her sin.*

Suppose that there is a society in this State that out of its own purse and magnanimity saves all the fugitive slaves that run to us, and protects our colored fellow-citizens, and leaves the other work to the government, so called. Is not that government fast losing its occupation, and becoming contemptible to mankind? If private men are obliged to perform the offices of government, to protect the weak and dispense justice, then the government becomes only a hired man, or clerk, to perform menial or indifferent services. Of course, that is but the shadow of a government whose existence necessitates a Vigilant Committee.

What should we think of the Oriental Cadi even, behind whom worked in secret a Vigilant Committee? But such is the character of our Northern States generally; each has its Vigilant Committee. And, to a certain extent, these crazy governments recognize and accept this relation. They say, virtually, 'We'll be glad to work for you on these terms, only don't make a noise about it.' And thus the government, its salary being insured, withdraws into the back shop, taking the Constitution with it, and bestows most of its labor on repairing that. When I hear it at work sometimes, as I go by, it reminds me, at best, of those farmers who in winter contrive to turn a penny by following the coopering business. And what kind of spirit is their barrel made to hold? They speculate in stocks, and bore holes in mountains, but they are not competent to lay out even a decent highway. The only *free* road, the Underground Railroad, is owned and managed by the Vigilant Committee. *They* have tunnelled under the whole breadth of the land. Such a government is losing its power and respectability as surely as water runs out of a leaky vessel, and is held by one that can contain it.

I hear many condemn these men because they were so few. When were the good and the brave ever in a majority? Would you have had him wait till that time came? — till you and I came over to him? The very fact that he had no rabble or troop of hirelings about him would alone distinguish him from ordinary heroes. His company was small indeed, because few could be found worthy to pass muster. Each one who there laid down his life for the poor and oppressed was a picked man, culled out of many thousands, if not millions; apparently a man of principle, of rare courage, and devoted humanity; ready to sacrifice his life at any moment for the benefit of his fellow-man. It may be doubted if there were as many more their equals in these respects in all the country — I speak of his followers only — for their leader, no doubt, scoured the land far and wide, seeking to swell his troop. These alone were ready to step between the oppressor and the oppressed. Surely they were the very best men you could select to be hung. That was the greatest compliment which this country could pay them. They were ripe for her gallows. She has tried a long time, she has hung a good many, but never found the right one before.

When I think of him, and his six sons, and his son-in-law, not to enumerate the others, enlisted for this fight, proceeding coolly, reverently, humanely to work, for months if not years, sleeping and waking upon it, summering and wintering the thought, without expecting any reward but a good conscience, while almost all America stood ranked on the other side — I say again that it affects me as a sublime spectacle. If he had had any journal advocating '*his cause*,' any organ, as the phrase is, monotonously and wearisomely playing the same old tune, and then passing round the hat, it would have been fatal to his efficiency. If he had acted in any way so as to be let alone by the government, he might have been suspected. It was the fact that the tyrant must give place to him, or he to the tyrant, that distinguished him from all the reformers of the day that I know.

It was his peculiar doctrine that a man has a perfect right to interfere by force with the slaveholder, in order to rescue the slave. I agree with him. They who are continually shocked by slavery have some right to be shocked by the violent death of the slaveholder, but no others. Such will be more shocked by his life than by his death. I shall not be forward to think him mistaken in his method who quickest succeeds to liberate the slave. I speak for the slave when I say that I prefer the philanthropy of Captain Brown to that philanthropy which neither shoots me nor liberates me. At any rate, I do not think it is quite sane for one to spend his whole life in talking or writing about this matter, unless he is continuously inspired, and I have not done so. A man may have other affairs to attend to. I do not wish to kill nor to be killed, but I can foresee circumstances in which both these things would be by me unavoidable. We preserve the so-called peace of our community by deeds of petty violence every day. Look at the policeman's billy and handcuffs! Look at the jail! Look at the gallows! Look at the chaplain of the regiment! We are hoping only to live safely on the outskirts of *this* provisional army. So we defend ourselves and our hen-roosts, and maintain slavery. I know that the mass of my countrymen think that the only righteous use that can be made of Sharp's rifles and revolvers is to fight duels with them, when we are insulted by other nations, or to hunt Indians, or shoot fugitive slaves with them, or the like. I think that for once the Sharp's rifles and the revolvers were employed in a righteous cause. The tools were in the hands of one who could use them.

The same indignation that is said to have cleared the temple once will clear it again. The question is not about the weapon, but the spirit in which you use it. No man has appeared in America, as yet, who loved his fellow-man so well, and treated him so tenderly. He lived for him. He took up his life and he laid it down for him. What sort of violence is that which is encouraged, not by soldiers, but by peaceable citizens, not so much by laymen as by ministers of the Gospel, not so much by the fighting sects as by the Quakers, and not so much by Quaker men as by Quaker women?

This event advertises me that there is such a fact as death — the possibility of a man's dying. It seems as if no man had ever died in America before; for in order to die you must first have lived. I don't believe in the hearses, and palls, and funerals that they have had. There was no death in the case, because there had been no life; they merely rotted or sloughed off, pretty much as they had rotted or sloughed along. No temple's veil was rent, only a hole dug somewhere. Let the dead bury their dead. The best of them fairly ran down like a clock. Franklin — Washington — they were let off without dying; they were merely missing one day. I hear a good many pretend that they are going to die; or that they have died, for aught that I know. Nonsense! I'll defy them to do it. They haven't got life enough in them. They'll deliquesce like fungi, and keep a hundred eulogists mopping the spot where they left off. Only half a dozen or so have died since the world began. Do you think that you are going to die, sir? No! there's no hope of you. You haven't got your lesson yet. You've got to stay after school. We make a needless ado about capital punishment — taking lives, when there is no life to take. *Memento mori!* We don't understand that sublime sentence which some worthy got sculptured on his gravestone once. We've interpreted it in a grovelling and snivelling sense; we've wholly forgotten how to die.

But be sure you do die nevertheless. Do your work, and finish it. If you know how to begin, you will know when to end.

These men, in teaching us how to die, have at the same time taught us how to live. If this man's acts and words do not create a revival, it will be the severest possible satire on the acts and words that do. It is the best news that America has ever heard. It has already quickened the feeble pulse of the North, and infused more and more generous blood into her veins and heart than any number of years of what is called commercial and political prosperity could. How many a man who was lately contemplating suicide has now something to live for!

One writer says that Brown's peculiar monomania made him to be 'dreaded by the Missourians as a supernatural being.' Sure enough, a hero in the midst of us cowards is always so dreaded. He is just that thing. He shows himself superior to nature. He has a spark of divinity in him.

> 'Unless above himself he can
> Erect himself, how poor a thing is man!'

Newspaper editors argue also that it is a proof of his *insanity* that he thought he was appointed to do this work which he did — that he did not suspect himself for a moment! They talk as if it were impossible that a man could be 'divinely appointed' in these days to do any work whatever; as if vows and religion were out of date as connected with any man's daily work; as if the agent to abolish slavery could only be somebody appointed by the President, or by some political party. They talk as if a man's death were a failure, and his continued life, be it of whatever character, were a success.

When I reflect to what a cause this man devoted himself, and how religiously, and then reflect to what cause his judges and all who condemn him so angrily and fluently devote themselves, I see that they are as far apart as the heavens and earth are asunder.

The amount of it is, our '*leading men*' are a harmless kind of folk, and they know *well enough* that *they* were not divinely appointed, but elected by the votes of their party.

Who is it whose safety requires that Captain Brown be hung? Is it indispensable to any Northern man? Is there no resource but to cast this man also to the Minotaur? If you do not wish it, say so distinctly. While these things are being done, beauty stands veiled and music is a screeching lie. Think of him — of his rare qualities! — such a man as it takes ages to make, and ages to understand; no mock hero, nor the representative of any party. A man such as the sun may not rise upon again in this benighted land. To whose making went the costliest material, the finest adamant; sent to be the redeemer of those in captivity; and the only use to which you can put him is to hang him at the end of a rope! You who pretend to care for Christ crucified, consider what you are about to do to him who offered himself to be the saviour of four millions of men.

Any man knows when he is justified, and all the wits in the world cannot enlighten him on that point. The murderer always knows that he is justly punished; but when a government takes the life of a man without the consent of his conscience, it is an audacious government, and is taking a step towards its own dissolution. Is it not possible that an individual may be right and a government wrong? Are laws to be enforced simply because they were made? or declared by any number of men to be good, if they are *not* good? Is there any necessity for a man's being a tool to perform a deed of which his better nature disapproves? Is it the intention of law-makers that *good* men shall be hung ever? Are judges to interpret the law according to the letter, and not the spirit?

What right have *you* to enter into a compact with yourself that you *will* do thus or so, against the light within you? Is it for *you* to *make up* your mind — to form any resolution whatever — and not accept the convictions that are forced upon you, and which ever pass your understanding? I do not believe in lawyers, in that mode of attacking or defending a man, because you descend to meet the judge on his own ground, and, in cases of the highest importance, it is of no consequence whether a man breaks a human law or not. Let lawyers decide trivial cases. Business men may arrange that among themselves. If they were the interpreters of the everlasting laws which rightfully bind man, that would be another thing. A counterfeiting law-factory, standing half in a slave land and half in a free! What kind of laws for free men can you expect from that?

I am here to plead his cause with you. I plead not for his life, but for his character — his immortal life; and so it becomes your cause wholly, and is not his in the least. Some eighteen hundred years ago Christ was crucified; this morning, perchance, Captain Brown was hung. These are the two ends of a chain which is not without its links. He is not Old Brown any longer; he is an angel of light.

I see now that it was necessary that the bravest and humanest man in all the country should be hung. Perhaps he saw it himself. I *almost fear* that I may yet hear of his deliverance, doubting if a prolonged life, if *any* life, can do as much good as his death.

'Misguided!' 'Garrulous!' 'Insane!' 'Vindictive!' So ye write in your easy-chairs, and thus he wounded responds from the floor of the armory, clear as a cloudless sky, true as the voice of nature is: 'No man sent me here; it was my own prompting and that of my Maker. I acknowledge no master in human form.'

And in what a sweet and noble strain he proceeds, addressing his captors, who stand over him: 'I think, my friends, you are guilty of a great wrong against God and humanity, and it would be perfectly right for any one to interfere with you, so far as to free those you wilfully and wickedly hold in bondage.'

And, referring to his movement: 'It is, in my opinion, the greatest service a man can render to God.'

'I pity the poor in bondage that have none to help them; that is why I am here; not to gratify any personal animosity, revenge, or vindictive spirit. It is my sympathy with the oppressed and the wronged, that are as good as you, and as precious in the sight of God.'

You don't know your testament when you see it.

'I want you to understand that I respect the rights of the poorest and weakest of colored people, oppressed by the slave power, just as much as I do those of the most wealthy and powerful.'

'I wish to say, furthermore, that you had better, all you people at the South, prepare yourselves for a settlement of that question, that must come up for settlement sooner than you are prepared for it. The sooner you are prepared the better. You may dispose of me very easily. I am nearly disposed of now; but this question is still to be settled — this negro question, I mean; the end of that is not yet.'

I foresee the time when the painter will paint that scene, no longer going to Rome for a subject; the poet will sing it; the historian record it; and, with the Landing of the Pilgrims and the Declaration of Independence, it will be the ornament of some future national gallery, when at least the present form of slavery shall be no more here. We shall then be at liberty to weep for Captain Brown. Then, and not till then, we will take our revenge.

SELECTED BIBLIOGRAPHY

The standard edition of Thoreau's works is the twenty-volume *Writings of Thoreau* (Boston, 1906) but it is gradually being superseded by the CEAA approved *Writings of Henry D. Thoreau* (Princeton, 1971–) as it appears. The *Collected Poems of Henry Thoreau* (Chicago, 1943; Baltimore, 1964) and the *Correspondence of Henry David Thoreau* (New York, 1958) contain material not in the earlier standard edition. Other scholarly editions include the *Variorum Walden* (New York, 1962), the *Annotated Walden* (New York, 1970), and the *Variorum Civil Disobedience* (New York, 1967).

The most sympathetic and satisfying biography is Henry Salt's *Life of Henry David Thoreau* (London, 1890). William Ellery Channing's *Thoreau, the Poet-Naturalist* (Boston, 1873, 1902), Frank Sanborn's *Life of Henry David Thoreau* (Boston, 1917), and Edward Emerson's *Henry Thoreau as Remembered by a Young Friend* (Boston, 1917) all have the advantage of personal acquaintance with Thoreau on the part of the author, but only the last-named demonstrates any artistry in its writing. Henry S. Canby's *Thoreau* (Boston, 1939) has good critical insights but is not always factually accurate. Walter Harding's *Days of Henry Thoreau* (New York, 1965) is the most detailed biography; Sherman Paul's *Shores of America* (Urbana, 1958), the best account of Thoreau's intellectual development; and Milton Meltzer and Walter Harding's *Thoreau Profile* (New York, 1962), the only pictorial biography. Joel Porte's *Emerson and Thoreau* (Middletown, 1966) concentrates on the relationship of the two men. Robert Stowell's *Thoreau Gazetteer* (Princeton, 1970) is a very useful compilation of maps and photographs of Thoreau's travels in Concord and elsewhere.

A judicious general critical analysis of Thoreau's writing is Joseph Wood Krutch's *Henry David Thoreau* (New York, 1948). Walter Harding's *Thoreau Handbook* (New York, 1959) is a comprehensive survey of all Thoreau scholarship and a general introduction to his writings. Wendell Glick's *Recognition of Henry David Thoreau* (Ann

Arbor, 1969) is the most comprehensive anthology of Thoreau criticism. More specialized critical studies include John Christie's *Thoreau as World Traveler* (New York, 1965) on the influence of Thoreau's reading in travel books; Ethel Seybold's *Thoreau: The Quest and the Classics* (New Haven, 1951) on his studies in the Greeks and Romans; Leo Stoller's *After Walden: Thoreau's Changing View on Economic Man* (Stanford, 1957); Eugene Timpe's *Thoreau Abroad* (Hamden, 1971) on his international fame; and Walter Harding's *Henry David Thoreau: A Profile* (New York, 1971), a collection of psychological studies. Perry Miller's lengthy introduction to *Consciousness in Concord* (the so-called "lost journal"; Boston, 1957) is an erinacious attack on Thoreau that has aroused much discussion. Three specialized studies of *Walden* are Stanley Cavell's *Senses of Walden* (New York, 1972), a profound philosophical analysis; Reginald Cook's *Passage to Walden* (Boston, 1949), primarily on Thoreau's relationship to Nature; and Charles Anderson's *Magic Circle of Walden*, a belletristic analysis.

Francis Allen's *Bibliography of Henry David Thoreau* (Boston, 1908) is the standard early bibliography. It has been supplemented by William White's *Henry David Thoreau Bibliography, 1908–1937* (Boston, 1939) and Christopher Hildenbrand's *Bibliography of Scholarship about Henry David Thoreau, 1940–1967* (Fort Hays, 1967). Walter Harding compiles "Additions to the Thoreau Bibliography" in the quarterly *Thoreau Society Bulletin* (Geneseo, 1974–) and these have been cumulated in his *Bibliography of the Thoreau Society Bulletin Bibliographies, 1941–1969* (Troy, 1971).

INDEX OF TITLES